the
AMERICANA ANNUAL

1989

GROLIER

AN ENCYCLOPEDIA OF THE EVENTS OF 1988
YEARBOOK OF THE ENCYCLOPEDIA AMERICANA

This annual has been prepared as a yearbook for general encyclopedias. It is also published as *Encyclopedia Year Book*.

Grolier Enterprises, Inc. offers a varied selection of both adult and children's book racks. For details on ordering, please write:

Grolier Enterprises, Inc.
Sherman Turnpike
Danbury, CT 06816
Attn: Premium Department

Contents

Feature Articles of the Year

The Alphabetical Section

Entries on the continents, major nations of the world, U.S. states, Canadian provinces, and chief cities will be found under their own alphabetical headings.

The Year in Review

The 1988 Nobel Peace Prize was awarded to the United Nations peacekeeping forces, which, according to the Norwegian Nobel Committee, "represent the manifest will of the community of nations to achieve peace through negotiations."

"History teaches us that enmities between nations . . . do not last forever. However fixed our likes and dislikes, the tide of time and events will often bring surprising changes in the relations between nations and neighbors."

On June 10, 1963, in his famous commencement address at American University, President John F. Kennedy announced that the United States, Great Britain, and the Soviet Union had agreed to talks on the banning of nuclear-weapons tests. His speech, which elaborated a "strategy of peace" to prevent nuclear holocaust, led to a historic treaty signing that August.

Twenty-five years later, "the tide of time and events" brought together U.S. President Ronald Reagan and Soviet General Secretary Mikhail Gorbachev to ratify another major treaty—one to eliminate intermediate-range nuclear forces. And beyond the improvement in superpower relations, world affairs throughout 1988 appeared to support Kennedy's view of history. Enmities persisted, but the course of events seemed guided by an undercurrent of "surprising changes."

The litany of cease-fires, peace talks, and other breakthroughs—however tenuous—covered many of the world's

trouble spots. Iran and Iraq agreed to a truce in the Persian Gulf war and opened talks aimed at a final peace. The Soviet Union began withdrawing its troops from Afghanistan. An agreement was reached to end the war in Angola. Parties in the Cambodian conflict held direct negotiations. And in Nicaragua, while peace seemed far off, the Sandinista regime and "contra" rebels agreed to a truce and held several rounds of talks. Perhaps the most intractable problem was that in the Israeli-occupied territories, where Palestinian demands for an independent state—and Israel's response—remained heated.

Democratic reform and popular sovereignty were themes as well. Furthering his program of *perestroika* (restructuring), Mikhail Gorbachev effected sweeping changes in the Soviet political system. In Chile, voters in a national plebiscite said "no" to a new term for hard-line President Augusto Pinochet. South Korea got a popularly elected president, a measure of stability, and the spotlight of the Summer Olympics—marred only by a drug scandal. Pakistan's President Zia ul-Haq died in a plane explosion, and opposition leader Benazir Bhutto was elected the first woman leader of a Muslim nation. In other elections, Canada returned Prime Minister Brian Mulroney to office, endorsing his free-trade pact with the United States; France reelected President François Mitterrand; Mexico made Carlos Salinas de Gortari its new president; and Israel's religious right made a strong showing. In China, where reform continued, Li Peng was confirmed as premier. Japan sensed the end of an era as Emperor Hirohito fell ill.

Natural disasters seemed especially devastating in 1988. An earthquake in Soviet Armenia left some 25,000 people dead; flooding in Bangladesh left 28 million people homeless; Hurricane Gilbert left Jamaica and parts of Mexico in shambles; and North America suffered its worst drought since the 1930s. Man-made disasters included the crash of a Pan Am 747 over Lockerbie, Scotland, killing all 259 people on board and others on the ground; a bomb was suspected.

In the United States, the year's biggest headlines went to the presidential election. Vice-President George Bush, calling up the successes of the Reagan years yet emerging as a political force in his own right, rolled to victory over Massachusetts Gov. Michael Dukakis on November 8.

As the Reagan era drew to a close, supporters noted the longest sustained economic expansion since the 1960s, while critics pointed to ever-mounting budget and trade deficits. Legislative highlights of the year included an overhaul of the welfare system, a major antidrug law, and an expansion of Medicare to cover "catastrophic" medical costs.

In a breathless moment on September 29, some 32 months after the tragedy of the space shuttle *Challenger,* America returned to space with the launching of *Discovery.*

"Takeover" was the watchword on Wall Street. *Phantom of the Opera* held Broadway spellbound. Disney's *Who Framed Roger Rabbit* charmed movie audiences. Steffi Graf won the Grand Slam of tennis. And, coming back to surprises, the Los Angeles Dodgers won the World Series.

THE EDITORS

Chiang Ching-kuo, the 77-year-old son of the late Chinese Nationalist leader Chiang Kai-shek and the president of Taiwan since May 1978, died January 13. Family members, dignitaries, and citizens of Taiwan joined in the official mourning.

© Richard Tomkins/Gamma-Liaison

January

1 In New Year's Day college football action, the University of Miami earns the unofficial national championship by defeating Oklahoma, 20–14, in the Orange Bowl.

11 Representatives of the United States and Canada sign a key amendment to an extradition treaty and a new agreement on the passage of U.S. icebreakers through the Arctic.

12 The National Assembly of Suriname elects Ramsewak Shankar as the nation's new president.

13 Taiwan's President Chiang Ching-kuo dies of a heart attack. Vice-President Lee Teng-hui assumes the office.

Amid continuing violence, Israel deports four Palestinians charged with instigating the riots that broke out the previous month in occupied territories.

Japan's Prime Minister Noboru Takeshita discusses trade and other economic matters with President Reagan in Washington.

The U.S. Supreme Court rules, 5–3, that public-school officials have broad powers to censor school newspapers and other "school-sponsored expressive activities."

15 A North Korean woman claiming to be a government agent confesses publicly to having helped blow up a Korean Air Lines passenger plane in November 1987.

16 At a summit meeting of Central American presidents, Daniel Ortega of Nicaragua agrees to direct talks with contra rebels, the lifting of a six-year-old state of siege, and other concessions.

18 A military rebellion in Argentina, the second in nine months, ends in an unconditional surrender.

24 Former professor Leslie Manigat is named the winner of Haiti's disputed January 17 presidential election.

25 President Reagan delivers his seventh State of the Union message, promising a vigorous final year in office.

26 Australia marks the bicentennial of its settlement. Some 2 million people attend festivities in Sydney harbor.

31 The prime ministers of Greece and Turkey, Andreas Papandreou and Turgut Ozal, meet in Switzerland and agree to work toward resolving bilateral disputes.

The Washington Redskins defeat the Denver Broncos, 42–10, in Super Bowl XXII.

February

2 The U.S. Federal Bureau of Investigation (FBI) defends a surveillance effort, revealed January 27, aimed at opponents of administration policy in Central America.

3 The U.S. House of Representatives rejects, 219–211, President Reagan's request for at least $36 million in aid to the Nicaraguan contras.

The U.S. Senate unanimously confirms Judge Anthony M. Kennedy as an associate justice of the Supreme Court.

8 The U.S. presidential primary season begins with the Iowa caucuses.

An international panel of historians concludes that Austria's President Kurt Waldheim had been aware of war crimes by his German army unit during World War II, but that he had not committed any crimes.

11 In Washington, DC, Lyn Nofziger, former political director to the Reagan White House, is convicted of illegal lobbying under the federal ethics law.

12 Two U.S. warships are intercepted and bumped by Soviet naval vessels in the Black Sea.

13 Leaders of the European Community (EC) conclude a three-day emergency summit in Brussels with accords on agricultural policy, aid to poorer members, and funding.

President Reagan and Mexico's President Miguel de la Madrid begin their sixth summit and sign an agreement allowing greater access to U.S. markets of Mexican-made textiles.

The XV Olympic Winter Games open in Calgary, Canada.

A crowd of 60,000 jams McMahon Stadium in Calgary, Alta., Canada, February 13, for the opening ceremonies of the XV Winter Games. A record 1,793 athletes from 57 nations participated in the Olympic contests.

© Heinz Kluetmeier/"Sports Illustrated"

© Timothy Ross/Picture Group

Panama was in the midst of a government crisis after President Eric Arturo Delvalle unsuccessfully tried to remove Gen. Manuel Antonio Noriega as the nation's de facto leader on February 26. A general strike called by Noriega opponents followed.

15 A Palestine Liberation Organization (PLO) ship on a protest voyage to Israel is damaged by a mine explosion in the Cypriot port of Limassol.

Finland's electoral college reelects President Mauno Koivisto to a six-year term.

17 U.S. Marine Lt. Col. William Higgins, the head of a UN truce observer unit in Lebanon, is kidnapped while driving near the southern port city of Tyre.

18 President Reagan submits to Congress a $1.09 trillion budget for fiscal 1989.

21 Businessman George Vassiliou is elected president of Cyprus in a runoff against rightist Glafkos Clerides.

24 The government of South Africa imposes sweeping new restrictions on 17 leading antiapartheid groups.

25 Roh Tae Woo, who won election in December 1987, is sworn in as president of South Korea.

26 Panama's President Eric Arturo Delvalle is ousted by the National Assembly after he moved to fire de facto leader Gen. Manuel Noriega. On February 5, Noriega was indicted by the United States on charges of drug trafficking.

27 Armenian nationalists suspend demonstrations in two Soviet republics after receiving assurances that General Secretary Mikhail Gorbachev would study their grievances.

29 Rioting breaks out in Dakar, Senegal, when President Abdou Diouf is declared the winner of the previous day's election. A state of emergency is declared.

March

2 Leaders of the 16 nations of the North Atlantic Treaty Organization open a two-day summit, their first since 1982, in Brussels, Belgium.

4 U.S. Secretary of State George Shultz concludes a week of Middle East shuttle diplomacy, with little result.

The Soviet Union reports that 31 people died in ethnic fighting in the Azerbaijan Republic on February 28.

8 Vice-President George Bush sweeps the South in "Super Tuesday" Republican presidential primaries. Massachusetts Gov. Michael Dukakis tops the Democratic field.

10 Indonesia's legislature elects President Suharto to a fifth five-year term.

11 After some ten days of missile attacks by Iran and Iraq into each other's capital cities, a cease-fire negotiated with the help of Turkey's Prime Minister Turgut Ozal takes effect.

14 Amid worsening street violence and deepening financial crisis, unpaid government workers join protests against the Panamanian regime.

16 President Reagan orders 3,200 U.S. troops into Honduras as a show of support for its government in the face of an alleged Nicaraguan invasion.

A U.S. grand jury indicts Lt. Col. Oliver North, former National Security Adviser John Poindexter, and two other key figures in the Iran-contra affair.

Three people are killed and 50 injured in a one-man attack at the Belfast funeral of three Provisional Irish Republican Army (IRA) members. The IRA members were slain March 6 by British security forces in Gibraltar.

17 Israel's Prime Minister Yitzhak Shamir ends a four-day U.S. visit, having refused to support a Middle East peace plan proposed by the Reagan administration.

20 The ruling party of El Salvador's President José Napoleón Duarte suffers defeat in legislative elections.

23 The Nicaraguan government signs a 60-day truce with contra rebels, pledging ongoing negotiations, the release of 3,300 prisoners, and freedom of speech.

28 To quell any further Palestinian protests, the Israeli army announces that it will seal off the entire West Bank and Gaza Strip for three days.

U.S. BUDGET DOLLAR

Where it comes from

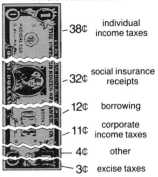

- 38¢ — individual income taxes
- 32¢ — social insurance receipts
- 12¢ — borrowing
- 11¢ — corporate income taxes
- 4¢ — other
- 3¢ — excise taxes

Where it goes

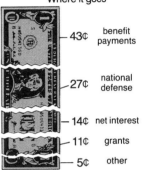

- 43¢ — benefit payments
- 27¢ — national defense
- 14¢ — net interest
- 11¢ — grants
- 5¢ — other

fiscal year 1989

By March the U.S. presidential primaries and caucuses were in full swing. On Super Tuesday, March 8, voting occurred in 20 states. For the Republican side, Vice-President George Bush, left with Mrs. Bush, won more primaries than any U.S. politician ever had on a single day. Massachusetts Gov. Michael Dukakis captured the most delegates among the Democrats.

April

1 President Reagan signs legislation approving $47.9 million in humanitarian aid for the Nicaraguan contras.

4 The Arizona Senate convicts Gov. Evan Mecham on charges of official misconduct and removes him from office.

The Kansas Jayhawks defeat the Oklahoma Sooners, 83–79, to win the National Collegiate Athletic Association (NCAA) men's college basketball championship.

5 The United States begins sending an additional 1,300 troops to Panama to bolster security at its bases there.

8 The government of Honduras declares a state of emergency in the nation's two largest towns amid anti-U.S. rioting over the arrest of an alleged major drug trafficker three days earlier.

9 During the 20-day annual session of China's National People's Congress, Li Peng is confirmed as premier.

11 At the 60th Academy Awards ceremony in Los Angeles, *The Last Emperor* wins nine Oscars, including best picture.

13 Christian Democrat Ciriaco De Mita is sworn in as prime minister of Italy, succeeding Giovanni Goria.

14 Afghanistan, Pakistan, the USSR, and the United States sign accords on the withdrawal of Soviet troops from Afghanistan and the creation of a neutral Afghan state.

In accord with an agreement mediated by the United Nations and signed in Geneva on April 14, the USSR began withdrawing its troops from Afghanistan on May 15. Soviet troops, below, *march in a homecoming parade in Termez.*

Five people are killed in a bomb explosion outside a club for U.S. Navy personnel in Naples, Italy.

16 Khalil al-Wazir, the military chief of the PLO, is shot and killed in a raid, believed to be carried out by Israeli commandos, on his home in Tunisia.

18 U.S. ships and planes sink or disable six Iranian vessels in the Persian Gulf. The battle follows the destruction of two Iranian oil platforms in retaliation for the crippling of a U.S. frigate by a mine blast April 14.

An Israeli court convicts John Demjanjuk, the alleged "Ivan the Terrible," of participating in Nazi death-camp murders during World War II. He is sentenced to death.

19 A West German court convicts Abbas Ali Hamadei, a Lebanese Shiite Muslim, for the 1987 kidnapping of two West Germans in Beirut. He is sentenced to 13 years in prison.

20 The hijackers of a Kuwaiti Airways jet—seized April 5 en route from Bangkok to Kuwait and diverted to Iran, Cyprus, and Algeria —release their 31 remaining hostages in exchange for free passage out of the country.

25 Syria's President Hafez al-Assad and PLO Chairman Yasir Arafat meet in Damascus for the first time since 1983.

26 Vice-President Bush clinches the Republican presidential nomination with a win in the Pennsylvania primary.

27 Canada's Prime Minister Brian Mulroney arrives in Washington for his fourth annual summit with President Reagan and addresses a joint session of Congress.

© Contrasto from Picture Group

Ciriaco De Mita, 60-year-old leader of Italy's Christian Democratic Party, was sworn in April 13 as premier of the nation's 48th government since World War II.

May

1 The Provisional IRA claims responsibility for the killing of three off-duty British servicemen in the Netherlands.

2 Israeli forces move into southern Lebanon en masse in search of Palestinian guerrillas.

3 Representatives of the United States, Cuba, Angola, and South Africa meet for the first time for a two-day conference in London on the issues of Angola and Namibia.

4 Three Frenchmen who had been held hostage in Lebanon for three years are set free.

5 Amid widespread labor unrest, Polish riot police raid the Lenin Steel Mill near Krakow, ending a nine-day strike.

On the New Caledonia island of Ouvea, French commandos free 23 hostages held by Melanesian separatists.

7 Pope John Paul II arrives in Montevideo, Uruguay, beginning a 12-day tour of South America.

Winning Colors, a filly, wins the Kentucky Derby.

8 France's Socialist President François Mitterrand easily wins election to a second seven-year term.

Rodrigo Borja Cevallos of the Democratic Left Party is elected president of Ecuador.

9 Wilfried Martens is sworn in as prime minister of Belgium, ending a five-month government impasse.

15 The Soviet Union officially begins withdrawing its more than 100,000 troops from Afghanistan.

18 A ten-day siege by Indian troops at the Golden Temple of Amritsar, the holiest Sikh shrine, leaves 46 dead.

22 Hungary's General Secretary Janos Kadar is ousted at a party conference and replaced by Premier Karoly Grosz.

24 President Reagan vetoes a comprehensive trade bill passed by Congress in April.

Rodrigo Borja Cevallos of the Democratic Left (ID) Party was elected president of Ecuador May 8. The 52-year-old lawyer had failed in his two previous runs for the post.

AP/Wide World

© Tass from Sovfoto

Strolling in Moscow's Red Square, General Secretary Mikhail Gorbachev introduces visiting Ronald Reagan to a young Muscovite. The president was in the USSR from May 29 to June 2.

Some 30 African heads of state open the 24th annual summit of the Organization of African Unity (OAU) in Addis Ababa, Ethiopia, marking the body's 25th anniversary.

25 Panamanian strongman Gen. Manuel Noriega rejects a U.S. proposal to give up power in exchange for the dropping of drug-trafficking indictments against him.

26 The government of Vietnam announces that it will withdraw 50,000 of its troops from Cambodia by year's end.

The Edmonton Oilers win hockey's Stanley Cup championship.

27 Syrian troops move into southern Beirut, Lebanon, to quell fighting between rival Shiite Muslim militias.

June

1 During a five-day summit in Moscow, U.S. President Reagan and Soviet leader Gorbachev exchange ratification documents for the 1987 intermediate nuclear forces (INF) treaty.

3 Denmark's Conservative Prime Minister Poul Schlüter and a new three-party government are sworn in.

6 Black workers in South Africa begin a massive three-day strike to protest a proposed new labor law.

7 Gov. Michael Dukakis (MA) clinches the Democratic presidential nomination with a win in the California primary.

8 After weeks of student protests, violence erupts between South Korean police and protesters at ten universities.

9 At a three-day summit, the Arab League vows "all possible support" for the Palestinian uprising in Israel.

14 U.S. federal agents reveal a multibillion dollar scandal involving the bribery of Defense Department aides.

White House chief of staff Howard Baker announces that he will be stepping down July 1.

Meeting in Vienna, Austria, members of OPEC decide to maintain current production quotas for six months.

18 Turkey's Prime Minister Turgut Ozal is wounded by a gunman while delivering a speech in Ankara.

19 Leaders of the seven major industrial democracies meet in Toronto, Canada, for their 14th annual economic summit.

20 Haiti's President Leslie Manigat is ousted in a military coup. Lt. Gen. Henri Namphy declares himself president.

21 The Los Angeles Lakers defeat the Detroit Pistons to win the National Basketball Association (NBA) championship.

23 The U.S. Department of Agriculture reports that 50% of the nation's agricultural counties have been designated as disaster areas because of drought conditions.

26 A new Airbus A320, considered by some the most advanced commercial jetliner on the market, crashes during a demonstration flight in France.

28 At a special Communist Party conference, Soviet General Secretary Gorbachev proposes an overhaul of the political system, incuding the strengthening of the post of president.

29 The U.S. Supreme Court upholds, 7–1, the federal law that provides for special prosecutors to investigate possible wrongdoing by high-ranking federal officials.

30 In defiance of papal orders, dissident Archbishop Marcel Lefebvre consecrates four bishops in Switzerland. The Vatican excommunicates Lefebvre and the four others.

Following reports of off-duty cocaine use by three White House guards, the White House announces random drug testing for employees of the executive office of the president.

© 1988 Touchstone Pictures and Amblin Entertainment, Inc.

"Who Framed Roger Rabbit?" was released by Disney on June 22 in time to become a summer blockbuster. The film represented a $45 million experiment in which animated characters and human actors, including Bob Hoskins, right, share top billing.

As the summer began, 50% of the agricultural counties of the United States were suffering from drought conditions following the driest spring since 1934.

AP/Wide World

July

An angry crowd of 10,000 took to the streets of Tehran, Iran, in a July 7 funeral march for the victims of Iran Air Flight 655, shot down by a U.S. warship in the Persian Gulf four days earlier. President Ali Khameini spoke at the procession, vowing revenge against the United States.

1 President Reagan signs legislation expanding the Medicare program to provide protection for the elderly and disabled against the costs of "catastrophic" illness.

3 A U.S. cruiser in the Persian Gulf shoots down an Iranian commercial airliner after mistaking it for an attack plane. All 290 persons on board the aircraft are killed.

4 Sweden's Stefan Edberg wins the men's singles tennis title at Wimbledon. West Germany's Steffi Graf took the women's crown two days earlier.

6 Up to 166 workers are feared dead in the explosion of an oil platform in the North Sea.

8 Great Britain announces the signing of an arms agreement with Saudi Arabia valued at some $12 billion.

During the 13th congress of Taiwan's ruling Nationalist Party, President Lee Teng-hui is elected chairman.

11 Three gunmen linked to a Palestinian terrorist group open fire on a Greek ferry, killing nine people and wounding 80.

Soviet General Secretary Mikhail Gorbachev begins a six-day official visit to Poland, his first since taking power.

12 President Reagan names former Gov. Richard Thornburgh of Pennsylvania to succeed Edwin Meese III as U.S. attorney general. Meese announced his resignation July 5, claiming that he was cleared of wrongdoing in an independent prosecutor's report.

13 Carlos Salinas de Gortari of the long-ruling Institutional Revolutionary Party is declared the winner of Mexico's July 6 presidential election. Opposition parties charge fraud.

15 William J. McCarthy is elected president of the Teamsters union, succeeding Jackie Presser who died July 9.

18 Iran accepts a United Nations plan to end the Persian Gulf war. Iraq demands direct talks as a precondition to truce.

21 At the Democratic National Convention in Atlanta, Gov. Michael S. Dukakis of Massachusetts accepts the party's presidential nomination. On July 12, Dukakis named Sen. Lloyd Bentsen of Texas as his vice-presidential running mate.

25 Opposing factions in the ten-year-old Cambodian war open four days of peace talks, their first, in Bogor, Indonesia.

26 Retired Gen. Sein Lwin emerges as the head of Burma's ruling party. He succeeds Ne Win, who stepped down July 23.

27 Thailand's Premier Prem Tinsulanonda declines a new term. Acting Deputy Premier Chatichai Choonhavan is named to the post.

31 Jordan's King Hussein announces that his government is surrendering all claims on the Israeli-occupied West Bank to the Palestine Liberation Organization (PLO).

August

4 A bill requiring U.S. companies to provide 60 days' notice of major layoffs or closings becomes law, after President Reagan took no action on it in the ten days allowed him.

U.S. Rep. Mario Biaggi (D-NY) and five others are convicted of racketeering in the Wedtech defense contract scandal.

5 James A. Baker III announces his resignation as U.S. secretary of the treasury, effective August 17. President Reagan names Nicholas F. Brady to the post.

7 A 22-week-long strike by 9,000 U.S. movie and television writers ends with ratification of a four-year contract.

8 After a series of U.S.-mediated peace talks, Angola, South Africa, and Cuba declare a truce in Angola and Namibia.

9 President Reagan names Lauro F. Cavazos as U.S. secretary of education, succeeding William J. Bennett, who resigned.

10 U.S. Secretary of State George Shultz concludes a nine-day, nine-nation tour of Latin America that included an assassination attempt against him in Bolivia on August 8.

17 Pakistan's President Mohammed Zia ul-Haq, U.S. Ambassador Arnold L. Raphel, and 28 others are killed in a midair plane explosion over eastern Pakistan.

Diplomats from more than 70 nations, including 30 heads of state, were among the 100,000 mourners at the August 20 funeral for Pakistan's late President Zia ul-Haq in Islamabad. President Zia was killed in a midair plane explosion August 17.

© Anis Hamdani/Gamma-Liaison

18 At the Republican National Convention in New Orleans, Vice-President George Bush and Sen. Dan Quayle (IN) accept the party's nominations for president and vice-president.

19 Burma's ruling party names Attorney General Maung Maung as the nation's new leader. He replaces Sein Lwin, who was forced to resign August 12 amid widespread public protests after less than three weeks in office.

20 Eight British soldiers are killed and 28 injured in a bus bombing by the IRA in Northern Ireland.

President Lazarus Salii of Palau, a Pacific island republic, is found shot to death at his home in the capital city of Koror.

21 Thousands of protesters march in Prague, Czechoslovakia, to mark the 20th anniversary of the Soviet-led invasion.

An earthquake along the India-Nepal border in the Himalayas leaves at least 650 dead and thousands injured.

22 The government of Burundi announces that at least 5,000 people have been killed in a week of ethnic violence.

23 President Reagan signs into law a revised comprehensive trade bill designed to open foreign markets and expand U.S. trade.

25 Peace talks between Iran and Iraq open in Geneva, five days after a UN-negotiated cease-fire took effect.

West Germany arrests a former U.S. Army sergeant and seven others on suspicion of operating a spy ring.

28 Three Italian jets collide during an air show at the U.S. Air Force base in Ramstein, West Germany, killing some 50 people and injuring 350.

31 After meeting with government officials, Lech Walesa, the leader of Poland's banned Solidarity trade union, calls on the nation's workers to end two weeks of strikes.

© Tom Lubin/Sygma

Student-led demonstrations precipitated the July 23 resignation of longtime Burmese leader Ne Win and the August 12 resignation of his successor, Sein Lwin. The unrest continued, however, as protesters demanded an end to one-party rule.

September

Sweden's Mats Wilander defeated Ivan Lendl for the men's singles title at the U.S. Open tennis championships. The win made Wilander the top-ranked men's player in the world.

AP/Wide World

3 Iraq's Foreign Minister Tariz Aziz denies widespread reports that his nation's army has used poison gas in a major drive against Kurdish rebels in northern Iraq. During recent weeks, more than 100,000 Kurds have fled across the border into Turkey.

Singapore's ruling People's Action Party of Prime Minister Lee Kuan Yew wins 80 of 81 seats in general elections for Parliament.

6 In Bangladesh, weeks of flooding reportedly have left three quarters of the nation under water, with 28 million people homeless.

7 Two Soviet cosmonauts return safely to earth after being stranded in orbit for 25 hours with a dwindling supply of air.

The U.S. Securities and Exchange Commission charges the Wall Street firm of Drexel Burnham Lambert and the head of its junk-bond department, Michael Milken, with insider trading and other violations.

11 Sweden's Mats Wilander wins the men's U.S. Open singles tennis title. The day before, West Germany's Steffi Graf took the women's crown, becoming the first player in 18 years to win the Grand Slam.

12 Hurricane Gilbert, the worst storm ever recorded in the Western Hemisphere, batters Jamaica and continues its destructive course across the Caribbean and Mexico.

17 Haiti's President Henri Namphy is ousted in a coup.

The XXIV Summer Olympic Games open in Seoul, South Korea.

18 The head of Burma's armed forces, Gen. Saw Maung, seizes power in a military coup against the month-old government of President Maung Maung.

Prime Minister Ingvar Carlsson of Sweden and his Social Democratic Party are returned to power in general elections.

19 Poland's Premier Zbigniew Messner and his 19-member cabinet announce their resignation—the first by a Polish government since World War II—amid discontent over the economy.

20 The 43rd session of the UN General Assembly opens in New York.

23 Following the expiration of Lebanese President Amin Gemayel's six-year term, Christian and Lebanese factions form rival regimes, raising fears of renewed communal violence.

29 The space shuttle *Discovery,* with five astronauts aboard, lifts off from Cape Canaveral, FL, ending a 32-month hiatus in U.S. space flight.

The peacekeeping forces of the United Nations are named the winner of the 1988 Nobel Peace Prize.

The International Monetary Fund and World Bank conclude their three-day joint meeting in West Berlin, reaffirming U.S.-backed monetary and world debt policies.

During the summer and early fall several Western states of the United States were struck by the worst forest fires in some 30 years. At Yellowstone National Park, above, fires burned within feet of the campgrounds.

October

1 In a Kremlin shake-up, General Secretary Mikhail Gorbachev assumes the Soviet presidency, which he plans to invest with broad powers. He succeeds Andrei Gromyko, who was retired.

3 Lebanese kidnappers release an Indian-born educator, Mithileshwar Singh, who had been held hostage for 20 months with three Americans.

Libya and Chad resume diplomatic relations and formally end their long border war.

5 In a national plebiscite, Chilean voters overwhelmingly reject a new term for President Augusto Pinochet Ugarte.

6 Algeria's President Chadli Benjedid declares a state of siege after two days of mass rioting by disenchanted youths.

10 Czechoslovak Premier Lubomir Strougal, an advocate of Soviet-style reforms, and his cabinet are forced to resign.

13 President Reagan signs into law the first major revision of the U.S. welfare system.

19 An emergency session of Yugoslavia's Communist Party Central Committee, called amid rising Serbian nationalism and discontent over the economy, ends after three days with no solutions.

20 The Los Angeles Dodgers complete a four-games-to-one defeat of the Oakland Athletics in the World Series.

21 Israeli warplanes strike targets in southern Lebanon in retaliation for a suicide car bombing two days earlier that killed seven Israeli soldiers.

Former Philippines President Ferdinand Marcos and his wife Imelda are indicted by a U.S. grand jury on racketeering charges.

22 The 100th U.S. Congress adjourns at 3:16 A.M. after pushing through a major antidrug bill as well as legislation on tax reform, insider trading, and other issues.

25 President Reagan signs legislation creating a cabinet-level Department of Veterans Affairs.

26 During a four-day visit to Moscow by West German Chancellor Helmut Kohl, Soviet leader Gorbachev states that "all persons whom the West considers political prisoners" will be released by year's end.

30 In the second-largest corporate merger in U.S. history, Kraft accepts a $13.1 billion takeover offer from Philip Morris.

November

4 The Soviet Union announces that it is temporarily suspending its withdrawal of troops from Afghanistan because of a worsening military situation.

Israel's Prime Minister Yitzhak Shamir (right), *whose Likud bloc won a narrow plurality in November 1 parliamentary elections, courted the nation's far-right religious parties, who made a surprisingly strong showing.*

After his victory at the polls, President-elect George Bush and his wife Barbara spent a long weekend vacationing in Florida. He did take time to consider appointments to his cabinet and presidential team.

Britain's Prime Minister Margaret Thatcher concludes a three-day visit to Poland with a journey to Gdansk to meet with Lech Walesa and other Solidarity leaders.

The U.S. Department of Labor reports an October unemployment rate of 5.2%, the nation's lowest in 14 years.

6 In a national referendum, French voters overwhelmingly approve a peace treaty for the colony of New Caledonia that could lead to independence.

8 Republican Vice-President George Herbert Walker Bush is elected the 41st president of the United States, soundly defeating Democratic Gov. Michael Dukakis of Massachusetts. The Democrats retain their majorities in both houses of Congress.

10 The U.S. Department of Energy announces the selection of Texas as the site of the planned $4.4 billion Superconducting Super Collider, or atom smasher.

11 The speaker of West Germany's parliament, Philipp Jenninger, resigns amid controversy over his speech the night before commemorating the 50th anniversary of *Kristallnacht* ("Night of Broken Glass"), the Nazi pogrom against Jews.

15 The Palestine National Council, the legislative body of the PLO, proclaims an independent Palestinian state and votes to accept UN Resolution 242, recognizing the existence of Israel.

The Soviet Union successfully launches, orbits, and lands its first space shuttle, *Buran*.

16 The opposition Pakistani People's Party, headed by Benazir Bhutto, wins that nation's first open legislative elections in more than a decade.

17 Britain's Prime Minister Margaret Thatcher concludes her last official meeting with President Reagan in Washington.

18 Beginning a three-day visit to India, Soviet leader Mikhail Gorbachev reaffirms his desire for closer bilateral relations.

21 Canada's Prime Minister Brian Mulroney and his Progressive Conservative Party are returned to power in general elections, ensuring passage of the U.S.-Canada free-trade pact.

U.S. Rep. Robert Garcia (D-NY) is indicted on bribery and extortion charges related to the Wedtech scandal.

©Lorraine Parow

On November 21, Brian Mulroney, 49, became Canada's first Conservative prime minister in the 20th century to be reelected to a second consecutive term.

23 In an unprecedented televised address, South Korea's former President Chun Doo Hwan apologizes for corruption and human-rights abuses during his eight years in power.

South Africa's President Pieter W. Botha reduces the sentences of the "Sharpeville Six," five men and a woman convicted on circumstantial evidence of involvement in a 1984 lynching, from death to prison terms of 18-25 years.

25 President Reagan vetoes a bill to extend federal lobbying restrictions to former members of Congress and their top aides and to tighten the rules for former administration officials.

26 U.S. Secretary of State George Shultz denies an entry visa to PLO chairman Yasir Arafat, scheduled to address the UN General Assembly in New York, on grounds of his "associations with terrorism."

28 Members of the Organization of the Petroleum Exporting Countries (OPEC) agree on a production quota of 18.5 million barrels per day, intended to drive the price of oil to $18 per barrel.

30 After a six-week takeover battle, the food and tobacco giant RJR Nabisco agrees to a $25.07 billion offer by the New York investment firm of Kohlberg Kravis Roberts. It is by far the largest takeover deal in U.S. corporate history.

U.S. Senate Republicans reelect Robert Dole (KS) as minority leader. The day before, Senate Democrats named George Mitchell (ME) as the new majority leader.

December

1 The Supreme Soviet (nominal parliament) of the USSR approves constitutional changes, proposed by General Secretary Gorbachev in June, that reorganize the nation's political system.

3 Israel returns four hijackers to the Soviet Union after their surrender at a Tel Aviv airfield the day before. The gunmen had commandeered a school bus in the southern USSR and had been granted a plane in exchange for the children.

4 The Argentine government announces that loyalist forces have put down a rebellion, the nation's third in 20 months, by mutinous army soldiers.

Carlos Andres Pérez of the ruling Democratic Action party is elected president of Venezuela.

6 The U.S. space shuttle *Atlantis* successfully completes a secret four-day military mission.

7 In a speech to the UN General Assembly in New York, Soviet leader Gorbachev pledges to reduce his nation's military forces by 500,000 troops by 1991. Later in the day he meets with President Reagan and President-elect Bush.

8 In their deepest ground attack in Lebanon in five years, Israeli troops raid a Palestinian guerrilla base near Beirut.

9 Japan's Finance Minister Kiichi Miyazawa resigns in an ever-widening and highly publicized stock-trading scandal.

12 A collision involving three trains during the morning rush hour in London leaves 33 persons dead and 113 injured.

14 In a major policy shift, U.S. Secretary of State George Shultz announces that the United States will begin a "substantive dialogue" with the Palestine Liberation Organization (PLO).

In protest of government economic policies, more than seven million Spanish workers stage a one-day general strike.

AP/Wide World

15 The Canadian Supreme Court strikes down a Quebec law that bars the posting of signs in any language but French.

19 Seven weeks after inconclusive parliamentary elections, Israel's two major parties, Likud and Labor, agree on a coalition government headed by Likud's Prime Minister Yitzhak Shamir.

Sri Lanka's Prime Minister Ranasinghe Premadasa of the ruling United National Party is elected president.

21 A Pan Am 747 bound from London to New York blows apart in the air and crashes in the Scottish village of Lockerbie, killing all 259 persons aboard and at least 11 on the ground.

Soviet cosmonauts Vladimir Titov and Musa Manarov return safely to earth after a record 365 days in space.

The giant Wall Street firm of Drexel Burnham Lambert agrees to plead guilty on six felony counts of federal securities law violations and to pay a $650 million fine.

22 Representatives of Angola, Cuba, and South Africa sign final accords on the independence of Namibia and the phased withdrawal of Cuban troops from Angola.

24 Japan's most sweeping tax overhaul in 40 years wins final approval in the upper house of Parliament.

26 After days of clashes with African students, thousands of Chinese march in the city of Nanjing shouting racist slogans.

28 South Korea agrees to a North Korean proposal for political and military talks to ease tension between the rival nations.

29 Amid widespread public unrest over government price increases on consumer goods, police in the Sudanese capital of Khartoum open fire on street demonstrators.

A U.S. federal commission proposes shutting down 86 military bases and partly closing five more to save $5.6 billion.

30 Yugoslavia's Prime Minister Branko Mikulic and his cabinet resign over Parliament's refusal to pass an economic law.

31 India's Rajiv Gandhi ends a three-day visit to Pakistan, the first by an Indian prime minister since 1960.

The southern Soviet republic of Armenia was left in ruins by an earthquake on December 7. At least 25,000 persons were killed and some 500,000 left homeless.

THE 1988 U.S. ELECTIONS

About the Author: Robert Shogan has been national political correspondent in the Washington Bureau of the *Los Angeles Times* since 1973. Previously he was an assistant editor of *The Wall Street Journal* and a correspondent for *Newsweek* magazine. Mr. Shogan's books include *None of the Above: Why Presidents Fail & What Can Be Done about It,* a study of the American presidency.

By Robert Shogan

For the better part of the past two decades U.S. presidential elections have seemed to be getting steadily bigger, longer, and costlier. The 1988 campaign represented not just a continuation of this trend but a magnification of it. No fewer than 13 men—seven Democrats and six Republicans—sought the nation's highest office, investing tens of millions of dollars and tens of thousands of hours. In large part the reason for this burst of activity was the constitutionally imposed two-term limit on presidents, which kept Ronald Reagan from trying to succeed himself. This was the first presidential election in which no incumbent could run since the reforms in campaign financing regulations and convention delegate selection procedures went into effect in 1972. The net result was the most wide open and sustained campaign ever seen in both parties.

The Democratic Candidates, Caucuses and Primaries, and Convention. Among the Democrats, the competition was driven by the party's almost desperate desire to regain the White House, after losing four of the last five elections. And each of the candidates offered his own formula for accomplishing this.

Former Arizona Gov. Bruce Babbitt boasted of his ties to the West, where recent Democratic presidential standard-bearers had been unable to penetrate. Massachusetts Gov. Michael S. Dukakis claimed the governing skills gained in his state house, particularly citing Massachusetts' surging economy. Missouri Congressman Richard Gephardt's stock in political trade was trade, more particularly the huge deficit in U.S. exports which he pledged to adjust by forcing other nations to treat American products more fairly. Tennessee Sen. Albert Gore, who turned 40 on March 31, 1988, offered youth and, even more important, an appeal to his native South. Former Colorado Sen. Gary Hart rested his case on new ideas, much as he had done in 1984, but his candidacy had been tarnished badly in 1987 by disclosure of a weekend dalliance with a Miami model. Black leader Jesse Jackson was by far the most compelling orator of the group but he had to contend with voter bias against his race and opposition to his liberal views. Illinois Sen. Paul Simon presented himself as a milder liberal than Reverend Jackson and placed great stress on his lack of pretention.

With none of these candidates strong enough to dominate the field the early caucuses and primary contests were indecisive. Gephardt, who had made the trade issue the foundation

George Herbert Walker Bush, 64, the Republican vice-president of the United States since 1981, was chosen as the nation's 41st chief executive on Nov. 8, 1988.

© Richard Sobol/1987

Jockeying for the Democratic nomination began early, with seven candidates (official or undeclared) in the running by late summer 1987. Left to right: Sen. Albert Gore, Jr. (TN); Rep. Richard A. Gephardt (MO); Gov. Michael S. Dukakis (MA); Sen. Joseph Biden, Jr. (DE)—who soon dropped out; the Rev. Jesse Jackson; former Gov. Bruce E. Babbitt (AZ); and Sen. Paul Simon (IL). Former Sen. Gary Hart (CO), who already had withdrawn, reentered the race in December.

for a strong populist appeal for economic change, finished first in the Iowa caucuses February 8 with 31% of the vote. But his 4% margin of victory over runner-up Simon was not great enough to give him momentum. Dukakis won the first primary, in New Hampshire, February 16, next door to his own state, with 36% of the vote, while Gephardt finished second with 20%. Babbitt, who had finished fifth in Iowa, was eliminated after running sixth in New Hampshire. Simon finished third in New Hampshire and Hart seventh and though both stayed in the race for a while, their candidacies no longer were taken seriously.

More important than Dukakis' victory in New Hampshire, which had been expected, was the lead he was building up in fund-raising. Aided by his position as governor of a thriving industrial state, and his support from the affluent Greek-American community, Dukakis was raising money at a rate more than twice as fast as any of his competitors. This was of critical importance in the so-called Super Tuesday mega-primary, involving contests in 20 states, 14 of them in the South or in border regions.

The Democratic nominee, Massachusetts Gov. Michael Dukakis, was accused by the Bush campaign—and, inevitably, by political cartoonists—of being weak on national defense.

© Brookins/"Richmond Times-Dispatch"

Super Tuesday had been designed by Southern Democratic politicians hoping to use the weight of Southern delegates to push the party toward nominating a conservative, preferably one from the South. But as it turned out, Dukakis, a liberal from New England, was the major beneficiary of the sprawling contest because his financial resources permitted him to invest heavily in television advertising. Dukakis finished first in the biggest Southern states, Florida and Texas, as well as in his home state which also held its primary that day, and in neighboring Rhode Island, and won more delegates than anyone else. Gore and Jackson also did well. The only white Southerner competing, Gore carried six states including his own Tennessee. Jackson, appealing mainly to the big black Democratic vote in the South, carried five states. But Gephardt, who had been regarded as the early front-runner after his Iowa victory, carried only his own state of Missouri. His populist message was smothered by the televised attacks of Dukakis and Gore, who accused him of "flip-flopping" on issue positions. Gephardt dropped out of the race after finishing third in the Michigan caucuses on March 26.

The Super Tuesday results made Dukakis the clear front-runner with Gore and Jackson as his main challengers. But Gore, who had concentrated his efforts in the South, was little known outside his home region. As for Jackson, though he was able to get more white votes than he had attracted in 1984, he had difficulty gaining sufficient white support to compete on equal terms against Dukakis. The high-water mark for Jackson's candidacy was the Michigan caucuses in which he defeated Dukakis and raised the hopes of his supporters and fears of his opponents that he might overcome the obstacle of race and win the nomination. But Dukakis rallied and soundly defeated Jackson in the Wisconsin primary April 5, with Gore finishing third. The New York primary two weeks later was fought bitterly, with New York City Mayor Ed Koch suggesting that members of the city's big Jewish population would "have to be crazy" to vote for Jackson because of the candidate's past anti-Semitic remarks and associations.

AP/Wide World

© Trippett/Sipa Press

The Dukakis campaign was managed by veteran political organizer John Sasso and Harvard law professor Susan Estrich, above. The Rev. Jesse Jackson, left, representing a key party constituency, finished second to Dukakis in delegate votes and had a large say in the platform.

To balance the ticket, both politically and geographically, Dukakis chose conservative Sen. Lloyd M. Bentsen, Jr. (center) of Texas as his running mate. The 40th Democratic National Convention, held July 18–21 in Atlanta, ended on a note of unity and optimism. Dukakis-Bentsen had a wide lead in the polls against the GOP opposition.

After Dukakis won the New York primary with 51% of the vote to 37% for Jackson, Gore, who finished third with only 10% of the vote, dropped out of the race. Dukakis' nomination now was assured though Jackson continued to compete against him for the rest of the campaign until the California and New Jersey primaries on June 7 which Dukakis won, gaining enough delegates to clinch a mathematical majority at the convention. With the nomination assured, Dukakis acted to strengthen his chances for November. On July 12, a week before the Democratic Convention opened in Atlanta, the nominee-to-be announced that he wanted Texas. Sen. Lloyd Bentsen to be his running mate. As a Southern conservative, Bentsen was expected to help the Massachusetts governor's bid for support in the South generally and particularly in Texas, the state Bush claimed as his home and without whose votes no Democrat had won the White House in the 20th century.

At the convention itself, unity and victory were the watchwords. Dukakis agreed to make concessions to Jesse Jackson about party rules and his role in the fall campaign to gain his support. In his acceptance speech, seeking to avoid the sort of controversy which had hurt Democratic standard-bearers in the past, Dukakis declared that the campaign was about "competence," not "ideology." Dukakis' speech was judged a success and the candidate left Atlanta with a significant lead in the polls over the GOP opposition.

". . . this election is not about ideology. It's about competence."

**Michael S. Dukakis
Democratic Convention**

The Republican Candidates, Caucuses and Primaries, and Convention. But the Republicans had just begun to fight after sorting out the results of their nominating contest. Just as the Democratic preconvention battle had been dominated by the search for the leader best equipped to break the Republican hold on the White House established under President Reagan, Republicans focused on choosing the nominee best qualified

to maintain Reagan's base of support. Though Reagan's prestige had been shaken by the Iran-contra scandal in 1987, his popularity among Republican voters remained high. Thus, with the exception of former Secretary of State Alexander Haig, who at times seemed relatively critical of Reagan's policies and who never received significant support, the Republican contenders each stressed aspects of their background that would help them appeal to Reagan voters.

Vice-President George Bush could claim closer identification with the Reagan administration than any of his rivals, and no one could question his unstinting loyalty to the president. Supporters of Kansas Sen. Robert Dole contended that through his role as Senate Republican leader, Dole had done more to implement the Reagan program than anyone except the president himself. As a former governor of Delaware, Pierre duPont was the only one of the Republicans who had experience as an executive, which was Reagan's initial background in politics. Backers of New York Rep. Jack Kemp argued that his early advocacy of the dramatic tax cuts underlying supply-side economics made him the most credible proponent for extending Reagan's policies of economic growth. And finally there was television evangelist Pat Robertson, who by plunging into politics as an outsider like Reagan himself, was well positioned to echo Reagan's anti-Washington themes.

Bush was unfortunate in that the first significant contest in the race, the Iowa caucuses, took place in a state where President Reagan was relatively unpopular among Republicans, who disliked his farm policies. This resentment carried over to Bush, and helped bring about his third-place finish in the caucuses with only 19% of the vote. Dole, who benefited from his roots in neighboring Kansas, came in first with 37% while Robertson, aided by a strong turnout of religious conservatives, finished second with 25%. Kemp was fourth, duPont fifth, and Haig sixth.

On the Republican side, Vice-President Bush easily locked up the nomination, far outpolling his opponents, left to right: the Rev. Pat Robertson; Sen. Robert Dole (KS); Rep. Jack R. Kemp (NY); and Alexander M. Haig, Jr., in the primaries and caucuses. Former Delaware Gov. Pierre duPont IV also made a brief try for the GOP nod.

The 34th Republican National Convention, held August 15–18 in New Orleans, marked the full "coming out" of George Bush as a political figure in his own right. After a sentimental farewell by President Reagan on opening night, the new standard-bearer roused the GOP faithful.

"This election isn't only about competence. . . . The truth is, this election is about the beliefs we share, the values that we honor, and the principles that we hold dear."

**George Bush
Republican Convention**

In the next big contest, the New Hampshire primary, the political environment was markedly different. Bush, helped by Reagan's popularity in the Granite State and the active support of its governor, John Sununu, came in first with 38% to 28% for Dole who finished second. Dole further damaged himself after the polls closed when he accused Bush of lying about his record in a nationally televised interview. Kemp's third-place finish allowed him to stay in the race but duPont, who finished fourth, dropped out, joining Haig who had quit even before the votes were cast. Robertson, who finished fifth in New Hampshire, promised to redeem himself with a victory in the South Carolina primary March 5, on the eve of the Super Tuesday contests in the South. But he succeeded only in building up the importance of the contest for Bush who won easily there with 48% of the vote. Kemp, after finishing fourth, dropped out of the race.

With the momentum from South Carolina, Bush swept the Super Tuesday contests, winning all 16 of the Republican contests that day. Though Robertson and Dole stayed in the race until after the Illinois primary, the contest was in reality over. And Bush clinched the nomination with a win in the Pennsylvania primary April 26.

The Issues and the Campaign. Vice-President Bush paid a price for his early success. With the Republican campaign over he dropped out of the news while Democrat Dukakis continued to win headlines, and approval, for his almost weekly victories in Democratic delegate contests over the controversial Jesse Jackson. This imbalance contributed to Dukakis' early lead in the polls over Bush, whose candidacy some observers now regarded as almost hopeless. But Bush and his advisers had a plan to counter Dukakis' early surge

based on the overriding reality governing the 1988 contest for the presidency. With the nation at peace and the economy apparently having withstood the shock of the October 1987 stock-market crash, there was no critical issue. The election thus boiled down to a fundamental choice between continuity and change. Against this backdrop Bush and his advisers set out to depict Dukakis as a liberal so far removed from what Bush called the American "mainstream" that the idea of change would be too risky for voters to accept.

Taking advantage of the fact that Dukakis was as yet little known on the national scene, and that he was reluctant to define himself ideologically, the Bush campaign set out to do that defining job for him, in terms that suited Bush's political interests. Even before the Republican convention opened in New Orleans on August 15, Bush and his surrogates launched an unrelenting assault seeking to depict the Democratic standard-bearer as far out in left field. To support this indictment the Republicans cited a variety of evidence drawn from Dukakis' nearly ten years as governor of Massachusetts. He was condemned for vetoing a law that would have required a recitation of the pledge of allegiance in the state's schools and for defending the state's prisoner furlough law that permitted Willie Horton, a convicted murderer, to escape while on furlough and attack brutally a Maryland couple. Bush also accused Dukakis of spending too freely and taxing too heavily as governor and of inexperience in foreign affairs and defense policy. In addition to overseeing the attack on Dukakis, Bush helped himself at the GOP convention with a strong acceptance speech in which he for the first time established himself as a political figure in his own right and promised to make the United States "a kinder, and gentler, nation."

AP/Wide World

James A. Baker III resigned as President Reagan's treasury secretary in August to manage the Bush campaign. After the election, Bush named him secretary of state in the new cabinet.

The one sour note at the convention was sounded over Bush's choice of Indiana Sen. Dan Quayle as his running mate. The 41-year-old Quayle's youth and inexperience made it hard even for some Republicans to understand this decision. And allegations that Quayle had used family influence to get into the National Guard and thus avoid the possibility of serving in Vietnam aroused concern that he would be a serious political liability. But even the widely shared misgivings about Quayle's qualifications failed to offset the damage Bush was able to do to Dukakis by his unrelenting attacks on the Democratic standard-bearer.

The Bush offensive compounded the difficulties facing the Dukakis campaign. The Democratic candidate's basic difficulty was his inability to get across a strong message to the voters—a compelling reason why he should be elected president. Dukakis and some of his advisers seemed to believe, as he had suggested in his acceptance speech, that competence, his ability to manage the nation's affairs, was a sufficient reason. But others argued that in time of peace and prosperity the voters needed a more powerful motive to switch parties and urged that Dukakis appeal to the middle-class concerns about the future by offering a brand of economic populism. Not until the last few weeks of the campaign did Dukakis decide to pursue consistently populist themes. Meanwhile,

© Dennis Brack/Black Star

Bush's selection of a running mate—41-year-old conservative Sen. J. Danforth Quayle of Indiana—raised some eyebrows at the convention. Bush introduced him as a "dynamic young leader," but the choice became a major campaign issue.

© Don Wright/"The Miami News"

Never was the "Pledge of Allegiance" more in the news than during the 1988 campaign. The Bush team repeatedly condemned Governor Dukakis for vetoing a bill that would have required recitation of the pledge in Massachusetts' schools.

ambivalent about his own message, the candidate was slow and ineffective in responding to Bush's attacks on him, allowing Bush to define Dukakis and the agenda of the campaign.

In these circumstances the Democrats pinned their hopes of reversing the Republican tide on the three scheduled televised debates—two between the presidential candidates and the third between their running mates. In the first debate, September 25, at Winston-Salem, NC, Dukakis gave a good account of himself, particularly when he accused Bush of questioning his patriotism by raising the pledge of allegiance issue. "I resent it," Dukakis declared. "I'm in public service today because I love this country." Polls showed that most viewers believed Dukakis had won, but his victory was not decisive enough to help him make major inroads in Bush's lead.

The debate between the vice-presidential candidates on October 5 in Omaha, NE, was in some ways the most emotional and dramatic because the questions from the panel of reporters seemed to reflect serious doubts about Quayle's credentials. At one point the hard-pressed Quayle sought to liken his experience in Congress to that of John Kennedy's, who like Quayle served in the House and Senate before seeking the White House. Bentsen responded with probably the most-quoted remark of the entire campaign: "Senator, I served with Jack Kennedy," Bentsen told Quayle. "I knew Jack Kennedy. Jack Kennedy was a friend of mine. Senator, you're no Jack Kennedy."

The debate was clearly a setback for Quayle but it had little direct effect on Bush's own candidacy. This served to increase the importance for Dukakis of his final debate with Bush on October 13 in Los Angeles. But as it later was revealed, Dukakis fell ill on that day and his performance against Bush was listless and stiff. Many felt that he lost the debate in answering the first question about how he would react if his wife, Kitty, were "raped and murdered." Dukakis offered a mechanical defense of his opposition to capital punishment, showing little passion either for the welfare of his wife or the principle he professed to believe in.

(Continued on page 35.)

The candidates held two face-to-face televised debates, on September 25 and October 13. By most accounts, Dukakis won the first and Bush the second.

AP/Wide World

Voter Turnout

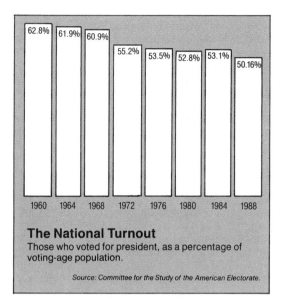

The National Turnout
Those who voted for president, as a percentage of voting-age population.

Source: Committee for the Study of the American Electorate.

1960 — 62.8%
1964 — 61.9%
1968 — 60.9%
1972 — 55.2%
1976 — 53.5%
1980 — 52.8%
1984 — 53.1%
1988 — 50.16%

© Bob Mahoney/Picture Group

In 1988 the United States held a presidential election and only half the eligible voters showed up at the polls on November 8. By official count 91,609,655 Americans cast their ballots for president. That figure constituted 50.16% of the eligible electorate, the lowest voter turnout since 1924. Outside of the states of the old Confederacy, the turnout was the lowest since 1824.

About 1 million fewer voters cast their ballots for president in 1988 than did in 1984, despite an increase of 8 million in the number of Americans eligible. It was the first time such a decrease was recorded since 1944 when millions of Americans were abroad and fighting a war and only the second time this trend has occurred in the 20th century. George Bush's 26.6% share of the eligible was the lowest percentage for an elected president in an essentially two-candidate race in the 20th century.

The turnout decline of 2.95 percentage points from 1984's 53.11% of eligible vote represents a resumption of the nearly three-decades-long decline in voter turnout, interrupted only by a small (0.5% point) rise in 1984 due to the massive voter registration campaigns of that year. Turnout has declined since 1960 by 12.6 percentage points or more than 20% of the electorate. Similar declines have occurred during midterm elections. From 1984 to 1988 more than 20 million former voters dropped out of the political process. If one counts both its presidential and midterm elec-

tions, turnout in the United States is now the lowest of any democracy in the world. (Switzerland had a 48% turnout for its most recent presidential election. But Switzerland decides most of its major policy issues by referendum and conducts most of its important administrative business on the canton or local level.)

A Dual Problem. The evidence suggests that what is becoming the United States' unique turnout problem is, in fact, two distinct and separate problems, each with its own demographic profile: 1. The problem of low voter turnout or why the United States, even when it achieved its highest level of voter participation since women were enfranchised in 1920 (62.8% in 1960), still had a lower rate of voter participation than most other democracies; and 2. The problem of declining voter participation or why, since 1960, when many registration barriers have been removed and the major demographic factors which are supposed to affect turnout—declining personal mobility, increased age, and greater education—all would have argued for higher turnout, turnout had declined by 20%.

"NEXT TIME I WANT TO VOTE **FOR** SOMEONE"

© 1988 by Herblock in "The Washington Post"

The failure of the presidential candidates to discuss the issues and define their agendas was cited as a reason for the low voter turnout on Nov. 8, 1988—only 50.16%.

The demography of the nonvoter in 1960 was almost exclusively poorer, more minority, younger, more unemployed, more urban and rural underclass, and more southern than the nation of voters. Since 1960 the demography of the nonvoter involves every class and income level with the exception of blacks who, until 1988, were increasing their rate of participation thanks to their enfranchisement in the South in the mid-1960s, and people aged 55-70 who have maintained a constant high level of voting.

Causes of Decline. Research indicates that the causes of *low* voter turnout in 1960 lay in two clusters: 1. A lack of class politics—the poor in the United States lack the class consciousness of the poor in other societies; the two major parties are heterogenous and thus do not reflect clear class interests. As a result of these factors and the complex nature of the American government, citizens do not find their vote as instrumental in achieving policy results aimed at their needs and desires as citizens do in countries with ideological, homogeneous parties, and parliamentary systems. 2.

Structural barriers—including at that time the disenfranchisement of blacks and the complex registration system that makes voting in the United States, unlike most other democracies, a two-step act. In the United States one must both register and vote. In almost every other democracy, the state conducts registration; all the individual has to do is vote.

Because the character of American parties and the poor has not changed and because barriers to black participation have been eliminated and registration requirements have been eased substantially, the cause of today's declining voter turnout lies neither in law nor in the general political structure of American society. Rather, research suggests it lies with an increasing feeling on the part of the individual citizen that one vote does not make any difference, a decline in identification with and partisanship for either of the major political parties, and a decline in the use of newspapers as the primary source of information about politics and public affairs. Research also indicates that there are two large groups of nonvoters—those of middle age who are alienated and angry about the conduct, course, and coverage of American politics and younger voters who are growing increasingly indifferent to politics.

Some of the problems were evident in the 1988 presidential campaign in which the candidates avoided commitment to discussion of major issues, conducted their campaigns largely through seven-second sound bites and demagogic commercials, and seemed unable to transcend programmed speeches. In addition the political parties offered no relevant issues or themes for debate in 1988. Some reasons for the apathy may lie deeper—in the political system itself; in inadequate family, public, and civic education; in less societal and more self-seeking values; in the rise of television; in the weakening of the American political parties; in a decline in the perceived honesty of government members and in the effectiveness of government; and in a lack of a shared national direction.

But for whatever reason, the trend toward decline continues and unless it is addressed and arrested, elected leaders will continue to come to office with an increasingly minority mandate and increasingly tenuous hold on the right to govern.

CURTIS B. GANS

Editor's Note: Curtis B. Gans is director of the Committee for the Study of the American Electorate, a nonpartisan, nonprofit organization researching the causes and potential cures of low and declining voter turnout in the United States.

© Halstead/Gamma-Liaison

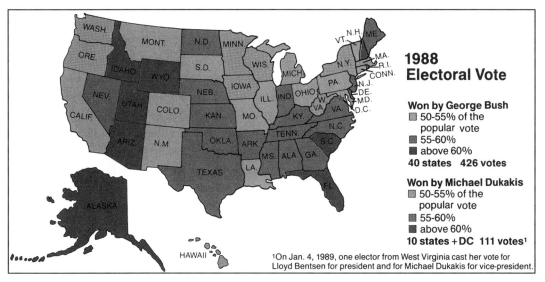

1988 Electoral Vote

Won by George Bush
- ▨ 50-55% of the popular vote
- ▩ 55-60%
- ■ above 60%

40 states 426 votes

Won by Michael Dukakis
- ▨ 50-55% of the popular vote
- ▩ 55-60%
- ■ above 60%

10 states + DC 111 votes[1]

[1]On Jan. 4, 1989, one elector from West Virginia cast her vote for Lloyd Bentsen for president and for Michael Dukakis for vice-president.

The Results. Though Dukakis and Bush both campaigned vigorously for the next three weeks until Election Day, November 8, a comparison of poll results right after the debate with the election returns suggests that few voters changed their minds during this closing interval. In becoming the 41st president of the United States, Vice-President Bush won 54% of the popular vote and carried 40 states with 426 electoral votes. He defeated Governor Dukakis in every quadrant of the country and carried eight of the ten largest states—losing only New York, a traditional Democratic stronghold, and Dukakis' home state of Massachusetts.

In defeat Dukakis could console himself with the fact that the ten states he carried were nine more than Democrat Walter Mondale won in 1984. In addition to New York and Massachusetts, Dukakis won Hawaii, Washington, and Oregon in the West; Minnesota, Wisconsin, and Iowa in the Midwest;

The president-elect and first-lady-to-be, joined by some of their grandchildren, wave to friends and supporters on election night in Houston.

Rhode Island, West Virginia, and the District of Columbia. He won no states in the South or the Rocky Mountain West.

Widespread criticism of the presidential campaign as negative and superficial was supported by turnout figures which indicated that 50% or fewer of eligible voters cast ballots, breaking a 40-year mark for low turnout (*see* page 33).

George Bush was the first vice-president to gain the White House since Martin Van Buren in 1836. But he was also the first new president since John Kennedy in 1960 not to bring in added strength for his party in the Congress. The Republicans lost three seats in the House, where Democrats emerged with a 260 to 175 majority and one seat in the Senate which the Democrats will control by a 55 to 45 margin. Among the Democratic newcomers to the Senate were three former governors —Nebraska's Robert Kerry, who defeated Republican incumbent David Karnes; Virginia's Charles Robb, who replaced retiring Republican Paul S. Trible, Jr., and Nevada's Richard Bryan who defeated Republican incumbent Chic Hecht. Other

© Lester Sloan-"Newsweek"/Woodfin Camp & Assoc.

Californians did vote "yes" on reducing insurance rates.

STATE REFERENDUMS: "Yes" or "No"

Voters entering the polling booth on November 8 had to know more than which candidate to vote for or which party they preferred. With 230 referendums and initiatives on the ballot in 41 states, they also had to make "yes" or "no" decisions on social and economic issues ranging from AIDS and abortion to gun control, nuclear energy, state lotteries, taxes.

In California—which led the way with 29 different propositions—voters called for a 20% rollback in automobile and home-insurance rates. As the State Supreme Court took up the matter, consumer groups and insurance companies across the United States waited to see if the initiative might trigger the kind of nationwide movement that followed the tax-slashing Proposition 13 ten years earlier.

The taxpayers revolt itself seemed to be losing steam in 1988, as voters in Colorado, South Dakota, and Utah turned down proposals to limit spending or roll back taxes. Even in California, voters approved a measure to ease spending limits on schools.

Among other notable issues dealt with by voter initiatives around the country were:

• Abortion: Arkansas, Colorado, and Florida voted for prohibitions on state-financed abortions; Arkansas voters also adopted a measure protecting life from the time of conception.

• Nuclear Energy: Voters in Massachusetts rejected a proposal to close the two nuclear power plants in the states; voters in Nebraska defeated a proposal to withdraw from an agreement with other states to place a low-level radioactive waste site in Nebraska.

• Language: Arizona, Colorado, and Florida, all states with large Hispanic populations, adopted measures making English the state's official language.

• Gun Control: Voters in Maryland upheld a state law banning cheap handguns.

• AIDS: Californians rejected a measure requiring doctors to report to the state anyone testing positive for the AIDS virus.

• Lotteries: State lotteries were approved by voters in Idaho, Indiana, Kentucky, and Minnesota.

Democrat Charles Robb, former governor of Virginia and son-in-law of the late President Lyndon Johnson, won election to the U.S. Senate and was seen as a rising young star in the party.

Democratic new faces were Joseph Lieberman in Connecticut, who defeated Republican incumbent Lowell Weicker, and Wisconsin businessman Herbert Kohl, who replaced retiring Democrat William Proxmire.

The election also brought five new Republicans to the Senate. In Florida, Congressman Connie Mack narrowly defeated Rep. Buddy MacKay to succeed retiring Sen. Lawton Chiles (D); Congressman Trent Lott of Mississippi was selected to fill the seat held by retiring Democrat John Stennis; Conrad Burns defeated Montana's Sen. John Melcher; Vermont Congressman James Jeffords was elected to replace retiring Republican Sen. Robert Stafford; and in Washington, Slade Gorton, who lost a close Senate reelection campaign in 1986, was returned to his former position.

In the gubernatorial races, the Democrats gained seats in Indiana and West Virginia from the Republicans, while the GOP took one previously Democratic governorship from the Democrats, in Montana. This left the Democrats with 28 of the nation's 50 governorships, a net gain of one.

Immediately after the votes were counted and the long and costly run for the White House came to an end, George Bush began the task of assembling a new administration. His first appointment was former Treasury Secretary James A. Baker III, a close friend who had served as his campaign manager, as secretary of state. On the question of whether or not the voters had given him a mandate, the president-elect said that he felt the "vote was convincing enough . . . that it gives a certain confidence to the executive branch of the government that [he] hope[s] will carry over and influence the Congress," with whom he is pledged to work.

See also BIOGRAPHY section for profiles of the candidates; UNITED STATES—*Domestic Affairs.*

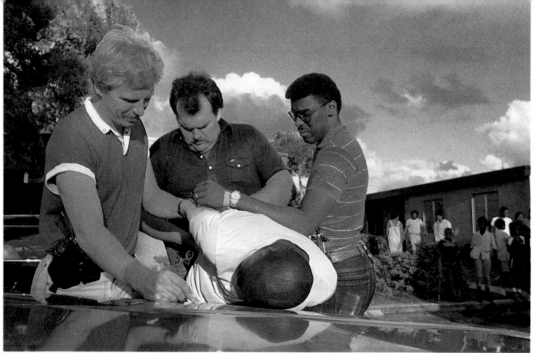

© Steve Starr/Picture Group, Inc.

WAR ON DRUGS

by Marc Leepson

About the Author. Marc Leepson, a free-lance writer in Middleburg, VA, is a regular contributor to Congressional Quarterly's *Editorial Research Reports*. The author of the book *Executive Fitness,* which was published by McGraw-Hill in 1982, Mr. Leepson has written for a variety of newspapers and magazines, including *The New York Times, The Washington Post, The Baltimore Sun,* and *The Christian Science Monitor*.

President Ronald Reagan took office in 1981 promising to plunge the United States into an international war against illegal drugs. The "war" received strong support from Congress and the American public and had a few victories. But the fight against the importation, sale, and use of heroin, marijuana, and cocaine went sour. Billion-dollar drug cartels based in Latin America were flooding the country with illegal drugs, and drug-related violence was at an all-time high.

Although the administration characterized the fight against drugs in positive terms, there was near universal agreement that the war was less than successful. "We're winning some battles, but it's difficult for me to say we're winning the war, especially when we consider (the extent of) drug dealing and use in our streets and our homes," said Health and Human Services Secretary Otis R. Bowen. "I don't know how I can honestly be very optimistic about the war on drugs."

The lack of optimism came at a time when the government was spending billions—more than $21 billion since 1981, according to the Office of Management and Budget—to combat drugs, when U.S. troops were dispatched to South America to cooperate with local officials to cut off supplies, and when unprecedented amounts of cocaine and marijuana were being seized by law-enforcement officials. Even though those pro-

grams seemed to be putting barely a dent in the illicit-drug traffic, the administration vowed to continue the war. In May 1988, for example, President Reagan—characterizing the drug problem as "a national emergency"—called for the death penalty for murder cases involving narcotics traffickers. William von Raab, the U.S. Customs commissioner and a strong proponent of stepping up the war, suggested that the United States go "on a war footing" to stop the importation of illegal drugs and adopt a series of stronger drug-fighting procedures, including setting up courts to specialize only in drug cases.

Photo page 38: *Members of a special investigation unit of the Fort Lauderdale (FL) police department arrest a suspected drug dealer. As the war on drugs escalated, several international drug kingpins were apprehended.*

Positive News: Record Drug Seizures and Declining Use.

There were some victories in the war against drugs during 1988. As had been the case in recent years, law-enforcement agencies confiscated unprecedented amounts of illegal drugs and arrested several international drug kingpins. In April, for example, federal and local officials announced a series of arrests in Hong Kong, Newark, NJ, and San Francisco, CA, of those involved in a major heroin-smuggling Asian cartel. The next month federal agents in San Francisco made the largest-ever seizure of marijuana and its concentrated derivative, hashish, when they confiscated some 30 tons of Southwest Asian hashish and 15 tons of Southeast Asian marijuana hidden beneath the deck of a barge under the Golden Gate Bridge. That month also saw the conviction in Jacksonville, FL, of Carlos Lehder Rivas, reputedly the leader of a Colombian organized crime group responsible for shipping most of the cocaine into the United States. After a seven-month trial, Rivas and an American codefendant, Jack Carlton Reed, were found guilty of conspiring to smuggle 3.3 tons of cocaine into the United States between 1978 and 1980.

The other main piece of positive news in the war on drugs involved drug consumption. National surveys released in 1988 indicated that, in general, drug use among Americans declined in 1987, the last year for which complete statistics were available. The annual survey of high-school seniors conducted for the federal government by the University of Michigan's Institute for Social Research is one example. The 1988 study found that 10.3% of the seniors interviewed reported using cocaine at least once during the preceding 12 months. That marked the end of a ten-year upward trend, which had peaked in 1986 when 12.7% of the seniors said they had used the drug during the previous year. As for marijuana, 36.3% of the seniors reported using the drug once during the previous 12 months—a 12-year low.

Other surveys, however, indicated a continued strong demand for cocaine, especially among the poor and the young who typically use a relatively inexpensive smokable form of the drug, known as crack. And even though marijuana use may be down, illicit production of marijuana in the United States remained a multibillion-dollar business. According to the U.S. Drug Enforcement Administration (DEA), there were as many as 150,000 commercial marijuana growers in the United States in 1987 and illegal marijuana crops added up to some 7.7 million lbs (3.5 million kg), worth about $10 billion.

© J. Sloan/Gamma-Liaison

While in the White House, Nancy Reagan staged her own campaign against drugs. The first lady encouraged Americans, especially schoolchildren, to "just say no" to drugs.

© Steve Starr/Picture Group, Inc.

The War on Drugs: A Customs official with help from her dog, above, confiscates 11 lbs (5 kg) of coke at a major entry point into the United States; a cocaine lab in the jungles of Peru, center, is discovered, inspected, and destroyed; a member of the Miami Vice Task Force, right, seizes a large quantity of marijuana at dockside. The U.S. Customs Service, part of the Treasury Department, "cooperates with other federal agencies and foreign governments in suppressing the traffic in illegal narcotics."

Internationally, the production of coca, marijuana, and opium-poppy crops grew substantially in 1987 in most drug-producing countries, according to a report released in March 1988 by the U.S. State Department. "Drug production and trafficking unfortunately remain big business, and drug-abuse levels all over the world continue to rise," the report noted. The report listed growth of as much as 10% in opium production in Afghanistan, Burma, Laos, Thailand, and Mexico and similar rises in coca-leaf production in Bolivia, Colombia, and Peru, and in marijuana production in Mexico and Colombia. There were reductions of coca production only in Ecuador and of marijuana in Jamaica and Belize.

The Social Cost. Drug use may be slowing down, but it remains a significant social problem in virtually all of the large U.S. cities. The main culprit appears to be crack, which has replaced heroin as the most abused drug among poor and working-class families. "The impact of crack is like a nuclear explosion on a family," said Kevin McEneanery, the director of clinical services at Phoenix House, the large New York City drug-treatment center. McEneanery and others were alarmed at the devastating effects of crack addiction not only among men, but also among increasing numbers of young women. "The 20-year-old woman with two children is a much different victim than the 17-year-old male," McEneanery said.

Law-enforcement officials believe that the crack market in the United States is controlled to a large extent by Jamaican drug gangs, many of whom are armed with automatic weapons and hand grenades. There are about 40 such gangs with 10,000 members in the country, according to Stephen Higgins, direc-

© Greg Smith/Picture Group, Inc.

© P. Chauvel/Sygma

tor of the U.S. Treasury Department's Bureau of Alcohol, Tobacco and Firearms. The gangs have been responsible for more than 1,000 drug-related killings nationwide.

A drug-related crime wave hit many of the big U.S. cities in 1988. In Washington, DC, for example, there were nearly twice as many homicides as in the previous year. About three fourths of the murders in Washington, police officials believed, were related to cocaine and crack trafficking. A similar rise in drug-related violence perpetrated for the most part by young drug gangs trafficking in crack hit throughout New York City's lower income areas, particularly in upper Manhattan. "They have decided they cannot run drug businesses without killing," said William K. Hoyt, Jr., an assistant district attorney who heads the city's Homicide Unit. "There have always been killings in the drug business, but these gangs believe that if they can intimidate everybody they can operate openly and flourish."

A similar situation existed in Oakland, CA, where police reckoned that drugs, primarily crack, are sold openly on more than 100 street corners. The hundreds of drug dealers in Oakland, many of whom are armed with machine guns, police believe, were responsible primarily for a 100% increase in the number of murders in the city in 1987–88.

The social problems of drugs are not confined to the inner cities. Experts say that unprecedented amounts of drugs are being bought and sold in suburban areas across the United States. They point to the fact that arrests for drug trafficking and admissions to drug-treatment programs in suburban areas increased rapidly in the last few years. In Prince William County, VA, which is 25 mi (40 km) southwest of Washington,

"There is an urgent need for improved international cooperation . . . to counter all facets of the illicit drug problem, in particular production, trafficking, and financing of the drug trade."

Toronto Economic Summit: Political Declaration June 20, 1988

DC, for example, drug arrests doubled in 1987 compared with the year before, and in 1988 were up nearly 75%. "If we took the whole police force and assigned them to get rid of the drug problem, I don't know whether we could do it," said Sgt. Ron Sullins, the county police department's vice and narcotics supervisor.

Stepping Up the War. The seeming intractability of the drug problem comes despite stepped-up efforts on the part of the federal government both in the United States and overseas to try to win the war against illegal drugs. Agents of the Drug Enforcement Administration, for example, worked with authorities in Bolivia to destroy hundreds of coca-leaf processing laboratories. In the United States the Department of Justice declared war on the domestic marijuana crop in July by unveiling "Operation Stop Crop," which included using National Guard troops to eradicate large-scale marijuana operations.

The federal government also inaugurated a "zero tolerance" program in 1988, in which agents seized millions of dollars in assets of those arrested for drug trafficking and possession. In Detroit, for example, U.S. Customs Agency officials seized 136 vehicles and arrested 82 persons who had tried to bring marijuana or hashish into the United States from Canada. The U.S. Coast Guard was ordered to confiscate all boats found to contain any amount of illegal drugs. In May the Coast Guard impounded a $2.5 million yacht after finding one tenth

Crack, below left, is a mixture of cocaine powder and baking soda. Known as the drug of the 1980s, crack is considered a major problem, especially among the poor and the young, in some 20 U.S. cities. Marijuana, below right, is a psychoactive drug consisting of the dried leaves and flowers of the cannabis plant. Although marijuana use seems to be down in the United States, the illegal marijuana crop totals some 7.7 million lbs (3.5 million kg).

© Omar Bradley/Picture Group, Inc.

© James Pozarik/Gamma-Liaison

of an ounce (2.8 grams) of marijuana on board. The yacht later was released after its owner paid a fine, and the zero tolerance policy was softened. The Customs Service and Coast Guard adopted new guidelines calling for the confiscation of vessels only when there was evidence they were being used to import illegal drugs into the country.

The use of the Coast Guard underscored a debate that was waged throughout 1988: whether or not to use U.S. military forces in the war on drugs. Those who favored using the military argued that there was a lack of coordination among the government agencies in the antidrug fight and that turning the job over to the military would streamline the process. Both the Senate and House versions of 1988's Defense Authorization Bill contained provisions greatly stepping up the military's role in stopping the importation of drugs by sea and air. But there was significant opposition to the idea—dubbed by some as "panzers versus pushers"—both in Congress and in the Pentagon. Defense Secretary Frank Carlucci, for example, testified before Congress that getting the military involved in the drug war would affect adversely the Pentagon's main mission: to defend the nation. Sen. William S. Cohen (R-ME) called the idea "a purely emotional response to a deep-seated social problem" that was "bound to fail."

The House-Senate conference committee convened to iron out differences in the two chambers' versions of the Defense Authorization Bill agreed with the critics and dropped virtually all of the antidrug provisions from the final measure. The conference report indicated that Congress believed that the military should not have the power to arrest citizens accused of drug smuggling. The conferees instead suggested that the best way to fight the drug problem was to focus on lessening demand in the United States. The final bill designated the Department of Defense as the "lead executive agency" in the air and sea surveillance of the nation's borders, and instructed the military to share information about potential drug smugglers with state and local law-enforcement agencies.

After weeks of heated debate, Congress passed a comprehensive drug bill just prior to adjourning on October 22. The bill establishes a variety of treatment and education programs to reduce drug consumption as well as various penalties and sanctions for the casual drug user. The new legislation also permits but does not mandate the death penalty for murders committed by people who had been involved in at least two continuing criminal operations involving drugs or for someone who kills a police officer while committing a drug-related crime.

Debate Over Whether or Not to Legalize Drugs. There also was a rekindling in 1988 of an old debate over whether or not drugs should be legalized. "Why not end this modern prohibition and devise some sort of legalization?" a *New York Times* editorial asked rhetorically. "Why not destroy the enormous profits that have spawned a new generation of organized crime, corrupting foreign states and our own justice system?" The editorial did not favor legalization. But Kurt L. Schmoke,

© Brent Jones

A "just say no" poster illustrates the negative aspects of drug use. A survey conducted for the U.S. government and released in 1988 showed the end of an upward trend in drug consumption by high-school seniors.

Demonstrators march in San Francisco in support of the legalization of marijuana. Proponents of some form of drug legalization have suggested that cocaine and marijuana be placed in the same legal category as tobacco and alcohol. Opponents believe that such legalization would increase drug abuse. The 1988 platforms of both the Democratic and Republican parties came out against the legalization of illicit drugs.

© Bill Nation/Sygma

the mayor of Baltimore, among others, endorsed the concept. "Now is the time to fight on the only terms the drug underground empire respects—money," Schmoke told the U.S. Conference of Mayors in April. "Let's take the profit out of drug trafficking."

Calls for the consideration of some form of selected drug legalization also came from—among others—Mayor Marion Barry of Washington, DC; Reps. Steny H. Hoyer (D-MD) and Fortney Stark (D-CA); William F. Buckley, Jr., editor of the *National Review;* the economist Milton Friedman; the criminologist Ernest van den Haag; and Ethan A. Nadelmann of Princeton University.

Some of those in favor of legalization suggested that drugs such as cocaine and marijuana should be placed in the same legal category as alcohol and tobacco. "A sensible policy," an April 1988 editorial in *The Economist* suggested, "might be to treat . . . alcohol, tobacco, [and] marijuana the same, with licensing, taxes, and quality control." A "main weapon," the editorial said, "should be tax: high enough to deter consumption, and varied enough to move people from the worst drugs."

The new support for legalization was opposed strongly by administration officials, members of Congress, and others. Dr. Donald Ian Macdonald, the director of the White House Drug Abuse Policy Office, for example, spoke out against any form

of legalization. Crime rates might fall if drugs were legalized, Macdonald said, "but all the other consequences of drug use would get worse. Legalization makes drugs more available, more acceptable, and more used." Commissioner William von Raab of the Customs Service termed the legalization of cocaine "madness." Instead of legalizing drugs, von Raab said, the nation should "look for additional ways to punish drug traffickers and users alike, and take steps to put some meaning back into the lives" of those who are attracted to drugs.

Rep. Charles B. Rangel, the New York Democrat who chairs the House Select Committee on Narcotics Abuse and Control, also strongly opposed legalization. "Many of the problems of drug abuse will not go away just because of legalization," Rangel said. "Even in a decriminalized atmosphere, money would still be needed to support habits. Because drugs would be cheaper and more available, people would want more and would commit more crime."

Opinion Polls and the Presidential Election. Opinion polls indicated that combatting drug abuse was the top concern of voters in 1988. A New York Times/CBS News poll conducted in May, for example, reported that 16% of those queried said that drugs constituted the most important problem facing the country—no other issue was named by more respondents. Similarly, a Washington Post/ABC poll released that month found that 26% of those asked said that drugs were the most important problem currently facing the country. No other issue—including the federal budget deficit, the economy, poverty, the threat of war, or unemployment—was cited by more than 8% of the respondents.

The fact that there was deep public concern about drugs was by no means lost on the two presidential candidates, Republican Vice-President George Bush and Democratic Massachusetts Gov. Michael S. Dukakis. Both made fighting drugs an issue in the election.

Vice-President Bush conceded that the Reagan administration's drug program had not been effective, and endorsed stepping up the ongoing war significantly. "We should have tougher penalties for those who poison our kids with drugs," Bush said in a May campaign speech. Bush also called for the death penalty in murder cases involving drug trafficking, and challenged the Democrats to get tough on drugs.

Governor Dukakis also spoke out strongly against drugs during the campaign. He criticized the administration's anti-drug program, saying that if elected he would wage "a real, not a phony, war against drugs." He added: "How can we possibly be serious about fighting a war on drugs, when we're cutting Coast Guard patrols by 55%?" Dukakis pledged that, if elected, he would step up the war against drugs and move it "to the top of our foreign-policy agenda." Dukakis also vowed to provide more help for drug abusers.

As 1988 drew to a close, the drug problem remained. The new administration must face the challenge of implementing the ideas suggested during the campaign and developing its own program to make any headway in the war on drugs.

"We believe that . . . every arm and agency of government . . . should at long last be mobilized and coordinated with private efforts under the direction of a national drug 'czar' to halt both the international supply and domestic demand for illegal drugs now ravaging" the United States.

**Democratic Party
Platform
July 19, 1988**

"The Reagan-Bush administration has set out to destroy it [the worldwide narcotics empire]. . . . We are determined to finish the job. . . . We support strong penalties, including the death penalty for major drug traffickers. User accountability for drug usage is long overdue."

**Republican Party
Platform
Aug. 16, 1988**

© J.K. Atlan/Sygma

"I have a dream that one day this nation will rise up and live out the true meaning of its creed."

Martin Luther King, Jr.
Aug. 28, 1963

"Brothers and sisters, this dream of freedom from poverty, racism, war, and violence is not a utopian fantasy. Now is the time to fulfill the promise of democracy."

Coretta Scott King
Aug. 27, 1988

BLACK AMERICANS
AN UPDATE

By U.S. Rep. Mervyn M. Dymally

Martin Luther King, Jr., had hoped to see the day when all God's children might be free at last. If his life had not been taken that April in Memphis, TN, in 1968, what would he feel, looking about his country in the late 1980s? Have black people joined God's other children in that land of freedom whose vision King's eloquence placed so indelibly in the mind of each black person of his era? A sense of bittersweetness likely would be Martin Luther King's most intense emotion as he looked out over today's United States: sweetness because more black Americans enjoy a higher standard of living than at any other time in the history of the country; bitterness because an alarming percentage of black people, particularly the youngest, are locked in a cycle of economic deprivation so strong that its consequences will be felt in the United States well into the next century. Black America in the late 1980s is a fragile study in extremes.

There have been positive changes. A substantial part of the black community in the late 1980s has earned a level of economic, intellectual, and political freedom that few blacks enjoyed during King's time.

On Aug. 27, 1988, Americans gathered in the U.S. capital, inset page 46, to commemorate the 25th anniversary of the March on Washington and to reflect on the meaning of Dr. Martin Luther King, Jr.'s "I have a dream" speech, page 46. The speech was a high point of the 1963 march, below, which drew some 250,000 persons to Washington in support of civil rights.

© Henley & Savage/After Image

About the Author. Mervyn M. Dymally was elected to his fifth term as a member of the U.S. House of Representatives in November 1988. During the 100th Congress which ended in 1988, he was chairman of the Congressional Black Caucus. A former teacher of exceptional children, Congressman Dymally served in the California legislature (1962-75) and as the state's lieutenant governor (1976-79).

Income. There long has been a middle class among blacks, but until quite recently it contained few members. In 1960, five years after King led the Montgomery, AL, bus boycott that brought him to national consciousness as a civil-rights leader, only 13 black households in 100 were of the middle class. Now, if a household income of at least $20,000 is taken as the entry point to the middle class, 29 black households in 100 are of the middle class. And five households of every 100 earn more than $50,000 per year, placing them in the upper class as defined by the federal government.

The greatest rate of entry to the middle and upper classes by blacks occurred between 1961, when President John F. Kennedy created the President's Committee on Equal Employment Opportunity, and 1975, when the first in a string of economic recessions ushered in an era of lowered expectations. Significantly, 80 out of every 100 black middle-class households are families rather than single persons living alone. That these new middle and upper classes are achievements of the civil-rights movement is indicated by the average ages of members of the two classes: 44 and 48, respectively. These are people who were able to take advantage of each civil-rights reform as it happened.

What these people have done with their money does not differ in any radical way from what non-black members of these classes have done. Perhaps most significantly, they have used their money to buy housing for their families in neighborhoods that are secure and are located near good schools. In practice, this has meant that these black households have moved either to racially mixed neighborhoods or to neighborhoods containing mainly other affluent blacks. The middle class has been at the forefront of both residential and workplace integration. Certain workplaces have been especially consistent in supporting entry of blacks into well-paid profes-

sional slots. IBM, Xerox, AT&T, and Hewlett-Packard are among the companies blacks have found most supportive of their professional recruitment and advancement. There are now at least 799,000 black managers or executives. In recent years, the number of blacks in these categories has grown at more than 12% per year.

Education. Education has played a very significant role in the growth of the black middle class. While some middle-class blacks still hold well-paid blue-collar jobs in factories, the larger portion of the black middle and upper classes is made up of white-collar workers in positions requiring college-level training. The educational advances of black people since Martin Luther King's time have been dramatic.

The actions of Dr. King and his colleagues, together with the national tone of concern over denial of civil rights which was set by President Lyndon Johnson, opened the doors of educational institutions to black people, and they passed through those doors willingly. The Civil Rights Act of 1964 denied federal funds to institutions, including educational institutions, that practiced discrimination. The Economic Opportunity Act established the College-Work Study Program, providing the financial assistance that made college attendance for blacks a viable possibility. In 1965 the Higher Education Act created Equal Opportunity Grants, making it even easier for those of low income to attend college. In the same year, the Elementary and Secondary Education Act provided funds to promote the racial integration of public elementary and secondary schools, and the Head Start Program was created to prepare educationally disadvantaged children for ele-

Photo page 48: Good housing for all blacks was a prime objective of the civil-rights era of the 1960s. Since that time, more and more blacks have been able to buy housing in secure, racially mixed neighborhoods or in neighborhoods containing mainly other affluent blacks.

Education has played a key role in the gains made by blacks. By 1988, more than 36% of blacks between the ages of 25 and 34 had completed at least one year of college.

© Brent Jones

© Billy E. Barnes/Click-Chicago

© Martha Everson/Picture Group

© Jacques Chenet/Woodfin Camp & Associates

In recent years, the number of blacks in managerial or executive positions has increased at the rate of 12% annually. Many large corporations now sponsor special programs to hire and promote black employees.

mentary school. The extension of the GI Bill to Vietnam veterans in 1968 allowed many blacks, who were overrepresented among Americans fighting that war, to enter college. Further pressure to allow black access to quality schooling was brought in 1969 by the Department of Health, Education, and Welfare when it found that several states continued to discriminate on the basis of race in their public schools. That finding required the states in violation to put into effect concrete plans by which discrimination would be abolished in their schools or risk a cutoff of federal funds.

By 1960, the first positive effects of the 1954 Supreme Court decision outlawing school segregation (in the case of *Brown v. Board of Education of Topeka, Kansas*) only were beginning to be felt. In that year, the high-school completion rate for blacks was 38%. By 1970, it had climbed to 56%, and by 1980 to 74.3%. Today it stands at nearly 81% for blacks in the 20–24 year age range.

Those completion rates have been accompanied by strong improvements in the scores of black students on the Scholastic Aptitude Test, a measure used by many colleges to determine preparedness for college. Between 1978 and 1988, black scores on the test's verbal portion improved on a national average by 21 points while white performance declined by one point. On the mathematics portion of the test, blacks improved their scores by 30 points while white scores increased by five points.

Growing preparedness and financial opportunity, together with the imposition of legal restrictions on institutional discrimination, made it possible for increasing numbers of blacks to attend at least some college. Between 1964 and 1970, the number of blacks entering college more than doubled, from 234,000 to 522,000. By 1980, the number had more than doubled again, to 1,107,000. Now more than 36% of blacks between the ages of 25 and 34 have completed at least one year of college. That compares with less than 15% in 1968.

Political Strength. As opportunities have opened to some blacks by virtue of their access to more and better education, so too has black political strength grown by virtue of improved access to the polls. Perhaps the most striking, if unheralded, political achievement of blacks in recent years has been their votes to return the U.S. Senate to Democratic control in 1986. Examination of voter data shows that in each of the states electing a new Democrat to the Senate in that transitional year, the black vote made the margin of difference. Those same voters in the 1988 Democratic presidential primaries made Jesse Jackson the strongest contender next to Michael Dukakis. There are sufficient numbers of blacks of voting age presently concentrated in key states to determine the outcome of future presidential races, if those potential voters actually do vote and vote as a bloc.

Black political representation has grown steadily since Martin Luther King's time. In 1968 there were only about 1,000 black elected officials in the whole United States. By

There has been a dramatic increase in the number of blacks holding political office. In 1988, Kurt L. Schmoke, top, a graduate of Yale and Harvard, was serving as mayor of Baltimore; Andrew Young, bottom right, a former U.S. representative and UN ambassador, was mayor of Atlanta; and William H. Gray III, bottom left, a five-term congressman from Pennsylvania, was chairman of the U.S. House budget committee.

© Lynn Johnson/Black Star

1970 there were 1,469; by 1980, 4,912. In 1987, the last year for which complete data are available, there were 6,681 blacks holding office at some level in the country; 23 of those were in the U.S. Congress, the largest number in U.S. history. In 1968, black Americans in the Congress numbered ten. In 1962 there were only four. There has been a similar growth in black leadership of major cities. In 1970 there were 81 black mayors in the country. As of 1987, there were 303. Among these were mayors of some of the largest U.S. cities, including Chicago, Los Angeles, Philadelphia, Detroit, Baltimore, Washington, New Orleans, and Atlanta.

The positive changes are very fragile. These undeniable advances would have to be a great joy to Martin Luther King were he alive today. Many of those advances are products of his efforts. King also would be the first to say today that his dream has been fulfilled only tenuously for some, and that it is more remote than ever for others. The wealth of the black community is air-thin. Educational stagnation is a growing source of concern, and black political representation is short of its potential.

Wealth. While incomes have risen for middle- and upper-class blacks, the margin between financial security and financial disaster is frighteningly narrow. Middle-class blacks discovered that the hard way in the late 1970s and early 1980s. When the recessions of that period hit, many formerly financially comfortable blacks found they had nothing to fall back on. Many had been employed in high-paying blue-collar jobs that were eliminated as the economy contracted. Others were white-collar federal government employees who, owing to their lack of seniority, found themselves victims of executive branch efforts to trim the size of the government work force.

The maintenance of income within black households is more dependent on a pooling of resources than is the case

among white households. Seventeen percent of black high-school children who work contribute most or all of their earnings to family expenses, versus about 3% of white students who work. Among black middle-class married couples where the wife works, an average of half the family's income is provided by the wife, compared to one third for comparable white families. Moreover, the median income of black middle-class married households is thousands of dollars lower than the median income of comparable white households, meaning that the loss of one paycheck in a black middle-class household quickly can move the family from middle-class status to the edge of poverty.

White households have more wealth, that is, assets over and above wages, to fall back on in time of need than do black families. In 1984, the last year for which figures are available, the median net worth of white households was $39,135, while for black households it was a mere $3,397. These differences hold even among the very poor. The median net worth of households with income under $10,000 was $8,443 for white households but only $88 for black households. There is no safety net under blacks who recently have entered the middle class.

Educational Stagnation. With the gradual loss of high-paying blue-collar jobs as an avenue to prosperity for blacks, the importance of education to achieve prosperity is underscored. Unfortunately, the strong gains in this area seen through the 1960s and up to the mid-1970s have been eroding. By percentage, the peak year of black enrollment in college was 1978, when blacks constituted 9.4% of the student body. In 1986, this percentage share had shrunk to 8.6%. The percentage of baccalaureate degrees earned by blacks has declined from 6.4 in 1977 to 5.9 in 1985. In 1977, blacks earned 21,037 master's degrees; in 1985, they earned only 13,939. The number of

Chicago youth, below left, line up to apply for a job through the Mayor's Office of Employment and Training. The front stoop, as shown at right, long has been a gathering point for urban residents. In spite of the many advances enjoyed by blacks in the last 25 years, serious problems remain. High unemployment, especially among black teenagers, and long-standing slum conditions are two examples.

The Rev. Jesse Jackson, below, who won some 6.6 million votes in the 1988 Democratic primaries, has emerged as a leading spokesman for blacks. For some years now, Jackson has encouraged blacks to exert their political potential by registering to vote and then going to the polls.

doctoral degrees awarded to blacks also has not improved. In 1977, blacks earned 1,253 doctorates; in 1985 they earned 1,154. The doors to educational institutions, opened wide for blacks during the civil-rights era, are beginning to swing shut once again. Such factors as increasing tuition and a decline in financial assistance are responsible for the change.

Unrealized Political Potential. It is ironic that at a time when there are more black elected officials than at any other time in the country's history, black politicians are daunted frustratingly in their efforts to keep the momentum of progress going in the black community. The black mayors have joined their white counterparts in pointing out that the growth of poverty in their cities is their single biggest concern.

In the U.S. Congress, blacks have achieved such seniority that in 1988 they chaired several key House committees and subcommittees, including the Budget Committee and the Education and Labor Committee. But rather than being able to advance the cause of civil rights from these important positions, the representatives have been lucky just to slow the deterioration of previous advances.

There have been severe threats to continued federal protection against institutional discrimination. In fact, the Justice Department, attempting to pursue a policy of color blindness, often has been the adversary rather than the champion of extended opportunity for blacks. And black elected officials have not been able to do more than slow implementation of the policy. The Commission on Civil Rights, created during the Eisenhower administration to extend civil rights, now so

often has taken positions limiting the expansion of civil rights that Congress has all but put the commission out of existence. Congress has done this by cutting its funds.

Looking beyond threats to the legal foundation for civil-rights extension, it is clear that the financial foundation is threatened as well. Funds previously available to help black and other poor students attend college have been exchanged for loans, greatly increasing the indebtedness of those who do attend college, and dissuading many from entering college. Programs that once aided poor blacks in their effort to climb out of poverty-programs like federal support for low-income housing, food stamps, and prenatal and early childhood health care for the impoverished have been restricted or cut back. In the 1980s, black elected officials have been busy allaying a barrage of threats to previously won advances. There has been scant opportunity to further advance the cause of civil rights.

What Lies Ahead? As the United States moves out of the 1980s and turns its face toward a new century, the overriding task in the black community, and in the American community at large, may well be to overcome the developing gulf between classes. After years of progress in allaying poverty, it now appears that the black community has been divided by the circumstances of the 1980s between those who have "made it" and those who face the real prospect of never "making it." In Martin Luther King's time, there was a strong community tie between the haves and the have-nots in the black community. That social structure was part of what made it possible for poor blacks to move out of poverty. With the physical, educational, and workplace separation of affluent from impoverished blacks, that important social relationship is now in question. Against the legacy of nearly a decade of indifference toward civil rights at best, and outright hostility toward them at worst, the rekindling of Dr. King's dream of freedom for all God's children will be America's challenge for the 1990s.

© Don Heiny/Picture Group

Blacks and whites join together, left, in a demonstration against racism. Dr. King's dream of an end to all racial bigotry remains unfulfilled.

Headaches:
The Number One Pain Problem.

"Lord, how my head aches! What a head have I!
It beats as it would fall in 20 pieces."

Romeo and Juliet by William Shakespeare

By Jenny Tesar

About the Author. Jenny Tesar, a free-lance writer living in Connecticut's Fairfield County, specializes in the fields of science, medicine, and technology. She is the author of *Introduction to Animals,* a part of the Wonders of Wildlife series, and *Parents as Teachers.* A computer enthusiast, Ms. Tesar has written a variety of educational programs.

At one time or another, almost everyone experiences the pain so vividly described by Juliet's nurse in the Shakespearean classic. For most people, such pounding aches are a fleeting discomfort, soon dispelled by rest, aspirin, or ice packs. But for others, the pain is chronic, recurring frequently and with such intensity that the sufferers cannot function normally in everyday life.

According to the National Headache Foundation, industry annually loses an estimated $50 billion due to absenteeism and medical expenses caused by headache. Sufferers make 8 million doctor's office visits each year and spend more than $400

million on over-the-counter pain relievers for headaches. But these statistics understate the problem, for most people neither miss work nor see a doctor when they get a headache. Indeed, a poll conducted by Louis Harris & Associates suggests that headaches are probably the most common physical complaint. The poll found that 73% of American adults suffered from one or more headaches during the 12 months prior to the survey.

The malady, while perhaps more prevalent today because of the stresses of modern life, is not of recent origin. Ancient peoples were bedeviled by headaches, too. More than 5,000 years ago, a Sumerian poet described how "headache roameth over the desert; blowing like the wind, flashing like lightning." Despite their wide prevalence throughout the ages, it has been only during the past few decades that headaches have been studied intensively as a set of unique diseases. But this research has broadened greatly the medical community's understanding of the ailment, leading to more effective diagnosis and treatment. Today, most headaches can be prevented, usually by the victim alone, and almost all headaches that do occur can be treated effectively by a physician.

Mysterious Causes, Multiple Triggers. The National Headache Foundation recognizes 21 types of headache, each with its own symptoms, precipitating factors, methods of treatment, and means of prevention. For simplification, these categories can be organized into three main groups: muscle contraction, vascular, and traction and inflammatory.

About 90% of all headaches are muscle contraction or tension headaches, characterized by a dull ache and a feeling of tightness around the head or neck. Emotional stress, fatigue, or depression is generally at the root of tension headaches. The majority of tension headaches are mild, lasting no more than a few hours. But some forms are severe and persistent, recurring over periods of weeks or even years.

Vascular headaches, which comprise about 10% of headaches, are characterized by changes of pressure in the blood vessels that supply the brain. The vessels constrict, then dilate, producing a throbbing pain that often is synchronized with the beating heart. Until recently, vasodilation, i.e., the widening of the cavity of blood vessels, was believed to be the cause of this headache. Today, however, many researchers believe that imbalances of brain chemicals such as serotonin, endorphins, and prostaglandins play a role, and that changes in electrical activity in the brain actually trigger the headache. One hypothesis suggests that a vascular headache results when there is a decrease in blood levels of serotonin, a neurotransmitter that switches nerve impulses on and off. As a result, serotonin-controlled circuits in the brain receive insufficient supplies of the chemical and begin misfunctioning.

The most infamous vascular headaches are migraines. The name comes from the Greek *hēmikrania*, meaning "half the skull," and refers to the fact that migraines usually are confined to one side of the head. In addition to severe, throbbing pain, people in the midst of a migraine attack may suffer from

Demons use various torture techniques to cause a headache in the 19th-century etching by George Cruikshank (page 56).

"You have spent your life in trying to discover the North Pole, which nobody on earth cares tuppence about, and you have never attempted to discover a cure for the headache, which every living person is crying aloud for."

**George Bernard Shaw
Upon meeting explorer
George Nansen**

nausea, vomiting, dizziness, sweating, and sensitivity to light and sound. Attacks are intermittent and may last from several minutes to a day or longer. A wide range of factors, including emotional stress, changing hormone levels during menstruation, excessive hunger, changes in altitude or weather, certain foods, and allergies, may trigger an attack. There also is a genetic component: Some three quarters of people with migraines have a family history of the ailment.

Migraines afflict three times as many women as men. But few women experience cluster headaches, a type of vascular headache in which attacks usually occur daily for a period lasting for 6 to 12 weeks, followed by a remission period of months or even years. Each headache is accompanied by excruciating pain on one side of the head. Some current evidence indicates that alcohol consumption may trigger cluster headaches.

An estimated 1% of headaches are traction and inflammatory headaches, caused by infection or some organic problem, such as high blood pressure, an aneurysm, or a brain tumor. Because this type of headache is a symptom of disease or injury, it is essential that it receive prompt medical attention. Ignoring such headaches may result in irreversible and even life-threatening damage.

Headache diagnosis is complicated by the fact that many headaches have symptoms that do not fall neatly into one or another of the three categories. It is possible, for instance, for an aneurysm headache—a precursor to a stroke—to mimic a migraine headache. Therefore, it is wise for people to seek professional help if their headaches occur frequently, require daily use of pain relievers, or are severe enough to prevent them from performing normal activities.

Preventing and Relieving Headaches. People of ancient times viewed headaches as a punishment from above. They performed incantations to appease the gods and concocted potions to lessen the pain. Some of their elixirs were precursors of the drugs of today. The ancient Egyptians used opium as a painkiller and the Greeks used willow-bark extracts containing chemicals similar to aspirin.

But many headache treatments of ages past were far from benign. From Neolithic times until as late as the 17th century, people practiced trephining, i.e., cutting a hole in the skull "to let the pain out." Abul Kasim (Abulcasis), an eleventh-century Spanish-Arabian physician and medical writer, tried to relieve a patient's pain by placing a hot iron against the temple. If this did not work, he would make an incision in the temple and place a piece of garlic under the skin. Then there were the quacks who through sleight of hand "removed" headache stones from their patients' heads, playing on the victims' knowledge that mineral stones caused kidney and gallbladder pain.

Although the medical profession still does not understand all the causes and origins of headaches, it has developed an array of preventives and treatments that make it possible to help an estimated 90% of headache sufferers.

". . . a permanent pain of the head, liable to be increased by noises, cries, a brilliant light, drinking of wine or strong smelling things which fill the head . . ."

**Paulus Aegineta
Greek surgeon
7th century**

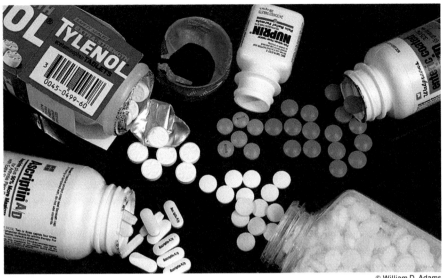

Medication. Drugs are the primary line of treatment for headaches. Mild muscle contraction headaches generally can be relieved by such nonprescription medications as aspirin and aspirin substitutes (e.g., the ibuprofen compounds).

In their search for relief, headache sufferers frequently turn to over-the-counter painkillers, aiding the rapid growth of a $400-million-a-year industry.

Ergotamines are probably the drugs most often prescribed for treatment of migraines and cluster headaches. But ergotamines can cause nausea and other side effects, and some physicians are turning to other compounds. Beta blockers and calcium-channel blockers, which are used to treat cardiac ailments, have been found useful in relieving migraines. Prednisone, methysergide, and lithium carbonate are often the drugs of choice for treatment of cluster headaches.

When large amounts of some medications are taken on a daily basis over an extended period of time, people may experience a rebound phenomenon: As the effects of the drugs wear off, the blood vessels relax, or dilate, producing more headache, which is viewed as a signal to take more medicine. This cycle—in which the relief of one headache sets the stage for the next—also can occur with migraine victims who make frequent use of vasoconstricting drugs.

Biofeedback. The term biofeedback describes a method of training patients to use relaxation techniques in order to control certain bodily functions that previously were considered involuntary. These functions include blood pressure, skin temperature, and muscle tension. The training is accomplished through instrumentation that monitors these functions. The patient will, hopefully, utilize these skills in controlling physical symptoms, including headache. Patients with headache are instructed in two types of biofeedback training—thermal and electromyographic (EMG) feedback. The thermal biofeedback training involves patients practicing relaxation techniques and imagery in order to increase the temperature of their fingers. It is believed that this training results in a new conditioned reflex, the adaptation-relaxation reflex. Most headache specialists believe that this reflex can be the mech-

anism responsible for successful use of biofeedback in treating migraine.

EMG training involves relaxation of the muscles in the upper part of the body, including facial, neck, and shoulder muscles. Through a series of relaxation exercises, the patient is aware of when a muscle is tense, and the effect of muscle tension on headache pain. In EMG biofeedback training, the patient is attached to a monitor that produces an annoying sound when the muscle tenses. Through relaxation training, the patient reduces the sound and, in turn, reduces muscle tension, and, ultimately, the severity of the headache.

Oxygen Therapy. Cluster headaches, which often occur at night or upon waking, may be triggered by the gradual increase in the blood's carbon dioxide level that occurs during sleep. This increase in carbon dioxide makes the blood vessels dilate, causing the pain. Inhaling pure oxygen through a mask connected to an oxygen tank counteracts this, and has been an effective therapy for aborting cluster headaches. This treatment is not used widely, but it has far fewer contraindications and side effects than ergotamines and other drugs.

Acupuncture. Most Westerners remain dubious about the validity of acupuncture—the ancient Oriental practice of inserting slender needles into specific areas of the body to relieve pain. Nonetheless, there is some significant evidence supporting the method's effectiveness. For example, in a study conducted at the National Hospital for Nervous Diseases in London, England, 59% of a group of migraine and muscle-tension headache sufferers reported that acupuncture treatments resulted in a reduction in frequency and severity of their headaches. Scientists at The University of Texas Health Science Center in Dallas suggest that acupuncture works by causing an increase in blood levels of endorphins, opiate-like chemicals released in the brain that apparently raise the body's pain threshold, making the person less sensitive to pain. Overall, however, the treatment is not used widely for headache sufferers, and the results are equivocal.

Exercise. A routine that includes regular daily exercise helps maintain good health, decreases stress, and makes people feel better. Headache sufferers often report that they have fewer attacks when they feel physically fit. This may be due to the fact that exercise stimulates the production of endorphins. Also useful are deep breathing exercises, neck rolls, and other exercises designed to help people relax. However, in some cases, exercise can aggravate headache. Therefore, persons should weigh carefully its benefits.

Diet. Strenuous dieting or skipping of meals can cause hunger headaches. Caffeine can cause caffeine withdrawal headaches. Excessive alcohol can cause hangover headaches. Monosodium glutamate, a food additive that enhances the flavor of food, can cause the so-called Chinese restaurant syndrome headache. Sodium nitrate, a preservative used in processed meats, can cause "hot dog headaches." And foods as diverse as chocolate, aged cheese, nuts, chicken liver, and citrus fruit can trigger migraines. Some studies conducted in recent years have shown that up to 75% of migraine sufferers

Editor's Note. The author and editors are grateful to Dr. Seymour Diamond, executive director of the National Headache Foundation in Chicago, for reviewing the article. The foundation, a major resource center for headache sufferers, publishes a quarterly newsletter.

Photos © Dan McCoy from Rainbow

Treatments for headache include thermal and electromyographic (EMG) biofeedback. In thermal biofeedback, patients practice relaxation techniques and imagery so as to produce an adaptation-relaxation reflex. In EMG training, below, a patient is attached to a monitor and encouraged to relax to reduce muscle tension and, ultimately, the severity of the headache.

are allergic to five or more foods. When patients adhered to diets that eliminated or greatly reduced such "triggers," they suffered fewer, less severe headaches.

Brightening Prospects. Today there is definite cause for optimism among the many headache sufferers. Hundreds of clinics specialize in the diagnosis and treatment of headaches, and headache research is being conducted extensively throughout the world. New technologies are enabling scientists to explore brain anatomy and function much more clearly and precisely than ever before. For instance, neuromagnetic techniques allow scientists to study the magnetic fields that are generated by electrical activity within the brain. Changes in these magnetic fields enable scientists to calculate the precise location of electrical activity within the brain, and to pinpoint abnormal electrical signals. The techniques are still experimental and the results are preliminary. However, they may hold tremendous promise in helping physicians identify and treat the underlying causes of headaches.

Headaches never will be eradicated completely, but as advances in knowledge bring scientists closer to a complete understanding of the problem, relief from pain will be easier, quicker, and more effective.

See also MEDICINE AND HEALTH.

"Oh! that the Healer's art and skill could dissipate this pain, this ill."

Anonymous

© David Moore/Black Star

AUSTRALIA AT 200
A Land Worth Living In

By R. M. Younger

About the Author. As an author, editor, and photographer, R. M. Younger has traveled to every corner of his native Australia. His many writings include *The Changing World of Australia* (1963), *Australia and the Australians* (1970), and the trilogy *Australia! Australia! A Bicentennial Record* (1987). Mr. Younger is a former director of the Australian News and Information Bureau in New York City and a former manager of the North American-Australian Tourist Commission in San Francisco.

On Jan. 26, 1988, before more than 2 million spectators, 11 square-rigged sailing ships entered the harbor of Sydney, Australia. The fleet had left England the previous July, reenacting the 15,000-mi (24 000-km) voyage of Australia's first European settlers. The festivities in Sydney Harbor marked the 200th anniversary of the arrival of the "First Fleet," headed by Capt. Arthur Phillip and carrying 1,030 felons and those sent to watch over them. Today a modern, lavishly endowed, rapidly changing society, Australia was founded in 1788 as an open-air jail.

The reenactment of the First Fleet's arrival kicked off a year-long bicentennial celebration in the "Land Down Under." The 11 tall ships were followed by a "great parade of sail" that brought 200 vessels to Sydney Harbor from some 40 countries. Blimps, helicopters, and skywriters dominated the

sky as the celebrants blew plastic horns, waved Australian flags, and sang "Waltzing Matilda." That night, a dramatic fireworks display was presented over the famous Sydney Harbor Bridge.

During the remainder of the year, the anniversary was celebrated with more than 30,000 special events across the nation. There were special concerts by the Sydney Symphony Orchestra as well as a new musical based on Manning Clark's six-volume *History of Australia*. On April 30 in Brisbane, Queen Elizabeth II opened Expo 88, a six-month A$450 million world exposition. Called the "crown jewel" of Australia's bicentennial celebrations, the fair was completed on time and within budget. The Australian government considered Expo a "significant opportunity" to try to increase its exports and thereby reduce its trade deficit. Forty-three nations and 25 international corporations were represented at the fair. With "Leisure in the Age of Technology" as the theme, Expo emphasized the joy of living in the technological age. Accordingly, the U.S. pavilion was a celebration of sport and recreation and the related application of science and technology; the Swiss pavilion included an indoor ski slope with fresh-made snow; the Japanese pavilion, Expo's most expensive one, featured a high-energy aerobics show; and the popular Fuji pavilion offered a three-dimensional computer-graphics generated movie projected on the ceiling. In addition, some 25,000 street-entertainment acts were booked for Expo.

During the queen's three weeks in Australia, she officially dedicated Australia's new Parliament House in Canberra on May 9. The A$1.1 billion extravaganza had taken eight years to build. Other openings during the year included the Stockman's Hall of Fame and Outback Heritage Centre in Longreach (Queensland), created as a tribute to the nation's pioneers and pioneering spirit; and the Australian Maritime Museum in Sydney. Other events ranged from a transcontinental hot-air balloon contest and the Around Australia Air Race to local earthworm races.

In celebrating the 200th anniversary of its European settlement, Australia expressed pride in its material achievements and unbroken political stability, while also taking stock of the road ahead. It seemed a fitting time both to bask in the nation's distinctive heritage and to weigh future prospects. For Australia has remained a largely unfinished nation—a paradoxical society. It is a nation searching for greater abundance through improved productivity and seeking to maximize human values, yet still torn between competing views on many issues fundamental to its direction and still reluctant to offer any political group more than passing commitment. As the bicentennial fervor took hold, Australians were given little respite from the warnings and urgings of those who wanted the anniversary to hasten a more purposeful national resolve to tackle many worrisome issues.

In economic terms, these issues included an unemployment rate persistently above 7%, undefeated inflation, and international earnings insufficient to pay for the high standard of living. Grudgingly, policymakers have been forced to a

A "great parade of sail," a 200-gun salute, and a massive fireworks display (page 62) were part of the festivities in Sydney, Jan. 26, 1988, beginning a year-long celebration honoring Australia's 200th birthday. To encourage tourism during the bicentennial year, koala Dundee, below, was the official symbol of the national airline.

Qantas Airlines

Qantas, A Cut Above The Rest.

Sipa Press

© Chris Sattleberger/Gamma Liaison

A monorail, above, *circled the site of Expo 88, a world exposition held in Brisbane, April 30– October 30. Since "Leisure in the Age of Technology" was the fair's theme, the U.S. pavilion,* right, *paid tribute to baseball and other American sports. The fair was considered a crowning achievement of the bicentennial celebrations. Another highlight was the formal dedication May 9 of the new Parliament House in Canberra, page 65 bottom. Britain's Queen Elizabeth II ceremoniously unlocked the doors of the building, 61 years to the minute after her father, King George VI, had unveiled a provisional parliament building. Some Australians, especially the Aborigines, considered the nation's partying superfluous. On the birthday itself, January 26, a group of 15,000 Aborigines and their supporters,* page 65 top right, *marched in a Sydney park to protest 200 years of discrimination by white settlers.*

clearer recognition of the economic realities of global competitiveness and the rise to unprecedented levels of the nation's foreign debt. Export returns have been strong (especially from wool and gold), but the nation's appetite for imported products has continued to raise the debt. To help remedy the situation, the welcome mat was put out for international visitors, and 1988 proved a record year for tourism, with more than 2 million travelers from abroad.

The bicentennial also caught Australians reconsidering the impact of their settlement on the original Australians—the Aboriginal peoples. The search continued for a sounder

course in Aboriginal policy, whereby the debt of long neglect might be repaid. But the path toward this goal remained elusive, even as the government intensified its efforts to give the Aboriginal community clearer involvement in federal support programs.

For their part, Aboriginal groups pressed Land Rights claims and gained greater respect for Aboriginal identity and cultural values. The bicentennial, however, did not create a celebratory mood among the Aborigines, whose leaders declared 1988 a Year of Mourning. Their protest struck a sympathetic note with many white Australians. Minister of Education John Dawkins called the celebration "a tasteless and insensitive farce." The national teachers' union told its members to boycott any school bicentennial observances that did not consider the plight of the Aborigines.

"As well as celebrating our present achievements, we can remember . . . what we owe to the people who have been before us, the Aborigines who have lived on this continent for some 40,000 years," said Prime Minister Robert Hawke just prior to the Australia Day festivities.

Britain's Prince Charles, representing the throne at the Sydney Harbor commemoration, also took note of the controversy. "A country free enough to examine its own conscience," he said, "is a land worth living in, a nation to be envied."

© Wildlight/Black Star

© Steve Liddell/Horizon

Australia today is a land of diversity. Nearly 60% of its area is pastureland, and the livestock industry, top, is a multibillion dollar one. With an urban population of about 85%, suburban towns, such as the one above, are home to 65% of the people.

Land and Life-Style. Perhaps no other people in all the world spend more time, or derive more pleasure from, analyzing themselves and their nation than do Australians. Their image of Australia as a "Land of Oz" is not new, and dedication to it runs deep. Lively, ingenuous ways, a generally uncomplicated life-style, and a liberal dose of conviviality—barbecues, beer drinking, legalized gambling, and the like—

are central elements of the national identity. With a climate that encourages open-air living, love of sport is pandemic.

But Australia and Australians are difficult to categorize—highly urbanized yet harboring a latter-day frontier spirit, one foot in the Space Age and one foot in the realm of the Golden Fleece, where 190 million sheep are raised. Impressions depend on time and place, and whatever is said about this vast nation-continent may be true: The awesome grandeur of unending deserts, untouched rain forests, huge cattle ranches, and open farmlands contrasts with a few great coastal cities that spread from central skylines to red-roofed suburbs.

Throughout its history, Australia has undergone sudden bursts of growth—with attendant national exuberance—interspersed with four- or five-year periods of economic slowing—with accompanying feelings of dismay or even inadequacy. Australians remain high-profile individuals who readily substantiate visitors' preconceptions, often exhibiting Paul Hogan's (the star of the *Crocodile Dundee* movies and international spokesman for Australian tourism) air of ingenuousness and friendliness, coupled with a detached outlook encouraged by the nation's distance from the rest of the world.

Yet at their bicentenary, Australians could not be regarded as an out-of-touch or unworldly people; satellite communications had seen to that. Rather, they were extracting the most from a California-style way of life. Here, in effect, California—with the addition of huge desert areas—has been rolled out over an entire continent to produce a nation paying homage to the automobile and tract housing, its families owning their

The many beautiful and unique features of Australia's landscape include Ayers Rock, top, a giant sandstone monolithic mountain of terracotta color located in the Northern Territory, and Russell Falls, above, on the Russell River in Mount Field National Park, Tasmania.

By 1988, there were 16.5 million people and 190 million sheep in Australia. The people are known for their ingenuous ways and friendly personalities. The sheep account for 30% of the world's total wool output.

own homes, using credit cards at great shopping centers, watching sports events and soap operas on television, and eating at fast-food restaurants. Australians generally are a house-proud people who mow their suburban lawns while cherishing a romantic myth of the bronzed, larger-than-life backcountry horseman who in fact is an ever-shrinking fragment of the national scene. Suburbia has become home to two out of three Australians, and in the 1980s women have come to outnumber men for the first time, adding to a strong feminist base.

Politics, Economy, and Defense. One of the prominent features of the bicentennial celebrations was a strong link with British royalty. During 1988, all of the Royal Family except the Queen Mother and the youngest members traveled to Australia to participate in commemorative events. This was only appropriate. The firm structure of the Australian culture and political outlook developed from British institutions and law, administered as closely as possible to the original form but conditioned by the free-wheeling spirit and empathy with the underdog that accompanied the opening of a land where spaciousness was a shaping influence.

In their dedication to constitutional monarchy and parliamentary tradition, Australians maintain a society that is open, democratic, egalitarian (at least in outlook), and money-oriented. Its cities are without beggars and, while hiding some poverty, are graced with an exceptionally high proportion of well-cared-for houses. Maintaining city prosperity has been a key feature of the nation's political outlook for many years. The suburban idyll has been made possible through a restrictive tariff structure that supports manufacturing and an interlocking system of wage determination based on official arbitration.

Unfortunately, election-winning formulas have not always resulted in sound measures for coping with increasing competition in a changing world. Such a failure has resulted in the current impasse over a cost structure that gives high wages to

unionists while dangerously eroding the nation's ability to pay its massive import and overseas interest bills with exports. The situation first appeared under the big-spending Labor regime of Prime Minister Gough Whitlam in 1972–75, at which time commentators began to label Australia the land of Big Government, Big Unionism, and Big Business.

The situation scarcely improved in the late 1970s. Under Liberal Prime Minister Malcolm Fraser, deficits grew in the domestic budget and—with exports failing to match the rise in imports—in international accounts as well. A 30-year-long rise in prosperity stalled in 1980 with the drop in world commodity prices. A new right-wing Labor regime headed by former trade unionist Robert Hawke gained power in 1983, reaching a tacit accord with the union movement. The bicentennial in 1988 marked the fifth year of the Hawke government, which had carried Australia well down the road to corporate statism.

During this period, the free-wheeling, strike-prone unions that had long countered easygoing capitalism emerged as a powerful and elaborate politicized structure (headed by the Australian Council of Trade Unions). The latter worked in close concert with the Hawke government to inspire what the magazine *The Economist* in 1987 described as the pervading "coziness of the corporate state." This coziness reduced the number of strikes but had the effect of perpetuating uncompetitive production costs. Even when the government's own Industries Assistance Commission pointed to the serious distortions wrought by exorbitant labor costs, the government—in the face of union concern—ignored the commission's remedial recommendations. Inflation, meanwhile, remained well above OECD (Organization for Economic Cooperation and Development) levels. The "accord" with the union movement virtually guaranteed government backing for price-related wage increases and, thereby, an unending wage-price spiral.

© James Pozarik/Gamma Liaison

Laborite Robert Hawke, above, a 59-year-old former Rhodes scholar who has headed Australia's government since March 1983, considered the bicentennial an appropriate time to "remember the past and what we [the Australians] owe to the people who have been before us."

Australians love their sports, especially tennis. A A$70 million tennis center, below, was completed in Melbourne in late 1987.

Sipa Press

CHRONOLOGY

1642 Abel Tasman sights and names Van Diemen's Land (now Tasmania) during a voyage delineating the broad limits of "New Holland."

1770 Captain James Cook charts the eastern coastline, claiming the area for Great Britain and naming it New South Wales.

1788 British First Fleet arrives on January 26 and Port Jackson (now Sydney) is founded as a penal settlement.

1813 An expedition crosses the Blue Mountains west of Sydney.

1834 "Unauthorized individuals" move into an unsettled area (later Melbourne), leading to rapid expansion of sheep grazing.

1851 Gold is found in Bathurst, west of Sydney, in February, and later in the year in Victoria; gold rushes to many locations begin.

1856 Elective governments are introduced, with secret vote by ballot and manhood suffrage.

1868 Great Britain ends the transport of convicts to Australia.

1872 A transcontinental (north-south) telegraph opens, linking Darwin, Australia, with Singapore.

1892 Rich goldfields are discovered at Kalgoorlie and Coolgardie in western Australia.

1901 The independent six-state Commonwealth of Australia is inaugurated on January 1 with Melbourne as the temporary capital.

1907 A minimum wage system is established.

1914 German possessions in the south Pacific are seized by Australia during World War I.

1927 The federal parliament is transferred from Melbourne to Canberra.

1928 The first U.S.-Australia flight is completed on June 9 by Australians Charles Kingsford Smith and Charles Ulm and Americans Harry Lyon and James Warner.

1939 Australia declares war on Germany and sends forces overseas.

1940 Australia and the United States exchange ministers, marking Australia's first direct diplomatic link with a nation other than Great Britain.

1941 War is declared on Japan on December 9 following widespread Pacific attacks.

1942 Darwin is bombed by Japan on February 19. U.S. armed forces arrive and Pacific Command headquarters are established by Gen. Douglas MacArthur.

1947 A large-scale government-sponsored immigration program begins.

1951 The ANZUS Pact, linking Australia and New Zealand with the United States, is signed.

1967 Barriers to migrants from Asian countries are eased under administrative instructions.

1975 On November 11, Governor-General Sir John Kerr dismisses the Labor Party government of Prime Minister Gough Whitlam and dissolves both Houses of Parliament to resolve the deadlock over the budget's nonpassage in the Senate.

1986 Enactment of the Australia Act ends the nation's few remaining formal links with Britain's legal system.

1988 Queen Elizabeth II opens the Parliament House in Canberra on May 9.

One of the ironies was that the Australian Labor Party, long regarded by the business community as irresponsible for its opposition to capitalist principles, became acceptable to the nation's corporate leaders for its "competent business management." This view was reinforced in 1988, when the succession of federal budget deficits finally was broken. The Labor regime thus proved able to work with big business, while the Liberals and their political allies—traditional champions of the private sector—failed to fire corporate enthusiasm. The role reversal, and in particular the Labor government's firm, pragmatic approach to economic and related social issues, was summarized in a 1987 newspaper headline: "Hard Labor, Soft Liberals."

Despite Labor's advantageous position and its superb political machine, 1988 federal by-elections and state elections showed that the party remained vulnerable to concerted attacks by those who support free enterprise. Meanwhile, the underlying issue of the government's element in economic activities remained. More than 40% of overall economic activity was in government hands, and efforts to privatize major entities met with strong resistance.

In the area of defense, Australian policy has undergone a major shift. As Australia has become more closely attuned to the Asian region in the economic and social spheres, its military involvement virtually has been eliminated. Since the end of the Vietnam War and the era of strengthened defense capacity of ASEAN (Association of Southeast Asian Nations), Australia has retreated effectively from a military role in the region.

The central question in Australian defense policy long has revolved around the issue of "forward defense" versus "home defense," or the extent to which the country should maintain a shield beyond its own northern limits. The current position focuses on a "strategy of denial," emphasizing self-defense. Critics regard this approach as overly restrictive and defensively oriented.

However, the emphasis on self-defense and the corresponding decline in Australia's contribution to overall Western alliance defense has its counter in a close compact with

Since the early 1970s, a significant number of Australia's immigrants have been arriving from Vietnam and other Asian nations, giving rise to new urban ethnic districts, including a Vietnam center in Sydney, below.

© Michael Coyne/Black Star

the United States, especially pertaining to communications bases for satellite monitoring.

Social Issues. In their introspective mood in 1988, Australians not only faced difficult economic and political issues, but they also pondered deep social concerns. In less than two generations, an easygoing homogeneous Anglo-Celtic society had become a complex community of highly varied ethnic groups. The national daily, *The Australian,* saw the nation of 16 million as having become a microcosm of the world.

Setting immigration guidelines always has been at the heart of Australian national policy-making. The strategy laid down in 1901 was designed to prevent any influx from Asian lands, and Britain was almost the sole source of immigrants until World War II; large-scale multiethnic immigration from Europe began in 1947. With an annual intake equaling 1% of the total population, after a single generation one person in four had at least one parent born abroad. During that period, naturalization of new settlers was the goal, "assimilation" the watchword. From the mid-1970s, the emphasis on citizenship was less apparent; the prevailing mood focused on "multiculturalism."

The federal parliament in 1988 provided active support for multiethnicity, passing a motion assuring "equal status" for any ethnic group—an approval which to many seemed to ignore the complications of introducing behavior patterns from vastly different societies. Multiculturalism appeared to arouse some public disquiet, with increasing numbers of citizens seeing a threat to "true" Australian identity.

Since the early 1970s, a significant number of Australia's immigrants have been arriving from Vietnam and other Southeast Asian countries. By 1988, Asians accounted for more than 30% of the arrivals and 3% of the overall population. While general tolerance prevailed, some hardening of attitudes now was apparent. There seemed to be new reservations about whether the large-scale migration from Asia should be allowed to continue.

Underlying most comment was a broadly perceived need to move Australia forward in terms of productivity and competitiveness. On the issue of immigration, there were calls for greater attention to work-related and entrepreneurial skills among persons selected for admission. Overall, it seemed, the nation's easy options were fading. There was a recognized need for more purposeful education policies that emphasize practical work skills and, more broadly, for measures to raise productivity through the modernization of industry. A parallel need was for an increase in household savings to boost economic growth and productivity. Such moves were seen as necessary to achieve what one economist hoped might be "a cathartic economic shakeout" as Australia moved beyond its 200th year. After two centuries of growth, expansion, and increasing opportunities for the individual, Australia combines with its frontier spirit, Oz image, and stable democratic principles a deeply entrenched confidence in the future.

See AUSTRALIA, page 127.

A Statistical Profile

Population
1901	3,825,000
1950	8,307,000
1987	16,248,800

Immigration
1901	17,800
1950	152,500
1987	103,659

Gross National Product
1900–01	A$419,000,000
1950–51	A$6,806,000,000
1986–87	A$260,367,000,000

© George W. Peters/The Port of Miami

SMOOTH SAILING
for the Cruise Industry

By Phyllis Elving

Soaring atriums of glass and brass. Private verandas. Croquet courts and swim-up bars. Is this any way to build a cruise ship?

For a new generation of passenger liners, the answer seems to be yes. Ships entering service these days sport features undreamed of a few years ago—and more people than ever before are boarding to take a look. Some 3.5 million North Americans chose cruise vacations in 1988, up 14% over 1987 and more than double the passenger totals of five years earlier. That escalating growth curve has resulted in an unprecedented flurry of shipbuilding and given birth to a whole new branch of the travel business: travel agents dealing in nothing but cruises.

The industry in question is a vastly changed one from that of even a decade ago. The advent of jet travel in the 1950s signaled the end of cruising as a point-to-point form of transportation. Cruise ships look different today, thanks to new technology and materials. They go to different places. And they offer a wider range of voyages, to a broader audience

A fleet of cruise ships lines the docks of Miami, waiting to pick up passengers for excursions to the Caribbean and beyond. Miami today is the world's most crowded port for cruise liners, serving 24 ships.

About the Author. Phyllis Elving is a free-lance travel writer and editor. As editor of *Pacific Travel News,* the official magazine of the Pacific Area Travel Association, for 12 years, she traveled throughout Asia and the Pacific. Ms. Elving has written and edited several travel books for Sunset Books.

than ever before. Most dramatic of all has been the focus on the cruise ship as a destination in itself, a self-contained floating resort that competes for business with shore resorts as much as with other cruise ships.

On passenger liners today you can pursue fitness and relaxation at exercise and massage centers or do mental gymnastics at computer workshops. You can play croquet on the new *Royal Viking Sun,* or play golf at the world's most famous courses via a two-story computerized golf simulator. Swimming pools are expected shipboard amenities, but when Club Mediterranée launches a new cruise-sailing ship in 1989, it will have a mesh pool that can be lowered right into the sea.

Casinos have become a standard shipboard feature in the last decade. They are a major source of revenue for some lines, and they have been getting bigger and more plush all the time. Shipboard entertainment is more elaborate, too, thanks to newly sophisticated sound and lighting systems that allow Broadway-type productions or Vegas-style revues. And if you do not feel like leaving your cabin, you may be able to watch the show on closed-circuit TV. On Royal Caribbean Cruise Line's huge new *Sovereign of the Seas,* you can use your cabin TV for everything from ordering room service to signing up for shore excursions.

Shipboard claustrophobia is fading. The new liners are taller and more open, offering such features as interior atriums, skylights, glass-walled sterns, and cabin windows instead of portholes. New technology has made for a better ride, too. Cunard Line's *Queen Elizabeth II* became the first to

Royal Caribbean Cruise Line

"Sovereign of the Seas," left, *the world's largest cruise ship, was launched in January 1988 by the Royal Caribbean Cruise Line. The $200 million vessel, which contains five nightclubs and two movie theaters, can carry up to 2,282 passengers and 750 crew members. The main lobby, below, is an atrium five decks high with glass elevators and towering fountains.*

© Susan Greenwood/Gamma-Liaison

boast vibration-absorbing rubber-mounted engines after being refurbished in 1987.

One more way in which cruise ships are trying to be competitive with land resorts is in the matter of cost. While the tab for a day afloat can run anywhere from $100 to $1,000, cruise companies are quick to point out that that figure includes meals, entertainment, transportation, and accommodations. And it would be higher were it not for the fact that most cruise ships are registered in foreign countries, enabling their owners to pay lower taxes and hire foreign (nonunion) crews.

A Matter of Style. Choice is a key word today—in ships and their amenities, in ports of call, even in ambiance. Explains Rich Skinner, spokesman for Holland America Line-Westours, "We see our market [customers] as 'relaxers'—the kind of people who would vacation at a spa in Palm Springs. Other lines are oriented toward people who vacation at Disney World or Las Vegas. Or they might be sports-oriented." In 1974, Miami-based Carnival Cruise Lines began advertising its Caribbean liners as "Fun Ships." Carnival offered shorter, less expensive, livelier cruises to appeal to a new, younger passenger—and the response has enabled the line to add four new ships since 1980, with three more on order.

Cruise length has had a lot to do with the broadening of the market. No longer is a cruise vacation limited to those who have the money and the leisure time to set sail for a month. Now passengers even can sample shipboard life on one-day "cruises to nowhere." And while those leisurely 101-day sails circumnavigating the globe still *are* available, trips of three days to a week are standard. Fly-cruise programs give quick access to cruising waters and also make it possible to buy single segments of long cruises. To attract new passengers and

More than 55% of North American cruise passengers travel to the Caribbean, below left, *but other destinations are growing in popularity. A Royal Viking Line ship,* below, *takes the inside passage in southeast Alaska.*

Good food and cool refreshments, whether a buffet luncheon with a Mexican theme or a fruity drink in the late afternoon, are among the major attractions of a cruise vacation.

keep the old ones coming back, cruise lines have scoured the world looking for offbeat ports of call. And to take travelers to places the superliners cannot reach—or to offer alternative styles of cruising—a new class of smaller ship has emerged. Among the more unusual of these ships are the sail-cruise vessels of Windstar Sail Cruises, which operate with a computerized sailing system in Caribbean, French Polynesian, and Mediterranean waters.

"Theme cruises" have proven popular for many lines. Passengers with an interest in wine, Wall Street, or watercolors can be entertained and instructed on the ship along with like-minded fellow passengers. Some cruise lines offer special programs and incentives for families or for single travelers. Premier Cruise Lines—the official cruise line of Disney World —even has promoted a single parents' cruise program. As for the destinations themselves, one region of emerging importance in 1988 was South America's Amazon River. Sitmar Cruises' 925-passenger *FairWind* became the biggest cruise ship ever to make regular stops at the city of Manaus in Brazil, 1,000 mi (1 609 km) upriver, when it began a series of Amazon cruises. The Mediterranean also has increased in importance, regaining much of the cruise traffic it had lost after the 1985 terrorist hijacking of the Italian liner *Achille Lauro* off the coast of Egypt.

The Caribbean has remained the destination of choice for more than 55% of North American cruise passengers. Despite the large number of cruise ships sailing the Caribbean, the area as yet shows no sign of waning in popularity. Fair seas and low prices seem likely to keep customers coming. Port growth reflects the popularity of the Caribbean. The region is served by the four busiest ports in North America: Miami, Port Canaveral, Tampa, and Port Everglades. Miami has more than doubled its cruise traffic since the late 1960s, with 24 passen-

ger liners using its port facilities. Within the next 15 years, say port officials, Miami will top the 4 million figure for annual passenger totals. In preparation, $100 million is being spent on new cruise terminals and a high-span access bridge. Another rapidly growing U.S. port is San Diego. Now in 11th place among North American ports in terms of traffic, the California city is moving up in the ranks as a takeoff point for cruises to Mexico—the second most popular cruise destination.

New and Revised. Cruise lines took delivery of more new ships in 1988 than ever before in a single year. Royal Caribbean Cruise Line started things off on a grand scale with the inaugural of the world's biggest cruise liner, the 2,282-passenger *Sovereign of the Seas*. Other new ships included Norwegian Cruise Line's 1,534-passenger *Seaward*, Royal Cruise Line's 990-passenger *Crown Odyssey*, Royal Viking Line's 740-passenger *Royal Viking Sun*, Epirotiki Lines' 500-passenger *Odysseus*, Crown Cruise Line's 500-passenger *Crown del Mar*, Seabourn Cruise Line's 212-passenger *Seabourn Pride*, Windstar Sail Cruises' 148-passenger *Wind Spirit*, and Clipper Cruise Line's 138-passenger *Yorktown Clipper*. The old Matson line *Monterey* came back after extensive refurbishing by Aloha Pacific Cruises, which put the American-registered 600-passenger ship into service in Hawaii. Several existing ships were taken over by different lines: American Star Lines' 380-passenger *Betsy Ross*, the former Bergen Line *Leda*; Regency Cruises' 800-passenger *Regent Sun*, former Royal Cruise Line's *Royal Odyssey;* and Premier Cruise Lines' 1,600-passenger *Star Ship Atlantic*, former Home Lines Cruises' *Atlantic*.

Whatever the destination, whatever the ship, sundecks and a saltwater pool are essential to the cruise experience.

© Bob Gelberg/The Image Bank

A cruise in the 80s isn't just for lounging around. On-deck aerobics classes have become popular in the last decade, though some travelers still prefer the old standby—shuffleboard.

The pace is not expected to slow in 1989, when Carnival Cruise Lines will inaugurate its fifth ship of the decade, the 2,050-passenger *Fantasy*. Princess Cruises will add the *Star Princess*, a 1,400-passenger ship (formerly announced as Sitmar's *FairMajesty*), Seabourn Cruise Line will take delivery of the 200-passenger *Seabourn Spirit*, and Club Med will launch a 416-passenger, five-masted cruise-sailing ship. Holland America Line will introduce its 1,500-passenger *Westerdam*, Home Lines' former *Homeric*, enlarged and refurbished, while Norwegian Cruise Line will take over the *Royal Viking Star*, renamed *Norwegian Star*. Still more ships have been announced for 1990 and onward, including a 3,000-passenger Tikkoo Cruise Lines vessel called *Ultimate Dream*. Carnival, Holland America, Princess, and Norwegian Cruise Line all have multiple ships on order.

Fear of too many cruise ships has not kept new lines from setting up business. Aloha Pacific Cruises, American Star Lines, and Seabourn Cruise Line were all new in 1988. Sea Venture Cruises is a new company awaiting a 350-passenger ship to begin Alaska service in 1989, and Crystal Cruises is a new subsidiary of Japan's NYK Line shipping company, planning to launch a 960-passenger world-range ship in 1990. Carnival Cruise Lines has announced plans for a new line of ships for the deluxe trade, hoping to carry over its success in the entry-level market. At the same time, a trend toward consolidation has continued as lines strive to achieve the "economy of scale" that was the industry catch phrase of 1988. Sitmar Cruises was purchased by Princess Cruises' parent company

Holland America Line

P&O, with full merger planned. A new holding company was formed by Royal Caribbean Cruise Lines and Admiral Cruises (itself the product of a 1986 merger), and Holland America Line acquired Windstar Sail Cruises. Late in 1988, Carnival Cruise Lines announced its purchase of Holland America Line; the two companies planned to maintain separate identities.

Nighttime cruise ship entertainment has become more elaborate, with sophisticated sound and lighting systems allowing Broadway-type productions and Las Vegas-style revues.

The Future. The question facing the cruise industry in 1988 was whether it could sustain the growth needed to fill all the new ships in the years ahead. Cruise Line International Association (CLIA), a marketing body representing 32 cruise companies, points out that only 5% of the U.S. population as yet has ever taken a cruise. That leaves a huge untapped pool of potential cruisers, says CLIA—30 million, by its calculations. This optimistic view has its share of proponents. One indication is the fact that there were perhaps 700 cruise-only travel agencies doing business in the United States by the end of 1988—compared with just ten five years prior. Even in a recession, says Holland America Line's Skinner, studies indicate that the cruising industry would show growth: "The perception now is that travel is a right, not a privilege."

Investors and cruise-line executives have their fingers crossed that the future will in fact be as rosy as CLIA predicts. Meantime, the consumer should be the clear winner as cruise companies scurry to close the gap between passenger demand and the new capacity levels. Their efforts to fill ships are likely to translate into a proliferation of fare discounts and ever more imaginative cruise offerings and shipboard amenities.

HIRSCHFELD 3

IRVING BERLIN at 100
stealing an extra bow

By John Milward

About the Author. John Milward is a free-lance writer
and critic. His work ap-
pears regularly in a variety
of publications, including
the *Philadelphia Inquirer,
New York Newsday,* the
Chicago Tribune, and *USA
Today.* Mr. Milward's
book, *The Beach Boys
Silver Anniversary,* was
published by Doubleday in
1985.

When the world paused to celebrate the centennial birthday of Irving Berlin on May 11, 1988, the dizzying sweep of
the 20th century was for a moment contained in the story of a
Russian immigrant who emerged from New York's Lower
East Side to help define the American popular song.

"Irving Berlin has no place in American music," said the
late Jerome Kern. "He is American music."

On the night of Berlin's birthday, performers gathered at
New York City's Carnegie Hall to pay tribute with a concert
of his songs. Berlin chose to celebrate in his East Side home
with his wife of 62 years. Berlin always has guarded his privacy, but as the vocalists filled the night with the words and
music that since long ago have been imbedded in America's

© Ken Regan/Camera 5

musical consciousness, it once again was clear that the composer is among the most public personalities of all.

Berlin's active career spanned from his first published song in 1907 ("Marie from Sunny Italy"), to his last Broadway show (*Mr. President,* 1962). The range of his catalog of more than 1,000 songs strains the imagination: How could one person conjure everything from the World War I doughboy's lament, "Oh, How I Hate to Get Up in the Morning," to Ethel Merman's brassy signature tune from *Annie Get Your Gun,* "There's No Business Like Show Business?" "White Christmas," for one, defies the notion that it was written by a former singing waiter who required an assistant to translate the melody into notes on a musical score. At the moment of its creation (for Bing Crosby's 1942 film *Holiday Inn*), "White Christmas" entered the realm of folklore, a tune as bound to the holiday as Santa Claus, and one that will be sung as long as the season it celebrates remains merry.

The enduring popularity of Berlin's songs can be attributed to his primary philosophy: "Keep it simple." He believed that a tune's title should be placed prominently, and that the work must touch the heart. As one of the first songwriters to compose both words and music, he believed the two must be joined as one. His four primary rules: "Easy to sing, easy to say, easy to remember, and applicable to everyday events."

Background. Berlin's biography fits the memorable criterion of his songs: It is a classic manifestation of the American Dream. He was born Israel Baline in Temun, Russia, the youngest of eight children. When he was 4, his family fled to the New World, their home literally burning in their wake. Settled into New York's teeming Lower East Side, the youngster barely had begun school when his father died and he took to the streets to help the family survive.

He sold newspapers and sang in the street. At the age of 14 he left home and found a night job singing from the balcony of Tony Pastor's Music Hall on 14th Street, and later was a singing waiter at the Pelham Cafe in Chinatown. He learned

Leading stars and celebrities, including (l-r) Rosemary Clooney, Frank Sinatra, Leonard Bernstein, Shirley MacLaine, Walter Cronkite, and Isaac Stern, gathered at New York's Carnegie Hall on May 11, 1988, for "A Gala Evening Celebrating Irving Berlin's 100th Birthday."

to play the piano by ear, but as he could play only in the key of F-sharp, he forever would use a transposing piano to shift keys. He composed harmonies through trial and error. (Israel Baline became Irving Berlin when "Marie from Sunny Italy" was credited mistakenly to "I. Berlin," and the young songwriter decided to go all the way by changing his first name to "Irving," which he considered more American.)

In 1909, Berlin got a $25-per-week job writing lyrics for a music publisher and immersed himself in the songwriting world known as Tin Pan Alley. Two years later, he came to define that world when he became an international celebrity after writing "Alexander's Ragtime Band," a tune that sparked a dance craze, introduced the mass audience to the world of jazz, and sold more than 1 million copies of sheet music. Because the tune was written under the old 75-year copyright law—current law calls for songs to be protected for 50 years beyond the life of the composer—Berlin has lived to see his first famous song pass into the public domain.

After "Alexander's Ragtime Band," however, the boy who had come to the United States in steerage never again had to worry about money. The copyrights of the hundreds of songs he wrote for Broadway shows, Hollywood musicals, and as stand-alone standards are among the most profitable in the history of popular music. In 1919 the composer formed his own music publishing company—the Irving Berlin Music Company—and two years later participated in the building of Broadway's Music Box Theater to house his own musical showcases.

The 1920s saw Berlin develop his touch for ballads, some of which reflected his courtship of Ellin MacKay, whose well-to-do father opposed their 1926 marriage. The early 1930s found him composing one of his greatest ballads, "How Deep Is the Ocean," and coining a holiday standard, "Easter Parade." In 1935 he wrote the first of many film scores, *Top Hat,*

Fred Astaire and Ginger Rogers (right) starred in "Top Hat," the first motion picture for which Irving Berlin wrote the score. Song hits from the movie classic include "White Tie and Tails," "Top Hat," and "Cheek to Cheek."

Credit: All sheet music, Frank Driggs Collection

Culver Pictures

Irving Berlin (right) *wrote the music and Ethel Merman* (left) *did the singing for the Broadway musicals "Annie Get Your Gun" (1946) and "Call Me Madam" (1950). The former introduced "There's No Business Like Show Business" and the latter "You're Just in Love."*

in which Ginger Rogers and Fred Astaire introduced, among other tunes, "Cheek to Cheek."

Berlin did not take his success lightly, and the gratitude of the multimillionaire who rose from poverty is reflected in a song that has all but become the nation's second national anthem, "God Bless America." It originally was written for a musical revue (*Yip, Yip, Yaphank*) that he composed while serving in the Army during World War I. The song was introduced formally by Kate Smith on Armistice Day in 1939. Berlin assigned the song's copyright and the resulting royalties to the Boy Scouts and Girl Scouts of America. Berlin's patriotism was reflected further in his score for *This Is the Army,* a show with which Berlin toured for 3½ years during World War II. For a man who became increasingly reclusive later in life, a prominent image of Berlin remains his appearance in the filmed version of the play, singing his song from World War I, "Oh, How I Hate to Get Up in the Morning."

Without a doubt, Berlin's most successful Broadway musical was *Annie Get Your Gun* (1946), which was based on the sharpshooting exploits of Annie Oakley. Its songs ranged from the folky "Doin' What Comes Natur'lly" to the sentimental "The Girl That I Marry" and the wryly comic "Anything You Can Do." Finally, of course, there was the song that toasted the footlights in much the same way that "God Bless America" celebrated the country: "There's No Business Like Show Business."

Irving Berlin long ago resisted Hollywood's request to produce a filmed biography. "My songs are my story," he said, and his tale lies in our collective memory. Each time "Blue Skies" or "Puttin' on the Ritz" or "Let's Face the Music and Dance" is sung, or hummed, or whistled, one cannot help but imagine the composer stealing an extra bow.

People, Places, and Things

High Flyers. *On a bright Saturday in April, the ultralight pedal-driven craft "Daedalus 88," top, broke the distance record for human-powered flight by soaring 74 mi (119 km) from Heraklion, Crete, to the island of Santorini. Montreal's Cirque du Soleil, above, dazzled audiences on a year-long North American tour. Le Cirque features 27 acrobats, mimes, daredevils, and clowns—most of whom started out as street performers—in a unique blend of magic, mystery, and theater.*

Rebirths and Revivals. *A taste for nostalgia and show tunes brought cabaret music back in style. At the forefront of the revival was pianist-singer Michael Feinstein, below left, who took his act from the cozy oak room of New York's Algonquin Hotel to the Broadway stage. Hockey superstar Wayne Gretzky, below right, began a new life during the summer, when he married Hollywood starlet Janet Jones and—to the horror of Edmonton Oiler fans—got traded to the Los Angeles Kings. Skateboarding, bottom, a sport perhaps more associated with California culture, reached a new level of popularity. Once confined to the surfer set, then a teen fad, skateboarding entered a new era of jumping ramps, organized competition, and all-important "thrasher" clothes. There were an estimated 20 million riders in 1988—not all of them kids.*

© Walter McBride/Retna Ltd.

UPI/Bettmann Newsphotos

© Mark Richards/Picture Group

© Susan Biddle/The White House

Attention-Getters. *In late April, on the occasion of her 75th birthday, former U.S. First Lady Lady Bird Johnson, above, was honored by Congress and the president for her environmental and humanitarian work. In the East Room of the White House, President Reagan awarded her a congressional gold medal. Also in late April, art dealers from around the world flocked to Sotheby's in New York for the auction of objects, right, owned by the late American pop artist Andy Warhol. The 10,000 items—ranging from statues to cookie jars—fetched a total of $25.3 million. It was one of the most extensive estate sales in history. And in October, at the peak of the presidential campaign and World Series, more attention seemed to focus on three gray whales, below, trapped in an Arctic ice pack at Point Barrow, AK. As the battered giants gulped for air through holes in the ice, an army of scientists, Eskimos, environmentalists, and oil-company officials organized a massive rescue effort—including the U.S. and Soviet governments. After 19 days, a Soviet icebreaker cut a path to open water. The two whales who survived swam to freedom.*

© D. Kirkland/Sygma

© Charles Mason/Black Star

© Elaine Henderson

Past and Present. *During late June, some 7,500 uniformed "troops" and 60,000 spectators gathered in the fields of Gettysburg, PA, above, for a reenactment of the Civil War's infamous Battle of Gettysburg. The reenactment opened a 17-day observance marking the 125th anniversary of that critical and bloody confrontation. At the site of another Civil War battle—Manassas National Park in Virginia, right—a new fight broke out in 1988. When developers announced plans in January for a giant shopping mall on adjacent land where the headquarters of General Lee once stood, a group of Civil War buffs organized the Save the Battlefield Coalition to block construction. The coalition won, as Congress voted to bar the mall. In Washington, DC, the early 19th-century Blair House, below, on Pennsylvania Avenue was reopened in June after an extensive restoration. The memorabilia-filled, four-story residence—containing more than 100 rooms—is used to house heads of state and government on official visits to the United States.*

AP/Wide World

© Bill Ballenberg/"Time" Magazine

The Alphabetical Section

At 11:37 A.M., Sept. 29, 1988, America returned to space. Thirty-two months after the fatal explosion of the space shuttle "Challenger," the redesigned shuttle "Discovery" lifted off from Cape Canaveral and roared into a new era of U.S. space flight. On board were five astronauts with previous shuttle experience—*opposite page:* Mission Commander Frederick H. Hauck *(left front);* Pilot Richard O. Covey *(right front);* and Mission Specialists David C. Hilmers *(left rear),* George D. Nelson *(center rear),* and John M. Lounge. After a successful four-day mission, "Discovery" returned safely to earth at Edwards Air Force Base, CA.

On Day 3 of the flight, the astronauts held a televised memorial for the crew of "Challenger." Said Hilmers: "Many emotions well up in our hearts. Joy for America's return to space; gratitude for our nation's support through difficult times; thanksgiving for the safety of our crew; reverence for those whose sacrifices made our journey possible." Said Lounge: "Gazing outside, we can understand why mankind has looked toward the heavens with awe and wonder since the dawn of human experience."

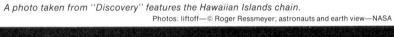

A photo taken from "Discovery" features the Hawaiian Islands chain.

Photos: liftoff—© Roger Ressmeyer; astronauts and earth view—NASA

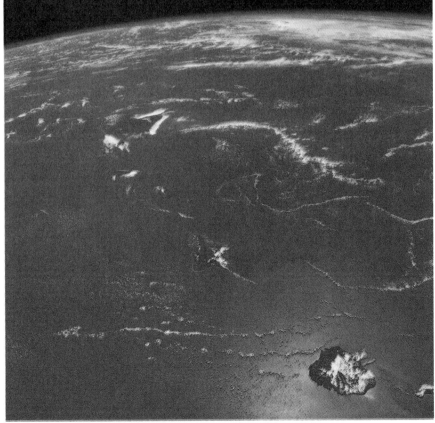

ACCIDENTS AND DISASTERS

AVIATION

Jan. 2—A West German airliner crashes into a hill near Izmir, Turkey, killing all 16 persons aboard.

Jan. 18—A Chinese airliner crashes in southwestern China; all 108 aboard are killed.

Feb. 8—A West German jet is struck by lightning and crashes near Duesseldorf, killing 21 persons.

March 8—Seventeen soldiers are killed when two Army helicopters collide near Fort Campbell, KY.

March 17—A Colombian airliner crashes shortly after takeoff near Cucuta. All 137 aboard are killed.

May 6—Thirty-six are left dead when a Norwegian plane crashes and burns near Norway's coast.

June 12—A DC-9 jet crashes while trying to land at Posadas, Argentina. All 22 aboard are killed.

July 3—A U.S. Navy warship shoots down an Iranian commercial airliner in the Persian Gulf, mistaking it for an attacking F-14 fighter jet. All 290 aboard the plane are killed.

Aug. 17—Pakistan President Muhammad Zia ul-Haq, U.S. Ambassador Arnold L. Raphel, and 28 others are killed when their plane explodes and crashes shortly after takeoff in eastern Pakistan.

Aug. 28—At an air show at Ramstein Air Base near Frankfurt, West Germany, three jets from a precision flying team of the Italian Air Force collide and crash. Fifty-nine persons are left dead and many are injured seriously.

Aug. 31—Fourteen are killed when a Delta jet crashes and burns shortly after takeoff at Dallas-Fort Worth International Airport, TX.

Sept. 9—A passenger plane crashes and explodes near Bangkok, Thailand, killing 75 and injuring six.

Oct. 17—A Uganda Airlines jet crashes near Leonardo da Vinci Airport outside Rome, Italy, killing 31.

Oct. 19—An Indian Airlines jet strikes a tree and explodes near Ahmadabad, India, killing 130.

Oct. 19—Thirty-four are left dead when a passenger plane slams into a hill near Gauhati, India.

Oct. 25—A Peruvian airliner crashes in the Andes near Juliaca, Peru, killing 22 and injuring 50.

Dec. 11—A Soviet military transport plane crashes on a rescue mission to earthquake-devastated Armenia, killing 78.

Dec. 21—A Pan Am Boeing 747 en route from London to New York City crashes into the town of Lockerbie, Scotland; all 259 aboard are killed and 11 of the town's residents are missing. A terrorist act is suspected.

FIRES AND EXPLOSIONS

Jan. 25—A fire breaks out in a coal mine in northern Mexico, killing 41 miners.

March 22—A fire sweeps through Lashio, Burma, leaving 113 dead and 20,000 homeless.

April 10—An accidental fire causes explosions lasting several hours at an army ammunition depot between Rawalpindi and Islamabad, Pakistan. At least 93 persons are killed.

June 1—An explosion in a coal mine near Borken, West Germany, leaves 51 dead.

June 22—A tent fire at a campground near a monastery in Asyut, Egypt, kills 47 Christian pilgrims.

July 7—An oil rig off the east coast of Scotland explodes, killing 165 oil workers in the worst rig disaster in North Sea history.

Dec. 11—Illegal fireworks for sale at a street market in Mexico City, Mexico, explode and cause a fire, killing 62 persons and injuring 83.

LAND AND SEA TRANSPORTATION

Jan. 24—Ninety people are killed and 66 seriously injured in the derailment of an express train in Yunnan Province, southern China.

May 14—A pickup truck traveling the wrong way on a highway near Carrollton, KY, collides with a school bus, rupturing the bus' gas tank. Twenty-seven teenagers are killed.

June 4—A freight train holding 120 tons of explosives blows up in Arzamas, USSR, killing 83.

June 27—Due to brake failure, a commuter train rams another train at the Gare de Lyon rail station in Paris, France. Fifty-six are killed and 32 injured.

July 8—A train derails while crossing a bridge in southern India and plunges into a lake. One hundred ten are killed.

Aug. 6—An overcrowded ferryboat capsizes in the Ganges River in the eastern state of Bihar, India. Four hundred are feared dead.

Aug. 16—A passenger train traveling from Leningrad to Moscow, USSR, derails and bursts into flame, killing 22 and injuring 107.

Sept. 17—As many as 120 are feared dead in Monterrey, Mexico, after four buses carrying people fleeing Hurricane Gilbert turn over in floodwaters.

Oct. 24—An interisland ferry sinks during a typhoon southeast of Manila, Philippines; 360 is killed.

Nov. 9—An oil tanker breaks in two and catches fire during an Atlantic storm off the coast of Newfoundland; all 27 crewmen are feared dead.

Dec. 12—A commuter train crashes into another train stopped ahead of it in south London, England. Thirty-three are feared dead.

Dec. 31—At least 51 are left dead when a boat carrying partygoers to watch fireworks at Copacabana Beach, Brazil, sinks near Rio de Janeiro.

STORMS, FLOODS, AND EARTHQUAKES

Feb. 19—A tropical storm strikes Rio de Janeiro, Brazil, leaving at least 275 dead.

March 13 (reported)—At least 57 persons are left dead when the coastal city of Quelimane, Mozambique, is hit by a cyclone.

Aug. 2—Extensive flash flooding along China's eastern coast leaves 264 dead and 50 missing.

Aug. 20—An earthquake registering 6.5 on the Richter scale shakes eastern India and Nepal, leaving at least 1,000 persons dead; it is the most severe quake in the region since 1950.

Sept. 1—At least 680 are dead in the aftermath of severe flooding in Bangladesh caused by monsoons.

Sept. 17—More than 100 are left dead and 750,000 homeless after Hurricane Gilbert sweeps through the Caribbean, doing the worst damage in Jamaica, Yucatán, Haiti, and the Dominican Republic.

Oct. 3—A week of flooding in India's northwest leaves at least 1,000 dead and many more homeless.

Oct. 23—At least 111 are killed when Hurricane Joan sweeps through Central America for six days. Fifty are reported dead in Nicaragua, 21 in Costa Rica, four in Panama, 25 in Colombia, and 11 in Venezuela.

Nov. 6—An earthquake registering 7.6 on the Richter scale strikes Yunnan Province in southwestern China, killing 938.

Nov. 24—Five days of heavy rains and flooding in southern Thailand leave almost 1,000 persons dead.

Nov. 29—A powerful cyclone strikes coastal areas of Bangladesh and eastern India, killing 2,000.

Dec. 7—One of the worst earthquakes in Soviet history, measuring 6.9 on the Richter scale, strikes Armenia. Entire towns are destroyed and some 25,000 are killed.

MISCELLANEOUS

March 13—Soccer fans rushing to escape a stadium during a hailstorm cause a stampede at Katmandu, Nepal; 90 are killed and dozens injured.

June 4—A two-week heat wave in India causes the deaths of more than 450 persons.

June 23—A landslide strikes the village of Catak, Turkey, killing 300.

July 7—The roof of a department store in Brownsville, TX, collapses during a severe rainstorm, leaving 16 dead and 47 injured.

Oct. 3—Forty persons are feared dead after a landslide buries several farms south of Medellín, Mexico.

Dec. 5—A rumor that a school building in Yaounde, Cameroon, is about to collapse causes a panic. At least 60 students are killed when they jump out windows or are trampled to death.

ADVERTISING

Nineteen eighty-eight was a tense year in the U.S. advertising industry, and one in which the states rather than the federal government became the dominant force in seeking new advertising regulation. But it was also a year of high visibility for the U.S. advertising business, most notably for negative political advertising and its key role in the presidential campaign.

Conflicts. New tensions in the advertising business put it on the front pages of newspapers several times during the year. The siege mentality of the tobacco industry led to one of the year's more dramatic ad account shifts when RJR Nabisco, whose cigarette brands include Winston and Camel, fired one of its agencies, Saatchi & Saatchi Advertising. The reason was that Saatchi, without giving RJR Nabisco the warning it wanted, had created a commercial for another client, Northwest Airlines, in which the airline's no-smoking policy was greeted enthusiastically by passengers. Agencies have been caught before in conflict situations between two advertisers in the same industry, but never before between two companies in different industries and at cross-purposes.

RJR Nabisco's strong reaction was only one reflection of the new feverishness with which the cigarette companies were battling antismoking forces. Philip Morris, whose Marlboro brand is the nation's largest-selling cigarette, launched an aggressive ad campaign emphasizing the economic influence and political clout of the population of smokers. RJR itself introduced a new "smokeless" cigarette in test markets in Phoenix, Tucson, and St. Louis, but the company immediately came under fire from antismoking forces who labeled the product a nicotine delivery system that needed to be regulated.

If the RJR clash over Northwest Airlines was unprecedented, so was the angry walkout by top executives, and many of their staffers, at an agency subsidiary. That's what happened at Lord, Geller, Federico, Einstein, which had been acquired a year earlier in the takeover of the U.S.-based JWT Group (the J. Walter Thompson and Lord Geller agencies) by the London-based WPP Group. The Lord, Geller executives, who were sued by WPP in a case not yet decided, left because they saw their autonomy being challenged by the new owners and were set up in business by Young & Rubicam, a rival of J. Walter Thompson. The $120 million IBM account, the entirety of which had been at Lord, Geller (creator of the Charlie Chaplin campaign for the IBM PC), left for two other agencies. The walkout at Lord, Geller and RJR Nabisco's firing of Saatchi were by-products of the wave of agency and advertiser mega-mergers of recent years.

Ad Volume. Total U.S. advertising spending was expected to reach $118.8 billion in 1988, an 8.4% increase over 1987, according to the McCann-Erickson agency. Late 1987 projections had called for a 9.0% increase, but local retail advertising came in lower than anticipated. All told, local advertising in 1988 was expected to increase 7.0% to $52.5 billion, while national advertising was projected to rise 9.4% to $66.4 billion.

One surprise was the strong upfront market for the 1988–89 network television season. The nearly $3.2 billion that advertisers committed in advance to the new prime-time season set a record, edging out the previous year's $3.1 billion. This was quite unexpected in a year when a six-month strike by the Writers Guild of America delayed the season and even the Summer Olympics delivered disappointing audience ratings. NBC's viewer ratings for the Seoul Games were 22% lower than ABC's for the 1984 Los Angeles Games, and the network reportedly was offering sponsors free air time to compensate for the shortfall.

Government and Legal. Regulation at the state rather than federal level continued to put the greatest unexpected pressure on the U.S. advertising industry. The new force generally did not come from state legislatures, as had been the case in 1987 (when, for example, Florida lawmakers passed—but later repealed—a 5% tax on most services, including advertising). Rather, it was state attorneys general who, perceiving that the U.S. Federal Trade Commission (FTC) in the Reagan administration had grown ineffective in monitoring advertising claims, took up the cause of establishing firmer guidelines. The National Association of Attorneys General first began looking at airline advertising, then turned to rental-car advertising, and was expected to look into such other areas as new-car sales and food health claims.

At the national level, Congress passed a bill that would have reintroduced limits affecting children's television programming, including restrictions on the amount of advertising that could appear. But the bill was vetoed by President Reagan.

Bigger and Bigger. The size and reach of advertisers and ad agencies continued to expand. Philip Morris—whose products include Marlboro cigarettes, Miller beer, Jell-O, and Maxwell House Coffee—had edged into the top spot among the largest U.S. advertisers in 1987, with U.S. expenditures of $1.6 billion. Its acquisition of Kraft Inc. in late 1988 made it far and away the largest advertiser, with spending approaching $2 billion. With the improvement in U.S.-Soviet relations, several U.S. agencies, including Young & Rubicam and Ogilvy & Mather, forged ties with top agencies in the USSR.

STEWART ALTER
"Adweek"

In Geneva, April 14, Afghanistan and Pakistan signed three UN-mediated agreements, calling for the withdrawal of Soviet troops from Afghanistan and other terms. The United States and the USSR agreed to serve as guarantors of the pacts.

AFGHANISTAN

The most momentous event in Afghanistan during 1988 was the Soviet commitment to withdraw its military occupation forces from the country. As the Soviet retreat progressed, anticommunist forces took over much of the countryside and many lines of communication. Although the pro-Soviet Kabul regime maintained a shaky control over the major cities, by year's end its days seemed numbered. With its military, political, and ideological hold weakening, the USSR concentrated on retaining its dominant economic grip.

Military Developments. On Feb. 8, 1988, Soviet leader Mikhail Gorbachev pledged to remove his troops from Afghanistan. When a United Nations (UN) agreement was signed in Geneva on April 14, it called for a Soviet withdrawal to begin on May 15, to be 50% accomplished by August 15, and to be completed by Feb. 15, 1989. An important factor in speeding the Soviet departure was the *mujahidin* (''holy warriors'') guerrilla resistance's use of U.S.-produced Stinger antiaircraft missiles, which denied Soviet forces their accustomed air supremacy.

On May 15, the first 1,500 Soviet troops departed Jalalabad for Kabul in a convoy of 300 tanks and armored personnel carriers. After a farewell parade in the capital, they crossed into the USSR at Termez. Logistical problems and intense *mujahidin* attacks delayed later convoys, but the Soviets met the August 15 deadline for withdrawing half their forces, leaving an acknowledged 50,000 troops still posted in six of the 31 Afghan provinces.

The spotty performance of Kabul-regime troops in repelling *mujahidin* assaults and protecting their retreating allies led to the use of new Soviet military tactics and weapons. Soviet artillery specialists were left in Jalalabad and other cities to advise the Kabul forces. Successful *mujahidin* offensives against regional centers, such as Koteh-ye-Ashrow in Wardak Province in June, were answered by artillery strikes and by carpet bombing from Soviet strategic air force TU-16s based in the USSR. Civilian casualties here and at Qalat, Kunduz, and other towns taken by the *mujahidin* in July and August forced the resistance to abandon these gains and to call off a planned late-summer, full-scale assault on Afghanistan's second-largest city, Kandahar. In October and November, the Soviets began to deploy TU-26 (Backfire) bombers, SS-1 (SCUD) surface-to-surface missiles, and 30 MiG-27 ground-attack fighters against the *mujahidin*, but the tide of battle continued to run in the resistance's favor.

The most dramatic *mujahidin* success came in August, when a chance rocket blew up a fuel and ammunition dump at Kalagay, about 100 mi (160 km) north of Kabul. The blast destroyed two years' supply of ordnance and killed up to 710 Soviet soldiers and civilians.

Rocket and truck-bomb attacks on Kabul and other cities increased during the year, causing many civilian casualties. The *mujahidin* acknowledged strikes on Soviet and regime military and civilian installations but claimed that attacks on bazaars and other civilian targets were Soviet operations designed to discredit the resistance.

Regime moves to prop up its defenses included forming People's Democratic Party of Afghanistan (PDPA) members into military units, raising local militias, giving soldiers a fivefold-to-tenfold pay increase, and promoting dozens of colonels to the rank of general. These measures did not raise the army's sagging morale, nor did they halt the high desertion rate.

Politics. President Najibullah's main political goal in 1988 was the surface democratization of his regime without the loss of real PDPA control. He tried to buy legitimacy by a policy of "national reconciliation" and by offering various concessions. A cease-fire, already in effect on paper during 1987, was extended for another six months in January 1988 but did not lower the heightened level of actual combat. An amnesty for *mujahidin* prisoners who vowed to stop fighting was declared. Death sentences on resistance field commanders such as Ahmad Shah Massoud were lifted.

A program to encourage the return of 5 to 6 million refugees living in Pakistan and Iran was intensified, and "Freedom Hotels" were set up to house them pending resettlement. Non-PDPA (and even anti-PDPA) rule in villages was accepted, provided only that lip-service loyalty to the Kabul regime was given. Various "opposition" parties, including those saying they represented noncommunist workers, peasants, and clergy were welcomed. Concessions were made to various classes formerly subject to discrimination: women, businessmen, landowners, and clergy.

In May, the Revolutionary Council, which acted as the legislature, was abolished, and there were nationwide elections to a new, bicameral National Assembly under provisions of the 1987 Constitution. It was claimed that 1.6 million Afghans, representing 74% of the enfranchised population, elected 51 senators and 210 deputies, of whom 22.6% were PDPA, 15.4% were from the PDPA-dominated National Front (NF), 6% were from registered opposition parties, and 56% (sic) had no party affiliation. An additional 13 senate and 22 deputy seats were reserved for (but not taken by) antiregime groups. The results were suspect because they showed that only 2.2 million of the 14 million Afghan population were deemed eligible to vote.

To downplay the PDPA role in government, Najibullah appointed a "nonparty" prime minister, Mohammed Hassan Sharq, long known as a leftist and suspected of being a KGB (Soviet security) agent. Sharq put together a cabinet of 30 ministers (in place of the 60 in the preceding cabinet), of whom 18 claimed not to be PDPA members.

Demoralization in the faction-ridden PDPA peaked in October when up to 50 ranking party members were arrested, presumably for coup plotting, and the leader of the Khalqi ("masses") group, Interior Minister Sayed Mohammed Gulabzoy, was sent off to Moscow as ambassador. Most (more than 60%) of the party's claimed membership of 205,000 was concentrated in the various police, security, and army units protecting the regime.

By November, even the Moscow press was carrying articles admitting that the regime had lost control in the countryside.

Meanwhile, the *mujahidin* had set up a provisional government in exile in Pakistan, but real political control over much of the country rested with various regional commanders. These commanders set up autonomous local civilian administrations in the areas under their control. The relative influence of the seven Pakistan-based exile leaders, who since 1980 had been the channels for getting weapons into *mujahidin* hands, declined as the field commanders' stature grew.

Economy. The Afghan economy continued to deteriorate during 1988. A Swedish relief group in Pakistan estimated that agricultural production in 1988 was about half that of 1979, with one third of all farmland out of production, the irrigation system in ruins, orchards and vineyards cut down, and herds reduced by 55% for cattle, 66% for sheep and goats (Afghanistan's main herds), and 45% for horses. One million new oxen would be needed for plowing in 1989.

The UN calculated that it would take at least three years and cost $1.5 to $4 billion to bring Afghanistan back up to self-sufficiency in agriculture. In the absence of firm government control, one of the easiest cash crops was the opium poppy. In the chaos of the war, Afghanistan by 1988 had emerged as the largest opium producer in southwest Asia.

The USSR, faced with the loss of its political, ideological, and military investments in Afghanistan, worked hard to preserve its economic stake. Between 1977 and 1987 the share of Afghan trade with developing and capitalist countries had fallen from 72% to 32% of the total, while that with the Soviet Union alone had climbed from 25.6% to more than

---

AFGHANISTAN • Information Highlights

Official Name: Republic of Afghanistan.
Location: Central Asia.
Area: 250,000 sq mi (647 500 km²).
Population: (mid-1988 est.): 14,500,000.
Chief Cities (March 1982): Kabul, the capital, 1,127,417; Kandahar, 198,161; Herat, 155,858.
Government: Najibullah, general secretary, People's Democratic Party (appointed May 1986) and president; Mohammed Hassan Sharq, prime minister (named May 1988). *Legislature*—bicameral National Assembly.
Monetary Unit: Afghani (50.6 afghanis equal U.S.$1, May 1988).
Gross National Product (1986 U.S.$): $3,080,-000,000.
Foreign Trade (1986 U.S.$): *Imports,* $851,000,000; *exports,* $536,000,000.

A member of the "mujahidin" resistance cleans his rifle while catching a little TV. Despite the Geneva agreements, fighting between the Soviets and the resistance continued. Although the Soviets introduced new military tactics and more weapons, the resistance were holding their own in Afghanistan's war.

60%. Afghanistan received 81% of its foreign aid from the USSR—equal to more than 70% of the Kabul state budget. Despite the deteriorating military situation, several big new Soviet projects were planned, including a string of hydroelectric power stations and improvement of the port facilities at the Soviet border town of Hayratan. Aid agreements with the USSR worth $100 million were signed in August.

Moscow put special emphasis on economic links with the nine Afghan provinces bordering the USSR, where 95% of the trade was already with the USSR, and Soviet aid to the region jumped by 300% between 1987 and 1988. There was widespread speculation that Moscow wanted to build a buffer area of economic prosperity and pro-Soviet political orientation there in case the current Kabul regime fell. In addition, there was an intense drive to establish aid and trade links between many Soviet republics and oblasts and all 31 Afghan provinces.

Trying to curry favor, the Najibullah regime wooed private enterprise by promising to return property to refugee landowners and by facilitating loans from the state. The USSR made its own contribution of 50 million rubles for Afghans who wanted to start private businesses.

The USSR also offered to contribute $600 million (in rubles) worth of consumer goods and light industrial products to the UN relief fund for Afghanistan. It refused, however, to join a U.S.-sponsored training program to locate and defuse the 10 million to 20 million land mines that remained in the country.

Diplomatic and Foreign Affairs. The most important international development affecting Afghanistan in 1988 was the signing in Geneva on April 14 of the UN peace accords, according to which the USSR would withdraw its military forces within a year. Ironically, a main belligerent (the *mujahidin*) and the overwhelming majority of Afghans who support them were not represented at the negotiations or the signing, and the resistance categorically refused to accept the accords as binding. The signatories were Pakistan and Afghanistan, with the USSR and the United States signing as coguarantors.

The agreements had five important provisions: Pakistan's and Afghanistan's mutual noninterference in each other's internal affairs; voluntary repatriation of Afghan refugees in Pakistan; withdrawal of all Soviet troops from Afghanistan by Feb. 15, 1989; a promise by the United States and the USSR to respect Afghanistan's neutrality and nonaligned status; and monitoring of the fulfillment of the agreements by a UN force.

The United States announced at the time that there was also an unwritten understanding that the United States and the USSR each had the right to continue arming its respective Afghan friends in "symmetry." The USSR later denied any such agreement and threatened to halt its withdrawal if Pakistan and the United States continued to arm the *mujahidin*.

Despite the accords, Pakistan and Afghanistan each accused the other of aggressive acts: Pakistan complained of more than 100 transborder strikes by aircraft bearing Afghan markings between April and September, and of more than 70 bombings by Afghan agents in Pakistan; the Afghans and Soviets charged Pakistan with violating the Geneva accords by continuing to arm the resistance and with employing Pakistani troops and artillery in direct support of the *mujahidin* on Afghan soil.

The Kabul regime enjoyed little international recognition. India, however, in May gave President Najibullah a warm reception during a three-day state visit.

On December 7, Soviet leader Gorbachev asked the UN to supervise a cease-fire that would permit the safe withdrawal of the occupational forces. Ignoring its Afghan allies, Moscow then held peace talks alone with resistance leaders in Saudi Arabia and Pakistan.

ANTHONY ARNOLD
Hoover Institution, Stanford

AFRICA

For the continent of Africa, the year 1988 marked several significant birthdays. The Organization of African Unity (OAU) celebrated its 25th anniversary in 1988. Established in 1963 as a symbol of African freedom and as a framework for cooperation among African countries, the OAU has held annual meetings of heads of state, debated issues of continental importance, particularly decolonialization and the elimination of apartheid in South Africa, and supported efforts by Africans to mediate conflicts in their region.

Another birthday was that of the UN Economic Commission for Africa (ECA), set up 30 years earlier. Since its birth in 1958, the ECA has become a voice for African views on major economic issues facing the continent. It drew up the Lagos Plan of Action, which African heads of state supported at the 1980 meeting of the OAU. The plan set out a long-run development strategy for the continent based on the eventual creation of an Africa-wide common market which would promote trade, investment, and growth.

These celebrations, though appropriate, were muted. The OAU had much to be proud of—its continuing existence over a quarter century with such a large, diverse, and at times fractious membership was an achievement. The ECA also had succeeded in focusing the attention of Africa and the world on key problems impeding economic progress on the continent. But much of Africa remained troubled in 1988. While good progress was made in resolving some long-running conflicts, others continued. And economic problems showed no sign of diminishing. Added to these problems were those of debt, disease, and natural disasters which continued to plague the continent.

Conflicts and Negotiations. A number of hopeful political trends were apparent by the end of 1988. Negotiations were at last underway between the protagonists in several of Africa's chronic conflicts. The United States mediated a series of meetings between the South Africans, the Cubans, and the Angolans that led to an accord on the withdrawal of the South African and Cuban troops from Angola together with a timetable for political independence for Namibia. The Sudanese government began discussions with the leader of the guerrilla movement fighting in the south of the Sudan. The Polisario, long challenging Moroccan control over the Western Sahara, began negotiations with Moroccan officials. Ethiopia and Somalia as well as Morocco and Algeria, long hostile neighbors, renewed diplomatic relations.

But renewed diplomatic relations between governments and negotiations between political and military adversaries provided no guarantee that peace would be restored in those areas. The conflict in Angola was an especially complex one to resolve and one of the main protagonists—the Angolan insurgency group, the National Union for the Total Independence of Angola (UNITA)—was not included in the main negotiations. And mutual distrust between the South Africans and the Cubans had made agreement on a timetable for the final withdrawal of Cuban troops difficult. Nevertheless, the success of the negotiations gave some hope that the coming year would see fewer conflicts in Africa than in the recent past.

Several prolonged and bloody conflicts continued with no sign of negotiation or peace. The Eritreans, fighting for their independence from Ethiopia for the past quarter of a century, had some military successes against Ethiopian troops during 1988, destroying tanks and reportedly capturing, killing, or wounding 20,000 soliders. The Ethiopian government's response to Eritrean successes was to step up its military pressure rather than to seek a negotiated solution to their conflict.

The South African-supported insurgency movement in Mozambique, Renamo (Mozambican National Resistance), continued its attacks on Mozambican military and civilian targets. A U.S. government-funded report on atrocities by Renamo was published in 1988 and dampened overt foreign support for the guerrilla movement. But fighting in Mozambique continued.

Conflict also broke out in Somalia as a Somali guerrilla group sought to topple the Somali government. And an ethnic-based massacre took place in Burundi, when soldiers of the minority Tutsi tribe murdered several thousand Hutu tribesmen in retaliation for several murders by Hutus of Tutsis. Ethnic tensions have remained high in Burundi since the large-scale massacres in that country in the early 1970s.

Economic Problems. Much of sub-Saharan Africa remained in the grip of an economic crisis during 1988, although some improvements in economic conditions were anticipated. The International Monetary Fund (IMF) projected a growth rate of 3% for Africa in 1988, the highest since 1980. Also in 1988, food production in Southern Africa was up over 1987 but drought in Ethiopia again threatened hunger there. Moreover, the Sudan and the Sahelian countries of Africa faced a severe locust infestation that threatened the first good harvests they had had in several years.

The locust infestation was centered in the Sudan and occurred as a consequence of good 1988 rains in part of that country. Because of conflict and economic dislocations in the Sudan, however, Sudanese government officials and foreign experts were slow to begin spraying against the locusts. As a result, locust destruction could turn out to be severe and periodic infestations could threaten crops in the Sahel in coming years.

More than two dozen countries sought to deal with their economic problems through structural adjustment programs, undertaking a variety of reforms in their economic policies and public institutions supported by loans from the IMF and the World Bank. A number of reform programs were beginning to bear fruit, with agricultural production rising in response to higher prices for farm products combined with favorable weather. In Ghana, the country implementing the broadest and most sustained program of reforms, overall economic growth had exceeded 5% annually for 1985–88. But by the end of 1988, it was clear that most of sub-Saharan Africa had a long way to go before economic recovery and sustained growth could be achieved. A review of Africa's economic-recovery programs conducted by the United Nations focused on the continuing shortages in resources available to those governments implementing reform programs. Without sufficient resources, it was argued, reforms would fail to promote recovery and growth.

Some hope could be drawn from the fact that Japan committed itself to a major increase in its aid to sub-Saharan Africa, and negotiations on the ninth replenishment of the International Development Association (IDA), the soft loan window of the World Bank, began in 1988. Sub-Saharan Africa has benefited from an increasing amount of concessional aid from the IDA and hopes were that that aid would increase further once the IDA ninth negotiations were completed in 1989.

During 1988, the problem of foreign debt emerged as a major concern of many African leaders. The total debt owed by sub-Saharan African countries to the rest of the world amounted to $125 billion, a small proportion of all the debt of developing countries. It was roughly equal to the total debt of Brazil. But for many African countries, their foreign debt represented a heavier burden for them than the debt of Brazil did for Brazil. An increasing number of African governments had to seek debt reschedulings and several—the Sudan, Liberia, Sierra Leone, and Zambia—stopped paying some of their debts, including their debts to the IMF, altogether. African leaders met under OAU auspices and called for an international conference of Africa's creditors and African debtors to discuss the debt problem.

Major creditor nations like the United States rejected the idea of an international conference. However, at the Toronto economic summit of the major industrial democracies and later at a meeting in Paris, major creditor nations proposed a "menu" of concessional debt-relief measures for low-income African countries, to be implemented in upcoming rescheduling agreements. These measures included cancellation of one third of debt-servicing payments, subsidies on interest rates on debt, and longer repayment periods. However, the impact of these various proposals remained unclear since these proposals have yet to be implemented and may require in some cases that debts be repaid more rapidly. Few Africans regarded these proposals as sufficient to relieve their heavy debt burdens.

Other Problems. AIDS remained a grave threat to the populations of many African nations, particularly those of Central Africa. Estimates that 15% to 20% of the sexually active age groups in urban areas were infected with the AIDS virus continued to be made. However, it also appeared that the rate of increase in infection had slowed considerably. A growing number of African governments were willing to acknowledge that AIDS was a problem in their countries and had begun education campaigns to encourage safe sex. Posters, television advertisements, and, in an effort to reach illiterate members of their populations, songs and films were used to warn of the threat of AIDS. In September the Third International Conference on AIDS met in a small Tanzanian town to discuss the economic effects of the disease.

As if the Sudan did not have enough problems, with its conflicts, economic decline, and infestation of locusts, the capital city, Khartoum, and other areas along the Nile, were struck by massive floods, leaving thousands homeless.

In West, Central, and Southern Africa, the dumping of toxic wastes by Western industrialized companies—sometimes under false pretenses or as a result of bribing local officials—became a hot issue in 1988. Toxic-waste dumps were discovered in ten countries. Africans were outraged at what they saw as yet another tragedy visited upon them, this time by foreigners. Several nations acted to prevent the African coastline from becoming a disposal site. Those responsible for dumping the wastes in Nigeria and Guinea were forced to remove them but the question remained—how many toxic-waste sites in Africa had not yet been discovered?

Foreign Relations. One of the most interesting changes affecting Africa in 1988 was in Soviet policies. The USSR actively cooperated in promoting negotiations between Angola, its client state, the Cubans, and South Africa. It also appeared to be backing away from its support of liberation movements and violence as a means to resolve conflicts in Southern Africa. These changes appeared to signal a fundamental shift in Soviet policies, away from regional confrontations with the United States, toward a more cooperative posture. Only time will tell how deep or permanent these changes really are.

U.S. policies in Africa were much the same as in previous years, with two exceptions. U.S. policy in promoting negotiations in Southern Africa became much more active as Chester

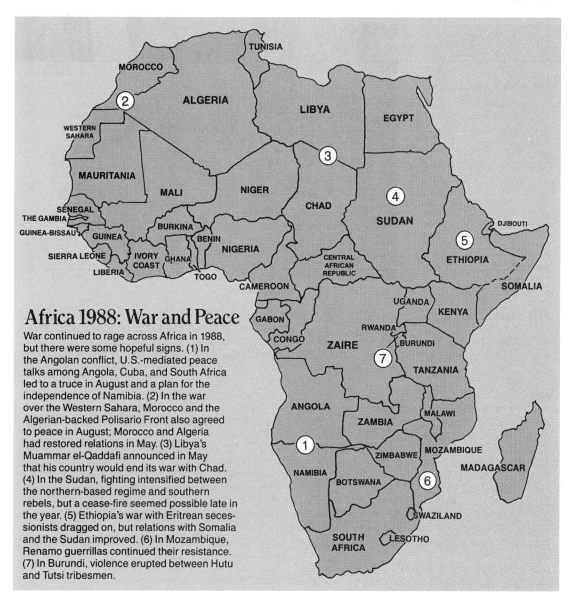

Africa 1988: War and Peace

War continued to rage across Africa in 1988, but there were some hopeful signs. (1) In the Angolan conflict, U.S.-mediated peace talks among Angola, Cuba, and South Africa led to a truce in August and a plan for the independence of Namibia. (2) In the war over the Western Sahara, Morocco and the Algerian-backed Polisario Front also agreed to peace in August; Morocco and Algeria had restored relations in May. (3) Libya's Muammar el-Qaddafi announced in May that his country would end its war with Chad. (4) In the Sudan, fighting intensified between the northern-based regime and southern rebels, but a cease-fire seemed possible late in the year. (5) Ethiopia's war with Eritrean secessionists dragged on, but relations with Somalia and the Sudan improved. (6) In Mozambique, Renamo guerrillas continued their resistance. (7) In Burundi, violence erupted between Hutu and Tutsi tribesmen.

Crocker, the assistant secretary of state for Africa, mediated a series of discussions among key protagonists. And, due largely to domestic budgetary stringencies, U.S. economic assistance to sub-Saharan African countries remained at roughly $850 million, 25% below its peak of 1985.

Papal Visit. A September visit by Pope John Paul II to Southern Africa provided a spiritual lift for that region. He was received especially warmly in war-torn Mozambique and his visit focused world attention on the suffering of not only Mozambicans but of the economic and political problems of this unfortunate region. However, the pope's visit was not without surprises or controversy. In Maseru, Lesotho, a bus load of Catholic pilgrims en route to see the pontiff was held hostage by hijackers demanding to meet the pope and Lesotho's King Moshoeshoe II. The bus crashed on the grounds of the British chancery and was stormed by South African security forces. Three hijackers and a 14-year-old hostage were killed.

Although the pope had not planned to stop in South Africa itself, his plane was forced by bad weather to land in Johannesburg. A number of Africans complained that he did not take a sufficiently critical position on South African racial discrimination and regional destabilization policies. The fallout from the pope's visit is a further reminder that peace and tranquility will continue to be elusive in this part of the world as long as governments follow policies that deny basic rights to their own people.

CAROL LANCASTER
Director, African Studies Program
Georgetown University

U.S. Secretary of Agriculture Richard Lyng details the nation's drought conditions in early July. As the situation worsened throughout the summer—the hottest in 52 years—grain crop estimates were revised downward repeatedly.

AP/Wide World

AGRICULTURE

Even with modern technology, agriculture was still vulnerable to bad weather in 1988. Severe drought ravaged the breadbaskets of North America, reducing U.S. corn production and Canadian wheat output by one third.

In North Dakota, springs went dry following several years of dry weather, and many cattle ranchers decided to quit ranching. Heat seared the Midwest, leading climatologists to wonder whether the anticipated "greenhouse effect," in which the earth's average temperatures will rise, was not already being manifested.

Weather was also a problem in Argentina, China, Bangladesh, sub-Saharan Africa, and elsewhere, causing a drop in world grain production.

Asian hog and chicken producers worried that they might not be able to obtain their feedstuffs in the usually dependable American market. American grain reserves proved more than adequate to cover a year of drought, but world grain and soybean prices rose sharply. U.S. consumer groups demanded an end to U.S. grain export subsidies, although domestic food prices rose no more than 2% as a consequence of the drought.

Weather, wars, and inadequate agricultural growth created demands for large-scale food aid—for Afghan refugees in Pakistan, Mozambican refugees in Malawi, drought victims in Tunisia, Angola, and Mozambique, refugees in Zambia, North Vietnamese, and displaced persons in Uganda.

World agriculture on the whole continued its technological and structural advance. Meat and dairy products, which comprised more than half the total value of agricultural production in industrial countries in 1988, were becoming increasingly mass-produced foods.

Taiwan and South Korea, for example, were moving to large livestock confinement operations which contrasted with the tiny farms that produced fruits, vegetables, and field crops. Biotechnology was becoming widely applicable in improving genetics, nutrition, and pest and disease control.

U.S. agriculture continued its recovery from the recession of the early 1980s, despite the drought which reduced production of many crops. Among the positive indicators were increased farmland values (Midwestern land had recovered as much as half of its lost value). Farm debt was down. Farm financial institutions had been buttressed to withstand the strains of previous bad loans.

Governments of industrial countries wished to reduce the costs of agricultural programs. The heads of 12 European Community (EC) governments initiated a system of "automatic price stabilizers" which would reduce future government outlays. The Reagan administration repeated its goal of minimizing U.S. government influence on agricultural markets. Multinational conferences focused on reducing government subsidies to agriculture.

But by a new measure of government's direct and indirect subsidies to agriculture, governments were spending more, not less. According to this new "producer subsidy equivalent," the U.S. government was subsidizing 36% of American farmers' income, up from 17% five years earlier. The European Community's Common Agricultural Program was subsidizing 50% of European farmers' incomes (up from 29%) and Japan's government was subsidizing 78% (up from 67%) of its farmers' income.

Trade Policies. In 1988 several dramatic breakthroughs enhanced agricultural trade. A free-trade agreement between the United States and Canada was expected to erase trade

barriers between these two countries over the next decade. The European Community was moving vigorously to end all its internal trade barriers by 1992. The United States signed a new agreement which ended Japan's long-standing reluctance to import substantial amounts of meat and fruit from the United States. Japan agreed to remove its quotas over three years, blunting the immediate economic impact by relying on higher protective tariffs. These tariffs would, in turn, be reduced in the more distant future. Korea agreed to admit 14,500 tons of U.S. beef under tariff, with revenues from the tariff to go directly to Korean beef producers.

U.S. Exports. U.S. agricultural exports of $34 billion in fiscal year 1988 were sharply higher than the $28 billion in 1987. The rise was due to higher world grain prices, reduced supplies among competitors, more animal exports, and increasing consumer demand.

The European Community (EC) remained the largest market for U.S. agriculture, and the 1988 outlook was for continued growth of exports to Europe. There were increased exports of oilseeds, fruits, and nuts, offsetting U.S. declines in the EC market share of feed grains, food grains, and cotton. However, the EC had decided to ban imports of meat treated with hormones, making it likely that the United States would lose much of its remaining European market for meat and meat products.

East Asia was a second large market, absorbing about one third of total U.S. agricultural exports, and prospects appeared good for future growth in this market. Japan, in particular, was ranked as the country with best prospects for increasing agricultural imports from the United States, because the Japanese had become interested in Western-style foods. Also, like Westerners, they were seeking good health through better diets. In a concurrent trend, American convenience foods were increasingly attractive to Japanese women, half of whom worked outside the home. In addition, the Japanese are expected to buy more products at lower consumer prices resulting from expanded U.S. exports of high-value foods such as beef.

The Japanese were not the only customers. U.S. exports to China were expected to show a large gain over the previous year. By offering good prices in 1988, the United States was also quietly becoming the principal wheat supplier to Mexico.

Meanwhile, the character of total U.S. exports changed slightly, with the resurgence of high-value agricultural products such as prepared meats, dairy products, wheat flour, and refined sugar, and raw foods such as eggs, fruits, nuts, and fresh vegetables. The United States and the European Community were in tight competition in world markets for many of these products.

The United States and the USSR worked toward a new grain agreement under which the USSR (the biggest importer of U.S. wheat) presumably would buy huge amounts of wheat, corn, soybeans, and soybean meal. USSR negotiators were reluctant to sign another five-year agreement, because they had high hopes that under USSR reforms Soviet production soon would reduce import needs. The United States was the major source of the Soviet imports in fiscal year 1988; these imports included 22 million tons of wheat and 10 million tons of feed grains.

Other Major Exporters. The Soviets shared a five-year agreement with Canada as well, but Canada's sales were delayed during 1988 due to the drought shortfall. Australia and Argentina also were obliged to wait for a late wheat crop in 1988 to fulfill export obligations. A 19% decline in Australian acreage reduced production by 23%, and reduced wheat exports by a projected 33%. Australia, like the United States, achieved an agreement with Japan permitting more beef exports to Japan.

The European Community had only limited export sales of new crop wheat and barley. EC production of wheat in 1988 was estimated at 74 million tons, up from 71 million in 1987. Feed grain production was also up from 79 million tons in 1987 to 81 million in 1988. Red meat and pork production edged upward, but confinement pork producers in the Netherlands and Denmark faced limits on further growth because of the unsolved problem of animal-waste disposal (the same environmental problem faced producers in other populous countries such as Taiwan and South Korea).

The Soviet Union. Although Soviet agriculture had been targeted for major reforms in 1988, the Soviet agricultural economy performed well enough compared to the previous year. Thanks to above-average July rain in grain areas, the Soviets harvested their fourth largest grain crop of the previous ten years. Meat, milk, and egg production was up slightly, and fertilizer production was above planned levels. However, consumer demand for a better diet also was increasing.

Soviet General Secretary Mikhail Gorbachev continued his vigorous advocacy of agricultural reform. He told the Communist Party's Central Committee in July 1988 that agricultural resources were not being used efficiently, and that among the basic changes to be made was a vast reorganization of the agricultural bureaucracy. Collective and state farms were being broken into smaller units. Producers' cooperatives were permitted to be established as subdivisions within larger farms. The government even authorized individual farmers to rent land, part of a full-scale return to family farming. These farmers are able to purchase tractors, trucks, and other equipment, and to hire workers at wage levels paid by the govern-

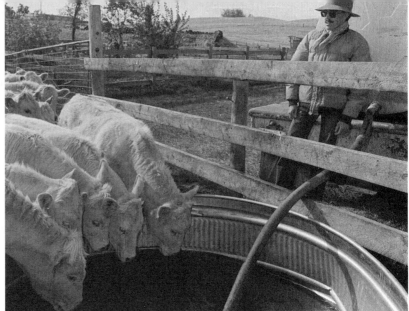

The drought was no less devastating in Canada than in the United States. Wells were running dry, pastures were parched, and farmers were suffering. Wheat production, for example, was down by about one third.

© Randy Fiedler

ment. Eventually, Soviets hope to make agriculture self-financing. Gorbachev indicated that his new rural policies were intended to return the country to traditional rural values that had been disrupted by Stalin's violent collectivization.

China. Despite floods in several southern and far northern provinces, China's grain output in fiscal year 1988 was up slightly from the previous year, but well below the record level of 1984. In 1988, China became a "net importer" (importing more goods than exporting) of U.S. agricultural products. Furthermore, China's exports of corn were down by 40 million bushels, as Japan and South Korea shifted their corn purchases to the United States.

After much debate in China about the underlying causes for this slowdown in grain production in recent years, the government increased some grain and oilseed crop prices. It also provided bonuses to farmers using fertilizer, and worked to reform the marketing system. As a result wheat production was expected to increase in the future. China again was expected to export soybeans, though as a producer it fell to third place behind the United States and Brazil. As the world's largest cotton producer, China experienced a sharp recovery from low production in 1987.

India. India, like China, reemerged as a large importer of grain after having become a significant exporter. Below-normal monsoon rains in 1987 reduced India's grain production and depleted grain reserves, requiring large imports of wheat and corn, some from the United States. Although India had made large strides in productivity, the poor 1987 season demonstrated that it would continue to be an occasional importer as well as an occasional exporter of food and feed grains.

Other Asian Countries. In 1988, Japan, Taiwan, and South Korea continued to move to-ward large-unit production of pork, dairy products, and poultry, increasing output to meet growing domestic demand. East Asian countries collectively had a surplus of rice, mainly because consumers were diversifying diets away from traditional foods. These countries again imported large amounts of feedstuffs for livestock, and soybean oil for human consumption, largely from the United States.

Taiwan and South Korea agricultures were caught in the paradox of modernized production systems feeding into inefficient traditional marketing systems. Food demands increased—but at price levels that did not yield adequate incomes for many small farmers. In Taiwan, the pull of off-farm jobs placed farm families under stress, while in Korea small farmers tended to be underemployed. Farmers voting in both countries became important in election politics; government officials listened responsively to farmers' demands for health insurance and adequate farm prices.

Africa. Millions of people in sub-Saharan African countries suffered malnutrition and hunger partly as a consequence of war, weather, and pests, but also because most African governments resisted positive agricultural development. For most Africans, the challenge of finding enough food grew more serious.

Latin America. Food shortages worsened also in parts of Latin America, and the United States continued to find large markets in Latin America for its wheat and other grains. The United States maintained demands for tropical products such as coffee and bananas. In addition, Southern Hemisphere producers, especially in Chile, became more firmly established as U.S. sources of "winter" fruits and vegetables.

See also FOOD.

DONALD F. HADWIGER
Iowa State University

ALABAMA

Relations between Republican Gov. Guy Hunt and the overwhelmingly Democratic legislature—Senate (30D-5R) and House of Representatives (89D-16R)—took top billing over the presidential election in Alabama in 1988.

Electoral Results. On November 8, Alabama was one of the first of the 40 states that ultimately ended up in George Bush's victory column. From the first postconvention polls through those conducted only a few days before the election, Vice-President Bush was shown to be in a commanding lead for the state's nine electoral votes. Also, for the first time more Alabama voters identified themselves as Republicans than as Democrats in public-opinion polls.

In the U.S. congressional contests, all of Alabama's incumbents—5D-2R—won reelection in November. E.C. Hornsby (D) was elected chief justice of the state Supreme Court.

In local elections about 150 blacks won municipal council seats. Many more opportunities for blacks became available as a result of litigation in federal court requiring district rather than at-large elections in areas where due to racially polarized voting, blacks previously had had difficulty winning. An additional 64 Republicans also were elected to local offices.

Flag Controversy. While the rest of the nation was preoccupied by the campaign debate over requiring schoolchildren to pledge allegiance to the American flag, Alabama was embroiled in a controversy over the Confederate flag, which flies atop the state capitol. On February 2, State Rep. Thomas Reed, president of the state NAACP chapter, and other black legislators were arrested for trying to climb a fence around the capitol in order to take the flag down. The arrested legislators' case was continued indefinitely.

Meanwhile, on September 30, Representative Reed was convicted of extortion in connection with efforts to win an early release from prison for a convicted murderer. Reed, the senior black member of the legislature, was sentenced to four years in prison and was expelled from the House of Representatives, where he had served since the 1960s.

Legislative Controversies. On February 8 an education task force designated by House Speaker Jimmy Clark made a report in which it suggested that, by making modest increases in the amount of state income tax paid by the more affluent, the state's per pupil spending could be brought up to the regional average. No new taxes were adopted during the regular legislative session, however, and it adjourned on May 5 with neither an education nor a general-fund budget having been passed. The first of the two special sessions to be called by Governor Hunt convened on August 30. A $2.44 billion education budget (funded from existing tax sources) passed in this session, along with a companion measure providing a 7.5% pay raise for classroom teachers and school workers. Legislative failure to pass the general-fund budget necessitated the second special session, which enacted such a budget only a few days before the state's new fiscal year began on October 1. Balancing the general-fund budget required the enactment of new taxes (primarily on gambling) which, it was estimated, would bring in about $35 million in additional revenue annually.

Questions pertaining to ethical conduct occupied the legislature during 1988. Senators and lobbyists called off a beach retreat to be paid for by a coalition of interest groups after unfavorable public and media reactions.

School Siege. National attention was focused on Tuscaloosa on February 2 when James Harvey entered the private West End Christian School and held children and teachers hostage until persuaded by Governor Hunt to release them by the false promise of a pardon. Harvey was charged with 84 counts of kidnaping. He pleaded guilty and was sentenced to life imprisonment.

Drought and Tornado. In the summer, Governor Hunt declared a drought disaster in each of the state's 67 counties. The Muscle Shoals area of northern Alabama was hardest hit, with a 50% deficit in rainfall. Farmers in all Alabama counties were eligible for drought-relief funds made available by the U.S. Congress in August. By the time the federal aid became available, renewed rains had provided significant relief for a majority of the state's crops threatened by drought. In fact, soybean, cotton, and peanut yields were expected to be in excess of 1987 figures.

On November 20 a powerful tornado swept through Tuscaloosa, damaging more than 100 houses and causing several injuries.

WILLIAM H. STEWART
The University of Alabama

ALABAMA • Information Highlights

Area: 51,705 sq mi (133 915 km²).
Population (July 1, 1987): 4,083,000.
Chief Cities (July 1, 1986 est.): Montgomery, the capital, 194,290; Birmingham, 277,510; Mobile, 203,260; Huntsville, 163,420.
Government (1988): *Chief officers*—governor, Guy Hunt (R); lt. gov. Jim Folson, Jr. (D). *Legislature*—Senate, 35 members; House of Representatives, 105 members.
State Finances (fiscal year 1987): *Revenue,* $7,077,000,000; *expenditure,* $6,333,000,000.
Personal Income (1987): $48,753,000,000; per capita, $11,940.
Labor Force (June 1988): *Civilian labor force,* 1,875,200; *unemployed,* 129,000 (6.9% of total force).
Education: *Enrollment* (fall 1986)—public elementary schools, 518,982; public secondary, 214,753; colleges and universities, 216,060. *Public school expenditures* (1986–87), $1,802,000,000 ($2,610 per pupil).

ALASKA

The major issue in Alaska in 1988 was the continued depression in oil prices and related activities that affected the declining real-estate market and continuing high levels of business failures. Some of the failures included major financial institutions of the state. Also adversely influenced was the state's fiscal year 1990 budget. Gov. Steve Cowper and state legislators were at loggerheads at the end of the year, especially regarding revised revenue projections due to continuing reductions in market prices for Alaska crude oil.

The Election. Voter turnout in the November 1988 presidential election did not meet Lt. Gov. Stephen McAlpine's projection of 72%, but did exceed 61% of the registered voters in the state. While the statewide vote went to Republican presidential candidate George Bush by a 24% margin and gave incumbent Republican Don Young a resounding victory in his race for reelection to the U.S. House of Representatives, it was the amendment and initiatives on the ballot that apparently caused the high turnout. Voters in Alaska overwhelmingly supported an amendment requiring preference for Alaska residents on public construction projects, voting for the measure by an 84% to 16% margin. Voters defeated an initiative aimed at overturning the recent restructuring of the University of Alaska system.

As a result of the election, Republicans controlled the Alaska Senate by a 12 to eight margin. However, given the vagaries of Alaska politics, the organization of the Senate, which took place immediately following the election,

resulted in a coalition comprising all 20 members of the Senate. This result effectively eliminated, for the first time in state history, minority-party representation in its organization. The state House of Representatives, while remaining in nominal control of the Democratic Party, almost certainly would be organized again by a coalition consisting of rural, or "bush caucus," members, and representatives of either party from the more urbanized districts in the state.

Economy. A decline in the market price for Alaska crude oil continued to affect Alaska's economy. In addition to its budget problems, the state experienced an out-migration of population as employment opportunities decreased, beginning in 1986. Alaska Department of Labor statistics, as well as those provided by the municipality of Anchorage, indicated that while the decline continued, it did so at a much slower pace in 1988 than in 1987. Anchorage, Alaska's largest city, had experienced a net loss in population of approximately 30,000 since 1986, with two thirds of that loss occurring in 1987. Unemployment rates in Anchorage were equivalent to those of 1984, about 7.8%. However, unemployment in other areas of the state remained higher than that of Anchorage. The bad news concerning the 1988 totals, according to the Anchorage municipality, was that this latest out-migration consisted mostly of families, unlike that of 1987, which consisted mostly of single males who had been employed in oil-related industries and construction. Furthermore, there was concern that the latest decline in oil prices could cause more unemployment, which could trigger more out-migration.

Environment. Arctic Alaska was the center of international interest for two weeks in October, as the plight of three California gray whales trapped by rapidly forming ice became known. A rescue effort that included the appearance of two ice-breaking ships donated by the USSR, as well as equipment, time, and

Alaska's Corrections Commissioner Susan Humphrey-Barnett attends the dedication of the state's new $48 million, 412-bed, maximum-security prison, located in Seward.

© Fran Dorner/NYT Pictures

money donated by the Alaska National Guard, the North Slope Borough, and oil-industry representatives, received worldwide media attention. The irony of the rescue, which saved two of the three whales, was that its primary success was due, not to modern equipment used or attempted, but to the efforts of several Inupiat Eskimos wielding chain saws donated for that purpose (*see* page 86).

An internal report by officials of the Fish and Wildlife Service of the U.S. Department of the Interior indicated that oil development in northern Alaska had caused much more environmental damage than the government had predicted.

Prison Construction. Alaska's first maximum-security prison opened in Seward in June. The 412-bed prison would house Alaskan inmates that prior to its completion had been forced to serve their time in facilities in other states.

Carl E. Shepro, *University of Alaska*

ALBANIA

In 1988, Albania continued the trend of recent years toward a mild easing of domestic restrictions and a significant improvement of its relations with other countries.

Domestic Affairs. Albanian leaders rejected publicly the possibility of introducing reforms similar to those taking place in the Soviet Union. They denounced the "insults and libels" suffered by the Soviet leader Stalin as a result of *glasnost* and warned that *perestroika* was leading the USSR to "barefaced capitalism." However, increased popular criticism of inefficiency and corruption in the Albanian government, cultural media, and economic sector was permitted, and Albanians were urged to free themselves from "old official and obsolete molds."

Economy. In December 1987, Niko Gjyzari, chairman of the State Planning Commission, declared that the main goals of the 1987 state economic plan had been reached, especially in the areas of mining, agriculture, and living

---

ALBANIA • Information Highlights

Official Name: People's Socialist Republic of Albania.

Location: Southern Europe, Balkan peninsula.

Area: 11,100 sq mi (28 750 km²).

Population (mid-1988 est.): 3,100,000.

Chief City (mid-1985): Tiranë, the capital, 215,857.

Government: *Head of state,* Ramiz Alia, chairman of the Presidium (took office November 1982) and first secretary of the Albanian Workers' Party (April 1985). *Head of government,* Adil Carçani, chairman, Council of Ministers—premier (took office January 1982). *Legislature* (unicameral)—People's Assembly, 250 members.

Monetary Unit: Lek (7 leks equals U.S.$1, July 1988).

Gross National Product (1986 est. U.S.$): $2,700,-000,000–$2,900,000,000.

---

standards. However, Gjyzari admitted serious shortfalls in oil and chrome production, engineering, and coal extraction. The draft budget for 1988 projected a 13% rise in income over 1987 and a 5% rise in expenditures. Wage differentials were approved for skilled and difficult jobs and bonuses were offered for overproduction and production improvements.

Foreign Affairs. Albania conspicuously improved its ties with a large number of countries. In August 1987, Greece announced that it was abolishing the "state of war" that had existed with Albania since 1940. In subsequent months, a series of new agreements was signed by the two nations. In September 1987, Albanian Deputy Foreign Minister Sokrat Plaka visited Athens to discuss a wide range of bilateral issues with prominent Greek officials. The following month, a cultural exchange agreement was signed in Tirana, and in November 1987 the Greek foreign minister signed an outline agreement for economic and commercial cooperation between the two countries. In April 1988, Albania and Greece signed their first post World War II accord to encourage cross-border trade.

At the beginning of October 1987, Albania and West Germany formally established diplomatic relations; negotiations had been going on since 1983. Later that month, West German Foreign Minister Hans-Dietrich Genscher visited Tirana to discuss "developing bilateral relations in all spheres." In November 1987, Albania was given authorization to receive DM 6 million (about $10.7 million) in West German goods without the obligation to pay for them. And the new West German ambassador, Friedrich Kronek, arrived in Tirana on Jan. 7, 1988.

In the latter half of 1987, Albania also established diplomatic relations with Jordan, Canada, Uruguay, and Bolivia, and agreed to do so in the future with the Philippines and East Germany.

Two-way recriminations continued over the status and activities of the Albanian ethnic population in the Yugoslav autonomous province of Kosovo. Head of State Ramiz Alia charged that the Albanians had been "quarantined, isolated, and exposed to segregation." Yugoslavia accused Albania of stirring the Kosovo Albanians to violence against local Serbs and to secession. It also charged serious Albanian underutilization of the new Titograd-Shkodër railroad line, resulting in huge financial losses for Yugoslavia. Nevertheless, in December 1987, the two countries signed a new trade protocol and planned to discuss a cultural agreement.

In February 1988, Albanian Foreign Minister Reis Malile attended a high-level conference of six Balkan states in Belgrade. Albania refused, however, to attend the 1988 Summer Olympic Games in Seoul, South Korea.

Joseph Frederick Zacek
State University of New York at Albany

ALBERTA

During 1988, Albertans' attention was divided among the oil and gas industry, business generally, weather, agriculture, politics, a band of Indians, and the world of sports.

Sports. Residents of Alberta, generally, and Calgary, in particular, were elated in mounting the 1988 Winter Olympics. Despite serious preliminary problems, many dealing with ticket distribution, the games, which were held in Calgary, Feb. 13–28, 1988, were considered an overwhelming success and realized a profit of some C$46 million. The sum would be devoted to the promotion of amateur sport and athletics throughout Canada. Particularly popular was the movement across Canada of the Olympic flame by thousands of randomly chosen Canadians. (*See also* SPORTS—*The XV Winter Games,* page 500.)

For the first time in history, Edmonton held both the National Hockey League's Stanley Cup and the Canadian Football League's Grey Cup in 1988. The Edmonton Eskimos had captured the Grey Cup in November 1987, and the Oilers retained the Stanley Cup in May 1988. Oiler fans were disturbed greatly, however, when the team's star, Wayne Gretzky, was traded to the Los Angeles Kings (*see* page 85). Efforts by the Eskimos to retain the Grey Cup in 1988 were unsuccessful. Meanwhile, Lethbridge captured the year's Canadian curling championship.

Business and Industry. Early in the year the oil and gas industry, of primary importance to the province, showed signs of recovery after several poor years. Declining prices following the cessation of hostilities between Iran and Iraq in the Persian Gulf war created some gloom at year's end. Otherwise, business was good in Alberta, especially in residential, retail, and some office construction. However, office vacancies remained high and seemed likely to continue so. The West Edmonton Mall, the world's largest, which includes an amusement park and a trendy hotel, proved a powerful tourist attraction and inspired rejuvenation of the city's center.

Agriculture and Forestry. Although southern Alberta suffered severely from the drought that affected much of North America, grain production in central Alberta was good and northern Alberta had the best crops in several years. Higher prices compensated for lower-than-average yields. In areas of poor return, government assistance alleviated widespread rural distress.

Despite drought conditions, forest-fire ravages were not as serious as first feared. Stubborn blazes in the Slave Lake and Central Foothills regions did prove troublesome. Some new processing plants were being planned or already were under construction as the year ended.

Politics. Federal elections held on November 21 gave Alberta five new seats in the House of Commons as a result of population growth. Following the November balloting, Alberta's federal parliamentary representation consisted of: 25 Conservatives, one member of the New Democratic Party, and no Liberals.

On the provincial scene, the Liberal Party, dormant for many years prior to the 1986 election, chose Edmonton's Mayor Laurence Decore as its new leader. However, he had to wait for a general or by-election to gain a seat in the provincial legislature. His colleagues chose Alderman Terry Cavanagh to serve as Edmonton's mayor until an election is held in 1989.

Lubicon Cree Indians. In 1899 the federal government signed Treaty No. 8 with most Indians in what is now Northern Alberta and Saskatchewan, promising them reservations at the rate of 128 acres (52 ha) per individual. The Lubicon band, residing between the Peace and Athabasca rivers, however, was missed. Negotiations regarding the size and location of the Lubicon reservation have occurred between the Indians and representatives of the federal and provincial governments since the 1940s. Until 1988, such talks had been unsuccessful.

In mid-October 1988, a group of Lubicons set up a blockade of some 95 sq mi (246 km²) of territory northwest of Edmonton, which the Indians claim as their ancestral homeland. On October 20 the blockade was broken by the Royal Canadian Mounted Police; 27 persons were arrested. Two days later, Alberta's Premier Donald Getty and Lubicon Chief Bernard Ominayak met in the town of Grimshaw and agreed to grant the Indians the land title they had been seeking. The pact, which must be ratified by the federal government, left unanswered the tribe's claim to jurisdiction over resources on almost 4,000 sq mi (10 360 km²) of oil-rich land.

JOHN W. CHALMERS
Historical Society of Alberta

ALBERTA · Information Highlights

Area: 255,286 sq mi (661 190 km²)
Population (June 1988): 2,393,000.
Chief Cities (1986 census): Edmonton, the capital, 573,982; Calgary, 636,104; Lethbridge, 58,841.
Government (1988): *Chief Officers*—lt. gov., Helen Hunley; premier, Don Getty (Progressive Conservative). *Legislature*—Legislative Assembly, 79 members.
Provincial Finances (1988–89 fiscal year budget): *Revenues,* $9,819,000,000; *expenditures,* $10,489,-800,000.
Personal Income (average weekly earnings, June 1988): $463.24.
Labor Force (August 1988, seasonally adjusted): *Employed* workers, 15 years of age and over, 1,194,000; *Unemployed,* 8.1%.
Education (1988–89): *Enrollment*—elementary and secondary schools, 481,700 pupils; postsecondary—universities, 48,200; community colleges, 23,200.
(All monetary figures are in Canadian dollars.)

ALGERIA

Violent riots rocked Algeria for a week in October 1988 as a round of labor strikes escalated into a rampage against government property and policies. Mobs of people took to the streets to vent their anger against food shortages, high unemployment, elite privilege, and austerity measures brought on by falling oil and natural gas prices. The army restored order only at the cost of 159 lives, according to the official death toll; hundreds were reported wounded and 3,000 were arrested. Although centered in Algiers and its outskirts, the disturbances spread to several other towns.

President Chadli Benjedid declared an unprecedented state of emergency on October 6 before promising in a nationally televised address on October 10 to heed the desire for political change. He pointed to the already scheduled December convention of the National Liberation Front, the country's sole political party, as the forum for a searching national debate, and also called for a referendum in early November to approve minor constitutional reforms. The referendum was approved November 3 by 92% of voters, a result seen as a show of support for Benjedid's policies. And on November 5 a new prime minister, Kasdi Merbah, was appointed. He dismissed most leading figures in the previous government and named 14 new cabinet ministers, pledging political and economic changes.

Foreign Affairs. Until the devastating outburst in October 1988, the president had attended primarily to regional and Arab world policy, apparently secure in the progress of his project of Greater Maghreb cooperation. ("Maghreb," Arabic for "west," is the traditional name for the North African region lying between the Mediterranean Sea and the Sahara.) Algeria restored diplomatic relations with Morocco in May, allowing Benjedid to host the first summit meeting of the five North African states stretching from Mauritania to Libya.

Regional politics began to evolve in November 1987 when Zine El Abidine Ben Ali assumed power in Tunisia. Algeria promoted a rapprochement between Tunisia and Libya in the apparent hope that smoothed relations there might lead Libya to join the "Fraternity Treaty" that has bound Algeria, Tunisia, and Mauritania since 1983. Despite a resumption of diplomatic and economic ties between Tunisia and Libya, Muammar el-Qaddafi's government remained aloof from the treaty, pressing Algeria instead to reconsider its long-standing proposal for a union. In June, Algeria did agree to further talks about a future union pending other developments in regional cooperation.

The real breakthrough occurred, however, to the west in the exchange of ambassadors and reopening of the border with Morocco, ending

ALGERIA · Information Highlights
Official Name: Democratic and Popular Republic of Algeria.
Location: North Africa.
Area: 919,591 sq mi (2 381 740 km²).
Population (mid-1988 est.): 24,200,000.
Chief Cities (Jan. 1, 1983): Algiers, the capital, 1,721,607; Oran, 663,504; Constantine, 448,578.
Government: *Head of state,* Chadli Benjedid, president (took office Feb. 1979). *Head of government,* Kasdi Merbah, prime minister (appointed Nov. 5, 1988).
Monetary Unit: Dinar (6.237 dinars equal U.S.$1, July 1988).
Gross Domestic Product (1986 est. U.S.$): $59,000,000,000.
Foreign Trade (1986 U.S.$): *Imports,* $9,177,-000,000; *exports,* $7,831,000,000.

a 12-year-old rift occasioned by the war over Western Sahara. The reconciliation created diplomatic pressure that induced the Polisario Front (the Algerian-backed liberation movement contesting Morocco's annexation of Western Sahara) to accept a United Nations-sponsored plan to conduct a referendum to determine the status of the territory.

Algeria hosted an Arab summit meeting on the Palestinian uprising in the West Bank and the Gaza strip in June. Immediately thereafter, the five-nation Greater Maghreb summit took place. It instituted a new regional commission which convened in Algiers in July to set up five subcommittees, each chaired by a different state, to promote further steps toward economic integration. The government also conducted week-long sensitive negotiations with the hijackers of a Kuwaiti airliner which it permitted to land at Algiers airport in April. All 32 passengers and crew members were released unharmed.

Economics and Politics. Throughout 1988, Benjedid took modest political and economic measures to deal with the pressures that were building in the economy. He appointed a new minister of agriculture, the engineer-economist Mohamed Rouighi, in an effort to stimulate rural production in the face of declining revenues to import needed foodstuffs. Shortages of semolina, used to prepare the national dish called couscous, eventually helped to spark the riots. He appointed a new minister of education to cope with an overcrowded, understaffed school system. The national energy company sought out new export contracts, signing supply agreements with Greece and Turkey, and new resources, entering joint ventures with Italian and Spanish companies for gas exploration. Credit agreements worth more than $800 million with France and Japan eased the pressure on the import side, but not enough to avert the austerity policies that sparked the October strife.

See also MOROCCO.

ROBERT A. MORTIMER,
Haverford College

Withdrawing from Angola in accord with a U.S.-mediated agreement, South African forces cross the Okavango River, marking the Angola-Namibia border.

© Juhan Kuus/Sipa Press

ANGOLA

After several months of talks during 1988, an agreement was reached between Angola, Cuba, and South Africa to end the 13-year Angolan civil war, a war that had cost nearly 60,000 lives. The U.S.-mediated agreement, reached in mid-November and concluded and signed in December, called for Cuba to withdraw its estimated 50,000 troops from Angola and for South Africa to grant independence to Namibia, a former German colony which it has ruled for 70 years. In the key initial breakthrough early in August, the three nations agreed to a cease-fire and South Africa began removing its troops from southern Angola.

The Agreement. Two related accords were signed on December 22. In the first, signed by all three nations, South Africa agreed to surrender control of Namibia, and UN Security Council Resolution 435 (adopted in 1978)—a timetable for Namibian independence—would go into effect on April 1, 1989. A 9,000-member UN force would be set up to supervise elections for a constituent assembly on November 1; South Africa would remove nearly all of its 50,000 troops in Namibia by July 1; and independence would be reached upon adoption of a constitution by the assembly. The second accord, signed only by Angola and Cuba, provides a detailed timetable for the withdrawal of Cuba's approximately 50,000 troops in Angola.

Some 3,000 would be removed by April 1, 1989, the balance incrementally over the next 27 months.

South Africa's Role. Within Angola, South Africa had been operating against the guerrilla forces and bases of the South West African People's Organization (SWAPO) and had been supporting Jonas Savimbi's rebel Union for the Total Independence of Angola (UNITA). In spring 1988, the military balance in Angola shifted with the arrival of an estimated 12,000 additional Cuban soldiers (bringing the number of Cuban troops in Angola to near 50,000).

The Cubans were able to set up a 280-mi (450-km) military frontline as close as 15 mi (24 km) from the Namibian border. As a result, more South African soldiers were killed. The South African military recognized that it faced the prospect of protracted fighting and that it would continue to suffer losses in an unpopular war. This, coupled with the hard-pressed South African economy and U.S. diplomacy, led to a reassessment of South Africa's policy toward Namibia and Angola.

The Soviet Union's Role. An important additional factor was that the Soviet Union, which was spending close to $1 billion a year in military aid to the government of President José Eduardo dos Santos (Popular Movement for the Liberation of Angola, or MPLA), began prodding the Angolans to end the 13-year-old war. Indeed Soviet-African affairs specialists were observers at some of the 1988 peace talks.

UNITA's Role. Jonas Savimbi's UNITA, which had been fighting in the Angolan civil war since Angola won independence from Portugal in 1975, was excluded from the negotiations because both the MPLA government and the Cubans refused to participate if UNITA was present. Nonetheless, UNITA approval of any final agreement remained essential to a smooth end to the Angolan civil war.

PATRICK O'MEARA
Indiana University

ANGOLA • Information Highlights

Official Name: People's Republic of Angola.
Location: Western Africa.
Area: 481,351 sq mi (1 246 700 km²).
Population: (mid-1988 est.): 8,200,000.
Chief City (1982 est.): Luanda, the capital, 1,200,000.
Government: *Head of state and government,* José Eduardo dos Santos, president (took office 1979). *Legislature*—People's Assembly.
Gross Domestic Product (1987 est. U.S. $): $4,700,-000,000.

ANTHROPOLOGY

In 1988, fossil discoveries challenged traditional views of early tool use, anthropologists took a new look at the roots of homicide and warfare, and an Israeli cave yielded clues to the evolutionary relationship between Neanderthals and modern humans.

Toolmakers. An analysis of delicate fossil hand bones found in South Africa indicates that members of a "dead-end" line of hominids—the evolutionary family that includes modern humans—were capable of making and using tools about 1.8 million years ago. The more traditional view holds that at that time the first direct ancestor of modern humans, *Homo habilis,* was the only stone-toolmaker.

Tools no longer can be considered one of the secrets to evolutionary success for early human ancestors, said Randall L. Susman of the State University of New York at Stony Brook, who studied the hand bones. Most of the fossils he examined belong to a group of hominids known as *Paranthropus,* which evolved at the same time as the Homo lineage but became extinct about 1 million years ago. Nearly 30 bone and stone tools also were found with the hominid remains.

A small number of early Homo remains are also in the South African deposit, leading some anthropologists to suggest that the tools may have been made by our direct ancestors and then borrowed by *Paranthropus.* Nevertheless, there is general agreement that the now-extinct *Paranthropus* species described by Susman had a "precision grip" equal to that of *H. habilis.*

Violence and Homicide. A primitive New Guinea society called the Gebusi was found to have one of the highest murder rates ever reported, about 40 times greater than the homicide rate in the United States. Gebusi social life is generally peaceful, reported Bruce M. Knauft of Emory University in Atlanta, but on occasion there is unrestrained aggression that frequently results in a death.

This pattern may be a critical aspect of the evolution of human violence, in Knauft's opinion, since simple societies such as the Gebusi with no power hierarchies among adult men have predominated for most of the history of modern humans. Gebusi murders usually involve the killing of a person branded as a sorcerer for allegedly causing the death of someone who succumbed to disease. Gebusi clans are obligated to encourage their women members to marry into other groups; members of clans holding out on this obligation, Knauft suggests, often are targets of sorcery murders.

In a related study, Napoleon Chagnon of the University of California at Santa Barbara reported that, among the Yanomamo Indians of the Amazon rain forest, nearly half the men over the age of 25 have killed someone and 30% of males die violently. Killings usually result from violent feuds between villages. Yanomamo men kill, according to Chagnon, to achieve high social status in their polygamous society; killers enjoy more wives and children than men who have not killed.

Modern Human Origins. The dating of burnt flints from an Israeli cave indicated that modern *Homo sapiens* lived in the Middle East around 92,000 years ago, about 50,000 years earlier than most previous estimates. According to a team of French and Israeli scientists, the new date suggests that a primitive form of modern humans inhabited southwest Asia before the Neanderthals, whose remains in the same region date to approximately 60,000 years ago. This supports the notion that modern *H. sapiens* originated in Africa and colonized the globe while other groups, such as the Neanderthals, became extinct. Neanderthals, said the researchers, probably migrated to the Middle East from Europe as Ice Age glaciers descended, but were not ancestors of modern humans.

Some anthropologists maintained the flint dates reinforce the view that Neanderthals were a separate species rather than a closely related subspecies of *H. sapiens*. Others argued that there is too much anatomical similarity between Neanderthal and early *H. sapiens* remains in Europe for the two groups to have been separate species. An alternative proposal holds that Neanderthals and early *H. sapiens* interbred in the Middle East and eventually produced the line of fully modern *H. sapiens*.

BRUCE BOWER, *"Science News"*

ARCHAEOLOGY

Important archaeological discoveries in the Eastern and Western Hemispheres during 1988 gave new insights into the way of life of ancient peoples.

Eastern Hemisphere

Farming Village. An archaeological site in northern Syria yielded the remains of one of the earliest and largest known village settlements in the world. Occupied from 9500 B.C. to about 5000 B.C. with one 500-year period of abandonment, the settlement witnessed the important transition in human existence from nomadic hunting and gathering to sedentary farming. Analysis of excavated material from the site indicated gradual shifts from hunting and gathering to crop domestication and then to animal herding. This discovery contradicts the long-standing theory that domestication of crops and animals occurred simultaneously during a sudden agricultural revolution that swept the Near East around 8000 B.C. Lush wild vegetation and huge herds of migrating gazelle

allowed the earliest settlers to remain in the village year-round, also challenging the notion that a sedentary lifestyle emerged only with farming.

London's Past. Archaeologists flocked to London, England, to find out what lies buried beneath hundreds of buildings being torn down to make way for new offices. By late 1988 more than 60 excavations had been completed, turning up more than a million artifacts from the city's 2,000-year history. Among the finds were animal-bone dice left by the Romans 20 centuries ago, a Roman warehouse believed to be the best-preserved structure of its kind in northern Europe, and a Roman amphitheater uncovered in the heart of London's financial district. Recent excavations also show that the Saxons founded a separate settlement just west of London, bypassing the Roman walls in favor of a more open site. This explains why London bears no archaeological traces of the Anglo-Saxon period.

Clay Tablets. A collection of 1,100 clay tablets, containing letters to the last rulers of a city destroyed in 1726 B.C., were discovered in

Syria. By deciphering the cuneiform inscriptions, researchers hope to uncover the history of Shubat Enlil, once the capital of a powerful northern Mesopotamian kingdom in the Near East. The tablets were uncovered during the excavation of an enormous palace. Some of the tablets already deciphered are letters from neighboring rulers to the king of Shubat Enlil suggesting that the kingdoms exchange captured spies. Another contains one of the earliest descriptions of a monarch's use of cavalry to police the countryside.

Roman Wall. Archaeologists digging on a slope of the Palatine Hill in Rome, Italy, unearthed what they contend is a defensive wall built when the city was founded. They maintain that this and other finds nearby in the Forum show that Rome became an advanced urban society in the 7th and 6th centuries B.C., significantly earlier than many previous estimates. Further work suggested that a large, naturally formed gully near the wall was modified into a defensive ditch in the 7th century B.C. and filled in about one century later as part of an extensive construction project. It is un-

© Etienne Bol

Excavations in the heart of two European capitals yielded important archaeological finds in 1988. Scores of digs in London, left, have provided new insights into various phases of the city's 2,000-year history. In Rome, below, the discovery of a defensive wall in the ancient Roman Forum has challenged existing theories on the founding of that city.

AP/Wide World

certain whether the wall and ditch confirm legends that the foundation of Rome was a specific historical act, but evidence at the site nevertheless reveals the complex nature of early Roman society.

Assyrian Tomb. A Sudanese archaeologist and his coworkers discovered the burial chamber of an Assyrian queen in Nimrud, Iran. Nimrud was one of the Assyrian empire's four great cities and reached its peak during the 9th century B.C. The queen's tomb yielded numerous artifacts, including gold necklaces and earrings, flakes of gilding, and a finely crafted pin with the shapes of a woman and a hawk. Perhaps most impressive is a golden pomegranate the size of an egg. The queen's ceramic casket is in an alcove of the tomb. Her name has not yet been determined, but she appears to have been an important ruler. Near the entrance to the tomb lies the skeleton of a servant in a shallow grave.

Western Hemisphere

Clovis People. In an apple orchard in Washington state, archaeologists uncovered the first undisturbed collection of artifacts belonging to the Clovis people, generally assumed to have been the earliest settlers of North America about 11,500 years ago. The find includes 12 Clovis points, the largest collection of the distinctively shaped stone spear points ever found. Several of the carefully flaked points are about 9 inches (23 cm) long, nearly twice the length of Clovis points found at other sites. Investigators also found stone scrapers, fleshers, and several pieces of antler apparently sharpened for use as tools. The ancient remains were probably a cache that Clovis people buried and intended to reclaim. The expertly fashioned points simply may have been artistic expressions, or they could have been used in initiation rites or religious ceremonies.

Moche Tomb. The richest cache of pre-Columbian artifacts ever excavated in the Americas turned up in an ancient Peruvian tomb. The 1,500-year-old burial contains the remains of a warrior-priest of the Moche civilization, a culture that dominated the north coast of Peru from about A.D. 100 to 700. Other tombs under excavation confirm the site as a burial area for a succession of high-ranking Moche officials. Among the treasures recovered by archaeologists are a solid gold crown, a gold face mask, a ceremonial rattle made of hammered sheet gold, and gold-and-turquoise ear ornaments with detailed decorations. More than 1,000 pots, bowls, beakers, and jars also were found. The warrior-priest appears to have been a supreme figure shown in decorations on previously recovered Moche ceramics. He is surrounded in his tomb by several other bodies —apparently servants, wives, or concubines— and even his faithful dog.

Sunken Ship. The sunken hull of an old wooden vessel found in a cove once used by the pirate Blackbeard is the remains of a massive twin-masted ship that apparently was abandoned, according to archaeologists who surveyed the wreck. The vessel is believed to date to between 1780 and 1820, more than 60 years after Blackbeard was captured and beheaded. It was about 62 ft (19 m) long and weighed 110 tons (100 MT). Underwater investigators at the North Carolina cove found a dime-sized token with "Carolus," Latin for Charles, written backward across it, indicating that some type of stamp or impression was made from a coin. After "Carolus" comes the Roman numeral "II," or possibly "III." The token may refer to Charles III, who ruled Spain at the time, but the nationality of the vessel has not been established.

Maya Port. A huge seawall, extensive docks, and a variety of trading goods—including turquoise, obsidian, and ceramics—from central Mexico and Central America were discovered on an island only 650 ft (198 m) in diameter off the north coast of Yucatan. According to a team of archaeologists from the United States and Mexico, the island, known as Isla Cerritos, was the chief port for the inland Maya capital of Chichen Itza, which was a power center in northern Yucatan from A.D. 900 to 1200.

Ancient Canal. Archaeologists discovered an ancient canal in the Sonora Desert of Arizona that may have been a major source of drinking water for a now-vanished society of native Americans known as the Hohokam. The six-mile- (10-km-) long structure channeled water from the Santa Cruz River through a floodplain to a Hohokam village site just north of present-day Tucson. The site was a focal point for a system of scattered agricultural villages inhabited from about A.D. 800 to 1400.

Slave Life. Dates were established for nine sites on a colonial plantation founded in Virginia in 1619. A distinctive type of unglazed pottery made by black slaves was uncovered only at sites occurring after the 1680s. Investigators concluded that masters and servants stopped living in the same main house and using the same household goods around 1680, thus necessitating pottery-making by slaves in their separate residences. This change in plantation life set the stage for what were to become separate slave quarters upon the major influx of black slaves at the end of the 17th century. Black servants or slaves and white indentured servants regularly shared living space before 1680, suggesting to the researchers that it was not until the end of the century that race became the predominant criterion for slave status and that slavery emerged as a full-blown institution.

BRUCE BOWER
"Science News"

ARCHITECTURE

With full predictions of a downturn in the volume of construction, U.S. architects in 1988 seemed to be turning inward to question their future roles and mission. Issues discussed at the annual convention of the American Institute of Architects (AIA) in New York City included everything from getting better control of the construction process to housing for the homeless and those who simply cannot afford the current high price of houses. "Designing good buildings is not enough," said AIA President Ted Pappas. "Architects must help shape the future of their communities."

Professional and public controversy over a major high-rise in New York City—whose height would cast shadows on Central Park and whose appearance, said critics, did not suit its surroundings—led to the dismissal of internationally known architect Moshe Safdie (*see* BIOGRAPHY). Construction began on Philadelphia's new Justice Center (Hellmuth Obata & Kassabaum and others, architects) in a form drastically reduced from the original proposal after much protest that it would have overshadowed City Hall. Rowes Wharf, a massive complex of hotels, apartments, and offices by architects Skidmore, Owings & Merrill, was completed in Boston.

Styles. Concern with finding good clients did not diminish architects' increasing preoccupation with style. While many critics heralded the end of the predominant emphasis on historic styles seen in Post-Modernism, few could point to any viable substitutes. Certainly, many of the outstanding buildings of the year, such as Rowes Wharf and the Becton Dickinson headquarters—a suburban office building with a country-villalike design by Kallman, McKinnel & Wood—exhibited the style. So, too, did many speculative office buildings just reaching completion with domes, pinnacles, huge cupolas, and sloped roofs. Examples included a 19-story flared-top structure outside Denver dubbed by architect Anthony Pellecchia as Il Campanile. Robert A. M. Stern Architects, a pioneer in the Post-Modern idiom, won a competition for the Norman Rockwell Museum in Stockbridge, MA, with a Federal Revival structure clad in white clapboard and green trim. But what did the critics find wrong with Post-Modernism? Author Tom Wolfe described it as the first style since the advent of modernism that people could understand. "Art that is understandable to ordinary mortals," he said, "undercuts the [art establishment's] special position."

One alternative was termed Deconstructivism, and several of its proponents were the subject of an exhibition at New York's Museum of Modern Art promoted by architect Philip Johnson. Deconstructivism, in its most advanced form, produces buildings that seem to be literally deconstructed—tenuously related groups of beams, walls, floors, and roofs as if seen after an explosion. The Los Angeles chapter of AIA gave one of its awards to an unbuilt residence in Santa Monica that would have incorporated ten pieces of discarded machinery intended, according to Morphosis, Architect, to suggest decay, tension, and risk. Another architectual firm working in the Deconstructivist style, the office of Metropolitan Architecture led by Rem Koolhaas, credits its main sources of inspiration as Russian Suprematism and the International Style "in attempting to balance idealized abstraction and material sensuousness." According to Wolfe, the art establishment was regaining control.

The joint winners of the year's Pritzker Prize, considered the Nobel of architecture, might have suggested that modernism was back. Both Gordon Bunshaft and Oscar Neimeyer were confirmed practitioners of that style. But, as one critic pointed out, the prize

Rowes Wharf, Boston's new complex of hotels, apartments, and offices, joins the underutilized waterfront to downtown.

American Institute of Architects
1988 Honor Award Winners

IBA Social Housing, Berlin, West Germany; Eisenmann Robertson Architects and Groetzebach, Plessow & Ehlers; "a strong symbol for the free world . . . sets up a rhythm and plays against it, raising low-cost housing to the level of art"

Monterey Bay Aquarium, Cannery Row, Monterey, CA; Esherick Homsey Dodge and Davis; "poetic waterside aquarium . . . celebrates both the life in the sea and the life its coastal community has drawn from the sea"

Guest House, Minnesota; Frank O. Gehry and Associates Inc. and Meyer, Scherer & Rockcastle, Ltd.; "a house interpreted as sculpture"

Library and Science Building, Westover School, Middlebury, CT; Gwathmey Siegel & Associates Architects; "brings order, clarity, and freshness to its private-school campus"

Residence in the Dominican Republic, La Romana, Dominican Republic; Hugh Newell Jacobsen, FAIA; "bright and beautiful house by the sea . . . an elegant celebration of the Dominican vernacular"

Tegel Harbor Housing, Berlin, West Germany; Moore Ruble Yudell; "Throughout the project, buildings *make* space instead of occupying it . . . establishing a . . . relationship with the river and the neighborhood"

Kate Mantilini Restaurant, Beverly Hills, CA; Morphosis; "a challenging example of both the art of architecture and the use of art in architecture"

8522, Culver City, CA; Eric Owen Moss-Architect; commercial office space in old warehouse captures "in simple materials the essential spirit of architecture"

United Airlines Terminal 1 Complex, O'Hare International Airport, Chicago, IL; Murphy/Jahn; "visually exciting and elegant . . . an uplifting experience worthy of the great transportation centers of the past"

Jacob K. Javits Convention Center, New York, NY; I.M. Pei & Partners and Lewis, Turner Partnership; "a latter-day Crystal Palace in the challenging urban context of New York"

The Menil Collection, Houston, TX; Piano + Fitzgerald, Architects; "quietly elegant art museum is wonderfully understated . . . at once deferential and inviting, self-effacing yet celebratory"

Carnegie Hall Restoration, New York, NY; James Stewart Polshek and Partners; "sensitive additions and renovations" that retain "the spirit and character of the original while enhancing and enriching it"

The High Museum at Georgia-Pacific Center, Atlanta, GA; Scogin Elam and Bray Architects, Inc.; art museum within a narrow greenhouse space is "an elegant and beautiful envelope . . . a wonderful sequence of spaces that provide a variety of experiences"

United Gulf Bank, Manama, Bahrain; Skidmore, Owings & Merrill; 12-story bank headquarters incorporates "a wonderful sense of light" and "dramatic transitional experiences"; "responsive both to the climate and culture of its site"

Feinberg Hall, Princeton University, Princeton, NJ; Tod Williams Billie Tsien and Associates; dormitory tower is "a disciplined and elegantly crafted place of habitation . . . a small gem"

---

is given for career accomplishments and, as such, does not necessarily reflect current style.

Construction Trends. Many of the issues that had concerned architects in the past seemed to recede in importance. Energy conservation, which promised everything from wide-open to totally sealed buildings, became less of an issue with the fall in the price of oil. Fast-track construction, by which architects finish the design of buildings even as they are being built, lost much of its luster with the decline in inflation and the rise in awareness of the many practical problems.

On the other hand, the preservation of historic buildings and the adaptation of older buildings of any kind continued to dominate the architectural scene. Many felt that such activities soon would replace new buildings as the primary focus of design and construction activity. Outstanding examples included a whole street of houses from different historic periods in Collegeville, PA, remodeled by Dagit Saylor Architects for dormitories and the fine arts department of Ursinus College; the conversion of a 64-year-old coal yard into a boy's club in Jersey City, NJ, by architects Oppenheimer, Brady & Vogelstein; and the renovation of a 1929 Spanish Revival drive-in market in Los Angeles by Levin & Associates. When architects were not designing new uses for existing buildings, they often were designing structures that linked them together. Such was the case at Western Wyoming College, where joint-venture architects Sasaki Associates and Anderson Mason Dale linked a loose grouping of 1960s buildings with a massive new one featuring a string of houselike roof monitors.

New types of buildings and adaptations of old ones both created pressures to revise building codes. In many cases, it was argued, existing codes simply do not recognize the more complex design requirements of contemporary structures, often forcing drastic and unnecessary alterations. In particular, many codes do not recognize the requirements of increasingly popular multiuse buildings, which combine hotels, offices, and stores in one structure—such as Rowes Wharf. One suggested solution was "safety equivalencies," which would dictate the desired result but only the bare essentials of means. Such provisions were being incorporated in the building codes of Boston, for example.

Architects tried new residential building types to fit increasingly unconventional lifestyles. One loftlike building in San Diego, designed by architect-developer Ted Smith, groups "undesignated" rooms around kitchens, thereby encouraging communal living. And serious architects were not afraid of some fun. Michael Graves, for example, unveiled plans for the Dolphin and Swan convention hotels adjacent to Orlando's Walt Disney World; each building would be topped by a five-story statue of its namesake. The most fanciful building planned was a $585 million hotel-casino in Atlantic City, NJ, said by architect Francis Dumont to be modeled on the Taj Mahal but more resembling an Indian carnival.

CHARLES K. HOYT, *"Architectural Record"*

ARGENTINA

As the 1989 presidential campaign got under way, Argentina faced turmoil in the military, labor unrest, and a massive foreign debt.

Politics and Government. Early in July, the nation's two major political parties chose their standard-bearers for presidential elections scheduled for May 28, 1989. In the first presidential primary ever held by the Justicialist (Peronist) Party, Carlos Saúl Menem, the populist governor of La Rioja province, edged out party president Antonio Cafiero. Eduardo Duhalde, a congressman representing Buenos Aires province, won the vice-presidential nomination. As for the governing Radical Civic Union, Eduardo Angeloz, the governor of Cordoba province, easily won the primary balloting. Angeloz enjoyed the support of most of the party's leaders, including President Raúl Alfonsín, who was barred by the constitution from seeking a second term. Juan Manuel Casella, a former governor of Buenos Aires, was chosen as Angeloz' running mate.

Throughout most of the year, President Alfonsín was pressured over the issue of amnesty for military personnel involved in human-rights abuses during the "Dirty War" of 1976–83. By judicial interpretation, a 1987 "due obedience" law was extended in May to two generals and a colonel involved in human-rights cases. The 1987 law absolved junior- and middle-level officers of human-rights violations because they did not have the authority to disobey or change orders issued by their superiors. If that interpretation were applied to the 40 or 50 cases of military personnel not absolved by the due obedience law, fewer than a dozen officers would face trial. Among these were former Gen. Carlos Guillermo Suárez Mason, who was extradited from the United States in May to face trial on 39 charges of murder. Nevertheless, the military continued its insistence on amnesty for all of those charged with crimes against humanity and pardons for those already convicted. In October the government denied that an amnesty was being negotiated.

In mid-January 1988, dissident army Lt. Col. Aldo Rico, who was under house arrest for organizing an April 1987 rebellion, escaped from custody and immediately attempted another rebellion. He and 100 supporters held out for three days at Monte Caseros on the border with Brazil and Uruguay. Minor mutinies were reported at five army posts and an air-force base in Buenos Aires. The uprising was put down easily by units loyal to the Alfonsín administration. Rico, 428 officers, and a handful of civilians identified with the ultrarightist Alerta Nacional were arrested. In the wake of the incident, President Alfonsín ordered a purge of extremist middle-ranking officers. Army Commander Gen. Dante Caridi, whose removal Rico demanded, was confirmed in of-

AP/Wide World

After a military revolt in January 1988—the second in nine months—Argentina's President Raúl Alfonsín declared that "democracy is consolidated, and we have put our house in order." There was another such uprising in December.

fice. In April the Senate approved a law that barred the armed forces from involvement in politics and bolstered civilian control over the military. And members of the armed forces later were granted 60% salary increases.

During the first week in December, however, some 500 rebel soldiers staged yet another uprising. The three-day rebellion, led by Col. Mohammed Ali Seineldín, centered on the Villa Martelli army based south of Buenos Aires, where the rebels established a stronghold. President Alfonsín, who had cut short a trip to the United States to deal with the crisis, finally announced on December 4 that Colonel Seineldín had been arrested and the uprising brought to an end without any concessions by the government. But Army Commander Caridi, whose removal was one of Seineldín's demands, resigned later in the month.

Earlier, a federal appeals court reviewing the verdicts of a military tribunal on retired officers charged with negligence in the 1982 Malvinas (Falklands) war upheld a 12-year prison

sentence for Lt. Gen. Leopoldo Galtieri, increased the term to 12 years for Brig. Gen. Basilio Lami Dozo, and lowered that of Navy Admiral Jorge Anaya to 12 years. All three were junta members at the time of the war.

Economy and Labor. In inaugurating a new session of the legislature on May 1, President Alfonsín revealed that the key feature of his economic policy for his remaining months in office would be a reduction of the fiscal deficit, which grew to 10% of the gross domestic product (GDP) in 1987 and was projected at about 7% for 1988. His plan called for a curb on spending through a gradual withdrawal of subsidies from all state industries except the national railways. Alfonsín also announced that U.S.$300 million would be pumped into agriculture, following a disastrous 73% slump in the trade surplus during 1987. In addition to a reliance on agricultural exports, the president identified the oil and gas sectors as sources of growth. A natural-gas discovery off the Tierra del Fuego coast was hailed as the most important hydrocarbon find of the decade.

On April 14, President Alfonsín signed a bill that significantly increased the power of labor unions. Under the new law, syndical officials could be fired only with a court order and unions were given control over their welfare funds, estimated at $1 billion. On August 20 the nation's teachers ended a six-week strike, after the labor ministry ruled that their dispute would have to be settled by arbitration.

To protest economic austerity measures announced by the government on August 1, the 12th general strike against the Alfonsín regime was held on September 9. A rally in Buenos Aires turned violent, as street gangs took to looting and vandalism. A 13th general strike was called three days later to protest police brutality in quelling the violence.

Foreign Debt. No progress was made in relieving the pressure of Argentina's $55 billion foreign debt, on which interest due in 1988 was about $5 billion. Alfonsín's efforts to have part of the debt principal written off and to convince commercial banks to freeze interest payments at a pre-1982 rate of 4% were rejected by international financiers. With its cash reserves depleted and a projected 1988 export surplus of only $2.2 billion, Argentina was forced to seek fresh foreign loans.

In October, with $1.3 billion in interest payments overdue, emergency steps were taken. Price increases and exchange rates were fixed until February 1989. Inflation, which had soared to a monthly rate of 30% in July, would be held below 10% per month for the remainder of the year. Trade barriers would be dismantled. Rates on public services and salary increases would be limited to 4%.

On the strength of these measures, the World Bank mobilized a $700 million loan for the nation's banking, trade, and industry sectors and two investment loans of $550 million for electricity and low-cost housing. Pending the issue of new standby credit from the International Monetary Fund (IMF), members of the Bank of International Settlements in October granted a $500 million bridge loan. Also in October, Argentina's Central Bank Director Daniel Marx obtained $3 billion in fresh loans from U.S. creditor banks for interest due in late 1988 and early 1989.

Foreign Affairs. Given the turmoil at home, President Alfonsín spent a surprising amount of time abroad during 1988. In Spain on February 1, he signed a four-year, $3 billion economic-aid package. During an April visit to Brazil, Alfonsín furthered the integration process by signing an accord—called the most important ever between the two countries—that committed both nations to the peaceful use of nuclear energy. On the road again in May, Alfonsín concluded a deal in China for the coproduction of medium-range missiles. He attended the August 10 inauguration of Ecuador's President Rodrigo Borja; discussions with other leaders following the ceremonies focused on the situation in Central America. And in late October, President Alfonsín joined counterparts from Brazil, Colombia, Mexico, Peru, Uruguay, and Venezuela in Punta del Este, Uruguay, to consider future relations with the United States and other topics.

At the request of Argentina in February, the Organization of American States (OAS) urged Great Britain to call off military exercises planned for the Malvinas (Falklands) in March. The exercises were held on schedule, and Argentina requested a meeting of the UN Security Council to inform it of the threat to international peace. On March 17, Foreign Minister Dante Caputo joined with representatives of 30 other countries in criticizing the British operation or calling for direct bilateral negotiations over the dispute. On September 20, Caputo was elected president of the 43rd session of the UN General Assembly.

LARRY L. PIPPIN, *University of the Pacific*

ARGENTINA • Information Highlights

Official Name: Argentine Republic.
Location: Southern South America.
Area: 1,068,297 sq mi (2 766 890 km²).
Population (mid-1988 est.): 32,000,000.
Chief Cities (1980 census): Buenos Aires, the capital, 2,922,829; Cordoba, 970,570; Rosario, 794,127.
Government: *Head of state and government,* Raul Alfonsín, president (took office Dec. 10, 1983). *Legislature*—Senate and Chamber of Deputies.
Monetary Unit: Austral (15.46 australs equals U.S.$1, Nov. 29, 1988).
Gross Domestic Product (1986 U.S.$): $77,200,-000,000.
Economic Indexes (1987): *Consumer Prices* (1980 = 100), all items, 592,933.9; food, 600,543.6. *Industrial Production* (1980 = 100), 98.
Foreign Trade (1987 U.S.$): *Imports,* $5,819,000,000; *exports,* $6,360,000,000.

ARIZONA

The impeachment of Gov. Evan Mecham and the national elections dominated the news in Arizona during 1988.

Impeachment. On Feb. 5, 1988, Evan Mecham (R) became the first Arizona governor to be impeached. The charges against Mecham ranged from illegally concealing a $350,000 campaign loan and misuse of a state protocol fund, to obstructing justice in a state investigation of an alleged death threat made against a disloyal member of his staff. In an anguished, emotional state House of Representatives, the vote was 46 to 14 for impeachment. Dropping the charges on the campaign loan, the Senate voted to convict on the obstruction of justice charge (21 to 9) and the misuse of the protocol fund (21 to 6). Mecham later was indicted and tried on criminal charges and acquitted.

The impeachment made unnecessary a recall campaign that had been launched shortly after Mecham's election. The Arizona Supreme Court ruled that a recall election (more than enough signatures for the election had been obtained) was unnecessary, and Secretary of State Rose Mofford, a Democrat, followed the normal pattern of succession to become the new governor. Mofford is the first woman to hold the state's highest elective office.

Elections. Angry Mecham supporters, with the former governor's blessing, retaliated in the Republican primary election by unseating, among others, the powerful Speaker of the House, Joe Lane, and the president of the Senate, Carl J. Kunasek, both of whom had voted for impeachment. Despite the Mecham backlash, Democrats managed to pick up two seats in both the state House and the Senate in the general election. But Republicans held on to their control of the state legislature, maintain-

ing majorities in the Senate (17 to 13) and the House (34 to 26).

Perhaps weary of politics in a year of political turmoil within the state, only 44.6% of Arizona's voters turned out on November 8, casting 61% of their ballots for George Bush and 39% for Michael Dukakis. The state's incumbent congressional delegation—John Rhodes (R), Morris Udall (D), Bob Stump (R), Jon Kyl (R), and Jim Kolbe (R)—won reelection, as did U.S. Sen. Dennis DeConcini (D).

Eight propositions also were placed before voters. The most controversial was a hotly contested, in this heavily Hispanic state, "Official English" standard. The proposition requires that all government transactions be conducted only in English. The measure passed by less than one percentage point.

Also approved were propositions to avoid another Mecham debacle by requiring a runoff election when no candidate for office receives

Secretary of State Rose Mofford, a Democrat, succeeded to the governorship of Arizona following the impeachment of Republican Gov. Evan Mecham. She is the first woman to hold the office of governor in Arizona.

a majority of the vote; to drop "male" from qualifications for state offices; and to place city magistrates under the scrutiny of a judicial commission. Among the four propositions defeated was one to raise the salaries of state legislators from $15,000 to $25,000.

Defense. The first Soviet observers arrived at Davis-Monthan Air Force Base in Tucson to witness the destruction of ground-launched cruise missiles as required under the terms of the new Intermediate Nuclear Force (INF) Treaty.

Geology. State sources revealed the discovery of an extensive underground cavern near the town of Benson. Kartchner Cave, so named for the rancher who owned the land, remains virtually undisturbed in pristine condition. It has been sold to the state and will be preserved as a state park and major tourist attraction.

JAMES W. CLARKE
University of Arizona

ARKANSAS

Weather played a major role in Arkansas during 1988. The year opened with residents in the Delta counties recovering from flooding that caused more than $20 million in damage. The summer followed with the most severe drought in recent years. As the year drew to a close, record rain caused new flooding. That, coupled with a series of tornadoes that killed six people, kept the forces of nature in the forefront of public attention, along with politics, the economy, and educational reform.

Politics. Gov. Bill Clinton called the General Assembly into special session on two occasions. In the first special session legislators failed to pass a bill requiring financial disclosures by lobbyists; the governor responded by submitting the proposal directly to the voters at election time. In the second session, lawmakers removed a number of restrictions on banking in the state, and enacted new regulations governing patient care in nursing homes.

In the "Super Tuesday" presidential primary on March 8, Arkansas joined with ten other southern states, all of which held elections on the same day in an effort to stimulate interest and increase voter participation. Sen. Albert Gore, Jr., from neighboring Tennessee, won the Democratic primary and George Bush the Republican. In the general election in November, Arkansas voters supported Bush by a large margin. They also approved three amendments to the state constitution—one establishing a process for disciplining judges; another creating a new juvenile court system, and a third prohibiting the use of public funds for abortions except when the mother's life is in danger. Also passed were a referendum authorizing the Soil and Water Commission to issue $250 million in bonds, and Governor Clinton's lobbyist disclosure law.

Economy. Led by an upswing in farm revenues, particularly for rice, cotton, and soybeans, the state's economic outlook improved considerably in 1988. The fiscal year ended with a $28.5 million surplus in the state treasury and with Arkansas' business climate ranked ninth in the nation. This improvement came despite barge traffic on both the Mississippi and Arkansas Rivers being stalled for several days due to low water levels caused by the summer drought.

Broilers continued to be the state's leading farm product, and the value of farm land increased for the first time in more than five years. Governor Clinton joined with the governors of Louisiana and Mississippi to sign an agreement to attract international investors to the lower Mississippi River Valley. A nine-member "Lower Mississippi Delta Development Commission" also was appointed at the federal level to prepare a ten-year plan for assessing the needs of those living in poverty in the region.

Education. The Businessmen's Council, composed of the state's 19 wealthiest citizens, commissioned the Carnegie Foundation to do a comprehensive study of the state's education system. That report, entitled *In Pursuit of Excellence* and designed to assist in efforts to promote economic development in the state, called for sweeping changes. In addition to encouraging increased consolidation of small districts, the commission also urged that school officials place greater emphasis on early childhood education, making kindergarten attendance mandatory, and increase offerings in foreign languages, math, and science. Colleges and universities were encouraged to increase their summer-school offerings and conduct periodic review of faculty members with tenure.

C. FRED WILLIAMS
University of Arkansas at Little Rock

ARKANSAS • Information Highlights

Area: 53,187 sq mi (137 754 km²).
Population (July 1, 1987): 2,388,000.
Chief Cities (1980 census): Little Rock, the capital (July 1, 1986 est.), 181,030; Fort Smith, 71,626; North Little Rock, 64,288; Pine Bluff, 56,636.
Government (1988): *Chief Officers*—governor, Bill Clinton (D); lt. gov. Winston Bryant (D). *General Assembly*—Senate, 35 members; House of Representatives, 100 members.
State Finances (fiscal year 1987): *Revenue,* $3,888,000,000; *expenditure,* $3,473,000,000.
Personal Income (1987): $27,481,000,000; per capita, $11,507.
Labor Force (June 1988): *Civilian labor force,* 1,130,500; *unemployed,* 88,500 (7.8% of total force).
Education: *Enrollment* (fall 1986)—public elementary schools, 306,851; public secondary, 130,587; colleges and universities, 79,182. *Public school expenditures* (1986–87), $1,137,000,000 ($2,795 per pupil).

ARMS CONTROL

At the June 1, 1988, summit meeting in Moscow, U.S. President Ronald Reagan and Soviet General Secretary Mikhail Gorbachev exchanged the instruments of ratification for the INF (Intermediate Nuclear Forces) Treaty, and the agreement immediately went into effect. The treaty was precedent-shattering in two respects.

It was the first time that the United States and the USSR had agreed to destroy some of their weapons. All prior agreements about arms either had placed ceilings on the manufacture of certain types of weapons—such as the SALT I limitation of ABMs to 100 for each nation—or they had prohibited weapons in particular places—such as the prohibition of weapons in the Antarctic region.

Specifically, the treaty requires the United States and the USSR to eliminate all of the intermediate-range and short-range missiles, those having ranges from approximately 300 to 3,400 mi (483–5 472 km), and prohibits each side from possessing such weapons hereafter. Facilities related to the use of the missiles also must be eliminated. The nations were allowed 18 months to destroy the shorter-range missiles, and three years to destroy the intermediate missiles. Checking to ensure that no more such missiles are being produced may extend until May 31, 2001.

Treaty Verification. The INF Treaty established the unprecedented on-site inspection rights of both parties so that each can verify that the other is in compliance with the treaty. Employing 200 inspectors, 200 monitors, and 200 air crew members, both sides will engage in five separate types of inspections.

The initial inspection is called the baseline inspection. During a 60-day period in the late summer Soviet inspectors visited 26 sites in the United States and NATO nations. American inspectors visited 126 sites in the Soviet Union, and seven more in East Germany and Czechoslovakia. The purpose of the dual inspections was to verify the initial numbers of missiles in each nation's arsenal. Upon completion of this first phase of the INF-required inspections, the Pentagon announced that each nation's numbers matched what had been claimed to be true by Moscow and Washington.

The second type of inspection is called the close-out inspection. This check is to verify that bases, and other missile support facilities, except production plants, no longer contain any of the prohibited missiles.

The third kind of check is termed elimination inspections. This involves the destruction of the INF missiles. According to the treaty, each side must provide a 30-day notice of the date when missiles will be destroyed, so that observers can be present to verify the destruction. At the Soviet site of Kapustin Yar, American inspectors observed the initial destruction of three SS-20 missiles in late August. After that date periodic destruction of both U.S. and USSR missiles occurred.

For 13 years after the treaty enters into force, the United States and the USSR are entitled to engage in a number of short-notice inspections. During the first three years of the treaty 20 such inspections a year are permitted. For the first five years after the elimination of all the weapons, 15 on-site inspections of short notice are permitted. For the last five years of the 13-year period, ten inspections a year are permitted.

For 13 years, continuous monitoring of production facilities is provided. It is called portal monitoring of production. In the case of the Soviet Union, American inspectors began checking the Votkinsk Machine Building Plant. Part of their task is to ensure that the plant

Soviet inspectors were on hand for the destruction of 41 ground-based Cruise missiles at a U.S. Air Force base in Arizona beginning in mid-October. The dismantling was part of the U.S.-Soviet Intermediate Nuclear Forces (INF) treaty.

produces no more SS-20s, although the building of the SS-25 mobile ICBM may continue. For their part, Soviet inspectors took up a monitoring watch at the Hercules Plant Number One at Magna, Utah, where Pershing IIs were built.

START. With the successful conclusion of the INF Treaty negotiations, Moscow and Washington concentrated anew upon the next major nuclear-weapons agreement, START (Strategic Arms Reduction Talks). As with the INF Treaty, a START agreement would involve both the elimination of weapons, generally estimated at between 30% and 50% of the strategic arms, and various kinds of on-site inspection plans to assure compliance.

Although the Reagan administration would leave office without completing a START agreement, President-elect George Bush indicated the START negotiations in Geneva would continue along the lines previously laid out.

ABM Treaty. Negotiated in 1972 by President Nixon, the ABM Treaty was a subject of debate in 1988. Some in the Pentagon, fearing the Soviets were cheating on the treaty, hoped that President Reagan would label the Krasnoyarsk radar a "material breach" of the treaty, instead of a "significant violation." The former action would have enabled the United States to withdraw formally from the treaty and move ahead more directly with SDI (Star Wars) activities. The president pleased the arms-control community by refusing to instigate the Pentagon proposal.

The Krasnoyarsk radar was a problem because U.S. military experts claimed it was in violation of the ABM Treaty, as it was perceived to be part of a prohibited Soviet Star Wars defense system. The Soviets stated that the radar was part of their peaceful outer space exploration program. The argument about the radar was important because the official U.S. position was that the START Treaty should be held up until the radar installation was dismantled. From Moscow's perspective, the START agreement was linked to continued U.S. willingness to abide with the strict interpretation of the ABM Treaty.

Nuclear Weapons Tests. Since the 1960s the United States and the USSR have agreed not to test nuclear weapons in deep space, in the atmosphere, or underwater. Underground testing, in a way which prevents the leakage of radioactive debris from the explosion, is permitted. The agreement was termed the Partial Nuclear Weapons Test Ban Treaty. Part of the explanation for permitting the underground testing was the desire by both nations to continue the testing and development of new weapons, and part of the reason was that the United States did not feel there was adequate means to monitor cheating on underground tests.

In 1974 the United States and the USSR signed, but the U.S. Senate did not ratify, the Threshold Ban Treaty, which placed a cap of 150 kilotons upon the size of an underground nuclear-weapon test. A companion treaty, also not ratified by the Senate, placed a ceiling of 150 kilotons on nuclear explosives used for peaceful purposes, such as excavation.

U.S. Senate ratification of the treaties was being held up because of concern over whether explosions smaller than 150 kilotons can be detected. However, early in the fall of 1988, experimental tests were conducted in the Nevada desert near Las Vegas and near the Soviet city of Semipalatinsk. The tests were staged to determine whether newly developed monitoring equipment could monitor the weaker explosions. The tests were part of an agreement reached at the Moscow summit to carry out what was termed the Joint Verification Experiment (JVE). The tests were designed to help settle a debate between the Soviet and American governments. According to the Russians, a series of seismograph instruments, similar to those which measure earthquakes, were sufficient to detect clandestine nuclear-weapons tests. U.S. government experts, however, were dubious; their position was that it may be necessary to employ more intrusive means of monitoring tests. One such procedure, called Corrtex, involves drilling a separate shaft—to hold monitoring equipment—near the shaft containing the nuclear weapon to be tested.

Pending the outcome of these and other experiments, there is support for what could be the final treaty on underground nuclear-weapons testing. This is called the Comprehensive Test Ban Treaty, because under its stipulations all nuclear-weapons testing would be prohibited. Should such an agreement be adopted by the two military superpowers, they then would face the difficult diplomatic task of persuading other nations to give up the modernization of their forces by forgoing nuclear-weapons testing and development.

Other Arms Negotiations. The United States and its NATO allies sought to redress the Warsaw Pact's superiority in conventional forces—such as tanks and artillery—by means of arms talks with the Russians. The negotiations, which did not reach final agreement during the year, were called the Conventional Stability Talks. The use of chemical weapons in the Iran-Iraq war, which at times produced heavy casualties, spurred efforts to develop international limitations of such chemical agents as nerve gas and blister gas.

In June the United Nations marked the 20th anniversary of the Non-Proliferation Treaty, a multilateral agreement designed to prevent the spread of nuclear weapons. At the time there were 136 adherents to the treaty.

ROBERT M. LAWRENCE
Colorado State University

"Family Portrait" (also called "The Bellelli Family") was part of the first major Edgar Degas retrospective in 50 years. The show began the year at the Grand Palais in Paris, inaugurated Ottawa's new National Gallery of Canada in May, and then moved to New York City's Metropolitan Museum of Art in October.

Courtesy of the Metropolitan Museum of Art, Lent by Musée d'Orsay, Paris

ART

The globalization of art, a trend for some years, proceeded with the rush of a breaking ice jam during 1988. Thawing relations between the West and the Communist bloc countries brought a flood of Soviet and Chinese art to U.S. museums and galleries, while Western dealers hurried to Moscow and Beijing to set up auctions and scout talent for the first time since the Communist revolutions there.

Blockbuster museum shows were less in evidence than in previous years. But the auction action, led by Japanese and European buyers, continued its frenzied upward spiral with hardly a pause after the October 1987 stock market plunge. An apparently insatiable lust for art drew artists, dealers, and collectors from all countries into a single expanding market that seemed to devour everything. Analysts were divided between those who were sure that the art market was solid, and those who were certain that it was a bubble mostly kept afloat by the illusion of scarcity.

Auctions. For the first time, contemporary art surged ahead of Impressionist and Post-Impressionist works in the auction market. Sotheby's May 2 auction of 74 contemporary works set a record, bringing in a total of $25.9 million. At that sale, Jackson Pollock's 1955 painting *Search* sold for $4.8 million, a record for a post-World War II work. The previous record was set by the same painting when it sold for $2.57 million in the spring of 1987.

Kazuo Fujii, the Tokyo dealer and gallery owner who bought *Search*, was one of the first Japanese dealers to stock Impressionist works

in the 1960s. In 1988 he led the assault on contemporary art, acquiring works by George Segal and Jean Arp, as well as another Jackson Pollock, *No. 31, 1949*, for $3.5 million.

Another auction record fell when Jasper Johns' 1962 painting *Diver* sold at Christie's for $4.18 million, the highest price ever paid for a work by a living American artist. It was surpassed in November when Johns' *False Start* (1959) brought in $17 million. Many individual artists' auction records were broken in 1988. Franz Kline's *Ninth Street* sold for $1.8 million, double its presale estimate. Cy Twombly's untitled 1967 painting brought $990,000; Richard Diebenhorn's *July* went for $1.2 million; Andy Warhol's *210 Coca Cola Bottles* sold for $1.43 million, and his *Marilyn Monroe (20 Times)* for $3.96 million.

Although contemporary paintings created the most excitement, Impressionist and early modern works also drew high prices. The highest price ever paid at auction for a piece of sculpture was $10.12 million for Edgar Degas' bronze, *Little Ballerina of 14 Years*, which went from the estate of Belle Linsky to an unidentified buyer at Sotheby's. Claude Monet's painting *Camille in the Meadow* was sold at Sotheby's in London for $24.3 million, four times the previous record at auction for a Monet. The Museum of Modern Art (MoMA) in New York sold its Matisse *Still Life with Lemons on a Flowered Background* for $5.72 million, more than twice its estimate. And Georgia O'Keeffe's *Black Hollyhock with Blue Larkspur* sold for $1.98 million. Still another record fell with the sale of Picasso's blue-period *Motherhood* (1901). Its $24.8 million price was the highest ever paid for a work of

20th-century art. The top price for all art works remained the $53.9 million paid in 1987 for Van Gogh's *Irises*. The Van Gogh mania of 1987 abated in 1988, but his 1890 portrait of *Adeline Ravoux* brought $13.8 million, six times its 1980 price, at Christie's in May.

The estates of two flamboyant personalities went on the market in 1988. Christie's, in conjunction with Butterfield & Butterfield of San Francisco, sold the contents of Liberace's five homes for the benefit of the late pianist's foundation for young artists. The 22,000 items, including his Baldwin Model L mirrored grand piano, brought in $2 million. Meanwhile, Sotheby's auctioned off the vast and eclectic collection of the late Andy Warhol. The ten-day sale brought in $25.3 million, including $23,000 for two cookie jars.

Antiquities also were bought at record prices during 1988. The highest, at a December Sotheby's sale, was the $2.09 million paid for a 3,000-year-old marble head from the Greek Cyclades islands.

And the heat of the auction market drew a variety of other art objects to the salesrooms. A 14th-century Ming vase, for example, sold for $2.18 million, a record for a Chinese work of art and for any ceramic piece.

In Moscow in July, Sotheby's held the first international art auction in Soviet history. The 119 modern paintings exceeded all expectations by bringing in a total of $3.4 million, one third of which went to the Soviet Ministry of Culture and 60% of which went to the artists. Grisha Brushkin's oil *Fundamental Lexicon* brought in $416,000, a record for a work by a living Soviet artist. Modern Soviet art went on the auction block in the United States for the first time, too, in an October sale conducted by Guernsey's in New York.

Exhibitions. Major museum shows of 1988 reflected the United States' improved political relations with the Soviet Union and China. The Art Institute of Chicago and the Metropolitan Museum in New York organized "Dutch and Flemish Paintings from the Hermitage," in exchange for an equal number (51) of Impressionist and early modern works sent for exhibition in Moscow and Leningrad.

Modern works by Russian and Soviet artists were seen during the summer at the Hirshhorn Museum in Washington, D.C. "Russian and Soviet Paintings 1900–1930," from state museums in Moscow and Leningrad, gave Americans a chance to see the full range of Russian styles from revolutionary Constructivism and Expressionism to the social realism of the Stalinist period. Modern Russian works also were prominent in a Museum of Modern Art show surveying "The Modern Poster."

Chinese paintings of the 19th and 20th centuries were shown at the Metropolitan Museum in a two-part exhibit that ran from February through September. All works were from the 471 paintings collected by Robert Hatfield Ellsworth and donated to the Metropolitan in 1986. The collection and its accompanying three-volume ($850) publication will be major scholarly resources for this little-known period in Chinese art.

Courtesy of the Art Institute of Chicago, Lent by the Hermitage, Leningrad

"A Bouquet of Flowers," left, *by Jan van Huysum (1682–1749) was one of 51 masterpieces on display in "Dutch and Flemish Paintings from the Hermitage." A gold, ceramic, and stone Buddha reliquary,* below, *from the Ming Dynasty was included in "Son of Heaven: Imperial Arts of China."*

© Don Hamilton/"Spokesman Review," Spokane, Washington

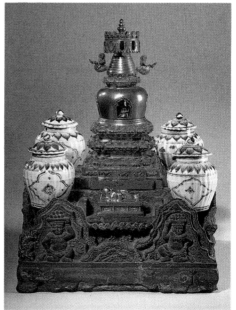

Today's Antique Market

Antiques of different styles are displayed at an antique show booth. Such shows are growing in popularity throughout the United States.

© Jacqueline Sideli Antique Shows

If you are one of those lucky people who own a rare, old, top-quality *objet,* you have made a good investment, as prices for choice antiques are at an all-time high. The competition for the best in the decorative arts is very lively. Since the severe drop in the stock market in October 1987, many investors prefer to buy something more tangible and profitable than stock certificates, whose value they cannot control. Overseas interest also adds to the increasingly high prices that select antiques can command. The fall of the U.S. dollar has enabled Europeans and Japanese to afford treasures in the American antique market.

To meet the needs of amateur and professional collectors, there has been a sharp increase in the number of antique shows. At the most comprehensive and prestigious one in the United States, the yearly Winter Antiques Show held at the Seventh Regiment Armory in New York City, some of the country's foremost dealers display and sell their prize furniture, porcelain, rugs, prints, silver, art, and quilts. Not at all a place for bargains, the 1988 show carried items as diverse as a rare American flag with a field of 34 stars, circa 1862, and a complete room of Empire furniture made for Marie Louise, the second wife of Napoleon. Smaller, specialized shows also are popular. These may feature silver and jewelry, original prints and fine art, quilts, or porcelain.

Auction activity also is feverish. Attendance has doubled in recent years, and auction houses have had record-breaking sales. In October 1987, Sotheby's in New York, the largest auction house in the world, indicated it had gained approximately 20,000 new private clients since the early 1980s. Christie's in London, the second-largest auction house, reported the number of registered bidders had risen as much as 82% in the area of American decorative arts alone.

For the first time, some examples of American decorative arts are bringing significantly higher prices at auction than their European and Asian counterparts. In 1987 collectors and dealers paid record-setting prices for an 1840s quilt ($176,000); a turn-of-the-century leaded glass window ($242,000); a 1780s needlework sampler stitched by a ten-year-old girl ($198,000); and a jeweled gold box ($411,500) made by Tiffany & Company in 1914.

Defying the stereotype of antique buying and selling as the province of older folks, well-heeled Yuppies are spending big bucks to indulge their love of beautiful things. Even dealers are getting younger. Some professionals entering the field are in their 20s and 30s.

Fledgling collectors, or those with a piggy-bank budget who dream of finding a significant bargain or making a discovery in a "Junque" shop or flea market, probably will be disappointed. With so many publications, including price guides, about antiques now available, dealers generally know the value of what they are selling and price their wares accordingly. It works both ways; collectors also know how much they should be paying. Nevertheless, if you relish the idea of owning a rusty railroad lantern or take a fancy to a scratched brass finial—buy it. Although it may not be rated a blue-chip antique, it will be a fabulous find to you.

GLADYS HANDELMAN

In Seattle, a show of 221 Chinese artifacts spanning 2,000 years opened in July and ran to the end of the year. Most of the works in the exhibit, titled "Son of Heaven: Imperial Arts of China," never before had been seen outside China. In Beijing, meanwhile, at the Museum of the Revolution, Chinese art lovers were introduced to contemporary American art through an exhibit of 100 Neo-Expressionist works by Frederick Brown of Greensboro, GA.

The international spirit also infused the contemporary art scene during 1988. A retrospective of works by 43-year-old German soul-searcher Anselm Kiefer started in Chicago, moved to Philadelphia and Los Angeles, and ended up in New York in the fall. Kiefer, a protégé of the late Joseph Beuys, produces gargantuan canvases heavy with spiritual and political innuendos in a grimly impressive style reminiscent of contemporary German film style.

Larger (and happier) crowds flocked to the 50th-birthday retrospective of British painter David Hockney, which opened in Los Angeles and traveled to New York and London. Hockney, who lives in California, documents the sun-splashed poolside life in a way that seems to accept the glamour and the trash equally. His designs for the Los Angeles Music Center Opera production of *Tristan and Isolde* added to Hockney's reputation as an innovative scenic designer.

The most important show by an American artist in 1988 was Frank Stella's retrospective at the Museum of Modern Art in January. His exuberant, shaped and painted aluminum reliefs made the tradition of American abstraction seem still vitally new.

Jasper Johns, whose *Diver* broke auction records in May, represented the United States at the Venice Biennale when it opened in June. This retrospective, covering work from 1974 to 1986, won Johns the international jury's award as the best living artist in the Biennale. The show went to the Philadelphia Museum in the fall.

Other contemporary artists who had major shows in 1988 included Philip Guston and Richard Diebenkorn, whose works on paper were seen at MoMA; and the late Andy Warhol, whose series of paintings of automobiles was shown at the Guggenheim Museum in New York.

Other major exhibits brought forward artists or periods that have been out of the limelight in recent decades. The Metropolitan Museum began the year with a Jean Honoré Fragonard show that revealed a haunting and melancholy side to this 18th-century charmer. The Metropolitan ended the year with a show of "Painting in Renaissance Siena: 1420–1500," the first major show of Sienese art in the United States.

The government of Greece helped organize two beautiful and scholarly shows in 1988.

Courtesy of the Metropolitan Museum of Art,
Lent by Timkin Art Gallery, San Diego, The Putnam Collection

"Blindman's Bluff, With the Pink Parasol," left, *was seen in a major New York exhibit devoted to Jean Honoré Fragonard (1732–1806). The anointing horn of Charles IX,* below, *was part of "Sweden: A Royal Treasury 1550–1700," marking the 350th anniversary of the Swedish settlement of North America.*

© Sven Nilsson, courtesy of the Minneapolis Institute of Arts

"The Human Figure in Early Greek Art" opened at the National Gallery in Washington and went on to the Nelsen-Atkins Museum in Kansas City. The other exhibition, "Holy Image, Holy Space," brought Byzantine icons and frescoes to the Walters Art Gallery in Baltimore.

Many of the major shows of 1988 were of early modern work that is both popular with the public and available to curators. Among these shows was a major Degas retrospective —the first in 50 years—which went from Paris to the new National Gallery of Canada in Ottawa and then the Metropolitan Museum of Art in New York. A Georgia O'Keeffe show opened at the National Gallery of Art and traveled to Chicago, Dallas, and New York. Works by the Futurist painter Umberto Boccioni were assembled at a major show at the Metropolitan Museum in the autumn. And Georges Braque was represented in a survey at the Guggenheim.

In Washington, DC, the National Gallery mounted a comprehensive Paul Gauguin exhibition, later seen at the Art Institute of Chicago. The Hirshhorn opened a retrospective of Alberto Giacometti in the autumn.

Perhaps the most controversial show of 1988 was MoMA's "Deconstructivist Architecture," which drew heavy media attention and mixed reviews. Cocurator Philip Johnson (with Mark Wigley of Princeton University) seemed to be trying to create a new architectural movement, much as he had in 1932 when, with Henry-Russell Hitchcock, he put together the show at MoMA that launched the "international style."

Museums. While traditional museums continued to expand, several new museums of unusual design or purpose opened during the course of the year.

In Minneapolis, a 7-acre (3-ha) sculpture garden on downtown parkland opened in September. A joint project of the Walker Art Center, the city's park board, and the University of Minnesota's Landscape Arboretum, the park includes 40 sculptures, all designed to endure —and even invite—public use and handling. A central attraction is a giant spoon holding a cherry (its stem is a fountain), which serves as a bridge to an island in a man-made pond. The work is by Claes Oldenburg and Coosje van Bruggen. Other works include Frank Gehry's 22-ft- (6.7-m-) high "Standing Glass Fish"; Meg Webster's "Glen," a plant-filled earthen crater; and sculptures by Isamu Noguchi, Mark di Suvero, and Henry Moore.

The American Museum of the Moving Image (AMMI) opened in September in Astoria, NY, on the site of the former Paramount Pictures production facility. Dedicated to film, television, and video, the museum has two screening rooms which opened with a month-long series of films in "Glorious Technicolor." AMMI's galleries house the ephemera of the moving image arts, everything from Mickey Mouse paraphernalia to the costumes of the stars. Just five days after the opening of AMMI, the British Film Institute opened its Museum of the Moving Image in London. The

"The Siesta," below, was one of 230 works in a Paul Gauguin exhibition—the first one covering the full range of his art in 80 years—at the National Gallery in Washington and the Art Institute of Chicago. "Sky Horizon," right, a 35-ft (11-m) black steel sculpture by the late Louise Nevelson (who died in April) was installed at the National Institutes of Health in Bethesda, MD.

© Ron Solomon

After a five-year, $6 million renovation, the Walters Art Gallery in Baltimore was reopened in May. In the grand upstairs galleries, left, neoclassical plasterwork and mahogany wainscots were restored and the walls upholstered in vivid colors.

two museums are unrelated except as the products of "an idea whose time has come."

Two museum projects in Massachusetts were in the news. The Peabody Museum of Salem opened its $8 million Asian Export Wing in May. The Peabody, which now includes an Oriental garden, houses the largest collection of objects brought to America through trade with the Orient. The second Massachusetts museum project was a visionary $50 million plan for a vast contemporary art center to be built in North Adams, a mill town in the northwestern part of the state. The Massachusetts Museum of Contemporary Art, or Mass MoCA as it is called, will include a convention center, shops, a hotel, restaurants, and condominiums, as well as exhibition space, all centered around the 28 buildings of an abandoned factory complex. Pushed by Gov. Michael Dukakis, the state legislature voted a $35 million bond issue to get the project started.

Mass MoCA is the brainchild of Thomas Krens, the energetic curator of the Williams College Museum of Art in Williamstown, MA, since 1980. In January 1988, Krens was appointed director of the Guggenheim Museum in New York. Kirk Varnedoe, an alumnus of Williams College, was appointed curator of painting and sculpture at MoMA in February, and the art world began to speak of a "Williams mafia." In addition to Krens and Varnedoe, the directors of five other major museums (Los Angeles County, San Francisco Fine Arts, Chicago Art Institute, Toledo Museum, and the Brooklyn Museum) are graduates of Williams College.

In California, several important museum projects were underway in 1988. In Santa Monica, architect Frank Gehry created an inventive new museum from an old ice warehouse. It is part of the Edgemar mall, a complex that will include retail and office spaces as well as the museum. Although not yet complete, the museum presented its first show in July, an installation by David Bunn.

The Japanese Pavilion of the Los Angeles County Museum neared completion in the fall. Toshio Nagamura, a Japanese banker, led the fund drive to which more than 500 Japanese corporations and individuals contributed a total of $4 million.

Armand Hammer, head of Occidental Petroleum and owner of a $250 million art collection, stunned the art world in January by announcing that he would build the $30 million Armand Hammer Museum of Art and Cultural Center. The Los Angeles County Museum of Art, of which Hammer is a longtime trustee and supporter, was expecting to receive his collection. Hammer's "boutique museum," as it sometimes is called, is scheduled to open in 1990.

Two of the United States' proudest old museums completed major building projects during 1988. In Baltimore, the Walters Art Gallery underwent radical renovation and reopened triumphantly in May. The Art Institute of Chicago opened a vast new wing, the Daniel and Ada Rice Building, with "The Art of Paul Gauguin" show in September.

MARILYN L. SCHAEFER
New York City Technical College

© Chip Hires/Gamma-Liaison

Monsoon rains caused widespread and devastating floods in Bangladesh during 1988. By early September, three quarters of the Asian nation was under water, more than 2,500 persons were dead, and some 28 million were homeless.

ASIA

The year 1988 was an eventful one in Asia, highlighted by growing pressures for democracy throughout the region, improving prospects for the resolution of bitter conflicts in Afghanistan and Cambodia, and the Summer Olympic Games (*see* page 494) in Seoul, South Korea.

Challenges of Nation-Building. Much of the region continued to experience the rapid economic growth that has characterized the global economy in the 1980s. Yet, as the case of South Korea has shown, economic prosperity is no guarantee against political unrest. In 1988 authoritarian regimes throughout the region were giving way to growing pressures for democracy. For South Korea and its newly elected government of President Roh Tae Woo (*see* BI-OGRAPHY), the Olympic Games represented an opportunity to showcase the progress the nation has made politically as well as economically.

The South Korean experience was paralleled elsewhere in the region. On Taiwan, the death of President Chiang Ching-kuo in January marked the transition to a new generation of leadership under native Taiwanese Lee Teng-hui. For the new president, the first year in office was characterized by growing popular unrest and political activism despite growing economic affluence. Meanwhile, on mainland China, Communist leaders attempted with only modest success to cope with inflationary pressures and a population restive for political progress.

Even in prosperous Singapore there were signs of change, as the nation's veteran leadership under Prime Minister Lee Kuan Yew prepared to step aside. In September legislative elections, the ruling party won its usual majority of seats, but the government's efforts to suppress opposition activities aroused widespread criticism and tarnished the republic as a model of development.

But the year's most violent unrest took place in Burma, where longtime ruler Gen. Ne Win was forced to step down in August after weeks of widespread rioting. At first the military regime attempted to retain power by suppressing discontent but, as the protests continued, elections were promised. In the meantime, opposition forces began to organize in an effort to oust the regime and release the country from nearly 30 years of economic stagnation and isolation.

In some countries, political unrest has been the consequence of deep-seated religious and racial tensions. In Sri Lanka, the bitter civil war between majority Sinhalese and separatist Tamils continued in 1988 despite the pressure of an Indian peacekeeping force and President Julius Jayewardene's efforts to conciliate the rebels. In India, communal tensions between Hindus and Sikhs did not subside, contributing to growing popular discontent against the ruling Congress (I) Party government of Prime Minister Rajiv Gandhi. Communal tensions also may have been a factor in Pakistan, where the death of President Zia-ul Haq in a suspicious plane crash in mid-August fueled political uncertainty.

Resolving Conflicts. The paradoxical mixture of hope and uncertainty that characterized internal developments in Asia also affected the arena of international politics, as 1988 witnessed significant progress toward the resolution of several regional disputes.

In April, in an agreement reached at Geneva, the Soviet Union promised to remove its

troops from Afghanistan, thus ending its nearly decade-long occupation. But many observers doubted whether the settlement would bring an end to the bitter civil war between Islamic rebels and the fragile pro-Soviet regime in Kabul, especially since the United States and Pakistan signaled their intention to continue providing assistance to the rebel forces.

Meanwhile, there were growing prospects for a negotiated settlement in Cambodia, where Vietnamese occupation troops were propping up a pro-Hanoi regime against resistance forces supported by China and the members of the Association of Southeast Asian Nations (ASEAN). Most of the progress has been in form rather than substance, but negotiations in France and Indonesia during 1988 produced the outlines of a possible agreement.

A major factor behind such developments was the continuing peace offensive by Soviet leader Mikhail Gorbachev. During 1988, Moscow continued its apparent effort to defuse the sources of regional conflict in Asia and provide a basis for improved relations with China and the United States. For months China rejected Gorbachev's bid for a summit meeting, insisting that Vietnamese troops first must be withdrawn from Cambodia. But in the fall, after Soviet and Chinese officials met to discuss a solution to the conflict in Indochina, China's Deng Xiaoping announced that a high-level meeting with Soviet leaders could take place in early 1989.

Gorbachev's diplomatic initiatives did not stop there. In a speech given in August, he offered to remove Soviet military forces from Vietnam in return for a U.S. withdrawal from its bases in the Philippines. Washington dismissed the offer as a propaganda gesture and in October signed an agreement with Manila to renew base rights until the early 1990s.

Regional Economic Cooperation. In May representatives of 15 Pacific Basin nations gathered in Osaka, Japan, for the sixth meeting of the Pacific Economic Cooperation Conference (PECC). The conference reached a joint position rejecting trade protectionism and calling for collective action at the December negotiations of the General Agreement on Tariffs and Trade (GATT). The representatives also took preliminary steps toward creating a permanent economic cooperation structure in the Pacific.

WILLIAM J. DUIKER
The Pennsylvania State University

ASTRONOMY

For more than a century, scientists have tried unsuccessfully to establish links between activity on the sun and weather on the earth. In 1988 astronomers Harry van Loon and Karin Labitzke announced the strongest correlation yet, a synchronization between the number of spots on the sun and the temperature of the stratosphere near the earth's north pole. There, when the winds blow from the west, as they do every few years, they are coldest when sunspots are fewest. This relation has persisted over at least three 11-year sunspot cycles, but a full explanation for it remains to be found.

Also during 1988, the first firm link was found between the sunspot cycle and the sun's energy output. Data from three artificial satellites taken over an eight-year period indicated that the sun is 0.04% brighter when solar activity is high (as it is now) than when it is low.

Pluto. With Pluto making its closest approach to the sun (an event that occurs only once every 248 years), scientists increased their understanding of this distant and mysterious planet in 1988. To learn more about the diameters, densities, and atmospheres of Pluto and its recently discovered moon, Charon, they took advantage of the fact that each passed directly in front of and behind the other. For example, scientists determined within a few percent accuracy that Pluto's and Charon's diameters are 2 284 and 1 192 km (1,419 and 741 mi), respectively. Results published by planetary scientists William McKinnon and Steve Mueller indicated that 68%–80% of Pluto's mass is contained in a rocky core occupying the inner three quarters of the planet. The core is surrounded by a water-ice shell 210 to 320 km (130 to 200 mi) thick, topped by a few kilometers of methane ice.

Also discovered in 1988 was Pluto's atmosphere, detected when the planet passed between the earth and a star on July 9. As astronomers watched, the star's light dimmed gradually, a telltale sign that an atmosphere is present. Composed of methane evaporated from Pluto's surface, this tenuous atmosphere exerts a surface pressure only 0.001% that of the earth's.

McKinnon theorized that Pluto probably formed near Neptune and was captured by it in a so-called resonance orbit (one in which collisions between the two bodies are impossible). But another study showed that Pluto's orbit is "chaotic"; that is, the precise motion of the planet cannot be predicted on a time scale longer than 20 million years—only 0.4% the age of the solar system. Thus, the jury remains out on the origin of this enigmatic world.

Extrasolar Planets. Over the last few years, several claims have been made for the discovery of planet-like objects around other stars. However, follow-up investigations have disproved the existence of such "extrasolar planets." The latest and best candidate was announced at the August 1988 meeting of the International Astronomical Union. According to astronomer David Latham, the object is some 10–20 times more massive than Jupiter and orbits the star HD 114762 every 84 days (about

the time the planet Mercury takes to revolve around the sun). But until this object's mass is better determined it remains unclear whether the object is a huge planet or a failed star (one so small that its nuclear fires could not ignite).

Pulsar Murder. One of the most interesting objects discovered in recent times is the pulsar PSR 1957 + 20, so named because it emits periodic pulses of radiation. Pulsars are neutron stars; this one is about 20 km (12 mi) across and contains mass equivalent to the sun's. Spinning on its axis 622 times per second, PSR 1957 + 20 is unique in having a companion, one that blocks its pulses every 9.16 hours. From observations of this blocking, astronomers conclude that the companion, which contains only 23 Jupiter masses, will not last long by cosmic standards. In much less than a billion years, radiation from the pulsar will have blasted this tiny body into oblivion. Astronomers believe that mass collected from such companions is responsible for the fantastic spinning rates of these so-called millisecond pulsars.

The Edge of the Universe. Records for the most distant known object fell several times during 1988. Among radio-emitting galaxies, first cousins to the famous quasars (probably very distant galaxies with exceptionally bright cores), the latest record-holder is 4C 41.17, which might lie 15 billion light-years away. Among quasars, the most luminous of all objects, the new record-holder is an object called 0051–279; it could be 20% farther away than 4C 41.17.

There even was evidence that the limit of the visible universe had been reached. J. Anthony Tyson and colleagues obtained images that revealed myriads of faint, exceptionally blue galaxies—an indication that these systems are undergoing their first burst of star formation. From counts of these galaxies at ever dimmer levels, the group concluded that the galaxies began to form stars when the universe was only about an eighth its present age (20 billion years, perhaps) and continued doing so for billions of years thereafter.

The detection of light from stars that formed even before the galaxies themselves was claimed by astronomers from Nagoya University in Japan. Exploring a previously neglected region of the electromagnetic spectrum, the scientists may have recorded radiation from very massive stars that flourished a mere 100 million years after the universe was born. Their observations at wavelengths between 0.5 and 1 mm did not directly detect light from these short-lived stars but radiation from silicate and carbon dust the stars ejected and warmed.

The presence of such material in an infant universe would answer a perplexing question: Where did the heavy elements in the present universe come from, since they could not be produced at the birth of the universe itself? And the fossil remains of that first stellar generation—black holes or neutron stars—might account for mass that is known to exist in the universe but whose identity is unknown.

Gravitational Lensing. In 1936, Albert Einstein discovered that gravity bends electromagnetic radiation (light and radio waves) in a manner not too dissimilar to a glass lens. Thus, if a massive body is aligned exactly between the earth and a more distant object, we should see the latter distorted into a ring. This is precisely what was found by astronomer Jacqueline Hewitt and colleagues in 1988, during observations of the radio source MG 1131 + 0456 with the Very Large Array telescope in New Mexico. The lensing body itself remained unidentified.

Gravitational lenses can make visible objects that otherwise would go undetected. During a recent search for lenses, many more quasars than expected turned up close to galaxies. This is explained as a consequence of nearby galaxies concentrating the light of quasars lying nearly along our line of sight.

Gravitational lenses also can form multiple images of a single object. In 1988 two cases were announced in which a foreground galaxy caused a quasar to be imaged as a four-leaf clover. Because of the sun's motion around the center of our galaxy, the perfect alignment needed to produce such symmetrical configurations can persist for only a few hundred years.

Observatories. For European astronomers desiring to build the world's largest telescope, 1988 was a very good year. In September a consortium of eight nations ordered four mirror blanks, each 8 m (315 inches) in diameter. When the light from all of them is combined in the Very Large Telescope, it will have a collecting area of 200 m² (2,150 sq ft)—about one quarter the size of a baseball diamond. This $220 million instrument is expected to be completed in ten years and will be located on a mountain in Chile.

The year 1988 may have been a watershed for confronting a problem of astronomical proportion—the pollution of the sky. Optical observatories are suffering from the proliferation of outdoor lighting. The situation is equally bleak at radio wavelengths, as special frequencies are invaded by commercial satellites and such everyday devices as mobile telephones. Even space itself is full of dangers, particularly debris from satellites and rockets that could strike and destroy orbiting observatories.

On the negative side, the 300-ft (91-m) radio-telescope in Green Bank, WV, one of the world's most powerful, collapsed under mysterious circumstances in mid-November. Experts estimated that the accident would set back astronomical research for years.

LEIF J. ROBINSON, *"Sky and Telescope"*

AUSTRALIA

In political terms, Australia's bicentennial year (*see* feature article, page 62) proved somewhat less felicitous for Prime Minister Robert J. Hawke and his Australian Labor Party (ALP) government than its festive atmosphere betrayed. Overall, the economy performed unexpectedly well, and no major foreign policy changes were in evidence.

Politics and Government. Three by-elections during the year showed ALP voter support down by 8–12% from the previous year; the party lost two seats and narrowly retained the other. Then in September the government's heavily promoted package of referendums for major constitutional change suffered a stunning rejection by voters. In addition to suffering setbacks at the federal level, Labor was defeated in the most populous state, New South Wales, for the first time in 12 years, and the ALP clung to power in Victoria with a reduced majority.

A degree of factionalism was apparent within the ranks of both the ALP and the opposition Liberal Party. In March the ALP's national president, Michael J. Young, resigned amid controversy after his acceptance of a part-time consultant job with Qantas, the state-owned airline. Open disagreements between Prime Minister Hawke and Treasurer Paul Keating on leadership and policy issues led to speculation of Hawke's early retirement—a prospect at least delayed by a strong showing of support for the prime minister at the ALP Conference in June. New controversy erupted in August when Foreign Minister Bill Hayden was named the country's new governor-general, beginning in February 1989. His appointment, recommended to Britain's Queen Elizabeth II, stirred controversy because in the 1970s Hayden publicly had advocated cutting ties with the Commonwealth. Meanwhile, Liberal Party and opposition leader John Howard

suffered a decline in popular support and al-most constant challenge to his leadership.

Immigration and the nation's Aboriginal people were prominent domestic issues during 1988. A report released in June by a government advisory panel recommended a significant increase in the immigration level, with a greater emphasis on immigrants with needed labor skills. In August opposition leader Howard called for a reassessment of the number and source of immigrants, specifically questioning existing levels of Asians. (About 40% of the nation's 130,000 immigrants in 1987 were from Asian countries.) A public opinion poll on the issue showed that 77% of Australians agreed with his views. On the Aborigine issue, Prime Minister Hawke called for a reconciliation treaty by the middle of 1990; Howard said the proposal was at odds with a "one-Australia" concept.

Economy. Fears of a recession after the stock market crash of October 1987 gave way to a growing sense of optimism in 1988. The gross domestic product (GDP) rose by 3.6% in fiscal 1987–88 (ended June 30, 1988); the business sector performed well; the rural sector basked in excellent seasonal conditions and improved returns; tax revenues were buoyant enough to yield a handsome budget surplus and to end federal borrowing; and consumer demand remained expansionary. Unemployment stood at 7.5%, and inflation fell below 7%. Personal borrowing grew, unchecked by higher interest rates. A boom in commercial and residential construction went hand-in-hand with a surge in property values.

Key elements of the government's economic policy included continued restructuring of industry to maintain investment levels and reduce deficit spending on imports, and a firm monetary policy combined with lower tariffs and wage controls to increase productivity. In May the government introduced a sweeping reform package, including a cut in corporate taxes from 49% to 39%, an average 20% cut in import duties, and individual tax cuts in 1989 tied to wage restraints. The budget for 1988–89, introduced in August, forecast a surplus of A$5.5 billion, real economic growth of 3.5%, and a drop in inflation to 4.5%.

Foreign Affairs. Following the resignation of Bill Hayden, incoming Foreign Minister Gareth Evans visited several Southeast Asian capitals in October. In Jakarta, Indonesia, he signed an agreement on the sharing of tax revenues from the potentially oil-rich Timor Gap off northwest Australia.

On May 31, customs officials in Sydney discovered some 12 tons of weapons apparently being smuggled to Indian militants on Fiji. Later reports suggested they had been loaded in Sri Lanka by Indian soldiers.

R.M. YOUNGER
Author, "Australia and the Australians"

AUSTRALIA · Information Highlights

Official Name: Commonwealth of Australia.
Location: Southwestern Pacific Ocean.
Area: 2,967,896 sq mi (7 686 850 km²).
Population (mid-1988 est.): 16,500,000.
Chief Cities (June 30, 1986, provisional): Canberra, the capital, 285,800; Sydney, 3,430,600; Melbourne, 2,942,000; Brisbane, 1,171,300.
Government: *Head of state,* Elizabeth II, queen; represented by Bill Hayden, governor-general (took office February 1989). *Head of government,* Robert Hawke, prime minister (took office March 11, 1983). *Legislature*—Parliament: Senate and House of Representatives.
Monetary Unit: Australian dollar (1.2065 A$ equal U.S.$1, Nov. 7, 1988).
Gross Domestic Product (1987 est. U.S.$): $196,000,-000,000.
Economic Indexes (1987): *Consumer Prices* (1980 = 100), all items, 176.2; food, 166.9. *Industrial Production* (June 1986, 1980 = 100), 99.
Foreign Trade (1987 U.S.$): *Imports,* $26,978,-000,000; *exports,* $26,455,000,000.

AUSTRIA

Politically and economically 1988 was a year of stability for Austria. Controversy over President Kurt Waldheim's activities during World War II subsided during the year. Official ceremonies on March 11 to 13 commemorated the 50th anniversary of Hitler's seizure of Austria (the *Anschluss* in 1938).

Government. On February 8 an international commission of historians appointed by the government presented a 200-page report detailing its investigation of war crimes charged against President Waldheim. The commission found that although Waldheim had known of the crimes and had misrepresented his war record, there was no evidence of his personal culpable behavior or his participation in war crimes. The publication of the report led to calls for Waldheim's resignation, but there were many who defended the president, including Vice-Chancellor and Foreign Minister Alois Mock of the People's Party and former Foreign Minister Karl Gruber. In a televised address to the nation, Waldheim said that he was happy the commission had issued a clear statement that he was not guilty of war crimes, and insisted that "knowledge is not a crime." He adamantly refused to resign.

In an effort to defuse the situation the Social Democratic-People's Party government coalition agreed that Waldheim would not speak at the official ceremonies commemorating the *Anschluss,* but would speak before them on national television. In his address, Waldheim recognized that there were many who had welcomed the Nazis. He apologized for war crimes committed by Austrians, but stressed that the nation should not suffer collective guilt for its history during World War II. Chancellor Franz Vranitzky delivered the main address at the ceremony in the Hofburg the next day.

Foreign Affairs. Pope John Paul II paid a visit to Austria June 22–27, met several times with President Waldheim, celebrated Mass before large groups, visited the old Mauthausen concentration camp, and met with leaders of the Jewish community. Also in June, President Waldheim was received royally in Saudi Arabia. Earlier Jordan's King Hussein had visited Austria.

On April 13, West Germany and Austria signed an agreement aimed at combating international terrorism, organized crime, and illegal drug trafficking. The agreement also set up a mechanism that would permit cross-border searches.

The planned establishment by the European Community (EC) of a single internal market by 1992 has caused concern in Austria about vital trade relations. The country is a member of the European Free Trade Association (EFTA), which is Austria's second largest market, taking about 11% of its exports. (The EC itself is Austria's largest market; it buys some 60% of the country's exports.) Many Austrians believe that joining the larger community ultimately would prove more beneficial than the present EFTA membership.

Membership would entail some basic changes in the Austrian economy. The country would have to accept the EC's tariff structure, as well as becoming subject to hundreds of EC regulations covering such areas as cross-border transport, technical standards, the adjustment of fiscal arrangements, and business privileges. In addition, Austria would have to increase its level of farm subsidies under the EC's Common Agricultural Policy. To apply for EC membership also might cause problems with the Soviet Union in regard to Austria's required status of neutrality. While no decision was made in 1988, Austria was seeking closer relations with the EC and was aligning its standards to meet the community's norms.

Economy. A major tax reform, effective on Jan. 1, 1989, has replaced the previous ten tax brackets with five, and lowers the basic level of taxation by 19%. The corporation tax, presently at a maximum of 55%, would be cut to a maximum of 30%. Additional revenue was expected through the ending of special tax allowances, termination of some state subsidies, and an increase in taxes levied on gambling, tobacco, and insurance policies.

A partial privatization of state-owned industries, which began in 1987, continued, with the state retaining 51% of company shares. Privatization notably has affected Austrian Air Lines, the national oil and electricity companies, and some banks.

The Austrian schilling remained stable and closely linked to the West German mark. Projections indicated that the budget deficit would be reduced substantially by the end of 1988.

See also EUROPE.

ERNST C. HELMREICH, *Professor of History Emeritus, Bowdoin College*

AUSTRIA • Information Highlights

Official Name: Republic of Austria.
Location: Central Europe.
Area: 32,375 sq mi (83 850 km²).
Population (mid-1988 est.): 7,600,000.
Chief Cities (1981 census): Vienna, the capital, 1,531,346; Graz, 243,166; Linz, 199,910; Salzburg, 139,426; Innsbruck, 117,287.
Government: *Head of state,* Kurt Waldheim, president (took office July 1986). *Head of government,* Franz Vranitzky, chancellor (took office June 16, 1986). *Legislature*—Federal Assembly: Federal Council and National Council.
Monetary Unit: Schilling (12.52 schillings equal U.S. $1, Nov. 2, 1988).
Gross Domestic Product (1985 U.S.$): $66,260,-000,000.
Economic Indexes (1987): *Consumer Prices* (1980 = 100), all items, 130.9; food, 126.3. *Industrial Production* (1980 = 100), 111.
Foreign Trade (1987 U.S.$): *Imports,* $32,679,-000,000; *exports,* $27,171,000,000.

AUTOMOBILES

Detroit's Big Three automakers—Chrysler Corporation, Ford Motor Company, and General Motors (GM)—entered the 1989-model year with high expectations: a fifth straight year of more than 15 million car and truck sales (including imports) in the United States. Sales in the 1988-model year, which ended September 30, reached about 15.6 million—10.6 million cars and a record 5 million trucks, vans, and utility vehicles.

The optimistic forecasts from the Big Three came despite admitted concerns about the economic policies of a new U.S. president, rising interest rates, and a possible return of cyclical downturns in auto-industry sales (as in the early 1980s). For that matter, each of the Big Three predicted modest declines in 1989-model-year volume. Ford was projecting 15.4 million units while GM and Chrysler both expected a 15.0 million total.

Ford's more exuberant outlook was traced to the fact that in 1988 its Ford Division outsold GM's Chevrolet Division in both cars and trucks for the second consecutive year. Ford's triumph over Chevrolet in car deliveries alone was its first since the 1960s. For 1989, Ford expected total car sales to reach 2.3 million, including 1.6 million by the Ford Division and 700,000 by Lincoln-Mercury. Ford truck sales, the company said, also would reach the 1.6 million mark, reflecting the continuing surge in consumer demand for light pickups, minivans, and four-wheel-drive utility vehicles.

Chrysler, which posted robust sales gains in 1988 (after its purchase of American Motors—AMC—in August 1987), expected its car sales to drop by about 100,000 units, to 1.1 million. But the No. 3 automaker, experiencing record-breaking sales of its minivans and of the Jeep units inherited from AMC, saw its volume of truck sales hold steady at nearly one million. Chrysler made headlines in May with its decision to install airbags as standard equipment on several of its car lines and extend them to all of its domestically manufactured cars by 1990.

The 1989 outlook was more of a question mark for giant GM, whose share of the car market fell from 37.5% (3.7 million units) in 1987 to about 36.0% (3.5 million) in 1988. GM did join Chrysler and Ford in raising truck sales, however, notching a 13% boost from 1.4 million to more than 1.6 million units. GM executives, promising a Chevrolet drive to regain the top sales position over Ford in 1989, also announced a long-range program to reverse the market-share attrition plaguing the No. 1 automaker and reclaim at least 40%.

The Big Three forecasts for 1988 and 1989 included about 3.1 million imported cars and 650,000 foreign-sourced trucks. Imported car sales ran close to 3.2 million in 1987 while foreign-sourced truck sales totaled 850,000 units,

only to plunge in subsequent months because of the surge in demand for domestic units.

The 1989 Models. Underscoring an industry-wide reemphasis on power and performance, Ford prepared to revive an engine-supercharger feature on its restyled Ford Thunderbird and Mercury Cougar cars. A supercharged engine, producing 210 horsepower in Ford's V-6 powerplant, had not been offered on a U.S.-built car since before World War II. At the same time, Ford's popular Taurus midsize line unveiled a Super High Output (SHO) series with an engine produced by Yamaha of Japan rated at 220 horsepower.

GM, facing a carryover design year for the most part, also turned to engine enhancements to boost buyer interest. A new 3.3-liter V-6 engine was introduced by Oldsmobile and Buick. Chevrolet's Corvette two-seater luxury coupe debuted a $50,000 ZR1 model equipped with a 390-horsepower V-8 engine and a six-speed manual transmission. Chevrolet added a hatchback sedan to its best-selling line, the Corsica and Beretta compacts. Chevy's imports were consolidated under the "Geo" nameplate, embracing the following makes: Metro, a minicompact car previously imported from GM partner Suzuki of Japan as the Sprint; Tracker, a new four-wheel-drive utility vehicle also produced by Suzuki; Spectrum, assembled in Japan by Isuzu as a sedan but due to be replaced in the fall of 1989 by the Storm, a new sports coupe; and Prizm, the new name for the Nova subcompact built at the Toyota-Chevrolet plant in Fremont, CA. Chevrolet also planned to join the year-old GM10 family of midsize front-drive cars in the spring of 1989 with the Lumina series four-door sedan. Sedan editions of the GM10 Buick Regal, Oldsmobile Cutlass Supreme, and Pontiac Grand Prix Coupes—two of which (the Cutlass and Grand Prix) had disappointing 1988 sales—were on tap for the 1990-model year.

Chrysler rolled out two new compact series —the Dodge Spirit and Plymouth Acclaim—as

The 1989 Ford Thunderbird features a V-6 engine, a five-speed manual transmission, and an antilock braking system.

Public Affairs, Ford Division

The 1989 Mercury Cougar, right, is lower and wider than recent cars of the same line. Like the Thunderbird, the Cougar has a 3.8 liter V-6 engine.

For 1989, Chevrolet introduced a hatchback to its best-selling model, the Corsica. With the folding rear seat down, the cargo capacity of the Corsica approaches that of many wagons.

eventual replacements for the aging Dodge Aries and Plymouth Reliant K-cars. A four-speed electronic automatic transmission was unveiled for the Chrysler New Yorker, and the long-promised Maserati TC two-seater coupe finally arrived from Italy. Chrysler also rolled out its amalgamation of the American Motors line under the Jeep/Eagle label. Eagle cars included the Premier midsize sedan, assembled in Ontario; the Medallion compact series, imported from Renault; and a new Mitsubishi-exported subcompact called the Summit.

Among discontinued domestic cars, the most notable was Pontiac's Fiero two-seater coupe. The Fiero helped resurrect the GM Division but fell victim to quality problems and a sluggish market for two-seater models.

Imports and "Transplants." Foreign automakers, stung by a higher-price trend caused by the U.S. dollar's weakness against Japanese and European currencies in the first half of 1988, reinforced their position by opening more domestic "transplant" assembly facilities and moving into upscale market segments.

Although Volkswagen closed its ten-year-old Golf/Jetta assembly plant in New Stanton, PA, three new assembly points serving North America commenced production late in the year: Mitsubishi-Chrysler Diamond Star at Normal, IL; Toyota at Georgetown, KY; and Hyundai at Bromont, Quebec. Significantly, all three of the new plants were to produce "upmarket" cars, with the Toyota and Hyundai facilities producing compact-sized models and Diamond Star producing sports coupes.

Hyundai, the largest of the three South Korean automakers exporting to the United States, named its new family-sized car the Sonata and prepared to move upscale a year ahead of the marketing launches of two new full-size cars from Japan in the $30,000 segment —the Nissan Infiniti and Toyota Lexus.

The 1989-model year was launched by the U.S. debuts of two highly-touted cars from Europe—the Peugeot 405 and Audi 100/200. Mazda joined the growing minivan market. And BMW targeted the upscale power-and-performance market with a 12-cylinder entry called the 750iL, priced at $69,000.

MAYNARD M. GORDON
Editor, "Motor News Analysis"

WORLD MOTOR VEHICLE DATA, 1987

Country	Passenger Car Production	Truck and Bus Production	Motor Vehicle Registrations
Argentina	158,743	34,573	5,344,000
Australia	303,000	20,500	8,959,700
Austria	6,958	3,747	2,831,062
Belgium	293,995	41,456	3,727,311
Brazil	700,043	220,195	11,937,283
Canada	809,927	825,187	14,689,446
China	12,000	385,000	3,574,463
Czechoslovakia	172,000	50,000	3,120,168
France	3,051,830	441,380	24,403,000
East Germany*	220,000	47,000	3,739,199
West Germany	4,373,629	260,445	28,975,349
Hungary	–	13,113	1,761,361
India	147,952	138,449	2,705,300
Italy	1,713,300	199,312	23,856,000
Japan	7,891,087	4,358,087	47,972,338
South Korea	793,125	186,614	1,309,434
Mexico	142,436	90,079	7,475,515
The Netherlands	125,247	26,676	5,413,859
Poland	302,150	61,500	4,875,000
Spain	1,402,572	301,899	11,405,987
Sweden	431,777	70,045	3,497,297
United Kingdom	1,142,985	246,727	19,916,944
United States	7,098,910	3,810,672	176,191,339**
USSR	1,329,000	900,000	20,200,000
Yugoslavia	288,079	36,422	3,162,076
Total	32,910,745	12,769,078	499,730,724***

Production figures include vehicles manufactured locally and not assembled from "knockdown" kits supplied by foreign producers. South Africa assembled 278,751 cars, trucks, and buses in 1987. * Includes East Berlin. ** U.S. total does not include Puerto Rico, which has 1,384,965 vehicles. *** World total includes 386,307,614 cars and 113,423,110 trucks and buses. Other countries with more than one million registrations include: Greece, 2,004,889; Colombia, 1,196,403; Bulgaria, 1,263,126; Taiwan, 1,486,570; Thailand, 1,486,270; Venezuela, 1,959,927; Indonesia, 2,193,111; Malaysia, 1,652,789; Saudi Arabia, 4,268,407; New Zealand, 1,750,916; Nigeria, 1,405,000; Denmark, 1,841,209; Finland, 1,828,949; Norway, 1,875,000; Portugal, 1,605,000; Switzerland, 2,896,723; Turkey, 1,677,815; and South Africa, 4,319,684. Source: Motor Vehicle Manufacturers Association of the United States, Inc.

BANGLADESH

Continuing political unrest and widespread flooding overshadowed other events in Bangladesh during 1988.

Politics. After declaring a national emergency and dissolving parliament in late 1987, President H. M. Ershad in January 1988 called for fresh parliamentary elections to be held on March 3. The main opposition groups, led by the Awami League (AL) and Bangladesh Nationalist Party (BNP), both vowed to boycott the elections, calling again for Ershad's resignation.

Prior to the parliamentary polls, on February 10, local council elections were marred by violent clashes between contending factions; more than 100 people were killed. The police and military were unable to provide adequate security at all polling stations, putting into doubt the government's ability to hold peaceful parliamentary elections.

Some members of the ruling Jaitya Party (JP) openly expressed policy differences concerning the parliamentary elections. Two cabinet members, the party treasurer, and a former member of parliament all resigned their posts, stating that it was wrong to hold elections without the participation of the opposition. The mainline opposition followed through on its threat to boycott the March 3 balloting, though many smaller opposition parties did take part.

The results showed a landslide for the JP—238 out of 281 contested seats, giving it a total of 256 out of 300. Violence broke out at a number of polling places, and the AL and BNP charged widespread voting fraud. Observers concluded that while President Ershad had obeyed the constitution in holding the elections within 90 days of dissolving parliament, he had damaged further his credibility and his ability to restore peace and order.

After the election, the president took steps apparently intended to divide the mainline opposition. Six prominent members of the BNP were expelled in late July on charges that they had called an illegal party council session and were conspiring with the JP to split the party. In the fractionalized AL, according to some sources, President Ershad worked to widen differences between the party leader, Sheikh Hasina, and other members. And in a move to undercut increasingly vocal Muslim fundamentalists, the JP-dominated parliament on June 7 passed a constitutional amendment making Islam the national religion.

Opposition groups for the first time took their campaign to Washington, where lobbyists tried to convince the Reagan administration and Congress to tie aid to Bangladesh to the restoration of democracy. They met with sympathy but no success.

Floods. Heavy monsoon rains in the latter part of August created the worst flooding Ban-

BANGLADESH · Information Highlights

Official Name: People's Republic of Bangladesh.
Location: South Asia.
Area: 55,598 sq mi (144 000 km²).
Population (mid-1988 est.): 109,500,000.
Chief City (1981 census): Dhaka, the capital, 3,430,312.
Government: *Head of state,* Hussain Mohammad Ershad, chief executive (assumed power March 24, 1982) and president (Dec. 1983). *Head of government,* Mizanur Rahman Chowdhury, prime minister (took office July 1986). *Legislature*—Parliament.
Monetary Unit: Taka (31.5 taka equal U.S.$1, June 1988).
Economic Indexes: *Consumer Prices* (Dhaka, February 1988, 1980 = 100), all items, 208.6; food, 213.5.
Foreign Trade (1987 U.S.$): *Imports,* $2,271,000,000; *exports,* $1,083,000,000.

gladesh had suffered in 70 years. Affecting as much as three quarters of the country, the floods left more than 2,500 people dead from drowning, hunger, snake bites, and a variety of diseases; up to 28 million people were left homeless; at least three quarters of the year's food crops were destroyed; water supplies were polluted; roads, railways, bridges, dikes, and buildings throughout the country suffered massive damage. As President Ershad observed, it was a crippling blow to the nation's long-term development, wiping out the hard-won progress of the previous two decades. Urgent appeals for assistance were made to the United Nations, other relief organizations, and individual nations. Millions of dollars in aid were pledged, but the flooding left thousands of villages and families inaccessible.

Economy. Even before the floods, Bangladesh's domestic economy was beset by stagnant growth, low demand in rural areas, and declines in personal income and private investment. The Asian Development Bank embarked on its first private investment scheme in Bangladesh, a $1 million venture with Padma Textile Mills, and was considering other such projects. Such investments, along with some $2 billion in aid from the World Bank Consortium, are aimed primarily at increasing employment and reducing poverty in rural areas.

Foreign Relations. Relations with the United States remained strained in 1988, largely because of the domestic political scene. Although Washington was troubled by the lack of democratization, it did not curb aid to the Ershad government.

Major problems also persisted in Indo-Bangladesh relations. India was reluctant to renegotiate a three-year water sharing agreement that expired in May, and Bangladesh continued to feel that India was aiding an ongoing tribal insurrection in the Chittagong Hills.

See also ASIA.

ARUNA NAYYAR MICHIE
Kansas State University

BANKING AND FINANCE

Though worries abounded that the U.S. banking system would suffer from the October 1987 stock-market crash, investors actually sought the protection of federal deposit insurance and flooded banks with money. Indeed, buoyed by a vigorous U.S. economy, the fortunes in the nation's banking industry improved, and any problems were overshadowed by the troubles at the nation's 3,100 savings and loan associations (S&Ls), which took on near-crisis proportions.

The Thrift Industry. Lax regulation by federal and state governments in the early 1980s, excessive speculation in Texas real-estate ventures, and the collapse of the energy and real-estate sectors in the Southwest finally hit with a vengeance in 1988. At the beginning of the year, one third of the savings and loan (S&L) industry was in trouble, with more than 500 S&Ls hopelessly insolvent, and another 400 near insolvency. The latter figures compared with a mere 11 failed and 16 "problem" (near insolvency) thrifts as of the beginning of the decade.

At first, the Federal Home Loan Bank Board, the industry's prime regulator, said it would cost $22.7 billion to liquidate or find merger partners for the sick thrifts. But to the chagrin of the agency, it found that the imbedded losses were more than twice what it had expected. By the fall, the bank board had more than doubled those estimates to $50 billion, with many private economists predicting that the cost could go as high as $100 billion.

Though cash for bailing out sick thrifts was limited, the regulators nevertheless began an aggressive program, announcing a string of billion-dollar assistance packages. Eventually the bank board liquidated or merged some 220 institutions. Instead of injecting cash into the sick thrifts—the normal process—it .issued promissory notes and offered investors blanket guarantees against future losses on loans and other assets. While the agency was only able to get a few hundred million dollars of new cash from outside investors, it issued nearly $39 billion in federal assistance.

The centerpiece of the bank board's program was the so-called Southwest Plan, under which it hoped to liquidate or merge almost 150 insolvent thrifts in Texas and surrounding states. Though the agency dealt with more than 60 of the institutions in 1988, critics warned that the deals were thin. With few exceptions, investors put up very little of their own money and the agency provided vast amounts of government aid. In many cases, buyers of sick thrifts had no prior S&L experience.

By far, the most significant deal of the year was the sale of the nation's largest insolvent thrift, the $30 billion American Savings and Loan Association of Stockton, CA, to the Rob-

AP/Wide World

Twelve of Texas' 150 insolvent S&Ls were sold to an investment group headed by William E. Gibson (right). The new consolidated thrift was called the American Federal Bank.

ert M. Bass Group of Fort Worth, TX. The Bass Group agreed to put up $500 million of its own funds, while the bank board agreed to inject $1.7 billion in federal guarantees—the costliest bailout for a single thrift on record.

By the fall, sentiment was growing in Congress that a taxpayer rescue of the industry might be unavoidable. Thirty percent of thrifts were unprofitable, recording losses that swamped the relatively meager earnings of the profitable sector. Losses were piling up at a rate of more than $1 billion per month. Most experts agreed that the healthy segment of the industry would not be able to pay for the mistakes of the insolvent institutions and that President-elect George Bush together with Congress would have to deal with the thrift problem beginning early in his first term.

The Commercial Banks. By contrast, the problems at commercial banks were modest. After huge write-downs of Third World loans by the money-center banks resulted in record losses in 1987, bank profits rebounded. Much of the recovery was concentrated among the

emerging superregional banks that lend to local businesses and do not participate in the international arena. Because many state legislatures have passed laws permitting banks in adjoining states to merge with their banks, but have kept out of the big New York City, Chicago, and California banks, the superregional banks have flourished.

The money-center banks, saddled with huge portfolios of troubled Third World loans, have found few new profitable businesses. And a recalcitrant Congress has been unwilling to let the commercial banks into new areas, such as securities underwriting and insurance.

Faced with a squeeze on their earnings, the big banks had to cope with yet another obstacle. The Federal Reserve Board and other federal regulators finalized new regulations that will require all banks to hold higher levels of capital. Though most of the superregional banks and small commercial banks already meet those requirements, almost all of the money-center banks fall short. As a result, they began selling off their ancillary operations to raise new cash, effectively shrinking the size of their institutions.

But the regional banks and the small commercial banks had their problems. The effects of the depressed farm and energy sectors continued to take a high toll, as up to 250 banks failed or needed federal assistance in 1988, 25% above the record of 203 set in 1987. The problem bank list remained high at about 1,500, but had declined from around 1,600 at the beginning of the year. By way of perspective, the number of problem banks totaled only 217 in 1980—a year that saw only ten failures. Federal regulators expected 1988 to represent the high-water mark, predicting that the number of failures then would begin to decline. Still, L. William Seidman, chairman of the Federal Deposit Insurance Corporation (FDIC), predicted that the government's insurance fund would suffer the first loss in its history.

The biggest banking institution to fail in 1988 was the $32.5 billion First Republic Bank Corporation of Dallas, that had 41 subsidiary banks. With a $4 billion cash infusion from the FDIC, First Republic was bought by the NCNB Corporation, a superregional bank based in North Carolina. The year also was marked by the first successful hostile takeover of a major bank. The Bank of New York won a grueling $1.45 billion takeover of the Irving Bank, after more than a year of resistance.

Legislation. Though many lawmakers recognized the banks' need for new business opportunities, Congress could not reach a consensus over whether to remove a 55-year-old wall between banking and securities underwriting erected by the Glass-Steagall Act of 1933 and permit banks to underwrite corporate stocks and bonds. In his final year in Congress, Sen. William Proxmire (D-WI), the chairman of the Senate Banking Committee, got a bill through the Senate that gave banks broad new securities powers, including the right to underwrite mutual funds and corporate debt. But the bill was stalled in a divided House of Representatives.

Only modest legislation—including a measure that requires issuers of credit cards to disclose more prominently their interest rates and finance charges and a bill that requires greater disclosure of terms on home-equity loans—was passed as Congress rushed to adjourn before the elections.

Finance. For the corporate and individual borrower, it was an uncertain year. Interest rates fell sharply in January and February. But then, the Federal Reserve Board got nervous over a resurgence of inflation. Economic growth was strong, unemployment low, and industrial output high—a classic equation for higher prices.

Moreover, Federal Reserve Chairman Alan Greenspan, a long-time Republican, was being watched carefully to see if he would steer a politically independent course at the central bank in an election year. Greenspan asserted his independence. Beginning in March, the Fed started to push its federal funds rate up in five successive credit tightenings from an average weekly low of 6.38% in February to about 7.8% in July. Then in early August, it sent a strong signal to the markets that it was intent on stopping any new inflation by raising the discount rate one half of a percentage point to 6.5%. This meant that the rates rose on home-equity loans, car loans, and other consumer borrowings. But at the same time, rates paid on deposits increased proportionally. Six-month certificates of deposit (CDs) rose from a February low of about 6.60% to 8.51% by November. Long-term rates did not move up as much. The Treasury's 30-year bond rose from about 8.40% in February to about 8.90%.

For investors, the higher-interest rate environment, plus the uncertainty of the stock market, meant a preference for savings over securities. Banks and other federally insured institutions increased their short-term time deposits by almost $115 billion from October 1987 through October 1988.

Perhaps the consumer financial product of the year was the home-equity loan, on which interest payments are deductible up to $100,000. Since the deductibility of credit-card interest is being phased out, consumers replaced credit cards and other debt with home-equity lines. In all, the Federal Reserve estimated that these borrowings rose more than $15 billion from January through October to $90 billion.

See also INTERNATIONAL TRADE AND FINANCE; UNITED STATES—*The Economy.*

NATHANIEL C. NASH
Washington Bureau, "The New York Times"

BELGIUM

For Belgium, 1988 was marked by two major conflicts, the first over control of the governmental majority and the second over control of the nation's dominant business firm.

Politics. The status of officials in regions containing numbers of both Walloons and Flemings provoked Prime Minister Wilfried Martens' resignation in 1987. As in the past, Mayor José Happart of the commune of Voeren in Flanders refused to speak Flemish to prove his bilingualism, as the law requires. Although deposed by the Council of State, his local council repeatedly has reinstated him. Socialists, unhappy with Martens' proposals to reduce top tax rates to 50% and questioning sale of state-owned stock, supported Happart.

Martens continued in a caretaker capacity, but loss of seats by his Flemish Christian Democrat Party (CVP) in the December 1987 elections suggested he would not retain the premiership. Yet following the failure by rival leaders to form a coalition, the 52-year-old Martens was sworn in once again as prime minister on May 9, 1988.

The new cabinet—Martens' eighth—leaned center-left, however, compared with the previous center-right, five-party government. The Socialists, who gained five seats in the 1987 election, replaced the Liberals in the coalition. To gain entry into the cabinet, they agreed that, after the October 1988 municipal elections, Happart's position and that of the other mayors in the border towns between Wallonia and Flanders would be reviewed by a bipartisan panel. Those elections reflected support for Martens. Happart was reelected, assuring continuance of the linguistic controversy.

In the new cabinet there were five vice-premiers, one each from the CVP, the Walloon Christian Democrats, the French and Flemish Socialist parties, and the Flemish nationalist Volksunie party. The coalition held 150 of the 212 seats in the House, controlling the two thirds majority required for constitutional revisions, such as those the linguistic issue would require. The 16 votes provided by the Volksunie thus would play a crucial role.

Economy. The new cabinet indicated it would support the continued devolution of national powers to the regions of Wallonia, Flanders, and bilingual Brussels. The economic decline of Wallonia, compared with the growing prosperity in the North, will make progress toward federalism more difficult, however.

Austerity measures were continued with the aim of reducing the budget deficit from 8% to 7% of the gross national product by 1989. Reductions in top tax rates would be balanced by tax increases on such items as liquor and cigarettes.

The near-successful bid of Italian business magnate Carlo de Benedetti to gain control of the Société Générale de Belgique (SGB), the huge Belgian holding company, shocked the Belgians. The SGB has holdings in some 1,200 companies worldwide; about 30% of Belgium's business revenues pass through its hands. De Benedetti just failed to muster enough shares to take over the company. Negotiations led to his agreement to reduce his stake in SGB in return for being named a vice-president and being given control of at least three seats on the board of directors.

In 1987, Belgian wages ranked seventh highest in the world. Unemployment continued to drop in 1988 from more than 12% in 1986. Continued growth in the banking industry came primarily from wholesale activities on the international market and among professionals, as Belgium provided the third largest venture capital market in Europe. Of the major industries in Belgium, the chemical industry now produces more than 20% of the nation's manufactured goods, and uses more than 40% of the total research and development funds.

Belgium's foreign trade has been concentrated almost entirely within the European Community (EC). In an attempt to expand trade, Belgium now is trying to establish stronger trade relations with countries outside Western Europe, particularly those in the Middle East, Eastern Europe, and China.

Other. Belgium supplied minesweepers to protect oil transports in the Persian Gulf during the Iraq-Iran war. Within NATO it opposed modernization of short-range nuclear missiles, favoring negotiations for missile reduction. Two U.S. cruise missile sites in Belgium were visited by 20 Soviet inspectors in August, under terms of the treaty to eliminate medium-range nuclear weapons in Europe. Four members of the Communist Combatant Cells were sentenced to life imprisonment for bombings in 1984–85.

J. E. HELMREICH, *Allegheny College*

BELGIUM • Information Highlights

Official Name: Kingdom of Belgium.
Location: Northwestern Europe.
Area: 11,780 sq mi (30 510 km²).
Population (mid-1988 est.): 9,900,000.
Chief Cities (Dec. 31, 1986): Brussels, the capital, 973,499; Antwerp (including suburbs), 479,748; Ghent, 233,856; Charleroi, 209,395; Liège, 200,891; Bruges, 117,755.
Government: *Head of state,* Baudouin I, king (acceded (1951). *Head of government,* Wilfried Martens, prime minister (formed new government Oct. 1985). *Legislature*—Parliament: Senate and Chamber of Representatives.
Monetary Unit: Franc (37.47 francs equal U.S.$1, Nov. 1, 1988).
Gross National Product (1986 U.S.$): $114,900,-000,000.
Economic Indexes (1987): *Consumer Prices* (1980 = 100), all items, 144.5; food, 142.3. *Industrial Production* (1980 = 100), 107.
Foreign Trade (1987 with Luxembourg, U.S.$): *Imports,* $83,231,000,000; *exports,* $83,100,000,000.

BIOCHEMISTRY

The 1987–88 period was another banner year for biochemists.

Protein Synthesis. For about two decades, scientists have known that DNA, the genetic material, contains a master code that directs protein synthesis in cells. Proteins are composed of amino acids and serve a variety of functions essential for life. Many of the details of the master genetic code have been known since 1967, but one important aspect of protein synthesis was unclear until 1988.

It is well known that the genetic code consists of groups of three bases, the chemicals that make up DNA. Different combinations of bases specify each of the 20 amino acids as they are assembled into proteins. First, however, the master code in DNA is transcribed into a related material called messenger RNA. The transcribed code in the latter molecule is then "read" by other related molecules called transfer RNA (tRNA), which have bound amino acids assembling them in the proper order to make a particular protein. There is a different tRNA for each of the 20 amino acids. However, biochemists had been baffled by how a particular tRNA could select a particular amino acid for binding.

By manipulating the structure of a tRNA that binds the amino acid alanine, Dr. Paul Schimmel and his student Ya-Ming Hou at the Massachusetts Institute of Technology discovered in 1988 that a tiny piece of the tRNA determined its function. The piece consisted of two bases stuck to each other. When it was removed, the tRNA became nonfunctional; it no longer recognized any amino acid. If the piece was inserted into a tRNA that normally recognized the amino acid cysteine, it recognized alanine instead. The same thing happened when the piece was introduced into the tRNA that normally recognized the amino acid phenylalanine. By late 1988, studies were under way to determine the bases in additional tRNAs by which other amino acids are recognized.

Alzheimer's Update. A prominent feature of the brains of patients of the generative disorder known as Alzheimer's disease (AD) is the presence of plaques in which amyloid protein accumulates, thereby interfering in normal brain function. By 1987, it had seemed that biochemists had pinpointed the cause of AD, but that turned out not to be the case.

In early 1987, scientists reported that some AD patients showed an abnormal duplication of the gene encoding a protein precursor from which amyloid protein is derived, suggesting that the extra copies of the gene would cause excessive production of amyloid protein. However, in October 1987 that possibility was ruled out when several scientists, in studies involving more than 100 AD patients, reported finding no evidence for gene duplication. Thus, for a time, it seemed that the amyloid gene did not play a role in the brain disorder.

In February 1988, however, biochemists discovered that the protein precursor encoded by the amyloid gene also contains a structure similar to known inhibitors of enzymes called proteases. Proteases are known to break down proteins, suggesting that the excessive amyloid deposition so characteristic of AD actually may be the result of too little breakdown rather than too much production. In July 1988, scientists discovered that the amyloid precursor protein resembles heparan sulfate proteoglycan (HSPG), which is the most common component of brain cells. HSPG normally undergoes turnover but in AD patients it apparently is degraded incompletely by the protease and gives rise to amyloid protein that accumulates in the brain. Studies were under way late in 1988 to identify the reasons for the incomplete degradation of HSPG in AD.

Other Developments. In the mid-1980s, scientists discovered that retinoblastoma (RB)—a highly malignant tumor that grows in the retina of the eye—is caused by a loss or inactivation of the RB gene. Now research shows that loss of the RB gene also contributes to the development of two additional types of cancer, breast cancer and small cell lung cancer. Although it has not been determined how the RB gene protects against cancer development, it is speculated that the protein encoded by the RB gene normally suppresses cell division and thus its loss causes cells to grow out of control. It is known that the protein is located inside the cell nucleus and binds avidly to DNA and may regulate the expression of other genes. Efforts were made in 1988 to transfer the RB gene into cells that lack it to see if their cancerous properties could be reversed. These transfer experiments may have implications for treating breast cancer and small cell lung cancer.

Biochemists also succeeded in defining the function of heat-shock proteins (HSP). Cells make HSP in response to heat or other stress. It also is known that other HSP exist in unstressed cells. However, the function of HSP had remained unclear. Two groups of scientists independently reported in 1988 that one family of HSP helps move proteins within a cell from their site of synthesis to a compartment across its membrane where they may be required. Apparently, HSP assist other proteins through a membrane by grabbing and unfolding them so that they can pass through in the straightened shape. On the other side of the membrane, another group of HSP assists in refolding of the proteins. It also is speculated that HSP might readjust incorrectly folded proteins by unfolding them and allowing them to refold correctly. This may be an important step in heat-stressed cells since proteins are unfolded by heat and must be refolded correctly to function.

PREM P. BATRA, *Wright State University*

BIOGRAPHY

A selection of profiles of persons prominent in the news during 1988 appears on pages 136–47. The affiliation of the contributor is listed on pages 591–94; biographies that do not include a contributor's name were prepared by the staff. Included are sketches of:

BENTSEN, Lloyd Millard, Jr.

If seeming presidential is a criterion for being Number 2 in the U.S. government, then Texas Sen. Lloyd Bentsen, the defeated vice-presidential candidate, passed that test with flying colors. Appearances aside, Bentsen's admirers contended that the senator's long experience in Washington would make him eminently qualified to understudy Michael S. Dukakis, who chose him as his running mate on the 1988 Democratic ticket. Moreover, Senator Bentsen's reputation as a conservative on economics and foreign affairs provided a pragmatic complement to Governor Dukakis' more liberal orientation.

His differences with Dukakis were evident on a range of issues. In the national-security area, Bentsen had voted for aid to the contra forces opposing the left-wing regime in Nicaragua, a policy that Dukakis vigorously opposes, and had supported funding for the MX and Midgetman missiles, weapon systems that Dukakis campaigned against. On social and economic matters, Bentsen had voted for prayer in schools, for mandatory balancing of the budget, and against federal financing of abortions, all positions opposite to Dukakis'.

Background. Lloyd Millard Bentsen, Jr., was born Feb. 11, 1921, in Mission, TX. His father, Lloyd, Sr., known in the lower Rio Grande Valley as Big Lloyd, was a millionaire landowner with the political connections that often go with great wealth. After earning a law degree from the University of Texas and serving as a World War II bomber pilot, Bentsen entered politics, winning election as county judge when he was only 25. In 1948 he sought and gained a seat in the U.S. House of Representatives, which he left after three terms to go back to Texas and make his fortune as head of an insurance holding company.

Having earned millions, Bentsen returned to politics in 1970, successfully challenging liberal incumbent Democratic Sen. Ralph Yarborough in a bitter primary. He went on to defeat George Bush, then a young Republican congressman, in the general election. Bentsen sought the 1976 Democratic presidential nomination as a candidate of the center, but soon abandoned the quest in the face of competition from another self-styled centrist, Jimmy Carter. Instead, Bentsen settled for winning reelection to the Senate, a success that he repeated in 1982.

When the Democrats regained control of the Senate in the 1986 elections, Bentsen became chairman of the powerful Senate Finance Committee; in that role he helped push through Congress such major legislation as the trade bill, the plant closing law, and catastrophic health insurance. In 1988, Texas law allowed him to run successfully for a fourth Senate term even though he was also a candidate for vice-president.

Bentsen and his wife, Beryl Ann, have three children, Lloyd III, Lan, and Tina.

ROBERT SHOGAN

BUSH, George Herbert Walker

When George Bush was elected 41st president of the United States on Nov. 8, 1988, he could point to an array of credentials gained in previous public service that his admirers claimed established his preeminent readiness for the responsibilities of the Oval Office. Yet despite the vice-president's successful campaign for the presidency and the breadth of his experience, even his partisans conceded that prior to his nomination to the top spot, the 1988 Republican standard-bearer had had trouble establishing a clear political identity for himself.

This ambiguity reflected not just Bush's service as vice-president, an office whose occupant is expected to submerge his own convictions, but also the varied circumstances of his early life. Bush's roots are in New England, where the Yankee elite regarded the world along traditional Republican lines, placing great emphasis on fiscal responsibility, but also giving great weight to individual rights.

But as a young man fresh out of the Navy, Bush moved to Texas. There he established himself in the oil business and politics, and was exposed to the growth-oriented outlook of the Sunbelt; economic beliefs there were more freewheeling than in the East, while attitudes toward civil rights and other social issues were more restrictive. In the process of adjusting from one region and one set of political and social values to another, Bush avoided taking firm philosophical positions. Instead of ideological consistency, Bush has looked to personal relationships fostered by his family name and connections, as well as his own industriousness and ingratiating personality, as the cornerstones of his political career.

Another factor in Bush's life that inhibited him from developing a distinctive viewpoint was the nature of the positions he held in government. With the exception of his two terms as a congressman from Texas, Bush has spent most of his public life in jobs where he was governed by policies established by a higher authority. Following two terms in the House, from 1967 to 1971, and a failed bid for the Senate in Texas in 1970, Bush served during the next six years as U.S. ambassador to the United Nations, chairman of the Republican National Committee, envoy to China, and then chief of the Central Intelligence Agency (CIA).

With his nomination as the party's presidential candidate and his well-received acceptance speech, his backers were convinced that at last Bush would move out of Reagan's shadow and begin to define his views and his political personality. "You must see me for what I am," Bush told the convention delegates, "the Republican candidate for president of the United States."

On the personal side, Bush's social standing and wealth—his net worth has been estimated at about $1 million—combined with his occasionally stilted speech and manners, have made him the target of humor that ranges from mild derision to crude ridicule. He has been

described as excessively deferential and overly effusive; during the 1984 campaign he was depicted in the Doonesbury cartoon strip as having put his manhood in a blind trust. In response, his admirers contend that Bush proved his manhood during World War II when, as an 18-year-old Navy pilot, he was awarded the Distinguished Flying Cross for a bombing mission after his plane was all but shot to pieces by the Japanese.

Background. Born in Milton, MA, on June 12, 1924, George Herbert Walker Bush grew up in affluent Greenwich, CT. His father, Prescott, served as a U.S. senator from Connecticut. Bush was graduated from the Phillips Academy prep school in Andover, MA, and attended Yale University, graduating Phi Beta Kappa in 1948.

By the time he left the CIA in 1976, Bush considered himself ready for the presidency and, without any other responsibilities, used his freedom to get an early start on the 1980 campaign. An intensive grass roots organizing effort led him to a stunning victory over the favored Ronald Reagan in the January 1980 Iowa caucuses. But Reagan came back to defeat Bush in the New Hampshire primary, and ultimately won the nomination. Bush was chosen as his running mate in part because he was considered a moderate and, it was believed, could broaden Reagan's appeal in the general election campaign.

Bush's campaign criticism of Reagan's supply-side tax cut proposals, which he labeled as "voodoo economics," stirred resentment of him among some Republican conservatives; this lingered even after the big Republican victory in 1980. But Bush labored to mend these fences by demonstrating his loyalty to the president. Eventually he won the warm backing of Reagan for his presidential ambitions, along with at least grudging acceptance of his candidacy from most conservatives.

Bush and his wife, Barbara, maintain their official residence in Washington, DC, and a voting residence in Texas. They are the parents of five grown children.

See also feature article on U.S. elections, page 24.

ROBERT SHOGAN

CAMPEAU, Robert

When a retail sale makes the first page of *The New York Times,* it probably has nothing to do with markdowns on designer shoes. In March 1988, Robert Campeau, the daring 64-year-old Canadian real-estate tycoon, made headlines with a bold, leveraged takeover of Federated Department Stores. Federated, headquartered in Cincinnati, OH, is one of the largest networks of stores in the United States, and includes the renowned Bloomingdale's chain. With a final offer of C$8.2 billion, the total cost of the deal, which covered the Federated debt plus acquisition costs, came to C$10.9 billion—the largest non-oil takeover in U.S. history until that time.

Campeau already had astounded American retail and financial markets in late 1986 with a leveraged C$4.9 billion takeover of Allied Stores Corp. in New York City; this was the largest Canadian takeover of a U.S. company. With the combined acquisitions of Allied and Federated, Campeau now is head of one of the most extensive retailing empires in the United States.

An unsuccessful foray into a non-real-estate enterprise in 1980 may have been the motivation for Campeau's interest in doing business in the United States. Campeau, of French-Canadian descent, attempted to acquire Royal Trustco, an entrenched financial institution in Toronto, the financial center of Canada; however, the English-speaking establishment prevented it. He stated in a 1988 interview, "The United States is a refreshing atmosphere to do business in; it doesn't matter what your name is."

Campeau is reputed to enjoy his celebrity status, and gives princely parties for 300 or more in his opulent Toronto mansion.

Background. Robert Campeau was born on Aug. 3, 1924, in the mining town of Sudbury, Ont. He was one of seven surviving children, with seven other siblings born who did not live past infancy. His father was an

AP/Wide World

Robert Campeau

auto mechanic, and Campeau showed an early skill with both mechanics and carpentry.

At the end of eighth grade Campeau left school to add to the family income. Still under 16, he was not yet of legal age to work, so he used the baptismal records of a deceased brother to get a job sweeping floors at an Inco Ltd. smelter. Later he trained as a machinist. He moved on to a paper mill near Ottawa, and became a manager by the late 1940s.

Campeau built his first house in 1949 for his wife and child, but before moving in decided to sell it when he found he could make a $3,000 profit. From this modest start as a home builder, he built about 20,000 homes in the Ottawa area during the next 30 years. His company also built an estimated 40% of the office space that the federal government now occupies in Ottawa.

In 1983, Campeau moved to Toronto from Ottawa with his second wife, Ilse Luebbert. They have two sons and a daughter. He also has three children from a previous marriage.

GLADYS HANDELMAN

CHER

Just a few years ago, it would have been impossible to believe that sequinned pop star Cher would earn an Oscar as best actress. Yet in 1988 she did just that, winning for her alternately comic and touching work in *Moonstruck.* As bookkeeper Loretta Castorini, she falls in love with the nutty kid brother of her fiancé, a romance that transforms Loretta from an unambitious creature of habit to a liberated beauty, a change that mirrors the remarkable growth of the 42-year-old entertainer herself.

Background. Cherilyn Sarkisian was born on May 20, 1946, in El Centro, CA, the daughter of bank manager Gilbert and former model Georgia, who were separated when Cher was one. Singing in local clubs as a teenager, Cher dropped out of high school in order to pursue acting. However, while recording background vocals in 1964, she met songwriter Salvatore "Sonny" Bono. Not only did she marry him, she gave up acting to sing with him professionally. As Sonny and Cher, they cut two

AP/Wide World

Cher

records before "I Got You, Babe," released in June 1965, became a three-million-copy smash. They followed it with other hits, including "The Beat Goes On" and "A Cowboy's Work Is Never Done." A daughter, Chastity, was born in 1969.

With equally stunning success, the couple branched into television with the hour-long variety series "The Sonny and Cher Comedy Hour" in 1971. At the same time, Cher recorded several solo hits. Unfortunately, after three years, the TV show was cancelled when Sonny and Cher suffered marital difficulties and were divorced. Each tried a solo show; both failed. They briefly reunited professionally to put the show back on the air in 1976. In the meantime, Cher had married rock star Gregg Allman the year before, gave birth to a son, Elijah Blue Allman, in 1976, and divorced Allman the next year. Turning to Las Vegas after the new series failed, Cher finally decided to devote herself full time to her first love, acting.

In 1982, she costarred on Broadway and on film as a member of a James Dean fan club in *Come Back to the 5 & Dime, Jimmy Dean, Jimmy Dean.* The following year, she landed a supporting role and an Oscar nomination as Meryl Streep's friend in *Silkwood.* Both performances showed that Cher could play nonglamorous, compassionate women, a fact underscored by her acclaimed performance as the mother of a disfigured boy in *Mask* in 1985.

In quick succession, the box office hits *The Witches of Eastwick* and *Moonstruck* made her a bankable star as well. As if the transformation from singer to actress were not enough, Cher proved that she still had what it takes to cut a hit record. She made a blockbuster return to the airwaves in 1987 with her album *Cher,* which stayed on the record charts well over half a year and has been certified gold.

JEFF ROVIN

DE MITA, Ciriaco

On April 13, 1988, Ciriaco De Mita became premier of Italy's 48th government since the end of World War II. The dour 60-year-old Southerner, who was little known outside Italy, took over as head of the same coalition of Christian Democrats, Socialists, Social Democrats, Republicans, and Liberals that have composed all Italian governments since 1981.

De Mita's taking on of the premiership ended a month-long crisis caused by the resignation of his protégé, Giovanni Goria, whose coalition government had split over the decision to resume construction of a nuclear-power plant. The Socialists and Social Democrats opposed further nuclear construction—as did the majority of Italy's voters in a referendum in November 1987.

Three days after De Mita's accession as premier, terrorists assassinated his closest adviser, Sen. Roberto Ruffilli. Like Ruffilli, De Mita has advocated constitutional reforms that would make decision-making more efficient. One of these is the abolition of secret voting in Parliament, a practice that often has been used (even by his own party) to bring down governments without warning. De Mita also would like to institute joint parliamentary committees to smooth out legislative differences between the coequal Chamber of Deputies and Senate. His other priority was to get Italy's huge budget deficit under control. De Mita's main goal, however, would be to stay in power until the next scheduled elections in 1992—no easy task in the face of the undisguised hostility of former Premier Bettino Craxi, leader of the increasingly strong Socialist Party.

Background. Son of a tailor, Ciriaco De Mita was born Feb. 2, 1928, in the mountain village of Fusco in Avellino province, east of Naples. A pensive person whose chief pastime is playing cards, he studied law at Milan's Catholic University. Joining the Christian Democratic Party in 1950, he first was elected to Parliament from his home district in 1963. He combined party politics with service in the government in the 1970s, heading at different times the ministry for the development of the South, the ministry of industry, and the ministry of foreign trade. In 1982 he was elected national secretary of the Christian Democratic Party.

As leader of his party, De Mita has preferred to work behind the scenes. He has managed to deprive some of the regional party barons of their control of patronage. Some observers believe that these disgruntled bosses pushed him into the premiership as punishment.

See also ITALY.

CHARLES F. DELZELL

DUKAKIS, Michael Stanley

When, in the address accepting the 1988 Democratic presidential nomination, Michael S. Dukakis declared: "This campaign is not about ideology, it's about competence," he defined the theme that had been the hallmark of his political career for nearly three decades. Yet despite this credo, which helps in large measure to explain why his party chose the Massachusetts governor as its standard-bearer in 1988, the U.S. electorate rejected him as its 41st president on November 8.

During 1988 the Democrats were in transition, struggling to find a new faith to replace their outworn dependence on government activism. The Massachusetts governor, who could claim to have demonstrated in his own state how to achieve the benefits of government without stirring the bitter ideological controversies that had hurt Democrats in past national elections, seemed like the ideal man to come to the aid of his party.

Reinforcing Dukakis' claim to competence were his deliberative manner and well-controlled personality, which made him appear to be a sort of political "Mr. Goodwrench." Personal traits acquired during his political career in Massachusetts added to this impression. Dukakis possessed the resiliency to rebound from defeat, notably after his abortive first effort to win a second term as governor in 1978. And he could learn from his mistakes; associates said he demonstrated this quality by becoming more flexible and less arrogant when finally he did gain a second term in 1982.

Background. In his drive for the Democratic presidential nomination, Michael Stanley Dukakis made

much of the fact that he was the child of Greek immigrants. In fact, his upbringing in the affluent Boston suburb of Brookline, MA, where he was born on Nov. 3, 1933, and where his father had a successful medical practice, was far more comfortable than the circumstances in which many first generation Americans grew up.

As a student at Swarthmore College, a "D" grade in physics ended any thought of his pursuing a medical career like his father. But Dukakis' other grades were good enough to earn him highest honors when he was graduated in 1955. After two years of service with the U.S. Army in Korea, he entered Harvard Law School, graduating in 1960.

As a young man, Dukakis was far more interested in practicing politics than practicing law; this inclination was stimulated by the excitement generated in his home state by the presidency of its native son, John F. Kennedy. In 1962, with the help of a group of young reformers, like himself inspired by the energy of the New Frontier, Dukakis won election to the state legislature. In four terms there, he displayed a distinct preference for solving nuts-and-bolts problems rather than getting caught up in ideological disputes. Avoiding the great controversies then raging over civil rights and the Vietnam war, Dukakis instead focused on such matters as rent control, billboard limits, and pushing through the nation's first no-fault auto-insurance law.

In 1970, Dukakis won the Democratic nomination for lieutenant governor. He lost the November election, but this experience helped prepare him to run for governor, as did a stint as moderator of the popular public television program *The Advocates.* Helped along by the public reaction against the Republicans in the wake of Watergate, Dukakis won the state house in 1974. But soon he ran into trouble; the state was hit hard by a nationwide recession, and for Dukakis the problem was aggravated by a campaign pledge he had made not to raise taxes. Ultimately Dukakis broke that promise to meet the state's financial needs. But resentment created by that turnabout and aggravated by his often high-handed and self-righteous governing style led to his defeat when he sought renomination in 1978. He then taught at Harvard's Kennedy School of Government (1979–82).

Stunned by his 1978 setback, but nonetheless determined to vindicate himself, Dukakis tried again for the governorship in 1982; this time he succeeded. By most accounts he returned to office far more willing to compromise and more sensitive to others than he had been in the past. He was also much luckier. This time, instead of having to confront a recession when he took office, he was able to take advantage of a national economic recovery then beginning to gather force. Business boomed and unemployment dropped, conditions which, as a presidential candidate, Dukakis proudly hailed as the "Massachusetts Miracle." He made the promise of "good jobs and good wages" the cornerstone of his campaign, a pledge buttressed by the prosperity enjoyed in his home state. Most analysts gave Dukakis credit for reforming the state's welfare system and tightening enforcement of the tax code, but some contended that the so-called miracle had less to do with Dukakis' management skills than with economic trends.

Dukakis married the former Katharine Dickson, known as Kitty, in 1963. The couple have a son, John, 30, by Mrs. Dukakis' first marriage, and two daughters: Andrea, 23, and Kara, 20.

See also feature article on U.S. elections, page 24.

ROBERT SHOGAN

EISNER, Michael Dammann

Since becoming chairman and chief executive officer of the Walt Disney Company in September 1984, Michael Eisner has emerged as perhaps the most creative and successful executive in the American entertainment industry. Inheriting an empire that had been in decline since the death of its founder in 1966, Eisner has managed to restore the Disney magic and reanimate the pub-

lic's enchantment. From fiscal 1983 through 1987, annual revenues doubled to $2.9 billion, with profits and stock value increasing nearly fivefold.

Eisner's creative and managerial energy have worked wonders in every realm of the Disney kingdom. With a new generation of family and adult releases—including the 1987–88 hits *Three Men and a Baby* and *Good Morning, Vietnam*—the Disney movie studio, Touchstone Pictures, has risen to number 1 in Hollywood. In addition, *Who Framed Roger Rabbit,* a $45 million film mixing cartoon characters and human actors and produced through the joint efforts of Walt Disney Co. and Steven Spielberg's Amblin Entertainment, opened amid much hoopla during the summer of 1988. On television, recent Disney favorites have included the sitcom *Golden Girls;* two cartoon shows, *The Adventures of the Gummi Bears* and *DuckTales;* and the *Disney Sunday Movie*—in which Eisner appears each week as the host.

Meanwhile, at the Disney theme parks in California, Florida, and Japan—which account for 60% of company revenues—total attendance in 1987 exceeded 50 million. In 1988, as Tokyo Disneyland celebrated its fifth anniversary, the Florida park was getting $1.4 billion in new attractions, and Euro Disneyland, scheduled to open outside Paris in 1992, was under construction. Add to that the fastest-growing pay-TV station in the United States, hotel complexes, expanded consumer retailing, and other ventures, and the Disney empire under Chairman Eisner appears to have entered a new Golden Age.

Background. Michael Dammann Eisner was born into an affluent Jewish family on March 7, 1942, in Mt. Kisco, NY, and grew up in a luxurious apartment on Manhattan's Park Avenue. He attended the Lawrenceville School in New Jersey and Denison University in Ohio, where he majored in literature and theater. His first job after college was as a page at NBC television in New York, but he moved soon to the programming department at CBS. Eisner's talents were recognized more fully at ABC, where he was hired as assistant to the na-

Michael Eisner

AP/Wide World

tional programming director. By the time he left in 1976, he had risen to senior vice-president for prime-time production and development.

Eisner entered the movie industry as the president of Paramount Pictures, where a string of hits—including *Saturday Night Fever* and *Terms of Endearment*—made him the hottest young executive in Hollywood. In 1984, after a bitter takeover battle at Disney, the chief stockholder—Roy Disney, Walt's nephew—persuaded the 42-year-old Eisner to head the company.

One of the movie industry's highest-paid executives, Eisner lives with his wife, Jane, and three children in a million-dollar home in Bel Air, CA.

GORBACHEV, Raisa

Style and charm are not qualities most Westerners associate with the wives of Soviet leaders, who typically remain firmly in the background. But Raisa Gorbachev, the wife of Soviet Communist Party General Secretary Mikhail Gorbachev, has captured media attention with just these traits. The image she presents—educated, well dressed, and attractive—seems tailored to her husband's image as a reformer of the Soviet system.

Raisa Gorbachev's importance appears to extend beyond image, however: She is said to have considerable influence with her husband. In a 1987 interview with Tom Brokaw of NBC News, Gorbachev stated that he and his wife "discuss everything"—including Soviet affairs at the highest level. That remark was deleted when the interview was broadcast in the Soviet Union, where the Soviet first lady's prominence at times has sparked gossip, criticism, and resentment.

Nor has her reception been universally favorable in the West, where some observers have found her a dogmatic proponent of Soviet philosophy. Considerable media attention also was directed at a supposed rivalry with Nancy Reagan, said to have begun when Raisa Gorbachev upstaged the wife of the U.S. president by attending the 1986 summit meeting in Iceland. (Mrs. Reagan, told that Mrs. Gorbachev would remain in Moscow, stayed home.) Relations between the two women were strained during the Gorbachevs' December 1987 visit to Washington, but appeared smoother when the Reagans traveled to Moscow in June 1988.

Background. Information about Raisa Gorbachev's background is sketchy. Her official biography states that she was born Raisa Maksimovna Titorenko in 1934 in Rubtsovsk, Siberia. Her father was a railway worker, and she reportedly grew up in Stavropol in the North Caucasus. She studied Marxist-Leninist philosophy at the prestigious Moscow M. V. Lomonosov State University and there met her future husband, also a student. They were married soon after her graduation in 1956 and returned to Stavropol, where Mikhail Gorbachev was first secretary of the local Young Communist League.

Over the next twenty-odd years, as her husband rose steadily through the party ranks, Raisa Gorbachev taught school; raised a daughter, Irina; and, in 1967, earned the equivalent of a doctorate. Her thesis dealt with peasant customs and attitudes, and it was notable for its use of surveys and field investigations, sociological techniques that were then new in the Soviet Union.

The Gorbachevs moved to Moscow in 1978. Under the aegis of Yuri Andropov (chairman of the KGB and, from 1982 to 1984, general secretary of the Communist Party), Gorbachev continued to gain in power and influence. Raisa Gorbachev, meanwhile, taught Marxist-Leninist philosophy at Moscow State University. She first drew international attention in 1984, when she accompanied her husband on an official visit to Great Britain. Charmed by her stylish and outgoing manner, the press called her "Soviet realism's answer to Princess Diana." She resigned her teaching post when her husband became general secretary of the party in 1985 and from then on has been seen frequently at his side. In 1986 she joined the presidium of the Soviet Cultural Fund.

ELAINE PASCOE

JACKSON, Jesse Louis

By winning some 6.6 million votes in the 1988 Democratic presidential primaries, the Rev. Jesse Jackson emerged as a force to be reckoned with in U.S. politics. Although his final tally fell short of the 9.7 million votes won by Massachusetts Gov. Michael Dukakis, Jackson's strong showing early in the year demonstrated his ability to appeal to a wide range of voters and fueled speculation that he might become the first black presidential nominee.

A gifted and compelling speaker, Jackson was a controversial candidate. He was criticized for exaggerating the poverty of his upbringing and his closeness to the Rev. Martin Luther King, Jr.; for past positions that included support of Cuban leader Fidel Castro and Palestine Liberation Organization leader Yasir Arafat; and for past statements that included a reference to New York City as "hymietown."

But Jackson, saying that he had matured as a politician, presented a toned-down image in 1988 and stressed stands against drugs and for housing and other programs to aid the disadvantaged. The approach was successful: While some two thirds of Jackson's support came from black voters, he also took more than 12% of the white vote—more than 2 million votes.

Background. Jesse Louis Jackson was born Oct. 8, 1941, in Greenville, SC. As an undergraduate at North Carolina Agricultural and Technical State College, he was an honor student, football quarterback, and a leader in the campus civil-rights movement. After graduation in 1964, he attended Chicago Theological Seminary but left shortly before graduation to join Martin Luther King, Jr.'s, Southern Christian Leadership Conference (SCLC). Doctor King chose Jackson to head the Chicago branch of Operation Breadbasket, a program that used boycotts and other tactics to prompt integration at major companies. He became national director of the program in 1967.

Jackson was ordained a Baptist minister in 1968, a few months after King's assassination. In 1971, he left SCLC to form his own group, Operation PUSH (People United to Save Humanity). Based in Chicago, the organization continued the work of Operation Breadbasket and campaigned for black pride with the slogan "I am somebody." A companion program, PUSH-Excel, focused on high dropout rates and other problems in inner-city schools.

Jackson emerged on the international scene in 1979 with trips to South Africa, where he led antiapartheid rallies, and the Middle East, where he met with Yasir Arafat. In 1983 he toured Europe, mounted a voter registration drive in the United States, and in November entered the race for the 1984 Democratic presidential nomination. His campaign was bolstered when, in January 1984, he traveled to Syria and secured the release of a U.S. Navy pilot whose plane had been shot down over Lebanon.

Although he made strong showings in New York and other states, Jackson's 1984 campaign failed to appeal to a broad range of voters. He won a total of 3.15 million votes, of which just 650,000 were cast by whites. Jackson kept his organization, which he called the Rainbow Coalition, alive after the campaign. Over the next four years, he continued to be an outspoken civil-rights leader and to travel and speak abroad.

In 1988, when it became clear that Jackson would not win the nomination, speculation shifted to the vice-presidential slot. Jackson supporters hoped as well to get the Democrats to adopt several liberal platform planks at the Democratic National Convention in July. At the gathering, however, they settled for a package of smaller concessions, including changes in party structure and rules that, they hoped, would work to their candidate's advantage in future campaigns.

Jackson married Jacqueline Lavinia Brown in 1964. They have five children and live in Chicago.

See also feature articles on U.S. elections, page 24, and black Americans, page 46.

ELAINE PASCOE

KENNEDY, Anthony McLeod

The appointment of Anthony Kennedy to the U.S. Supreme Court marked a decidedly calm climax to a turbulent eight-month political battle over the future direction of the court. Kennedy, President Ronald Reagan's third choice to fill a Supreme Court vacancy created by the retirement of Justice Lewis F. Powell in June 1987, was regarded as a moderate conservative and won Senate confirmation by a vote of 97–0 on Feb. 3, 1988. His style and temperament—restrained, courteous, and affable—appeared to match his performance on the bench as a federal appeals court judge in California. While clearly right of center, Kennedy demonstrated flexibility and pragmatism in writing some 500 opinions during more than 12 years as an appellate judge.

In taking his place on Feb. 18, 1988, as the 104th justice in the high court's history, he restored the court to full strength and inherited a pivotal vote on key issues. President Reagan's first choice for the vacancy, Robert H. Bork, was rejected by the Senate following a protracted political fight. The president's second choice, Douglas H. Ginsburg, withdrew after admitting he smoked marijuana while a law professor. Kennedy's nomination prompted little opposition, most of it over his former membership in all-male, all-white private clubs. Kennedy was regarded as something of an enigma, with little known about his views on such controversial issues as abortion rights, affirmative action, and church-state relations. He is the third Reagan appointee to join the high court, following Justices Sandra Day O'Connor and Antonin Scalia.

Background. Anthony McLeod Kennedy was born in Sacramento, CA, on July 23, 1936, the son of parents active in Republican politics. His mother, Gladys, was a prominent civic booster. His father, Anthony J. Kennedy, was a politically connected lawyer and lobbyist in Sacramento. At the age of 10, the future justice took a year off from school to serve as a page in the California State Senate. He was graduated, Phi Beta Kappa in political science, from Stanford University in 1958 and from Harvard Law School in 1961. His ambition was to be a judge. In 1963, while a lawyer in San Francisco, he married Mary Jeanne Davis, who has taught elementary school.

Kennedy took over his father's law practice in Sacramento when his father died of a heart attack in 1963. He worked for a time as a statehouse lobbyist there, representing among others Schenley Industries Inc., the liquor distillers. Kennedy also developed working ties to Ronald Reagan when he was governor of California, and to Reagan's then-executive secretary and future U.S. attorney general, Edwin Meese III. Kennedy was appointed a federal appeals court judge in 1975 by President Gerald R. Ford.

Kennedy also has taught constitutional law at McGeorge School of Law at the University of the Pacific in Sacramento. He and his wife have two sons and a daughter.

JIM RUBIN

LACROIX, Christian

Haute couture's latest superstar, Christian Lacroix, entered the pantheon of fashion luminaries with his Spanish collection, designed for the House of Patou in 1985. Subsequent collections shown in 1986–87 sealed his triumph. Lacroix's extensive art history background enables him to use the past to create contemporary fashions that have been characterized as wild, witty, and totally fresh. Skirt lengths are often mid-thigh, and outfits can feature bustles, flounces, and crinolines. His innovative "pouf" or "bubble" dress has been copied widely. Other Lacroix penchants include whimsical hats and bizarre accessories. His palette is a riotous array of bright, emphatic colors in an unlikely alliance. Lacroix believes that *haute couture* should be a "laboratory of ideas," and his bold experiments may have changed the course of recent fashion history.

AP/Wide World

Christian Lacroix

Lacroix began his fashion career in the late 1970s as assistant fashion coordinator at Hermès, the leather specialists. Then followed a position as assistant for accessories to designer Guy Paulin. His breakthrough came in 1981 when he won a competition to become chief designer for the couture house, Jean Patou. After six years he left to form the House of Lacroix. Both his first signature collection in July 1987 and his first line of luxury ready-to-wear three months later strengthened his position as a preeminent designer. Although Lacroix's designs have been praised widely, he has his detractors. A *Newsweek* fashion reporter wrote that he was "pushing high fashion to ludicrous lengths," and called his clothes "often outlandish."

The designer's first mass ready-to-wear collection, shown in March 1988, was generally well received. His 1988 fall and winter couture collection was softer, simpler, and more diversified. Colors were muted, and skirt lengths and shapes ran the gamut.

In 1986 the Chambre Syndicale de la Couture Parisienne, a leading trade group, gave Lacroix the Golden Thimble, the industry's most prestigious award, and the following year the Council of Fashion Designers of America honored him for his inspiration to other designers. He was awarded a second Golden Thimble in 1988. True to his vision of fashion as theater, Lacroix's adventurous costumes for a new production of *Gaîté Parisienne* which premiered in Tampa, FL, in January 1988, garnered rave reviews.

Background. Christian Lacroix was born on May 17, 1950 in Arles, France, and grew up in a comfortable middle-class home. His father, an engineer who designed oil-drilling equipment, also enjoyed drawing Arlesian women when they dressed up and promenaded on bullfight days. Emulating his father, Lacroix declared his intention, at the age of five, to become a "couture-drawer."

Lacroix attended the University of Montpellier for three years where he studied the classics, and majored in French and Italian painting and the history of costume. In 1973 he went to Paris to study fashion history at the École du Louvre, hoping to become a museum curator. Shortly after he arrived there he became enamored of Françoise Rosensthiel. Already in the fashion business, she was impressed with his fashion drawings and encouraged him to become a designer.

GLADYS HANDELMAN

Andrew Lloyd Webber

LLOYD WEBBER, Andrew

Not only did Andrew Lloyd Webber's 1988 show, *The Phantom of the Opera,* have the highest advance sale of all time, collecting more than $16 million in the three months before it opened, but it was the composer's third hit show running simultaneously on Broadway and in London. The others were *Cats* and *Starlight Express.* Only once before had a composer achieved that triple crown; that was in 1983, when Lloyd Webber himself had *Evita, Joseph and the Amazing Technicolor Dreamcoat,* and *Cats* playing at the same time in both theater capitals.

Based on a 1911 novel by Gaston Leroux, Lloyd Webber's *The Phantom of the Opera* opened in London in 1986, and premiered in New York in January 1988. It went on to win seven Tony Awards, including best musical.

Background. Andrew Lloyd Webber was born in South Kensington, London, England, on March 22, 1948. His parents both were musicians. His late father, William, was a composer and the director of the London College of Music, and his mother, Jean, taught piano. His younger brother, Julian, is a renowned cellist. Andrew studied music at London's Westminster School and at the Royal College of Music. He plays the piano, violin, and French horn.

Lloyd Webber and record producer-lyricist Tim Rice collaborated on the lighthearted musical *Joseph and the Amazing Technicolor Dreamcoat* in 1967. The show told the biblical story in a variety of musical styles, ranging from country to jazz to 1950s rock to calypso. Intended for just a choral performance by St. Paul's Junior School, the work was heard by a music critic, whose enthusiasm led to other performances and finally a stage version. Far more important was the team's next effort, the rock opera *Jesus Christ Superstar.* Originally produced as a record album, the frenetic, iconoclastic retelling of the New Testament made music charts around the world; especially popular was the song "I Don't Know How To Love Him." The London stage version ran for eight years, and the musical reached Broadway in 1971. Lloyd Webber and Rice followed this success with the equally controversial *Evita,* a musical that romanticized the reign of Argentina's dictator Juan Perón and his ambitious wife Eva.

On his own, Lloyd Webber next set T.S. Eliot's *Old Possum's Book of Practical Cats* to music as *Cats,* and enjoyed his biggest international hit to that time. The show, in which cats in an alley tell their life stories, produced the hit song "Memory." Lloyd Webber's musical about a train race, *Starlight Express,* once again drew upon various musical genres such as country and doowop. However, its success is attributable largely to its spectacular staging and actors racing around the set on roller skates. *The Phantom of the Opera* was next, and audiences responded to the beauty-and-the-beast love story between the deformed Phantom and the young opera singer Christine.

Lloyd Webber is the father of Imogen and Nicholas by his first wife, Sarah Jane Tudor Hugill. His second wife, Sarah Brightman, created the role of Christine in London and on Broadway.

JEFF ROVIN

LOUGANIS, Gregory Efthimios

Amid the scandal of steroids, the demise of amateurism, the pranks and boasting of visiting athletes, and the multimillion-dollar commercialism of the 1988 Seoul Olympics, even the most cynical of critics could not ignore the display of courage, competitive grit, and sheer athletic excellence—in short, the demonstration of true "Olympic spirit"—by U.S. diver Greg Louganis.

Having won gold medals in both the springboard and platform events at the Los Angeles Games in 1984, the modest, soft-spoken 28-year-old entered the 1988 Seoul Games as the overwhelming favorite to become the first man to repeat as a double winner in Olympic diving. As it turned out, both events were ultimate tests of his athletic ability and his will to succeed. In the springboard competition, the veteran competitor missed a dive in the qualifying round and struck his head on the board. After taking four stitches in the scalp, he not only dived twice more that night to qualify, but he came back the following night to win the gold. A week later in the platform finals, Louganis faced a surprising challenge from a diver half his age, 14-year-old Xiong Ni of China. Trailing by 85.56 points going into his last dive, Louganis knew he would need a near-perfect score to win. In what U.S. diving coach Ron O'Brien called "probably the biggest dive of his career," Louganis executed an almost flawless reverse three-and-a-half somersault (considered the most difficult dive in the sport) and eked out the victory by a mere 1.14 points. In one of the memorable moments of the 1988 Games, he collapsed in tears on the shoulder of his coach.

In recognition of his inspiring performance, Louganis was named winner of the U.S. Olympic Committee's "Olympic spirit" award.

Background. Adversity was nothing new to Gregory Efthimios Louganis. Of Samoan and northern European ancestry, he was born in 1960 to unwed teenage parents and adopted at an early age by Peter and Frances Louganis of San Diego, CA. Teased by classmates because of his shyness and an early reading disability, Louganis took refuge in gymnastics and dancing. The latter was encouraged by his mother, who "didn't want klutzes," and the former by a doctor, who thought the exercise would help cure his asthma. When he began practicing acrobatics off the diving board of the family pool, his father enrolled him in diving classes in nearby La Mesa.

In 1975, after performing well in junior competition, Louganis came under the tutelage of two-time Olympic gold medalist Dr. Sammy Lee. Under Lee's guidance, the up-and-coming 16-year-old won a silver medal in platform diving at the 1976 Olympics in Montreal. In 1978 he accepted a scholarship to the University of Miami, transferring to the University of California at Irvine in 1981 in order to train under O'Brien. He was graduated in 1983 with a bachelor's degree in theater. With the exception of the 1980 Olympics, in which he did not participate because of the U.S. boycott, the 5'9" (1.75-m), 165-lb (75-kg) Louganis has won virtually every major international

diving championship of the 1980s. His many awards include the 1984 Sullivan Memorial Trophy as the amateur athlete "who has done the most ... to advance the cause of sportsmanship."

Late in 1988, the gold medalist announced his retirement from diving to pursue a career in acting.

MORRISON, Toni

Toni Morrison's *Beloved,* a powerful novel about slavery, generated such strong emotions that when it did not win the National Book Award for 1987 or the National Book Critics Circle Award in 1988, a letter of protest, signed by many of America's most important black writers and critics, appeared in *The New York Times.* Morrison, deeply touched by the support, said that "It made me feel blessed." *Beloved,* which confronts painful truths about the burden of slavery and its continued haunting of black and white America, subsequently was awarded the 1988 Pulitzer Prize in fiction.

Background. Chloe Anthony (Toni) Wofford was born on Feb. 18, 1931, in Lorain, OH, to George and Ramah (Willis) Wofford. Her parents' strength helped sustain the family through the miseries of the Depression. In 1949, after doing outstanding work in high school, she went to Howard University, where she found kindred spirits in the theater group, the Howard University Players. In 1953 she went on to Cornell University to do graduate work in English. After receiving her M.A. degree, she taught at Texas Southern and at Howard University. While at Howard, she married a Jamaican architect, and became the mother of two sons. It also was during this time that she began to write fiction.

In 1964, Morrison was divorced, left teaching, and went to Random House as an editor. The short story she developed into her first novel, *The Bluest Eye* (1970), quickly brought her recognition as a writer of great promise. It is a touching and violent story of young black girls growing up in a small town in Ohio. The sharp observations, compassionate insights, and poetic language are dazzling. In *Sula* (1973), Morrison sustained a more elaborate plot as she traced two women from the misadventures of their childhood to the tragedies of their

Toni Morrison

adult lives. *Song of Solomon* (1977) was a major literary event; Morrison moved to a masculine viewpoint successfully, and told of a quest for self and identity with universal significance. *Tar Baby* (1981), a sensuous and dramatic love story, is more philosophical in tone, and deals in almost symbolic terms with the tragic impasse in relations between whites and blacks.

In her various writings, Morrison speaks to the hearts of her readers. She brings a compassionate understanding that allows one to understand the most troubling of her characters. And she beautifully celebrates the black community that has survived cultural, economic, and social disruption. Each one of her novels has been more ambitious, taking on greater technical risks, more problematic social relations, and deeper human relations than her previous work. Toni Morrison has established herself as one of America's major living writers.

JEROME STERN

NORIEGA MORENA, Manuel Antonio

Few world leaders have caused the United States more headaches in recent years than Panama's dictator and the commander of its 16,000-member Defense Force, Manuel Antonio Noriega Morena. General Noriega's behavior, allegedly including the brutal treatment, even murder, of political opponents and the acquisition of a vast fortune through the international drug trade, embarrassed the administration of President Ronald Reagan. This was particularly true because of the close ties between the two nations in regional defense matters as well as the president's frequent boasting of his success in promoting democracy in the Caribbean.

Hoping to drive Noriega from power, the United States tried tough economic sanctions, which badly crippled Panama's economy but did not unseat the general. Neither strikes nor barracks revolts loosened his grip on Panama. A U.S. court indicted him in February 1988 on drug-connected charges, but it was unlikely he ever would be tried as long as he remained in Panama. President Reagan authorized covert actions against him, but Noriega's popularity mandated caution. Meanwhile, Noriega purged the military of unfriendly officers, exiled hundreds of citizens, and got the legislature to "depose" President Eric Arturo Delvalle, who went into hiding. (*See also* CENTRAL AMERICA—*Panama.*)

Background. Manuel Antonio Noriega Morena was born in Panama in 1934, to parents of Colombian descent. He was graduated from the Instituto Nacional and hoped to attend medical school, but his family was too poor. Instead, he accepted a scholarship to a military school in Lima, Peru. On graduation he joined Panama's national guard as a sublieutenant, commencing a lifelong military career. Early on, he fell under the protective wing of Capt. Omar Torrijos; in return Noriega supported Torrijos in the 1968 barracks revolt that overthrew President Arnulfo Arias. In 1969, Noriega played a key role in preventing a countercoup against his sponsor, now commander in chief of the National Guard and dictator of Panama. Noriega was promoted to lieutenant colonel and head of Panama's military intelligence, a position making him very valuable to President Richard Nixon and the Central Intelligence Agency (CIA).

Following Torrijos' 1981 death in a plane crash, Noriega became chief of staff of the Panama National Guard, and in August 1983 he assumed the post of commanding general. He brought the smaller navy and air force into a combined Panama Defense Force under his command, securing $32 million from the United States to modernize the unit.

Noriega is 5'5" (1.7 m) tall, with a stocky build, dark hair, and pockmarked complexion. He is a vegetarian whose hobbies are dancing, reading, judo, and porcelain collecting. He is married to the former Felicidad Sierio; they have three daughters. Noriega is believed to have immense wealth, including a Paris apartment, a French chateau, and rich collections of art and cars.

THOMAS L. KARNES

QUAYLE, James Danforth

On Nov. 8, 1988, the U.S. electorate selected Republican James Danforth Quayle, Indiana's second-term junior senator, as the nation's new vice-president.

With the unexpected announcement that he had been selected as George Bush's vice-presidential running mate in August, Senator Quayle suddenly was thrust from obscurity into the center of a political storm. The tempest that broke over Quayle's head had less to do with his staunchly conservative views than with his personal life and background, particularly his decision as a young man in 1969 to enter the National Guard. Critics charged that Quayle used the influence of his wealthy and powerful family to get in the Guard and claimed that his motive was to avoid combat service in Vietnam.

The controversy was ironic because one reason the 41-year-old Quayle had been chosen for the ticket was his membership in the generation that had come of age during the turbulent Vietnam era.

Background. James Danforth Quayle was born on Feb. 4, 1947, in Indianapolis, IN, the grandson of the late Eugene Pulliam, conservative founder of a publishing empire that included the *Indianapolis Star.*

He grew into a young man regarded by friends as charming and affable but considered by critics to be something of a playboy who got by on his good looks and family connections. After graduating from DePauw University, Quayle served in the National Guard for six years, working about one weekend a month. Meanwhile he was graduated from Indiana University School of Law, served as an aide in the Indiana statehouse, and subsequently became associate publisher of the *Huntington Herald-Press,* owned by his father.

Entering politics in 1976, Quayle won election to the House of Representatives; after serving there two terms he moved up to the Senate by defeating veteran Democratic incumbent Birch Bayh in a bitter campaign. In 1986 he easily won reelection. In the Senate he was known as a hard-liner on defense issues. He vigorously supported the Strategic Defense Initiative and, for a time, opposed the Euromissile Treaty negotiated by President Reagan with Soviet General Secretary Gorbachev, though he eventually voted for the pact. On domestic issues, he generally joined with most other conservatives in opposing gun control and federal funding for abortion, and led the fight for Senate confirmation of conservative Judge Daniel Manion to the U.S. Court of Appeals. Probably his most significant achievement was the 1982 Job Training Partnership Act, coauthored with Democratic Sen. Edward Kennedy of Massachusetts, which was designed to replace the Comprehensive Education and Training Act in providing help for workers laid off in industries hurt by foreign competition.

Quayle and his wife, Marilyn, whom he met in law school, have three children: Tucker, 14; Benjamin, 12; and Mary Corinne, 10.

ROBERT SHOGAN

ROCARD, Michel Louis Léon

When Socialist President François Mitterrand named Michel Rocard as his prime minister May 10, 1988, a new message went out to the world: France would pursue moderate, pragmatic, free-market, pro-Western alliance policies built on a new consensus between left- and right-wing political parties. Even Rocard's critics conceded he was well qualified to implement that message.

Rocard, quick-witted and headstrong, still hopes to become president of France. But in his typically straightforward manner, he often says: "I just don't know when." Rocard's presidential ambition is known to deeply annoy Mitterrand. Rocard's personality and his ability to get along with Mitterrand would be tested severely, analysts predicted, following the ending of a tense, two-year power sharing arrangement between

AP/Wide World

Michel Rocard

Mitterrand and the outgoing neo-Gaullist leader, Jacques Chirac.

Despite the long Mitterrand-Rocard rivalry and their differences of opinion over many issues, the Socialist program drew nationwide support in parliamentary elections June 12. The results allowed Rocard to form a new Socialist minority government, the first in the history of the Fifth Republic.

Background. Pragmatism, leftist ideals, and the tendency to be something of a maverick have marked Rocard since his school days. Friends say this perhaps is because of his being Protestant in a predominantly Roman Catholic nation. The son of a distinguished scientist who helped develop France's atom bomb, Michel Louis Léon Rocard was born Aug. 23, 1930, in Courbevoie near Paris. He was graduated from Paris' Louis-le-Grand lycée and the École Nationale d' Administration (ENA), France's elite graduate school for civil servants. As a student, Rocard was active in the Socialist Party. After graduating from ENA near the top of his class as an *inspecteur des finances,* and rising rapidly in the civil service, he continued as a leftist by taking the helm of the tiny Unified Socialist Party in 1967.

Two years later, he was elected a deputy from Yvelines, a department that includes Versailles, near Paris. This followed his first, unsuccessful bid for the presidency, when he obtained only 3.6% of the votes. In 1974, he and his followers joined the Socialist Party then reorganizing under Mitterrand's leadership. A year before the 1981 presidential election, Rocard mounted his second bid for the presidency within the Socialist Party. Although he stepped aside when Mitterrand announced his candidacy, his ambitiousness was thought by critics to undermine Mitterrand's leadership of the party. Annoyed with the challenge but mindful of Rocard's popularity with Socialists, Mitterrand appointed him to the relatively minor post of minister for planning and regional development and, two years later, as minister of agriculture. Amid new disagreements with Mitterrand, Rocard resigned from the government in 1985.

In 1986, amid doubts over whether Mitterrand would seek reelection, Rocard began his third presidential campaign but quickly shelved the plans when it became clear Mitterrand would run. Rocard then campaigned actively for the president.

In 1977, Rocard was elected mayor of the Yvelines town of Conflans-Sainte Honorine, a position he still held in 1988. He resides there with his second wife, Michèle Legendre, a sociology professor; they have three sons and one daughter. An author of several books on economics and politics, Rocard sails and skis avidly.

See also FRANCE.

AXEL KRAUSE

ROH Tae Woo

In the 18 months from mid-1987 to the end of 1988, Roh Tae Woo underwent a political conversion that changed the course of modern South Korean history—from the confidant and designated successor of a military dictator, to politician, to democratic coup-maker, to popularly elected president, to national stabilizer.

Amid violent political unrest in early 1987, the former general was chosen by his longtime friend, the strongman President Chun Doo Hwan, to be the candidate of the ruling Democratic Justice Party (DJP) in presidential elections. The voting would be conducted under the existing constitution, thereby assuring victory for the DJP candidate. On June 29, however, in an historic speech, Roh broke with President Chun and endorsed the demands of the opposition—direct election of the next president, release of political prisoners, and restoration of democratic rights. A draft constitution incorporating these changes was approved overwhelmingly in a popular referendum in October, and direct presidential elections were held on December 16. Largely because of a split between the two opposition candidates, the 55-year-old Roh won the balloting with 35.9 % of the vote.

In South Korea's first peaceful transition of power since becoming independent in 1948, Roh was sworn in as president on Feb. 25, 1988. Pledging democratic reforms and promoting a populist image, he promptly released more than 7,000 political prisoners and later met with opposition leaders in hopes of quelling student unrest. Despite continued outbreaks of violence and the DJP's loss of a legislative majority in April elections, Roh's political fortunes were given a boost by the success of the 1988 Seoul Olympics (of which he had been the chief organizer from 1983 to 1986).

Roh Tae Woo

AP/Wide World

In addressing the United Nations General Assembly on October 18, he called for a six-nation "consultative conference for peace" to bring an end to the division of the Korean peninsula. The meeting would include North and South Korea, China, Japan, the United States, and the USSR.

Background. Roh Tae Woo was born on Dec. 4, 1932, in a village outside Taegu, the same city that produced President Chun. Roh's father was killed in an automobile accident, and he was raised by his mother. An uncle sent him to the prestigious Kyonbuck High School in Taegu, where he became friends with Chun. With the outbreak of the Korean War, they both entered the Korean Military Academy, graduating in 1955. They served together in Vietnam during the 1960s, with Roh returning to Korea in 1974. By 1979 he had been elevated to the rank of general, with command of the First Division.

In December 1979, seven weeks after the assassination of then President Park Chung Hee, a group of military officers led by Chun staged a military coup against the new regime and—with the crucial support of a regiment led by General Roh—wrested control. As Chun consolidated power, suppressed the opposition—a campaign that included the military violently suppressing a 1980 uprising in the city of Kwangju—and implemented martial law, Roh was placed in key positions. After heading the Defense Security Command (a military network responsible for political surveillance), he retired from the military in 1981 and held a series of cabinet posts: minister of political affairs (1981); minister of sports (1982); and minister of home affairs (1982). He left the cabinet in 1983 to head the Seoul Olympic Organizing Committee.

Roh and his wife, Kim Ok Sook, live in the South Yonhidong section of Seoul. They have two children.

See also KOREA.

Reviewed by HAROLD C. HINTON

RONSTADT, Linda

The unpredictable Linda Ronstadt, drawing upon her Mexican heritage, surprised fans and music critics alike in 1988 by creating a mariachi album and accompanying tour, *Canciones de mi Padre* (*Songs of My Father*). Sung entirely in Spanish, the album went gold; the popular concert tour ran for most of the year—including a successful 18-performance stop on Broadway; and Ronstadt strengthened her reputation as a versatile singer willing to take considerable professional risks.

Background. Linda Ronstadt was born on July 30, 1946, in Tucson, AZ, into a house which always was filled with music. Her father—who managed a hardware store—wrote songs, sang, and played guitar and piano. Her mother also sang and played the ukelele, and records by Mexican and country artists were heard constantly. The young soprano gave her first public performances when she was still a teenager, singing folk songs with sister Suzie and older brother Pete on local TV shows.

After dropping out of the University of Arizona in 1964, Ronstadt followed her friend, guitarist Bob Kimmel, to Los Angeles, hoping to establish a career in music. There, with guitarist-keyboardist Kenny Edwards, they formed the group The Stone Poneys and played the local music clubs. Under contract to Capitol Records, the folk-pop trio released three moderately successful albums. The highlight of their recording career was the top-ten single "Different Drum," composed by The Monkees' Mike Nesmith and released in November 1967.

The group disbanded late in 1968, and Ronstadt cut several solo albums. By the early 1970s, her albums regularly went platinum (selling more than one million copies each). She won two Grammy Awards and had a succession of hit singles, including "You're No Good" and "When Will I Be Loved?."

Not content with being a best-selling singer, Ronstadt accepted producer Joseph Papp's offer to star in his 1980 stage production of Gilbert and Sullivan's *The*

Linda Ronstadt

Pirates of Penzance. Although the theater world initially was aghast, Ronstadt's soaring voice and doe-eyed innocence were perfect for Mabel, the major-general's daughter who falls in love with an apprentice pirate. She also starred in the 1983 film version.

In yet another startling change of pace, Ronstadt teamed with the arranger Nelson Riddle to record three albums of standards by the likes of George Gershwin and Cole Porter. The first of these was the 1983 smash hit *What's New.* Then, in 1984, she took her boldest step yet, starring in Papp's New York production of Puccini's opera *La Bohème,* singing the lead role of the seamstress Mimi. Just before undertaking the labor of love *Canciones de mi Padre,* Ronstadt teamed with Dolly Parton and Emmylou Harris for the enormously popular country album *Trio.*

Never married, Ronstadt has been linked romantically to rock star Mick Jagger, California's former governor Jerry Brown, and filmmaker George Lucas.

JEFF ROVIN

SAFDIE, Moshe

While Canada may be far removed from the architect Moshe Safdie's native Israel, it is there that he has made his mark on the North American continent—first with his precast-concrete prototype housing complex, Habitat 67, at Expo 67 in Montreal, and most recently with the National Gallery of Canada in Ottawa, which opened on May 21, 1988. To bring the massive gallery (some 350,000 sq ft, or 32 500 m²) into human scale, Safdie organized the plan around two courtyards that provide orientation as well as natural light—one of the trademarks of his designs—inside the three-story building. These courtyards, surrounded by arched walls that appear to be built from heavy stone blocks, reflect a heavy Mediterranean influence. Indeed it is this mix of tradition and ritual with futuristic innovation—as seen in the segmented glass-and-metal ceiling of the gallery's 128-ft-(39-m-) high Great Hall—that best characterizes the architect's work. From without, the pink and gray granite building is more restrained than some of Safdie's earlier designs (most notably the Columbus Center in New York City, which has aroused controversy over its massive

size and relationship to its surroundings). The gallery's truncated-pyramid roof forms seem to echo those of Ottawa's older, dignified structures. Other Canadian projects being handled by Safdie include the Musée de la civilisation in Quebec, which was to open in fall 1988; the $236 million Toronto Ballet-Opera complex, a commission he won in 1988; and a major addition to the Montreal Museum of Fine Arts.

Background. Moshe Safdie was born in Haifa, Israel, on July 14, 1938. As a boy, he lived on a *kibbutz* (collective farm) and for a while attended the Reali School in Haifa. Then, at age 16, he moved with his family to Canada. After graduating from Westmount (Quebec) High School in 1955, he enrolled in the School of Architecture at McGill University in Montreal. A gifted student, he won ten scholarships and prizes before obtaining his Bachelor of Architecture degree in 1961.

In association with a Montreal architectural firm, Safdie began work on Habitat 67—an outgrowth of his McGill thesis on urban housing—in 1964. The success of that project firmly established his reputation and put him in high demand—especially in his native Israel. Since opening an office there in 1970, he has undertaken a wide variety of projects in Jerusalem: major renovations in the old city; Hebrew Union College; a children's memorial next to the Holocaust Museum; and a master plan for the holiest Jewish monument, the Wailing Wall. Other projects around the world have included the Cambridge Center Complex in Massachusetts; the North Station area in Boston; Coldspring New Town in Baltimore, MD; Tampines New Community in Singapore; and Robina New Town in Gold Coast, Australia.

Safdie holds the Order of Canada and has won the Governor General Gold Medal. He has taught at Harvard University since 1978, and divides his time between his offices on two continents. Described as highly articulate, well-read, and "informal" in attitude, the gray-haired architect was married for the second time in 1981, to the former Michal Ronnen. He has two children from that marriage and two from his first marriage.

CHARLES K. HOYT

SALINAS DE GORTARI, Carlos

Dr. Carlos Salinas de Gortari, a former teacher, took office on Dec. 1, 1988, to serve a single six-year term as president of Mexico, after being elected July 6 in the most competitive presidential election in 20th-century Mexican history. Even though 40-year-old Dr. Salinas claimed only a 50.5% victory margin, opposition candidates maintained that this unprecedented low margin was fraudulent.

The new president's selection as the candidate of the Institutional Revolutionary Party (PRI) had caused massive defections from the PRI, led by his chief electoral rival, Cuauhtémoc Cardenas of the National Democratic Front. As minister of budget and planning (1982–87), Salinas had devised the economic austerity strategy that produced massive declines in real income and significant political opposition from the left and the right.

As president, he would be forced to move quickly to assert strong personal control over his government and the PRI to prove that he is not a weak leader, while also reversing the fracturing of the political system. A technocratic pragmatist, he was expected to introduce needed democratic reform to pacify the left and the right, making the system more pluralistic. PRI dissidents would be encouraged to return to the fold, while more opposition political victories would be recognized.

Salinas also was expected to continue the International Monetary Fund-guided economic policies of the previous administration, while adopting a more leftist nationalistic foreign policy stance for domestic consumption. Privatization of state enterprises, encouragement of foreign investment, and quasi-monetarist economic policy, tempered by domestic political demands, probably would continue. He would seek means of inducing controlled economic growth and reducing

the costs of servicing the foreign debt. To blunt leftist criticisms of these policies, he was expected to be very nationalistic in foreign policy.

Background. Carlos Salinas de Gortari, whose parents were government employees, was born in Mexico City on April 3, 1948. He received a degree in economics from the University of Mexico and later earned a master's degree in public administration, a master's in political economy and government, and a doctorate in political economy and government, all from Harvard University. After a brief stint as a legislative aide to a congressman, he served in the PRI "think tank," the treasury secretariat, and the planning and budget secretariat. He is identified closely with his mentor, Miguel de la Madrid, who selected him as the PRI candidate, and with Mexico's probusiness, pro-U.S. wing.

He is married and the father of three children.

DONALD J. MABRY

WINFIELD, David Mark

A week before the opening of the 1988 major league baseball season, the long-simmering feud between Dave Winfield, right fielder of the New York Yankees, and George Steinbrenner, outspoken owner of the team, exploded into the headlines. The trigger was the March 28 publication of excerpts from the book *Winfield: A Player's Life* in *The New York Daily News.* Winfield's criticisms of Steinbrenner convinced the Yankee owner to redouble efforts to trade his hard-hitting outfielder. Those efforts were thwarted, however, because of veto rights granted Winfield in his ten-year, $23 million contract with the Yankees, signed in 1980.

Winfield answered the persisting trade rumors with a sizzling start that included 29 runs batted in (RBIs) in April, tying the major league record for the month. A .398 batting average and seven home runs over the same span earned him recognition as the American League's Player of the Month. In 1988, the 6'6" (1.98-m), 220-lb (100-kg) slugger was named to the all-star team for the 12th consecutive year and had 100 RBIs for the sixth time in seven seasons with the Yanks. He finished the year with a .322 batting average, 25 home runs, and 107 RBIs. He also won his eighth Gold Glove for defensive excellence. Winfield reached a career milestone with his 350th home run on July 27.

Dave Winfield

UPI/Bettmann Newsphotos

Background. David Mark Winfield was born in St. Paul, MN, on Oct. 3, 1951—the day Bobby Thomson hit his famous pennant-winning home run for the New York Giants. Winfield and his brother, Steve, were raised by their mother and grandmother after the separation of Frank and Arline Winfield when David was three. Upon graduating from Central High School in St. Paul, Winfield earned a scholarship to the University of Minnesota, where he was a three-sport star. Drafted by professional teams in football, basketball, and baseball, he accepted the $50,000 signing bonus offered by baseball's San Diego Padres and in 1973 advanced directly to the major leagues without playing in the minors.

Four years after his career began, he founded the David M. Winfield Foundation, a nonprofit organization dedicated to helping underprivileged children. The following year, 1979, Winfield led the National League with 118 RBIs and 333 total bases, finished third in home runs with 34, and placed third in the voting for most valuable player (MVP). He later achieved career peaks with 37 home runs in 1982 and a .340 batting average in 1984.

Though he turned 37 the day after the 1988 season ended, Winfield maintains a trim athletic physique through rigorous off-season workouts, coupled with abstinence from drinking and smoking. He enjoys photography, art, travel, fishing, designing his own clothes, and decorating his homes in Teaneck, NJ, and St. Paul. Winfield married the former Tonya Tucker on Feb. 18, 1988. He also has a daughter, Lauren Shanel.

DAN SCHLOSSBERG

WITT, Katarina

The queen of the 1988 Winter Games in Calgary, East Germany's Katarina Witt made Olympic history by becoming only the second woman to repeat as the singles figure skating champion and the first since the great Sonja Henie in 1936. (Henie's gold medal that year was her third in a row.) The competition in Calgary was billed as a showdown between the 22-year-old defending gold medalist and the 1986 world champion, Debi Thomas of the United States. At the end of the first two phases of the competition—the compulsory figures and short program—Witt trailed her American rival by a slim margin. The drama of the free-skating event was heightened by the fact that both skaters would be performing to the same music—from the tragic final scene of Bizet's opera *Carmen*. Wearing a dazzling red and black gypsy-style costume, Witt turned in an irresistibly elegant and artistically captivating performance, while opting for more cautious jumps than she knew Thomas would attempt. Witt thus earned superior scores for "artistic impression," but her total for "technical merit" left room for the American to move ahead. But when Thomas faltered in her own performance, stumbling several times, the 5'5" (1.65 m), 112-lb (51-kg), East German beauty had won her second Olympic gold medal.

Background. Katarina Witt was born on Dec. 3, 1965, in the town of Staaken, East Germany, near Berlin. She began skating at the age of 5, when her mother took her to the local sports club and signed her up for lessons. Witt began entering formal competitions in 1972 and immediately showed promise. At age 11 she moved into the training group of Jutta Müller, the celebrated coach of a number of world-class skaters.

In 1981, at the age of only 15, Witt won the first of eight consecutive East German championships, and two years later she captured the first of six straight European titles. In the winter of 1984, she scored a string of spectacular victories, winning the European, world, and Olympic crowns. Living and training in the southern city of Karl Marx Stadt, she continued her competitive career and retained each of her titles—with the exception of the 1986 world championship—through 1988.

An aspiring actress, Witt has been enrolled at the Berlin Drama School since 1986. She retired from competitive skating after Calgary and became a "sports envoy" for UNICEF.

BIOTECHNOLOGY

The year 1988 saw more dramatic advances in the use of biological systems for the development and improvement of agricultural, industrial, and medical processes.

Food Production. With the rapid expansion of the world population, food production remains a high priority. Until now yields of the main cereal crops have been improved only by the hybridization of genetically diverse strains, followed by selective breeding of offspring with desirable traits. In 1988, however, working with corn tissue, Dr. Carol Rhodes and associates at the Sandoz Crop Protection Corporation in California were able to enzymatically digest away the nonliving wall around each cell and grow the naked cells (protoplasts) in tissue culture. To the culture medium they added circular pieces of DNA (plasmids), which contained a bacterial gene that makes cells resistant to kanamycin. This chemical compound normally kills any corn plant exposed to it. After the protoplasts absorbed the plasmids, the cells grew, divided, and formed embryos, each of which developed into an adult corn plant that was resistant to kanamycin.

This achievement will permit the introduction of other genes, regardless of the species from which they come, into corn and other cereal plants. Scientists will be able to choose genes that increase plant yields and thereby boost world food production.

In animal food production, a number of laboratories have been engaged in transferring the growth hormone gene from one fish species to another. One such experiment, by Dr. D. A. Powers and colleagues at Johns Hopkins University in Baltimore, resulted in the transfer of the rainbow trout growth-hormone gene to carp eggs. During development, the genetically altered carp produced both carp and rainbow trout growth hormones. When adult, the fish were about one third larger than normal carp. Similar experiments are under way to increase the size of catfish, northern pike, and striped bass—all important food sources.

Human Protein in Mouse Milk. Among the recent advances in genetic engineering has been the transfer of the human gene for tissue plasminogen activator (TPA) to a strain of mice. TPA is a naturally occurring enzyme that has been used successfully to dissolve blood clots in heart attack victims. Of potentially great significance was the discovery that the milk of the genetically altered strain of mice contained an appreciable amount of TPA. Scientists at Integrated Genetics, the Massachusetts biotechnology company where the experiment was conducted, hope the same kind of results can be obtained using cows, sheep, or goats. If so, a variety of human genes could be transferred to these animals, and large quantities of such drugs as insulin (used in treating diabetes), human growth hormone (retarded physical development), and blood clotting Factor 8 and Factor 9 (hemophilia) could be extracted. Obtaining these drugs from animals is expected to be more efficient than the current method of obtaining them from genetically engineered bacteria.

Tracking Engineered Microbes. Some agricultural biotechnology programs require the inoculation of soil with genetically engineered microbes, raising the fear that such organisms might spread through the soil and upset the ecosystem of the area. Until recently, no information has been available on the distance that such bacteria move from where they are placed.

Now, however, such field studies are being conducted. In one such investigation, two genes from the bacterium *Escherichia coli* were transferred to *Pseudomonas fluorescens,* a bacterium that lives on the roots of crop plants. Naturally occurring *P. fluorescens* do not contain these genes and, therefore, are easily distinguishable from the genetically engineered forms. At the Clemson University (SC) research station, wheat seeds were coated with the engineered bacteria and planted in a test plot. Soil samples taken over a four-month period showed that the bacteria remain localized and present no threat to the ecosystem.

Rejuvenating Oil Fields. Normally about 50% of the oil in an oil field goes unrecovered because of the loss of pressure in each well as oil is removed and because oil tends to clog the pores of the surrounding rock, preventing the remaining oil from seeping into the well. Scientists have found that bacteria of the genera *Bacillus* and *Clostridium* occur naturally in wells. As part of their normal metabolism, some species release gases that raise the pressure in the well and secrete chemical solvents that loosen the oil from the pores of the surrounding rock. The U.S. Department of Energy has started a program to culture carefully selected bacterial strains and inject them into an aging, five-acre (two-hectare) oil field in Oklahoma. They are expected to diffuse slowly through the surrounding rock and rejuvenate the field.

Patenting an Engineered Animal. As a result of a series of rulings by the U.S. Supreme Court and the U.S. Patent and Trademark Office, the patenting of organisms has progressed from "nonnatural man-made microorganisms" in 1980 to a "transgenic nonhuman eukaryotic animal" in 1988. The latter patent was granted to Harvard University on April 12 for a mouse strain in which the cells were engineered to contain a cancer-predisposing gene sequence (activated oncogene), making the mice especially susceptible to cancer-causing substances (carcinogens). The animals can be used to test low doses of suspected carcinogens and the effectiveness of substances thought to protect against the development of cancer.

Louis Levine, *City College of New York*

On May 10 in El Alto near La Paz, Bolivia, at an altitude of 13,450 ft (4 100 m), Pope John Paul II said Mass for some 300,000 Aymara Indian peasants. In his homily the pontiff called for a new respect for the family unit.

BOLIVIA

Bolivia's governing party, the National Revolutionary Movement (MNR), surmounted a severe internal crisis in September 1988 when it nominated Gonzalo Sanchez de Losada, minister of planning in the government of President Victor Paz Estenssoro, as its candidate in presidential elections scheduled for May 1989. Under the Bolivian constitution, Paz Estenssoro cannot succeed himself.

Politics. An intraparty split between supporters of Sanchez de Losada and Foreign Minister Guillermo Bedregal had become so rancorous that Paz Estenssoro, a founder of the MNR in 1952 and its lifetime chief, summoned those two candidates and a third, Bolivia's ambassador to Peru, Nuflo Chavez Ortiz, to the presidential palace in August to issue a personal plea for party unity. The plea came in the face of the growing strength of opposition parties, which swept municipal elections in December 1987.

The principal opposition candidates are Gen. Hugo Banzer Suarez, a former president and the leader of the conservative Nationalist Democratic Action (ADN), and Jaime Paz Zamora of the populist Leftist Revolutionary Movement (MIR). In the municipal elections, ADN finished first, with MIR close behind.

Economy. Paz Estenssoro's MNR was in trouble for all the wrong reasons, in the view of Reagan administration officials. Since assuming office in 1985, Paz Estenssoro had checked runaway inflation, restored economic growth to a severely depressed economy, cut the government's deficit, pared down bloated publicly owned corporations, made progress in reducing Bolivia's $3 billion foreign debt, and cracked down on the country's flourishing illicit drug trade.

But the austere measures of Paz Estenssoro's New Economic Policy (NEP)—including a wage freeze and deregulation of prices and interest rates—have drawn strong opposition from businessmen and labor organizations. Protest marches and nationwide strikes have marked Paz Estenssoro's regime, and they continued throughout 1988. Passage of a strong antidrug-trafficking law in July and the destruction of thousands of acres of coca plants raised the ire of Bolivia's powerful cocaine-trade barons and thousands of peasants who depend on the cultivation of the coca leaf for their livelihood. An August bomb attack against the caravan of visiting U.S. Secretary of State George Shultz, who was to deliver a speech supporting government efforts to combat the cocaine trade, was believed to be carried out by drug traffickers.

The results of NEP, however unpopular the program, have been spectacular. From a high

---

BOLIVIA • Information Highlights

Official Name: Republic of Bolivia.
Location: West-central South America.
Area: 424,162 sq mi (1 098 580 km²).
Population (mid-1988 est.): 6,900,000.
Chief Cities (mid-1986 est.): Sucre, the legal capital, 88,774; La Paz, the actual capital, 1,033,288; Santa Cruz de la Sierra, 457,619; Cochabamba, 329,941.
Government: *Head of state and government,* Victor Paz Estenssoro, president (took office Aug. 6, 1985). *Legislature*—Congress: Senate and Chamber of Deputies.
Monetary Unit: Bolivianos (2.350 bolivianos equal U.S.$1, May 1988).
Gross Domestic Product (1987 est. U.S.$): $3,870,-000,000.
Economic Index (February 1988): *Consumer Prices* (La Paz, 1980 = 100), all items, 8,236,626; food, 8,422,445.
Foreign Trade (1987 U.S.$): *Imports,* $1,018,000,000; *exports,* $566,000,000.

of 14,000% in 1985, the inflation rate dropped to 10.7% in 1987 and ran at an annual rate of about 12% in the first half of 1988. The economy, which shrank 23% from 1980 to 1985, was expected to grow 2.3% in 1988 and 4% in 1989. The government deficit, as a portion of gross domestic product (GDP), fell from 28% in 1985 to a projected 6.1% in 1988. Sanchez de Losada is a strong supporter of NEP; the leftist MIR seeks its abolition.

RICHARD SCHROEDER
Formerly, "Visión" Magazine

BRAZIL

In 1988 Brazil's economic headaches permeated its political and foreign-policy concerns. Meanwhile preparations for direct presidential elections in 1989 began.

Politics and Government. On January 6, Mailson Ferreira da Nobrega was sworn in as President José Sarney's fourth finance minister in three years. Nobrega promised to proceed with talks on Brazil's $116 billion foreign debt and to reach an agreement with the International Monetary Fund (IMF). He also stated that he would follow Sarney's priorities of fighting inflation and reducing both the budget deficit and the state's role in the economy.

On September 2 the Constituent Assembly approved Brazil's eighth constitution since

Members of Brazil's Constituent Assembly celebrate after approving the draft of a new constitution, September 2. The nation's eighth charter was put into effect October 5.
AP/Wide World

1822, after 578 days of debate and an estimated 39,000 amendments. The 245-article charter, which went into force on October 5, called for a bicameral legislature to play a major role for the first time since the 1964 military coup. Even though the armed forces yielded power in 1985, the increasingly unpopular Sarney had ruled without consulting Congress on key issues.

The new constitution maintains a presidential system, yet bestows greater powers on state and municipal governments. It embraces a mix of socially liberal and conservative measures. For instance, the fundamental law expands civil liberties, welfare benefits, the freedom of workers to strike, and the right of *habeas data* (a citizen's right to see his own personal records). But the charter does not tamper with the established power structures —notably, it invests the military with the right to intervene in governmental affairs in the interest of national security.

A source of legislative-executive tension sprang from the Congress' newly acquired power to dominate public finances control in order to keep a lid on federal spending. The charter charges the legislature with the task of preparing the budget. While the Assembly asked for easier terms for local governments to pay their foreign debts, the executive insisted that these terms would strain public-sector borrowing and fuel already rampant inflation which was at an annual rate of 600%. Congress further enhanced its own budgetary powers by permitting itself to rewrite executive proposals provided that it does not exceed total expenditures. In an act of resurgent nationalism, the new charter also restricts foreign companies' explorations for oil, gas, and minerals. Additionally, the document gives amnesty to certain small business debts and caps real-interest rates at 12% per year.

Mounting economic problems and the suppression of strikers at the Volta Redonda steel complex sparked a huge antigovernment protest vote in the November 15 municipal contests. The leftist Partido dos Trabalhadores captured the mayorships of key state capitals, including São Paulo. Meanwhile the cogoverning PMDB lost in all but two state capitals.

Economy. A year after declaring a moratorium on commercial bank interest payments in February 1987, Nobrega announced its end and petitioned the IMF for an additional $6.5 billion in credits. The country found the moratorium too costly: Private-trade credit had dwindled, export-credit agencies cut their financing of Brazil's inputs, and Brazil missed opportunities to negotiate more attractive interest rates on loans. The rescheduling of the debt called for banks to lend Brazil $5.2 billion over the next 18 months. To attain this target, the financial institutions had several options available; for instance, they could tie loans to trade, accomplish debt-for-equity swaps, lend to new

BRAZIL · Information Highlights

Official Name: Federative Republic of Brazil.
Location: Eastern South America.
Area: 3,286,475 sq mi (8 511 970 km²).
Population (mid-1988 est.): 144,400,000.
Chief Cities (1985 est.): Brasília, the capital, 1,576,657; São Paulo, 10,099,086; Rio de Janeiro, 5,615,149; Belo Horizonte, 2,122,073.
Government: *Head of state and government,* José Sarney Costa, president (took office April 21, 1985). *Legislature*—National Congress: Senate and Chamber of Deputies.
Monetary Unit: Cruzado (512.46 cruzados equal U.S.$1, Nov. 14, 1988).
Gross National Product (1986 U.S.$): $270,000,-000,000.
Economic Indexes (1987): *Consumer Prices* (São Paulo, 1980 = 100), all items, 53,009; food, 57,875. *Industrial Production* (September 1986, 1980 = 100), 125.
Foreign Trade (1986 U.S.$): *Imports,* $15,586,-000,000; *exports,* $22,392,000,000.

borrowers, and take exit bonds that would release them from future reschedulings. After the 18-month period, Brazil then would pay $20.9 billion in interest due to the banks.

Brazil held its first debt-conversion auction on March 29. Under the plan, the government would auction off $150 million in Brazilian cruzados to creditors each month. In March they swapped $186 million in debt payments due to them for investment in stipulated areas of the country—reserving half of the money to promote progress in the hugely underdeveloped Northeast and the Amazon. Banks could convert their credits and interest into companies or conversion funds at a discount fixed by the auction. Foreign banks sought Brazilian companies that outperformed the national economy—such as paper and pulp and petrochemicals.

On June 22, Brazil reached a preliminary accord on debt rescheduling with its major creditors. The pact, which anticipated repayment of Brazil's $61 billion debt over 20 years, also provided $5.2 billion in new loans to be repaid over 12 years. The agreement stipulated that only interest would be paid in the first eight years, while principal payments plus interest would be repaid in the last 12 years. A payment of 2% would begin in 1997 and would climb to 10% in the final two years. Brazil's foreign obligations totaled roughly $121 billion—more than that of any other developing nation. Nobrega praised the pact as "the best debt accord that any Third World country has ever had."

Inflation, which reached 24% in September, was predicted to reach 800% by the end of 1988, more than doubling 1987's record of 366%. Sarney's two abortive price freezes did not restrain spiraling prices even as they further disrupted the economy.

Brazil compiled a $16 billion trade surplus for 1988—up from $11.15 billion the year before.

The first clash between the Congress and the executive branch took place over the 1989 budget submitted for legislative approval in October 1988. The draft, endorsed by Sarney, included austerity measures that transferred financial responsibilities to state governments. State governments protested the requirement that they pay the national treasury 25% of the principal and interest due in 1989 on their foreign debts—valued at $2.7 billion.

In late October, 800,000 federal and state employees as well as the staff of the state-owned Banco do Brasil launched a strike to protest low salaries and disturbing economic forecasts. Although the scale of the strike was unprecedented, the government continued to function normally. Ironically the protest showed what millions of Brazilians already believed—that is, that thousands of civil servants in the bloated bureaucracy were unnecessary.

Foreign Affairs. Bilateral relations with the United States were strained in 1988. In January the United States protested a projected sale of Brazilian arms to Libya. Brazilian Foreign Minister Roberto Costa de Abreu Sodre confirmed that a Libyan delegation sought to buy $2 billion worth of "defensive" weapons, including armored cars, battle tanks, and short-range missiles. Even though military items constitute an important source of foreign exchange—some experts rank Brazil's arms industry as the fifth or sixth largest in the world—the deal never was consummated.

Secretary of State George Shultz visited Brazil April 5–7 to talk with Sarney and Sodre. They agreed to work out a solution to the trade dispute over pharmaceutical patents. In addition, Sodre backed U.S. efforts to pressure Nicaragua to make democratic changes. Nonetheless, relations deteriorated later in the year. In July, President Reagan ordered the imposition of trade sanctions against $200 million worth of Brazilian exports for Brazil's alleged refusal to provide patent protection to U.S. pharmaceutical and fine chemicals companies.

Also, Brazil's computer protectionist law entered into its fifth year as the new constitution confirmed the exclusion of foreign microcomputers from the greatly expanding Brazilian market. On October 27, Brazil charged that the United States violated its pledge, in the so-called Uruguay Round of trade negotiations, not to introduce new restrictive measures.

In mid-October, Sarney flew to Moscow to meet for the first time with USSR's Mikhail Gorbachev. In addition to essentially ceremonial talks in which the two leaders pledged to continue the struggle against fascism, they signed declarations on trade in machinery and equipment, on cooperation in peaceful space research, and on peace and international cooperation. Gorbachev intended to visit Brazil in March 1989.

GEORGE W. GRAYSON
College of William and Mary

BRITISH COLUMBIA

An uneasiness on the part of some Cabinet colleagues with the political style of Premier William Vander Zalm of the Social Credit Party and his low public-approval ratings overshadowed other political events in British Columbia (B.C.) in 1988.

Political Affairs. Premier Vander Zalm, reacting to the Supreme Court of Canada's decision in January that struck down federal curbs on abortion as unconstitutional, refused the use of public funding for abortions except where a mother's life was threatened. This policy sparked some initial dissension within the Social Credit Party caucus and was overturned in March by the chief justice.

Further controversy erupted as rumors abounded of interference by the premier's office on behalf of Vancouver businessman Peter Toigo in the sale of B.C. Enterprise Corporation assets, including the Expo 86 lands. Hong Kong billionaire Li Ka-Shing proved to be the successful bidder for the Expo site, and a Royal Canadian Mounted Police investigation into the financial relationship between Vander Zalm and Toigo found no evidence of a breach of law.

A special report by the provincial Ombudsman was released in August that found evidence of inappropriate interference by the premier's principal secretary in the licensing for a Vancouver Knight Street pub and led to the resignation of the principal secretary.

A second report into the covert surveillance of the pro-choice abortion movement found it to have been inappropriate and that the then attorney general, Brian Smith, erred. A later Ombudsman's report into complaints of improper interference in the operation of the Parole Board cleared the premier of any intentional attempt at influence. Despite the controversies, Vander Zalm received an overwhelming endorsement of his leadership at the October meeting of the Social Credit Party.

David C. Lam was appointed as the province's 25th lieutenant governor.

By-Election and Cabinet Changes. A June 8th by-election in Boundary-Similkameen, a seat held by Social Credit for 22 years, resulted in the election of the New Democratic Party candidate, Bill Barlee.

In the final week of the spring sitting of the legislature, Attorney General Brian Smith resigned his portfolio. A few days later, Minister of Economic Development Grace McCarthy also resigned. A restructuring of the Cabinet on July 6 saw the departure of Stephen Rogers and an overall increase in the size of the Cabinet from 17 to 22 members. Two new ministries, one for International Business and Immigration and one for Regional Development, were created. Deputy ministers were reassigned with six new appointees from outside B.C. public service. The B.C. legislature approved the Meech Lake accord in June.

Budget and Provincial Policy. The provincial budget for 1988–89 estimated general fund expenditures at C$11.8 billion with a deficit of C$395 million. Two special funds, a Budget Stabilization Fund and a Privatization Benefits Fund, were created as part of a deficit-reduction strategy.

The privatization of Crown corporations and other government operations continued with C$741 million obtained from the sale of the mainland natural gas division of B.C. Hydro.

Negotiations with the 29,000-member B.C. Government Employees Union broke down in September and resulted in a week-long strike. The union and the government later agreed to a three-year contract with protection for members threatened by privatization.

NORMAN J. RUFF, *University of Victoria*

BRITISH COLUMBIA • Information Highlights

Area: 365,946 sq mi (947 800 km²).
Population (Sept. 1988): 2,989,200.
Chief Cities (1986 census): Victoria, the capital, 66,303; Vancouver, 431,147; Prince George, 67,621; Kamloops, 61,773; Kelowna, 61,213.
Government (1988): *Chief Officers*—lt. gov., David C. Lam; premier, William Vander Zalm (Social Credit Party). *Legislature*—Legislative Assembly, 69 members.
Provincial Finances (1988–89 fiscal year budget): *Revenues,* $11,405,000,000; *expenditures,* $11,800,000,000.
Personal Income (average weekly earnings, July 1988): $458.10.
Labor Force (September 1988, seasonally adjusted): *Employed* workers, 15 years of age and over, 1,350,000; *Unemployed,* 10.7%.
Education (1988–89): *Enrollment*—elementary and secondary schools, 535,400 pupils; postsecondary—universities, 38,500; community colleges, 26,100.
(All monetary figures are in Canadian dollars.)

BULGARIA

In 1988, Bulgaria scaled back the ambitious domestic changes it had announced in 1987 and took steps to improve relations with its Balkan neighbors.

Domestic Affairs. On Jan. 28–29, 1988, a special meeting of more than 3,000 members of the Bulgarian Communist Party was held in Sofia. It originally had been scheduled for December 1987, for the purpose of ratifying the radical changes in the party and state structures proposed by President and Communist Party General Secretary Todor Zhivkov in July 1987, in loyal imitation of the drastic reforms then under way in the Soviet Union. However, in October 1987, Zhivkov had been summoned to Moscow and apparently cautioned to restructure at a more gradual pace, to avoid the risk of destabilizing his country.

Consequently, the special party meeting in January endorsed the general notion of "modernization" but approved only a few minor changes in the national economy and party operation. It called for a gradual loosening of central economic controls and more self-management by state enterprises, but left private enterprise illegal. It declared in favor of "qualitative change" within the party but reaffirmed its "leading role." It confined itself to expressing support for limiting leading party officials to a maximum of three five-year terms in office, a change already approved by the party's Central Committee.

Chudomir Alexandrov, a reformist leader who had been regarded widely as a possible successor to the aging Zhivkov, became a vocal critic of the slackening pace of change. A showdown came in July when Zhivkov expelled Alexandrov and his supporters from the party's Central Committee.

Foreign Affairs. Foreign Minister Petur Mladenov attended a conference of the foreign ministers of the six Balkan states held in Belgrade, Yugoslavia, on Feb. 24–26, 1988. It was the first meeting of officials from all six countries since the early 1930s and had been advocated enthusiastically by Bulgaria. Its announced purpose was to ameliorate bilateral differences and to develop cooperation in such areas as the economy, trade, tourism, and environmental protection. Mladenov reiterated Bulgaria's familiar international position in favor of eliminating all nuclear and chemical weapons from the Balkans.

Also in February, Bulgaria tried to mend its damaged relations with two of its immediate neighbors. After the pollution of the Bulgarian town of Ruse by a cloud of chloric acid from a chemical plant across the border in Romania, the two countries agreed to initiate measures to prevent such cross-border atmospheric pollution. Mladenov and Turkish Foreign Minister Mesut Yilmaz also agreed to try to repair Turkish-Bulgarian relations, injured by reciprocal polemics over Bulgaria's alleged mistreatment of its large ethnic Turkish minority.

In its report made public in March 1988, the Organization of Economic Cooperation and Development listed Bulgaria, along with Hungary and Poland, among the three east European Communist countries whose foreign debts "warrant careful monitoring."

See also special report, page 227.

JOSEPH FREDERICK ZACEK
State University of New York at Albany

BURMA

Burma in 1988 was a nation in violent turmoil due to the confrontations between protesters and government forces that were endemic since March. Whether the violence—and the mounting fatalities—would push Burma toward democratic elections and reform, toward civil war, or, more likely, merely reconsolidate the military rule that has governed so disastrously since 1962, was unclear as 1988 ended.

Rising Protest. Deepening economic woes and the government's abrupt decision to demonetize (declare worthless) most of the Burmese currency in September 1987 wiped out three fourths of the money supply overnight. While designed to cripple Burma's flourishing black market, demonetization had the more general effect of wiping out individuals' life savings.

The first political riots of 1988 followed that move. Yet, few were prepared for the savage clashes, starting in March, that would cost more than 8,000 lives by November.

The round of violence opened with a brawl March 12 in a Rangoon tea shop between students and residents. When it resumed the next night the army opened fire, killing eight students. Army-student clashes spread to several campuses, and by March 18 there was open fighting in the streets of Rangoon. The universities closed, but when they reopened in May, the demonstrations and protests reemerged. What seemed to keep the struggle alive was not the initial dispute, but the brutality of the army crackdown. More than 200 students had been killed, 41 of whom had suffocated in a police van. The army's harshness, coupled with grim economic conditions, served to discredit the one-party government of Gen. U Ne Win and embolden the opposition to demand free and open elections.

On July 23, Ne Win resigned his formal position as head of the ruling Burma Socialist Programme Party (BSPP) and called for a referendum on whether multiparty elections should be held. Though Ne Win thereafter held no official posts for the first time in 26 years, the 78-year-old strongman still was presumed to be the de facto power behind his successors.

BULGARIA • Information Highlights

Official Name: People's Republic of Bulgaria.
Location: Southeastern Europe.
Area: 42,823 sq mi (110 910 km²).
Population (mid-1988 est.): 9,000,000.
Chief Cities (April 1985): Sofia, the capital, 1,114,759; Plovdiv, 342,131; Varna, 302,211.
Government: *Head of state,* Todor Zhivkov, chairman of the State Council and general secretary of the Communist Party (took office July 1971). *Head of government,* Georgi Atanasov, chairman of the Council of Ministers (took office March 1986).
Monetary Unit: Lev (1.31 leva equal U.S.$1, July 1988).
Gross National Product (1986 U.S.$): $61,200,-000,000.
Economic Index: *Industrial Production* (1987, 1980 = 100), 132.
Foreign Trade (1986 U.S.$): *Imports,* $15,249,-000,000; *exports,* $14,192,000,000.

Ne Win's resignation raised hopes for an orderly move toward democratic elections, but these were dashed when the BSPP replaced him with U Sein Lwin, the security chief responsible for the crackdown on the students. Revolts resumed and soon spread to more than 30 cities. Sein Lwin again called out the army, which responded brutally, killing an estimated 3,000 people. Nevertheless, many times that number rallied to the opposition, including, for the first time, Buddhist monks. Martial law was declared August 3, but the fighting continued. After 17 days in power, Sein Lwin was forced to step down August 12.

On August 19, U Maung Maung, one of two civilians in Ne Win's government, became Burma's first civilian president in 26 years. Maung Maung lifted martial law five days later. In an effort to end a general strike that paralyzed the government, he promised to consider establishment of a Western-style democracy and recommended a referendum on elections which was approved September 10 by the BSPP. He also released 2,700 political prisoners.

The opposition, apparently emboldened by bringing down the ruthless Sein Lwin government, refused to be mollified by these steps. They demanded that a neutral interim government be formed until elections could be held. The general strike went on and the riots continued. Massive demonstrations of more than 200,000 people in Mandalay and more than one million in Rangoon took place September 5. On September 18, Maung Maung was ousted by a military coup led by Gen. Saw Maung. The new army coup savagely crushed most of the overt opposition to the government though it was not until October 3 that the general strike concluded. Sabotage continued.

The military government endorsed elections but set conditions that would prevent them from occurring in a timely fashion. Political parties were allowed to register with the government and almost 100 did so.

The National League for Democracy, led by U Aung Gyi, appeared to be the main op-

position. Its most likely candidate, Aung San Sui Kyi, is the daughter of nationalist hero Aung San, who was assassinated in 1947.

All of the parties were hamstrung in their political organization by the government's ongoing censorship, harassment of party workers, and the ban on demonstrations and meetings.

Insurgencies. A legacy of British colonial policies of divide and rule, ethnic strife has been endemic since Burmese independence. Yet under the federal constitution, rights for indigenous groups and some degree of local autonomy existed. That constitution and the federal system fell along with the government in 1962 when Ne Win took over.

In 1988 all of Burma's indigenous ethnic groups except the Chins were in open revolt. Armed insurgents, estimated to number 25,000, were organized under the broad political umbrella of the National Democratic Front. Since 1987 they had been struggling for a federal solution to their grievances for two reasons: Army victories had demoralized their movement, and crackdowns on their smuggling of opium, gems, and other goods had deprived them of much of their income. However, due to the national government's disarray and an upsurge in fresh recruits, their political demands may have hardened.

Economic Conditions. Burma began 1988 appealing to the United Nations for "least developed nation" status. That dubious distinction was granted, allowing Burma to convert some loans to aid. The once prosperous and mineral-rich nation was forced to acknowledge that its citizens had an annual per capita income of only $180. This encouraged the government to loosen some controls on the state monopolies. The most devastating blow to consumers was a tenfold increase in the price of rice in 1988. The government had allowed private trading in rice, but set the prices so low that little was planted.

Though thought to have one of the world's largest untapped reserves of onshore oil, Burma's oil production has been only half that needed to keep its faltering economy functioning. With foreign exchange reserves down to $5 million by November, prospects for imports were nil. Exports had been halted since August, but the artificially high exchange rate damaged export prospects even before the political chaos ensued. Corruption and the black market further distorted the economy.

Foreign Relations. Japan, West Germany, and the United States cut off all aid to Burma following the army massacres of unarmed civilians in September. However, precisely because Burma pursued such an isolationist foreign policy for three decades, little leverage existed externally for quelling the violence or rebuilding the economy. Only Japan was a significant aid donor, and its aid had been cut back severely before the political violence began.

LINDA K. RICHTER, *Kansas State University*

BURMA • Information Highlights

Official Name: Socialist Republic of the Union of Burma.
Location: Southeast Asia.
Area: 261,216 sq mi (676 550 km²).
Population (mid-1988 est.): 41,000,000.
Chief Cities (1983 est.): Rangoon, the capital, 2,458,712; Mandalay, 532,895.
Government: *Head of government,* Gen. Saw Maung (took power Sept. 18, 1988). *Legislature* (unicameral)—National Assembly.
Monetary Unit: Kyat (6.576 kyats equal U.S.$1, July 1988).
Gross Domestic Product (1986 est. U.S.$): $7,097,-000,000.
Economic Index (Rangoon, 1986): *Consumer Prices* (1980 = 100), all items, 135.0; food, 128.1.
Foreign Trade (1987 U.S.$): *Imports,* $306,000,000; *exports,* $222,000,000.

BUSINESS AND CORPORATE AFFAIRS

Among many major trends and developments in U.S. business and corporate affairs during 1988, the most significant was the overall economic climate—the longest period of peacetime prosperity in the nation's history. Not only was this a continuing boon to the business community, but it appeared to be the decisive factor in the presidential election.

Underlying all the political rhetoric and negative campaigning were real differences between the economic policies of the two candidates. The key question for many voters was, "Am I better off today than I was eight years ago?" A majority answered "yes" and cast their ballots for Vice-President George Bush. The outcome of a U.S. presidential election can have a considerable impact on business and corporate affairs. The immediate reaction of the business community was not exactly what many expected. The stock market declined, and concerns about the federal deficit and declining value of the dollar continued despite Bush's election.

The U.S. economy was in its sixth year of stable economic growth. The gross national product (GNP) was growing at an annual rate of 2.2% in the third quarter; inflation was running between 4% and 5%; corporate profits continued to climb; and unemployment was down to 5.2% in October. As in 1987, however, not all regions of the country were sharing equally in the economic growth and prosperity. The East and West coasts were booming in many respects, but the country's midsection and oil-producing regions still had some weak spots. Much of the farm belt was hurt badly by the summer drought, the worst since the dustbowl era of the 1930s.

Perhaps the best business news of 1988 concerned the stock market. On "Black Monday," Oct. 19, 1987, the Dow Jones Industrial Average dropped 508.32 points and closed at 1,738.74; exactly one year later it closed at 2,137.27. The dire economic predictions made in the aftermath of the crash proved to be wrong and, for the most part, business activity continued across the country as if Black Monday never happened.

The Global Economy. The economic world is changing rapidly, and no one can predict with certainty how the transition from a primarily national economy to a global economy will affect the U.S. business community. The United States continued to carry a sizable foreign trade deficit, but the shortfall was down significantly from previous years. The continuing decline in the value of the dollar was a major factor in that regard, encouraging exports and discouraging imports. Meanwhile, significant steps were being taken to lower international trade barriers in certain areas of the world. The U.S. Congress passed the Canada Free-Trade Agreement Implementation Act which would eliminate most tariffs between Canada and the United States over ten years beginning on Jan. 1, 1989. In Canada, however, the measure was a source of heated debate.

Action taken by the European Community (EC) during 1988 may have a major impact on the global economy. The 12 member nations agreed on new measures to implement a "unified internal market" by 1992, whereby people, goods, services, and capital can move among nations unhampered by political boundaries or economic barriers. The U.S. business community was concerned that when the walls came down among the 12 EC nations, external walls simply could replace the internal ones to impede the influx of U.S goods and services. In addition, the European Community Commission will be empowered to review any proposed merger that would draw 25% or more of its revenue from outside a single EC country. If the commission concludes that a merger poses a threat to EC competition, it could block the deal. The prospect of such action prompted a takeover frenzy involving more than $20 billion during 1988. The commission

Personal computer pioneer Steven Jobs, who cofounded Apple Computer, introduced NeXT, a computer workstation designed for the university market.

declared that it had a "fundamental stake in the existence of free and open international trade" and dismissed the fears of a looming European protectionism as "senseless and groundless."

Merger Mania and Leveraged Buy-Outs. With all the mergers and leveraged buyouts that took place in 1987, a general slowdown in such activity was expected in 1988. Quite the opposite was true. There was so much activity and some of the takeover bids were so large that *The Wall Street Journal* headlined 1988 as the "year of the megadeals." While many of the largest deals in 1987 occurred in the transportation industry, activity in 1988 focused on the food and tobacco industries.

The biggest deal of the year—and indeed in U.S. corporate history—was a $25 billion buyout of RJR Nabisco, the food and tobacco giant, by the Wall Street investment house of Kohlberg Kravis Roberts & Company (KKR). Underscoring the efforts of U.S. tobacco companies to diversify in the face of a decline in smoking, Philip Morris, another cigarette and food giant, made a successful offer of $13.1 billion in cash in its attempt to take over Kraft Food Company. Meanwhile, Pillsbury for two months fought a takeover bid by the British conglomerate Grand Metropolitan. In mid-December, however, after a court struck down its "poison pill" antitakeover defense (*see* glossary below), Pillsbury agreed to Grand

Met's $5.68 billion offer. Carl Icahn, one of the masters of the takeover game, was defeated in his $14.2 billion bid for Texaco.

Successful takeovers concluded in 1988 included Nestle's $4.5 billion buyout of the British confectioner Rowntree; Tootsie Roll's $65 million takeover of Charms; Hershey's $300 million takeover of Cadbury Schweppes' three U.S. candy plants; and the buyout of Montgomery Ward from its parent Mobil Oil for $3.8 billion by a private management group. In the meantime, Safeway agreed to a takeover bid of $4.25 billion; the increasing concentration among supermarkets was worrying government officials.

But not all takeover bids are successful, as companies have ways to defend themselves. In 1988, J.C. Penney planned to borrow $700 million to finance an employee stock purchase as a defense against a takeover. Ramada planned to sell its hotel and restaurant businesses and distribute the proceeds to shareholders as a move to prevent a takeover; the plan would leave Ramada with its expanding casino business, its most consistently profitable unit. And Kroger countered takeover bids with a $4.6 billion restructuring that included a $40 cash dividend for each share of common stock.

In addition to the wave of takeover battles, the year 1988 also saw a number of large-scale mergers. Maytag purchased the Chicago Pacific

Merger Mania: A Glossary of Terms

The growth of corporate mergers and takeovers in recent years has brought with it some colorful descriptive language. Such terms include:

arbitrager: a securities specialist who buys large amounts of stock in companies threatened by takeover, gambling that the takeover effort will be successful or that other suitors will bid for the firm. The resulting short-term change in the price of the stock enables the arbitrager to make a large profit.

corporate raider: an individual or company that bids a very large amount of money for controlling interest in a firm, especially where the buyout is opposed by management.

crown jewels: the most valuable assets of a firm targeted for takeover. These assets may be sold by the existing management either to make the company less attractive to raiders, or to pay off debts incurred after an attempted takeover.

golden parachute: generous severance benefits guaranteed to a firm's top management officials in the event that they lose their jobs due to a takeover.

greenmail: an agreement by a target firm to buy back shares of its stock owned by a potential raider at a price greater than the market value of the stock.

junk bonds: bonds issued by a company to finance its takeover defense strategies. These are actually loans sometimes secured by the firm's assets, and are called "junk" bonds because the company very likely will have trouble paying them back. Because of their risk, they offer high yields to attract investors.

leveraged buyout: a practice where the money used by investors to buy a company is obtained by borrowing, in which case the investors later may have to sell off part of the company's operations to repay the debt. This practice also allows management to buy all shareholders' stock and take the firm private.

pac-man defense: tactic used by the target company in which it launches a takeover attempt against the raider.

parking: an illegal practice where a raider has arbitragers buy and hold large blocks of the stock of a company in which it has an interest. The raider then owns a large amount of the target company's stock indirectly before it openly purchases the 5% which legally requires it to make its bid public.

poison pill: provisions made by the target firm that would make a takeover more expensive for a corporate raider or would decrease the value of the firm if bought.

proxy fight: practice employed by raiders in which they solicit shareholders' proxies to gain a voice at the target firm's annual meeting, including the election of the board of directors.

scorched-earth defense: the tactic of selling off major assets of a firm (*see* crown jewels) in order to make the firm unattractive to raiders.

shark repellents: measures used by a target company to make the firm more difficult for a raider to acquire; for example, requiring a "super majority" of 80% to 95% shareholder approval before a raider can buy out a company.

tender offer: a bid made by a raider offering to buy a certain amount of a company's stock at a specific set price. Usually this price is higher than market value, to encourage stockholders to sell, and the offer usually expires on a set date.

tin parachute: generous severance benefits guaranteed to a firm's employees in the event that they are laid off by new management after a takeover. This measure is often used as a "poison pill."

white knight: a buyer encouraged by a target firm to bid against the original raider, either because his offer would be more generous to shareholders and management or because his corporate philosophy is closer to that of the target firm's management than is that of the raider.

Corporation, owner of the Hoover Company, in a friendly $1 billion deal. Ames Department Stores bought the troubled discount-stores division of Zayre for $800 million, creating the country's third largest cut-price retailer. Rupert Murdoch bought Triangle Publications—including *TV Guide*—in a $3 billion deal. Also in the publishing field, Maxwell Communications acquired Macmillan Publishing in a $2.62 billion leveraged buyout during the year.

Despite all the takeovers and mergers, many of the largest U.S. corporations remained relatively immune from a change in ownerships. In the case of Hershey Foods and Campbell Soup, for example, 50% or more of stock is owned by individuals or groups not vulnerable to takeover. IBM and Exxon are still too big to be bought out. The Ford Company, The Washington Post, Dow Jones, and The New York Times each have a class of supervoting stock that keeps control among descendants of the founder or builder of the business. AT&T, General Motors, and General Electric are protected from takeovers because, it is felt, the federal government would not permit such giant companies to be exposed to the risk of leveraged buyouts.

Nevertheless, all the speculative activity in the takeover "binge" created its own frenzy on Wall Street. As investors became increasingly frightened, many takeover stock prices and bond prices went down. A number of state governments passed laws impeding takeovers, although legislation introduced in the 100th U.S. Congress to place various restrictions on takeovers was not passed.

Airline Deregulation. The 1978 Airline Deregulation Act, which ended U.S. government control over airline fares and routes, was designed to bring competition and lower fares. But ten years after the act was signed into law by President Jimmy Carter, chaos reigned. To begin with, the cost of air travel no longer had anything to do with how many miles one flew. For example, in October 1988 the round-trip fare from Pittsburgh to London with certain restrictions was $298, while the cost of flying round trip from Pittsburgh to Washington, DC, without any restrictions was $230. If one lives at the right place and can fly at the right time, there were real bargains; otherwise, high fares prevailed. That trend has become increasingly pronounced as individual airlines have accounted for a growing percentage of flights at specific "hub" airports—another development since decontrol. The most extensive restructuring of airline fares in a decade went into effect in November. The airlines eliminated the three-to-seven-day advance-purchase fares used mostly by business travelers, and increased the lowest and most widely used discount fares, the Maxsavers, by an average of about 8%. All in all, a decade of air travel without strict government controls has created unprecedented congestion at airports, increasing concern about aviation safety, a decline in services, and a virtual end to entrepreneurship in the aviation industry.

Business Frauds. A number of major U.S. companies and their executives were indicted for, or convicted of, criminal fraud during 1988 (*see also* CONSUMER AFFAIRS and CRIME). Sunstrand was fined $127.3 million for procurement fraud in contracts with the U.S. Department of Defense, and it was suspended as a government contractor. The fine was the largest ever levied against a U.S. defense contractor. A federal jury ruled that the three Hunt brothers were required to pay more than $130 million in damages for conspiring to corner the world's silver market in 1979 and 1980. The Eastman Kodak Company began to disburse $200 million to an estimated 3.4 million people who bought its instant-picture cameras from 1976 to 1986; Kodak had announced in 1986 that it would no longer produce film for those cameras because it had been found guilty of violating patents of the Polaroid Corporation.

Employee Benefits. The continuing escalation in the cost of employee benefits caused considerable concern in the U.S. business community during 1988. Certain benefits, such as Social Security, workmen's compensation, and unemployment compensation are paid out on a continuing basis, but retiree health- and life-insurance benefits represent substantial future obligations. For example, General Motors' retiree health- and life-insurance obligation of $280 million represented 23% of its net income of $3.55 billion in 1987. The Financial Accounting Standards Board, the private-sector institution to which the U.S. Securities and Exchange Commission has delegated the responsibility of establishing standards for financial reporting, presented new proposals in 1988 that could require the nation's largest companies to add as much as $2 trillion in new obligations to their financial statements to cover retiree health- and life-insurance obligations. (*See also* special report, page 318.)

Names in the News. Ira C. Herbert was named president of Coca-Cola Company. The Du Pont Company named Edgar S. Woolard, Jr., as its new chairman and chief executive officer. Ralph S. Larsen was named Johnson & Johnson's new chief executive officer.

In a major product promotion, Steven Jobs unveiled his first new computer since he was forced out of the Apple organization in 1985. His new company brought out NeXT, a sleek, black computer system developed for the education market. Its ability to perform complex financial calculations and facilitate industrial-design tasks also was expected to impress the business market.

See also STOCKS AND BONDS; UNITED STATES—*The Economy*.

STEWART M. LEE, *Geneva College*

CALIFORNIA

The November 1988 election set campaign-expense records in California, and the state suffered through a second season of severely dry weather.

The Election. The ratio of California's Democrats to Republicans in the U.S. Congress remained the same following the November general election. Republican incumbent Pete Wilson of San Diego defeated challenger Leo McCarthy of San Francisco in the most expensive U.S. Senate contest in the state's history. In the U.S. House of Representatives, California's Democratic delegation retained its 27–18 edge over the Republicans. The state legislature retained a Democratic majority in both houses. Speaker Willie Brown of San Francisco fought off a challenge from both Republicans and dissident moderate Democrats to retain his office. The Bush-Quayle ticket won the state's 47 electoral votes.

The election also produced the longest ballot since 1922, involving 29 propositions. The total dollars spent on five measures regarding auto insurance, only one of which passed, also set a spending record on ballot issues. The approved initiative, requiring rate reduction on all property and casualty insurance, was challenged in the state Supreme Court by the insurance industry.

Voters approved nine measures obligating the state for $6 billion in principal and interest for bonds to pay for classrooms, libraries, prisons, and water systems, plus another $5.9 billion for water-plant and housing programs. Another measure guaranteed a minimum appropriation to schools, which also would receive any annual surplus in the general fund.

An initiative was approved requiring testing for AIDS and other communicable diseases of persons charged with certain cases of sexual assaults, but another proposal requiring doctors to report persons possibly exposed to the AIDS virus to local health officials was rejected by a 2 to 1 majority. Legislators had been anxious throughout 1988 to pass legislation relative to AIDS, but Gov. George Deukmejian vetoed four bills which, he said, duplicated existing state or federal programs.

Growth Control. Slow growth advocates, who were in full cry in 1987, suffered serious defeats at the polls in 1988, especially in fast-growing Orange, Riverside, and San Diego counties. Developers and builders spent heavily to oppose control measures, but the public also seemed unimpressed by results to date. Around the state, only 15 of 32 measures passed, while 15 of 17 were passed in 1987. Several measures to control oil drilling or facilities construction were approved, however.

Celebrity Mayors. Sonny Bono, 53, singer and entertainer, was elected mayor of Palm Springs in a landslide. His platform called for bringing more business to the wealthy winter-resort city. Clint Eastwood, mayor of Carmel, chose not to run for a second term.

Nuclear Power. In March the Nuclear Regulatory Commission voted, 5-0, to allow the re-starting of the Rancho Seco nuclear-power plant near Sacramento, closed since 1985 to meet new safety regulations. Area voters rejected a proposal to close the plant permanently and instead supported an 18-month trial operation.

Higher Education. To meet enrollment projections, the University of California announced plans to add three new campuses to the present nine in the next 12 years. The plans would require regental and legislative approval, and controversy was expected as to locations and the possibility of expanding, instead, existing campuses. The California State University trustees approved a 20th campus for that system at San Marcos.

Environment, Weather, Geology. After a two-year effort and under strong federal pressure, the legislature adopted a measure requiring local agencies to reduce smog pollution by 5% a year, or have a state agency take over the task until federal air standards were met. A second act would raise standards of the vehicle inspection program. While the package complied with federal demands, there was skepticism as to whether the goals were realistic.

Most of the state experienced the second year of below-average rainfall, including the area of the Sierra Nevada, from which the state's three largest urban areas receive much of their water. Only mild water-saving rules, however, were considered necessary.

Late in the year, geologists discovered two major faults deep below some of the most developed areas of metropolitan Los Angeles, apparently increasing the risk of earthquakes.

CHARLES R. ADRIAN
University of California, Riverside

CALIFORNIA · Information Highlights

Area: 158,706 sq mi (411 049 km²).
Population (July 1, 1987): 27,663,000.
Chief Cities (July 1, 1986 est.): Sacramento, the capital, 323,550; Los Angeles, 3,259,000; San Diego, 1,015,000; San Francisco, 749,000; San Jose, 712,080; Long Beach, 396,280; Oakland, 356,960.
Government (1988): *Chief Officers*—governor, George Deukmejian (R); lt. gov., Leo McCarthy (D). *Legislature*—Senate, 40 members; Assembly, 80 members.
State Finances (fiscal year 1987): *Revenue,* $70,336,000,000; *expenditure,* $62,481,000,000.
Personal Income (1987): $492,989,000,000; per capita, $17,821.
Labor Force (June 1988): *Civilian labor force,* 14,175,700; *unemployed,* 770,600 (5.4% of total force).
Education: *Enrollment* (fall 1986)—public elementary schools, 3,045,684; public secondary, 1,332,305; colleges and universities, 1,733,554. *Public school expenditures* (1986–87), $16,130,-000,000 ($3,751 per pupil).

Cambodia's Defense Minister Koy Buntha (right) and Gen. Le Ngoc Hien (left), the head of Vietnamese forces in Cambodia, offer a salute during June 30 ceremonies in Phnom Penh marking the departure of 300 Vietnamese officers. Their removal was part of Vietnam's plan to withdraw 50,000 troops by year's end.

AP/Wide World

CAMBODIA

A pattern of diplomatic and military stalemate began to change in 1988, after ten years of Vietnamese occupation of Cambodia. During the early months of the year, the Vietnamese did not mount their usual dry season offensive against the resistance. In addition, Prince Norodom Sihanouk, leader of the resistance, held his second meeting with Hun Sen, head of the Vietnamese-backed Phnom Penh regime. Vietnam announced it would withdraw 50,000 of its 120,000 troops from Cambodia, and in December it claimed to have done so.

Meanwhile, in July, leaders of the four Cambodian factions—the regime, the non-Communist Sihanouk group, the Communist Khmer Rouge, and the non-Communist Khmer Rouge National Liberation Front—met in Jakarta, Indonesia, with representatives of eight Southeast Asian nations. The meeting seemed to reflect a growing desire on the part of most of the parties to end the conflict and reestablish a nonaligned Cambodia.

Politics. After the Jakarta conference, Sihanouk announced that he would meet again with Hun Sen. Stating that he and Hun Sen could form the nucleus of a new nonaligned government, Sihanouk pointed out that his own forces (fewer than 15,000) combined with those of Hun Sen (about 40,000) would far outnumber the Khmer Rouge Resistance, who had about 25,000 troops. China was supporting the Khmer Rouge because they were a useful weapon against Vietnam.

Sihanouk's public statements throughout the year indicated that he believed Vietnam really wanted a neutral, nonaligned Cambodia to be formed. He said he considered the Khmer Rouge the main stumbling block to such a solution. He plainly had not forgiven the Khmer Rouge for their reign of terror in the 1970s, in which they are believed to have massacred up to one million Cambodians, including members of Sihanouk's own family. Nor had he forgiven them for their repeated clashes with his own resistance group in the 1980s. Sihanouk also expressed growing contempt for the other non-Communist resistance group led by his former minister, Son Sann.

Economics. Having barely scraped through a major drought in 1987, the Cambodian people faced another very difficult year in 1988. Preliminary estimates indicated that rice and other food crops would be only a little better than in 1987. The Phnom Penh regime seemed to be learning to manage the economy more effectively, but without foreign aid and an active smuggling trade with Thailand, there still would be major shortages of almost everything.

Ten years of Soviet and Vietnamese aid had restored only partially the modest industrial base that was built before 1970 and then destroyed in subsequent wars. In 1988 the resistance groups continued to threaten roads and railroad lines in many provinces. The government was banking heavily on restoring the once prosperous rubber plantations.

Foreign Relations. In October, Prince Sihanouk met with President Reagan in Washington DC. On November 3, the United Nations General Assembly passed a resolution calling for the withdrawal of foreign troops from Cambodia and "no return to practices of the past." This was understood to refer to the Khmer Rouge dictatorship of the 1970s. Meanwhile, China sought to make their Khmer Rouge clients more acceptable as partners in a coalition government by offering to have the most feared Khmer Rouge leaders retire to China.

PETER A. POOLE
Author, "Eight Presidents and Indochina"

CAMBODIA • Information Highlights

Official Name: Cambodia.
Location: Southeast Asia.
Area: 69,900 sq mi (181 040 km²).
Population (mid-1988 est.): 6,700,000.
Chief City (1986 est.): Phnom Penh, the capital, 700,000.
Government: *Head of state,* Heng Samrin (took office 1979). *Head of government,* Hun Sen, prime minister (took office Jan. 1985).
Monetary Unit: Riel (4 riels equal U.S.$1, 1984).

CANADA

For Canadians, 1988 was a year of surprises, some of them pleasant. The Canadian economy performed better than that of any other major economic power. The Calgary Winter Olympics were a success; the Seoul Summer Olympics brought Canada unexpected humiliation. The Conservatives, seemingly doomed in 1987, won an almost unprecedented second mandate that guaranteed that Canada's economy would be governed by a comprehensive trade agreement with the United States. To many Canadians, this made 1988 a watershed year in their country's history.

Free Trade. The Canada-U.S. Trade Agreement, initialed on Oct. 4, 1987, was signed at separate sites by President Ronald Reagan and Prime Minister Brian Mulroney on Jan. 2, 1988. The agreement promised a ten-year transition to the elimination of all tariffs between the adjoining economies, including free access for U.S. financial and service industries and U.S. markets for Canadian natural resources. During the transition, both countries would continue to negotiate the elimination of remaining restrictions that one side or the other considered to be an unfair trading advantage.

The signatures were sufficient ratification for Canada, though the U.S. Congress, operating under its prearranged "fast-track" procedure, needed only short debates to produce huge majorities to ratify the agreement. In Canada, parliamentary debate was limited to the legislation required for implementing the treaty. Mulroney's Conservative government could muster backing from most business groups, seven provinces (eight after Conservatives defeated Manitoba's New Democratic Party, or NDP, regime) and most privately owned media. Ontario, Prince Edward Island, the Liberals and the NDP, organized labor, most farm groups, and about half the population were opposed. Supporters promised easier access to U.S. markets, opportunities for vigorous entrepreneurs, and a gust of healthy U.S. competition. They also argued that the deal gave Canada its only safe haven in a world of protectionist trading blocs.

Opponents warned of loss of sovereignty, the threat to social and regional development programs that would be labeled unfair by U.S. interests, and the certainty that the United States would not have accepted a deal that would increase Canada's trade surplus. With the agreement, opponents argued, U.S. parent firms would have no reason to keep branch plants or jobs north of the border. Nor would the Canada-U.S. Auto Pact survive the erosion of its safeguard clauses.

Mulroney's huge House of Commons majority flattened Liberal and NDP opposition to the 123 pages of free-trade legislation, allowing only five days of debate and voting 177 to 64 in favor at the end of August. Liberal opposition leader John Turner threatened a roadblock in the Liberal-dominated Senate of Canada, a tactic Mulroney denounced as undemocratic since Canadian senators are appointed. Pollsters, however, found that most voters wanted an election on the issue.

Preelection Politics. Getting ready for an election dominated the 1988 political agenda, although Mulroney was not required legally to call an election until September 1989. Canada's parliaments can run five years, but only fear of defeat would drive a prime minister to wait past

THE CANADIAN MINISTRY

M. Brian Mulroney, prime minister
Harvie Andre, minister of consumer and corporate affairs
Henry Perrin Beatty, minister of national defence and acting solicitor general of Canada
Pierre Blais, minister of state for agriculture
Benoît Bouchard, minister of transport
Lucien Bouchard, secretary of state of Canada and acting minister of the environment
Pierre Cadieux, minister of labour
Jean Charest, minister of state for youth and fitness and amateur sport
Joseph Clark, secretary of state for external affairs and acting minister of justice and attorney general of Canada
John C. Crosbie, minister for international trade
Robert R. de Cotret, minister of regional industrial expansion and minister of state for science and technology
Paul W. Dick, associate minister of national defence
Jake Epp, minister of national health and welfare
Tom Hockin, minister of state for finance
Otto J. Jelinek, minister of supply and services and acting minister of public works
Monique Landry, minister for external relations
Douglas Lewis, minister of state for Treasury Board and acting president of Treasury Board
Elmer M. MacKay, minister of national revenue
Shirley Martin, minister of state for transport
Marcel Masse, minister of energy, mines, and resources
Charles J. Mayer, minister of state for grains and oilseeds
Donald F. Mazankowski, deputy prime minister, government house leader and president of Privy Council for Canada and minister of agriculture
John McDermid, minister of state for international trade and minister of state for housing
Barbara J. McDougall, minister of employment and immigration
William H. McKnight, minister of Indian affairs and northern development and minister of western economic diversification
Gerald S. Merrithew, minister of veterans affairs and minister for the purposes of the Atlantic Canada Opportunities Agency Act
Lowell Murray, leader of the government in the Senate and minister of state for federal-provincial relations and acting minister of communications
Frank Oberle, minister of state for science and technology and acting minister of state for forestry
Thomas E. Siddon, minister of fisheries and oceans
Bernard Valcourt, minister of state for small business and tourism and Indian affairs and northern development
Monique Vézina, minister of state for employment and immigration and minister of state for seniors
Gerald Weiner, minister of state for multiculturalism and citizenship
Michael H. Wilson, minister of finance

Canapress Photo

Opponents of Canada's free-trade agreement with the United States—an issue that prompted national elections—demonstrate in the streets of Ontario. The opposition parties, organized labor, farm groups, and others all were against the pact.

the fourth year. Mulroney was entitled to be afraid: His Progressive Conservatives (PCs) had run a poor third in opinion polls taken well into early 1988, and the year began with fresh scandals affecting cabinet ministers Marcel Masse and Michel Côté. The latter, heavily indebted to firms doing business with the government, swiftly resigned.

However, times had changed. The prime minister's office, now supervised by civil servant Derek Burney, managed the crises skillfully. Deputy Prime Minister Don Mazankowski, shrewd and likable, took over day-to-day management of the government and House of Commons, and the prime minister was free to travel Canada and the world. The media seemed embarrassed to be muckraking, and public opinion showed more indifference to scandals than before.

The government suddenly seemed to have a full program of its own making: election reform, antipornography legislation, a $4 billion program for day-care, reinforcement of official bilingualism and multiculturalism, and the privatization of Air Canada, the big state-owned flag carrier. While each item provoked noisy and prolonged debate, the Conservatives now controlled the political agenda.

It was the Liberals' turn for trouble. Reconfirmed as leader in 1986, John Turner lagged far behind his party in popularity, and his antifree-trade stand—condemned by the business community—made it tough to wipe out the Liberals' $4 million debt or to raise a $10 million campaign fund. In April a Montreal-based attempt by former supporters to oust him failed.

So did a rebel movement in his own caucus. Liberal fortunes slumped, especially in the traditional party stronghold of Quebec. French Canada, once deeply protectionist, had been persuaded that U.S. markets could be conquered easily while language would be a sufficient barrier to the pervasive American culture. Robert Bourassa, Quebec's Liberal premier, shared free-trade views and many other political ideas with Prime Minister Mulroney. Turner's support for the government's 1987 Meech Lake package of constitutional reforms, heavily favored by Bourassa, was neutralized by noisy Liberal opposition in Manitoba and New Brunswick. While Liberals everywhere were in trouble, in Quebec, the province they had swept in 1980, they appeared to be utterly eclipsed by the Mulroney-Bourassa coalition.

Though Ed Broadbent's New Democratic Party kept out of trouble and moderated its unpopular opposition to the North Atlantic Treaty Organization (NATO), the NDP lost more ground than the Liberals, especially as its burst of Quebec support in 1987 collapsed in the face of Mulroney's invigorated, pro-free-trade policy. By summer 1988, the NDP was back in its usual third place, falling from 40% in the polls to 25% in a year. Defeat of the NDP government by the PCs in Manitoba on April 26, after a voter revolt against high auto-insurance premiums, was a factor.

By summer, the PCs were close behind the Liberals in the polls. On June 20 the Conservatives easily won a by-election in Lac St-Jean, Quebec. Lucien Bouchard, a former Quebec

Four weeks before the November 21 elections, Liberal leader John Turner (below, at left) scored a major success in a televised debate with Conservative Prime Minister Brian Mulroney, breaking the campaign wide open. The New Democratic Party of Ed Broadbent (corner below) trailed badly. In Quebec (right), traditionally a Liberal stronghold, proponents of free trade restored the Conservative momentum—ultimately leading to a big victory on Election Day.

© Jim Merrithew/Picture Group

Canapress Photo

© Richard Hartmier

separatist and Mulroney's ambassador to France, campaigned as "M. Net" (Mr. Clean), but $4 million in campaign promises influenced the results—as did the issues: Meech Lake and free trade. On September 6, Nova Scotia voters confirmed federal PC popularity by reelecting narrowly a scandal-plagued Conservative provincial government. Being a Tory was no longer a burden.

Parliament, in session since August 1987, wrestled inconclusively with day-care, abortion, immigration, and excessive bank charges —and more decisively with free trade. Meanwhile, the prime minister was free to tour the country, announcing grants for AIDS research, cleanup of the St. Lawrence River, a park for Toronto, and other preelection benefits ranging from $900,000 for the ethnic media to $400 million for a heavy oil-upgrader at Lloydminster on the Saskatchewan-Alberta border. The biggest single item in a $12 billion preelection list was $3.2 billion to reopen Hibernia, Newfoundland's high-cost offshore oil develop-

CANADIAN GENERAL ELECTIONS						
Party	**Seats**			**% Popular Vote**		
	1980	**1984**	**1988**	**1980**	**1984**	**1988**
PC	103	211	170	33	50	43
LIB	147	40	82	44	28	32
NDP	32	30	43	20	18	20
Other	—	1	—	3	4	5
TOTAL	282	282	295	100	100	100

ment. Pushed by the U.S. example, Ottawa ended five years of negotiations with Japanese-Canadians interned during World War II: The government tendered an apology and $291 million in compensation, including $21,000 for each surviving internee. Other groups promptly surfaced to demand compensation for their historic grievances.

While imminent elections allegedly had nothing to do with this government activity, they coincided with a dramatic improvement in Conservative popularity.

Election 1988. On October 1 the prime minister asked Governor-General Jeanne Sauvé to issue writs for Canada's 34th federal election on November 21. Polls showed the Tories well ahead in public support, with few voters undecided and the Liberals and NDP battling for second place. The prime minister, however, had to shepherd his volatile majority through seven weeks of campaigning. For the first month, Mulroney's handlers "low-bridged" the prime minister, keeping him from spontaneous contact with voters or the media. Liberal John Turner, in contrast, fought as an underdog, risking everything on impromptu and occasionally accident-prone contact with the public. The NDP, waging a nationwide campaign for the first time, relied on Ed Broadbent's popularity and political experience.

On October 24 and 25, the ritual of leaders jetting to media events was interrupted by three-hour television debates in French and English. In French, Turner scored the most points, though no leader shone in his second language. The English-language debate on the second night broke the campaign open. An aggressive John Turner seized on the free-trade agreement and proclaimed it as a threat to Canada's identity as a nation. Mulroney was thrown on the defensive, and Broadbent was eclipsed. Post-debate polls showed Liberal fortunes soaring. Support for the free-trade agreement fell.

Across much of Canada, the free-trade issue turned the campaign into a referendum. By forcing the networks to schedule the debates a month before the election, however, the Conservatives had time to mobilize a counterattack. Business allies and free-trade enthusiasts flooded the media. Emmett Hall, a retired judge and architect of Medicare, rejected Liberal and NDP claims that social programs were at risk. Simon Reisman, Canada's free-trade negotiator, called Turner a traitor. Lucien Bouchard led a chorus of Quebec voices claiming that Ontario opponents to free trade were trying to deny prosperity to French Canada. Under the barrage, Conservative fortunes and free-trade support both recovered. In an election of apparently violent swings of opinion, the Conservatives emerged on election eve with their momentum restored, while John Turner had established his party as the main vehicle for antifree-trade sentiment.

New electoral boundaries and more constituencies—295 instead of 282—favored the Conservatives. So did business, the stock market, and an improving economy.

Election day, Monday, November 21, ended with the Conservatives holding 170 seats, the Liberals 82, and the NDP 43. Liberals gained in Atlantic Canada and Manitoba; the Conservatives swept Quebec and dominated a supposedly antifree-trade Ontario. The NDP, once again denied a breakthrough, gained in the West to win more seats than ever in its history.

For Brian Mulroney, it was a historic triumph: He was the first prime minister since 1953 to win a consecutive majority and the first Conservative since 1891 to do so. A renewed mandate would allow the Conservatives to put a more enduring stamp on Canada through key appointments to the Supreme Court, the Canadian Broadcasting Corporation, and other bodies. The government would be free to buy nuclear submarines, impose a national sales tax, privatize Canada's crown enterprises, and, above all, to lay out the "level playing field" of the Canada-U.S. trade agreement, which was approved at year's end.

External Affairs and Defense. Politics also affected Canadian defense and foreign policy more than usual in 1988. An apparent swing in Canadian sympathy toward Arabs justified tough talk to Israel about its management of the occupied territories. A government accused earlier of truckling to France in an Atlantic fishing dispute seized French trawlers and made harsh noises. At the United Nations, Canada scolded South Africa for its racial policies, though the government stopped short of further sanctions. The annual Mulroney-Reagan meeting, in April, was disappointing, producing nothing from the lame-duck president but a promise to look again at the issue of acid rain. The seven-nation economic summit, held in Toronto in June, occurred as Canada sustained a healthy economy. Stephen Lewis, a former NDP activist who had improved Canada's Third World links, was replaced as UN ambassador by a former Liberal and Mulroney friend, Yves Fortier, in August. Another former Liberal and early architect of the free-trade initiative, Donald S. MacDonald, went to London as high commissioner to the United Kingdom.

While the vigorous rearmament plans proposed in the 1987 defense policy paper seemed a little anachronistic to the peace-minded in a new era of world détente, distributing contracts was good politics. At Saint John, N.B., in May, Mrs. Mila Mulroney helped launch HMCS *Halifax,* the first new Canadian warship in 17 years. Earlier, the prime minister announced plans to double the frigate program to 12. The additional ships also would be built at K. C. Irving's Saint John Dry Dock. West Coast shipyards shared a minesweeper contract. A Calgary firm contracted to build 820 all-terrain troop carriers (at double the price of the Swedish originals). New rifles, trucks, radios, antisubmarine helicopters, and antiaircraft weapons promised contracts, jobs, and political gratitude. On the other hand, resistance from U.S. officials and from disarmament groups repeatedly delayed a decision on whether an $8 billion nuclear-powered submarine contract would go to French or British consortia.

Prime Minister Mulroney signed a treaty-in-principle on September 5 guaranteeing compensation, land rights, and political power to the Dene Indians and Métis (mixed-blood people) of the Mackenzie Valley in the Northwest Territories. Other native groups also pressed claims.

Canapress Photo

World peace and Canadian pride both were served in August by dispatch of a 499-member Canadian signals and service unit as part of the UN peacekeeping operation on the Iran-Iraq border. By the end of the year, most of the troops were safely home. Recognition of UN peacekeepers through the 1988 Nobel Peace Prize reminded Canadians that they had shared in 15 UN missions from Kashmir to Cyprus and that 78 Canadian soldiers had died.

Laws and Constitution. Armed by the 1982 Charter of Rights and Freedoms, the Supreme Court ruled 5-2 in January that Canada's abortion law was too restrictive, vindicating Dr. Henry Morgentaler after his 20-year struggle for abortion on demand. Attempts to find a new compromise failed in the House of Commons when all three choices offered by the government were rejected. The antiabortion position was defeated 118-105, with 23 women members of Parliament (MPs) united with Liberals and New Democrats. The Supreme Court also upheld pre-1905 federal laws guaranteeing francophone rights in Alberta and Saskatchewan, though both provinces took up the court's invitation to enact their own, more restrictive legislation. Quebec's Premier Bourassa, sensitive to court challenges to his own province's laws restricting English, endorsed these new laws to the indignation of prairie francophones.

Native groups blockaded roads, bridges, and an air force runway at Goose Bay to focus attention on their claims to compensation, land, and political power. In May the Dene Indians and Métis (mixed-bloods) of the Mackenzie Valley won their settlement: 15,000 people would share $500 million, full rights over 3,900 sq mi (10 100 km²), surface rights over 68,000 sq mi (176 120 km²), and a share of royalties from resource development. In October, Alberta's Lubicon band forced the government to promise a land reserve by proclaiming independence from Canada.

In February, Svend Robinson, an NDP MP from British Columbia, became the first member of Parliament to publicly proclaim his homosexuality. He was reelected in November. Efforts by the United Church, Canada's biggest Protestant denomination, to allow ordination of gay clergy, led to a favorable compromise in Victoria, B.C., in August, but

---

CANADA · Information Highlights

Official Name: Canada.
Location: Northern North America.
Area: 3,851,792 sq mi (9 976 140 km²).
Population (mid-1988 est.): 26,100,000.
Chief Cities (1986 census): Ottawa, the capital, 300,763; Montreal, 1,015,420; Toronto, 612,289.
Government: *Head of state,* Elizabeth II, queen; represented by Jeanne Sauvé, governor-general (took office May 14, 1984). *Head of government,* M. Brian Mulroney, prime minister (took office Sept. 17, 1984). *Legislature*—Parliament: Senate and House of Commons.
Monetary Unit: Canadian dollar (1.2001 dollars equal U.S.$1, Dec. 7, 1988).
Gross Domestic Product (1987 U.S.$): $412,800,-000,000.
Economic Index: *Consumer Prices* (1987, 1980 = 100), all items, 155.5; food, 147.5.
Foreign Trade (1987 U.S.$); *Imports,* $87,578,-000,000; *exports,* $94,402,000,000.

the controversy raged unabated among the United Church's congregations. Few other denominations wanted to consider the issue.

People and Diversions. For Canadians fed up with politics, house prices, and the weather, spectator sports were a major diversion in 1988. Weather endangered the Calgary Winter Olympics with high winds and low snowfall, but there were few hitches in the two-week spectacle. As usual, Canada's high medal hopes were dashed. Brian Orser had to settle for silver in men's figure skating, but second place in the women's competition, behind the incomparable East German Katarina Witt, was a triumph for Ottawa's Elizabeth Manley. Calgary also realized $32 million in profits from games that were as commercialized as they were efficient.

Propelled by "the Great One," Wayne Gretzky, the Edmonton Oilers ended the hockey season with the usual Stanley Cup. Gretzky's marriage to Hollywood starlet Janet Jones gave Edmonton a near-royal wedding on July 16 but only a month later the hockey star had been traded to the Los Angeles Kings for a reputed $16 million. Trading an aging star was a smart move for Oilers' owner Peter Pockling-ton, but it was a hard blow to national pride. (*See* page 85.)

A harder blow came at the Seoul Olympics when sprinter Ben Johnson's 9.79-second victory in the 100-meter race was disallowed because evidence of extensive steroid use was found in his urine. Furious faultfinding and denials led to the appointment of Charles Dubin, an Ontario judge, to head a federal royal commission to study drug use by athletes, and overshadowed gold-medal performances by Lennox Lewis in superheavyweight boxing and by Carolyn Waldo and Michelle Cameron in synchronized swimming.

DESMOND MORTON
Erindale College, University of Toronto

The Economy

During 1988 the Canadian economy, in its sixth year of expansion, was growing at an estimated annual rate of 4.4%. Growth was posted in all parts of the country except Manitoba and Saskatchewan, where severe drought had forced the provincial economies into contraction.

Expansion in domestic consumption, foreign trade, and capital investment helped fuel the growth. By midyear the level of total real spending by individuals and businesses had increased by 3.5%. Retail sales in August grew for the fourth consecutive month, up by 5% from July. Sales for department stores were up 2.3%, grocery, confectionary, and sundry stores up 1.8%, and used cars up 10.2%. Simultaneous expansion of foreign trade gave further stimulus to total demand. In July, Canada's trade surplus soared to $1.9 billion, the highest since October 1985. By August, trade had expanded further as exports led by autos, metals, and alloys rose to $12.3 billion, $1.3 billion higher than in July. In the meantime, despite the higher imports of capital goods and automobiles, the overall trade surplus for the first eight months remained at $7.7 billion, close to the $8.0 billion of a year earlier.

Manufacturing firms increased their production to meet the surging domestic and foreign demand for goods. The value of their monthly factory shipments, having reached the peak value of $26 billion by March, the highest since August 1987, settled at $24 billion by August 1988. The monthly ratio of inventories to shipments, which peaked in July, also declined in August. New orders, after two months of decline, posted a 2.7% increase in August while the backlog of unfilled orders rose by .5%. In addition, expansion in corporate profit margins due to a sharp run-up in the prices of industrial materials, particularly pulp, paper, and metal, caused many firms to launch capital projects.

The Labor Market and Inflation. The boisterousness of the economy was reflected aptly by the Canadian labor market. In September alone 62,000 additional jobs were created in the community, business, and personal-services sector, while an extra 41,000 workers were absorbed by the construction industry. Some sluggishness, however, was apparent in the trade sector where employment dropped by 24,000, while another 16,000 workers were laid off in transportation, communication, and utility enterprises. Yet the country's overall unemployment rate for September was 7.8%, marginally up from a seven-year low of 7.6% in June.

Unionized workers were taking fatter pay pockets. In Ontario, wages rose 5.6% in the second quarter while the national annual average wage was up 4.5%. This partly confirmed the fears of the Bank of Canada about wage-price pressure on the economy. Late in the year the projected rate of increase in the consumer price index was revised to 4.0% from 3.8% forecast in May 1988. The Bank of Canada's response to this threat of inflation pushed the prime lending rate to 11.25% in August, the highest in two years. This was expected to have an adverse effect on overall consumer demand, especially in such interest-sensitive sectors as autos, household appliances, and housing.

Housing. Residential construction, in general, was on the wane. In the first eight months of 1988, housing starts averaged 217,500 units, down 13.4% from 215,125 in the same period a year earlier. September housing starts were down further to 208,000 from 219,000 in August.

R. P. SETH
Mount Saint Vincent University

Canapress Photo

The spectacular new National Art Gallery of Canada, located on Ottawa's Nepean Point, opened in May. The C$117 million, three-story facility was expected to admit 750,000 visitors in 1988, triple the number of visitors to the old building.

The Arts

Communications Minister Flora MacDonald announced in April that the Canadian Broadcasting Corporation (CBC) would get a new C$380 million broadcast center in Toronto to replace the 24 different facilities it currently was using. Construction began in October and was scheduled to finish in 1992. MacDonald also sought to increase government funding of CBC to allow for increased Canadian TV programming. She proposed financial rewards for private stations that exceeded their quota of Canadian content and financial penalties for those that fell short. But artists, whose biggest employer is CBC, wondered what effects both inflation and the November general election would have on any plans. A major undertaking by CBC was its C$11.2 million TV miniseries, *Chasing Rainbows,* in seven two-hour episodes that took 18 months to film. A romantic comedy set in 1917–22, it was written by Douglas Bowie and produced by Mark Blandford.

Visual Arts. In Ottawa, the striking new C$117 million National Art Gallery of Canada building was opened in May. Designed by architect Moshe Safdie (*see* BIOGRAPHY), it has room to store or exhibit 40,000 works. Its inaugural international exhibition was "Degas," the first retrospective of that artist in 50 years. The new museum also mounted "Master Drawings from the National Gallery of Canada" which had opened first at the Vancouver Art Gallery. A cooperative effort by the national galleries of Ottawa and Washington, the show included some 100 drawings by such European masters as Rembrandt and Van Gogh.

The Art Gallery of Ontario exhibited 50 works by Hans Holbein, all borrowed from the collection of Britain's Queen Elizabeth II. The same gallery showed 104 works by U.S. artist

Ellsworth Kelly and mounted "Phenomena," 41 paintings by Paterson Ewen which then went on tour. A second Ewen show, "Paterson Ewen: the Montreal Years," opened at the Mendel Art Gallery in Saskatoon and then traveled to three other cities. "Looking for Bianca Cappello," a collection of Jennifer Dickson's paintings and photographs, originated in Toronto. "Treasures of the Holy Land," at the Royal Ontario Museum, included the Dead Sea Scrolls.

Calgary's Winter Olympics Arts Festival included an exhibition of native Indian works called "The Spirit Sings: Artistic Traditions of Canada's First Peoples." Some of the artifacts dated from the 16th century. "The Expressionist Landscape," a major exhibition of landscape painting by leading North American avant-garde artists from 1920 to 1947, originated in Birmingham, AL, and then moved to the Vancouver Art Gallery. The focus of the exhibition was British Columbia artist Emily Carr. The Vancouver gallery also showed another B.C. artist, in "Ian Wallace: Selected Works 1969–1987."

Performing Arts. The death and rebirth of the 59-year-old Vancouver Symphony Orchestra made headlines in 1988. In February the 84 musicians were told that the orchestra would be disbanded because of accumulated debts of C$1.7 million. A few days later they played their final concert, many of them ending in tears. Public support had been slipping, and conductor Rudolph Barshai had not proved popular; his contract had not been renewed. At a meeting in Montreal, the Association of Canadian Orchestras discussed the financial problems at the Vancouver Symphony and warned of others, but it showed optimism about possible cures. In May the orchestra's creditors agreed to forgive what they were owed, and

members of the Vancouver Symphony Society voted overwhelmingly to try to revive the orchestra. A new five-year contract was signed with the musicians, and Peter McCoppin, who was named music adviser and conductor, planned a new season. Each performance would fall into one of four categories: "Masterworks" for standard symphonies, "Musica Viva" for contemporary works and little-known classics, "Mostly Mozart," and "Light Classics." Vancouver Mayor Gordon Campbell gave vigorous support as the symphony staged free summer concerts and galas to sell itself to the public. Grants from the city, provincial, and federal governments, combined with brisk ticket sales, guaranteed a new season.

The Stratford (Ont.) Festival—the biggest resident theater company in North America—started its second 35 years with the same two Shakespeare plays, *Richard III* and *All's Well That Ends Well*, that had launched the company in 1953. The 1988 *Richard III,* starring Colm Feore, was directed by Brian Rintoul; *All's Well That Ends Well* was directed by Peter Moss. The Stratford's busy season (13 productions) included two musicals, *Irma La Douce* and *My Fair Lady.* The latter starred the festival's artistic director, John Neville, as Professor Higgins. The former was choreographed and directed by Jeff Hyslop. To mark the centenary of T.S. Eliot's birth, Stratford presented his play *Murder in the Cathedral.* And an unusual but effective double bill saw the pairing of Sophocles' *Oedipus,* starring Stuart Hughes, with Sheridan's *The Critic.* Robin Phillips, who directed both, drew deft parallels between tragedy and comedy. During the summer, the British actor and director David William was named to succeed Neville as the Stratford's artistic director.

The 1988 highlight of Canadian television was the seven-part miniseries "Chasing Rainbows." It was the world's first series shot with high-definition (HDTV) equipment.

© Bruce Macaulay/CBC

The Shaw Festival at Niagara-on-the-Lake, Ont., presented the first revival of Shaw's 50-year-old political fantasy *Geneva.* The festival's artistic director, Christopher Newton, directed the production, with Herb Foster playing Midlander and Wendy Thatcher as Begonia. The season opened with another Shaw play, *You Never Can Tell,* directed by Newton and starring Douglas Rain and Frances Hyland. *Once in a Lifetime,* the 1930 comedy by George S. Kaufman and Moss Hart, received a sparkling rendition, with direction by Duncan McIntosh and starring Tony van Bridge, Dan Lett, and Nora McLellan. Other presentations included J. B. Priestley's *Dangerous Corner,* Harley Granville-Barker's *The Voysey Inheritance, Peter Pan,* and a stage adaptation of Tolstoy's *War and Peace.*

Lotfi Mansouri, director of the Canadian Opera Company in Toronto, resigned after 12 years to direct the San Francisco Opera. The former company gave Canada's first performance of Dmitri Shostakovich's opera *Lady Macbeth of Mtsensk.* The International Opera Festival in Montreal presented a lavish C$7 million production of *Aïda,* featuring a cast of 1,000 and real tigers and elephants. The National Ballet of Canada toured Newfoundland and the Maritime provinces with a company that included Karen Kain and Veronica Tennant. Earl Stafford was the guest conductor. The Anna Wyman Dance Theatre of Vancouver performed at World Expo 88 in Brisbane, Australia. Dancer and choreographer Judith Marcuse took her Vancouver ballet company across Canada with a varied program. And the Royal Winnipeg Ballet toured Jacques Lemay's ballet, *The Big Top.*

Film. Animator Frederic Back of Montreal won his second Hollywood Oscar in the animated short-film category for *The Man Who Planted Trees,* about conservation. Attracting big crowds, Montreal's World Film Festival opened with the world premiere of *Stick,* a South African film about white soldiers attacking blacks. Toronto's Festival of Festivals also drew big crowds and featured director David Cronenberg's horror film *Dead Ringers.* Vancouver's eighth International Film Festival showed more than 130 films from 37 countries. In Ottawa, former CBC Vice-President Pierre DesRoches was named executive director of Telefilm Canada, the federal agency that helps finance TV films. Because of problems with tax laws and with financial difficulties at Telefilm Canada, the federal government postponed its plans for a Canada Film Year. In Ottawa, a film on the artist Degas by Harry Rasky of Toronto was shown at the National Gallery of Canada in conjunction with the "Degas" exhibition there. And the Canadian Centre for Advanced Film Studies, founded by director Norman Jewison, opened in Toronto.

DAVID SAVAGE, *Free-lance Writer*

CARIBBEAN

Caribbean economic integration took a significant step forward in 1988 when the 13 member countries of the Caribbean Economic Community (CARICOM) began dismantling long-standing barriers to intraregional trade.

The 13 member countries of CARICOM, all English-speaking and all but one (Montserrat) independent former British colonies, agreed in July at a summit meeting in Antigua to remove tariff and nontariff barriers to interisland trade, except for 17 products from the smaller countries of the group which might be injured by import competition.

Economic integration has been a goal of CARICOM since its founding in 1973. Over the years, however, free trade within the region has been hampered by the unilateral imposition of import restrictions to protect nascent industries or to conserve foreign exchange reserves.

As a result of the unilateral controls, trade within the community, which has a combined population of 5.5 million, fell from $593.3 million in 1981 to $295 million in 1986. It recovered to $317 million in 1987 and is expected to continue to rise under the free-trade agreement.

CARICOM members include the independent nations of Antigua-Barbuda, the Bahamas, Barbados, Belize, Dominica, Grenada, Guyana, Jamaica, St. Kitts-Nevis, St. Lucia, St. Vincent and the Grenadines, Trinidad and Tobago, and the British crown colony of Montserrat. Cuba, Haiti, the Dominican Republic, and Puerto Rico are not members.

CBI. The U.S.-sponsored Caribbean Basin Initiative (CBI) entered its fifth year of operations to a mixed reception in both the United States and the basin. The CBI, which took effect on Jan. 1, 1984, for a 12-year period, provides duty-free entry to the United States for a broad variety of products made in the Caribbean and Central America.

A study issued in 1988 by the U.S. General Accounting Office (GAO), an arm of the Congress, found that the CBI had helped to foster trade and investment opportunities in the region, but had not generated broad-based economic growth, nor alleviated debt problems or generated lasting employment opportunities.

A second report, published by the U.S. International Trade Commission (ITC) in September, said that despite the duty-free program, U.S. imports from CBI beneficiary countries actually were declining. The ITC reported that the value of U.S. CBI imports fell from $8.8 billion in 1983 to $6.1 billion in 1986 and to $6.0 billion in 1987. In the latter year, U.S. exports to the region reached $6.7 billion, giving the United States a trade surplus with the beneficiary countries. The slump in Caribbean exports to the United States continued through the first half of 1988, falling by 1.2%, compared to the first half of 1987.

In 1988, U.S. legislators tried to extend the life of the CBI beyond its scheduled expiration date of 1995, and to broaden the coverage of products granted duty-free status. The legislation—known as the CBI-II bill—failed to win congressional approval, but the Congress, in an omnibus trade bill signed by President Ronald Reagan in August, declared its belief that the Caribbean Basin was a critical region for the United States and expressed its intent to strengthen the CBI. The trade bill also increased the amount of ethyl alcohol (ethanol) that could be exported duty-free to the United States from the Basin. U.S. farm groups had opposed the ethanol provision.

Economy. The Caribbean economies remained mired in recession and debt problems throughout 1988. The tourism industry and, to a lesser extent, light manufacturing, were bright spots on the economic horizon, but agriculture—especially the sugar industry—continued in decline.

A 1988 study by the Caribbean Tourism Research and Development Center showed that foreign exchange earnings from tourism rose by 60% between 1980 and 1986. Indications are that the trend has continued upward since then. Tourist arrivals in the region were up 6% between May and December of 1988, compared with the same period a year earlier.

Agricultural exports to the United States, on the other hand, plummeted 26% to $1.7 billion in 1987 and in the period from October 1987 to April 1988, fell by 16.8%. The Caribbean sugar industry suffered a sharp setback when the United States cut its sugar import quota for 1988 to the lowest level in more than a century. In September, however, the United States increased the quota by one third to compensate for a sugar-beet crop shortfall due to the U.S. summer drought.

An international donors group of 22 nations coordinated by the World Bank pledged a $3 billion, three-year aid package for the Caribbean in mid-1988, calling the medium-term economic outlook for the Caribbean countries "promising," provided sufficient external assistance was made available.

Drugs. A report by the U.S. Customs Service, published in September, said that 80% of the cocaine that reaches the United States travels on Caribbean routes and that 75% originates in Colombia. The U.S. House Select Committee on Narcotics and Drug Abuse conducted a fact-finding visit to the area in early December.

Under heavy pressure from the United States, many Caribbean governments have increased drug interdiction efforts in recent years. The United States, nonetheless, has been critical of drug-law enforcement in the Caribbean, and U.S. officials have accused some high Caribbean officials, such as Prime Minister Lynden Pindling of the Bahamas, of direct involvement in the drug trade. Pindling

Hurricane "Gilbert" left Jamaica in shambles after striking the island on September 12. Prime Minister Seaga called it "the worst natural disaster in our modern history." Some 500,000 Jamaicans were left homeless, and the banana and poultry industries were wiped out.

AP/Wide World

Jamaica

The most powerful hurricane in recorded history swept across the Caribbean in September 1988, leaving a trail of death and destruction in Jamaica, the Cayman Islands, and Mexico's Yucatán Peninsula.

Hurricane *Gilbert*'s winds reached 155 mi (250 km) per hour, making it a category 5 hurricane, with a record low barometric pressure of 26.13 inches (66.4 cm). The previous low of 26.35 inches (66.9 cm) was recorded in 1935 when a violent storm battered the Florida Keys.

There was widespread damage and destruction in Mexico, but, proportionately, Jamaica bore the brunt of the hurricane. Half a million people—nearly one quarter of the island's population—were left homeless and four out of five structures in Jamaica suffered damage. At least 38 people were killed in the storm. Jamaican officials said that more than $500 million in immediate disaster relief was needed to replace homes, farms, and tourist facilities destroyed by *Gilbert.*

In the wake of the storm, emergency assistance poured into Jamaica from the United States and from neighboring countries. The World Bank and the Inter-American Develop-ment Bank dispatched survey teams to draw up plans for longer-term reconstruction, the cost of which, according to Jamaica's Prime Minister Edward Seaga, could reach as much as $7 billion.

With parliamentary elections due to be held by April 1989, public opinion polls showed Seaga's Jamaica Labor Party (JLP) trailing the opposition Peoples National Party (PNP), led by former Prime Minister Michael Manley, in the contest to control the island's 60-seat legislature.

The economy appeared to be the central issue of the campaign. According to a report issued by the International Monetary Fund (IMF) in August, the Seaga government, following IMF-approved austerity programs, had cut inflation from 25% in 1985 to 7% in 1987. The country recorded real economic growth of 5.5% in 1988. Nontraditional exports reached $285 million, an increase of 65% over 1987, and debt rescheduling helped produce a balance of payments surplus of $190 million.

The austerity programs, however, proved to be unpopular. Sharp cutbacks in central government expenditures erased several thousand jobs, and many Jamaicans said they had seen few benefits from the economic turnaround.

RICHARD C. SCHROEDER

---

called such accusations "imprudent and without foundation." In their July summit meeting in Antigua, Caribbean leaders drafted a letter to President Reagan protesting the "derogation" of the sovereignty of Caribbean nations by U.S. drug officials.

Dominican Republic. President Joaquin Balaguer turned 81 on September 1. Although Balaguer is nearly blind and suffers from various ailments, he remained firmly in control of the government. In June, amid rumors of a coup, he replaced his defense minister, Gen. Antonio Imbert Barrera, with another military man, Gen. Elias Wessin y Wessin.

Balaguer's ambitious public-works projects led to a shortage of cement during the year. The country's chronic energy shortage continued. Tourism emerged as the leading industry, accounting for $570 million in foreign exchange earnings, double the income from the traditional mainstays, sugar, coffee, and cocoa.

See also CUBA; HAITI.

RICHARD C. SCHROEDER
Formerly, "Visión" Magazine

Participants in the March signing of a Nicaraguan cease-fire agreement included (l–r): *Defense Minister Humberto Ortega, President Ortega, João Baena Soares of the OAS, Cardinal Obando, and contra leaders Alfredo Cesar and Adolfo Calero.*

CENTRAL AMERICA

The unraveling of U.S. policy in Central America gathered greater speed in 1988. The turning point in U.S. relations with Central America had occurred in August 1987 when the five Central American presidents met and signed a peace agreement that, in part, stood in opposition to U.S. policy, and the U.S. government would not support it. But by the end of 1988 it would be difficult to determine just what the U.S. Central American policy had become.

Despite six years of effort by the Ronald Reagan administration, the Sandinistas still held power in Nicaragua in 1988. They had been weakened in many ways, but their security scarcely was threatened. Probably no friends were gained for the United States when Colin Powell, U.S. national security adviser, toured Central America warning the governments that they would suffer if they did not help President Reagan win support for the rebel Nicaraguan contras. In February, Congress voted down an administration aid package for the contras. Then, the next month, the contras, probably resigned to the political divisions in Washington, startled their American supporters by signing a cease-fire with the Nicaraguan government. On numerous occasions the two warring factions even met and held peace talks. Failing to get additional military aid for the contras through Congress in 1988, Reagan announced in October that he would leave the issue for the next president.

After years of massive aid from the United States, El Salvador's government barely hung on. The right wing was resurging at the polls despite its inflating record of human-rights violations. President José Napoleón Duarte was stricken with cancer, and just whom the United States should support became a critical question. Although enjoying a troop advantage of ten to one, El Salvador was not eliminating the guerrillas. The economy depended almost exclusively upon the whims of the U.S. government.

The Reagan government spent much of the year trying to drive Manuel Noriega out of Panama; each new attempt merely seemed to make the dictator stronger and more popular at home. (*See* special report, page 176.)

For six years Honduras has carried out faithfully its function as America's "launching pad" in Central America. But the continued presence of thousands of refugees from Nicaragua and elsewhere, plus the arrival of 3,200 more American troops, greatly disturbed the Honduran people.

Even the United States' usually close friendship with Costa Rica was strained when Reagan's contra support conflicted with President Oscar Arias' efforts to restore feelings of pride in Central Americanism.

The Central American debt crisis was aggravated by a quarrel between the United States and members of the Inter American Development Bank (IDB) over voting methods. Specifically, the United States wanted to be able to veto a loan if one other member agreed.

The United States was withholding its substantial contribution until the issue was settled.

Belize

After nearly seven years of independence from Great Britain, Belize finally appeared to be on the road to settling its dispute with Guatemala over matters of sovereignty and boundaries. The Guatemala struggle highlighted the indecision hampering the young nation's growth. At the end of May, commissioners from the two nations, plus British observers, met in Miami for two days of treaty talks. Discussions were held on several later occasions. No details were released, but it was assumed generally that a year might be spent establishing rules for a joint plebiscite. The foreign minister of Belize observed that there would be no territorial cession on his nation's part. The political turmoil in Guatemala could prove the largest obstruction to a prompt settlement.

The opposition People's United Party was generally successful in the March municipal elections, causing the ruling United Democratic Party, led by Prime Minister Manuel Esquivel, to make public its concern for some of its divisions. Major cabinet shifts took place, and a new party paper, *People's Pulse*, appeared.

The prime interest rate, which had been as high as 20% in 1985, was reduced from 12% to 8% on Aug. 1, 1988, in an effort to stimulate investment.

The sugar harvest in 1988 exceeded 1987's by about 11%, but was still only half the potential capacity for lack of investment. Drought in the United States probably accounted for the increase. Cool weather brought citrus production down about 20%. The future of banana marketing looked excellent; a new port was under construction at Big Creek and was to be completed in 1990. This will mean that bananas for the first time can be shipped directly from Belize to Great Britain and not by way of Honduras, greatly increasing the profit potential of the industry. Considering this step, the World Bank was lending more than $5 million to growers to double banana acreage.

Costa Rica

Record numbers of tourists visited Costa Rica in 1988. They found a peaceful and pleasantly comfortable land where even the rural and civil guards, which had replaced the army, had changed to less military-looking navy and gray uniforms. Nonetheless, a large and growing number of economic problems gnawed at the popularity of President Arias Sánchez and even threatened the stability of the nation.

Many thousands of refugees, mostly from Nicaragua, but many from Panama as well, overwhelmed the social services of the state; the pressure of their numbers grew daily. Some of these exiles were Nicaraguan contras who once had used Costa Rica as a base for the reconquest of their country from the Sandinistas.

Other problems were essentially domestic: a 6% currency devaluation, austere tax adjustments, and rising food and utility costs. Shortages of low-cost housing still continued, in spite of President Arias' promise to construct 80,000 units during his term of office. Little progress at all had been made until 1988; con-

Visitors inspect Poás Volcano in central Costa Rica. Increased investment and promotional campaigns have caused an upswing in the nation's tourism industry. A record number of people traveled to the republic during 1988.

Roberto D'Aubuisson, the founder and former leader of El Salvador's rightist Republican National Alliance (ARENA), drew enthusiastic crowds during the 1988 campaign. The ruling Christian Democrats lost major ground to the ARENA in National Assembly and municipal elections in March.

© Ron Kinney/Black Star

struction began to move ahead, but often the homes were too expensive for many of the lower-income groups to buy. Substantial unemployment too often had been attacked by putting large numbers of persons on the government payroll. Over all the other problems hung the $5 billion of foreign debt that would not go away.

Another major concern for the nation was its relations with the United States. Although the State Department denied it, Costa Rica apparently was being punished by Washington for its strict neutrality in the Nicaraguan civil war. U.S. aid dropped from $217 million in 1985 to $180 million in 1987.

Perhaps the largest stumbling block was that Arias' peace plan requires Honduras to give up its role as a staging area and military base for the United States. Previously Arias had refused to grant asylum to former President Ferdinand Marcos of the Philippines and had forced the abandonment of a Central Intelligence Agency (CIA) airstrip in Costa Rica. Arias' measures were well-received internationally and were in line with traditional Costa Rican neutrality, but when they appeared to threaten aid from the United States, some of President Arias' opponents made political capital of them.

Costa Rica has no serious race problem; nevertheless the government was working closely with specialists to preserve and expand the usage of the languages of some 20,000 Indians, members of a dozen ethnic groups. The aim was to restore a pride of "Indianness" to villagers threatened by squatters and lumber interests. Some six ancient languages were still in use; the University of Costa Rica was preparing bilingual materials in such languages as Malecu. Proof of Indian heritage was also important in establishing rights to Indian lands.

El Salvador

The Christian Democrats, President José Napoleón Duarte's ruling party, suffered a stunning defeat by the rightist Republican National Alliance (ARENA) in the March elections. (Voters chose members of the National Assembly as well as municipal officials in more than 200 towns.) In the 60-seat Assembly, ARENA jumped from 13 seats to a slight majority, and the Christian Democrats dropped from 33 to 23. ARENA even captured the mayoralty of the capital city of San Salvador for the first time in more than 20 years.

Instead of Roberto D'Aubuisson, the former leader and founder of ARENA, the party selected Alfredo Cristiani as its presidential candidate for the 1989 elections. Cristiani, who is a graduate of Georgetown University and a wealthy coffee planter, announced that D'Aubuisson would not be in his cabinet.

The Christian Democrats faced another crisis when it was revealed that the president had incurable cancer and might not be able to continue in office. In June, President Duarte went to Washington's Walter Reed Hospital, and in August started receiving chemotherapy treatment. Although gravely ill, the 62-year-old chief executive continued to govern and hoped to finish out his term.

In the face of his terminal illness, Duarte could find solace in some of his past efforts. He could claim some success for his program of land redistribution, and bank and export nationalization. His party might be a shambles, but there had been no coup against him; his people still respected the ballot; the army was less repressive. His failure lay in not bringing about all of the wide-ranging reforms that his nation—and the United States—wanted of him.

Most of El Salvador's budget continued to come from the United States. The $400 million aid package in 1988 brought the U.S. aid total to more than $3 billion in the decade so far. Inflation was still about 25% in 1987. For ten consecutive years the per capita gross national product had declined. Since 1980 exports had dropped 44%, and imports had risen 11%. The drought in 1988 even forced the importation of cotton and beans, items normally exported. Yet many lands were empty of crops because their owners feared expropriation. Unemployment exceeded 40%.

In September, President Duarte asked the United States to grant temporary refuge to nearly 500,000 Salvadorans (10% of El Salvador's population) illegally residing in the United States. Duarte argued that they would support the political left if forced to go home; furthermore, their return greatly would increase unemployment in El Salvador and sharply reduce the funds that they send home from their American earnings—an amount estimated at $350 to $600 million per year. The U.S. Congress was considering the request.

In spite of the military spending of $100,000 per rebel in eight years, the civil war continued. The 6,000 to 8,000 guerrillas were tougher and more dedicated than the army, which numbered 50,000. The rebels demonstrated that they could win most battles—in November they hit the national guard headquarters in the capital—and they could be a nuisance in many ways, but they were not winning much popular support or many permanent bases.

Guatemala

In March 1988, President Marco Vinicio Cerezo, without consulting business interests, signed an agreement with labor for broad wage raises, price controls on basic goods, and recognition of peasant organizations. The next month his Christian Democratic Party swept the nation's municipal elections. These developments appeared to have made the radical right determined to stop Cerezo's gains. In May, triggered by talk that the government was considering cultural ties with Cuba and discussions with leftist leaders, a few army officers rebelled. Lacking the support of any high-ranking officers, the uprising failed, but the president was forced to end his talks with the rebels and increase the military budget.

His troubles continued. He resorted to measures of austerity to remedy old economic mistakes; these were pleasing to few people and provoked many strikes. Church officials and Western diplomats agreed that human-rights violations were increasing, as rural areas reported more torture, kidnappings, and murder. (According to the Center for the Investigation, Study, and Promotion of Human Rights, 75 people were assassinated in Guatemala in September alone.)

Guatemala's human-rights record was one of the worst in the hemisphere. Greater freedom of the press had followed President Cerezo's inauguration in January 1986, but in June 1988 death squads threatened "communist" journalists, and several writers fled the country.

The government had begun to improve the nation's poor infrastructure, bringing water to some towns for the first time, and expanding road- and school-building programs. But Guatemala continued to have one of the worst land distribution programs in Central America. For the first time the Catholic Church took a strong stand in urging government support for the small farmer. The church urged adoption of fair prices and wages, protection of the peasants, granting of state-owned land to small farmers, and guarantees of peasants' land titles. But the government accomplished little as it encountered stiff resistance from coffee planters and buyers. Most farm workers still earned less than one dollar a day.

A related problem was the presence of Guatemalan Indians in Mexico. Perhaps more than 200,000 fled their nation's strife in the early 1980s, abandoning hundreds of villages. Many since have drifted home, and Guatemala warned the others that they could lose their land if they do not return. The Mexican government reported that only 40,000 Guatemalans remained in Mexico, many of whom had jobs uncovering ancient Mayan ruins. While there was not enough work to go around, the Indians stayed because they felt safer, and many had Mexican-born children.

Like Costa Rica, Guatemala began a bilingual-education program, but with much greater handicaps. Guatemala has a very large Indian

CENTRAL AMERICA · Information Highlights					
Nation	Population (in Millions)	Area (sq mi)	(km²)	Capital	Head of State and Government
Belize	0.2	8,865	22 960	Belmopan	Minita Gordon, governor-general Manuel Esquivel, prime minister
Costa Rica	2.9	19,653	50 900	San José	Oscar Arias Sánchez, president
El Salvador	5.4	8,124	21 040	San Salvador	José Napoleón Duarte, president
Guatemala	8.7	42,042	108 890	Guatemala City	Marco Vinicio Cerezo Arévalo, president
Honduras	4.8	43,278	112 090	Tegucigalpa	José Azcona Hoyo, president
Nicaragua	3.6	49,998	129 494	Managua	José Daniel Ortega Saavedra, president
Panama	2.3	30,193	78 200	Panama City	Manuel Noriega, military leader

population and a high degree of illiteracy. Guatemalans speak 23 languages, many of them derived from Mayan. The government, as of 1988, trained 14,000 first-grade teachers in a new curriculum with Spanish as a second language.

Honduras

When Honduran-born Juan Ramón Matta escaped from a Colombian prison in 1986, he returned to Honduras, where he lived a life of ease. Called a "modern Robin Hood" by some Hondurans, he was better known to U.S. drug officials for his ties to the notorious Medellin Cartel of Colombian drug lords. He previously had escaped from a Florida prison in 1971, and U.S. marshals wanted him back to finish his term and to face new drug trafficking charges. On April 5, Honduran police took him from his home. He was flown to the Dominican Republic, and then to the United States. A U.S. marshal called the capture a "major milestone in the war on drugs." U.S. officials stated that Matta controlled 80% of the cocaine trade in the United States and that he was worth $2 billion. Matta's lawyer denied that the action was extradition and called it plain kidnapping.

That this was more than a simple criminal case to the Hondurans was made evident two days later when more than 1,000 Hondurans (mostly students) demonstrated and stoned the U.S. embassy in Tegucigalpa. They set fire to the annex and some took part in its looting. Guards fired on the crowd; four Hondurans were killed and a number were wounded.

The demonstration followed one by students a few weeks before, objecting to the arrival of about 3,200 U.S. troops in Honduras. Increasingly, the Hondurans were telling the world that they no longer wanted their nation to be the United States' "aircraft carrier" in Central America or to bear the brunt of criticism from the rest of Latin America. Concern for Matta was merely an opportunity to show their feelings.

Since 1983 the United States had paid Honduras more than $1.2 billion for the use of the land in the fight against the Nicaraguan Sandinistas. Many Hondurans sought an end to the arrangement, made especially unpalatable by the continued presence of some 6,000 contras on Honduran soil.

The U.S. government quickly denied the rumor that the Southern Command eventually would be moved to Honduras from highly combustible Panama (that arrangement expires in 1999). Meanwhile, Honduras and the United States were holding talks concerning a new treaty, which greatly worried many Central Americans.

Late in the year Honduras strongly urged the United States to begin removing the thousands of contras; Honduras no longer could feed the Nicaraguans and wanted the United States to recognize its responsibility. Tegucigalpa claimed that refugees from Guatemala, El Salvador, and Nicaragua totaled more than 250,000 people, who not only drained funds but also created deep social and cultural tensions.

Further aggravating the economy was the October strike of 40,000 civil servants asking

© Cindy Karp/Black Star

The Honduran government declared a state of emergency in Tegucigalpa (right) after anti-American rioting broke out in April. The rioters were protesting the capture of a reputed drug dealer wanted by officials in the United States.

In October, Hurricane Joan swept across Bluefields on Nicaragua's Caribbean coast. With winds over 125 mph (200 km/hr), the storm took more than 100 lives and destroyed thousands of homes. The government declared a state of emergency.

for higher wages and job stability, the first such action by government employees in 50 years.

Nicaragua

For virtually his full two terms in office, Ronald Reagan struggled to rid the hemisphere of Sandinistas. It was clear that his goal was not accomplished and that his successor, President-elect George Bush, would inherit the problem.

The movement for peace then lay with the Central American presidents, led by Costa Rica's Oscar Arias. These leaders encouraged the opening of discussions between the two Nicaraguan factions in April at Managua, the first time in years that most of the contra representatives had been in the capital.

By August 1988, a year after the signing of the peace pact, the nations had complied with that document in greatly varying degrees. Only Costa Rica had met all its obligations. Honduras' record was the worst. Nicaragua's was mixed; the government released nearly 1,000 political prisoners, lifted the state of emergency, and relaxed restrictions on radio and the press. But the last concession soon had the appearance of a game, and when the opposition newspaper *La Prensa* became too critical for the Sandinistas' taste, its newsprint supply was cut sharply and editors were warned.

A cease-fire was signed in March and generally observed, but tensions remained high. Several rounds of peace talks took place, usually falling short because the contras wanted reform guarantees that the government would not make.

In July the Sandinistas suddenly adopted a renewed hard line; a rock-throwing protest was broken up by tear gas, and people were dragged off a bus and jailed. Blaming the United States for the demonstration, the Nicaraguan government expelled the American ambassador and several staff members. Radio stations and papers were shut down.

That same month the contras reorganized their leadership, Col. Enrique Bermúdez getting recognition as the new leader. Bermúdez, who once had worked for President Anastasio Somoza, was condemned roundly by many of the contras' regional commanders for corruption and dictatorial behavior. Several of these same leaders soon were removed from their posts, and Colonel Bermúdez began lobbying for renewed military aid and an end to peace talks.

Nicaragua's economy continued to worsen. Several devaluations of the córdoba were made during the year. Inflation sometimes reached four figures. Wages were raised 500% in eight months, but the price of rice went up 900%. Unemployment reached 30%; industrial production dropped 35% in a year; large numbers of doctors, engineers, and teachers gave up their careers or left the country.

Sadly, in October, Hurricane Joan smashed into Nicaragua, leveling the department of Bluefields, killing possibly 100, and leaving thousands homeless. Far less damage was done to neighboring states. The Nicaraguans received aid from the Red Cross and Cuba but refused help from the United States.

THOMAS L. KARNES
Arizona State University

175

Focus on Panama

Manuel Antonio Noriega re-mained Panama's strongman despite U.S. pressure to drive him from office. The 54-year-old general, who became chief of staff of Panama's national guard following the 1981 death of Omar Torrijos, was indicted by Florida grand juries on drug charges in February 1988.

© Sygma

Events in Panama in 1988 demonstrated once again the close relationship that has existed between the tiny isthmus republic and the United States since Panama's independence from Colombia in 1903.

The Panama Canal. U.S. President Theodore Roosevelt helped Panama achieve a "bloodless revolution" by stationing U.S. battleships around the country to keep the Colombian military at bay. In return, the United States won sovereignty over a 10-by-50-mi (15-by-80-km) strip of land through which to build a canal connecting the Pacific and Atlantic Oceans. The canal was completed in 1914. Meanwhile, by treaty right, presence, and commerce stimulated by the canal, the United States acquired overwhelming influence in the affairs of Panama, and treated the nation as a colony or mandate. In the first years there were few tensions between the states, but over time a Panamanian sense of nationhood developed, and the citizens sought greater recognition, as well as profits from the canal.

In the 1930's, U.S. President Franklin Roosevelt's Good Neighbor program took cognizance of these new feelings and volunteered changes in the 1903 treaty, giving Panama more sovereignty and income. Yet each new generation in Panama sought more concessions from the U.S. government. Riots broke out in 1959 and again in 1964 over the sovereignty issue. The 1964 riots centered partially on the U.S. refusal to fly the Panamanian flag alongside the U.S. flag in the canal zone; four U.S. soldiers and 21 Panamanians were killed during the rioting. The U.S. government responded by easing U.S. controls in the isthmus and by increasing the rents paid to Panama for the canal zone. Other U.S. observers, including members of Congress, contended that U.S. money and skill had built the canal, and therefore it never should be alienated.

After decades of divisiveness and debate, the United States and Panama signed the Torrijos-Carter treaties in 1978. These treaties provided for the gradual relinquishment of U.S. ownership and control of the Panama Canal during the period from 1978 to the year 2000. In the interim, commissioners from the two nations are to direct the administration of transit. The Canal Zone was abolished, and matters concerning defense, revenues, international status, American bases, and other details were agreed upon. Following the ratification of the treaties, the changes generally have occurred as planned.

Political and Social Development. Population growth has slowed since the 1960s, but increasingly heavy urbanization has wrought great changes in the employment picture. In the late 1980s, almost one half the rural people were between the ages of ten and 19; many migrated to the cities, aggravating problems of both food production and urbanization. Re-

sulting unemployment was substantial. Per capita gross domestic product doubled between 1960 and 1980, but the foreign debt increased at an incredible rate, by 1988 resulting in a severe crippling of the nation's credit.

The Rise of Noriega. In 1968 a revolt led by Gen. Omar Torrijos placed the military more firmly in control of the nation. He died in a plane crash in 1981, and Gen. Manuel Antonio Noriega took his place (*see* BIOGRAPHY). Noriega often proved useful to the administrations of U.S. Presidents Richard Nixon and Ronald Reagan, but by 1988 he had become an irritant in the relationship between the two nations. His political opponents charged that he exploited his position to protect the drug trade between Colombia and the United States, making himself very rich in the process. In February, Florida grand juries indicted him on counts related to the drug charges, and demands for his resignation escalated.

In late February, Panamanian President Eric Arturo Delvalle announced that he was removing Noriega as head of the military, but Noriega refused to step down. Instead, the Noriega-controlled National Assembly unanimously voted to replace Delvalle, who subsequently went into hiding. Cuba, Paraguay, and Nicaragua recognized the new president, while most of Latin America and the United States pretended that Delvalle still held power. U.S. policy was obsessed with driving Noriega out of Panama, or at least out of office, but several deals with the dictator failed, and it became clear that much of the effort only made Noriega more popular at home. Most of the Panamanian business community opposed him, however, and staged a general strike in February. The United States suspended aid and froze Panamanian assets and payment on various obligations in the belief that a sick economy might bring about Noriega's overthrow. But the measures hurt the Panamanian masses much more than they did Noriega. The Reagan administration eased measures when it finally realized that economic pressures achieved no better results than did dealing with Noriega.

The Standoff. In April, Panama's military broke a dockworkers' strike and assumed control over many public services. Noriega cashiered some officers and stepped up recruiting of the poor into the military in order to ease unemployment. But the shortages of credit and goods hurt; virtually every American nation and even President Delvalle urged the United States to remove the various sanctions.

By mid-1988 much of Panama had been affected by these events. Most liquid assets fled the country; shops closed early or totally; restaurants had no food. Streets were deserted at night. Investment disappeared along with construction, once responsible for 30,000 jobs.

The nation was saved from bankruptcy by an unexpected source—the U.S. Treasury. The monthly payroll for the U.S. military and civilian workers in Panama was some $40 million, much of which was spent locally. The United States scarcely could justify withholding those payments. Then some foreign banks lent funds to Panama, and local businessmen brought cash back from hiding in Miami. The Noriega government bloated the civil service to 130,000 employees, and provided them with partial pay; their checks became a form of currency, three fourths of an employee's check being accepted for grocery bills and the cash balance for such things as utilities. By June the banks had reopened and were permitting partial withdrawals, although many banks discounted government checks by as much as 20%.

The government tried to protect the poor with free food and various welfare programs. But the middle classes had to help themselves, and there was not much they could do when jobs were lost or payrolls not forthcoming. It was the damage to these groups that made the Reagan government's position untenable. Noriega and his immediate followers seemed to be beyond reach. Crippling the middle classes could turn them against the United States.

Effects on the Canal Zone. Regularly, increased tensions between the United States and Panama stirred emotions about the future of the Panama Canal; events of 1988 supported that thesis. About 1,100 workers and their families still lived in the former Canal Zone, since 1979 a part of Panama proper. Their concerns, combined with the Panamanian demonstrations, prompted the Reagan administration to increase substantially the number of troops at some of the nine Panamanian bases still occupied by the U.S. military. Their arrival made the Panamanians nervous. Only minor incidents took place, however.

Throughout all the turmoil the canal continued to maintain normal operations under its joint management. But other changes were taking place that damaged the appearance of Panama's ability to continue good service. For example, the Panama Railroad, which the United States ceded to Panama in 1979, had fallen on bad times. Strikes were common, and port fees were among the highest in the world, driving traffic down. In spite of the loss of business, the payroll had tripled. Japanese shippers were upset by poor service and were considering other options; U.S. commerce ceased using the line because of its bad safety record and increasingly avoided Panama entirely by moving goods across the United

The closing of Panama's banks on March 4—at the height of the U.S.-Noriega standoff—caused severe problems for the nation's citizens and brought the economy to a virtual halt. Many Panamanians were perplexed by their inability to cash their social-security checks.

© Christopher Morris/Black Star

States in containers. Noriega's followers charged that the changes in transit methods and much of the strained relationship resulted from a U.S. plot to destabilize Panama and thus justify breaking the canal treaties.

New U.S. Policies. The United States increasingly saw Noriega as a threat to the security of the Western Hemisphere, even though he had been instrumental to the U.S. intelligence community in the past. U.S. lawmakers sought a solution which would force Noriega out without also bringing about revolution in Panama, or destroying its economy.

Among the diplomatic schemes devised by the United States to rid Panama of Noriega was an offer to drop the drug-trafficking indictments and end the economic sanctions if Noriega would resign by August 12, leave Panama in September, and remain in exile until after the completion of the Panamanian presidential election in May 1989. Democratic congressmen, as well as Noriega, ridiculed the plan, and the talks fell through.

President Reagan ruled out the use of force, although some members of his administration urged it and even advocated kidnapping the general for trial in the United States. The president did, however, authorize covert activity, partially nullified by almost immediate press leaks. Presumably, covert action would include such measures as psychological warfare, aid to dissenting troops, and more economic pressure. But the precedent of the administration's failure to achieve its goals in Nicaragua—at great expense—weakened that option. Lack of congressional support for another such adventure, plus Reagan's reticence to make waves during the U.S. presidential election, made it seem that the president would save the problem for his successor.

Central American Opinion. Many Central Americans would oppose new unilateral intervention by the United States. Most Central American leaders who have little fondness for Noriega preferred that struggles of this sort be treated in some form of regional consultative process as provided by existing treaties. Regional public opinion is important in Central America, and pressure from the neighboring states could be persuasive.

Panama's people were divided fiercely, but the anti-Noriega factions lacked leadership. President Delvalle briefly visited Washington in July for assurances of continued American support. If he received any, it was not publicly conveyed to Panamanians. At home he usually remained in hiding, and had been supplanted by a pro-Noriega acting president.

One political option died with Arnulfo Arias Madrid in August. In spite of his advanced years (86), he had been spoken of as a likely candidate to run for president against Noriega in 1989. (The latter would have had to resign his military command to be eligible to run.) Arias had been elected three times—the first time in 1941—and had been thrown out by the army three times; in 1984 he lost by probable fraud. Ironically, the United States had backed the revolt against Arias in 1941 because of his fascist leanings, but in 1988 would have welcomed his candidacy.

Meanwhile, hundreds of Panamanians were in exile, and many professionals had migrated. The economy was at its lowest level in decades, and business leaders felt that 20 years of progress had been destroyed. Many Panamanians were disillusioned with U.S. policy, and even some opponents of Noriega faulted the United States for many of their problems.

THOMAS L. KARNES

CHAD

Chad's two-decade-old civil war appeared to be ending in 1988 as President Hissein Habré's political rivals were in disarray. There was a struggle for leadership in the Transitional Government of National Unity (GUNT), the main opposition party. Although Libya's President Muammar el-Qaddafi publicly pronounced support for GUNT's nominal leader Goukouni Oueddei, he had ceased to provide much monetary or military support long before he announced, in May, an end to Libya's attacks on Chad. Habré's solidification of authority throughout the country enabled the badly neglected agricultural sector to begin to recover. Especially important was the improvement in the cotton harvest, the state's major export. Foreign assistance also had enabled the rebuilding of much of the capital city of Ndjamena.

Foreign Affairs. The disastrous campaign of 1987 which cost Libya an estimated 10% of its army and more than $1 billion in equipment, and Libya's growing isolation, convinced Qaddafi to end the war. On May 25, 1988, he recognized Habré's regime and was withdrawing Libyan troops. This action was welcomed not only by Habré's government but also by the French, who had supplied most of Chad's logistical support but were fearful of being drawn into the conflict. Troops of the Libyan-supported Islamic Legion were active along the border with Sudan and air and minor ground action was endemic.

The situation deteriorated until a series of meetings between representatives of Chad and Libya resulted in the resumption in October 1988 of diplomatic relations between the two states and a continuation of the cease-fire agreement of September 1987. But the agreement postponed any final decision on which state should control the mineral-rich Aouzou Strip which Libya had occupied since 1973.

The French government showed no indication of removing its 1,000-man logistic and air force personnel from Chad. The United States, which had sent more than $32 million in military equipment in 1987, continued to supply advanced weapons.

Domestic Affairs. Health services were almost nonexistent and the school system was a shambles; only 50% of the nation's students were attending. A grant of $22 million from the International Development Association (IDA) targeted the educational system. Two further IDA credits totalling $45 million were designated to improve public finance and pay for priority imports. The French government in August promised to finance most of Chad's priority projects.

HARRY A. GAILEY
San Jose State University

CHAD • Information Highlights

Official Name: Republic of Chad.
Location: North-Central Africa.
Area: 495,753 sq mi (1 284 000 km²).
Population: (mid-1988 est.): 4,800,000.
Chief City: Ndjamena, the capital.
Government: *Head of state and government,* Hissein Habré, president (seized control June 7, 1982).
Monetary Unit: CFA franc (316.620 CFA francs equal U.S.$1, July 1988).

CHEMISTRY

Developments in chemistry in 1988 included ultrafast studies of chemical reactions, new experiments on carbon clusters, and a surprising prediction regarding molecular structure.

Ultrafast Studies. Chemical bonds are made and broken in the course of chemical reactions. Normally these events take place far too rapidly to be timed, although knowledge of such times would be of great scientific interest. New developments in laser technology, however, now are making such measurements possible. In 1988 a team of scientists at the California Institute of Technology was able to time the breakup of cyanogen iodide (ICN) into the fragments I and CN. The scientists used two ultrafast pulses of laser light, the first to start the reaction and the second to detect the CN product. They found that the bond between I and CN persisted for about 200 femtoseconds after the first flash of light was absorbed. A femtosecond is a millionth of a billionth of a second, or 0.000000000000001 second.

The Cal Tech team also examined the reaction in which a hydrogen atom (H) attacks carbon dioxide (CO_2) to form a hydroxyl (OH) radical and carbon monoxide (CO). In this reaction, a "collision complex" is first formed and then breaks up into the products. The scientists found that the intermediate complex lasts for about five millionths of a millionth of a second, which in chemical terms is a surprisingly long period of time.

Carbon Clusters. Back in 1985, a team of scientists working at Rice University in Texas discovered that remarkably stable clusters of 60 carbon atoms were produced when graphite was vaporized by laser pulses. At the time, the scientists proposed that the clusters were composed of sheets of graphite wrapped into a sphere, rather like a soccer ball in shape. They named such clusters "buckminsterfullerene" in honor of the late R. Buckminster Fuller, the inventor and designer who made use of structures of similar "geodesic" shape.

Later experiments have tended to support this "soccer-ball" shape for the 60-carbon clusters, attributing their stability to their unusual three-dimensional network of bonds. In 1988 the model was strengthened further by ex-

periments in which the carbon clusters were combined with lanthanum, potassium, and cesium ions. When the clusters were subjected to intense laser irradiation, they tended to lose two-carbon fragments rather than the ions of the metals. This appears to indicate that the metal ions were trapped inside the hollow spheres and not attached on the outside.

It has been speculated that 60-carbon clusters even may exist in interstellar space. They may be responsible for certain otherwise unexplained features, called diffuse stellar lines, observed in spectra obtained from outer space.

Structural Theory. For some time a group of West German scientists has been performing quantum mechanical calculations on molecules that possess what they call "rule-breaking" structures. In 1988 they turned their attention to one such compound, called tetralithiosilane. This compound contains four lithium atoms and a silicon atom. Chemists might expect the lithium atoms to be placed around the central silicon atom in a symmetrical way, so that the molecule would have a tetrahedral shape. New calculations, however, indicate that this is probably not the true molecular arrangement. The calculations indicate that the most favorable form of the molecule has all the lithiums on the same side, with considerable freedom to change their positions. This latter property of flexible position is known as "fluxional character."

Other Developments. The chemical bond between fluorine and carbon is very strong. As a result, fluorocarbons such as Teflon generally are assumed to be chemically inert and, as a result, nontoxic as well. Experiments by chemists in Scotland, however, now have called this assumption into question. The experiments disclosed that one such fluorocarbon called perfluorodecalin, which sometimes is used in artificial blood, can react with organic compounds even under relatively mild conditions. This discovery also casts doubt on the inertness of other fluorocarbons, as well.

Back in 1962 the assumed chemical inertness of the noble gas xenon was disproved by the discovery of a compound called xenon hexafluoride, opening up the area of noble-gas chemistry. In 1988 a scientist at McMaster University in Ontario produced the first example of a chemical bonding between another noble gas, krypton, and nitrogen. Previously krypton had been known to bond only with the highly reactive element fluorine. The newly observed compound of krypton and nitrogen, however, is stable only below $-50°$ C ($-58°$ F).

One question that has bothered some researchers is the way in which water molecules are arranged at a water surface. According to a number of theoretical studies, the hydrogen atoms in the molecules should be pointed down toward the liquid. These theories now appear to have been confirmed by scientists working at Columbia University and at the IBM Watson Research Center in New York.

New types of plastics continue to be developed, especially for high-technology uses. In 1988, for example, British scientists made polyacetylene semiconductor devices that perform far better than previous devices. The new devices, however, remain inferior in performance to currently available inorganic semiconductor devices. New electricity-conducting plastics also were reported. For developments in superconductivity, *see* PHYSICS.

PAUL G. SEYBOLD, *Wright State University*

CHICAGO

Chicagoans will remember 1988 for its searing heat and drought, the first night baseball game at Wrigley Field, and political jockeying for another mayoral election. The struggling Sears company put its headquarters, the 110-story Sears Tower—the world's tallest building —up for sale for more than $1 billion.

Heat. Like much of the U.S. midsection, Chicago had its hottest and driest year on record. From June to September, weather records toppled like dominoes. The three-month period had an average daily high temperature of 87.2° F (30.7° C), a full degree above the previous record set in 1955. Other records fell as well, according to the U.S. Weather Service. Chicago had seven days with temperatures above 100° F (37.8° C), the most ever and well in excess of the yearly average (one day). Seven days had all-time high temperatures, and 47 days had temperatures of 90° F (32.2° C) or above, tying the old record. June 4 was the hottest day in city history—104° F (40° C).

Chicagoans retreated indoors to the cool of air conditioning, venturing outside only to go to work, take care of necessary chores, or water lawns. Rainfall well below average from May through July gave the city parched lawns and withered flowers. Water and electric bills soared. Ironically, the city's first real downpour came in the fourth inning of the first night baseball game at Wrigley Field.

Baseball. An era in major-league baseball came to an end on August 8, when the National League Chicago Cubs played their first night game at 74-year-old Wrigley Field. Since 1948, Wrigley Field had been the only unlighted ballpark in the major leagues. (The first major-league night game was played in 1935.) Chicago aldermen had long bowed to community pressure, refusing to allow the installation of lights at the stadium. Opponents of night baseball, led by a group known as Citizens United for Baseball in the Sunshine (CUBS), feared that noise, traffic, and rowdy fans would disrupt the evening serenity of the neighborhood.

In February 1988, after the Cubs ownership (The Tribune Company) threatened to move

AP/Wide World

After 6,852 day games and decades of debate, an era in baseball history ended at Chicago's Wrigley Field on Aug. 8, 1988—the night the lights went on. Since 1947, Wrigley had been the only unlighted ballpark in the major leagues.

the team out of the city, the City Council passed an ordinance to allow the installation of lights at Wrigley. Under a compromise plan, the team would play only a limited number of night games there—seven in 1988 and 18 in each subsequent year until 2002. A sellout crowd of 39,008 was on hand for the first one—against the Philadelphia Phillies. As fate would have it, with the Cubs leading 3-1, the rains came and the game was called.

On the South Side, meanwhile, the American League Chicago White Sox were promised a new, state-financed stadium across the street from 70-year-old Comiskey Park, where they now play. The new stadium—scheduled for completion in 1991—and a more favorable lease for the White Sox were approved by the state legislature, 60–55, on July 1.

Politics. Democratic Mayor Eugene Sawyer kept busy trying to solidify his tenuous political base in the face of a court-ordered mayoral election in April 1989 for the unexpired term of the late Harold Washington. Sawyer, a black who was elected interim mayor in December 1987 by a coalition of black and white aldermen, faces primary opposition from two black aldermen. Some white aldermen also were expected to enter the race in the hope that a split of the black vote might land them in the mayor's chair.

ROBERT ENSTAD, *"Chicago Tribune"*

CHILE

Hundreds of thousands of Chileans paraded through the streets of Santiago and other cities on Oct. 6, 1988, celebrating the rejection by voters of a bid by Gen. Augusto Pinochet Ugarte to perpetuate himself in power. The economy improved and human rights remained a central issue in foreign relations.

Politics and Government. In the October 5 plebiscite, Chileans voted either "yes" in favor of Pinochet or "no" if they favored new presidential elections. Under the 1980 Constitution, which General Pinochet himself helped draft, a victory would give him a new eight-year term (until 1997). If he were rejected, Pinochet would remain president until March 1990, but elections for his successor would be held in December 1989. Pinochet also would remain commander of the army until 1995.

Some 7.2 million Chileans went to the polls, with 54.7% (nearly 4 million) voting "no" and 43.0% (about 3.1 million) voting "yes". (The rest were blank or voided ballots.) The 72-year-old Pinochet reportedly was surprised by the outcome but announced the following day that he accepted the "verdict of the citizenry" and would abide by the terms of the 1980 Constitution. Even the opposition was surprised by the size of its victory. A 16-party coalition, united under an umbrella organization called the Command for the No, had seized upon the plebiscite as an opportunity to end 15 years of often repressive military rule and rallied their countrymen to cast a "vote of conscience." General Pinochet, meanwhile, on August 24 lifted the state of emergency that had been in effect since he took power in 1973, and on September 1 issued a decree permitting the return of 430 political exiles.

Despite Pinochet's defeat, there was considerable uncertainty as to the political future of the country. The uncertainty went beyond Pinochet's intentions. The opposition itself was divided and had rallied behind no single figure who could represent all parties in the December 1989 election. Also unclear was the receptiveness of the military to political reform. The day after the plebiscite, Patricio Aylwin, leader of the Christian Democratic Party and the chief spokesman for the "no" coalition, called for an

181

AP/Wide World

Chile's 72-year-old President Augusto Pinochet Ugarte was defeated in his bid for a new eight-year term. In an October 5 plebiscite, 54.7% of Chileans voted "no."

accord with the armed forces to ensure a smooth "transition to an authentic democracy." Few believed that the four-man government junta would agree to wholesale changes in the Constitution, but the commander of the Air Force did say he was willing to negotiate changes in the amendment procedure.

Also on the day after the plebiscite, Pinochet's 16-member cabinet tendered its resignation. Pinochet rejected the resignation, but on October 21 he replaced nine members. Among them were the interior minister, foreign minister, and government secretary-general. Among those retained were Defense Minister Patrício Carvajal, Finance Minister Hernan Buchi, and Economics Minister Manuel Concha.

In September the Chilean Human Rights Commission reported that 15,405 persons had been murdered since the September 1973 coup that brought General Pinochet to power; another 2,206 were missing and 1,180 had been sent into internal exile.

Economy. The high price of copper—$1.47 per pound in October 1988, compared with $.63

in October 1987 and $.83 in October 1986—along with increased exports of manufactured goods and agricultural products enabled Chile to reduce its foreign debt by $899 million during the first six months of 1988. As of July, the nation's debt stood at $18 billion, down from $23 billion in mid-1985. Exports through August totaled $4.5 billion, according to Director of Economic Relations Manuel Casanueva, an increase of 38.1% over 1987. The trade surplus in 1988 was likely to reach $1.85 billion, up from $1.25 billion in 1987. And Casanueva predicted that overall economic growth in 1988 would reach 6%, up from 5% in 1987.

While there was concern that an expanded money supply and consumer spending might stimulate inflation, the rate of inflation from October 1987 to September 1988 was only 10%. An increase to 15.6% was expected by December, but that was still considerably lower than the 20.8% recorded in 1987.

The National Statistics Institute reported that 145,400 new jobs were created in the first four months of 1988, reducing unemployment to 8.6%—the lowest for a four-month period in 14 years. A shortage of skilled industrial workers led the Ministry of Labor to launch a new training program, by which businesses that train apprentice workers get tax exemptions. And on May 1, President Pinochet announced a 24% increase in the minimum wage, a 25% increase in the family income supplement for lower-income groups, and a 10%–15% wage increase for public employees.

Foreign Policy. While U.S. officials congratulated Chile for "carrying out a peaceful, orderly, and impartial plebiscite," Washington did not abolish import duties imposed on Chilean products in December 1987; duty-free trade status on many items was withdrawn at that time because of Chilean violations of worker rights. The United States in 1988 also continued to seek Chilean cooperation in extraditing two men for the 1976 murder in Washington of former Chilean Ambassador Orlando Letelier. On the positive side, Chilean frigates and destroyers joined U.S. ships in military maneuvers in the South Pacific in September and October.

Another sign that Chile wanted to improve its human-rights image was Pinochet's ratification in mid-September of conventions adopted by the Organization of American States (OAS) and United Nations aimed at preventing torture.

Relations with Argentina improved to the point that ships from the two countries participated in rescue maneuvers in the Beagle Channel in August; further joint maneuvers were proposed for early 1989. The Beagle Channel had been the focus of dispute between the two nations until a solution was reached in 1985.

NEALE J. PEARSON
Texas Tech University

CHILE • Information Highlights

Official Name: Republic of Chile.
Location: Southwestern coast of South America.
Area: 292,259 sq mi (756 950 km²).
Population (mid-1988 est.): 12,600,000.
Chief Cities (July 31, 1985): Santiago, the capital, 4,099,714; Concepción, 280,713.
Government: *Head of state and government,* Gen. Augusto Pinochet Ugarte, president (took power Sept. 1973). *Legislature*—Congress (dissolved Sept. 1973).
Monetary Unit: Peso (247.21 pesos equal U.S.$1, official rate Nov. 1, 1988).
Gross Domestic Product (1986 U.S.$): $16,400,-000,000.
Economic Index (Santiago, 1987): *Consumer Prices* (1980 = 100), all items, 375.7; food, 355.6.
Foreign Trade (1987 U.S.$): *Imports,* $4,023,000,000; *exports,* $5,102,000,000.

CHINA, PEOPLE'S REPUBLIC OF

Meeting in March 1988, the National People's Congress (NPC), China's highest legislative body, accepted the resignations of a number of elderly and relatively conservative colleagues of paramount leader Deng Xiaoping and confirmed as their replacements a group of young, technically more competent individuals who set out an ambitious agenda of economic reform. By October, however, this agenda was placed effectively on hold by the Chinese Communist Party (CCP) Central Committee's Third Plenum, acting in response to a series of nagging economic problems. While the political succession put in place during the spring appeared to hold, the new leaders' latitude in pursuing reform was constrained severely. Although there is no question that economic and political reform will go forward, it will do so at a considerably more measured pace than had been planned.

The Economy. The economic news from the People's Republic in 1988—nearly ten years since leader Deng Xiaoping launched China's economic reform program and open-door policy—was mixed. Midyear figures showed that the overall growth in gross national product (GNP) was running at 11%, leading planners to project that the target of 7.5% for the year

likely would be exceeded. Industrial production grew at a rate of 17.5% during the first three quarters. Despite drought and flooding during the summer, total grain production was projected at nearly 400 million tons—short of the goal of 405 million tons, but not so far short as weather-related disasters had led pessimists to predict.

But there was bad news as well. Concern over inflation—a serious problem in late 1985 —began to resurface late in 1987. By fall 1988, the problem seemed to many to be spiraling out of control. The rate of inflation is not easy to determine, since there is no consumer price index in China. Food prices in China's cities rose especially sharply, with some items doubling and even tripling in price during the course of the year. Since the average urban family spends more than half its income on foodstuffs, the effect was magnified for these people. Their situation was exacerbated by the government's reluctance to raise the wages of state workers to compensate for increases in the cost of living. By midyear the Chinese press was admitting to a double-digit annual inflation rate. Unofficial estimates ranged from 24% to 80%.

But only one in four Chinese live in the city and work for the state. In the countryside, real income continued to rise and inexpensive food was widely available. The strong reaction of Beijing's political leaders to the problem of inflation thus reflected concerns that went be-

At the annual legislative session of the National People's Congress in March, Li Peng was confirmed as China's premier. In his keynote address, he declared his support for the ongoing reform movement but warned against hasty change.

AP/Wide World

Economic reforms have made consumer products more available, but by 1988 inflation had become a serious problem. Food prices in China's cities rose sharply, with some items doubling or tripling in price.

© Don Heiny/Picture Group

yond the urban shopping basket. First, the dissatisfactions of urban residents figure much more importantly in political decision-making than do the dissatisfactions of rural residents. City dwellers live closer to the seats of power and are engaged in occupations that will make or break China's modernization efforts. If they choose to take to the streets in protest against erosion of their standard of living, as some did during the late spring and summer months, the government and party are likely to give disproportionate attention to their concerns.

Second, the problem of inflation extended well beyond the urban consumer. Indeed, some of its manifestations called into question the government's ability to solve the problem even after resolving in October to give it priority. For one thing, inflation was fueled by a nearly 25% increase in the state wage package during the year, with the addition of subsidies to offset the rising cost of food.

Also contributing to the problem was the fact that China has no equivalent to U.S. Treasury notes as a means of financing government operations not covered by tax revenues. Instead, the government prints money to finance these operations. As a result, the money supply grew by about 40% during 1988.

Finally, the government seemed unable to regulate savings and investment. Despite the announcement of a policy to tighten credit, loans by state-owned banks exceeded quotas by a significant amount, and the interest rate, although raised to discourage potential borrowers, was still less than 10%. Similarly, the rate of interest paid to savers was raised in September, but the new rate of 9% was still lower than the rate of inflation. As a result, in quick succession, consumers emptied their savings accounts and cleared department store shelves of consumer durables. In Harbin, for example, during a two-day period in late July, there was a $3.4 million run on local banks and a 200% increase in sales of electrical appliances.

Chinese with whom one spoke during the fall were in fact concerned about the cost of living, but most of them regarded it as a short-term problem capable of resolution. More troublesome for them was the growing problem of corruption, for which they saw no possible solution. In June the Chinese Academy of Social Science carried out a survey on the subject. Eighty-three percent of urban residents polled said that they believed political leaders are corrupt. More troubling was the finding that, among the political leaders surveyed, 63% admitted to engaging in corruption.

Corruption often takes the form of bribery —a particularly pervasive problem in a society that functions on *guanxi* or "connections." It also takes the form of embezzlement. During the year the official press reported cases of embezzlement involving as much as $100,000—a substantial figure in a society where the average per-capita income still stands at less than $500 per year.

In terms of its effect on economic reform, however, the most pernicious form of corruption in China today is profiteering. Despite the introduction of "market forces" into an economy that had been planned totally, economic decision-making still is vested in the hands of local and central bureaucrats. The key actors in this new, mixed economy are more often government officials spending state funds than they are entrepreneurs spending their own capital. Hoarding scarce commodities and reselling them for personal gain is a temptation into which these bureaucratic players are falling more and more frequently.

Political Response. The March meeting of the NPC came just as these economic clouds were beginning to gather on the horizon. While Deng Xiaoping retained his position as head of the Central Military Commission—his only remaining official post—several of his cohort of post-Mao political leaders resigned their positions. Peng Zhen, 86, stepped down as chair-

CHINA · Information Highlights

Official Name: People's Republic of China.
Location: Central-eastern Asia.
Area: 3,705,390 sq mi (9 596 960 km²).
Population (mid-1988 est.): 1,087,000,000.
Chief Cities (Dec. 31, 1985 est.): Beijing (Peking), the capital, 5,860,000; Shanghai, 6,980,000; Tianjin, 5,380,000.
Government: *General Secretary of the Chinese Communist Party,* Zhao Ziyang (chosen Oct. 1987); *Head of Government:* Li Peng, premier (took office Nov. 1987); *Head of State:* Yang Shangkun, president (took office March 1988). *Legislature* (unicameral)—National People's Congress.
Monetary Unit: Yuan (3.80 yuan equal U.S.$1, official rate, 1988).
Gross National Product (1987 est. U.S.$): $286,000,-000,000.
Foreign Trade (1987 U.S.$): *Imports,* $43,392,-000,000; *exports,* $39,542,000,000.

man of the NPC, and Li Xiannian, 78, stepped down as president. They and others who resigned with them had been associated with a relatively cautious approach to reform that favored central control, a measured pace, and a heavy dose of skepticism about Western influence. Their resignations removed a relatively conservative group who had relinquished their positions in the CCP five months earlier.

Yang Shangkun, 81, one of the few military figures in the new administration, was named China's new president. Wan Li, 72, with experience in both urban and rural economic planning, was appointed chairman of the NPC. And, as expected, the Congress confirmed the appointment of Li Peng, 60, as premier.

Observers of the Chinese scene were intrigued by apparent differences in approach between Premier Li and party leader Zhao Ziyang. At a meeting of the Central Committee just prior to the NPC, Zhao delivered a bold speech in which he called for a speeding up of wage and price reform and an expansion of foreign investment in China's coastal provinces. Li Peng, by contrast, with his training in the Soviet Union as a student, was seen as adopting an approach that favors central planning and avoids bold experimentation. His keynote address at the Congress was interpreted as more cautious than Zhao's and his appointment as a concession to the departing conservatives. In his press conference at the conclusion of the Congress, Premier Li took the opportunity to refute this interpretation and to affirm the unity of his and Zhao's approach to reform.

Whether or not Zhao and Li represent different schools of thought, by midsummer there could be no doubt that a debate was underway within the party's Politburo. Meeting as they often do in August at a seaside resort north of Beijing known as Beidaihe, party leaders weighed the implications of a series of strikes, bank runs, buying sprees, and some public demonstrations of dissatisfaction with economic conditions. Emerging from these meetings, Zhao told visiting Japanese journalists that price reform was to be put on hold and that state ceilings on the prices of most commodities would remain in place. In a formal meeting four days later, however, the Politburo passed a five-year program of price and wage reform that appeared to endorse rapid and extensive decontrol. Finally, on August 30, the State Council—the "cabinet" of the Chinese government—issued a six-point decision calling for no further price reform for the rest of 1988 and 1989; for stiff controls on investment in fixed assets, credit, and the printing of money; and for a crackdown on corruption.

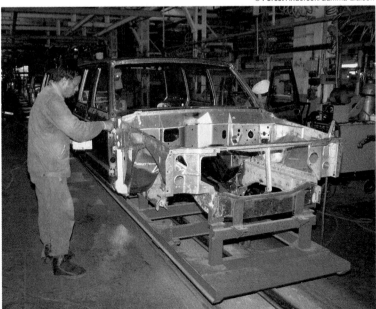

China's industrial production was especially strong in 1988, growing 17.5% in the first three quarters. There was a fledgling market for private automobiles.

The debate was resolved in late September at a plenary meeting of the Central Committee. The communiqué from this meeting stated that an "improvement of the economic environment and a rectification of the economic order" were to constitute the focus of reform for the next two years. Though caution won out over boldness, Zhao, the chief spokesman for boldness, seemed to emerge still firmly in control of his position as party head. By late fall there were signs that the party and government response had been effective. Inflation slowed, and public confidence in the economy seemed to be returning.

Trade and Foreign Investment. Zhao's efforts at promoting trade and investment in what some call China's "gold coast" have begun to pay off. As part of the program announced in March, trade and investment decision-making were decentralized further and, for the first time since 1949, domestic and foreign clients were permitted to purchase land in selected coastal cities.

The latter move—anathema to an earlier, more orthodox generation of leaders—was made more acceptable through the vehicle of what are called "use rights." By this system, title to use rights is bought and sold, while nominal ownership of the land itself remains in the hands of the state. The system is self-consciously modeled after the way land is traded in Hong Kong.

Foreign investment in China over the previous ten years reached approximately $16 billion in 1988, of which about two thirds came from Hong Kong. Figures released in late sum-

mer showed that U.S. investments since 1979 had totaled $2.76 billion and that Japanese investments had totaled $1.86 billion. During the first half of 1988, Japanese firms committed themselves to more than 500 new projects in China. If they come to fruition, they will bring more than $2 billion in new Japanese investments in the People's Republic.

Substantial new credit was extended to China by three international lenders during 1988. A package of loans totaling $6 billion was announced by Japanese Prime Minister Noburu Takeshita during his visit to Beijing in late August. In October the Asian Development Bank approved some $50 million in new credits, and the Soviet Union announced plans to lend China more than $80 million in conjunction with a railway construction project on their common border.

With total foreign trade continuing to expand, China projected a rough balance between imports and exports for 1988. The Chinese currency is not freely convertible outside of China, and China's trading partners pressed for a revaluation of the yuan. While it was officially valued at 3.80 to the U.S. dollar, the yuan was being traded at more than twice that figure in newly established "currency swapping centers" that allow certain approved joint ventures to trade foreign currency for Chinese currency at negotiated rates.

Hong Kong, Japan, the United States, and West Germany (in that order) continued to be China's major trading partners. New players include Taiwan, with whom two-way trade was projected at more than $2 billion in 1988, and

© Don Heiny/Picture Group

The continued expansion of the Chinese business sector was evidenced by the construction of new office buildings in Beijing, right, and other cities.

On September 7, China launched its first experimental meteorological satellite from a site in Taiyun, Shanxi Province.

South Korea, at $2.5 billion. The bulk of trade from those two nations, as well as a limited amount of their investment, pass through Hong Kong. Trade with the Soviet Union also was on the rise in 1988, projected to reach a total of $1.3 billion—a fourfold increase over the level in 1981.

Figures published in 1988 showed that some $5 billion of Chinese exports in recent years have been in arms sales to Third World countries. Half of these shipments went to Iraq, a third to Iran. These sales have made China the fourth-ranking supplier of arms on the international market after the Soviet Union, the United States, and France. Although Washington protested that Chinese weapons were being used against U.S. warships in the Persian Gulf and were a destabilizing influence in that strife-torn region, Beijing remained reluctant to cut off their sale. Profits from these sales help China's balance of trade, serve as an important source of foreign exchange, and augment the dwindling budget share of the Chinese army, which manufactures the arms and supervises their sale. Moreover, they allow China to exert an influence in a part of the world in which the Soviet Union long has been active.

Foreign Relations. The most important development in China's international relations during 1988 took place in its bilateral ties with the Soviet Union. Given the similarities between China's reform program and the reforms underway in the Soviet Union under General Secretary Mikhail Gorbachev, it would seem natural that the two nations would draw closer to one another. Indeed, China's then Foreign Minister Wu Xueqian (succeeded by Qian Qichen in April) acknowledged this affinity in a meeting with Soviet planners in January, and the Chinese press commented favorably on the unprecedented open conference on reform held by the Communist Party of the Soviet Union in mid-1988.

Despite the overcoming of past ideological divisions, Beijing held firm to its position that the Soviets must act to remove "three obstacles" before normalization of relations can proceed: their support of Vietnam's occupation of Cambodia, their occupation of Afghanistan, and their stationing of troops and missiles on China's northern border. During the year progress was made on two of these fronts, as Moscow announced plans for the withdrawal of its troops from Afghanistan, and Vietnam set a timetable for its withdrawal from Cambodia. Soviet and Chinese diplomats met in Beijing in July to discuss the terms of a Cambodian settlement. While no significant breakthrough occurred, there were signs during the fall that the Chinese were prepared to be flexible in their support of the factions ranged against the Hanoi-supported regime in Phnom Penh.

With the groundwork for formal contact beginning to take shape, Deng finally responded (during a meeting with Finnish President Mauno Koivisto in October) to Gorbachev's thrice-repeated suggestion that he and Deng meet. Deng said that he thought a summit likely would take place in 1989. The last meeting between top Chinese and Soviet leaders took place in 1959, between Mao Zedong and Nikita Khrushchev.

Chinese officials took pains to point out that, even if such a meeting were to result in a normalization of relations between the two states and the two Communist parties, it would not constitute a significant shift in Chinese foreign policy, nor weaken China's extensive ties with the United States, Japan, and Western Europe. Western observers agreed that China would have little to gain from such a shift of emphasis, since Beijing has so much at stake both economically and strategically in its links to the West.

See also TAIWAN.

JOHN BRYAN STARR, *Yale-China Association*

CITIES AND URBAN AFFAIRS

U.S. cities in 1988 continued to face dwindling federal support, along with such social problems as homelessness and drug abuse.

Federal Aid. The U.S. Congress in 1988 failed to appropriate funds for Urban Development Action Grants (UDAGs), effectively killing the program. UDAGs were designed to stimulate private-sector investment in inner cities, and they were very popular with mayors and local business leaders. Over 11 years, $4.6 billion in UDAGs were distributed, stimulating an estimated $27 billion in private investment and creating approximately 550,000 jobs—more than half of which went to low- and moderate-income workers. But when specific programmatic trade-offs had to be made to meet federal deficit-reduction goals, the UDAG program lost out. More than $216 million in UDAGs were approved for fiscal year (FY) 1988, but only a small, diminishing amount of money will be distributed in FY 1989.

Other urban programs also fell victim in the deficit-slashing exercise. Congress cut $500 million from its sewage treatment grant program, turning almost all new sewage facility construction back to the states and localities; this program had distributed $45 billion in federal funds since 1972. Further cuts also were imposed in housing assistance. These actions came on top of the termination of the revenue-sharing program in 1987, a loss of $4.6 billion to local governments.

Thus, as the Reagan presidency drew to a close, the majority of local governments were not receiving direct federal assistance. The only large program remaining for federal aid to cities was the Community Development Block Grant (CDBG) program, which was to distribute about $3 billion in FY 1989. For U.S. cities, the "Reagan revolution" has meant the end of most forms of direct federally assisted municipal aid. The budget for the U.S. Department of Housing and Urban Development (HUD) declined from $35.7 billion in FY 1980 to less than $14 billion by FY 1989 (from about 7% of the federal budget to less than 1%); this was the steepest reduction for any cabinet department during those years. HUD did announce that it would designate 100 special "enterprise zones," but no federal money was involved.

Urban leaders generally do not foresee the revival of national urban programs. During the presidential campaign of 1988, urban issues seemed to take a backseat to many others. One reason for this may have been the declining electoral influence of inner cities. Less than 12% of the 1988 vote was cast in large cities, compared with almost 60% in suburbs and small towns. The Election '88 committee of the National League of Cities had little if any influence on either candidate, and the George Bush administration, even with a Democratic-controlled Congress, was not expected to raise funding levels for urban programs.

The place of cities in the intergovernmental system has changed fundamentally in the 1980s. Whereas city officials during the 1960s and 1970s forged direct links to federal administrators, most federal dollars now go through state administrative agencies, which distribute them down through the system. In the opinion of one former mayor, "The states tend to siphon off major portions and trickle down what is left according to a politically popular formula."

An indication of the conflict in the intergovernmental system emerged in 1988 over the distribution of federal antidrug money. Under the 1986 Antidrug Abuse Act, the states were to submit plans to the U.S. Justice Department for the distribution of funds to local governments. Most states were slow in following this process, and in 1988 the National League of Cities, the U.S. Conference of Mayors, and the National Association of Counties lobbied Congress to send the money directly to local governments. They narrowly lost their fight, however, in the face of a counterlobby by the National Governors' Association and National Conference of State Legislators.

Many city officials were concerned not only that they were last in the intergovernmental hierarchy, but that the federal government continued to impose "unfinanced mandates." For example, communities were required to carry liability insurance, and the Environmental Protection Agency required cities to reduce lead levels in drinking water, but no funds were made available for these purposes.

Social Problems. In 1988 a general awareness of the problems posed by a permanent, isolated, and expanding urban "underclass" intensified. A leading scholar has called the growth of the urban underclass "one of the most important social transformations of the last quarter of the 20th century." The families and individuals making up the underclass—numbering in the millions—are chronically poor and unemployed, exhibiting high rates of drug addiction and crime. One federal response in 1988 was the passage and signing of an omnibus drug bill (*see* feature article, page 38).

Homelessness continued to be an urban problem of crisis proportions. Advocacy groups estimated the number of homeless at 3 million or more, and the problem showed no sign of easing. Out of a national stock of 4 million public housing units, 70,000 are lost each year due to age and poor maintenance—far exceeding the approximately 20,000 federally assisted units constructed in 1988. But the housing shortage confronts both the poor and nonpoor, as condominium conversions drive up rents in the remaining units. In such cities as New York, San Francisco, and Boston, vacancy rates average only 1–2%.

Cities and states have undertaken a variety of programs to expand housing supplies. Several states have enacted housing trust funds, which provide money to developers or non-profit organizations to build low-cost housing. Seattle voters approved a bond issue to raise local funds for low-income housing. The National Corporation for Housing Partnerships urged local governments to issue low-income housing bonds, but bond issues were actually down in volume during the year. Several cities have developed programs which link commercial and for-profit residential development to low-income housing construction. San Diego initiated a program to preserve existing single-room occupancy (SRO) units and adopted new building regulations to make construction of new SROs affordable. However, these programs supplied only a tiny proportion of the needed units—perhaps 1% or less.

DENNIS R. JUDD
University of Missouri-St. Louis

COINS AND COIN COLLECTING

Perhaps the most significant events of 1988 as far as commemorative coinage was concerned were the Winter and Summer Olympic Games. Olympic fever has, in recent years, prompted governments to strike coins to satisfy the demand for artistic, intrinsically valuable souvenirs of the competitions. Among the countries releasing coinage to commemorate the 1988 games were Cook Islands, Niue, Panama, Portugal, Switzerland, and the United States, as well as the host nations Canada and the Republic of Korea.

The U.S. Mint was authorized to strike a total of 1 million gold $5 coins and 10 million silver $1 coins to commemorate participation by American athletes in the 1988 competition. A surcharge included in the price of the coins was designated for contribution to the U.S. Olympic Committee. The obverse of the 1988 U.S. Olympic $5 piece was designed by Elizabeth Jones, chief sculptor-engraver of the U.S. Mint; much-honored sculptor Marcel Jovine created the $5 reverse. The work of sculptor Patricia Lewis Verani was chosen for the silver $1 Olympic coin obverse, while that of U.S. Mint assistant sculptor-engraver Sherl J. Winter was selected for the reverse.

Other coins issued in 1988 included a regular-issue Australia 50-cent piece noting the discovery of Australia by Europeans in 1788. The reverse features a sailing ship in front of an old map of the region. Portugal announced the first set in a new series of legal-tender commemorative coins honoring its 15th- and 16th-century explorers, who, by venturing into the unknown, led the way for the discovery of America in 1492. Another series of coins was released by Israel to mark its 40th anniversary.

1988 U.S. Olympic gold $5 coin

1988 U.S. Olympic silver $1 coin

1988 Australian platinum bullion coin

New Coinage and Mint Status. Bullion coin producers saw increased competition as two more countries began bidding for a share of the precious-metals investment market. Great Britain introduced a 22-karat-gold ''Britannia'' in the latter part of 1987, and Australia unveiled a new platinum legal-tender coin dubbed the ''Koala.'' Canada added platinum and silver versions of its Maple Leaf bullion coins.

Since late 1974, the West Point Bullion Depository has produced coins for circulation, special numismatic issues, medals, and American Eagle gold bullion coins. It was granted full Mint status on March 31, 1988. The San Francisco Assay Office, at which coinage operations were suspended from March 1955 until 1965, was restored to full Mint status on the same date.

In 1987 coin hobbyists and professionals had been vocal about their desire for a change in the designs of U.S. circulating coinage. Letters and petitions led to introduction of the American Coin Redesign Act in October 1987; hearings were conducted before the U.S. Senate Committee on Banking, Housing, and Urban Affairs in April and September 1988. Advocates stress the need for artistic coinage that expresses U.S. culture and history.

MARILYN A. REBACK
Associate Editor, ''The Numismatist''

In Bogotá, April 7, Colombia's President Virgilio Barco Vargas, right, and U.S. Attorney General Edwin Meese discuss the drug-trafficking issue.

AP/Wide World

COLOMBIA

The situation in Colombia during 1988 could be summed up by a single headline: "Economy Healthy Amid Violence." The year was marked by the continued escalation of violence by guerrilla groups and the drug "Mafia"; by a healthy if not robust economy; and by the first election of local officials in the nation's history.

Politics. Direct elections of mayors and state legislators, held on March 13, produced mixed results. Only 48% of eligible voters went to the polls, compared with 61% in the 1986 presidential balloting. The elections were regarded as a test of the old-line political parties—the Liberals and Conservatives—against the challenge of the leftist Union Patriotica (UP). The results confirmed continued dominance by the old guard, as Liberals won 420 and Conservatives won 412 of the 1,008 contested mayoralties. The Conservatives scored a major triumph in Bogotá with the election of Andres Pastrana, son of former President Misael Pastrana Borrero, as mayor.

In January, Andres Pastrana had been kidnapped by the "extraditables" (members of the drug cartel fighting extradition to the United

States). He was released unharmed, but later that month Attorney General Carlos Mauro Hoyos, a leading antidrug crusader, was brutally slain. At midyear, the Supreme Court suspended the issuance of extradition permits pending a new law validating the 1979 extradition treaty with the United States.

Violence and kidnapping were not limited to the drug cartel, however, as attacks by various guerrilla groups—both rightist and leftist—increased during the year. On May 29, prominent opposition leader Alvero Gómez Hurtado of the Social Conservative Party was kidnapped by an urban cell of the leftist M-19 group; he was released two months later. The government announced that there were 9,808 violent deaths during the first six months of the year.

Economy. The nation's economy remained strong, although the escalating violence appeared to be affecting agricultural production (down 15%) and petroleum exports. Industrial production was up 5.3% for the first five months, compared with 5.1% in 1987. Exports during the first half were up 7.7% over 1987, despite a 12% decline in coffee exports. Foreign investment rose 177.3% during the first four months. Exports of cocaine were estimated at $300 billion in 1987, of which $135 billion worth went to the United States.

Foreign Relations. Drugs remained the major issue between Colombia and the United States. The release from custody in January of suspected drug kingpin Jorge Luís Ochoa touched off loud U.S. protests and restrictions on imports of Colombian products. The threat of retaliatory action by the Organization of American States forced Washington to lift the restrictions.

Colombia strengthened ties with Argentina and Brazil during the year, signing an economic integration agreement with the former and exchanging head of state visits with the latter.

ERNEST A. DUFF
Randolph-Macon Woman's College

COLOMBIA • Information Highlights

Official Name: Republic of Colombia.
Location: Northwest South America.
Area: 439,734 sq mi (1 138 910 km²).
Population (mid-1988 est.): 30,600,000.
Chief City (Oct. 15, 1985): Bogotá, the capital, 3,982,941.
Government: *Head of state and government,* Virgilio Barco Vargas, president (took office Aug. 1986). *Legislature*—Parliament; Senate and House of Representatives.
Monetary Unit: Peso (320.00 pesos equal U.S.$1, Oct. 26, 1988).
Gross National Product (1987 est. U.S. $): $34,000,000,000.
Economic Index (Bogotá, 1987): *Consumer Prices* (1980 = 100), all items, 403.7; food, 430.9.
Foreign Trade (1987 U.S.$): *Imports,* $3,907,000,000; *exports,* $4,642,000,000.

COLORADO

Colorado voters generally endorsed the political status quo in 1988, keeping Republicans in control of the state legislature and reelecting all six incumbent U.S. Representatives—three Republicans and three Democrats; meanwhile, the sagging economy showed some improvement.

Politics. In the 6th District, three-term Republican incumbent Dan Schaefer was challenged vigorously by former Republican State Sen. Martha Ezzard, who switched to the Democrats in 1987. Ezzard raised nearly $500,000, but Schaefer won a fourth term in the heavily Republican district with 63% of the vote. The 2d District race was almost a mirror image of the 6th. Incumbent Rep. David Skaggs (D) and his Republican challenger, David Bath, served together as Democrats in the Colorado House before Bath switched to the GOP. But Bath had trouble raising money and Skaggs' well-financed campaign won a second term also with 63% of the vote. Colorado's four other incumbent U.S. Representatives— Democrats Pat Schroeder and Ben Campbell, and Republicans Hank Brown and Joel Hefley —won by even larger margins.

Democrat Michael Dukakis fought hard for Colorado's eight electoral votes, visiting the state five times. But Bush, who campaigned in Colorado seven times, won with 52.8% to 45.6% for Dukakis. The Bush victory did not have much of a local "coattail" effect. Democrats picked up one seat in the state Senate and two in the state House of Representatives. But the GOP kept control over both chambers with a 24-11 Senate majority and a 39-26 House edge.

For the sixth time since 1970, Colorado voters rejected a far-reaching tax-limitation plan. The 1988 version, amendment 6, was defeated by more than 57% of the voters after opponents warned it would force extensive cuts in public services. Voters also rejected amendment 7, which would have allowed the state to resume paying for abortions for indigent women. Such payments stopped in 1984, when voters narrowly approved a constitutional amendment banning them. The 1988 rematch between pro-life and pro-choice forces was more decisive— the proposal to restore abortion funding was crushed by almost 59% of the vote.

Amendment 1, which establishes English as the official language of Colorado, won handily with 59% of the vote. Opponents, especially Hispanics, charged the proposal smacked of racism, but backers successfully argued it would promote cultural unity. Legal experts said the amendment was largely symbolic because it does not restrict the use of bilingual ballots or bilingual-education programs.

Denver's Mayor Federico Peña, reelected in 1987, narrowly missed an unscheduled electoral test in 1988, when a petition for his recall fell short of the required number of signatures. The petitioners accused Peña of mismanaging city operations and his ambitious plans for Denver's development.

Economy. On the economic front, Colorado continued to recover slowly from the slump triggered by falling prices for oil and other natural resources. Major employers such as Data General Corp., Union Pacific Resources, and Chevron USA announced new cutbacks in their Colorado work forces. On the bright side, Cray Research picked Colorado Springs as the site for a new production facility for its upcoming Cray-3 supercomputer, which should create about 1,000 new jobs by 1990. Martin-Marietta Corp. captured a $508 million contract to develop a computer complex to support the Strategic Defense Initiative in Colorado Springs that was expected to provide 1,500 more jobs by 1992.

In September state officials announced that the Colorado unemployment rate stood at 5.9%. While that figure was still higher than the national unemployment rate of 5.4% for September, it was much better than the 9.1% recorded in March 1987, the state's highest rate in more than 40 years. Part of the drop in the jobless rate was caused by unemployed Colorado residents moving to other states. But Colorado also posted actual job gains due to improvements in the state's tourism and farm economies, as well as manufacturing.

In June, voters in suburban Adams County approved a plan allowing Denver to annex almost 50 sq mi (130 km²) to build a new metropolitan airport, which civic leaders hope will provide a further economic boost.

Sports. The Denver Broncos lost the 1988 Super Bowl for a second consecutive year as the Washington Redskins flattened them 42–10. The Broncos then went on to have a very disappointing 1988 season, finishing with a 8–8 record and without a play-off berth.

BOB EWEGEN, *"The Denver Post"*

COLORADO · Information Highlights

Area: 104,091 sq mi (269 596 km²).

Population (July 1, 1987): 3,296,000.

Chief Cities (July 1, 1986 est.): Denver, the capital, 505,000; Colorado Springs, 272,000; Aurora, 217,990; Lakewood, 122,140.

Government (1988): *Chief Officers*—governor, Roy Romer (D); lt. gov., Michael Callihan (D). *General Assembly*—Senate, 35 members; House of Representatives, 65 members.

State Finances (fiscal year 1987): *Revenue,* $6,723,000,000; *expenditure,* $5,456,000,000.

Personal Income (1987): $51,369,000,000; per capita, $15,584.

Labor Force (June 1988): *Civilian labor force,* 1,691,700; *unemployed,* 105,100 (6.2% of total force).

Education: *Enrollment* (fall 1986)—public elementary schools, 386,304; public secondary, 172,111; colleges and universities, 181,907. *Public school expenditures,* (1986–87), $2,123,000,000 ($4,129 per pupil).

COMMUNICATION TECHNOLOGY

In 1988 significant advances were made in the technologies that underlie modern communication. The Integrated Services Digital Network (ISDN) took further steps toward realization with a series of successful trials and demonstrations. The growing size and complexity of communication networks stimulated the development of automated management systems. Progress in microelectronics and microprocessing also continued, with developments in integrated circuits and photonics setting records for circuit capacity and speed of operation.

Transmission and Switching. The first demonstration of ISDN operation was conducted in early 1988, utilizing 64 kbs (kilobits per second) for transmission of voice, data, facsimile, and desktop conferencing. ISDN trials were underway or being planned in 20 U.S. local exchanges and more than a dozen other countries.

A new commercial mobile cellular telephone system using digital technology was demonstrated by AT&T Bell Laboratories. The system uses only one third the bandwidth of the present 30 kHz (kilohertz) analog system, allowing it to carry three times as many calls per radio channel. Since it can handle digital data, it gives cellular radio access to ISDN.

A local area computer network (LAN) capable of transmitting information between computers at a rate of 1.4 Gbs (gigabits per second) was introduced by Scientific Computer Systems Corporation. It can transfer the contents of an entire encyclopedia in less than three seconds.

TAT-8, the first transoceanic optical fiber cable system, was completed in 1988, connecting the United States, Great Britain, and France. With an initial capacity of 280 Mbs (megabits per second), it can support 8,000 phone circuits. Bit-compression techniques eventually will increase the capacity by five times. A similar cable across the Pacific, HAW-4/TPC-3, neared completion. It will connect California with Hawaii, Guam, and Japan.

The U.S. Federal Communications Commission approved plans for TAT-9, a transatlantic light-guide cable with an even greater capacity—1.7 Gbs, capable of carrying 80,000 simultaneous phone calls. It will be built by a consortium of nine countries and is expected to be completed by 1991 at a cost of $400 million.

Network Management. With the rapid growth of communication networks, the need for automatic, computer-aided management systems has become urgent. Automatic configuration of lines and switches; systems for measuring performance, locating problems, and effecting quick restoration of service in case of trouble; and software programs for a multiplicity of supervisory functions have begun to make their appearance. Intensive development also is underway in the field of Operating Systems, which make use of supervision and measuring equipment controlled by computers embedded in the network and guided by programs known as Expert Systems (ES). In this new approach to network management, ES program modules incorporate the life experience, problem-solving techniques, reasoning power, and intuition of technicians skilled in the design, operation, and maintenance of communication facilities. As of 1988, at least half a dozen Expert Systems were being employed.

Facsimile (FAX) Machines. Although the transmission of pictures and text over telephone lines is not new, the introduction of lower-priced (as low as $800) and improved FAX machines had a major impact on business communications in 1988. Up to one million units were sold in the United States during the year, while in Japan—the principal manufacturing source—more than 2.5 million were in use. FAX equipment combines a telephone line and a small, simple machine into which the page to be transmitted is inserted. The pictures or printed words are scanned automatically and converted into electrical signals corresponding to the point-by-point density of each element. A page can be copied and transmitted across the United States in less than one minute.

Microelectronics and Microprocessors. The IBM Corporation developed a bipolar heterojunction transistor with a silicon collector and emitter and a silicon-germanium base. The new structure will increase the useful frequency range of bipolar transistors from the present upper limit of 25 GHz to as high as 50-75 GHz.

Researchers at AT&T Bell Laboratories reported a new electro-optical effect of potentially great importance in high-speed lasers, light detectors, and modulators. In a gallium arsenide semiconductor sandwiched between two layers of other materials, the light absorption can be switched from zero (on) to complete (off) by applying a small voltage. The light absorption in this mechanism—called a "quantum well"—is about 50 times greater than for any other effect so far used. As a superfast optical shutter, it has potential applications in lightwave transmission and optical computers.

Researchers continued efforts to incorporate more circuit functions and memory capabilities in tiny semiconductor chips—the heart of modern computers. With the present technique of photolithography, which employs ultraviolet light, the width of the lines that form the circuits is about 1.5 microns (millionths of a meter). X rays, however, which are shorter in wavelength than ultraviolet light, could print lines finer by a factor of ten. This would allow nearly one billion circuits to be engraved on a single chip.

M.D. FAGEN
Formerly, AT&T Bell Laboratories

COMPUTERS

The distinctions among types of computers blurred during 1988 as companies introduced desktop supercomputers, super minicomputers more powerful than minisupercomputers, and workstations able to run personal computer software. Steven Jobs, former head of Apple Computer, introduced the NeXT Computer System, intended primarily for university students. Based on the Motorola 68030 processor, NeXT uses a variation of Unix as its operating system and a new laser technology for storing text, photographic images, and other details.

More Powerful Chips. The "brain" of a personal computer is a silicon chip, or microprocessor, not much bigger than the head of a thumbtack. Over the years microprocessors have become ever more powerful, reaching the point that they may become the processing units of mini- and mainframe computers.

Intel Corporation has dominated the microprocessor market, most recently with its 80286 and 80386 chips. These are the centerpieces of the IBM PC (personal computer) and IBM PS/2 series and their myriad clones. Intel's next-generation chip, the 80486, is expected to be introduced by early 1989. With more than one million transistors, it will have the number-crunching power of some mainframes, thus ushering in the era of personal mainframes.

Still greater computing power is promised by advocates of RISC (reduced instruction set computer) technology. The RISC concept was developed by IBM in the 1970s, but it is only now taking off. As general-purpose microprocessors have evolved and become more powerful, they also have become more complex; today's chips contain hundreds of instructions that rarely are used. Eliminating these instructions from the chip and putting them in software results in greater speed at lower cost. That is the premise behind RISC. Fewer functions are built into the circuits of a RISC chip, and the execution of instructions is streamlined.

Motorola and Intel were among the companies introducing RISC chips in 1988, and a price war developed as competition heated up. At summer's end, LSI Logic began selling its Sparc chips for as little as $79, a drastic reduction from the $600 charged by some firms.

Operating Systems. An operating system (OS) comprises the programs that enable a computer to manage its internal housekeeping tasks. The OS interacts with memory, controls input and output functions, and communicates with the user. The most widely used operating system in personal computers has been the Disk Operating System (DOS), a version of which is used in IBM PCs, PS/2s, and their clones.

The year 1988 saw the introduction of several versions of the new OS/2 operating system, jointly developed by IBM and Microsoft. Designed to work with IBM's PS/2 series, OS/2 provides access to very large amounts of RAM (random access memory) and allows users to run several programs simultaneously. Its value will be realized better with the introduction of "Killer Apps." These powerful new

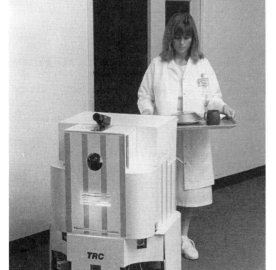

Like their human colleagues, robots are moving from the manufacturing sector into service jobs. HelpMate, left, developed by Transitions Research Corp., delivers meals to hospital patients. "Robin," below, developed by Odetics, Inc. for nuclear-plant use, walks on six legs and can change a light bulb or lift a 300-lb (136-kg) object.

Computer Viruses

As biological viruses run rampant through large segments of the human population, their electronic counterparts are spreading among computers. Known as computer viruses, these are bits of computer codes rather than living microorganisms. But they share important characteristics with human infections. First, they replicate themselves and spread from one program to another. Second, they may lie dormant for months or even longer, then suddenly attack. Third, they are capable of wreaking incredible destruction.

Computer viruses—there are hundreds of varieties—originate with programmers who write the code. Typically, the code is attached surreptitiously to existing software, such as a popular utility or word-processing program. The program is then disseminated, perhaps via an electronic bulletin board or a company's computer network. Once inside a new host, the virus reproduces. Then, at a preset time, the virus is activated.

Some viruses are innocuous. Many, however, are designed to destroy or scramble data and programs or damage monitors and disk drives. To add insult to injury, the virus often taunts its victim with a final message on the screen: "Gotcha!"

Although the phenomenon of computer viruses dates back to the 1970s, only recently has alarm over them become widespread. This is due to the growing number of computer users who have suffered from infections, as well as the publicity given several incidents. In one case, a recently fired employee planted a virus in his former company's computer system that once each month would wipe out all records of sales commissions. The company lost 168,000 records before discovering and disabling the program. In September the former employee was convicted of harmful access to a computer and faced a possible ten-year prison term.

In another case, the so-called SCORES virus, designed to sabotage a private computer company in Texas, was introduced—either deliberately or accidentally—into thousands of personal computers as well as data processing systems at the U.S. National Aeronautics and Space Administration, Environmental Protection Agency, and other government agencies, destroying files and delaying projects.

Defense against viruses is difficult, though certain precautions, such as tightening security controls over electronic networks, can be taken. And as in the world of medicine, vaccines are available. These are programs that help detect viruses lurking on disks and vaccinate against future infections.

JENNY TESAR

applications packages will have standardized command structures, enabling a user to move from one program to another without having to learn an entirely different set of commands for each program.

Computer Security. People's increasing dependence on computer systems has created a growing awareness of the need for greater protection of data against loss, theft, and fraud. In January 1988, President Ronald Reagan signed into law the Computer Security Act of 1987, which requires the National Bureau of Standards to develop security standards and guidelines for all government computer and telecommunications systems except those classified for national security reasons.

Many security experts are alarmed at the ease with which unauthorized people can gain access to computers. For instance, in April it was disclosed that, using international phone links, a West German citizen had gained access to 30 unclassified computers belonging to the U.S. Defense Department and other military organizations around the world.

Technologies to combat such problems range from software that controls data-base access to hardware that encodes data or scrambles it when a phone line is tapped. Government agencies and private organizations are issuing electronic "smart cards" to employees, who must enter the cards into the computer in order to gain access to information.

Video Terminals: Health Issues. Two research projects in 1988 provided new evidence that looking at video display terminals (VDTs) for long periods of time can affect people's health. In one study, subjects who worked an average of six hours a day on VDTs for more than four years experienced difficulty in focusing their eyes, particularly on near objects. It was not established how long such problems persist after work on VDTs ceases.

The second study found that women who spent more than 20 hours a week at VDTs during the first three months of pregnancy experienced twice as many miscarriages as did pregnant women who did not use VDTs. Whether this was caused by the VDT or working conditions was not determined. Some suspect that the culprit is low-level electromagnetic radiation emitted by the terminals. This fear received new support when an international team of researchers reported that magnetic fields of the type emitted by VDTs can cause "significant developmental abnormalities" in chicken embryos.

Physicians recommend frequent breaks and annual eye checkups for workers who use VDTs for long periods. Some localities have passed laws requiring companies to subsidize eye examinations and any corrective lenses required because of working on VDTs.

JENNY TESAR, *Free-lance Science Writer*

Connecticut's Attorney General Joseph I. Lieberman, a 42-year-old Democrat who also had served in the state legislature, narrowly defeated Sen. Lowell P. Weicker, Jr., a liberal Republican who was seeking a fourth term.

CONNECTICUT

Republican George Bush, who was reared in Greenwich and whose father, Prescott Bush, represented the state in the U.S. Senate from 1952 to 1963, easily won Connecticut's eight electoral votes in the November presidential election. Bush won 53% of the votes cast compared with 47% for Democrat Michael Dukakis.

The big surprise of the election was the defeat of Republican Lowell P. Weicker, who had served 18 years in the U.S. Senate and was seeking a fourth six-year term. Weicker was upset by Democrat Joseph I. Lieberman, Connecticut's attorney general, by a narrow margin. In previous elections, Weicker successfully had won voter support with his reputation as a moderate Republican who often bolted from following his party's wishes in the Senate. However, Lieberman's campaign strategy of avoiding identification with his party's liberal wing apparently captured Connecticut voters, who were in a conservative mood as reflected by their choice of George Bush for president.

The state's U.S. representative delegation in Washington remained evenly divided politically as all six incumbents were reelected. They were Democrats Barbara B. Kennelly, Sam Gejdenson, and Bruce A. Morrison and Republicans Christopher Shays, John G. Rowland, and Nancy L. Johnson. The Democrats retained firm control of the state legislature.

Legislature. The 1988 session of the General Assembly adopted a record $6.3 billion budget, a 12% increase in spending over the 1987–88 fiscal year. Legislators also adopted a 5% pay raise for themselves in 1989, a $60 million tax exemption for large corporations, a $1.6 billion bonding package for cities and towns, a $34.4 million bailout for the city of Bridgeport, and a package of building inspection reforms.

In September, Gov. William O'Neill ordered state agencies to cut spending by 3% to offset a projected budget deficit.

Settlement. A settlement totaling more than $41 million was announced on November 4, resolving all claims and litigation stemming from the deaths and injuries resulting from the April 23, 1987, collapse of a half-finished apartment building at L'Ambiance Plaza in Bridgeport. Most of the money would go to the families of the 28 men killed and to the 16 workers injured in the accident. The settlement was worked out by a mediation panel made up of two judges and was approved by state and judicial officials December 1. For reasons of insufficient evidence, federal authorities also decided not to press criminal charges and to forgive all but

---

CONNECTICUT • Information Highlights

Area: 5,018 sq mi (12 997 km²).

Population (July 1, 1987): 3,211,000.

Chief Cities (July 1, 1986 est.): Hartford, the capital, 137,980; Bridgeport, 141,860; New Haven, 123,450; Waterbury, 102,300.

Government (1988): *Chief Officers*—governor, William A. O'Neill (D); lt. gov., Joseph J. Fauliso (D). *General Assembly*—Senate, 36 members; House of Representatives, 151 members.

State Finances (fiscal year 1987): *Revenue,* $7,595,000,000; *expenditure,* $6,666,000,000.

Personal Income (1987): $68,291,000,000; per capita, $21,266.

Labor Force (June 1988): *Civilian labor force,* 1,761,800; *unemployed,* 53,000 (3.0% of total force).

Education: *Enrollment* (fall 1986)—public elementary schools, 321,823; public secondary, 147,024; colleges and universities, 159,040. *Public school expenditures* (1986–87), $2,493,000,000 ($5,552 per pupil).

$430,000 of $5.1 million in fines levied by the Occupational Safety and Health Administration against contractors for safety violations.

Strikes. Workers at the Electric Boat submarine shipyard in Groton went on strike in July after members of the Metal Trades Council, a coalition of ten unions, rejected a contract offer. Also on strike in 1988 were jai-alai players from frontons in Hartford and Bridgeport. The former walkout was settled on October 12; the latter one continued into December.

Academia. During the year, there were changes at the top among the state's colleges and universities. In July, Wesleyan University appointed Stanford University faculty member William M. Chace to succeed Colin G. Campbell as president. Trinity College President James F. English announced that he would retire in July 1989. English had become president of Trinity in 1977 after a 26-year career at Connecticut Bank and Trust Company. Humphrey Tonkin, an English-literature scholar, was selected in October as president of the University of Hartford.

ROBERT F. MURPHY, *"The Hartford Courant"*

CONSUMER AFFAIRS

"As a consumer, I am not delighted by the cornucopia of goods available to me. Instead, I am angry that I can't begin to make a systematic comparison and thus a rational choice. And so I buy haphazardly, as other consumers do." These words, spoken by a concerned consumer named Ellen C. Webb, reflected an apparently rising level of frustration in the U.S. buying public regarding both the proliferation of products and the increasing complexity of many products. More and more consumers are depending on the Consumer Union's monthly magazine *Consumer Reports* for guidance. More often than not, however, American consumers just are paying their money and taking their chances.

Consumer Fraud. The proliferation and complexity of products are just two problems confronting consumers. Another is consumer fraud. Three major fraud cases made news in 1988. Early in the year, the Hertz Corporation conceded that it had defrauded motorists and insurance companies by charging them inflated and sometimes fictitious collision-repair costs. Hertz was fined $6.85 million—the largest known fine ever imposed on a corporation in a criminal consumer-fraud case—and ordered to make restitutions totaling at least $13.7 million to the victims.

A former chief executive and a former vice-president of the Beech-Nut Nutrition Corporation were fined $100,000 each and sentenced to one year and one day in jail for permitting the distribution of phony apple juice intended for babies. The juice was marketed as 100% pure but actually was made from a flavored concentrate that contained little or no apple juice.

And the Chrysler Corporation—which in 1987 was embarrassed by revelations that it had sold as new automobiles with disconnected odometers that had been driven by company executives—came under fire again. In August the company agreed to reimburse some 39,500 people who had bought Chrysler cars that had been test-driven with disconnected odometers. And in September, Chrysler was charged by the New York attorney general's office with violating the state's "lemon law." Under that law the company had bought back 400 defective automobiles, but then it allowed New York dealers to resell them without warning purchasers. Chrysler agreed to pay up to $2 million in a settlement that New York Attorney General Robert Abrams called the first of its kind in the nation.

Federal Consumer Activity. Federal legislation, passed by Congress and signed into law by President Ronald Reagan in 1987, that limits the length of time banks can hold deposited checks, began going into effect on Sept. 1, 1988. Under the provisions, checks drawn on banks in the same region of the Federal Reserve System must be cleared within three business days (two beginning on Sept. 1, 1990). Cashier's checks, certified checks, and government checks must be made available for withdrawal by 9 A.M. on the day after deposit.

In October 1988, Congress passed and President Reagan signed a bill that requires banks, retail stores, and other issuers of credit cards to disclose to consumers such information as annual fees, interest charges, method of calculating unpaid balance, late fees, over-the-limit fees, and other details. Nearly 106 million Americans in 1988 held approximately 800 million credit cards.

In late October the Consumer Product Safety Commission approved a ban on lawn darts, which had been responsible for many injuries. It also agreed to extend its ban on the sale of three-wheeled all-terrain vehicles.

Product Liability. The U.S. Congress in 1988 took up another hotly debated consumer issue —product liability. Consumer groups and product manufacturers were divided deeply over a bill that would establish the first federal product-liability laws, preempting conflicting state statutes with a federal standard. The drive for federal legislation stemmed from hefty increases in the premiums manufacturers pay for product liability insurance. Proponents of the measure said it would bring them relief from state laws that are stacked against them. Consumer advocates argued that the measure would make it harder for persons injured by defective or dangerous products to sue manufacturers for just compensation. By year's end, no final action had been taken on the bill.

STEWART M. LEE, *Geneva College*

FBI Director William Sessions (right) *attends a mid-April congressional hearing on the status of organized crime in the United States. Georgia's Democratic Sen. Sam Nunn,* left, *chaired the investigation.*

AP/Wide World

CRIME

Which U.S. presidential candidate would best control crime? That question played a major role in the 1988 campaign, as Republican Vice-President George Bush and Democratic Gov. Michael Dukakis (MA) attacked each other on such crime issues as control of drugs (*see* feature article, page 38), prison furloughs, and capital punishment. Each candidate, reflecting the public mood, tried to outdo the other in terms of his "toughness" toward criminal offenders and sympathy for crime victims. The 1960s stress on compassion for lower-class criminals and its emphasis on rehabilitation now were seen clearly by political office-seekers as unappealing to voters. Being viewed as "soft on crime" has become a serious political handicap.

Prison Furloughs. The notorious case of William Horton, Jr., a convicted murderer who was allowed to leave a Massachusetts prison on a weekend pass and then raped a Maryland woman and brutally beat her fiancé, haunted the Dukakis campaign. The Bush forces enlisted the fiancé to express publicly his outrage at Horton's furlough. Dukakis was criticized also for failing to apologize to the Maryland couple, a matter that was taken to indicate his "astounding lack of sensitivity and a lack of human compassion toward crime victims and their families." Bush argued that Dukakis and the "liberal Democratic leadership" were "so blinded by their ideology that they can't see the human costs of this kind of social experiment." It also was pointed out that 60 of the Massachusetts prisoners allowed out on temporary passes were still at large.

Dukakis, stung by the epithet "the furlough king," counterattacked: "You don't think I'm going to let Bush get away with this furlough business, do you?" he said. "[I]t's obviously an attempt to divert attention from his [Bush's] failure every time he's been given an assignment involving law enforcement and drugs." Dukakis admitted that "the Horton incident was a tragedy" but pointed out that the program, which had been instituted during an earlier Republican administration in Massachusetts, was changed as a result. He also argued that nearly one quarter of the prisoners in federal institutions, including some convicted drug traffickers and murderers, had received furloughs during the previous year. In Massachusetts, the overall escape rate was 0.5% for the 10,835 inmates granted furloughs between 1982 and 1987. In addition, 39 other states had furlough programs. Under the California program when Ronald Reagan was governor, two convicts had committed murder while on furlough in 1972, but the program has not been changed.

Bush pointed out that Massachusetts had the only program that extended furloughs to first-degree murderers who were not eligible for parole. Dukakis in turn stressed that under his governorship, Massachusetts had the second-largest four-year drop in crime of any state, down 13% while the rate for the nation as a whole was rising. Moreover, he indicated, Massachusetts also had the lowest homicide rate of any major industrialized state.

Capital Punishment. The death penalty was another subject on which Bush (in favor) and Dukakis (opposed) disagreed. According to a comprehensive study by the U.S. Bureau of Justice Statistics on the application of capital punishment from 1976 (when it was reinstated by the U.S. Supreme Court) to 1987, there had been 224,400 reported cases of murder and non-negligent manslaughter, and 217,120 ar-

Mario Biaggi (D-NY) is surrounded by his wife and his lawyer as he resigns from Congress. Earlier he had been convicted of racketeering, conspiracy, and extortion.

rests for these crimes. During the same period, 2,743 persons were sentenced to death and 93 (about one in thirty) were executed. Almost one third of those sentenced to death were removed from death rows for new trials, new sentences, or commutations, or else died before their execution date. Prisoners executed during 1987 had spent an average of seven years and two months on death row. Some 62% of death row inmates currently are being held in Southern states, 18% in the West, 15% in the Midwest, and 5% in the Northeast. About 50% are 33 or older. As of late 1988, 37 states had capital punishment laws.

Blacks are overrepresented strikingly on death rows, making up 41.4% of the total (compared with 12% of the U.S. population). Writing in *The Wall Street Journal,* Christopher Mulder maintained that blacks are victims of a pattern of discrimination in criminal justice that focuses on the race of the victim. The death penalty was sought in 49% of the cases of capital murder in which a black killed a white, Mulder pointed out, but in only 11% of the cases in which a black killed a black. He suggested that white judicial officials tend to identify with victims who belong to their own group more readily than with those who do not, even in the absence of conscious prejudice. He also argued that the makeup of juries in capital cases has a significant effect: Blacks are excluded disproportionately from capital cases because they are more likely than whites to oppose the death penalty.

Gun Control. Despite the tough stances of the presidential candidates on crime control,

the U.S. House of Representatives in October rejected legislation that would have imposed a nationwide seven-day waiting period for the purchase of a handgun. This measure, supported by President Ronald Reagan, had been recommended by many law enforcement authorities as a way to reduce the incidence of homicide. The waiting period was intended to give local police time to run background checks on potential handgun purchasers to provide a cooling-off period that might prevent some crimes of passion. But the so-called "Brady amendment"—named after White House Press Secretary James Brady, who was injured seriously in the 1981 assassination attempt against President Reagan—was defeated on the House floor by a 228–182 vote. Following the vote, Dewey Stokes, president of the Fraternal Order of Police, contended that the lobby effort in favor of the measure had been overcome by congressional campaign contributions from the 2.8-million-member National Rifle Association, which vigorously opposed the amendment.

In 1986, Congress had placed curbs on the sale of armor-piercing bullets, which pose a threat to law-enforcement officers. In 1988, it also banned the manufacture, sale, or possession of firearms with plastic or ceramic frames that could evade detection by X-ray machines or metal detectors. The measure was anticipatory, since no such guns had yet been manufactured. The new law requires all guns to have at least 3.7 oz. (105 g) of metal so that they can be detected by airport magnetometers.

In May, Maryland became the first jurisdiction in the United States to ban cheap handguns known as "Saturday night specials." The measure goes into effect at the beginning of 1990. Proponents of the bill had called upon Brady's wife, Sarah, and Coretta Scott King, wife of the slain civil-rights leader, to promote passage of the legislation. Mrs. Brady claimed that in the past 20 years, Saturday night specials had been used to kill 250,000 persons and injure 1.5 million others. James Brady himself praised the measure: "I'd like to see other states, like dominoes, fall into line," he said. "Thumbs up for Maryland." The state attorney general, however, said that the law will have minimal impact unless the federal government and neighboring states also ban the guns.

Toy guns also came under attack during the year, after incidents in which police officers, mistaking such toys for real guns, killed three youths. By year's end, a dozen cities and the state of Connecticut had regulated the manufacture of realistic toy guns, and some companies began altering their designs. Psychologists have suggested that toy guns, as well as war toys, lead to violent behavior. They point to research showing increased violence in children after playing with such toys. One researcher, for example, found that play with "He-Man" and "Master of the Universe"

dolls doubled the incidence of antisocial and violent behavior versus play with "Cabbage Patch" dolls. "We are transmitting an unhealthy message," he said, "encouraging children to have fun pretending to murder each other." Another psychiatrist insisted that "the message of toy guns is that you solve problems by pulling a trigger." Other specialists, however, claim that the results of research on toy guns is suspect because of the small number of subjects and the subjective definition of aggression. And a spokesman for the Hasbro company, which makes an army doll called "G.I. Joe," voiced the opinion of many manufacturers: "The reality is," he said, "that children have played fantasy games involving the triumph of good over evil for centuries."

Crime Rates. The National Crime Survey (NCS), based on interviews with a random sample of the U.S. population, reported a 1.8% increase in the incidence of crime during 1988, ending a five-year decline in annual NCS totals. Even with the increase, however, crime levels were 16% lower than in 1981, the peak year. The slight increase, according to Alfred Blumstein of Carnegie-Mellon University, was the result of a greater concentration of lower-income groups in younger segments of the population, "where the crime goes on." People in the West were most likely to be the victims of crime, while residents of the Northeast were the least likely.

In a May report, the U.S. Bureau of Justice Statistics noted that statistics from the United Nations, International Police Organization (Interpol), and World Health Organization showed a rate of violent and property crimes several times higher in the United States than in various other countries. Crimes of violence (homicide, rape, and robbery), for example, were found to be four to nine times more frequent in the United States than they are in Europe. The United States reported a homicide rate of 7.9 per 100,000 population, compared with—for example—1.2 in Denmark, 0.8 in Ireland, 3.0 in Portugal, and 1.1 in Switzerland.

White-Collar Crime. Legislation passed by Congress just prior to adjournment in October increased the penalties for insider stock trading, the white-collar crime most in the spotlight during 1988. The measure, titled the Insider Trading and Securities Fraud Act of 1988, made securities firms civilly liable for triple the amount of illegal profits should they "knowingly or recklessly" fail to supervise staff and prevent trading on insider information. The maximum fine was increased from $500,000 to $2.5 million per violation. In addition, investors who traded at the time that insiders were reaping illegal profits could seek damages for their losses. The bill also provided for bounties to informants of up to 10% of the fine or penalty in a particular case, and authorized the Securities and Exchange Commission to cooperate with foreign countries investigating frauds by their citizens or others in the United States.

The measure was the first congressional response to the insider trading scandals that began with the 1986 case against merger specialist Dennis L. Levine. In October 1988, Stephen Sui-Kuan Wang, Jr., a former Morgan Stanley & Company analyst who allegedly gained $200,000 in a multimillion-dollar insider trading scheme, was sentenced to a three-year prison term, to be followed by two years of probation. Wang was accused of passing confidential information about his company's investment banking deals to a Taiwanese businessman.

The previous month, the federal government filed a civil suit charging the Wall Street firm of Drexel Burnham Lambert and Michael Milken, the head of its junk bond division, with civil violation of securities laws. The company was accused of insider trading, stock manipulation, hiding the true ownership of stocks, and keeping phony books. Milken was accused of buying stock when he had inside information about takeovers. In December, Drexel agreed to plead guilty on six related criminal charges and pay a $650 million fine.

The U.S. Sentencing Commission during 1988 released recommendations for restructuring the sentencing of white-collar criminals. By the recommendations, punishment would be calculated on the basis of a complex formula that multiplies the loss caused by the crime times the probability that the offender will be caught. Critics claimed that the formula would render punishment so insignificant that in most cases it would deter prosecutors from pursuing white-collar criminals. During the year a number of federal judges ruled that the sentencing guidelines in general were unconstitutional. In June, the U.S. Supreme Court agreed to review the matter.

Organized Crime. Twenty defendants said to make up the entire membership of the Lucchese organized-crime family in New Jersey were acquitted in August after one of the longest criminal trials in U.S. history. The defendants were charged with running a criminal enterprise that included the sale of cocaine, credit-card fraud, gambling, and loan-sharking. The trial lasted 21 months, produced more than 40,000 pages of testimony, and was believed to cost millions of dollars.

Forensic Criminology. The ability to analyze DNA (deoxyribonucleic acid) from a single human hair was reported during the year. Hair is one of the most common clues left at crime scenes. The new technique also can be applied to samples of human tissue, semen, or blood when the sample is too small or too poorly preserved to be studied by traditional means.

See also PRISONS.

GILBERT GEIS
University of California, Irvine

CUBA

The most important policy decision adopted by the Cuban government in 1988, the 30th year of the Castro revolution, was to continue along its own socialist path and to reject *perestroika* and *glasnost*, the renovating ideological and administrative changes advocated by the Soviet Union under Mikhail Gorbachev. This policy line, forcefully stated by President Fidel Castro, was underlined by a vigorous campaign to "rectify errors and negative tendencies," which Havana said were the results of an experiment in economic liberalization abandoned two years earlier.

Domestic Affairs. Even though the Cuban economy declined in 1988, mainly because of lower agricultural and industrial output and the low world market price of sugar, the country's main export, there were no serious efforts to arrest that decline. The government's only new economic initiative was to revive the experiment of "mini-brigades" terminated in the late 1970s as unproductive and antieconomical. In 1988 these same work gangs of "volunteers" from factories and offices were given the task of building apartment houses, schools, and other installations.

Insisting that Cuba "must safeguard its independence," Castro, in his July 26 speech marking the anniversary of the revolution, said that the "outstanding characteristic of the (Cuban) revolution is that it has not copied anyone . . . and does not have to rectify anything whatsoever. We are not going to deviate from (our) path a single inch." Despite this implicit criticism of the Soviet reforms, and another, more explicit, of the Soviet participation in the Seoul Olympic Games, which Cuba boycotted in support of North Korea's claim to cohost the games, the Cuban president insisted that his relations with Moscow were good. He said he had spoken about the issue to General Secretary Gorbachev who, Castro reported, assured him that there was no need for Cuba and the USSR to "do things the same way." Ideological differences with Havana notwithstanding, the Soviet Union gave no indication that it would curtail its economic aid to Cuba. This aid totals about $3.5 billion a year—exclusive of military assistance.

Even though the Cuban news coverage of the political and economic reforms in the Soviet Union was very limited and selective, it seemed unlikely that the Cuban people could be isolated for long from the winds of change blowing from Moscow through the Communist world. Soviet publications describing the Gorbachev reforms were sold out within minutes after they were put on sale.

According to Havana, Cuba's 1987 domestic commercial production fell by 3.2% and sugar production by 3.9%. Partial 1988 production figures indicated that Cuba produced between 7.3 and 7.5 million tons of sugar, slightly more than the harvest of 7,231,000 tons in 1987. Castro asserted that in 1989 the country must produce more than 8 million tons of sugar to resolve its foreign currency shortfall.

Foreign Relations. On the diplomatic front, Cuba moved to solve two old and difficult problems: its military presence in Angola and its dismal human-rights record. In 1975, Castro sent thousands of soldiers to Angola to help that country's pro-Soviet government repel a South African invasion. The Cubans stayed, and over the years fought alongside Angolan government troops against both South African raids into Angola and antigovernment Angolan rebels. Late in 1987, Angola, faced with a major South African attack on the town of Cuito Guanavale, requested Cuban reinforcements. Fresh Cuban troops, including squadrons of MiG 23 fighters, arrived in Angola in the first weeks of 1988. In February the Cubans, by that time 50,000 strong, pushed the South Africans back into Namibia with heavy losses. As the fighting died down, diplomatic talks aimed at reaching a peaceful solution to the Angolan-Namibian crisis received a new impetus, encouraged by the United States, with the Soviet Union in the wings supporting the U.S. effort. By mid-December, negotiators for Cuba, Angola, South Africa, and the United States reached agreement on a timetable for the removal of Cuban troops from Angola and independence for Namibia.

In September a special United Nations Commission, empowered to assess the human-rights conditions in Cuba, visited a number of the country's prisons and talked to scores of political prisoners, some jailed for more than 20 years. Representatives of the International Red Cross and of other human-rights organizations visited Cuba for the same purpose. Their preliminary findings were that while some reforms had taken place in Cuban jails, violations of human rights continued and citizens were still receiving very high prison sentences for even minor antigovernment activities.

Cuban-U.S. relations remained unchanged, with Castro waiting for the new U.S. adminis-

---

CUBA • Information Highlights

Official Name: Republic of Cuba.
Location: Caribbean.
Area: 42,803 sq mi (110 860 km²).
Population (mid-1988 est.): 10,400,000.
Chief Cities (Dec. 31, 1986 est.): Havana, the capital, 2,036,799; Santiago de Cuba, 364,544; Camagüey, 265,588; Holguín, 199,861.
Government: *Head of state and government,* Fidel Castro Ruz, president (took office under a new constitution, Dec. 1976). *Legislature* (unicameral) —National Assembly of People's Power.
Monetary Unit: Peso (0.748 peso equals U.S.$1, July 1988).
Foreign Trade (1986 U.S.$): *Imports,* $9,173,000,000; *exports,* $6,298,000,000.

tration to make the next move. Restrictions on importing and exporting books, films, phonographs, and other informational material to and from Cuba, in force since 1962, were eliminated by a trade bill signed into law by President Reagan in August. Cuba reestablished diplomatic relations with Ecuador and was moving toward the reestablishment of ties with Colombia. The European Community, at Cuba's request, also agreed to establish diplomatic relations with the Havana government.

GEORGE VOLSKY, *University of Miami*

CYPRUS

During 1988, UN Secretary-General Javier Pérez de Cuéllar's efforts to reconcile the Greek Cypriot majority with the Turkish Cypriot minority led to a resumption of talks between the two communities. However, the island remained split in two as it had been since 1974 when Turkey invaded and occupied about 37% of Cyprus' territory. The occupied zone was unilaterally proclaimed the "Turkish Republic of Northern Cyprus" in 1983, but received international recognition only from Turkey. In 1988 the UN Peacekeeping Force—numbering about 2,100 troops—continued to be stationed on the island, along with about 4,000 British army and air force personnel.

Elections. The first of two presidential elections was held on Feb. 14, 1988, with participation only by Greek Cypriots; incumbent President Spyros Kyprianou lost his bid for a third term. A runoff election was held February 21 between the two top contenders, Glafkos Clerides, who had served as acting president in 1974, and George Vassiliou, a multimillionaire businessman running as an independent. With the help of the Cypriot Communist party, AKEL, Vassiliou won.

Plan for Reunion. Vassiliou's chief aim was to seek reconciliation with the Turkish Cypriots and an end to the occupation. While espousing the concept that Cyprus should be recast as a unified federal republic with separate local administrative areas for the Greek and Turkish Cypriots, he emphasized the need for the "three freedoms." These were that all Cypriots would have freedom to travel, to secure property, and to settle anywhere on the island. Equally, he called for the withdrawal of the approximately 29,000 Turkish troops of occupation and of the settlers—estimated at 60,000 to 65,000—that the Turks had brought in from the mainland. He emphasized that the roughly 200,000 Greek Cypriots who had fled from the north during the 1974 invasion should be allowed to return home. Vassiliou also called for the demilitarization and nonalignment of the island, which he said would benefit both communities. The Turkish Cypriot leadership, however, saw his initiatives as a Greek Cypriot attempt to dominate the whole island.

Intercommunal Talks. Vassiliou and Rauf Denktas, leader of the Turkish Republic of Northern Cyprus, met in Geneva in August 1988 under the auspices of Pérez de Cuéllar to resume intercommunal talks which had collapsed early in 1985. Though the Cyprus government did not recognize Denktas' title as president in northern Cyprus, the two men seemed cordial publicly; and they set June 1, 1989, as the date by which to reach an agreement. They met again in Nicosia beginning in September 1988, and in November held discussions at the UN in New York, where Denktas' unfavorable attitude about the "three freedoms" and the implementation of other reforms became a stumbling block. A further meeting was held in Nicosia in December.

Terrorism. Attention was fixed on Cyprus in April, when a hijacked Kuwaiti airliner made a forced landing at Larnaca airport. The hijackers killed two hostages before airport officials gave them fuel to go on to Algiers.

Economy. As in prior years, the unoccupied areas prospered while the economy in the north, faced with occupation and new settlers from Turkey, stagnated. With his government promoting foreign investments, Vassiliou said in November that Cyprus eventually would apply for membership in the European Community.

GEORGE J. MARCOPOULOS
Tufts University

CYPRUS • Information Highlights

Official Name: Republic of Cyprus.
Location: Eastern Mediterranean.
Area: 3,571 sq mi (9 250 km²).
Population (mid-1988 est.): 700,000.
Chief Cities (1982 est.): Nicosia, the capital, 149,100; Limassol, 107,200.
Government: *Head of state and government,* George Vassiliou, president (took office Feb. 1988). *Legislature*—House of Representatives.
Monetary Unit: Pound (0.486 pound equals U.S.$1, July 1988).
Gross Domestic Product (1984 est. U.S.$): $2,400,-000,000.
Economic Index (1987): *Consumer Prices* (1980 = 100), all items, 143.5.
Foreign Trade (1987 U.S.$): *Imports,* $1,484,000,000; *exports,* $608,000,000.

CZECHOSLOVAKIA

The rise to power of Czechoslovakia's new Communist Party chief Miloš Jakeš in December 1987 was followed by a change of government leaders in October 1988. Lubomir Strougal, a reform-minded moderate, was replaced as premier by Ladislav Adamec, considered to be more conservative. New ministers of foreign affairs and internal affairs also were appointed, and a noted hard-liner, Jan Fojtík, became the party's chief ideologist.

On October 27, for the first time in four decades of Communist rule, the formation of the Czechoslovak state in 1918 was celebrated in the streets of Prague. In August a mass protest marked the 20th anniversary of the Soviet invasion.

The Economy. In July 1988 a new law on state industrial enterprises went into effect, and some 30% of enterprises had converted to the new system by late in the year. The law provides for the election of managers and workers' councils by the employees of the respective enterprises who could vote for the managers' recall. But the right to nominate managerial candidates and to initiate managers' recall was retained by the state. Economic performance was to be evaluated according to how well it satisfied the needs of the consumers rather than how it fulfilled production targets. Employee remuneration was to be determined by the quality, quantity, and social importance of products and services. But prices continued to be set by the state. Enterprises were directed to fulfill their tasks in consonance with the policy of the Communist Party, and party organizations remained "the political nuclei" of each enterprise's workers' collective. New laws also were enacted to provide slightly better conditions for the operation of citizens' cooperative ventures.

In view of the many restrictive provisions included in the new laws, it seemed doubtful that this kind of "restructuring" really could do what it was supposed to do for the country's economy, whose performance continued to be rather mediocre. Although in the first half of 1988 increases over the corresponding period of 1987 were registered in industrial production (2.8%), construction (3.5%), labor productivity in industry (2.7%) and construction (3.7%), freight transportation (5.6%), and foreign trade (2.2%), production costs remained too high and the technical level of a great many products remained well below world standards.

Religious Affairs and Human Rights. After protracted negotiations agreement finally was reached between Czechoslovakia and the Vatican on the appointment of three new bishops. Even so most of Czechoslovakia's 13 dioceses still remained without functioning bishops. Nor has there been any really significant improvement in state-church relations. In April, Prague's archbishop, Cardinal František Tomášek, felt it necessary to write a letter to the premier complaining about the "repressive and unjust character of the state's religious policy." The most blatant act of government repression occurred in March when a peaceful gathering of some 2,000 Slovak Catholics in the Slovak capital, Bratislava, was dispersed brutally by riot police and water cannons. A petition protesting religious discrimination was signed by some 550,000 Czechs and Slovaks.

Haunted by the memories of the "Czechoslovak Spring"—the 1968 reform movement halted by a Soviet-led military intervention—the Communist regime resisted attempts to liberalize the system and force more respect for human rights. Even so, on August 21 some 10,000 people in Prague staged a massive protest demonstration to commemorate the 20th anniversary of the Soviet invasion.

International Relations. Among the international accords signed by Czechoslovakia in 1988 were agreements with China and Bulgaria on long-term economic, scientific, and technological cooperation. An agreement also was signed with West Germany on inland shipping.

EDWARD TABORSKY
University of Texas at Austin

CZECHOSLOVAKIA • Information Highlights

Official Name: Czechoslovak Socialist Republic.
Location: East-central Europe.
Area: 49,371 sq mi (127 870 km²).
Population (mid-1988 est.): 15,600,000.
Chief Cities (Jan. 1, 1986 est.): Prague, the capital, 1,193,513; Bratislava, 417,103; Brno, 385,684.
Government: *Head of state,* Gustáv Husák, president (took office 1975). *Head of government,* Ladislav Adamec, premier (took office 1988). *Communist party,* general secretary, Miloš Jakeš (took office 1987). *Legislature*—Federal Assembly.
Monetary Unit: Koruna (9.140 koruny equal U.S.$1, July 1988).
Economic Indexes (1987): *Consumer Prices* (1980 = 100), all items, 111.0; food, 114.3. *Industrial Production* (1986, 1980 = 100), 118.
Foreign Trade (1987 U.S.$): *Imports,* $23,391,-000,000; *exports,* $22,958,000,000.

DANCE

The dance world appeared to be in a celebratory mood in 1988, emphasizing festivals, galas, and anniversaries. The season also was marked by historic events. The Soviet Union permitted its dancers for the first time to perform as guest artists in the repertories of American companies, and the Paris Opera Ballet School, the symbolic cradle of classical dance, made its debut in the United States.

For all the surface gaiety, the deaths of leading dance personalities cast a shadow. Robert Joffrey died after a long illness, 32 years after he founded the Joffrey Ballet. Gerald Arpino, the company's associate director, succeeded him as artistic director. Arpino, also the troupe's resident choreographer, pledged to continue Joffrey's policy of promoting new works and reviving major 20th-century ballets.

The death of Sir Frederick Ashton, England's greatest choreographer and a former director of the Royal Ballet, removed a giant of 20th-century ballet. Other key dance figures who died in 1988 were Hugh Laing, whose dramatic power in Antony Tudor's works made him a star in American Ballet Theatre (ABT); La Meri, the American dancer who was an expert on ethnic forms; William Carter, formerly a leading dancer in ABT and the New York City Ballet; and Arnie Zane, the experimental choreographer and dancer.

Controversy surrounding the death on Dec. 29, 1987, of Patrick Bissell, a principal dancer in ABT, marked the beginning of the year. Speculation about substance abuse in the ballet world mounted (to subside later) after Bissell's death officially was ruled as drug-related. The season's artistic side was happier, however.

Soviet Presence. The unprecedented flow of Soviet dancers to the United States obviously stemmed from the Soviet Union's policy of *glasnost*. Thus, Nina Ananiashvili and Andris Liepa, young stars of the Bolshoi Ballet, were able to spend three weeks with the New York City Ballet in New York. They performed in three George Balanchine works, the kind of plotless ballets once condemned in Russia. The Kirov Ballet, the Bolshoi's rival, sent Altynai Assylmuratova and Faruk Ruzimatov to perform in New York with ABT in the 19th-century classic *La Bayadère*. In December, Susan Jaffe of ABT danced in Leningrad with the Kirov.

Maya Plisetskaya, the senior Bolshoi ballerina, and a group of Bolshoi dancers spent three weeks in Boston at a Soviet-American music and dance festival organized by Sarah Caldwell, director of the Opera Company of Boston. Mikhail Baryshnikov, who defected from the Kirov in 1974, appeared at a gala honoring the 62-year-old ballerina. Although past her prime, Plisetskaya won over audiences with her strong presence in her own ballets. These works were considered mediocre choreographic illustrations of literary sources *(Anna Karenina, The Sea Gull, The Lady with a Small Dog)* and shrewd vehicles for Plisetskaya's superstar personality. A new choreographer, Andrei Petrov, made a better showing with *Sketches,* from Gogol's stories.

The Moscow Classical Ballet, another new Soviet group, served fleetingly as a showcase for Yekaterina Maksimova, a popular 49-year-old Bolshoi ballerina, and introduced two young virtuosos, Ilghiz Galimullin and Vladimir Malakhov. The Georgian State Dancers and Pavel Virsky's Ukrainian Dance Company,

© Martha Swope

Helene Alexopolous and Alexandre Proia are featured in "Ives, Songs," a major new work by Jerome Robbins that was performed by the New York City Ballet during 1988.

two Soviet folk ensembles, returned to the United States after a long absence.

Ballet Premieres. American ballet troupes presented more new productions than usual. Christian Lacroix, the French fashion designer, rightly was credited with the huge success of a new staging of Léonide Massine's 1938 *Gaîté Parisienne.* ABT's gala for this occasion was filled with an audience in Lacroix gowns whose bright colors and fantasy were echoed in the costumes onstage. Choreographic ingenuity marked ABT's world premieres. Mark Morris' *Drink to Me Only with Thine Eyes* matched the wit of its music, Virgil Thomson's *Études.* Clark Tippet cleverly explored ballet conventions in *Bruch Violin Concerto No. 1.* Agnes de Mille turned to folk dance for inspiration in *The Informer,* a tale of betrayal in Ireland. Tudor's *Gala Performance* was revived.

The Joffrey Ballet again stimulated interest by staging *Cotillon,* a 1932 Balanchine "lost" ballet that had not been performed since 1946. Tina LeBlanc and Edward Stierle, two young stars emerging from the Joffrey ranks, were outstanding in the work. Although today's audiences could not be convinced that this was a major Balanchine work, its perfumed imagery of young people at a ball served to reveal a different Balanchine from the more abstract choreographer of later years.

James Kudelka, a talented Canadian who has worked previously with the Joffrey Ballet, created *Concerto Grosso,* a ballet set to music by the Canadian composer Jean Papineau-Couture that explored different patterns in partnering.

The New York City Ballet celebrated its 40th anniversary in November. Earlier, in the spring, it staged a three-week festival devoted to American composers. The American Music Festival, conceived by Peter Martins, presented 22 new works, 15 ballets from the repertory, one company premiere, and a work danced by the School of American Ballet, the company school. Premieres came from 15 choreographers. Joseph Duell, Balanchine, and Jerome Robbins were represented by earlier ballets. Critical opinion was divided on the festival, which was very well attended. The choreography was uneven but excitement was generated by the participation of musicians such as Leonard Bernstein, Morton Gould, and Ray Charles.

The most successful premieres were Martins' *Black and White* and *The Waltz Project,* Paul Taylor's *Danbury Mix,* Lar Lubovitch's *Rhapsody in Blue,* and William Forsythe's *Behind the China Dogs.* Other festival choreographers were Eliot Feld, Laura Dean, Violette Verdy, Jean-Pierre Bonnefoux, Robert Weiss, Christopher d'Amboise, Robert La Fosse, Miriam Mahdaviani, Bart Cook, Richard Tanner, and Ib Andersen.

The City Ballet earlier performed a major new Robbins work, *Ives, Songs.* A figure identified with the composer Charles Ives looked back at turn-of-the-century America.

Forsythe, the American director of the Frankfurt Ballet in West Germany, seemed ubiquitous. The San Francisco Ballet came to Washington, DC, with a lavish new *Swan Lake* and the East Coast premiere of Forsythe's *New Sleep.* The choreographer's signature style— fierce energy applied to classical steps danced in an off-center manner—was seen also in his premiere for the City Ballet, in the New York City debut of the Frankfurt Ballet, and in *In the Middle, Somewhat Elevated,* performed by the Paris Opera Ballet at the Metropolitan Opera House.

Cheered at the City Ballet, Forsythe was booed by a more conservative audience at the Met. The Paris Opera Ballet met further resistance with the American premieres of experimental and imaginative dance-theater pieces such as Maguy Marin's *Leçons de Ténèbres* and Robert Wilson's version of *Le Martyre de Saint Sébastien,* created in 1911 by Gabriele D'Annunzio. Rudolf Nureyev, the troupe's director, was honored by a 50th birthday gala that brought together many of his former partners.

A complete success was scored by the young pupils of the Paris Opera Ballet School, whose purity and refinement come down from the school's 17th-century origins. The students presented an all-day classroom demonstration and performed in *Soir de Fête* and *Les Deux Pigeons.*

Other visitors to the United States included the Royal Danish Ballet, the National Ballet of Canada, the Royal Spanish National Ballet, and DV8, a new experimental British group, that shocked some with its violent movement.

Modern Dance. The First New York International Festival of the Arts, a month-long event, included modern-dance troupes from abroad. Pina Bausch presented *Victor* and *Carnations;* Daniel Larrieu staged *Waterproof* in a swimming pool.

Major activity in modern dance came from American companies. The Martha Graham Dance Company offered the new *Night Chant* and a reconstruction of *Deep Song* (1937), a powerful solo inspired by the Spanish Civil War. Dan Wagoner's *To Comfort Ghosts* stood out in its poetic sensibility. Among other premieres were Erick Hawkins' *Cantilever Two,* Merce Cunningham's *Eleven,* Paul Taylor's *Brandenburgs* and *Counterswarm,* and Alvin Ailey's *Opus McShann.*

Ailey received the Kennedy Center Honors, while the Samuel Scripps-American Dance Festival Award went to Hawkins. Charles (Honi) Coles won the Capezio Award.

ANNA KISSELGOFF
"The New York Times"

© Susan Gregg/The News-Journal Papers

Delaware politicians continued a state tradition by gathering on Return Day (two days after the November elections) to bury a hatchet—literally and figuratively. Winners included incumbent Gov. Michael Castle (second from right).

DELAWARE

Return Day, a unique Delaware tradition, marked the end of the long 1988 election campaign for residents of the Diamond State. This celebration, held two days after the general election, traditionally marks the time when returns were gathered by horseback and officially announced. More recently, Return Day almost has reached the stage of becoming a state holiday as politicians gather in Georgetown, DE. Winning and losing candidates ride together in an open carriage. A symbolic hatchet is buried to signify the ending of the election competition and the beginning of a new era in the governing process.

Election 1988. There were few surprises for Delawareans on Return Day as most races turned out as predicted. The state's voters held to a tradition of awarding Delaware's three electoral votes to the winning presidential candidate, in this case, Republican George Bush. U.S. Sen. William V. Roth, Jr., (R) defeated incumbent Lt. Gov. S. B. Woo (D) by a margin of 62% to 38%. Woo had made history in 1984 by becoming the highest ranking Chinese-American elected statewide official in the United States. Michael N. Castle (R) overwhelmed his opponent, Jacob Kreshtool (D), by a margin of 71% to 29% to gain four more years as governor. Congressman Thomas R. Carper (D) won his fourth term in the U.S. House of Representatives by defeating political newcomer James P. Krapf, Sr., (R) by 67% to 33%.

The race for the independently elected position of lieutenant governor featured two nonincumbents. Dale E. Wolf (R), running as a teammate with Governor Castle, defeated his opponent Gary E. Hindes (D) by a margin of 53% to 47%.

Incumbent County Executive Rita Justice (R) became the state's only major officeholder to suffer defeat. She was repudiated by the voters of New Castle County, as they elected State Auditor Dennis E. Greenhouse (D) to the executive post by the margin of 73% to 27%.

DELAWARE • Information Highlights

Area: 2,045 sq mi (5 295 km²).
Population (July 1, 1987): 644,000.
Chief Cities (1980 census): Dover, the capital, 23,512; Wilmington, 70,195; Newark, 25,247; Elsmere, 6,493.
Government (1988): *Chief Officers*—governor, Michael N. Castle (R); lt. gov., S. B. Woo (D). *General Assembly*—Senate, 21 members; House of Representatives, 41 members.
State Finances (fiscal year 1987): *Revenue,* $1,980,000,000: *expenditure,* $1,553,000,000.
Personal Income (1987): $10,751,000,000; per capita, $16,696.
Labor Force (June 1988): *Civilian labor force,* 352,800; *unemployed,* 10,600 (3.0% of total force).
Education: *Enrollment* (fall 1986)—public elementary schools, 64,807; public secondary, 29,603; colleges and universities, 33,895. *Public school expenditures* (1986–87), $413,000,000 ($4,776 per pupil).

Split control was retained in the Delaware General Assembly as the Democrats held their margin of 13 to eight in the Senate, and the Republicans increased their hold on the House by one seat for a 23 to 18 edge. Daniel S. Frawley (D) was reelected as the mayor of Wilmington, defeating his opponent Donald R. Smythe (R) by a margin of 60% to 40%.

Legislative Session. The eyes of the nation's business leaders were on Delaware as the General Assembly considered major legislation regulating corporate takeovers. The measure, which was passed and signed into law, established rules that make the hostile takeover of a corporation more difficult.

350th Anniversary. King Carl XVI Gustaf and Queen Silvia of Sweden were the leading group of dignitaries to visit the state to celebrate the 350th anniversary of the founding of New Sweden, in what is now Wilmington. The colony, founded in 1638, became the first permanent European settlement in the Delaware Valley and one of the earliest in North America. A reenactment of the landing of the first settlers was carried out by the Swedish Navy.

Sports. The University of Delaware became a major site for the training of world-class figure skaters as a major new Ice Skating Science Development Center was opened there. Six pairs of skaters trained in Delaware were members of the U.S. Olympic team competing at the 1988 Winter Games in Calgary.

JEROME R. LEWIS
University of Delaware

DENMARK

On May 10, 1988, the Danes went to the polls for the second time in eight months to elect a new Folketing (parliament). The ostensible reason was a resolution passed by parliament on April 14, providing that captains of foreign naval vessels calling at Danish ports be given a letter stating that Denmark does not tolerate nuclear weapons on its territory in times of peace and that they were to abide by this injunction. The measure, which was backed by the three socialist parties and the Radical Liberals but opposed by the cabinet, was problematic for Denmark's membership in the North Atlantic Treaty Organization (NATO) because of the U.S. and British policies of not disclosing whether or not their vessels are carrying nuclear weapons. Prime Minister Poul Schlüter called for an election to bring public opinion to bear.

Election returns showed the Progress Party to be the biggest victors, advancing from nine to 16 seats, while the parties that had supported the resolution lost seven seats. The four-party coalition in the cabinet—the Conservative Party, Center Democrats, Liberals, and the Christian People's Party—ended up with the same number of seats overall (70 seats out of 179) as before, and still lacked a majority. Following three weeks of negotiations, a new minority cabinet, commanding 67 seats, took office on June 3. Once again headed by Poul Schlüter of the Conservative Party, the new cabinet consisted of eight other members of that party, five members of the Radical Liberal Party, and seven members of the Liberal Party.

In his speech opening the new session of parliament on June 7, the prime minister emphasized that the guidelines regarding nuclear weapons on foreign vessels calling at Danish ports would be in force, but captains were to be left free to confirm or deny their presence.

Economic Affairs. Throughout 1988, efforts were made to maintain a tight fiscal policy in spite of a deficit on the balance of payments, while stimulating exports and holding down domestic consumer demands. A stringent wage policy and encouragement of private-sector savings were also aims of the government.

On October 1, Denmark became the first member country of the European Community to open its borders to other EC members, making it possible for the Danes to get loans in foreign currencies and to place their money in foreign banks.

The Faeroe Islands. The Faeroe Islands, part of the Kingdom of Denmark, in the spring celebrated the 40th anniversary of its gaining local autonomy in several areas of government. The population of 46,000 continued to face difficulties arising from the introduction of the new Law of the Sea Convention, mandating 200-mi (322-km) economic zones abutting islands as well as landmasses. Faeroese fishermen, in the main confined to their own zone, have seen their catches reduced and their incomes lowered. An agreement with the Soviet Union concerning fishing in each other's waters has alleviated the situation but is a source of controversy.

ERIK J. FRIIS
"The Scandinavian-American Bulletin"

DENMARK • Information Highlights

Official Name: Kingdom of Denmark.
Location: Northwest Europe.
Area: 16,629 sq mi (43 070 km²).
Population (mid-1988 est.): 5,100,000.
Chief Cities (Jan. 1, 1985 est.): Copenhagen, the capital, 1,358,540; Århus, 194,348; Odense, 136,803.
Government: *Head of state,* Margrethe II, queen (acceded Jan. 1972). *Head of government,* Poul Schlüter, prime minister (took office Sept. 1982). *Legislature* (unicameral)—Folketing.
Monetary Unit: Krone (6.885 kroner equal U.S.$1, Nov. 7, 1988).
Gross National Product (1986 U.S.$): $78,700,-000,000.
Economic Indexes (1987): *Consumer Prices* (1980 = 100), all items, 157.8; food, 152.0. *Industrial Production* (1980 = 100), 122.
Foreign Trade (1987 U.S.$): *Imports,* $25,444,-000,000; *exports,* $25,576,000,000.

DRUGS AND ALCOHOL. *See* WAR ON DRUGS, page 38; SPECIAL REPORT/MEDICINE AND HEALTH—*The Problems of Alcohol*, page 351.

ECUADOR

Politics in economically troubled Ecuador took a leftward turn in 1988 with the election of Rodrigo Borja Cevallos, a social democrat, as president.

Borja, 52, won a runoff election on May 8 against populist Abdala Bucaram Ortiz, a former mayor of Guayaquil, Ecuador's largest city. The two men had finished at the top of the balloting in the first electoral round held on January 31. Out of the running following that race were conservative Sixto Duran Ballen of the governing Social Christian Party and Frank Vargas Pazzos, a former Air Force officer who had led two unsuccessful attempts to overthrow the government of President León Febres Cordero.

On August 10, Febres Cordero, a strong advocate of free-market economic policies, handed over the presidential power to Borja, whose Democratic Left Party favors more government involvement in the Ecuadoran economy. It was the second consecutive peaceful transition from one elected government to another in Ecuador, which for decades has been plagued by political instability. Febres Cordero had defeated Borja in a runoff election in 1984.

To assure a legislative majority, Borja formed an alliance with the left-of-center Christian Democrat Party. The 30 legislative seats of Borja's Democratic Left, together with the seven seats held by the Christian Democrats, gave the coalition a majority in the 71-member national congress.

Nationalization. Borja moved quickly to reassure the country he would not change radically the mix of public and private firms in Ecuador. In a press conference shortly before his May 8 victory, he said, "I reiterate that we do not have any plans to make properties state-owned. This is for the simple reason that we believe that state ownership is not sufficiently effective. . . ."

Nonetheless, within a month of taking office, Borja announced plans for the government to assume control of the country's major oil fields and the main pipeline that transports crude oil from the interior to refineries on the coast. Government spokesmen insisted that this was not an instance of nationalization, but followed the terms of a contract with Texaco, which holds a 37.5% interest in the oil facilities. The contract, the spokesmen said, calls for Ecuador to assume full control of the pipeline by October 1989 and of the oil fields by July 1990. Texaco is to receive payment of a reported $300 million in the transfer.

Oil and Debt. In a parallel action, the Borja government said it would seek an increase in its oil production quota from the Organization of the Petroleum Exporting Countries (OPEC) because of the economic crisis facing the country. Ecuador's normal quota was 210,000 barrels a day, which OPEC temporarily increased to 310,000 barrels in 1987 to allow Ecuador to repay oil borrowed from Venezuela and Nigeria when the main pipeline was ruptured by an earthquake. Ecuador was seeking to extend the temporary quota beyond its scheduled expiration date.

With prices declining on the international oil market, Ecuador's budget was in critical condition. The country's energy minister said that 1988 budget projections were based on a minimum price of $17 a barrel for oil, which had dropped into the $11-a-barrel range by midyear. As a result, Borja pronounced Ecuador's $9.2 billion foreign debt as "unpayable," and urged Latin American cooperation to resolve the region's external debt problem.

Unrest. Borja's ascendancy to the presidency did little to quell the social unrest in the country. Ecuador's economy was virtually stagnant, with an economic contraction of 5% in 1987 due to earthquake damage, and an inflation rate of 55%. Strikes, which had plagued the latter part of the Febres Cordero presidency, continued. At the end of August, the government imposed an economic austerity program, devaluing the currency, doubling the price of gasoline, and instituting tighter controls on currency-exchange transactions. Nonetheless, as labor agitation mounted, Borja was forced to grant wage increases in several key sectors.

Foreign Affairs. Borja seemed determined to pursue a middle-of-the-road diplomatic course. He restored diplomatic relations with Nicaragua, which had been broken off by Febres Cordero. He also said Ecuador anticipated continued good relations with the United States.

RICHARD C. SCHROEDER
Formerly, "Visión" Magazine

ECUADOR • Information Highlights

Official Name: Republic of Ecuador.
Location: Northwest South America.
Area: 109,483 sq mi (283 560 km²).
Population (mid-1988 est.): 10,200,000.
Chief Cities (mid-1986 est.): Quito, the capital, 1,093,278; Guayaquil, 1,509,108; Cuenca, 193,012.
Government: *Head of state and government,* Rodrigo Borja Cevallos, president (took office August 1988). *Legislature* (unicameral)—Chamber of Representatives.
Monetary Unit: Sucre (511 sucres equal U.S.$1, financial rate, Oct. 19, 1988).
Gross National Product (1986 U.S.$): $13,100,-000,000.
Economic Index (1987): *Consumer Prices* (1980 = 100), all items, 461.9; food, 591.8.
Foreign Trade (1987 U.S.$): *Imports,* $2,052,000,000; *exports,* $1,989,000,000.

EDUCATION

In 1988 the fifth anniversary of *A Nation at Risk*—a landmark federal report that found a "rising tide of mediocrity" in U.S. education—evoked heated debate on the effects of subsequent reform. Before leaving office on September 20, Secretary of Education William J. Bennett issued reports on model elementary and secondary school programs. Other major reports in 1988 focused on urban schools, "geographic illiteracy," and education levels in the work force. Bennett's successor was Lauro F. Cavazos, the nation's first Hispanic-American cabinet secretary.

Debate Over Reform. On April 26, at a White House observance marking the fifth anniversary of *A Nation at Risk,* Secretary Bennett submitted to President Ronald Reagan a report evaluating the effects of school reforms since 1983. According to the new report, titled *American Education: Making It Work,* "We are doing better than we were in 1983. . . . But we are certainly not doing well enough fast enough. We are still at risk." The second part of the report identified "the five fundamental avenues of reform" needed to improve U.S. schools: "strengthening content, ensuring intellectual opportunity, establishing an ethos of achievement, recruiting and rewarding good teachers and principals, and instituting accountability throughout our education system."

Secretary Bennett's report was met with severe criticism by a number of education groups and politicians. National Education Association (NEA) President Mary Futrell called the report a "cover-up for the Reagan administration's failure to help improve America's schools." Federal aid to public schools, she said, fell by one third (from 9.2% in 1981 to 6.2% in 1988) during the Reagan years. According to Futrell, President Reagan's first education secretary, Terrel H. Bell, was excluded from the anniversary ceremony because he advocated "what the White House doesn't want to hear: excellence costs."

Teachers protesting the White House ceremony applauded U.S. Sen. Lowell P. Weicker (R-CT), who called Bennett "the secretary of ignorance." American Federation of Teachers (AFT) President Albert Shanker called Bennett's views a misguided return to the 1930s. "Instead of leading your troops," he wrote in an open letter to the secretary, "you keep shooting at them."

Meanwhile, both the AFT's Shanker and the NEA's Futrell offered reform proposals of their own. Shanker's plan, issued in April, proposed innovative schools-within-existing-school-buildings that would be taught by concerned teachers and attended by a normal range of students whose parents approve—and

a hands-off principal who supports—alternative approaches. Futrell's proposal, issued in March, urged each state to designate one district as an "experimental, living laboratory to fundamentally restructure America's schools." In response to the latter plan, Secretary Bennett commented, "It's rather ironic to hear a call for reform from the organization that has done the most to resist [it]."

NEA and AFT officials were elated by a Rand Corporation study, issued in May, which found that teachers unions were not obstacles to reform but committed agents of change.

A study issued in May by the Carnegie Foundation for the Advancement of Teaching, titled *A Report Card on School Reform,* found that the 13,500 teachers surveyed were "dispirited" about U.S. school reform since 1983. Half the teachers gave it a grade of C; 29% gave it a B; and 20% gave it a D or F. Carnegie President Ernest L. Boyer said that five years of school reform had left teachers "more responsible but less empowered." The challenge now, he said, is to "make teachers full participants in the process."

Curricula. Long an advocate of tougher core curricula in U.S. schools, Secretary Bennett in late December 1987 described in detail the courses he considered essential for high-school students. His ideal curriculum, proposed for a fictional James Madison High School, would include four years of English; three years each of social science, mathematics, and science; two years each of foreign language and physical education; and one year of art and music history.

A similar proposal, made in August 1988 for a fictional James Madison Elementary School, called for a return to classic children's literature, a greater emphasis on writing skills, foreign language instruction by the fourth grade, and exposure to the fundamentals of art and science.

College Costs. In August the College Board reported that college tuition would rise by an average of 7% in 1988–89. Annual costs at four-year, private schools would average $11,330, while fees at four-year public schools would average $4,445 for in-state students. Bennington College in Bennington, VT, was said to be the nation's most expensive school.

Geographic Illiteracy. In a study commissioned by the National Geographic Society (NGS), Americans aged 18–24 ranked sixth in a nine-country survey of basic geographic knowledge. According to the sampling, 75% of Americans could not find the Persian Gulf; 45% did not know where Central America is; only one third could locate Vietnam; one in four could pick out the world's biggest country or largest ocean; only half knew that Nicaragua is the battleground between Sandinistas and contras; and only 14% could identify the United States on a world map. Americans did worse

on the 1988 test than they did in a similar survey 41 years earlier. The study was conducted by the Gallup Organization.

Said NGS President Gilbert M. Grosvenor upon issuing the results in July, "We've lost . . . our young adults to geographic illiteracy. . . . More than 75% of our students have had no geography" in public school.

Troubled Urban Schools. A report issued in March by the Carnegie Foundation for the Advancement of Teaching, titled *An Imperiled Generation: Saving Urban Schools,* found that school systems in six major U.S. cities had unacceptably high dropout rates, old and indecent facilities, and ineffective leaders mired in regulations. "Many people have simply written off city schools as little more than human storehouses to keep young people off the streets," the report said. "The harsh truth is that the reform movement has largely bypassed our most deeply troubled schools."

Among the solutions suggested in the report were decentralizing bureaucracies; making individual schools more accountable for student achievement; dividing large schools into units of no more than 450 students; putting students between kindergarten and fourth grade into an ungraded "basic school"; making high-school schedules more flexible for students with jobs; and building partnerships with parents, colleges, and businesses. Without major federal and other efforts, the report declared, generations of young Americans will be "doomed to frustrating, unproductive lives."

Meanwhile, a 1987 poll of high-school students in Baltimore found that 64% knew someone with a handgun in school; 60% knew someone who had been shot, threatened, or robbed at gunpoint in school; and half of male students said they had carried a handgun at

least once. An alarming increase in guns at schools throughout the United States has been attributed to more drug trade, a spillover of street crime onto school grounds; television violence; and ease of purchase.

Bankruptcy and State Intervention. In late July, a New Jersey judge authorized the state takeover of Jersey City's 29,000-student school system. A report the previous month had documented widespread political patronage, corruption, and mismanagement in the city's 36 public schools. Among the findings were a dropout rate of more than 50%, an absenteeism rate of 20–25%, and a 74% failure rate on the High School Proficiency Test among ninth graders.

State intervention in academically bankrupt school districts was a hotly debated issue in 1988, as Kentucky, Texas, and New Mexico also considered such moves. The shift from local to state control had begun in the 1960s, with a series of legal rulings against the financing of schools through property taxes. By 1986 the states were supplying half of local school budgets, up from 39% in 1966. In addition, reform pressures have led to more direct state control over curriculum, high-school graduation requirements, standardized testing, and other matters. Some observers believe that curricula and other decisions no longer should be left to local whim. Others fear state rigidity, excessive paperwork, and less sensitivity to children's needs.

The National Conference of State Legislatures in July called for a stronger state role, including establishment of student-performance goals, linking of student performance to funding, public comparison of test results among districts, providing technical and other assistance, and taking over academically bankrupt districts.

Open Schools. One school-reform plan with a growing number of supporters encourages parents to enroll children in public schools of their choice outside their neighborhood, even if busing is required. By such "open enrollment," good schools attract more students and get more money, forcing weak schools to improve or close down. The basic plan, first used for desegregation in the 1970s, has been implemented in the south Bronx, NY, parts of Massachusetts, and Minnesota. By 1990, Minnesota will give its 700,000 students the option of enrolling in any public school in the state; up to $4,000 in state aid will be transferred with each student. Advocates of open-school programs see it as a brand of consumerism that improves public schools and a better alternative than a voucher system, which would move public money to private schools.

Changes in Chicago. The Chicago public school system, called the "worst" by state legislators, was the target of a major reform bill passed in December. The city's 594 public

U.S. Public and Private Schools

	1988–89	1987–88
Enrollment		
Kindergarten through Grade 8	32,800,000	32,200,000
High school	13,100,000	13,500,000
Higher education	12,600,000	12,300,000
Total	58,500,000	58,000,000
Number of Teachers		
Elementary and secondary	2,700,000	2,600,000
Higher	700,000	700,000
Total	3,400,000	3,300,000
Graduates		
Public and private high school	2,812,000	2,737,000
Bachelor's degrees	989,000	1,001,000
First professional degrees	74,000	75,000
Master's degrees	290,000	294,000
Doctor's degrees	34,000	34,000
Expenditures		
Public elementary-secondary school	$180,100,000,000	$168,600,000,000
Private elementary-secondary	15,800,000,000	15,100,000,000
Public higher	85,200,000,000	81,300,000,000
Private higher	46,900,000,000	42,700,000,000
Total	$328,000,000,000	$307,700,000,000

schools had 420,000 students, of whom 69% lived below the poverty line, 45% dropped out, and 9% had limited English proficiency. Some 40% of high-school students there were failing two or more courses per year. The teachers union had been unusually strike-prone, and the bureaucracy had 42,167 employees, almost half of whom were not teachers. The city's school budget in 1988 was $1.9 billion, compared with $719 million in 1971, when there were 27% more students. In June the *Chicago Tribune* charged school administrators with "institutionalized child neglect" and urged the use of vouchers, allowing parents to send their children to the city's private schools (where standardized test scores are well above average). Defensive public-school administrators pointed out that parochial schools have more supportive parents and can reject problem students.

The reform, signed into law December 12, removes incumbent members of Chicago's board of education. New members will be appointed by Chicago's mayor, who will select from nominees chosen by a citizens' screening committee. Local councils consisting of parents, teachers, and community residents will be established for each of the city's schools. Each council hires the school principal, exercises some control over spending, and has the authority to fill teaching vacancies. Principals have renewable four-year contracts; tenure is abolished.

Politics and the Administration. Secretary Bennett's resignation took effect on September 20. President Reagan named 61-year-old Lauro F. Cavazos, the president of Texas Tech University, as Bennett's successor. Cavazos was unanimously confirmed (94–0) by the U.S. Senate, but critics saw the appointment of a Texan and Hispanic as an election year ploy in behalf of Vice-President Bush. Following the election it was announced that Cavazos would retain the post in the Bush administration.

In a Gallup poll conducted in April, 78% of respondents ranked quality of education first among 13 major issues in the 1988 presidential election. A poll in August revealed the chief specific concerns about the nation's public schools: drug use, poor discipline, lack of financial support, a need for better teachers, poor curricula, and low standards. Some 90% of respondents (94% of those with children in public schools) urged AIDS education; 73% favored a nationwide exam for high-school graduation (up from 50% in 1958); 88% agreed that "developing the best educational system in the world" would most aid America's strength in the next 25 years; and 64% said they would pay more taxes for better schools (up 6% from 1983).

Better-Educated Work Force. A survey reported by the U.S. Labor Department in March found that the U.S. work force was more educated in 1988 than in 1978. According to the survey, one in four workers in 1988 was a college graduate (compared with one in five in 1978); an additional 20% had one to three years of college (compared with 16%); 40% had high-school diplomas (same); and only 5% had no high-school diploma (24%). College graduates in the work force included 26% whites (21%), 15% blacks (10%), and 13% Hispanics (9%). High-school dropouts in the work force fell to 8% of whites (14%), 23% of blacks (40%), and 40% of Hispanics (52%). The work-force jobless rate was 1.7% for college graduates, 3.7% for workers with one to three years of college, 5.4% for high-school graduates, and 9.4% for high-school dropouts. The jobless rate for black college graduates was more than twice that of white college graduates, 3.3% versus 1.5%. Of the 66% of U.S. working-age women who held jobs (up from 56.1%), 80.6% (up from 70.8%) had a college degree.

Great Britain. One of the most controversial legislative proposals of Britain's Conservative government, the Education Reform Bill, became law on July 29 when it received Royal Assent. It was seen as the nation's most far-reaching educational reform since 1944. Its provisions included:

• a national core curriculum for elementary and secondary schools in English, math, and science; foreign languages, history, technology, and geography; music, art, and physical education;

• national assessment at ages 7, 11, 14, and 16 to monitor student progress;

• allowing parents to vote to "opt out" of local authority control in favor of a centrally administered Grant Maintained Schools Trust;

• open enrollment, allowing schools to accept as many students as space and teaching staff permit;

• tighter financial control of Britain's 47 universities and the abolishment of tenure for new faculty members;

• the transfer of 29 polytechnical and 346 other colleges from local to national control;

• the creation of new city technology colleges (secondary-school level) targeting the needs of industry and trade.

Advocates of the reform had been disillusioned with the effects of progressivism and egalitarianism in British schools during the 1960s and 1970s. Studies had found that the average British 14-year-old was one year behind German students of the same age, while the bottom 40% were two years behind. All in all, fully one fourth of Britain's secondary schools were judged to be unsatisfactory. Critics of the new law saw the reform as politically motivated, taking power from Labour Party-controlled local authorities and strengthening the Conservative grip.

FRANKLIN PARKER
Northern Arizona University

Bilingualism

© Bart Bartholomew/NYT Pictures

A new plan for bilingual education in the Los Angeles school system (above), the United States' second largest, calls for teaching most courses in students' native language until they learn English.

Bilingual education—various forms of instruction in two languages—has existed as a common way of schooling throughout the world for many centuries. While such instruction was used to some degree in the United States in the 19th century, it was introduced more formally in 1963 in Miami, FL, in response to the needs of the Cuban-American community and through the support of English-speaking parents who wanted their children to learn Spanish.

In the United States today bilingual education refers to the use of two languages, one of which is English, as mediums of instruction for all curricular subjects. While originally designed mainly for non-English-speaking students, increasing numbers of classes provide bilingual instruction for both majority and minority students who choose to attend. Federal and state legislation and court decisions have provided incentives for development of special instruction for language-minority students (those who come from a home in which a language other than English is spoken), with such programs having expanded throughout almost all of the states.

The original federal legislation, the Bilingual Education Act of 1968, or Title VII of the Elementary and Secondary Education Act, was designed to assist language-minority children of low-income families who were non- or limited-English-speaking as well as language-minority children who were not succeeding academically even though fluent in English. Reauthorized four times, the Bilingual Education Act of 1988 continues to provide special services for limited-English-proficient students of all socioeconomic backgrounds for those school districts that choose to apply for funds. Twelve states (Alaska, Arizona, California, Connecticut, Illinois, Iowa, Massachusetts, Michigan, New Jersey, Texas, Washington, and Wisconsin) mandate bilingual education for language-minority students through state legislation, and 12 additional states (Colorado, Indiana, Kansas, Maine, Minnesota, New Hampshire, New Mexico, New York, Oregon, Rhode Island, South Dakota, and Utah) have legislation explicitly permitting bilingual instruction.

Types. Many different types of bilingual-program models have been developed to meet the greatly varying needs of students. Four major models are transitional, maintenance, two-way, and immersion. Transitional ("early-exit") bilingual education is a segregated model, offered only to language-minority students who are limited in English proficiency. It

is typically a two-to-three-year program, designed to teach English as a second language and to continue students' subject mastery and cognitive development in native language. Transitional classes are especially important for older students, who cannot afford to lose time in subject-area instruction while learning basic English.

In contrast, maintenance ("late exit") bilingual programs place less emphasis on exiting students from native-language classes as soon as possible. Instead, students receive subject-area instruction in both languages equally for as many grades as the school system can provide. In the United States most maintenance programs end in the sixth grade with secondary-level instruction taught only in English, mainly for lack of bilingual-teacher resources. Research has shown that with no native-language instruction, it takes a student five to eight years to become fully proficient in all aspects of second language needed for schooling. This process can be shortened through the transfer of academic skills from first to second language in a maintenance bilingual program, as students generally begin to succeed in academic achievement after three to five years of schooling in both languages. In a transitional program, native-language instruction helps significantly. However, younger students sometimes are exited too early, causing their long-term academic achievement to suffer.

Two-way bilingual programs, a third model, are another form of the maintenance type, with English-speaking students added to the classes. In the beginning stages of implementation, two teachers instruct each language group separately in native language for a portion of the day, with second language activities that are meaningful to the students provided in all subject areas. As both language groups grow in their second-language proficiency, they work together at all times, with half of their curriculum taught in each language. This integrated model avoids isolation of the minority group, increasing self-esteem and intercultural understanding.

The fourth major program model, immersion, first was developed in Canada for speakers of English to learn French by being schooled in both languages. It has been so successful in developing proficiency in both languages as well as continuing students' strong academic achievement that immersion programs have mushroomed in Canada, even spreading to provinces where there are few French speakers. U.S. immersion programs now are growing in number, with more than 68 schools implementing bilingual-immersion classes in Spanish, French, German, or Cantonese, and English. This model is not to be confused with structured immersion in the United States, in which the curriculum is taught exclusively in English, with the minority language not supported in school.

Early total immersion, one variation, initially provides all instruction in the minority language for kindergarten and first grade, introduces the majority language in second grade, and by fourth grade teaches half the day in one language and half in the other. Late total immersion, a second variation, provides the immersion experience in a minority language at seventh- or eighth-grade level. A third variation, partial immersion, is equivalent to maintenance, with students studying half a day in one language and half in the other for as many years as the school system can provide. Increasing numbers of two-way immersion classes, a fourth variation, now are developing in the United States.

Aims. In all types of bilingual programs, there are three instructional aims: (1) continuing development of the first language, (2) acquisition of the second language, and (3) instruction in all subject areas (e.g., mathematics, science, social studies) using both first and second languages. The program models may differ as to the time each language is introduced or ended in the curriculum, the amount of instructional time in each language, and the degree of integration of minority and majority students. While transitional bilingual programs are the most widespread in the United States, integrated two-way models are growing in popularity as more English-speaking parents choose to have their children participate in bilingual classes. In program evaluations, immersion, two-way, and maintenance bilingual programs have been the most successful in long-term high academic achievement of both minority and majority students.

Most language-minority communities in the United States have endorsed the importance of the development of students' first language literacy and school skills, either through formal public or private schools, or through informal home and community instruction, wherever possible. Research clearly shows that first language literacy and cognitive development significantly aid second language acquisition for school purposes. Sociologists have found that, contrary to the fears expressed by some monolinguals, bilingual schooling increases harmonious relations between ethnic groups and facilitates language minorities' acculturation to and successful participation in the new society.

VIRGINIA P. COLLIER

The Reagans hosted a state dinner for Egypt's President Hosni Mubarak (far left) and wife Susan (far right) in late January 1988. During his visit, and throughout the year, Mubarak sought a greater role as a Middle East peacemaker.

EGYPT

The government's struggle against internal dissent, especially from Muslim fundamentalists, continued during 1988. President Hosni Mubarak's efforts to reintegrate Egypt into the Arab world continued, while he simultaneously maintained attempts to keep the Middle East peace process alive. Egyptians were delighted that one of their countrymen, Naguib Mahfouz, won the 1988 Nobel Prize in literature; he was the first Arabic writer to be so honored (*see* LITERATURE—*Overview*).

Domestic Affairs. Throughout 1988 periodic clashes between police and Islamic fundamentalist demonstrators erupted, resulting in continued arrests and trials by special courts. In April, 33 Islamists were put on trial; they were accused of attempting to assassinate two former cabinet ministers and a newspaper editor. (The name of the organization to which they reportedly belonged was Those Redeemed from Hell.) During the year the Islamic demonstrators joined university students in several protests in support of the Palestinian uprising in Israel. In January ten people were killed at Rafah in Sinai when Egyptian security forces fired on demonstrators protesting against Israeli policies. Egyptian authorities accused Iran of using one of its diplomats to set up a sabotage group and to recruit adherents among Egyptian Muslim fundamentalists. In May, Libya also was charged with organizing underground terror groups; Libyans were implicated at a trial of 15 people accused of planning to bomb foreign airline offices in Cairo.

At the other end of the political spectrum, a group called Egypt Revolution was implicated in plans to murder several American and Israeli diplomats. In February, 20 people, including Khalid Abdel Nasser—son of late President Gamal Abdel Nasser, who led Egypt from 1952 to 1970—were indicted for complicity in organizing and financing the group's subversive activities. (Egypt Revolution opposes the 1979 peace treaty with Israel.) The group was said to include physicians, civil servants, and businessmen who intended to assassinate foreign diplomats; this would have demonstrated that Egypt was insecure and undermined relations between Egypt, Israel, and the United States. While membership in Egypt Revolution was not widespread, public reaction to the indictment showed that there was still much sympathy for the ideas of the former president.

In another decision, the Court of Ethics in April ordered confiscation of assets worth some 18 million Egyptian pounds (about $12.6 million) from the late President Anwar Sadat's brother, Ismat al-Sadat. He was accused of obtaining the fortune through illicit deals.

The growing dangers of environmental deterioration became ever more obvious during 1988. As a result of growing drought in central Africa, there was a serious decline in the volume of water stored behind the High Nile Dam at Aswan. The loss of water already had caused a drop in electric power supplied by the dam's turbines. If water supplied from Ethiopia was insufficient again, there was danger that the country would face a major food shortage in 1989–90. At the other end of the Nile, in the delta where the river enters the Mediterranean, it became clear that the sea was cutting into rich agricultural regions and that in many areas the ground was sinking. Scientists at the U.S. Smithsonian Institution announced in 1988 that about one million people now living in areas likely to be flooded will lose their land in the next century.

Foreign Affairs. President Mubarak greatly improved Egypt's relations with the Arab

world during 1988. Throughout the year he traveled to Iraq and the Arab Gulf States. He also traveled to the United States and Western Europe. As a result, Tunisia and South Yemen resumed diplomatic relations with Egypt after an eight-year hiatus following Egypt's peace agreements with Israel. This left only Syria, Libya, Algeria, and Lebanon (among the 20 Arab League states) without diplomatic ties to Cairo by late 1988. In July, Egypt was readmitted to the Arab League's Educational, Culture and Scientific Organization (to take effect in December).

Mubarak's role as a regional peacemaker was demonstrated in October when he became an intermediary between Palestine Liberation Organization (PLO) Chairman Yasir Arafat and Jordan's King Hussein. The two leaders were brought together by Mubarak after a two-year estrangement. A meeting was held in October between the Egyptian, Jordanian, and PLO leaders in southern Jordan, where Hussein agreed to accept the PLO as the "sole, legitimate representative of the Palestinian people." Following the PLO's proclamation in mid-November of an independent Palestinian state and the U.S. decision to hold talks with the PLO—both of which were rejected by Israel—Mubarak offered to visit Israel if it "would lead to solving the [Arab-Israeli] problem."

In his U.S. visit during January, Mubarak discussed with U.S. President Ronald Reagan and U.S. congressional leaders Egypt's concern about the Palestinian uprising in Israel's occupied territories and the urgent need for an international peace conference. He proposed a six-month moratorium on violence by both the Israelis and the Palestinians. During March, Egypt and the United States signed a "memorandum of understanding," placing Egypt on equal footing with Israel and NATO countries in competition for U.S. weapons contracts and military research. Improved relations with Italy were demonstrated by the first joint war games between the two countries. Egypt also wooed the Soviet Union by reopening the So-

viet cultural center in Cairo which had been closed for more than six years.

Relations with Israel improved as a result of the international arbitration panel decision awarding to Egypt the long-disputed Taba area on the Red Sea. The 765-yard (1200-m) long beach resort area had been disputed since the 1979 peace treaty. In compliance with an American request, Egypt agreed to delay implementation of the decision until after the November 1 Israel election.

DON PERETZ
State University of New York, Binghamton

ENERGY

Heightened awareness of the "greenhouse effect" (the trapping of heat by gases released into the atmosphere) and the role of burning fossil fuels in that global warming phenomenon found their way into many energy forums during 1988. At the same time, there was a significant breakthrough in the efficiency of photovoltaic solar cells, leading many to call for expanded solar research to help meet the world's energy needs with minimal effects on the environment.

Continued disarray among members of the Organization of the Petroleum Exporting Countries (OPEC) and a decline in oil prices as supplies reached glut levels led to the realization that worldwide conservation efforts, coupled with better utilization of other fuel sources, had weakened severely the stranglehold so long enjoyed by OPEC countries.

Largely due to strong industrial growth, but certainly exacerbated by a record cold winter and a record hot summer, there was unprecedented U.S. demand for electricity—and a record number of appeals to consumers to curb usage—as utilities scrambled to stretch available supplies. This crunch was particularly acute in the northeast, where utilities were forced to impose voltage reductions ("brownouts") ten times during the summer.

Many observers expected energy to emerge as a major issue in the 1988 presidential campaign. But with media attention focused largely on crime, drugs, defense, and the overall negative tone of the campaign, energy remained on the back burner.

Electricity. U.S. demand for electricity grew by nearly 5% in 1988, with peak levels exceeding those expected in the early 1990s. The growth was particularly dramatic in Alaska (18%), Washington (14.5%), and Vermont (11%). Utilities were able to meet the increased demand, but only through such means as reducing voltage, "wheeling" (shipping large amounts of electricity from one part of the country to another), and buying huge amounts of electricity from Canada. There also was increased use of cogeneration and electricity pro-

---

EGYPT • Information Highlights

Official Name: Arab Republic of Egypt.
Location: Northeastern Africa.
Area: 386,660 sq mi (1 001 450 km²).
Population (mid-1988 est.): 53,300,000.
Capital: Cairo.
Government: *Head of state*, Mohammed Hosni Mubarak, president (took office Oct. 1981). *Head of government*, Atef Sedki, prime minister (took office November 1986). *Legislature* (unicameral)—People's Assembly.
Monetary Unit: Pound (0.7 pounds equal U.S.$1, July 1988).
Gross Domestic Product (1987 U.S.$): $34,000,-000,000.
Economic Index (1987): *Consumer Prices* (1980 = 100), all items, 295.0; food, 320.7.
Foreign Trade (1987 U.S.$): *Imports*, $11,941,000,-000; *exports*, $4,352,000,000.

duced by small, private companies, and a renewed call for additional conservation.

The North American Electric Reliability Council, a forecasting group representing virtually all Canadian and U.S. utilities, warned that several areas in the United States faced acute shortages in the near future unless some corrective measures were begun almost immediately. With no utility willing to undertake large power-plant construction because of time and cost uncertainties, there was a much greater emphasis on creative solutions to the dilemma of future supplies. There seemed to be more willingness to explore regional construction, where utilities from several states would band together and build a plant for their joint use, and a move toward increased reliance on Canadian supplies. The latter solution ran into some rough sailing, however, when Canada announced that it was rethinking some of its long-term energy contracts with the United States because of its own faster-than-expected growth in demand.

Oil. Throughout the year, OPEC tried repeatedly to reach accords on production quotas and price fixing. Each time an agreement seemed near, oil prices would rise; as each potential agreement failed to materialize, prices would fall. The overall trend clearly was downward, however, and prices that had hovered in the $20 range through most of 1987 began dropping in December and continued falling through all of 1988. OPEC Secretary-General Subroto of Indonesia warned that continued production disagreements could lead to prices as low as $5 per barrel.

OPEC production throughout 1988 was well above the "ceiling" quota of 17.4 million barrels per day, frequently hitting peak levels of 21.5 million barrels. With worldwide demand for OPEC oil averaging about 19 million barrels per day, the overflow created an enormous glut. Finally in late November, OPEC oil ministers agreed to limit production to 18.5 million barrels per day, hoping to push prices to $18 per barrel. But one minister stated that this quota was not official, causing speculation that the agreement would not hold.

Much of OPEC's overproduction resulted from the August cease-fire in the Iran-Iraq war. Both countries were battered badly during the course of the eight-year conflict, and both needed revenues to rebuild. Iraq, which at 2.7 million barrels per day already had been exceeding its 1.54 million barrel quota, seemed likely to increase its daily output. Iran, however, was unlikely to be able to exceed its quota of 2.4 million barrels because of its heavily damaged facilities. Each was given a 2.64-million quota at the November meeting.

Although lower oil prices would help the overall U.S. economy and temper inflation, they would be disastrous for developing countries that rely heavily on oil exports for their revenues. Likewise, lower prices would not be welcomed by U.S. oil-producing states, whose economies already were battered by the price collapse of the early 1980s. By 1988, however, the situation in these states showed signs of improving. Large U.S. and European oil companies had regrouped, streamlined operations, and built up huge capital reserves. They once again were increasing acquisitions and explorations in the belief that oil prices would be headed up.

The long-term outlook for oil prices continued to hinge on OPEC. The Canadian Energy Research Institute projected a number of scenarios, ranging from the collapse of OPEC—which could result in prices below $9 per barrel in the 1990s, climbing to no more than $16 by the year 2000—to full accord among the OPEC countries—which could result in prices as high as $27 per barrel by 2000.

In the United States, according to the Energy Information Administration, demand for oil continued to grow in 1988, increasing by approximately 310,000 barrels per day (about 2.1%) to 17 million. This was the highest level since 1980 but still less than 1978's record demand of 18.8 million barrels per day. Demand was expected to grow approximately 1.2% in 1989. Domestic production, however, already at its lowest level in ten years, was expected to continue declining. This trend will lead to a greater reliance on imported oil and, according to the Government Accounting Office, could result in another oil crisis during the 1990s. Imports were expected to increase from 6 million barrels per day in 1987 to 7 million in 1988 and 7.4 million in 1989—representing 38%, 39%, and 41%, respectively, of total U.S. demand. Even the latter percentage would be lower than the 1973 preembargo figure.

The surplus and low price of oil helped keep U.S. gasoline plentiful and priced at levels close to those of 1987, averaging approximately $1 per gallon. In fact, according to the American Automobile Association, when inflation is taken into account, the price of gasoline in 1988 was nearly the same as in 1970, when the actual price was about 36 cents per gallon.

Natural Gas. U.S. demand for natural gas remained at approximately 17 trillion cubic feet (480 billion m^3) in 1988, but many environmentalists and energy analysts called for increased reliance on this domestic fuel as a means of reducing the greenhouse effect. Because burning natural gas releases fewer "greenhouse gases" than does burning coal or oil, and because the U.S. Department of Energy estimates a 60-year supply in the continental United States, this fuel seemed a logical choice for the 1990s.

Although the contribution of natural gas to U.S. energy consumption has declined from 30% to 23% since 1973, there were signs that the industry was beginning a comeback. Gas

demand by such large energy consumers as steel mills and the petroleum refining industry has been on the rise, increasing by 28% and 20%, respectively, in 1987.

Nuclear. Nuclear power continued to produce an increasing share of U.S. electricity requirements—approximately 17.7% in 1987 and nearly 20% in 1988. By year's end, there were 109 plants licensed in the United States and more than 410 worldwide. While nuclear power supplied approximately 16% of the world's electricity, it supplied about one third of that used in Western countries. In some nations, such as France and Belgium, nuclear power supplies more than two thirds of the electricity demand. Although fears about the greenhouse effect led some to call for increased reliance on nuclear power (because nuclear fission releases none of the gases produced in fossil fuel combustion), few analysts thought this likely because of the experience utilities have had with cost overruns. Critics again raised questions of nuclear-plant safety.

Controversy continued to surround the U.S. nuclear-power industry in 1988, and the future of several plants was uncertain. In Sacramento, CA, voters narrowly defeated a proposal to close permanently the troubled Rancho Seco plant, and instead gave it an 18-month trial period to improve. In Massachusetts, a referendum to shut down the state's two nuclear plants, Pilgrim and Yankee Rowe, was defeated 68%–32% in November. The Pilgrim plant, idle since 1986 because of maintenance and management problems, was approved for restart by the Nuclear Regulatory Commission (NRC) in December.

Even though the NRC issued clarifications of its emergency planning requirements, this issue continued to be the stumbling block for both the beleaguered Seabrook plant in New Hampshire and the Shoreham plant in New York. Massachusetts Gov. Michael Dukakis continued his opposition to the idle Seabrook plant, and nearby communities in Massachusetts removed their emergency notification sirens. In January, largely because of the financial drain of the facility, its main owner, Public Service Company of New Hampshire (PSNH), filed for bankruptcy, becoming the first utility in modern times to take that step. By year's end, a bankruptcy court was considering several options, including a plan by PSNH to restructure and remain independent, a proposal from Vermont and Maine utilities to merge with PSNH, and offers from other New England utilities to buy the service territory and non-Seabrook assets of PSNH. The NRC determined in December that, regardless of PSNH's bankruptcy, the plant was qualified to receive a license for low-power testing.

In New York, Gov. Mario Cuomo proposed a novel solution to the controversial Shoreham nuclear plant on Long Island: The state would pay one dollar for the plant with the understanding that it would be dismantled immediately. In exchange for the $5.3 billion asset, its owner, the Long Island Lighting Company (LILCO), would be guaranteed federal tax write-offs of $2.5 billion, plus rate increases of 5% annually for the next seven years. The plan was nearly as controversial as the plant itself, however, with some legislators and officials hesitating to abandon an operating facility at the expense of U.S. taxpayers. By year's end, there was no clear resolution of the situation.

In 1987, for the first time in history, a kilowatt-hour of nuclear electricity became more expensive than an equal measure of coal electricity. Although nuclear fuel held a substantial cost advantage over coal fuel, operating and maintenance expenses pushed total costs slightly higher—2.18 cents versus 2.07 cents per kilowatt-hour. Both remained significantly cheaper than other sources, however, as natural gas cost 2.89 cents and oil cost 3.74 cents per kilowatt-hour.

Research into a number of new, safer reactor designs was stepped up in 1988, some involving passive safety systems in the traditional water-cooled design, others relying on gas or liquid sodium as their primary coolant.

Solar Technology. In 1988, Congress appropriated $149 million for research and development of alternative energy sources and another $154 million for energy conservation research —in both cases more than requested by the administration. Only about $35 million of this was directed to photovoltaic research, however, a substantial drop from $150 million in 1981. Fortunately, private sources have continued funding this research at increasing levels.

One of the Department of Energy's solar research projects, conducted at Sandia National Laboratories in New Mexico, scored a breakthrough early in 1988 with the development of a photovoltaic solar cell that is 31% efficient. The 30% barrier once was considered the maximum, and the breakthrough led to speculation of possible 35%-38% efficiencies. This compares with 34% efficiency for fossil-fuel burning plants and opens the door to future widespread use of the sun for generating electricity.

The costs of existing—and improving—photovoltaic solar technology have been dropping dramatically for more than a decade, but solar-produced electricity still costs about four times as much as that produced through conventional means. As this cost differential decreases and as efficiencies increase, there is a very real possibility that by the year 2000, solar could be supplying 1%—6 billion watts—of the country's electricity supply, or enough to meet the needs of three million people.

ANTHONY J. CASTAGNO
Energy Specialist

ENGINEERING, CIVIL

Civil engineers could look back at the achievements of 1988 with a sense of accomplishment. Nonetheless, two 1987 tragedies, the collapse of a bridge in New York and that of an apartment building under construction in Connecticut, prompted many engineers to reflect upon the wisdom of some current practices and procedures.

Civil engineers took special notice of a report released by the National Council on Public Works Improvement in Washington, DC. At the behest of President Ronald Reagan, the council evaluated the state of the U.S. infrastructure and assigned grades to its main components: highways, mass transit, aviation, water resources, water supply, wastewater, solid waste, and hazardous waste. Averaged together, the infrastructure earned a solid ''C,'' with the highest scorer, water resources, earning a ''B'' and hazardous waste finishing last with a ''D.'' The report set very clearly and publicly the agenda for an entire profession and lent extra weight to the serious business of halting the deterioration of the existing infrastructure, as well as raising the quality of new structures being designed and built.

Bridge Safety and Construction. Some 600 files and 65,000 documents were reviewed by engineers participating in the New York State investigation into the Schoharie Creek Bridge collapse. The Schoharie Creek Thruway Bridge collapsed April 5, 1987, under the onslaught of a near record-breaking flood that was 63,000 cubic ft per second (cfs) greater than that which the bridge had been designed to withstand. Concurring with earlier findings, the final report blamed scour, the process by which the rush of violent waters erodes the ground out from under a bridge's footings. This natural process culminated in disaster because errors in the initial design of the pier foundations also led to errors in repair. In addition, because specifications had not been followed accurately, the riprap, an underwater foundation made of irregularly shaped stones, had not been placed around the bridge piers properly. And finally, because the as-built drawings erroneously showed metal sheeting around the riprap, improper maintenance procedures were followed.

Many engineers and officials called for a reevaluation of current inspection procedures, and recommendations for improvements emerged. Future tragedies might be averted if inspectors have bridge design experience, are personally familiar with the design approach of the bridge under inspection, and either perform or are present at all underwater inspections of submerged structural items. Structural integrity checks at least once every ten years, installation of scour indicator systems, and other measures also were suggested.

While much attention was taken up by the evils of underwater bridge deterioration and how better to detect it, engineers Stewart C. Watson and David G. Stafford concluded that most of the world's cable-stayed bridges built within the last 30 or 40 years are in serious danger because of premature corrosive degradation of their cables. The annals of their survey tell of a seven-year-old German bridge which in its third year had to have all of its cable tendons replaced because of corrosion, and the locked coil strand cables of a French bridge enshrouded in clouds of rust after being hit by a hammer. Although the cables of every bridge inspected had been covered by some sort of cable protection, Watson and Stafford reported that almost all of those were inadequate.

Stafford and Watson's findings warn that corrosion, the chief cause of cable deterioration, eventually can weaken a cable-stayed bridge cable to the breaking point. Once the cable snaps, progressive collapse may follow. Careful to affirm that they believe in cable-stayed bridge design, the engineers generated significant controversy, which should further their professed goal of bringing cable-corrosion problems to the attention of both bridge designers and owners.

Engineers chose a cable-stayed design for a new bridge over the Fraser River in Vancouver, B.C.; the bridge was expected to be completed by year's end. With a 1,115-ft (340-m) main span and 453-ft (138-m) side spans, the bridge is to be the world's longest used solely for rail transit; the Skytrain light rail system, which debuted at the 1986 World's Fair, will be in use. Those making the river crossing will ride in aluminum cars with linear induction motors over automated guideways. Installation and final testing of the system should be complete by 1990.

Connecticut Apartment Disaster. Reforms were proposed in Connecticut by an advisory committee appointed after the April 1987 collapse of the L'Ambiance Plaza apartment building under construction in Bridgeport; the proposals shifted more quality control responsibility to civil engineers. The committee called for a halt to the lift-slab construction method that was used at the site where 28 lives were lost until controlling regulations are added to the state building code. Also proposed were independent reviews of plans and specifications for buildings above a certain height or square footage or those with maximum occupancies exceeding 1,000. The committee recommended that the engineer of record or a qualified replacement review shop drawings, daily construction logs, and the construction progress regularly. The committee also stipulated that only architects and engineers with code-enforcement experience should serve as state building inspectors.

New Projects. Meanwhile in Chicago, substantial progress was made in 1988 on what soon would be the world's tallest concrete building. Standing some 967 ft (296 m) tall, the postmodern high rise at 311 South Wacker Drive has a post-tensioned floor system and was being constructed of concrete mixed with microsilica to add extra strength. The top-down method of construction used at the site meant that the underground excavation could proceed simultaneously with the tower-frame construction, saving significant time.

In 1988, Boston's $744 million Southwest Corridor project—a massive urban and community revitalization effort that relocated three high-speed railroad tracks and an elevated section of Boston's 80-year-old Orange Line—was named 1988's outstanding civil engineering achievement by the American Society of Civil Engineers. Hailed as the largest public construction project in Massachusetts' history, the Southwest Corridor project originated in the 1950s as an urban-highway plan, but was transformed in the late 1960s as the public began to recognize the merits of mass transit. After Gov. Francis W. Sargent signed a highway moratorium in 1969, the Massachusetts Bay Transportation Authority took over the land cleared for the 12-lane interchange; three sets of tracks were relocated here, using the federal money that had been budgeted for the highway. Three new rail stations also were built and 52 acres (21 ha) of parkland were added.

In 1988 privatization was given a boost in the field of transportation. Engineers, in cooperation with a private corporation, helped to change a Virginia law barring private ownership of roads to make way for the construction of a 15-mile (24-km) limited-access extension to Loudoun County's Dulles Toll Road. Unique because its owners, developers, and sponsors are a publicly traded New York City corporation, the extension also has given the civil engineers involved a chance to create their own market—a necessity these days, since the decline in public funds means falling demand for design services.

During 1988 the Albuquerque District of the Corps of Engineers began a ten-year, $53.3 million program to rehabilitate New Mexico's community irrigation systems, called acequias. Based upon simple technology, the state's 700 acequias range from small open irrigation flumes running water overland to only a few farms to major channels with diversion dams that serve large villages.

In Columbus, OH, engineers rapidly advanced the design work for $200 million worth of improvements to that city's wastewater treatment system, thereby completing in two years what normally would take three and a half years. A July 1, 1988, deadline for compliance with the Federal Clean Water Act's discharge standards was the motivation for the rushed improvements to the system's two treatment plants, 25 pumping stations, and almost 3,000 miles (4 828 km) of sewers. Thanks to the engineers' quick work, the city was able to escape exorbitant fines for noncompliance.

MARION H. HART, *Free-lance Writer*

ENVIRONMENT

Again in 1988, concern over ozone and radon dominated U.S. environmental news. Debate rekindled over another long-standing concern, global warming—spurred in large measure by the summer's record U.S. drought. Research identified a new danger in acid rain, and U.S. legislation tackled some nagging problems concerning endangered species, medical wastes, and ocean dumping.

Ozone. The recent discovery that a seasonal hole forms in the stratospheric-ozone layer above Antarctica set in motion a worldwide program to investigate its causes and potential environmental repercussions. These studies confirmed in 1988 that the problem of ozone destruction extends far beyond the southern polar skies.

In the first quarter of the year, three groups of researchers published similar estimates of global stratospheric-ozone losses. University of Illinois scientists published the first, in January, based on data collected by the Total Ozone Mapping Spectrometer (TOMS) aboard the Nimbus-7 weather satellite. Their work indicated that global stratospheric ozone fell about 5% between 1979 and 1986. That figure was comparable to another reported in January by National Oceanic and Atmospheric Administration (NOAA) scientists using ground-based instruments. But the most compelling evidence came on March 15, when an international "ozone-trends panel" comprising more than 100 experts released a report confirming a global drop in stratospheric ozone.

Depending on how and where the measurements were made, the drop ranged from 2.3% to 6.2% in the Northern Hemisphere during winter, according to an August report by the ozone-trends panel. However, the panel noted, since this post-1978 decline also coincides with a periodic fall in the solar-activity cycle, much of the ozone drop may be due to lower ultraviolet light emissions. As a result, the panel predicted little further drop in global stratospheric ozone—at least until 1991, when the sun's ultraviolet emissions are due to fall again.

NOAA scientists in 1988 also found the first solid evidence of ozone-destroying chlorine reactions above the North Pole. While the chemicals and their proportions recorded there in February were similar to what has been reported in the Antarctic ozone hole, the magnitude of the Arctic's ozone loss was only one fifth as great.

AP/Wide World

Beaches on Long Island, NY (above), as well as in New Jersey and other Eastern states, were closed temporarily during the summer after medical wastes—from syringes to prescription bottles and even vials of blood—washed up on shore.

Ironically, while evidence of significant stratospheric-ozone loss throughout the Northern Hemisphere was reported during 1988, the Antarctic hole turned out to be far less serious than anticipated. Unlike 1987, when ozone losses over the South Pole peaked in September at about 50%, the greatest drop in stratospheric ozone concentrations during 1988 was a mere 15%.

National Aeronautics and Space Administration (NASA) scientists studying the TOMS data believe that the lower-than expected seasonal thinning of ozone above the Antarctic resulted from unusual regional upper-atmosphere weather patterns. Ordinarily a strong vortex of stratospheric winds cordons off ozone-destroying chemicals, holding them at its center. In 1988 it was suspected that unusual wind patterns made the vortex less efficient in holding the pollutants together long enough for the ozone-destroying chemical reactions to occur.

Ozone Protection. In 1987 an international ozone-protection agreement was reached to tackle some of the primary human-generated pollutants believed responsible for falling stratospheric ozone levels. But the Montreal Protocol, as the agreement is called, will not go into force until the treaty is ratified by at least 11 nations representing two thirds of global CFC consumption. On March 31, 1988, Mexico became the first nation to ratify it. Three weeks later, the United States followed suit. By November, 14 of the Protocol's 47 signers had ratified it.

The U.S. Environmental Protection Agency (EPA) proposed regulations on August 1 to limit domestic CFC production to the levels specified in the Montreal Protocol. But concerned that the treaty's halving of CFC production by 1999 would not be sufficient to protect stratospheric ozone, EPA Administrator Lee M. Thomas on September 26 proposed amending the treaty to ban all use of CFCs and halons (three chlorine- or bromine-based chemicals important in fire fighting). Citing results of a new EPA analysis, Thomas said that data now show the risk to ozone posed by human-generated air pollutants to be "alarming," even worse than had been anticipated a year earlier. In particular, the new study pointed to risks posed by methyl chloroform, a common industrial solvent not scheduled for regulation.

At least one U.S. industry during 1988 responded to the new ozone findings and adapted its practices. In mid-April, manufacturers of disposable foam products used for food (such as plates and cups) announced that they would voluntarily halt use of products made with CFCs by year's end.

Radon. A seven-state EPA study, released in September, suggested that dangerous levels of radon, a natural radioactive pollutant emitted by soil and water, may pollute more homes and apartments than previously had been suspected. In 1987, EPA's survey of ten other states found indoor radon levels exceeding four picocuries per liter (pCi/l)—the level at which EPA recommends homeowners to consider corrective action—in one out of every five homes tested. The new survey found similarly high contamination in one out of every three homes tested. A four pCi/l radon environment poses about the same cancer risk as smoking half a pack of cigarettes daily, according to Richard Guimond, director of EPA's radiation programs. The highest radon levels were found in North Dakota, where a "hot spot" similar to Pennsylvania's infamous Reading Prong was identified. Responding to the survey, Assistant Surgeon General Vernon J. Houk issued a "na-

tional radon health advisory," recommending that all U.S. homes be tested for the pollutant and that corrective action be taken where levels are high.

The most comprehensive report on radon health effects was published in January 1988 by the National Academy of Sciences (NAS). After reviewing a host of scientific studies, NAS concluded that radon may initiate 350 lung-cancer deaths among every one million persons receiving a lifetime exposure equal to "one working-level month" (WLM)—roughly the dose a person might receive from living for two years in a house containing four pCi/l.

Greenhouse Warming. For U.S. farmers, the summer of 1988 was the driest in more than 50 years. It also may have been the hottest on record, according to NASA climate expert James Hansen. In fact, he told a Senate panel that the heat and drought of 1988 may have been the first symptoms of a climatic global warming due to the "greenhouse effect."

Even before the parching 1988 drought took hold, other climatologists were asking whether a greenhouse warming had begun. It long has been known that if "greenhouse" gases—those, like methane and carbon dioxide (CO_2), that trap infrared radiation—are allowed to build up in earth's atmosphere, the climate will warm. Researchers at the University of East Anglia in Norwich, England, reported that globally, five of the past seven years have been the hottest ever recorded.

While most climatologists believe it is still too soon to tell if the observed warming is part of a continuing, long-lasting trend—fostered by greenhouse gases—a research paper by NASA's Hansen released in August noted that until recently, abnormally hot summers occurred only about twice every six years. While Hansen said he could not firmly attribute 1988's heat to a greenhouse warming, he said the string of so many hot summers since 1980 suggests a greenhouse warming has begun.

One way to slow a global warming is to capture with trees more of the CO_2 emitted by fossil-fuel burning. And in October, the Washington, DC-based World Resources Institute announced a first-of-a-kind CO_2-conserving deal it helped arrange. Applied Energy Services (AES) of Arlington, VA, announced that it was donating $2 million toward a ten-year project to plant 50 million trees in Guatemala—the number calculated as necessary to absorb all the CO_2 that an AES coal-fired power plant in Connecticut will generate over its 40-year expected life. CARE, an international relief and development organization, the U.S. Peace Corps, the Guatemalan government, and the U.S. Agency for International Development each pledged comparable financing or assistance. While trees in the United States would have had the same CO_2-sequestering effect, CARE proposed planting them in Guatemala so that the project also would help save tropical forests and teach forest conservation to 40,000 local farmers.

Another way to slow a greenhouse warming is to reduce the atmospheric buildup of nitrogen oxides (NOx), a class of combustion pollutants that also contributes to acid rain and smog ozone. On October 31, a total of 25 nations—including the United States—drafted an NOx-limiting treaty in Sophia, Bulgaria. Nations ratifying it will pledge to limit their future NOx emissions to 1987 levels.

Acid Rain. In the past, concerns over acid rain have tended to center on its ability to burn plants and lethally acidify waters. But in late April 1988, the New York City-based Environmental Defense Fund (EDF) issued a new study showing that at least in the eastern United States, acid rain was fostering another important aquatic change: oxygen depletion.

Ordinarily nitrogen is a fertilizer. But when its levels are too high, the overgrowth of algae ("algal blooms") and other planktonic plants it fosters quickly can consume most of the dissolved oxygen, suffocating other water life and cutting sunlight's transmission to species near the seafloor.

Using data from state and federal agencies, EDF showed that nitrogen deposited by acid rain into several major water bodies, including the Chesapeake Bay—the nation's largest estuary and a major spawning ground for ocean fish—accounted for at least 25% of that attributable to human activities. EDF studies showed algal blooms are endangering these waters increasingly and that the nitrogen from acid rain undoubtedly was a major contributor.

On November 1 the United States and 24 other nations signed an international protocol to freeze the rate of emission of nitrogen oxide, a major source of acid rain.

Asbestos. In recent years, cancer-causing asbestos has been found to contaminate many structures, including schools and homes. In an EPA study released in March, federal officials estimated that one in five commercial U.S. buildings contain easily broken asbestos, the type posing the greatest health hazard. In fact, of the 733,000 buildings estimated to contain this hazard, 43% may have "significantly damaged" asbestos. When construction materials containing the mineral are damaged, asbestos can become airborne and inhaled. Though the mineral was most prevalent in large apartment buildings, EPA officials said that few residents were at risk.

Water Quality. Temporary summer closings of Eastern U.S. beaches made news in 1988, as medical wastes washed ashore in New York and New Jersey. Bathers encountered hypodermic syringes, prescription bottles, used bandages, sutures—even vials of blood, some of which later tested positive for hepatitis and AIDS. Nobody claimed responsibility for these

wastes, apparently dumped in the ocean illegally. But among the more positive outgrowths of the episodes was the passage and presidential approval of two new pieces of legislation: the Ocean Dumping Reform Act and the Infectious Waste Tracking Act.

Radioactive Wastes. The U.S. government had planned to begin storing large quantities of high-level nuclear wastes generated by the Defense Department in a $700 million underground vault near Carlsbad, NM, in October. It was to be the nation's first permanent storage facility for these dangerous wastes. But in mid-September, Energy Department officials announced that they were delaying indefinitely the plant's start-up. Known as the Waste Isolation Pilot Plant (WIPP), this facility was chosen specifically for its geology, salt beds 2,150 ft (655 m) below ground. Being ductile, the salt should collapse and encapsulate any wastes stored in it. Moreover, underground salt tends to accumulate where there is no water. But concern about the plant's future began surfacing late in 1987, when water was found leaking into the supposedly bone-dry facility. Once inside the salt, water turns to brine. Engineers feared that the brine could corrode waste canisters and generate a radioactive-waste slurry which could be carried out of the site—potentially even to the surface.

Forest Fires. The 1988 U.S. drought took its toll on forests, converting their trees into dried kindling. More than 4.3 million forested acres (1.7 million ha) were lost to unintentional forest fires during the year—twice the total for all of 1987 (until then, globally the hottest year on record). Yellowstone National Park was hit particularly hard in 1988, when 20% of its forests were charred.

While the fires looked devastating, they were not catastrophic to the forests. In fact, U.S. Forest Service officials said, Yellowstone's losses were so high only because the park had not experienced enough fires in the recent past. Certain species—such as lodgepole pine—depend on fires to reproduce. Fires also provide a kind of housekeeping function, cleaning out the dead wood and opening old stands to new growth. So, while the fires were temporarily disfiguring, they were expected ultimately to help the overall ecology.

Less beneficial are the estimated 2%–5% of earth's land surface *intentionally* set ablaze each year—largely to clear tropical lands for agriculture. By diminishing the planet's tree cover, the conversion of forest to agriculture not only removes a major storage system for carbon dioxide—and thereby contributes to the atmospheric accumulation of a greenhouse gas—but also is eliminating the only acceptable habitat for many of earth's species. In April, atmospheric chemists from NASA's Langley Research Center in Hampton, VA, reported an additional drawback to intentional burning.

They found that microbes in soil recently ravaged by forest fires increase as much as tenfold their production of nitric oxide (a contributor to acid rain) and nitrous oxide (a "greenhouse gas"). The accelerated production can last up to six months.

Threatened Species. In April, the African Wildlife Foundation (AWF) reported census data showing only 750,000 African elephants still remaining by year-end 1987—not quite 58% of the number recorded nine years earlier. AWF estimated that another 10% of these animals would die in 1988.

Driving the rapid destruction of these animals is the escalating price of ivory—as much as $68 per pound in 1988, compared with just $2.45 in the 1960s. As many older males already have been slaughtered, poachers now are turning to young males, breeding females, and the old matriarchs who lead elephant families. Because the young learn survival skills from the females—instruction that may take 12 years—the poachers' increasing focus on females threatens greatly to disrupt elephant society and the ability of those who are not hunted to survive, according to Cynthia Moss, director of the Amboseli Elephant Research Project in Kenya.

To help reduce the market for African-elephant artifacts, the U.S. Congress passed and President Reagan signed a bill requiring the government to impose sanctions on any country dealing in illegal ivory. It prohibited importation of ivory from countries not adhering to provisions of the Convention on International Trade in Endangered Species (CITES) and provided $25 million to help African countries develop tougher anti-poaching strategies.

In May, the World Wildlife Fund and American Association of Zoological Parks and Aquariums sued the U.S. government to block importation of two Chinese giant pandas by the Toledo Zoo, charging that these "rent-a-panda" deals not only violate CITES' intent, but also commercially exploit a species in danger of extinction. They particularly objected to the Toledo deal because it would have imported animals from a Chinese captive-breeding facility—in violation of China's policy to lend only nonbreeding animals. In September —before the lawsuit was settled—China essentially resolved the matter by indefinitely banning such short-term loans of pandas to U.S. zoos.

On October 7, President Reagan signed a reauthorization of the Endangered Species Act —three-and-a-half years after the bill first was proposed. The measure doubled funding for protection of endangered species, increased protection of rare plants, cut the backlog of species to be listed as threatened or endangered, and offered protection to species awaiting resolution of their status.

JANET RALOFF, *"Science News"*

ESPIONAGE

Many events in 1988 cast a spotlight on the shadowy world of espionage. The Soviet Union spied on the United States more than ever in 1988, according to the head of the U.S. Central Intelligence Agency (CIA), William Webster. Espionage incidents occurred in the Middle East. Existing spy cases remained in the news. Additionally, two of the century's most notorious spies died during the year.

The Conrad Case. The worst spy case in 1988 began with information from East bloc officials working secretly for the West that a Warsaw Pact spy ring was operating in Western Europe. These officials were caught and executed in their own countries, but their reports led to the arrest of an American, Clyde Lee Conrad, in West Germany on August 23.

Conrad was a sergeant in the 8th Division, attached to the North Atlantic Treaty Organization (NATO) from 1974 to 1985. With clearance to handle classified documents, he had access to contingency plans for the 8th Division in NATO's overall European defense strategy. He was accused of passing information to agents of Hungarian intelligence for more than a decade. His motive was said to be money.

The Conrad case was disturbing partly because the sergeant had been a decorated Vietnam War veteran. He had received an honorable discharge in 1985, and the Army had hired him as a trusted civilian expert. He allegedly transmitted the last batch of secret documents to his East bloc contacts in Vienna in July 1988, only a month before his arrest.

At the same time, two Hungarian members of the spy ring were arrested in West Germany and Sweden. They were caught with clandestine radios and ciphers for receiving and sending messages. A search was mounted across Europe for others in this spy ring.

Conrad's espionage case created a crisis for NATO, which had to withdraw its compromised contingency plans and draw up new ones.

More Military Spying. Another sergeant who had won a commendation in Vietnam was found guilty of attempted espionage in July 1988. Daniel Richardson was serving at the Aberdeen Proving Ground when he passed information to American agents, thinking that they were Russians.

Glen Michael Sauter, another espionage suspect, was a petty officer in the U.S. Navy when discharged in 1982. He had disappeared from Old Dominion University in Norfolk, VA, in 1986. He surfaced in Moscow in July 1988, proclaiming himself a victim of FBI harassment; the Russians granted him asylum.

FBI Library Surveillance. A widely debated spy story led from American libraries to a House subcommittee in Washington, DC. On June 20, 1988, the subcommittee heard testimony about the Federal Bureau of Investigation (FBI) asking librarians to help stop Soviet espionage. At issue was the presumed national interest versus library users' right to privacy. Under the FBI's Library Awareness Program, which had been in place since the late 1970s, librarians in many large cities were asked to report on people with foreign accents who had asked for assistance in locating technical materials.

James H. Geer, assistant FBI director, said that Soviet agents already had stolen many library microfiche bearing technical information, used libraries to hold clandestine spy meetings, and attempted to recruit some librarians. The FBI established the program to keep librarians alert to the danger, Geer added.

A new U.S. Embassy compound under construction in Moscow (right) was found in 1987 to be riddled with listening devices, apparently planted by the KGB. In October 1988, President Reagan called for the complete dismantling of the building.

Many librarians condemned the Library Awareness Program. They argued that the FBI exaggerated microfiche thefts, that the clandestine spy meetings were doubtful, and that no known recruits were made in libraries. Witnesses pointed out that the American Library Association forbids releasing the names of any library users except to obey court orders.

U.S. Representative Don Edwards, a former FBI agent, charged that the Library Awareness Program violated constitutional rights to privacy. He said it was doing more "damage to our society" than any spies the FBI might unmask.

Canadian Connection. Canada expelled eight Soviet officials and diplomats on June 21, 1988. As a reason behind the expulsions, Canadian Prime Minister Brian Mulroney cited "improper and unacceptable behavior" (a common euphemism for espionage). The charges were based on evidence from Yuri Smurov, a Russian with the International Civil Aviation Organization, who had defected in Montreal. Smurov said that the Soviet spies worked for the KGB (Soviet civil intelligence) and the GRU (Soviet military intelligence). According to Smurov, Russian officials had ordered the spies to penetrate Canadian intelligence. They were to gather classified information on Canada's naval strength in the Arctic. Industrial spying was also high on their list of espionage assignments. Moscow denied the charges, and expelled five Canadian diplomats from the USSR. The Canadians expelled four more Russians. The affair died down, but Mulroney stood by his charges.

European Cases. West Germany arrested six accused Soviet spies in March 1988 and provided data that led the Swiss to seize an East bloc engineer suspected of espionage. West Germany was shaken by a spy-for-love scandal. A woman working for the Development Aid Ministry was accused of showing secret documents to her lover who was suspected of being an operative of Czech intelligence.

In September 1988, Great Britain expelled three Czechs on spy charges, accusing them of conspiring to set up an espionage ring in Britain. Czechoslovakian authorities, denying any knowledge of the affair, expelled two British military attachés in retaliation.

Israeli Cases. The U.S. Justice Department stated in February 1988 that an accomplice of Jonathan J. Pollard was being sought. (Pollard had received a life sentence in 1987 for spying for Israel). On March 24, after a seven-month trial, Mordechai Vanunu was found guilty in Israel on spying and treason charges for describing Israel's secret atomic installation to a British newspaper; he received an 18-year prison sentence. (The Vanunu affair had been surrounded by controversy ever since October 1986, when Israeli agents seized him in Rome and carried him back to Israel.)

Islamic Espionage. Three Islamic nations held spy trials in January 1988. Iran executed four men accused of spying for Iraq. Syria executed two men as spies for Israel. An Afghanistan court sentenced Alain Guillo, a French journalist, to ten years in jail. The prosecutor claimed that Guillo had entered Afghanistan from Pakistan and spied for *mujahidin* rebels fighting to overthrow the Soviet-backed regime in Kabul.

Supreme Court Decision. On Oct. 17, 1988, the U.S. Supreme Court upheld the conviction of Samuel Loring Morison. A former intelligence analyst, Morison was found guilty of espionage because he had provided a British publication with classified photographs of American space projects. Morison's challenge of his original conviction was based on the claim that he was acting as a "whistle-blower," and not as a spy. Although the conviction had held up in the Court of Appeals in April, two of the three judges found that the prosecution had raised important First Amendment questions. But the Supreme Court refused to hear the case, upholding the conviction.

Moscow Embassy. On Oct. 27, 1988, President Reagan called for the dismantling of the new U.S. embassy in Moscow. In 1987 it had been found to be riddled with secret listening devices, apparently planted by the KGB while sections of the embassy were being worked on at a Russian factory. One suggested remedy was to have new sections built in the United States and shipped to the Soviet capital for assembly.

Deaths. The two notorious spies who passed from the scene in 1988 were Klaus Fuchs and Kim Philby.

Klaus Fuchs died on January 29 in East Germany. He was an atomic scientist who did nuclear research in Britain, and worked on the U.S. atomic bomb project at Los Alamos during World War II. In 1949, he was unmasked as a spy for the Russians. After nine years in a British jail, he was expelled to East Germany, where he continued nuclear research until his death.

Harold ("Kim") Philby died on May 11 in the Soviet Union. He had a notable career in British intelligence while spying for the KGB, and seemed on his way to becoming director of MI6 (the British intelligence agency). In 1951, he was the "third man" who warned spies Guy Burgess and Donald Maclean to escape to Moscow before being arrested. Under suspicion by his British colleagues, Philby himself escaped in 1963. He later said MI6 allowed him to escape to prevent a London trial that would have been a scandal for the organization. He joined the KGB in Moscow, and remained a consultant on British intelligence for Russia until his death.

VINCENT BURANELLI
Coauthor, "Spy/Counterspy"

ETHIOPIA

Ethiopia in 1988 endured extraordinary military setbacks in its 26-year war with Eritrean secessionists in the north. President Mengistu Haile-Mariam responded by curtailing famine relief to northern civilians, having the air force bomb civilian targets, and negotiating an end to the state of war with Somalia.

Civil War. The Eritrean People's Liberation Front (EPLF), which along with the Eritrean Liberation Front (ELF) has been battling for secession for almost 30 years, killed 4,000 Ethiopian soldiers, captured 14,000, routed 2,000 others, and took three Soviet advisers prisoner in a spectacular military offensive in the town of Afabet between March 17–19. Also in the north, the Tigre People's Liberation Front (TPLF), which advocates secession for the region of Tigre, captured the town of Axum, one of Ethiopia's ancient capitals. President Mengistu declared that the government was facing "grim battles" and called on Ethiopians to "unite" against the rebels. In the following months, Ethiopian planes dropped bombs on civilian villages, killing hundreds.

It was reported in August that a number of middle-level military leaders were executed because of military defeats caused by Ethiopian rebels.

Famine. With more than 7 million people at risk from famine as a result of drought that hit the country again in 1987, the government ordered all foreign relief workers out of Tigre and Eritrea on April 6, 1988. Hoping to limit support for the insurgents, foreign relief agencies were ordered to turn over their operations to the government. UN Secretary General Javier Perez de Cuellar announced on May 31 that Mengistu had agreed to allow the UN to monitor Ethiopia's distribution of food to the north.

The government went ahead with plans to continue the relocation of families from the drought-stricken north to the southwest. Some 800,000 peasants had been resettled by late 1988, and 400,000 more were to be moved by the end of 1989. With the resettlement scheme calling for the eventual movement of 1.2 million, this would conclude the program.

Foreign Affairs. Facing an entirely new and disastrous situation in the north, Mengistu acted to improve relations with states Ethiopia had been confronting.

The first move was with Somalia when on April 4, 11 years after Somalia invaded Ethiopia's Ogaden region which led to war between the two countries, both states agreed to resume diplomatic relations. In a signed accord they also agreed to an exchange of prisoners of war, the ending of support to all liberation movements, the withdrawal of military forces ten miles (16 km) from each side of the border, the creation of a demilitarized zone around the border areas, and minor frontier adjustments.

ETHIOPIA • Information Highlights

Official Name: Ethiopia.
Location: Eastern Africa.
Area: 471,776 sq mi (1 221 900 km²).
Population (mid-1988 est.): 48,300,000.
Chief Cities (1984 census): Addis Ababa, the capital, 1,412,577; Asmara, 275,385; Dire Dawa, 98,104.
Government: *Head of state,* Mengistu Haile-Mariam, president (took office Sept. 10, 1987). Legislature —Parliament (National Shengo, established Sept. 9, 1987).
Monetary Unit: Birr (2.07 birr equal U.S.$1, May 1988).
Gross Domestic Product (1987 est. U.S. $): $5,400,000,000.
Economic Index (Addis Ababa, 1986): *Consumer Prices* (1980 = 100), all items, 130.0; food, 131.7.
Foreign Trade (1987 U.S.$): *Imports,* $1,097,000,000; *exports,* $477,000,000.

They did not agree on who had legal sovereignty over the Ogaden, or on what to do with civilian refugees. The compact allowed Ethiopia to shift troops from the border area to the rebellious north.

During the same period Ethiopia and the Sudan began a series of talks aimed at improving their strained relations. The Sudan has given support to Ethiopia's rebels while Ethiopia has supported southern rebels opposed to the Sudanese government. In January, military support from the Sudan aided in the EPLF's attack on a relief column which destroyed 176 tons of relief food being sent to drought victims in the north. In June, Mengistu pressed for improved ties with the United States, but his plea was rejected.

Heads of state from more than 30 African nations attended the 24th annual summit of the Organization of African Unity in Addis Ababa, Ethiopia's capital, May 24–28.

Domestic Politics. In 1988, Ethiopia increased the price paid to farmers for part of their grain harvest and allowed them to sell the balance themselves. It also lifted internal controls on the movement of food inside the country allowing a limited free market to develop. Ethiopia, however, retained its commitment to a collectivized agricultural society by the year 2000.

Seven members of the family of former Emperor Haile Selassie, including his daughter and four granddaughters, were released from prison after 14 years.

In June the patriarch of the Ethiopian Orthodox Church, Abuna Tekle Haimanot, died of an unspecified illness.

Ethiopia boycotted the 1988 Summer Olympics held in Seoul, South Korea, in September in sympathy with North Korea's boycott. Since Ethiopia has some of the best long-distance runners in the world, it was a move not welcomed by Ethiopia's population.

See also AFRICA; SUDAN.

PETER SCHWAB
State University of New York at Purchase

ETHNIC GROUPS

The year 1988 was a mixed one for U.S. ethnic minorities, who are expected to make up one third of the population by the early 21st century. For the most prominent groups—blacks, Hispanics, and American Indians—advancement was signaled by several major court cases, new civil-rights legislation, and increased prominence in politics. But a report by a panel of leaders in business, education, and government indicated that the United States was backsliding in efforts to gain equality for minorities. The report, released in May, was prepared by a group that included former presidents Gerald Ford and Jimmy Carter and had been formed by the American Council on Education and the Education Commission of the States. It found that gaps between minorities and the white majority in education, income, health, and other areas had narrowed in the early 1970s but had grown from 1975 to 1985.

In 1988 the U.S. Congress ended a four-year battle over one aspect of minority rights by overriding President Ronald Reagan's veto of the Civil Rights Restoration Act. The central issue in the fight was whether an institution that accepted federal funds would be bound by antidiscrimination statutes in all programs or in only those programs funded. In 1984, in a case involving Grove City College, the Supreme Court had ruled that only funded programs were affected, a position the administration backed. The goal of the 1988 law was to extend the statutes to entire institutions.

Blacks. The 25th anniversary of the March on Washington and the 20th anniversary of the death of civil-rights leader Martin Luther King, Jr., provided an opportunity for blacks to assess their progress toward equality. While they could draw encouragement from the strong showing of the Rev. Jesse Jackson (*see* BIOGRAPHY) in the race for the 1988 Democratic presidential nomination, the consensus was that progress had been mixed at best. (*See* feature article, page 46.)

Two developments in New York State drew national attention. In August, Yonkers, the state's fourth-largest city, was ruled in contempt for failing to implement a court-ordered housing desegregation plan. Daily fines that would have bankrupted the city were halted a few weeks later, when the city council dropped its opposition to the plan's concept and voted to seek revisions in its specifics.

The Hudson River town of Wappingers Falls was the site of a furor over a criminal case that revolved around racial issues. Late in 1987, a black teenager, Tawana Brawley, charged that she had been assaulted sexually by five or six whites, including a white police officer. The Brawley case quickly became a cause célèbre among blacks, drawing prominent activists and extensive publicity. How-ever, Brawley and her lawyers refused to cooperate with a state grand jury, accusing the state of a cover-up. After a seven-month investigation, the grand jury concluded in October that Brawley's story had been fabricated.

Hispanic Americans. With the U.S. Hispanic population up 34% from 1980—and much of it concentrated in such key states as California, Texas, New York, and Florida—the presidential candidates of both parties bid for the Hispanic vote in 1988. Hispanic political leaders, meanwhile, continued to express concern over employment, education, and income levels—areas in which Hispanics, like blacks, lagged behind the national average. The year also saw charges that the U.S. Immigration and Naturalization Service discriminated against Hispanics, at times harassing U.S. citizens of Hispanic descent. And the FBI, the agency chiefly responsible for enforcing national civil-rights laws, lost a discrimination suit by more than 250 of its own Hispanic agents.

Native Americans. The U.S. Bureau of Indian Affairs (BIA), charged with providing a range of services for Indians on reservations, came under fire on several fronts in 1988, including failure to provide good education. Debate on the future of the BIA continued, with Director Ross O. Swimmer advocating a gradual move to self-determination for the tribes and eventual abolition of his agency. The plan was opposed by many Indians who felt that, even with its faults, the BIA was better than nothing.

In another development, Indian groups were incensed when President Reagan, during his trip to Moscow in May, said that the United States might have erred when it "humored" Indians by setting up reservations.

Several land-claim cases also drew national attention. In August, the Pullyap tribe dropped its claim to some of the most valuable land in Tacoma, WA, in exchange for $162 million in land, cash, and jobs—one of the largest settlements ever in an Indian land-claim case. Meanwhile, Congress considered a bill that would return to the Sioux a part of the Black Hills taken by the federal government in 1877.

The year's largest land settlement came in Canada, however. On September 5, the government agreed to cede some 260,000 sq mi (670 000 km²) in northern Canada to Indians, Eskimos, and people of mixed ancestry, and to give these groups a voice in the development of another 1.1 million sq mi (2.8 million km²).

Asian Americans. Asian immigration and investment continued to rise in the United States. Redressing an old wrong, Congress voted in August to extend an apology and pay $20,000 to each of 60,000 Japanese-American survivors of World War II internment camps. Canada adopted a similar plan in September.

ELAINE PASCOE
Author, "Racial Prejudice"

EUROPE

At the beginning of 1988, it appeared to many Europeans that the year would bring economic recession, provoked by the worldwide stock market crashes of October 1987. These fears proved unwarranted. European industry resumed the steady recovery begun in 1981, encouraged by falling oil prices and sporadic improvements in the American trade imbalance.

Confidence in the long-term prospects for economic growth was strengthened further by the progress of the leaders of the European Community (EC) in preparing for the creation, by 1993, of a totally integrated market among their 12 countries. At the same time, political confidence seemed justified by the lessening of Cold War tensions between the Western and Eastern blocs.

Western Europe's Economic Strength. In spite of massive losses in stock values at the end of 1987 throughout Western Europe, the expected falloff in consumer spending—which might have triggered recession—did not occur. The European central banks eased credit for the first half of 1988. Some governments made goods cheaper by reducing the rates of the value-added tax. Even the fall in stock prices was seen to have had a positive aspect, restoring stock values to more realistic levels and reducing inflationary pressures. The inflation rate was expected to remain at about 3% in the EC as a whole, and no member was likely to exceed 5%. West Germany remained a model of excellence, with an expected trade surplus of $70 billion and virtually no inflation.

Although unemployment remained high, the level in the EC stabilized at 11%, while high unemployment benefits permitted most of Europe's 19 million unemployed to take some part in the increased consumer spending which rose by 2.7%. From a record Christmas buying spree in 1987 to a surge of automobile purchases in the summer, Europe's consumers were enjoying an extravagance not entirely justified by the community's 2% growth rate.

Toward a Single European Market. Within the European Community, preparations continued for the totally integrated market which the community leaders had agreed to establish by the end of 1992. By 1987, all EC members had approved the Single European Act, the first important revision of the original Treaty of Rome founding the community. The act provided for streamlined voting procedures in the Council of Ministers, for an increase in the powers of the European Parliament, and for abolition of all existing trade barriers in the community. Access to a market of 320 million consumers thus was to be extended not only to industrial and agricultural enterprises but also to such sectors as banking, insurance, and private services. A major step toward market freedom was taken in June when the EC finance ministers agreed on a timetable for complete freedom of capital movement, a measure calculated to save $26 billion in the cost of financial services. Private companies, increasingly aware of both the opportunities and dangers facing them in 1993, continued large-scale restructuring, often through international mergers carried out as the result of hostile takeovers of vulnerable rivals.

Little progress was made on EC financial reform, especially on the reduction of agricultural expenses, which reached $32 billion in 1987. Agreement finally was reached at an emergency summit meeting in Brussels in February 1988 to restrict agricultural production by cutting prices on products in surplus. To help the poorer regions of southern Europe and Ireland prepare for 1993, subsidies for regional development were to be doubled.

In June the community took the historical move of opening formal relations with the East European economic bloc, the Soviet-led Council for Mutual Economic Assistance, thus making possible diplomatic relations between the community and individual East European countries. The same month, at their summit meeting in Hanover, the EC leaders maintained the new momentum by agreeing to study the creation of a community central bank and a common currency and by reappointing the activist Jacques Delors as commission president.

Finally, fearing being left outside a possibly protectionist community after 1992, Norway, Austria, and Turkey began to explore the possibility of becoming full community members.

Terrorist Threats to Political Stability. In this calm economic climate, political crises were solved quickly. Socialist President François Mitterrand was reelected easily in France in May. In spite of labor unrest, the Christian Democratic Party in Italy, under the leadership of Prime Minister Ciriaco De Mita, increased its vote in local elections in June. A five-month political crisis in Belgium was solved by reappointment of Christian Democratic Premier Wilfried Martens. When Conservative Danish Premier Poul Schlüter called elections in May to fight off opposition to Denmark's role in Western defense, his coalition was returned with exactly the same representation as before.

Europe's terrorists were determined, however, to disturb the prevailing stability. Basques in both France and Spain engaged in bombings in their quest for an independent state. Left-wing groups in Italy murdered a leading Christian Democratic senator. Middle Eastern terrorists killed or wounded some 100 people on a Greek tourist ferry. And in Northern Ireland, the Irish Republican Army stepped up its attacks against British soldiers, killing more than 30 in its attempt to force the British out of Ireland.

F. ROY WILLIS
University of California, Davis

The Eastern Bloc

Soviet General Secretary Gorbachev (front) reviews Polish troops upon his arrival in Warsaw for a June summit of the Warsaw Pact nations. Poland's Gen. Wojciech Jaruzelski (left) was a staunch supporter of Gorbachev's reformist policies, but some other Eastern European leaders were less enthusiastic.

© Wojtek Laski/Sipa Press

In 1987, Soviet leader Mikhail Gorbachev proclaimed, in apparent acceptance of the growing lack of unity and uniformity in Eastern Europe, "In the past it used to be said that the orchestra was conducted by Moscow and that everybody else listened. That is no longer the case." That was certainly not the case in 1988, when provocative changes came thick and fast in the region, but the Soviets, preoccupied with their own internal problems, neither sanctioned nor condemned them.

Some of the turmoil could be attributed to the freer climate for dissent and experimentation that flowed from Moscow itself. But the basic stimulus was provided by the deteriorating economic conditions in what used to be called "the Soviet bloc." Hundreds of thousands of East Europeans signed petitions and participated in strikes, demonstrations against their Communist governments, and ethnic confrontations. The authorities responded with some immediate concessions to popular demands and promises of future reforms, but with forceful repression, too.

The range and degree of disturbance varied greatly from country to country. At one end of the spectrum, East Germany, the most productive and prosperous member of the East European socialist bloc, dogmatically and successfully resisted economic and political changes. And Albania, divorced from the bloc since 1961, cautiously edged away from some 40 years of fanatically dogmatic Marxist rule at home and self-imposed isolation from the rest of the world. In Poland, negotiations between

General Wojciech Jaruzelski's Polish United Workers' (Communist) Party and Lech Walesa's banned Solidarity union seemed permanently deadlocked, with the nation paralyzed and sliding into ever-greater poverty. And Yugoslavia, which—under its charismatic national leader Tito—had separated itself from the Soviet bloc in 1948, had to face almost every variety of problem simultaneously.

In 1988, Marxian socialism seemed finally to be played out within the Socialist commonwealth, in default on its rosy economic promises and unable even to provide the basic material essentials of life to its adherents. Decades of rigid command economics had resulted in chronically sick economies, with low productivity, diminishing exports, massive international debts, soaring inflation, acute shortages of consumer staples and energy, and a steadily falling standard of living. Attempts by the regimes to cope with the disaster by initiating drastic austerity programs only destabilized conditions further. Waves of strikes occurred in Poland, Romania, and Yugoslavia. Party and government buildings were occupied and ransacked. The alarmed authorities rescinded their decisions on prices and wages and promised to "refresh and strengthen socialism" by introducing more free-market policies, legalizing more private and cooperative enterprises, encouraging more joint ventures with Western companies, and seeking new capital investment, a rescheduling of foreign-debt payments, and additional loans from abroad.

Other varieties of protest owed more, perhaps, to the influence of the Soviet Union's own ongoing reform program. Although the restless masses of Eastern Europe generally welcomed Soviet-style *glasnost* and *perestroika,* the East European Communist leadership, with its vested interest in the old Brezhnev ways, gave them a mixed reception. Poland, Hungary, and Yugoslavia were the most enthusiastic. All three had been experimenting with greater degrees of political, economic, and intellectual liberalization for years, earlier than the Soviets themselves. Stolidly orthodox East Germany, boasting the highest standard of living in the bloc, rejected "openness" and "restructuring" as unnecessary. Romania's Communist dictator, Nicolae Ceauşescu, ruling over a country plagued with severe economic hardship and harsh political repression, called them "a betrayal of socialism." Czechoslovakia and Bulgaria fell between these extremes. Both the regime and people of Czechoslovakia, acutely mindful of their own remarkably similar attempt at reform, "Prague Spring," and its disastrous end in 1968, reacted cautiously. The party and government opted for slow economic modernization but rejected "uncontrolled *glasnost"* and refused to share power or even initiate a dialogue with non-Communists. Bulgaria, after a radical liberalization of its party and governmental structures and economy in 1987, fell back, apparently on Soviet advice, to a more modest and gradual approach to reform.

Almost everywhere in Eastern Europe, organized opposition groups (such as Charter 77 in Czechoslovakia and Solidarity in Poland), students, workers, and the aroused masses took to the streets. They chanted once unthinkable slogans such as "freedom!," "democracy!," "down with Ceauşescu!," "Dubček! Dubček!," and "Russians go home!" They demanded respect for human and civil rights, full religious freedom, restrictions on police authority, and even environmental protection. Above all, they called for a greater role in government.

In due course, as in the Soviet Union itself, even the specters of age-old ethnic hostility and separatism and nationalism, considered taboo and long repressed under Communism, made their appearance within and between some of the states of the bloc. In Czechoslovakia, well-publicized pilgrimages of tens of thousands of Catholic Slovaks were construed by some experienced observers of Eastern Europe as a reaffirmation of dormant Slovak nationalism against their federal partners, the Czechs. Resentment over the alleged mistreatment of the Serbian and Montenegrin ethnic minorities by the Albanian ethnic majority in the Kosovo autonomous province of Yugoslavia stirred up passionate expressions of nationalism among the large Serbian population of the country. Such resentment also supported the rise of a Serbian "new Tito," Slobodan Milosević, and damaged relations with neighboring Albania, thought to have encouraged its kinsmen. Similarly, the alleged repression of 2 million Hungarians in Romanian Translyvania brought mass protests and patriotic demonstrations in Hungary and bitter denunciations by the Hungarian Socialist Workers' (Communist) Party of the Communist leaders of "brotherly" Romania. Particularly alarming to the ruling elites was evidence that a well-organized and growing network of dissenters existed throughout Eastern Europe, with ties to kindred groups in the Soviet Union itself and with spokesmen in the West. Its members expressed solidarity and coordinated their protests on various occasions.

The party and governmental hierarchies hastily made some initial concessions, betraying serious internal rifts in the process. Large numbers of officials of all ranks were dismissed and replaced by new incumbents believed to be more suitable to the critical times. Sometimes they were individuals with known sympathy for reform, sometimes hard-liners. Those dismissed included the aged party leaders of Czechoslovakia and Hungary, Gustáv Husák and János Kádár, the Polish and Czechoslovak prime ministers, Zbigniew Messner and Lubomír Strougal, the entire council of ministers of Czechoslovakia, and the entire party politburo in the autonomous province of Vojvodina in Yugoslavia. The Communist leadership promised political democratization in the future and even made grudging attempts at a broader accommodation with major religious bodies, especially the Roman Catholic Church in Poland, Hungary, and Czechoslovakia, and the Protestant Evangelical Church in East Germany. But when popular protests became too broad and too violent, they sent in police and military forces to dispel them.

At year's end, the Communist rulers of Eastern Europe had managed temporarily to placate or coerce their challengers and were still in charge and upholding the "leading role" of their parties. The Soviet Union consistently had maintained a low profile in the area. But the forces of opposition and the problems and grievances that animated them were still in place, too. It remained to be seen if the Communist regimes would be able to reform themselves rapidly enough to avert a crisis in which their very existence would be threatened.

JOSEPH FREDERICK ZACEK

FAMILY

From housing rights to infant mortality to teen pregnancy, issues that affect families received fresh attention in 1988. The concerns of working parents appeared particularly important, with child-care proposals figuring in the U.S. presidential campaign and bills on child care and parental leave pending in Congress.

Family Size. A U.S. Census Bureau report released during the year showed that the size of the average U.S. family has continued to decline, dropping to 3.19 members in 1987 from 3.21 the year before. The decline has been steady since 1940, when the average family size was 3.76, and has been attributed to several factors—later marriages, an increased divorce rate, fewer children.

Census figures showed marriage and birth rates remaining low. The marriage rate for 1987 was 9.9 per 1,000 people, the lowest since 1977. The birthrate for the same year was 66.1 for each 1,000 women between the ages of 15 and 44, about half the rate at the peak of the baby boom in the 1950s. But with women of the baby-boom generation reaching prime child-bearing years, the number of births was increasing.

The divorce rate was also down, to 4.8 per 1,000 people in 1987 from a high of 5.3 per 1,000 in 1981. Meanwhile, the number of unmarried couples living together continued a steady rise, topping 2.3 million in 1987.

Income. Economically, families were better off, according to a Congressional Budget Office study. But the report showed a growing gap between rich and poor. Using a measure that took into account inflation and family size, the study compared median family income in 1970 and 1986 and found a 20% increase. However, the improvement was distributed unevenly, and the report credited much of the increase to the rise of two-worker families. Families headed by single parents had little increase or, among some groups, a decline in median income. Elderly families showed the biggest improvement, up 50%, while families headed by people under 25 showed a decrease of 18%.

Another study, released by the Census Bureau, showed an average family income of $34,924 in 1986. But for the one family in six headed by a single woman, the average was $13,500. Some 20% of the nation's children were living in poverty in 1987, the bureau said, and nearly one fourth of all children lived in single-parent homes.

Nationally, just 35% of single mothers received child support from absent fathers. State child support enforcement programs, aided by the federal Office of Child Support Enforcement, continued to work to collect court-ordered payments. But a congressional welfare-reform proposal called for still stiffer measures: identifying the fathers of all newborns and registering their Social Security numbers; setting state guidelines for support payments; and, after 1994, withholding child support from the absent parent's pay.

Child Care and Parental Leave. With more than half of new mothers staying in the job market, and with two-income and single-parent families accounting for some 10 million children under the age of six, issues of child care and parental leave moved to the forefront in

With the number of two-income and single-parent families on the rise, more and more men are taking on the role of "working father." One way of meeting the dual responsibility is to take the child to work. At the offices of Domino's Pizza, left, the idea is encouraged.

A family in Philadelphia was denied an apartment because it
turned out to be one of the 25%
in the United States that had a
"no children allowed" policy.
Federal legislation passed in
1988 bars such housing bias.

© Dan Miller/NYT Pictures

1988. There were increased calls for employers to provide such benefits, as well as more flexible working schedules (*see* LABOR—*Benefits in Flux,* page 318).

In the face of stiff opposition from business, Congress scaled back House and Senate bills requiring employers to provide unpaid parental leave. The new House version, for example, called for leaves of ten rather than 18 weeks for new parents, and exempted firms with fewer than 50, rather than 15, employees. Both the House and Senate debated the matter in the fall but took no final action.

Among some 100 child-care proposals introduced in Congress, there were two leaders. One was a Democratic plan to provide $2.5 billion to states to set up and expand day-care programs or to distribute as vouchers to low- and moderate-income families; the other was a Republican proposal for block grants to states, tax exemptions, and tax credits for employers who set up child-care centers. Supporters of the two plans pledged to work toward a compromise bill, but final action did not occur in 1988.

Housing. Discrimination against families with children in the sale or rental of housing became illegal under a federal law signed by President Ronald Reagan on September 13. The law, which was to take effect 180 days after the signing, included provisions for strict penalties for violators and was expected to end a widespread pattern of such discrimination: According to one widely cited survey, 25% of all rental units did not allow children, and 50% restricted the access of families with children. Exempted from the law were apartments and housing developments designed for the elderly —those in which all residents were 62 or over or in which at least 80% of the units had at least one occupant 55 or older.

Teenage Parents. The National Center for Health Statistics released figures showing that from 1970 to 1985 (the most recent year for which it had data), the birthrate among teenagers had dropped significantly, from 68.3 per 1,000 to 51.3. However, more than half the teenage mothers in 1985 were unmarried, making them vulnerable to poverty. The birthrate was highest among girls from low-income families and those with low academic skills.

The role of teenage fathers was beginning to receive more attention, and several programs were under way to encourage their involvement with their children. One, administered by the Bank Street College of Education in New York City, provided job training and referrals, counseling, and parenting classes to 400 teen fathers in eight cities. After two years, 74% of the fathers were providing some financial support for their children and 82% had daily contact with them.

Infant Mortality. Citing unacceptably high infant mortality rates, a congressional commission in August called for greatly expanded Medicaid and employer health-insurance payments for prenatal and well-baby care. The commission's report said that babies born in 18 other industrialized countries had a better chance of surviving the first year than those born in the United States, and that chances were better among those born in Czechoslovakia and Bulgaria than among U.S. blacks.

The national Centers for Disease Control (CDC), meanwhile, said that the infant mortality rate was declining but acknowledged that the United States would not meet its goal of reducing the rate from 10.6 per 1,000 live births to 9 by 1990. Another goal likely to be missed, the CDC said, was ensuring that 90% of women received prenatal care in the first three months of pregnancy. The projection for 1990 was that 23.6% of all mothers, and 38.5% of black mothers, would go without such care, which is considered important to infant survival.

ELAINE PASCOE, *Free-lance Writer*

FASHION

Fashion in 1988 was in a state of retreat and retrenchment. The slink, the pouf, and the miniskirt, designed to entice reluctant consumers back into stores, only succeeded in driving them further away. The increasing cost of clothing, the impracticality and, for most women, the inappropriateness of these extreme styles were the catalysts for a virtual consumer boycott that forced manufacturers to reach back to the classic designs that were the backbone of real women's wardrobes.

Silhouette. The silhouette relaxed, moving away from the body, not in the oversized, exaggerated way of several years past, but in a slightly rounded oval or cocoon shape. There also was a return to a simplicity and purity of line free of frills, ruffles, or bows. Hemlines came down again, giving the consumer a variety of wearable lengths that ranged from mid-knee to mid-calf. Some leading designers—notably Ralph Lauren and Giorgio Armani—even showed ankle-length skirts for day, done in the softest fabrics and with a simplicity of styling that gave them a timeless grace. Exaggerated femininity was taking a backseat to comfort, wearability, and practicality, combined with classic good taste.

Coats. Coats were "hot" in 1988. Easily worn over the slimmed-down, uncluttered silhouette, they became an important wardrobe component. The classics, including the reefer, trench, and balmacaan were strong, but the newest looks were tenty or cape-like in shape or were smock- or cocoon-shaped. They often sported oversized shawl collars or hoods and many were three-quarter length. The traditional colors—navy, black, and neutrals—dominated; fashion excitement was in new, hot colors—violet, acid green, shocking pink, fuchsia, or cobalt blue. Most interesting were the duffel coats and shearlings done in these vibrant colors. Even Mongolian lamb, the year's "fun fur," came up fuchsia in Donna Karan's line and in voltage yellow at Fendi. Another coat trend was the lavish use of real or fake fur trims. Collars, cuffs, and hems of beaver, raccoon, or Persian lamb were design elements on dress and casual coat styles.

The 1988 fashion scene included Giorgio Armani's daytime, ankle-length skirt, left, and the more mannish trouser that featured easy pleating and a high waistband, right. Both styles were considered extremely feminine and graceful.

© Cavalli/Sipa Press   © Matteini/Sipa Press

© Daniel Simon/Gamma Liaison

Designing attractive and comfortable clothes for working women has become a major objective of today's designers and manufacturers. Accordingly, not only the suit but also the coatdress, above—especially those that could be worn after five as well as to the office—were big successes. Other fashion innovations of the year were the vivid-colored coat, worn with or without a fez-shaped hat.

Professional Look. Catering to the needs of the increasing number of working women, manufacturers concentrated more on apparel for a professional look. Suits were a large part of every line with new looks created using coordinated fabrics, patterns, or textures for the jacket and skirt. While the blazer was still an important basic, the newer jackets were fitted and shorter, often cropped at the waist like a bolero or waiter's jacket. Some were banded at the bottom for a slightly blouson effect, and many had cardigan necklines to accommodate more feminine blouses that featured neckline draping or soft collars.

Dresses stripped of froufrou became the fashionable alternative to the suit in many working women's wardrobes. Favorite looks considered appropriate for the office as well as chic enough for after-five professional or personal functions were the chemise and the coatdress, which was done in a variety of single- and double-breasted versions.

Pants. Pants, meant as an alternative to 1987's miniskirt, continued to be strong, and the types ranged from slim cuts in knitted fabrics to full, flowing palazzo pajamas. Most prevalent were mannish trousers in menswear fabrics that had easy pleating or high-rise waistbands to give a more feminine look; many were teamed with the newer cropped jackets to create sophisticated pantsuits for urban women. Fuller trousers or culottes in jerseys of cashmere, wools, and other soft fabrics were gathered at the waist and flared at the hem to give the appearance of a skirt and, for evening, there were elegant wide and full palazzo paja-

© Barthelemy/Sipa Press

© Mario Ruiz/Picture Group

Menswear turned to a conservative yet relaxed style. Such a look often featured crisp, spread-collar shirts paired with the traditional foulard tie.

mas in velvet, chiffon, or other luxe fabrics. As with skirts, there were a variety of lengths from mid-knee to shoe topper but both Donna Karan and Giorgio Armani cropped their pants in a new way—just above the anklebone. There also was a revival of the jumpsuit in versions ranging from the tailored mechanics' type to more fancy halter-topped evening ones in crepes, velvet, or taffeta.

Fabrics. The classic fabrics—flannel, tweeds, linens—were ubiquitous in keeping with the restrained trend of fashion, but there were some new faces. Cashmere was the fabric of choice of most designers; "boiled" wool, the traditional fabric of Tyrolean peasant jackets, went into coats and jackets; and lace was a primary evening fabric as well as a trimming on blouses, dresses, and accessory items.

Accessories. Accessories were increasingly important wardrobe extenders promoted to update and add color and interest to basic fashions. Bright scarves and shawls in bold patterns were draped over suits and coats or tied at the necklines of simple sweaters or dresses. Pearls, fashion perennials, came in all lengths, sizes, and colors and often were mixed with gold chains or gemstones. Charm bracelets were back and heavy link necklaces and bracelets, bangles, and fancy, bejeweled wristwatches were important jewelry trends. But the most popular jewelry item was the pin. Big and bold or in groups of small "scatter" pins, they adorned lapels, pockets, hats, collars, and cuffs.

There were fur and felt hats shaped like fezzes, toques, and oversized berets, as well as high-crowned coachman's toppers to add pol-ish to suits and coats; more casual sportswear looks took to knitted hoods or helmets.

Footwear was down to earth with the basic pump being the key shoe. Done in polished leathers, suede, or reptile, it came in flat to medium heel heights and a wide range of colors. For versatility and practicality there often were included or available bows or ornaments to clip on for a change in look; newly built-in comfort features were stressed for working women. And for the many pants looks, demi-boots in easy-to-wear heel heights were pump alternatives.

Menswear. Menswear in 1988 tended to be a conservative blend of English tailoring wedded to American ease. Suits in hard-finished tweeds or flannels had the crisp look of Saville Row but were less fitted with lightly sloped shoulders and roominess across the chest. Straight cut shirts with spread collars were another indicator of the new ease of tailoring while ties in traditional foulards and stripes solidified the conservative look.

Coats were square and boxy and often collared in beaver; accessories were low-keyed essentials such as narrow belts, classic watches, dark unpatterned socks, and hearty shoes like oxfords of boot leather, brogues, or monk straps.

Sportswear was home on the range in authentic Western gear. Denim and corduroy jeans, frontier jackets, checked or plaid flannel shirts, and shearling coats were accessorized with ten-gallon hats, bolo ties or neckerchiefs, cowboy boots, and leather belts with hammered silver buckles.

ANN M. ELKINS, *"Good Housekeeping"*

FINLAND

While the reelection of Mauno Koivisto of the Social Democratic Party as president of Finland was expected, nevertheless, it was a preeminent national event. The election was especially significant as it was the first time that Finns cast direct ballots for a candidate, as well as for electors in the electoral college.

Politics. President Koivisto's reelection to a second six-year term was held over two days, January 31 and February 1. He won handily over four rival candidates: Paavo Vaeyrynen, chairman of the Center Party and a former foreign minister, got 20.1%; Prime Minister Harri Holkeri, head of the National Coalition Conservative Party, obtained 18.1%; Kalevi Kivistö, a Eurocommunist, got 10.4%; and Jouko Kajanoja of the Communist Democratic Alternative received 1.4%. With Koivisto having garnered 47.9% of the vote, and a majority needed for election, the final selection (according to the new electoral rules) had to be made by the 301-member Electoral College. Harri Holkeri subsequently transferred 45 of his electoral votes to the incumbent. President Koivisto began his second term with a speech to Parliament in which he vowed to continue his policies of the previous six years.

Following the election no changes were planned for the four-party coalition cabinet headed by Prime Minister Harri Holkeri, which is comprised of members of the Social Democratic Party, National Coalition Party (conservatives), Rural Party, and Swedish People's Party. However, several unsuccessful attempts were made during the year to bring the Cabinet down. The fourth attempt was a no-confidence motion on October 5 in which the Cabinet was criticized for its tax-reform plans and its 1989 budget propoals. The opposition said the plans and proposals favored the rich.

A third Communist party was born on May 21—the Communist Labor Party. Headed by Markus Kainulainen, the new party claims that the other two Communist parties have not been faithful to their original revolutionary ideology.

Visit by President Reagan. Ronald Reagan became the first sitting U.S. president to visit Finland. He and Mrs. Reagan stopped in Helsinki for three days, May 26–28, prior to their summit meeting in Moscow a few days later. The American presidential couple was received warmly. President Reagan conferred with President Koivisto and other government officials, and saluted Finland's contributions to world peace in a speech in Finlandia Hall.

Year of Friendship. During 1988 the 350th anniversary of the founding of the New Sweden colony in the state of Delaware was celebrated. Numerous Finnish-Americans participated. (In 1638, Finland had been a part of the Swedish realm.) A Year of Friendship was declared, both in Finland and the United States, with prominent Finnish dignitaries taking part in the Delaware celebration.

Women Ministers. Following a decision by the Finnish Lutheran Church to admit women to the pastorate, 94 women were ordained in churches throughout the country on March 6, 1988.

Cultural Affairs. Finnish composer Magnus Lindberg was awarded the Nordic Council Music Prize for 1988. Lindberg won the prize, amounting to 125,000 Danish kroner (about $30,000), for his composition *Kraft* (*Power*).

Finland also marked the 500th anniversary of the first printed Finnish book, the *Missale Aboensis*. Printed in Germany, in 1488, the work was a prayer book in Finnish churches.

ERIK J. FRIIS
The Scandinavian-American Bulletin

FLORIDA

Launched from Florida's Cape Canaveral, the U.S. space shuttle *Discovery* catapulted five astronauts into space on Sept. 29, 1988—32 months after the *Challenger* catastrophe suspended the United States manned space flight program. Although the *Discovery* encountered several technical problems before lift-off, the mission was pronounced a success.

Lottery. Florida also launched its first state lottery in 1988. Instant scratch-off tickets were sold beginning in January, and computerized games went on-line in April, including the weekly Lotto jackpot that made millionaires of more than a dozen people before the year's end. In September, a Winter Springs real-estate agent won more than $55 million—the second largest lottery payoff in U.S. history.

Elections. In the presidential race, Florida voters preferred George Bush over Michael Dukakis by a 3-2 margin. Republican Rep. Connie Mack won the closest U.S. Senate race in Florida history; his opponent was Democrat Rep. Kenneth (Buddy) McKay.

On the night of the election, Mack had gone to bed thinking he had lost the election. But a count of the votes which included the absentee ballots proved Mack the winner by a 30,000-vote margin. His opponent demanded a recount, but later acceded to Mack's win.

For the first time since the Reconstruction, Republicans were elected to the state cabinet. They were Jim Smith, a former attorney general who had switched parties, and former legislator Tom Gallagher. Smith became secretary of state while Gallagher was elected treasurer-insurance commissioner.

Nine of the 11 proposed constitutional amendments were passed by voters. The most heated campaign involved the proposal to limit non-economic damages to $100,000 in accident and negligence cases, pitting doctors against lawyers. Floridians ignored their physicians' advice that passing the amendment would ease the health-care crisis and reduce insurance rates. Almost $15 million was spent by proponents and opponents of the amendment; it was the second costliest campaign in the state's history.

An amendment that would make English the official language in Florida passed by an overwhelming five-to-one margin. The amendment, which gives the state power to mandate use of English in all governmental and legal documents and transactions, is expected to meet tough court challenges.

Other amendments passed would create state departments for the elderly and for veterans, and would allow crime victims to testify at most trials on the impact of the crimes to them. Florida voters defeated an amendment that would have extended the four-year terms of county judges to six years.

Legislation. Two major bills involving taxes and car insurance were passed by the 1988 legislature. The services tax that had been passed in 1987 was criticized so highly that Gov. Bob Martinez asked for it to be repealed and that,

In a close, but major, win for the GOP, Rep. Connie Mack, the 48-year-old grandson of the baseball legend, defeated Rep. Buddy McKay in Florida's race for the U.S. Senate.

in its place, another penny be added to the sales tax. The legislature followed his wishes. Penalties for not carrying auto insurance were stiffened and liability insurance—in addition to personal injury protection—was made mandatory effective Oct. 1, 1989.

Other key new laws would permit counties to add an extra day to the state's optional 48-hour waiting period for handgun purchases, and would allow minors to attend horse- and dog-racing tracks, as well as jai-alai frontons.

Environment. The Wilderness Society warned that the Key Deer National Wildlife Refuge in the Florida Keys and the Loxahatchee National Wildlife Refuge in Palm Beach County were among the nation's most threatened wildlife areas, due to rampant development. "Migrating waterfowl are landing in poisoned marshes, development is destroying vital wetlands and dams, and irrigation projects are choking off essential sources of water," the society's report said. In addition, about 20% of the endangered, tiny Key deer population is killed by traffic each year and there are fewer than 300 left, the report revealed.

The opposite is true with the Florida alligator. Because the reptile's population has grown so rapidly, the state approved a month-long hunt in September 1988 that netted almost 3,500 alligators.

GREG MELIKOV
State Desk, "The Miami Herald"

FLORIDA • Information Highlights

Area: 58,664 sq mi (151 939 km²).
Population (July 1, 1987): 12,023,000.
Chief Cities (July 1, 1986 est.): Tallahassee, the capital, 119,480; Jacksonville, 610,030; Miami, 373,940; Tampa, 277,580; St. Petersburg, 239,480.
Government (1988): *Chief Officers*—governor, Bob Martinez (R); lt. gov., Bobby Brantley (R). *Legislature*—Senate, 40 members; House of Representatives, 120 members.
State Finances (fiscal year 1987): *Revenue,* $17,394,000,000; *expenditure,* $15,426,000,000.
Personal Income (1987): $187,365,000,000; per capita, $15,584.
Labor Force (June 1988): *Civilian labor force,* 6,142,200; *unemployed,* 295,200 (4.8% of total force).
Education: *Enrollment* (fall 1986)—public elementary schools, 1,120,938; public secondary, 486,382; colleges and universities, 483,964. *Public school expenditures* (1986–87), $6,037,000,000 ($4,056 per pupil).

FOOD

Adventurous consumers, resolute dieticians, and innovative food suppliers teamed up to make 1988 a watershed year of liberation from traditional diets. It became clear that food consumers finally had broken from their cultural moorings, and were seeking not just low prices and quality, but also variety, safety, convenience, and improved health. People belonging to non-European cultures—while keen to preserve traditional foods—were crowding into "fast food" establishments such as McDonald's and Kentucky Fried Chicken, and frequenting restaurants serving European cuisines. U.S. consumers continued their trend of sampling foods from other cultures.

Food consumers increasingly were committed to good health. In greater numbers they listened to what dieticians and other authoritative advisers had affirmed for many years: Good nutrition is indeed a road to improved health.

The giant U.S. food companies were intensely competitive in their research labs and at the supermarket. In addition to their advertising budgets, they were spending millions of dollars to rent shelf space to display new products in the grocery stores. In light of these trends, it should be noted that such major U.S. companies as RJR Nabisco and Kraft were the subjects of late in the year merger/buyout attempts (*see* BUSINESS AND FINANCE).

In this exciting environment, past practices were no longer a guide to dietary behavior. Beef producers manifested the prevailing attitude by reshaping their product to fit various health demands rather than questioning whether new health guides were valid.

New Products. Two major forces brought a rush of new food products. One of these forces was a new technology which reduced the need for refrigerated storage. "Frozen foods are on the way out," said one industry expert. "They are being replaced by shelf-stable, possibly irradiated foods." The other force was the decisive shift to microwave cooking. One food giant, Pillsbury, anticipated that its 1988 microwave food product sales would reach $225 million (industry-wide microwave food sales were nearing $1 billion) and Pillsbury was spending 60% of its research budget on microwave products.

Successful microwave cookery was a skill to be learned in classes offered at department stores, schools, and community centers, or to be learned from microwave recipe books. Companies were seeking wrappings that could overcome the sogginess of microwaved foods.

Included among the new microwave products in 1988 were "shelf-stable" foods in packages rather than in the traditional tin cans. Many of these foods had been vacuum-sealed to eliminate oxygen and then precooked in steam or hot water. Some were also irradiated

to destroy microorganisms. These packages could be carried to work or on outings, and prepared in two minutes (as compared with a five-minute preparation time needed for traditional frozen meals).

Food Safety. New processes generated some new fears. It was thought that irradiation of food might disrupt bonds between molecules, allowing cells to recombine to form toxic chemicals called "radiolytic products." Environmentalists were concerned about the long-term health effects of widespread use of radioactive materials in food processing.

Outbreaks of food poisoning were on the rise, partly because of the unperfected "quick-fix" foods, but also because centralization of the food industry had resulted in greater delivery distances, and had made it possible for an occasional batch of contaminated food to reach large numbers of consumers. However, a factor inflating the number of occurrences of food poisoning was improved detection methods that could identify food specifically as the cause of many illnesses.

There were concerns in 1988, as in earlier years, that Third World countries were being used as the dumping ground for contaminated foods—for example, that European food radiated during the 1986 Chernobyl nuclear accident in the USSR was being exported to Africa. But consumers in some rapidly developing countries were becoming safety-conscious: In Taiwan a new Consumers Federation successfully lobbied for a food-labeling law (stating ingredients and expiration date), and started a magazine to publish early warnings of adulterated or unhealthy products.

Fresh eggs were suddenly suspect for consumers in the northeastern United States. In the summer of 1988, the U.S. Centers for Disease Control issued an advisory that the area's eggs no longer should be eaten raw (as in milk shakes), though they were safe when cooked. A few specific seafoods also were placed in suspect categories.

Nutrition and Health. Definite changes in food choices were reported in a U.S. Department of Agriculture (USDA) study comparing present choices with those from a survey 15 years earlier. Beef, pork, and lamb, which earlier comprised three fourths of all meat consumption, now made up only two thirds. Americans were eating more cereal products, fruits and vegetables, fish, poultry, and cheese. They were eating fewer eggs and potatoes.

The dietary changes were caused by many factors. Price advantage was a factor in choice of poultry over other meats. People also were attracted by upscale value-added products such as boneless breast fillets. Health goals rose in importance in 1988. According to Food Marketing Institute surveys, 27% of shoppers said they were concerned about fat in their foods (as compared with 16% in 1987, and only 9% in

Perhaps as never before, consumers throughout the world sampled foods from other cultures. American ''fast foods'' were available almost everywhere. In Beijing, China, left, people lined up for Kentucky Fried Chicken. And in Moscow, below, adventurous Soviets tasted American-style pizza.

1983). Finally, people clearly had become more knowledgeable about health and nutrition issues.

But health messages that had changed some diets for the better also had accelerated the search, especially among teenagers, for magic diets and pills that would burn off fats and build muscular bodies. While Americans were shifting to more nutritious diets, there was criticism in the USSR that Soviet citizens still had not been moved from their fatty diets.

World Hunger and Malnutrition. Droughts, flooding, and other natural disasters caused some severe food shortages in 1988, but in some cases societies found means to prevent widespread hunger. Unfortunately other governments ignored hunger among their citizenry and even hindered efforts of international agencies to import sufficient food.

Thousands of starving refugees fled to unfriendly Ethiopia from Sudan's drought and civil war. Newspaper reports charged that Ethiopian President Mengistu Haile Mariam was bent on starving insurgents in his provinces of Eritrea and Tigré, and that the government of Sudan was diverting international food aid from the needy Southern famine areas to the regime's supporters in the North. United Nations Secretary Javier Pérez de Cuéllar won limited access in Ethiopia for UN observers but not full access for food-relief groups.

In May, Vietnamese leaders appealed to the United Nations for food aid, stating that 8 million people in North Vietnam were short of food, ''at the edge of starvation.'' By contrast, Bangladesh people who fled massive floods largely were saved from the famine and disease that typically accompanied such natural catastrophes.

Natural catastrophes, it seems, were less to be blamed than uncaring governments. Pockets of hunger were evident even in the prosperous United States. National and state governments generally lacked enthusiasm for hunger relief; vigorous volunteer groups organized ''soup kitchens'' in cities throughout the nation.

IT'S FRESH

FIRST AMERICAN PIZZA IN MOSCOW

ASTROPIZZA

Photos AP/Wide World

A World Food Conference held in Brussels concluded that a major crisis centered around the fact that there was too much food production in the developed nations; concurrently, the crisis of hunger was due to inadequate economic and financial structures. Many economists who once felt that market forces would generate adequate amounts of food had become convinced of the need for structural policies to improve marketing, technology, and credit, and also to accelerate employment growth.

See also AGRICULTURE.

DONALD F. HADWIGER
Iowa State University

FRANCE

France's political life in 1988 was dominated by presidential and parliamentary elections and, before the settlement of issues, violence in the South Pacific colony of New Caledonia. Socialist President François Mitterrand, in winning a second seven-year term, was able to regain powers that had become diluted under a two-year power-sharing arrangement with conservative Prime Minister Jacques Chirac. Mitterrand projected the image of a strong, competent leader throughout the year, according to observers. His prime minister, Michel Rocard (*see* BIOGRAPHY), in contrast, governed amid criticism from the left wing of the Socialist party, sporadic strikes, and weak support in the National Assembly. Rocard's major achievement was the New Caledonia settlement.

Politics. The year began with a well-publicized forecast by a French magazine that President Mitterrand, if he decided to run for reelection, would win easily. The poll, published on January 2 by *Paris Match,* ultimately proved correct. But it and similar surveys appeared at a time when Mitterrand, 71, still was hesitating about running. His main opponents appeared to be, and ultimately were, conservative Prime Minister Jacques Chirac and former Prime Minister Raymond Barre, also a conservative. Michel Rocard, another Socialist, led Chirac in the *Paris Match* poll, but trailed Barre.

On the whole, the campaign was dull. This reflected a convergence to the political center by the three mainstream political groups: the Socialists; Chirac's ruling Gaullist Rally for the Republic (RPR); and its junior coalition partner, the Union for French Democracy (UDF), a center-right party. As the elections approached, however, Chirac began attacking Mitterrand increasingly even though they continued to govern under a power-sharing arrangement known as "cohabitation."

Although Mitterrand, as president, remained firmly in control of foreign policy, Chirac on March 1 criticized him for stating his opposition to the modernization of North Atlantic Treaty Organization (NATO) conventional weapons. In two newspaper interviews, Mitterrand had said that it would be unwise for France to support an upgrading of NATO battlefield weapons. "At a time when the two superpowers are reinforcing their dialogue," he said, "people expect Europe to give out positive signals." Chirac, intensifying his campaign for the presidency, boasted that it was he, not Mitterrand, who had been responsible for upgrading France's own nuclear forces. Responding through a spokesman, Mitterrand said that he merely had expressed the view that the modernization was not urgent.

In his April 6 election manifesto, "A Letter to All the French," candidate Mitterrand emphasized the importance of a fully open European market by 1992; a strong and independent French defense; and increased spending on education, job training, and research. Encouraged by the polls, Mitterrand continued to polish his image as a head of state who would unite all French citizens, an assertion also made by Chirac. In positions aimed at distancing himself from the right, Mitterrand favored reinstitution of a "wealth tax" on France's richest citizens, while repeatedly stressing the rights of immigrants.

In the first round of the elections on April 24, with a voter turnout of about 82%, Mitterrand led all other candidates with 34.0% of the vote. He thus would face Chirac, the runner-up, in the second round two weeks later. The premier's 19.9% of the popular vote was viewed as a major setback for the RPR, which had been expected to win as much as 24%. Both Chirac and Barre, who was backed by the UDF and won 16.6% of the vote, lost votes to Jean-Marie Le Pen, the leader of the extreme right-wing National Front. Le Pen made a surprisingly strong showing, garnering 14.4% of the vote. The centerpiece of his campaign was a call for the ouster of immigrant workers as a solution to France's economic and social problems. Le Pen's performance, which he described as a "political earthquake," solidified his position as the fourth power in French politics because he displaced the Communists, who continued to slip badly at the polls. The Communist Party's candidate, André Lajoinie, obtained only 6.7% of the vote, the worst showing in the party's history. About 30.8 million votes were cast.

Mitterrand, who made few personal appearances, said that if reelected he would name a new premier to reflect the "presidential" majority. Because the Chamber of Deputies was dominated by a coalition of the RPR and the UDF, Mitterrand's signal to the country was

---

FRANCE • Information Highlights

Official Name: French Republic.
Location: Western Europe.
Area: 211,208 sq mi (547 030 km²).
Population (mid-1988 est.): 55,900,000.
Chief City (1982 est.): Paris, the capital, 8,706,963.
Government: *Head of state,* François Mitterrand, president (took office May 1981). *Chief minister,* Michel Rocard, prime minister (took office May 1988). *Legislature*—Parliament: Senate and National Assembly.
Monetary Unit: Franc (5.88 francs equal U.S. $1, Dec. 5, 1988).
Gross Domestic Product (1986 U.S.$): $724,-100,000,000.
Economic Indexes (1987): *Consumer Prices* (1980 = 100), all items, 167.3; food, 167.3. *Industrial Production* (1987, 1980 = 100), 104.
Foreign Trade (1987 U.S.$): *Imports,* $157,913,-000,000; *exports,* $142,488,000,000.

"A United France is on the March" was the campaign slogan of Socialist President François Mitterrand, whose supporters (right) elected him to a new seven-year term on May 8. His defeat of Prime Minister Jacques Chirac ended two years of power-sharing. Reflecting his centrist leanings, Mitterrand named moderate Socialist Michel Rocard (bottom) as prime minister. Rocard became the first premier in the 30-year history of the Fifth Republic from a nonmajority party in parliament. One of the year's surprises was the showing of Jean-Marie Le Pen (below, left), of the extreme right-wing National Front. Le Pen got nearly 15% of the vote in the first round of the election.

© A. Nogues/Sygma

© Nahassia/Rea/Picture Group

© B. Bisson/Sygma

In France's South Pacific colony of New Caledonia, Melanesian separatists (or Kanaks) confront French police, protesting the May 5 "massacre" in which French commandos attacked a cave on the island of Ouvea and freed 23 French hostages. An agreement later was reached on the future of the colony.

AP/Wide World

clear: readiness to appoint a new prime minister who would have the support of both the Socialists and centrists. One issue that generated acrimony between Mitterrand and Chirac was the scheduling of a televised debate. Chirac opposed Mitterrand's refusal to debate before the first round of balloting. One debate took place on April 29, with widespread agreement that it broke little new ground.

Meantime, events thousands of miles away became central to the campaign. On April 22, Melanesian separatists in the French South Pacific colony of New Caledonia killed several policemen and took 27 French hostages. The separatists, members of the Kanak Socialist National Liberation Front (FLNKS), were demanding that the presidential and New Caledonian municipal election results be declared void; that France withdraw its troops from the island of Ouvea, where the initial killings and kidnappings took place; and that negotiations open on the question of independence.

In the days just prior to the second round of France's election, two spectacular events captured public attention. First, three Frenchmen who had been held hostage in Lebanon for three years were released in Beirut on May 4. The hostages were welcomed back to France on May 5 by Prime Minister Chirac, who had been trailing Mitterrand in opinion polls. Chirac also thanked Iran for its role in helping win the release of the captives and said that their freedom opened the way for a normalization of relations with Iran, broken in the summer of 1987.

On May 5 in New Caledonia, French commandos attacked a cave in Ouvea and freed 23 remaining French hostages, but the dawn raid also resulted in the deaths of 15 separatists and two French commandos. Chirac offered his "warm congratulations" to the French forces.

Mitterrand, who had been more receptive to the Kanak's call for self-government than Chirac, said he was "very sad" about the death toll and that he always preferred conciliation and mediation. Other Socialist leaders blamed Chirac for dragging the territory into violence for political reasons. The FNLKS said "the massacre" would reinforce Kanak opposition to French rule, which dated back 135 years.

In the second round of voting on May 8, as the polls predicted from the beginning, Mitterrand easily won his second seven-year term as president, with 54.0% of the 30.9 million votes cast to Chirac's 46.0%. Mitterrand's margin of victory was the largest since that obtained by Georges Pompidou in 1969. On May 10, Mitterrand named Rocard, a moderate Socialist, to succeed Chirac as prime minister. Rocard thus became the first premier in the 30-year history of the Fifth Republic to head a government that did not command a majority in parliament.

The choice of Rocard, according to most observers, further underscored President Mitterrand's centrist leaning. On May 12, amid widespread speculation that new parliamentary elections would be called soon, Rocard named a cabinet dominated by veteran Socialist politicians, but with some non-Socialists in secondary posts. Some UDF leaders, including former President Valéry Giscard d'Estaing, said they would not vote in parliament to censure the new government but would consider legislation on a case-by-case basis. As expected, the parliament was dissolved on May 14, and legislative elections were called for June; 575 seats in the 577-member National Assembly would be contested.

Following the two rounds of voting on June 5 and June 12, however, neither the Socialists nor the rightist coalition were able to obtain a majority, the first time since the Fifth Republic

240

was founded in 1958 that voters failed to install an absolute Assembly majority. The Socialists captured 276 seats; the UDF-RPR alliance won 271 seats; the Communists took 27; and the National Front retained one. Mitterrand asked Rocard to form a new, minority government, which was sworn in on June 28. Socialists filled the major cabinet positions, while centrists and independents were given lesser posts.

Prime Minister Rocard achieved his first major success on June 26, when he announced that an agreement had been reached in New Caledonia for the future of the colony's administration and that a plan for self-determination would be submitted to French voters in a referendum November 6. Although the 37% voter turnout disappointed Rocard, the new law was approved. It calls for a vote in New Caledonia in 1998 to decide whether the archipelago will become independent or remain part of France. The plan also calls for a ten-year transition period characterized by increased local self-government and French aid.

Economy. The National Statistics Institute announced that France's gross domestic product (GDP) had expanded 2.2% in 1987, basically unchanged from 1986, amid widespread expectations that a mild pickup would occur later in 1988. The nation's trade deficit grew to 31.4 billion francs (U.S. $5.6 billion) in 1987, up from 500 million francs ($89 million) in 1986, while consumer prices inched up 3.1%, compared with 2.1% in 1986. Both the trade deficit and inflation were expected to worsen somewhat during the course of 1988.

The unemployment level reached about 11%, or 2.5 million people, as the year began, and it did not begin to fall (slightly) until the autumn, when the expected expansion of GDP began. Socialist Finance Minister Pierre Beregovoy, who replaced Edouard Balladur, a key Chirac strategist, predicted that France would enter 1989 with a growth rate of between 3.0% and 3.5%. French and U.S. private banks supported that scenario, described by Banque Paribas as "like a sailing boat righting itself after a squall." Investments also began to accelerate early in 1988 amid private forecasts that they would rise by 11% in 1988 and 8% in 1989.

The growing optimism was reflected in the Paris Bourse, which continued to outperform most other European stock exchanges, notably in the immediate wake of Mitterrand's reelection. By early October, Smith Barney, a New York investment bank, predicted that the Bourse "may be one of Europe's top performers in 1989." A major factor, the bank stated, was Mitterrand's determination to maintain a stable franc within the European Monetary System (EMS). Despite a falling U.S. dollar and since the last devaluation in January 1987, the franc throughout most of 1988 was stabilized close to its central EMS parity rate of 3.37 francs to the West German mark. French officials repeatedly denied rumors of devaluation as the mark strengthened throughout the year.

In the business world, Renault, the giant state-owned automaker, announced on March 22 that 1987 profits had totaled 3.6 billion francs ($600 million) on sales of 147.51 billion francs ($24.6 billion), reversing six straight years of losses. The results were regarded as a major triumph for Chairman Raymond Levy and his predecessor, Georges Besse, who started the company's restructuring in 1985 and was assassinated a year later.

In his first speech to the National Assembly, Prime Minister Rocard on June 29 announced a moderate program for the economy. Reflecting a shift toward the center, Rocard said that the government's goals were not "those of one half of France against the other, but those of all the French." One of the few specific policies he outlined was the reinstitution of the wealth tax, which had been scrapped by the Chirac government. He also repeated a call for a guaranteed minimum income and emphasized that France remained committed to the European Community's goal of a single integrated market by 1992. Rocard

AP/Wide World

A new glass pyramid in the western courtyard of the Louvre in Paris serves as the main entrance to the museum and the center of an underground complex of auxiliary services. The giant pyramid, designed by I. M. Pei, was not received kindly—to say the least.

pledged to pursue an economic "rigor . . . to guide us toward a new rate of growth."

Commenting on the 1992 plan, Rocard said that France was beset by "fears" and "difficulties," but his speech did little to dispel the mood of the country at midyear, described by the magazine *Le Point* as in a state of "dereliction." The magazine said France's future was "devoid of projects and ideas," while the daily newspaper *Le Monde* described the country as a "rudderless ship." Rocard's spokesmen, brushing off the criticism, said the government planned a major legislative program in the autumn.

But by mid-October, the government and the nation faced a wave of sporadic strikes that had started quietly and spread gradually, mainly in the public sector. Primarily the strikers were seeking higher pay, arguing that wage increases had not kept up with inflation since France adopted a tough austerity policy in 1983. But the government remained firm, conceding some very modest increases in several sectors only. Among those who went on strike were nurses, prison guards, Renault workers, teachers, postal and electric utility employees, and municipal bus and subway crews. The government's goal was to keep inflation to about 2.8% in 1988, amid speculation that the strikes would erode confidence in the franc.

With some of the strikers slowly returning to work, the franc was supported by more good news at the end of October: The seasonally adjusted trade balance had shown a surplus of 400 million francs (about $65 million) in September, turning around from a deficit of 9 billion francs (about $1.5 billion) in August. Analysts attributed the surplus to an even industrial trade balance and improved agricultural exports. Beregovoy said it was "a good figure for France's foreign trade" but warned of over-optimism. The Organization for Economic Cooperation and Development (OECD), in its year-end review of member countries, projected France's seasonally adjusted trade deficit at $9 billion in 1988, down slightly from $9.5 billion in 1987, and remaining at that level in 1989 and 1990. That projection, an improvement over the midyear figures, was expected to keep downward pressure on the franc throughout 1989, observers said. Other OECD projections published in December showed France's GDP slipping to 3% growth in 1989 from an estimated 3.5% in 1988, with consumer prices falling slightly from 2.5% in 1988 and 1989 to 2.25% in 1990. The unemployment rate will continue at just under 11% through 1990, OECD said, adding that "the growth of unit labor costs is likely to be among the lowest in the OECD area" (comprising North America, Europe, and the Pacific region).

In a November interview, Rocard said that his policy of austerity, or "rigor," might be eased, but not before the spring of 1990.

Foreign Affairs. France and West Germany on Jan. 22, 1988, formally established joint councils on defense and economic issues. Agreements were signed in Paris by President Mitterrand and West German Chancellor Helmut Kohl during ceremonies marking the 25th anniversary of a friendship treaty signed by predecessors Charles de Gaulle and Konrad Adenauer. The joint defense council, to be based in Paris, will seek to improve cooperation on military strategy, troop deployment, and weapons procurement; the two allies also agreed to establish a 4,000-troop joint brigade stationed in Boeblingen, West Germany. The joint economic council will seek to strengthen ties and coordinate policy. French officials emphasized that the councils were but a first step in bringing the two nations closer together. German officials said they hoped that, as a result, France would continue moving closer to the unified NATO military command from which it withdrew in the 1960s.

Rocard, shortly after being named prime minister, announced that France would begin the process of restoring diplomatic relations with Iran. The move fulfilled a pledge made by the previous Chirac government in connection with the release of the three remaining French hostages held in Lebanon. In his announcement, Rocard said that no written account of the negotiations had been found, but that France would keep its word to restore ties, settle the outstanding balance on a $1 billion 1974 loan from Iran, and renew other commercial relations. Despite denials by Chirac and Rocard, media accounts continued to report that the deal for the release of the hostages had involved direct payments, which some Arab diplomats estimated at more than $6 million. Formal relations were restored on June 16.

As 1988 ended, two French girls, who had been held hostage by Palestinians for more than a year, were released in Libya.

President Mitterrand on June 8 announced that the French government would cancel one third of the debts owed to it by the poorest Third World nations. The debt was about 1 billion francs ($167 million).

France reacted harshly to comprehensive trade legislation signed by President Ronald Reagan in Washington on August 23. Following similar statements by the European Community Commission in Brussels, the Rocard government described the legislation as "particularly insupportable and unacceptable." Government spokesmen said the United States was abandoning its commitment to multilateral trade liberalization. Edith Cresson, Rocard's minister for European affairs, said that "reciprocity is the basis of our policy on access to markets and related issues, and we intend to press for reciprocal advantages. . . ."

AXEL KRAUSE
"International Herald Tribune," Paris

The 5,600-seat bingo parlor at Florida's Big Cypress Seminole Indian Reservation is the largest in the world. U.S. Indian tribes now sponsor more than 100 gambling operations, most of them high-stakes bingo. Legislation passed in 1988 calls for federal regulation of high-stakes bingo and other types of gambling on Indian reservations.

© Red Morgan/"Time" Magazine

GAMBLING

The commercial gambling industries in the United States generally have experienced strong growth during the 1980s. In 1987, casinos in Nevada and Atlantic City, NJ, generated gross gaming revenues (win) of $6.4 billion. State lotteries grossed $6.6 billion after payout of prizes. Horse racing, horse offtrack-betting, greyhound racing, legal bookmaking, and jai alai accounted for another $3.4 billion in gross win. Legal bingo, charitable gambling, and gambling on Indian lands accounted for $1.7 billion in gross win. In total, legal-gambling industries in the United States generated consumer spending (gross operator win after payment of prizes and operator losses) of $18.4 billion in 1987, nearly doubling the 1982 figure of $10.4 billion.

Casinos. Gross revenues generated by slot machines and other gaming devices in casinos have been a major source of growth. In 1987, slot machines generated $3.6 billion in total casino win in Nevada and Atlantic City, about 56% of the total casino revenues.

Public corporations are replacing individual entrepreneurs as the typical owners and operators of the American casino. As of 1987, the 27 (of 155) casino operations owned by public corporations in Nevada generated 49% of gross gaming revenue, and in Atlantic City, nine of the 12 casinos were owned by public corporations. (Two of the remaining three were owned by the Donald Trump organization.) Corporate casinos, along with improved state regulatory processes in Nevada and New Jersey, have improved the perceived legitimacy of the casino gambling industry. Improved image and the willingness of governments to turn to casino gambling for job creation and new tax revenue led to a number of attempts to legalize casinos in new jurisdictions in the 1980s. However, by 1988, such attempts had failed in Florida, Minnesota, Colorado, and Arkansas. Voters in the city of Detroit also rejected such a motion in August 1988.

Lotteries. Aggregate lottery sales (before payout of prizes) in the United States in 1987 exceeded $12 billion. At that time, 27 states and the District of Columbia ran lotteries through government agencies or lottery commissions. Since the introduction of the first modern U.S. lottery in 1963, lotteries have evolved from passive games, where a person would buy a ticket and wait up to three months to see if the ticket won, to games where the player selects his or her own numbers, or where the outcome is determined instantly on a scratch-out ticket. Extremely large jackpots have been part of the attraction of lotteries, especially lotto, and casino slot machines.

Voters in Virginia approved a state lottery in 1987, and five states—Idaho, Indiana, Kentucky, Minnesota, and North Dakota—held referenda on the subject in 1988. The motion was rejected in North Dakota only.

Horse Racing. Total revenues for the parimutuel horse-race industry barely kept up with inflation between 1982 and 1987. Market saturation, high tax rates, competition from other commercial gambling, and the difficulties of attracting new bettors are cited as reasons for the slower growth. Virginia voters approved parimutuel betting in 1988.

Other Forms. Poker parlors, which operate legally on a local option basis in California, are beginning to resemble Las Vegas facilities. Low-stakes blackjack can be found in Oregon and North Dakota, and the Canadian provinces of Manitoba, Alberta, and British Columbia have introduced low-stakes casinos, where the net proceeds accrue to charitable organizations. Finally, because of the lack of state jurisdiction on Indian reservations, gambling operations, especially commercial bingo, on tribal lands have become a growing business.

WILLIAM R. EADINGTON
University of Nevada—Reno

The Conard-Pyle Company, West Grove, PA

© Nor'East Miniature Roses Inc., Rowley, MA

For the first time, two miniature rose varieties were chosen as winners of the All-America Rose Selections Award. "Debut," left, features deep-red and creamy white flowers up to 2 inches (5.08 cm) across; "New Beginning," right, is an orange-red and yellow blend.

GARDENING AND HORTICULTURE

Between 1986 and 1987, U.S. gardeners increased spending by 23% for both indoor and outdoor garden activities, according to a 1987–88 Gallup Organization survey conducted for the National Gardening Association. The survey found that the money spent increased to $17.491 billion for 1987 from $14.206 billion in 1986. The percentage of U.S. households involved in doing their own lawn and garden care increased to 59% (53 million), and 41% (37 million) were involved in growing houseplants, both up by one million households.

The U.S. floral symbol, the rose, is the most popular flower in the nation, according to a Gallup Organization survey conducted for the All-America Rose Selections, Inc. The survey found that 23 million households spent nearly $400 million during 1987 on growing roses.

Award Winners. The All-America Rose Selections Award (AARS) 1989, for the first time in its 50-year history, was announced for four outstanding new varieties. Two of the winners were miniature roses, great for small-space and container gardens. "Debut," a showy, red-blend miniature rose, produces blooms of 20 large petals with deep red at the outer edge, softening to creamy white and almost yellow at the petal base. The blooms may be 2 inches (5.08 cm) across. "Debut" was introduced by the Conard-Pyle Company, West Grove, PA, and hybridized by Jacques Mouchotte, Selection Meilland, Antibes, France. "New Beginning," a colorful orange-red and yellow blend miniature rose, blooms profusely throughout summer and into late fall and shows excellent vigor and disease resistance. "New Beginning" was developed and introduced by F. Harmon Saville, Nor'East Miniature Roses Inc., of Rowley, MA. The two other AARS winners were a white floribunda, "Class Act," and "Tournament of Roses," a coral-pink grandiflora named the official commemorative rose of the Pasadena "Tournament of Roses" Centennial in 1989. The latter two roses were hybridized and introduced by William A. Warriner, Jackson and Perkins Co., Medford, OR.

The All-America Selections (AAS) judged eight flowers as 1989 AAS Award winners from the 33 flower trial gardens across the United States. "Orchid Daddy," an Fl grandiflora petunia, produces 3-inch (7.62-cm) blooms with heat and weather tolerance, and was the first plant ever to receive both the AAS Bedding Plant Award and the AAS Flower Award. Others receiving AAS Awards included: "Early Sunrise," an early-blooming coreopsis; "Tango," a bright-orange impatiens; "Golden Gate," a compact, dwarf French marigold with 2- to 2.5-inch (5.08- to 6.35-cm) blossoms; "Telstar Picotee," a heat-tolerant dianthus exhibiting crimson blossoms with white edge borders; and "Clown Mixture," a torenia with deep rose, white, blue-violet, and mid-blue blossoms. "Novalis Deep Blue" verbena was chosen for three improved qualities over other verbenas: more flowers, a longer blooming season, and a compact dwarf growth habit. "Sandy White" verbena was selected for pure white umbels the color of fresh snow.

New Product. Sharpshooter, a new environmentally safe broad-spectrum vegetation killer, was introduced by Safer, Inc., Wellesley, MA, after receiving federal Environmental Protection Agency (EPA) approval for consumer and commercial use. Sharpshooter's active ingredients are potassium salts of saturated fatty acids. According to Dr. Michael Atkins, chairman of Safer, "the introduction of Sharpshooter will revolutionize the herbicide industry and provide consumers and commercial users with an effective, safe alternative to petrochemical-based weed-control products. Sharpshooter does not leave harmful residues in the soil and is nontoxic to people, pets, and wildlife."

RALPH L. SNODSMITH
Ornamental Horticulturist

GENETICS

It has been known for some time that the pattern of development of at least one dominant human genetic disease—Huntington's chorea—depends on which parent contributed the gene. Huntington's chorea is a disorder characterized by progressive deterioration of the nervous system, leading to constant thrashing and writhing movements, insanity, and death. The gene that causes this disease is dominant, but if it is inherited from one's father, symptoms begin during adolescence; if one's mother is the source of the gene, symptoms do not appear until middle age.

An explanation for this and similar phenomena may come from a recent discovery in mice, where it was found that genes inherited from a female have more methyl (CH_3) groups attached to them than do the same genes inherited from a male. It also was found that the amount of methylation of a gene is related to its level of activity: The less methylated gene tends to be active, the more methylated gene tends to be inactive. If the same situation exists in humans, the difference would explain the delayed onset of Huntington's chorea when the gene is inherited from one's mother.

The parental determination of a gene's activity level has been called *imprinting*. An especially interesting aspect of this process, also found in mice, is that if a male inherits a particular gene from his mother, the gene will be in a highly methylated state. His progeny, however, whether male or female, will have the same gene in a much reduced methylated form. Thus, the degree of gene methylation depends on the type of gamete (sperm or egg) that was the source of the gene.

Male-Producing B Chromosomes. In addition to their basic complement of chromosomes, many species of plants and animals have been found to carry extra, or supernumerary, chromosomes. For most species, the role of such B chromosomes is unknown, and not all members of a species have them. B chromosomes are unknown in humans.

The role of the B chromosome is particularly interesting in the wasp species *Nasonia vitripennis*. In this organism, as in many other wasp and bee and ant species, females normally are produced from fertilized eggs, and males normally develop from unfertilized eggs. When that is the case, the chromosomes of a male are all maternal in origin and half in number of those found in females.

Some *N. vitripennis,* however, have a B-type chromosome called *psr* (paternal sex ratio). When females mate with males that have *psr,* they produce only male offspring. This unusual condition has been investigated by Dr. Uzi Nur and his associates at the University of Rochester. A study of eggs that had been fertilized by *psr*-containing sperm demonstrated that the set of normal chromosomes introduced by the sperm became condensed, failed to divide, and eventually was ejected from the egg. The B chromosome, on the other hand, did divide and was distributed normally during subsequent divisions of the egg. As a result, all of the "fertilized eggs" developed into males that carried the *psr* B chromosome.

It is clear that a continuation of this process ultimately would lead to the extinction of the species because of the production of only males. However, in natural populations of this wasp, the highest observed percentage of males carrying the *psr* chromosome is 20%. Studies are now under way to determine what environmental or genetic factors prevent the spread of *psr* to all males of the species.

Uniparental Disomy. Uniparental disomy is the term used for the presence of two identical chromosomes in a genome that are derived from one parent. It was unknown in humans until 1988, when Dr. J. E. Spence and his colleagues at the Baylor College of Medicine in Houston announced the first such verified case. It involved a female patient suffering from cystic fibrosis (CF), a genetic disease that occurs in individuals homozygous for the recessive CF gene—located on chromosome 7.

A detailed analysis revealed beyond doubt that both members of the patient's chromosome-7 pair came from her mother. It was hypothesized that this condition arose as a result of faulty formation of both sperm and egg. The sperm was formed without a chromosome 7, while the egg was formed with two such identical chromosomes. The fusion of these gametes resulted in a fertilized egg with the normal number of chromosomes (46) but with two identical copies of chromosome 7. It is believed that most cases of uniparental disomy are lost through spontaneous miscarriages.

Untranslated Segment of mRNA. It has been assumed for a long time that any messenger RNA (mRNA) molecule reaching a ribosome contains only those coding sequences needed to specify the amino acid sequence of the resultant protein. In 1988, however, Dr. W. M. Huang and his colleagues at the University of Utah Medical Center reported an unexpected finding in the mRNA transcribed from the T4 viral gene for the enzyme topoisomerase. This enzyme changes the geometric form of the virus' DNA in preparation for its replication. The researchers found that a 50-nucleotide region of the mRNA was not translated into the resultant topoisomerase. It was hypothesized that the mRNA molecule folds in a hairpinlike configuration that is bypassed during the translation process. Although this was the first and only example yet of an untranslated segment of a fully formed mRNA, the discovery added another factor to be considered in the model of the DNA-RNA-protein process.

LOUIS LEVINE, *City College of New York*

GEOLOGY

The year 1988 saw continued advances in the field of geology, as scientists probed the inner earth, learned more about the crustal plates, and made significant fossil discoveries.

Earthquakes. A major earthquake—measuring 6.9 on the Richter scale, with an aftershock of 5.8—devastated several cities in the Armenian SSR on December 7, including Leninakan, Kirovakan, and Spitak. More than 25,000 people were killed, thousands were injured, and about half a million were left homeless. The quake occurred in a zone where several of the plates of the earth's surface converge. Earlier, on August 20, an earthquake measuring 6.5 on the Richter scale struck parts of Nepal and India, killing more than 980 people. The quake's epicenter was located north of Dharbanga, India, and the tremors were felt across a wide region. Damage in Nepal was confined largely to Bihar state and eastern Nepal, where hundreds were killed and thousands left homeless. It was the strongest quake to have hit the Himalayas in half a century. Another major quake occurred on November 6, when a temblor of magnitude 7.6 rocked southwestern China, killing about 1,000 people and leaving 100,000 homeless.

A moderate quake (4.5 on the Richter scale) shook a wide area of Southern California on June 26. The earthquake was centered near Upland, CA, and felt 50 mi (80 km) away; there were no reports of injuries or damage. And a major temblor, magnitude 7.2, rocked Alaska on March 6. It was centered offshore about 210 miles (340 km) south of Cape Yakataga; no casualties or destruction were reported.

Fossils. Geologists in Iowa discovered a large fossil bed containing the oldest well-preserved land vertebrates ever collected in North America. The 35-million-year-old fossil cache contained the remains of the oldest known amphibian. Meanwhile, a new fossil bird found in Spain was thought to be the oldest known flyer, an intermediate between *Archaeopteryx,* the oldest known bird, and modern birds. And in Charleston, SC, scientists collected fossils of the largest known flying seabird. Apparently related to pelicans and cormorants, the species lived about 30 million years ago, had a wingspread of 18 ft (5.5 m), and may have weighed up to 90 lbs (41 kg).

In Colorado, paleontologists recently uncovered 6-ft (1.8-m) pelvic bones of what may be the largest known dinosaur. And two exceptionally large dinosaurs—"supersaurus" and "ultrasaurus"—were shown to be unusually large specimens of the known species *Brachiosaurus* instead of being distinct species of supergiants, as originally proposed.

Debate continued over mass extinctions and the demise of the dinosaurs. A new theory proposes that the ocean's plankton was killed off by the immediate cooling effect of a meteorite impact 65 million years ago. That event, according to the theory, may have spawned an extreme global heat wave that helped wipe out about half the existing species of plants and animals. This occurred at the Cretaceous-Tertiary (K-T) boundary. Some scientists believe that the presence of an iridium layer at the K-T boundary indicates that an extraterrestrial object hit the earth, causing the extinction of the dinosaurs and many other Cretaceous organisms. And it now is suggested that the explosive impact of the meteorite may have fractured the earth's crust and triggered massive outpourings of lava that aided the mass extinctions. The geologic record indicates that 11 known episodes of lava flooding correlate well with 11 known mass extinctions.

Plate Tectonics and Earth Structure. The discovery of massive, deeply buried rocks beneath the flat plains of the U.S. Midwest suggests that a vast mountain range, possibly the size of the Himalayas, may have cut across eastern Ohio more than 1 billion years ago. Geophysical surveys have revealed very thick stratified rock formations about 2 mi (3.2 km) beneath the surface. These structures, 4 to 6.5 mi (6.4 to 10.5 km) thick and some 100 mi (160 km) wide, were on the earth's surface about 1.3 billion years ago. Similar deep-seated structures in southern Illinois appear to be layered volcanic formations from which molten rock originated to form a major portion of the North American crustal plate. Certain of the formations in eastern Ohio dip as much as 24 mi (39 km) below the surface. They are thought to be great subsurface faults generated when crustal plates collided with each other and pushed up mountains in the process. Certain of these deeply buried rocks are sedimentary in origin. And since subsurface sedimentary structures can be reservoir rocks for oil and natural gas, these basement rocks could represent an untapped source of fossil fuels.

A new theory challenges traditional thinking about the formation of the earth about 4.6 billion years ago. The traditional view is that the earth originally condensed into a cold, solid mass out of an immense, rotating cloud of gas, dust, and rock. Radioactivity and gravity then heated the core materials. According to the new theory, the materials at the center of the newly formed earth were hot nearly from the beginning. This conclusion was reached by geologists at the Rensselaer Polytechnic Institute through spectral analysis of light reflected from distant asteroids, the same sort of primordial material from which the earth was formed. The analysis revealed that certain asteroids had been subjected to powerful blasts of intense light, perhaps from the young sun, early in the history of the solar system.

WILLIAM H. MATTHEWS III,
Lamar University

246

Dinosaurs: A New Look at Some Old Bones

Dinosaurs long have been among the most popular and widely studied of all fossils. These great reptiles appeared in the late Triassic, some 225 million years ago, and became extinct at the end of the Cretaceous Period 65 million years ago. Their remains have been found on all continents and they represent the largest animals to have lived on land.

Recent studies have provided new insights as to the nature—and ultimate extinction—of these so-called "terrible lizards." Even the techniques of discovering and studying dinosaur remains have changed. Scientists have developed a "sonic geophysical imaging" system that uses sound waves to get an accurate picture of buried bones. Bones are differentiated from the surrounding rock by the length of time it takes sound waves to pass through each material. This method was used, for example, to unearth Seismosaurus, a plant-eater that measured at least 110 ft (33.5 m) long and weighed 40 tons (36 MT) or more.

Western scientists also gained new insights from hundreds of dinosaur fossils, representing 22 species, recently excavated in China's Sichuan Province and on loan to Seattle's Burke Museum.

The Nature of Dinosaurs. Dinosaur eggs recently have been examined by computerized axial tomography, or CAT scanning. This has

© Mark A. Philbrick/Brigham Young University Public Communications

Geologist Wade Miller, above, holds a 150-million-year-old dinosaur egg found in Utah. Computerized axial tomography, or CAT scanning, produced images of the embryo—the earliest ever found. Scientists also were able to reconstruct the embryo of Orodromeus makelai, below, based on studies of the skeleton from one of 19 fossilized eggs found in Montana.

Museum of the Rockies

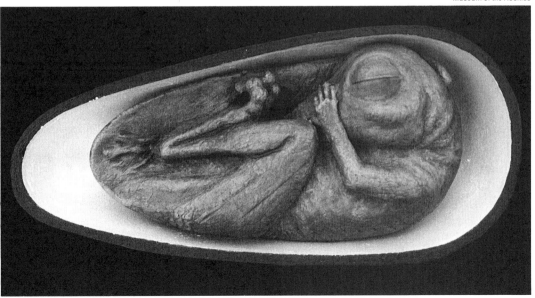

© Robert Harbison/"The Christian Science Monitor"

"Yangchuanosaurus shangyuensis" was one of 22 species on display in "Chinasaurs: The Dinosaurs of Sichuan" at Seattle's Burke Museum. The skeletons were 95% complete.

produced images of a dinosaur embryo in a 150-million-year-old egg found in Utah. It is probably the oldest known dinosaur embryo. A study of dinosaur eggs from Montana shows that some young dinosaurs were able to walk about immediately after hatching; others remained in the nest where they were fed by their parents.

Dinosaur eggs also have provided clues to the nesting habits of dinosaurs. Eggshells found in western Colorado occurred in at least six layers of nests. This suggests that certain species preferred isolated nesting sites and used them repeatedly. In the Gobi Desert of Mongolia, where the first dinosaur eggs were found more than 65 years ago, egg fragments were found upright and packed in strawlike plant fibers. The nest, similar to some modern-day birds' nests, contained bones believed to

be the remains of small animals used to feed dinosaur offspring.

All dinosaurs may not have been egg layers, for neither Brontosaurus eggs nor baby Brontosaurus remains have been found. Studies of 40 to 50 brontosaur skeletons show that the brontosaur pelvic canal was wide enough to bear young alive. The small pelvises of most other dinosaurs would have prevented live birth.

Some paleontologists believe that the dinosaurs never died out completely, but evolved into birds. A fossil braincase from a small, meat-eating dinosaur may help unravel this mystery. Found in Alberta, Canada, the fossil is part of the skull of a troodon dinosaur. Delicate bone structures preserved in the braincase resemble those in modern birds. Another skull found in Montana in 1942 provides further clues to the dinosaur-bird relationship. It recently has been reclassified as a baby tyrannosaur because its braincase is riddled with air canals. Birds also have extensive air canals in the braincase of their skulls.

Some fossil evidence suggests that unlike modern-day cold-blooded reptiles, dinosaurs were warm-blooded. Researchers know that dinosaurs roamed to the ends of the continents toward both poles into regions of considerable cold. Their distribution suggests warm blood to withstand low temperatures.

Were dinosaurs "loners?" Recent findings indicate they were gregarious. One such find is a grave of five sheep-sized baby ankylosaurs that apparently were buried by a sandstorm some 75 million years ago.

Extinction Theories. But despite these advances, the ultimate mystery remains: What killed the dinosaurs and certain other life forms 65 million years ago? One theory proposes a collision between Earth and an asteroid with a force equal to a hydrogen bomb explosion of 100 million megatons. Vaporized rock formed a dust cloud that blocked sunlight for five years. Plants could not grow and dinosaurs were deprived of their main source of food. It also has been suggested that "Nemesis," a death star, triggered a shower of comets causing periodic extinctions. And some scientists believe that both cometary impacts and volcanic eruptions created toxic air and acid rain, asphyxiating and burning plants and animals. There is also some indication that mass extinctions might be triggered by reversals of Earth's magnetic field. Another theory suggests that the dinosaurs died out gradually because of changes in sea level, drastic changes in food supplies, and increased competition for food and space.

WILLIAM H. MATTHEWS III

GEORGIA

In the presidential election year of 1988, Georgians watched political developments statewide and nationally. Georgia, likewise, was watched by the nation as it hosted the Democratic Convention and contended for the position of host to the 1996 Summer Olympics.

Politics. Georgia was involved in the presidential primary race early—from when Georgia Democratic Sen. Sam Nunn was considered a potential front-runner to the final nomination of the Democratic candidate at the national convention in Atlanta. After Nunn decided against running for president, Georgians, in the Super Tuesday primary in March, selected George Bush as their Republican choice and split the vote between Albert Gore and Jesse Jackson on the Democratic side.

Democrats spent an active, fun-filled convention week in late July in Atlanta. The city had prepared for conventioneers by completing major beautification projects and organizing a schedule of elaborate social events. Preconvention media attention focused on the small size and limited capacity of the convention site, the World Congress Center. While the location was praised for creating an intimate "television-style presentation," it forced fire officials to block access to convention delegates on several evenings when the hall was full.

As had been expected, in the general election Georgians chose George Bush over Michael Dukakis by a wide margin. Fourth District Congressman Pat Swindall (R), accused of lying to a grand jury about negotiations over a loan with an alleged drug dealer who had pleaded guilty to money laundering, was defeated easily by his Democratic challenger, Ben Jones. All other congressional incumbents were reelected.

Indictments. Two Fulton County commissioners, Reginald Eaves and Charles Williams, were indicted by federal officials on charges that they extorted money in exchange for influence on rezoning matters. Eaves, who was found guilty, was appealing his sentence late in 1988, while Williams, who pleaded guilty, was serving time in a federal facility.

General Assembly. AIDS legislation, environmental issues, and budgetary allocations were the primary concerns of Georgia legislators. An AIDS bill, imposing criminal penalties for knowingly spreading the virus and strengthening confidentiality by extending to AIDS-related information the same protection afforded to psychiatric information, passed both houses.

Environmentalists applauded passage of a bill directing the Department of Natural Resources to locate sites of former landfills and to attach a notice to land deeds regarding the existence of such sites. In addition, environmental activists successfully lobbied for passage of a right-to-know bill, whereby state employees

---

GEORGIA · Information Highlights

Area: 58,910 sq mi (152 576 km²).
Population (July 1, 1987): 6,222,000.
Chief Cities (July 1, 1986 est.): Atlanta, the capital, 421,910; Columbus, 180,180; Savannah, 146,800.
Government (1988): *Chief Officers—governor,* Joe Frank Harris (D); lt. gov., Zell Miller (D). *General Assembly—*Senate, 56 members; House of Representatives, 180 members.
State Finances (fiscal year 1987): *Revenue,* $10,241,000,000; *expenditure,* $9,061,000,000.
Personal Income (1987): $88,977,000,000; per capita, $14,300.
Labor Force (June 1988): *Civilian labor force,* 3,150,100; *unemployed,* 201,600 (6.4% of total force).
Education: *Enrollment* (fall 1986)—public elementary schools, 777,991; public secondary, 318,434; colleges and universities, 195,123. *Public school expenditures* (1986–87), $3,153,000,000 ($3,167 per pupil).

---

can learn if they are working with hazardous materials and the involved risks.

The assembly approved a record-high budget of $6.25 billion, of which the biggest share (51%) was designated to education; also included was $14 million to purchase land adjacent to the World Congress Center for construction of a new domed athletic stadium.

Atlanta. For the third consecutive year, Atlanta was ranked the nation's best business location by top-level corporate executives. Indeed, several extravagant development announcements supported the impression of continued business activity. A service station in midtown Atlanta sold for $3.8 million, and a 9.5 acre (3.8 ha) property in the downtown area sold for $47.5 million. Atlanta developer John Portman announced plans to build a 60-story office structure in the heart of the city. It would be the tallest building in the Southeast. Universal/MCA Corporation unveiled plans for a 20,000-seat amphitheater in southwest Atlanta. Among Atlanta's historic black colleges, Clark College and Atlanta University agreed in June to a merger. With all this activity, it was not surprising to learn that Hartsfield International Airport became the world's busiest.

Media. The resignation of Bill Kovach, editor of the *Atlanta Constitution,* prompted one public demonstration and numerous protest letters. Kovach, former Washington bureau chief of *The New York Times,* resigned citing "a lack of mutual trust" between him and management. Among the 250 demonstrators who marched in support of Kovach were journalist Hodding Carter III, novelist Pat Conroy, cartoonist Doug Marlette, and Lillian Lewis, wife of U.S. representative John Lewis.

Olympics. Supported by a strong recommendation from the U.S. Olympic Committee, Atlanta was designated a nominee to host the 1996 Summer Olympics. It now must compete internationally with other interested cities.

KAY BECK, *Georgia State University*

GERMANY

In 1988 the two German states—the Federal Republic of Germany (FRG), or West Germany, and the German Democratic Republic (GDR), or East Germany—continued to improve bilateral relations. The GDR's policy of allowing its citizens to visit the Federal Republic continued, and more than five million East Germans, or almost 30% of the country's population, traveled to the West German side. The two states signed a new transit agreement in September, by which the FRG, beginning in 1990, will increase its payments to East Germany for the use of access routes to West Berlin to about $500 million annually. The GDR will use the funds to modernize the *autobahns* (highways) leading to West Germany and to build new border-crossing facilities. The two states also reached agreement on several environmental issues, but negotiations over cleaning up the Elbe River, one of Europe's most polluted waterways, stalled over the question of where to draw the exact boundary between the two states.

In November, for one of the few times in their histories, the two German states acknowledged their common legacy of the Third Reich and the Holocaust. In ceremonies throughout both countries, the 50th anniversary of *Kristallnacht* ("Crystal Night," or "Night of Broken Glass")—a nationwide pogrom that marked the beginning of the Nazi persecution of Jews—was commemorated.

In West Germany the main ceremonies were held in Frankfurt, the home of Germany's second largest Jewish community (after Berlin's) prior to the Third Reich. A new Jewish museum was inaugurated, and memorial services were attended by President Richard von Weizsäcker and Chancellor Helmut Kohl together with German and other European Jewish leaders. A major political controversy broke out, however, at a special memorial session of parliament on November 10, when Speaker Philipp Jenninger of the governing Christian Democratic Union (CDU) delivered a speech interpreted by many as a justification of Nazism. Dozens of members walked out of the parliament chamber and demanded Jenninger's resignation. He did step down the following day but insisted his speech had been misinterpreted.

In East Germany, which only recently acknowledged its responsibility to pay reparations to survivors of the Holocaust, the cornerstone for a new synagogue was laid in East Berlin. The GDR invited 40 leaders of American Reform Judaism for the anniversary ceremonies, which also included a special session of the legislature.

Federal Republic of Germany (West Germany)

The year 1988 was a difficult one for Chancellor Helmut Kohl and his CDU. The party suffered declines in two state elections, actually losing power in Schleswig-Holstein, and

West Germany's Chancellor Helmut Kohl (second from left) *and wife Hannelore* (far right) *visited Moscow for four days in October. Soviet leader Mikhail Gorbachev* (second from right) *said the "ice has been broken" in bilateral relations.*

AP/Wide World

saw its support in public-opinion polls drop to 40%. The debacle in Schleswig-Holstein was caused in part by a major political scandal which had led to the suicide of former state Premier Uwe Barschel in September 1987. In 1988, the CDU in another northern state, Lower Saxony, was shaken by revelations that proceeds had been skimmed from state-run gambling casinos and directed into the party's treasury. The Social Democrats by the end of the year were pressing for new elections there; if the CDU were to lose power in Lower Saxony, it would also lose its majority in the Bundesrat (upper house of the national parliament).

The Bavarian wing of the party, the Christian Social Union (CSU) lost its leader in October 1988, when Franz Josef Strauss died suddenly of a heart attack. Strauss had been one of the dominant political figures in West German politics for 40 years. He had served in several national cabinets as defense and foreign minister and since 1978 as the chief executive (premier) of his native Bavaria; in 1980 he was the CSU's candidate for chancellor.

The major beneficiary of the CDU's troubles in 1988 was the Free Democratic Party (FDP), the junior partner in the coalition government. Support for the FDP in opinion polls increased throughout the year, and Foreign Minister Hans-Dietrich Genscher, the titular head of the party, remained the most popular political leader in the country. There were signs, however, that the FDP was beginning to move away from the Christian Democrats and toward its partner from 1969–1982, the Social Democrats. In the city-state of Hamburg, the Free Democrats formed a coalition with the SPD, the first since 1982. In October the party selected Count Otto Lambsdorff as its new national chairman. Lambsdorff, who had resigned as economics minister in 1984 because of his involvement in a party finance scandal, has been a sharp critic of Kohl's economic policies.

Meanwhile, the major opposition party, the Social Democrats (SPD), rebounded strongly from its poor performance at the 1987 general election. By the end of 1988, the SPD's national support had grown to 43%—higher than the CDU's. In May the SPD scored a stunning victory in Schleswig-Holstein, taking over sole control of the state government for the first time in the history of the Federal Republic. During the course of the year, the SPD moved more toward the center of the political spectrum. One of its leaders, Oskar LaFontaine, once the favorite of the left wing, advocated a reduction in the workweek with a corresponding drop in wages and salaries as a way to reduce unemployment. While LaFontaine incurred the wrath of the party faithful, his national popularity increased sharply. Hans-Jochen Vogel, the SPD's parliamentary leader,

---

WEST GERMANY • Information Highlights

Official Name: Federal Republic of Germany.
Location: North-central Europe.
Area: 95,977 sq mi (248 580 km²).
Population (mid-1988 est.): 61,200,000.
Chief Cities (June 30, 1986): Bonn, the capital, 290,800; West Berlin, 1,868,700; Hamburg, 1,575,700; Munich, 1,269,400.
Government: *Head of state,* Richard von Weizsäcker, president (took office July 1, 1984). *Head of government,* Helmut Kohl, chancellor (took office Oct. 1982). *Legislature*—Parliament: Bundesrat and Bundestag.
Monetary Unit: Deutsche mark (1.7453 D. marks equal U.S.$1, Nov. 14, 1988).
Gross National Product (1986 U.S.$): $908,300,-000,000.
Economic Indexes (1987): *Consumer Prices* (1980 = 100), all items, 121.0; food, 117.0. *Industrial Production* (1980 = 100), 107.
Foreign Trade (1987 U.S.$): *Imports,* $228,096,-000,000; *exports,* $293,843,000,000.

---

also received high marks for his ability to unite the party.

In spite of increasing conflict among its various factions, the Green Party in 1988 retained the support of about 8% of the electorate, well above the 5% minimum needed for representation in the national parliament. The party also received about 8% of the vote at the March state election in Baden-Württemberg, but could gain the support of only 3% of the voters in Schleswig-Holstein. Since many Green voters prefer the Social Democrats as their second choice, the party does best where the SPD has little chance of winning an absolute majority, as in Baden-Württemberg. However, where the Socialists have a good chance of winning, as in Schleswig-Holstein, the Green vote drops.

The Fundamentalist ("Fundis") faction in the Green Party continued to oppose any cooperation or coalition with the Social Democrats. The Fundis also wanted the party to concentrate more on mobilizing citizens to take part in strikes and demonstrations against government policies. The Realist faction, however, continued to support cooperation with the Socialists and opposed party sponsorship of mass protests.

Economy. Led by a surge in exports, as well as strong domestic demand and increased business investment, the West German economy in 1988 grew by almost 3.5% in real terms, the highest level since 1979. The strong performance surprised many economists and even the Kohl government, which at the beginning of the year was anticipating a growth rate of about 2%. A record level of exports—more than $300 billion—produced a trade surplus of $73 billion, an increase of some 4.2%.

For the third consecutive year, West Germany maintained its position ahead of Japan and the United States as the world's largest trading nation. The success of the German "export machine," however, prompted renewed

demands from the United States, France, and other neighbors that the Federal Republic stimulate its economy to increase imports and decrease the trade surplus. The Kohl government did pass a major tax-reform law, which it hoped would increase consumer spending. The government's 1989 budget also increased spending by about 5%, the highest level since 1981.

Inflation in 1988 remained low at about 1.5%, but the strong economy did little to reduce unemployment: About 8.5% of the work force was jobless, only a slight drop from 1987.

Environment. Concern over environmental issues remained strong throughout 1988. In addition to the widespread opposition to nuclear power plants and the deterioration of Germany's fabled forests by acid rain, several new problems attracted nationwide attention. In May the government of North Rhine-West-

At the U.S. Air Force Base in Ramstein, West Germany, three Italian jets collided during an August 28 air show. One of the planes crashed in the crowd, killing 67 civilians.

AP/Wide World

phalia, West Germany's largest state, indicted several feed-lot operators for illegally injecting calves with a "hormone cocktail," composed mainly of estrogen, designed to speed growth. The scandal soon spread to other parts of the country, and by late summer a consumer boycott cut sharply into the sale of meat. More than 14,000 calves were seized and destroyed by state authorities.

Pollution in the North Sea reached record-high levels in 1988 and was responsible in part for the near extinction of the seal population. By the end of September, nearly all of the 5,000 seals identified in the spring had died. Many of the nation's North Sea beaches were closed after large concentrations of salmonella bacteria were found. Local sewage plants and passenger ships were the major sources of the pollution.

Government action on the environment in 1988 included a ban, which took effect in February, on leaded gasoline and the introduction of a mandatory 25-cent deposit on plastic bottles. The latter measure was criticized sharply by soft-drink bottlers.

"Noise pollution" from low-altitude training flights by NATO jet fighters also became a major environmental and political issue in 1988. Many communities protested to German and NATO authorities, demanding restrictions on such flights as exist in other NATO countries. When in April a NATO fighter nearly crashed into a nuclear-power plant, demands for some German control over such flights spread from environmental groups and local governments to the national political parties. Both the SPD and the Greens called for an end to low-level training flights over populated areas.

In late August the nation was shocked by the collision of three Italian military stunt planes, one of which crashed into a crowd of spectators, at the annual air show at the Ramstein U.S. Air Base. The accident, which killed 67 civilians (including 57 Germans), prompted Defense Minister Rupert Scholz to ban all military stunt flying in the country. The government was criticized for not having taken such action sooner, but Bonn officials responded that they had little control over NATO military bases or German airspace. The disaster thus prompted a nationwide debate over limits on West Germany's sovereignty.

Foreign Policy. West Germany's relations with the Soviet Union improved significantly during 1988. In October, Chancellor Kohl paid his first official visit to Moscow since Soviet General Secretary Mikhail Gorbachev came to power in 1985. Shortly before his trip, a consortium of West German banks completed arrangements for a $1.7 billion line of credit, the largest Western loan in history to the Soviet Union. The money would be used exclusively to improve Soviet food-processing and con-

sumer-goods industries, a top priority for the Gorbachev regime. Since 1984, German banks have lent about $5 billion to the Soviet Union.

During Kohl's visit, agreements were reached on a wide range of political, economic, and scientific projects. Among them was a plan to send a West German astronaut to the orbiting Soviet space station Mir. Bonn also agreed to help modernize some 200 light industrial and food-processing concerns and to assist the Soviet atomic energy agency in the construction of a high-energy nuclear reactor. Also during the chancellor's visit, the Kremlin announced that it would release all political prisoners before the end of 1988.

In early August the Soviet Union released Mathias Rust, the young West German pilot who had flown a single-engine plane to Red Square in May 1987 and later was sentenced to four years in prison.

But improvement in Bonn's relations with the Soviet Union and other Eastern European countries was seen most clearly in the sharply increased flow of ethnic German émigrés from all corners of the Soviet bloc. For decades the Federal Republic had urged Poland, the Soviet Union, and Romania to allow all nationals who, by virtue of language, ancestry, or education, professed to be German, to resettle in West Germany. To the surprise of many German leaders, the Soviet bloc countries in 1988 relented. More than 200,000 were allowed to leave for West Germany, and it was estimated that a total of about 2 million eventually would settle in the Federal Republic.

German Democratic Republic (East Germany)

In 1988 the "new thinking" of Soviet leader Mikhail Gorbachev continued to have an unsettling effect in East Germany. While one of the most economically prosperous of the Soviet bloc states, the GDR has remained a bastion of ideological orthodoxy throughout most of its history. The aging leadership of the ruling Socialist Unity (Communist) Party (SED) has shown little enthusiasm for the winds of change coming from Moscow. Some party officials have been openly critical of *glasnost,* seeing little relevance for East Germany. (*See* special report on Eastern Europe, page 227.)

Erich Honecker, the 76-year-old general secretary of the SED, was expected to step down from his party post in October 1989, on the occasion of the 40th anniversary of the GDR's founding. While he was expected to stay on as chairman of the State Council, the top governmental body, the question of his successor as party chief was complicated in September 1988 by the unexpected death of Hans Felfe, widely regarded as a leading candidate. Another possible successor, Günter Mittag, the GDR's chief economic planner, was in ill

© Chris Niedenthal/"Time" Magazine

A monolithic bastion of Communist ideology, East Germany in 1988 resisted the winds of reformism coming from Moscow. Some party officials openly criticized "glasnost."

health. Gorbachev's favorite was reported to be Hans Moldrow, the head of the Dresden party organization.

The GDR leadership in 1988 remained divided over how to deal with the nation's growing number of peace, environmentalist, and human-rights groups, most of which operate under the protection of the Protestant church. The Honecker faction within the SED favored a moderate, tolerant approach, while the hard-line faction, centered in the party bureaucracy and state-security agencies, wanted the regime to crack down on dissenting groups and expel their leaders to West Germany or West Berlin. In January 1988 the state-security agency hindered the participation of church-related peace and human-rights activists at the annual rally to honor the founders of the German Communist Party. Some of the demonstrators were arrested, jailed, or expelled to West Germany. In March, however, Honecker met for the first time in ten years with the leader of the country's Protestants and apologized for the incident, explaining that he was not informed properly because the official responsible for church matters had been out of the country at the time of the rally. But the pendulum of state reaction swung back in April, when some church publications were censored. Later in the year, however, two well-known dissidents who had been expelled to West Germany were allowed to return.

Economy. For the third consecutive year, the GDR's economy in 1988 failed to meet the growth targets of the current Five-Year Plan.

EAST GERMANY · Information Highlights

Official Name: German Democratic Republic.
Location: North-central Europe.
Area: 41,826 sq mi (108 330 km²).
Population (mid-1988 est.): 16,600,000.
Chief Cities (Dec. 31, 1985): East Berlin, the capital, 1,215,600; Leipzig, 553,700; Dresden, 519,800.
Government: *Head of state,* Erich Honecker, chairman of the Council of State. *Head of government,* Willi Stoph, chairman of the Council of Ministers. General Secretary of the Socialist Unity (Communist) Party, Erich Honecker (took office 1971). *Legislature* (unicameral)—Volkskammer (People's Chamber).
Monetary Unit: DDR mark (1.80 DDR marks equal U.S.$1, July 1988).
Gross National Product (1986 U.S.$): $187,500,-000,000.
Economic Index (1987): *Industrial Production* (1980 = 100), 131.
Foreign Trade (1986 U.S.$): *Imports,* $27,414,-000,000; *exports,* $27,729,000,000.

Real growth fell from 3.0% in 1987 to about 2.5% in 1988, well below the 4% called for in the plan. A drop in exports due to strong competition from Asian countries such as South Korea and Taiwan and a poor harvest were the major factors in the weak economic performance.

The GDR continued to have difficulty in making the transition from a "smokestack" to a high-tech economy. Its computer, industrial robot, and biotechnology enterprises, for example, lagged well behind their Western counterparts. A three-year plan to speed up the modernization process was begun in 1988, and 16 selected industrial conglomerates *(Kombinate)* were given greater independence from central planners and encouraged to generate their own investment capital and export markets.

The consumer-goods sector of the economy suffered from numerous shortages in 1988. In June the Politburo, the ruling body of the Communist party, admitted to the nation's inadequate supplies of clothing, radios, home furniture, and cosmetics. While East Germans have one of the highest standards of living in the Soviet bloc, they remain well behind the Federal Republic. Items that are commonplace in West Germany, such as automatic washing machines and food freezers, remain in short supply in the GDR. Newer consumer products such as microwave ovens, instant cameras, video recorders, home computers, and compact disc players are very rare. And for the delivery of a new Trabant or Wartburg automobile, East Germans still have to wait from 11 to 14 years.

Unlike other countries in the Socialist bloc, however, many GDR citizens can turn to their relatives in West Germany for assistance in acquiring scarce consumer products. In September the government made it easier for East Germans to receive coveted "West marks" from the Federal Republic.

Foreign Policy. The GDR in 1988 attempted to expand and improve its ties with other Western countries. In February, Honecker became the first GDR leader to make an official state visit to France. After decades of insisting that it had no responsibility for the crimes of the Nazi era and refusing to make reparations to Jews who had been victimized by those crimes, the Honecker government in January agreed to pay reparations to Jewish survivors of the Third Reich. In October, Honecker met with the president of the World Jewish Congress, Edgar M. Bronfman, to discuss the compensation question.

In reaching out to the world Jewish community, the GDR sought, among other things, to improve trade relations with the United States. In particular, the regime hoped for elevation by Washington to most-favored-nation trading status. Honecker's goals before stepping down as party leader were to pay official visits to London and Washington and, in general, to make the GDR a fully accepted member of the international community. However, the issues of the Berlin Wall and unresolved U.S. claims on property seized by the Communists after 1945 remain significant obstacles to the accomplishment of his goals.

West Berlin

Political stability and robust economic growth characterized the divided city in 1988. Since 1985, more than 250 new companies and 42,000 new jobs have been created there. The city's population, after decades of decline, went over the 2 million mark in 1988 and continued to rise at an annual rate of about 20,000. As in West Germany, however, unemployment remained high, at about 11%. The city also is still dependent on large subsidies from the Federal Republic. More than half of its annual budget, for example, is covered by grants from Bonn.

In September the annual meeting of the International Monetary Fund (IMF) and the World Bank brought more than 14,000 delegates from 151 countries to West Berlin. It was the largest international conference ever held on German soil. The meeting also attracted the attention of the city's radical left political groups, including some terrorists. Shortly before the conference, a leading official in the West German finance ministry responsible for organizing the meeting narrowly escaped assassination. In West Berlin, groups from the left-wing counterculture staged numerous demonstrations, charging that the IMF and World Bank were exploiting underdeveloped countries. Several banks and business establishments in the city were vandalized during the demonstrations.

DAVID P. CONRADT
University of Florida

The Duke and Duchess of York —Prince Andrew and the former Sarah Ferguson—had their first child August 8. Named Beatrice Elizabeth Mary, the child became fifth in line to the British throne. The entire royal family came under especially intense scrutiny throughout the year.

© H.R.H. The Duke of York/Rex Features Ltd. from RDR Productions, Inc.

GREAT BRITAIN

With the arrival of the New Year in 1988, Margaret Thatcher became the longest-serving British prime minister of the 20th century. Since she was the first woman ever to serve as prime minister, admirers were forced to scramble for regal analogies to describe Margaret of the 3,000-plus days. "You've got to put her in the same category as Bloody Mary, Elizabeth I, Queen Anne, and Queen Victoria," said her former lord chancellor, Lord Hailsham. Given her propensity to refer to the ministers and bureaucrats who constitute Her Majesty's government as "my government," some critics worried that Thatcher was taking on royal airs. In fact, never in British history has a woman who did not wear a crown so dominated the politics and imagination of the nation.

Thatcher Center Stage. So dominant was Thatcher that Michael Heseltine, her former defense secretary, accused her of running an authoritarian regime, abandoning cabinet government, and promoting a cult of personality. Some critics claimed she used her womanhood as a device to get her own way and was unreasonable, emotional, and excitable. Senior aides dismissed the criticism, but agreed that Thatcher loves confrontation. U.S. President Ronald Reagan recalled a summit meeting in which a fellow head of state strongly criticized Thatcher. Reagan caught up with her afterward to soothe her feelings and assure her the man had been out of line. Replied an unruffled Thatcher, "Women know when men are being childish."

In October, Thatcher declared her intention to run for a fourth term. She has enjoyed good health and will be 67 when her current term is up in 1992.

Foreign Affairs. Thatcher has become the senior leader of the Atlantic alliance, but her prickly, confrontational style still can frustrate her continental colleagues. She traveled extensively throughout 1988—from South Africa to the United States, Poland, Australia, and half a dozen other nations. All of this was part of a carefully plotted, meticulously briefed effort to project Thatcher as a major player on the world stage. Her longevity and forcefulness gave the United Kingdom a voice in world affairs far beyond its economic and military might.

Thatcher demonstrated a deft hand as a go-between for Reagan and Soviet leader Mikhail Gorbachev on arms control. After a chilly start, she developed a solid working relationship with Gorbachev that, coupled with her close, personal relationship with Reagan, allowed her to play a valuable role as a superpower middlewoman. In June, after ceremonially ratifying a reduction in intermediate nuclear forces (INF) with the Russians in Moscow, Reagan paid a final presidential visit to London to brief Thatcher personally and warmly thank her for the role she played in securing the INF treaty. Reagan long has been one of her greatest fans, and no British prime minister since Winston Churchill has made so strong, and largely favorable, an impression on Americans. Thatcher paid a farewell call on Reagan in Washington in mid-November.

Economy. Not since Prime Minister David Lloyd George was accused of running a presi-

dential-style government has Britain had such an interventionist leader. Thatcher's unrestrained style produced its share of problems. Throughout 1988, the ailing National Health Service was seldom off the front pages. She replaced the property tax with a community charge, or poll tax, which critics and supporters alike called unwise and inequitable. Driving relentlessly ahead with plans for the privatization of publicly owned industry—including British Steel in 1988—Thatcher brought an end to the socialist era in Britain, but had yet to build a solid consensus for her entrepreneurial alternative. Most polls showed the British had little personal affection for her and no great love for her policies.

Economically robust, Britain experienced a strong real growth rate of about 4% during 1988. Encouraging, too, was a steady decline in unemployment; by October the jobless rate had fallen to 7.7%. Also in October, however, the balance of payments deficit reached a record high. Inflation in the 12 months ending with October totaled 6.4%, the highest level since July 1985.

The European Community. The end of Thatcher's third term would coincide with the 1992 target date set for the realization of a genuine common market in Europe. As that date neared, conflicts emerged between Thatcher, who would like to see integration limited to a relaxation of trade barriers, and her continental partners, who envision a more far-reaching union. Thatcher spent much of 1988 fighting a solitary battle against most of her partners in the European Community (EC) who are determined to have a Europe in 1992 that is more unified politically as well as economically. Thatcher was adamant that the new Europe rest on a foundation of cooperating sovereign states with control over their own economies. "We have not successfully rolled back the frontiers of the state in Britain," she said, "only to see them reimposed at a European level with a European superstate exercising a new dominance from Brussels."

As far as Prime Minister Thatcher was concerned, the dream of a United States of Europe with a common currency, a central bank, and a harmonized tax structure was the stuff of fairy tales. She grew very uneasy as she watched her old foes, the trade unions, line up solidly behind the concept of a strong, centralized pan-European government. She was certain they would take the rather vague talk about a "social dimension" for the new unified EC and use it to erase the tough legal restraints on union activity she pushed through parliament. She saw the tougher health and environmental laws of some neighbors bringing more regulation to an economy she wanted to keep as free as possible from government intervention. While her opponents accused her of being anti-European, Thatcher and her supporters insisted she was only introducing a note of realism to a process that has grown increasingly utopian.

Domestic Politics. Thatcher's domination of the British political scene in 1988 owed as much to the weakness of the opposition as it did to her strength. The Labour Party had yet to recover from its landslide defeat in 1987. Public opinion polls show support for the party steadily dwindling, and even some of Labour leader Neil Kinnock's followers were beginning to question his leadership. With public support for unions declining along with union membership, the Labour Party was not able to escape the view that it was dominated by the unions. And, as the country has shifted to the right, the Labour Party still seemed wedded to aging left-wing policies like public ownership of industry and unilateral disarmament.

Kinnock sought to strengthen the opposition's eroding support by ordering a major policy review that would coopt some of the elements of Thatcherism and move Labour more toward the center of the political spectrum. But the difficulty inherent in trying to hold traditional supporters while reaching out to new voters became glaringly apparent when, in a matter of weeks, Kinnock twice changed his position on the crucial question of disarmament, alienating old allies and confusing new voters in the process.

Northern Ireland. Despite her political dominance, even Prime Minister Thatcher was unable to solve the major domestic problem that has dogged Britain for decades: the bitter struggle between Catholics and Protestants in Northern Ireland. At the start of the year, morale of the outlawed Irish Republican Army (IRA) was at rock bottom, its public support diminished by a terrorist bomb that had killed 11 innocent civilians in the town of Enniskillen.

A pair of legal decisions stemmed the ebb of sympathy. An appeals panel upheld the 1975

GREAT BRITAIN • Information Highlights

Official Name: United Kingdom of Great Britain and Northern Ireland.
Location: Island, western Europe.
Area: 94,525 sq mi (244 820 km²).
Population (mid-1988 est.): 57,100,000.
Chief Cities (mid-1986 est.): London, the capital, 6,775,200; Birmingham, 1,004,100; Glasgow, 725,000; Leeds, 710,900; Sheffield, 534,300.
Government: *Head of state,* Elizabeth II, queen (acceded Feb. 1952). *Head of government,* Margaret Thatcher, prime minister and First Lord of the Treasury (took office May 1979). *Legislature* —Parliament: House of Lords and House of Commons.
Monetary Unit: Pound (0.5460 pound equals U.S.$1, Dec. 14, 1988).
Gross National Product (1987 U.S.$): $556,800,-000,000.
Economic Indexes (1987): *Consumer Prices* (1980 = 100), all items, 152.4; food, 139.9. *Industrial Production* (1980 = 100), 130.
Foreign Trade (1987 U.S.$): *Imports,* $154,389,-000,000; *exports,* $131,133,000,000.

British soldiers carry the coffins of two comrades killed after straying into an IRA funeral in Belfast, Northern Ireland, on March 19. The violent struggle over Northern Ireland remained the major domestic problem facing the Thatcher government.

AP/Wide World

convictions of six Irish Catholics charged with planting bombs that killed 21 people in two Birmingham pubs. New information had raised doubts about the evidence in the case and fueled claims by the so-called Birmingham Six that they had been beaten into confessing. At the same time, British officials refused to prosecute a group of Royal Ulster Constabulary (RUC) officials accused of covering up a shoot-to-kill campaign against suspected terrorists in the early 1980s. Legal authorities conceded that justice had been ''perverted'' by police in the course of investigating six 1982 killings by the RUC. A book about the investigation written by a former police official, John Stalker, who was removed from the case because he had been too diligent in his pursuit of police wrongdoing, shot to the top of the best-seller list and left little doubt that there had been at least an unofficial shoot-to-kill policy.

In March three IRA terrorists were shot and killed by British agents in Gibraltar. Though the three admittedly were planning to bomb a changing-of-the-guard ceremony in Gibraltar, the fact that they were unarmed at the time they were shot fueled charges that the British were pursuing a shoot-to-kill policy. The weeks that followed saw an escalation of violence on both sides. As thousands gathered in Belfast's Milltown cemetery for the funerals of the three slain IRA commandos, a deranged Protestant gunman attacked the mourners with hand grenades and a pistol, killing three and wounding more than 50. Days later, two off-duty British soldiers who accidentally strayed into a funeral procession for one of the Milltown victims were pulled from their car, beaten, and shot.

Throughout the summer, the violence continued and the death toll mounted. In August the IRA blew up a busload of British troops, killing eight and wounding 27, the largest number of fatalities in a single terrorist assault in a decade. The British began examining a series of measures to counter the IRA. Troops were redeployed to key areas along the Irish-Ulster border. Intelligence efforts were stepped up, and plans were made to expand antiterrorist laws to include the financial godfathers who fund terrorist activities.

Determined to counter terrorism even if it meant circumventing the civil liberties of suspected terrorists, the government banned the direct broadcasting of statements by the outlawed IRA as well as its legal political arm, Sinn Fein, and several outlawed Protestant groups. Suspected terrorists had the right to remain silent in court, but a new law allowed judges to instruct juries to weigh a suspect's silence in making a decision.

Its armories well stocked with heavy weapons supplied by Libya, the IRA seemed committed to escalating the violence. And its small, committed cadre—probably no more than 40 active gunmen supported by a network of 150 volunteers—was prepared for a long struggle. While no one expected an end to the violence anytime soon, a few hopeful signs of movement toward reconciliation between the warring factions began to appear.

One of the brightest developments was an embryonic effort to integrate the school system now segregated by religion. Though barely 2,000 of Ulster's 340,000 students were in integrated schools, the British government in 1988 took the first steps toward creating a genuinely pluralistic system of education in Northern Ireland. The government will provide financial aid to schools open to students regardless of reli-

gion. It also will support a central organization to promote and coordinate integrated education. For the first time in history, promoting integrated education will be official government policy.

The Royal Family. Britain's royal family, always a source of fascination, came under intense scrutiny in 1988. What began with the tabloids leering at the supposedly rocky marriage of Charles and Diana, the prince and princess of Wales, ended with the quality press probing the ties that bind Britain to its monarchy. In the process, a flood of books, magazines, and television shows probed life inside the palace and spotlighted the pop-star quality of the prince and princess. Noting the genuinely important role the monarchy plays as a focus of national identity, some observers worried that the constant glare of publicity could reduce the royal family to little more than soap-opera stars and, ultimately, condemn them to the fate of the aristocracy: irrelevance. Said Cambridge royal historian David Cannadine, "There's a question of how much attention the monarchy can stand." David Starkey, an expert on the modern monarchy at the London School of Economics, agreed: "The royal family, particularly its younger members, has become dangerously glitzy. Di is indistinguishable from Joan Collins."

Some observers dismiss the uproar as the ripples from a disaffected heir to the throne looking for a meaningful role. Prince Charles, who turned 40 in November, had ended 1987 with an outraged speech criticizing plans to build modern glass-and-steel high-rises in London's Paternoster Square adjoining St. Paul's Cathedral, the Christopher Wren masterpiece where he and Diana were married. He accused architects and planners of doing more to deface London than the German air force in World War II. His opposition effectively stalled the project and touched off a national debate, including a flood of rebuttals from architects and city planners who said the prince was ill-advised and naive. Still, no one could dispute the fact that he had become a major influence in British architecture.

His thoughtful efforts throughout 1988 firmly established Charles as a maverick with a strong interest, and no small financial leverage, in reviving the inner cities and encouraging small business. He also emerged from the tabloid rantings as an intellectual with a keen understanding of the pressures facing a modern monarchy. Not since the abdication of Edward VIII (1936) had the British monarchy undergone such intense scrutiny as it did in 1988. And no member of the royal family was more aware than Charles of its fragility. "Something as curious as the monarchy won't survive unless you take account of people's attitudes," he has said. "After all, if people don't want it, they won't have it."

Other. Many of the architectural problems that concern Prince Charles resulted from a property boom in London that sent prices soaring. Even the exclusive tailor shops on Savile Row felt the pressures of development as the demand for office space forced many to move, while others fought to turn Savile Row into a protected historical district. In other parts of Britain, development was welcomed as a source of jobs and income for depressed areas. London's Tate Gallery opened a branch in Liverpool in a refurbished factory that became an instant landmark. Glasgow, a Victorian boomtown and the second city of the British empire before it entered a period of postindustrial decline, spruced itself up and became a showcase for art as urban development.

On London's south bank of the Thames, construction began on a replica of the Globe Theater, not far from the original where many of Shakespeare's plays first were performed.

In midsummer, the giant Piper Alpha drilling platform in the North Sea exploded in the worst offshore oil disaster in history. The tragedy raised troubling questions about the safety of offshore drilling in the North Sea, where more than 400 people have died since 1965. The massive explosion ripped apart a gas-compressing unit and touched off a series of smaller explosions on the Occidental Petroleum rig. It killed 168 men. Only 64 men managed to get off the towering inferno alive. Insurance claims by individuals, reconstruction costs, and lost production made Piper Alpha the most expensive industrial disaster in history.

The year's worst tragedy, however, occurred on December 21, when a Pan Am 747 jumbo jet en route from Heathrow Airport outside London blew apart in midair and crashed over the southern Scottish town of Lockerbie. All 259 people on board the plane, as well as 11 more on the ground, were killed. After a week of intensive investigation, British experts concluded that the explosion had been caused by a bomb.

Perhaps the most amazing event in Britain in 1988 was the startling progress of a book called *A Brief History of Time* to the top of the best-seller list, where it stayed for much of the year. Its author, a 46-year-old physicist named Stephen Hawking, is paralyzed by a progressive, incurable disease. Unable to speak, he communicates through a computerized voice synthesizer attached to his wheelchair. Hawking, who holds Isaac Newton's chair as Lucasian Professor of Mathematics at Cambridge University, is one of a number of scientists pursuing a grand unification theory that would link the general theory of relativity and quantum mechanics. His book, an improbable best-seller, details his personal physical struggle as well as his purely cerebral search.

GERALD C. LUBENOW
London Bureau Chief, "Newsweek"

The Arts

Despite the budget cuts that forced state-supported arts organizations to search out corporate assistance, the maxim "the show must go on" was alive and well in Great Britain in 1988.

Theater. The London stage enjoyed good health, considering there were fewer U.S. tourist dollars and cuts in government subsidies. A lack of cash flow, however, meant less risk-taking, and there were few new plays. Among the entries were *Hapgood*, Tom Stoppard's first play in six years, that combined espionage and quantum physics, mounted at the Aldwych Theatre. The Globe featured Peter Shaffer's *Lettice and Lovage*, a comedy about two formidable women, starring Maggie Smith. The costly production by British standards ($5.4 million) of *Ziegfeld*, about the colorful U.S. stage producer, met with strong critical disapproval, as did the musical biography *Winnie*, about Winston Churchill during World War II.

Noteworthy revivals included J. M. Barrie's *The Admirable Crichton*, starring the redoubtable octogenarian Rex Harrison, at the Haymarket Theatre Royal; and an outstanding production of Chekhov's *Uncle Vanya*, featuring Michael Gambon.

There was a change in leadership at the National Theatre in the summer of 1988 when Sir Peter Hall stepped down after 15 years as director, with Richard Eyre replacing him. The theater was renamed the Royal National Theatre to celebrate its 25th anniversary. Late in the year Sir Peter inaugurated the Peter Hall Company with a well-received presentation of Tennessee Williams' *Orpheus Descending*. It starred Vanessa Redgrave.

The Royal Shakespeare Company, after some inconsistent productions, scored two hits: *The Merchant of Venice*, with Antony Sher as Shylock; and a powerful production of *Titus Andronicus*.

Music. An amalgam of talents could be credited for the English National Opera's (ENO's) winning production of *The Barber of Seville*, most especially Jonathan Miller's controversial staging and Della Jones' dazzling Rosina. David Pountney's fresh staging of *Hansel and Gretel*, set in 20th-century England, imparted a psychological interpretation that was rich both theatrically and musically. ENO garnered more plaudits for *The Magic Flute* in a new production by the widely heralded opera director Nicholas Hytner.

Important staff changes were made at the Royal Opera House, Covent Garden, with Jeremy Isaacs named general director, and Paul Findlay, opera director. The fashionable but critically and financially beleaguered company began the season with a disappointing *Parsifal*, with Peter Seiffert in the title role and Bernard Haitink conducting. Grace Bumbry took the stage in the title role of *Tosca*, conducted by James Lockhart. The first female conductor at the Royal Opera, Sian Edwards, bowed with *The Knot Garden*, a new production by Nicholas Hytner. Stuttgart, West Germany, sent a production of *Anna Bolena* featuring Dame Joan Sutherland in her debut with the company. And Russian director Yuri Lyubimov directed *Das Rheingold*, the prologue to a new *Ring*, to be completed in 1991.

Royal Festival Hall was the venue in October 1988 for a 15-minute performance of a reconstruction of the first movement of Beethoven's planned *Tenth Symphony*, pieced together by Dr. Barry Cooper, a professor of music at the University of Aberdeen in Scotland. Dr. Cooper discovered the material while doing research on a book about Beethoven.

Britain's Queen Elizabeth II and Prince Philip greet cast members of Shakespeare's "The Tempest" on the occasion of a Royal Gala celebrating the 25th anniversary of London's prestigious National Theatre.

One of the dance highlights of the year was the Rambert Dance Company's performance of "Pulcinella" (right), choreographed by Richard Alston.

© Catherine Ashmore/Dominic Photography

Critical reaction was mixed—it appeared that Beethoven's Tenth was not deemed as good as his esteemed Fifth.

Dance. The Royal Ballet mounted several notable productions, including Peter Wright's *Giselle; Manon,* choreographed by Kenneth MacMillan; and the eagerly awaited revival of *Ondine,* Frederick Ashton's masterpiece. New works by the Contemporary Dance Trust included *Hang Up* by Jonathan Lunn and *Giant Steps* by Darshan Singh.

The London Festival Ballet's repertory offered Christopher Bruce's *Cruel Garden,* based on the life of García Lorca. Richard Alston's *Rhapsody in Blue* and *Pulcinella* were presented at a Royal Gala in the presence of the Duchess of York by the Rambert Dance Company. Second Stride performed Ian Spink's highly touted *Weighing the Heart.*

Eminent visiting troupes included the Australian Ballet, the Kirov Ballet, and the Dance Theater of Harlem.

Fine Arts. A jewel of an exhibition at the Royal Academy (RA), "Old Master Paintings from the Thyssen-Bornemisza Collection," featured Caravaggio's *St. Catherine of Alexandria* as well as 17th-century Baroque paintings. The RA followed with "Cézanne: The Early Years 1859–72," a first-time exhibit of the modern master's paintings and drawings from age 20 to 33. The exhibit offered a rare opportunity to observe the process of self-discovery. "Henry Moore," a major retrospective of Britain's preeminent 20th-century sculptor, ended the year at the Royal Academy.

Nicholas Serota became the new director of the Tate Gallery. The Tate presented a fascinating exhibit, "Late Picasso," which included paintings, sculpture, drawings, and prints—with sex and death the continuing themes. Following the Picasso show, there was an exciting retrospective of David Hockney's works organized by, and first shown at, the Los Angeles County Museum of Art in California. Whitechapel Art Gallery exhibited a blockbuster retrospective of a major British commemorative sculptor: "Michael Sandle: Sculpture & Drawings 1957–88."

Film and Television. The biggest news in both the film and television industries went beyond the success or failure of any individual creative endeavor.

In film, the phenomenon of the U.S.-inspired multiscreen cinema complex surfaced in 1988 with a glittering opening in Nottingham of Britain's largest and grandest movie theater. Showcase Cinemas, with 11 screens, was built by Boston's National Amusements, Inc., for $10 million. Both U.S. and Canadian movie operators are building elaborate multiscreen complexes in 20 midsize British cities. The industry hoped that the sparkling decor, comfortable seats, concession stands, and free parking increasingly would attract a film audience that declined to a post World War II low in 1984, but since then has been growing.

Prime Minister Thatcher kept an election promise she made in 1987 to do something about "the deep public concern over the display of sex and violence on television"; U.S. programs are considered chief offenders. Mrs. Thatcher appointed Sir William Rees-Mogg to become chairman of the Broadcasting Standards Council, a new watchdog agency. Broadcast industry spokesmen had concerns over creeping censorship that ultimately could affect news and public affairs programs.

GLADYS HANDELMAN
Free-lance Writer

GREECE

During 1988, Greek-Turkish relations improved slightly, but Greece's socialist government went through severe internal crises.

Greek-Turkish Relations. Greek Prime Minister Andreas Papandreou met with Turkish Prime Minister Turgut Ozal at Davos, Switzerland, in January. Though both are members of NATO, Greece and Turkey have had serious differences over Cyprus and the control of sea, mineral, and air rights in the Aegean Sea. The two men conferred again in March at a NATO meeting in Brussels; and Ozal paid a visit to Greece in June, the first time a Turkish prime minister was there officially in 36 years. These meetings were positive steps but they did not result in any fundamental agreements.

Papandreou's Woes. Papandreou and his ruling party, the Panhellenic Socialist Movement (PASOK), came under increasing criticisms. In June he reorganized his cabinet for the 14th time since coming to power in 1981. His appearances with his constant companion, Dimitra Liani, became a political scandal. In deteriorating health, the 69-year-old Papandreou flew with the 34-year-old Liani to London, where he underwent heart surgery on September 30. An announcement before the operation that he would divorce his American-born second wife, the former Margaret Chant, further eroded public confidence. Papandreou's return to Greece with Liani on October 22 found the government enmeshed in financial scandals, including one based on the dealings of George Koskotas, chairman of the Bank of Crete. Allegations of impropriety abounded in this case and in other cases. (Even Papandreou's son George, the minister of education and religion, was implicated.) Charged with embezzlement and fraud, Koskotas in early November fled to Brazil and later in the month moved to the United States, where he was arrested and held for an extradition hearing.

GREECE · Information Highlights

Official Name: Hellenic Republic.
Location: Southwestern Europe.
Area: 50,942 sq mi (131 940 km²).
Population (mid-1988 est.): 10,100,000.
Chief Cities (1981 census): Athens, the capital, 885,737; Salonika, 406,413; Piraeus, 196,389.
Government: *Head of state,* Christos Sartzetakis, president (took office March 1985). *Head of government,* Andreas Papandreou, prime minister (took office Oct. 1981). *Legislature*—Parliament.
Monetary Unit: Drachma (146.50 drachmas equal U.S.$1, Dec. 19, 1988).
Gross National Product (1986 U.S.$): $39,500,-000,000.
Economic Indexes (1987): *Consumer Prices* (1980 = 100), all items, 366.4; food, 355.7. *Industrial Production* (1980 = 100), 106.
Foreign Trade (1987 U.S.$): *Imports,* $13,154,-000,000; *exports,* $6,509,000,000.

In Greece the 15th cabinet restructuring of Papandreou's term was announced on November 16, followed by further changes within the next 24 hours, and then even more changes after that. A parliamentary inquiry, established in mid-November, steadily uncovered evidence of corruption. PASOK plummeted in public opinion polls. By year's end the government seemed in disarray and unprepared to lead the nation toward parliamentary elections scheduled for June 1989. Constantine Mitsotakis of the opposition New Democracy party called for immediate elections.

The Economy. New Democracy accused the government of having mishandled the economy which was beset by strikes, a huge budgetary deficit, high inflation, and other problems. The government claimed the economy was improving, and Parliament in mid-December narrowly approved Papandreou's $27.9 billion budget (with a projected deficit of $9.6 billion) for 1989. He had said that the government would resign if the budget were voted down.

Greece and the European Community. Greece assumed the rotating presidency of the

AP/Wide World

Greece's Prime Minister Andreas Papandreou, 69, underwent successful heart surgery in September. Before the operation, he announced that he would be divorcing his wife of 37 years. His frequent appearances with 34-year-old girlfriend Dimitra Liana (left) created a scandal.

European Community (EC) on July 1 for a six-month term, but Papandreou's illness decreased initiatives by the Greek government. At a gathering of EC leaders held on Rhodes on December 2 and 3, he appeared with Liani, causing the Greek press to pay more attention to his private life than to the substance of the EC meeting.

Armed Attacks. During the year Greece saw a number of bombings and attacks. Among these were the killing of the U.S. defense and naval attaché, Capt. William E. Nordeen, on June 28. A secret radical organization called November 17 (named after a failed 1973 student uprising) claimed responsibility. On July 11 a group opened fire on the cruise ship *City of Poros,* resulting in more than 100 casualties. The same day a car exploded in a suburb of Athens, killing two. These two incidents were linked to Palestinian issues, but the Palestine Liberation Organization denounced both. Other bomb explosions in 1988 included four in Athens in December, just as the EC leaders were assembling at Rhodes.

Greece and the U.S. Bases. Before his first electoral victory in 1981, Papandreou had called for the removal of American bases from Greece. During 1988 his government negotiated with the United States on the possible retention of the bases, subject to a later referendum.

Flight of Daedalus. On April 24, Kanellos Kanellopoulos, a trained cyclist, flew a human-powered aircraft, "Daedalus 88," from Crete over the Aegean to Santorin (Santorini), a distance of more than 74 miles (119 km) in just under four hours. The feat, which doubled the record for human-powered flight, followed the path of the mythic Daedalus who escaped a Cretan prison on wings of wax and feathers (*see* page 84).

Reburial of Princess Andrew. The mother of Britain's Prince Philip, Princess Andrew of Greece (1886–1969), who had become a Greek Orthodox nun in later life, was reburied beneath a church on the side of the Mount of Olives in Jerusalem on August 3. It was her dying wish that she be buried there near the tomb of her aunt—also an Orthodox nun—the Grand Duchess Elisabeth Feodorovna, who was killed during the Russian Revolution.

GEORGE J. MARCOPOULOS, *Tufts University*

HAITI

Tumult continued unabated in Haiti, the poorest and most troubled of the Caribbean countries, during much of 1988.

Manigat Government. Following the violent cancellation of Haiti's first presidential election in 30 years on Nov. 29, 1987, the country's ruling body, the provisional National Council of Government (CNG), presided over tightly controlled balloting on Jan. 17, 1988. The vic-

Photos AP/Wide World

Leslie Manigat (above left) was elected president of Haiti on January 17 but was ousted in a coup, led by Lt. Gen. Henri Namphy, on June 20. Namphy was deposed on September 18 and replaced by Lt. Gen. Prosper Avril (below left).

tor was Leslie Manigat, a middle-of-the-road university professor who had spent more than two decades in exile during the dictatorship of François Duvalier and his son, Jean-Claude. Manigat was inaugurated on February 7, two years to the day after Jean-Claude Duvalier had abandoned the presidency and fled Haiti.

The January 17 election, which was boycotted by the principal opposition figures and in which only an estimated 10% of the electorate participated, seemed to bring about no essential change in the Haitian power structure, which continued to be dominated by the army under the military commander, Lt. Gen. Henri Namphy, who had headed the provisional government after the flight of Duvalier.

Military Rule. In June, Manigat tested his presidential prerogatives by dismissing Namphy from his army post. On June 20, in a bloodless coup, Namphy seized the presidential palace and sent Manigat into exile in the neighboring Dominican Republic. Full military rule was restored as Namphy declared himself pres-

ident, abolished the elected National Assembly, reshuffled the top army command to eliminate dissidents, and suspended constitutional guarantees, jailing numerous civilian opposition figures.

Violence mounted in the wake of Namphy's coup. In September the army stepped up its attacks on opposition forces, burning two Roman Catholic Churches, killing at least nine civilians, and wounding 77 others. The assaults on the churches and on an outspoken priest, Father Bertrand Aristide, were blamed widely on the reemergence of the Tontons Macoute, the dreaded Duvalier paramilitary secret police. Involvement of high military officers in illicit drug trafficking helped fan popular unrest, local observers said, and led foreign governments to cut off the last remnants of aid to the stricken country.

Discontent with Namphy finally filtered down to the lower ranks of the military and on September 18, a revolt apparently led by a group of noncommissioned officers deposed Namphy and installed Lt. Gen. Prosper Avril, the head of the presidential guard, as provisional president. Avril, like Namphy and many other ranking army officers, had been a trusted adviser of the Duvalier dictators, but he moved quickly to assure Haitians—and foreign governments—of his democratic intentions. In his first few days in power, Avril sacked a key military officer, Col. Jean-Claude Paul, who was under indictment for drug dealing in the United States; a few weeks later, Paul died suddenly under suspicious circumstances. Avril also held a series of meetings with civilian opposition leaders, who pronounced themselves cautiously optimistic about an eventual return to stability.

Foreign governments, including the United States, also expressed restrained hopes for an end to the chaos of the past two years. But a renewal of substantial foreign assistance, on which Haiti's revival depends, was questionable as 1988 drew to an end.

RICHARD C. SCHROEDER,
Formerly, "Visión Magazine"

HAWAII

An unexpected flood, the indictments of Hawaii residents Ferdinand and Imelda Marcos (the former Philippine president and his wife), and election-year politics made news in Hawaii during 1988.

The Flood. A New Year's Eve (1987) flood hit the island of Oahu with devastating effect, particularly on the east end, where many expensive homes and automobiles were tumbled like toys down the hillsides. More than 13 inches (33 cm) of rainfall were recorded during the single night of the "once-in-500-years" flood, but no lives were lost. Multimillion-dollar damage suits were filed against the city fathers, however, because of alleged failure to keep storm drains and runoff systems operative.

The Marcos Indictment. Political intrigue was in play late in the year when Hawaii's third president in exile in the post World War II era was indicted by a federal grand jury. Former Philippine President Ferdinand Marcos, who has been living in Hawaii since early 1986, and his wife Imelda were named in a New York City grand jury indictment on charges involving fraud and embezzlement. President Ronald Reagan refused to interfere in the grand-jury case.

The Election. Honolulu Mayor Frank L. Fasi (R) emerged victorious in his reelection bid. He first had won election in 1968, but was defeated in 1980, coming back in 1984 after changing political parties. The mayor's reelection was attributed in part to his strong criticism of housing speculators.

Hawaii voters were in the minority in awarding their electoral votes for the presidency to Democrat Michael Dukakis, and they sent incumbent U.S. Sen. Spark Matsunaga (D) back to Washington along with incumbent U.S. representatives Daniel Akaka (D) and Patricia Saiki (R).

Economy. Tourism, Hawaii's leading industry, continued at a record-setting pace (more than 6 million visitors) in 1988, and entrepreneur Christopher Hemmeter continued building luxury resorts to meet the demand.

Concerns about Hawaii's housing shortage, particularly in the "affordable" category (the average price of a home was more than $226,000 at midyear), were a hot topic during the election campaign as well as around dinner tables. Japanese billionaire Genshiro Kawamoto fueled the flames by buying more than 165 homes and apartments over a two-year period, presumably removing them from the local market so that he could resell them to his Japanese friends and other speculators. But the adverse publicity accompanying Kawamoto's mass purchases dampened the entire Japanese home-buying spree of the past several years. Some plush residences in Waialae-Kahala, which had been sought avidly by the Japanese, were going begging on the market.

Legislature. Despite a mandate under the state constitution that it give a refund to taxpayers if there were a large budget surplus, the legislature provided only a $1-per-person rebate. Legislators promised to use the several hundred million dollars in excess funds for needed projects, including a program to provide more affordable housing.

Air Disaster. An Aloha Airlines Boeing 737 lost a large portion of its upper fuselage while flying interisland April 28, causing a stewardess to be swept to her death and terrifying the remaining 94 passengers and crew before a "miracle landing" was made at Kahului, Maui. The incident resulted in mass purging of older aircraft from the Aloha Airlines fleet and in lengthy investigations and hearings by the Federal Aviation Administration.

CHARLES TURNER
Honolulu

HONG KONG

During 1988 attention in Hong Kong was focused on the "White Paper" (policy document) on representative government and a Basic Law draft. Lisa Mingchuen Wang, Hong Kong's popular TV entertainer, was elected to China's National People's Congress.

Political Affairs. The "White Paper" was tabled in the Legislative Council (Legco) on February 10. After heated debates, the Legco voted to support the paper's proposals, including the replacement of two appointed Legco seats with two indirectly elected seats in 1988, and the introduction of direct elections of ten of the Legco's 56 members in 1991. The Heung Yee Kuk (Rural Consultative Council) burnt the "White Paper" in protest of not being allocated an indirectly elected seat in the Legco as a functional constituency.

On April 28, 1988, the 176-member Basic Law Drafting Committee released a draft of the Basic Law, which outlines procedures for the establishment of the Hong Kong Special Administrative Region. Although the draft promises to protect civil liberties, it contains numerous qualifiers. For example, one of its sections promises freedom of speech, press, assembly, and religion but these may be restricted, when necessary, to maintain national security, public order, public health, and morals. The draft also gives China's legislature the final power to interpret and amend the Basic Law. Hong Kong residents were given five months to give their comments to the 58-member Basic Law Consultative Committee (BLCC). A total of 73,327 submissions were made, which the BLCC said it would consider in making revisions. However, many local people felt that their input would make little difference in the final document.

Economy. Hong Kong overtook Rotterdam, The Netherlands, as the world's busiest container port. The first berth of a sixth terminal was completed in May 1988, and its second and third berths were scheduled to open in 1989. Tourism was Hong Kong's third-largest foreign exchange earner; about 4.5 million visitors contributed $3.3 billion to the economy in 1987.

The Hong Kong Convention and Exhibition Centre in Wanchai District, consisting of two luxury hotels, an apartment block, an office block, and two exhibition halls, was completed in 1988. The construction of a 6.4-mi (4-km) tunnel linking Kowloon and Sha Tin New Town began in the summer. Hong Kong University of Science and Technology, the territory's third university, with a capacity for 10,000 students, was being constructed at Tai Po Tsai, near Clearwater Bay.

In February the U.S. government decided to remove Hong Kong from the generalized system of preferences, effective Jan. 2, 1989.

Link with China. In 1988 reexports of goods to and from China constituted almost 80% of Hong Kong's reexports, and more than one million people travelled by cross-border coaches between Hong Kong and China.

More Hong Kong manufacturers now are setting up factories in Shenzhen Special Economic Zone to capitalize on its cheap labor and land. Hong Kong accounted for 70% of Shenzhen's total investment in 1988. Since the Shanghai Economic Zone was established in 1982, Hong Kong has become the zone's largest export market, largest source of external investment, and second largest trading partner after Japan in 1988.

Chinese business interest in Hong Kong continued to increase; about 2,000 China-funded companies were operating in the territory in 1988, double the number in 1985.

DAVID CHUENYAN LAI
University of Victoria, British Columbia

Shirley McVay Wiseman, president of the National Association of Home Builders, inspects the blueprints of a new home in Lexington, KY. U.S. housing starts were expected to total some 1.5 million units in 1988.

NAHB

HOUSING

As in the previous several years, the performance of the U.S. housing market in 1988 was mixed. The production and sale of single-family homes held up quite well on a national basis, and home prices advanced at a faster pace than the overall rate of inflation. On the other hand, the multifamily housing sector—primarily apartment buildings for rent—was quite weak. On a regional basis, the performance of both the single-family and multifamily housing markets was very uneven.

Several major studies issued during 1988 documented the growing seriousness of two housing problems in the United States. First, low-income renters were having a harder and harder time finding decent rental housing that they could afford, a problem dramatized by a growing number of homeless families. Second, young Americans were having a harder and harder time buying their first homes. These problems spurred development of new national policy options during 1988, paving the way for the introduction of major legislation in 1989.

Total Production. Housing production in the United States, measured by starts of new units, fell by 8% in 1988 to 1.49 million units. This was the second consecutive annual decline of roughly the same magnitude, and the 1988 production level was the lowest since the recession year of 1982.

The housing sector was in relatively weak condition as 1988 began, and the production level (on a seasonally adjusted basis) fluctuated within a narrow range during most of the year. Late in the year, tightening labor markets and other factors were placing greater upward pressure on interest rates, presaging a further decline in housing activity during 1989.

Single-Family Housing. The production and sale of single-family homes held up well in 1988 despite the fact that the stock-market crash of October 1987 wiped out hundreds of billions of dollars of household wealth. Indeed, the stock-market debacle had positive consequences for the single-family market. It resulted in large declines in both short- and long-term interest rates but did not provoke a general economic recession. Furthermore, large fluctuations in both the stock and bond markets served to reinforce interest in homes as a long-term investment.

After bottoming out in March, interest rates ratcheted upward during 1988, with long-term fixed-rate home mortgages exceeding 11% by the end of the year. But interest-rate developments had relatively little impact on single-family housing activity, as the adjustable-rate mortgage (ARM) was the lifeline of the single-family market. Buyers could get ARMs with initial interest rates about 2½ percentage points below prevailing rates on the traditional fixed-rate mortgage. And even though the spread between short-term and long-term rates in other components of the U.S. financial markets virtually disappeared as 1988 came to a close, the initial rate advantage on ARMs was still substantial. ARMs accounted for nearly two thirds of all home loans written in the United States during 1988.

Multifamily Housing. The market for residential structures with two or more units was quite weak in 1988, as the production of rental housing slipped badly. Indeed, starts of new multifamily housing fell below 400,000 units, down 40% from the 1984–85 level and about equal to the level during the 1981–82 recession.

The multifamily housing market was plagued by very high vacancy rates. The national rental vacancy rate was about 8%, the highest in more than 20 years, and the rate for structures with five or more units was above 11%. There was some improvement in the south-

ern part of the country, where earlier over-building had been most serious, but the situation worsened in the West and Northeast.

Completion of new rental units slowed during 1988, reflecting a sharp decline in starts since 1985, and there was some improvement in the pace of new-unit rentals. However, market fundamentals remained quite weak as the year came to a close, and the Tax Reform Act of 1986, which sharply reduced incentives for investment in rental housing, remained intact.

Regional Markets. Housing activity declined to some degree in all major regions of the United States during 1988, with the exception of the Pacific Coast. In general, markets that had been robust in the previous few years cooled down, while markets that had been contracting sharply approached their lows. Reductions in housing starts were recorded in New England and the Middle Atlantic regions, although activity in these areas generally remained high by historical standards. A buildup of inventories of unsold new homes in the Northeast caused builders to cut production and led to a sharp slowdown in the appreciation of home prices. The industrial Midwest turned in a relatively solid performance. A resurgence of U.S. export markets and an associated surge of capital investment clearly helped the economy of this part of the country and gave new support to the housing market. Housing markets in the "oil patch" states of Texas, Louisiana, Oklahoma, and Arkansas remained very weak, although the degree of decline was much smaller than during the 1984–87 period. The volume of housing starts leveled off late in the year but at a very low volume. This part of the country accounted for only about 5% of total U.S. housing starts in late 1988, down from more than 20% as recently as 1983.

National Housing Policy. Two major reports dealing with the condition of housing in the United States were issued early in 1988. The Center for Housing Studies at Harvard University released "The State of the Nation's Housing," and the National Housing Task Force, a blue-ribbon group established as part of a congressional effort to reexamine U.S. housing policy, issued "A Decent Place to Live." Both reports noted that relatively high levels of housing construction, home sales, and remodeling expenditures during the previous five years had deflected national attention from critical housing problems facing growing numbers of Americans. They focused on a widening gap between the "housing haves and the have-nots," identifying some of the biggest losers in the housing market as young families trying to buy their first homes and low-income households unable to find decent, affordable rentals. They also noted the growing problem of homelessness, stressing that more and more of the homeless population was made up of people with jobs and families with children.

The National Housing Task Force developed a broad range of policy options to deal with problems encountered by potential first-time home buyers and low-income renters, as well as the special problems of the homeless and other disadvantaged groups. Congressional staffs began drafting components of a major legislative package, based largely on Task Force recommendations.

Introduction of housing-policy legislation was expected early in 1989. While bipartisan congressional support seemed likely, budgetary considerations would be a major constraint. The perspectives of the George Bush administration on national housing policy were not developed fully during the presidential campaign, but many felt it would be more favorably disposed to expansion than was the Reagan administration. In December, Bush named conservative Republican Jack Kemp, who was giving up his U.S. House seat, as his secretary of housing and urban development.

International. Housing activity worldwide benefited from the surge in liquidity and the drop in interest rates that followed the stock market collapse of October 1987.

In Canada, housing starts were expected to total between 210,000 and 230,000 units in 1988, representing a decline from 1987. Home prices were rising at about 9% annually, a retreat from the double-digit rates of mid-1987. The home ownership rate during 1988 stood at about 63%, similar to the U.S. figure.

In Japan, where home ownership patterns reflect the nation's agricultural traditions, a population flow to the cities during the 1960s and early 1970s yielded a substantial decline in home ownership rates; reversing that trend, the rate rose to 63% by 1983. Rigorous conservation laws and tax policies keep lands out of the housing market, causing a rapid escalation of prices. Japanese housing starts in 1987 reached nearly 1.7 million units and were expected to top 1.9 million in 1988. The typical single-family house in Japan is less than two thirds the size of the average new home in the United States.

In West Germany, high housing costs and low, subsidized rents keep the home ownership rate to only about 40%; stagnant population growth also contributes to a sluggish market. In 1988 housing completions, which had fallen every year since 1984, were expected to show a small increase to about 235,000 units.

In Great Britain, the government of Prime Minister Margaret Thatcher actively has promoted the privatization of public (council) housing stock and reduced subsidies on rental housing. By the 1980s, the home ownership rate there also rose to 63%. Total housing starts in 1988 were forecast at 220,000–230,000, up less than 5% from 1987.

KENT W. COLTON and DAVID F. SEIDERS
National Association of Home Builders

The Remodeling Trend

Faced with the high cost of building a new house or buying a better one, millions of U.S. homeowners have turned to remodeling. A healthy economy and lower interest rates for borrowing, often through the popular home-equity loan, have made this possible. With a need for more amenities—or just to confront the ravages of time over timber—homeowners in 1987 paid $93.7 billion for remodeling and restoration. This figure was more than double the amount spent five years earlier, according to estimates by the National Association of Home Builders' Remodelors Council.

Currently, remodeling is most prevalent in areas where land is scarce and costly, or where there are many older houses. A recent study by the trade magazine *Remodeling* revealed that "remodeling is the strongest from Boston to Washington, as well as the California coast and most major urban areas in the United States." Working couples have found it a hardship to move even farther away from the workplace because of increased commuting time. A more palatable alternative, especially for families that are settled in their neighborhoods, has been to enhance their present homes.

Having one's house painted has proven to be the most basic home improvement. According to the National Association of the Remodeling Industry, the alterations most popular in 1987 were new windows, kitchens, and additions; the third choice usually involved basement and attic conversions or the addition of a second story for more living space. The trend toward installing luxury bathrooms with whirlpool tubs continued unabated. The average homeowner spent from $15,000-$20,000 to add approximately 300 sq ft (28 m²) or a 16' (5 m) by 18' (5.5 m) room. The costs of labor and materials varied in different parts of the country.

Homeowners believe improvements are a sound investment; they generally can recoup about 72% of their expenses when it is time to sell, depending on the neighborhood and how long after the remodeling they live in the house, indicated a spokesperson for *Remodeling* magazine. The popularity of rental housing also contributed to the rehab phenomenon. With the increasing number of new apartment buildings and unusually high rents in some areas, owners have had to polish up their properties to keep abreast of the competition. According to a 1986 study by William C. Apgar, Jr., of the Joint Center for Housing Studies of MIT and Harvard, "Rehab expenditures by

© Hazel Hankin/Stock, Boston

Many U.S. homeowners are performing renovations themselves, due to rising costs and a shortage of contractors.

rental property owners more than doubled from 1982 to 1986 . . . sharp increases in rent levels now are making investment in existing rental units profitable again."

Homeowners with high hopes for creating instant improvements generally have had to put their plans on hold. Finding a contractor to give a house a mini or a major facelift is difficult. The demand for contractors, electricians, plumbers, carpenters, masons, and landscapers far exceeds the supply. Unfortunately, the prospects are dim for turning this shortage of skilled workers into a sufficient supply. With a shrinking pool of teenagers in the population, enrollment in vocational programs which traditionally have furnished the building industry with the workers it needs has dwindled.

Do-It-Yourself. The dearth of help (and its high cost when it can be found) galvanizes many homeowners to join the growing ranks of do-it-yourselfers. Men and women who once shrank from changing a light bulb are getting into the trenches to fight fuse failure, combat

This Old House

The host of PBS-TV's "This Old House," Bob Vila (left), discusses a renovation project with homeowners. The program is the most popular half-hour series on PBS, with a weekly audience of more than 11 million. It owes much of its appeal to its realism: Each project takes place in a privately-owned home, and not everything goes smoothly.

© WGBH Boston

wood rot, and attack leaky faucets. Some Mr. and Ms. Fix-Its are going beyond maintenance and repair to undertake more complex and costly renovations. With no contractors in sight, getting the job done and "done right" for less money is paramount, say determined homeowners. Beleaguered do-it-yourselfers have a mountain of resource materials to help them. Books and manuals abound. Homeowners who catch the fix-it fever can find answers to their questions in such magazines as *The Family Handyman, Home Resource Magazine,* and *Practical Homeowner.*

Budding builders also are going back to school to make the grade. Self-help courses are popular at community colleges and local home-improvement centers, where eager students can learn everything from the basics of tiling to decoding building plans. Even VCRs are becoming a medium for helping people create their "house beautiful." An array of videotapes can be found in lumberyards and through mail order. Neophytes are able to see the process involved in such projects as "How to Install Drywall."

Homeowners have had an active interest in enhancing their domestic investment for many years, as manifested by the popularity of *This Old House,* the award-winning half-hour series on PBS, which has broadcast 26 programs each season since 1979. The show's wisdom also is available on videotape and in book form. The host of the series, Bob Vila, and his master carpenter, Norm Abram, have become friends to a weekly audience of more than 11 million viewers.

During 1988, home improvement tips and techniques also were available on ABC's new late-morning television program *Home,* which premiered in January. Overall it deals with a number of topics, but for a continuing feature *Home* bought a $167,000 two-bedroom house that needed transforming. Viewers saw step-by-step remodeling as well as interior decorating—with advice from experts on contractors, interior design, and real estate.

Either unable or unwilling to trade up, homeowners are having a busy time making the most of the houses they already have.

GLADYS HANDELMAN

Hungary's Premier Károly Grósz, left, *succeeded János Kádár as general secretary of the Communist Party on May 22. In November, Grosz gave up the premiership to concentrate on his new party responsibilities.*

AP/Wide World

HUNGARY

Hungary experienced far-reaching changes in 1988, including its first new political leadership in more than 30 years.

Domestic Affairs. The major event of the year was an extraordinary national conference of the Hungarian Socialist Workers' (Communist) Party held May 20–22. It was preceded by a flurry of public meetings called by the Hungarian Democratic Forum and other opposition groups demanding democratization.

At the party conference, János Kádár, the party's general secretary since 1956, was replaced by Károly Grósz, the country's premier. Kádár and a group of his loyal associates were dropped from the party's politburo. They were replaced by individuals known for their reform sympathies, including Imre Pozsgay, leader of the Patriotic People's Front, and Reszö Nyers, a noted economic planner. About 40% of the party's Central Committee also was replaced. In June, a Kádár ally, Károly Németh, retired as president and the Grand National Assembly elected Bruno Ferenc Straub, a non-Communist, to succeed him. Imre Pozsgay also was confirmed as minister of state (first deputy premier) and charged with implementing the new regime's reform program. In late November, Grósz resigned as premier to concentrate on his party post. Politburo member Miklos Németh was nominated as the new premier, and Rezsoe Nyers, another Politburo member, was named state minister responsible for economic issues.

Grósz indicated that new, pragmatic changes would include greater openness and

further liberalization in party and governmental procedures and improvement of Hungary's sluggish economy through greater reliance on free-market forces and increased economic ties and more joint ventures with the West.

In October, Grósz pushed through a series of laws reintroducing private enterprise to Hungary. Effective Jan. 1, 1989, joint stock companies were legalized and a national stock exchange was revived. The limit on the number of employees permitted for private enterprises was raised to 500, with no limit for foreign-owned companies.

Nevertheless the new regime adopted a tough stance toward open political dissent. Earlier, on March 15, the 140th anniversary of the outbreak of the Hungarian revolution of

---

HUNGARY • Information Highlights

Official Name: Hungarian People's Republic.
Location: East-central Europe.
Area: 35,919 sq mi (93 030 km²).
Population (mid-1988 est.): 10,600,000.
Chief Cities (Jan. 1, 1987): Budapest, the capital, 2,093,487; Debrecen, 214,836; Miskolc, 211,156.
Government: *Head of state,* Károly Németh, president of the presidential council (took office June 1987). *Head of government,* Miklos Nemeth, premier of the council of ministers (took office November 1988). Secretary general of the Hungarian Socialist Workers' Party, Károly Grósz (took office May 1988). *Legislature* (unicameral)—National Assembly.
Monetary Unit: Forint (54.012 forints equal U.S.$1, July 1988).
Economic Indexes (1987): *Consumer Prices* (1980 = 100), all items, 159.2; food, 151.4. *Industrial Production* (1980 = 100), 115.
Foreign Trade (1987 U.S.$): *Imports,* $9,886,000,000; *exports,* $9,602,000,000.

1848, more than 10,000 persons had been permitted to march in Budapest shouting "Democracy!," the largest antigovernmental demonstration since 1956. In June, however, when some 500 people assembled to commemorate the 30th anniversary of the hanging of Imre Nagy, prime minister during the revolution of 1956, they were met with police beatings and arrests.

Foreign Affairs. Hungary's major foreign problem continued to be the treatment of some 2 million ethnic Hungarians in Romania. In January 1988 the Hungarian government announced that in 1987 about 6,400 ethnic Hungarians had fled Romania and been granted asylum in Hungary. In early June, a high-level meeting of representatives of the two countries in Budapest over alleged repression of the Hungarian language and culture in Romania was inconclusive. On June 27, perhaps as many as 50,000 people demonstrated in Budapest to protest Romania's planned destruction of thousands of ethnic Hungarian villages in Transylvania. In August, Grósz met with Romanian President Nicolae Ceauşescu in Arad, Romania, but was unable to gain any concessions from him.

In July, General Secretary Grósz visited the United States, meeting with President Reagan and other top officials.

See also special report on Eastern Europe, page 227.

JOSEPH FREDERICK ZACEK
State University of New York at Albany

ICELAND

The coalition government formed in July 1987 was brought down in September 1988 when Iceland's three main political parties (Independent, Progressive, and Social Democratic) failed to reach an agreement on measures necessary to stabilize the economy. A wage and price freeze went into effect while discussions regarding a new government took place. A new coalition, headed by former For-

eign Minister Steingrímur Hermannsson, leader of the Progressive Party, was formed later in the month.

Presidential elections were held on June 25. Although the opposition candidate, Sigrun Thorsteinsdottir of a minority fringe party, had advocated a more politically active role for the president, the incumbent, Mrs. Vigdís Finnbogadóttir, was returned overwhelmingly for a third term.

Economy. The favorable economic climate of the previous two years deteriorated and inflation for the year was expected to rise to 25%. Gross domestic product (GDP) rose slightly but national income dropped as a result of a worsening of the terms of trade, caused by falling fish prices abroad, especially in the United States. Real disposable incomes were thought likely to fall by 1%.

There was a general recession in export production as prices abroad failed to keep pace with high capital costs and interest rates at home. The woolen industry was affected particularly badly, and many firms were forced to lay off workers. Fur farming, especially of foxes, also ran into difficulties. The króna was devalued three times, by 6% in February, 10% in May, and 3% in October after the new government took office.

A strike by members of a 10,000-strong Reykjavík union in support of a pay-claim closed offices and shops in the capital for three weeks in May. Pickets at the international airport at Keflavík prevented passengers from leaving the country for several days. Following the settlement of the dispute, the income-tax-free threshold and social security payments were raised. Further union action was made illegal until March 1989.

Unemployment remained negligible (about 0.4%), while job vacancies stood at about 3% of the work force. A pay-as-you-earn income tax system and simplification of customs tariffs and sales-tax classifications were introduced early in the year.

Fish catches were good and the total value of catches seemed likely to exceed that of 1987. Many fish processing plants, however, were running at a serious loss due largely to the low markets in the United States and the continuing weakness of the U.S. dollar.

General. Four European aluminum producers formed a company to investigate the feasibility of establishing a new aluminum smelter at Straumsvík in southwest Iceland, near the existing smelter owned by Alusuisse.

The Althing (parliament) voted in favor of legalizing the sale of beer with an alcoholic content of more than 2.25% beginning in March 1989. The action ended Iceland's ban on beer which had been in force since 1915. The National Art Gallery moved into new premises in central Reykjavík.

ANNE COSSER, *Reykjavík*

ICELAND • Information Highlights

Official Name: Republic of Iceland.
Location: North Atlantic Ocean.
Area: 39,768 sq mi (103 000 km²).
Population (mid-1988 est.): 200,000.
Chief Cities (Dec. 1, 1987): Reykjavík, the capital, 93,425; Akureyri, 13,856.
Government: *Head of state,* Vigdís Finnbogadóttir, president (took office Aug. 1980). *Head of government,* Steingrímur Hermannsson, prime minister (took office Sept. 1988). *Legislature*—Althing: Upper House and Lower House.
Monetary Unit: Króna (46.8 krónur equal U.S.$1, August 1988).
Gross Domestic Product (1986 U.S.$): $3,900,-000,000.
Foreign Trade (1986 U.S.$): *Imports,* $1,589,000,000; *exports,* $1,376,000,000.

IDAHO

An acrimonious legislative session was followed by an election in which voters removed from office the state Senate's top leader and the House's second-in-command, while Gov. Cecil Andrus (D) continued to push for increased education support. The state's starting pay for public-school teachers dropped to the lowest in the nation. Although the legislature refused to raise tax revenues enough to meet Andrus' budget requests for public schools and higher education, a strong economy made it appear toward year's end that unexpected revenue could help prevent another showdown in the coming year.

The pending legislative realignment mirrored a shift in attitude within the Idaho Supreme Court as a new justice was seated. Economic growth was tempered by continuing drought in the agricultural south and by congressional failure to pass wilderness legislation defining the extent of future timber harvests in the wooded North.

Legislature. Following a year of harmony between the Republican legislature and Democrat Andrus, relations soured as legislative leaders declared a year of stability in taxes and appropriations. When Andrus went on statewide television to solicit support for his veto of a $356 million public school appropriation— which he considered too low—House Speaker Tom Boyd (R) and Senate President James Risch (R) followed immediately to make the case for it. Andrus was forced to let the legislative majority have its way.

Legislators also refused to approve most of Andrus' proposals getting tougher with child abuse but ended a three-year battle over telephone deregulation by passing compromise legislation.

Election. Andrus campaigned for Democratic opponents to top legislative leaders, and Senate President Risch, long a power to be

reckoned with throughout the state, was defeated in his Boise district in the November 8 general election. House Majority Leader Jack Kennevick (R) also was defeated, and Democrats picked up three seats in the Senate, giving Republicans a 23–19 majority.

State voters also approved a constitutional amendment authorizing a state lottery and overwhelmingly returned to office 2d District Congressman Richard Stallings, the First Democrat elected to three successive terms in the conservative district. In the 1st District, GOP incumbent Larry Craig also won easily.

Judiciary. Early in the year, Andrus appointed Boise lawyer Byron Johnson to replace the late Charles Donaldson on the Idaho Supreme Court. Johnson, considered the most liberal candidate among the four names sent to Andrus by the state Judicial Council, was expected to shift the five-member court from a conservative to a liberal disposition, but evidence of that was still scarce late in the year.

Economy. Although continuing drought threatened southern farms, national economic growth and a renewed electronic microchip business in the Boise area drove unemployment down and income up. Personal income tax payments in September were 16% higher than a year earlier.

JIM FISHER, *"Lewiston Morning Tribune"*

ILLINOIS

Illinois voters stayed with the winner for the third presidential election in a row as they gave George Bush a narrow 94,999-vote margin over Michael Dukakis out of nearly 4.7 million votes cast in the state.

Chicago gave the Massachusetts governor a 400,000-vote margin, although Bush won a plurality in eight of the city's 50 wards. The vice-president overcame the city vote by a strong showing in the suburbs and downstate Illinois.

There was little else for Republicans to cheer about in Illinois. Democrats maintained control of the Illinois General Assembly, picked up one congressional seat, and trounced efforts by some "new" Republicans to win office in Cook County. The Republican county slate was led by Edward Vrdolyak, former chairman of the Democratic Party of Cook County, who lost a bid for clerk of the Circuit Court to Democrat Aurelia Pucinski.

The Drought. The summer drought that devastated the nation's heartland reduced Illinois' 1988 corn yield by an estimated 50% and caused untold other crop losses. The state is one of the nation's leading producers of corn and soybeans.

The impact of the long dry spell could extend into 1989 crop production, experts said, because the moisture level of Illinois farmland remained below normal levels. A side effect of

---

IDAHO • Information Highlights

Area: 83,564 sq mi (216 432 km²).

Population (July 1, 1987): 998,000.

Chief Cities (1980 census): Boise, the capital (July 1, 1986 est.), 108,390; Pocatello, 46,340; Idaho Falls, 39,590.

Government (1988): *Chief Officers*—governor, Cecil Andrus (D); lt. gov., C. L. Otter (R). *Legislature*—Senate, 42 members; House of Representatives, 84 members.

State Finances (fiscal year 1987): *Revenue,* $1,868,000,000; *expenditure,* $1,605,000,000.

Personal Income (1987): $11,847,000,000; per capita, $11,868.

Labor Force (June 1988): *Civilian labor force,* 484,200; *unemployed,* 26,100 (5.4% of total force).

Education: *Enrollment* (fall 1986)—public elementary schools, 149,613; public secondary, 58,778; colleges and universities, 45,260. *Public school expenditures* (1986–87), $513,000,000 ($2,555 per pupil).

AP/Wide World

Robert Michel (R) was elected to a 17th term as U.S. representative from Illinois' 18th District. He later was chosen for a fifth term as House minority leader.

ILLINOIS • Information Highlights

Area: 56,345 sq mi (145 934 km²).
Population (July 1, 1987): 11,582,000.
Chief Cities (July 1, 1986 est.): Springfield, the capital, 100,290; Chicago, 3,009,530; Rockford, 135,760.
Government (1988): *Chief Officers*—governor, James R. Thompson (R); lt. gov., George H. Ryan (R). *General Assembly*—Senate, 59 members; House of Representatives, 118 members.
State Finances (fiscal year 1987): *Revenue,* $20,632,000,000; *expenditure,* $18,821,000,000.
Personal Income (1987): $190,430,000,000; per capita, $16,442.
Labor Force (June 1988): *Civilian labor force,* 5,808,200; *unemployed,* 403,600 (6.9% of total force).
Education: *Enrollment* (fall 1986)—public elementary schools, 1,249,340; public secondary, 575,845; colleges and universities, 692,092. *Public school expenditures* (1986–87), $6,270,000,000 ($3,980 per pupil).

the drought was to force commercial navigation on the Mississippi River to come to a near halt as low water levels made it difficult for barges to navigate. It prompted Governor Thompson to ask federal officials for permission to divert billions of gallons of water from Lake Michigan to the water hungry Mississippi. Governors of other Great Lakes states opposed the proposal and the plan was never put into effect.

New Jobs. On the same day that Gov. James R. Thompson and Chrysler Corp. Chairman Lee Iacocca marked the grand opening of the new Diamond-Star auto plant in downstate Normal, Illinois lost its bid for the Department of Energy's new $4.4 billion superconducting super collider. Thompson and the state's congressional delegation had lobbied hard for the super collider to be built at the prestigious Fermilab in west suburban Chicago. The selection of George Bush's home state of Texas for the project came just two days after the national election, prompting Illinois Sen. Alan Dixon (D) to charge the decision was based on politics. Twenty-one of the state's House members asked President Reagan to appoint a commission to investigate the matter.

The Diamond-Star grand opening is probably Thompson's most visible accomplishment in trying to bring jobs to Illinois during his 12 years as governor. The state gave $80 million in incentives for the $650 million plant, which is a joint venture of Chrysler and Japan's Mitsubishi Motors Corp. It is scheduled to be turning out 240,000 cars per year by 1990, and should employ about 3,000 workers in Normal. Diamond-Star's first models were the Plymouth Laser and the Mitsubishi Eclipse subcompact sports coupe.

Winnetka Tragedy. In May the affluent and normally tranquil North Shore Chicago suburb of Winnetka was shaken by a bizarre shooting spree and two violent deaths. On the morning of May 20, Laurie Dann, a 30-year-old area resident with a history of mental problems, walked into the Hubbard Woods Elementary School carrying a revolver. Entering a second-grade classroom, she opened fire, killing one eight-year-old boy and wounding four other children. Leaving the school, Dann went to a nearby house, where she confronted Philip Andrews, a student at the University of Illinois; he struggled with her and was shot in the chest. The police arrived and a daylong siege of the house followed. At dusk police officers stormed the residence and found that the disturbed woman had ended her own life with a gunshot wound to the head.

Police later learned that on the same morning as the Hubbard Woods incident, Dann had tried to burn down another school in nearby Highland Park, and had set fire to a home in Winnetka where she had been employed as a baby-sitter; she also had planted food laced with arsenic at two Northwestern University fraternities and at other homes where she had worked on the North Shore. The family whose house she had tried to burn recently had given her notice, and had children attending the Hubbard Woods School.

ROBERT ENSTAD, *"Chicago Tribune"*

The relaxed manner of India's Prime Minister Rajiv Gandhi belied his mounting political problems in 1988. The 44-year-old leader faced an increasingly vociferous opposition.

AP/Wide World

INDIA

With the continuing decline in the personal popularity and credibility of Prime Minister Rajiv Gandhi in 1988, India's "Rajiv Revolution" seemed to be losing much of its steam. Further evidence of this could be seen in the increasing dissension in the ruling Congress(I) party, election reverses, the existence of opposition governments in several states, and unusually extensive—if still unsuccessful—efforts of opposition parties to form a national front against the ruling party. Terrorism and violence, especially in the Punjab state, continued. The economic picture, as usual, was mixed, with continuing heavy deficits and an adverse balance of payments, but there also was some evidence of better prospects ahead. The four-year drought ended, but the life-giving rains also brought floods, disease, and heavy loss of life in many parts of the country. Gandhi continued to be active in international affairs, but India's relations with most of its South Asian neighbors were far from satisfactory.

The Faltering "Rajiv Revolution." In his message to the nation on Jan. 25, 1988, on the eve of India's 39th Republic Day, President Ramaswami Venkataraman referred to "communal riots in various parts of the country," "religious fundamentalism and communalism," "the cult of terrorism," and "pulls of subnational loyalties" as forces that were impeding the progress of the nation. Increasing numbers of Indians were alienated from Gandhi and the Congress(I) government because of lack of progress in checking these alarming trends. But many more were alienated by the evidence (real or perceived) of Gandhi's growing isolation from his people (in part, perhaps, for security reasons), and from almost everyone in public life except his own inner circle of

constantly changing advisers; his growing loss of credibility and reputation; and his alleged increasing arrogance, imperiousness, and authoritarianism. Internal dissensions in the Congress(I) became increasingly apparent. In the summer, 30 Congress(I) members of Parliament publicly complained about Gandhi's failure to hold party elections and to tackle the problem of corruption.

Public dissatisfaction was reflected in the outcome of by-elections in seven states on June 16, in which the Congress(I) lost five out of seven parliamentary seats and six out of 11 seats in state legislative assemblies. In the most highly publicized contest, in Allahabad, a city in Uttar Pradesh (the ancestral home of the influential Nehru family, to which Indira Gandhi was born), Gandhi and other top Congress(I) leaders campaigned vigorously, but lost nonetheless. The Congress(I) candidate, Sunil Shastri (son of former Prime Minister Lal Bahadur Shastri), was defeated decisively by Vishwanath Pratap Singh, a leading political opponent who once had served as finance and defense minister in Gandhi's cabinet.

Gandhi tried to strengthen his position by two major shakeups in his Council of Ministers —a practice he had followed some 23 times. In the first shakeup, on February 14, he brought 13 people into the government; four were given cabinet posts. His desire to strengthen his position in the Hindi-speaking heartland in north India was shown by the fact that eight of the 13 new ministers were from Uttar Pradesh and Bihar—megastates which generally were regarded as badly run but which returned nearly one fourth of the members of the Lok Sabha (the lower house of the national Parliament). Two of the new ministers were former chief ministers of Bihar and Madhya Pradesh who recently had been removed from these posts. A

noteworthy addition was Dinesh Singh, once a close associate of former Prime Minister—and Rajiv's mother—Indira Gandhi. Singh, who at one time was estranged from the Gandhi family, became a federal minister for the first time in 17 years.

On June 16, in the wake of his electoral setbacks, Gandhi engineered the dismissal of the Congress(I) chief ministers of Uttar Pradesh and Maharashtra, and made ten major changes in his ministry. Among the new ministers were two Congress veterans, P. V. Narasimha Rao, who returned to his former post of foreign minister, and S. B. Chavan, who was named minister of finance.

In August a poll reported in a well-known journal, *India Today,* indicated that only 38% of the 10,000 Indians polled believed that Gandhi was doing a good job. It suggested that if a general election were held immediately and the opposition fielded a single slate of candidates, Gandhi would face defeat, but that if the opposition remained disunited, as it always had been, the Congress(I) would win a majority of Lok Sabha seats.

Opposition parties tried to capitalize on the growing disillusionment with Gandhi and the Congress(I), but even the non-Communist parties could not bury their differences deep enough to present a formidable opposition to the ruling party. On March 8 opposition parties joined in their first nationally organized protest, in the form of a *band* (strike). They demanded Gandhi's resignation and called for national elections to be held well in advance of the mandatory date of December 1989. The *band* virtually closed down many major cities, but it was really effective in only seven states where non-Congress governments were in power. During the strike, 50,000 persons were arrested, and at least ten died in street violence.

Throughout 1988, various opposition parties announced agreements to unite against the Congress(I). V. P. Singh and two powerful non-Congress chief ministers—N. T. Rama Rao in Andhra Pradesh and Ramakrishna Hegde in Karnataka—played leading roles in these political alliances. Only one of these unity efforts seemed to have any prospect of more than limited and temporary success. In late July the formation of a national front of four centrist parties (collectively labeled the Samajwadi Janata Dal, or Socialist People's Party) was announced. The front anticipated that at least three more centrist parties could be persuaded to join. It was hailed by opponents of Gandhi and the Congress(I) as perhaps the first serious threat to the Congress(I) in more than a decade, but it ran into difficulties from the outset. It suffered what appeared to be a major setback only a few days after its formation was announced, when an uproar over alleged wiretapping in Karnataka led to

the resignation of Hegde as chief minister. Hegde denied any involvement in the wiretapping of Karnataka state officials, but he accepted responsibility and resigned. Instead of ending his political career, however, his resignation eventually worked in his favor, and gave a new lease on life to the National Front.

Accords and Disasters. Two long-festering insurgencies ended in August. The Indian government signed an agreement with leaders of a tribal insurrectionary movement in the state of Tripura, which borders on eastern Bangladesh. The guerrilla war in Tripura had been going on for eight years, and had resulted in the loss of at least 2,000 lives. In the Darjeeling district of West Bengal, the Gurkha National Liberation Front (GNLF), which had been agitating for two years for a separate Gurkhaland state, signed two separate agreements, one with the government of India, which had been acting as mediator of the dispute (or, as the West Bengal government claimed, as agitator), the other with the West Bengal government. In return for a promise of greater autonomy (well short of a separate state), the GNLF agreed to end the guerrilla war and to instruct its followers to surrender their weapons.

Disasters are commonplace in Indian life, but at least four attracted unusual attention: More than 1,000 casualties resulted from heavy flooding in at least eight states. On August 6 a ferry boat on the flood-swollen Ganges capsized, killing about 400 people; it was described as the worst disaster of its kind in India's history. On August 20 a devastating earthquake measuring 6.5 on the Richter scale killed about 1,000 people (its epicenter ran along the India-Nepal border and caused extensive damage from southern Nepal to the Bangladesh port of Chittagong). On October 19, 164 persons were killed in two separate plane crashes. Hundreds also were killed by a late November cyclone. (*See also* ACCIDENTS AND DISASTERS.)

Crisis in Punjab. Punjab remained the center of widespread terrorism and violence during 1988. More than 2,000 people were killed in that troubled state during the year. The Indian government seemed to be unable to deal with the continuing crisis. Militant Sikhs (adherents of an Indian religion that combines elements of Hindu and Muslim beliefs) continued to dominate the state. Already vested with emergency powers in Punjab, the Indian government was given even more extraordinary powers in the Constitution Act, or 59th Amendment, which became operative in March.

On May 14, Indian paramilitary forces, aided by units of the Indian army, moved into the Golden Temple complex in Amritsar to oust Sikh militants. The operation, called "Black Thunder," was reminiscent of the tragic "Operation Bluestar" in June 1984, in which several hundred people died. This time casualties were less than 50, mainly because

In mid-May, after militant Sikh separatists shot and wounded a district police chief, thousands of government troops surrounded the Golden Temple at Amritsar, the holiest Sikh shrine. The siege was lifted on May 18, after the remaining militants surrendered. At least 46 people were killed during the incident.

AP/Wide World

the Indian forces were ordered to exercise restraint and the Sikh militants were not as uncompromising as in 1984. On May 15 about 146 people, mostly Sikh extremists, surrendered, and a few days later the siege was lifted and the last 46 Sikh militants surrendered. But even as "Black Thunder" ended, Sikh extremists were killing scores of Hindus in various parts of Punjab, and the violence continued throughout 1988. On July 25 two influential moderate Sikh religious leaders were assassinated—Sohan Singh, head priest of the Golden Temple, and Bhan Singh, secretary of the committee which governed the gurdwaras (shrines).

On September 21, Prime Minister Gandhi visited Punjab for the first time in three years. Speaking to small communities, he appealed to moderate Sikhs to resist extremism, a counsel that terrorized moderates could accept only at great risk. Because of extraordinary security measures (his mother had been assassinated by her Sikh bodyguards in 1984), Gandhi was unable to speak to many Sikhs personally. His promise of economic incentives and hints of political concessions seemed to be quite inadequate. On the eve of his trip Gandhi announced the release of more than 130 of the approximately 350 people who had been imprisoned without trial after the Indian assault on the Golden Temple complex in 1984. But he did not defer to the demands of Sikh leaders, including moderates, for an immediate and impartial investigation of the anti-Sikh riots and killings in New Delhi and elsewhere that had followed Indira Gandhi's assassination.

On August 3 the Supreme Court of India upheld a lower court conviction of two of three Sikhs—Satwant Singh and Kehar Singh—who had been condemned to death for their role in Mrs. Gandhi's assassination, but overturned the death sentence of a third, Balbir Singh. On October 12 a district judge signed a warrant authorizing the hanging of Satwant Singh and Kehar Singh, which occurred early in 1989.

The Economy. In his address at the opening of the budget session of the Indian Parliament on February 22, President Venkataraman called attention to the economic consequences of "one of the worst climatic setbacks in memory, namely, the widespread drought in most parts of the country and the floods in the eastern region." Among the consequences were a shortfall of 7 to 10% in food-grain production, and a decline in foreign-exchange reserves. He pointed out, however, that in spite of these adverse conditions, imports in 1987–88 increased by 135% over the previous year and exports by 247%. Industrial production was greater than in the previous year, raising the overall growth rate to 2% in 1987–88. In most of these respects economic conditions were considerably better for the remainder of 1988, with the prospect of a growth rate of nearly 7% for the fiscal year ending on March 31, 1989.

The central budget for 1988–89, presented to the Parliament by Finance Minister N. D. Tiwari on February 29, envisioned outlays of approximately $22 billion, an increase of 17% over 1987–88, and an uncovered deficit of about $5.75 billion. Substantial increases in funds were projected for agriculture, water resources, rural development, transport and communications, fertilizer subsidies, and defense (the last to $10 billion).

Midterm assessments of the seventh Five Year Plan (1985–90) indicated that the average growth rate likely to be achieved would be 4.3 to 4.5%, a fairly impressive rate in view of the relative stagnation of agriculture during the first three years of the plan.

On May 23, Prime Minister Gandhi presided over a meeting of the Planning Commission, plus the finance, agricultural, and home ministers, to review the revised framework of

the eighth Five Year Plan (1990–95). Gandhi said that this plan would be employment-oriented, with emphasis on agricultural development and increased use of science and technology.

To achieve its economic objectives, India had no choice but to continue to rely on substantial external economic assistance. In May it was announced that India would receive a record amount of $3 billion from the World Bank and its soft-loan affiliate, the International Development Association, nearly $1 billion more than in 1987–88. In June the Aid India Consortium made a commitment of $6.3 billion to India for fiscal 1988–89, including $3.9 billion on concessional terms. This was an increase of 16% over 1987–88. In the same month, Japan announced an extension of its 28th Overseas Development Aid concessional loan to India, amounting to some $1 billion.

Foreign Policy. In spite of his preoccupation with internal and regional affairs, Rajiv Gandhi made a number of visits abroad in 1988 to Sweden, the United States, West Germany, Jordan, Turkey, Yugoslavia, Spain, and China.

During a November visit to India, Soviet leader Mikhail Gorbachev joined Prime Minister Gandhi in urging the United Nations to help establish a coalition government in Afghanistan and in signing an agreement for the USSR to build two nuclear reactors for an Indian power plant, to be financed largely by a Soviet loan.

India's relations with at least three of its South Asian neighbors often were strained. It continued to criticize Pakistan for alleged support of the Sikh extremists in Punjab, in the form of weapons, training, and other kinds of assistance. Documents seized from Sikh extremists when Indian forces moved into the Golden Temple complex in May were said to have provided concrete evidence of Pakistani support to Sikh guerrillas. Some Indians even went so far as to accuse Pakistan of mounting

a sustained campaign to destabilize India. The effects on Indo-Pakistan relations of such major developments as the beginning of Soviet withdrawal from Afghanistan, the death of Pakistani President Zia ul-Haq in a plane crash on August 17, and the creation of a civilian government under Benazir Bhutto in Pakistan after November 19 elections, were difficult to assess. As 1988 ended, Gandhi went to Pakistan to meet with Prime Minister Bhutto.

On official levels, India's relations with Sri Lanka remained close and cordial. Sri Lankan President Junius Jayewardene was welcomed warmly when he went to New Delhi in late January, but in both India and Sri Lanka there was continuing criticism of the presence of large numbers of Indian troops in Sri Lanka. The troops were there as a peacekeeping force charged with enforcing acceptance by Sri Lankan Tamils of the controversial Indo-Sri Lankan accord of July 1987. In this capacity they were to counter the armed resistance of the main Tamil extremist group, the Liberation Tigers of Tamil Eelam (LTTE). In June, India began a phased withdrawal of its forces. The Indian government welcomed President Jayewardene's efforts to draw more Sri Lankan Tamils into the political process by holding November elections to an integrated regional council in the Northern and Eastern provinces, where the majority of the Sri Lankan Tamils live.

In 1988, Bangladesh suffered from its worst floods of the century, with three fourths of the country partially submerged at one time. Many people in Bangladesh blamed India for the catastrophe, saying that India should have cooperated with neighboring countries in regulating the flow of the Ganges and the Brahmaputra rivers, which flow through Indian territory into Bangladesh. This delicate issue was discussed with high Indian officials by the president of Bangladesh, Lieut. Gen. H. M. Ershad, during a visit to New Delhi on September 29. Gandhi and other Indian officials told him that the issue should be dealt with bilaterally and not on a regional basis. They adhered to this position in spite of strong pressures for a regional solution. As a prominent Indian journalist wrote, "India fears other countries will gang up on it if it deals with the issue on a regional basis."

Indo-American relations improved considerably during the year, although Indians were still critical of U.S. relations with Pakistan, and especially of continued U.S. military assistance to that country. During a visit to India in April, U.S. Secretary of Defense Frank Carlucci confirmed reports that the United States was willing to cooperate in the field of high defense technology, and the secretary signed several specific agreements with Indian defense officials.

NORMAN D. PALMER, *Professor Emeritus*
University of Pennsylvania

INDIA • Information Highlights

Official Name: Republic of India.
Location: South Asia.
Area: 1,269,340 sq mi (3 287 590 km²).
Population (mid-1988 est.): 816,800,000.
Chief Cities (1981 census): New Delhi, the capital, 5,157,270; Bombay, 8,243,405; Calcutta, 3,283,148.
Government: *Head of state,* Ramaswami Venkataraman, president (took office July 25, 1987). *Head of government,* Rajiv Gandhi, prime minister (took office Oct. 31, 1984). *Legislature*—Parliament: Rajya Sabha (Council of States) and Lok Sabha (House of the People).
Monetary Unit: Rupee (14.99 rupees equal U.S.$1, Nov. 16, 1988).
Gross National Product (1987 U.S.$): $200,000,000,000.
Economic Indexes (1987): *Consumer Prices* (1980 = 100), all items, 184.4; food, 184.7. *Industrial Production* (1980 = 100), 159.
Foreign Trade (1987 U.S.$): *Imports,* $16,370,000,000; *exports,* $11,087,000,000.

INDIANA

Hoosier Republican J. Danforth Quayle's election as vice-president of the United States helped make 1988 a historic year in Indiana politics. Highway funding dominated debate in the General Assembly's short session, and severe drought headlined news stories during the year.

Election. Republicans and Democrats shared victories in the record-setting 1988 elections in Indiana, where voter turnout was higher than predicted. In the largest-ever margin of victory for a U.S. senator from Indiana, incumbent Republican Richard G. Lugar overwhelmed John F. Wickes, Jr., by more than 700,000 votes to become the state's first Republican senator to be elected to a third term since 1956. George Bush and Dan Quayle carried 88 of Indiana's 92 counties to defeat Democrats Michael Dukakis and Lloyd Bentsen by more than 400,000 votes. On December 12 outgoing Gov. Robert D. Orr named Dan Coats, a 45-year-old, four-term U.S. congressman, to fill Quayle's Senate seat until the 1990 elections. A special election would be held to fill the vacant House seat.

GOP Lt. Gov. John M. Mutz failed in his bid to continue his party's 20-year control of the governorship. As a result of massive ticket-splitting, Democratic Secretary of State B. Evan Bayh, the son of former Sen. Birch Bayh, became the state's third-youngest governor ever, carrying 69 of 92 counties by approximately 125,000 votes. Bayh's victory highlighted an apparent Democratic resurgence in the state over the last four years. Democrats reduced Republican control of the upper house of the state legislature to a two-vote margin and managed an unprecedented 50-50 Democratic-Republican split in the lower house. Democrats also retained six of Indiana's ten U.S. representative seats.

Statewide referenda on three constitutional propositions also produced mixed voting patterns. More than 60% of Hoosier voters approved the removal of a 137-year-old constitutional ban on state lotteries and other forms of gambling. Bitterly debated for almost a decade, the repeal returns the issue to the General Assembly where bills on a state lottery, casino gambling, and pari-mutuel betting were pending. Voters also agreed to a reduction in the number of criminal cases appealed directly to the Indiana State Supreme Court, thus decreasing the court's caseload. With traditional conservatism, however, voters refused to allow elected county officials to serve more than two consecutive terms.

Legislature. In a somewhat lackluster session that was overshadowed by the political campaign in Indiana, state legislators passed bills that raised workers' compensation benefits, provided information and imposed civil and criminal penalties to curb the spread of AIDS, and banned civil enforcement of surrogate mother contracts. Responding to an outcry from virtually all segments of the Hoosier population, the General Assembly also voted 98-1 and 50-0 to ban local measured service telephone rates for three years and approved measures to allow the use of state funds to pay for

AP/Wide World

Democrat Evan Bayh (right), Indiana's 33-year-old governor-elect, receives congratulations from his father, former Sen. Birch Bayh, and his half brother, Christopher.

INDIANA • Information Highlights

Area: 36,185 sq mi (93 720 km²).
Population (July 1, 1987): 5,531,000.
Chief Cities (July 1, 1986 est.): Indianapolis, the capital, 719,820; Fort Wayne, 172,900; Gary, 136,790.
Government (1988): *Chief Officers*—governor, Robert D. Orr (R); lt. gov., John M. Mutz (R). *General Assembly*—Senate, 50 members; House of Representatives, 100 members.
State Finances (fiscal year 1987): *Revenue,* $9,037,000,000; *expenditure,* $8,342,000,000.
Personal Income (1987): $76,961,000,000; per capita, $13,914.
Labor Force (June 1988): *Civilian labor force,* 2,828,100; *unemployed,* 129,000 (4.6% of total force).
Education: *Enrollment* (fall 1986)—public elementary schools, 653,613; public secondary, 313,167; colleges and universities, 250,185. *Public school expenditures* (1986–87), $2,978,000,000 ($3,379 per pupil).

indigent private-school students' textbooks and classroom fees. Also approved was the assessment of fees to telephone customers to pay for 911 emergency service. In a break with tradition, legislators enacted a law enabling the state to borrow money to pay for highway construction through the sale of bonds up to $300 million.

The Economy. In 1988, Indiana experienced its worst drought in 50 years. A record-breaking number of rain-free weeks and high temperatures caused heavy damage to the state's agricultural economy. Corn yields were down from 123 bushels per acre (50 bu per ha) in 1987 to 78 bushels (32 bu per ha) in 1988; soybean production dropped by 30% from the preceding year; and all 92 counties qualified for various federally funded disaster-relief programs.

The state's overall economy, however, continued to grow. With a gain of 80,000 new jobs during 1988, Indiana outpaced the nation in increased employment—with more than a 4% gain compared to 3% for the nation as a whole —and in growth in personal income.

Sports. During the summer, Indianapolis reaffirmed its position in the amateur sports world by hosting the U.S. Olympic trials in track and field, canoeing and kayaking, and diving.

LORNA LUTES SYLVESTER
Indiana University, Bloomington

INDONESIA

Amid concern over mounting foreign debt, Indonesia in 1988 continued economic reforms to lessen its heavy dependence on oil exports. President Suharto, running unopposed, was elected to a fifth consecutive term in March.

Economy. The World Bank projected Indonesia's external debt, the largest in Asia, at $50 billion for 1988–89 and more than $60 billion by the year 2000. The government estimated that debt service would consume 36.8% of its budget in 1988–89.

INDONESIA • Information Highlights

Official Name: Republic of Indonesia.
Location: Southeast Asia.
Area: 741,097 sq mi (1 919 440 km²).
Population (mid-1988 est.): 177,400,000.
Chief Cities (Dec. 31, 1983 est.): Jakarta, the capital, 7,347,800; Surabaya, 2,223,600; Medan, 1,805,500; Bandung, 1,566,700.
Government: *Head of state and government,* Suharto, president (took office for fifth five-year term March 1988). *Legislature* (unicameral)— House of Representatives.
Monetary Unit: Rupiah (1,706.0 rupiahs equal U.S.$1, Nov. 1, 1988).
Gross National Product (1987 U.S.$): $59,000,-000,000.
Economic Index (1987): *Consumer Prices* (1980 = 100), all items, 183.8; food, 180.
Foreign Trade (1986 U.S.$): *Imports,* $10,718,-000,000; *exports,* $14,805,000,000.

The 1988–89 budget loosened some of the spending restrictions imposed after the 1986 collapse in oil prices, and the government continued efforts to increase non-oil exports. Reforms introduced late in 1987 were designed to liberalize import and export procedures. In a sign that these and other reforms were taking hold, non-oil exports were expected to be up 40% in 1987–88. However, a drop in world oil prices during 1988 clouded the economic picture.

Politics. The People's Consultative Assembly, which meets every five years, elected Suharto to his fifth consecutive term on March 10 and then turned to the choice of a vice-president. The post holds little power, but it was thought that the person chosen eventually might succeed the 66-year-old leader. Sudharmono, Suharto's chief of staff, had the backing of the president and his Golkar coalition but was viewed coolly by the army. In an unusual move, Jailani Naro, the head of the small Muslim-based United Development Party, also stood as a candidate. In the end, Naro withdrew and Sudharmono was chosen by consensus.

Suharto made a number of changes in government before and after the election. Gen. Benny Murdani, widely viewed as the second most powerful person in the country, was replaced as head of the armed forces by Gen. Try Sutrisno in February. Murdani was named defense minister in a late March cabinet shuffle that retained 19 ministers and brought in 19 new ones. Named foreign minister was Ali Alatas, Indonesia's former ambassador to the United Nations. President Suharto also restructured several economic ministries to promote reform.

East Timor remained closed to journalists and other outsiders, as it had been since its annexation in 1976. A low-level insurgency there was said to be mostly under control.

Foreign Affairs. Indonesia and China reportedly were moving closer to normalizing diplomatic relations, frozen since the mid-1960s. Since 1985, China has provided a growing market for Indonesian exports, and it has urged that the two countries open trade offices in each other's capitals. However, obstacles remained. The initial chill developed over questions about China's role in a 1965 coup attempt, the crushing of which brought Suharto to power. Indonesia continued to insist that China apologize for its alleged involvement and meet other conditions. Another roadblock was Indonesia's support of Vietnam in its dispute with China over the Spratly Islands in the South China Sea. In March, China seized six atolls in the Spratlys, prompting Indonesian alarm.

U.S. Secretary of State George P. Shultz visited Indonesia in July.

ELAINE PASCOE, *Free-lance Writer*

INDUSTRIAL PRODUCTION

U.S. industrial output grew rapidly in 1988, thanks to strong capital investment at home and a revival of economic growth in major industrial countries.

Industrial production rose nearly 8% in Japan, almost 6% in Canada, and close to 3.5% in Western Europe. This was in sharp contrast with 1987, when growth in Japan was only 1.1% and in Europe, 1.9%.

In 1987–88, U.S. industrial production quickened its pace, posting a 5.4% gain for 1988 and 3.8% for 1987. Mining output rose nearly 3% after a 0.3% increase in 1987, but it still was 15% off the 1981 level. Utilities showed a 3.5% gain, double the 1987 increase. Manufacturing industries stepped up production by 5.8%, after a 4.3% gain in the preceding year. By comparison, manufacturing output had gained only a little more than 2% in 1985 and 1986.

Especially strong in the manufacturing sector was the nonelectrical group. All nonelectrical industries contributed to this group's 11.9% gain. Engine and farm equipment producers showed nearly a 15% gain; construction equipment production was up 13%; metalworking machinery and general industrial machinery makers raised output nearly 12%; and office and computing equipment producers registered an 11% gain.

In the electrical and electronic group, the stellar performance was the electronic component industry with an 11% gain. U.S. truck production rolled up a 6.7% gain to a record 4.1 million units in 1988, but car production edged down 0.9% to 7.1 million units. The popularity of vans, classified as trucks, accounted for the 4% gain registered in the Federal Reserve Board's index for the motor vehicle and parts industry.

There also were declines in the manufacturing sector, however. Basic chemicals were off nearly 2%, an exception within the strong chemical industry group. In the clay-stone-glass group, cement production was down by almost 4%, while leather and leather products continued its decline with a 2% loss in output.

While defense equipment production declined, a few segments improved on their 1987 records. Electronic equipment output increased by more than 3%, transmission equipment by nearly 2%, and the output of missiles, truck trailers, engineering instruments, and industrial trucks posted smaller gains. Tank production was cut back the most, by 18%.

Brisk demand from machinery makers and foreign customers pushed steel production to its highest point in years. After rising 9.2% in 1987, raw steel output in 1988 rose more than 13%, reaching 100 million tons. That claimed almost 90% of capacity, up from the 79.5% capacity utilization in 1987. The industry once again was profitable, thanks partly to quotas on steel imports that limited foreigners' share of the market to 20%. In fact, foreign steel claimed only 18% of the market.

While the dollar depreciation in 1987 boosted exports of manufactured goods by 11%, reviving economies in the industrialized countries helped step up the demand for U.S. manufactured products by 27% in 1988 to a total of some $250 billion. Exports of capital goods rose 28%, reflecting increases for aircraft, electrical and industrial machinery, power-generating machinery, and office and computing machinery. Consumer goods exports rose 30%. Even foreign manufacturers who had been producing in the United States for the U.S. market started to export. Among these were Honda, which shipped 6,000 cars to Japan; Toshiba, which began exporting projection televisions from its U.S. subsidiary; and Sharp Electronics, which shipped U.S.-made microwave ovens to Europe.

Employment and Productivity. Over the previous ten years U.S. manufacturing employment had declined by nearly 5%, reflecting in large part productivity gains that averaged 3% over the same period. Also contributing to the decline throughout the 1980s was the slow growth of manufacturing output: Gains averaged less than 2.5% annually. Manufacturing

U.S. Industrial Production			
	Percent Change 1986 to 1987	Index (1977 = 100) 1987 level	Percent Change 1987 to 1988
Total Production	3.8	129.8	5.4
Mining	0.3	100.7	2.9
Utilities	1.7	110.3	3.5
Manufacturing	4.3	134.7	5.8
Consumer Goods	3.0	127.8	4.2
Business Equipment	3.6	144.5	9.1
Defense and Space Equipment	3.8	188.9	−1.6
Durable Goods Manufacturing	3.7	133.1	6.4
Lumber and products	5.0	130.3	4.5
Furniture and fixtures	6.1	152.8	5.3
Clay, glass and stone products	0.7	119.1	2.1
Primary metals	8.7	81.2	9.4
Fabricated metal products	2.7	111.0	8.5
Nonelectrical machinery	5.3	152.7	11.9
Electrical machinery	4.0	172.3	4.8
Transportation equipment	1.3	129.2	2.0
Nondurable Goods Manufacturing	5.1	136.8	4.8
Foods	2.5	137.8	3.1
Tobacco products	6.7	103.5	0.2
Textile mill products	6.1	115.9	0
Apparel products	4.1	107.4	1.6
Paper and paper products	5.8	144.4	4.0
Printing and publishing	6.9	172.1	6.3
Chemicals and products	6.1	140.2	8.1
Petroleum and products	1.0	93.5	2.3
Rubber and plastic products	8.0	163.6	6.4
Leather and products	−2.3	60.0	−2.0
Source: Board of Governors of the Federal Reserve System			

output surged in 1983–84 as the economy recovered from the recession, and picked up again in the 1987–88 period as the dollar depreciated against other currencies and made U.S.-produced goods more competitive in domestic and world markets. With output rising faster than productivity, factory employment in 1988 managed a 2.4% increase to 19.5 million.

Mining. Mining output rose in 1988 as domestic crude oil production increased 4.5% to a rate of 8.7 million barrels a day. Coal mines stepped up output by 3.5% to 952 million tons. As for metal mining, copper mines delivered a 10% increase, and zinc and iron ore production also rose. Domestic mines raised iron ore output almost 21% in 1987 and 15% in 1988.

Construction. After slowing considerably in 1987, construction activity decreased slightly in 1988. Residential construction held up fairly well despite a 10% drop in housing starts that followed a similar decline in 1987. Housing starts totalled 1.46 million in 1988. Single-family home building remained relatively steady as it had for the past six years, with starts averaging more than 1 million. The big losses in housing starts were in apartment construction; apartment building starts dropped 17% in 1988.

Business construction was off by 1% from the 1987 pace. The only categories to show increases in 1988 were hospitals, miscellaneous buildings that include amusement and recreational structures, and, contrary to expectations, office construction. Disappointingly, industrial construction was off by 1.7%. Sharp drops were in hotels and motels, and educational facility construction.

Public construction declined fractionally, with large drops in conservation and development and military facilities. Construction of sewer systems and streets and highways were among the main props that buoyed public-sector construction in 1988.

Business Investment. After increasing investment 2.7% in 1987, U.S. business stepped up the pace of spending on new plants and equipment by 10% in 1988, bringing the total for the year to $429 billion. Manufacturing industries raised capital investment by nearly 12%, with primary metals producers leading with better than 20% increases. Electrical machinery manufacturers showed an 18% growth in investment for the year. Motor vehicle producers trimmed expenditures by 5.6% in 1988, after a 14.6% cutback in 1987. The aircraft industry increased investment by 2% in 1988, following a 6.7% drop in 1987. The durable goods sector showed a strong overall investment increase of 9% for 1988, compared with just 2.7% for 1987.

Employees on Nonagricultural Payrolls
(in thousands)

	1987	1988*	Percent Change
Good-producing industries	24,784	25,537	3.0
Mining	721	733	1.7
Construction	4,998	5,286	5.8
Manufacturing	19,065	19,518	2.4
Durable goods	11,218	11,502	2.5
Lumber and wood products	740	758	2.4
Furniture and fixtures	518	537	3.7
Stone, clay, and glass products	582	587	0.9
Primary metal industries	749	781	4.3
Fabricated metal products	1,407	1,452	3.2
Machinery, except electrical	2,023	2,133	5.4
Electric & electronic equip.	2,084	2,120	1.7
Transportation equipment	2,048	2,040	−0.4
Instruments & related products	696	712	2.3
Miscellaneous mfg. industries	370	383	3.5
Nondurable goods	7,847	8,017	2.2
Food and kindred products	1,624	1,645	1.3
Tobacco manufactures	54	53	−1.9
Textile mill products	724	726	0.3
Apparel & other textile goods	1,100	1,097	−0.3
Paper & allied products	679	689	1.5
Printing & publishing	1,507	1,562	3.6
Chemicals & allied products	1,026	1,062	3.5
Petroleum & coal products	165	167	1.2
Rubber & misc. plastics products	823	871	5.8
Leather & leather products	144	146	1.4

*Preliminary
Source: Bureau of Labor Statistics

Value of New Construction Put in Place in the United States
(Billions of 1982 dollars)

	1987	1988*	Percent Change
Total new construction	349.0	345.9	−0.9
Private construction	283.0	280.0	−1.1
Residential buildings	171.3	171.2	−0.1
Nonresidential buildings	78.2	77.4	−1.0
Industrial	11.6	11.4	−1.7
Office	22.5	22.9	1.8
Hotels and motels	6.3	5.5	−12.7
Other commercial	24.7	23.6	−4.5
Religious	2.6	2.4	−7.7
Educational	2.9	2.3	−20.7
Hospital and institutional	5.1	5.9	15.7
Miscellaneous buildings[1]	2.5	3.4	36.0
Telephone and telegraph	2.6	7.0	−7.9
All other private[2]	2.4	1.7	−29.2
Public construction	66.0	65.9	−0.2
Housing and redevelopment	1.3	1.3	0
Industrial	1.2	1.2	0
Educational	7.5	8.8	17.3
Hospital	1.9	1.9	0
Other public buildings[3]	9.5	9.4	−1.1
Highways and streets	19.8	20.9	5.6
Military facilities	3.7	3.3	−10.8
Conservation and development	4.8	4.2	−12.5
Sewer systems	8.3	9.4	13.2
Water supply facilities	3.3	3.3	0
Miscellaneous public[4]	4.7	4.1	−12.8

Source: Bureau of the Census   * preliminary
[1] Includes amusement and recreational buildings, bus and airline terminals, animal hospitals, and shelters, etc. [2] Includes privately owned streets and bridges, parking areas, sewer and water facilities, parks and playgrounds, golf courses, airfields, etc. [3] Includes general administrative buildings, prisons, police and fire stations, courthouses, civic centers, passenger terminals, postal facilities. [4] Includes open amusement and recreational facilities, power generating facilities, transit systems, airfields, open parking facilities, etc.

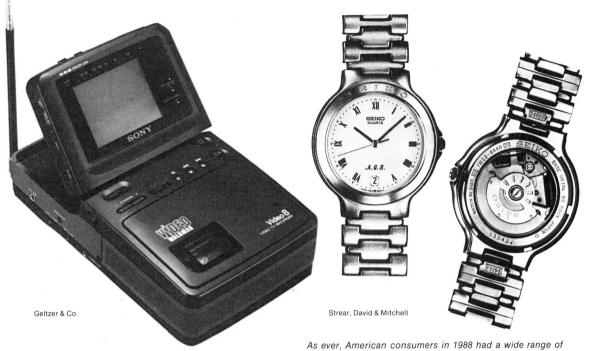

Geltzer & Co.

Strear, David & Mitchell

As ever, American consumers in 1988 had a wide range of new products to choose from. Sony introduced the Video Walkman, above left, a 2.5-lb (1.1-kg) portable 8-mm VCR and color TV. Seiko brought out the first automatic self-generating quartz watch, above, which eliminates the need for a battery or winding. And from Australia came the long-armed Universal shower head, left.

Gemini Distributors

The paper industry posted the largest investment increase—25%—in the nondurable goods group. Food followed with a 15% hike, and chemicals producers raised their capital expenditures by 12% in 1988. The increase for nondurable goods producers came to 14%, after a modest 1.8% growth posted for 1987.

Capital spending in other sectors also rose in 1988. Railroads showed an 18% gain, after cutting back 11% in 1987. Airlines invested almost 16% more than in 1987, when they posted

a 4% increase. Mining industry outlays were up almost 10%. Even public utilities showed a gain of 3%, reversing a like spending drop in 1987. Capital spending by the trade and services sector rose 9% in 1988, compared with 2.9% in the previous year.

International Production. Spurred by strong export growth, capital investment, and healthy consumer demand, U.S. production at year's end was 5.1% higher than at the end of 1987. Production growth for most other industrial countries was also strong, with a 9.2% gain registered for Japan, 8.0% for Australia, 6.9% for Italy, 5.7% for Switzerland, 5.4% for France, 5.1% for Canada, 3.8% for the United Kingdom, 3.6% for West Germany, 2.6% for Belgium, 1.8% for Spain, and 0.9% for the Netherlands. Sweden showed a 1.1% decline in its industrial production between year's end 1987 and year's end 1988.

Industrial output in the Soviet Union slowed considerably as the introduction of stricter quality-control requirements compounded difficulties posed by interruptions of raw material supplies and transportation bottlenecks. The disaster at Chernobyl in 1986, not to mention the catastrophic earthquake in Armenia in December 1988, placed extra demands on resources that otherwise could have been used to modernize industry. Estimates put the increase in industrial output at 1.5% for 1987 compared with a 2.5% gain in 1986. The output

Industrial Production: International Overview 1980 = 100						
	1982	1983	1984	1985	1986	1987	1988*
Industrial Countries	97	99	106	109	111	114	119
Australia	98	92	99	103	108	104	106
Austria	98	98	104	109	110	110	108
Belgium	98	99	102	104	105	107	109
Canada	90	95	104	108	110	115	122
Denmark	102	106	117	122	128	123	126
Finland	104	107	111	116	117	122	126
France	98	99	100	101	102	104	107
Germany	94	95	98	102	104	104	107
Ireland	104	112	124	127	131	146	156
Italy	95	92	95	97	99	103	106
Japan	101	105	115	119	119	123	132
Luxembourg	95	100	114	121	125	125	124
Netherlands	94	97	101	105	106	107	106
Norway	99	108	117	111	126	134	141
Spain	98	101	102	104	107	111	115
Sweden	97	101	109	111	111	116	117
Switzerland	94	94	98	102	107	107	N/A
United Kingdom	98	102	103	108	110	114	117
United States	95	101	112	115	114	120	126

Source: International Monetary Fund
*Preliminary Estimate

gain for 1988 was estimated not to be much better than in the preceding year.

Introduction of increasingly productive machinery and equipment is the key to a long-lasting improvement in the Soviet economy, according to General Secretary Mikhail Gorbachev. Thus, it was disappointing that in 1987 the machine-building sector—the key to modernization plans—registered no increase in output. This led to a shortfall in equipment for investment, resulting in a failure to meet production plans in major industries such as metals and chemicals. And production difficulties plagued the Soviet bloc in general. According to Soviet estimates, industrial output in the Eastern bloc countries increased at an average rate of 3.5% in the 1981–87 timespan.

AGO AMBRE
U.S. Department of Commerce

INSURANCE, LIABILITY

The liability crisis that plagued U.S. businesses, professionals, and municipal governments in the mid-1980s continued to ease in 1988. Many policyholders who had been denied coverage or priced out of the market several years before once again were able to buy protection from lawsuits.

But even as the nation's 3,555 property-casualty insurers emerged from their most recent cyclical depression, there were signs that the 1985–86 crisis had left permanent scars on the liability system. Orthopedic surgeons and obstetricians in many parts of the country still found it hard to obtain medical-malpractice coverage. Manufacturers refrained from making potentially harmful drugs or other products for fear of losing their product-liability coverage. Day-care centers discovered that their policies were less extensive than they had been before the crisis. And affordability was still a problem, as premium rates remained high.

For these reasons, the heated debate that has pitted liability insurers and their policyholders against consumers and their advocates continued in 1988. The insurers blamed the nation's system of tort law, the branch of the legal system that allows individuals to be compensated for damages caused by another's wrongful acts. They said that the lure of huge jury awards encouraged consumers and lawyers, who received a percentage of the final award, to sue for damages. On the other hand, lawyers and consumer advocates blamed the insurers for the lack of adequate and affordable liability coverage, the result, they said, of the industry's financial mismanagement.

In 1988, lawmakers sought in vain to change the liability system in ways that would satisfy both sides of the debate. A proposal that would have established the country's first product-liability law fell victim to intense opposition by trial lawyers and consumers. For their part, the insurers succeeded in killing a proposal to limit the industry's exemption from antitrust laws, a concession it enjoyed because of the need to pool nationwide actuarial data to set premium rates.

But while efforts to reform the liability system foundered on the federal level, sweeping changes were made by the states. By October, all but eight states had made changes in tort law, such as caps on awards for "pain and suffering" and penalties for filing frivolous lawsuits. Two states—California and Alaska—passed insurance referendums in the November 8 election. The California referendum would roll back insurance rates by 20% for property and casualty insurance; it passed by a narrow margin and immediately was challenged in court by the insurance industry. The Alaska referendum, which would restrict the amount of damages that could be collected in a civil suit, passed by a wide margin.

Meanwhile, the outcome of several liability cases during 1988 seemed destined to have an important impact on the issue. The tobacco industry for the first time in history was found partially liable for the death of a smoker. The June 13 decision against Liggett Group Inc. appeared likely to produce a wave of "smoker liability" litigation. There also was action in another landmark case, involving A.H. Robins Co., maker of the Dalkon Shield, a defective birth-control device. In October, some of the more than 200,000 women injured by the shield began to receive compensation. And late in the year, the U.S. Supreme Court agreed to rule on the constitutionality of punitive damages, which insurers said violate the 8th Amendment's prohibition against excessive fines. If the high court were to accept this argument, it would hand the insurance industry its most important victory to date.

MARY H. COOPER
"Editorial Research Reports"

The American country style, with an emphasis on such items as quilts, rag rugs, and collectibles, remains extremely popular in decorating circles throughout the United States.

© Hedrich Blessing

INTERIOR DESIGN

Interior decorating, a profession that is only a century old, keeps taking on more and more characteristics of the older world of fashion. Leading decorators are now media celebrities and the field's fads and foibles are part of the news.

Two strong, dissimilar trends that have been apparent for at least a decade dominated U.S. interior design in 1988. These were: old-world opulence for the wealthy in East coast cities, especially New York, and the American country style, popular throughout the nation with people of all economic classes.

Blair House. Nevertheless, many U.S. design aficionados regarded the June 1988 reopening of the deeply traditional Blair House, the national guest house for distinguished visitors in Washington, DC, as the decorating event of the year. Located across the street from the White House, this complex of townhouse buildings underwent a major architectural restoration and redecoration. Under the direction of Chief of Protocol Selwa Roosevelt and Curator Clement Conger, the eminent decorators Mario Buatta and Mark Hampton shared the job of furnishing some 50 major rooms; each was in full charge of half that number.

They created in Blair House a showcase of late 18th- and early 19th-century Anglo-American decoration. It is the stuff of which Winterthur Museum in Winterthur, DE, Colonial Williamsburg in Virginia, and countless house museums and art-museum period rooms are made. It is also the stylistic basis of much of the residential work that Hampton, Buatta, and many of the nation's other top designers do.

To many Americans, the style of Blair House is the only way in which to decorate; however, the supply of Georgian and Federal furniture gets scarcer and pricier each year. The small but highly visible core of decorating clients whose homes fill the coffee-table magazines has begun to turn to later, more opulent 19th-century styles. Favored are William IV, Beidermeier, and other neoclassical styles, as well as exotic revival styles including Jacobean, Rococo, Moorish, and Egyptian. Accompanying this florid furniture are rich textiles, layered window treatments, and patterned walls and floors, just as in Victorian days.

The Country Style. At the opposite design pole is American country style, a look that seems so natural and suitable that it is surprising Americans did not decorate this way always. The look has proliferated in the past ten or 15 years, fueled by the U.S. bicentennial, and is based less on real farmhouses than on farmhouses in books and movies.

American country breaks down clearly into three subgroups. One is sweet and pretty with flowery cotton fabrics and rugs and white-painted wicker. Another is lean and contemporary, incorporating a few strong elements of American folk art. The third aims for a quaint old-time effect using dark calicos and golden oak furniture and a clutter of "collectibles," such as trivets and hand tools. Old decoys, hooked and rag rugs, and quilts appear in all three modes.

American country style can be achieved on any budget and often is done successfully by amateurs. This benefit, along with an intrinsic aura of homines, helps to account for the lasting appeal of the look. Many design watchers think American country decorating will not peak for many years to come.

ELAINE GREENE
Free-lance Design Reporter

INTERNATIONAL TRADE AND FINANCE

As 1987 drew to a close, a group of 33 economists from 13 countries, assembled by the Institute for International Economics in Washington, issued a warning that there is still "something seriously wrong with the world economy." Stock markets had crashed around the globe on Oct. 19, 1987. Earlier that year, bond prices had nose-dived. And the twin deficits in the United States, those of the federal budget and international payments, remained massive. Economists and the financial community were nervous.

But the economy did not collapse. Nor did the financial system unravel or the U.S. dollar plummet on the foreign-exchange markets. And so, as 1988 progressed, everyone heaved a collective sigh of relief, and the world economy marched forward. As the International Monetary Fund (IMF) put it in an October 1988 publication, "The performance of the world economy in the past two or three quarters has been considerably more satisfactory than was expected. . . . Output in the industrial countries has grown strongly, world trade has been robust, and inflation appears to have remained under control."

International Economic Coordination. The scare in the securities markets actually may have done some good. It certainly brought stock prices down to levels which many analysts considered more realistic by such measures as the ratio of stock prices to corporate earnings. The fright also prompted the Group

of Seven industrial democracies (the United States, Japan, West Germany, France, Great Britain, Canada, and Italy) to lay aside their squabbles and agree on measures to prevent a slump. West Germany and six other European central banks joined in cutting key interest rates on Dec. 3, 1987, a move designed to strengthen the U.S. dollar. Just before Christmas they united in a statement declaring that the dollar had fallen far enough and implying that they would intervene in the currency markets to keep it from dipping much further. Early in 1988 they made their point by driving up the dollar on the foreign-exchange markets with massive interventions. But there were no sweeping policy changes that would help erase the huge U.S. trade deficit.

The Group of Seven's concerted efforts helped keep the dollar reasonably stable during the winter. In June the seven heads of government met in Toronto for their annual economic summit, and the get-together was relatively cheery. The West German economy had pepped up. The Japanese balance of payments surplus had fallen somewhat. And the U.S. merchandise-trade deficit showed a favorable trend. Less upbeat was a surge in commodity prices that raised the risk of higher inflation.

Generally, there was less cause for the seven presidents and prime ministers to be critical of one another. Among other things, this summit was notable for the absence of "Japan-bashing." The leaders of the other six nations did not take verbal pokes at Japan's economic behavior. After all, the Japanese economy was booming. Domestic demand for goods and ser-

In Long Beach, CA, August 23, President Ronald Reagan signed the Omnibus Trade and Competitiveness Act of 1988. Members of California's congressional delegation (l–r)—Sen. Pete Wilson, Rep. Glenn Anderson, and Sen. Alan Cranston—joined U.S. Trade Representative Clayton Yeutter at the ceremony. The legislation is intended to end unfair foreign trade practices.

vices had risen dramatically, drawing in more imports. The Japanese had removed many government nontariff barriers to trade, though business sometimes still colluded to keep out foreign competition. And further, Japan announced measures to double foreign aid over the next five years. "The Japanese have a growing sense that Japan should play a greater role in affairs outside of Japan," said Michihiko Kunihiro, the chief cabinet counselor on external affairs.

Japan's movement to center stage at the summit was mostly welcome. However, the United States was not keen on a new proposal by Japanese Finance Minister Kiichi Miyazawa for relieving the international debt burden of the "middle-income" nations, such as Brazil and Mexico. The plan called for debtors to transfer some currency reserves into an IMF account that would be used to repay bank loans. With this assurance of repayment, banks then would negotiate with each debtor to turn parts of its debt into securities and to reschedule other parts. The United States opposed the plan because it did not entirely square with the initiative proposed in 1985 by then U.S. Treasury Secretary James A. Baker III.

The finance ministers at the summit did work out a deal to provide poor nations in sub-Saharan Africa with some form of debt relief. They assigned the task of working out details to the Paris Club, a group of the major creditor countries that deals with government-owned debts. Under the plan, some countries simply may forgive debts. Others may reduce interest rates or stretch out payments. Or a nation could offer a mix of all three techniques.

The Group of Seven was less successful in tackling the question of farm subsidies. The United States, which at one time hoped for the elimination of such subsidies, sought a strong statement from the Group of Seven to prod negotiators in the latest talks aimed at reducing trade barriers, being held under the aegis of the General Agreement on Tariffs and Trade (GATT). But the European Community and Japan, where farmers have strong political clout, maintained that farm subsidies should be reduced only slowly. The issue was taken up again at the midterm review of the GATT negotiations in Montreal in early December. Participants were able to settle on negotiating outlines for ten of 15 topics and an actual package of trade concessions on tropical products. However, the United States and the community deadlocked on agriculture again. It was agreed that further talks would be delayed until April 1989 in Geneva.

In Washington, three years of political wrangling on Capitol Hill over trade ended on August 23, when President Reagan signed into law the Omnibus Trade and Competitiveness Act of 1988. The legislation was intended to help restore U.S. economic competitiveness and to end unfair foreign-trade practices. During the long legislative process, the bill was stripped of most of the strong protectionist measures in the original House and Senate versions. Nonetheless, business executives and others abroad still were concerned that the new law could lead to a more restrictive U.S. trade policy. Although certain provisions require a tougher White House trade stance, most have loopholes that will allow the president or the U.S. trade representative to avoid taking action. If, for example, it is decided that retaliation against unfair foreign trade practices would hurt national security or that the costs of protecting domestic industry from full import competition outweigh the benefits, then no action is required.

The joint annual meeting of the IMF and the World Bank in West Berlin in late September turned out to be something of a "nonevent," but for street demonstrations by leftist and other groups. With the U.S. facing an election in November and sending to Berlin a new treasury secretary, Nicholas F. Brady, no major decisions were expected and none were made. The finance ministers and central bankers of the key industrial nations talked happily about the healthy status of the world economy and proclaimed that the current exchange level of the U.S. dollar—which had risen during the summer—was about right in relation to the West German mark and the Japanese yen. Despite such talk, the dollar weakened once again after the election of George Bush as president. On the day before Thanksgiving, the dollar could be bought in New York for 121.03 yen, a 40-year low. The Bank of Japan and other central banks intervened heavily to support the dollar, but it continued to slip on foreign-exchange markets.

World Debt. A major topic for discussion in West Berlin was the $1.2 trillion in developing country debts. Many of these countries were suffering from what was termed "debtor fatigue." They were fed up with servicing their debts, arguing that the payments were restraining severely domestic growth. The United States and other industrial countries earlier had agreed to a $75 billion increase in the capitalization of the World Bank, which would enable it to step up its loans to developing countries. However, the United States especially opposed any plan for debt relief that would cost its treasury any money. It preferred sticking with the Baker initiative, which calls for economic reform in debtor countries, supported by $20 billion in new loans from commercial banks and additional sums from multilateral agencies to promote economic growth. However, the commercial banks generally were making no more extra loans than required under rescheduling agreements. In fact, the banks overall reduced the amount of credit risk outstanding with developing countries.

In 1987 the debtor nations, ranging from extremely poor to middle-income nations, paid some $29 billion more in interest and principal payments to wealthy industrial nations than they received in new investment, loans, and foreign aid. That trend continued in 1988. Aware of such trends, the managing director of the IMF, Michel Camdessus, was critical of the U.S.-dominated management of the debt crises, and numerous private economists proposed alternate measures for trimming the debt burden of the developing countries.

The latest figures, for 1987, showed that the well-to-do countries contributed $41 billion in foreign aid to the poorer countries. Making allowances for inflation and changes in the foreign-exchange rate of the dollar, this represented a decline of 2% from 1986. Total resource flows to developed countries reached $84 billion in 1987, versus $82 billion in 1986; this corresponded to an apparent decline in real terms of about 10%. But if large prepayments of bank debt by South Korea and heavy short-term inflows of private funds to Taiwan were taken into account, the resource flow to the poor countries showed a slight increase in real terms in 1987.

By the end of 1988, the total external debt of the developing countries reached about $1.18 trillion. That compared with a figure of just $602 billion in 1980. For the same countries, the ratio of debt-service charges to exports of goods and services stood at 155% as of Sept. 30, 1988; that compared with 114% in 1980 and a peak of 185% in 1986. Thus, while there has been some improvement in the ability of the developing nations to service their debts, there also appears to be a greater reluctance to do so.

A study by the Organization for Economic Cooperation and Development (OECD), looking at the problems of the middle-income Latin American debtors, commented: ". . . a renewed effort is needed by debtors, creditors, and official agencies to identify how the growth process can be restarted." Countries such as Brazil, Argentina, and Mexico still suffered from huge budget deficits, financed partially by the creation of new money that soon produces extreme inflation.

One interesting development in 1988 was the increasing use of various techniques for reducing the debt, such as swapping debt for equity (or other stakes) in local businesses. Such swaps have cut more than $6 billion from Brazil's $121 billion foreign debt. Altogether, such schemes may have wiped $15 billion to $20 billion in loans off commercial bank ledgers since 1985.

Camdessus, at the IMF gathering in West Berlin, also called for a greater IMF role in the international coordination of currency exchange rates, a job now handled by the Group of Seven. He even talked of the dollar being replaced in some degree as the world's leading reserve currency by Special Drawing Rights, a bookkeeping currency maintained by the IMF for transactions among governments or with the IMF.

The Japanese again broached their plan for debt relief, and it got nowhere. The U.S. influence in the World Bank was shown when its president, Barber Conable, recommended $1.25 billion in new loans for Argentina before an economic adjustment program had been negotiated with the IMF. By the usual practice, the IMF takes the leading role in working out such a program with a debtor nation. However, James Baker, at that time campaign manager for Vice-President Bush, gave Conable the go-ahead.

With its own international-payments deficit, the United States slid further into debt. At midyear 1988, the total financial assets which foreigners held in the United States exceeded their total liabilities to the United States by a record $537 billion. That represented a net increase of $579 billion in foreigners' holdings of U.S. financial assets in four-and-a-half years. Foreigners were buying up real property at a strong $53.6 billion annual rate in the second quarter. The most spectacular development in the first half of 1988, however, was the fact that foreign investors added $47.6 billion to their holdings of U.S. government securities, or nearly 78% of the $61.2 billion total increase in such securities during that period. For the most part, those purchases were made by foreign central banks, who bought dollars on the foreign exchange markets and invested them in U.S. government securities.

Production and Trade. The world output of goods and services, according to IMF estimates, grew about 3.8% in 1988. In the United States, still the world's most powerful economy, growth slowed during the 1st quarter of 1988, but economists still were expecting a gain in national output of about 4% in real terms for the year. Even West Germany, which had been criticized widely in 1987 for its reluctance to stimulate its economy further, enjoyed growth of about 3.5%. Great Britain was booming— about 4% real growth. The Japanese economy expanded by about 5.5%. Helped by higher commodity prices, Canada and Australia enjoyed increases in national output of 4–5%. The growth rate of the newly industrializing countries of East Asia (South Korea, Taiwan, Hong Kong, and Singapore) ran about 8–9%. Some of the small Latin American economies, such as Chile and Colombia, experienced rapid growth. But the "big three" Latin nations (Mexico, Brazil, and Argentina), hit by lower oil prices, domestic economic mismanagement, and the lingering impact of the debt crisis, contracted by 1–2%.

One of the important economic events of 1988 was the free-trade agreement between

Canada and the United States. Signed on Jan. 2, 1988, by President Reagan and Prime Minister Brian Mulroney, the accord will eliminate, over a ten-year period, tariffs and many other trade barriers between the two nations. In the United States the implementing legislation was passed by Congress, and signed into law by President Reagan on September 28.

In Canada the bill was passed easily by the House of Commons, where Mulroney's Progressive Conservative Party had a huge majority. But John Turner, the leader of the opposition Liberal Party, asked that the Senate (whose members are appointed and where the Liberals had a majority) hold up the legislation until the people of Canada had an opportunity to express their opinion. After several weeks and an improvement in the outlook for the Tories in public-opinion polls, Prime Minister Mulroney called an election for November 21. The Liberals and a third party, the left-of-center New Democratic Party, made their opposition to free trade the heart of the campaign. Public opinion seemed to fluctuate, but when the votes were counted the Conservatives had won. After the election, Turner promised that he no longer would use the Senate to block the free-trade bill.

Canadian tariffs on dutiable imports from the United States were averaging 9.9%, whereas U.S. tariffs on dutiable imports from Canada were averaging 3.3%. Some tariffs were so high as to prohibit or discourage trade across the border, but bilateral trade between the two nations was still the largest in the world —about $150 billion. Under the free-trade agreement, some tariffs were to be removed completely at the start of 1989. A second group of tariffs were to be reduced at a 20% annual rate over five years. And a third group of tariffs, on the products of more sensitive industries, were to come down at a 10% rate over ten years. The agreement also removed various obstacles to commerce in the service, energy, liquor, and agriculture industries. Economists predicted that free trade, creating a continental market of 272 million people, will boost national output in the United States by 1% and in Canada by 3%. It also was expected to add thousands of jobs in both countries, as well as to make industry more competitive.

But the agreement raised concerns that the world could be splitting into continental trading blocs—those of North America, Europe, and East Asia. President-elect Bush spoke of the need for a special trade deal with Mexico, which further would accentuate economic "continentalism." Many world leaders were keen to see the latest round of GATT talks succeed and trim trade barriers for all of its 96 contracting parties.

According to a study by GATT, the volume of world merchandise trade expanded by 5% in 1987 and was growing by about the same rate in 1988. That was well above the rate of growth in the two preceding years, putting the volume of world trade at least one quarter higher than in the recession year of 1982. The value of world merchandise exports increased by 16.5% in 1987 to $2.475 trillion. The most dynamic category of trade in 1987, and apparently 1988, was manufactured goods.

Stocks and Bonds. The world's stock markets did pretty well in 1988. From Dec. 31, 1987, to Nov. 30, 1988, stock prices in the United States (Dow Jones industrial average) were up 11.85%. In the United Kingdom, the gain was 3.89%; West Germany 29.32%; France 48.06%; Canada 7.28%; Australia 12.61%; Switzerland 25.94%; Japan 39.86%; Italy 21.9%; Singapore 26.17%; and Hong Kong 16.71%.

Despite the October 1987 crash, the Dow Jones industrial average produced a 16% (11% in real terms) average annual compound rate in total investment return during the Reagan years, 1981–88. The bond market's 11% real rate of total return for the same years was the highest of any presidency since Warren Harding's.

All in all, the world economy in 1988 provided some good cheer. But debts—domestic and foreign in the United States and the external debts of the developing countries—prompted a steady flow of worrying words from economists.

See also EUROPE; STOCKS AND BONDS; UNITED STATES—*The Economy.*

DAVID R. FRANCIS
"The Christian Science Monitor"

IOWA

For the first time in 24 years the Democrats gained Iowa's electoral vote in 1988. The popular vote was 55% for Michael Dukakis, and 45% for George Bush.

There was no race for governor or the U.S. Senate. In the U.S. congressional delegation races, all incumbents—James Leach (R) in the 1st District; Tom Tauke (R) in the 2nd; Dave Nagle (D) in the 3rd; Neal Smith (D) in the 4th; Jim Lightfoot (R) in the 5th; and Fred Grandy (R) in the 6th—were reelected. Neal Smith, Iowa's senior congressman, was returned for a 16th term, with 72% of the vote.

The Democrats retained control of the Iowa General Assembly. Of the 150 seats, 25 in the Senate and all 100 in the House were on the ballot, but 26 positions were uncontested. The Democratic margin in the Senate in 1989 would be 30 to 20. In the House, Democrats would hold 61 seats to 39 for the Republicans.

Politics and Government. The Iowa General Assembly in 1988 was again in the hands of the Democrats, while Republican Terry Branstad continued in his second term as governor.

IOWA • Information Highlights

Area: 56,275 sq mi (145 753 km²).
Population (July 1, 1987): 2,834,000.
Chief Cities (July 1, 1986 est.): Des Moines, the capital, 192,060; Cedar Rapids, 108,390; Davenport (July 1, 1984 est.), 102,129.
Government (1988): *Chief Officers*—governor, Terry E. Branstad (R); lt. gov., Jo Ann Zimmerman (D). *General Assembly*—Senate, 50 members; House of Representatives, 100 members.
State Finances (fiscal year 1987): *Revenue,* $5,481,000,000; *expenditure,* $5,075,000,000.
Personal Income (1987): $40,348,000,000; per capita, $14,236.
Labor Force (June 1988): *Civilian labor force,* 1,501,100; *unemployed,* 61,000 (4.1% of total force).
Education: *Enrollment* (fall 1986)—public elementary schools, 323,536; public secondary, 157,750; colleges and universities, 155,369. *Public school expenditures* (1986–87), $1,679,000,000 ($3,740 per pupil).

Nevertheless, the legislative session was marked by a spirit of cooperation between the Democratic-controlled House and Senate, and the Republican governor's office.

The major accomplishments of the session included: no increase in the sales or income taxes, but higher taxes on cigarettes and tobacco, as well as gasoline. These increases were signed into law by Governor Branstad. The temporary income-tax reform was made permanent. The legislature did restore a portion of the $25 million to the social welfare program that had been item vetoed by the governor.

Agriculture and the Economy. The summer of 1988 was the driest in Iowa since the dust bowl years of the 1930s. As a direct result of the drought, the corn and soybean harvests in Iowa were reduced drastically. Corn production was 37% below that of 1987 for a total of 811 million bushels, 78 bushels per acre. Soybean production totaled 228 million bushels, an average of 29 bushels per acre.

The Iowa economy in 1988 ran well ahead of 1987 in several areas. All economic indicators demonstrated significant improvement for the second year in a row. Much of the increase took place outside the Des Moines area, unlike the situation in 1987. The unemployment rate in Iowa declined in 1988, reaching a low of just under 4%. Meanwhile the state's population continued to decline, but at a slightly slower rate than in the previous two years.

Education. The SAT and ACT scores of Iowa high-school students ranked first in the nation. Minimum teacher salaries in Iowa were just above $18,000, but the average for Iowa teachers was still about 35th in the nation.

The Iowa Board of Regents, after a nationwide search, appointed Hunter Rawlings III president of the University of Iowa. Tuition at the three state-supported universities was increased by an average of more than 10%.

RUSSELL M. ROSS, *University of Iowa*

IRAN

For Iran 1988 brought significant internal political changes, and a cease-fire in the long and destructive Gulf War with Iraq. (*See* page 289.)

In July, Iran's leader, Ayatollah Ruhollah Khomeini, who long had sworn to fight on until Iraq was defeated, suddenly agreed to a UN-sponsored cessation of hostilities. This was not the only surprise of the year. In January the militant Khomeini had conceded that on occasion religious dogma might have to give way to other considerations. In September he was ordering the importation and sale of consumer goods and saying, "People should be free to run businesses."

Political Changes. Apparently with the Ayatollah's approval, the country was coming under the control of a triumvirate with no official character or constitutional name, consisting of the Ayatollah's 42-year-old son, Ahmad Khomeini, President Ali Khamenei and the speaker of the *Majlis* (parliament), Ali Akbar Hashemi Rafsanjani, who is the strongest of the three. These men were all, at least in the Iranian context, "moderates;" their rise weakened the power of Premier Mir Hosein Musavi-Khamenei and (to some extent) of Hosein Ali Montazeri, Khomeini's designated successor.

Iran's aging leader, the Ayatollah Khomeini, votes in May parliamentary elections. Power began shifting to three younger "moderates," including his son, Ahmad (right).

AP/Wide World

The Gulf War

An August 1988 cease-fire between Iran and Iraq seemed to signal an end to the eight-year Gulf War (although a peace treaty had yet to be arranged by the close of the year). A year earlier, in August 1987, the UN Security Council had passed Resolution 598 calling for a cease-fire, but though Iraq promptly had accepted (it had been trying to end the war since 1982), the Iranian response was evasive and conditional. So in January 1988 it seemed likely that the conflict would drag on indefinitely. Western analysts had coined the maxim "Iraq cannot win and Iran cannot lose." Indeed, neither happened—each side held approximately the same territory in 1988 as it had held in September 1980.

The year began with land warfare still in progress, as was the "tanker war" in the Gulf. In December 1987 there were 34 attacks on commercial shipping, making it the worst month since the tanker war began in 1984. The total number of attacks for 1987 was 187—71 more than in 1986—making 1987 the worst year.

In late December 1987 and in January 1988, Syria's Foreign Minister Farouk al-Shara toured the Gulf states and shuttled between Damascus and Tehran in a mediation effort that proved fruitless, and clearly was unwelcome to Iraq.

Iranian Difficulties. However, the war was placing an increasing strain on Iranian resources. Toward the end of 1987, Iranian President Ali Khamenei proclaimed a so-called "financial *jihad*"—in plainer terms, a semivoluntary levy on wealthier Iranians. In January it appeared that it was not proving possible to mobilize sufficient volunteers for the long-heralded final attack on Basra; by February any major Iranian offensive was manifestly no longer in the cards. Indeed, by this time Iraq had more men under arms than Iran—an extraordinary achievement, Iran's population being three times larger. Two small attacks on Basra in March and April were repulsed easily. Iran, which at the time still held some Iraqi territory, would have done much better to accept a cease-fire at that point, rather than six months later.

Recapture of Faw. The most striking military event of the spring was the recapture by Iraq on April 18 of its southern oil port of Faw (or Fao) which Iran had taken two years previously. Faw was defended only lightly by second-string troops. Though the retaking of this unusable port was not a costly victory, it may

have been the last straw, in conjunction with other setbacks in April, that convinced the Ayatollah's key advisers that a cease-fire was unavoidable. Iraq had another success at Fish Lake, near Basra, in May, and an overwhelming victory at Majnoun Island on June 25 which liberated the last important piece of southern Iraqi territory in Iranian hands.

Central and Northern Fronts. Iranian rebel forces of the *mujahidin,* based in Iraq and supported by Iraqi troops, advanced into Iran on June 19 and seized the largely deserted town of Mehran. They held it for several days before withdrawing to Iraq. On the northern front, Iranian Revolutionary Guards, supported by Kurdish guerrillas, captured the towns of Khormal and Halabja in Iraqi Kurdistan after heavy fighting (March 13–16). On March 16 and 17, Iraqi aircraft bombed Halabja and the nearby area with chemical weapons—including mustard gas—killing some 5,000 people, mostly Kurdish civilians. This act was condemned widely and led to a UN Security Council resolution in May condemning (though only in general terms) the use of chemical weapons.

War of the Cities. Raids on civilian targets, in abeyance since November 1987, resumed on February 27 when Iraqi aircraft bombed four Iranian cities. Iranian jets raided Basra the next day. Such exchanges continued daily until March 10, with some sporadic attacks through April. The Iraqi attacks, which numbered 56 as against Iran's 25, were much more destructive, especially when Iraq fired 200 Soviet-made Scud-B missiles against Tehran. Some 1,200 people were killed in these attacks on cities, more in Iran than in Iraq.

The Tanker War. Throughout 1988 there were many incidents in which Iraq continued to raid Iranian oil terminals and tankers carrying Iranian oil, while Iranian gunboats raided ships trading with Iraq or the Gulf states. When a U.S. frigate, the *Samuel B. Roberts,* was damaged badly by a mine on April 14, with ten wounded, the reaction was strong. U.S. naval units destroyed two Iranian oil platforms in the central Gulf and sank or damaged several ships. Iran claimed that there were 44 casualties. On April 29, U.S. President Ronald Reagan announced a change in the "rules of engagement" to permit U.S. ships to protect neutral shipping as well as U.S.-flag ships. The number of Iranian attacks seemed to diminish.

The "Vincennes" and Flight 655. On July 3 an Iran Air passenger plane, Flight 655 from Bandar Abbas to Dubai, was shot down by a

missile fired from the U.S.S. *Vincennes*. Of the 290 passengers killed, four fifths were Iranian. The *Vincennes* was at the same time in combat with five Iranian patrol boats, and U.S. military spokesmen claimed that the downing of the plane was a mistake made in the heat of battle. Iran's failure at the UN Security Council meeting (July 16–20) to secure a resolution placing sole responsibility on the United States for the tragedy, showed how weak its international position had become. On July 18, Iran finally announced its acceptance of Security Council Resolution 598 (calling for an immediate cease-fire and other steps toward peace), and the Ayatollah's public statement on the subject —which constituted a complete about-face— was read for him on Iranian television on July 20. There was a little more military activity, but UN Secretary-General Pérez de Cuéllar managed to secure the agreement of both sides to a cease-fire effective August 20. This was surprisingly well observed for the remainder of the year.

On September 26, the last of 89 U.S. convoys passed through the Strait of Hormuz. The policy initiated in July 1987 had been completely successful.

The cease-fire was not followed by any diplomatic settlement; the armistice formally remained that and no more. Four meetings at intervals of the two sides under UN auspices achieved nothing, coming to nought over Iraq's demand that its boundary with Iran should be on the east bank of the Shatt-al-Arab.

Reflections. Thus ended, in a draw, after one month short of eight years, the Iraqi-Iranian War, the bloodiest war since World War II. Masses of enthusiastic young Iranians were sent up against effective Iraqi defenses, and thus slaughtered. The use of poison gas, the occasional and rather ineffective bombing of cities, as well as the heavy censorship imposed by both sides, were also reminiscent of World War I. Western countries showed curiously little interest in the Gulf War prior to 1984; from then until 1988 the dangers to shipping in the gulf riveted Western attention. But the war, like most wars, was decided on land, not at sea.

Iraqi President Saddam Hussein demonstrated that religious fanaticism does not make a state invincible, and that the Shiite brand of Islamic fundamentalism, so greatly feared, was not the threat to other states that had been thought. Iraq, Saudi Arabia, the Gulf emirates, all warded off the dangers from religious fanaticism with no more than some unpleasant incidents.

The costs of the war, human and material, were enormous. Estimates vary widely. The U.S. Central Intelligence Agency estimated that Iran lost some 600,000 men, with 1.5 million in total casualties; Iraq's casualties were approximately half of those figures. Before the war, Iraq possessed ample foreign exchange reserves, but it ended the war with an external debt of some $60 billion. Iran's foreign debt, by contrast, is quite small. These figures do not include the costs of reconstruction.

ARTHUR CAMPBELL TURNER

In a new political testament issued at the end of December 1987, Khomeini stipulated that his power should not be inherited by a single clerical leader (that is, not by Montazeri), but by an elected committee of three or five persons. The action, not surprisingly, evoked rumors that the aged Khomeini was terminally ill and soon would die. Such rumors—which

were not new—continued throughout the year, especially as Iran embarked on policies flatly contrary to what the Ayatollah earlier had espoused.

Even before Khomeini's decision to accept a cease-fire, other voices had been raised in opposition to the war, notably those of the dissident religious leader Ayatollah Sayed Tabatabai Qomi and former Premier Mehdi Bazargan.

Elections. Elections to the *Majlis* were held in two stages on April 8 and May 13, and the new parliament convened on May 28. In the elections the ''reformists''—those favoring more state control of the economy—gained ground, but this seemed in practice to have little political importance. Rafsanjani, the powerful moderate, was reelected speaker of parliament, and on June 2 Khomeini made him acting commander-in-chief, with a special mission to coordinate the armed forces. This prepared the way for a fusing of the Revolutionary Guards with the regular army, and some steps in that direction were taken during the following months.

IRAN • Information Highlights

Official Name: Islamic Republic of Iran.
Location: Southwest Asia.
Area: 636,293 sq mi (1 648 000 km²).
Population (mid-1988 est.): 51,900,000.
Chief City (1986 census): Tehran, the capital, 5,770,000.
Government: *Supreme faqih,* Ayatollah Ruhollah Khomeini. *Head of state,* Ali Khamenei, president (took office Oct. 1981). *Head of government,* Mir Hosein Musavi-Khamenei, prime minister (took office Oct. 1981). *Legislature* (unicameral)—Islamic Consultative Assembly *(Majlis).*
Monetary Unit: Rial (71.381 rials equal U.S.$1, August 1988).
Gross National Product (1987 U.S.$): $86,400,000,000.
Foreign Trade (1986 est. U.S.$): *Imports,* (est.) $10,000,000,000; *exports,* $7,800,000,000.

Hosein Musavi, prime minister of Iran since 1981, was reelected by the *Majlis* on June 30. An opponent of the new course of policy, he tried to resign in September, but peremptorily was ordered by Khomeini to remain.

Foreign Relations. Saudi Arabia broke diplomatic relations with Iran on April 27 because of Iran's resistance to Saudi insistence on controlling Iranian pilgrim traffic to Mecca. Saudi Arabia is determined to prevent a repetition of the disorders created by Iranians there in 1987. Diplomatic links were restored, however, with France, Canada, and Britain.

Economy. Morale in Iran was low after eight years of costly and unsuccessful war. The economy was in desperate shape. For the first time, Iran began to default on foreign debts. Still undecided was the contest between hardliners—perhaps a minority—who want to maintain the Islamic revolution in all its purity at whatever cost, and those, the most prominent being Khamenei and Rafsanjani, aided by Khomeini, who think Western economic aid and technology an impressive necessity. Iran was back to facing the questions of imported technology and economic development that were so prominent under the Shah.

ARTHUR CAMPBELL TURNER
University of California, Riverside

IRAQ

The most important event of the year for Iraq was the cessation of its eight-year war with Iran. (*See* special report, page 289.) The Baath Party regime of Saddam Hussein Takriti remained in power, with enhanced prestige.

Liberalization. On February 4 a decree gave the National Assembly new powers to investigate the action of cabinet ministers and recommend their dismissal, punishment, or promotion. In the past the National Assembly had been a virtual rubber-stamp institution with functions limited to the making of jejune comments on government's actions. It was difficult to estimate how important its newly enhanced powers would prove in practice. They at least may be useful in directing attention to

lack of competence in particular cabinet members.

Ministerial Reshuffles. On January 16, Ibrahim al-Shawi, justice minister, was appointed minister of higher education and scientific research, and replaced at justice by Akram al-Qadir Ali, chairman of the State Consultative Council. On February 22, Col. Hussein Kamil was appointed head of a new body intended to supervise the military use of industry; on June 13, Colonel Kamil also was made minister of the combined ministries of industry and minerals, the previous holders of these two portfolios being dismissed. On May 11 Health Minister Sadiq Hamid Allush was relieved of his post for "negligence of duty," and 18 senior officials in the ministry also were dismissed.

Pardons and Amnesties. The Revolutionary Command Council (RCC), inner ruling group of Iraq, on April 27 announced pardons for persons who already had served one year in prison for "economic crimes," provided their original sentences were for less than ten years. There also was an amnesty for some undergoing life imprisonment and for some draft evaders.

Internal Problems. The lower marshlands between the Tigris and Euphrates, north of Basra, had become something of a haven for draft evaders and deserters in 1987 and early 1988. In February the government claimed that a military sweep had cleaned out the area.

Critics of government appeared to be becoming a little more daring. On February 3 a group of Iraqi opponents of the regime issued a statement accusing security forces of an ongoing campaign to eliminate political enemies. They pointed to the murder in the Sudan (February 3) of a prominent Shiite cleric, exiled from Iraq since 1969, and to other similar acts of violence in London and Oslo, Norway.

Iraq's major internal problem is that of relations with its large Kurdish minority, a problem with international ramifications. (*See* MIDDLE EAST.) Strong U.S. disapproval of the Iraqi use of chemical weapons against the Kurdish town of Halabja on March 16 led to Secretary of State George Shultz's being refused a meeting with Hussein in June; and U.S.-Iraqi relations grew even cooler in the fall.

Gulf War's Aftermath. The national euphoria which greeted the armistice of August 20 (increased by an unprecedented release of consumer goods) was followed, almost inevitably, by disillusionment in later months. There was no lifting of censorship or of the ban on foreign travel. Iraq, of course, faces a heavy task in making up the losses of war. But it now appears that its oil reserves are enormously larger than estimated hitherto (100 billion barrels as against 70); and a crucial OPEC decision at Vienna in November granted Iraq a production quota equal to Iran's.

ARTHUR CAMPBELL TURNER
University of California, Riverside

IRAQ • Information Highlights

Official Name: Republic of Iraq.
Location: Southwest Asia.
Area: 167,923 sq mi (434 920 km²).
Population (mid-1988 est.): 17,600,000.
Chief City (1981 est.): Baghdad, the capital, 3,400,000.
Government: *Head of state and government,* Saddam Hussein, president (took office July 1979).
Monetary Unit: Dinar (0.311 dinar equals U.S.$1, August 1988).
Gross National Product (1987 est. U.S.$): $40,000,-000,000.
Foreign Trade (1986 est. U.S.$): *Imports,* $9,500,-000,000; *exports,* $7,450,000,000.

IRELAND

Political relations between the Irish and British governments suffered a series of reverses in 1988 owing to the continuing struggle over Northern Ireland. To the dismay of many Irish citizens, the British cabinet decided in January against prosecuting members of the Royal Ulster Constabulary (RUC), who had been implicated in a "shoot-to-kill" policy in the north during 1982. (Six unarmed men had been killed in three separate incidents under the RUC policy.) Several days after the cabinet's announcement, the British Court of Appeal turned down the appeal of six Irishmen imprisoned in British jails for their involvement in bombing Birmingham pubs in 1974.

Anglo-Irish relations deteriorated further after March 6, when undercover British security forces in Gibraltar shot and killed three members of the provisional Irish Republican Army (IRA) who were engaged in a car-bomb operation. Although unarmed at the time, the two men and one woman were shot down before they had time to surrender. Joining in the outcry against what many considered to be an act of murder, Prime Minister Charles Haughey expressed his government's grave concern over the attack and criticized the British forces for not having tried to arrest the suspects. The burial of the three IRA victims in Belfast triggered a new cycle of violence in the north and gave greater urgency to the meeting of the Anglo-Irish Conference in London on March 25. On this occasion Ireland's Minister for Foreign Affairs Brian Lenihan discussed security and other matters with Britain's Secretary of State for Northern Ireland Tom King. Both indicated the talks were encouraging.

In its own campaign to curb the provisional IRA, the Irish government prosecuted Dessie O'Hare, known as "the Border Fox" for his guerrilla activities in the north. A suspect in some 27 killings on both sides of the border, O'Hare pleaded guilty to charges of kidnapping and firearms offenses, and on April 13 he was sentenced to 40 years in prison. In a bid to improve the government's ability to combat terrorism, Minister for Justice Gerry Collins approved a major reorganization of the Garda (the republic's police force).

On May 13 the government negotiated a new arrangement with Britain for the extradition of terrorist suspects from Ireland. Anxious to avoid the appearance of succumbing to British pressure, Ireland's Attorney General John Murray insisted on the receipt of formal evidence of a suspect's complicity in criminal acts before any extradition could take place. This controversial agreement was put to a severe test June 13, when a Dublin court refused to extradite a well-known provisional IRA operative, Patrick McVeigh, who recently had been released from a prison near Dublin. Accused by British authorities of carrying out a series of bombings in Britain from 1981 to 1983, McVeigh won his freedom on a legal technicality and promptly went into hiding. The court's verdict exposed the limits of the extradition accord and provoked some critical comments from Prime Minister Thatcher.

A wave of bombings and other attacks on British security forces in the north in June, July, and August made it clear that the IRA was still capable of waging deadly guerrilla war despite some losses among its active units. The most effective IRA attack—a bus bombing on August 20—killed eight British soldiers.

Economy. On the economic front, high taxes and unemployment rates continued to cast a pall over the country. Ireland's VAT (value added tax) of 25% stood at the top of the European Community (EC). And with at least 19% of the labor force out of work, and relatively few good jobs available to young people, the incentive for emigration loomed large. Officials expressed concern over census figures that showed a sharp rise in emigration during the decade. Had it not been for this outward flow, the population would have risen an estimated 169,000 instead of only 97,200 by 1986. One bright spot in this gloomy picture was the inflation rate, which stood at 1.8% for the first half of the year—the lowest level in 25 years. With Ireland scheduled to join the other 11 members of the EC in an unrestricted system of capital circulation in 1992, many people wondered how this would affect them.

Other. On January 15 the country lost one of its most eminent statesmen and jurists, Sean MacBride, aged 83, a veteran of the old IRA and a cowinner of the Nobel Peace Prize in 1974 for his work in promoting human rights around the world.

In soccer, Ireland defeated England, 1-0, in the World Cup competition on June 12.

L. PERRY CURTIS, JR., *Brown University*

IRELAND • Information Highlights

Official Name: Republic of Ireland.
Location: Island in the eastern North Atlantic Ocean.
Area: 27,135 sq mi (70 282 km²).
Population (mid-1988 est.): 3,500,000.
Chief Cities (1986 census): Dublin, the capital, 920,956 (incl. suburbs); Cork, 173,694; Limerick, 76,557.
Government: *Head of state,* Patrick J. Hillery, president (took office Dec. 1976). *Head of government,* Charles Haughey, prime minister (took office March 1987). *Legislature*—Parliament: House of Representatives (Dail Eireann) and Senate (Seanad Eireann).
Monetary Unit: Pound (0.6702 pound equals U.S.$1, Nov. 1, 1988).
Gross National Product (1986 U.S.$): $21,700,-000,000.
Economic Indexes (1987): *Consumer Prices* (1980 = 100), all items, 191.1; food, 171.8. *Industrial Production* (1980 = 100), 146.
Foreign Trade (1987 U.S.$): *Imports,* $13,627,-000,000; *exports,* $15,978,000,000.

ISRAEL

The uprising of Palestinian Arabs in the occupied West Bank and Gaza and elections for the 12th Knesset (parliament) dominated events in Israel during 1988. Progress toward a peace settlement was stymied by continued divisions within the national unity government and the emergence of Likud as the strongest party in the November balloting. The uprising of Palestinian Arabs continued throughout 1988, gaining wide support and intensifying the deep divisions within Israel over policies toward the territories. (*See* special report, page 294.)

Election and Domestic Affairs. The uprising and Israel's stance on peace negotiations were major issues in the campaign for Knesset elections on November 1. A total of 27 parties were authorized to participate in the elections. Kach, a militantly nationalist party led by Rabbi Meir Kahana, was disqualified as racist by the High Court of Justice for advocating the deportation of Arabs from all areas held by Israel.

Fifteen different parties secured at least the 1% of votes required to obtain a Knesset seat, although the two dominant parties, Likud and Labor, between them captured nearly two thirds of the votes. The 120 Knesset seats were divided as follows: the right-wing Likud bloc, 40; the center-left Labor Party, 39; four extreme-right religious parties, 18; three extreme-right secular parties, 7; the far-left and Arab bloc, 8; and parties traditionally allied with Likud, 8.

Because no party acquired a majority of seats, forming a government required some coalition agreement. After consultation with all party leaders, President Chaim Herzog called on Prime Minister Yitzhak Shamir, leader of the Likud bloc, to form a government. Shamir negotiated with the four religious parties and with two militantly nationalist groups; he also consulted with Labor's Shimon Peres about a new national unity coalition, but the offer was

---

ISRAEL • Information Highlights

Official Name: State of Israel.
Location: Southwest Asia.
Area: 8,019 sq mi (20 770 km²).
Population (mid-1988 est.): 4,400,000.
Chief Cities (Dec. 31, 1985 est.): Jerusalem, the capital, 457,700 (including East Jerusalem); Tel Aviv-Jaffa, 322,800; Haifa, 224,600.
Government: *Head of state,* Chaim Herzog, president (took office May 1983). *Head of government,* Shimon Peres, prime minister (took office Sept. 14, 1984). *Legislature* (unicameral)—Knesset.
Monetary Unit: Shekel (.6656 shekels equal U.S.$1, Dec. 28, 1988).
Gross National Product (1986 est U.S.$): $21,000,-000,000.
Economic Indexes (1987): *Consumer Prices* (1980 = 100), all items, 39,937.5; food, 38,908.7. *Industrial Production* (May 1988, 1980 = 100), 127.
Foreign Trade (1987 U.S.$): *Imports,* $11,910,-000,000; *exports,* $8,475,000,000.

---

rejected. Terms demanded by the religious parties for cooperation with Likud included a revision of the nation's laws defining a Jew, recognizing only the authority of the orthodox rabbinate. The religious parties also insisted on stricter interpretation and enforcement of legislation pertaining to sabbath restrictions and other Orthodox Jewish observances. These demands raised a storm of protest among non-Orthodox Israelis and Jews worldwide, who feared that the influence of the religious parties would become too powerful. Delegations of Reformed and Conservative Jewish leaders from the United States and Britain converged on Israel to warn Prime Minister Shamir that assent to these conditions would undermine financial and political support from Jews abroad. Thus, while the Arab uprising had been the dominant issue at the outset of the campaign, the increase in strength by the ultraorthodox parties made the religious question prominent in the aftermath of the elections.

Finally on December 19, after seven weeks of wrangling, Likud and Labor agreed on a new coalition government, to be led by Prime Minister Shamir. Under the arrangement, a four-

Following inconclusive parliamentary elections on November 1 and weeks of negotiations, Yitzhak Shamir (left), leader of Israel's Likud bloc, and Shimon Peres (right), leader of the Labor Party. agreed to form a new coalition government.

AP/Wide World

The Palestinian Issue

The Palestinian issue again became the focus of international attention during 1988 as a result of an uprising against Israeli occupation in the West Bank and Gaza. It dominated proceedings of the Arab League summit in Algiers during June, was a prominent theme in the campaign leading to the Israel Knesset election on November 1, led to a decision by Jordan's King Hussein to sever ties between Jordan and the occupied territories, and culminated in the declaration of independence on November 15 by the Palestine National Council at its 19th extraordinary session in Algiers.

The *Intifada*. The *intifada,* as the uprising was called by Palestinians, began during December 1987 in Gaza as a spontaneous demonstration of youths in a refugee camp who were protesting against the death of several Arabs killed by an Israeli driver in an automobile accident. The demonstration quickly spread throughout Gaza to the West Bank and to Arab Jerusalem, turning into a protest against the occupation and Israeli policies in the territories. A Unified National Leadership emerged, comprised of representatives of groups affiliated with the Palestine Liberation Organization (PLO), including Fatah, the Popular Front for the Liberation of Palestine, the Democratic Popular Front, the Palestine Communist party, and an Islamic fundamentalist organization. The PLO leaders in Tunis had played no direct role in initiating the *intifada,* but later liaison was established between them and the Unified National Leadership.

Observers concluded that the uprising resulted from frustration with 20 years of occupation, severe Israeli policies in the territories, deteriorating conditions in the increasingly crowded refugee camps, and intensification of Palestinian national consciousness.

During 1988, Palestinians generally refrained from using "hot" weapons against the occupation forces. Rather, they resorted to throwing stones, iron bars, and an occasional Molotov cocktail; they also hurled insults at the Israeli soldiers. As the *intifada* gained popular support, other measures of civil resistance were adopted—including an economic boycott of Israeli products, nonpayment of Israeli taxes and fees, mass resignations by Israeli-appointed Arab police and other government officials, and periodic strikes which shut down commercial, educational, and other facilities. At times facilities were closed by order of the *intifada* leadership, and at other times on orders from the Israeli military authorities. The objectives of the uprising included the end of occupation, the release of political prisoners, and the establishment of an independent Palestinian state in Gaza and the West Bank.

Israeli security forces in the territories were unable to suppress the *intifada* despite a variety of measures. These included mass arrests of demonstrators and others suspected of "subversive" activities and their imprisonment without trial, and the increasingly frequent deportation to neighboring Arab countries of suspects. Schools, universities, stores, and other facilities were closed. Local committees established to provide services cut off by the uprising were banned. Curfews were enacted. Destruction of homes belonging to suspects and sieges of unruly villages were condoned. Economic sanctions were leveled. Diverse forms of physical force against demonstrators were used routinely. By the end of the year, nearly 300 Palestinians had been killed by Israeli forces. Israeli casualties were minimal.

The *intifada* became a focal point of political and social change among the Palestinian Arab community in the territories. New, young, radical leaders emerged to replace many in the traditional older generation who were often conservative in their political and social perspectives. Morale in the Arab community was raised. Palestinian consciousness galvanized a feeling of previously unknown national unity. The *intifada* ended the feasibility of the "Jordan option," a scheme in which King Hussein would assume responsibility for the future of the West Bank and Gaza in peace negotiations.

Within Israel the *intifada* had extensive repercussions. It became a dominant issue in the election campaign for Israel's 12th Knesset. As a result of strikes by Arabs from Gaza and the West Bank employed in Israel, there were labor shortages in construction, agriculture, and other economic sectors. Exports to the territories, valued at about $1 billion, were diminished greatly. The Jewish labor sector was affected because of the additional time army reservists had to serve in the occupied territories. In April it was believed that Israel attempted to strike a blow at the *intifada* by assassinating Abu Jihad, the PLO's most senior military figure, at his home in Tunis. Jihad had been a possible heir to Yasir Arafat as PLO leader. Israeli officials neither denied nor claimed responsibility for the assassination.

Inter-Arab Affairs. As a result of the *intifada,* King Hussein undermined the "Jordan option" in July by renouncing all claims to the

occupied territories and responsibilities for the inhabitants. Between 1949 and 1967 the West Bank, including East Jerusalem, had been part of the Hashemite Kingdom. (Gaza was under Egyptian occupation.) After the Israeli occupation, Jordan had continued to provide salaries to many officials in the West Bank, passports to its Arab residents, and a variety of other forms of assistance. Several seats in Jordan's parliament were held by West Bankers. Even Israel unofficially recognized a measure of Jordanian responsibility in the West Bank, permitting use of the Jordan dinar along with Israeli currency.

When King Hussein announced that he was turning over to the PLO full responsibility for the occupied territories and their population, Palestinians in the territories and in Jordan received the announcement with mixed feelings. Even those who opposed the "Jordan option" were concerned about the economic impact of losing Jordanian assistance.

The *intifada* dominated proceedings of the Arab League summit in Algiers during June. The meeting, convened to deal with the uprisings, was the second summit in seven months and the best-attended in more than a decade. Attention shifted from the Iraq-Iran war (the major theme at the previous summit) back to the Palestine problem. The PLO came to the summit requesting extensive financial aid to support the *intifada,* but left disappointed because no specific allocation was ordered. Instead, a joint committee of the PLO and six other league members was designated to deal with assistance to the uprising and to make collective decisions. The PLO leaders charged that withholding financial aid was a dereliction of duty toward the uprising.

Declaration of Independence. As the year progressed, there was increasing discussion within the PLO about declaring an independent Palestinian state, about establishing a government in exile, and about allowing some form of recognition for Israel. The Unified Leadership in the occupied territories had issued several statements calling for establishment of an independent state coexisting with Israel. Pressure from the territories and increased international discussion of the issue led to open debate within the organization.

Bassam Abu Sharif, a close adviser to PLO chairman Arafat, indicated a radical change in policy during June at the Arab summit in Algiers. Abu Sharif emphasized several points: The Israelis, like the Palestinians, were seeking lasting peace and security, and these goals could be achieved only through direct talks between the PLO and Israel. The PLO accepted UN Security Council Resolutions 242 and 338

AP/Wide World

A young Palestinian waves the outlawed Palestinian flag at a February protest in the Israeli-occupied West Bank.

(resolutions which recognized the state of Israel), but had made no public pronouncement on acceptance because the resolutions contained no reference to Palestinian national rights. The Palestinians were willing to accept a short, mutually-agreed-upon interim period during which the occupied territories might be placed under an international mandate. The Palestinians agreed to international guarantees for the security of all states in the region, including Israel and Palestine—an arrangement that could be established in direct talks through a UN-sponsored international conference. The Palestinians were willing to accept a UN buffer force on the Palestinian side of the border with Israel to ensure security to both countries. Abu Sharif's statement received favorable response in Western Europe, but was regarded with skepticism by both Israel and the United States because Chairman Arafat would neither endorse nor reject it.

After several postponements the 500-member Palestine National Council, considered the PLO's parliamentary body, convened in Algiers in mid-November to sanction officially proposals for an independent state. In a speech to the

council on November 15, Arafat proclaimed "in the name of God, in the name of the people, of the Palestinian people, the establishment of the state of Palestine on our Palestinian nation, with its capital in holy Jerusalem."

The council called for the pursuit of a peaceful resolution to the conflict with Israel based on Resolutions 242 and 338 and claimed a willingness to negotiate with Israel in the context of an international peace conference, provided Israel recognized Palestinian rights. The council rejected terrorism and the use of violence except in the territories to resist Israeli occupation. The council also recognized the special relationship between the Palestinian and Jordanian peoples, and planned a confederation of the two countries to be approved in a referendum after establishment of Palestinian independence.

Although militant minority factions denied that the resolutions implied recognition of Israel, they stated that they would remain within the PLO and not disrupt the spirit of national unity generated at the council meetings.

Israel denounced the council resolutions. Official U.S. reaction was tepid. U.S. spokesmen, while finding some "positive elements" in the Algiers meetings, rejected the idea of an independent Palestinian state, and any other unilateral decisions concerning the occupied territories.

By the end of November more than 70 nations did recognize the declaration of independence and indicated willingness to establish diplomatic exchanges with the new state. In addition to most of the Arab states, China and the Soviet Union endorsed it. In Western Europe, however, only Greece was willing to grant full recognition.

Arafat was invited to address the UN General Assembly at its regularly scheduled meeting in December in New York. The U.S. government refused to issue a visa, however, so the Assembly meeting was moved to Geneva. In his speech, Arafat indicated that the PLO was eager for direct contacts with the United States, and he spelled out in further detail many of the points adopted at the November meeting of the National Council in Tunis. But the Reagan administration was not satisfied, contending that the PLO position on recognition of Israel was still too ambiguous. Through the intervention of Sweden, a delegation of American Jews was invited to Stockholm for clarification of the PLO position in parleys with Arafat. As a result of that meeting and a subsequent Geneva press conference by Arafat, U.S. Secretary of State George Shultz announced that the PLO had met the preconditions for a dialogue; talks began in Tunis the next day. Israel, to no one's surprise, rejected Arafat's declarations; Prime Minister Shamir proclaimed that he would never negotiate with the PLO and called on the United States to renounce its own decision to do so.

Don Peretz

member inner cabinet—composed of Shamir (Likud); Peres (Labor), who would shift from foreign minister to finance minister; Defense Minister Yitzhak Rabin (Labor); and Moshe Arens (Likud), the new foreign minister—was expected to control the major government decisions.

Economic issues, although secondary in the campaign, still were significant. The nation was beset by a number of major strikes during the course of the year. Among the most serious were strikes by physicians, nurses, and health workers, which created a crisis in the public-health system. Meanwhile, debts incurred by agricultural cooperatives, collectives, and other settlements led many to the verge of bankruptcy; several key industries were plagued with financial troubles; and the large Labor Confederation (Histadrut) holding company, Koor, which controlled some 300 industrial firms, faced a similar crisis in October, when it was unable to meet interest payments on loans from U.S. banks.

The months-long and highly publicized court trials of John Demjanjuk and Mordechai Vanunu both were concluded in 1988. Demjanjuk, who was accused of collaboration with the Nazis in the murder of Jews during World War II, was found guilty in April and sentenced to death. Vanunu, who was charged with treason and espionage for revealing Israeli atomic secrets in a British newspaper article, was found guilty in March and sentenced to 18 years in prison.

Foreign Affairs. Contacts leading toward reestablishment of relations with the Soviet bloc were continued throughout 1988. In January the Soviet Union agreed to permit an official Israeli delegation to visit Moscow, and in June, Prime Minister Shamir held his first meeting with Soviet Foreign Minister Eduard Shevardnadze at the United Nations in New York. Contacts with Hungary, initiated in 1987, were strengthened by Shamir's visit to Budapest in September 1988. Despite contacts with the Soviet bloc, Shamir continued to reject the concept of an international peace conference, favored by Moscow, as the way to achieve a Middle East settlement.

See also Middle East.

Don Peretz
State University of New York, Binghamton

AP/Wide World

In mid-June, two months after taking office, Italy's Prime Minister Ciriaco De Mita (left) made an official visit to Washington. President Reagan thanked him for Italy's agreement to provide a base for a squadron of U.S. fighter planes.

ITALY

Italy continued to advance among the world's industrial powers in 1988, while in domestic affairs, Italy's Parliament enacted important reforms in its voting system, and the Communist Party continued to decline.

Domestic Affairs

When 1988 began, Prime Minister Giovanni Goria's five-party coalition of Socialists, Christian Democrats, Social Democrats, Republicans, and Liberals was still in office. It had been formed on July 26, 1987.

On February 10, Goria submitted his resignation following his failure to get his budget approved. But President Francesco Cossiga persuaded him to seek again a vote of confidence in parliament on the budgetary issue.

Goria's respite did not last long. Soon his coalition government split apart when Goria decided to resume construction of a nuclear-power plant. The Socialists and Social Democrats opposed further nuclear construction—as had the majority of Italy's voters in a referendum in November 1987. On March 11, Premier Goria resigned. This time his resignation was accepted.

Premier Ciriaco De Mita. President Cossiga now turned to Ciriaco De Mita, the powerful secretary of the Christian Democratic Party. On April 13, after a month of negotiations, De Mita managed to form a new government (Italy's 48th since World War II). It was composed of the same five parties (the *pentapartito*) that had been in Goria's government.

De Mita, who comes from Avellino province in southern Italy, hitherto had been little known outside of his own party circles. Some observers doubted if his jealous party rivals would allow him to continue very long as party secretary in addition to being premier. (*See* BIOGRAPHY—*De Mita, Ciriaco.*)

Reforms in Parliament. Premier De Mita's most urgent problem was to gain parliamentary approval of his budget—a difficult task because of the 140-year-old tradition of secret voting in Italy's Parliament. This voting practice often has enabled opposition Communists and even renegade members of the premier's own party to scuttle his proposals and to bring down the government. There was almost no way to impose party discipline on these dissidents, known in Italy as "snipers."

A bill to eliminate the practice of secret voting would have to surmount the hurdle of a secret vote. Nevertheless, on October 13, such a procedural reform measure was enacted by the Chamber of Deputies by a narrow majority of seven. The Senate was expected to ratify it later. Premier De Mita had threatened to resign if he lost on this issue. Had that happened, there was a good chance of early elections, a prospect that had little appeal to either Christian Democrats or Communists.

The new procedure would require lawmakers to vote openly on the national budget and all other financial issues. In a compromise move, secret voting will be retained for such issues as civil rights, abortion, and divorce. The action by the Chamber of Deputies marked a turning point in Italian political life, many observers believed. The new voting procedure

may help governments to survive longer than the usual six months or so.

Communist Party Decline. The big loser under the new voting system in Parliament will be the Communist Party, which already was slipping at the polls and now was deprived of a parliamentary tool that had given it considerable leverage. In the 1976 parliamentary elections the Communist Party had reached its peak, polling 34.4% of the votes cast. It has been declining ever since. Thus, in the 1987 parliamentary elections, it dropped to 26.6%, while in local elections on May 29, 1988, it fell to only 21.9%—barely more than Bettino Craxi's rapidly growing Socialist Party. (Former Premier Craxi had presided over the longest-running government—from 1984 to 1987—in Italy's post-World War II history.)

Craxi's party, along with the Radicals and Greens, steadily had been winning votes at the expense of the Communists. Craxi hoped to achieve in Italy what President François Mitterrand had done in France—make the Socialists the main voice of Italy's Left.

In the wake of these local elections, the Italian Communist Party chose a new leader—52-year-old Achille Occhetto—to succeed the ailing 70-year-old party hack, Alessandro Natta. Occhetto, who came from the party's centrist faction, has called for a "new course" that he hoped would broaden the party's appeal beyond the working class to include employees in the public sector.

Most observers felt, however, that the only practical way for the Communists to win an effective share of political power in Rome was through a deal with Craxi's Socialists. Craxi made no secret of his desire to dislodge the Christian Democrats from their 43-year-long hegemony over Italy's postwar governments. He wanted to head an alternative Center-Left coalition government made up of the Socialists, Republicans, Social Democrats, and a democratized and less powerful Communist party. But he would not be ready for such a challenge until after the next parliamentary elections. If his Socialists could push ahead of the Communists, he might be willing to deal with them.

Meanwhile, Craxi was doing his best to whittle away at Communist strength. He took advantage of Mikhail Gorbachev's policy of *glasnost* (openness) and posthumous rehabilitation of some of Stalin's purge victims to launch a critical reexamination of the actions of the late and once revered Italian Communist Party secretary, Palmiro Togliatti. Craxi's exposé aroused further disillusionment among Italian Communists, some of whom were prepared to concede that Togliatti often had collaborated closely with Stalin's repressive acts.

In addition to Craxi's offensive, there were other explanations for the Italian Communist Party's steady decline in recent years. Thus far, members had failed to transform their party into a modern reformist political movement and they had lost much of the cultural dominance they used to exercise over a broad strata of Italian society. Gorbachev's *perestroika* (restructuring) also had caused some Italian party members to lose faith in the old Communist economic prescriptions.

The Mafia and Terrorism. A sense of guarded optimism prevailed at the start of 1988 with regard to the Mafia's international drug trafficking, as well as to the problem of political terrorism. Major crackdowns on organized crime in Sicily and southern Italy, followed by mass trials, seemed to have paid off. But this sense of relief came to a sudden end in the autumn when the Mafia launched a vicious counter-offensive. During a two-week period, 18 people were slain. The killing, on September 25, of Judge Antonio Saetta, a senior appellate court judge in Palermo, violated what had been considered a Sicilian taboo. The Mafia never had killed a sitting judge before. Violence also occurred in Calabria, Naples, and elsewhere.

Some terrorist acts were directed against U.S. military personnel. On April 14 in Naples, five people, including an American sailor, were killed and 15 others were wounded when a bomb exploded in a U.S.O. club. In this case, the suspect was a member of the left-wing Japanese Red Army who already was wanted for an attack on the U.S. Embassy in Rome in June.

On April 16, Italian Sen. Roberto Ruffilli, a close ally of Premier De Mita, was shot and killed at his home in Forli by a faction of the Red Brigades. In February an Italian court convicted *in absentia* the Arab terrorist Abu Nidal, and sentenced him to life imprisonment for the 1985 Rome airport massacre.

The Shroud of Turin. On October 13 the Roman Catholic Church announced that the Shroud of Turin, kept for the last 410 years at the Cathedral of Turin, was not authentic. The shroud has been venerated by millions of Christians over the centuries as the burial cloth of Jesus. New radiocarbon dating tests showed that the linen dates only to the period between 1260 and 1390. Nevertheless, Catholics were encouraged to continue their veneration of the shroud as a pictorial image of Christ.

Economy. By 1988 many Italians were taking pride in their country's rapid climb to the status of a great power in the world economy. Italy was not only one of the industrialized "Big Seven" in the free world, but according to some calculations (if the underground or "black" economy is included), Italy's gross national product (GNP) of approximately $800 billion was ahead of Britain's and about one sixth that of the United States. On a per capita basis, Italy's income was about $13,200, compared with $17,000 in the United States. In 1988, Italy's rate of increase in GNP was about 3.8%. Inflation, which in 1980 reached 21%, was down to about 4.5% by late 1988.

But there were also severe problems. The budget deficit was about 11% of GNP. Italy also carried a huge national debt—93% of GNP. Luckily, this was an *internal* debt owed to Italian banks. Moreover, Italy enjoyed a much higher rate of saving than did the United States—23% of income compared with 4%. Unemployment in September was at 14%, although the "black" economy attenuated this national average. Unemployment remained much higher in the South than in the North.

Italy's population has stabilized and emigration has stopped. Italy began importing laborers in 1988. (There were about 1 million foreign workers, many coming from North Africa and the Philippines.) Italy's standard of living has improved. During the past three decades, life expectancy has risen by ten years. There was one automobile for every 1.5 inhabitants, and one telephone for every 47 people.

Somewhat belatedly, Italy has become more concerned about the problems of toxic pollution of the environment. The country was dismayed to learn of attempts to dispose of Italian toxic wastes by shipping them to Third World countries.

Italy exported to the United States about $17 billion in goods during 1988—three times more than it did ten years ago. There was a $6 billion surplus in Italy's trade account with the United States. The process of privatization of the large public sector of Italy's economy continued. Alfa Romeo was sold to Fiat in 1987. In January the government agreed to terms for the privatization of the investment bank Mediobanca.

Passing of a Political Generation. The year 1988 saw the deaths of several figures who had played prominent roles in Italian politics in previous decades. Giuseppe Saragat, who had served as president from 1964 to 1971, died on June 11 at age 89. In 1947, during the Cold War, he broke with the pro-Communist Socialists of Pietro Nenni and formed the Socialist Party of Italian Workers, which later became the Social Democratic Party. Dino Grandi, who held several high-ranking positions (including foreign

minister) in the Fascist regime of Benito Mussolini but helped orchestrate Mussolini's downfall in 1943, died on May 21. Two founder-members of the neofascist Italian Social Movement (MSI), Giorgio Almirante and Pino Romualdi, also died in May. And Giuliano Pajetta, a veteran member of the Italian Communist Party Central Committee and a former member of Parliament, died in August.

Foreign Affairs

Italy's foreign policy in 1988 rested on the twin pillars of the NATO alliance and membership in the European Community.

Italy and NATO. When Spain declined, in February, to agree to the continued basing of 72 American F-16 fighter-bombers at Torrejon, the Italian government volunteered to provide a base for them in Calabria. Despite objections from Moscow and from many Italian leftists, as well as hostility from some Catholic bishops in southern Italy, Parliament gave its approval at the end of June for the relocation in 1991 of the U.S. 401st Tactical Fighter Wing, the cost of relocation to be paid by NATO.

When Italy's Premier De Mita met with U.S. President Ronald Reagan in Washington in June, the latter expressed his gratitude to Italy for its strong commitment to NATO and for taking in the "homeless" American squadron.

European Community. Italy is committed firmly to a policy of global free trade and looked forward with confidence to the establishment of the single European market in 1992. There will be some wrenching problems for Italy to adjust to the new rules, however—particularly in the South, which will continue to need subsidies from the more affluent members of the European Community.

Gorbachev's USSR. The Italian government welcomed the policies of *perestroika* and *glasnost* espoused by Mikhail Gorbachev in the Soviet Union. In mid-October, Premier De Mita made a state visit to Moscow. A return visit to Italy by General Secretary Gorbachev was expected. De Mita announced that Italian banks would extend $800 billion of credits to the Soviet Union for trade. Despite the desire for more trade with the USSR, Italy remained wary of Soviet efforts to weaken the NATO alliance.

Mediterranean World. Italy has special interests in the Mediterranean basin and was concerned especially about the rapidly increasing population along its southern rim and the pressure this puts on Italy. The persistent problem of terrorism in the area caused Italy to favor an early solution to the Palestinian problem, but in a way that safeguards the security and independence of Israel.

CHARLES F. DELZELL
Vanderbilt University

ITALY • Information Highlights

Official Name: Italian Republic.
Location: Southern Europe.
Area: 116,305 sq mi (301 230 km²).
Population (mid-1988 est.): 57,300,000.
Chief Cities (Dec. 31, 1986): Rome, the capital, 2,815,457; Milan, 1,495,260; Naples, 1,204,211.
Government: *Head of state,* Francesco Cossiga, president (took office July 1985). *Head of government,* Ciriaco De Mita, prime minister (sworn in April 13, 1988). *Legislature*—Parliament: Senate and Chamber of Deputies.
Monetary Unit: Lira (1,283.75 lire equal U.S.$1, Nov. 30, 1988).
Economic Indexes (1987): *Consumer Prices* (1980 = 100) all items, 211.0; food, 199.4. *Industrial Production* (1980 = 100), 103.
Foreign Trade (1987 U.S.$): *Imports,* $125,004,-000,000; *exports,* $116,595,000,000.

Japan's Crown Prince Akihito—posing with his wife, Princess Michiko—was formally asked by the cabinet to assume the duties of emperor when his father, the 87-year-old Emperor Hirohito, fell ill in September. Akihito, 55, ascended the throne upon Hirohito's death on Jan. 7, 1989.

AP/Wide World

JAPAN

As the nation kept a vigil through the worsening condition of 87-year-old Emperor Hirohito, Japanese seemed to realize they were passing through an important transition. The Showa era, as his reign is called, had begun in December 1926, when 25-year-old Crown Prince Hirohito succeeded his father, Emperor Yoshihito. Thus began a reign that lasted 62 years, the longest in recorded Japanese history. The era had witnessed dramatic changes in Japanese life: a promising development of parliamentary democracy in the 1920s; a plunge into militarism, aggression, and war in the 1930s and 1940s; a disastrous defeat in World War II and military occupation from 1945 to 1952; and spectacular reconstruction and growth—to the point of becoming a major economic world power—in the 1960s, 1970s, and 1980s.

Hirohito's death came on the morning of Jan. 7, 1989, and Crown Prince Akihito immediately became Japan's 125th emperor.

Meanwhile, government officials and business leaders in 1988 were referring to Japan's entry into a "third revolution." The first involved the opening up and modernization of Japan during the Meiji Era (1868–1912). The second, during the post-World War II period, was identified with demilitarization, democratization, and reconstruction. And the third, many Japanese predicted, would see a restructuring of the economy—with emphasis on increasing domestic demand and decreasing dependence on exports—and the internationalization of the society.

Domestic Affairs. In speeches throughout 1988, Prime Minister Noboru Takeshita stressed the need for Japan to create a "global village." As the world's second-largest free economy, he said, Japan must emphasize "spiritual affluence." In an aging society, the results of economic growth should be reflected in people's daily lives. And, he stressed, Japan must make "the maximum contribution in forging a world economic order in the interest of global prosperity and world peace." The trouble was that his restructuring program involved not only a tax cut (to boost domestic demand) but also the politics of tax reform, which preoccupied the Takeshita government all through the year.

Party Politics. In October 1987 the majority Liberal-Democratic Party (LDP) had given outgoing Prime Minister Yasuhiro Nakasone the power to nominate his successor. He chose from among the so-called "three new leaders" —Kiichi Miyazawa, Shintaro Abe, and Noboru Takeshita. His choice was Takeshita, who assumed the presidency of the LDP on October 31 and was elected as the 74th Prime Minister of Japan by both houses of the Diet on November 6. Prime Minister Takeshita promptly formed a cabinet, with one of his party rivals, Miyazawa, as finance minister. Sosuke Uno was named foreign minister, and Hajime Tamura became head of the Ministry of International Trade & Industry (MITI). His other rival, Abe, took the important post of secretary-general of the LDP.

In late December 1987, when the 112th regular session of the Diet convened, the LDP and its allied conservative independents controlled 307 of the 512 seats in the (lower) House of Representatives and 143 of the 252 seats in the (upper) House of Councillors. The Japan Socialist Party (JSP), leading the opposition, held 86 seats in the lower house and 42 seats in the upper house. Other opposition parties included the Clean Government Party (Komeito), the Democratic Socialist Party (DSP), and the Japan Communist Party (JCP).

When the Diet reconvened on Jan. 25, 1988, Prime Minister Takeshita unveiled a drastic tax-reform plan, including a 1.3 trillion yen (about $10 billion) cut in the income tax and the imposition of a 3% indirect consumption levy, or value-added tax (VAT). Takako Doi, the first woman to lead a major Japanese party (the JSP), immediately announced that all opposition parties would oppose the VAT. She urged the LDP to proceed with the income-tax cuts but to allow voters to decide on the VAT.

According to public-opinion polls in late March, the LDP tax plan was taking its toll on the party's popularity. Approval ratings for the Takeshita cabinet declined from more than 58% in November to just over 52%. The tax issue also divided Japan's business community. Representatives of powerful industry groups called for tax reform, including the creation of a VAT. But Nobutsugu Shimizu, the head of Japan Chain Stores Association, representing some 3,500 retailers, said he was "absolutely" opposed to the new tax.

The 150-day regular session of the Diet was adjourned on May 25 without a settlement of the tax issue. On July 19 an extraordinary session was called, but periodic boycotts by the opposition parties slowed progress.

In the delay, the LDP, government, and business establishment were rocked by a widening stock scandal involving the Recruit Cosmos company. The first major figure to fall victim was Finance Minister Miyazawa, who allegedly bought shares in the real-estate subsidiary before it went public. Miyazawa denied wrongdoing but resigned December 9. Five days later, Hisashi Shinto, chairman of Nippon Telegraph and Telephone, resigned amid charges that he had taken money from Recruit in exchange for favors.

Miyazawa's resignation was part of a deal with the opposition parties to ensure that the upper house of Parliament would pass the tax reform; the lower house had passed it November 16. Final approval of Japan's most sweeping tax overhaul in 40 years came on December 24. National and local income-tax rates were lowered, corporate tax rates were decreased, and the 3% VAT was imposed.

Takeshita promptly announced the appointment of Tatsuo Murayama, one of the architects of tax reform, as the new finance minister. Then on December 27, in an effort to restore trust, Takeshita shuffled his cabinet. The new appointees included Hiroshi Mitsuzuka as head of MITI; Tsutomu Hata as minister of agriculture, forestry, and fisheries; and Takashi Hasegawa as minister of justice—who would oversee government investigations into the Recruit scandal. But three days later Hasegawa resigned over political donations he had received from the company; former Tokyo Supreme Court judge Masami Takatsuji was named to the post.

Economy. In the first quarter of 1988, according to the Economic Planning Agency (EPA), Japan's economy grew at the fastest pace (2.7%) in a decade. As a result, the adjusted annual growth rate for fiscal 1987 (ended March 31, 1988) was 4.9%, well above the official target of 3.7%. Even more importantly, the ratio of current-account surplus to gross national product (GNP) dropped from 4.5% in fiscal 1986 to 3.5% in fiscal 1987. Japan's GNP in calendar year 1987 amounted to 311.5 trillion yen (about $2.4 trillion). The total reflected a strong 5% increase in domestic demand and a 0.7% drop in external demand.

On April 7, 1988, the regular session of the Diet passed a budget for fiscal 1988. General-account expenditures totaled 56.7 trillion yen (about $456 billion). Outlays for public works were raised 20% from the previous year, with the aim of expanding domestic demand. Expenditures on defense rose 5.2%.

The National Land Agency reported that land prices nationwide rose an average of 21.7% in the fiscal year (ending March 1988), outpacing the previous year's increase of 7.7%. General inflation, however, remained modest; the consumer price index stood at 101.4 in May 1988 (May 1987 = 101.2; 1985 = 100).

Foreign Affairs. In travels throughout the world during 1988, Prime Minister Takeshita called for greater promotion of cultural exchange and strengthening of diplomatic bonds to achieve peace. Japan, he announced, planned to expand its official development assistance (ODA) program.

In a June speech at the third special session on disarmament at the United Nations, Takeshita proposed a five-point action program: (1) diplomatic efforts to solve regional disputes, such as the Iran-Iraq war and the Cambodia conflict; (2) international cooperation to prevent disputes; (3) participation in efforts toward peaceful solution of disputes; (4) assistance to refugees; and (5) increased contributions to reconstruction assistance.

Finance and Trade. Such unusual diplomatic efforts doubtless reflected Japan's economic power and a kind of defense against criticism of its trade policies. On May 2 the Finance Ministry announced that in fiscal 1987 Japan recorded a trade surplus of $94.28 billion. The ministry hastily added that the figure represented a drop of $7.36 billion from the year before. Exports in fiscal 1987 reached a record $233.39 billion (up 10.5%), but imports soared to a record $139.11 billion (up 26.9%). By the end of May 1988, foreign exchange reserves reached an all-time high of $87.24 billion.

On the eve of the summit meeting of major industrial democracies in Toronto, June 19–21, the cabinet formalized a five-year program to offer more than $50 billion in ODA. The Foreign Ministry announced that ODA totaled $7.5 billion in 1987, about 0.31% of Japan's GNP

During an 18-day tour of the Far East, U.S. Secretary of State George Shultz (left) held talks in Tokyo with Japan's Foreign Minister Sosuke Uno on July 19. Trade issues continued to dominate U.S.-Japanese relations throughout the year.

that year. In a meeting with Canada's Prime Minister Brian Mulroney in Toronto, Takeshita unveiled a program of debt relief for the poorest nations of the world. According to the proposal, repayments on the $5.5 billion Japan had lent to least-developed countries in the past decade (the first of which were due in 1988) would be switched to grants. Japan's plan was received cautiously by the other six nations represented at the summit.

U.S. Relations. On Jan. 13, 1988, in Washington, Prime Minister Takeshita held his first meeting with U.S. President Ronald Reagan. The two leaders were accompanied by Foreign Minister Uno and Secretary of State George Shultz, respectively. Takeshita emphasized Japan's determination to fulfill its global responsibilities by continuing the restructuring of the Japanese economy, boosting domestic demand, and further opening Japan's markets to foreign competition.

On March 3 the Washington Metro system rejected a bid for a subway extension submitted by a joint venture involving the Kajima Corporation of Japan. The action resulted from a new U.S. law banning the participation of Japanese firms in projects financed by U.S. federal funds as long as the construction market in Japan is closed to outsiders. On March 29, after talks between Deputy Chief Cabinet Secretary Ichiro Ozawa and U.S. Trade Representative Clayton Yeutter in Washington, an agreement was reached on the participation of foreign firms in Japanese public works. Projects accessible to U.S. firms fell into three categories: (1) the new Kansai International Airport in Osaka; (2) plans to acquaint foreign

corporations with bidding procedures; and (3) construction supported by private or joint government-private sectors.

On June 20, Japan and the United States announced agreement on another problem that had been festering for several years. In cabinet-level negotiations in Tokyo with Trade Representative Yeutter, Agriculture Minister Takashi Sato agreed that Japan would expand beef import quotas by some 50% over three years. Japan also would move toward removing quotas on oranges by April 1991 and on orange juice by 1992.

Meanwhile, on April 22, Japanese officials and business leaders expressed great dissatisfaction over passage in the U.S. House of Representatives of an omnibus trade bill intended, in part, to open foreign markets. A section of the legislation was aimed at any nation engaged in "unfair trade practices." Another section provided sanctions specifically against the Toshiba Corporation, a subsidiary of which had violated a regulation against exporting sensitive machinery to the USSR. Said Chief Cabinet Secretary Keizo Obuchi, "The measure will adversely affect Japan-U.S. relations and the world economy." Hajime Tamura, the head of MITI, openly expressed the hope that President Reagan would veto the legislation.

The U.S. president did exercise his veto power (because of a totally unrelated clause in the bill), but on August 23 he signed similar legislation. Many Japanese felt that their nation had been singled out for attention because of the U.S. budget and trade deficits.

Soviet Relations. Throughout 1988 there was lively speculation in the Japanese press

over the possibility of a visit to Tokyo by Soviet General Secretary Mikhail Gorbachev. In September, however, Japanese officials learned that they would be hosting Soviet Foreign Minister Eduard Shevardnadze instead, December 19–21. His meeting with Foreign Minister Uno would be the first ministerial contact between the two nations in two and a half years. The Japanese hoped that a long-delayed peace treaty would be a major topic of discussion, but an ongoing territorial dispute remained an obstacle. Although Tokyo has maintained normal diplomatic relations with Moscow, discussions of a peace treaty had been hampered by what the Japanese called the "Northern Territories" issue. This had to do with the small Kurile islands (located just north of Hokkaido), which since World War II have been occupied by Soviet forces. On July 30 in Moscow, former Prime Minister Nakasone had engaged Gorbachev in a discussion of the claim. Although the general secretary continued to brush aside the problem, by the end of the year there were signs that the Soviets might reconsider.

Northeast Asia. Prime Minister Takeshita visited Seoul, South Korea, February 24–25, to attend the inauguration of President Roh Tae Woo. The two leaders agreed to set up a bilateral committee (called the "Wisemen Group") to discuss cultural, political, and economic issues. Takeshita emphasized Japan's readiness to help in any way to assure the success of the 1988 Olympic Games in Seoul. Foreign Minister Uno traveled to Seoul on March 20 for a follow-up visit with his South Korean counterpart, Choi Kwang Soo. The two ministers agreed to expand economic relations between the two countries. Uno promised Prime Minister Lee Hyun Jae that Tokyo would try to improve the status of the 675,000 Koreans living in Japan.

Japan welcomed Roh's call for an end to the bitter confrontation between the two Koreas.

North Korea remained the only country with which Japan had no diplomatic relations. Sanctions against even informal contacts with Pyongyang were imposed in February, when evidence showed that North Korean agents had been involved in the bomb destruction of a South Korean civilian airliner. Tokyo lifted those sanctions in September, but Pyongyang's detention since 1983 of two Japanese fishermen on espionage charges remained an obstacle to normal relations.

Prime Minister Takeshita visited China for six days in late August to celebrate the tenth anniversary of the signing of the Sino-Japanese peace treaty. In talks in Beijing with his counterpart, Li Peng, the prime minister pledged support for 42 Chinese modernization projects over a five-year period (1990–95). In October, MITI officials led a mission to China to study investment in environmental projects, and China's Foreign Minister Quan Qichen traveled to Tokyo for reciprocal celebrations of the treaty anniversary.

India. On April 15 in Tokyo, Takeshita and India's Prime Minister Rajiv Gandhi praised the signing of agreements in Geneva that paved the way for the pullout of Soviet troops from Afghanistan. Takeshita declared that relations with India were one of the pillars of Japanese diplomacy and that Tokyo strongly would promote economic cooperation with India.

Middle East. Tokyo also welcomed the August announcement by UN Secretary-General Javier Perez de Cuellar of a cease-fire between Iran and Iraq. MITI promptly announced that Japan was ready to extend yen-denominated loans to help repair their war-ravaged economies.

In Israel during late June, Foreign Minister Uno reiterated Japan's position that Israel should recognize the Palestinian right to self-determination and should withdraw from occupied areas. Israel's Prime Minister Yitzhak Shamir in turn expressed concern about the anti-Semitic literature being published in Japan (see RELIGION—*Judaism*). The discussions marked the first official visit to Israel by a Japanese foreign minister. Before his stop in Jerusalem, Uno had met with officials in Jordan, Egypt, and Syria to discuss the possibility of regional peace.

South Pacific. On July 5, Prime Minister Takeshita returned to Japan from a four-day visit to Australia, his seventh overseas trip since taking office. With his Australian counterpart, Robert Hawke, Takeshita agreed on a plan to expand bilateral cooperation, to increase official development aid (ODA) to the South Pacific region, and to promote dialogue among the newly industrializing economies of Asia. He also conveyed former Prime Minister Nakasone's idea of establishing a Pacific league of parliamentarians.

ARDATH W. BURKS, *Rutgers University*

JAPAN • Information Highlights

Official Name: Japan.
Location: East Asia.
Area: 143,749 sq mi (372 310 km²).
Population (mid-1988 est.): 122,700,000.
Chief Cities (Oct. 1, 1986 est): Tokyo, the capital, 8,354,615; Yokohama, 2,992,926; Osaka, 2,636,249; Nagoya, 2,116,381.
Government: *Head of state,* Hirohito, emperor (acceded Dec. 1926). *Head of government,* Noboru Takeshita, prime minister (took office Nov. 1987). *Legislature*—Diet: House of Councillors and House of Representatives.
Monetary Unit: Yen (123.8 yen equal U.S.$1, Nov. 9, 1988).
Gross National Product (1987 U.S.$): $2,400,000,-000.
Economic Indexes (1987): *Consumer Prices* (1980 = 100), all items, 115.3; food, 113.6. *Industrial Production* (1980 = 100), 126.
Foreign Trade (1987 U.S.$): *Imports,* $139,110,-000,000; *exports,* $233,390,000,000.

Jordan's King Hussein (center), Egypt's President Hosni Mubarak (left), and Palestine Liberation Organization Chairman Yasir Arafat discuss relations between Jordan and the PLO at the king's Red Sea beachfront palace October 22.

AP/Wide World

JORDAN

King Hussein was tested during 1988 in economic matters and, strikingly, in the tangled area of Jordan's relations with the West Bank and the Palestinians.

Economic Issues. The economy experienced increasing problems. Unemployment, estimated at 8%, was inconveniently high. Already in October 1987 it had been announced that after the end of the year no more work permits would be issued to foreigners. Unemployment seemed to be worsened by the reluctance of Jordanians to accept low-level jobs. Official figures in September estimated that there were 32,000 unemployed junior college and university graduates as against 18,000 unemployed unskilled workers.

One basic reason for Jordan's current difficulties was a reduction in subsidies from wealthier Arab states. Much, however, had gone well with the 1986–90 five-year national development plan. Some 224 schools were under construction, far exceeding the 115 at first envisaged. Water, electricity, education, and health projects were making rapid progress.

JORDAN · Information Highlights

Official Name: Hashemite Kingdom of Jordan.
Location: Southwest Asia.
Area: 35,475 sq mi (91 880 km²).
Population (mid-1988 est.): 3,800,000.
Chief Cities (Dec. 1986): Amman, the capital, 972,000; Zarqa, 392,220; Irbid, 271,000.
Government: *Head of state,* Hussein I, king (acceded Aug. 1952). *Head of government,* Zayd al-Rifa'i, prime minister (appointed April 4, 1985). *Legislature*—Parliament: House of Representatives and Senate.
Monetary Unit: Dinar (.47 dinar equals U.S.$1, Dec. 14, 1988).
Economic Index (1987): *Consumer Prices* (1980 = 100), all items, 129.6; food, 119.5.
Foreign Trade (1987 U.S.$): *Imports,* $2,703,000,000; *exports,* $734,000,000.

West Bank. The most striking development of the year, by far, was a series of major and unforeseen policy changes at the end of July by which Jordan largely severed its connections with the West Bank. This area, once part of the Palestine Mandate, had been taken over in 1948 by King Abdullah (Hussein's grandfather), and it was administered as part of the Hashemite Kingdom until 1967, when it was lost to Israel in the Six-Day War. But Jordan continued to claim the area as part of its territory, included it in all statistical data, and (with a good deal of tacit Israeli cooperation) carried on some administrative activities there.

None of this earned Jordan much Arab goodwill. Jordan had to swallow the recognition by the Arab League Summit at Rabat in 1974 of the Palestine Liberation Organization (PLO) as the "sole legitimate representative of the Palestinian people," a decision essentially reaffirmed by the emergency Arab League meeting at Algiers in June 1988—a meeting occasioned by the preceding six months of violence in the West Bank.

On July 28 the Jordanian cabinet terminated the West Bank development plan, a vast $1.3 billion scheme first promulgated in August 1986. Adequate funding from other Arab states had not been forthcoming. The plan, viewed favorably by the United States and Israel, was opposed by the PLO, which did not see it as being in its interests. Secondly, on July 30 a royal decree dissolved the House of Representatives, lower house of the National Assembly (the Senate remained unaffected and continued to function). Half of the 142 seats represented West Bank constituencies or Palestinian refugees.

Finally, in a televised speech in the evening of July 31 the king announced that Jordan was giving up its efforts to administer the Israeli-occupied West Bank, saying "Jordan is not Palestine." On August 4 the government announced that it would discontinue paying the

salaries of 18,000 civil servants, teachers, and other professionals in the West Bank, though there would be severance and retirement provisions. Later it appeared that Jordanian passports would continue to be issued to Palestinian Arabs, though for shorter terms.

Much speculation and comment followed this remarkable about-face, but it seemed clear that Jordan rationally was abandoning a line of policy that had been very costly as well as unproductive and was thrusting on the PLO the responsibilities that that body so long had claimed.

These changes appeared to end the "Jordanian option," or involvement, as an approach to Arab-Israeli peacemaking, but later developments suggested that this gambit could not be totally precluded. King Hussein, President Hosni Mubarak of Egypt, and PLO leader Yasir Arafat (whom Hussein had denounced in February 1986) had a cordial meeting at Aqaba, Jordan, on October 22. In mid-November Jordan was one of the nations that quickly recognized the independent Palestinian state proclaimed in Algiers by the PLO.

See also ISRAEL—*The Palestine Issue;* MIDDLE EAST.

ARTHUR CAMPBELL TURNER
University of California, Riverside

KANSAS

The Kansas economy remained fairly stable in 1988, despite sluggish agricultural and oil industries. State revenues consistently exceeded estimates, creating a larger than anticipated surplus.

Agriculture. The 1988 Kansas wheat crop totaled 319.6 million bushels, down 13% from 1987. This was the lowest production since 1981, averaging 34 bushels per acre. The total number of acres harvested, 9.4 million, was the lowest since 1972, the result of government crop acreage reduction programs. While Kansas was not hit as hard by drought as other states in the Midwest, a lack of moisture and hot weather took their toll.

For the fifth consecutive year, Kansas led the nation in sorghum grain production with a yield of 60 bushels per acre, in spite of being 29% lower than 1987. The 1988 corn crop was estimated at a total of 138 million bushels, down 3% from 1987 while the soybean crop totaled only 48.3 million bushels, down 28% from the previous year.

Farm income for 1987 (the last full year for which statistics are available) totaled $7.3 billion. Due in part to increases in other farm income and government payments, this total was up 5% from 1986, but farm production expenses were also up 2%.

Legislation. A number of significant issues were addressed by the 1988 Kansas legislature, many of which were related to an estimated tax windfall of approximately $135 million created by changes in the federal income-tax laws. A tax-revision package would return about $35.4 million of the windfall to taxpayers by lowering state income-tax rates from 8% to 2%. Approximately 105,000 Kansans with low income will be dropped from the tax rolls; senior citizens and the blind will receive double exemptions.

In April, U.S. District Judge Richard Rogers of Topeka ordered the state to reduce prison overcrowding by 400 inmates, leading to legislative action on the issue. Construction and expansion projects totaling $23.2 million were approved, with an additional $15.8 million appropriated to expand community corrections programs.

One of the issues discussed most heatedly was aid to the state's 303 public-school districts. Ultimately state aid was increased by more than $32 million after compromises were made that decreased the large cuts that would have resulted for the state's four largest school districts.

Other legislation included a division of assets bill to lessen the burden of long-term care for the surviving spouse, a cap on damage awards in some types of lawsuit in an effort to control costs of liability insurance, and a sales-tax exemption on the purchase of manufacturing machinery.

Elections. George Bush easily defeated Michael Dukakis in the Kansas vote for president, and all five incumbents in the U.S. House of Representatives—Pat Roberts (R), Jim Slattery (D), Jan Meyers (R), Dan Glickman (D), and Bob Whittaker (R)—were reelected easily. Republicans retained their majorities in both the Kansas House and Senate.

Sports. In April the University of Kansas Jayhawks, led by senior forward Danny Manning, won the NCAA basketball tournament by defeating Big Eight rival Oklahoma 83-79.

PATRICIA A. MICHAELIS
Kansas State Historical Society

KANSAS • Information Highlights

Area: 82,277 sq mi (213 098 km²).

Population (July 1, 1987): 2,476,000.

Chief Cities (July 1, 1986 est.): Topeka, the capital, 118,580; Wichita, 288,060; Kansas City, 162,070.

Government (1988): *Chief Officers*—governor, Mike Hayden (R); lt. gov., Jack D. Walker (R). *Legislature*—Senate, 40 members; House of Representatives, 125 members.

State Finances (fiscal year 1987): *Revenue,* $4,112,000,000; *expenditure,* $3,629,000,000.

Personal Income (1987): $37,450,000,000; per capita, $15,126.

Labor Force (June 1988): *Civilian labor force,* 1,306,700; *unemployed,* 56,700 (4.3% of total force).

Education: *Enrollment* (fall 1986)—public elementary schools, 291,564; public secondary, 124,527; colleges and universities, 143,311. *Public school expenditures* (1986–87), $1,541,000,000 ($4,137 per pupil).

Kentucky's Gov. Wallace Wilkinson (center) joined Kaneyoshi Kusunoki (left), president of Toyota Motor Manufacturing, U.S.A., Inc., and Schoichiro Toyoda, president of Toyota Motor Corporation, in October at the dedication ceremonies of Toyota's new $800 million Georgetown, KY, plant.

AP/Wide World

KENTUCKY

In the November 1988 elections Kentucky voters gave George Bush 731,446 votes (56%) to Michael Dukakis' 579,077 (44%), with Bush getting nine electoral votes. While Kentucky generally votes Democratic in state elections, it has not voted for a Democratic president from a northern state since Franklin Roosevelt. There was no U.S. Senate race in Kentucky in 1988, and all incumbents—four Democrats and three Republicans—won reelection to the U.S. House of Representatives. The state legislature remained heavily Democratic, with no significant change.

Politics. The political scene was dominated by Gov. Wallace Wilkinson and the legislature. Wilkinson, a businessman who previously had not held elective office, was determined to set the agenda for the state. The legislature, however, which has been growing more independent in recent years, was determined equally to avoid his control.

Governor Wilkinson, who made a state lottery a major theme of his campaign in 1987, gained legislative approval for placing the lottery on the ballot as a constitutional amendment. The voters approved the lottery by a margin of more than 60%. In addition to the lottery amendment, the voters also approved a constitutional amendment designed to prohibit coal companies from strip mining on land where they own the mineral rights under "broad form deeds," written in the 19th century.

The legislature rejected pressure from the governor to approve a constitutional amendment designed to permit governors to serve a second consecutive term. Kentucky is one of two remaining states banning gubernatorial succession. Virginia is the other.

Election Reform. After the *Louisville-Courier Journal* published a series of articles describing how funds are raised for campaigns, and how votes are bought in some counties, the legislature passed a package of reforms. Several reforms were designed to crack down on, and raise the penalties for, the buying of votes. Another provision was aimed at discouraging wealthy candidates from loaning large sums of money to their campaigns, and recouping the funds from contributors.

Economic Development. There is general agreement in Kentucky that more adequate funding for education and other purposes requires a broader tax base, derived from greater economic development. Several years ago the state provided major incentives to the Toyota company to build an automobile factory in Scott county. In 1988 the Toyota factory opened, and the first cars rolled off the assembly line.

KENTUCKY • Information Highlights

Area: 40,410 sq mi (104 660 km²).
Population (July 1, 1987): 3,727,000.
Chief Cities (July 1, 1986 est.): Frankfort, the capital (1980 census), 25,973; Louisville, 287,460; Lexington-Fayette, 213,600.
Government (1988): *Chief Officers*—governor, Wallace Wilkinson (D); lt. gov., Brereton Jones (D). *General Assembly*—Senate, 38 members; House of Representatives, 100 members.
State Finances (fiscal year 1987): *Revenue,* $6,926,000,000; *expenditure,* $6,334,000,000.
Personal Income (1987): $44,945,000,000; per capita, $12,059.
Labor Force (June 1988): *Civilian labor force,* 1,709,700; *unemployed,* 133,700 (7.8% of total force).
Education: *Enrollment* (fall 1986)—public elementary schools, 446,901; public secondary, 195,877; colleges and universities, 144,562. *Public school expenditures* (1986–87), $1,790,000,000 ($3,107 per pupil).

Education. There was support in the legislature for raising taxes, primarily to improve education. These efforts did not succeed due to opposition from the governor, who had campaigned as an opponent of tax hikes.

The outlook for increased spending for education brightened because of judicial action near the end of the year. A state circuit judge ruled that the legislature had failed to conform to the state's constitutional requirement for an "efficient" school system. Since the state had failed to provide sufficient aid to the poorer school districts where funding for education is low, the judge said that some children are "condemned to an inferior education." Legislative action on this issue was delayed, however, when the issue was appealed to the Kentucky Supreme Court.

Highway Tragedy. A church-sponsored outing for teenagers ended in tragedy on May 14, 1988, when Larry Mahoney drove his pickup truck the wrong way on an interstate highway and crashed into a bus, killing 27 people. Mahoney, age 34, had a blood alcohol content twice the state's legal limit.

MALCOLM E. JEWELL
University of Kentucky

KENYA

After a year of international pressure to strengthen his human-rights record, President Daniel T. arap Moi released several political prisoners in January. The following month Moi dissolved parliament and called for new elections, which were held on March 21. While this greatly strengthened his political position, the economic position of the country remained very weak.

Elections. The preliminary selection of candidates was characterized by two constitutional changes. Rather than voting by secret ballot, members of the ruling party, KANU, voted by queuing behind pictures of the candidate of their choice. In addition, if candidates received 70% or more of the party vote, they were elected directly to parliament. Since registered voters outnumber KANU members, the electoral process effectively disenfranchised a significant proportion of the population in the 61 constituencies in which candidates were returned directly to parliament.

Queue voting also replaced secret ballots in the March election, in which 30% of the incumbents were defeated. A prominent loser was Justus Ole Tipis, who until January had served as the powerful minister of state for internal security in the office of the president. Martin Shikuku, an outspoken critic of the Moi government, also was defeated.

Cabinet Reshuffle. Immediately following the elections, Moi demoted Mwai Kibaki, who had served as vice-president since Jomo Ken-

---

KENYA • Information Highlights

Official Name: Republic of Kenya.
Location: East Coast of Africa.
Area: 224,961 sq mi (582 650 km^2).
Population (mid-1988 est.): 23,300,000.
Chief Cities (1985 est.): Nairobi, the capital, 1,162,189; Mombasa, 442,369.
Government: *Head of state and government,* Daniel T. arap Moi, president (took office Oct. 1978). *Legislature* (unicameral)—National Assembly, 188 elected members, 12 appointed by the president.
Monetary Unit: Kenya shilling (18.085 shillings equal U.S.$1, June 1988).
Gross Domestic Product (1986 U.S.$): $5,000,-000,000.
Economic Index (1986): *Consumer Prices,* (Nairobi, 1980 = 100), all items, 215.2; food, 187.1.
Foreign Trade (1987 U.S.$): *Imports,* $1,756,000,000; *exports,* $961,000,000.

---

yatta's death in 1978. Kibaki, now minister of health, and other Kikuyu politicians have found their power declining as Moi has surrounded himself with individuals whose major sources of political strength come from their close relationship to the president. Josephat Karanja, the new vice-president, is such a person.

Moi also expanded his government by adding five new ministries to the 24 already in existence and by enlarging the number of MPs who serve in the government, thus ensuring an increasingly docile parliament.

Limiting Public Criticism. Shortly after the new parliament met, it enacted a constitutional amendment that gave the president the power to dismiss judges and members of the Civil Service Commission at will. The amendment also extended from 24 hours to two weeks the length of time suspects or individuals "about to commit a capital offense" can be held without a charge. While "imagining" the death or overthrow of the president is already a capital offense, under the amendment, "thinking seriously" about murder, armed robbery, or treason is as well.

Economy. Business confidence boomed following the March elections as property values and the black market value of the Kenya shilling increased. Many investors viewed Moi's consolidation of power as an opportunity to develop special relationships with members of the government without having to worry about criticism from parliament. Kenya's international position continued to deteriorate, largely due to depressed coffee earnings, Kenya's major source of foreign exchange. As foreign exchange reserves fell to record lows, new exchange controls were introduced and imports were restricted. Furthermore, in an effort to reduce the growth in the money supply and thereby reduce inflation, the Central Bank increased interest rates 1% to 15%.

WILLIAM CYRUS REED
Wabash College

South Korea's outgoing President Chun Doo Hwan (center) and his wife Lee Soon-ja welcome his newly inaugurated successor, Roh Tae Woo, to the presidential mansion, Feb. 25, 1988. Late in the year, Chun was under fire for alleged corruption and abuse of power during his rule. Although Chun apologized to the nation, the new president named a special unit to investigate his friend.

AP/Wide World

KOREA

The year's most important developments in the divided peninsula occurred in South Korea: the inauguration of a new president committed to political liberalization; the election of a new National Assembly in which the government party controlled only a minority of the seats; and the hosting of the XXIV Summer Olympic Games.

Republic of Korea (South Korea)

Politics and Government. After his election in December 1987, former Gen. Roh Tae Woo was inaugurated as president of the Sixth Republic on Feb. 25, 1988 (see BIOGRAPHY). His announced program, which was democratic and even populist in tone, reduced tensions with the opposition if not actually winning it over. One of his first acts was to announce a general amnesty for more than 7,000 criminal and political prisoners; another 1,000 or more political prisoners remained in jail.

During the ensuing election campaign for the National Assembly—much as in the 1987 presidential campaign—the two major opposition parties, Kim Dae Jung's Party for Peace and Democracy (PPD) and Kim Young Sam's Reunification Democratic Party (RDP), failed to unite. The April 26 balloting produced some surprising results. President Roh's ruling Democratic Justice Party (DJP) failed to win a majority of seats, as had been expected, though it did win a plurality (125 out of 299). The PPD won 70 seats, and the RDP won 59.

The National Assembly, which opened May 30, was thus a lively and often turbulent body. Five committees, each representing all the parties, were formed for such purposes as investigating alleged corruption and abuses of power

under former President Chun Doo Hwan; curbing the Agency for National Security Planning (the formidable political police); and reopening the notorious case of the Kwangju massacre (the May 1980 military suppression of a popular uprising in Kwangju). Televised hearings late in the year, featuring the testimony of Chun and other former high officials, held the nation transfixed.

Largely through cooperation between the DJP and the opposition, the Assembly took a number of constructive steps during the year. One was the elimination of abuses, including torture, formerly practiced by the police. Another was planning for the introduction of local elected government (local offices previously had been appointive). And there was considerable progress toward an independent judiciary. Chief Justice Kim Yong Chul, who was regarded as too political, resigned in June, but President Roh's nominee for the post then was rejected by the Assembly.

President Roh clearly was eager to conciliate the opposition, as exemplified in April by the government's expression of regret for the Kwangju massacre. One of his main objectives was to promote a level of political calm sufficient to permit the Olympic Games to proceed without disruption. On the whole, he was successful in this. The Games, held from September 17 to October 2 under very tight security, witnessed no serious demonstrations, terrorist incidents, or pressures from North Korea.

Nevertheless, the militant opposition, consisting largely of leftist students, was far from inactive during 1988. In June and in August, for example, radical students attempted to march to the Demilitarized Zone (DMZ) to promote contact—and ultimately reunification—with North Korea, and a U.S. military withdrawal; both times they were stopped by police. The militants lost much of their earlier support from

the urban middle class and labor, which largely had accepted the new political system. After the Olympics, however, the student radicals made former President Chun the main target of their demonstrations, calling for his arrest and trial, and this proved to be a more popular cause than attacks on President Roh himself. The radicals continued to demand the overthrow of Roh, but for this they found little support. Industrial workers began to express disgruntlement with their long hours, poor working conditions, strict discipline, and low wages relative to productivity. The increasingly liberal political atmosphere was paralleled by an increase in the frequency of strikes.

In short, while the general political trend was less turbulent than it might have been, it was still a source of concern to the DJP. In August one of its leaders even advocated a change from a presidential to a parliamentary constitution, which, he said, would facilitate the maintenance of political and social order.

In December, President Roh replaced most of his cabinet and appointed a new prime minister, Kang Young Hoon, in an effort to separate himself from former President Chun.

Economy. After a sharp upturn in early 1988, the South Korean economy slacked off somewhat under the impact of rising labor costs, strikes, and the appreciation of the won. Growth for the year was approximately 9% in real terms—a very respectable figure, although lower than the preceding few years. The inflation rate stood at 7%–8%.

President Roh established a commission to study the restructuring of the economy so as to reduce the role of the government, cut the trade surplus, promote domestic demand, and improve living standards. Overall, however, the economy would continue to be export-driven. A minimum-wage law and a system of worker's pensions had been introduced at the end of 1987. The eight large government corporations were to be partially privatized through the sale of stock to persons with no more than middle-class incomes. The private sector continued to be dominated, however, by a small number of huge family holding companies (*chaebol*). One of the largest of these, Hyundai, suffered a three-week strike in the middle of the year by workers who, although enjoying a rising wage level, resented the firm's unusually paternalistic management style. Other companies also experienced a growing frequency of industrial disputes.

In spite of the strength of the won, South Korea's exports continued to grow rapidly, and the favorable trade balance established in 1986 persisted. Nevertheless, the business community was apprehensive about the effects of further currency appreciation and resentful of U.S. pressures for more rapid increases. These pressures reflected South Korea's $9.6 billion trade surplus with the United States (versus a

AP/Wide World

Widespread demonstrations by South Korean students, which had led to democratic reform in 1987, continued in 1988. Former President Chun was the main target.

$5.2 billion deficit with Japan) in 1987, an amount half again as large as the overall South Korean surplus of $6.3 billion ($47.3 billion in exports, $41.0 billion in imports). The trade surplus for 1988 was expected to exceed $10 billion.

These surpluses were all the more remarkable inasmuch as they accumulated in the face not only of the appreciation of the won but also the gradual reduction of South Korea's import tariffs. Government efforts to liberalize imports were controversial for reasons that were partly economic and partly political. The resentment was directed mainly against the United States, the principal source of outside pressure for import liberalization. The opening of the South Korean market to U.S. cigarettes was followed by the country's first antismoking campaign. U.S. beef imports continued to encounter strong resistance from South Korean farmers. And American-made camera film encountered opposition from South Korean manufacturers and distributors.

There were a number of encouraging developments in the field of foreign trade. The cease-fire in the Iran-Iraq war aroused hopes for a further lowering of oil prices and a resumption of lucrative construction contracts for South Korean firms and sent the Seoul stock market soaring. South Korean banks were beginning to emerge as significant international lenders. The

Hyundai Motor Company opened its first overseas automobile assembly plant, in Canada. The participation of most Communist countries in the Seoul Olympics seemingly brought nearer the beginning of trade with the Soviet Union, Eastern Europe, and even Vietnam—a development much desired by both the government and the business community of South Korea. Hungary opened a trade office in Seoul in June, with the Soviet Union and China reportedly planning to do the same. A sizable "unofficial" trade—upward of $2 billion annually—already had been achieved with China (via Hong Kong) and was expected to continue growing. Travel, including tourism, to and from the Communist countries also was getting under way.

Foreign Affairs. South Korea hoped that the Olympic Games would signal the country's economic and diplomatic "coming out" in the world community, much as the 1964 Tokyo Olympics had done for Japan. Understandable concern over the possibility of disruption by North Korean, Arab, or other terrorists—or even an actual attack by North Korea—led to massive security precautions. Among these were the placing on alert status of the 43,000 U.S. troops stationed in South Korea and the deployment of two U.S. aircraft carriers off the coast.

"Sports diplomacy" did much to improve South Korea's foreign relations in 1988. The Olympics clearly enhanced the nation's visibility and image on the world scene. Only six states—North Korea, Cuba, and Ethiopia being the most important—boycotted the Games. President Roh was able to make significant progress in his "Nordpolitik" campaign, an effort to forge ties with the Communist countries. In September he became the first South Korean president to hold talks with Soviet officials, in Seoul. Moscow took an effusive attitude toward the Olympics and made an important cultural contact by sending the Bol-

---

SOUTH KOREA • Information Highlights

Official Name: Republic of Korea.
Location: Northeastern Asia.
Area: 38,023 sq mi (98,480 km²).
Population (mid-1988 est.): 42,600,000.
Chief City (1985 census): Seoul, the capital, 9,639,110.
Government: *Head of state,* Roh Tae Woo, president (formally inaugurated February 1988). *Head of government,* Kang Young Hoon, prime minister (appointed December 1988). *Legislature*—National Assembly.
Monetary Unit: Won (728.3 won equal U.S.$1, June 1988).
Gross National Product (1987 U.S.$): $118,000,-000,000.
Economic Indexes (1987): *Consumer Prices* (1980 = 100), all items, 148.8; food, 144.6. *Industrial Production* (1980 = 100), 234.
Foreign Trade (1987 U.S.$): *Imports,* $41,000,-000,000; *exports,* $47,300,000,000.

---

shoi Ballet to Seoul. In September, Hungary became the first Communist country to grant diplomatic recognition to the Republic of Korea. And relations improved with other nations as well, such as Japan. Prime Minister Noboru Takeshita visited Seoul in February and reportedly agreed to help South Korea normalize relations with China. Later, at the time of the Olympics, the two major Japanese opposition parties, the Japan Socialist Party and the Japan Communist Party, which had been very critical of political developments in South Korea, sent delegations to Seoul.

On the whole, the bittersweet relationship with the United States, South Korea's only ally, was not improved by the Olympics. Some Koreans objected to the tone of television coverage by the National Broadcasting Company (NBC) and the behavior of some U.S. athletes; some Americans disliked the tight security and the allegedly unsportsmanlike conduct of some Korean athletes and audiences. These issues hardly would have been noticed, however, if it had not been for the continuing existence of

South Korea underwent extensive construction and redevelopment in preparation for the 1988 Summer Olympics in Seoul. The total cost was estimated at $3.1 billion. Athletes from a record 160 nations participated.

AP/Wide World

more basic problems. Radical students were not the only South Koreans who continued to blame the United States for having divided the country in 1945, supported a series of military governments, and stood in the way of the widely desired unification with North Korea. Many favored South Korean control over the Combined Forces Command, currently headed by a U.S. general. There was widespread concern over the suspected deployment in South Korea of hundreds of U.S. tactical nuclear warheads, whose number Washington would not reveal and whose very presence it would "neither confirm nor deny." In the Yongsan area not far from Seoul, a complex of official U.S. housing, athletic facilities, and military installations was an offense to many Koreans. And U.S. pressures for import liberalization and increased South Korean financial support for U.S. forces in the country (which already amounted to $27,000 per soldier) were resented widely.

On the other hand, the U.S. connection, including the presence of troops, still was accepted by the South Korean public as a whole. Opposition leader Kim Dae Jung, never considered pro-U.S., said publicly while in the Philippines that the U.S. bases there were important to the stability of the region and should be retained. The annual U.S.-South Korean joint military exercises, known as Team Spirit, were held as usual in March. U.S. Secretary of Defense Frank Carlucci, during a June visit, said that U.S. forces would stay in South Korea but only as long as needed and wanted by their hosts. The following month, U.S. Secretary of State George Shultz expressed optimism during an official visit regarding security for the Olympics and praised a recent overture by President Roh to North Korea. Shultz also indicated that the United States was willing, at Seoul's request, to resume unofficial contacts with the North (which had been suspended in January). President Roh made an official visit to the United States in October, during which he made a speech before the United Nations General Assembly (becoming the first Korean leader ever to address that body) and held talks at the White House with President Ronald Reagan.

Democratic People's Republic of Korea (North Korea)

Because of the closed, totalitarian nature of North Korea's Communist regime, little was known of developments there in 1988 except in the field of foreign affairs, where Pyongyang's position tended to deteriorate.

Domestic Affairs. Although the aging "Great Leader," Kim Il Sung, remained in overall command, his son and intended successor, Kim Jong Il, reportedly was in charge of daily operations. There was some reason to believe,

however, that the younger Kim's political position was being affected adversely by the poor state of the economy, management of which was his responsibility. A political succession, possibly involving a struggle for power, appeared to lie not far in the future.

Foreign Affairs. Pyongyang had claimed the right to cohost the 1988 Olympic Games, but the International Olympic Committee (IOC) would allow only five events to be held in North Korea. During visits by Soviet Politburo member Viktor M. Chebrikov and Chinese President Yang Shangkun—marking North Korea's 40th anniversary (September 9)—North Korea's big Communist allies reportedly conveyed the message that they did not want Pyongyang to disrupt the Games, since their own athletes would be participating. To the disappointment of Seoul, the IOC, the international sporting community, and even many of its own citizens, North Korea boycotted the Olympic Games.

After the sabotage of a South Korean airliner by a confessed North Korean agent in November 1987, the United States and Japan both suspended informal contacts with North Korea in January 1988; Washington officially listed it as one of the nations guilty of state-sanctioned terrorism. To ease tensions in advance of the Olympics, Japan lifted diplomatic sanctions in September. And in late October, on the urgings of South Korea's President Roh, the United States resumed limited contact. Pyongyang, however, continued to export arms to numerous troublesome states in the Third World, notably Iran.

Mainly for economic reasons, the North Korean regime apparently wanted to expand its international contacts, but it seemed at a loss to know how. It resented the presence of U.S. forces in South Korea, as well as Washington's efforts to promote "cross-recognition" of the two Koreas and the admission of both to the United Nations—moves which seemed to threaten a permanent division of the peninsula. Hungary's recognition of South Korea was viewed in Pyongyang as a betrayal. A number

Delegates from North (left) and South (right) Korea met in Panmunjom in mid-October to discuss a possible reunification conference. The meeting ended inconclusively after two hours. A similar conference had occurred in August.

AP/Wide World

of North Korea's West European creditors were unhappy over Pyongyang's nonpayment of interest, and Austria went so far as to close its embassy. Even the Soviet Union, while it continued to send limited shipments of advanced weapons, was unenthusiastic about North Korea's poor economic performance and its unbending attitude toward the South.

The Two Koreas

As in previous years, the relationship between North Korea and South Korea consisted of two contradictory elements: the threat of outright military conflict and intermittent political contacts.

Continuing Confrontation. On Nov. 29, 1987, Korean Air Flight 858, en route from Baghdad to Seoul, crashed in the sea off Burma; all 115 persons aboard were killed. Two North Korean agents who had left the flight in Abu Dhabi attempted suicide after being apprehended in Bahrain. One, a woman named Kim Hyon Hui, survived and was sent to South Korea. After a month in custody, she confessed to having planted a bomb aboard the aircraft on orders originating with Kim Jong Il. Her confession apparently was motivated more by repentance than by coercion and was accepted widely as genuine. The purpose of the sabotage apparently had been to disrupt the South Korean presidential election and discourage foreigners from traveling to South Korea for the Olympics via Korean Air.

Another threat from the North, a potentially more serious one, failed to materialize. Since late 1986, North Korea had been constructing a dam north of the DMZ that had been viewed by official Seoul as having the capability to release enough water to flood the city, perhaps at the time of the Olympics. To counter that threat, South Korea began con-

structing the so-called Peace Dam across the Pukhan River north of Seoul. By the time of the Olympics, however, it appeared increasingly unlikely that the North Korean "water bomb," or any other form of direct pressure, would be unleashed against the South, at least in the near future.

North-South Contacts. As an interim approach to the division of the peninsula, pending ultimate unification, South Korea has favored a "German" solution, based on a North-South treaty; Seoul has been proposing a North-South summit conference since 1981. North Korea, meanwhile, long has been demanding the withdrawal of U.S. forces from the South, followed by a confederation between the two sides; Pyongyang apparently believes that these two steps would maximize the chance of a political collapse of the South Korean government.

In mid-1988 the Seoul regime expressed new interest in establishing contacts with the North. By doing so, it hoped to appease the rising public demand for progress toward unification, to preempt student radicals threatening to disrupt the Olympics, and to minimize the chances of interference by the North. In June, therefore, South Korean Prime Minister Lee Hyun Jae proposed the resumption of North-South talks, which had been suspended since January 1986. And on July 7, President Roh made a major statement in favor of trade, travel, and diplomatic cooperation between the two sides.

Pyongyang rejected these ideas, proposing instead that the full memberships of both National Assemblies meet, first in Pyongyang and later in Seoul, to discuss a nonaggression pact and cohosting of the Olympics. Although Pyongyang clearly refused to concede legitimacy to the Roh government by negotiating directly, there were elements of flexibility in its over-

ture. In particular, the termination of the U.S.-South Korea security tie, including the withdrawal of U.S. troops, was treated as a result, rather than a precondition, of the desired non-aggression pact. In August delegations representing the two National Assemblies met at Panmunjom, but the talks broke down, mainly over Seoul's rejection of Pyongyang's continuing demand to cohost the Olympics. The representatives met again after the Games, but discussions of a full meeting of National Assemblies proved inconclusive.

Meanwhile, as early as August, President Roh had begun trying to involve the United Nations—in which both Koreas are represented as observers rather than full members—in the reunification process. On October 18, Roh made a major address to the General Assembly, in which he renewed the proposal for a North-South summit and advocated a "consultative conference for peace" composed of the United States, the Soviet Union, China, Japan, and the two Koreas. The latter idea was based in part on a similar proposal advanced by Soviet General Secretary Mikhail Gorbachev in September. North Korean Deputy Foreign Minister Kang Sok Ju addressed the General Assembly the following day, stressing the familiar demands of a U.S. troop withdrawal and a North-South confederation.

In a brief meeting with President Reagan on October 20, Roh urged the United States to resume informal contacts with North Korea (limited trade, travel, and diplomatic exchange), which had been suspended after the Korean Air Lines sabotage. The White House complied.

HAROLD C. HINTON
The George Washington University

KUWAIT

No country in the Persian Gulf region had better reason than Kuwait to welcome the August 1988 cease-fire in the Iran-Iraq war. Small, extremely rich and vulnerable, and adjacent to both combatants, Kuwait had led a precarious existence during the eight years of war. It had endured sporadic Iranian attacks, and been the target of terrorist incidents.

Hijacking. The most spectacular terrorist attack of 1988 concerned a Kuwaiti airliner and lasted April 5–16. The plane, en route from Bangkok, Thailand, to Kuwait, was over the Arabian Sea when a group of hijackers, thought to be pro-Iranian Shiite Muslims from Lebanon, took over and forced it to fly to Mashhad, Iran, later to Cyprus, and finally to Algeria. There were 112 passengers on the plane, including three members of the Kuwaiti royal family. In the course of the plane's wanderings, more than half of the passengers were released; two were murdered. The hijackers' demand was for the release by Kuwait of 17 convicted

---

KUWAIT • Information Highlights

Official Name: State of Kuwait.
Location: Southwest Asia.
Area: 6,800 sq mi (17 820 km²).
Population (mid-1988 est.) 2,000,000.
Chief Cities (1985 est.): Kuwait, the capital, 44,335; Salmiya, 153,369; Hawalli, 145,126.
Government: *Head of state,* Jabir al-Ahmad Al Sabah, emir (acceded Dec. 1977). *Head of government,* Saad al-Abdallah Al Sabah, prime minister (appointed Feb. 1978). *Legislature—* National Assembly (dissolved July 1986).
Monetary Unit: Dinar (0.2798 dinar equal U.S. $1, Nov. 29, 1988).
Gross Domestic Product (1987 U.S.$): $16,900,-000,000.
Economic Index (1987): *Consumer Prices* (1980 = 100), all items, 126.6; food, 110.2.

---

terrorists who had been involved in terrorist acts in Kuwait in 1983. The Algerian government eventually negotiated release of the remaining hijackers to depart to a destination that was not disclosed. The 17 prisoners in Kuwait were not released.

Arms Deal. Kuwait in 1988 sought to bolster its defenses by purchasing arms from abroad. On July 7 the Reagan administration sent to Congress a proposal to sell Kuwait $1.9 billion worth of arms, including 40 F-19 fighter planes, Maverick-D and Maverick-G missiles, and other arms. The proposal soon ran into difficulty in Congress. In the resulting compromise, Kuwait secured most though not all of the arms it had sought. However, it had to accept certain restrictions on their use. Kuwait also concluded arms deals with the USSR and Egypt.

British Petroleum. Kuwait's foreign investment program received a jolt in August when it was ordered by the British government to divest itself of some of its holdings in British Petroleum (BP). Kuwait had acquired large holdings in BP in 1987 and by early 1988 these amounted to 21.7% of BP stock. After an investigation by Britain's Monopolies and Mergers Commission, Kuwait was ordered to lower its holdings to 9.9% of BP stock over a period of one year.

Diplomacy. Kuwait's Premier Saad al-Abdallah Al Sabah arrived in Washington July 11 for a four-day official visit. On September 28 the emir of Kuwait, Jabir al-Ahmad Al Sabah, addressed the UN General Assembly on a three-point plan for dealing with Third World debt.

Internal Affairs. A series of cabinet changes made in February brought several new appointees into the Kuwaiti government. In June the unofficial stock market was closed. Past speculation in this market had led to excessive debts and bankruptcies. Stocks which were being traded there were transferred to the official market.

ARTHUR CAMPBELL TURNER
University of California, Riverside

LABOR

The world labor scene in 1988 produced two surprises worthy of special note: The unemployment rates of the United States and Canada, unlike those of most other industrial nations, continued to decline; and in Poland the Solidarity labor organization, pronounced dead after its suppression by the government in the early 1980s, reemerged as a movement with mass support.

United States

"America's great job-generation machine . . . will run out of steam in 1988," wrote the human-resources expert of the Conference Board, a leading business research organization, in January. In the same vein, most economic forecasts then predicted an increased unemployment rate for the year, one ranging from 6% to 7%.

The economy, however, performed better than the economic forecasters. By September the number of civilian jobs rose to 115.3 million, a 2.5 million increase over 12 months earlier, equaling or surpassing the job expansion of six out of the prior eight years. Moreover, the civilian unemployment rate, which averaged 6.2% in 1987, hovered around 5.5% for most of the year, a low level not achieved since 1974. The percentage of the civilian population at work climbed to 62.4% in September.

More than 20 million of the employed worked part-time, two thirds of them by

<hr/>

Labor Hall of Fame

During 1988, a privately sponsored Labor Hall of Fame was established in the headquarters of the U.S. Department of Labor to honor posthumously Americans who contributed to the welfare of working people. The Friends of the Department of Labor (FDL), a private, nonpartisan group, funded the hall, which was to open to the public on Jan. 11, 1989. The initial honorees are:

Cyrus S. Ching (1876–1967), an industrialist who served as director of the Federal Mediation and Conciliation Service.

John R. Commons (1862–1945), a labor economist who was a professor at the University of Wisconsin (1904–32).

Samuel Gompers (1850–1924), the first president of the American Federation of Labor (1886–94, 1896–1924).

Frances Perkins (1880–1965), U.S. secretary of labor (1933–45).

<hr/>

choice. While total employment increased by 32% since 1974, the number of part-time workers swelled by 68%, most of them women in the service sector.

The unemployment rates of adult white men and adult white women both fluctuated closely around the 4% mark, but otherwise unemployment was distributed unequally in the population. The rate for black adults was more than double that of whites, with black women faring the worst. Regionally, the New England labor market did the best, with the jobless rate shriveling below 2% in Vermont. Meanwhile, areas in a few states, particularly Texas, still had double-digit unemployment.

Earnings and Costs. The average hourly pay of nonsupervisory workers in the private sector in September was $9.37, compared with $9.02 a year earlier; their average weekly earnings (including those of part-time workers) were $325, compared with $312 a year earlier. In real (inflation-adjusted) terms, however, their wages stagnated. Average weekly earnings ranged from a high of $544 for miners down to $185 for employees in retail trades, which have large numbers of part-timers. For all full-time wage and salary workers, the average weekly pay came to $382 in the second quarter.

Taking into account earnings and all benefits, including holidays and vacations, employee compensation costs in the private sector rose 4.5% in the 12 months ending September 30, just over one percentage point higher than in the comparable period a year earlier. The benefits portion of the compensation package increased by 6.7% in 12 months, twice the rate of the previous 12-month period, mainly because of higher health-benefit premiums.

Collective Bargaining. In that September-to-September period, unionized workers averaged more benefits and lower wage increases than did nonunionized workers, but the cost of the total compensation package was the same for both groups, 4.5%. In addition, the unionized workers started from a 1987 earnings base that among full-time wage and salary workers was 33% higher than that of workers not covered by union agreements.

Strikes were rare in 1988. The number of idle days lost in major work stoppages was about the same as the all-time low of 1987, when strikes caused the loss of only 0.02% of working time in large enterprises.

Unions. Nearly 17 million Americans were members of labor unions at the start of 1988, approximately the same number as a year earlier. However, membership declined proportionately, from 17.5% to 17.0% of the increased number of wage and salary workers. Among full-time workers, the proportion was higher—19.4%, which was still a 0.5% decline for the year.

Union leaders saw hope for the future in an August Gallup poll, in which 61% of all persons

surveyed and 67% of those from 18 to 24 years old, answered "yes" to the question, "Do you approve of unions?" It was the highest union approval level recorded by Gallup in nearly 20 years.

The American Federation of Labor–Congress of Industrial Organizations (AFL-CIO), with 14 million members, gained two affiliates during the year: the 28,000-member Brotherhood of Locomotive Engineers, which had been independent since its founding in 1864, and the 55,000-member International Longshoremen & Warehousemen's Union, which prior to 1950 was a CIO affiliate.

In major leadership changes, John N. Sturdivant, 50, was elected president of the American Federation of Government Employees, and William J. McCarthy, 69, was named president of the International Brotherhood of Teamsters. McCarthy succeeded Jackie Presser, 61, who died in July. The 1.7-million-member Teamsters union faced a civil trial in February 1989 on a U.S. Justice Department suit seeking to oust the union leadership because of purported ties to organized crime.

Presidential Election. At a meeting of its general board in August, the AFL-CIO endorsed the Democratic ticket, as did almost all the federation's affiliates. The major exception was the Teamsters union. Various exit polls found that from 57% to 69% of union members voted for Dukakis-Bentsen. However, two thirds of all congressional and gubernatorial

William J. McCarthy on July 15 was elected president of the International Brotherhood of Teamsters, with 1.7 million members the largest labor union in the United States. McCarthy, 69, had been a Teamster for 52 years and had served as the union's top official in New England for some two decades. He succeeded Jackie Presser, who died July 9.

AP/Wide World

candidates endorsed by the AFL-CIO were elected, an outcome that ensured continued labor influence in the legislative process despite its support for the losing presidential candidate.

Federal Legislation. The U.S. Congress in 1988 passed several measures on labor's agenda. Among them were laws establishing "catastrophic" health insurance, toughening U.S. trade policies against restrictive practices by foreign countries, and requiring a 60-day notice for plant closings and large-scale layoffs. Under the new trade law, the persistent denial of worker rights was deemed an unreasonable trade practice that could cause an offending country to lose export privileges to the United States.

A major defeat for labor was the failure of Congress to increase the federal minimum wage, which has been frozen at $3.35 per hour since 1981. A bill to raise the minimum by 40 cents annually for three years failed even though Vice-President Bush, to the dismay of some supporters, gave his endorsement to an unspecified increase in the minimum wage if it were tied to a subminimum "training" wage for new workers. That bill died in the session's last days. So did two other labor-supported bills, one providing $2.5 billion for child-care programs, the other giving workers the right to take up to ten weeks unpaid leave upon the birth, adoption, or illness of a child or during their own serious illness.

NLRB. President Reagan in January 1988 appointed James M. Stephens, 41, a former aide to Sen. Orrin G. Hatch (R-UT), to be chairman of the five-member National Labor Relations Board (NLRB), the agency that administers federal laws affecting union-management relations. Stephens succeeded Donald L. Dotson, who left at the expiration of his term in December 1987.

Unions had criticized the board sharply under Dotson for what they regarded as its systematic undermining of laws protecting the worker's right to organize. On the other side, the National Right to Work Committee, which seeks to outlaw labor-management agreements making union membership a condition of employment, attacked the Stephens appointment as "outrageous . . . in the eyes of the 68% of Americans who oppose compulsory unionism."

ILO Standards. U.S. representatives long have used the month-long annual conference of the International Labor Organization (ILO) in Geneva as a platform to criticize dictatorial countries for violating its worker-rights standards, which usually are incorporated into treaty-like documents called "conventions." But the U.S. government itself had ratified only a few ILO standards after joining the organization in 1934, and none at all in the previous 35 years. That moratorium ended in 1988, when

the Senate approved and President Reagan signed two ILO conventions. One requires health and safety conditions on board ships; the other requires tripartite (government, worker, employer) consultations on ILO-related issues.

Canada

From a recession peak of 12.8% in late 1982, Canada's unemployment rate gradually has moved downward. It dipped below 8% for most of 1988 and reached 7.8% in September (7.4% for men, 8.3% for women). Employment expanded by 2.8% in the 12 months that ended in September, just under the rate of a year earlier. With 12,375,000 persons employed, the proportion of the population holding down jobs reached 61.5% in September, about a percentage point lower than the ratio in the United States. Real hourly income rose slightly, as a nominal 5% increase in earnings almost was matched by a rise in consumer prices. Collective bargaining negotiations settled in the second quarter provided for compensation increases averaging 4.5%.

The number of union members—3,841,000 —grew 1.6% over the 1987 level but continued a gradual decline as 'a percentage of the non-agricultural work force—from a peak of 40% in 1983 to 36.6% in 1988. Unions affiliated with the Canadian Labour Congress (CLC) accounted for 58% of all Canadian unionists. At its 17th biennial convention in May, the CLC unanimously reelected Shirley Carr, the daughter of a Nova Scotia coal miner, to her second two-year term as president. The 2,800 convention delegates cheered her declaration that the CLC would take a "war footing" in the November general election behind the opposition New Democratic Party, which the CLC helped found in 1961, and against Conservative Prime Minister Brian Mulroney. The CLC vigorously attacked Mulroney for supporting the U.S.-Canada free-trade agreement, denounced as a threat to Canadian jobs as well as to the country's extensive system of social benefits.

International

Despite a healthy 3.5% economic growth rate, Western Europe, unlike North America, continued to show unhealthy unemployment rates: nearly 11% overall. Moreover, much of the unemployment appeared to be long-term. Of Western Europe's 19 million jobless, two fifths had been out of work for one year or more (compared with one out of 12 in the United States).

On the other side of the globe, Japan boasted an unemployment rate a few tenths of a percentage point below the 1987 average of 2.7%. Only Sweden (1.6%) and Switzerland (0.6%) did not have to feel envious. In contrast, Belgium, France, the Netherlands, and Spain all registered double-digit rates. West Germany maintained roughly the same level as in 1987, just under 8%. Great Britain's 8% in August and September was its best in seven years.

Wage increases in West Germany, Italy, Japan, and Great Britain outpaced price increases, but elsewhere they barely kept up or fell behind. In France, which enjoyed an economic growth rate of more than 3%, the militant 900,000-member French Democratic Federation of Labor (CFDT) declared, "They have to share this prosperity with us." The CFDT joined with other labor groups in a spasm of public-sector strikes involving nurses, customs officers, radio and television operators, and transport workers, all demanding wage hikes larger than the 2.2% offered by the government. At the end of November the government had to use troops and military trucks to ferry strike-bound suburban commuters into Paris.

In Japan, where strikes are a rarity, the annual spring labor negotiations resulted in wage increases of 4.4% for workers in large firms—short of the 7–10% demanded by unions but nearly a percentage point higher than the 1987 spring increase. Later in the year most large firms also handed out bonuses, which in 1987 added 4.3% to salaries.

Privatization. At least 56 governments around the world were involved in moves to disengage themselves from such state-owned operations as banks and telecommunications. Since privatization usually means a change in employer-employee relations, it often provokes a negative reaction from unions.

The European Trade Union Institute (ETUI), the research arm of the European Trade Union Confederation, in May published an analysis of privatization in Western Europe, where about one job in four was in the public sector and where most governments (led by Great Britain) had some form of privatization underway or on the drawing board. On the one hand, European unions opposed the private ownership of public "services such as post and telecommunications, railways, gas and water supply, (which) are natural monopolies," according to the ETUI study. Some privatization schemes, it charged, only "cream off the most lucrative and innovative services, . . . leaving for the public sector all that is of no interest to private entrepreneurs." On the other hand, most of the unions did not take an across-the-board position against privatization outside the "monopoly" sector and accepted the inevitability of governments getting out of the business of producing such things as cars, ships, and steel. When that happens, the ETUI report said, the priority concern "is to safeguard in the privatized companies the levels of employment, pay and conditions, and the forms of industrial democracy which prevailed prior to privatization."

During a November visit, Britain's Prime Minister Margaret Thatcher dismayed Polish officials by speaking out on behalf of Solidarity and traveling to Gdansk to meet with Lech Walesa, head of the trade union.

AP/Wide World

European Unity. The European Community (EC) goal of establishing an integrated Europe by the end of 1992 has sparked controversy about what that evolution will mean for workers. Ernst Breit, president of the 8-million-member German Trade Union Federation, warned that 1992 could bring widespread "social dumping" by transnational corporations moving their firms to southern Europe, where labor costs are lower, unions weaker, and statutory labor requirements fewer (e.g., no mandatory worker representation on company boards, as in West Germany).

Responding to such concerns, Jacques Delors, the president of the EC Commission, assured a British union meeting in September that 1992 will mean much more than the creation of a barrier-free market of goods, services, and capital. "I propose establishment of a platform guaranteeing basic social rights, such as the right of every worker to be covered by a collective agreement and creation of a European company statute which will include the participation [on company boards] of European workers and their representatives." Britain's Prime Minister Margaret Thatcher promptly showed her disapproval of such proposals by repeating her criticisms of those "who see European unity as a vehicle for spreading socialism."

Revival in Poland. Suppressed by the government in the early 1980s, the Solidarity labor movement in Poland moved underground and into what the government hoped, and many observers believed, would be oblivion. But in 1988, Solidarity emerged from the catacombs, first in the spring through a series of endorsed strikes, and then in the fall by more strikes and demonstrations—all demanding that the government restore freedom of association by allowing Solidarity to operate openly.

The government promised "round table" talks but was torn on how to cope, especially because it now had in place a large labor apparatus of its own. To its discomfort, Prime Minister Thatcher, during an official visit to Poland in November, spoke out publicly as an advocate of Solidarity. She also became the first Western head of government to visit with the Solidarity leadership in Gdansk. There, before a crowd of 5,000 outside the main gate of the Lenin Shipyard, Solidarity's birthplace in 1980, Thatcher told Solidarity leader Lech Walesa: "Nothing can stop you." Later, in a gesture of openness, the government allowed Walesa to appear on Polish television for the first time in five years.

The outcome of Solidarity's struggle may have implications throughout the Communist world. In Hungary, two small unions emerged for the first time in 1988, one for motion-picture workers, the other for scientific workers. But these were exceptions. The policy of *glasnost* (openness) still had not touched labor policy in the Soviet Union, where free trade unions remained still illegal. Nor had reforms in the People's Republic of China allowed for the free and open organization of labor.

World Labor Solidarity. At its congress in Melbourne, Australia, in March, the International Confederation of Free Trade Unions (ICFTU) rededicated itself to promoting freedom of association for workers throughout the world. The 800 delegates and observers represented unions from 109 countries with 87 million members, compared with 46 million when the ICFTU was founded in 1949. Speakers, including John Vanderveken of Belgium, who unanimously was reelected secretary-general, called special attention to two labor leaders who were absent because their governments had denied them permission to attend: Vethamuthu David, the general secretary of the Malaysian Trades Union Congress, and Lech Walesa.

Robert A. Senser, *Free-lance Labor Writer*

Benefits in Flux

© Michael L. Abramson/Woodfin Camp & Assoc.

Employer-sponsored fitness programs were once perks reserved almost entirely for senior executives. That exclusiveness is changing slowly. More and more companies are providing exercise rooms and fitness centers right at the workplace for all employees. Such centers are not the only new benefit being offered to employees by corporate America. More and more corporations are initiating programs to promote good health or "wellness," including stop-smoking clinics; classes to help employees control stress; and child-care assistance for employees. This variety of benefits is so diverse and new that it has not been grouped yet under a commonly accepted label or term or completely documented. Like the older and more traditional benefits, these new ones are a direct employer response to employee needs.

The two traditional types of benefits—pensions and various kinds of insurance (especially health)—are still by far the dominant ones. The returns on these reach the employee away from the job. Most of the emerging new benefits reach people right at work or at least nearby. A third category of benefits—education assistance—has existed for some time and affects the employee both at work and away from the job. In addition, many corporations long have supported company physicians and nurses as well as annual physical examinations for at least its key employees.

Health and Exercise Programs. The new corporate health and wellness programs tend to be in the preventive medicine field. Corporate giants, including General Motors (GM), IBM, and Johnson & Johnson, have set the pace. GM has expanded routine blood-pressure and hypertension screening of workers into a substantial wellness program that wins high acclaim from the United Automobile

Workers (UAW). At GM's Hydramatic plant in Warren, MI, for example, many autoworkers start or end each shift with a visit to a 24-hour wellness center supplied with Nautilus machines, stationary cycles, and other equipment, and staffed with three trainers certified in exercise, nutrition, and diet planning. A preliminary study by the Institute of Aerobics Research in Dallas indicated that worksite exercise programs not only improve employee fitness but also reduce absenteeism. In one company, absenteeism among program participants dropped nearly 50% in a year. Another company reported a drop in sick leave of 4.7 hours per employee enrolled in the program.

Where a worker once was suspended or fired for alcohol or drug addiction, there is a growing emphasis today on counseling, treatment, and prevention. Where acute job pressures once were recognized only as an executive affliction, some employers now have set up classes for all their workers on how to cope with stress. Corporate stress-management programs now include everything from group counseling, to classes in the Oriental art of t'ai chi ch'uan, to hypnosis, to simple humor. Meanwhile the emphasis on stress management has led to the development of a number of new antistress products for the corporate market.

In the "no smoking" era of the 1980s, many employees are getting help to break the nicotine habit. Their firms are offering stop-smoking sessions to those who want to stop. Corporations engage specialized agencies like Smoke Enders and Smoke Stoppers to conduct "group behavior" seminars that promote an antismoking atmosphere. In addition, a Toronto entrepreneur has developed "The Last Pack," a self-help kit of aids to discourage

smoking. During a six-month period, his company sold 4,000 of the $150 kits to several major companies.

In a slightly different area, companies also are adopting programs focusing on such issues and disorders as child abuse and spouse beating. Deborah Anderson, executive vice-president of Responses to End Abuse of Children Inc., believes that "family violence costs employers millions of dollars annually in lower productivity, turnover, absenteeism, and excessive use of medical benefits." Such new programs are an extension of those aimed at drug users and alcoholics.

Child Care. The employee need that has gained nationwide recognition since the mid-1980s is child care. By 1988, 3,300 corporations were offering child-care assistance programs, compared with only 100 a decade earlier, according to the Conference Board, a business-research organization. In its own survey, the U.S. Department of Labor found that 25,000 of the public and private workplaces with ten or more employees sponsor day-care centers for their workers' children, and that another 35,000 provide financial assistance specifically for child care.

More and more potential employees are asking about day care, maternity leave, and flexible time. This trend is stimulated by the massive entry of future mothers into the job market. Today 70% of the women between 25 to 34, prime childbearing years, are in the labor force, compared with 45% in 1970.

Ann McLaughlin, secretary of labor in the final year of the Reagan administration, summarizing the report of a special task force she appointed, called child care "an issue with vast implications for the health of the American economy and the well-being of American workers and their families." Her department's report came as Congress was considering more than 100 bills addressing the problem. Though the task-force report did not take a position on the need for legislation it concluded that responding to child-care needs requires flexibility, rather than a sweeping "one size fits all" solution. Translated, that read as an alert for caution on a legislative approach.

The National Association of Manufacturers (NAM) insists that the decision on what kind of child care to offer, if any, must be left to the individual employer rather than being mandated by law, because the economic feasibility of such programs varies from company to company. Recognizing that the pressures for action by Congress were strong, however, the NAM in April urged that federal initiatives be limited to offering incentives (such as tax concessions) to encourage the voluntary involvement of employers, employees, and communities in child-care programs. Although the debate thus focused not on whether there should be new legislation but on its contents, the 1988 congressional session adjourned without taking final action on the issue. (*See also* FAMILY.)

Cost. The major cause of employer concern is cost. According to the U.S. Bureau of Labor Statistics, slightly more than one fourth of employee compensation is in some form of benefit, including those legally required. The U.S. Chamber of Commerce estimates that the benefit cost is even higher. As a result of a nonrandom mail survey, the Chamber calculated that for its own member firms employee benefits in 1986 accounted for 39.3% of total payroll, the highest level in the 32-year history of the survey. Legally required employee taxes (e.g., for unemployment compensation and Social Security) and payments for holidays, sick leave, vacations, rest periods, and other time not worked accounted for most (22.5%) of the 39.3%. The two traditional benefit staples, retirement plans and health insurance, made up the great bulk of the other payroll costs—about 15% in all. Child care came to 0.6% of payroll, about one half of the Chamber's growing "miscellaneous benefits" category.

Many employers have modified their health insurance plans in order to contain costs. According to a survey of 240 large firms, 80% of hospitalization plans paid all room and board costs in 1982, but only one third did so five years later; 43% required no employee contributions in 1982, but only 29% did so in 1987. Circle K, a convenience store chain, announced it would limit insurance coverage for health problems arising from "certain personal life-style decisions regarding the use of alcohol, drugs, self-inflicted wounds, and sickness due to AIDS."

In an attempt to cope with both rising costs and changing employee needs, more companies have introduced a measure of employee choice into benefits through "cafeteria" plans. These allow employees to select from a menu of employer-provided benefits. The flexibility is especially useful to two-career families. By reducing her medical-, dental-, and disability-insurance coverage and piggybacking on her husband's insurance, a working wife can apply the savings to other benefits.

With the corporate world facing a growing challenge to attract and retain the most qualified and productive employees and with the costs of employee benefits escalating rapidly, it is evident that employee benefits will remain in flux for the foreseeable future.

ROBERT A. SENSER

LAOS

During 1988, Vietnam reportedly withdrew half of the 40,000 troops it had stationed in Laos, and the Laotian government enacted a law designed to promote foreign investment. Both developments were part of an overall campaign, led by Vietnam, to improve relations between Indochina (Vietnam, Laos, and Cambodia) and the West. The campaign was aimed at attracting Western capital and technology and gaining access to Western markets.

Politics. During the year, the ruling Lao People's Revolutionary Party (LPRP) held a series of elections for people's representatives at the district, provincial, municipal, and national levels. After district elections in June—Laos' first nationwide balloting since the Communists seized power in 1973—the party admitted that it had done a poor job in selecting candidates. In some districts, people even petitioned to have their representatives replaced.

Economy. The purpose of the elections was to revitalize the government and make it possible to implement economic reforms laid down by the Fourth Party Congress in 1986. Much of the Laotian population engages in subsistence farming, and the land is divided into steep mountains and small, isolated valleys. One of the priorities, therefore, is to build more roads to move surplus food to areas of scarcity. Fertilizer is needed to increase crop yields, and the government seeks to develop industries based on agriculture to increase crop values. The regime also has sought to persuade tribes living on the upper slopes of mountains to abandon slash-and-burn farming, which causes massive soil erosion. Public data has indicated little progress in any of these areas, although the government did claim in June that most parts of the country were self-sufficient in food.

Foreign Affairs. Laotian leaders continued to support Vietnam's efforts to end the Cambodian conflict in terms that would satisfy Hanoi. Laos also held a series of talks with Thailand on reducing border conflicts and increasing trade. Laos and the United States continued to cooperate in the search for the remains of U.S. servicemen killed in the Indochina war.

PETER A. POOLE
Author, "Eight Presidents and Indochina"

LAOS · Information Highlights

Official Name: Lao People's Democratic Republic.
Location: Southeast Asia.
Area: 91,430 sq mi (236 800 km²).
Population (mid-1988 est.): 3,800,000.
Chief City: Vientiane, the capital.
Government: *Head of state:* Phoumi Vongvichit, temporary president; *Head of government,* Kaysone Phomvihan, chairman. *Legislature* (unicameral)—national Congress of People's Representatives.

LATIN AMERICA

During 1988 several Latin American countries took important steps to open up societies and economies that had been closed and inward looking for decades. The trend was seen in major political changes in such countries as Argentina, Brazil, Chile, and Mexico; in the lowering of traditional trade barriers in Mexico and the Southern Cone countries of Argentina, Brazil, and Uruguay; and in an emerging consensus on the need for fresh approaches to the international debt problem and a stronger emphasis on restarting economic growth. The definitive impact of these changes may not be obvious for several years, but many analysts believe that 1988 may be seen as the year in which Latin America began to emerge from a decade of economic and social doldrums.

Politics. In Mexico, the monolithic government Institutional Revolutionary Party (PRI), which had not faced a serious national political challenge since it was founded nearly 60 years earlier, barely won a July presidential election in balloting that opponents charged was marked by widespread fraud. In October, Chilean voters opted to end the 15-year military dictatorship of Gen. Augusto Pinochet, a decision the military government said it would respect. Brazil adopted a new constitution providing for direct popular elections, bringing to a close more than two decades of military rule. And in Argentina, the Peronist Party, debilitated by a decade of military rule, appeared to be gathering strength and positioning itself for a strong showing in presidential elections scheduled for 1989.

Trade. The era of import substitution policies, which have dominated Latin American trade since the end of World War II, showed signs of drawing to a close. Mexico's accession to the General Agreement on Tariffs and Trade (GATT) in 1986—and that of several other Latin American countries since then—launched a series of reductions in tariff and nontariff barriers and a new emphasis on export diversification, including several new trade liberalization agreements between the United States and Mexico. Brazil effectively jettisoned 40 years of import substitution in 1988 and took steps to open its markets to more imports. Economic integration in the Southern Cone moved ahead with the April signing of new trade liberalization agreements among Argentina, Uruguay, and Brazil.

The U.S. trade deficit with Latin America grew slowly, rising from $13.2 billion in 1986 to $14.6 billion in 1987. But many Latin American governments were critical of U.S. trade policies, saying they ran against the trend of trade liberalization in the hemisphere. The U.S. Omnibus Trade Bill signed by President Ronald Reagan in August 1988, aimed at making U.S. exports more competitive in world markets,

Chile was one of several Latin American countries in which the democratic process made breakthroughs in 1988. The nation's long-suppressed opposition rallied forces and voted "no" to another eight years of rule by Gen. Augusto Pinochet.

AP/Wide World

was called "protectionist" in several inter-American forums. U.S. officials, on the other hand, said the bill sought reciprocity and equal treatment for goods sold overseas and in the United States.

U.S. exclusion of three Latin American countries—Chile, Nicaragua, and Paraguay—from the duty-free privileges of the U.S. Generalized System of Preferences (GSP) also drew protests. The Reagan administration said the exclusions were in response to abuse of workers' rights in the three countries.

One positive note for Latin America during the year was an increase of 40% in the U.S. sugar import quota, which had fallen to its lowest level in more than a century. The increase permitted the Dominican Republic to export an additional 53,000 tons of sugar to the United States in 1988, and allowed Brazil to increase its exports by 44,000 tons. Paradoxically, the quota increase did not reflect a change in U.S. trade policy so much as an expected shortfall in U.S. sugar beet production due to the summer-long drought in the U.S. farm belt.

Economy. Political openings and trade liberalization augur well for a longer-term improvement in Latin American social and economic evolution, many observers believe. But in the shorter term, the region still staggers under a crushing foreign-debt burden, which continues to drain capital and impede domestic investment in new productive facilities. External sources of capital investment still are slow to grasp the reality of Latin America's long-term economic potential, the observers say.

In the words of Enrique Iglesias, the new president of the Inter-American Development Bank (IDB), "Nineteen eighty-seven was a year of deterioration. This year will be substantially worse. The adjustment process continues, but we still have a long way to go." Natural disasters, such as Hurricane Gilbert,

which wreaked havoc in the Caribbean and Mexico during September, added to the region's woes. But one of the major stumbling blocks to the region's recovery, in Iglesias' view, is the lack of long-range vision and planning, both within and outside the area. "We have all been kidnapped by crisis thinking," Iglesias said.

International Organizations. Iglesias, a former foreign minister of Uruguay, became president of the IDB on April 1, replacing Antonio Ortiz Mena of Mexico, who retired after leading the bank for 17 years. The cause of Ortiz Mena's resignation was believed to be a dispute with the United States over control of IDB lending. The United States has withheld new funding from the bank until it is given more power over loan policy. Iglesias' first task was to reach an agreement with the United States in order to expand the IDB's resources.

The Organization of American States (OAS) also had a budget crisis during the year, because of the failure of the United States and a few Latin countries to meet their financial commitments to the organization. OAS officials said that if fresh funding were not forthcoming, the OAS might have to reduce its 1,000-person secretariat by as much as 25%.

U.S. Policy. U.S. relations with Latin America figured prominently in the 1988 U.S presidential campaign. Both major candidates agreed that attention must be given to find creative new solutions to the Latin American debt and that multilateral approaches to regional problems should be stressed. The candidates diverged on U.S. policy in Central America, however, with Republican George Bush arguing for continued military aid to the anti-Sandinista "contra" forces in Nicaragua and Democrat Michael Dukakis rejecting such aid.

RICHARD C. SCHROEDER
Formerly, "Visión" Magazine

LAW

The Reagan administration's efforts to place a conservative imprint on the U.S. Supreme Court took some interesting twists and turns during 1988. After two unsuccessful tries, President Ronald Reagan succeeded in winning unanimous (97–0) Senate confirmation of his third choice, Anthony M. Kennedy (*See* BIOGRAPHY), to fill a high court vacancy created in June 1987. Kennedy, a 51-year-old Californian who had served 12 years on the Ninth Circuit Court of Appeals, succeeded Lewis F. Powell to become the 104th justice in U.S. history.

Meanwhile, Chief Justice William H. Rehnquist, promoted to that position by President Reagan in 1986, emerged in a more dominant and not always predictable role as leader of the court. In perhaps the term's most memorable decision, Rehnquist led the majority in upholding the federal law that allows independent prosecutors to investigate alleged wrongdoing in the executive branch. Rehnquist also was the author of a handful of other majority opinions that belied his reputation as the anchor of the court's right wing.

Nonetheless, many court observers saw hints of a rightward turn for the future. The 1987–88 term generally lacked the kind of high-profile, divisive cases that split conservatives and liberals along predictable lines. Moreover, Kennedy missed more than half the term, and his role had yet to take clear shape. But the justices did serve notice that a controlling conservative coalition could be developing. In an announcement that sent shock waves through the civil-rights community, five justices agreed to consider overturning a key 1976 ruling that permits a post-Civil War law to be used as a potent weapon against private racial discrimination. That issue was to be explored in the court's 1988–89 term. Voting to take a fresh look at the 1976 precedent were Kennedy, Rehnquist, and Justices Sandra Day O'Connor,

Byron R. White, and Antonin Scalia. The more liberal members—Justices William J. Brennan, Thurgood Marshall, Harry A. Blackmun, and John Paul Stevens—warned that the court appeared to be turning its back on minorities.

In the lower courts, an important chapter was written in the saga of "Baby M," as the legal system continued to struggle with the issue of surrogate motherhood. There also were headline-capturing cases of a black teenager whose charge that she was assaulted came into question and of the so-called "preppie murder" in which a young woman died during an apparent sexual escapade.

In international law, the year's highlights included adverse rulings against the United States in its effort to close the United Nations observer mission of the Palestine Liberation Organization.

United States

Supreme Court. There were signs that the shifting center on the court was inching to the right. Justice O'Connor, the first of three Reagan appointees who was hailed a year earlier as an increasingly independent and moderate force, sided with the liberal Justice Brennan fewer times in the 1987–88 term than did Chief Justice Rehnquist. Also, the five generally more conservative members voted together in most of the 13 cases decided by 5–4 splits.

In one of the term's most closely watched cases, however, Justice Scalia was the lone dissenter as a 7–1 majority upheld the so-called Special Prosecutor Law. Enacted in the wake of the Watergate scandal, the law permits a special court to appoint independent counsels to investigate alleged crimes by high-ranking government officials. A handful of Reagan administration aides were targets of such investigations. The court said that the law does not violate the constitutionally mandated separa-

The White House, Feb. 18, 1988: Chief Justice William Rehnquist, far right, administers the oath of office to the Supreme Court's newest member, Anthony M. Kennedy, as Mrs. Kennedy holds the Bible. Kennedy's appointment had been confirmed unanimously by the Senate.

tion of powers between the executive, legislative, and judicial branches (*Morrison v. Olson*). The power of the executive branch also was tested in a decision in which the court said that the Central Intelligence Agency (CIA) can be sued by a fired homosexual employee. The court rejected the CIA's claim that its director has absolute discretion over agency employment practices (*Webster v. Doe*).

Two other cases involving governmental legal immunity attracted considerable attention. The court held that government contractors cannot be sued when products they make cause death or injury as long as the products were designed to meet government specifications and contractors disclosed any known hazards (*Boyle v. United Technologies*). And the justices ruled that the federal government may be sued for monetary damages when a vaccine it licenses causes the disease it is intended to prevent (*Berkovitz v. U.S.*). The court also ruled that state judges, and presumably federal judges as well, may be sued for monetary damages when administrative decisions they make violate someone's constitutional rights (*Forrester v. White*).

It was a busy term for free-speech cases. The court ruled that public figures cannot collect for the emotional distress they suffer when made the target of even pornographic parody or satire that no reasonable person would take seriously. With Rehnquist writing the opinion, the court threw out a legal victory that the Rev. Jerry Falwell had won over *Hustler* magazine and its publisher, Larry Flynt (*Hustler v. Falwell*). The court ruled that public-school officials have sweeping authority to censor student publications produced as part of the curriculum (*Hazelwood School District v. Kuhlmeier*). It also held that communities have the power to ban pickets from demonstrating in front of a particular home, although pickets still may have the right to march through an entire neighborhood along public streets. The ruling specifically barred antiabortion protesters from demonstrating at the home of a doctor who performed abortions (*Frisby v. Schultz*). In another First Amendment case, the justices ruled that states may not impose stringent regulations on fund-raising companies that solicit contributions for charities, such as requiring them to tell potential contributors what fees they collect (*Riley v. National Federation of the Blind*). The court also said that states may not ban lawyers from advertising by mailing solicitations to potential customers (*Shapero v. Kentucky Bar Association*).

In the area of criminal law, the court ruled that states may not execute convicted killers who were under 16 when they committed their crimes if the state's death penalty law does not establish a minimum age for those eligible for execution (*Thompson v. Oklahoma*). The court held that a state law designed to protect child

AP/Wide World

Robert Reynolds, a Hazelwood, MO, high-school principal, displays a copy of the school paper after learning that the Supreme Court had decided in his favor and ruled that school officials can censor student publications.

victims of sexual assault by allowing them to testify in court behind a one-way screen violated the Sixth Amendment rights of defendants to confront their accusers. The justices also ruled that police do not need a court warrant before searching through garbage left at curbside outside a home (*California v. Greenwood*). And the court upheld the federal mail and wire fraud convictions of a former *Wall Street Journal* reporter and two others in a stock market insider-trading case involving advance knowledge of articles on companies (*Carpenter v. U.S.*).

In a ruling on church-state relations, the court upheld a law providing federal money to religious groups for encouraging teenagers to abstain from premarital sex (*Bowen v. Kendrick*). The court also ruled that development within a national forest does not violate the religious rights of an Indian tribe's members even if it irrevocably alters what the tribe considers to be holy ground (*Lyng v. Northwest Indian Cemetery*).

In a key civil-rights decision, the court said that workers may use statistics in trying to prove that their employer's subjective management decisions illegally discriminate against them (*Watson v. Fort Worth Bank & Trust*).

The court allowed states and cities to ban sex discrimination against women and minorities by large private clubs where business lunches and similar activities take place (*New York State Club Association v. New York City*).

In a major defeat for labor unions, the court ruled that workers in the private sector who are covered by a union contract and who are required to pay the equivalent of dues even though they are not union members may not be assessed for any expenses not linked to collective bargaining (*Communications Workers v. Beck*). The court also upheld a federal law denying food stamps to striking workers and their households unless they are poor enough to qualify before going on strike (*Lyng v. International Union*).

In a significant business case, the court allowed manufacturers to stop supplying discount dealers if they want to protect other, more favored distributors from price competition (*Business Electronics v. Sharp Electronics*). On a related issue, the court handed discounters a big victory by upholding most imports of so-called gray market goods—the trademarked foreign-made products such as watches and cameras that retailers buy from independent distributors overseas and sell in the United States at bargain prices (*K Mart Corp. v. Cartier Inc.*).

Overruling a major 1895 precedent, the court said that Congress is free to tax all interest on state and municipal bonds. The decision, upholding a relatively minor tax provision passed by Congress in 1982, raised fears among state and local officials that additional federal taxes could be in the offing.

Local Justice. One of the most closely watched courtroom battles—the so-called Baby M case—concluded when surrogate mother Mary Beth Whitehead-Gould won unsupervised visitation rights to see her daughter. A judge in New Jersey granted Mrs. Whitehead-Gould the right to spend time alone with Melissa Stern, who turned two years old in 1988 and had become the symbol of a still-developing legal and moral controversy. Melissa's father, William Stern, and his wife, Elizabeth, agreed not to appeal the judge's ruling in the case that sparked worldwide debate on reproduction technologies. The Sterns, who have custody of Melissa, had wanted to delay unsupervised visits by Mrs. Whitehead-Gould until Melissa was at least six years old. The court order on visitation rights concluded a battle that began when Mrs. Whitehead-Gould agreed to be artificially inseminated with Stern's sperm and then, after giving birth to the child, decided to refuse the $10,000 surrogate fee and keep the baby. The New Jersey Supreme Court ruled that surrogacy-for-pay is illegal and restored Mrs. Whitehead-Gould's parental rights, but upheld custody for the Sterns.

Two unrelated cases with troubling racial overtones touched off legal and political maneuvering in New York. In one, the Yonkers City Council—faced with multimillion dollar contempt fines causing worker layoffs—ultimately yielded to a federal judge's order to adopt a housing desegregation plan. The turnabout climaxed a protracted fight stemming from U.S. District Judge Leonard Sand's ruling in 1985 that for decades Yonkers intentionally had fostered segregated public schools and housing. Four of the city's seven councilmen defied the judge's desegregation order for weeks before the community's impending bankruptcy prompted acquiescence by a council majority.

The center of another highly publicized case was Tawana Brawley of Wappingers Falls, NY, a black teenager who claimed she was raped by a gang of white men. Brawley disappeared for four days in late 1987 and was found in a garbage bag with racial epithets penned on her body. Months of investigation by law enforcement officials and the news media produced doubts that an attack had occurred, and on October 6 a New York State grand jury concluded that Brawley had concocted the story. The teenager had refused to testify before the grand jury, while her lawyers charged a coverup by the white establishment. Critics of the Brawley family advisers said the lawyers were engaging in a politically motivated charade that could stir racial animosity.

In a New York trial that attracted widespread notoriety and was dubbed "The Preppie Murder Case," Robert E. Chambers, Jr., 21, pleaded guilty to killing Jennifer Levin during a 1986 sexual encounter in New York City's Central Park. Chambers was sentenced to 5–15 years in prison for the strangulation death of Ms. Levin. Chambers also decided not to fight a $25 million civil-damage suit filed against him by the young woman's parents.

In Richmond, VA, a federal appeals court upheld the espionage and theft convictions of former U.S. intelligence analyst Samuel Loring Morison. He was sentenced to two years in prison for giving secret satellite photographs of a Soviet ship to a British magazine.

The U.S. Army's ban on homosexual soldiers was declared unconstitutional by a federal appeals court in San Francisco. The court ruled in favor of Perry Watkins, 39, of Tacoma, WA, who enlisted in the Army at age 19 and said on a medical form that he had homosexual tendencies. The ruling was expected to be appealed to the Supreme Court.

The stage also was set for a high court ruling on drug testing in the workplace. Conflicting federal appeals court rulings struck down testing for railroad employees and upheld the tests for customs service workers seeking drug enforcement jobs.

JIM RUBIN, *The Associated Press*

International Law

In 1988 the United States became involved in two potentially far-reaching disputes involving its legal obligations as host country to the United Nations.

PLO Mission Controversy. In the first case, the Justice Department ordered the Palestine Liberation Organization (PLO) to close its observer mission to the UN as required by the U.S. Anti-Terrorist Act of 1987. That act banned the establishment or maintenance of PLO offices anywhere in the United States.

Under the 1947 Headquarters Agreement between the United States and the UN, however, the United States is committed "not (to) impose any impediments" to any person or group invited to UN headquarters. In 1974 the General Assembly invited the PLO to participate as an observer in the UN's sessions and in its work. Accordingly the UN took the view that the American order to close the PLO office violated the Headquarters Agreement. The General Assembly held four separate debates to protest the American move and UN Secretary-General Javier Pérez de Cuéllar asked the Reagan administration to submit the controversy to arbitration under Section 21 of the Headquarters Agreement, which provides for arbitration of U.S.-UN disputes involving the treaty. When the administration declined, the General Assembly asked the World Court for an advisory opinion as to whether the United States was obliged legally to go to arbitration. On April 26 the World Court's 15 justices ruled unanimously that the Headquarters Agreement required the United States to go to arbitration.

Meanwhile, however, the Justice Department had taken the case to Federal District Court in New York where it asked Judge Edmund Palmieri to rule on whether the Anti-Terrorist Act required the closing of the PLO Observer Mission. Until Judge Palmieri rendered an opinion, the United States told the UN, it would be "premature" to enter into arbitration. Judge Palmieri ruled on June 29 that the Justice Department could not close down the PLO office because Congress, in drafting the Anti-Terrorist Act, had shown a "lack of clarity" about its intentions. If Congress adopts a law that appears to be inconsistent with an international obligation, the ruling said, then the congressional intent to overturn the international obligation must be very clear. Since it was not clear in this case, the international obligation prevails.

After a bitter battle between Justice Department officials who wanted to appeal Judge Palmieri's ruling to a higher court and State Department officials who wanted to let it stand, the Reagan administration decided in September not to appeal. Speaking for the UN secretary-general, a UN official welcomed the decision and declared that the UN's dispute with the United States had ended.

Exclusion of Arafat. But less than three months later a similar dispute erupted. The chairman of the PLO. Yasir Arafat, asked for an American visa so that he could address the 43d General Assembly's debate on Palestine on December 1. To the UN's surprise and indignation, Secretary of State George Shultz rejected the request, declaring that Arafat "knows of, condones, and lends support to" acts of terrorism and that his presence in the United States would jeopardize security.

Most governments reserve the right to exclude persons who threaten the security of their nationals. Had there been compelling evidence that Arafat's presence in New York for a day or two would pose a threat to Americans, the U.S. decision to bar him might have been accepted at least by some UN member nations. Without such evidence, the entire General Assembly except Israel criticized the Reagan administration for again violating its agreement "not (to) impose any impediments" to persons invited to UN headquarters.

On November 30 the General Assembly adopted a resolution deploring the U.S. decision to bar Arafat and urging Washington to change its position. Two days later, in the face of Washington's refusal, the Assembly voted 154 to 2 to move its session to Geneva so that Arafat could address it. Ironically, concessions made by Arafat in Geneva led the United States to open talks with the PLO in December. After that dramatic policy shift, the whole visa dispute quickly was forgotten.

Other. In another development the UN Security Council published a report by a team of UN investigators that charged that Iraq had used poison gas in the war against Iran "repeatedly" and "on an intensive scale." Iraq denied the charge, countering that Iran had used gas against Iraqi cities. The use of chemical weapons by one or both countries renewed the widespread calls to strengthen the 1925 Geneva Protocol that bans their use.

The 20 nations with decision-making rights under the 1959 Antarctic Treaty completed a major new international treaty elaborating a regime for the handling of mineral exploitation in Antarctica. The treaty, called the Antarctic Mineral Convention, allows companies to prospect for minerals providing they use techniques with "a relatively light impact on the environment." However, "full-scale exploration . . . involving major blasting or drilling" can take place only in certain areas.

At year's end President Reagan issued an executive proclamation extending the territorial waters of the United States from 3 mi (5.5 km) to 12 mi (22 km). The extension by the United States was in accord with the limits permitted by international law.

JANE K. ROSEN, *"Manchester Guardian"*

LEBANON

The violence between Lebanon's various political and religious factions—and the tug-of-war between Lebanon's allies and detractors—were harbingers of the political chaos that ensued later in 1988, when Lebanon's existence as a state was called into question.

The Crisis of the Presidency. In 1988, Lebanon experienced its worst political crisis since gaining independence from France in 1943. Although Lebanon already was partitioned for most practical purposes before September, the facade of the presence of the Lebanese state had remained intact. The erosion of the authority of the president, the parliament, and the military not only raised the question of whether the Lebanese republic could be restored in some form, but also of whether the Lebanese state even existed any longer.

The crisis began in September, when the parliament failed to elect a president to succeed incumbent President Amin Gemayel. The absence of a head of state lead to the formation of two rival governments with two competing cabinets: the transition government appointed by Gemayel and led by Gen. Michel Aoun, and the Syrian-supported government of Salim al-Hoss, who had been minister of education and acting prime minister under the Gemayel regime. The crisis intensified in October with the failure to elect a speaker of parliament. In November the Muslim defense minister in the Salim al-Hoss government dismissed the Army's Christian commander, Gen. Michel Aoun. The cumulative effect of this progressive deterioration was to lay bare the extent to which the entire country already has undergone "de facto" partition.

The failure to elect a new president helped to trigger the crises in the parliament and the army. Under a 1943 agreement that distributes power among the country's 17 recognized religious groups, the president must be a Maronite Christian, the prime minister a Sunni Muslim, and the speaker of the parliament a Shia Muslim. The constitution limits each president to one six-year term, and requires him to appoint a transition government headed by a prime minister if the parliament fails to elect his successor before his term expires.

Syria's Role. In August problems over the presidential elections began to surface. Syria, a power broker among Lebanon's Muslim factions, attempted to tighten its grip on Lebanon. Syria, which had some 25,000 troops in Lebanon and controlled roughly 65% of the country, wanted to use the election to break a two-and-a-half-year deadlock between Syria, the Lebanese Christians, and the Lebanese Muslims. The Lebanese Forces (LF), the political movement that controls the Christian enclave in Lebanon, had revolted against the Syrian-sponsored Tripartite Agreement.

Syria sought to end the stalemate by insisting that the presidential election grant Lebanon's Muslim population more political power. Syria's President Hafez Assad refused to agree to the election of a president who would perpetuate the political status quo.

The situation was aggravated by a disagreement between President Gemayel and the LF over who qualified as an acceptable consensus candidate. Gemayel's position was that Syrian influence in Lebanon was inevitable, while the LF worried about the security of the Christian community. The Muslims had given their proxy to Syria on the matter of suitable presidential candidates. Gemayel had stated his willingness to discuss the Lebanese presidential elections with Assad, but Assad refused to see him. The LF preferred the continuation of de facto partition of Lebanon over a loss of control over the Christian community's security. These differences notwithstanding, no faction in the Christian community was willing to allow the Syrians to dominate Lebanon. In mid-August, Syria announced its support of former President Suleiman Franjieh to succeed Amin Gemayel. The Christians were almost unanimous in their rejection of Franjieh, who was deeply unpopular among most Lebanese, including his fellow Christian Maronites. Most Lebanese associated his tenure as president—between 1970 and 1976—with widespread corruption and the widening of factional divisions.

Syria responded to the rejection by increasing pressure upon the Christian community. The Syrian-supported Muslim and Druze opposition groups declared that they would not agree to elections unless the Christians first agreed to specific constitutional reforms that redistributed political power in the Muslims' favor. But many Christian Lebanese saw Franjieh less as an ally than as a pawn of Syria.

The Syrians believed that the presidency was so important to the Maronites that they would make significant political concessions in order to retain control of it. But the Maronites were not willing to share political power with Syria. Maintaining the security of their enclave was more important to the Christians than maintaining control over the presidency.

Since the Syrians were able to coerce the deputies residing in West Beirut to vote their way, the LF called for a boycott of the meeting of parliament to vote on Gemayel's successor scheduled for August 18. The Christian-backed boycott foiled Syria's attempt to have Franjieh elected because the Muslims alone could not muster a quorum for the vote.

The United States' Role. As the Syrian role in Lebanese elections increased over the summer of 1988, Lebanese Muslims and Christians urged the United States to become more involved in order to neutralize the Syrians. In mid-September, U.S. Assistant Secretary of State Richard Murphy was dispatched to Da-

AP/Wide World

Muslim religious leaders led a rally in Beirut on October 23, the fifth anniversary of the bombing of a U.S. Marine base that killed 241 American servicemen. Lebanon in 1988 continued to be racked by factional violence and political chaos.

mascus to press for a compromise candidate. After some 16 hours of discussions, Murphy succeeded in persuading the Syrians to back away from Franjieh. The August 18 parliamentary boycott demonstrated that he could not be elected, anyway. Assad also dropped the demand of reform before the election. However, of a list of ten possible candidates that Murphy presented to Assad, only one, Mikhail Daher, a 60-year-old member of parliament and close associate of Franjieh, was acceptable to Assad. On September 19, Murphy told the Christian leaders in Lebanon that they must accept Daher or suffer "dire consequences." The Christians rejected the Daher candidacy, and combined pressures from Syria and the United States could not intimidate the Christians.

On September 21, just two days before Gemayel's term was to expire, Assad invited him to Damascus for a meeting. Gemayel asked Assad to choose a third Lebanese candidate (or to allow Daher to accompany him to East Beirut so that Gemayel could "sell" him to the Christians), and to change the venue—to a neutral zone—of a parliamentary meeting to elect his successor. Assad refused.

Available evidence suggests that Gemayel and Assad did, in fact, reach an agreement on Gemayel's successor. Gemayel agreed to appoint Daher as head of a "transition government." Obviously Gemayel could not openly do this, as no one in the Christian community would have accepted Daher. Therefore he tried to promote Daher indirectly by eliminating any other possible candidate. When he returned to Beirut from Damascus, he first asked Pierre Helou to form a government, but the Muslim ministers refused to serve; Helou had to bow out. During a crisis meeting on the last night of his term, Gemayel asked Dany Chamoun to try to form a government. Chamoun later reported that the only possibility was to name Selim al

Hoss prime minister, with Chamoun as deputy. This arrangement was contrary to the understanding among the Christian leaders that if no president were elected, the prime minister would be a Maronite. Finally with only minutes left in his term, Gemayel asked if anyone would object if Michel Aoun were asked to form a government. Gemayel apparently expected Samir Geagea, the leader of the LF, to oppose Aoun, thereby providing Gemayel with the opportunity to propose Daher. Geagea met with Aoun privately. The two concluded that Gemayel had been trying to paralyze the formation of a government in order to appoint Daher as the only alternative. They agreed that as a first step the LF would take over Gemayel's independent power base, since it exposed the Christian enclave to a Syrian military attack. If Gemayel could betray the Christian community politically by agreeing to Syria's candidate for president, he could also do so militarily. Therefore Geagea agreed to support Aoun. The two men returned to announce complete agreement on a transition, which apparently took Gemayel by surprise.

With less than ten minutes remaining in his presidency, Gemayel named Aoun to head a transition government. Aoun was thought to be acceptable to Syria, but Syria refused to recognize the new government and threw its support to the West Beirut-based government of former acting Prime Minister Hoss, a Muslim, which continued to function even though its sanctioned term expired with Gemayel's.

The Christian members of parliament asked the patriarch of the Maronite Christians to choose candidates to present to the United States which would try to sell the least objectionable to Syria and to Lebanon's Muslims. In December the Syrians rejected this list.

The Crisis of the Parliament. Parliament's failure to elect a successor to Hussein al-Hus-

seini, whose one-year term expired October 18, accelerated Lebanon's drift toward permanent partition. The parliament had been the only major forum where Christian and Muslim leaders continued to meet and cooperate.

The attempt to elect a speaker was aborted when deputies from East Beirut failed to show, denying a quorum, and Muslim deputies from East Beirut boycotted the session because it was held in the old Parliament Building in West Beirut, which they considered unsafe.

Parliament remained paralyzed because Muslim and Christian deputies could not agree on how to handle the void in the absence of clear constitutional guidance. The Muslims wanted to extend Husseini's incumbency as caretaker. The Christians insisted that the oldest member of parliament, Shia deputy Kazem al-Khalil, should act as speaker.

The Crisis of the Army. The potential for serious friction between the two rival governments lay in efforts by both cabinets to gain control of the institutions of the central government. On November 9 the Muslim minister of defense in the Hoss government, Adel Osseiran, dismissed Michel Aoun as army commander and announced the appointment of Muslim Maj. Gen. Sami Khatib as acting commander.

Although the Lebanese Army split in 1984 into Christian and Muslim units, officers continued to adhere to the tradition of not engaging in politics. But the Khatib appointment raised the possibility of the army being formally split into two rival "national" armies.

Four Christian-commanded brigades (totalling 15,000 men) were under Aoun's command. Another five brigades (18,000 men) either sided with various militias or remained on the sidelines. Two others disintegrated altogether.

The Growing Partition. The clearest evidence of "de facto" partition was that the failure to elect a new president and speaker did not produce any dramatic changes in the day-to-day operations of the government. Since the beginning of the conflict in 1975, the central government has performed fewer and fewer functions. The remaining functions it performed were decentralized to several locations over the past decade. This enabled the popula-

tion who must transact government business to do so in their own sector without having to travel through potentially dangerous areas.

This was one reason why the Lebanese pound, a well-known barometer of trouble, appeared barely to be affected by the latest crisis, at least early in the year. The value of the pound, which had nosedived from five to the U.S. dollar in 1984 to more than 600 to the dollar earlier in 1988, remained stable. After falling from 400 to 420 to the dollar it settled back to 410 almost immediately.

Even the emergence of two competing caretaker governments did not change significantly the situation in operational terms from what it was before Gemayel's term ended. The cabinet under Gemayel had been estranged from the president ever since he had refused to support the Tripartite Agreement with Syria in 1986.

Terrorism and Factional Violence. Underscoring the political chaos in Lebanon were the high levels of terrorism and factional fighting throughout 1988. On February 17, U.S. Lt. Col. William Higgins, who was attached to a United Nations unit, was abducted by an Iranian-backed Shiite Muslim group. Several hostages in Lebanon were released during the year, but more than a dozen were still in captivity at the year's end (*see* TERRORISM).

Interfactional violence claimed thousands of casualties. At least 51 people died during a four-day battle between rival Shiite militias in Southern Lebanon in early April. A car bombing (one of many during 1988) in Tripoli on April 24 killed at least 66 people; no group took credit for it. A car bomb planted outside a Christian Phalangist Party office on May 30 killed 20 people. During May, two Shiite groups fought for control of a section of Beirut; the death toll was estimated at between 300 and 400 people. The fighting ended when Syrian troops were deployed to the area to enforce the peace. Fighting in Southern Lebanon between the Palestine Liberation Organization (PLO) and a Syrian-backed PLO dissident faction claimed at least 174 lives in June and July.

On August 17—in response to the mounting political crisis—Christians and Muslims exchanged artillery fire across the "Green Line" (a border that separates Christian East Beirut and Muslim West Beirut) for the first time in 16 months. Another artillery exchange took place on September 22. On December 7, Lebanon's central bank, located in West Beirut, was rocked by a rocket-propelled grenade.

Cross-Border Raids. In 1988 the PLO continued to launch attacks against the Israelis from their bases in Lebanon. Israel retaliated with several military raids into the "Israeli Security Zone," an area of Southern Lebanon in which Israel has maintained a military presence since 1985.

LEWIS W. SNIDER
The Claremont Graduate School

LEBANON · Information Highlights

Official Name: Republic of Lebanon.
Location: Southwest Asia.
Area: 4,015 sq mi (10 400 km²).
Population (mid-1988 est.): 3,300,000.
Chief Cities (1980 est.): Beirut, the capital, 702,000; Tripoli, 175,000.
Government: *Head of transitional government,* Michel Aoun (installed Sept. 1988). *Legislature* (unicameral)—National Assembly.
Monetary Unit: Lebanese pound (512 pounds equal U.S.$1, Dec. 12, 1988).
Foreign Trade (1985 U.S.$): *Imports,* $2,200,000,000; *exports,* $482,000,000.

LIBRARIES

During 1988 librarians reacted in outrage to the Federal Bureau of Investigation's (FBI's) "Library Awareness Program." Under the program, the FBI asked librarians to report "suspicious looking foreigners" who were using nonclassified scientific and technical materials. The librarians so contacted were primarily in large academic and public libraries, but concern was widespread in the library community because of a potential threat to the privacy of all library users and the confidentiality of library records. Both print and television journalists drew public attention to the issue and congressional hearings were held in 1988.

Children and Libraries. On a happier note, the American Library Association (ALA) and the National Commission on Libraries and Information Science, with major support from the Readers Digest Foundation and J. Walter Thompson, launched a campaign to stop illiteracy where it starts—in the home. The campaign, with the theme "The Best Gift You'll Ever Give Your Child—A Library .Card," urged parents and other care givers to encourage children to sign up at the library. Two major corporations, Sears and McDonald's, also encouraged their customers to participate.

The importance of introducing children and young adults to information in all its forms is stressed in new guidelines issued by the American Association of School Librarians (AASL) and the Association for Educational Communications and Technology (AECT). *Information Power: Guidelines for School Library Media Programs* was introduced to the educational community through a teleconference in April 1988. Produced by the University of South Carolina, the teleconference involved sites in every U.S. state and many Canadian provinces. More than 10,000 persons participated.

Video. The Carnegie Corporation of New York, which had financed the construction of 1,681 public libraries between 1880 and 1920, gave ALA $500,000 to purchase video equipment for those Carnegie libraries, to conduct workshops on the use of video for public librarians generally, and to publish materials to help librarians build and manage video collections. A 1987 ALA survey found that more than 62% of U.S. public libraries loan videocassettes, and the percentage is higher in larger libraries.

Nonprint Materials. Although most people associate libraries with books, the addition of videocassettes to libraries is not a revolutionary development. Videocassettes are just a recent entry in a long line of nonprint materials that have been acquired and loaned by libraries. For example, a 1986 survey of public libraries serving populations of 25,000 or more found that 96.4% of them loaned musical records or tapes and 22% loaned compact discs.

More than 76% loaned books-on-tape; some 67% loaned 16mm films, and more than 57% loaned art prints. The same survey found that more than 43% had microcomputers for public use and some 40% made software available. Both of the latter practices are growing rapidly.

CD-ROM. Academic library use of the very latest information technology was promoted through a teleconference in April sponsored by the Association of College and Research Libraries. Produced by Oakton Community College in Illinois, the 2½-hour broadcast on CD-ROM went to more than 400 sites in the United States. (CD-ROMs are a new form of data storage that use laser technology to record vast amounts of data on a small disk for retrieval by a microcomputer. A single CD-ROM holds the equivalent of 250,000 printed pages.) The broadcast sought to educate more than 10,000 participants on the use of a technology that is assuming a major role in all libraries.

Individual libraries and groups of libraries have their catalogs on CD-ROM. Also, many reference tools—indexes, directories, encyclopedias—are available in this format.

Associations. The ALA held its 107th annual conference in New Orleans, LA, July 9–July 14, 1988. A total of 16,530 participants attended. President Margaret Chisholm presided. Dr. F. William Summers of Florida State University was inaugurated president at the end of the conference and Patricia W. Berger of the National Bureau of Standards was welcomed as president-elect.

The Canadian Library Association's 43rd annual conference in Halifax, N.S., attended by 1,242 librarians, was built around the theme: "Libraries in the Information Marketplace." President Bill Converse was succeeded by Vivienne Monty, head of the Government and Business Library at York University in Downsview, Ont.

MARY JO LYNCH
American Library Association

LIBRARY AWARDS OF 1988

Beta Phi Mu Award for distinguished service to education for librarianship: Samuel Rothstein, professor emeritus, University of British Columbia

Randolph J. Caldecott Medal for the most distinguished picture book for children: John Schoenherr, *Owl Moon* (story by Jane Yolen)

Melvil Dewey Award for recent creative professional achievement of a high order: Herbert Goldhor, professor emeritus, School of Library and Information Science, University of Illinois

Grolier Award for unique contributions to the stimulation and guidance of reading by children and young people: Lucille Cole Thomas, former director, School Library Services for Elementary Schools, New York City Board of Education

Joseph W. Lippincott Award for distinguished service to the profession of librarianship: Henriette D. Avram, assistant librarian for processing services, Library of Congress

John Newbery Medal for the most distinguished contribution to literature for children: Russell Freedman, *Lincoln: A Photobiography*

Libya's leader Col. Muammar el-Qaddafi (left) bids farewell to Tunisia's President Zine El Abidine Ben Ali in Tunis in February. The two leaders also conferred in Tripoli in August, and an improvement in relations between the two nations resulted.

AP/Wide World

LIBYA

Libya's already slumping national economy suffered from a precipitate decline in oil prices in 1988, as well as from an infestation of locusts that seriously damaged crops in several parts of the country. The downward spiral of oil revenues, in conjunction with international criticisms of Libyan policies that virtually had isolated the country, prompted Libyan leader Col. Muammar el-Qaddafi to revise some political and economic practices in an attempt to allay both internal and external hostility. As a result, Libya's relations with its immediate neighbors and with other Arab states generally improved during 1988. Nevertheless, evidence of Libyan assistance to a variety of revolutionary movements around the globe persisted. In light of these activities, the United States continued to denounce Libya as a supporter of international terrorism.

Oil revenues, which had exceeded $20 billion annually at the beginning of the 1980s, dropped to only $4.5 billion in 1987 and were expected to total only $3.3 billion in 1988. This rapid diminution of petroleum income made it difficult for the government to honor its commitments to internal development and also curtailed purchases of goods and services abroad, provoking an increase in dissatisfaction with the regime. Throughout the year, Qaddafi took political and economic steps designed to assuage the poorly organized but potentially dangerous domestic opposition. In a dramatic gesture in March, he personally bulldozed the prison in which four hundred political detainees had been held. Shortly thereafter, he recommended the abolition of capital punishment and invited Libyan exiles to return to their country without fear of retribution. At the end of August, Qaddafi imposed restrictions on the powers of the Revolutionary Committees, which he said had treated political dissidents too harshly. He also proposed abolishing the police and armed forces, replacing them with a voluntary "people's army."

At the same time, the government responded to the specifically economic discomfort occasioned by the declining price of oil. Many state controls on the economy were eased in the hope of quelling the growing unrest over shortages and the complete absence of many commodities. Moves toward the privatization of state businesses, which had met with some successes in other North African countries, also were initiated in a break with trends that had prevailed in Libya since the revolution.

In order to lessen its international isolation, Libya joined other North African countries in the course of 1988 to explore plans that would promote regional integration and cooperation. Relations with Tunisia improved markedly following the replacement (November 1987) of Tunisian President Habib Bourguiba, a frequent critic of Qaddafi, by Zine El Abidine Ben Ali. Qaddafi and Ben Ali met in Tunis in February and in Tripoli in August to discuss issues of mutual concern, including the exploitation of offshore oil fields in the Gulf of Gabès.

The reopening of the Tunisian-Libyan frontier in early 1988 proved advantageous to both countries. In the months that followed, the severe shortages of commodities in Libya drew more than 250,000 Libyans to Tunisia in search of products unavailable in their own country. These consumers pumped more than $100 million into the Tunisian economy, most of it in the southern, and least economically developed, part of the country. At the same time, some 15,000 unemployed Tunisian workers found jobs in Libya.

A similar relaxation of tensions with Egypt took place at the end of March, when Saudi Arabia successfully mediated a withdrawal of Libyan troops from positions along the Egyptian border. Nevertheless, in June, when Qad-

dafi made his first visit to an Arab League summit in a decade, he refused to endorse the readmission of Egypt to the League.

Plummeting oil revenues greatly restricted Libya's ability to sustain its costly war with Chad. This, coupled with the fact that events in Chad had raised fears of Libyan expansionism among the North African countries with which Libya sought to improve relations, led Qaddafi to declare an end to the 13-year war in May. On the occasion of the 25th anniversary of the founding of the Organization of African Unity, the Libyan leader recognized the government of Chadian President Hissein Habré, promised to repatriate Chadian prisoners of war, and proposed a financial aid plan for the reconstruction of northern Chad, the region of the country most devastated during the fighting. In October, Libya resumed full diplomatic relations with Chad, pledging to negotiate a resolution of the question of sovereignty over the Aouzou Strip, a mineral-rich territory along the Libyan-Chad border claimed by both countries, but occupied primarily by Libya.

In addition to these efforts to break Libya's diplomatic isolation, Colonel Qaddafi also acted as an intermediary in several matters involving the Palestinians. In April he arranged a round of talks between the feuding Palestine Liberation Organization (PLO) Chairman Yasir Arafat and Syrian President Hafiz al-Assad. Two months later, as Syrian-backed Palestinian guerrillas prepared to overrun the Beirut positions of PLO soldiers loyal to Arafat, a delegation of Libyan officers arranged and oversaw the evacuation of the latter to secure positions in south Lebanon.

These indications of Libyan willingness to act responsibly on the international scene helped to foster new commercial projects. Turkish Prime Minister Turgut Ozal visited Libya during the summer, accompanied by scores of Turkish bankers and businessmen anxious to open new ventures with Libya, Turkey's third largest petroleum supplier. A number of European entrepreneurs also traveled to Libya in the hope of generating new business. Still under construction by a South Korean firm is "the great man-made river project" by which water will be piped from Sawknah in the interior to Tripoli and other points along the coast.

During 1988, Libya also renewed diplomatic ties with a number of African states with which it had severed relations in recent years. Charges of Libyan meddling in the internal affairs of African states lingered, however. In January and February, both Uganda and Senegal made allegations of Libyan interference, but could not offer conclusive proof. Later in the year, French officials accused Libya of carrying out a terrorist bombing in the former French colony of Djibouti. Prior to the end of the fighting with Chad, Libya supplied extensive armaments that the Sudanese army needed for its campaign against rebels in the south in return for the freedom to operate against Chadian forces that had crossed the border into Sudan's Darfur province.

In October 1988, Sudan, increasingly dependent on Libya for help in its civil war, signed an agreement that envisioned an eventual union between the two countries; in mid-November Sudanese Prime Minister Sadiq al-Mahdi visited Tripoli for talks with Qaddafi.

At various times during the year, critics of Colonel Qaddafi accused Libyan operatives of assassinating opposition figures in exile in Europe and of participating in an attack on a Greek cruise ship, while a Pakistani court convicted a former Libyan intelligence officer of conspiring to hijack an American airliner in late 1986. The Libyan government also was alleged to have provided arms and explosives to the Irish Republican Army, smuggled weapons to the island nation of Fiji, and funneled missiles and other weapons to Iran. As a result of these practices, Libya found it increasingly difficult to acquire weapons through legitimate international channels. Under U.S. pressure, Brazil, which had been a major source, rejected a planned multibillion-dollar Libyan purchase, while the Soviet Union and China also declined to renew Libya's arsenal.

Despite the accumulation of evidence linking the Berlin disco bombing that had triggered the American air raid on Libya in April 1986 with Syria, the United States continued to insist that Libya had been responsible for the attack. In January the Reagan administration extended its two-year-old antiterrorist sanctions against Libya. U.S.-Libyan relations deteriorated further as 1989 began when U.S. warplanes shot down two Libyan fighters that displayed "clear hostile intent" in international waters off the Libyan coast. At the same time the United States was becoming increasingly concerned over its belief that a chemical plant in Libya was built to manufacture chemical weapons.

KENNETH J. PERKINS
University of South Carolina

LIBYA • Information Highlights

Official Name: Socialist People's Libyan Arab Jamahiriya ("state of the masses").
Location: North Africa.
Area: 679,359 sq mi (1 759 540 km²).
Population (mid-1988 est.): 4,000,000.
Chief Cities (1984 census): Tripoli, the capital, 990,697; Benghazi, 485,386.
Government: *Head of state,* Muammar el-Qaddafi (took office 1969). *Legislature*—General People's Congress (met initially Nov. 1976).
Monetary Unit: Dinar (0.293 dinar equals U.S. $1, June 1988).
Gross Domestic Product (1986 est. U.S.$): $20,000,-000,000.
Foreign Trade (1986 U.S.$): *Imports,* $5,000,000,000; *exports,* $5,000,000,000.

Photos AP/Wide World

Nobelist Naguib Mahfouz of Egypt

U.S. Poet Laureate Howard Nemerov

LITERATURE

Overview

The world of letters in 1988 paid tribute to several great authors, both living and dead. Two Nobel laureates in English-language literature—the poet, playwright, and critic T.S. Eliot and the playwright Eugene O'Neill—were honored on the centennials of their births. Fans of the novelist Upton Sinclair and mystery writer Raymond Chandler also held 100th birthday commemorations. Among living greats, Egypt's Naguib Mahfouz became the first Arabic writer to be awarded the Nobel Prize in Literature. Toni Morrison (*See* BIOGRAPHY) won the Pulitzer Prize in fiction for her 1987 novel *Beloved;* earlier in the year, a group of 48 black writers and critics signed a statement of "thanks" to Morrison for her life's work and of protest to the literary community after *Beloved* was overlooked for the National Book Award. Howard Nemerov was named U.S. poet laureate, taking over from Richard Wilbur in the fall.

Centennials. Widely regarded as the premier poet of his time, a seminal voice of 20th-century modernism, and a spokesman for the "lost generation" after World War I, Thomas Stearns (T.S.) Eliot was born on Sept. 26, 1888, in St. Louis, MO. He later renounced his U.S. citizenship and settled in England for the rest of his life; he died there in 1965. In 1988 the centenary of Eliot's birth was marked by lectures, readings, and exhibitions in both the United States and Great Britain. Highlighting the occasion was the publication of *The Letters of T.S. Eliot: Volume I, 1898–1922,* edited by his second wife, Valerie Eliot.

Born on Oct. 16, 1888, in a New York City hotel, Eugene Gladstone O'Neill came to be regarded as America's first playwright of distinction and still is acclaimed as its finest. Many of his nearly 30 long plays—including such classics as *Desire Under the Elms* (1924), *The Iceman Cometh* (1939), *Long Day's Journey into Night* (1940–41), and *A Moon for the Misbegotten* (1941–43)—evinced the same darkness and tragedy that characterized his adult life. O'Neill died in 1953 in a Boston hotel room. The centennial of his birth in 1988 was commemorated by special performances, readings, and seminars throughout the United States.

Nobelist. The 77-year-old novelist, playwright, and screenwriter Naguib Mahfouz was honored as the recipient of the 1988 Nobel Prize. In its formal announcement, the Swedish Academy of Letters said that Mahfouz, "through works rich in nuance—now clear-sightedly realistic, now evocatively ambiguous—has formed an Arabian narrative art that applies to all mankind." The author of nearly 40 novels, a dozen short-story collections, several plays, and more than 30 screenplays, Mahfouz is compared with such 19th-century realists as Dickens and Balzac for his depictions of life in Cairo. His novels include the untranslated trilogy *Al-Thulathiyya* (1957), the 1,500-page saga of a Cairo family spanning 27 years and the two World Wars; *The Children of Gebelawi* (1959), a controversial religious work; and the highly political *The Thief and the Dogs* (1961). Although his works are highly popular in the Arab world, his books were banned for a time in many Arab countries because of his support for the 1979 peace treaty between Egypt and Israel.

U.S. Poet Laureate. Howard Nemerov, the 68-year-old poet, novelist, literary critic, and professor of English at Washington University in St. Louis, was named in May as the third poet laureate of the United States. He assumed the one-year post in September, succeeding Richard Wilbur, but continued to teach at Washington University. Nemerov's many awards include the 1978 Pulitzer Prize and National Book Award in poetry for his *Collected Poems* (1977).

American Literature

Since the 1950s, much of the best American fiction has been introspective and personal. Male authors have explored their adolescent angst, marital conflicts, and mid-life crises. Then women authors began telling their side of the story, and the effect was liberating. The struggles of individuals to find meaningful lives led to insights into the contradictions, hypocrisies, and inadequacies of our culture.

Novels. In 1988 the travails of the individual still were being explored, especially in that subgenre dealing with privileged, unhappy young people. Michael Chabon's *Mysteries of Pittsburgh* tells of a college graduate's summer of discovery of his real self and his father's sins. Jay McInerney's *Story of My Life* is about a rich, destructive young woman. To some critics, however, these books seemed self-indulgent; the quests of the main characters lead inevitably into narcissism.

A similar problem besets the middle-aged protagonist of Frederick Exley's *Last Notes From Home*, the final novel in his trilogy. Even John Updike's *S.*, a series of letters from a woman whose search for peace takes her to an ashram in Arizona—and the third of Updike's novels inspired by Nathaniel Hawthorne's *The Scarlet Letter*—is not entirely successful in creating a character with enough depth and passion to sustain interest.

A number of books signaled the return of the family to American fiction, not as a study in pathology but as an intricate network of human needs. Anne Tyler's *Breathing Lessons* pictures a complex of relationships energized and controlled by a forceful woman at the center. Bobbie Ann Mason's *Spence + Lila* lovingly recreates the texture of the lives of a rural

couple who have been married 40 years. Reynolds Price's *Good Hearts* returns to his beloved characters, Rosacoke Mustian and Wesley Beavers, who now have been married 30 years. Alice Adams' *Second Chance*, a story of aging political activists in northern California, evokes the family created not only by marriage and kinship, but by friendship and shared experiences.

Bleaker views of modern American life have not disappeared. Laurence Naumoff's *The Night of the Weeping Women*, Frederick Barthelme's *Two Against One*, and the brutal junkyard life of Carolyn Chute's *Letourneau's Used Auto Parts* convey visions of sterility and loss.

Novelists also were reexamining the individual's relationship to tradition and the past. The most striking example was Jane Smiley's *The Greenlanders*, an imaginative saga of medieval Scandinavia, focusing on the decline of a settlement beset by marauders, disease, and supernatural terrors. Paul West's *The Place in Flowers Where Pollen Rests*, Louise Erdrich's *Tracks*, and Clarence Major's *Painted Turtle: Woman With Guitar* all deal with the painful dilemmas of Native Americans, uprooted from the traditions that nurtured their people for centuries and thrust into a secular world that provides no spiritual sustenance.

Several writers seemed more inclined to explore their heritage than to free themselves from its burdens. William Kennedy's *Quinn's Book* mythologizes the history of Albany, NY, with a rich array of characters and plots. In Larry McMurtry's *Anything for Billy*, a Philadelphia writer of pulp fiction goes West and gets involved with a Billy the Kid figure. Susan Dodd's *Mamaw* imagines the mother of Frank and Jesse James. Roberto Fernandez's *Raining*

Anne Tyler's acclaimed 11th novel, "Breathing Lessons," examines the subtleties, complexities, and vicissitudes of marriage: "the way that everything—and nothing—changes." The story takes place in one day, on a 200-mile car trip.

© Diana Walker   Courtesy of Knopf

Backwards is more skeptical, showing how the Cuban community in Miami is caught in a mythology of a past which prevents it from seeing itself truly.

Don DeLillo's *Libra* questions how we know the past at all. A fictional reconstruction of the assassination of President John Kennedy, the book persuasively puts the reader inside the head of Lee Harvey Oswald, his mother, his wife, Jack Ruby, and various government agents to suggest that the CIA may have been part of an assassination plot. Whether or not such freedom from verifiable fact is a useful "way of thinking," as DeLillo argues, his characters ring with authenticity and insight in the finest tradition of the novel.

And at least four noteworthy works of 1988 made clear that the American novel remains untrammelled by any school. Alison Lurie's *The Truth About Lorin Jones* is a witty, satirical-realist assault on feminists and the art world. Jonathan Franzen's *The Twenty-Seventh City* is a zany, somewhat surreal thriller about a Bombay woman revolutionist who becomes police chief of St. Louis, MO. Jay Cantor's *Krazy Kat* is an evocation of the classic comic strip as philosophical novel. And Lawrence Shainberg's *Memories of Amnesia* takes place inside the head of a neurosurgeon suffering from progressive brain damage.

Short Story. Short fiction remains of major interest to American readers. Acute in their particularity, short stories are free to isolate intense moments and evoke the deepest sensations. Harold Brodkey's *Stories in an Almost Classical Mode* accomplishes this by an incredibly rich, almost baroque prose which elaborates and develops every feeling, thought, and idea. This collection of 30 years of his work enhances Brodkey's reputation as a masterwriter.

Raymond Carver's *Where I'm Calling From*, which appeared shortly before he died in August, is the antithesis of Brodkey's work. Carver's stripped language—crisp, resonant, exact—is an art of subtraction. The stories evoke events even smaller than an anecdote: A waitress becomes fascinated by a fat man; a couple takes care of their neighbor's apartment; a father defends his son. The consequences are not delineated; these are flashes that transform both character and reader. Brodkey and Carver form a polarity reminiscent of Faulkner and Hemingway, the rhetorical splendor of one versus the crisp precision of the other.

James Salter's *Dusk* represents the distinctive voice of another highly respected writer. Salter's subtlety and elegance contrast with the plenitude of Brodkey and the minimalism of Carver. Salter's stories are of people whose lives are surfaces of manners and culture, people who belong to exclusive clubs and own expensive horses but cannot escape the darkness in their lives. Mary Robison's *Believe Them* tends to deal with "newer money," the chic and comfortable who still grapple with emptiness and anguish.

But most contemporary short-story writers take on grittier subjects. Mary Gaitskill's *Bad Behavior* focuses sharply and perceptively on the underside of American life, the world of prostitutes and drug addiction. E. Annie Proulx's *Heart Songs and Other Sorrows* depicts a New England of "rusty oil drums, collapsed stacks of rotten boards," where a man is so bent on petty revenge that he destroys the only beauty in his life. Philip F. Deaver's *Silent Retreats* takes place in a Midwest where one character declares, "Pain is all that motivates." Larry Brown's *Facing the Music* deals with the hard lives of men in Mississippi. And Reginald McKnight's *Moustapha's Eclipse* reveals the ironies of racial tensions in Africa and the United States.

Poetry. American poetry long has suffered from popular neglect; with few exceptions, it has been bought and read only by a loyal but small literary audience. Now it also is suffering from serious critical neglect; poetry reviews in national magazines are few, brief, and often long-delayed. In reaction to low sales, lack of public interest, and virtually no promotion, the large bookstore chains provide little shelf space for serious poetry and are reluctant to deal with independent presses, the primary publishers of younger poets.

The year 1988 seemed a particularly difficult one for American poets. The older generation was respected but not celebrated. Richard Wilbur brought out his *New and Collected Poems;* it is fine work—rich, expressive, and moving—but few people know that he was the U.S. poet laureate (succeeded in September by Howard Nemerov). W. S. Merwin's *The Rain in the Trees* shows the continued vitality of another master who has explored man's relationship to nature. Thomas McGrath's *Selected Poems: 1938–1988* represents 50 years of work by the illustrious North Dakota poet.

But neglect has not stopped American poetry from being ambitious and fiery. A number of book-length poems were published in 1988. Robert Kelly's *The Flowers of Unceasing Coincidence* is fearlessly difficult. Leslie Scalapino's *Way* is a long invocation and meditation on a city of death. Elizabeth Socolow's *Laughing at Gravity: Conversation with Isaac Newton* is an imaginative work conjuring up the voices of Newton and an early translator who was Voltaire's rejected lover. Perhaps most successful of all, Donald Hall's *The One Day* is an eloquent, tightly constructed three-part work written in several antiphonal voices.

Steve Kowit's anthology *The Maverick Poets* blames "the pervasive style of late 20th century verse" for poetry's problems. Characterizing that style as "tepid, mannered,

© Rand Hendrix   © Nancy Crampton

Historian Barbara Tuchman, left, gives an account of the American Revolution in "The First Salute." Neil Sheehan, right, examines America's role in Vietnam through the eyes of career officer John Paul Vann in "A Bright Shining Lie."

and opaque,'' Kowit counters with the work of poets whom he describes as "spirited, outspoken, fiercely independent, and happily disinclined to run with the herd." They range from such well-known figures as Charles Bukowski, Lawrence Ferlinghetti, Allen Ginsberg, and Gary Snyder, to such younger voices as Alta, Antler, David Kirby, and Al Zolynas. Their liveliness, irreverence, and vigorous language suggest poetry's bright future despite all neglect.

History and Biography. Biography, once a polite literary form in which a trusted family member or literary executor gathered documents and interviews to create a properly respectful portrait of the esteemed subject, has fallen on strange days. In reviewing David Roberts' relentlessly intimate *Jean Stafford: A Biography,* Joyce Carol Oates coined the term "pathography," which she describes as a focusing on "dysfunction and disaster, illnesses and pratfalls, failed marriages and failed careers." Another striking example was Albert Goldman's *The Lives of John Lennon,* a portrait which fulfills Oates' definition by "wallowing in squalor and foolishness." The English writer Ian Hamilton's *In Search of J.D. Salinger* ran into another sort of trouble; Salinger's obsession with privacy tied the book up in court until an approved final version was permitted.

Some figures are so controversial that they simultaneously precipitate two biographies with differing perspectives: for example, Sidney Zion's *The Autobiography of Roy Cohn* and Nicholas von Hoffman's *Citizen Cohn.* Philip Roth's *The Facts: A Novelist's Autobiography* further confuses the notion of historical truth by claiming to give "the facts" but

also having Roth's fictional character, the ubiquitous Zuckerman, comment on the autobiography itself.

Such exemplary new biographies as Gerald Clarke's *Capote,* Judy Oppenheimer's *Private Demons: The Life of Shirley Jackson,* and Scott Donaldson's *John Cheever,* treat difficult subjects with a candor unthinkable a generation ago but also manage to be balanced and insightful. And parts of major, multivolume biographies, like Arnold Rampersad's *Life of Langston Hughes* and Joan Richardson's *Wallace Stevens,* make clear that biography still can give insight not only into its subject but also into the history of our culture.

One of the most chilling books of the year, Herbert Mitgang's *Dangerous Dossiers,* revealed that the FBI consistently has devoted extraordinary amounts of time and energy to spying on American writers, developing elaborate files on them, and prying into the most personal aspects of their lives.

Culture and Criticism. The diversity of American culture was recognized in several major works of 1988. Houston Baker's *Afro-American Poetics* and Henry Louis Gates, Jr.'s *The Signifying Monkey* explore the richness of the black experience and its contribution to American literature. Sandra M. Gilbert's and Susan Gubar's *No Man's Land* establishes women's role in creating 20th-century literature. And an entirely different America is scrutinized in Lewis Lapham's *Money and Class in America* and Nelson W. Aldrich's *Old Money,* revealing and highly critical accounts of the customs and attitudes of the upper-upper classes.

JEROME STERN
Florida State University

AMERICAN LITERATURE: MAJOR WORKS | 1988

NOVELS

Adams, Alice, *Second Chances*
Adams, Richard, *Traveller*
Barthelme, Frederick, *Two Against One*
Cantor, Jay, *Krazy Kat: A Novel in Five Panels*
Chabon, Michael, *The Mysteries of Pittsburgh*
Chute, Carolyn, *Letourneau's Used Auto Parts*
Crews, Harry, *The Knockout Artist*
DeLillo, Don, *Libra*
Dexter, Pete, *Paris Trout*
Dixon, Stephen, *Garbage*
Dodd, Susan, *Mamaw*
Douglas, Ellen, *Can't Quit You, Baby*
Edgerton, Clyde, *The Floatplane Notebooks*
Erdrich, Louise, *Tracks*
Exley, Frederick, *Last Notes From Home*
Fernandez, Roberto, *Raining Backwards*
Franzen, Jonathan, *The Twenty-Seventh City*
Gilchrist, Ellen, *The Anna Papers*
Greenberg, Joanne, *Of Such Small Differences*
Hawkes, John, *Whistlejacket*
Heller, Joseph, *Picture This*
Hoffman, Alice, *At Risk*
Kennedy, William, *Quinn's Book*
Kingsolver, Barbara, *The Bean Trees*
Kosinski, Jerzy, *The Hermit of 69th Street*
Kraft, Eric, *Herb 'n' Lorna*
Lurie, Alison, *The Truth About Lorin Jones*
Major, Clarence, *Painted Turtle: Woman With Guitar*
Mason, Bobbie Ann, *Spence + Lila*
McElroy, Joseph, *The Letter Left to Me*
McInerney, Jay, *Story of My Life*
McMurtry, Larry, *Anything for Billy*
Morris, Mary McGarry, *Vanished*
Naumoff, Laurence, *The Night of the Weeping Women*
O'Hehir, Diana, *The Bride Who Ran Away*
Paretsky, Sara, *Blood Shot*
Powers, J.F., *Wheat That Springeth Green*
Price, Reynolds, *Good Hearts*
Shainberg, Lawrence, *Memories of Amnesia*
Singer, Isaac Bashevis, *The King of the Fields*
Smiley, Jane, *The Greenlanders*
Smith, Lee, *Fair and Tender Ladies*
Tyler, Ann, *Breathing Lessons*
Updike, John, *S.*
Williams, Joy, *Breaking and Entering*
West, Paul, *The Place in Flowers Where Pollen Rests*
Woiwode, Larry, *Born Brothers*

SHORT STORIES

Brodkey, Harold, *Stories in an Almost Classical Mode*
Brown, Larry, *Facing the Music*
Canin, Ethan, *Emperor of the Air*
Carver, Raymond, *Where I'm Calling From*
Colter, Cyrus, *The Amoralist*
Deaver, Philip F., *Silent Retreats*
Dubus, Andre, *Selected Stories*
Dumas, Henry, *Goodbye, Sweetwater*
Ellison, Harlan, *Angry Candy*
Frucht, Abby, *Fruit of the Month*
Gaitskill, Mary, *Bad Behavior*
Klinkowitz, Jerry, *Short Season*
Martone, Michael, *Safety Patrol*
McKnight, Reginald, *Moustapha's Eclipse*
Oates, Joyce Carol, *The Assignation*
Prose, Francine, *Women and Children First*
Proulx, E. Annie, *Heart Songs and Other Sorrows*
Ravenel, Shannon, ed., *New Stories From the South: The Year's Best, 1988*
Robison, Mary, *Believe Them*
Salter, James, *Dusk*
Singer, Isaac Bashevis, *The Death of Methuselah*
Spencer, Elizabeth, *Jack of Diamonds*
Steele, Max, *The Hat of My Mother*
Updike, David, *Out on the Marsh*

POETRY

Adcock, Betty, *Beholdings*
Ashbery, John, *April Galleons*
Daniell, Rosemary, *Fort Bragg & Other Points South*
Dennis, Carl, *The Outskirts of Troy*
Flanders, Jane, *Timepiece*
Gernes, Sonia, *Women at Forty*
Gossett, Hattie, *Presenting . . . Sister Noblues*
Hall, Donald, *The One Day*
Harrison, Jeffrey, *The Singing Underneath*

Hongo, Garrett, *The River of Heaven*
Kelly, Brigit Pegeen, *To the Place of Trumpets*
Kelly, Robert, *The Flowers of Unceasing Coincidence*
Kowit, Steven, ed., *The Maverick Poets*
Levine, Philip, *A Walk With Tom Jefferson*
McGrath, Thomas, *Selected Poems: 1938–1988*
McPherson, Sandra, *Streamers*
Merwin, W.S., *The Rain in the Trees*
Merwin, W.S., *Selected Poems*
O'Hehir, Diana, *Home Free*
Pankey, Eric, *Heartwood*
Pastan, Linda, *The Imperfect Paradise*
Scalapino, Leslie, *Way*
Shapiro, Harvey, *National Cold Storage Company*
Skinner, Jeffrey, *A Guide to Forgetting*
Socolow, Elizabeth, *Laughing at Gravity: Conversation with Isaac Newton*
Swensen, Cole, *New Math*
Wilbur, Richard, *New and Collected Poems*
Wright, Charles, *Zone Journals*
Zeidner, Lisa, *Pocket Sundial*

HISTORY AND BIOGRAPHY

Bergman, Ingemar, *The Magic Lantern: An Autobiography*
Brian, Denis, *The True Hem: An Intimate Portrait of Ernest Hemingway by Those Who Knew Him*
Butscher, Edward, *Conrad Aiken: Poet of White Horse Vale*
Clarke, Gerald, *Capote: A Biography*
Donaldson, Scott, *John Cheever: A Biography*
Foner, Eric, *Reconstruction: America's Unfinished Revolution 1863–1877*
Gay, Peter, *Freud: A Life for Our Time*
Gelderman, Carol, *Mary McCarthy: A Life*
Goldman, Albert, *The Lives of John Lennon*
Hall, Michael G., *The Last American Puritan: The Life of Increase Mather 1639–1723*
Hamilton, Ian, *In Search of J.D. Salinger*
Hoffman, Nicholas von, *Citizen Cohn*
Kazan, Elia, *Elia Kazan: A Life*
McLaughlin, Jack, *Jefferson and Monticello*
McPherson, James M., *Battle Cry of Freedom: The Civil War Era*
Mitgang, Herbert, *Dangerous Dossiers: Exposing the Secret War Against America's Greatest Authors*
Morgan, Edmund S., *Inventing the People: The Rise of Popular Sovereignty*
Murphy, Bruce Allen, *Fortas: The Rise and Ruin of a Supreme Court Justice*
Oppenheimer, Judy, *Private Demons: The Life of Shirley Jackson*
Ramdin, Rom, *Paul Robeson: The Man and His Mission*
Rampersad, Arnold, *The Life of Langston Hughes: II, 1941–1967: I Dream a World*
Richardson, Joan, *Wallace Stevens: The Later Years, 1923–1955*
Roberts, David, *Jean Stafford: A Biography*
Roth, Philip, *The Facts: A Novelist's Autobiography*
Sheehan, Neil, *A Bright Shining Lie: John Paul Vann and America in Vietnam*
Tuchman, Barbara, *The First Salute: A View of the American Revolution*
Walker, Margaret, *Richard Wright: Daemonic Genius*
Zion, Sidney, *The Autobiography of Roy Cohn*

CULTURE AND CRITICISM

Aldrich, Nelson W., Jr., *Old Money: The Mythology of America's Upper Class*
Baker, Houston A., Jr., *Afro-American Poetics: Revisions of Harlem and the Black Aesthetic*
Gates, Henry Louis, Jr., *The Signifying Monkey: A Theory of Afro-American Literary Criticism*
Gilbert, Sandra M. and Susan Gubar, *No Man's Land: The Place of the Woman Writer in the Twentieth Century: The War of the Worlds*
Kaplan, E. Ann, *Rocking Around the Clock: Music, Television, Postmodernism, and Consumer Culture*
Lapham, Lewis H., *Money and Class in America: Notes and Observations on Our Civil Religion*
Nixon, Richard, *1999: Victory Without War*
Oates, Joyce Carol, *(Woman) Writer: Occasions and Opportunities*
Pagels, Elaine, *Adam, Eve, and the Serpent*
Reed, Ishmael, *Writin' is Fightin'*
Smith, Hedrick, *The Power Game: How Washington Works*
Terkel, Studs, *The Great Divide: Second Thoughts on the American Dream*
Vidal, Gore, *At Home: Essays 1982–1988*
Weart, Spencer R., *Nuclear Fears: A History of Images*
Wright, Robert, *Three Scientists and Their Gods: Looking for Meaning in the Age of Information*

Children's Literature

The children's book market continued to be strong, with increasing bookstore sales steadily influencing publishers' outputs. Noticeable 1988 trends included longer texts for picture books, an upswing in poetry offerings, and a gratifying number of attractive, compelling nonfiction books.

In fact, nonfiction came up the surprising winner in the Newbery Medal. Russell Freedman's *Lincoln: A Photobiography* won the American Library Association's prestigious award for literary merit. And the Caldecott Medal, awarded for book illustration, went to *Owl Moon*, written by Jane Yolen and illustrated by John Schoenherr.

Recommended Books. The river of baby books that poured forth in the last several years abated somewhat, replaced by stories designed for the opposite end of the picture-book spectrum. Stories with lengthy texts appeared in surprising numbers. Among them were Diane Stanley's *Shaka*, which tells the story of the 19th-century African military genius, and Alice Walker's *To Hell With Dying*. The latter, written originally as an adult short story, was wedded to illustrations and placed in a format suitable for younger readers.

The biggest children's publishing event of the year was the appearance of Maurice Sendak's newest book, *Dear Mili*. It is an intricately illustrated interpretation of a recently discovered Grimm story. Several other acclaimed illustrators also presented offerings. Anita Lobel fashioned a rich Italian setting for Steven Kroll's adventure *Looking for Daniela;* Barbara Cooney memorably evoked the rugged Maine coast in *Island Boy;* and Thomas Locker's *Family Farm*, about a family struggling successfully to keep their land, is graced with the artist's compelling, opulent paintings.

Good fiction for the middle grades traditionally is a somewhat scarce commodity. Picture books and books for junior-high students almost always are more plentiful. Still, each year notable titles appear. Among 1988's best were Betsy Byars' *Beans on the Roof*, a comic examination of a family of would-be poets; and Mollie Hunter's *The Mermaid Summer*, about two children who try to save their grandfather from a mermaid's curse. First-rate fantasy-adventure could be found in Michael Morpurgo's *King of the Cloud Forests;* and a smoothly written contemporary school story was Ilene Cooper's *Queen of the Sixth Grade.*

A number of substantial novels for junior-high readers appeared in 1988. Award-winning author Paula Fox presented a meticulous study of painful maturation in *The Village By the Sea*. Complex, exciting fantasy is found in Diana Wynne Jones' *The Lives of Christopher Chant;* and gritty realism about inner city violence turns up in Walter Dean Myers' *Scorpions*.

SELECTED BOOKS FOR CHILDREN

Picture Books
Ackerman, Karen, *Song and Dance Man*
Carrick, Donald, *Harald and the Great Stag*
Chaikin, Miriam, *Exodus*
Cherry, Lynne, *Who's Sick Today?*
Fleischman, Sid, *The Scarebird*
Johnson, Tony, *Yonder*
Levinson, Riki, *Our Home Is the Sea*
Siebert, Diane, *Mohave*

Fiction: Ages 9–12
Fine, Anne, *Alias Madame Doubtfire*
Herman, Charlotte, *Millie Cooper, Take a Chance*
Hurwitz, Johanna, *The Cold and Hot Winter*
Jukes, Mavis, *Getting Even*
Lasky, Kathryn, *Sea Swan*
Lowry, Lois, *Sam's Story*

Fiction: Young Teens
Cameron, Eleanor, *The Private Worlds of Julia Redfern*
Christopher, John, *When the Tripods Came*
Cole, Brock, *The Goats*
Klein, Norma, *Now That I Know*
Levin, Betty, *The Trouble with Gramary*
Lyon, George Ella, *Borrowed Children*
Perez, N. A., *Breaker*
Shusterman, Neal, *The Shadow Club*

Fiction: Young Adults
Davis, Jenny, *Sex Education*
Koertge, Ron, *The Arizona Kid*
Mahy, Margaret, *Memory*
Rylant, Cynthia, *The Kindness*
Swenson, May, and Knudson, R. R., *American Sports Poems*
Wolff, Virginia E., *Probably Still Nick*

Nonfiction
dePaola, Tomie, *Tomie dePaola's Book of Poems*
Fisher, Leonard Everett, *Pyramid of the Sun*
Freedman, Russell, *Buffalo Hunt*
Fritz, Jean, *China's Long March*
Haldane, Suzanne, *Face Painting*
Jaspersohn, William, *Ice Cream*
Larrick, Nancy, comp., *Cats Are Cats*
Opie, Peter and Iona, *Feathers from Mother Goose*
Patent, Dorothy Hinshaw, *Babies*
Simon, Seymour, *Volcanoes*
Wurmfeld, Hope Herman, *Boatbuilder*

Various contemporary issues continued to be explored in strong young adult books. The oppressive consequences of apartheid are the subject of *Somehow Tenderness Survives*, a collection of stories about southern Africa compiled by Hazel Rochman. The war in Vietnam is a powerful backdrop for Walter Dean Myers' *Fallen Angels*, which explores the effects of war on a 17-year-old youth who enlists in the service to avoid the dead-end streets of Harlem.

High quality nonfiction titles covered a variety of subjects. Eda LeShan's *When Grown-Ups Drive You Crazy* offers comforting advice to young people who are having difficulty getting along with their elders. The story of Washington's Vietnam War Memorial is told in Brent Ashabranner's *Always to Remember*, and all the excitement and artistry of a circus performance is captured in Hana Machotka's *The Magic Ring*.

DENISE MURCKO WILMS
Assistant Editor, "Booklist"

Canadian Literature: English

Anticipating the November general election, Canadian writers in 1988 produced many books about politics and political leaders.

Nonfiction. Prime Minister Brian Mulroney was the subject of Norman Snider's highly critical *Dark Kingdom: Brian Mulroney and the Transformation of Canada*. Equally critical of the Liberal Opposition leader was Greg Weston's *Reign of Error: The Inside Story of John Turner's Troubled Leadership*. More bland was Judy Steed's *Ed Broadbent: The Pursuit of Power*, about the New Democratic Party leader. Other political books included Ian MacDonald's *Mulroney*; newspaperman Charles Lynch's *The Lynch Mob*; Eddie Goodman's *Life of the Party*; Jeffrey Simpson's *Spoils of Power: The Politics of Patronage*; and *The Broadway Book of Canadian Political Anecdotes*, edited by Marc Bosc.

The year's top biographies included *Bible Bill*, by David R. Elliott and Iris Miller, about colorful William Aberhart, who became Social Credit premier of Alberta in 1935. *Odd Man Out: The Life and Times of Eric Kierans*, by Jamie Swift, traces the long career of the former federal cabinet minister. Bronwyn Drainie writes about her actor father in *Living the Part: The Turbulent Times of John Drainie*. And Paul Blanchard's *The Life of Emily Carr* details the career of a great painter.

Pierre Berton's latest popular history is *The Arctic Grail*, about northern exploration and the search for the Northwest Passage. *Echoes from a Frozen Land* by the late Donald B. Marsh (notes edited by his wife, Winifred Marsh) describes his missionary work among Inuit people in the Arctic. Ken Coates and William Morrison contribute *Land of the Midnight Sun: A History of the Yukon*. Basil M. Johnston's *Indian School Day* describes the wretched conditions at schools for native Indians in the 1940s. Jane Errington's *The Lion, the Eagle and Upper Canada* tells of early Canadians being torn between British and U.S. influences. Suzanne Zeller's *Inventing Canada* details how science during Victorian times helped Canada develop. Robert M. Stamp's well-illustrated *Kings, Queens & Canadians* documents Canadian interest in the British royal family from 1714 to the present. Poet Robin Skelton's *Memories of a Literary Blockhead* recounts his growing familiarity with Canadian literature since he arrived in Canada in 1962.

Peter Padfield, himself a sailor, produced the beautifully illustrated *Armada: A Celebration of the Four Hundredth Anniversary of the Defeat of the Spanish Armada 1588–1988*. Seventy years elapsed between the writing and the publication of Edwin Campion Vaughan's *Some Desperate Glory*, a diary of his experiences during World War I. Robert Bothwell's *Nucleus: The History of Atomic Energy of Canada Limited* is a well-researched work. *Wild Furbearer Management and Conservation in North America*, edited by Milan Novak, James A. Baker, Martyn E. Obbard, and Bruce Malloch, argues that trapping does not endanger animal species and should be allowed to continue. And the late Marshall McLuhan and his son, Eric McLuhan, coauthored *Laws of Media: The New Sciences*.

Poetry. *Ride Off Any Horizon II*, edited by Peter Christensen and Lorne Daniel, is a second collection of Western Canadian poetry. bill bissett, who scorns capital letters, contributes *animal uproar*. Don Bailey's poems in *How Will We Know When We Get There?* have an elegiac tone. Stephen Scobie's *The Ballad of Isabel Gunn* tells the true story of a Scottish girl who disguised herself as a man and got a job in Canada with Hudson's Bay Company as a means of joining her lover. Other notable volumes included Norm Sibum's *Eight Poems*, Sharon Thesen's *The Beginning of the Long Dash*, and Patricia Young's *All I Ever Wanted Was a Beautiful Room*.

Fiction. Robertson Davies' ninth novel, *The Lyre of Orpheus*, increases his international reputation. It is the last book in his Cornford trilogy, which began with *The Rebel Angels* and *What's Bred in the Bone*. At times funny and at times profound, it is, like its predecessors, influenced by the philosophy of Carl Jung.

Robert Harlow's *The Saxophone Winter*, his seventh novel, concerns a 14-year-old boy and his problems in the winter of 1938–39. Don DeLillo did enormous research for *Libra*, a novel based on the assassination of U.S. President John Kennedy. Margaret Atwood's *Cat's Eye* shows how a woman's childhood friends greatly influenced her. W. O. Mitchell's *Ladybug, Ladybug* concerns a retired professor and his housekeeper. Charles Templeton's *World of One*, set in the 1990s, is about a TV evangelist. Morley Callaghan contributes *A Wild Old Man on the Road*, and Hugh Hood's *Tony's Book* is the seventh volume in a planned series of 12. Among the year's notable short-story collections were Mavis Gallant's *In Transit*, W. P. Kinsella's *The Further Adventures of Slugger McBatt*, and Timothy Findley's *Stones*.

DAVID SAVAGE, *Free-lance Writer*

English Literature

Novels appeared from many of Britain's major writers during 1988; most particularly, a Graham Greene manuscript, titled *The Captain and the Enemy*, that had been lying unfinished for many years. Also published were Doris Lessing's *The Fifth Child*, a study of the appearance of unexplained evil, and Piers Paul Read's *A Season in the West*, a cool view of Western society and manners. From William

Britain's Doris Lessing produced another acclaimed novel in 1988, "The Fifth Child," about the sudden appearance of unexplained evil—in the form of a monster-child—in the lives of a young British couple in the 1970s. It was Lessing's 35th book.

© 1988 Miriam Berkley

Trevor came another subtle Anglo-Irish novel, *The Silence in the Garden*, and from Molly Keane the sharp *Loving and Giving*, also set in Ireland. Anita Desai took another look at East meeting West in *Baumgartner's Bombay*, and Kingsley Amis wrote the slyly misogynist *Difficulties with Girls*.

Other Fiction. In the fall, Edna O'Brien contributed her first novel in 11 years, *The High Road*, a further picture of women ravaged by love, and Anita Brookner's new work *Latecomers* was accounted her best work to date. Muriel Spark was back in a mood of black humor with *A Far Cry From Kensington*, while Alan Hollinghurst brought out a homosexual novel of humor and decadence, *The Swimming Pool Library*. Historian and polemicist E. P. Thompson contributed his first work of fiction, *The Sykaos Papers*, an extraterrestrial, philosophical mystery.

The Booker Prize short list of nominees, however, included other novels—*Utz* from Bruce Chatwin, *The Beginning of Spring* by Penelope Fitzgerald, *The Lost Father* by Marina Warner, *Oscar and Lucinda* by Peter Carey, *Nice Work* by David Lodge, and *The Satanic Verses* from Salman Rushdie. The £15,000 (about $26,000) prize went to Carey.

Nonfiction. This was a bumper year for biographies, with lives of writers, actors, politicians, and poets under scrutiny. The last volume of Martin Gilbert's marathon life of Sir Winston Churchill, *Never Despair: 1945–1965*, was greeted with great admiration. Also well received was Alistair Horne's *Macmillan 1894–1956: The Making of a Prime Minister*, although it was felt to diminish the reputation of Harold Macmillan. Among theatrical personalities, Melvyn Bragg's life of Richard Burton, *Rich*, was a popular hit, as was Anthony Holden's portrait of *Olivier*, a study which showed actor Laurence Olivier's personality in all of its complexity. Probably the liveliest event of the year was the publication of Michael Holroyd's first volume of the life of George Bernard Shaw. Brenda Maddox's

Nora, the first biography of the wife of James Joyce, aroused controversy and interest; and A. N. Wilson contributed a study of the life of Tolstoy. Many biographies and critical studies celebrated the 200th anniversary of the birth of Lord Byron, none more tenderly appreciative than *The Politics of Paradise: A Vindication of Byron*, by Michael Foot.

Letters and memoirs poured from the presses, none more extensive than volume six of the *Letters of Charles Dickens, 1850–1852*. Among other writers' correspondence, the *Durrell-Miller Letters, 1935–1980* celebrated the mutual admiration of Lawrence Durrell and Henry Miller, two good friends and celebrators of the flesh. The first volume of *The Letters of T. S. Eliot* came out on the occasion of the centenary year of the poet's birth.

Among the most interesting literary studies was Valentine Cunningham's *British Writers of the Thirties*, which laid bare the world of Auden, Waugh, and Elizabeth Bowen, among others. However, a poet who strayed into criticism, Seamus Heaney, provided the most arresting literary expression in his masterly series of essays that first had been given as the Eliot memorial lectures of 1986, entitled *The Government of the Tongue*.

Poetry. Most other poetry was overshadowed in 1988 by the publication of the *Collected Poems* of Philip Larkin, who was easily felt to be at the time of his death the most genuinely loved poet in Britain. Douglas Dunn's new collection of poems, *Northlight*, was greeted as a welcome return from the veteran poet who had recovered very recently from the death of his wife, the impassioned subject of his earlier *Elegies*. Among others, Kathleen Raine's *Selected Poems*, summing up forty years of dedicated craftsmanship, and Donald Davie's *Scorch or Freeze* were admired widely. The year also saw the Arvon International Poetry Competition won by Selima Hill for her convincing *The Notebook*, purporting to be the diary of a mental patient.

MAUREEN GREEN, *Free-lance Writer, London*

World Literature*

Non-English belles lettres during late 1987 and the first half of 1988 showed a remarkable consistency of quality throughout the major linguistic and geographic areas of the world, as well as in many of the smaller or more exotic ones. In terms of sheer number of notable new works, Asia led the way, followed by Africa, the German-speaking countries, and Russian-language literature.

Asia and the Pacific. Japan's only Nobel Prize winner, Yasunari Kawabata, loved the short-story form above all others, and *Palm-of-the-Hand Stories* presents the reader of English with 70 of them, just over half of the author's total output. Ranging in length from a few paragraphs to six pages, they exhibit a dazzling variety of styles and moods but focus on many of the same concerns which mark his famous novels: time's passage, love, loneliness, and the conflict between tradition and modernity. A much earlier classic of Japanese literature, Natsume Sôseki's compellingly squalid and self-conscious 1908 "antinovel" *The Miner,* also made its first appearance in English. Shûsaku Endô, the current president of the Japan PEN Club, brought out *Scandal,* a "psycho-philosophical mystery" which relies on a doppelgänger motif to explore the darker side of human nature. The younger generation of Japanese writers was ably represented by Yuko Tsushima (daughter of the famed late novelist Osamu Dazai), a selection of whose stories appeared in English as *The Shooting Gallery* and revealed a particular affinity for society's abandoned and exploited elements.

From China, new prose collections by Lu Wenfu (*The Gourmet and Other Stories*), Feng Jicai (*The Miraculous Pigtail*), and A Cheng (*The Three Kings*) brought readers in Europe

* Titles translated.

Colombia's Gabriel García Márquez, the 1982 Nobelist, saw the English debut of his "Love in the Time of Cholera."

© Helmut Newton

and the Americas an excellent sampling of the range of recent Chinese short fiction. India's esteemed novelist Raja Rao marked the 15th anniversary of his literary debut by publishing *The Chessmaster and His Moves,* the massive first volume of a projected trilogy covering an enormous range of philosophical, religious, and historical themes. Anita Desai's new novel *Baumgartner's Daughter* also spans two very different worlds (in this case Indian and German) and attempts some kind of understanding or reconciliation between them, although with a somewhat lighter touch and less cosmic concern than does Rao. Nirmal Verma's award-winning Hindi stories of Indian alienation at home and in Central European exile became available in English in 1988 as *The World Elsewhere.* From Pakistan, meanwhile, emerged *The True Subject,* a beautiful selection from famed Urdu poet Faiz Ahmed Faiz's finest work.

In a year when world attention focused on Korea for events both athletic and sociopolitical, the journalist and novelist Ahn Junghyo brought out *White Badge,* cleverly subtitled "A Novel of Korea" and concerned with matters of conscience, memory, and morality.

Africa and the West Indies. The Nigerian novelist Chinua Achebe, whose work many critics place on a par with that of 1986 Nobel laureate (and Achebe's countryman) Wole Soyinka, in 1988 brought out his first full-fledged novel in 20 years, *Anthills of the Savannah.* The story follows three principal characters through a series of epochal changes in their nation's government and society that test the nature of power, ambition, courage, conscience, and love. Cyprian Ekwensi, colorfully dubbed the Nigerian Defoe, continued his prolific career with two new books: *Jagua Nana's Daughter,* the sequel to 1960's bawdy *Jagua Nana*; and *For a Roll of Parchment,* a text first written in the 1950s (but now adapted) about the widespread African veneration for a foreign university degree. *Memory of Departure* is an extraordinary first novel by Tanzanian-born Abdurazak Gurnah, described by one critic as "a compelling study of one man's struggle to find a purpose for his life and a haunting portrait of a traditional society collapsing under the weight of poverty and rapid change."

From non-English-speaking Africa came two works by Sony Labou Tansi of the Congo: *The Volcano's Eyes* is an exuberant exercise in magical realism, full of crimes and wars and revolutions, and merging fantasy with fiction in its condemnatory tale of governmental corruption and general ignorance; *The Antipeople* takes a smaller target—the sanctimonious headmaster of a small teachers college in Zaire —and works far more successfully as a morality tale about a world of banal evil. *The World of "Mestre" Tamoda,* written in an Angolan prison during the 1960s by the soldier-poet-

novelist-diplomat Uanhenga Xitu, gathers three loosely related novellas depicting life in prerevolutionary Angola of the 1940s.

The most noteworthy new works from the Caribbean in 1988 were the lushly lyric and threateningly mysterious novel *Hadriana in All My Dreams* by the Haitian-born René Depestre; and *Your Handsome Captain*, a one-character play by Guadeloupe's Simone Schwarz-Bart dramatizing the sufferings of the "wretched of the earth."

Middle East. The monumental anthology *The Literature of Modern Arabia*, produced under the general editorship of Salma Khadra Jayyusi, offers English readers a truly first-rate gathering of recent texts from Saudi Arabia, Kuwait, Yemen, and the United Arab Emirates, among others. The emphasis is on writings of crisis and protest, identity searches, and attempts to return to an ancient heritage or adapt it in some meaningful way to the present. The 1988 Nobelist, Naguib Mahfouz of Egypt, saw two more of his novels rendered into English: *Respected Sir*, a slim 1975 work about overreaching ambition in pre-1950s Egypt; and *The Search*, an allegorical quest tale with dark Jungian undercurrents and a rich lode of Arabic-Islamic cultural symbolism. Egyptian-born Andrée Chedid's *Worlds Mirrors Magics* offers 21 stories, sketches, and reflections spanning 3,000 years and ranging in mood from tragedy to poignant romance to warm affection to light irony. Israel's Aharon Appelfeld examines post-Holocaust trauma in *The Immortal Bartfuss*, a tale of taciturn war survivors whose moral outrage and linguistic minimalism serve only to eliminate the consolation of friendship and companionship.

German. New novels by West Germany's Martin Walser and Gert Hofmann and by Austria's Friederike Mayröcker topped the list of creative works in German for 1988. Walser's *Hunt* extends its central metaphor of pursuit into several arenas, including business competition and the chase for sexual and political dominance. With *Before the Rainy Season*, Hofmann spins an exotic, panoramic tale of intrigue and danger in the lush setting of a South American rain forest. Mayröcker's *My Heart My Room My Name* offers a startling 350-page monologue cast as a single unending sentence, an alternately compulsive and confessional tirade spoken as much to fend off loneliness, silence, and fear as to convey either meaning or message.

Elsewhere in the German-speaking realm, *Medusa* by Switzerland's Gertrud Leutenegger and *Strange Farewell* by Hermann Lenz proved somewhat disappointing, given the quality and popularity of their earlier work. The Czech émigré Ota Filip solidified his metamorphosis into a German writer with *Homesickness for Procida*, covering 40 years in the seriocomic, adventure-filled life of a picaresque

Tass from Sovfoto

The Soviet author Chinghiz Aitmatov produced "The Block," an acclaimed novel about drug trafficking in the USSR and a sweeping reflection on the Stalin era and other issues.

refugee from Central Europe now uneasily resettled in the West. Günter Grass weighed in with *Stick Out Your Tongue*, the written and pictorial record of his six-month stay in India.

Russian. The prominent Soviet author (and deputy to the Supreme Soviet from his native Kirghizia) Chinghiz Aitmatov led the way for Russian-language literature in 1987–88 with the publication of his novel *The Block*, an unprecedented exposé of narcotics trafficking and abuse in the USSR and, more importantly, a philosophical reflection upon such matters as religion in an atheist state and the intolerance and inhumanity of the Stalinist legacy. Anatoli Rybakov's *Children of the Arbat* made its English-language appearance in early 1988, several months after its original Russian publication and two decades after its composition. Compared to Aitmatov's new book, however, its revelations about the Stalinist years seem rather tame, presenting no real challenge to current or recent ideological orthodoxy. From another era entirely but in a similar vein to Aitmatov came the first-ever English version of Evgeny Zamyatin's *A Godforsaken Hole*, set in czarist Russia and concerned with a corrupt, brutal, and hypocritical closed world.

The Queue by Anatoly Sorokin consists entirely of dialogue, from the intellectual patter of a self-professed writer, to the rhythms and colloquialisms of ordinary Russian speech, to the grunts and silences (rendered as blank spaces and pages) of the subliterate as they all wait in modern-day Russia's interminable lines to purchase foodstuffs and other necessities.

Abroad, two of the best-known Soviet exiles brought out English editions of their most recent work: 1987 Nobelist Joseph Brodsky's three-act play *Marbles* presents a classical dialogue (the setting is ancient Rome "two centuries after our era") between two prisoners debating such subjects as freedom, reality versus illusion, and the permanence of literature versus the transience of politics. Vassily Aksyonov brought out *Quest for an Island,* containing the title story and other short fiction as well as several dramatic works, most of them satiric.

Spanish and Portuguese. The outstanding Peruvian novelist Mario Vargas Llosa issued two important new books in 12 months, topping the year's literary news in Spanish America: *The Storyteller* employs a double narrative thread typical of the author's best early work, here interweaving a personal history of growing up in Lima and an itinerant storyteller's folkloric oral history of the Peruvian Amazon Indians; *Stepmother's Pet* presents an erotic tale of incest and corruptive innocence that is remarkable for both its sensuality and its sensitivity. *Iphigenia and Other Stories* gathers a number of recent and older prose selections by one of Spain's most honored authors, Gonzalo Torrente Ballester. The anthology *On Our Own Behalf* provides a first-rate collection of women's fiction from Catalonia in Spain. *Constancia and Other Stories for Virgins* brings the best of Mexican writer Carlos Fuentes' recent short fiction to the English-reading public, stories which all convey a certain mystery, magicality, and linguistic experimentation.

The sprawling frontier novel *Showdown* by Brazil's prolific Jorge Amado was rendered splendidly into English by Gregory Rabassa for the delectation of readers to the north. The novel *The Strange Nation of Rafael Mendes* by Brazil's Moacyr Scliar offers that same audience a more subtle but still wonderfully comic account of financial and sexual schemings in modern-day Brazil. Two of the most important *new* Portuguese works to appear in Brazil during 1988 were Nélida Piñon's entertaining novel *Caetana's Sweet Song* and Oswaldo França Junior's sweeping epic of rural modernization, *In Deep Waters.*

French and Italian. Robert Pinget produced one of the year's most readable serious novels in France, *The Enemy,* a disturbingly ambiguous tale exploring the nature of the writer's craft and his "exorcistic struggle against chaos." Patrick Modiano's *Repayment of Pain* is a fragmentary reminiscence of a flawed childhood and adolescence in a provincial town. Claude Mauriac at last brought his autobiographical "Time Immobile" series to a conclusion after 30 years with the tenth volume, *Uncle Marcel*; and Julien Green extended his much-praised 62-year *Journal* with a new installment covering the years 1981–84.

© Marcela Briones

Eduardo Galeano of Uruguay completed his trilogy on the history of the Americas—collectively titled "Memory of Fire" —with the 1988 publication of "Century of the Wind."

The most notable new title to emerge from Italy in 1988 was *When God Left the Church* by the talented Triestine author Fulvio Tomizza, a set of historically based accounts of the Inquisition's cruelties and abuses in the Istrian peninsula during the 16th century.

Other European. The 1979 Nobel laureate, Odysseus Elytis of Greece, saw his recent collection of verse and lyric prose *The Little Mariner* reach a worldwide audience with the publication of an English translation by Olga Broumas. The award-winning poet and playwright Paavo Haavikko of Finland issued his first new collection of verse in a decade, *Five Series about Rapidly Fleeting Life*; its five divisions alternately engage the themes of death and the relationship between money and power throughout human history.

The Czech prose writer Bohumil Hrabal brings off a risky experiment in his new novel, *Weddings in the House,* by telling the entire story through the point of view of a young and timid woman. Poland's multitalented Tadeusz Różewicz was honored with the publication of a deluxe two-volume edition of his collected plays and theatrical sketches, including such now-classic works of the European repertory as *The Card File.* The high esteem accorded the work of Serbian prose writer Danilo Kiš was enhanced by the appearance of the story collection *The Encyclopedia of the Dead* in a quality English translation. And lastly, the prolific Ismail Kadare of Albania brought out yet another French edition of a recent work, this time *Aeschylus or the Eternal Loser,* a literary manifesto couched in the form of an invocation to such Olympians as Aeschylus, Homer, and Shakespeare.

WILLIAM RIGGAN, *"World Literature Today"*

Los Angeles Dodger baseball fans wait on line for World Series tickets (later to learn that tickets would be sold by telephone only). In a banner year for L.A. sports, the Lakers won the NBA championship and the Dodgers won the Series.

LOS ANGELES

The worst skyscraper fire in the city's history, a new museum, gang warfare, and conflicts over transportation policy and redistricting by the county board marked developments in Los Angeles during 1988.

Fire. On the night of May 4, a fire broke out in the 62-story First Interstate Bank building, the tallest building in the state. Five mid-building floors were gutted, with an estimated $450 million in damages and one fatality. Nearly 300 firefighters struggled for four hours to put out the blaze. A new sprinkler system had been installed in the building, but it had not yet been turned on. The cause of the fire was not determined, but investigators did rule out arson.

Museum. In January, Armand Hammer, the 89-year-old head of Occidental Petroleum and owner of a $250 million art collection, announced plans to build a $30 million private museum on the city's West Side. Hammer had said for years that his collection eventually would be donated to the Los Angeles County Museum of Art. The new Armand Hammer Museum of Art and Cultural Center was scheduled for completion in 1990.

Crime. Violence by street gangs increased sharply during the year, as the burgeoning crack trade made such groups more willing to kill to protect their business. In search of new markets, the gangs moved into suburban areas, bringing a proliferation of "drive-by" shootings and other violent incidents. Gang-related homicides increased 12.3% in the first nine months of 1988. The city police launched major offensives, and a state law increasing the penalty for shooting from a moving vehicle was adopted, but law enforcement efforts proved largely unsuccessful.

Redistricting. In September the U.S. Department of Justice filed suit in federal court against Los Angeles County, claiming that the boundaries it established in 1981 for the election of county supervisors diluted the voting power of Hispanic voters. A similar suit had been filed the previous month by two public interest groups. Some 27% of the county's 7.5 million residents are Hispanic.

Transportation. A bureaucratic war was waged during the year, as the County Transportation Commission sought to create a new agency to build the second segment of the Metro Rail subway system. The commission proposed to exclude the giant Rapid Transit District, which was still in the process of building the first segment. The feud threatened to delay additional federal grants.

Clean Air. Two new state laws in 1988 aimed at a 5% annual statewide reduction in smog, through regulatory action by local agencies and strengthening of the vehicle inspection program. Also during the year, Mayor Tom Bradley proposed barring 18-wheel trucks from city streets during peak commuting hours. The Airport Commission approved a ten-year plan to reduce by 20% air pollution caused directly or indirectly by area airports. And the air quality management district for the greater Los Angeles area announced a plan that could produce clean air for the region within 20 years. According to testimony at legislative hearings, however, the cost would be enormous and the stringent regulations might have diminishing public support.

Sports. The Los Angeles Lakers became the first team in 19 years to repeat as champions of the National Basketball Association. Baseball's Los Angeles Dodgers won the World Series. And hockey fans cheered the arrival of superstar Wayne Gretzky to the Los Angeles Kings.

CHARLES R. ADRIAN
University of California, Riverside

LOUISIANA

The revolution promised by Gov. Charles E. (Buddy) Roemer in fiscal policies and politics for his troubled state was realized only partially in 1988. The legislature adopted a balanced budget proposed by Roemer, but his fiscal reform measures were watered down at a special session late in the year.

The Governor's Agenda. After defeating incumbent populist Gov. Edwin W. Edwards in the 1987 election, Roemer entered the governor's mansion in Baton Rouge in March, calling for major reforms to end Louisiana's economic malaise and promising to improve the state's poor image. Beset by low petroleum prices and plagued by a series of state scandals, Louisiana was ripe for improvements, according to Roemer.

With the assistance of a new, more conservative and business-oriented legislature, Roemer was able to balance the state's budget for the first time since the 1984–85 fiscal year. Also, several important acts to aid businesses were approved. The record high $8.29 billion budget was balanced through reductions in assistance to school boards, cities, and local social programs and through tripling the state's one-cent sales tax on food, gasoline, and utilities for one year.

The Legislature. Among the pro-business bills passed in the regular session of the legislature were ones to help shield manufacturers from product liability, to repeal mandatory union-scale wages on state construction projects, to create a business-oriented administrative system to handle workers compensation claims, and to cut jobless benefits and tighten qualifications for receiving such benefits. While the legislature doubled the hazardous-waste-disposal tax, it rejected most other environmental measures. To help protect the threatened redfish, which has become nationally popular as a Cajun delicacy in recent years, the state did ban commercial harvesting of the fish for three years.

Lawmakers also tightened regulations on campaign-contribution and reporting laws. In an attempt to improve the state's much criticized educational system, the legislature approved a plan for teacher-pay raises and for tougher evaluations, as well as small class sizes. While Governor Roemer obtained much of what he wanted, the legislators refused his pleas to merge many state boards and to create a single superboard for higher education.

Legislative Special Session. In the fall, the governor called a special session of the legislature to deal with a fiscal-reform package aimed at restructuring the state's tax system. He asked the legislature to shift the tax base away from dependence on oil and gas revenues and sales taxes, to place increased reliance on income taxes and local property taxes, and to transfer the cost of many public services paid for at the state level to local governments.

The most politically controversial element was the proposal to decrease the state's homestead exemption. Under the existing system, the owner of any home assessed at less than $75,000 paid no property taxes. That meant that the great majority of Louisiana homes were tax-free. Roemer proposed that the limit be reduced to $25,000, which would help local governments to increase their revenues. The homestead exemption, however, is an old political sacred cow in the Bayou State. While a majority of legislators supported the proposal, tax bills must be approved by two thirds of both legislative houses, and the House of Representatives fell ten votes short.

Louisiana was facing another massive deficit for the 1989–90 fiscal year, which would begin in July 1989, because the sales-tax hikes approved in the 1988 special session expire. Much of the deficit would affect state funds for local governments.

The Election. All eight of Louisiana's congressmen were reelected in 1988. Seven of the eight won victories or were unopposed in the state's open primary election in October. Winning their seats in the primary were Democrats Lindy Boggs, W. J. (Billy) Tauzin II, and Jerry Huckaby and Republicans Robert Livingston, Jr., and James McCrery, who had won an interim election to Roemer's vacant seat early in 1988. Two candidates—James A. Hayes (D) and Richard Baker (R)—ran unopposed in the primary. Only Clyde Holloway (R) in the 8th District was forced into a November 8 runoff, where he defeated Faye Williams, his Democratic challenger.

State Rep. Kathleen Blanco (D) became the first woman to be elected to the state's Public Service Commission. In August, New Orleans served as host for the 1988 Republican National Convention.

JOSEPH W. DARBY III, *"The Times Picayune"*

LOUISIANA • Information Highlights

Area: 47,752 sq mi (123 677 km²).
Population (July 1, 1987): 4,461,000.
Chief Cities (July 1, 1986 est.): Baton Rouge, the capital, 241,130; New Orleans, 554,500; Shreveport, 220,380; Houma (1984 est.) 101,998.
Government (1988): *Chief Officers*—governor, Charles E. Roemer (D); lt. gov., Paul Hardy (R). *Legislature*—Senate, 39 members; House of Representatives, 105 members.
State Finances (fiscal year 1987): *Revenue,* $9,257,000,000; *expenditure,* $8,460,000,000.
Personal Income (1987): $51,174,000,000; per capita, $11,473.
Labor Force (June 1988): *Civilian labor force,* 1,916,200; *unemployed,* 204,100 (10.6% of total force).
Education: *Enrollment* (fall 1986)—public elementary schools, 580,771; public secondary, 214,417; colleges and universities, 171,344. *Public school expenditures* (1986-87), $2,314,000,000 ($3,237 per pupil).

MAINE

Emerging from the presidential election of 1988 with their "As Maine goes . . ." slogan verified by the state's voters, Maine citizens gave the state's four electoral votes to the Republican candidates for president and vice-president, and returned a Democratic majority to the House and Senate. Sometime Kennebunkport resident George Bush of Walker's Point and his running mate carried the state by a 56% to 44% margin over the Dukakis-Bentsen ticket. In one of the state's more stunning examples of ticket splitting, however, the Democratic incumbent, Sen. George Mitchell, was returned to his seat by a majority of 81.3% over his Republican opponent, Jasper Wyman. Mitchell's margin is the largest in the state's recent history of Senate campaigns.

Former Gov. Joseph Brennan also was sent back to his 1st District congressional post; he won by a 63%–37% margin over his GOP opponent, Edward O'Meara. Second District Republican incumbent Olympia Snowe had no problem with her challenger, Kenneth Hayes, who got less than 34% of the vote.

Republican Gov. John McKernan, in the second year of a four-year term, will have to work with a state legislature controlled by Democratic majorities in both the Maine House and Senate. Maine voters approved referenda that included funding for the University of Maine and the addition of the so-called gender amendment to the Maine Constitution, initiating a rewriting project that will neutralize all masculine references in all state documents.

Economy. Contemplating his chances for reelection in 1990, Governor McKernan could look back on another thriving year for the state's economy. Although not as intense as the growth spurts of 1986 and 1987, the continued economic vigor of 1988 brought Maine through the months that followed the October 1987 stock-market plunge with scarcely a

AP/Wide World

It was a good year for Maine's George Mitchell. He not only was reelected to the U.S. Senate but his Democratic colleagues also selected him as the new majority leader.

tremor. Unemployment was at record lows, and economic growth rates averaged about 3%.

Early tourism figures for 1988 indicated a continued increase in the number of visitors. Mary S. Garcelon, state tourism specialist, reported a continued 10% rise in the indicators that measure visitor activity, and there were reports that officials from several coastal communities believed that their towns may have reached the saturation point. Responding to pleas from rural areas that steps be taken to ease development pressures, the legislature enacted a law requiring all communities to draft zoning plans designed to help control growth and protect sensitive natural resources. The state planned to help by opening a new office of Comprehensive Land Use Planning.

While many rural and coastal towns looked for ways to control random development, Portland, Maine's largest city, had expensive waterfront condominiums that were proving difficult to sell, and the "boutique boom" that had changed the city's streets had begun to slow down.

On the labor front, one of Maine's bitterest and longest strikes came to an end in October when Local 14 of the United Paperworkers International Union called in its pickets from the gates of the International Paper Company's mill in Jay. After 16 months, the union quit its effort, and many workers were without jobs.

At the Bath Iron Works, however, contracts were approved, and workers at the state's largest industry were geared up for one of the busiest times in the company's history as contracts for new Navy ships were approved and implemented.

JOHN N. COLE, *"Maine Times"*

MAINE • Information Highlights

Area: 33,265 sq mi (86 156 km²).
Population (July 1, 1987): 1,187,000.
Chief Cities (1980 census): Augusta, the capital, 21,819; Portland, 61,572; Lewiston, 40,481; Bangor, 31,643.
Government (1988): *Chief Officer*—governor, John R. McKernan, Jr. (R). *Legislature*—Senate, 33 members; House of Representatives, 151 members.
State Finances (fiscal year 1987): *Revenue,* $2,651,000,000; *expenditure,* $2,287,000,000.
Personal Income (1987): $16,558,000,000; per capita, $13,954.
Labor Force (June 1988): *Civilian labor force,* 607,100; *unemployed,* 22,200 (3.7% of total force).
Education: *Enrollment* (fall 1986)—public elementary schools, 143,671; public secondary, 68,081; colleges and universities, 46,230. *Public school expenditures* (1986-87), $718,000,000 ($3,650 per pupil).

MALAYSIA

Major news in Malaysia in 1988 involved events surrounding the power struggle within the United Malays National Organization (UMNO), the dominant Malay political party headed by Prime Minister Mahathir bin Mohamad, and a crisis within the judicial branch of government.

Problems Within UMNO. In February a Malaysian court declared UMNO, the dominant party in the ruling National Front coalition, illegal. The court ruled on a legal challenge brought by supporters of Tengu Razaleigh Hamzah, a former trade and industry minister who had challenged Mahathir for party leadership in 1987, claiming that some branches of UMNO were not registered properly.

Following the ruling, challengers to Mahathir unsuccessfully attempted to register a new party, UMNO Malaysia, headed by Malaysia's first prime minister Tunku Abdul Rahman. Mahathir, who also serves as the home and justice secretaries, soon moved to set up a new party, UMNO (Baru)—meaning new UMNO—which was registered and which then refused to take in all of the members of the original UMNO.

Another challenge, preventing UMNO (Baru) from acquiring the original UMNO's substantial assets of properties and shareholdings, was dealt a setback after Parliament amended the Societies Act to facilitate transfer of original UMNO assets to the new party. Nonetheless, new UMNO needs half of the old membership to maintain control of the assets. In August the Supreme Court dismissed an appeal by UMNO dissidents to reinstate the original party.

Mahathir's leadership style was an issue in a by-election in Johor Baru that gave the dissidents a wide margin of victory. A later by-election in Parit Raja gave a slim victory to the Mahathir forces, but by year's end several members of Parliament loyal to UMNO but critical of the prime minister had become independents.

Judicial Crisis. With the support of the Mahathir government, Parliament in March passed amendments to the constitution that diminished powers previously vested in the judiciary. One such change removed the courts' right to interpret the law. The government later suspended the lord president, or chief justice, and five other Supreme Court justices. In August the ruling king dismissed the lord president, and in October two of the five other justices were removed.

Economic and Diplomatic News. Malaysia's economic growth was a healthy 7–8% during 1988. The manufacturing sector was responsible primarily for the good showing, especially during the early months of the year. Domestic demand for manufactured goods revived in

1988 on the heels of a 1987 upturn in manufacturing exports. An upsurge in commodity prices particularly had helped plantation and mining interests. The national unemployment rate, however, was about 10%.

Malaysia and Singapore agreed to a new accord that provided Singapore with additional fresh water from Malaysia. Singapore also agreed to buy natural gas. In April, Malaysia and China signed a bilateral trade pact in Beijing.

During 1988 the Primary Industries minister, Datuk Lim Keng Yaik, visited various European capitals in an attempt to placate critics of Malaysia's logging policy. Malaysian and other environmentalists had claimed that the nation's timber industry threatened East Malaysia's tropical rain forest as well as the indigenous peoples' way of life.

The government indicated that it would accept no more Vietnamese boat people after April 1989 and would close the Pulau Bidong camp unless there were new agreements for resettlement of the refugees to a third country.

JAMES J. MCMAHON
Formerly, SUNY Buffalo/ITM, Malaysia

MANITOBA

Major news in Manitoba in 1988 centered on the provincial and federal elections and the dire agricultural situation, precipitated by lack of rain and hot weather.

Political News. Manitoba's political landscape changed dramatically during 1988. In February the government of New Democratic Party Premier Howard Pawley announced large increases in rates for its compulsory automobile insurance. Although this and other rate increases brought the government's popularity to a very low level, the NDP retained its one-seat majority in the legislature. This situation changed, however, on March 8 when James Walding, a backbench NDP member who previously had conflicts with Premier Pawley, voted against his own government's budget, bringing the government down and marking the

Manitoba's Conservative leader Gary Filmon, a 45-year-old former educator and businessman, became minority provincial premier after April 26 elections.

first time in the 20th century that a Canadian provincial government was defeated by an internal rebellion. Following the resignation of Pawley as party leader, the NDP on March 30 chose Gary Doer as the new leader.

During the ensuing election campaign, the NDP nearly collapsed. The Liberal Party capitalized on the problems of the NDP and also focused public attention on the unpopular actions of the federal Progressive Conservative (PC) government, which had antagonized Manitoba's voters during 1985–87 when it awarded several lucrative contracts to non-Manitoba firms, despite lower bids from Manitobans.

In the April 26 election, the NDP lost 18 seats and kept 12, and the opposition PCs lost five seats and gained four, dropping from 26 to 25. The big winners, however, were the Liberals, who had been virtually nonexistent in Manitoba politics for 30 years. They jumped from one seat in 1986 to 20 in 1988. Liberal leader Sharon Carstairs thus became Canada's first woman opposition leader. The PC leader, Gary Filmon, became premier.

Filmon, who supports Canada's new constitutional amendment, the Meech Lake Accord, was in no position to act on that issue, as both the Liberals and the NDP opposed it. By November the accord, which requires the consent of every province to pass, remained an unresolved issue.

Mrs. Carstairs' Liberal Party got another boost in September, when a backbench PC, Gilles Roch, joined the Liberals. Roch's constituents demanded that he resign and run in a by-election, but he rejected their demands.

The PCs began their campaign for the November 1988 federal election by setting up several new government facilities in Winnipeg. These included a national center for disease control and an animal research center. However, both Liberals and New Democrats pointed out that the overall value of these was less than that of the previous lost contracts. In the federal election, Manitoba's PCs won seven parliamentary seats, the Liberals, five, and the NDP, two.

Agricultural Problems. While Manitoba is not wholly dependent upon agriculture, the farm sector is still very important, and 1988 saw much bad news for farmers. For several years, rainfall had been below average, and in the first nine months of 1988, it reached only 67% of normal precipitation. The spring of 1988 was also unusually hot, and cereal production dropped drastically, especially in southwestern Manitoba. Combined with possible low farm prices, these variations, if they continued in 1989, could produce the worst agricultural crisis in Manitoba since the 1930s.

MICHAEL KINNEAR
The University of Manitoba

MANITOBA • Information Highlights

Area: 250,946 sq mi (649 950 km²).

Population (June 1988): 1,083,600.

Chief Cities (1986 census): Winnipeg, the capital, 594,551; Brandon, 38,708; Thompson, 14,701.

Government (1988): *Chief Officers*—lt. gov., George Johnson; premier, Gary Filmon (Progressive Conservative). *Legislature*—Legislative Assembly, 57 members.

Provincial Finances (1988–89 fiscal year budget): *Revenues,* $4,365,000,000; *expenditures,* $4,561,-000,000.

Personal Income (average weekly earnings, June 1988): $422.19.

Labor Force (August 1988, seasonally adjusted): *Employed* workers, 15 years of age and over, 497,000; *Unemployed,* 8.0%.

Education (1988–89): *Enrollment*—elementary and secondary schools, 219,400 pupils; postsecondary—universities, 20,150; community colleges, 4,300.

(All monetary figures are in Canadian dollars.)

MARYLAND

Marylanders voted 51% to 49% to commit the state's ten electoral votes to the George Bush-Dan Quayle ticket. Voter turnout registered 49.1%. Voters also returned Democrat Paul S. Sarbanes to the U.S. Senate and all the incumbents, six Democrats and two Republicans, to the House of Representatives.

Handgun-Control Law. Of considerable voter interest was a handgun-control law passed by the General Assembly in its winter 1988 session, and quickly petitioned for referendum by gun enthusiasts. Marylanders endorsed the law by a margin of 58% to 42%.

The law was intended to reduce the number of cheaply made handguns—"Saturday night specials"—available to street criminals and minors. The National Rifle Association (NRA), through the Maryland Committee Against the Gun Ban, poured $6.1 million into an effort to defeat the law, making it the most costly political campaign in Maryland history.

According to the new law, a nine-member board will be established consisting of three citizen members, the superintendent of the state police, and one representative each of a state prosecutor's association, the Maryland Association of Chiefs of Police, Marylanders Against Handgun Abuse, the NRA, and a Maryland gun manufacturer. They are charged with drawing up a roster of handguns that can be made and sold legally in Maryland. The law takes effect on Jan. 1, 1990, and applies to handguns made after 1984. It provides for fines and for appeal of the board's decisions.

Proponents of the law, including police officials and prosecutors, pointed to the growing number of crimes committed with cheap handguns. They also cited cases of teenagers using firearms—sometimes in school—to settle disputes fatally that a generation ago would have resulted only in fistfights and bloody noses.

The campaign took on a racial tone as black ministers lamented the toll of violence on young, black, urban males—while progun forces argued that the law would render low-income citizens unable to afford firearms to defend their homes. The 2nd Amendment was invoked, along with the threat of a ban on all guns.

Medical Ethics. At the request of the state's Office on Aging, the attorney general's office issued a comprehensive 46-page opinion to clarify state law on ending tube feeding of patients in the last stages of terminal illness or if permanently unconscious. In general, the opinion—the first of its kind in state history—equated artificial feeding with artificial breathing, and cited the legal precedents that grew out of the 1976 Karen Ann Quinlan case in New Jersey. Like the decision to turn off a respirator, the opinion said, the decision to stop tube feeding rests with a patient and his family, al-

though there are circumstances when a court should be involved.

Banking. The state negotiated a settlement with the Internal Revenue Service to pay a $14.8 million tax claim growing out of the 1985 Maryland savings and loan scandal. The state lost an appeal in federal tax court, and failed to secure passage in Congress of a special bill to escape liability. The state unwittingly acquired the liability along with the Maryland Savings-Share Insurance Corp. when it took over the failing private insurance fund to forestall a collapse of the state savings and loan industry.

Drug Controversy. Baltimore Mayor Kurt L. Schmoke provoked considerable, but short-lived, controversy during his first year in office by suggesting a national debate on the legalization of drug use. He argued that attempts to stop traffic in illegal drugs seemed to be failing and that resources might be better used both to educate people in the danger of drug use and to treat addicts. He did not suggest legalizing the private sale of drugs.

Amtrak Case. Ricky L. Gates, the former Conrail engineer who caused a major Amtrak crash in 1987, was sentenced to three years in federal prison on charges of lying to investigators after the accident. He already was serving a five-year prison term on a state charge of manslaughter by locomotive. The federal term would be served after the state sentence. Sixteen people were killed and more than 170 injured in the Jan. 4, 1987 crash.

Video Privacy. Maryland's 1988 video-privacy law imposes a penalty on retail video establishments of up to $500, and a jail term of up to six months, for releasing information about customer preferences. The law stems from a listing by a Washington publication in 1987 of the videocassette movies rented by Judge Robert H. Bork, whose nomination to the Supreme Court was rejected.

PEGGY CUNNINGHAM
"The Evening Sun," Baltimore

MARYLAND · Information Highlights

Area: 10,460 sq mi (27 092 km²).
Population (July 1, 1987): 4,535,000.
Chief Cities (1980 census): Annapolis, the capital, 31,740; Baltimore (July 1, 1986 est.), 752,800; Rockville, 43,811.
Government (1988): *Chief Officers*—governor, Donald Schaefer (D); lt. gov., Melvin A. Steinberg (D). *General Assembly*—Senate, 47 members; House of Delegates, 141 members.
State Finances (fiscal year 1987): *Revenue,* $9,700,000,000; *expenditure,* $8,714,000,000.
Personal Income (1987): $82,190,000,000; per capita $18,124.
Labor Force (June 1988): *Civilian labor force,* 2,464,500; *unemployed,* 108,700 (4.4% of total force).
Education: *Enrollment* (fall 1986)—public elementary schools, 456,045; public secondary, 219,702; colleges and universities, 238,880. *Public school expenditures* (1986–87), $2,880,000,000 ($4,659 per pupil).

MASSACHUSETTS

The presidential candidacy of Gov. Michael S. Dukakis affected many aspects of life in Massachusetts during 1988, but especially politics and government.

Dukakis won the Democratic nomination in July and left the convention with a nationwide 17% lead over Republican contender George Bush. During the ensuing campaign, Lt. Gov. Evelyn Murphy, the state's highest ranking elected woman official, served as acting governor whenever Dukakis was out of the state. The resulting press attention fueled speculation that Murphy almost certainly would be a candidate for governor if the office were vacated. That was not to be. Dukakis lost his bid for the presidency, although he carried his home state by a 54% to 46% margin.

In other contests the Democrats generally fared well. Edward Kennedy was reelected to a fifth full term in the U.S. Senate with no difficulty, and in the U.S. House of Representatives, the Massachusetts delegation would be made up of ten Democrats and one Republican.

The Legislature. Activity in the legislature, the center of political life in the Bay State, almost constantly was affected by Dukakis' bid for the presidency. In the spring, the legislature approved a bill that made Massachusetts the first state to guarantee health insurance to all residents, an achievement that Dukakis made a political issue, as he campaigned for universal health insurance for the nation.

Also, as the year wore on, it became apparent that there would be a major shortfall in state revenues, threatening to create a budget deficit. This was an issue critical to the Dukakis campaign, as he often claimed to have balanced every budget in his years as governor. Dukakis took several measures to shore up revenues, including tax increases and loans from state pension funds, and cut state aid to cities and towns. The aid cuts especially angered many lawmakers, but the Democratic state legislature went along with his actions. In early December, however, Dukakis acknowledged a $471 million budget deficit. Recognizing that there were "serious problems facing us," he outlined a savings package—including use of the state's $121 million "rainy day fund"—that appeared to avoid severe austerity measures.

Economy. Virtually every economic indicator for the state published during 1988 was interpreted in light of the presidential campaign. Dukakis had made the "Massachusetts Miracle"—the continued low unemployment and steady economic growth—the cornerstone of his national campaign. The state's economy showed few signs of faltering during the year. Unemployment hovered at 3%. The finance, wholesale, and retail sectors continued to grow, although there was some slowing in traditional manufacturing industries. The cost of

---

MASSACHUSETTS • Information Highlights

Area: 8,284 sq mi (21 456 km^2).
Population (July 1, 1987): 5,855,000.
Chief Cities (July 1, 1986 est.): Boston, the capital, 573,600; Worcester, 157,700; Springfield, 149,410.
Government (1988): *Chief Officer*—governor, Michael S. Dukakis (D); lt. gov., Evelyn F. Murphy (D). *Legislature*—Senate 40 members; House of Representatives, 160 members.
State Finances (fiscal year 1987): *Revenue,* $14,001,000,000; *expenditure,* $14,015,000,000.
Personal Income (1987): $112,085,000,000; per capita, $19,142.
Labor Force (June 1988): *Civilian labor force,* 3,216,700; *unemployed,* 110,200 (3.4% of total force).
Education: *Enrollment* (fall 1986)—public elementary schools, 559,418; public secondary, 274,500; colleges and universities, 417,562. *Public school expenditures* (1986–87), $3,698,000,000 ($4,856 per pupil).

---

living continued higher than the national average, however, fueled primarily by high housing costs. At midyear the average price of a single family home was $181,000, one of the highest in the nation. Housing-market analysts generally welcomed a cooling off of housing construction and sales which began during the last half of the year, pointing out that continued inflated housing prices could damage the economy in the long run.

The insurance industry—a major component of the state's economy—remained healthy, except in the area of auto insurance. There, a new round in the continuing struggle between car owners, state insurance regulators, and the insurance companies failed to resolve the complex and difficult issues that have for many years kept the state's auto-insurance premiums the highest in the country. One major auto-insurance underwriter, Allstate, refused to operate in the state in October.

Prisons. Dukakis' policies on crime were another major campaign issue, and his efforts to deal with overcrowded prisons were highlighted in 1988. In August there were serious disturbances at prisons in Lawrence and Billerica. Throughout the year a proposal to construct a prison in the small central town of New Braintree was much in the news.

Boston Harbor Pollution. Republican presidential candidate George Bush's dramatic appearance at Boston Harbor in September, where he charged that Dukakis had delayed the cleanup of the polluted waterway, drew new attention to the issue. Massachusetts finally began a multibillion-dollar, ten-year project to clean the harbor, the largest and costliest ever tackled by the state. Water bills in communities around Boston were expected to increase substantially over the ten-year period. Two huge sewage treatment plants also were scheduled for construction.

HARVEY BOULAY
Rogerson House

MEDICINE AND HEALTH

Medical news of 1988 often was dominated by ethical, moral, and legal dilemmas. The practice of infertile couples to hire surrogate mothers received a setback when the New Jersey Supreme Court ruled that such contracts are illegal. Later in the year, Michigan became the first state to pass a law making it a felony to arrange a surrogacy contract, though the new law later was interpreted to permit such contracts so long as the surrogate mother does not relinquish her maternal rights.

Another alternative for infertile couples is in vitro fertilization, the procedure that produces so-called test-tube babies. Doctors, insurance companies, and childless couples exploited by unscrupulous clinics have pressured the government and medical organizations to regulate the business. According to a report by the U.S. Office of Technology Assessment (OTA) in 1988, nearly half the nation's clinics conducting in vitro fertilization had not yet achieved a live birth. "What you have is a million couples desperate for a baby, and the evidence is the fertility clinics are promising results they can't achieve," said U.S. Rep. Ron Wyden (D-OR).

And as researchers continued to expand the frontiers of medical knowledge, new issues developed. The federal government suspended support of research using fetal tissue obtained from legal induced abortions and appointed an expert panel to provide advice on the issue. Although the use of fetal tissue offers potentially enormous benefits, including improved treatments for such ailments as diabetes and Parkinsonism, critics fear that such research would encourage and justify abortion.

In France, opponents of abortion raised such a storm when a revolutionary new abortion pill was introduced that Groupe Roussel Uclaf, the company that developed the drug, suspended distribution. Two days later, following widespread denunciation of the suspension by doctors, family-planning groups, and women's organizations, the French government ordered the company to resume distribution. The drug, RU 486 or Mifepristone, interrupts pregnancy by preventing the implantation of a fertilized egg on the uterine wall. The drug is more than 95% effective in ending pregnancy during the first seven weeks, and it is both safer and less expensive than surgical abortions.

Health Care. The Massachusetts legislature passed a health-care bill making the state the first to guarantee health insurance for all its residents. The bill, which will be fully effective by 1992, requires uninsured residents to pay for their insurance based on how much they earn. Companies will pay a surcharge to the state of about $1,680 per worker to help pay for the plan. However, companies that offer insurance

benefits to their employees will be allowed to deduct the cost of that insurance from the surcharge.

As of 1988, some 37 million Americans lacked health insurance, and although universal health insurance bills often have been introduced in Congress, they never have made much progress. To protect Medicare beneficiaries from the huge expenses of catastrophic illness, however, Congress did pass a bill that provides unlimited free hospital care after the recipient pays the first $564 annually. The recipient will pay a monthly premium of $4, plus a 15% surtax of the amount he or she paid in federal taxes, with a ceiling of $800.

The U.S. Department of Health and Human Services reported that the average hospital stay declined 22% from 1980 to 1985, from 7.35 days to 5.71 days. The decline was attributed to advances in medical technology, growing acceptance of outpatient treatment, the growth of health maintenance organizations, and other factors. Preliminary data indicated that the decline began to level off in 1986.

Diagnostic equipment designed for use in physicians' offices is improving office efficiency and cost effectiveness. For instance, a benchtop chemistry system developed by DuPont performs the 13 most frequently requested blood tests, printing out results in about ten minutes. The system eliminates not only the two- to three-day wait for the testing of blood samples by a commercial laboratory but also the need for follow-up visits or phone calls.

Cardiovascular Disease. Surgeon O.H. Frazier of the Texas Heart Institute in Houston successfully implanted an experimental pump into the heart of a heart-attack victim who otherwise faced certain death. The pump, known as a ventricular assist device, temporarily took over part of the injured heart's workload, allowing the damaged muscle to rest and recover. No larger than a pencil eraser, the pump has a turbine blade that rotates 25,000 times per minute as it pushes oxygenated blood from the left ventricle into the aorta.

Currently, some 230,000 Americans undergo coronary bypass surgery each year. The operation reroutes the flow of blood to the brain, bypassing blocked arteries—one of the most common causes of strokes. But almost since the time the operations first were performed in the late 1960s, there has been disagreement among surgeons on the criteria for determining whether the operation is justified. New fuel for the controversy came in mid-1988, when researchers for the Rand Corporation, who studied 386 such operations, reported that 14% of the operations were performed for inappropriate reasons and an additional 30% might have been inappropriate.

Traditionally, surgeons have used sections of a patient's leg vein to create the bypass.

Problems of Alcohol

The U.S. war on drugs held the center of the media spotlight during 1988 (*see* page 38). But most health experts agreed that the highly publicized "war" did not include a drug that is linked to a variety of extremely serious—and in some cases deadly—health and social problems: alcohol.

"Alcohol is the most widely used drug in America and it should not be excluded from the war on drugs," said Patricia Taylor, director of the Alcohol Policies Project, a Washington, DC, public-interest group. "Alcoholism and alcohol-related problems cost our nation over $120 billion a year in health-care costs, absenteeism, decreased productivity, and treatment—far more than any other health problem, including smoking."

Despite national campaigns against the dangers of alcohol, surveys indicated that alcohol use has remained essentially unchanged in recent years. Alcohol abuse is particularly troublesome among high-school and college students. A 1988 study by the National Institute on Drug Abuse indicated, for example, that more than 90% of high-school seniors have tried alcohol, and that some 4.6 million teenagers have "serious alcohol-related problems." The total number of Americans who are alcoholics or have serious drinking problems is estimated by experts to be about 15 million.

Although alcohol problems affect all economic and social groups, government studies report that alcohol abuse is the leading health and safety problem among black Americans. Even though blacks consume less alcohol per capita than whites, blacks experience disproportionately high rates of chronic liver disease (cirrhosis of the liver), esophageal cancer, and other alcohol-related health problems, according to a report by the National Institute on Alcohol Abuse and Alcoholism.

Among all Americans, alcohol abuse has been linked to one fourth of all suicides and is a major factor leading to divorce and other problems brought to family courts. In addition, the number of traffic deaths caused by drunken drivers is increasing. In 1986, the last year for which complete statistics are available, there were nearly 24,000 alcohol-related traffic deaths—a 7% increase compared with 1985, according to the U.S. Department of Transportation.

The problems of alcohol abuse seem particularly acute among teenagers and young adults. Young people account for a disproportionately high percentage of legally intoxicated drivers killed in car crashes, for example. And student drinking at colleges and universities appears to be increasing. At Princeton University, 45 students were treated for alcohol-induced illnesses following a night of parties in February 1988. Three months later, two of the parties' organizers received 30-day jail sentences for their roles in the incident. Also in February, an 18-year-old Rutgers University student died after drinking a large amount of liquor during a fraternity initiation.

U.S. colleges have hired full-time alcohol counselors and set up programs to try to combat the problem. Officials at Yale University, for example, beefed up the school's alcohol-education program in 1986 after a student died of alcohol poisoning. The expanded program "has not stopped the abuse of alcohol on campus," Betty Trachtenberg, Yale's dean of students, said. "It's a perennial problem."

Alcohol also is a significant problem in the military. Nine percent of American servicemen and women characterized themselves as "heavy drinkers" in a Pentagon survey of more than 17,000 members of the armed services released in July 1988. That figure compares with 12% in 1985. Nevertheless, with usage of marijuana and cocaine down significantly since the introduction of widespread drug testing, alcohol represented the leading drug problem in the military.

Health experts have expressed concern in recent years about the growing use by young people of a relatively new alcoholic beverage —the wine cooler. Coolers, a combination of wine and carbonated fruit juice, have been sold nationally only since the early 1980s. By 1987 the cooler market recorded some $1.7 billion in sales. Studies undertaken in the last three years indicated that as many as 80% of high-school students have tried coolers and that a large majority of elementary and high-school students do not understand that wine coolers are intoxicants. In fact, most brands of wine coolers contain larger amounts of alcohol per container than most brands of beer.

Children are said to be attracted to coolers for many reasons, including their taste. One expert notes that "the word 'cooler' evokes a refreshing, light beverage that's pleasant, airy, and stimulating." Added another expert, Diane Purcell, of a Chicago alcoholism treatment center, "You can go from lemonade to a lemon cooler in one easy step. You don't have to acquire a taste for alcohol."

MARC LEEPSON

Aspirin

The old standby for treating headaches, fever, muscle pain, and other minor ailments, the common aspirin tablet—325 milligrams of a salicylic acid derivative ($C_9H_8O_4$)—has been elevated to a new position of prominence in medicine and pharmacology. A number of studies in recent years have indicated that this commonplace drug—of which Americans consume $800 million worth each year—has potentially far-reaching therapeutic value by: bolstering the immune system against diseases ranging from cancer to the common cold; reducing the risk of cataracts; curbing high blood pressure; and protecting against the recurrence of strokes. Most notably of all, researchers reported in 1988 that aspirin substantially reduces the risk of heart attack.

In January 1988, U.S. scientists announced that a five-year study of 22,071 healthy male physicians aged 40 to 84 (an extremely low-risk group) indicated that taking a regular-strength aspirin every other day cut the risk of heart attack almost in half. It also reduced the percentage of heart attacks that are fatal. The study was the largest ever done to determine the effects of aspirin on heart disease.

Simultaneously, British scientists published the results of a similar six-year study involving more than 5,000 British physicians. They did not find any strong evidence to support the premise that aspirin reduces the risk of heart attack. But the British physicians took 500 milligrams of aspirin daily—more than three times as much as the American physicians. For that reason, neither the authors of the British study nor other specialists felt that these findings invalidated the U.S. study.

The two studies followed earlier research showing that aspirin helps reduce the risk of a second heart attack in people who have already suffered from one attack.

Americans suffer as many as 1.5 million heart attacks each year, of which 540,000 are fatal. They occur when clots block the arteries that carry blood to the heart. Essential to the formation of the clots are platelets, small cellular elements in the blood. Aspirin is believed to act by reducing the ability of platelets to form clots.

In some people, however, aspirin may decrease blood clotting too much, increasing the chance of a hemorrhagic stroke. This occurs when a blood vessel breaks and leaks blood into the brain; it is fatal 70% of the time. People with high blood pressure, neurological problems, or a history of stroke in their family especially are susceptible.

Heart specialists stress that the decision to take aspirin as a preventive measure should be made only upon consultation with a physician.

Now they increasingly are using internal mammary arteries from the chest. For reasons not yet understood, these arteries seldom develop the fatty deposits that cause blockage. Studies show that patients undergoing the newer operation live longer and have fewer heart attacks, fewer repeat bypass operations, and fewer complications than do patients receiving leg-vein grafts.

An alternative to bypass surgery is balloon angioplasty. In this procedure, a tiny balloon is inserted into a clogged vessel and then inflated, creating pressure that widens (opens) the vessel. An estimated 200,000 Americans underwent this procedure in 1988. Some patients with advanced atherosclerosis, however, remain at risk for future heart attacks or sudden death. Two studies indicated that dietary fish oils can help prevent restenosis, the recurrence of blockage within coronary arteries following balloon angioplasty. Although the results were promising, researchers cautioned that angioplasty patients should not take fish oil without first discussing it with their physicians.

The development of drugs that dissolve blood clots is dramatically altering treatment of heart-attack victims. Known as thrombolytic therapy, the treatment uses streptokinase, t-PA (tissue plasminogen activator), or a similar drug to break up the clot that blocks a coronary artery, stops the flow of blood, and causes a heart attack. Timing is crucial: Treatment must begin within a few hours of the start of an attack to prevent death or severe damage. Already the treatment, still in its infancy, is achieving up to a 50% reduction in in-hospital deaths from heart attacks.

Physicians long have recommended that adults lower fat intake to combat high blood-cholesterol levels, a major cause of heart attacks. Now they also are urging that diets of children be improved. Physicians at the University of Michigan reported that 25% of the schoolchildren they tested had elevated cholesterol levels. Public-health organizations recommended that fats should comprise no more than 30% of a child's daily calories, with only 10% derived from saturated fats.

Cancer. New evidence linked several specific types of papilloma viruses with cancer, particularly cervical cancer. These viruses have been found in the cervical cells of more than 90% of women with cervical cancer. It is not yet known if the viruses invade the cells before or after the cancer strikes, but most researchers believe the viruses contribute to the development of the disease. New tests that identify the viruses in samples of cervical tissue will enable physicians better to monitor infected patients, identifying and treating any cervical cancer that develops in its early stages, when it is highly curable.

A research team at the University of Utah Medical Center reported that more than half

The Nursing Shortage

An estimated 200,000 to 300,000 nursing vacancies across the United States have created serious problems for hospitals, nursing homes, and other medical facilities. There is no doubt that health care is being compromised because of this shortage. Many hospitals have closed wards, eliminated beds, and delayed admissions. Once admitted, patients find themselves waiting, perhaps in vain, for medications, assistance in walking, and other help. And they often are discharged early, before they should be, to make room for new patients.

A variety of factors have contributed to the shortage of nurses. Health-care facilities need more nurses than ever before, in part because of growing populations of elderly people, AIDS patients, and others who require a significant amount of care. Meanwhile, however, working conditions for nurses have deteriorated: In efforts to contain costs, hospitals have limited salaries for nurses while increasing their responsibilities, having them take over work previously done by other employees.

Since the early 1980s many nurses have left the field, and young people have been discouraged from choosing nursing as an occupation. According to Dr. Carolyne Davis, head of the Federal Commission on Nursing, nursing-school enrollment dropped 30% between 1984 and 1988. Women—who have dominated the nursing field—instead chose careers that offered better salaries and opportunities for advancement.

About 10% of U.S. hospitals are trying to meet their need for nurses by recruiting overseas. Approximately 10,000 foreign nurses work in the United States under visas that normally limit stays to five years. In May 1988 the federal government agreed to provide one-year extensions to foreign nurses at the end of their temporary work visas. A similar waiver was expected to be requested by hospitals and other employers of nurses in 1989.

Health-care facilities are offering a broad range of inducements to retain and recruit ex-

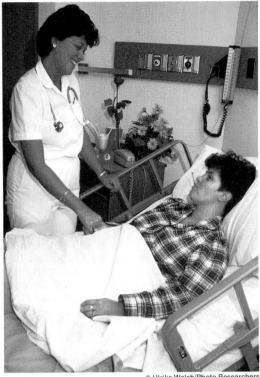

© Ulrike Welsh/Photo Researchers

perienced nurses. Heading the list are increasing salaries: Starting pay for a registered nurse now averages about $22,000, while experienced nurses with special expertise may earn as much as $55,000. Also of particular appeal to nurses is sufficient ancillary staff to handle paperwork and other tasks. Other perks include expanded day-care programs, elimination of mandatory overtime, subsidized housing, and expanded tuition programs.

While efforts are under way to solve the nursing shortage, growing shortages of laboratory technicians, medical technologists, therapists, and pharmacists also threaten the quality of health care.

the people who develop colon and rectal cancer have an inherited disposition to the disease. Environmental factors, particularly dietary factors, then come into play, changing benign polyps into cancerous tumors. Experts advised that people who have relatives with colon or rectal cancer get regular checkups and follow a low-fat, high-fiber diet.

The incidence of breast cancer among American women—already the highest in the world—continues to rise, killing 42,000 women annually. However, there is some indication that the increase (in known cases) may be explained at least partially by increased screening for the cancer. Meanwhile, an analysis prepared by researchers at the National Cancer Institute showed that annual mammograms significantly reduce deaths from breast cancer among women under age 50—a benefit previously proven for women over age 50. When breast cancer is detected and treated early, 90% of the affected patients can be cured.

A park ranger at the Fire Island (NY) National Seashore warns visitors of the danger of tiny ticks whose bites can cause Lyme disease. Named for the Connecticut town in which it was discovered, the disease was reported in some 33 states by summer 1988. The bacterial infection is difficult to diagnose because its symptoms are similar to those of several other ailments, including common flu.

© John S. Abbot/"Sports Illustrated"

Antiacne Drugs. Tretinoin, a derivative of vitamin A that has been used for almost two decades to treat acne, became newsworthy in 1988 for some of its other effects. A study conducted at the University of Michigan found that one tretinoin formulation, a cream sold under the name Retin-A, reversed some of the wrinkling and other damaging effects caused by sun exposure. To be effective, the Retin-A had to be applied daily for at least a year, then twice a week to maintain any improvement. There often were undesirable side effects, including redness, irritation, and peeling of the skin. The cream diminished only fine wrinkles, having no effect on deep wrinkles or natural aging.

A more potent form of tretinoin, Accutane, was reported to prevent skin cancer in patients with xeroderma pigmentosum, a rare, inherited disorder characterized by a high incidence of skin cancer. Here, too, patients experienced unwanted side effects, including skin abnormalities and high levels of triglycerides in their blood. Accutane also can cause severe birth defects, including facial deformities and mental retardation. Despite warnings against its use by pregnant women, at least 69 babies have been born in the United States with severe defects because their mothers took the drug. European nations have placed stringent curbs on distribution of Accutane, and an advisory committee to the FDA recommended that U.S. distribution also be restricted.

AIDS. The number of Acquired Immune Deficiency Syndrome (AIDS) cases continued to grow rapidly during 1988. The World Health Organization estimated that as many as 10 million people worldwide may be infected with viruses that cause AIDS, though the majority had not yet developed the deadly disease. By late 1988, AIDS had been diagnosed in some 76,000 Americans. The Centers for Disease Control (CDC) projected that 270,000 Americans will

have come down with the disease by the end of 1991; 179,000 will have died. And, said the CDC, the costs of caring for living AIDS patients will be staggering—anywhere from $5 billion to $13 billion annually.

Educational programs and media coverage have made the public aware of preventive measures, which are designed to avoid contact with the bodily fluids of infected individuals. Far more problematic has been the search for vaccines and cures. Optimistically, the earliest a vaccine might be available is 1995—"if all goes perfectly," says Dr. Anthony Fauci, director of the National Institute of Allergy and Infectious Diseases. Only azidothymidine (AZT) has been demonstrated to extend lives, though it is so toxic that many patients cannot take it for long periods. Furthermore, a British study found that when dosages were reduced in patients experiencing serious side effects, some of the patients suffered brain inflammations. However, a study conducted by researchers from the National Cancer Institute found that AZT caused IQ levels to rise in children whose brains had been damaged by the AIDS virus.

Other medications show promise, and advocates of AIDS patients greatly criticized the federal government for failing to make these experimental drugs available. The U.S. Food and Drug Administration (FDA), which must approve drugs before they can be marketed in the United States, agreed in July to allow Americans to import unapproved foreign drugs in small quantities for personal use. And in October, the FDA changed its approval procedures to make new treatments available more quickly to people suffering from AIDS and other life-threatening diseases. Only two phases of human tests are required to prove an AIDS drug effective and safe; the traditional third stage of human testing, which can take several years, is not required.

Pediatrics. The Office of Technology Assessment reported in 1988 that "the United States could do better in preventing health problems in infants and young children. The nation ranked 17th among industrialized countries in infant mortality—a position that has not improved since 1980. A significant number of young American children have not received all their recommended immunizations. Furthermore, low-income children bear more than their share of the burdens of illness and death." Strategies identified by OTA for improving children's health included: (1) increasing access to early prenatal care for poor women; (2) encouraging adherence to the schedule of well-child care visits required for complete immunization; (3) encouraging the use of child-safety restraints in automobiles; (4) improving poor children's access to physicians' care; and (5) expanding newborn screening to include tests for additional disorders.

The use of Ritalin and other stimulants to treat attention deficit disorder (ADD), commonly called hyperactivity, long has been a controversial issue. At least 13 lawsuits have been filed on behalf of U.S. parents distressed at the effect of such medications on their children, and experts question the appropriateness of giving the drugs to nonhyperactive children who have trouble paying attention. But new studies confirm earlier evidence of the drugs' effectiveness in treating ADD. In one study, 70 children with diagnosed ADD were given a mild stimulant and a placebo for alternating two-week periods. During the periods when they received the stimulant, 69% of the children showed improvement; only 3% seemed better with the placebo.

A procedure developed by French physicians enables doctors to evaluate and treat fetuses with much greater precision than ever before. The technique involves inserting a needle into the blood vessels of the umbilical cord. The needle can be used to draw samples of fetal blood, inject drugs, or give blood transfusions. A doctor in Boston reported that he used the technique to treat fetuses with severe Rh disease, generally a fatal ailment, and that 80% of the fetuses survived.

The American College of Obstetricians and Gynecologists released new guidelines on caesarean deliveries. Pointing out that caesarean operations put both the mother and her infant at increased risk, the organization recommended that women who have had one caesarean should try to have vaginal delivery in subsequent births. Studies indicate that as many as 80% of the women who have had caesareans later can have successful vaginal deliveries.

Hair Loss. The FDA in 1988 approved the prescription drug Rogaine which promotes hair growth in some men whose hair is thinning. It was the first such drug approved for sale in the United States. To reap the benefits, users must apply Rogaine consistently twice a day. The drug will not help men who are completely bald, nor will it restore the density of hair that a man had in his youth. Also, clinical studies found that after men used Rogaine for more than one year, they gradually continued to lose hair, although the drug seemed to slow the rate of loss.

Eye Chart. Conventional eye charts, which have letters that become progressively smaller, measure the eye's ability to focus. During 1988, however, doctors at Syracuse University and Cambridge University developed an eye chart with letters that remain the same size but become progressively fainter, testing the eye's ability to see faint images. This ability becomes impaired when increased pressure to the nerves at the back of the eye damage retinal cells. The new test can help doctors detect several common eye diseases at an early stage, when the chances of slowing or preventing blindness are greatest.

Dentistry

A survey conducted by the National Institute of Dental Research (NIDR) found that half of U.S. school-age children never have experienced tooth cavities or other signs of decay. Another survey conducted by CDC found that more than 65% of U.S. nine-year-olds are free of tooth decay. The gains in reducing tooth decay were credited to the increased use of fluoride in the nation's drinking water as well as in toothpastes and mouthwashes. But tooth decay remained a serious problem for some high-risk children, including those who are poor.

Microbiologists at Israel's Tel Aviv University reported finding a new antibiotic that effectively fights periodontitis, a bacterial disease that destroys the tissues surrounding and supporting the teeth. Early testing showed that the compound, named antibiotic TA, bound strongly to tooth surfaces and was released slowly while retaining its bactericidal activity. This adhesive quality, uncommon in antibiotics, makes the antibiotic TA compound especially attractive.

Periodontal disease afflicts more than 90 million Americans and is the main cause of tooth loss in people over age 35. Experimental procedures for treating the disease include the use of synthetic materials to rebuild parts of the jaw destroyed by bacterial secretions. Researchers also are testing procedures to regenerate connective tissue, which normally holds the teeth to the jawbone but which also is destroyed by the bacteria.

See also feature article, HEADACHE: THE NUMBER ONE PAIN PROBLEM, page 56.

JENNY TESAR
Medical and Science Writer

Mental Health

Mental-health researchers in 1988 continued to make advances in understanding the biology of mental illnesses, identifying genetic components, and developing new drugs for control or treatment. Brain-imaging studies were conducted as evidence grew that many major disturbances arise from brain dysfunctions that can be identified, described, and, when fully understood, controlled or treated.

Autism. Autistic persons display a severely impaired ability to learn to speak and interact socially, and they are often mentally retarded. A new finding offers the first strong evidence that autism is a developmental brain abnormality and is not, as some have thought, a psychosocial disorder resulting from poor parenting. The finding was obtained by investigators at the University of California at San Diego, using the radiological technique called magnetic resonance imaging (MRI). They scanned the brains of 18 autistic patients and found that in 14 of them a part of the cerebellum, in the lower back part of the brain, was about 25% smaller than normal. The cerebellum helps to control balance and muscle coordination. In the autistic patients, a segment called the neocerebellum had not developed properly. How this abnormality related to symptoms of autism, however, is not yet known.

Schizophrenia. At the National Institute of Mental Health (NIMH), researchers used MRI and other techniques such as computerized tomography (CAT scans) and positron emission tomography (PET) to examine the brains of schizophrenic patients. The results indicate small but possibly important differences in the cerebral cortex of schizophrenics. The cerebral cortex executes most of the higher mental processes of the brain. MRI scans showed a 20% reduction in gray matter (surface tissue) in the temporal lobes, the parts of the cerebral cortex that contain centers for hearing and memory. PET images of brain activity in the patients showed reduced levels of glucose metabolism in the mid-prefrontal cerebral cortex, which coordinates one's ability to attend to the outside world. Still another cortex abnormality, enlarged ventricles, appeared on CAT scans of some patients. These findings can help scientists determine what goes wrong in the schizophrenic brain and to sort out the different illnesses that are classified as schizophrenia.

Obsessive-Compulsive Disorder (OCD). Persons with OCD become preoccupied with worrisome ideas and develop compulsive, ritualized behaviors to cope with them. In 1988 the Food and Drug Administration approved a drug called clomipramine for experimental treatment of OCD, after a number of studies showed that the drug, an antidepressant, can help OCD sufferers who are not depressed as well as those who are. By late 1988, 27 U.S. and Canadian research centers were participating in the clinical trials of clomipramine. Two other drugs, fluvoxamine and fluoxetine, also may be effective against OCD. Like clomipramine, they influence the brain's ability to use the neurotransmitter chemical called serotonin.

In another approach found helpful against OCD, a patient is exposed in some way to the feared object or idea and then is discouraged or kept from carrying out the usual compulsive response. One such study of this so-called exposure and prevention approach found that three fourths of the OCD patients improved.

Finally, an intriguing study, using PET scans of the brains of OCD patients, linked the disorder to excessive metabolic activity in two small parts of the brain known as the basal ganglia and the orbital gyri, the latter being twin parts of the frontal cortex. These structures are known to depend greatly on serotonin.

Borderline Personality Disorder (BPD). Persons with BPD exhibit extreme behaviors such as self-injury, drug overdosing, and assaults on others. Mood extremes and sometimes brief psychotic episodes also are observed. In 1988 investigators at NIMH found that certain drug treatments produce modest but clinically important improvements in the mood and behavior of persons with BPD. Two drugs that had clear beneficial effects on anger, anxiety, and depression were the antidepressant tranylcypromine and the anticonvulsant carbamazepine. The latter also produced a dramatic reduction in the frequency and severity of out-of-control behaviors. As the investigators expand their clinical research, they hope to pinpoint the biological causes of the disorder and to learn what combination of drugs and psychotherapy can give the best relief.

Depression. In 1988 the NIMH initiated an ambitious national campaign to educate the public, primary care physicians, and mental-health specialists about symptoms of and treatments for depressive disorders. Called D/ART, for Depression/Awareness, Recognition, and Treatment, the program is sponsored in cooperation with agencies in the private sector. It includes the wide distribution of information materials, the broadcasting of public service announcements, the creation of a network of groups to implement the campaign, professional training through grants to universities and medical schools, and a worksite program designed to increase awareness in business and industry about depression and the effects it can have in the workplace.

Late in 1988, D/ART made a particular effort to improve public understanding of bipolar disorder (also called manic-depressive illness). This form of depressive disorder is marked by extreme mood swings and by alternating episodes of depression and intense activity.

LEWIS L. JUDD, M.D.
Director, National Institute of Mental Health

METEOROLOGY

Meteorological discussion in 1988 was dominated by debate about ozone depletion and the global warming trend. Two new meteorological satellites were launched in 1988. A tragic note was struck in the aftermath of two major hurricanes.

Air Chemistry. In 1988 researchers made good progress toward explaining the "hole" which has been appearing annually in the stratospheric ozone layer over Antarctica in August, September, and October. The hole was smaller in 1988 than in 1987, but nonetheless it represented a near-total depletion of ozone over the South Pole. In addition, studies indicated that the Arctic also was experiencing a depletion of a few percentage points.

Because the South Pole is more uniformly surrounded by land and ocean than the North Pole, the area has a more symmetrical atmospheric circulation. This symmetry isolates the stratosphere over Antarctica from the rest of the atmosphere, allowing enough cooling in the long polar night to produce ice clouds, a key to the destruction of ozone by chlorine and bromine atoms.

The amount of stratospheric chlorine and bromine is proportional to the chlorofluorocarbons (CFCs) and other halogen-based compounds released into the atmosphere. These chemicals—which are very useful as refrigerants, electronic-compound degreasers, plastic-foam-blowing agents, and fire retardants—are so inert that they diffuse all the way to the stratosphere before breaking down (and releasing chlorine and bromine). An international protocol was signed in Montreal in September 1987 to reduce consumption of the suspect chemicals slowly through 1998, but a new U.S. Environmental Protection Agency (EPA) report called for the "immediate" halt to their use. A group of manufacturers was trying to find replacements for the chemicals.

Another air-chemistry concern was the anticipated climatic change that many scientists believe is occurring as the result of increases in radiatively active trace gases (RATG) in the atmosphere. RATG, of which carbon dioxide is the best-known, are so named because they interact with the radiant heat energy passing through the atmosphere. Computer studies indicated that the greatest warming will occur at high latitudes in the winter. Also, more warming was predicted to take place over sea ice and land than over the ocean.

Satellites. In September two meteorological satellites were launched. The National Oceanic and Atmospheric Administration (NOAA) polar-orbit satellite NOAA-11 was launched from Vandenberg Air Force Base to join NOAA-9 (which it will replace) and NOAA-10. Among its seven instruments NOAA-11 carried a package for COSPAS/SARSAT, an international satellite-aided search and rescue project. NOAA's newest satellite also carried an improved instrument that should provide better estimates of the stratosphere's ozone content.

Also in September the "Wind and Cloud No. 1" experimental weather satellite was launched into polar orbit from Taiyuan, in north-central China. This was the first such sat-

Unusually dry conditions in the spring caused the Mississippi River to be at its lowest level since the 1930s. Giant barges filled with goods headed for market were delayed by the emergency, causing a vast traffic jam on the river.

ellite for the Chinese, who plan to launch several more by the mid-1990's. It was reported to have an imaging radiometer with a resolution comparable to the NOAA series.

Global Wobble. Week-to-month-long wobbles in the Earth's rotation were related to observations of persistent pressure systems, according to recent research. The surface pressure is proportional to the mass of atmosphere over a point, so if there were higher-than-average pressure over North America and lower-than-average pressure elsewhere, the Earth's center of mass would shift slightly and force a wobble in the rotation.

El Niño. During 1988 the tropical Pacific Ocean experienced a modest "La Niña," characterized by sea-surface-temperature changes and surface-pressure and wind changes which were the opposite of those in an El Niño. Thus, La Niña was characterized by a strengthening in the trade winds, and cooler-than-average sea-surface temperatures in the eastern and central Pacific.

Rainfall Roundup. Beginning in early to mid-spring a wide area from Maryland to Georgia to the Dakotas, and into the Canadian prairie provinces, experienced dry conditions. By mid-July large sections of this area were experiencing drought conditions which exceeded those of 1936; severe or extreme drought was reported in 62% of the corn- and soybean-producing area. The Mississippi River was at its lowest level since the 1930s, seriously hampering barge and towboat traffic. At Memphis, TN, the river was at its lowest level since records began in 1872. Rains partially made up the deficit in the late summer and fall (with significant boosts from several tropical storms), but selected areas, such as the Delmarva Peninsula —Delaware and parts of Maryland and Virginia —by 1988 had had three "dry" or "extremely dry" growing seasons in a row.

The Sahel in Africa had average or above-average rains during the growing season, as in 1987. Eastern Africa had good rains, resulting in the first flooding in Khartoum, Sudan, in over 30 years. Unfortunately, the deluge proved very favorable for desert locusts. For the first time since the early 1960s, swarms of locusts devastated large areas in Sudan, estimated to be in excess of 11,000 sq mi (28 490 km²). Yet, even though the weather was favorable for agriculture, the ongoing civil strife in parts of East Africa hampered locust-control, harvest, and marketing activities.

The Asian summer monsoon provided normal or better precipitation amounts throughout southern Asia. As in Africa, the result was scattered flooding. Bangladesh was particularly hard hit, with two thirds of the country in flood conditions at the worst. One culprit in the Bangladesh floods was a rapid melting of above-average snowpacks in the Himalaya Mountains.

The Philippines experienced relatively dry conditions during the summer due to a scarcity of tropical storms, with more storms appearing in October. Luzon was particularly hard hit by typhoon Ruby, which packed 120-knot winds at landfall. It was speculated that the change in tropical storms might be related to changes in sea-surface temperature related to La Niña.

Atlantic Hurricanes. The Atlantic hurricane season was more active than average, with 11 named storms, of which five became hurricanes. The record-setting Hurricane Gilbert reached tropical-storm strength on September 9 just east of the Antilles. On September 12, now grown to a dangerous class five hurricane, Gilbert devastated large sections of Jamaica, killing at least 38 Jamaicans and damaging 80% of the island's housing (*see* CARIBBEAN—*Jamaica*). The next day, west of Grand Cayman Island, Gilbert set a new record low pressure in the Western Hemisphere—885 millibars (26.13 inches of mercury)—with sustained winds of 175 knots. On September 14, the storm crossed the northern tip of the Yucatan Peninsula, and then slammed into the northern Gulf coast of Mexico on the evening of September 16. Resulting floods in both Mexico and Honduras raised the hurricane's death toll to at least 66 people.

Another rare event occurred on October 22, when Hurricane Joan crossed southern Nicaragua (from east to west). Such a southern landfall is rare, and caught many residents unprepared. Hurricane Joan left at least 186 people dead in its wake—more than 100 in Nicaragua alone, but casualties also were reported in Colombia, Costa Rica, Panama, and Honduras (*see* CENTRAL AMERICA).

Other Weather Highlights. Accompanying the drought, many states experienced the hottest summer since the beginning of U.S. climate summaries in 1895. Considerable attention was given to the heat as a sign that the global warming had begun. However, there was not yet a substantial indication that the globe had warmed as a whole.

Major winter storms occurred in the central United States in late January, mid-March, and early May. In all three cases, near-blizzard conditions extended from Colorado to the Great Lakes, with severe weather in the lower Mississippi Valley and Gulf Coast.

The main U.S. tornado season (April through July) only saw 527 twisters, which was two thirds the usual number. However, the year as a whole was nearly normal with 780 twisters reported. The extra tornadoes occurred in September, as a result of Hurricane Gilbert, and in November. November ranked second in number in 1988, rather than the usual ninth. The 88 fatalities from tornadoes were about one third of the usual number, with November having three times more than any other month.

GEORGE J. HUFFMAN, *University of Maryland*

Dr. Carlos Salinas de Gortari (center) of Mexico's long-dominant Institutional Revolutionary Party won the nation's July 6 presidential election—but by a surprisingly narrow margin. Opposition groups charged vote fraud, but Salinas took office on December 1.

© S. Dorantes/Sygma

MEXICO

In Mexico's political sphere, 1988 proved to be momentous with the narrowest of victories for the government's presidential candidate, the rise of a leftist movement as the second largest political force, and the advent of real opposition in the Chamber of Deputies. In the economic sphere, Mexico continued to stagger through hard times engendered by falling export income and the shift to a more market-oriented economy. In the face of its domestic challenges, Mexico adopted a low profile in foreign policy.

Politics. For the first time in more than a century, Mexico had a truly competitive presidential election, one in which the victory of Dr. Carlos Salinas de Gortari (*see* BIOGRAPHY), candidate of the ruling Institutional Revolutionary Party (PRI), was disputed for months after official results were announced.

Public opinion polls and political pundits had predicted that Dr. Salinas could win only by a narrow margin, but he had stated publicly that he wanted a credible victory margin. His low 50.74% of the official vote raised doubts about his victory. Past presidents had claimed a minimum 70% victory.

During the campaign, he faced stiff opposition from Cuauhtémoc Cárdenas and Manuel Clouthier, both of whom usually outdrew Dr. Salinas at political rallies. Cárdenas, son of the nation's most popular 20th-century president, former governor of Michoacán, and former PRI leader, was awarded 31% of the total vote and victories in four states and the Federal District. Cárdenas campaigned at the head of an antigovernment coalition of four political parties

and 24 civic action groups. Although often described as left-wing because of socialist parties' support, the National Democratic Front (FDN) received support across the political spectrum as Mexicans protested the severe economic austerity programs authored by Dr. Salinas when he was national budget director. Real wages had fallen by half since 1982. Cárdenas called for a moratorium on the foreign debt and income redistribution. Clouthier of the National Action Party (PAN), credited with almost 17% of the vote, tapped the conservative pro-business people unhappy with government policy but unwilling to vote for a leftist candidate. His campaign asserted that the government regularly lied to the Mexican people about the true status of the economy and was tied too closely to foreign interests. Cárdenas and Clouthier launched protest movements, lawsuits, and appeals to the electoral commissions in an unsuccessful effort to overturn the official results.

Events surrounding the campaign and the vote counting raised doubts about the validity of the returns. The mild-mannered, scholarly Dr. Salinas, even with the massive support of PRI and the government, ran an uninspiring campaign during which he was often greeted with boos and jeers. Cárdenas, on the other hand, drew huge crowds which responded enthusiastically to his nationalistic and anti-austerity message. He had the active support of numerous popular former PRI leaders. Clouthier, although less popular, also kept Salinas on the defensive.

A week before the July 6, 1988, election, Cárdenas' campaign manager was murdered, and four of Cárdenas' student campaign work-

ers were found murdered in August. On election night, the government quit announcing election returns, claiming that incoming telephone calls had overloaded its new, sophisticated computer system. When official returns were announced days later, Salinas had won unusually large percentages or all of the vote in some PRI-controlled districts. Many observers believed that PRI had manipulated vote totals to give Salinas a majority instead of the plurality he actually won, thus guaranteeing him a mandate. In his September comments to the press, the PRI commissioner to the Federal Electoral Commission asserted that the letter of the law was not followed in awarding deputyships.

Congressional returns also were disputed hotly. The FDN was awarded four of the 64 Senate positions, seating representatives from the Federal District and Michoacán. In the more important Chamber of Deputies, the FDN eventually was awarded 136 seats (29 by direct election, 110 through proportional representation), but three persons almost immediately switched to PRI. PAN was awarded 101 seats (38 by direct election, 63 by proportional representation). Both PAN and FDN vociferously argued that they had won more and disrupted outgoing President Miguel de la Madrid's State of the Union address as a protest measure. After months of public wrangling and private negotiations, PRI conceded 237 of the 500 seats to opposition political parties, thereby guaranteeing forceful opposition in the national legislature.

The electoral events promised the first major restructuring of the political system since PRI was founded in late 1928. Dr. Salinas had made it clear that Mexico would become a more democratic state, a promise he seemed to be fulfilling when he demanded that more opposition party victories be recognized. (Whether he could continue to open the system in the face of opposition from PRI political bosses and organized labor, a stalwart of the old regime, remained to be seen.)

Cárdenas, for his part, was charged with converting the FDN into a stable political party, a difficult task at best. The coalition was composed of the Authentic Party of the Mexican Revolution (a formerly conservative party he used for his presidential candidacy), the People's Socialist Party, the Mexican Socialist Party, and the Cárdenas Front for National Reconstruction. The left originally had united behind Heberto Castillo as the best hope of breaking PRI's stranglehold on the nation, but switched to Cárdenas when it became obvious that he was the strongest opposition candidate. Other people supported Cárdenas because he had name recognition. Perceiving that the FDN was a fragile organization, Cárdenas spent the last months of 1988 trying to build a permanent party organization.

PAN, now the third largest party, was better organized and appeared likely once again to become the major opposition party. Analysis of presidential electoral returns from the northern states, where PAN won numerous deputy seats, indicated that many PAN supporters voted for Cárdenas as the most effective protest measure.

Economic Policy. President de la Madrid continued his program of economic austerity, privatization, and anti-inflationary efforts. Federal expenditures were reduced, while tax collections increased, as the government reduced the amount of its deficit spending. Through the Pact of Economic Solidarity—an agreement among workers, farmers, and businessmen to hold the line on wages and prices—the inflation rate was reduced from 150% to just above 10% by late October 1988. Private capital investment grew as the government reduced its share of investment to 33%. The National Telegraph Company and the Mexican Postal System were converted to decentralized enterprises, which will not receive subsidies. Late in the year, the government sold Aeromexico (one of two government airlines) and two copper companies, and announced the impending sale of another 50 state-owned corporations, thus reducing the number of state enterprises to 350, down from a high of 1,155 in 1982. The timing of these moves ensured the completion of de la Madrid's economic program and gave a freer hand to his successor. Foreign-debt renegotiation yielded more favorable terms and, in March 1988, the nation was able to buy back more than $3.6 billion of foreign debt at a 30% discount.

Salinas is expected to encourage more foreign investment (currently 9% of all investment), a larger role for private enterprise in public-works programs, congressional caps on foreign loans, and a continued shift to a market economy. He also was expected to adopt programs to raise real wages in order to pacify government critics.

MEXICO • Information Highlights

Official Name: United Mexican States.
Location: Southern North America.
Area: 761,602 sq mi (1 972 550 km²).
Population (mid-1988 est.): 83,500,000.
Chief Cities (1980 census): Mexico City (Federal District), the capital (1983 est.), 9,663,360; Guadalajara, 1,626,152; Monterrey, 1,090,009.
Government: *Head of state and government,* Carlos Salinas de Gortari, president (took office Dec. 1988). *Legislature*—National Congress: Senate and Federal Chamber of Deputies.
Monetary Unit: Peso (2,280 pesos equal U.S.$1, floating rate, Nov. 7, 1988).
Gross Domestic Product (1986 U.S.$): $127,220,-000,000.
Economic Indexes (1987): *Consumer Prices* (1980 = 100), all items, 4,626.0; food, 4,440.3. *Industrial Production* (1980 = 100), 104.
Foreign Trade (1987 U.S.$): *Imports,* $12,742,-000,000; *exports,* $20,628,000,000.

Hurricane Gilbert wreaked havoc across the Yucatán Peninsula and parts of northern Mexico, left, September 16–17. According to the government, some 200,000 people were left homeless, and damage exceeded $880 million.

AP/Wide World

Economic Performance. The economy continued in recession but showed signs of improvement. Manufactured goods grew to represent 56% of all exports. Increases in the fishing industry made Mexico the 11th largest fishing nation in the world. The nation became self-sufficient in wheat, sugar, poultry, and rice production. The automobile industry once again became profitable. Tourism and the in-bond plant program grew, bringing much-needed foreign exchange. Petroleum and mining exports declined, however, as world prices continued to fall. In spite of its $12 billion in monetary reserves, Mexico obtained a $3.5 billion loan from the United States in October to offset export income losses. Lost oil export income cost $1.5 billion in 1988 and was expected to yield only $5 billion in 1989, threatening the possibility of economic recovery.

Social Policy. Expansion in the educational system in 1988 reached the point that primary education was available to all students, secondary schools to all urban students, and technical education was sufficient for current industrial needs. To address rural-housing deficiencies, the National Fund for Rural Housing was created in April. In a major change, the Basic Commodities Corporation (CONASUPO) was converted into a regulatory agency. Previously it had been an agency that directly competed with private enterprise by selling low-cost, subsidized food, clothing, and basic consumer items. To protect the poor, the government operated a rehydrated milk distribution program, a tortilla food stamp program, and a more active consumer protection program with a mandate to enforce price controls on basic foodstuffs. To combat the growth of drug abuse the nation launched a modest campaign through 12,000 committees and subcommittees of parents, teachers, and government officials.

Foreign Affairs. The meeting of President de la Madrid and U.S. President Ronald Reagan in February 1988 resulted in an agreement to disagree over such issues as illegal migration, Central America, drug trafficking, and protective trade practices. The United States was more concerned with Mexican economic survival than these issues. Mexicans were angry justifiably in April when the U.S. Senate voted to decertify Mexico because its members believed that Mexico was not cooperating with U.S. international policy. In fact, Mexico was the most cooperative nation, spending 60% of its justice department budget to combat drug trafficking and sacrificing numerous policemen and soldiers in drug wars. Mexican officials argued that the consumer nations, principally the United States, were responsible for the high level of drug trade. Washington eventually calmed the storm by pointing out that government policy is not set just by Senate votes. Complicating the issues were accusations by drug-enforcement agents in the United States that Mexican authorities have not been zealous enough in investigating the murder of Enrique Camarena Salazar, a U.S. drug-enforcement agent slain in Mexico in 1985. In September 1988, three men were convicted in a Los Angeles court of complicity in Camarena's murder, but others involved in the crime were still in Mexico and were thought to be shielded by corrupt Mexican officials.

Mexico continued to strengthen its ties with other Latin nations. The Group of Eight (Mexico, Argentina, Colombia, Peru, Uruguay, Brazil, Venezuela, and Panama) met in Mexico in June 1988 and in Uruguay in the autumn to plan strategies to deal with common problems such as international indebtedness, access to markets in industrial nations, and regional peace. Panama was excluded from these meetings as a protest against its strongman, Manuel Noriega. Mexico continued to support a negotiated settlement in Central America and nonintervention in the region's internal affairs. Joint consultations were held with Spain, Belize, and Guatemala.

DONALD J. MABRY
Mississippi State University

MICHIGAN

The November general election, a vote on casino gambling in Detroit, and a controversy over Detroit city records were major news stories in Michigan during 1988.

The Elections. Michigan was considered a "swing state" in the presidential elections, and both Vice-President George Bush and his Democratic challenger Gov. Michael Dukakis made several campaign trips through the state. President Ronald Reagan also visited the state twice in the weeks preceding the election to campaign for Bush, who eventually won Michigan's 20 electoral votes. In the U.S. congressional races, all of Michigan's incumbents (11 Democrats and seven Republicans) were reelected. Democrat Donald Riegle was returned to the U.S. Senate.

In a referendum on the abortion issue on the November ballot, "pro-life" forces scored a decisive victory when voters approved a ban on welfare abortions by a wide margin. The ban, which took effect in December, would halt an estimated 18,500 tax-paid abortions each year, which cost the state $6 million. The vote climaxed a bitter legislative and legal battle of several years' duration, as both Gov. James J. Blanchard and his predecessor, William Milliken, had vetoed repeatedly legislative bans on welfare abortions.

Surrogate Motherhood. The Michigan legislature enacted a law, effective September 1, outlawing motherhood for pay. The measure made anyone who is a party to a surrogate motherhood contract liable to misdemeanor charges. The broker of the agreement could face a felony charge. The action came after a case in which a Michigan woman bore twins under a surrogacy contract and then refused to surrender them to their father.

Detroit News. Detroit voters overwhelmingly rejected casino gambling in their city for the third time in 12 years in an August 3 primary vote. The vote was seen as a slap at Detroit Mayor Coleman A. Young, who had loaned $287,500 from his personal-campaign fund to help finance the pro-casino campaign.

In what was viewed as repudiation of Detroit's public-school policies and practices, city voters on November 8 elected four newcomers to the Board of Educaton and rejected two of three ballot funding proposals for the deficit-plagued district. Four "reform" candidates claimed seats on the 11-member board.

A confrontation between Detroit city officials and *The Detroit News* over city records led to the jailing of city attorney Donald Pailen for contempt of court. Upon orders from Mayor Young, Pailen defied a court order to release public documents on a $42.1 million land deal requested by the newspaper under the state Freedom of Information Act. Pailen was freed October 25 after the Michigan Supreme Court upheld lower court orders to release the documents, and he surrendered the information. The documents revealed that the city paid $35.8 million for secondhand machinery while condemning land for a new Chrysler Corporation facility and resold it for $1.7 million. Those involved said the original owners repurchased most of the stock for less than five cents on the dollar. A federal grand jury was investigating the matter as the year ended.

Outgoing U.S. Attorney General Edwin Meese approved a joint-operating agreement between *The Detroit News* and the *Detroit Free Press* on August 8. The action was challenged in court by a group of subscribers and advertisers. U.S. District Judge George H. Revercomb upheld Meese's decision, but the opponents appealed to a three-judge panel of the U.S. District Court of Appeals in Washington, DC.

The Roman Catholic Archdiocese of Detroit announced plans to close 43 Detroit parishes whose memberships had dwindled to the point that they no longer could support themselves. On a happier note, Detroit Archbishop Edmund Cusimir Szoka was named a cardinal in May.

Insurance. Michigan Blue Cross-Blue Shield came under fire from several sources. John C. McCabe, longtime board chairman, was forced out of his job shortly before the start of the year and was replaced by Richard E. Whitmer, senior vice-president. In March a state audit reported that losses resulting from gross mismanagement endangered the well-being of the state's largest health insurer. About 4.4 million state residents received health-care benefits from the corporation and nearly 500,000 were enrolled in its health-maintenance organizations. The audit urged restructuring or dropping of the health-maintenance organizations.

CHARLES W. THEISEN, *"The Detroit News"*

MICHIGAN • Information Highlights

Area: 58,527 sq mi (151 586 km²).

Population (July 1, 1987): 9,200,000.

Chief Cities (July 1, 1986 est.): Lansing, the capital, 128,980; Detroit, 1,086,220; Grand Rapids, 186,530; Warren, 149,800; Flint, 145,590; Sterling Heights, 111,960.

Government (1988); *Chief Officers*—governor, James J. Blanchard (D); lt. gov., Martha W. Griffiths (D). *Legislature*—Senate, 38 members; House of Representatives, 110 members.

State Finances (fiscal year 1987): *Revenue,* $21,493,000,000; *expenditure,* $18,791,000,000.

Personal Income (1987): $141,618,000,000; per capita, $15,393.

Labor Force (June 1988): *Civilian labor force,* 4,593,800; unemployed, 326,400 (7.1% of total force).

Education: *Enrollment* (fall 1986)—public elementary schools, 1,108,798; public secondary, 573,082; colleges and universities, 520,428. *Public school expenditures* (1986–87), $6,101,000,000 ($3,954 per pupil).

MICROBIOLOGY

Microbiological research during 1988 yielded advances in the fight against infectious diseases and a clearer understanding of the complexities of microbial life.

Rabies Vaccine. Rabies is a viral disease which attacks the nervous system of humans and other mammals, resulting in a painful and fatal illness. The virus is found in the saliva of infected animals and is transmitted through their bites. Rabies is associated most frequently with dogs, raccoons, skunks, bats, squirrels, and foxes.

A vaccine against rabies was developed by Louis Pasteur in 1885 and has been used effectively to protect dogs and other domestic animals from the disease. Only recently, however, has any attempt been made to rid the entire wild animal population in a given area of this incurable disease. The Wistar Institute in Philadelphia recently has developed a rabies vaccine that can be taken orally. It consists of the vaccinia (cowpox) virus, to which was added the rabies gene, whose protein product stimulates the immune system to form antibodies against the rabies virus.

Plans have been made to distribute food pellets containing the vaccine over large areas of isolated islands off the coast of Virginia. Then, wild animals on the islands will be captured and tested for antibodies against rabies. If the animals are found to have been vaccinated successfully using this procedure, the project will be extended to various regions known to contain rabies-infected animals. By this method, scientists hope eventually to rid the entire United States of the disease.

Prey to Parasite Transformation. In western North America, tree holes are alternately empty spaces during the dry summer season and miniature ponds during the rainy fall season. As such, they become complex ecological niches for their many inhabitants. At the University of California, Berkeley, Dr. J. O. Washburn and his associates have studied a fascinating life process involving the protozoan *Lambornellia clarki* and the larvae of the mosquito *Aedes sierrensis*. These two species survive the summer in tree holes as dessication-resistant cysts and eggs, respectively. With the fall rains, both the protozoans and the mosquito larvae become active, with the mosquito larvae feeding on the protozoans. As they feed and grow, the mosquito larvae secrete a chemical compound to which the protozoans react by becoming transformed into a parasitic stage. As parasites, the protozoans infect the mosquito larvae, ultimately killing them. This "induced parasitism" is an unusual example of antipredator defense in which prey becomes parasite and predator becomes host.

Periodontitis. Found mainly in adults over the age of 35, periodontitis is a bacterially induced gum disease which results in the destruction of the bone and connective tissue that support the teeth. If left untreated, it results in the loss of teeth. Hundreds of different bacterial species normally are found at periodontitis sites, but scientists have had difficulty determining precisely which ones cause the disease. It has been noted, however, that one species—*Bacteroides gingivalis*—is isolated repeatedly from diseased gums and that the concentration of this species at the disease site increases as the disease worsens.

In order to determine whether *B. gingivalis* actually causes periodontitis, Dr. S. C. Holt and his associates at the University of Texas Health Science Center at San Antonio implanted the bacteria in the gums of monkeys that had been found free of infection by this species. Twenty weeks later, *B. gingivalis* was found in the diseased gum areas where bone destruction had occurred. The results thus supported the hypothesis that *B. gingivalis,* most likely in addition to other bacteria, is a periodontal pathogen. Researchers hope that identifying the specific bacteria that cause periodontitis will be the first step in preventing their colonization of the gums.

Diploidy in Amoebae. A continuing problem in microbiological research is the determination of whether the chromosome complement of a particular single-cell species constitutes the haploid or diploid condition. In a haploid cell, each chromosome—and hence each gene—is represented only once, as in a human sperm or unfertilized egg cell. In a diploid cell, each chromosome and hence each gene is represented twice (in pairs), as in a fertilized human egg and all the cells derived from it.

All the molecules of a protein produced by a haploid cell must be identical because there is only one gene encoding the protein. In a diploid cell, however, if the paired chromosomes contain different forms (alleles) of a particular gene, the molecules of the protein produced will be of two varieties, each reflecting the gene code of its particular allele. Such protein molecule differentiation can be detected by a process called electrophoresis, in which suspended particles move through a fluid under the action of an electromotive force.

At the National Center for Scientific Research in France, Dr. M. L. Cariou and his colleagues conducted an analysis of five amoeba species of the genus *Naegleria*. They examined the electrophoretic pattern of 15 proteins and found different varieties for all 15 proteins in all five species. This was the first evidence of diploidy in these amoebae, suggesting that some kind of sexual process may occur regularly in them and that each of these single-celled species has evolved as a unit—much as the human species has.

LOUIS LEVINE
City College of New York

At a November meeting of the Palestine National Council in Algiers, right, PLO chairman Yasir Arafat joined other delegates in proclaiming an independent Palestinian state and accepting UN resolutions that recognize the existence of Israel. The Palestinian problem remained one of the world's most intractable.

© M. Attar/Sygma

MIDDLE EAST

As in many past years, the Middle East in 1988 was, to an extraordinary extent, the cynosure of the world's attention. And even though the underlying issues and problems in this troubled region generally change little from year to year, or even decade to decade, there were major shifts in focus during 1988. The preeminent problem ceased to be the long-running Iraqi-Iranian war, which came to a halt, and its place was taken by the Palestinian problem, which late in the year was the occasion of some major and most surprising policy shifts.

Iraqi-Iranian War. After nearly eight years, the war between Iraq and Iran was suspended, either temporarily or permanently, by a UN-mediated cease-fire on August 20. (*See* special report, page 289.) Hostilities ended, and both Iraq and Iran began to wrestle with the problems of reconstruction. The "tanker war," which had evoked a formidable naval presence in the Persian Gulf from the United States and more modest naval forces from several European states, also ended, and U.S. naval forces there were reduced (though not altogether withdrawn). Diplomatic exchanges between the two former combatants did not produce any substantive agreements before the end of the year, and substantial questions remained in abeyance. Iraq insisted, as a condition precedent to any further negotiations, that it should enjoy total freedom of navigation in the Shatt-al-Arab waterway and through the Strait of Hormuz. Iran wished to retain some control.

Perhaps the most regretted of many acts of violence during the last period of the Gulf War was the destruction by the U.S.S. *Vincennes* on July 3 of an Iranian passenger plane, killing all 290 people aboard—a tragic accident which was, however, strangely without any direct political consequences.

Palestinian Disturbances. After the suspension of the Iraqi-Iranian war, attention was concentrated largely on events in the Israeli-occupied Gaza Strip and West Bank—a term that Israelis find prejudicial, preferring "Judea and Samaria." (*See also* special report, page 294.) Since Dec. 9, 1987, Arabs living in those areas had demonstrated against the Israeli occupation and administration, consequences of the swift and overwhelming Israeli victory in the Six-Day War of June 1967. Also taken over at that time were the Sinai Peninsula, handed back to Egypt in fulfillment of the Egyptian-Israeli peace treaty of 1979, and East Jerusalem and the Golan Heights. The last two, unlike the West Bank and Gaza, had been directly incorporated into Israel; the West Bank and Gaza remained "administered areas."

At no time in the two decades since 1967 have the West Bank and Gaza been free of hostile incidents aimed at the occupying power and its agents, military or civilian. What was different in the series of events that began late in 1987 and continued throughout 1988 was their continuous and determined character. There was a new level of resistance to Israeli rule, with a virulence that bespoke a widespread popular resentment, even desperation, and

some degree of organization behind it. It became fashionable to call this long-drawn-out and fairly low-key rebellion the *intifada* (literally in Arabic "tremor" or "shaking," but often translated as "the uprising").

The leadership of the movement remained cloudy. The Palestine Liberation Organization (PLO) was perhaps the major beneficiary of the turmoil, especially toward the end of the year, but there was no reason to believe that the PLO instigated it. Rather, the *intifada* appeared to have been in part a protest against what the approximately 1.5 million Arab residents of the area saw as the ineffectiveness of the PLO in doing anything to aid them or change their condition in more than 20 years of occupation. This resentment also was directed at the neighboring Arab states. Despite their many statements of sympathy for the Palestinian cause, in many cases they feared and distrusted the PLO. King Hussein had ejected the PLO from Jordan after pitched battles, and it also had been ejected from Lebanon. The last straw, perhaps, was the Arab League meeting of November 1987 in Amman, Jordan, which was almost totally concerned with the Gulf War. The brief discussion there of the Palestinian issue occurred only at the insistence of Syria.

The typical pattern of incidents in the West Bank, occurring with infinite variations, was an attack by stone-throwing youths, evoking a response from Israeli troops attempting to maintain order. Israel adopted a policy of an "iron fist" response on January 19, and the casualties were extremely one-sided through the course of the year. By the end of December, just over 300 Arabs had died, and hundreds had been wounded. Israeli deaths, civilian and military, numbered about a dozen. At any one time, about 6,000 Arabs were in Israeli jails, most without prospect of trial.

The whole network of social and economic relations betewen Arabs and Israelis in the occupied areas changed beyond recognition within a few months. The Palestinians called a number of general strikes. They resorted to violence and intimidation against anyone who attempted to cooperate with the Israelis. About half of the Palestinians serving in the police force were pressured into resigning. Arson became common.

The Israeli government imposed a number of economic and other sanctions: restrictions on the amount of funds that could be moved into the West Bank, limits on the sales of commodities, control of individual movements, deportations, and extended school closings. None of these moves was entirely effective in controlling the turbulence. Nor did the assassination in Tunis on April 16, apparently by Israeli agents, of Khalil Wazir ("Abu Jihad"), Arafat's second-in-command and principal military aide, produce much benefit for Israel. Israeli troops managed to maintain a sullen surface

calm most of the time throughout most of the area, but no more than that. In the midst of all this, Israel on May 14 marked the marked the 40th anniversary of its founding, though there was not a great deal to celebrate.

Meanwhile, from February through June, U.S. Secretary of State George Shultz made four fruitless trips to the Middle East, and Assistant Secretary of State Richard W. Murphy also visited several times without effect. Their aim was to further the U.S. peace plan, first adumbrated in 1982, to achieve Arab-Israeli peace by means of an international conference and to gain some kind of autonomy for the Palestinians in association with Jordan. But this policy, which had seemed less relevant to the realities of the situation as time went on, became almost completely so in July, when King Hussein of Jordan renounced all responsibility for the West Bank, which Jordan had ruled from 1950 to 1967.

Arab League Meeting. Jordan's new policy had been foreshadowed at the Arab League emergency meeting, held in Algiers, June 7–9, to discuss the then six-month-old *intifada*. At the summit, King Hussein praised the uprising and declared that he was not in competition with the PLO. In sharp contrast with the previous meeting in Amman, the Algiers summit gave strong support to the PLO, though there was some caution about making specific financial commitments. A "two-state" solution of the Palestinian problem was endorsed.

Seventeen of the Arab League's 21 heads of state were present at Algiers, the best atten-

In the spring, in its perennial effort to rid the area of Palestinian guerrillas, Israel launched an incursion into its self-declared security zone in southern Lebanon.

AP/Wide World

dance in ten years. Egypt's full return to membership was delayed by the opposition of Syria. A note of comedy was provided by Col. Muammar el-Qaddafi of Libya, attending his first meeting in a decade, who directed sundry acts of rudeness at the kings of Jordan, Morocco, and Saudi Arabia.

Palestinian State Proclaimed. The pace of change quickened greatly in the fall. A four-day (November 12–15) meeting in Algiers of the Palestine National Council (PNC), regarded as the legislative body of the PLO, ended with a proclamation of the establishment of an independent Palestinian state and the acceptance of certain key UN resolutions (242 and 338) passed in 1967 and 1973. These resolutions contained an acceptance of the right of all states in the region "to live in peace within secure and recognized boundaries." The PNC at Algiers also renounced acts of violence—but only outside Israel. The ambiguities and evasions of the Algiers pronouncements were noticeable and kept the United States from accepting them. They also were rejected by Israel. Nevertheless, by the end of the year some 70 states had accorded recognition to the new hypothetical state.

United States and the PLO. The PLO's progression toward moderation in public statements continued rapidly. The refusal by Secretary Shultz (November 26) to allow Arafat a visa to attend the UN General Assembly session in New York, on the ground of his association with terrorism, was criticized widely, but the action may have served to pressure Arafat into making more concessions. At any rate, his speech in Geneva, where the General Assembly was moved expressly to hear him, was more explicit and conciliatory; statements at a meeting in Stockholm with some American Jews and at a press conference in Geneva were still more so. The outcome, a stunning policy reversal, was the announcement on December 14 by U.S. President Ronald Reagan, elaborated in a news conference by Secretary Shultz, that the United States would enter into a "diplomatic dialogue" with the PLO. Arafat's Geneva press conference was regarded as having met the conditions laid down by former U.S. Secretary of State Henry Kissinger in 1975, i.e., explicit recognition by the PLO of Israel and of the UN resolutions on the subject of Palestine. Discussions began within 24 hours in Tunis between the PLO and the U.S. ambassador to Tunisia.

Clearly, however great the change in the political climate, nothing really had been solved. Arafat said on December 21 that he continued to support the *intifada,* and others in the loose congeries of Palestinian organizations said explicitly that acts of violence within Israel would continue. The indecisive Israeli election of November 1 resulted in Yitzhak Shamir's continuance as prime minister and,

after seven weeks of negotiations, in a renewed Likud-Labor coalition government. But neither group would recognize a Palestinian state or yield territory to make such a state possible.

The Kurds. While the Palestinians were basking in the world's attention and enjoying enormous public relations success, another larger and more oppressed people, the Kurds, were suffering enormously greater hardships and brutalities. An ancient people numbering some 12 million, the Kurds—Sunni Muslim but not Arab or Persian—have for 1,000 years occupied a mountainous homeland known as Kurdistan in the region where Turkey, Iran, and Iraq meet. The largest number live in Turkey, with smaller numbers in Iran and Iraq. In Iraq, however, they make up about 20% of the total population.

The Kurds have a long history of rebellion against various oppressors—earlier, the Ottoman and Persian empires; today, their successor states. Largely for want of political cooperation, however, they have never approached the achievement of a Kurdish state. Iraqi Kurds conducted a long-running civil war against the Baghdad government in the 1960s and early 1970s until the Shah Mohammed Reza Pahlavi of Iran withdrew his support in 1975. During the Gulf War of the 1980s, both Iraq and Iran gave aid to the other side's Kurdish rebels, a gambit in which Iran was rather more successful. Kurds cooperated with Iranian troops, and Iraq was forced to divert some of its military forces to hold down the Kurdish north. There was a serious campaign in Iraqi Kurdistan during the spring of 1987.

As the Iraqi-Iranian war neared its end, Iraq, not surprisingly, turned savagely on its Kurdish rebels. They were bombed, their villages were destroyed, and part of their population was deported. The most serious attack on the Kurds began at the end of June, at which time Iran, about to conclude a treaty with Iraq and in a curious echo of 1975, informed its erstwhile Kurdish allies that it could no longer assist them.

As a result of an intensified Iraqi onslaught at the end of August (reportedly involving the use of poison gas), an estimated 60,000 Kurds fled into Turkey. Although Turkey did make reasonably generous attempts to provide emergency shelter and food for its unforeseen guests, it was something of an unwilling host.

The reports of Iraq's treatment of the Kurds incensed U.S. opinion, and both the Senate and House of Representatives passed legislation imposing sanctions on Iraq. The measure died, however, with the end of the congressional session in October.

Arms. A notable trend of 1989 was the purchase of arms by Middle East states from suppliers other than the United States. The major underlying reason was that the proposed U.S. arms sales to Arab countries generally run into

During the first seven months of the year—prior to the August cease-fire between Iran and Iraq—violence continued in the Persian Gulf. In April, in retaliation for a mining incident, U.S. warships destroyed key Iranian oil platforms.

political difficulties in Congress. In many cases the number of weapons is scaled down, or certain classes of weapons are eliminated. In June 1988, for example, the Senate eliminated advanced Maverick missiles from a $1.9 billion arms sale to Kuwait. In July, Great Britain and Saudi Arabia concluded one of the largest arms sales ever, including minesweepers and about 50 Tornado fighters among many other items. The deal was said to be worth more than $12 billion over ten years. Britain also was in the process of supplying arms to Kuwait, Egypt, the United Arab Emirates, Oman, and other states in the Gulf area. And the Arab countries have been turning to other suppliers as well, including France and China.

Among the most ominous developments in regard to arms in the Middle East was the growing proliferation of missiles. It was estimated that ten Mideast states in 1988 possessed a total of at least 1,200 surface-to-surface missiles with ranges of 25 to 1,800 miles (40 to 2 900 km). Missiles were used extensively by Iraq against Tehran in an April offensive.

Balance Sheet. The Middle East is never lacking in ominous developments and bad news, and 1988 certainly had its share. In addition to the festering Palestinian problem, Gulf violence, and dreadful fate of the Kurds, the year saw grave disorders in the Sudan; conflict between competing governments in divided Lebanon; and strife between North and South Yemen. Yet there were, on the credit side,

quite a number of favorable developments during 1988. Many of these might be subsumed under the general rubric of "the reluctant acceptance of unwelcome realities"—not something the Middle East has been typically good at. Yet the Iranian government finally did accept that it was beyond its power to defeat Iraq. The PLO edged toward moderation, and the United States acknowledged that it had done so. And a great many diplomatic links, severed for years, were restored. Egypt, treated as a pariah by other Arab states after peace with Israel in 1979, began to have normal relations with them again; in November, Algeria became the 14th Arab state to restore diplomatic relations with the Cairo government. Libya's Qaddafi and Iran's Ayatollah Khomeini were even heard singing the praises of a free-market economy.

In one of the year's most interesting developments, the five states of the Maghreb (in Arabic "the West")—Libya, Tunisia, Algeria, Morocco, and Mauritania—began to move toward closer cooperation. The key factor here was the Moroccan-Algerian rapprochement of May 1988, by which normal diplomatic relations were restored. The leaders of the five states met in Algiers on June 10 in a mood of goodwill and initiated work toward the creation of a "Greater Arab Maghreb."

See also article on individual countries.

ARTHUR CAMPBELL TURNER
University of California, Riverside

MILITARY AFFAIRS

Despite the adoption of the Intermediate-range Nuclear Force (INF) Treaty and the open discussion of the Strategic Arms Reduction Talks, or START, the world's two largest military powers continued to modernize their strategic forces with impressive weapons during 1988. However, in both Moscow and Washington, there were small signs that pointed to a lessening of tension between the two giants.

Strategic Nuclear Systems. The Soviets added SS-24 ICBMs (intercontinental ballistic missiles) to their arsenal. The SS-24 was designed to be carried on a railroad car to protect it from a "first strike" attack. A companion ICBM, the SS-25, was designed to be mounted upon a vehicle with off-road capability. The Soviets also were proceeding with production of a new intercontinental range jet bomber, the Blackjack. Typhoon class submarines were incrementally replacing older SLBM (submarine launched ballistic missile) carrying boats.

In the United States debate swelled over the utility of the B-1B bomber. According to congressional critics and General Accounting Office analysts, the 100-plane fleet suffers from a variety of problems. The worst defect was believed to be the inability of its electronic warfare system to negate Soviet defenses.

A new airplane, called the Stealth strategic bomber, made its official appearance at a roll-out ceremony in Palmdale, CA, late in the fall. The new craft incorporated a radical design intended to both absorb and scatter radar impulses, thus making it difficult for enemy defenses to detect and track the plane's path.

The debate as to whether the nation's 450 Minuteman IIs and 550 Minuteman IIIs should be replaced eventually by MX ICBMs deployed in a rail garrison mode, or by a new ICBM, the Midgetman, was not resolved. After the deployment of 50 MXs in fixed and hardened silos, Congress refused to fund further development unless the Reagan administration developed a new basing mode for the missile. In response, the Department of Defense suggested a plan that would have two missiles each carried in special railroad cars attached to 25 trains that would be disguised to look like ordinary commercial trains. The trains normally would be kept in specially constructed shelters within a garrisoned area such as an Air Force base. In time of increased tension the trains could be dispersed over 125,000 mi (201 163 km) of railroad track in the United States, and mingled with regular trains to confuse an enemy planning to strike them.

In contrast to the 100-ton MX with its ten warheads, the Midgetman would carry one warhead and weigh about 15 tons. Its small size would permit each missile to be carried on a vehicle towed by a tractor. This combination, called a hard mobile launcher, would have the capability to operate on roads, or across open terrain. In peacetime, the hard mobile launchers would be housed at Air Force bases. In wartime, they could be dispersed quickly off base so they could roam about the countryside. Like the rail garrison MX, the dispersed Midgetmen would prove difficult to target.

Arms-control enthusiasts supported the Midgetman because of its one warhead. This, they contended, would enable the weapon to threaten unacceptable damage after it survived an enemy attack, but would prevent it from being perceived as a first strike weapon designed to barrage an enemy in a disarming attack. Opponents of the Midgetman contended that with only one warhead per missile the system would be too expensive to build, and that there was still a need for the ten-warhead MX.

The United States continued modernizing its SLBM fleet by replacing older boats with the new Trident submarines, designed to carry the new D-5 missile.

Space Defense. Five years after U.S. President Ronald Reagan announced his vision for a defense system to protect the U.S. population against ballistic missile attack, the grandiose scheme had been reduced to much more modest proportions. The generally acknowledged problem with the Strategic Defense Initiative (SDI), popularly called "Star Wars," was that the Buck Rogers weapons, such as lasers and particle beam generators, it would depend upon would not be feasible technically for decades.

The original SDI plan was for such weapons to be carried aboard earth-circling satellites from which they could destroy almost all Soviet missiles. However, in Reagan's last year as president, the concept of SDI was changed substantially. The new plan was to orbit satellites carrying "kinetic kill vehicles," small projectiles that destroy a target by the force of impact. More important would be the system of ground-based interceptors which would be fired at Soviet warheads as they descended on their targets. This second concept was similar to the Anti-Ballistic Missile (ABM) force that might have been deployed if U.S. President Richard Nixon had not signed the ABM treaty with the Soviets in 1972. The purpose of the scaled-down program would be, according to U.S. Secretary of Defense Frank Carlucci, to complicate Soviet execution of an attack upon U.S. ICBMs in their underground silos. According to military experts, protecting the silos would be easier than trying to protect much more vulnerable targets, such as cities.

The general impression in the U.S. scientific community was that if American science could not develop laser and particle beam weapons, the less advanced Soviet scientific establishment could not do so either.

Problems in Nuclear Weapons Plants. A basic component of the U.S. nuclear-weapons program encountered grave problems in 1988.

The U.S. Department of Energy (DOE) revealed that several nuclear plants charged with making weapons-grade tritium and plutonium had been leaking dangerous levels of radioactive material into the environment for more than two decades. DOE's complicity in the matter was shown by the fact that it apparently had known about the leakages all along, yet failed to do anything to rectify the problems. Rep. Thomas Luken (D-OH), chairman of a panel that looked into the matter, said, "The allegations of DOE . . . constitute a statement that DOE was waging a kind of chemical warfare against the community. . . ."

DOE shut down nuclear reactors at the Savannah River Plant in Georgia in August. A plant in Ohio also was shut down temporarily, and plants in Washington and Colorado were closed partially.

In terms of national security, the stoppage of tritium production at Savannah River was viewed as the most critical threat. Tritium, an isotope of hydrogen, is necessary to maintain most nuclear warheads in a state of operational readiness. Since tritium decays at the rate of about 5½% a year, new tritium often has to be added to the warheads. According to DOE officials, the United States would need to start borrowing tritium from some warheads to maintain others if the Savannah River facility is not restored to operation by summer 1989. DOE hoped to have the Savannah River reactors operable again by that time.

Compounding the problems with the nuclear-weapons plants were accusations that security had been lax in regard to foreign visitors at the nation's nuclear weapons laboratories. The Lawrence Livermore Laboratory in California, and the Sandia and Los Alamos facilities in New Mexico were said to be involved in the problem.

Withdrawal and Reduction of Forces. For very different reasons, both the United States and the USSR engaged in partial withdrawal of their externally based military forces. The USSR began the withdrawal of its troops from Afghanistan (the Soviets had invaded that country in 1979). The most obvious motivation for the action was the inability of the Soviets to subdue the stubborn resistance of the *mujahedin* who opposed the occupation of their nation. A second reason was thought to be the stagnating Russian economy which was hard put to support the Afghan war effort. According to an UN-sponsored agreement, all Soviet troops were to be out of Afghanistan by February of 1989; however, the USSR troops slowed their withdrawal in the latter part of 1988.

After it appeared that Iran and Iraq were willing to engage in genuine peace negotiations to end their long war, the White House announced it was trimming down the U.S. naval force that had been operating in the Persian Gulf to protect oil tankers from Iranian attack. The occasional skirmishes between Navy patrols and Iranian gunboats were marked by a particular tragedy on July 3, 1988. The navy cruiser *Vincennes* fired a surface-to-air missile at what was thought to be an attacking Iranian plane; it was, in reality, an Iranian jetliner. All 290 crew and passengers were killed.

The Persian Gulf was not the only place where the United States was to reduce its military presence. The Spanish government negotiated the withdrawal of an F-16 squadron from the Torrejón air base near Madrid by 1991. In Manila the United States and the government of Philippine President Corazon Aquino were preparing for hard discussions about whether U.S. forces at the Subic Bay naval base and Clark Field air base could continue operations after 1991. Looking toward that date, the United States agreed in late 1988 to increase payments to the Philippines for the bases during the remainder of the treaty.

Military bases in the United States were eyed for cutbacks. In October, President Reagan signed a bill that would eliminate many obsolete military bases over a period of a few years.

Reduced Tensions. In Moscow, military strategists talked about new doctrines to guide development of the Soviet armed services. One such idea was that in the future the size and offensive capability of the Soviet military would be altered to reflect more of a defensive mentality. Also, it was suggested in Soviet military writings that the concept of "reasonable sufficiency" would moderate the numbers of troops and types of Soviet armaments which would be deployed in the 1990s. While Americans interested in arms control and better United States-USSR relations praised the new doctrinal rhetoric, the secretary of defense urged caution in accepting the Soviets at face value. According to Secretary Carlucci, ". . . we in the West have yet to see any slackening in the continued growth of Soviet military power."

As if in answer to Secretary Carlucci's complaint, General Secretary Gorbachev made a dramatic announcement before the United Nations in December. The Soviet leader said his country would reduce its troop strength by 500,000 and its tank force by 10,000 over a two-year period. While welcoming the cuts, U.S. and allied officials pointed out that even after the reductions the Soviet forces would hold a numerical advantage over NATO. For his part, President Reagan applauded the Gorbachev initiative by saying, "About the Soviet unilateral troop reduction, I can only say that if it is carried out speedily and in full, history will regard it as . . . significant."

See also ARMS CONTROL.

ROBERT M. LAWRENCE
Colorado State University

MINNESOTA

Mixed election results, the effects of the drought, Pillsbury's struggle to prevent a takeover, a beleaguered university, and adoption of a constitutional amendment permitting a state-run lottery were among major developments in Minnesota in 1988.

Politics. Democrat Michael Dukakis won the state's presidential vote, 54% to 46%, but Republican U.S. Sen. Dave Durenberger was reelected over Attorney General Hubert H. Humphrey, III, son of the late vice-president, 56% to 42%. The incumbent U.S. congressmen —five Democrats and three Republicans— were reelected, all by wide margins.

The lottery amendment won big, 58% to 42%, despite vigorous opposition. But the lottery still faced a struggle for statutory implementation in the 1989 legislature. Also approved were constitutional amendments permitting the use of six-person juries and establishing a trust fund to protect the environment. The fund will be financed by lottery earnings.

The Democratic-Farmer-Labor (DFL) Party retained an 81 to 53 margin of control of the state House of Representatives. The main issue was a charge by Independent-Republicans that the DFL had eliminated the homestead property tax, a claim that the DFL said was based on a distortion.

Minneapolis turned down four charter amendments aimed at changing city government. St. Paul rejected an amendment that would have made city-council actions in the human-rights field not subject to referendum, a move regarded as aimed at preventing the voters from nullifying council actions on gay rights.

Voter turnout fell to 68%, still the highest percentage in the nation, but below the state's record-breaking turnout of 75.4% in 1976.

Drought. The loss in crop yields resulting from the drought was offset partially by higher prices, but most of the state's farm belt still was feeling the drought's effect. Farmers and businesses dependent on agriculture faced an uncertain future heading into the 1989 planting season. With 80% of the state's topsoil moisture rated short to very short, farmers were hoping for bountiful rains.

Minnesota University. Troubles at the University of Minnesota, involving a cost overrun in the remodeling of the president's residence, alleged theft of student-aid funds, irregularities in the support of athletes, and the revelation of large unreported reserves, led to the resignation of President Kenneth H. Keller and the dismissal of Athletic Director Paul Giel. On December 1, Nils Hasselmo, vice-president for academic affairs at the University of Arizona, was named the university's 13th president.

Takeover. The Minnesota-based Pillsbury Company was the target of takeover by the British conglomerate Grand Metropolitan. Late in the year the outcome was uncertain; the Pillsbury management was maneuvering to turn back the $5.23 billion buyout effort, which had the support of many shareholders who stood to make substantial profit. Pillsbury was countering with a poison pill move that would hike the takeover price to $20 billion.

State Issues. Preparing for the 1989 legislature, the state faced these issues: lottery implementation, improvement in the process for selecting University of Minnesota regents, property-tax reform, increased funding for highways, reorganization of the state's mental-health system, state financing of light-rail transit in the Twin Cities, and changes in workmen's compensation.

ARTHUR NAFTALIN, *University of Minnesota*

MISSISSIPPI

Federal elections in which Republicans gained state victories in both the presidential and senatorial contests; two noteworthy legislative sessions; and continuing efforts to reform county government were items of major interest to Mississippians in 1988.

The Elections. In the "Super Tuesday" presidential primary held March 8, George Bush won 27 of 31 Republican state delegates while Jesse Jackson captured 24 of 40 Democratic delegates. Eight months later Bush received 60% of the votes cast in the state in the general election, making him the fourth Republican in the last five presidential contests to win Mississippi's electoral votes. Michael Dukakis, the Democratic presidential nominee, carried only 19 of 82 counties.

U.S. Rep. Trent Lott (R, 5th District) received 54% of the general election vote to defeat Rep. Wayne Dowdy (D, 4th District) in the contest for the Senate seat being vacated by John C. Stennis (D) after 41 years. Lott's vic-

© Carol Waddell/''Mississippi Press''

Trent Lott, his wife, and mother (right) celebrate his election to the U.S. Senate. The 47-year-old Mississippi Republican had served eight terms in the U.S. House.

tory assured the state of two Republican senators for the first time since Reconstruction. Long-term incumbent Congressmen Jamie Whitten (D, 1st District) and G.V. Montgomery (D, 3d District) were reelected easily, as was first-term black Congressman Mike Espy (D, 2d District), who increased measurably his level of white support. Larkin Smith (R, Gulfport) won the seat being vacated by Lott, and Mike Parker (D, Brookhaven) won the Dowdy seat.

Legislative Sessions. The first legislative session of Democratic Gov. Ray Mabus' term began in January with the House of Representatives under the leadership of a new speaker,

---

MISSISSIPPI • Information Highlights

Area: 47,689 sq mi (123 515 km²).
Population (July 1, 1987): 2,625,000.
Chief Cities (1980 census): Jackson, the capital (July 1, 1986 est.), 208,440; Biloxi, 49,311; Meridian, 46,577.
Government (1988): *Chief Officers*—governor, Raymond Maybus, Jr. (D); lt. gov., Brad Dye (D). *Legislature*—Senate, 52 members; House of Representatives, 122 members.
State Finances (fiscal year 1987): *Revenue,* $4,413,000,000; *expenditure,* $3,956,000,000.
Personal Income (1987): $27,013,000,000; per capita, $10,292.
Labor Force (June 1988): *Civilian labor force,* 1,143,900; *unemployed,* 89,600 (7.8% of total force).
Education: *Enrollment* (fall 1986)—public elementary schools, 356,052; public secondary, 142,587; colleges and universities, 101,104. *Public school expenditures* (1986–87), $1,200,000,000 ($2,534 per pupil).

Tim Ford (D, Tupelo). Lawmakers gave the governor's education program top priority, enacting a record-breaking teacher pay raise spread over two years and increasing funding for higher education. Under the plan, teacher salaries would be increased from an annual average of $20,000 to $24,550 by September 1989. The improvements would be financed through anticipated growth in state tax revenues and not through a tax increase.

Legislators also funded an organizational study of the executive branch of state government, but they rejected two other reform measures on the governor's agenda—calling a referendum on a proposed constitutional convention and mandating the county-unit system of centralized road management.

The county-unit question was resubmitted to a special session of the legislature in August, and that body enacted a compromise measure requiring all counties to vote in November on the unit plan. A centralized purchasing and inventory control system was made mandatory for all counties, whether they accept or reject the unit structure.

County Reform. In the November referendum mandated by the special legislative session, about 61% of the voters statewide favored adoption of the county-unit system. This vote translated into approval by 48 counties and rejection by 34, including 13 who had governing board members who were arrested as a result of the federal government's ongoing investigation of corrupt purchasing practices. A proposal to replace elected county superintendents of education with appointed superintendents was on the November ballot in 66 counties but was approved in only Coahoma County.

Other Items. Like much of the nation, Mississippi suffered an extended summer drought, leading the federal government to declare a number of counties eligible to receive disaster funds. Barge traffic on the Tennessee-Tombigbee Waterway grew, as low water levels on the Mississippi River led some shippers to choose this alternative route to the Gulf of Mexico.

Arkansas, Mississippi, and Louisiana governors signed an agreement in May to coordinate efforts to improve conditions in the Mississippi Delta region. In November, Mississippi was selected by the National Aeronautics and Space Administration as the location for a proposed $1.2 billion rocket plant. This facility, to be built on the Yellow Creek nuclear power plant site abandoned by the Tennessee Valley Authority in 1984, was expected to employ 1,400 persons in economically depressed northeast Mississippi and was scheduled for completion in 1992.

The state's economy improved, and the unemployment rate, while above the national average, declined during the year.

DANA B. BRAMMER
The University of Mississippi

MISSOURI

The Republican Party continued its recent domination of statewide politics in Missouri, with U.S. Sen. John Danforth and Gov. John Ashcroft winning reelection landslides. Danforth, 52, won a third term over Democratic State Sen. Jay Nixon. Ashcroft, 46, was elected to a second term, defeating Democratic State Rep. Betty Hearnes.

U.S. Rep. Gene Taylor retired after eight terms in Congress. He was succeeded by fellow Republican Mel Hancock. The state's eight other incumbent congressmen were reelected. U.S. Rep. Richard Gephardt (D) of St. Louis started fast in his bid for the presidency, winning the Democratic presidential caucus in neighboring Iowa on February 8. But on Super Tuesday, he won only Missouri's Democratic primary. He withdrew from the presidential race on March 28 in time to file for reelection to Congress.

George Bush won Missouri's 11 electoral votes in a hotly contested fall race, taking 52% of the vote in the state. Dukakis visited Missouri nine times after the Democratic convention, and his running mate, Lloyd Bentsen, visited the state on ten occasions. Bush traveled to Missouri seven times, his running mate, Dan Quayle, five, and President Reagan twice. Both sides invoked the name of Missouri's favorite son, Harry S. Truman, during the campaign. Democrats vowed to come from behind to win as Truman did in 1948, and Reagan, a former Democrat, claimed if Truman were alive, he also would have joined the GOP.

Missouri voters, traditionally stubborn in op-, posing tax increases, loosened their purse strings in August, easing a century-old barrier to passage of local bond issues. In the November election, however, voters rejected a proposed earnings tax that would have financed a new health-care program for people without insurance.

Courts. The 8th U.S. Circuit Court of Appeals upheld most provisions of a lower court

MISSOURI · Information Highlights

Area: 69,697 sq mi (180 516 km²).
Population (July 1, 1987): 5,103,000.
Chief Cities (July 1, 1986 est.): Jefferson City, the capital (1980 census), 33,619; Kansas City, 441,170; St. Louis, 426,300; Springfield, 139,360; Independence, 112,950.
Government (1988): *Chief Officers*—governor, John Ashcroft (R); lt. gov., Harriett Woods (D). *General Assembly*—Senate, 34 members; House of Representatives, 163 members.
State Finances (fiscal year 1987): *Revenue,* $7,761,000,000; *expenditure,* $7,095,000,000.
Personal Income (1987): $74,945,000,000; per capita, $14,687.
Labor Force (June 1988): *Civilian labor force,* 2,610,100; *unemployed,* 134,300 (5.1% of total force).
Education: *Enrollment* (fall 1986)—public elementary schools, 549,348; public secondary, 251,258; colleges and universities, 246,185. *Public school expenditures* (1986–87), $2,406,000,000 ($3,345 per pupil).

ruling on desegregation of the Kansas City schools. But the court overturned a 25% surcharge on the state-income tax of people working in the school district.

Crime. Two convicted killers, Gerald Smith and George C. "Tiny" Mercer, came within hours of being Missouri's first criminals to be executed since 1965. In each case, a stay was granted by the appeals court.

A bizarre case came to light when a naked man wearing a dog collar escaped from the Kansas City house of Robert Berdella. Human skulls and pictures of men being tortured were found in Berdella's home. He eventually pleaded guilty to six counts of murder, admitting that he drugged his prisoners with animal tranquilizers and tortured them before killing them.

Kansas City brothers George Kroh and John A. Kroh, Jr., whose real-estate development company went bankrupt in 1987, were found guilty of federal bank fraud. George Kroh pleaded guilty and then testified against his brother, who was convicted by a jury.

Business. Merger mania ruled in Missouri as it did nationally. Boatmen's Bancshares, Inc.

Missouri's Gov. John Ashcroft (center) and Sen. Kit Bond (right) join George Bush for a campaign rally at St. Louis' Union Station. The vice-president won the state's electoral votes, and its GOP governor captured a second term.

AP/Wide World

of St. Louis, already the state's largest bank-holding company, took over Centerre Bancor-poration, the third largest such company in the state. In a management buyout, Payless Cash-ways of Kansas City went private to fend off takeovers. Kansas City Southern Industries staved off a merger, with help from Hallmark Cards Inc. of Kansas City, which put up $78 million to keep the company in local hands. As the year drew to a close, Interco of St. Louis successfully fought a takeover battle.

Other News. Pulitzer Prize-winning poet Howard Nemerov of St. Louis was named the third poet laureate of the United States. St. Louis lost its National Football League team when the Cardinals opted to move to Phoenix, AZ.

On November 28, an explosion at a highway construction site killed six Kansas City fire-fighters. The men were battling an arson fire in one of two trailers loaded with ammonium ni-trate when the explosives ignited in a pair of blasts felt across the metro area.

STEPHEN BUTTRY
"The Kansas City Times"

MONTANA

Montana voters followed the national trend by supporting George Bush over Michael Du-kakis for the presidency, 52% to 48%; they also elected a new governor, Stan Stephens. Ste-phens, a Republican, beat Tom Judge, who was governor for eight years in the 1970s, 53% to 47%. Sen. John Melcher, a Democrat, was ousted by Conrad Burns, 52% to 48%. Rep. Ron Marlenee, a Republican, won his seventh congressional term in Montana's eastern-dis-trict, defeating Buck O'Brien, who was his Democratic challenger for the second time. The vote was 56% to 44%. Democrat Rep. Pat Williams easily retained his western-district seat, defeating Republican Jim Fenlason by 61% to 39%.

MONTANA • Information Highlights

Area: 147,046 sq mi (380 848 km²).
Population (July 1, 1987): 809,000.
Chief Cities (1980 census): Helena, the capital, 23,938; Billings, 66,798; Great Falls, 56,725.
Government (1988): *Chief Officers*—governor, Ted Schwinden (D); lt. gov., George Turman (D). *Leg-islature*—Senate, 50 members; House of Repre-sentatives, 100 members.
State Finances (fiscal year 1987): *Revenue,* $1,816,000,000; *expenditure,* $1,697,000,000.
Personal Income (1987): $9,992,000,000; per capita, $12,347.
Labor Force (June 1988): *Civilian labor force,* 412,200; *unemployed,* 26,600 (6.5% of total force).
Education: *Enrollment* (fall 1986)—public elemen-tary schools, 107,572; public secondary, 45,755; colleges and universities, 35,238. *Public school expenditures* (1986–87), $567,000,000 ($4,070 per pupil).

The campaigns took a back seat to fires and drought during most of the year, however.

Drought. Throughout the eastern two thirds of Montana, precipitation, river flows, and soil moisture were at record-low levels, thanks to a dry winter and spring and a record-hot sum-mer. In addition to dry-land grain and hay crops that did not thrive, forage withered in pastures, forcing ranchers to ship as many as 10% of their cattle out of state for the fall and winter. Nearly nonexistent topsoil moisture discouraged eastern Montana farmers from planting winter wheat, which normally would sprout in the fall and mature the next summer. Without moisture in the ground, many farmers opted to wait until spring to plant their fields with other crops.

Forest Fires. The summer heat dried forests and paved the way for one of the worst forest fire seasons in decades. Cooke City in southern Montana was evacuated for a week before the normally lucrative Labor Day weekend as a pair of wildfires from the adjacent Absaroka-Beartooth Wilderness to the north and a mas-sive fire from Yellowstone National Park to the south converged on the town. Firefighters kept the blaze out of town, though it swept as close as 10 ft (3 m) from some buildings.

West Yellowstone, MT, where the economy depends heavily on tourist trade from the na-tional park, was hurt by news of fire sweeping 500,000 acres (202 429 ha) in Yellowstone. Those associated with fire control made their headquarters at West Yellowstone and helped businesses make up for lost tourist trade.

The southern-Montana fires sparked heated debate over a controversial federal policy by which forest fires that start naturally in the park or wilderness are allowed to burn unchecked until they threaten lives and property. Cooke City and West Yellowstone residents con-tended that their towns and economies would have been spared any effect from the fires had they been extinguished when they were discov-ered.

Fires in August also burned to the town lim-its of Lame Deer in southeastern Montana and through forest land filled with recreation cabins south of Helena. Wildfire also roared along the western edge of Glacier National Park.

Hunting. Forest conditions conducive to fire prompted Gov. Ted Schwinden to ban hunting and close public lands to recreation a day be-fore many hunting seasons opened in Septem-ber. The land remained closed for more than a week, until rain lowered the chances of fire.

Taxes. A federal judge ruled that Montana illegally had collected a severance tax on coal mined on the Crow Indian Reservation in southeastern Montana. The judge ordered the state to pay the tribe the $30 million it had col-lected over the previous decade.

ROBERT C. GIBSON
"The Billings Gazette"

MOROCCO

Morocco played a strong hand in 1988 in advancing the concept of pan-Maghrebin unity. ("Maghreb," Arabic for "west," is the traditional name for the North African region lying between the Mediterranean Sea and the Sahara.) Morocco and Algeria reestablished diplomatic relations May 16 after a 12-year hiatus. A historic meeting June 10 in Algiers brought together—for the first regional conference since the early 1960s—the five government heads of Algeria, Libya, Mauritania, Morocco, and Tunisia. In August, UN Secretary-General Javier Pérez de Cuéllar proposed a referendum on who should control the Western Sahara, territory disputed between Morocco and the Polisario guerrilla front. Both sides agreed to abide by the results of the referendum. These events together bode well for future regional cooperation.

Foreign Affairs. After more than a decade of severed diplomatic ties between Morocco and Algeria caused by the latter's recognition of the Polisario's proclaimed Saharan Arab Democratic Republic (SADR) in 1976, the two countries reestablished diplomatic relations in May. This was followed almost immediately by the reopening of their borders and the creation of a joint Moroccan-Algerian commission intended to handle the practical details of future cooperation between the two countries. On June 11 the new commission completed its preliminary work and announced a formal framework for collaboration in five major areas: transportation, post and telecommunications, cultural exchanges, tourism, and the development of frontier regions.

Domestic economic, social, and political pressures in the two countries, along with an unfavorable international economic environment, have persuaded Moroccan and Algerian leaders of the need for greater bilateral and multilateral cooperation within the context of Maghrebin unity. Underlying these dramatic developments has been the recognition that the Western Sahara conflict needed resolution before other concrete economic and political steps could be taken.

Working through the newly created Maghreb Committee which was formed during the Algiers Arab summit in June, Morocco accepted the notion of a UN-sponsored referendum to determine the final political outcome of the Western Sahara. Private negotiations, completed in advance of public announcements on the subject, indicated a compromise solution which would give SADR regional autonomy within the larger Moroccan state rather than complete political independence. While the Polisario responded favorably to the renewal of relations between Morocco and Algeria and its implications for Maghrebin unity, it did not accept the notion of a predetermined outcome of

MOROCCO · Information Highlights

Official Name: Kingdom of Morocco.
Location: Northwest Africa.
Area: 172,413 sq mi (446 550 km²).
Population (mid-1988 est.): 25,000,000.
Chief Cities (1982 census): Rabat, the capital, 518,616; Casablanca, 2,139,204; Fès, 448,823; Marrakech, 439,728.
Government: *Head of state,* Hassan II, king (acceded 1961). *Head of government,* Azzedine Laraki, prime minister (appointed Sept. 30, 1986). *Legislature* (unicameral)—Chamber of Representatives.
Monetary Unit: Dirham (8.496 dirhams equal U.S.$1, July 1988).
Gross Domestic Product (1986 U.S.$): $11,900,-000,000.
Economic Indexes (1987): *Consumer Prices* (1980 = 100), all items, 178.8; food, 182.3. *Industrial Production* (1986, 1980 = 100), 112.
Foreign Trade (1986 U.S.$): *Imports,* $4,069,000,000; *exports,* $2,260,000,000.

a referendum which would leave the Western Sahara under Moroccan control.

Fighting continued in the territory in late 1988. Guerrillas staged a major attack in September involving several hundred casualties and the introduction, for the first time, of deadly and efficient Soviet-made missiles. Despite major Moroccan losses, King Hassan was determined not to let the attack disrupt renewed relations with Algeria (the Polisario's main supporter) or interfere with prospects of ending the economically draining war. In December, a missile attack occurred over Mauritania in a known guerrilla warfare area against two planes used by a U.S. government relief agency. One plane was downed, killing five crewmen.

Domestic Affairs. There were no major domestic crises and no significant protests or demonstrations by students, workers, or Muslim fundamentalists in Morocco in 1988, as had been the case in previous years. The economy improved somewhat although fundamental problems persisted. On September 1, Morocco received a new standby credit of $270 million from the International Monetary Fund (IMF) to cover financial obligations for 16 months through December 1989. The country continued to abide by the IMF's structural adjustment program (instituted in 1983) involving greater privatization of the public sector and reduction of government subsidies.

Part of the king's purpose in pursuing greater regional cooperation is to overcome domestic economic problems. Already thousands of Algerian tourists have crossed into Morocco to buy the many consumer goods not available at home. Additionally, agricultural and energy-related projects between both countries were being advanced and implemented. As one example, both countries agreed in September to construct a pipeline to carry Algerian natural gas across Morocco to Western Europe.

JOHN P. ENTELIS, *Fordham University*

MOTION PICTURES

The year 1988 was a controversial one in the world of motion pictures. The most dramatic instance revolved around the release of Martin Scorsese's *The Last Temptation of Christ,* based on the novel by Nikos Kazantzakis, and went beyond mere words to picket lines and demonstrations. Various religious groups denounced the film as blasphemous, in some cases even before representatives had seen it, because it allegedly rejected the view of Jesus Christ as infallible and incapable of harboring doubts about his martyrdom. The film's sequence depicting Christ fantasizing on the cross about leading a normal life that would include sex and a family was especially objectionable to some, although ultimately Christ concludes that that this fantasy is a temptation of the devil and that He must die to complete God's will.

The result of the protests had mostly the opposite effect from what was intended. The widespread media coverage gave the movie enormous free publicity, and there were long lines of the curious eager to learn what the fuss was about. The picket lines soon waned, but the protests did succeed in making some theater operators decide not to play the film.

In another controversy—the battle against coloring old black and white movies—the opposition to the practice won a partial victory. During his final months in office, President Ronald Reagan signed legislation that called for a 13-member National Film Preservation Board with the power to designate as many as 25 films a year as classics. Should such films be colored or otherwise altered "without the participation of the principal director, screenwriter, or other creators," accompanying information to that effect would be required.

Vice-President George Bush, in his criticism of Gov. Michael Dukakis for his membership in the American Civil Liberties Union (ACLU), created still another controversy impinging on the film industry. In the first presidental campaign debate, Bush denounced the ACLU's opposition to the Motion Picture Association of America (MPAA) rating system—which can prohibit underage children from attending a film—saying that he liked the ratings. The ACLU countered with a memorandum to its affiliates explaining that the organization did not oppose voluntary advisory systems, but indicating that the current sytem was not merely advisory, but also restrictive in that an X-rating removes the parents entirely from the decision-making process.

Costly Strike. For nearly six months of the year, a labor dispute was a prime topic in the movie and television industries. A strike by the Writers Guild of America lasted 22 weeks and brought delays in film production and television shows planned for the fall season. A crucial

TM & © 1988 Lucasfilm Ltd. All Rights Reserved. Courtesy of Lucasfilm Ltd.

Jeff Bridges plays the maverick 1940s automobile inventor and manufacturer Preston Tucker in the stylish "Tucker: The Man and His Dream," directed by Francis Ford Coppola.

issue, part of the infighting relating to changing industry patterns, was the matter of residuals. Producers and writers were at odds over how much the writers would be paid for films and television shows earning increasing profits abroad. When the final settlement came, there was no clear victory for either camp.

New Demographics. For many years Hollywood has tended to aim a large proportion of films at the teenage audience, which surveys have shown is the key to big box-office results. But a new survey by the MPAA was surprising. Things were changing; the percentage of older moviegoers was increasing.

Statistics revealed that the number of people over 40 years of age who went to the movies was 56% higher in 1987 than in 1986. Jack Valenti, president of the MPAA, asserted: "The movie world need no longer be girdled around by boundaries set by the very young."

There were signs that producers were beginning to free themselves from slavish adherence to the demands of the youth market. During the summer, numerous films were released that catered to adult audiences in addition to the fluff targeted for teenagers during vacation time.

Strong Performances. Many stars excelled in a variety of demanding roles in the year's

THE ACCIDENTAL TOURIST. Director, Lawrence Kasdan; screenplay by Frank Galati and Mr. Kasdan, based on the book by Anne Tyler. With William Hurt, Kathleen Turner, Geena Davis.

THE ACCUSED. Director, Jonathan Kaplan; screenplay by Tom Topor. With Kelly McGillis, Jodie Foster.

ANOTHER WOMAN. Written and directed by Woody Allen. With Gena Rowlands, Mia Farrow, Ian Holm, Blythe Danner, Gene Hackman, Betty Buckley, John Houseman.

AU REVOIR LES ENFANTS. Written and directed by Louis Malle. With Gaspard Manesse, Raphaël Fejtö, François Négret.

BABETTE'S FEAST. Director, Gabriel Axel; screenplay by Mr. Axel, from a novel by Isak Dinesen. With Stéphane Audran, Birgitte Federspiel, Bodil Kjer.

BEACHES. Director, Garry Marshall; screenplay by Mary Agnes Donoghue, based on the novel by Iris Rainer Dart. With Bette Midler, Barbara Hershey.

BETRAYED. Director, Costa Gavras; screenplay by Joe Eszterhas. With Debra Winger, Tom Berenger.

BEETLEJUICE. Director, Tim Burton; screenplay by Michael McDowell, Warren Skaaren. With Alec Baldwin, Geena Davis, Michael Keaton.

BIG. Director, Penny Marshall; screenplay by Gary Ross and Anne Spielberg. With Tom Hanks, Elizabeth Perkins, Robert Loggia, John Heard, David Moscow.

BIG BUSINESS. Director, Jim Abrahams; screenplay by Dori Pierson, Marc Rubel. With Bette Midler, Lily Tomlin, Fred Ward, Edward Herrmann, Michele Placido.

BILOXI BLUES. Director, Mike Nichols; screenplay by Neil Simon, based on his play. With Matthew Broderick.

BRIGHT LIGHTS, BIG CITY. Director, James Bridges; screenplay by Jay McInerney, based on his novel. With Michael J. Fox.

BULL DURHAM. Written and directed by Ron Shelton. With Kevin Costner, Susan Sarandon, Tim Robbins.

CLARA'S HEART. Director, Robert Mulligan; screenplay by Mark Medoff, based on the novel by Joseph Olshan. With Whoopi Goldberg.

CLEAN AND SOBER. Director, Glenn Gordon Caron; screenplay by Tod Carroll. With Michael Keaton.

COCOON: THE RETURN. Director, Daniel Petrie; screenplay by Stephen McPherson, from a story by Mr. McPherson and Elizabeth Bradley. With Don Ameche, Wilford Brimley, Hume Cronyn, Jack Gilford, Steve Guttenberg, Maureen Stapleton, Jessica Tandy, Gwen Verdon, Tahnee Welch.

COLORS. Director, Dennis Hopper; screenplay by Michael Schiffer. With Robert Duvall, Sean Penn.

COMING TO AMERICA. Director, John Landis; screenplay by David Sheffield and Barry W. Blaustein, story by Eddie Murphy. With Eddie Murphy, Arsenio Hall.

CROSSING DELANCEY. Director, Joan Micklin Silver; screenplay by Susan Sandler, based on her play. With Amy Irving, Peter Riegert.

A CRY IN THE DARK. Director, Fred Schepisi; screenplay by Robert Caswell and Mr. Schepisi. With Meryl Streep, Sam Neill.

DA. Director, Matt Clark; screenplay by Hugh Leonard. With Bernard Hughes, Martin Sheen, William Hickey.

DANGEROUS LIAISONS. Director, Stephen Frears; screenplay by Christopher Hampton, based on his play. With Glenn Close, John Malkovich, Michelle Pfeiffer.

DEAD POOL. Director, Buddy Van Horn; screenplay by Steve Sharon. With Clint Eastwood.

DEAD RINGERS. Director, David Cronenberg; screenplay by Mr. Cronenberg and Norman Snider. With Jeremy Irons, Genevieve Bujold.

DEAR AMERICA: LETTERS HOME FROM VIETNAM. Director, Bill Couturie; screenplay by Richard Dewhurst and Mr. Couturie. (Documentary, with readings by Robert De Niro, Michael J. Fox, Kathleen Turner, Ellen Burstyn, Howard Rollins, Jr., and Robin Williams.)

DIE HARD. Director, John McTiernan; screenplay by Jeb Stuart and Steven E. deSouza. With Bruce Willis, Bonnie Bedelia, Alan Rickman.

DIRTY ROTTEN SCOUNDRELS. Director, Frank Oz; screenplay by Dale Launer, Stanley Shapiro, Paul Henning. With Steve Martin, Michael Caine.

EIGHT MEN OUT. Written and directed by John Sayles, based on the book by Eliot Asinof. With John Cusack, Clifton James, Michael Lerner, Christopher Lloyd, Charlie Sheen, Mr. Sayles, and Studs Terkel.

EVERYBODY'S ALL-AMERICAN. Director, Taylor Hackford; screenplay by Tom Rickman, from the novel by Frank Deford. With Dennis Quaid, Jessica Lange, Timothy Hutton.

A FISH CALLED WANDA. Director, Charles Crichton; screenplay by John Cleese. With John Cleese, Jamie Lee Curtis, Kevin Kline, Michael Palin.

FRANTIC. Director, Roman Polanski; screenplay by Mr. Polanski and Gerard Brach. With Harrison Ford, Betty Buckley, Emmanuelle Seigner.

THE GOOD MOTHER. Director, Leonard Nimoy; screenplay by Michael Bortman, based on the novel by Sue Miller. With Diane Keaton, Asia Vieira.

GORILLAS IN THE MIST. Director, Michael Apted; screenplay by Anna Hamilton Phelan. With Sigourney Weaver.

HAIRSPRAY. Written and directed by John Waters. With Sonny Bono, Divine.

A HANDFUL OF DUST. Director, Charles Sturridge; screenplay by Tim Sullivan, Derek Granger, and Mr. Sturridge, from the novel by Evelyn Waugh. With James Wilby, Kristin Scott Thomas, Rupert Graves, Anjelica Huston.

HOTEL TERMINUS: THE LIFE AND TIMES OF KLAUS BARBIE. Director, Marcel Ophuls. (A documentary).

THE HOUSE ON CARROLL STREET. Director, Peter Yates; screenplay by Walter Bernstein. With Kelly McGillis, Jeff Daniels, Mandy Patinkin, Jessica Tandy.

IMAGINE: JOHN LENNON. Director, Andrew Solt. (A documentary).

THE LAND BEFORE TIME. Director, Don Bluth; screenplay by Stu Krieger, from a story by Judy Freudberg and Tony Geiss. Animation.

THE LAST TEMPTATION OF CHRIST. Director, Martin Scorsese; screenplay by Paul Schrader, based on the novel by Nikos Kazantzakis. With Willem Dafoe, Harvey Keitel, Barbara Hershey, Harry Dean Stanton, David Bowie.

MADAME SOUSATZKA. Director, John Schlesinger; screenplay by Ruth Prawer Jhabvala and Mr. Schlesinger, from the novel by Bernice Rubens. With Shirley MacLaine.

MARRIED TO THE MOB. Director, Jonathan Demme; screenplay by Barry Strugatz and Mark R. Burns. With Michelle Pfeiffer, Matthew Modine, Dean Stockwell.

MIDNIGHT RUN. Director, Martin Brest; screenplay by George Gallo. With Robert De Niro, Charles Grodin.

THE MILAGRO BEANFIELD WAR. Director, Robert Redford; screenplay by David Ward and John Nichols. With Chick Vennera, Sonia Braga, John Heard, Christopher Walken, Melanie Griffith.

MILES FROM HOME. Director, Gary Sinise; screenplay by Chris Gerolmo. With Brian Dennehy, Richard Gere, Kevin Anderson, Helen Hunt, John Malkovich.

MISSISSIPPI BURNING. Director, Alan Parker; screenplay by Chris Gerolmo. With Gene Hackman, Willem Dafoe.

MOON OVER PARADOR. Director, Paul Mazursky; screenplay by Leon Capetanos and Mr. Mazursky. With Richard Dreyfuss, Raul Julia, Sonia Braga.

MYSTIC PIZZA. Director, Donald Petrie; screenplay by Amy Jones, Perry Howze, Randy Howze, and Alfred Uhry. With Julia Roberts, Annabeth Gish, Lili Taylor, William R. Moses, Adam Storke, Conchata Ferrell.

THE NAKED GUN. Director, David Zucker; screenplay by Mr. Zucker, Jerry Zucker, Jim Abrahams, Pat Proft. With Leslie Nielsen, Priscilla Presley.

A NEW LIFE. Written and directed by Alan Alda. With Mr. Alda, Hal Linden, Ann-Margret, Veronica Hamel, Mary Kay Place.

A NIGHTMARE ON ELM STREET 4: THE DREAM MASTER. Director, Renny Harlin; screenplay by Brian Helgeland and Scott Pierce. With Robert Englund.

MR. NORTH. Director, Danny Huston; screenplay by Janet Roach, John Huston, and James Costigan, based on the novel *Theophilus North* by Thornton Wilder. With Anthony Edwards, Robert Mitchum, Lauren Bacall, Harry Dean Stanton, Anjelica Huston, Tammy Grimes, David Warner, Christopher Durang.

PASCALI'S ISLAND. Written and directed by James Dearden, based on the novel by Barry Unsworth. With Ben Kingsley, Charles Dance, Helen Mirren.

Baseball was a subject of two popular films of 1988. In "Eight Men Out," left, director and writer John Sayles explored the many-faceted story of the 1919 World Series fixing plot of the Chicago White Sox. In its scope, the movie went beyond the game to a story of America's dreams and disillusionment. "Bull Durham," below, featured Kevin Costner and Susan Sarandon as an over-the-hill player and a baseball groupie.

PATTY HEARST. Director, Paul Schrader; screenplay by Nicholas Kazan, based on the book *Every Secret Thing*. With Natasha Richardson.

PELLE THE CONQUEROR. Written and directed by Bille August, based on the novel by Martin Andersen Nexo. With Max von Sydow.

PUNCHLINE. Written and directed by David Seltzer. With Sally Field, Tom Hanks, John Goodman.

RAIN MAN. Director, Barry Levinson; screenplay by Ronald Bass and Barry Morrow. With Dustin Hoffman, Tom Cruise.

RED HEAT. Director, Walter Hill; screenplay by Harry Kleiner, Troy Kennedy Martin, and Mr. Hill. With Arnold Schwarzenegger, James Belushi, Peter Boyle.

ROCKET GIBRALTAR. Director, Daniel Petrie; screenplay by Amos Poe. With Burt Lancaster, Suzy Amis.

RUNNING ON EMPTY. Director, Sidney Lumet; screenplay by Naomi Foner. With Christine Lahti, Judd Hirsch, River Phoenix, Martha Plimpton, Jonas Abry.

SCROOGED. Director, Richard Donner; screenplay by Mitch Glazer and Michael O'Donoghue. With Bill Murray.

SHOOT TO KILL. Director, Roger Spottiswoode; screenplay by Harv Zimmel, Michael Burton, Daniel Petrie, Jr. With Sidney Poitier, Tom Berenger.

STAND AND DELIVER. Director, Ramon Menendez; screenplay by Tom Musca and Mr. Menendez. With Edward James Olmos.

STORMY MONDAY. Written and directed by Mike Figgis. With Melanie Griffith, Tommy Lee Jones, Sting.

SUNSET. Written and directed by Blake Edwards. With Bruce Willis, James Garner.

TALK RADIO. Director, Oliver Stone; screenplay by Mr. Stone and Eric Bogosian, based on Mr. Bogosian's play and the book *Talked to Death: The Life and Murder of Alan Berg*, by Stephen Singular. With Mr. Bogosian.

TEQUILA SUNRISE. Written and directed by Robert Towne. With Mel Gibson, Michelle Pfeiffer, Kurt Russell.

THINGS CHANGE. Director, David Mamet; screenplay by David Mamet and Shel Silverstein. With Don Ameche, Joe Mantegna.

TORCH SONG TRILOGY. Director, Paul Bogart; screenplay by Harvey Fierstein, based on his play. With Mr. Fierstein, Anne Bancroft, Matthew Broderick.

TRACK 29. Director, Nicolas Roeg; screenplay by Dennis Potter. With Theresa Russell.

TUCKER: THE MAN AND HIS DREAM. Director, Francis Ford Coppola; screenplay by Arnold Schulman and David Seidler. With Jeff Bridges.

TWINS. Director, Ivan Reitman; screenplay by William Davies, William Osborne, Timothy Harris, Herschel Weingrod. With Arnold Schwarzenegger, Danny DeVito.

THE UNBEARABLE LIGHTNESS OF BEING. Director, Philip Kaufman; screenplay by Jean-Claude Carrière and Mr. Kaufman. With Daniel Day-Lewis.

WHITE MISCHIEF. Director, Michael Radford; screenplay by Mr. Radford and Jonathan Gems, from the novel by James Fox. With Charles Dance, Sarah Miles, Greta Scacchi, Joss Ackland, Trevor Howard.

Photos © 1988 Orion Pictures Corporation. All Rights Reserved.

WHO FRAMED ROGER RABBIT. Director, Robert Zemeckis; director of animation, Richard Williams; screenplay by Jeffrey Price and Peter Seaman. With Bob Hoskins, Christopher Lloyd, Joanna Cassidy, Stubby Kaye, and animated characters.

WILLOW. Director, Ron Howard; screenplay by Bob Dolman, story by George Lucas. With Warwick Davis, Jean Marsh, Val Kilmer, Gavan O'Herlihy, Joanne Whalley, Billy Barty, Patricia Hayes.

WINGS OF DESIRE. Director, Wim Wenders; screenplay by Mr. Wenders and Peter Handke. With Bruno Ganz, Otto Sander, Peter Falk.

WITHOUT A CLUE. Director, Thom Eberhardt; screenplay by Gary Murphy and Larry Strawther. With Michael Caine, Ben Kingsley.

WOMEN ON THE VERGE OF A NERVOUS BREAKDOWN. Written and directed by Pedro Almodovar. With Carmen Maura.

WORKING GIRL. Director, Mike Nichols; screenplay by Kevin Wade. With Melanie Griffith, Harrison Ford, Sigourney Weaver.

A WORLD APART. Director, Chris Menges; screenplay by Shawn Slovo. With Barbara Hershey, Jodhi May, Linda Mvusi, Albee Lesotho.

new films. Jodie Foster was particularly brilliant as a rape victim who wants to see her attackers punished in *The Accused,* and critics remarked upon her steady growth as an actress. Sigourney Weaver went to great lengths for her impressive performance in *Gorillas in the Mist* as Dian Fossey, known for her research among gorillas and her stalwart (some might say obsessive) efforts to protect them from poachers before she was mysteriously murdered. In Rwanda, where the film was shot, Weaver, too, ventured among the gorillas and learned techniques for earning their trust.

Gena Rowlands gave a complex and moving performance as a woman learning to get in touch with her feelings and the reality of her life in Woody Allen's *Another Woman.* Shirley MacLaine played a character considerably older than herself in *Madame Sousatzka.* It was a flamboyant portrayal of a dominating piano teacher, the sort of star turn that often wins Oscar nominations. Although the praised *A World Apart,* dealing with apartheid in South Africa, did not have a long run, Barbara Hershey left an indelible impression as a fighter for racial equality. Diane Keaton won accolades for her portrayal of a mother fighting for custody of her daughter in *The Good Mother.* In *A Cry in the Dark,* based on a real-life case in Australia, Meryl Streep once again demonstrated her versatility with an engrossing and emotionally searing portrayal of a mother falsely accused of murdering her child.

The fortunes of actor Tom Hanks continued to rise. One of the year's most popular films was *Big,* in which Hanks charmed audiences as a boy who gets his wish to grow and proceeds to stumble into adult situations with which he must cope despite his adolescent mentality. He scored again as a stand-up comedian trying to make it to the top in *Punchline,* which also starred Sally Field.

Don Ameche continued his revived career in grand style playing a shoe-shine man who is mistaken for a Mafia don in David Mamet's clever *Things Change.* Another outstanding male performance was Forest Whitaker's depiction of musician Charlie Parker in *Bird,* the Clint Eastwood-directed drama about Parker's tragic life. Max Von Sydow was brilliant as a struggling immigrant father in the Danish import *Pelle the Conqueror.*

The most intricate assignments of the year went to Jeremy Irons and Bob Hoskins. Irons played two parts in David Cronenberg's bizarre *Dead Ringers*—twin brothers locked in psychological dependency. Hoskins had to act with animated characters in Robert Zemeckis' *Who Framed Roger Rabbit,* a film lauded for its technical virtuosity.

Not many actors get to play Jesus Christ on film. That distinction went to Willem Dafoe, who gave a sensitive title performance in Scorsese's *The Last Temptation of Christ.*

Director Martin Scorsese came under fire for "The Last Temptation of Christ." Labeled blasphemous by some religious groups, the film was not shown in many communities.

Noted Directors. Numerous directors of repute returned with new works. Francis Ford Coppola, whose last several films were not given the acclaim of his earlier efforts, made *Tucker: The Man and His Dream.* It had style and effervescence in its dramatization of the life of Preston Tucker (played with élan by Jeff Bridges), whose Tucker car was ahead of its time, much to the chagrin of the conventional auto industry. Sidney Lumet examined the residue from 1960s activism in *Running on Empty,* a drama set in the 1980s; Judd Hirsch and Christine Lahti played a couple still underground and wanted for their role in a protest bombing, while burgeoning star River Phoenix portrayed their son, striving to break away and face the future in the open. The civil-rights movement of the 1960s was recalled in Alan Parker's *Mississippi Burning.*

Constantine Costa-Gavras, known for his political films, unleashed *Betrayed,* a melodramatic look at racism in a right-wing fringe organization out to take over the government. Tom Berenger played a racist, with Debra Winger as the FBI agent investigating him and also falling for him. Another maker of political movies, Marcel Ophuls, unveiled his documentary *Hotel Terminus: The Life and Times of Klaus Barbie,* a fascinating four-and-one-half-hour inquiry into the historical and moral issues involving Barbie, his trial for World War II atrocities, and the complicity of those who used and protected him.

Barry Levinson directed Dustin Hoffman and Tom Cruise, playing brothers, in *Rain Man.* Mike Nichols directed Melanie Griffith, Sigourney Weaver, and Harrison Ford in

Working Girl. Lawrence Kasdan made *The Accidental Tourist,* starring William Hurt and Kathleen Turner. Garry Marshall teamed Bette Midler with Barbara Hershey in *Beaches,* offering Midler another chance at a dramatic role.

John Sayles turned to baseball with *Eight Men Out,* about the Chicago White Sox scandal of 1919. Another baseball film was the popular *Bull Durham,* directed by Ron Shelton and starring Susan Sarandon in an effervescent performance as a team groupie.

Jonathan Demme spoofed the Mafia with *Married to the Mob,* starring Michelle Pfeiffer. Martin Brest, another director with a light touch, costarred Robert De Niro and Charles Grodin in *Midnight Run,* an action-filled comedy about a bounty hunter and his quarry. Joan Micklin Silver, who has an eye for offbeat drama and comedy, scored with *Crossing Delancey,* a heartwarming story about a young Jewish woman (Amy Irving) from New York's lower East side who finds true love with a pickle salesman (Peter Riegert).

Moneymakers. True to form, numerous films that did not excite the critics did well at the box office. Eddie Murphy in *Coming to America* attracted his fans even though the story that featured him as an African prince was less than compelling. *Die Hard* gave Bruce Willis of television *Moonlighting* fame a chance to make a name for himself as an action hero. *Rambo III,* starring Sylvester Stallone in a repeat of his money-making role, was a high grosser, although it cost $60 million to make. Another popular attraction was Paul Hogan's reprise as the Australian outback hero in *Crocodile Dundee II.* One modest film liked by critics showed surprising success at the box office for a small-scale project. *A Fish Called Wanda* received enthusiastic word of mouth, largely because of John Cleese's delightful comic ability.

The general box-office picture was healthy. Despite the proliferation of videocassettes and home viewing, the total of some $4.6 billion in admissions spent by moviegoers in the first eight months of 1988 represented an increase of 8% over the same period in 1987.

New Horizons. Even as foreign-language films were having an increasingly difficult time competing with American products, programmers of film festivals and museums were casting an eye toward parts of the world where new talent and activity were observed. The Far East was an area that drew particular enthusiasm as the New York Film Festival showcased films from China, South Korea, and Taiwan. However, the outlook was for such films to get limited exhibition in major cultural centers, but not much exposure throughout most of the United States.

See also PRIZES AND AWARDS.

WILLIAM WOLF, *New York University*

MOZAMBIQUE

The central fact of life in Mozambique in 1988 was the unrelenting attacks by guerrillas of the Mozambique National Resistance (Renamo) which had cut rail lines and sacked countless villages.

Figures released by President Joaquim Chissano's government indicated that Renamo had forced closure of 595 clinics, 31% of the nation's health network, and more than 2,500 schools. Renamo, which has an estimated 25,000 followers, had killed an estimated 100,000 between 1986 and late 1988 and had forced almost one million persons to flee the country. In addition, local warlords and bandits murdered and stole from the farmers, most of whom stopped planting crops.

Mozambique, already impoverished by ill-conceived socialist programs and devastating droughts, has become the poorest state in Africa with a per capita income of $95 per year, half of the 1980 figure. Relief agencies, which have expended $22 million in trucks and tractors alone since 1984, were finding it almost impossible to feed the refugees in their camps because Renamo controlled the roads and was attacking the food convoys.

Foreign Policy. Renamo, originally supported by Rhodesia and South Africa, has been denounced by South Africa, which was training three battalions of Mozambique's ill-prepared army to guard Cabora Bassa Dam. The United States condemned Renamo, but did little officially to aid Chissano's government. However, its representatives joined an international conference in April 1988 which pledged $270 million to meet Mozambique's emergency needs.

Communist bloc states, Britain, Portugal, and Italy, in addition to South Africa, were involved in training and equipping the Mozambique army. Zimbabwe had 15,000 men guarding the vital railway to Beira and Malawi aided in keeping the route to Ncala open. Mozambique's Minister of Cooperation met South African President Pieter W. Botha in April to revive the Joint Security Committee provided for by the 1984 Nkomati Pact, and in September Botha promised to increase economic aid to Mozambique.

HARRY A. GAILEY, *San Jose State University*

MOZAMBIQUE • Information Highlights

Official Name: People's Republic of Mozambique.
Location: Southeastern coast of Africa.
Area: 309,494 sq mi (801 590 km²).
Population (mid-1988 est.): 15,100,000.
Chief City (1987 est.): Maputo, the capital, 1,006,765.
Government: *Head of state,* Joaquim A. Chissano, president (took office November 1986). *Head of government,* Mário da Graca Machungo, prime minister (took office July 1986). *Legislature* (unicameral)—People's Assembly.
Gross National Product (1987 est. U.S.$): $1,300,000,000.

Philip Glass' "The Making of the Representative from Planet 8" was presented at the Houston Opera House during the summer. The new opera also was staged in Washington, telecast nationally, and released on disc.

MUSIC

The year 1988 was a good one for notable moments. It was, for instance, the year of Irving Berlin's 100th birthday. The most prolific of popular songwriters, Berlin's more than 1,000 songs are by now part of the American grain. (*See* feature article, IRVING BERLIN AT 100, page 80.)

The year saw the 70th birthday of conductor and composer Leonard Bernstein, along with a generous series of musical celebrations to commemorate the day. It was the year singer-songwriter Tracy Chapman arrived on the scene, the year of the Irish rock band U2's new album *Rattle and Hum*, the year that African and Caribbean sounds and rhythms were welcomed into rock music.

This was the year for current history and science fiction to make their debuts in modern opera, and a great year for opera in general, as opera houses throughout the United States produced little-known works, new works, and newly envisioned versions of the old standards. And, the First New York International Festival of the Arts opened in 1988—a huge multiform effort that brought in musicians and composers from around the world.

Classical

New Music. Two musical styles remained in opposition in 1988: Minimalism, a form based on open, consonant tonality and repeated, slowly evolving phrases; and what might be called a "mainstream" classical language—a broad variety of styles taking in everything from academically rigid atonality to lush neo-Romanticism. In fact, neo-Romantic eclecticism seems to have the popular edge, because its blending of familiar form and language with novel touches strikes a chord among listeners who find Minimalism too simplistic and atonality and serialism too harsh.

Minimalist music has progressed beyond some of its original hallmarks. For instance, the notion of a slow evolution of musical themes over a seemingly endless time span has given way to a quicker progression of changes; and the early small ensembles have been replaced by full orchestras and even grand opera.

The major contributions to Minimalist music in 1987–88 were the opera *Nixon in China* by composer John Adams, with a libretto by Alice Goodman and staging by the iconoclastic Peter Sellars; and two new works by Philip Glass—his fourth full-scale opera, *The Making of the Representative from Planet 8*, and a theater piece, *1000 Airplanes on the Roof*. The Adams work actually was unveiled in late 1987; but 1988 was the year of its great impact, with performances in Washington, a national telecast, and a disc release.

Adams, Goodman, and Sellars grappled directly with the question of opera's contemporary relevance. Not only was the plot drawn from an event less than two decades distant and involving familiar political figures; but it also provides some broadly applicable observations on global politics, psychology, and the sweep of history. In this regard, the work has some recent predecessors, most notably An-

thony Davis' *X* (about civil-rights activist Malcolm X), and Philip Glass' *Satyagraha,* about Gandhi.

Philip Glass' latest opera, his fourth full-scale work, uses science fiction for its libretto: It is a collaboration with the English author Doris Lessing on the fourth book in her science-fiction series, *Canopus in Argos.* In addition to *The Making of the Representative from Planet 8,* Glass and Lessing also were at work on an operatic setting of the second book, *The Marriages Between Zones Three, Four, and Five. Representative* did not fare well when it was presented in Houston in July: Critics found Glass to be resting too heavily on his own well-worn stylistic conventions, and much of the setting was said to be lacking in operatic intensity. Glass' recent chamber opera, *The Fall of the House of Usher,* suffered similar criticism in May.

1000 Airplanes on the Roof, with a book by David Henry Hwang (who also had a Broadway Tony winner in 1988 with *M. Butterfly*) was far more successful than Glass' operas. A 90-minute monodrama with continuous musical accompaniment, the work opened in Vienna and went to Philadelphia's American Music Theater Festival in September, at the start of a North American tour. The protagonist (who can be played by either a man or a woman; the Philadelphia production alternated) describes an abduction by beings from another planet, while Glass' music—forward moving and chromatic, but still full of his distant musical thumbprints—conveys as much as Hwang's text about the speaker's perception and mental state, and about the abduction itself.

In mainstream composition, premieres abounded, and it seemed that audience resistance to new music at last may be breaking down. One of the most striking new works of the year, Bright Sheng's *Lacerations,* was presented by Gerard Schwarz and the New York Chamber Symphony in April. Sheng, a 32-year-old composer born in China and trained in New York, composed the piece as a searing portrait of China's Cultural Revolution. Like many of the most successful non-Minimalist works, its language has a modernist spareness, but also a distinctly emotional undercurrent. Its effect is immediate and haunting.

Also from firmly within the compositional mainstream, the composer William Bolcom won the Pulitzer Prize in music for his "12 New Études," a varied and technically demanding set of works for the piano.

There were, of course, hundreds of premieres by composers working in the non-Minimalist style. During the summer a generous dose of mainstream music was supplied by the First New York International Festival of the Arts, a sprawling celebration that featured ensembles from around the world and focused exclusively on the 20th century—in art, music, dance, theater, and film. Several new works were commissioned by the festival itself; others were brought along for American premieres by such diverse foreign ensembles as England's Electric Phoenix, a vocal ensemble, and Japan's Soundspace Arc.

Performers. In the world of performance, the early instrument movement gained further ground. Once limited to Renaissance and Baroque music, early instrument advocates moved on to Mozart about a decade ago, and are now redoing Beethoven. In London, Roger Norrington and Christopher Hogwood both were performing and recording the Beethoven Symphonies, with Norrington's versions regarded as decidedly the more exciting. Norrington, who conducted his brisk-paced, clear-textured Beethoven in Boston during the summer, now was offering a fresh new look at the music of Berlioz. Meanwhile, conductors of modern (that is, standard) instrument orchestras have been departing from standard interpretations. In 1988, David Zinman, for one, was embarking on a series of Beethoven Symphony performances with the Baltimore Symphony that was taking scholarly findings into account. So far, the results have been refreshing.

In New York, a complete cycle of Franz Schubert's works began in January at the 92nd Street Y. The series, which would include contributions from some of the world's finest soloists and chamber ensembles, is performing the works chronologically. Since there are more than 1,000, the series will end only in 1997, the bicentennial of Schubert's birth.

Opera. In the world of opera, critics have continued to lament the passing of the Golden Age of great singers, but audiences still have their favorites. Luciano Pavarotti, Placido Domingo, and Kiri Te Kanawa are among the era's reigning superstars. Eva Marton, Ghena Dimitrova, and Hildegard Behrens may join them within the next few years.

At New York's Metropolitan Opera, the two final installments of Wagner's "Ring" cycle were mounted, completing a three-year project. The whole cycle would be produced in spring 1989.

The most colorful opera was offered during the summer, however. The St. Louis Opera, for example, put on three comparative rarities —Mozart's *La Finta Giardiniera,* Barber's *Vanessa,* and Weber's *Oberon.* At Spoleto U.S.A. in Charleston, SC, Dvorak's *Rusalka* and Carl Heinrich Graun's *Montezuma* were given rare stagings. And, while Mozart's *Marriage of Figaro* is performed frequently, it rarely has been done as Peter Sellars staged it, in a laundry room in a New York skyscraper.

The Sellars production was one of several unusual Mozart stagings the director has offered at Pepsico Summerfare in Purchase, NY. For the last few years, this small festival has

Carl Heinrich Graun's "Montezuma" was produced with unusual staging at Spoleto USA in Charleston, SC, in 1988.

© William Struhs

been regarded as the liveliest and most adventurous summer series in the New York area. Sadly, it was announced that 1988 would be its last year; it was losing more money than its corporate sponsors were willing to spend.

Russian Visits. The effect of *glasnost* (Soviet openness) on the musical world has been impressive. Early in the year a large company of Soviet performers went to Boston to collaborate with U.S. colleagues on a festival called "Making Music Together," a three-week series that included premieres of works by Schnittke, Dmitriev, and other Soviet composers with familiar names, but, until now, unknown works. In exchange, the Soviet Union was scheduled to host a U.S. dance festival during 1989.

More Soviet soloists and conductors than usual arrived as guests of U.S. orchestras, including two highly regarded young players—the pianist Vladimir Viardo and the violinist Vladimir Spivakov—who have not been heard on U.S. shores in a decade. And 58 Russian students joined with 52 U.S. conservatory students to form the American-Soviet Youth Orchestra, which toured the United States in August, then visited Russia.

Both the Baltimore Symphony and the New York Philharmonic toured the Soviet Union. The Baltimore players ended their concerts with resident composer Christopher Rouse's orchestral version of "Twist and Shout," a rock tune that the Isley Brothers and the Beatles first made popular.

Celebrations. It was the year of Leonard Bernstein's 70th birthday (*see* special report, page 383), Elliott Carter's 80th, and Ned Rorem's 65th, all celebrated either with retrospectives or individual works on the programs of numerous orchestras and ensembles.

The biggest celebration of all, however, was given to Bernstein at Tanglewood, the Boston Symphony Orchestra's summer home, where Bernstein worked as a student under the festival's founder, Serge Koussevitzky. The concerts offered in Bernstein's honor lasted four days, and included several of his compositions. The last concert, a gala conducted by Bernstein and Seiji Ozawa, was attended by an audience of 14,000, and included a set of variations composed by Lukas Foss, John Williams, Leon Kirchner, John Corigliano, Jacob Druckman, and William Schuman.

Bernstein, of course, was continuing to conduct and record with a combination of youthful energy and the interpretive wisdom that age brings. His Mahler performances, both on tour with the Vienna Philharmonic and in his latest series of Deutsche Grammophon discs, were revelatory. He announced that he intended to collaborate with Martha Graham on a piece which would have a decidedly American theme.

End Notes. Financial concerns have become pressing throughout the musical world. The 1987 strike of the Detroit Symphony was settled before it could do much damage, but other orchestras have not been so lucky. The New Orleans Symphony cancelled its 1988 season, and the Oklahoma Symphony was disbanded. The Baltimore players opened their season with a walkout, which still was unresolved by late 1988. And, of course, the Pepsico festival is no more.

Leave-takings occurred in more than their usual number. Zubin Mehta announced that he would not renew his contract with the New York Philharmonic (it expires in 1991); Bruce Crawford, the general manager of the Metropolitan Opera, resigned his post in favor of a corporate job; Charles Wadsworth, founder of the Chamber Music Society of Lincoln Center, announced that the 1988 season (his 20th) would be his last, and cellist Fred Sherry was named his successor. And at the New York City Opera, Beverly Sills announced that she would retire in early 1989 and would be succeeded as general manager by the conductor Christopher Keene.

Together, these changes meant that every musical performance organization in New York's Lincoln Center underwent a major shakeup in 1988. Occasional games of musical chairs help to keep things lively, however, and New York was not the only city to see major managerial changes. In February, Terry McEwen announced his retirement as general director of the San Francisco Opera, and director Lotfi Mansouri was appointed to succeed him. Mansouri began his tenure with a promise to make opera less stodgy by mixing standard operatic fare with Broadway musicals in an operatic context—something Beverly Sills has done with some success at the New York City Opera.

ALLAN KOZINN
"The New York Times"

Leonard Bernstein at 70

It was a night to remember in Lenox, MA—in fact, *four* spectacular nights—of musical events to honor the versatile and brilliant conductor Leonard Bernstein on his 70th birthday. Endowed with diverse musical gifts, Bernstein is a world-class conductor, a gifted composer in both the classical and popular idioms, an excellent pianist, and a charismatic teacher. The fact that such luminaries as Seiji Ozawa, Michael Tilson Thomas, Beverly Sills, John Williams, and cellist Mstislav Rostropovich participated in the gala is an indication of his stature.

The actual birthday concert on August 25 was a star-studded fund-raiser for the Tanglewood Music Center, the Boston Symphony's summer education unit in Lenox, where the

© Joseph McNally/Sygma

maestro has been teaching since 1948. "Tanglewood is where I most wanted to celebrate my birthday," Bernstein said. "I can't think of any place in the world where I'm happier." The last concert of the weekend, and the only one conducted by the maestro in his active, emotive style, had 14,000 people in attendance and was televised, in part, live to Europe.

A native of Lawrence, MA, born on Aug. 25, 1918, of Russian-Jewish immigrants, Leonard Bernstein went to Harvard hoping to become a pianist. Upon graduation he attended the Curtis Institute of Music in Philadelphia with a focus on conducting. He also studied under Serge Koussevitzky, his mentor, at Tanglewood during the summers of 1940 and 1941.

Bernstein's debut in 1943 came unexpectedly. As a 25-year-old assistant conductor with the New York Philharmonic he replaced the ailing Bruno Walter, a guest conductor. Without benefit of rehearsal, Bernstein's performance of a difficult program was so extraordinary that it made page one of *The New York Times.* The next year was a prolific one, with premieres of his First Symphony *(Jeremiah),* the ballet *Fancy Free,* and a Broadway musical, *On the Town.* Then came the musicals *Candide, Wonderful Town,* and *West Side Story,* music for the film *On the Waterfront,* and the ballet *The Age of Anxiety.*

Bernstein became musical director of the New York Philharmonic in 1958, the first American-born conductor to head a leading symphony orchestra. In 1958, in a series of televised Young People's Concerts, his talent as a teacher was enjoyed by viewers of all ages. After resigning from the Philharmonic in 1969, he composed such works as the "theater piece" *Mass* (1971) and the ballet *Dybbuk* (1974).

AP/Wide World

Leonard Bernstein, above, conducts the last concert of a weekend gala at Tanglewood, celebrating his 70th birthday. Kitty Carlisle Hart, right with the maestro, was cochair of a pregala dinner on August 25, attended by throngs of well-wishers.

The Human Rights Now! concert, a six-week tour featuring (l-r) Youssou N'Dour, Peter Gabriel, Bruce Springsteen, Tracy Chapman, and Sting, was organized by Amnesty International to mark the 40th anniversary of the Universal Declaration of Human Rights.

AP/Wide World

Popular and Jazz

Another boom year for the record business was highlighted in 1988 by a number of aesthetically unrelated pop-music trends.

Singer-songwriters, particularly women, made a big comeback in 1988, spurred in part by Suzanne Vega's 1987 success with the hit single "Luka." Tracy Chapman, a black singer-songwriter from Boston, came out of nowhere to have a major hit single with "Fast Car" and to sell more than 2 million copies of her self-titled debut album. Singing songs that frequently touched upon the economic and social concerns of the lower classes, Chapman also underscored the traditional commitment that folk-based artists have had to social causes. Highlighting her auspicious year, Chapman was invited to join Bruce Springsteen, Sting, Peter Gabriel, and Youssou N'Dour on a Human Rights Now! tour, a six-week caravan that performed on five continents in support of Amnesty International.

Chapman was hardly the only new singer-songwriter on the scene, however. Well-received debut albums were released by Michelle Shocked (*Short Sharp Shocked*), Toni Childs (*Union*), and Julia Fordham (*Julia Fordham*). Some of the most highly touted young country artists—specifically, Lyle Lovett and Nanci Griffith—also wrote songs that occupied the borders between folk, rock, and country. John Hiatt, a veteran of the singer-songwriter world, made his second great album in as many years, *Slow Turning*.

Heavy metal, generally dismissed by critics and rarely heard on the radio, is a rock genre that has flourished since the early 1970s. The core audience for the music is adolescent boys, but some of the most successful recent bands have downplayed the genre's sledgehammer guitars to emphasize melody and glamor. Bands like Bon Jovi and Def Leppard have used this combination to bring females into their audience and sell millions of records; Leppard's *Hysteria* rode high on the charts throughout the year, while Bon Jovi's *New Jersey* was released to instant sales success. Aerosmith, a hard-rock band from the 1970s that was influenced heavily by the Rolling Stones, consolidated its comeback in 1988.

Metallica was one of the most stunning heavy metal successes of the year. The group's *. . . And Justice for All* leapt into the Top 10. In contrast to most of its heavy-metal competiton, Metallica has gotten significant critical support for songs that often deal with the horror of senseless violence. Its success, however, reaffirms the notion that heavy metal's popularity is derived more from courting the audience through live concerts than from appealing to older tastemakers.

The kings of the heavy-metal genre, Led Zeppelin, have not recorded since 1979 but never have disappeared from rock radio. The quartet regrouped to close an all-day concert in New York celebrating the 40th anniversary of Atlantic Records; the drums once powered by the late John Bonham were handled by his son Jason. Zeppelin's two principals, guitarist Jimmy Page and singer Robert Plant, each released solo albums and toured in 1988.

Another British group whose members have been going their separate ways is the Rolling Stones. That band's two main players, singer Mick Jagger and guitarist Keith Richards, released solo albums. Jagger's *Primitive Cool* drew mixed reviews and lackluster sales; the singer's first-ever solo tour traveled through Japan and Australia but avoided Europe and

America. Richards' *Talk Is Cheap,* his first recording project without the Stones, won kudos from critics and spurred speculation that the Stones would regroup for a new album and tour in 1989.

Rap music, which in some respects is black youth's equivalent to white heavy metal, continued to produce new stars—including Jazzy Jeff, Doug E. Fresh, Public Enemy, and Salt 'n' Peppa—and to sell plenty of records. Still, limited radio airplay and a tendency for many rappers to fail to produce follow-up hits made some suspect that the genre was beginning to peak.

Two teenage singers, Tiffany and Debbie Gibson, each launched numerous Top 10 singles from debut albums. The pair illustrated the spectrum of teen stardom. Tiffany generally is regarded as the creation of careful handlers, who steered her toward appropriate material (such as "I Think We're Alone Now," an old hit by Tommy James and the Shondells), and stoked the promotional fires by sending the singer on a lip-synch tour of U.S. shopping malls. In contrast, Gibson wrote all of the material on her first album (including the title track, "Out of the Blue"), displaying a definite talent that well could develop despite the starmaking machinery that threatens to overwhelm any young star.

Debbie Gibson, a talented teenage singer-songwriter from Merrick, NY, made a successful musical debut in 1988 with the hit album "Out of the Blue."

A number of mainstream rock acts also made career breakthroughs in 1988, including the Australian band INXS, which toured for much of the year in support of its hit album *Kick.* Another Australian band, Midnight Oil, found more modest success, doubly significant because of the political nature of many of its songs.

Many of the big stars of the 1980s continued their hot streaks with major albums and tours. U2 followed the massive success of *The Joshua Tree* by producing a movie (*Rattle and Hum*) that chronicled both the band's triumphant tour and the recording of studio tracks for the film's soundtrack.

Michael Jackson and Bruce Springsteen followed up their 1987 albums with major tours that dominated concert stages for much of 1988. Jackson's tour spent the year wandering from the United States to Europe and back again for a series of concerts that the singer said would be his last. Springsteen's initially limited tour was extended to include a series of European dates, and ultimately concluded after he and the E Street Band joined in on Amnesty International's Human Rights Now! tour. To kick off the latter, Springsteen released an EP of live concert material that included a version of Bob Dylan's "Chimes of Freedom," which became the closing number of the Amnesty shows.

Prince, the funk and rock musician who stirs controversy with his provocative lyrics, added to his string of critical kudos while the mass popularity he obtained with *Purple Rain* continued to wane. Still, some critics considered his *Lovesexy* album to be among the best of his career, and his highly theatrical tour was a major hit in Europe, if not in the United States.

Another tour that attracted much attention was the reunion of Frank Sinatra's "Rat Pack," a crew of Hollywood hobnobbers that gained gossip column notoriety in the early 1960s. In addition to Sinatra, the tour included Sammy Davis, Jr., and Dean Martin; after Martin dropped out for health reasons, Liza Minnelli became the third "rat packer."

Pop music was also in the movie theaters, with some of the year's best-selling albums soundtracks spawned by films. The soundtrack to *Dirty Dancing* continued to sell through 1988 and was one of the major hits of the year, with a second album of songs culled from the nostalgic film also doing good business. *Imagine,* a documentary on the life of the late John Lennon, also produced a soundtrack. The most highly regarded music movie of the year, however, was the Clint Eastwood-directed biography of seminal jazzman Charlie Parker, *Bird.* With the popularity of compact discs already prompting the reissue of classic jazz recordings, the film put a spotlight on the saxophonist who was one of the prime architects of bebop.

© Beth Gwinn/Retna

Grammy winner Randy Travis was at the forefront of a trend in country music toward younger, more traditional performers, while also achieving pop success.

Contemporary jazz continued to struggle with its past and a present that is not always receptive to new sounds. The small amount of jazz that made it onto commercial radio generally fell into a fusion style that mixed elements of rock and funk into a slick instrumental package. Jazz purists dismissed such music but generally were supportive of the surprise crossover hit of the year: Bobby McFerrin's *Simple Pleasures*. McFerrin, a supple vocalist who uses overdubs to create jazz-style a cappella music, scored a left-field hit with "Don't Worry, Be Happy."

A flock of players spearheaded by the Marsalis brothers—trumpeter Wynton and saxophonist Branford—continued to produce music devoted to reviving the bop style of the 1960s. Saxophonist Steve Coleman was one of a group of Brooklyn-based musicians who made waves with postmodern music directly linked to such traditions as bebop and computer-generated sounds.

New record labels were launched to introduce adventurous music to both jazz fans and others bored with instrumental new-age music. Pangaea, financed in part by the rock star Sting, released conceptual albums by the adventurous New York producer Kip Hanrahan as well as work by Argentina's Astor Piazzolla. The most notable record on CBS' revived Portrait label was *Virgin Beauty*, a well-received recording from a pioneer of avant-garde jazz, Ornette Coleman.

The jazz world mourned the death of the consummate arranger and pianist, Gil Evans, who oversaw the recording of such seminal Miles Davis records as *Kind of Blue* and *Sketches of Spain*. Evans was a master at or-

chestrating a tune while still giving players room to contribute their own individual style.

The improvisatory nature of jazz traditionally has combined elements of various types of music; today the same thing is happening in pop music through a movement that critics have dubbed "world beat." Talking Heads' *Naked* was indicative of the trend, incorporating Caribbean influences and African players into music that retained its intellectual New York edge. Furthermore, in the wake of Paul Simon's successful adaptation of South African pop for his *Graceland* LP, a variety of African musicians got a much wider hearing among Western pop fans.

The cross-pollination of musical influences is regarded widely as one of the most intriguing trends of the late 1980s. Among the styles gaining international audiences are soca from Trinidad and Antigua, which blends old-fashioned calypso and modern funk; soukous from Zaire, an effervescent Central African variation of the rhumba with an emphasis on the electric guitar; and zouk, a buoyant style of party music from the French Caribbean.

The world beat trend, helped by domestic releases of foreign albums, also has helped to bring a wide variety of musicians to American stages. One of the most unusual tours of the year was mounted by the Bulgarian State Radio and Television Female Vocal Choir, whose *Le Mystère des Voix Bulgares* became a favorite among followers of international sounds. The choir takes native folk music to ethereal extremes with crystal-clear voices blending to create a dense harmonic weave.

This interest in foreign rhythms undoubtedly helped Ziggy Marley find an audience for his reggae album, *Conscious Party*. Marley is the son of the late reggae superstar Bob Marley. Coincidentally, as the son's album was going gold, signifying sales of more than 500,000 copies, his father's *Legend* album passed the million mark.

Country music continued to be enlivened by a younger breed of performer grouped under the rubric of "new traditionalists." The smooth-singing Randy Travis continued to consolidate his position as the genre's top star when his *Old 8x10* achieved solid sales. K. T. Oslin, a singer virtually unknown until after her 40th birthday, released a successful second album, *This Woman*.

Britain continued to pepper the Broadway stage with musicals, including *Les Misérables*, Andrew Lloyd Webber's *Phantom of the Opera*, and *Starlight Express*. Stephen Sondheim offered *Into the Woods*, but one of the truly surprising successes was that of *Sarafina!*, a South African musical that included pop music in the mbaqanga style. Its success was a further confirmation of the increasing integration of international styles of music.

JOHN MILWARD, *Free-lance Writer and Critic*

Democrat Bob Kerrey, 45-year-old former Nebraska governor who lost a leg in the Vietnam war, was elected to the U.S. Senate. He easily defeated the GOP incumbent, Sen. David K. Karnes.

NEBRASKA

The year 1988 began with a cautiously optimistic attitude toward the farm economy. Farm debt had dropped from $11.2 billion in 1983 to under $8.75 billion, farm income and land values were rising, and recent crop yields had been high. By June, however, the drought that struck so much of the farm belt throughout the United States and Canada brought serious concern over whether the agricultural recovery could continue.

Fortunately for Nebraska farmers, the state was not one of the hardest hit areas, and the extensive use of irrigation provided an advantage in bringing the crops through the drought. The fall harvest, while meager in some heavily stressed areas, was near normal across the state.

The Election. As usual in an election year, there were a number of special issues on the ballot. In the May primary, voters gave members of the state legislature their first pay raise in 20 years—from $4,800 to $12,000 a year. In the November election, voters rejected an initiative to withdraw from the Central Interstate Low-Level Radioactive Waste Compact, a five-state regional compact that proposed to build a waste-disposal facility in Nebraska. At the same time, voters approved an amendment to the state constitution guaranteeing the right to keep and bear arms.

On October 5 the nation's political attention focused on Nebraska as senators Lloyd Bentsen (D) and Dan Quayle (R) held their vice-presidential debate in Omaha's Civic Auditorium. Nationally televised, the event generated much interest.

The key political contest, however, was over the Senate seat that had been filled by the appointment of David Karnes to complete the term of Sen. Edward Zorinsky, who died in 1987. Omaha Congressman Hal Daub challenged Karnes unsuccessfully in the Republican primary. All the political signs, however, pointed to the Democratic candidate, former Gov. Bob Kerrey, as the man to beat. Despite a campaign visit on Karnes' behalf by Vice-President George Bush, the incumbent was unable to overcome the popularity of Kerrey, who won with about 57% of the vote, even though Bush received 60% of the state's vote for the presidency. The Democrats also captured the 2nd-District seat in the House of Representatives vacated by Daub, as Peter Hoagland narrowly defeated Republican Jerry Schenken. Republican incumbents were re-elected in Nebraska's two other congressional districts.

Old Main Fire. Higher education lost one of its early landmarks on August 25 when Dana

---

NEBRASKA • Information Highlights

Area: 77,355 sq mi (200 350 km²).

Population (July 1, 1987): 1,594,000.

Chief Cities (July 1, 1986 est.): Lincoln, the capital, 183,050; Omaha, 349,270; Grand Island (1980 census), 33,180.

Government (1988): *Chief Officers*—governor, Kay Orr (R); lt. gov., William E. Nichol (R). *Legislature* (unicameral)—49 members (nonpartisan).

State Finances (fiscal year 1987): *Revenue,* $2,475,000,000; *expenditure,* $2,282,000,000.

Personal Income (1987): $22,845,000,000; per capita, $14,328.

Labor Force (June 1988): *Civilian labor force,* 821,900; *unemployed,* 27,300 (3.3% of total force).

Education: *Enrollment* (fall 1986)—public elementary schools, 185,282; public secondary, 81,857; colleges and universities, 100,401. *Public school expenditures* (1986–87), $864,000,000 ($3,437 per pupil).

College's Old Main, located in Blair in eastern Nebraska, was destroyed by fire caused by faulty electrical wiring. Built in 1886, Old Main held the record as the oldest educational building still in use in the state and was on the National Register of Historic Places.

Football. Cornhusker football, as usual, received enthusiastic support when the University of Nebraska team embarked on a successful season. The Cornhuskers' national second-place ranking tumbled when UCLA defeated them, 41-28, on September 10. Despite a series of unbroken victories thereafter, Nebraska was unable to climb to the top spot, but the 7-3 victory over arch-rival Oklahoma at the season's close brought the Big Eight championship and a spot against Miami in the Orange Bowl. The Cornhuskers were overwhelmed by the Hurricanes in the Orange Bowl, 23-3.

WILLIAM E. CHRISTENSEN
Midland Lutheran College

NETHERLANDS, THE

The year 1988 in the Netherlands passed without any major crises, but there was some uneasiness over the prospect of European economic unification, set for 1992.

Government and Politics. The national government remained in the hands of a coalition of the Christian Democratic (CDA) and conservative (VVD) parties, although Prime Minister Ruud Lubbers had to bring his personal prestige to bear in overcoming tension between the two parties over the government's ongoing social and political retrenchment program. Revision of tax rates brought the top bracket down from 72% to 50%, but the gravest difficulty faced by the government in the States General (parliament) was triggered by a relatively minor issue—a dispute over whether the nation's new passport was fraud-proof. When a commission of inquiry reported that Deputy Minister of Foreign Affairs René van der Linden and his

predecessor, Wim van Eekelen, now minister of defense, had misled parliament on the matter, both were forced to resign.

Reorganization of the nation's universities, all of which are funded by the state, continued to present problems. The final decision was to maintain low tuition rates for six years of study, considered sufficient for earning a doctoral degree, after which they would rise sharply. Although tuition was increased from 1,600 guilders (about $770) to 1,750 guilders (about $840), arrangements for government-sponsored loans ended a protest movement.

Another conflict set the government against medical specialists, whose permissible income was reduced sharply. Debate continued over a decision to make medical and hospital insurance compulsory for all—and with increased premiums—but the conservative party (the smaller partner in the governing coalition) bowed to a majority that included the Christian Democrats and the opposition Labor Party (PvdA). The leadership of the PvdA indicated a willingness to negotiate a new coalition government with either the CDA or VVD.

According to the government, federal spending in 1988 would decline by 2.3% to 168.03 billion guilders (about $80.8 billion), while revenue would drop by 9.1% to 144.36 billion guilders (about $69.4 billion). In March the two coalition partners agreed to a package of social and economic reforms that would set the trend for the second half of the government's term—until the election scheduled for 1990—and prepare the economy for European unification in 1992. The new package included major cuts in social security benefits and personal taxes, as well as reductions in welfare premiums and corporate taxes.

Foreign Affairs. Controversy over foreign affairs—in particular the installation of U.S. nuclear weapons—declined in the wake of improved relations between the United States and Moscow. The U.S. Pershing cruise missiles stationed at the Woensdrecht air base, the site of repeated demonstrations, were removed in accordance with the U.S.-Soviet treaty on intermediate-range nuclear forces.

Other. The nation was shocked by the discovery of the body of Gerrit-Jan Heijn, the head of the country's largest supermarket chain, who had been kidnapped in September 1987. The confessed murderer was an unemployed aerospace engineer.

Dutchmen were elated, however, at the victory of their national soccer team over the Soviet Union, 2–0, in the finals of the European soccer championship in June.

According to research by Dutch scientists, an epidemic that killed thousands of seals in the North Sea and Baltic Sea during the summer was caused by the canine distemper virus.

HERBERT H. ROWEN
Rutgers University

NETHERLANDS • Information Highlights

Official Name: Kingdom of the Netherlands.
Location: Northwestern Europe.
Area: 14,405 sq mi (37 310 km²).
Population (mid-1988 est.): 14,700,000.
Chief Cities (Jan. 1, 1987 est.): Amsterdam, the capital, 682,702; Rotterdam, 572,642; The Hague, the seat of government, 445,127.
Government: *Head of state,* Beatrix, queen (acceded April 30, 1980). *Head of government,* Ruud Lubbers, prime minister (took office Nov. 1982). *Legislature*—States General: First Chamber and Second Chamber.
Monetary Unit: Guilder (2.015 guilders equal U.S.$1, Dec. 30, 1988).
Economic Index (1987): *Consumer Prices* (1980 = 100), all items, 122.3; food, 115.2. *Industrial Production* (1980 = 100), 107.
Foreign Trade (1987 U.S.$): *Imports,* $91,317,000,000; *exports,* $92,882,000,000.

NEVADA

Nevada delivered its four electoral votes to Republican presidential contender George Bush. Despite early optimism by the Michael Dukakis camp that Nevada was winnable for the Democrats, Bush scored a 60% to 40% victory in the November election. Also highlighting Nevada politics in 1988 was the successful challenge by sitting Democratic Gov. Richard Bryan to freshman U.S. Sen. Chic Hecht (R).

The Elections. In the May presidential caucuses, Pat Robertson (R), with a strong grassroots organization, edged George Bush. On the Democratic side, Sen. Albert Gore won.

Nevadans continued their practice of ticket-splitting in the general election as Governor Bryan defeated Senator Hecht with a 51% to 47% margin, with 2% for neither candidate. The two contenders set a Nevada record by spending nearly $6 million in one of the nastiest campaigns in modern Nevada politics. Democratic Lt. Gov. Robert Miller would assume the governorship in January 1989. In the U.S. House of Representatives, three-term Republican Congresswoman Barbara Vucanovich fought off her most serious challenge in four campaigns, defeating Democrat James Spoo by a margin of about 17%. Freshman Democratic Congressman James Bilbray polled 65% of the vote in defeating Lucille Lusk.

There were few changes in the state legislature's composition, with the Republicans gaining one seat in the Senate for a 13–8 majority and the Democrats gaining one seat in the Assembly for a 30–12 margin. Senate Democrats elected the first black member of Nevada's legislative leadership, picking Sen. Joe Neal as minority leader.

Issues prevalent in state races included a commitment to keeping taxes low, support for improving education, and health costs containment. While none of the nine ballot questions stirred much controversy, Question Nine, an initiative proposing a constitutional amendment forbidding the imposition of a personal income tax, received 88% of the vote. To become law it must be passed again in 1990.

Economy. Gross sales taxes increased nearly 15% while gaming taxes increased about 14%, accounting for about 80% of the general fund revenues. Fiscal year 1987–88 ended with a state-budget surplus of more than $66 million and a contingency fund of $40 million. The unemployment rate dropped to 5.1% in September. Nevada led the nation in industrial-employment growth with a 7.4% increase in jobs between January 1987 and March 1988. Mining continued to boom with a 32.5% increase in jobs over 1987, and in 1988, Nevada was the nation's premier producer of gold.

The drought, which began in 1987, had a mixed effect, with the mild weather aiding tourism, thus increasing gaming and tourism revenues, while causing 1988 losses of more than $15 million to northern Nevada agriculture.

Explosions. In May a series of explosions destroyed the Pacific Engineering and Production Company, a rocket-fuel factory in Henderson. Two employees were killed in the blasts.

TIMOTHY G. HALLER
University of Nevada, Reno

NEW BRUNSWICK

The provincial highway patrol reached the end of its road in 1988. Spending restraint became the watchword in New Brunswick's fiscal policy. And one of the province's two French-language dailies folded.

The Highway Patrol. The New Brunswick Highway Patrol was abolished by the Liberal government of Premier Frank McKenna following eight dispute-filled years. A statement issued July 28 said that the duties of the patrol, created by Premier Richard Hatfield's Conservative government in 1980 to enforce highway traffic laws, would revert to the Royal Canadian Mounted Police (RCMP). Solicitor General Conrad Landry promised that the government would find new work for the patrol's approximately 160 full-time employees, including 130 uniformed officers.

Financial Matters and the Legislature. Finance Minister Allan Maher released a financial statement July 7 which he claimed showed a "substantial improvement" in New Brunswick's fiscal affairs. The operating deficit stood at C$103.8 million, very close to the $104 million projection made in 1987. Maher said the deficit would have been considerably lower but for accounting changes that resulted in write-offs of a number of loans and advances. He acknowledged that New Brunswick's net debt had climbed past the $3 billion mark—compared with $2.4 billion two years earlier.

In a budget presentation on April 6, Maher offered New Brunswickers a dose of spending

---

NEVADA • Information Highlights

Area: 110,561 sq mi (286 352 km²).

Population (July 1, 1987): 1,007,000.

Chief Cities (July 1, 1986 est.): Carson City, the capital (1980 census), 32,022; Las Vegas, 193,240; Reno, 111,420.

Government (1988): *Chief Officers*—governor, Richard H. Bryan (D); lt. gov., Robert J. Miller (D). *Legislature*—Senate, 21 members; Assembly, 42 members.

State Finances (fiscal year 1987): *Revenue,* $2,475,000,000; *expenditure,* $2,010,000,000.

Personal Income (1987): $16,484,000,000; per capita, $16,366.

Labor Force (June 1988): *Civilian labor force,* 582,700; *unemployed,* 31,800 (5.5% of total force).

Education: *Enrollment* (fall 1986)—public elementary schools, 112,164; public secondary, 49,075; colleges and universities, 46,796. *Public school expenditures* (1986–87), $538,000,000 ($3,768 per pupil).

NEW BRUNSWICK · Information Highlights

Area: 28,355 sq mi (73 440 km²).
Population (June 1988): 713,500.
Chief Cities (1986 census): Fredericton, the capital, 44,352; Saint John, 76,381; Moncton, 55,468.
Government (1988): *Chief Officers*—lt. gov., Gilbert Finn; premier, Frank McKenna (Liberal). *Legislature*—Legislative Assembly, 58 members.
Provincial Finances (1988–89 fiscal year budget): *Revenues*, $3,270,300,000; *expenditures*, $3,300,-000,000.
Personal Income (average weekly earnings, June 1988): $418.45.
Labor Force (August 1988, seasonally adjusted): *Employed* workers, 15 years of age and over, 283,000; *Unemployed*, 12.1%.
Education (1988–89): *Enrollment*—elementary and secondary schools, 138,400 pupils; postsecondary—universities, 15,460; community colleges, 2,220.

(All monetary figures are in Canadian dollars.)

restraint. Taxes were increased; services to the elderly and poor were decreased. He budgeted 1988–89 expenditures at $3.3 billion, with an operating deficit of $29.7 million—the lowest in seven years.

The budget presentation was the highlight of the legislature's spring session which ended May 18. It was the legislature's first session since the Liberals swept the long-entrenched Conservatives out of office in October 1987. Since there was no opposition—the Liberals having taken all 58 seats—the government allowed Conservative and New Democratic Party representatives to sit in on committee meetings.

Help for the Jobless. A $70 million, federal-provincial program to assist jobless young New Brunswickers find employment was unveiled in Fredericton on September 15. The federal government would contribute up to $49 million of the program's cost, the provincial government up to $21 million during a 2½-year period. It was aimed at about 17,000 persons between the ages of 15 and 24. Unemployment among New Brunswick youth was averaging 20% to 25%.

"Le Matin" Folds. Moncton's French-language daily newspaper *Le Matin* ceased publication in June. The paper's demise left *L'Acadie Nouvelle* of northeastern New Brunswick as the only Francophone daily serving the province's 250,000 French-speaking citizens.

JOHN BEST, *Canada World News*

NEWFOUNDLAND

Events in the fishing and oil industries dominated provincial news in 1988.

Fishing Disputes. In April and May a protracted Canadian-French dispute over fishing rights in waters claimed by both countries flared again. It began when a trawler from the French territory of St. Pierre-Miquelon was seized in the disputed zone by Canadian fishery officers. On board the trawler were 17 crew members, a member of the French Chamber of Deputies, two territorial government officials, and the mayor of St. Pierre, who was also a French senator. Retaliation came in May when the Newfoundland vessel *Maritimer* was seized for illegal fishing and was towed to St. Pierre. In Ottawa and Paris, calm eventually returned, and the desired result was achieved when the suspended bilateral talks resumed. At the September meeting of the Northwest Atlantic Fisheries Organization (NAFO) in Ottawa, the European Community announced that it was not going to cut back on what Canada regards as overfishing in the international waters beyond the 200-mi (322-km) zone.

Economy. The Newfoundland fishery had mixed economic results. While total landings were up, prices in the American market were down, and there were areas of the province where no fish were landed. In response to the latter situation, the federal and provincial government announced in September a special C$4.8 million assistance package for fishermen.

Energy's economic picture appeared on the upswing in 1988. The year began with Premier Brian Peckford assuming the energy portfolio. In July a $5.2 billion preliminary agreement covering preproduction costs for development of the Hibernia oil field was signed by the federal and provincial governments and a consortium of oil companies. The agreement meant $1.66 billion in federal loan guarantees, $1.04 billion in federal development grants, an $11 million grant from the Newfoundland government, and an exemption from Newfoundland's 12% retail sales tax. Another $95 million grant came from the Canada-Newfoundland Offshore Development Fund. The oil companies, led by Mobil Oil and Petro-Canada, pledged $20 million. The agreement would become final when necessary legal documents were signed in 1989.

The provincial government got into increasing difficulties over a joint project with Calgary

NEWFOUNDLAND · Information Highlights

Area: 156,649 sq mi (405 720 km²).
Population (June 1988): 567,600.
Chief Cities (1986 census): St. John's, the capital, 96,216; Corner Brook, 22,719.
Government (1988): *Chief Officers*—lt. gov., James A. McGrath; premier, A. Brian Peckford (Progressive Conservative). *Legislature*—Legislative Assembly, 52 members.
Provincial Finances (1988–89 fiscal year budget): *Revenues*, $2,664,144,000; *expenditures*, $2,925,-584,000.
Personal Income (average weekly earnings, June 1988): $444.75.
Labor Force (August 1988, seasonally adjusted): *Employed* workers, 15 years of age and over, 195,000. *Unemployed*, 17.7%.
Education (1988–89): *Enrollment*—elementary and secondary schools, 132,910 pupils; postsecondary—universities, 10,990; community colleges, 3,150.

(All monetary figures are in Canadian dollars.)

businessman Philip Sprung to build a gigantic greenhouse for the commercial production of cucumbers and tomatoes that cost the province more than $15 million in subsidies. By May, as the hothouse cucumber production proceeded, hostilities surfaced between Newfoundland and Nova Scotia over competition for mainland cucumber markets.

SUSAN MCCORQUODALE
Memorial University of Newfoundland

NEW HAMPSHIRE

The Seabrook nuclear power plant and politics dominated New Hampshire headlines.

Seabrook. Perhaps the year's biggest story was the bankruptcy of the Public Service Company of New Hampshire (PSNH), principal investor in the Seabrook plant. Following its failure to get an emergency rate increase and burdened with a $2.1 billion debt, late in January the company sought protection under Chapter 11 of the Federal Bankruptcy Code. It thereby became the first major investor-owned utility to file for protection since the 1930s. The $5.2 billion Seabrook plant was approved by the Nuclear Regulatory Commission in December to receive a license for low-power testing, but at year's end the reorganization process for PSNH was still moving slowly and the operational status of Seabook remained uncertain. This uncertainty concerned New England utility officials, who feared that the region lacked adequate generating capacity to meet the growing demand for electric power.

The Election. The nation's first presidential primary once again brought national attention to the state. All agreed that George Bush's seemingly faltering campaign received a major boost in the February primary by gaining 38% of the Republican vote to 28% for Sen. Robert Dole. Gov. John Sununu (R) received much of the credit for the Bush victory. Michael Dukakis did even better in the Democratic primary, receiving 37% of the vote to 20% for runner-up Rep. Richard Gephardt. Voter turnout set a record for a presidential primary, but it represented only half of the registered voters.

In May, Governor Sununu announced that he would not seek a fourth term, resulting in a series of realignments in major state offices— all held by Republicans. A hotly contested Republican primary in September brought victory for Rep. Judd Gregg (R) in the gubernatorial race and Charles Douglas (R) in the contest for Gregg's congressional seat. In the lively state campaign that followed, most candidates in both parties pledged to keep taxes at current levels and to follow generally conservative policies in other areas. The general election in November brought a Republican sweep of the major state and federal offices and continued the GOP's overwhelming domination of the

---

NEW HAMPSHIRE • Information Highlights

Area: 9,279 sq mi (24 032 km²).
Population (July 1, 1987): 1,057,000.
Chief Cities (1980 census): Concord, the capital, 30,400; Manchester, 90,936; Nashua, 67,865.
Government (1988): *Chief Officer*—governor, John H. Sununu (R). *General Court*—Senate, 24 members; House of Representatives, 400 members.
State Finances (fiscal year 1987): *Revenue,* $1,759,000,000; *expenditure,* $1,484,000,000.
Personal Income (1987): $18,529,000,000; per capita, $17,529.
Labor Force (June 1988): *Civilian labor force,* 609,200; *unemployed,* 12,100 (2.0% of total force).
Education: *Enrollment* (fall 1986)—public elementary schools, 109,948; public secondary, 53,769; colleges and universities, 53,886. *Public school expenditures* (1986–87), $503,000,000 ($3,386 per pupil).

---

state legislature. New Hampshire voters gave Bush 63% of the popular vote, a percentage exceeded only in Utah. The voter turnout of 71% of those registered exceeded the national average by 21%.

Economy. The economic boom that the state has enjoyed showed signs of slowing down. Unemployment figures remained among the lowest in the country, but the figure in July rose to 2.5% compared with 2% in June. Home sales slowed, and their high average price inhibited worker recruitment.

Other News. Northern New Hampshire was the source of three major stories. Receiving national attention was the series of 21 arson fires in the small town of Jefferson. On October 12 police arrested a suspect, a former volunteer firefighter, for 16 of the fires, and no additional fires were reported after that date. Second, in May, Diamond International announced the sale of 90,000 acres (36 450 ha) of timberland to interests controlled by developer Claude Rancourt. Fearing major changes in the region, conservation groups and the state cooperated in purchasing 45,500 of the original acreage (18 427 ha) to protect it from development. Finally, the state Department of Transportation selected a highway bypass route around North Conway, a town which has become a mecca for shoppers and tourists with the recent construction of scores of outlet stores and the expansion of its recreation facilities. During the summer, the area witnesses major traffic congestion, which the proposed bypass is intended to alleviate. The selected route is opposed by many area residents and likely will result in much discussion during 1989.

In October the Highway Hotel in Concord, which had served as Republican headquarters for many national and state campaigns, closed its doors. If its closure signified the conclusion of an era, President-elect Bush on November 17 announced the beginning of a new one by appointing outgoing Gov. John Sununu as his White House chief of staff.

WILLIAM L. TAYLOR, *Plymouth State College*

After one of the most expensive and acrimonious U.S. Senate contests in the country, Democratic incumbent Frank Lautenberg emerged victorious over Pete Dawkins.

NEW JERSEY

Environmental issues and electoral politics dominated the news in New Jersey in 1988.

Environmental Issues. The long-awaited report of the New Jersey Planning Commission, setting out a plan for economic development for the state over the next 20 years, was made public in January. Known as the State Development and Redevelopment Plan, it anticipated an additional 212 million sq ft (20 million m²) of office space, one million new jobs, and a population growth of 1.3 million. In order to prevent destruction of New Jersey's remaining rural areas, the report recommended that further growth be confined as much as possible to existing urban areas and major transportation networks. The plan proved controversial for a number of reasons. Local governments, for one, complained that too much leeway was given to legislative oversight. Furthermore, a poll conducted by the Eagleton Institute of Politics at Rutgers University revealed that 53% of New Jersey residents were of the opinion that there had been too much growth, too rapidly, throughout the state in the last decade, and that it was adversely affecting their personal lives.

Of particular concern was the impact of pollution and population growth on the Jersey shore. Several beaches in Hudson and Monmouth counties had to be closed for several days at the height of the summer's heat wave because of contaminated waste from New York City hospitals that had been dumped carelessly into New York Harbor. The cumulative effect of that and similar pollution problems in the summer of 1987 was a marked decrease in tourism along the shore, raising questions about the future of one of New Jersey's great natural resources. The rapid population growth in the coastal areas of Monmouth County was equally alarming. Gov. Thomas H. Kean's order banning further coastal development in the county was viewed by many as too little and too late.

Allied with environmental problems was the possibility of a crisis in public finance at the state level. Governor Kean's proposed $11.8 billion budget for fiscal 1988 was about 12% larger than that for 1987, and tax revenues were expected to rise by only 7%.

Electoral Politics. Two longtime powers in New Jersey were no longer on the scene for the 1988 congressional elections. Peter Rodino, who had represented the 10th District for 40 years and gained national fame as chairman of the House Judiciary Committee during the Watergate hearings, announced his retirement in large part so that his district, now heavily populated by minorities, could be represented by a black. This goal was accomplished when Democrat Donald Payne won the district in the fall election, making him the first black congressman in New Jersey history. Congressman James J. Howard of the 3d District died in late March.

Aside from the House contests, the fall elections featured a bitterly fought Senate race between Frank Lautenberg, the Democratic incumbent, and Republican Peter Dawkins. A West Point football hero, Rhodes scholar, retired brigadier general, and investment banker, Dawkins appeared unbeatable at first, but ultimately could not overcome the Lautenberg charge that he was from out of state, using New Jersey as a stepping-stone to a national political career.

Early in the presidential race, there was speculation that Governor Kean might be Vice-President George Bush's running mate on the

---

NEW JERSEY • Information Highlights

Area: 7,787 sq mi (20 169 km²).
Population (July 1, 1987): 7,672,000.
Chief Cities (July 1, 1984 est.): Trenton, the capital (1980 census), 92,124; Newark, 316,300; Jersey City, 219,480; Paterson, 139,160; Elizabeth, 106,560.
Government (1988): *Chief Officer*—governor, Thomas H. Kean (R). *Legislature*—Senate, 40 members; General Assembly, 80 members.
State Finances (fiscal year 1987): *Revenue,* $19,542,000,000; *expenditure,* $17,175,000,000.
Personal Income (1987): $156,145,000,000; per capita, $20,352.
Labor Force (June 1988): *Civilian labor force,* 4,024,400; *unemployed,* 146,800 (3.6% of total force).
Education: *Enrollment* (fall 1986)—public elementary schools, 742,324; public secondary, 365,143; colleges and universities, 295,353. *Public school expenditures* (1986–87), $6,302,000,000 ($6,120 per pupil).

Republican ticket, but Kean was passed over for Indiana Sen. Dan Quayle. The election results showed a continuation of New Jersey's split political personality. George Bush carried every county except Essex and Hudson, yet the Republicans could not pick up a Senate seat, and the congressional delegation tipped in favor of the Democrats by a margin of eight to six.

Other News. Judicial news of the year included the state Supreme Court ruling that surrogate motherhood contracts involving payment are illegal. In the Baby M surrogacy case, New Jersey's Superior Court granted broad visitation rights to the natural mother, Mary Beth Whitehead Gould. In October, New Jersey's Supreme Court ruled that the death penalty could be imposed only on those who intentionally commit murder.

The New Jersey Education Department in August imposed a partial takeover of the Jersey City school system, which the state considered to be grossly mismanaged.

HERMANN K. PLATT, *Saint Peter's College*

NEW MEXICO

A record number of New Mexicans voted in November, with a 75% turnout statewide. They supported Vice-President George Bush in his bid for the presidency with 52% of the votes against 48% for Massachusetts Gov. Michael Dukakis. Voters also returned incumbent Democratic Sen. Jeff Bingaman by more than a two-to-one margin over his Republican opponent, Bill Valentine.

Republicans carried two of New Mexico's three congressional districts at the polls. Joe Skeen (R) ran unopposed for a fifth term in the 2nd District in the southern part of the state. Steve Schiff (R), a district attorney in Albuquerque, defeated his opponent Tom Udall (D) in a close race in the 1st District, which includes the Albuquerque metropolitan area and several surrounding counties. With more than 70% of the vote, incumbent Bill Richardson (D) eclipsed his rival, Cecelia Salazar, in the 3rd District in northern New Mexico.

Democrats won a majority of the statewide races, gaining firm control of the state legislature. Issues in the various contests included education, the elderly, environmental concerns, and crime. Changes in the state constitution and the sport of hot-air ballooning also received widespread attention in 1988.

Constitutional Amendments. Voters approved seven amendments to the state constitution. Included among them were changes allowing judges in appellate, district, and some metropolitan courts to be appointed initially by the governor, rather than elected, as they had been since 1912. Also, overwhelming support was given to an amendment allowing the denial

---

NEW MEXICO · Information Highlights

Area: 121,593 sq mi (314 925 km²).
Population (July 1, 1987): 1,500,000.
Chief Cities (1980 census): Santa Fe, the capital, 48,953; Albuquerque (July 1, 1986 est.): 366,750; Las Cruces, 45,086.
Government (1988): *Chief Officers*—governor, Garrey Carruthers (R); lt. gov., Jack L. Stahl (R). *Legislature*—Senate, 42 members; House of Representatives, 70 members.
State Finances (fiscal year 1987): *Revenue,* $3,842,000,000; *expenditure,* $3,306,000,000.
Personal Income (1987): $17,812,000,000; per capita, $11,875.
Labor Force (June 1988): *Civilian labor force,* 692,300; *unemployed,* 59,900 (8.7% of total force).
Education: *Enrollment* (fall 1986)—public elementary schools, 191,037; public secondary, 90,906; colleges and universities, 80,271. *Public school expenditures* (1986–87), $903,000,000 ($3,537 per pupil).

---

of bail to persons convicted of a crime while they are appealing their conviction. The popular measure arose from the murder of nine-year-old Deanna Lynn Gore of Roswell by a previously convicted sex offender free on bail.

Environment. The scheduled opening of a storage site for low- and intermediate-level nuclear waste was postponed indefinitely both by opposition groups in the state and by congressional inaction. The U.S. Department of Energy had developed the Waste Isolation Pilot Plant (WIPP) site in ancient salt beds 2,150 ft (655 m) below ground near Carlsbad. Various groups opposed the site altogether citing, e.g., supposed seepage problems in the salt beds and difficulties in the safe transport of the waste, and called for a delay until the state received federal funding to build bypass roads for hauling waste around heavily populated areas.

Bills providing $200 million for a road system, $250 million to compensate the state for lost mineral royalties and for transference of the land above the site from the public domain, did not gain congressional approval.

School Paddling Rule. A case originating in New Mexico, *Miera v. Garcia*, that involved paddling by school officials reached the Supreme Court. On March 21 the court upheld a federal appellate ruling that excessive corporal punishment by school officials may violate constitutional rights. A nine-year-old third-grader had been scarred permanently from a severe paddling.

Ballooning. The annual International Balloon Fiesta, held in Albuquerque every October, continued as one of the major public events in the state. It features the largest mass balloon ascension in the world. Nearly 600 hot-air balloons of all descriptions took to the blue skies over Albuquerque at the 1988 festival. Several hundred thousand state residents and tourists viewed the week-long celebration.

MICHAEL L. OLSEN
New Mexico Highlands University

NEW YORK

Massachusetts Gov. Michael Dukakis carried New York's 35 electoral votes in his attempt to win the presidency—with 52% of the state's popular vote, compared with Vice-President George Bush's 48%. Sen. Daniel Patrick Moynihan won a third term over Garden City lawyer Robert McMillen by a record 67% to 32% margin. New York's 34-member U.S. House delegation would have 21 Democrats and 13 Republicans. Republicans retained control of the state Senate, while Democrats continued to dominate the Assembly.

"Decade of the Child." In his State of the State address early in 1988, Gov. Mario Cuomo proclaimed the beginning of "The Decade of the Child," outlining ambitious goals in health care, education, and economic security to protect "our state's most valuable resource, its children." By the end of the year, however, there had been little progress toward these goals, even as the public grew increasingly concerned about the social problems that seemingly threatened the state's youth. A January poll had indicated that New Yorkers saw economic problems as the most serious issue confronting the nation, despite low statewide unemployment and economic growth stronger than the national average. But by the end of October, New Yorkers were telling pollsters that drugs and crime were their main concerns.

Legislature. Governor Cuomo's call for expanded social programs—only a few of which he proposed specifically—drew little response from the legislature, in part because the state government surprisingly found itself financially strapped. Revenue growth was limited by the second year of a record $4.5 billion, four-year income-tax cut, and tax collections were down sharply due largely to changes in the federal tax code. Resulting political wrangling delayed adoption of the state budget until three weeks into the new fiscal year, and delayed the traditional July adjournment of the legislature. Cuomo's announcement in November that the state's $44.2 billion budget faced a $1.9 billion deficit, prompting a state hiring freeze, pointed to the likelihood of continuing restraint.

With state resources spread thin, and officials reluctant to raise taxes in an election year, voters were asked to approve the largest borrowing in state history: a $3 billion bond issue to pay for road and bridge repairs. It won approval by a ten-point margin in November.

Politics. The legislature's most powerful Republican, Senate Majority Leader Warren M. Anderson of Binghamton, retired at year's end, completing a 36-year career in state government, the last 13 at the Senate helm. Anderson's departure marked the end of a political tradition: GOP senators for the first time selected a downstate legislator, State Sen. Ralph J. Marino of Nassau County, as their new

---

NEW YORK • Information Highlights

Area: 49,108 sq mi (127 190 km²).
Population (July 1, 1987): 17,825,000.
Chief Cities (July 1, 1986 est.): Albany, the capital, 101,727 (1980 census); New York, 7,262,700; Buffalo, 324,820; Rochester, 235,970; Yonkers, 186,080; Syracuse, 160,750.
Government (1988): *Chief Officers*—governor, Mario M. Cuomo (D); lt. gov., Stan Lundine (D). *Legislature*—Senate, 61 members; Assembly, 150 members.
State Finances (fiscal year 1987): *Revenue,* $55,572,000,000; *expenditure,* $47,505,000,000.
Personal Income (1987): $320,930,000,000; per capita, $18,004.
Labor Force (June 1988): *Civilian labor force,* 8,555,600; *unemployed,* 289,300 (3.4% of total force).
Education: *Enrollment* (fall 1986)—public elementary schools, 1,713,465; public secondary, 894,254; colleges and universities, 1,014,497. *Public school expenditures* (1986–87), $14,568,-000,000 ($6,299 per pupil).

---

leader, indicating the shift of Republican strength from upstate to the New York City suburbs.

Governor Cuomo remained the state's most popular political figure and, in the aftermath of Dukakis' defeat by Vice-President Bush, was viewed by many as a potential 1992 presidential candidate. As he did after the Democratic defeat in 1984—and in campaign appearances throughout the nation in 1988—Cuomo insisted that he was not interested in the presidency.

Race Relations. Two occurrences overlaid by allegations of racism also drew New Yorkers' intense interest in 1988. In February, Governor Cuomo ordered Attorney General Robert Abrams to investigate allegations by a black teenager, Tawana Brawley, that she had been kidnapped and sexually assaulted by six white men, some of them linked to law enforcement. Brawley's legal and family advisers, however, refused to cooperate with the investigation, claiming it was fraught with prejudice against blacks. The Brawley case became the most publicized and costliest investigation in the state's history. After dominating headlines for many months, the saga wound down when a grand jury in October concluded that Brawley's story was fabricated. Abrams asked authorities to discipline the lawyers for the teenager, who moved with her family to another state.

Race also was an issue in Yonkers, the state's fourth-largest city, where a majority of the city council for many weeks refused to obey a federal court order to approve a plan increasing low-income housing in a predominantly white section of the city. Rebuffed by the U.S. Supreme Court, and facing municipal bankruptcy from the progressive fines levied by U.S. District Judge Leonard Sand, the councilmen eventually relented and agreed to allow the housing to be built.

REX SMITH, *"Newsday"*

On August 31, New York City Mayor Ed Koch (left) and New York Gov. Mario Cuomo (third from left) met with Jesse Jackson and other black leaders to try to heal differences that arose during New York's racially divisive primary. During the campaign the mayor seemed as irascible as ever, alienating some voters with harsh attacks against the Reverend Jackson.

AP/Wide World

NEW YORK CITY

The racketeering conviction and resignation of a senior New York congressman, a midsummer riot that raised a storm over police brutality, and washups of medical wastes that closed ocean swimming beaches during the hottest summer in years generated headlines in New York City in 1988. Perennial problems—homelessness, drug abuse, crime, and traffic congestion—also drew attention. But a new chancellor brought hope to a troubled public school system; New York's economy was still robust; and the Central Park Zoo reopened after a five-year, $35 million renovation.

Official Corruption. Representative Mario Biaggi, a Bronx Democrat who had served nearly 20 years in Congress, was found guilty, with five others, of corruption charges involving the Wedtech Corporation, a Bronx military contractor that paid millions in bribes for lucrative government business. It was Biaggi's second conviction in a year, and he resigned his seat in Congress rather than face expulsion.

Environmental and Social Problems. At intervals in the summer, ocean beaches in the area were closed because of washups of syringes, blood vials, and other medical wastes, whose source remained a mystery.

During a sultry August night of violence reminiscent of the 1960s, the police clashed with hundreds of demonstrators protesting a curfew at Tompkins Square Park in Manhattan's East Village. While some civilians hurled bottles, videotapes showed that it was the police who rioted. They rushed into crowds, clubbing and kicking bystanders. Police Commissioner Benjamin Ward acknowledged police failings, removed some commanders, and ordered new training and crowd-control procedures.

The winter, for some, had been even worse. Homeless people filled bus and rail terminals, and while there was plenty of room in city shelters, many of the homeless, fearing violence and harassment in shelters, preferred to brave the cold. At least six people froze to death during a January cold spell.

Crime. Despite police crackdowns, drug abuse, mostly of the smokable cocaine derivative crack, was blamed for countless robberies and 40% of the city's murders—including the killings of six police officers—and left whole neighborhoods in terror. One crack-addicted youth was charged with five murders. Overall, New York City homicides were at a near record-high level and robbery in the first six months of the year was up 8%.

In court, two 1986 crimes came to judgment. Robert E. Chambers, Jr., pleaded guilty to manslaughter amid jury deliberations on a murder charge and was sentenced to five to 15 years for killing Jennifer Levin in Central Park. In the Howard Beach, Queens, racial assault case, several white teenagers were convicted and sentenced. As the year drew to a close the trial of former Miss America Bess Myerson, who was charged with seeking to influence a judge in her companion's divorce case, and the trial of Joel Steinberg, who was charged with murdering his illegally adopted daughter, were dominating the headlines. Myerson and her two codefendants were acquitted December 22.

Other News. The city's economy was healthy but declining slightly after a decade of growth. Tourists, particularly Japanese, flocked to New York in record numbers. Office construction in Manhattan boomed, although the city's office-vacancy level was the highest since the 1970s. Employment was higher than at any time since the 1940s, but experts said problems with affordable housing and with education threatened the picture. Dr. Richard R. Green, former superintendent of Minneapolis schools, was named chancellor of New York's public-school system.

ROBERT D. McFADDEN
"The New York Times"

NEW ZEALAND

The declining state of the economy caused mounting apprehension that New Zealand was teetering on the edge of a severe depression.

Economy and Budget. The nation's gross domestic product (GDP) declined 1% in fiscal year (FY) 1987 (ending March 31, 1988). In opinion polls on the issues of greatest concern, unemployment topped the list by wide margins. In January the number of those out of work or on special schemes exceeded 100,000 (7.6% of the work force) for the first time since the depression of the 1930s. By midyear it had reached a post-World War II high, and by October the rate of 11.4% (152,000) was close to an all-time peak.

The Labour government of Prime Minister David Lange continued to press its monetarist noninterventionist policies, though it slowed the pace of change. By way of support, it pointed to declining interest rates—9% in FY 1987, the lowest since 1984—and to a dip in inflation—forecast as low as 5% by year's end. The government in May deregulated gasoline prices and electricity rates and declined to provide direct assistance to a struggling rural sector. Its 1988–89 budget, unveiled in July, called for a major program of asset sales to reduce debt. Including revenue from asset sales, the budget showed an NZ$2.2 billion (U.S. $1.45 billion) surplus; without it, there was a deficit of NZ$1.38 billion ($910 million). The proposed privatization program included sale of the Post Office, calculated to yield NZ$9 billion ($6 billion). In March the government announced the sale of its 70% stake in Petroleum Corporation of New Zealand for NZ$800 million ($528 million). With hefty increases in social welfare and education spending, the state's activities were expected to account for nearly 43% of GDP. Radical tax cuts went into effect in October, but the frequency of adjustments to national retirement benefits was reduced, and the short-lived revenue-sharing scheme with local government was phased out.

Politics and Administration. No by-elections were held during 1988, although the High Court overturned the 1987 Wairarapa election result, ousting the Labour member of Parliament (MP) and installing the National Party candidate by 34 votes. The Labour Party thus held 58 seats, the National Party 39. Polls consistently gave National a 13%–16% lead over Labour, and in September a cabinet reshuffle elevated Mike Moore to minister of external relations and trade and deputy minister of finance. In August, Prime Minister David Lange underwent surgery for a coronary lesion, but the following month he paid a short visit to the United States. The purpose of the trip was to attempt to repair the frayed relationship with the United States. He also addressed the UN and attended a variety of special functions.

Social Issues. An official survey revealed that while a sizable majority wanted more money spent on education and crime prevention, only 20% desired more public funds applied to implementing a bicultural society (including Maoris—who make up some 9%–13% of the population—and descendants of European settlers). The government's commitment to racial partnership and court decisions in favor of Maori land and fishing claims provoked widespread disquiet. A bill introduced late in the parliamentary session proposed progressive assignation of the fishing quota to Maori groups, so that 50% would be in their hands by the year 2008.

The reformist zeal of the government continued unabated. Major inquiries were held on social policy, education administration, the public hospital system, cervical cancer treatment, tertiary education, and local government.

GRAHAM BUSH
University of Auckland

NIGERIA

Gen. Ibrahim Babangida's third year in power witnessed some positive changes in the economy and definite progress toward civil rule.

Economic Development. In January 1988 a majority of Nigeria's creditors rescheduled $3.2 billion of commercial debt for 22 years instead of repayment by 1990. Babangida and the Armed Forces Ruling Council (AFRC) announced the names of 96 companies scheduled for privatization (divided into five categories varying from full privatization to those which would remain largely public). This measure and the Structural Adjustment Program (SAP) to control the currency, remove subsidies, and make cutbacks in state and federal expenditure convinced the World Bank in October to lend

© James Brooke/NYT Pictures

A new oil refinery in Port Harcourt was the first in a series of moves by Nigeria—an OPEC member—to diversify from the export of crude oil to refined petroleum products.

comprising 42 separate unions, was dissolved and a single administrator was appointed to oversee the restructuring of the union system.

AFRC slashed employment rolls in a number of industries. Heaviest retrenchment was in the Railway Corporation where 5,500 workers were laid off. The railway, electrical, and phone systems needed major capital expenditures which were not available. The railways had only 36 operative engines, compared with 173 in 1982. The Electrical Authority lost thousands of dollars each day yet could not supply the needs of urban Nigeria. Heavy rainfall caused widespread crop damage and increased the heavy erosion in many states. Flooding plagued Lagos, Kaduna, Port Harcourt, and Kano. In September, 300 villages in the Sokoto area were submerged by the Niger River. The Bagauda Dam, one of the nation's largest, collapsed in August.

Constitutional Changes. The AFRC in 1987 postponed the date of return to civil control to 1992. This was to ensure more time to construct a viable constitution. The 23 committees of the Constituent Assembly submitted their reports, and the first draft of the constitution was completed in October 1988. It called for a presidential system and continuation of the present federal structure. All local government ministries were abolished. State elections were projected for 1990 and elections for the federal executive and legislature two years later. Only two political parties to be formed in 1989 would be allowed to contest the elections. Politicians presently banned would not be allowed to participate and the two political parties must not have an ethnic, sectional, or a religious base.

Foreign Affairs. The major policy goal in 1988 was to convince foreign creditors to ease their demands and continue to provide funds. Better relations with Benin were signalled by the opening of the border at Semo. Ghana agreed to exchange prisoners. Babangida continued his opposition to apartheid in South Africa and his support of Hissein Habré's government in Chad.

Nigeria $1 billion and promise $500 million more by the end of 1988. The petroleum industry, which provides 90% of Nigeria's capital, continued to expand. A fourth refinery and six new oil wells opened. Petroleum production was stabilized relatively at 1.2 million barrels per day; however, OPEC's failure to agree on quotas allowed world prices to plunge and reduced profits. Nigeria's per capita gross income fell below $500.

Domestic Affairs. The AFRC in January 1988 ended a four-year freeze on wages, but due to budgetary limitations only one of its 19 states could raise salaries. Removal of subsidies for petroleum products resulted in a nationwide strike which was ended quickly by the government. The Nigerian Labor Congress,

HARRY A. GAILEY, *San Jose State University*

NORTH CAROLINA

North Carolina voters backed Republican presidential and gubernatorial candidates in 1988, but returned Democratic majorities for Congress and the state legislature. On the economic front, unemployment declined but the wage level remained low.

Election. James G. Martin became the first member of the GOP to be reelected governor in more than 100 years, and his margin of 12% helped elect James C. Gardner, the state's first Republican lieutenant governor in the 20th century. Two Republicans won judgeships in statewide votes, and the party would have 46 members (out of 120) in the House of Representatives and 13 (out of 50) in the state Senate —a record for the 20th century. The Council of State also remained Democratic, but by smaller than usual majorities. The entire congressional delegation (eight Democrats, three Republicans) was reelected. The Bush-Quayle ticket swept the state.

Legislature. The off-year session of the General Assembly resulted in a further erosion of gubernatorial powers. For example, the controller was transferred from the appointed Board of Education to the elected superintendent of public instruction. About $452 million was added to the budget, including $30 million for prisons and $7 million for local "pork barrel" projects. A 5% sales tax was imposed on mail-order purchases from out of state, and the intoxication standard for bus and truck drivers was lowered to .04%.

The Economy. Although state revenues grew less than the 6.3% estimated by the General Assembly, the economy remained strong. Unemployment fell to below 3% in July, and North Carolina ranked fifth in the nation in job growth. However, average earnings and income put the state 34th, and its factory wages —an average of $7.83 an hour—were second from the bottom. Establishment of direct flights from Raleigh-Durham to France and Mexico by American Airlines helped nearly double the traffic from that airport.

Robeson County. Long afflicted by triracial controversies, Robeson County remained much in the news. In a bitter referendum, voters narrowly supported the merger of all five of its school systems into one. The murder of Julian T. Pierce, a Lumbee Indian candidate for a judgeship, stirred accusations of assassination by white political foes, but an investigation indicated that he was shot by another Indian, who committed suicide three days later. On February 1, Eddie Hatcher and Timothy Bryan Jacobs, calling themselves Tuscarora Indians, seized the offices of the *Robesonian* newspaper in Lumberton and held the staff hostage at gunpoint for up to ten hours. In a surprise verdict, a federal jury freed both men on hostage-taking and related charges.

Weather. Tornadoes hit Wake and eight other counties on November 28, killing four, injuring scores, and leaving about 500 homeless.

Sports. The city of Charlotte dedicated a new coliseum and fielded the state's first professional basketball team, the Hornets.

H. G. JONES
University of North Carolina at Chapel Hill

NORTH DAKOTA

The drought of 1988 hit hardest in North Dakota, according to federal officials, evaporating $3.4 billion from the state's economy. George Bush won the presidential race in the state, but Democrats tightened their grip on state offices.

Drought. Parching summer weather cut 1988 crop yields in North Dakota to about one half of normal. Farmers harvested 78.2 million bushels of spring wheat, down 59% from 1987; 40 million bushels of durum, down 46% from a year earlier; 43.7 million bushels of barley, down 69%; 8 million bushels of oats, down 78%; and 12.6 million bushels of corn, down 73%. Economists estimated farmers suffered $1.1 billion in crop and livestock losses.

Reductions in related business activity brought the drought's impact on the state to $3.4 billion, economists said. Farmers, however, were to receive $411 million in federal drought aid, easing the drought's impact statewide. Gov. George Sinner ordered state agencies to cut spending by 4% in anticipation of drought-related declines in tax revenue.

Politics. Democratic presidential candidate Michael Dukakis and his running mate, Lloyd Bentsen, each visited sparsely populated North Dakota twice but could not salvage their campaign in the state. Vice-President George Bush beat Dukakis 57% to 43%. Eighty-year-old

U.S. Sen. Quentin Burdick (D), urged publicly even by some Democrats to retire, ran for another term and handily defeated Republican challenger Earl Strinden, 60% to 40%. U.S. Rep. Byron Dorgan (D) easily swept away Republican Steve Sydness, 72% to 28%.

Despite the poor economy, Governor Sinner topped his Republican challenger, Leon Mallberg, 60% to 40%. Attorney General Nicholas Spaeth (D) won reelection, as did Democratic incumbents Robert Hanson, the state treasurer, Insurance Commissioner Earl Pomeroy, Tax Commissioner Heidi Heitkamp, and Public Service Commissioner Bruce Hagen. Republicans lost control of two other offices they had held. Democrat Sarah Vogel captured 45% of the vote to become state agriculture commissioner, toppping Keith Bjerke (R) and incumbent Kent Jones, a Republican running as an independent. Democrat Jim Kusler became secretary of state defeating Republican Dave Koland, 52% to 48%. The office had been held by Republican Ben Meier, who retired after 34 years. The only Republican to hold his state office was Auditor Robert Peterson, who edged challenger Steve Pederson.

After the election, Democrats held 14 of 17 federal and statewide political offices. Democrats also won 14 of 26 state Senate seats up for election to strengthen their majority status. Republicans held the state House of Representatives, but their numbers were diminished.

Energy. A North Dakota firm purchased the nation's only commercial-scale synthetic fuels plant from the U.S. Department of Energy (DOE). Basin Electric Cooperative outbid seven other firms to win the Great Plains coal gasification plant, located near Beulah, ND. DOE took control of the plant in 1985 after private builders defaulted on government-guaranteed construction loans.

State Lottery. In June voters rejected for a second time a proposal to institute a state lottery.

JIM NEUMANN, *"The Forum," Fargo, ND*

NORTHWEST TERRITORIES

The signing of a land claims agreement-in-principle by the Dene (Indian) and Metis peoples of the Northwest Territories and the government of Canada was the most significant development in the Northwest Territories in 1988. The agreement was signed on September 5 by Prime Minister Brian Mulroney, Dene Nation President William Erasmus, and Metis Association President Michael Paulette.

The settlement provides full title to 3,900 sq mi (10 100 km²) of land, surface rights to 68,000 sq mi (176 120 km²), and C$500 million to the Dene-Metis. While resource royalties to the Dene-Metis under the agreement may be modest in the short term, there was good potential for future growth. Guaranteed participation in the management of land, water, and renewable resources will give aboriginals more environmental control and an economic base.

Energy Accord. An enabling agreement for a northern energy accord was signed between the governments of Canada and the Northwest Territories in September 1988. The agreement was aimed at devolution of powers in the energy field (particularly oil and gas) from the federal to the territorial government.

Economy. Economic conditions improved in the Northwest Territories in 1988, despite the final closing of the largest producing mine at Pine Point. There were increases in employment; retail sales; construction activity; tourism; mineral, oil, and gas exploration; and average earnings. The distribution of economic activity still heavily favored a few larger communities, however, and initiatives were under way to solve that uneven growth.

Legislation. Legislation passed during the year included: an act providing for the Northwest Territories Power Corporation under the jurisdiction of the territorial government; a bill promoting assistance to the victims of crime, including funding from surcharges imposed on persons convicted of the crimes; and amendments to the Labour Standards Act reducing the standard workweek to 40 hours.

ROSS M. HARVEY
Government of the Northwest Territories

NORWAY

Norway in 1988 endeavored to cope with a weakened economy related to low oil prices, high domestic prices and interest rates, and demands by various groups for higher salaries and government assistance. In September the choice of Lillehammer as the site of the 1994 Winter Olympics brought jubilation to the whole nation, but also a challenge to meet the high investments required.

Government. The minority government of Prime Minister Gro Harlem Brundtland remained in power despite some setbacks, largely because the four opposition parties to the right could not agree on a common program. In June the Storting (legislature) ended 20 years of dispute by voting to build a new international airport on the Hurum peninsula, some 37 mi (60 km) south of Oslo. The vote was a defeat for the government, which had promoted Gardemoen north of Oslo as the site. This defeat, together with the government's appointment of a highly paid woman to head the Postal Savings Bank—in contravention of the government's own wage policy—led to a strong protest and a partial restructuring of the cabinet.

Economy. In February the employers' association and the largest labor union federation reached an agreement to limit wage increases to 5% in 1988. The labor federation insisted, however, that the restriction must apply to all workers, and the government complied with follow-up legislation in March. The measure limited most unionized wage earners and all civil servants to increases of only one krone per hour. This drastic action, combined with the low export price of oil—Norway's most important product—dampened private demand. Unemployment was expected to reach 3% by year's end, the highest level since 1984.

The nation's leading commercial banks reported record losses in 1987 and expected similar losses in 1988, as many businesses failed and individuals could not keep up on loan payments. Public spending did not take up the slack. One positive result of this situation was some improvement in the balance of payments, also due in part to favorable world markets for metals and chemical and wood products. Increases in oil production were limited voluntarily to 7.5%, in support of OPEC's efforts to boost prices.

Environment. A series of incidents in 1988 served to raise the public's awareness of the dangers of pollution. Norway and its North Sea neighbors suffered a coastal invasion of red algae and saw thousands of dead seals wash ashore, probably killed by a pollution-caused virus. Norsk Hydro, Norway's largest company, was threatened with the closure of a big magnesium smelter because it could not meet government antipollution standards. Environmental protection groups opposed a postponement of the closure, believing that it would send the wrong message to other industries. And Norway was embarrassed when its honorary consul in Guinea, West Africa, was imprisoned temporarily because his company, the Klaveness shipping group, was accused of dumping ash containing dioxin.

Social Problems. The full costs of the shortened workweek, which went into effect on Jan. 1, 1987, became evident in 1988 as social institutions faced financial and staffing problems. For high-school teachers, unacceptable pay increase offers in 1987 prompted work slowdowns and other forms of strikes in 1988. And although they received somewhat more than the minimum offer and agreed to end their action for the time being, the issue was still a live one.

Because of a lack of qualified personnel—due to low pay—hospitals and nursing homes could not fill existing positions, let alone meet the need for expanded care. Because of inadequate child-care facilities, many mothers were not able to take paid jobs. Already burdened by heavy increases in social-welfare payments, cities faced numerous appeals for help at the same time that tax revenues were falling. This resulted in a squeeze on traditional services—such as maintenance of roads and other public areas, public transportation, support of the arts, and others—for which no satisfactory solution was found.

ELLEN NORBOM
Free-lance Writer

NORWAY · Information Highlights

Official Name: Kingdom of Norway.
Location: Northern Europe.
Area: 125,182 sq mi (324 220 km²).
Population (mid-1988 est.): 4,210,900.
Chief Cities (Jan. 1, 1988): Oslo, the capital, 450,808; Bergen, 209,912; Trondheim, 135,542.
Government: *Head of state,* Olav V, king (acceded Sept. 1957). *Head of government,* Gro Harlem Brundtland, prime minister (took office May 2, 1986). *Legislature*—Storting: Lagting and Odelsting.
Monetary Unit: Krone (7.1865 kroner equal U.S.$1, Sept. 28, 1988).
Gross National Product (1987 U.S.$): $82,629,-821,000.
Economic Indexes (1987): *Consumer Prices* (1980 = 100), all items, 179.5; food, 193.1. *Industrial Production* (1980 = 100), 135.
Foreign Trade (1987 U.S.$): *Imports,* $20,514,-000,000; *exports,* $20,615,000,000.

NOVA SCOTIA

During 1988, Nova Scotians participated in political elections, experienced a falling unemployment rate, and were excited by the bronze-medal-winning performance of native son Ray Downey, a light-middleweight boxer, at the Summer Olympics.

Government and Legislation. The Conservative Party led by John Buchanan, which had been hit by various scandals, sought and won its fourth consecutive mandate to rule Nova Scotia. This was a personal victory for John Buchanan, who became the longest reigning premier in Canada. Yet his party suffered a humiliating defeat in many constituencies, especially in Cape Breton where the party virtually was wiped out. Its standing in the House of Assembly dwindled from 40 seats held at election time to 28, while the Liberals increased their legislative strength from 6 seats to 21. The biggest surprise of the election was the failure of the New Democratic Party (NDP) to make a predicted breakthrough. Instead the party lost one seat while Alexa McDonough, its leader, barely managed to retain her seat.

Before going to the polls, the Conservative government had introduced 128 bills of which 78 were enacted. The new laws provided for the establishment of a body to advise the government on issues related to AIDS, the formation of a commission for achieving pay equity among public employees regardless of sex, and the creation of the Clean Nova Scotia Foundation for protecting the natural, physical, and environmental heritage of the province and enforcing a legal ban on all activities related to the exploration of gas and oil reserves over the area covered by Georges Bank. In the wake of the election, the government also announced many public projects, including a C$200 million Halifax harbor cleanup, a new power plant for Cape Breton, and an $8.8 million harness-racing track near Halifax International Airport.

Economy. During 1988, the Nova Scotian economy posted the most rapid growth among the Atlantic provinces. This was attributed to continuous expansion of the service, resource, and manufacturing sectors. Business and personal services showed a strong recovery from a slow 1987, resulting from an increase in summer tourism. During the first half of the year,

Canapress Photo

Nova Scotia's Premier John Buchanan was elected to a fourth term in September 6 provincial elections—but narrowly. His Conservative Party lost 12 seats in the Assembly.

retail trade grew by 6.8%, while the sales of motor vehicles were up by 21.4%.

Despite problems caused by the recent strength of the Canadian dollar, lumber production grew by 20% during the first half of the year. In coal mining, Cape Breton Development Corporation (Devco) experienced a rapid increase in demand for its coal due to a worldwide boom in steel making. The fishing sector remained strong and stable, despite a dramatic tumble in fish prices. Lobster landings hit record levels, and Nova Scotia mussel producers were starting to bounce back from the effects of toxic Prince Edward Island mussels in 1987. In manufacturing, capital expansion plans were announced by Michelin Tires and Lavalin Inc. In addition, Thyssen Industries of West Germany decided to locate a $58 million military-equipment manufacturing plant in Cape Breton. The boisterousness of the various sectors became so sharp that the unemployment rate declined from a 1987 high of 14.5% to 9.6% in July 1988.

R. P. SETH
Mount Saint Vincent University, Halifax

NOVA SCOTIA · Information Highlights

Area: 21,425 sq mi (55 491 km²).
Population (June 1988): 882,600.
Chief cities (1986 census): Halifax, the capital, 113,577; Dartmouth, 65,243; Sydney, 27,754.
Government (1988): *Chief Officers*—lt. gov., Alan R. Abraham; premier, John Buchanan (Progressive Conservative). *Legislature*—House of Assembly, 52 members.
Provincial Finances (1988–89 fiscal year budget): *Revenues,* $3,168,264,000; *expenditures,* $3,283,606,000.
Personal Income (average weekly earnings, June 1988): $416.02.
Labor Force (September 1988, seasonally adjusted): *Employed* workers, 15 years of age and over, 370,000; *Unemployed,* 45,000 (10.8%).
Education (1988–89): *Enrollment*—elementary and secondary schools, 170,700 pupils; postsecondary—universities, 24,950; community colleges, 2,350.

(All monetary figures are in Canadian dollars.)

OBITUARIES

UPI/Bettmann Newsphotos

NEVELSON, Louise

American sculptor: b. Kiev, Russia, Sept. 23, 1900; d. New York City, April 17, 1988.

One of the best-known women artists of the 20th century, Louise Nevelson caught the public imagination with her pioneering work in environmental sculpture. Her large, abstract, wood sculptures—box structures filled with odd pieces of furniture, wheels, doorknobs, and other found objects—earned her an international reputation in the 1950s and remain on display in the great museums of the world. The critic Hilton Kramer once described her works as "utterly shocking . . . , yet profoundly exhilarating in the way they open an entire realm of possibility."

In the 1960s and 1970s, Nevelson turned from the dark wooden assemblages to sculp-

© Ken Howard

AP/Wide World

L'AMOUR, Louis

American novelist: b. Jamestown, ND, March 22, 1908; d. Los Angeles, CA, June 10, 1988.

One of the world's most popular novelists, Louis L'Amour wrote a total of 101 books (86 novels, 14 short-story collections, and one nonfiction work); almost 200 million copies of his books are in circulation. His novels include such Western classics as *Hondo* and *The Burning Hills*.

L'Amour described himself as a storyteller in the old folk tradition. His tales are characterized by their fast-paced plotting, meticulous research, and plain-speaking characters. Many celebrate the breed of "hard-shelled men" who opened the American West. One element notable for its absence is violence, despite the six-

HOUSEMAN, John

U.S. theatrical producer, director, and actor: b. Bucharest, Romania, Sept. 22, 1902; d. Malibu, CA, Oct. 31, 1988.

John Houseman, one of American theater's major personalities, gained success at age 71 as Professor Kingsfield, the autocratic law professor of *The Paper Chase* (1973), a film role which brought him an Academy Award. The film led to the 1978 television series in which he also appeared. Much of his career, however, came prior to his encounter with Kingsfield. According to James Bridges, director of *The Paper Chase*, Houseman's influence was so great that "almost every major theater in America is run by a Houseman protégé."

Background. Jacques Haussmann was the son of a British mother and an Alsatian father,

tures employing brighter materials—metal and plexiglass—and brighter finishes—white and gold. Influenced by pre-Columbian and Futurist art, both her wall-mounted and freestanding works are compositional rather than figurative in form, and passionately independent in spirit. Her best-known sculptures include *Sky Cathedral* (1958), *Night Presence IV* (1972), and *Sky Gate, New York* (1978) at Manhattan's World Trade Center. In 1977–78 she executed the all-white Chapel of the Good Shepherd for Saint Peter's Lutheran Church in mid-Manhattan, and in 1979 the Louise Nevelson Plaza—an outdoor display of her black sculptures—was dedicated in lower Manhattan.

Background. One of four children, Louise Berliawsky left her native Kiev at age five in 1905, when her father moved the family to Rockland, ME. Her father ran a lumberyard, where the young girl would spend hours scav-

enging for odd pieces of wood. In 1920 she was married to Charles Nevelson, whose family was in the shipping business, and moved to New York. After studying acting and music, she spent two years at the Art Students League under the painter and etcher Kenneth Hayes Miller. Separated from her husband in 1931, she studied with Hans Hofmann in Munich and returned to New York in 1932 to become an assistant to the Mexican artist Diego Rivera. Although she began exhibiting her work as early as 1933, she did not have her own show until 1941 and did not earn a steady income from her art until the 1960s.

As stylized in her dress as in her art, as passionate in her belief in political freedom as in her pursuit of creative freedom, Nevelson worked energetically almost until the time of her death. She was survived by a son.

JEFFREY H. HACKER

---

shooters carried by his heroes. But "I don't like being pigeonholed," L'Amour said, and not all of his books are Westerns. *Last of the Breed* is set in modern-day Siberia, its hero an Air Force pilot taken prisoner after a forced landing.

Background. Louis Dearborn LaMoore was born in Jamestown, ND, on March 22, 1908. As a child, he listened to tales about his great-grandfather, who was scalped by the Sioux, and his grandfather, who fought in the Civil War. When Louis was 15, he left school to drift around the West, supporting himself at various kinds of manual labor and meeting people with tales of frontier life.

While serving in the tank corps in World War II, he entertained his fellow soldiers with Western yarns. One of his listeners suggested that he write his stories down, and in the late 1940s, L'Amour began selling them to the

pulps under the name Tex Burns. In 1951, "Tex Burns" published his first novel, *Hopalong Cassidy and the Riders of High Rock*. His first novel as Louis L'Amour was *Hondo*, in 1953. Over the next five years, L'Amour wrote 15 books for several publishers.

After coming under contract to Bantam Books in 1955, L'Amour kept up a three-book-a-year pace for the rest of his life, producing such best-sellers as *Guns of the Timberland, Shalako,* and *The Silver Canyon*. His last novel was *The Haunted Mesa* (1987), and he was working on his autobiography when he died.

L'Amour's awards and citations included the Congressional Medal of Honor (1983)—he was the first novelist to be so honored—and the Presidential Medal of Freedom (1984). L'Amour and his wife Katherine were married in 1956; they had a son and a daughter.

LINDA TRIEGEL

---

who was in the grain-trading business. Houseman was educated at the Clifton School in England and had a short-lived career as a grain merchant. He arrived in the United States in 1924, becoming a citizen in 1943.

His first major show-business break came in 1934 when the composer Virgil Thomson offered him the chance to direct his opera, *Four Saints in Three Acts*. A year later, Houseman began a productive collaboration with the actor-director Orson Welles. Among their first projects, organized through the Works Progress Administration's Federal Theatre Project, were the WPA Negro Theatre Project in 1935, which made history with a version of *Macbeth* set in Haiti, and the Classical Theatre in 1936. In 1937 the collaborators established the Mercury Theatre, known for its innovative productions of the classics, and they were involved in radio's Mercury Theatre of the Air.

Between 1943 and 1956, Houseman produced films for certain Hollywood studios, among them *The Bad and the Beautiful* (1952), which garnered several Academy Awards. He also directed various stage productions and was artistic director of the American Shakespeare Festival Theatre (1956–59), UCLA's Professional Theatre Group (1959–63), and was director of the drama division of New York's Juilliard School (1967–76), where he established the acclaimed Acting Company.

Houseman maintained his interest in opera as well, directing *Otello* and *Tosca* for the Dallas Civil Opera Company in the 1960s. He also was acclaimed for such television productions as *The Seven Lively Arts* (1957) and *Playhouse 90* (1958–59). In his later years, he became familiar to television audiences for his commercials and appeared in occasional films.

SAUNDRA FRANCE MCMAHON

The following is a selected list of prominent persons who died during 1988.
Articles on major figures appear in the preceding pages.

Addams, Charles (76), cartoonist; provided offbeat cartoons to *The New Yorker* during a 50-year period. His sense of the macabre was often evident as in one 1946 drawing depicting strange-looking residents of a Victorian house. He had 12 published books, the last of which was *Creature Comforts* (1982): d. New York City, Sept. 29.

Adler, Kurt (82), Viennese-born conductor; led the San Francisco Opera for 28 years as artistic director (1953–56) and general director (1956–81), making it into one of the leading opera ensembles in the world. Prior to emigrating to the United States in 1938, he conducted at opera houses in Germany, Italy, and Czechoslovakia: d. Ross, CA, Feb. 9.

Alvarez, Luis W. (77), physicist and winner of the 1968 Nobel Prize in Physics; he was a member of the team that developed the atomic bomb during World War II. He won the Nobel Prize for his use of bubble chambers to detect new subatomic particles. Other scientific work that he engaged in included the development of a type of radar to aid aircraft landings, the use of radiation from space to prove that there were no hidden chambers in the Chephren pyramid in Egypt, and more recently, with his son, support of the controversial theory that one or more extraterrestrial impacts killed off the dinosaurs and hundreds of other species 65 million years ago. Nearly all of his academic career was spent at the University of California at Berkeley: d. Berkeley, CA, Sept. 1.

Ameche, Alan (55), football player; was a running back for the Baltimore Colts (1954–60); he scored in overtime to defeat the New York Giants in the National Football League's 1958 championship game. He was an All Pro selection for four years: d. Houston, Aug. 8.

Anable, Gloria Hollister (87), explorer, scientist, conservationist; set a women's world record in 1931 for ocean descent in a bathysphere, going down 410 ft (125 m). A longtime associate of oceanographer William Beebe, she was on many of his voyages of the 1920s and 1930s. She also served with expeditions of the New York Zoological Society and worked in its laboratory: d. Fairfield, CT, Feb. 19.

Anderson, Herbert (74), physicist; a close associate of Enrico Fermi, he was a pioneer in the development of nuclear energy and the atomic bomb: d. Santa Fe, NM, July 16.

Armstrong, Henry (born Henry Jackson) (75), boxer; held three world titles simultaneously in 1938 as featherweight, lightweight, and welterweight. He began his career in 1931, and beginning in 1937 won 46 consecutive bouts. He was elected to the Boxing Hall of Fame in 1954: d. Los Angeles, CA, Oct. 24.

Aronson, James (73), editor, teacher, journalism critic; co-founded *The National Guardian*, a left-wing weekly, in 1948. He turned the publication over to his staff in 1967: d. New York City, Oct. 21.

Artukovic, Andrija (88), Yugoslav former leader of the Nazi puppet state of Croatia; he was extradited from the United States to Yugoslavia in 1986 after a long-disputed extradition process. He was condemned to death in Yugoslavia for mass murder committed during World War II, but had won a stay of execution and died of natural causes: d. Zagreb, Yugoslavia, Jan. 16.

Ashby, Hal (59), motion-picture director; his films include *Harold and Maude, Shampoo, Coming Home, The Last Detail, Being There,* and *Bound for Glory.* He also had been a film editor and in 1968 won an Oscar for editing *In the Heat of the Night:* d. Malibu, CA, Dec. 27.

Ashton, Sir Frederick (83), British ballet dancer, choreographer, director; he was for most of his career associated with the British Royal Ballet, joining that company in 1935 after study with Léonide Massine and an association with Dame Marie Rambert and Ida Rubinstein in Paris. Among his important early works for the Royal Ballet were *A Wedding Bouquet* and *Les Patineurs.* With the coming of World War II, he turned to ballets depicting struggles between good and evil, including *Dante Sonata* and *The Wise Virgins.* The postwar years brought *Symphonic Variations, Cinderella, Daphnis and Chloe, Ondine, La Fille Mal Gardée,* and *Monotones;* more recent works include *A Month in the Country, La Chatte Métamorphosée en Femme* and *Fanfare for Elizabeth.* Many of his ballets starred the ballerina Margot Fonteyn. Sir Frederick, who developed into one of the greatest classical choreographers, was director of the Royal Ballet between 1963 and 1970. In an early collaboration that is remembered as legendary, he was invited to New York in 1934 to choreograph *Four Saints in Three Acts,* an opera with music by Virgil Thomson and text by Gertrude Stein: d. Sussex, England, Aug. 18.

Astorga, Nora (39), Nicaragua's chief delegate to the United Nations (1986–88) and a Sandinista hero of the revolution that came to power in 1979 after overthrowing Gen. Anastasio Somoza Debayle. She also served for a time as a deputy foreign minister and was rejected in 1984 by the United States as Nicaraguan ambassador to the United States: d. Managua, Nicaragua, Feb. 14.

Barabas, Alfred J. (77), football halfback for Columbia University who scored the only touchdown in Columbia's 7–0 upset victory over Stanford University in the 1934 Rose Bowl game: d. Rockville, MD, Jan 7.

Barragán, Luis (86), Mexican architect, considered his country's greatest architect. He designed mainly houses, housing complexes, fountains, public plazas, and monumental gates. He won architecture's prestigious Pritzker Prize in 1980: d. Mexico City, Nov. 22.

Bell, Travers J., Jr. (46), founder (1971) and owner of the security firm Daniels and Bell, Inc., the only black-owned member of the New York Stock Exchange: d. New York City, Jan. 25.

Berlin, Ellin (85), novelist and wife of songwriter Irving Berlin; she wrote several articles for *The New Yorker* and four novels. She was a Roman Catholic debutante who rebelled against her wealthy father and married the Jewish songwriter: d. New York City, July 29.

Bible, Alan (78), U.S. senator (D-NV, 1954–75); best known for his advocacy of national parks: d. Auburn, CA, Sept. 12.

Bingham, Barry, Sr. (82), newspaper publisher; was owner of the Louisville, KY, *Courier Journal* and the *Louisville Times.* The family businesses also included Louisville television and radio stations and a printing company. He sold the papers and other businesses in 1986 because of family dissension: d. Louisville, KY, Aug. 15.

Boxer, Mark (born Charles Mark Edward) (57), British editor, cartoonist, and satirist; drew under the pen name of Marc and in his cartoons created the Stringalongs, a social-climbing couple: d. London, July 20.

Boyington, Gregory (Pappy) (75), Marine flying ace of World War II; commanded the Black Sheep Squadron, shot down 28 planes, and was awarded the Congressional Medal of Honor and the Navy Cross. In 1958 he wrote *Baa Baa Black Sheep,* a best-seller about his flying exploits: d. Fresno, CA, Jan. 11.

Bradshaw, Thornton F. (71), chairman of RCA between 1981 and 1985, when the company was sold to the General Electric Company. He was also a former chairman of Atlantic Richfield Company: d. New York City, Dec. 6.

Branton, Wiley (65), attorney; was the principal lawyer in the civil-rights case that desegregated the public schools in Little Rock, AR, in 1957. He was later dean of Howard University Law School (1978–83): d. Washington, DC, Dec. 15.

Charles Addams

Luis W. Alvarez

Sir Frederick Ashton

Luis Barragán

Photos, AP/Wide World

Brewster, Kingman, Jr. (69), president of Yale University (1963–77) and ambassador to Britain (1977–81). Since 1986 he had been the master of one of the colleges at Oxford University. An alumnus of Yale College, Harvard Law School, and a former Harvard Law professor, he presided over a turbulent period at Yale, involving student protests, increased minority enrollment, and the admission of women to the university: d. Oxford, England, Nov. 8.

Brownson, Charles B. (74), U.S. representative (R-IN, 1951–59); later founded the *Congressional Staff Directory*, a comprehensive reference work for congressional staff members: d. Washington, DC, Aug. 4.

Burk, Dean (84), chemist with the National Cancer Institute for more than 30 years; he retired in 1974. He won the Hildebrand Prize in 1952 for work on photosynthesis and the Gerhard Domagk Prize in 1965 for the development of procedures for distinguishing the difference between a normal cell and one damaged by cancer. He was also codeveloper of the prototype of the nuclear magnetic resonance scanner and a codiscoverer of biotin, a B-complex vitamin: d. Washington, DC, Oct. 6.

Butterfield, Charles William (Billy) (71), trumpeter; was with the Bob Crosby, Artie Shaw, and Benny Goodman bands as well as the World's Greatest Jazz Band, founded in 1968: d. North Palm Beach, FL, March 18.

Byrd, Richard E., Jr. (68), son of the famous admiral and Arctic explorer, he had accompanied his father on a journey to Antarctica in 1947: d. Baltimore, MD, Oct. 3 (found dead).

Caliguiri, Richard S. (56), mayor of Pittsburgh (1977–88); provided leadership during a period when the city began to diversify its economy following the decline of the steel industry: d. Pittsburgh, PA, May 6.

Campbell, William J. (83), the longest serving federal judge in the United States; he was appointed in 1940 by President Franklin D. Roosevelt. Before becoming a judge, he helped prosecute Al Capone on tax-evasion charges: d. Florida, Oct. 19.

Campion, Donald R. (67), Jesuit priest, author, and editor in chief of the Catholic weekly magazine *America* (1968–75): d. New York City, Dec. 11.

Caniff, Milton A. (81), cartoonist; wrote the comic strips *Terry and the Pirates* and *Steve Canyon:* d. New York City, April 3.

Carradine, John (born Richmond Reed Carradine) (82), actor; appeared in more than 200 films in a career spanning more than 50 years, often in character roles. He also appeared on the stage, touring with *Hamlet* in the 1940s. His last major role on Broadway was in the 1962 musical *A Funny Thing Happened on the Way to the Forum*. His first important film role was in *The Grapes of Wrath* (1940): d. Milan, Italy, Nov. 27.

Carter, William Alton 3d (Billy) (51), brother of former President Jimmy Carter, he took charge of the family peanut warehouse and farm in Plains, GA, when Jimmy Carter ran for president, but found life in the limelight difficult. He was the subject of investigations by the Internal Revenue Service and other government agencies: d. Plains, GA, Sept. 25.

Carver, Raymond (50), short-story writer and poet; his books were inhabited by working-class people, the people of Carver's background. He first gained attention with the short story, *Will You Please Be Quiet, Please?* in 1967: d. Port Angeles, WA, Aug. 2.

Castellano, Richard (55), actor; noted for his portrayal of Italian-Americans; won praise in the film *The Godfather* (1972) and for his performances in the Broadway stage and film comedy *Lovers and Other Strangers* (1970): d. North Bergen, NJ, Dec. 10.

Chiang Ching-kuo (77), president of Taiwan (1978–88); he had been the prime minister (1972–78). He was the son and political heir of Chiang Kai-shek, the Chinese Nationalist leader who fled mainland China following his defeat by the Communists in 1949. Chiang's death ended the era in which the Chinese who fled the mainland were the prime leaders of Taiwan: d. Taipei, Taiwan, Jan. 13.

Chinh, Truong (80), one of the last of the original group of militant Communist revolutionaries of Vietnam; he was general secretary of the Communist Party in Vietnam (1941–56) and again for six months in 1986. He was also head of the National Assembly (1960–76): d. Hanoi, Vietnam, Sept. 30.

Cohn, Al (62), musician; was a jazz saxophonist and arranger. He had a long association with saxophonist Zoot Sims; together they made the album *Al and Zoot* that won critical acclaim: d. East Stroudsburg, PA, Feb. 15.

Cournand, André F. (92), French-born physician and a Nobelist in medicine (1956). He was a professor of medicine at Columbia University from 1935 until his retirement in 1964, although he continued for a time thereafter as a special lecturer. His Nobel Prize, which he shared with others, was for perfecting a method of exploring the heart through catheterization: d. Great Barrington, MA, Feb. 19.

Cousins, The Rev. William Edward (86), Roman Catholic archbishop of Milwaukee (1959–77). Considered a liberal churchman, the archbishop was a central figure in a civil-rights controversy in the 1960s when he gave qualified support to a

Photos, AP/Wide World

Kingman Brewster, Jr.   Raymond Carver

liberal priest who advocated open housing laws and was a militant leader of civil-rights marches: d. Milwaukee, WI, Sept. 14.

Cunningham, Glenn (78), a former world record holder for the mile run; in 1979 he was named the greatest track performer in the history of Madison Square Garden in New York: d. Menifee, AR, March 10.

Daniel, Price (77), Texas politician; served as a state legislator (1939–43), U.S. senator (1953–57), governor (1957–63), and member of the Texas Supreme Court (1971–79). He also was an assistant to President Lyndon B. Johnson: d. Liberty, TX, Aug. 25.

Daniels, Billy (73), nightclub performer, actor, and singer; gained fame in 1948 with his recording of *That Old Black Magic*. He also made several movies and appeared on the stage: d. Los Angeles, CA, Oct. 7.

Dart, Raymond A. (95), Australian-born anatomist who in 1924 revolutionized the study of human origins with his discovery of the Taung child, a nearly complete skull of a three-year-old child found in Taung, South Africa. Dart claimed that the skull had a mixture of apelike and humanlike features, but was more human than ape. He called the species *Australopithecus africanus*. Later research determined that these creatures lived two to three million years ago, and work by Louis Leakey established the African genesis of early humans: d. Johannesburg, South Africa, Nov. 22.

Davis, Glenn (73), U.S. representative (R-WI, 1947–57; 1965–75); he was a strong supporter of President Richard Nixon: d. Arlington, VA, Sept. 21.

Dawn, Hazel (born Hazel Tout) (98), singer and actress in the early part of the 20th century; she was known as "The Pink Lady," from a musical of the same name in which she made her Broadway debut in 1911. She starred in the original *Ziegfeld Follies* and in silent films: d. New York City, Aug. 28.

Day, Dennis (born Eugene Denis McNulty) (71), singer and actor; became popular as the Irish tenor and comic foil on Jack Benny's radio and television shows: d. Bel Air, CA, June 22.

Dearden, Cardinal John (80), Roman Catholic churchman; served as archbishop of Detroit (1958–80). He was named a cardinal in 1969: d. Southfield, MI, Aug. 1.

Dell, Gabriel (born Gabriel del Vecchio) (68), stage and film actor; began acting on Broadway as one of the Dead End Kids, appearing in *Dead End* (1935) and later in the film version. He went on to appear in many films and stage plays, including *Luv* and *Prisoner of Second Avenue:* d. North Hollywood, CA, July 3.

Devereux, James P. S. (85), U.S. representative (R-MD, 1951–59) and a World War II hero for his defense of Wake Island against overwhelming Japanese forces in 1941. After 15 days of combat, he surrendered to avoid a bloodbath. He spent four years in Japanese prison camps and later was awarded the Navy Cross: d. Baltimore, MD, Aug. 5.

Diamond, I. A. L. (67), screenwriter and longtime collaborator with director Billy Wilder; won an Academy Award for *The Apartment* (1960): d. Beverly Hills, CA, April 21.

Divine (born Harris Glenn Milstead) (42), film actor; known for his transvestite roles in the films *Pink Flamingos, Lust in the Dust, Polyester, Female Trouble,* and *Hairspray:* d. Hollywood, CA, March 7.

Dodd, Bobby (Robert Lee) (79), football coach (1944–66) and athletic director (1950–76) at Georgia Tech; member of the National Football Hall of Fame: d. Atlanta, GA, June 21.

Dorati, Antal (82), Hungarian-born orchestra conductor; led the National Symphony in Washington (1970–77). He championed the music of Bartók. He made his conducting debut with the Budapest Royal Opera in 1924. From there he worked at the Dresden Opera and the Münster Opera. Between 1933 and 1941, he was a conductor with the Ballet Russe de Monte Carlo and between 1941 and 1945 was with the American Ballet Theatre. He later was with the Dallas Symphony, the

Minneapolis Symphony, the Royal Philharmonic in London, and his last full-time post was with the Detroit Symphony (1977–81): d. Gerzensee, Switzerland, Nov. 13.

Drees, Jack (71), radio and television sports broadcaster; announced the Chicago White Sox games (1968–72): d. Dallas, TX, July 27.

Drees, Willem (101), prime minister of the Netherlands (1948–58); instituted that nation's comprehensive welfare system: d. The Hague, Netherlands, May 14.

Drozak, Frank (60), president of the Seafarers International Union of North America (1980–88): d. Alexandria, VA, June 11.

Duggan, Andrew (64), actor; appeared in many Broadway productions in the 1940s and 1950s. He began working in television in the 1950s. His film credits include *Seven Days in May* (1964): d. Los Angeles, CA, May 15.

Dulski, Thaddeus J. (73), U.S. representative (D-NY, 1959–75). He helped write the legislation creating an independent U.S. Postal Service: d. Buffalo, NY, Oct. 11.

Duncan, John J. (69), U.S. representative (R-TN, 1965–88): d. Knoxville, TN, June 21.

Eames, Ray (72), a founder and partner of the California design firm, the Office of Charles and Ray Eames, that designed the Eames chair and had an influence on furniture and industrial design for 40 years: d. Los Angeles, CA, Aug. 21.

Eldridge, Florence (86), actress; best known for her stage performances, particularly in *Long Day's Journey into Night* (1956), with her husband Fredric March, a performance for which she won the New York Drama Critics award for best actress. She also appeared on stage with her husband and Tallulah Bankhead in *Skin of Our Teeth* (1942): d. Santa Barbara, CA, Aug. 1.

Estes, Eleanor (82), children's book author; won the prestigious John Newbery Medal in 1952 for *Ginger Pye:* d. Hamden, CT, July 15.

Evans, Gil (born Ian Ernest Gilmore Green) (75), Canadian-born jazz composer and arranger; he became second only to Duke Ellington as the most important composer and orchestrator in post-World War II jazz: d. Cuernavaca, Mexico, March 20.

Eyskens, Gaston (82), prime minister of Belgium (1949; 1958–61; 1968–72), he also served as finance minister in several administrations. A member of the Social Christian Party, he was elected to Parliament in 1939: d. Louvain, Belgium, Jan. 3.

Farida (Safinaz Zulficar) (68), former queen of Egypt; she married King Farouk in 1938, adopting the name Farida in accordance with a tradition that all members of the royal family have the same initial. The king divorced her in 1948 after she had had three daughters but no male heir: d. Cairo, Egypt, Oct. 16.

Faure, Edgar (79), French prime minister (1952; 1955–56); served in the National Assembly (1946–58), and held 11 cabinet posts in a career spanning more than 30 years: d. Paris, March 30.

Fennelly, Parker W. (96), actor on radio, film, and television; known especially for his portrayals of old Yankee characters: d. Peekskill, NY, Jan. 22.

Ferrari, Enzo (90), Italian racing-car enthusiast and founder and chairman of the car company that bore his name: d. Modena, Italy, Aug. 14.

Feynman, Richard P. (69), Nobel-Prize-winning theoretical physicist and a developer of quantum theories; his Feynman diagrams are now in universal use by physicists. He was involved with the Manhattan Project that built the atomic bomb at Los Alamos, NM, during World War II. After the war he taught at Cornell University and within four years had completed the work in quantum electrodynamics that won him the Nobel Prize in physics in 1965 (shared with two other scientists). In 1950 he went to the California Institute of Technology where he spent the rest of his life. His collaborations with fellow physicist Murray Gell-Mann brought about the discovery of new laws and the investigation of the weak force. His other major scientific achievements included the mathematical theory that explained the behavior of liquid helium near a temperature of absolute zero and his explanation of the behavior of electrons in high-energy collisions done at the Stanford Linear Accelerator Center: d. Los Angeles, CA, Feb. 15.

Ffolkes, Michael (born Brian Davis) (63), cartoonist for *Punch* and several other periodicals: d. London, Oct. 18.

Fidler, Jimmie (89), Hollywood gossip columnist; at his peak, he was heard on 486 radio stations, and his column appeared in 360 newspapers: d. Los Angeles, CA, Aug. 9.

Foreman, Percy (86), defense attorney; defended James Earl Ray, the accused assassin of Dr. Martin Luther King. He once estimated that he had tried 1,500 death-penalty cases, but only one of his clients was executed. In the Ray case, he had Ray plead guilty in exchange for a 99-year sentence: d. Houston, TX, Aug. 25.

Fornasetti, Piero (74), Italian artist and designer; internationally known for his black and white ceramics and furniture: d. Milan, Italy, Oct. 9.

Franco, Carmen Polo de (87), widow of the Spanish military ruler Francisco Franco in power from 1939 to 1975: d. Madrid, Spain, Feb. 6.

Frank, Melvin (75), film writer, producer, and director of some memorable romantic comedies of the 1940s and 1950s. He, along with his collaborator, Norman Panama, brought out such films as *Mr. Blandings Builds His Dream House, My Favorite Blonde, The Return of October, Road to Utopia, The Court Jester,* and *Road to Hong Kong.* The team also wrote and produced the Broadway musical *Li'l Abner* (1956; film 1959): d. Los Angeles, CA, Oct. 13.

Freeman, Paul Lamar, Jr. (80), U.S. Army four-star general; infantry commander in World War II and the Korean War. He also was a former commander in chief of the U.S. Army in Europe and the North Atlantic Treaty Organization Central Army Group (1962–65): d. Monterey, CA, April 17.

Frenay, Henri (82), a leader in the French Resistance during World War II: d. Aug. 6.

Frobe, Gert (born Karl-Gerhard Frobe) (75), German actor; played in nearly 100 movies including *Goldfinger* (1964), *Those Magnificent Men in Their Flying Machines* (1965), and *Is Paris Burning?* (1966): d. Munich, Sept. 5.

Fuchs, Klaus (76), German-born physicist; was imprisoned in Britain in the 1950s for passing nuclear secrets to the USSR. His case led to the uncovering of a nuclear espionage ring that led to the execution of Ethel and Julius Rosenberg in 1953. Upon his release from prison, he moved to East Germany: d. Jan. 28.

Fuller, S. B. (83), a door-to-door entrepreneur; he became the first black member of the National Association of Manufacturers: d. Blue Island, IL, Oct. 24.

Galbreath, John W. (90), real-estate developer and sportsman who owned the Pittsburgh Pirates baseball team (1946–85): d. near Columbus, OH, July 20.

Gerson, Noel Bertram (75), author of more than 325 books; wrote under his own name and several pseudonyms. His works include the "Wagons West" series and the "White Indian" series: d. Boca Raton, FL, Nov. 20.

Gibb, Andy (30), Australian-born popular singer; the younger brother of the threesome who made up the BeeGees: d. Oxfordshire, England, March 10.

Gillars, Mildred (born Mildred Elizabeth Sisk) (87), known as Axis Sally for her Nazi propaganda radio broadcasts to Allied forces in Europe and North Africa during World War II. She was an American who lived in Berlin. After the war, she was tried and imprisoned for 12 years for treason: d. Columbus, OH, June 25.

Gollan, Frank (78), physician; isolated the type MM poliomyelitis virus. In the early 1950s he was a leader in the development of

Andrew Duggan

Florence Eldridge

Richard P. Feynman

Andy Gibb

Photos, AP/Wide World

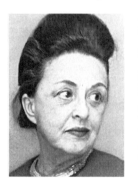

Sheilah Graham

Robert A. Heinlein

Carl Hubbell

Photos, AP/Wide World

Robert Joffrey

the heart-lung machine for use in open-heart surgery. He and his wife, both in deteriorating health, appeared to be suicides: d. Miami, FL, Oct. 5.

Goossens, Leon (90), British oboist; his exceptional talents caused several prominent composers, including Benjamin Britten and Francis Poulenc, to write music for him and thus to add to the repertory for the instrument: d. Tunbridge Wells, Kent, England, Feb. 12.

Graham, Sheilah (born Lily Shiel) (84), British-born Hollywood gossip columnist who rose from poverty in a London slum and who, along with Hedda Hopper and Louella Parsons, made up a powerful trio of Hollywood journalists. She was probably best remembered for her love affair with F. Scott Fitzgerald, of which she wrote in her first book, *Beloved Infidel* (1958). She wrote several other books, some of which centered on Fitzgerald: d. Palm Beach, FL, Nov. 17.

Granville Wrather, Bonita (65), a child film star of the 1930s; she later was an executive in the Wrather Corporation, a complex of oil, entertainment, and real-estate businesses founded by her husband. She won a 1936 Oscar nomination for *These Three* and appeared in more than 50 other motion pictures: d. Santa Monica, CA, Oct. 11.

Gross, Robert E. (83), cardiovascular surgeon; performed the first surgical correction (in 1938) of one of the most common congenital heart disorders in children, closing the opening between the aorta and an artery of the lung, which usually closes after birth. In 1948 he was the first surgeon to graft artery tissue from one person to another: d. Plymouth, MA, Oct. 11.

Hall, Al (72), jazz bassist; worked with many of the famous jazz musicians: d. New York City, Jan. 18.

Hamilton, Hamish (87), American-born British publisher; worked for Jonathan Cape publishers and Harper and Brothers before starting his own company in 1931. His first major success was John Gunther's *Inside Europe*, and he went on to build a distinguished house with a number of prominent authors: d. London, May 25.

Hansell, Haywood, Jr. (85), U.S. commander of American strategic bombing of Germany and Japan in World War II as an Army Air Force major general. He had joined the Army in 1928 and soon became a stunt pilot, working with the Air Corps Aerobatic and Demonstration team known as "The Men on the Flying Trapeze": d. Hilton Head, SC, Nov. 14.

Hargreaves, Roger (53), creator of Mister Men—figures with circles for heads, two dots for eyes, and a U for mouths, which appeared on countless items and inspired Mr. Men and Little Miss books: d. Kent, England, Sept. 12.

Hatem, George (born Shafick Hatem) (78), American doctor who spent more than 50 years in China as a leader in public health. He won the Albert Lasker Public Service Award in 1986: d. Beijing, Oct. 3.

Heinlein, Robert A. (80), science-fiction writer; a former aviation engineer, his fiction showed imagination and technical expertise. His stories often foreshadowed scientific and technical advances; he wrote of the atomic bomb before one was exploded. His most famous book is probably *A Stranger in a Strange Land* (1961): d. Carmel, CA, May 8.

Higgins, Colin (47), screenwriter and director; he wrote the film *Harold and Maude* (1971), which became a cult favorite; he also wrote and directed *Foul Play* (1978) and *9 to 5* (1980): d. Los Angeles, CA, Aug. 5.

Hinkle, Clarke (79), football star; played with the Green Bay Packers (1932–41). He was a four-time All-Pro player and a member of the Pro Football Hall of Fame: d. Toronto, OH, Nov. 9.

Holman, M. Carl (69), civil-rights activist and president of the National Urban Coalition (1977–88); he helped found the black journal *The Atlantic Inquirer* in 1960, and in 1962 joined the staff of the U.S. Commission on Civil Rights: d. Washington, DC, Aug. 9.

Holmes, John Clellon (62), novelist and poet; considered a spokesman of the Beat Generation. His novel *Go* (1952) was where the phrase first appeared. He was also a professor at the University of Arkansas (1976–87): d. Middletown, CT, March 30.

Howard, Trevor (71), British actor of stage and films. He began his career in the theater, appearing in Shakespearean roles and in 1935 in Sheridan's *Rivals*. His first film role came in 1943 in director Sir Carol Reed's *The Way Ahead;* he went on to do some of his most memorable work in Reed's films, including *The Third Man* (1950). He is probably best known for *Brief Encounter* (1946). In all he made more than 70 films: d. Bushey, England, Jan. 7.

Hubbell, Carl (85), baseball Hall of Fame pitcher; won 253 games for the New York Giants. A left-hander, he pitched only with the Giants, between 1928 and 1943, and was the National League's most valuable player in 1933 and 1936. He won 21 or more games each year from 1933 to 1937. Among outstanding examples of his pitching talent were a no-hitter against Pittsburgh in 1929, his first full season in the major leagues; an 18-inning, 1–0, victory over St. Louis in 1933; and the striking out in order in the 1934 All-Star Game of five of baseball's greatest hitters—Babe Ruth, Lou Gehrig, Jimmie Foxx, Al Simmons, and Joe Cronin—all of whom are now in the Hall of Fame: d. Scottsdale, AZ, Nov. 21.

Hung, Pham (born Pham Van Thien) (75), prime minister of Vietnam (1987–88). He joined the Indochinese Communist Party in 1930. After the defeat of the French in Vietnam in 1954, he rose rapidly in the Communist party, entering the politburo in 1956. He also served as a deputy prime minister and interior minister: d. Ho Chi Minh City, Vietnam, March 10.

Hurd, Clement G. (80), illustrator of children's books; he had done nearly 100 books. He was probably best known for *Goodnight Moon* (1947), which never has been out of print. Other books that he had illustrated include the "I Can Read" series for Harper and Row: d. San Francisco, CA, Feb. 5.

Iannelli, Fons (71), photojournalist who during World War II documented naval combat and who later became a leading magazine photographer. His war photos were collected in *U.S. Navy War Photographs,* edited by Edward Steichen and included in group shows at the Museum of Modern Art: d. Jersey City, NJ, Aug. 26.

Isbell, Marion W. (83), founder of the chain of Ramada motels: d. Scottsdale, AZ, Oct. 20.

Joffrey, Robert (born Abdullah Jaffa Bey Khan) (57), founder and artistic director of the Joffrey Ballet, a company that started as a touring group of six dancers. Between 1954 and 1962, Joffrey did much of the choreography for the group. Later, the company became the resident ballet company of City Center Theater in New York and began to gain a reputation as a repository of dance and as an innovative company where modern-dance choreographers could try their skills with ballet. Joffrey danced with Roland Petit's Ballets de Paris in New York early in his career and also gained a reputation as a teacher with American Ballet Theatre School and the High School of Performing Arts. Between 1957 and 1962 he was resident choreographer for the New York City Opera. His first major ballet was *Persephone* (1952). His *Astarte,* a rock ballet, was a hit in 1967: d. New York City, March 25.

Jonas, Charles Raper (83), U.S. representative (R-NC, 1953–73): d. Lincolnton, MD, Sept. 30.

Jordan, Jim (91), radio personality; played Fibber McGee in the show *Fibber McGee and Molly,* which ran on the NBC radio network from 1935 to 1957: d. Beverly Hills, CA, April 1.

Kiesinger, Kurt Georg (83), chancellor of West Germany (1966–69); he had joined the Nazi Party in 1933 but was soon disillusioned and had become an inactive member by 1934. He led his country during a time of economic difficulties, which necessitated a partnership between his Christian Democrats and the more left-wing Social Democrats. He held a seat in

Photos, AP/Wide World

Frederick Loewe   *Joshua Logan*   *Georgi Malenkov*   *John Mitchell*

parliament from 1949 until 1980: d. Tübingen, West Germany, March 9.

Killian, James R., Jr. (83), science administrator; chairman of the President's Science Advisory committee (1957–59); as such he worked on the creation of the National Aeronautics and Space Administration, which began operating in 1958. A science administrator, not a scientist, he earlier had served as president of Massachusetts Institute of Technology (1947–57): d. Cambridge, MA, Jan. 29.

Kluszewski, Ted (63), professional-baseball player; during 15 seasons as a major league first baseman, 11 of them with Cincinnati, he batted .298 and hit 279 home runs. He led the National League in home runs (49) in 1954, and retired from the game in 1961: d. Cincinnati, OH, March 29.

Krasner, Milton (84), cinematographer; won an Academy Award for *Three Coins in the Fountain* (1954): d. Los Angeles, CA, July 19.

Kuenn, Harvey (57), manager of baseball's Milwaukee Brewers (1982–83); as a player with the Detroit Tigers, he was the American League rookie of the year (1953) and batting champion (1959). During his playing career, he had a lifetime batting average of .303 in 15 seasons: d. Peoria, AZ, Feb. 28.

Laing, Hugh (born Hugh Skinner) (77), ballet dancer; born in Barbados; former star of American Ballet Theatre; he specialized in Antony Tudor ballets: d. New York City, May 10.

La Meri (born Russell Meriwether Hughes) (89), dancer, teacher, and dance ethnologist; considered the leading American authority on ethnic dance, particularly the dance of India and Spain: d. San Antonio, TX, Jan. 7.

Lassiter, Luther (Wimpy) (69), billiards player; he won six world billiards championships: d. Elizabeth City, NC, Oct. 25.

Lazarus, Ralph (74), chairman of Federated Department Stores (1967–82); he also had been president of the company whose many divisions included Abraham & Straus and Bloomingdales, beginning in 1957: d. Cincinnati, OH, June 18.

Leach, Wilford (59), theater director; he had been associated with New York's Public Theater, the New York Shakespeare Festival, and with La Mama, an experimental theater company. He won Tony Awards for the Broadway musicals *The Pirates of Penzance* (1981) and *The Mystery of Edwin Drood* (1986): d. Rocky Point, NY, June 18.

Lemnitzer, Lyman L. (89), four-star Army general and World War II hero. He served under Dwight Eisenhower in London during World War II. He later was a commander in the Korean War, first with the seventh Infantry Division and then with the Eighth Army in Korea. In 1955 he was promoted to commander of all U.S. and United Nations troops in Korea and Japan. In 1957 he became Army vice chief of staff under Gen. Maxwell Taylor, who soon retired. Lemnitzer then became chief of staff. From 1960 to 1962 he was chairman of the Joint Chiefs of Staff. He later served as Supreme Allied Commander in Europe before retiring in 1969: d. Washington, DC, Nov. 12.

Le Poulain, Jean (63), French stage actor and the administrative director of the Comédie Française, France's national theater (1986–88): d. Paris, March 1.

Linen, James 3d (75), publisher of *Time* magazine (1945–60) and president of Time Inc. (1960–69). In his early years with *Time*, he had been an advertising salesman: d. Greenwich, CT, Feb. 1.

Loewe, Frederick (86), Vienna-born composer; along with Alan Jay Lerner, his lyricist partner, he created the scores for the Broadway musicals *My Fair Lady, Camelot, Paint Your Wagon,* and *Brigadoon,* all of which became films, and for the film musical *Gigi* (1958), which won an Academy Award as best picture. A skilled pianist by age 4, Loewe became at age 13 the youngest piano soloist to appear with the Berlin Symphony Orchestra. He also began writing songs at an early age and at age 15 wrote the European hit *Katrina.* After coming to the United States in 1924, Loewe struggled for several years before selling his first song to Broadway in 1935. Loewe and

Lerner were first brought together in 1942. Though their early efforts were not successful, they continued to collaborate, and with *Brigadoon* (1947), they had a solid success. *My Fair Lady,* which opened in 1956, was hailed as a masterpiece. Their last major effort was *Camelot* (1960). Lerner died in 1986: d. Palm Springs, CA, Feb. 14.

Logan, Joshua (79), stage and film director; was often the coauthor, producer, or coproducer of his works. He studied at Princeton University and with the Russian actor, producer, and director Konstantin Stanislavsky in Moscow. Among his most prestigious stage hits were *South Pacific* (1949; film 1958) and *Mister Roberts* (1948). Other of his major stage productions, some of which he also directed on the screen, were *On Borrowed Time* (1938), *I Married an Angel* (1938), *Knickerbocker Holiday* (1938), *Charley's Aunt* (a revival, 1940), *Annie Get Your Gun* (1946), *Picnic* (1953; film 1955), *Fanny* (1954; film 1961), *Middle of the Night* (1956), and *The World of Suzie Wong* (1958). Other major films include *Bus Stop* (1956), *Sayonara* (1957), *Camelot* (1967), and *Paint Your Wagon* (1969): d. New York City, July 12.

Low, Carl (71), actor of stage, films, and television; appeared as Dr. Bob Rogers on the television soap opera *Search for Tomorrow* for more than 15 years: d. Nyack, NY, Oct. 19.

MacBride, Sean (83), French-born Irish revolutionary, lawyer, politician, and diplomat. He supported the causes of Irish nationalism, a united Europe, nuclear disarmament, and human rights. He won both the Nobel (1974, shared) and Lenin (1977) peace prizes, honored, respectively, for his work on behalf of human rights and nuclear disarmament. His father was executed by the British in 1916 for his part in the Easter Uprising in Dublin, and that year, at age 12, he and his mother returned from France to Ireland, and he joined the Irish Volunteers, forerunners of the Irish Republican Army. He was arrested many times by the British and imprisoned three times, in 1918, 1922, and 1930. MacBride ended his association with the IRA in 1937. He was admitted to the Irish bar that same year and quickly became the most successful trial lawyer in Dublin. Elected to parliament in 1947, he served until 1958 and was foreign minister (1948–51). He later was assistant secretary-general of the United Nations and UN commissioner for Namibia or South-West Africa (1973–76). At the time of his death he was president emeritus of the International Peace Bureau in Geneva, having headed the bureau (1972–85). He was a founder of Amnesty International in 1961 and served as its chairman until 1975: d. Dublin, Jan. 15.

Malenkov, Georgi (86), Soviet premier (1953–55); was a leading political figure in the USSR after the death of Josef Stalin, and for a brief period headed the Communist Party. He was expelled from the Communist Party in 1961: d. USSR, Jan. 1988 (announced Feb. 1).

Maravich, Pete (known as Pistol Pete) (40), basketball player; the greatest scorer in National Collegiate Athletic Association history; he scored a record 3,667 points at Louisiana State University (1968–70) for a career average of 44.2 points. During his ten years as a pro player in the National Basketball Association, he averaged 24.2 points per game. He was inducted into the Basketball Hall of Fame in 1987: d. Pasadena, CA, Jan. 5.

Marchand, Jean (69), Canadian Liberal Party politician and labor leader from Quebec province who was pivotal in the election of Pierre Elliott Trudeau when he pushed him forward as leader of the Liberal Party after the retirement of Lester Pearson. He served with the Trudeau government for eight of the nearly 16 years that Trudeau was in office. He later was a member of the federal Senate: d. near Quebec City, Canada, Aug. 28.

Matthews, Burnita S. (93), first woman to serve as a U.S. district judge; she was named to the federal district court in the District of Columbia by President Harry Truman in 1949: d. Washington, DC, April 25.

McClory, Robert N. (80), U.S. representative (R-IL, 1963–83); served on the Watergate panel that handled impeachment proceedings against President Richard Nixon: d. Washington, DC, July 24.

McCracken, James (61), operatic dramatic tenor; a major star of the Metropolitan Opera in the 1960s and 1970s: d. New York City, April 30.

Means, Gardiner (91), economist; in the 1930s, he developed the theory of "administrative prices," which explained why prices in certain corporations, particularly steel, oil, and automotive, did not always rise and fall in response to supply and demand: d. Vienna, VA, Feb. 15.

Meeker, Ralph (67), film and stage actor; starred on Broadway in *Picnic* (1953). His first Broadway part was in *Cyrano de Bergerac* (1947). He also was in *Mr. Roberts* (1948), *Cloud 7* (1958), *Something About a Soldier* (1962), and *Mrs. Dally* (1965); and he replaced Marlon Brando as Stanley in *Streetcar named Desire*. He was a member of the Lincoln Center Repertory Theater in 1963–64, and while with that group appeared in the original production of *After the Fall*. He also made a number of movies: d. Woodland Hills, CA, Aug. 5.

Méndez, Aparicio (84), president of Uruguay (1976–81); he was in fact a figurehead president as Uruguay was ruled during these years by the military: d. Montevideo, Uruguay, June 26.

Miki, Takeo (81), prime minister of Japan (1974–76); he advocated Japanese-American friendship prior to World War II. Elected to parliament in 1937 on the Liberal Democratic Party ticket, he was identified with the progressive wing of the party. He also served as foreign minister (1966–68) and deputy prime minister (1972–74): d. Tokyo, Nov. 14.

Mitchell, John N. (75), U.S. attorney general under President Richard Nixon; was jailed for his role in the Watergate scandals that forced the resignation of Nixon. He served 19 months for conspiracy, obstruction of justice, and lying under oath, leaving prison in 1979. A lawyer by profession, he was disbarred after the conviction: d. Washington, DC, Nov. 9.

Mohammed Ibn Abdel-Aziz, Prince (80), prince of Saudi Arabia; the oldest surviving brother of King Fahd. In 1977 he had ordered the execution of a granddaughter and her husband after the granddaughter defied a royal order to marry another man. The incident caused a furor when the British documentary, *Death of a Princess*, was shown on television, bringing the affair to public attention: d. Riyadh, Saudi Arabia, Nov. 25.

Morse, Richard S. (76), scientist and inventor; founded the National Research Corporation in 1940 to develop techniques and products. He developed high-vacuum machines and frozen orange juice concentrate. He worked as a U.S. government adviser and became director of research and development for the U.S. Army. He returned to his alma mater, the Massachusetts Institute of Technology, in 1961, retiring in 1977: d. Falmouth, MA, July 1.

Nef, John U. (89), economic historian; was associated with the University of Chicago for more than 50 years, beginning in 1929: d. Washington, DC, Dec. 25.

Newhouse, Norman R. (82), publishing executive; a member of a family that built an empire of 27 newspapers, 11 magazines, five publishing houses, and three cable television companies in several states: d. New Orleans, LA, Nov. 6.

Nichols, William (70), U.S. representative (D-AL, 1967–88): d. Washington, DC, Dec. 13.

Noguchi, Isamu (84), American sculptor; worked in stone, clay, and wood as well as newer materials, including stainless steel. The son of a Japanese father and an American mother, he lived in Japan from 1906 to 1918, when he returned to the United States to complete his education. He entered Columbia University as a premed student and also began sculpture classes at the Leonardo da Vinci Art School. In 1927 he received a Guggenheim Fellowship and went to Paris as an assistant to the sculptor Brancusi. He returned to New York in 1929 and had since traveled in Europe and Asia from time to time, maintaining homes in New York City and Japan. In 1938 he received his first major commission, creating a sculpture symbolizing freedom of the press at New York's Rockefeller Center. Other major commissions followed, including his Sunken Garden on the Yale University campus and the Billy Rose Sculpture Garden in Jerusalem. The Isamu Noguchi Garden Museum in Long Island City, Queens, NY, opened in 1985. He had worked in numerous media, including painting and ceramics, and had been involved in interior design and architecture: d. New York City, Dec. 30.

Norstad, Lauris (81), commander of United States (1956–62) and North Atlantic Treaty Organization (1956–63) forces in Europe; he served during the Berlin crisis of 1961. A West Point graduate and World War II veteran, as commander he worked for the strengthening of NATO in manpower, quality, and equipment. He established in 1961 a fast-moving multinational unit: d. Tucson, AZ, Sept. 12.

Ogilvie, Richard B. (65), Republican governor of Illinois (1969–73): d. Chicago, IL, May 10.

Oliver, Melvin James (Sy) (77), jazz composer and arranger: d. New York City, May 27.

Olson, James (64), chairman of American Telephone and Telegraph Company (1986–88); was with the Bell Telephone System for 44 years: d. Short Hills, NJ, April 18.

Onassis, Christina (37), Greek heiress to the Aristotle Onassis shipping empire, which she assumed control of in 1975 after her father's death. She was married four times, but all ended in divorce: d. Buenos Aires, Argentina, Nov. 19.

Orbison, Roy (52), popular rock singer and songwriter; had a number of hits in the late 1950s through the mid-1960s, including *Oh, Pretty Woman*, a rockabilly hit which he also wrote, and the ballads *Only the Lonely* and *Blue Bayou*. Other hits were *Running Scared, Crying, Dream Baby, In Dreams,* and *It's Over.* After his first wife's death in 1966, he stopped writing songs; later two of his three children by his first wife were killed in a fire. He performed through the 1970s but had no big hits, although other singers helped bring a new popularity to his songs. In 1985 he rerecorded a double album of his hits: d. Hendersonville, TN, Dec. 6.

O'Rourke, Heather (12), actress; probably best known for her performances in the films *Poltergeist* and *Poltergeist II:* d. San Diego, CA, Feb. 1.

Ortiz, Peter Julien (75), Marine officer; highly decorated by the French, British, and American governments for his feats in World War II: d. Prescott, AZ, May 16.

Pagels, Heinz (49), physicist and executive director of the New York Academy of Sciences; he was the author of several books on physics and cosmology for the general public, including *The Cosmic Code, Perfect Symmetry,* and *The Dreams of Reason:* d. near Aspen, CO, July 24.

Parish, Peggy (61), author of more than 30 children's books, including 11 on her best known character, the inept, literal-minded maid, Amelia Bedelia: d. Manning, SC, Nov. 18.

Passman, Otto (88), U.S. representative (D-LA, 1947–77); a conservative, he was opposed to civil-rights legislation and fought tirelessly against spending for foreign aid. In 1979 he was charged with taking illegal gratuities while in the House from wealthy Korean rice trader Tongsun Park; he was found not guilty after a lengthy trial: d. Monroe, LA, Aug. 13.

Paton, Alan (85), South African author and political leader; wrote the novel *Cry, the Beloved Country* (1948), made into a Kurt Weill-Maxwell Anderson Broadway musical in 1949 and into a film in 1952. He struggled against apartheid in his writings and as head of the Liberal Party. Although he maintained his liberal convictions, in recent years he was regarded as conservative as he opposed economic sanctions against South Africa: d. Durban, South Africa, April 12.

Patterson, Frederick D. (86), educator, founder of the United Negro College Fund, and president of the Tuskegee Institute in Alabama (1935–53): d. New Rochelle, NY, April 26.

Isamu Noguchi
© Neal Boenzi/NYT Pictures

Christina Onassis

Roy Orbison

Heather O'Rourke
Photos, AP/Wide World

Pendleton, Clarence M., Jr. (57), chairman of the U.S. Civil Rights Commission (1981–88). He switched to the Republican Party in 1980 and worked for Ronald Reagan in his bid for the presidency: d. San Diego, CA, June 5.

Phelps, William H., Jr. (85), Venezuelan ornithologist, explorer, and conservationist; he conducted several expeditions to unexplored parts of Venezuela and together with his wife and father built the foremost collection of birds in Latin America, consisting of 100,000 tropical bird specimens: d. Caracas, Venezuela, Aug. 13.

Philby, Harold Adrian Russell (Kim) (76), British-born double agent who betrayed his country and defected to the USSR in 1963 when his involvement in a Soviet spy ring was about to be revealed. He had worked for British intelligence for 30 years, becoming one of its leading agents. He, along with Guy Burgess and Donald Maclean, both of whom he helped to escape to Moscow in 1951, and the fourth man, Anthony Blunt, provided much valuable information to the Soviets: d. Moscow, May 11 (reported from London).

Pinero, Miguel (41), Puerto Rican-born playwright; began his first play, *Short Eyes*, in prison. It won the New York Drama Critics Circle award for best American play in 1974: d. New York City, June 17.

Ponge, Francis (89), French surrealist poet; gained fame through his "thing-poetry," detailed and long descriptions of objects. In 1972 he won the French Academy's grand prize for poetry: d. Le Bar-sur-Loup, France, Aug. 6.

Popper, Hans (84), Austrian-born pathologist; was internationally known as the father of hepatology, the study of the liver and its diseases. He was the author of 28 books: d. New York City, May 6.

Porter, Kenneth (91), air ace; was among the last American air aces of World War I: d. New York City, Feb. 3.

Pratt, Walter (Babe) (72), Canadian hockey player; began his 12-year career with the New York Rangers in 1935. He was elected to the Hockey Hall of Fame in 1966: d. Vancouver, B.C., Dec. 16.

Presser, Jackie (61), president of the International Brotherhood of Teamsters (1983–88). One of his successes occurred in the fall of 1987 when the union was readmitted to the AFL-CIO. He was sensitive to the Teamster image as a corrupt union tied to organized crime and attempted to change that view; however, at the time of his death he was under indictment for embezzlement and racketeering charges: d. Lakewood, OH, July 9.

Prinz, Rabbi Joachim (86), president of the American Jewish Congress (1958–66); was active in civil-rights causes. He had been a rabbi of the Jewish community in Berlin for 12 years prior to coming to the United States in 1937: d. Livingston, NJ, Sept. 30.

Provenzano, Anthony (71), organized crime leader and convicted murderer and extortionist. He was serving a sentence in a federal penitentiary in Lompoc, CA: d. near Lompoc, CA, Dec. 12.

Qoboza, Percy (50), South African journalist; was editor of several leading antiapartheid publications. He spent some time in the United States as a Nieman fellow at Harvard University (1975–76) and as editor-in-residence at the now defunct *Washington Star* (1980–81). In 1977 he was detained in South Africa for more than five months before being released without charge. At the time of his death he was with the Johannesburg-based *City Press:* d. Johannesburg, South Africa, Jan. 17.

Rabi, Isidor Isaac (89), physicist, born in Austria-Hungary, a pioneer in exploring the atom. He was awarded the 1944 Nobel Prize in physics for developing a method of measuring the magnetic properties of atoms, molecules, and atomic nuclei, making possible the precise measurements for the development of the atomic clock, the laser, and diagnostic scanning of the human body by nuclear magnetic resonance. During World War II, he helped in the development of radar and also served as an adviser on the Manhattan Project, which developed the atomic bomb. He later was an advocate of nuclear-arms control. He was chairman of the general advisory committee to the Atomic Energy Commission (1952–56) and also headed President Dwight Eisenhower's science advisory committee. He also originated the idea of Geneva's CERN nuclear research center and played a major part in the creation of the Brookhaven National Laboratory: d. New York City, Jan. 11.

Raines, Ella (67), actress; starred in film Westerns, dramas, and comedies of the 1940s. She also appeared in the television series *Janet Dean, R.N.* in 1953–54: d. Los Angeles, May 30.

Lord Ramsey (Arthur Michael) (83), archbishop of Canterbury (1961–74); the 100th archbishop; he was a proponent of worldwide Christian ecumenism and, as such, paid an official visit in 1966 to Pope Paul VI in Rome and in 1972 preached from the pulpit of St. Patrick's Roman Catholic Cathedral in New York City: d. Oxford, England, April 23.

Ramsey, Paul (74), professor of religion at Princeton University for nearly 40 years; was a recognized authority on medical ethics: d. Princeton, NJ, Feb. 29.

Raschi, Victor (69), baseball pitcher for the New York Yankees (1946–53); he won 132 games in a ten-year career before retiring in 1955. Known as the Springfield Rifle, he won six games in six World Series won by the Yankees. His career record was 132–66, with a 3.72 earned-run average: d. Groveland, NY, Oct. 14.

Reardon, John (58), baritone; champion of contemporary operatic works; appeared with the New York City Opera (1954–72) and sang several roles with the Metropolitan Opera beginning in 1965: d. Santa Fe, NM, April 16.

Rich, Irene (96), silent screen actress; made many films in the 1920s and the 1930s, including seven with the humorist Will Rogers. She was also a radio personality in the 1930s and made some talking films, including *Fort Apache* and *Joan of Arc*. She appeared on Broadway in *As the Girls Go* (1948–50): d. Hope Ranch, CA, April 22.

Richter, Curt P. (94), professor of psychobiology at Johns Hopkins Medical Institutions and a pioneer in the study of biorhythms. He was credited with the concept of the "biological clock": d. Baltimore, MD, Dec. 21.

Righter, Carroll (88), astrologer to many Hollywood film stars and a syndicated astrology columnist for 166 newspapers around the world: d. Santa Monica, CA, April 30.

Roberts, Bill (63), a founder of political consulting and a manager of Ronald Reagan's political career. He was one of the first people to turn political consulting from an amateur, part-time activity into a professional enterprise: d. Santa Monica, CA, June 30.

Robinson, Max (49), television correspondent; came to national attention in 1978 when he became a coanchor with Frank Reynolds and Peter Jennings on the ABC weeknight program *World News Tonight*. He remained on the program until 1983 when Jennings became the sole anchorman: d. Washington, DC, Dec. 20.

Roman, Ed J. (57), basketball player on the 1949–50 City College of New York team which won both the National Invitation Tournament and the National Collegiate Athletic Association tournament; he pleaded guilty to game fixing during the 1950–51 season. He later returned to City College and New York University to gain a masters and doctorate in psychology: d. Valhalla, NY, March 1.

Romney, Marion G. (90), senior member of the Mormon Church's Council of the Twelve Apostles, he was named to the Council in 1951 and for more than 45 years was a leading authority in the church: d. Salt Lake City, May 20.

Rooney, Arthur J., Sr. (87), founder of the Pittsburgh Steelers and a figure on the American sports scene for more than 50 years; he founded the club on an investment of $2,500 that he

Clarence Pendleton, Jr.

Jackie Presser

Lord Ramsey

Marion G. Romney

Photos, AP/Wide World

had won at a racetrack in one weekend. He brought the Steelers into the National Football League in 1933; it became a premier club of the league in the 1970s, winning the Super Bowl in 1975, 1976, 1979, and 1980: d. Pittsburgh, PA, Aug. 25.

Roosevelt, Franklin D., Jr. (74), U.S. representative (D-NY, 1949-55); the son of President Franklin D. Roosevelt, he also was undersecretary of Commerce (1963) and chairman of the Equal Opportunity Commission (1965): d. Poughkeepsie, NY, Aug. 17.

Rorem, C. Rufus (93), economist; was an early advocate of pre-paid health care; his studies led to the creation of Blue Cross and Blue Shield. In 1929 he began his career in the health-care field as a staff member of the federally sponsored Committee on the Costs of Medical Care: d. Cherry Hill, NJ, Sept. 19.

Rose, George (68), English actor; appeared often in the London theater and on Broadway in New York. He began his career with Britain's Old Vic Company. Later, with the Royal Shakespearean Company, he became known as a Shakespearean comic actor. From the 1960s onward, he appeared on Broadway in a variety of roles and over the years became known for his adeptness as a musical comedy actor in such musicals as *My Fair Lady, The Pirates of Penzance*, and recently in *The Mystery of Edwin Drood*: d. Dominican Republic, May 5.

Rosson, Harold G. (93), cinematographer; worked on the silent film *David Harum* (1915), an early color movie, *The Garden of Allah* (1936), *The Wizard of Oz* (1939), and *The Asphalt Jungle* (1950). He was married briefly to actress Jean Harlow: d. Palm Beach, FL, Sept. 6.

Rothchild, Baron Philippe de (85), a member of the Rothchild banking family; a wine expert, owner of Château Mouton-Rothchild wines: d. Paris, Jan. 20.

Rouse, Charlie (64), jazz tenor saxophonist: d. Seattle, WA, Nov. 30.

Roush, Edd J. (94), baseball player; won two National League batting championships, in 1917 and 1919. He batted higher than .300 in 12 of his 16 seasons as a major leaguer. In 1962 he was elected to the Baseball Hall of Fame: d. Bradenton, FL, March 21.

Ruben, Samuel (88), U.S. research scientist and inventor; known for his electrochemical work; his inventions led to more than 300 patents, including the alkaline battery: d. Milwaukie, OR, July 16.

Rukeyser, Merryle S. (91), financial columnist and editor; wrote for the Hearst Newspapers and the International News Service for more than 30 years: d. White Plains, NY, Dec. 21.

Ruska, Ernst (81), German electrical engineer; shared the 1986 Nobel prize in physics for his invention of the electron microscope: d. West Berlin, May 30.

St. Johns, Adela Rogers (94), journalist, author, and screenwriter; served as a journalist for the Hearst newspapers, as well as the International News Service. Her screenwriting assignments included Tom Mix Westerns. She also wrote for *Photoplay* magazine and published fiction in *The Saturday Evening Post, Good Housekeeping*, and other magazines: d. Arroyo Grande, CA, Aug. 10.

Saragat, Giuseppe (89), president of Italy (1964–71); originally a Socialist, he was a founder of the Social Democratic Party in Italy: d. Rome, June 11.

Sardinias, Eligio (Kid Chocolate) (77), Cuban boxing champion; in the early 1930s was a world champion in the featherweight and junior lightweight levels: d. Havana, Aug. 8.

Satterfield, David E. 3d (67), U.S. representative (D-VA, 1965–81): d. Richmond, VA, Sept. 30.

Scherer, Gordon (81), U.S. representative (R-OH, 1953–63): d. Cincinnati, OH, Aug. 13.

Schoenbrun, David F. (73), journalist for CBS News and part of the Edward R. Murrow team in the 1940s. He left CBS in 1964 and then was a free-lance broadcaster and television writer and the author of several books: d. New York City, May 23.

Schonfield, H. J. (86), British author of books on religion and the Bible. His best-known book was *The Passover Plot* (1965): d. London, Jan. 24.

Scott, Sheila (born Sheila Christine Hopkins) (61), British aviator; in 1971 she became the first woman to pilot a flight circling the world in a light aircraft by way of the North Pole: d. London, Oct. 20.

Seymour, Anne (79), stage, film, and television actress; also performed in more than 5,000 radio programs: d. Los Angeles, CA, Dec. 8.

Shannon, William V. (61), journalist and scholar; was U.S. ambassador to Ireland during the Carter administration. As a journalist he worked for the *New York Post* (1951–64) and *The New York Times* (1964–77). In 1981 he joined the faculty at Boston University, and he also began writing for the *Boston Globe* newspaper: d. Brookline, MA, Sept. 27.

Shaplen, Robert (71), correspondent and writer for *The New Yorker* magazine (1952–88); wrote articles and books on Asia. He earlier was an Asia correspondent for *Newsweek, Fortune*, and *Colliers* magazines: d. New York City, May 15.

Photos, AP/Wide World

Arthur J. Rooney, Sr.   *Gertrude Soule*

Shepley, James R. (71), president of Time Inc. (1969–80); he was hired by *Time* magazine in 1942, served as a war correspondent and was Washington bureau chief (1948–57): d. Houston, Nov. 2.

Sherif, Muzafer (82), Turkish-born social psychologist; widely known for his famous Robber's Cave experiment, a field experiment on intergroup conflict involving 22 boys at a summer camp who were placed in two competing groups. The experiment became the subject of a 1961 book, *Intergroup Conflict and Cooperation: The Robber's Cave Experiment*, and became a model for social psychologists and is often cited as the seminal study on intergroup relations. He taught and did research at Princeton and Yale universities and at various state universities. He retired from the University of Pennsylvania in 1972. With his wife and others, he wrote 17 books on social psychology: d. Fairbanks, AK, Oct. 16.

Shulman, Max (69), novelist, playwright, and humorist; created the Dobie Gillis character and worked on the television series that ran four years. He also wrote the novel *Rally Round the Flag, Boys* (1957) and cowrote the play *The Tender Trap*, which made its Broadway debut in 1955: d. Los Angeles, CA, Aug. 28.

Siegel, Rabbi Seymour (60), leader in Conservative Judaism; he was associated with New York's Jewish Theological Seminary for 41 years as both a student and teacher. The author of many articles, he helped bring about the ordination of women rabbis through his writings. An opponent of the Vietnam war, he moved toward neoconservatism more recently, although he remained a liberal with regard to theological matters: d. New York City, Feb. 24.

Sitwell, Sir Sacheverell (90), British poet and art critic; he was the last of the trio of Sitwell siblings that included Sir Osbert and Dame Edith, who were forces in the British literary world. Sir Sacheverell produced 50 volumes of poems and about 40 other books on travel, music, art, and architecture: d. England, Oct. 1.

Sorabji, Kaikhosru (born Leon Dudley) (96), English composer and critic; in 1940 he placed a ban on the performance of his music which lasted until 1976. His *Opus Clavicembalisticum* is thought to be the longest nonrepeating piano piece ever composed, lasting more than three hours. In the 1920s and 1930s he was active as an essayist and music critic: d. Dorchester, England, Oct. 15.

Soule, Gertrude (93), Shaker sect leader; was placed in a Shaker community at age 11 and chose to remain, signing the Shaker vow of celibacy at age 21. In the early 1950s, she became an eldress or spiritual leader and in 1957 was appointed to the Lead Ministry of the United Society of Believers: d. Canterbury, NH, June 11.

Spellman, Gladys Noon (70), U.S. representative (D-MD, 1975-81); was running for a fourth term when her heart temporarily stopped. Her condition later stabilized, but she remained in a coma. She had won reelection in 1980, but her seat was declared vacant in February 1981 and a special election was held: d. Rockville, MD, June 19.

Staley, Oren L. (65), first president (1955–79) of the National Farmers Organization, a group that grew out of farm price protests by Iowa farmers in the 1950s: d. Kansas City, KS, Sept. 19.

Steptoe, Patrick (74), British obstetrician who, along with his colleague Dr. Robert Edwards, inaugurated the test-tube-baby era when in 1978, through the procedure *in vitro* fertilization, one of his patients delivered a baby girl conceived in a laboratory dish: d. Canterbury, England, March 21.

Stevens, Siaka P. (82), president of Sierra Leone (1971–85): d. Freetown, Sierra Leone, May 29.

Strauss, Franz Josef (73), Bavarian premier (1978–88); headed the conservative Christian Social Union Party for 25 years and served as a member of the federal parliament from 1949 to

Photos, AP/Wide World

Gladys Noon Spellman   *Stuart Symington*   *Edward Bennett Williams*   *Mohammad Zia ul-Haq*

1978. He held various ministerial posts, but is best remembered as "the architect of rearmament" as defense minister (1956–62). He was later finance minister (1966–69): d. Regensburg, West Germany, Oct. 3.

Sullivan, Leonor K. (85), U.S. representative (D-MO, 1961–85); was a champion of consumers and the disadvantaged: d. St. Louis, MO, Sept. 1.

Symington, Stuart (87), U.S. senator (D-MO, 1953–77); was on both the Foreign Relations and Armed Services committees and was at first a supporter of military expenditures, although he later became increasingly critical of excessive defense spending and of the Vietnam war. Earlier in his career he had been an adversary of Sen. Joseph McCarthy. He also campaigned for the Democratic presidential nomination in 1956 and 1960: d. New Canaan, CT, Dec. 14.

Szeryng, Henryk (69), Polish-born violinist; was considered a part of the Romantic school of violin playing. Educated in diplomacy as well as in music, he taught at the National University in Mexico City beginning in 1943: d. Kassel, West Germany, March 3.

Thomson, Vernon (82), U.S. representative (R-WI, 1961–75); he earlier was a member of the State Assembly and was governor of Wisconsin (1957–59): d. Washington, DC, April 2.

Tiffeau, Jacques (59), French-born fashion designer; rose to prominence in the 1960s as a strong proponent of the miniskirt: d. Paris, Feb. 29.

Tinbergen, Nikolaas (81), Dutch-born British zoologist; shared the 1973 Nobel Prize in medicine. He was on the faculty of Oxford University from 1949 to 1974 and professor emeritus there until his death: d. Oxford, England, Dec. 21.

Uhlenbeck, George E. (87), Dutch-born physicist; codiscoverer of the electron's spin and a former president of the American Physical Society. He was a member of the faculty at Rockefeller University (1960–74): d. Boulder, CO, Oct. 31.

Ungar, Frederick (90), Austrian-born founder of the Frederick Ungar Publishing Company in New York City in 1940: d. Scarsborough, NY, Nov. 16.

Urquhart, Robert E. (87), British major general; commander at the Battle of Arnhem. He was portrayed by the actor Sean Connery in the 1977 movie *A Bridge Too Far*: d. Port of Menteith, Scotland, Dec. 13.

Vinson, Eddie (Cleanhead) (70), jazz alto saxophonist and singer; got his start in bebop and made his career in rhythm and blues: d. Los Angeles, CA, July 2.

Volk, Cardinal Hermann (84), Roman Catholic archbishop of Mainz, West Germany (1962–82); he was named a cardinal in 1973: d. Mainz, July 1.

von Balthasar, Hans (82), Swiss theologian; made a cardinal four weeks prior to his death by Pope John Paul II. He wrote an essay, *The Razing of the Bastions*, in 1952 that was considered one of the most important works published in preparation for the Second Vatican Council. He later wrote articles critical of the papal council's reforms: d. Basel, Switzerland, June 26.

Wainwright, Loudon S. (63), former columnist, reporter, and bureau chief for *Life* magazine. He was the author of *The Great American Magazine*, a history of *Life*: d. New York City, Dec. 12.

Wallich, Henry C. (74), U.S. economist who was a member of the Federal Reserve Board (1974–86): d. Washington, DC, Sept. 15.

Wankel, Felix (86), German inventor of the Wankel rotary engine: d. Lindau, West Germany, Oct. 9.

Weyer, Lee (51), National League baseball umpire (1962–88): d. San Mateo, CA, July 4.

Wien, Lawrence A. (83), lawyer, realtor, and philanthropist who donated millions of dollars to education and the arts: d. Westport, CT, Dec. 10.

Wilentz, David (93), New Jersey attorney general who prosecuted the accused Lindbergh baby kidnapper, Bruno Richard

Hauptmann, in 1935. He had become attorney general in 1934, and the case was the first criminal case he ever had tried. He went on to become a powerful Democratic politician in New Jersey: d. Long Branch, NJ, July 6.

Williams, Edward Bennett (68), lawyer; presided over the Washington, DC, law firm of Williams and Connolly. He was a celebrated trial attorney who strongly believed in the Constitution's 6th Amendment and a defendant's right to a fair trial, an idea that he explored in his book *One Man's Freedom* (1962). In addition to his law practice, he was the owner of the Baltimore Orioles baseball team and had been president of the Washington Redskins professional football team for 20 years: d. Washington, DC, Aug. 13.

Williams, G. Mennen (76), governor of Michigan (1949–61); he was later a member of the Michigan Supreme Court (1971–86), serving as chief justice for three years (1983–86). He also was assistant secretary of state for African affairs (1961–66) and ambassador to the Philippines (1968–69). Though he had been a Republican as a young man, he later became a Democrat and as governor established a record for the appointment of blacks and against racial discrimination: d. Detroit, MI, Feb. 2.

Williams, John J. (83), U.S. senator (R-DE, 1947–71): d. Lewes, DE, Jan. 11.

Williams, Roger J. (94), biochemist and nutritional expert; he was professor of chemistry at the University of Texas (1934–71) and also directed the Clayton Foundation Biochemical Institute at the university until 1985. He discovered the growth-promoting vitamin pantothenic acid, and later at the Institute he presided over the discovery of other vitamins and their variants: d. Austin, TX, Feb. 20.

Willman, Noel (70), British actor/director; best known in the United States for directing the Broadway stage production of *A Man for All Seasons* (1961): d. New York City, Dec. 24.

Wilson, Lois Burnham (97), founder of the Al-Anon Family Groups whose members are relatives and friends of alcoholics: d. Mount Kisco, NY, Oct. 5.

Woodhouse, Barbara (78), British dog trainer; became famous in Britain and the United States for her work with dogs through the television program, *Training Dogs the Woodhouse Way*. She wrote *No Bad Dogs—the Woodhouse Way*, which became a best-seller in 1982: d. Buckinghamshire, England, July 9.

Wootton, Barbara (Frances) (Baroness Wootton of Abinger) (91); British social scientist; wrote *Social Science and Social Pathology* (1959); was one of four women among the first life peers created in 1958: d. July 11.

Wright, J. Skelly (77), U.S. federal judge (1949–86); was a judge of the Federal District Court in New Orleans and then on the U.S. Court of Appeals for the District of Columbia. He played an important role in promoting racial desegregation of public schools and transportation in New Orleans and later played a role in the legal controversy surrounding the publication of the Pentagon papers in 1971: d. Westmoreland Hills, MD, Aug. 6.

Wright, Sewall (98), geneticist; considered the 20th century's foremost American evolutionary theorist, he established a mathematical basis for evolution. He was on the faculty at the University of Chicago and the University of Wisconsin (1955–60): d. Madison, WI, March 3.

Zia ul-Haq, Mohammad (64), president of Pakistan; he had assumed power following a 1977 coup in which he overthrew Zulfikar Ali Bhutto: d. in a plane crash in eastern Pakistan, Aug. 17.

Zumwalt, Elmo 3d (42), Vietnam veteran who was a victim of the Agent Orange sprayed in Vietnam. His father, an admiral in the U.S. Navy, had ordered the spraying of the defoliant, which is thought to cause cancer and other illnesses. Together they had written a book, *My Father, My Son*, published in 1986: d. Fayetteville, NC, Aug. 13.

OCEANOGRAPHY

Scientists from the United States, Canada, Japan, West Germany, Belgium, France, Sweden, and Great Britain continued their participation in the Ocean Drilling Program (ODP), a long-term international partnership that systematically is exploring the structure beneath the sea floor. In the most recent phase, an 18-month survey of the Indian Ocean, a drilling on the flanks of the Southwest Indian Ridge in a deep fracture of the rift system retrieved more than a quarter mile (400 m) of samples from the deepest layers of the ocean's crust. The samples, from an ancient magma chamber formed at least 12 million years ago, provided evidence of how molten magma rises from deep within the earth, cools, and then solidifies. The samples also may show how the circulation of cold seawater reacts with hot rocks deep within the earth's crust.

In another project, the area of the East Pacific Rise was mapped in close detail by a team from Hawaii with instruments capable of recording features as small as a house trailer. The results showed many places where the spreading centers overlap because of irregularities in the magmatic pulses released at such sites. Magma plumes, once thought to be fixed in position while crustal plates move over them, here are seen as flickering flames with spurts of magma from different deep sources, not coalescing into a single outflow.

Deposits in the hot springs found in 1985 on the mid-Atlantic ridge near 26°N latitude at a depth of 3 650 m (2.3 mi) were sampled in 1988 and shown to have high contents of gold and copper. The deposits resemble mineral-rich lodes on land and may have future economic significance. Interest has been expressed in leasing the cobalt-rich manganese crusts within the Hawaiian and Johnson Islands Exclusive Economic Zone (EEZ) of the United States, where the material lies in depths possibly suited for strip mining techniques. Environmentalists strongly oppose any such activity.

Currents. The Tropical Ocean and Global Atmosphere (TOGA) program continued to compile meteorological and oceanographic data from buoys throughout the oceans of the Southern Hemisphere. From such data, the complex system of the El Niño-Southern Oscillation (ENSO)—a current reversal and atmospheric pressure shift in the eastern Pacific—can be followed over time. Expanding knowledge of the equatorial warming mechanism which controls the system has made it possible to predict the changes in current. Three different numerical models successfully predicted the El Niño of 1986–87, suggesting that routine prediction may be feasible as the large-scale changes become better understood.

The upcoming international World Ocean Circulation Experiment (WOCE) will include direct measurement by satellite-tracked drifters and subsurface floats with strong support from sensors on earth-orbiting satellites. The purpose of WOCE is to create a better model of general oceanic and climatic circulation. The South Atlantic, where many water masses intermingle in complex relationships, will be examined in particular detail. The climatic effects of this circulation in the North Atlantic are pronounced because of heat exchanges across the Equator by the current systems.

Ocean Life. Coral species throughout the Caribbean—from Colombia and Venezuela as far north as the Florida coast near Palm Beach —were attacked in 1987 by a bleaching disease in which the coral's white skeleton becomes visible through its transparent tissue; the latter loses its algal symbionts and finally dies. Reefs in Australia have been affected by a similar disease. Scientists are monitoring closely the recovery of the coral reefs, which remain threatened by possible future outbreaks. The disease is thought to be related to high water temperatures and possibly to changes in ultraviolet light penetration.

The spiny starfish which infested Pacific coral reefs in 1968–1972 has begun to threaten parts of the Great Barrier Reef near Australia with a similar population explosion. Previous control programs in Micronesia, the U.S. Trust Territories, and Japan had negligible success, but studies in Guam show good recovery of coral when the basic reef structure remains intact after predation. Caribbean populations of spiny sea urchins were attacked by disease in 1983 and 1984, greatly reducing their numbers. The effect has been to alter the composition and abundance of algal species in the coral community and to cause some changes in the presence of algae-eating fish species. Such problems emphasize the delicate balance of the coral ecosystem and of interactions in the food chain.

In 1988 up to 90% of the young harbor seals around the North Sea were reported to be affected by a disease caused by canine distemper virus. The disease killed off large numbers of the seal populations previously found off the coasts of Denmark, Sweden, Norway, West Germany, The Netherlands, and Great Britain, and possibly could spread to the coasts of Canada and the United States. Some scientists believe that the dumping of toxic wastes may have increased the impact of the disease, although no clear evidence linking the virus to pollution was available presently. Sea pollution in various forms was widespread in 1988, affecting not only the eastern seaboard of the United States but also European beaches from the Mediterranean and the Bay of Biscay to the North Sea. (*See* ENVIRONMENT.)

DAVID A. McGILL
U.S. Coast Guard Academy

OHIO

Throngs of Ohioans got close-up views of the two 1988 presidential candidates as late campaigning centered on their pivotal Midwest state. George Bush then captured its 23 electoral votes with 2.41 million votes to Michael S. Dukakis' 1.93 million.

Democratic Sen. Howard M. Metzenbaum won a third term, while promising not to seek a fourth. He defeated George V. Voinovich, Cleveland's mayor since 1979, by 2.47 million ballots to 1.87 million. Key elements in the campaign were the winner's strong support from organized labor and the backfiring of a Voinovich commercial charging that the senator is soft on child pornography. Following his defeat, Voinovich seemed to have at least two political options—to run for another term as mayor or to seek Ohio's governorship in 1990.

Incumbent U.S. congressmen were reelected in 20 of Ohio's 21 districts. In the 5th District, state Sen. Paul E. Gillmor (R) defeated the son of retiring Rep. Delbert Latta in the primary and easily captured the House seat in November. In the 20th District, Rep. Mary Rose Oakar had survived easily a primary challenge by former Cleveland Mayor Dennis Kucinich.

Ohioans elected Alice Robie Resnick, a Toledo Democrat, to their Supreme Court. She would be the first woman to serve on the state's high court since 1928. As a result of the balloting, the state's Senate would have 19 Republicans and 14 Democrats. The House would have 59 Democrats and 40 Republicans. The Democrats lost one seat in each chamber.

Adverse publicity continued to rock Gov. Richard F. Celeste. The administrator of Ohio's Board of Employment Services resigned early in 1988 after criticism increased over charges that four women in the bureau had been harassed sexually, and proper official reaction had not followed. Celeste, whose second term ends in January 1991, cannot immediately seek a third term under Ohio law.

Economics. In September, Ford Motor Company and Nissan Motor Company of Japan announced plans to double the size of a Ford plant at Avon Lake, near Cleveland, to build minivans. Cost was estimated at about $900 million. Production of the vans was targeted for the 1992-model year. The venture, plus Honda Motor Company's building of a second plant at Marysville (begun in March 1988), would ensure Ohio's position as a principal vehicle-production state.

A National Research Council survey showed that 458,000 new jobs were created in Ohio between January 1984 and January 1988. The largest category was service jobs, 266,400. Other surveys revealed that 62,000 new jobs were established in Cleveland and 27,000 in Columbus in 1987 alone. Also boding well for

employers and workers was the fact that college enrollment in Ohio grew by 13,000 during the 1987–88 school year.

Environment. Contamination worries rose sharply when the federal Department of Energy's operations at its Fernald uranium processing plant and its uranium enrichment site at Piketon came under fire. A U.S. House Energy and Commerce Subcommittee hearing charged that large quantities of possibly lethal wastes were released over many years. Estimates of costs of cleaning up these and other similar sites ranged in the billions of dollars.

Marietta. The city of Marietta, at the Ohio and Muskingum rivers, observed its 200th anniversary with celebrations in the spring and summer.

JOHN F. HUTH, JR., *Cleveland*

OKLAHOMA

In the 1988 elections, Vice-President George Bush carried Oklahoma by a comfortable margin of 58%-42% and the congressional delegation remained as before, with two Republicans among the six members. Two members had no challengers. Republican James M. Inhofe of the 1st District in the Tulsa area struggled in his first reelection bid to win by 53%-47%. The other three congressmen won by landslides, capturing 65% or more of the vote.

In the only statewide contest for a state executive office, a seat on the Corporation Commission, Republican Bob Anthony, a prominent businessman, defeated Democratic legislator Charles Morgan. This Republican win of a major secondary office was an important development in a state where Democrats long have dominated the contests for lesser offices. In legislative contests, some prominent incumbents lost their reelection bids in the

Officials at the University of Oklahoma—(l-r) interim president David Swank, athletic director Donnie Duncan, and head football coach Barry Switzer—respond to an announcement by the National Collegiate Athletic Association that sanctions were being imposed against the university for recruiting violations.

AP/Wide World

primaries, possibly because of charges of pork-barrel politics that the state's leading newspaper, *The Daily Oklahoma,* publicized extensively. In the general elections, Democrats increased slightly their margin of control in both houses. These Democratic gains critically reduced Republican leverage in blocking appropriation bills that normally require special majorities in order to take effect immediately.

Two state questions passed by large margins. One expanded the power of judges to deny bail to those accused of a number of serious crimes, not just those accused of capital offenses. The other made the state labor commissioner an elective rather than an appointive office. The decision reversed a vote in 1975 when the office was made appointive in the aftermath of scandals associated with the then commissioner.

Economy. The precarious state of Oklahoma's economy persisted. Signs of improvement occurred but were modest and the future remained clouded. The downturn precipitated by the end of the oil boom in 1982 lingered. The Commerce Department's analysis of leading economic indicators in the fall found some increase in retail sales, but the construction index registered a downturn. Farm prices saw some improvement. Unemployment fell to 6%, but some of the improvement was due to declines in the work force due to emigration.

The oil industry continued in the doldrums. Another threat on the horizon was the ailing savings and loan industry. More promising was the opening of Remington Park, a new horse-racing track with pari-mutuel betting, in Oklahoma City.

Legislation. There were several bills designed to stimulate the economy and to implement economic development laws previously enacted. Teachers won a modest salary increase. Higher education fared especially well in spite of a tight budget. The state's ethics commission finally won funding. A special legislative session was held to deal with the issue of severely overcrowded state prisons. The Republican governor, Henry Bellmon, and the Democratic legislature resolved their differences with a $17.7 million funding measure for the state's prisons. On November 7 a state commission voted to boost legislators' pay from $20,000 to $32,000.

Higher Education. The State Regents for Higher Education drastically revised its formula for allocating funds to favor the two major universities in the state on the theory that they should be research institutions. There also was discussion of tightening admission standards.

HARRY HOLLOWAY
University of Oklahoma

OKLAHOMA • Information Highlights

Area: 69,956 sq mi (181 186 km²).
Population (July 1, 1987): 3,272,000.
Chief Cities (July 1, 1986 est.): Oklahoma City, the capital, 446,120; Tulsa, 373,750; Lawton (1980 census), 80,054.
Government (1988): *Chief Officers—governor,* Henry Bellmon (R); lt. gov., Robert S. Kerr III (D). *Legislature—*Senate, 48 members; House of Representatives, 101 members.
State Finances (fiscal year 1987): *Revenue,* $5,781,000,000; *expenditure,* $5,510,000,000.
Personal Income (1987): $41,069,000,000; per capita, $12,551.
Labor Force (June 1988): *Civilian labor force,* 1,529,600; *unemployed,* 94,800 (6.2% of total force).
Education: *Enrollment* (fall 1986)—public elementary schools, 417,287; public secondary, 175,896; colleges and universities, 170,840. *Public school expenditures* (1986–87), $1,490,000,000 ($2,701 per pupil).

ONTARIO

The Liberal government of Premier David Peterson eschewed any far-reaching legislative program for Ontario in 1988, preferring instead to follow through on earlier initiatives, including requirements for reduced auto-insurance premiums for unmarried males under 25 years

ONTARIO • Information Highlights

Area: 412,580 sq mi (1 068 580 km²).
Population (June 1988): 9,399,300.
Chief Cities (1986 census): Toronto, the provincial capital, 612,289; Ottawa, the federal capital, 300,763; Scarborough, 484,676; Mississauga, 374,005; Hamilton, 306,728; London, 269,140.
Government (1988): *Chief Officers—lt. gov.,* Lincoln Alexander; premier, David Peterson (Liberal). *Legislature—*Legislative Assembly, 130 members.
Provincial Finances (1988–89 fiscal year budget): *Revenues,* $37,427,000,000; *expenditures,* $37,-900,000,000.
Personal Income (average weekly earnings, June 1988): $484.15.
Labor Force (August 1988, seasonally adjusted): *Employed* workers, 15 years of age and over, 4,886,000; *Unemployed,* 5.1%.
Education (1988–89): *Enrollment—*elementary and secondary schools, 1,917,800 pupils; postsecondary—universities, 197,500; community colleges, 96,700.
(All monetary figures are in Canadian dollars).

of age. Certain dominant issues emerged, however, some impacting on the proposed free-trade treaty between Canada and the United States.

Legislation. Premier Peterson, who has become an outspoken opponent of the free-trade treaty despite the favorable response to the treaty by the Ontario business community, was especially sensitive to the fears of Ontario's automobile and wine industries. Initially, his opposition was tempered somewhat by the hope that the agreement would be rejected by the U.S. Congress, and in May he decided not to challenge federal legislation implementing the agreement, particularly the provisions regarding liquor and wine. Legislation introduced by the Ontario government in June, however, apparently sniped at the treaty, setting a 12-year timetable for the elimination of markups on foreign alcoholic beverages and creating new categories based on the content of domestic and imported grapes in wines sold in Ontario. Other June legislation seen as a challenge to the treaty involved the control of freestanding clinics and medical centers, giving preference to nonprofit and Canadian concerns.

Sunday shopping in the province also emerged as a volatile issue. The government introduced a bill to leave the regulation of Sunday shopping to municipalities, arguing that the province was too diverse for a universally applicable policy. Municipal politicians, faced with a growing lobby of churches, unions, and small businesses opposing Sunday shopping, denounced the government for abdicating its responsibilities.

Budget. The government's cautious approach was reflected further in the April 20 budget. Despite a thriving economy and increased revenues, taxes were raised by C$1.3 billion to cover increased social spending and to reduce the deficit. The sales tax was raised to 8%. The income tax was raised one percentage point and will go up another point in 1989. Taxes on wine, spirits, beer, and cigarettes also were raised. To pay for road construction, there was a one-cent-per-liter increase on unleaded gas and a four-cent increase on leaded gas. Total spending was projected at $37.9 billion, with a deficit of $473 million, the lowest in 19 years, bringing the accumulated deficit to $38.8 billion. A tax credit was given for first-time home buyers, and $900 million was to be spent over three years for school construction; other funds were provided for university and college construction. Treasurer Robert Nixon hoped to create 180,000 new jobs and reduce the unemployment rate to 5.1%.

Other Political Affairs. Health-care costs, up by $1.2 billion, in 1988 amounted to $12.7 billion, one third of total provincial expenditures. The treasurer warned that costs could go no higher without placing other programs at risk. As a result, hospitals were told to stay within their budgets and make cuts where necessary, although there was a temporary bailout for some hospitals in August. Doctors' fees were held to an increase of 1.75%.

© Canapress Photo Service

Ontario's Premier David Peterson (right) *and Michigan's Gov. James Blanchard met in Toronto on April 19 to sign six agreements, including a ''declaration of partnership'' between the state and the Canadian province.*

After the Supreme Court of Canada struck down the abortion-law provisions of the Criminal Code, the province agreed to end hospital abortion committees. The province also agreed to pay for abortions performed in hospitals.

The provincial education ministry offered new guidelines on school prayers after the Ontario Court of Appeal ruled against the compulsory recitation of the Lord's Prayer in public schools.

In November, Francophone school trustees went to court to try to force postponement of the November municipal elections because alleged errors had led to Francophones being enumerated as Anglophones. Also late in the year, Housing Minister Chaviva Hosek came under fire for failing to provide an adequate supply of low-and mid-priced housing, especially in southern Ontario.

PETER J. KING, *Carleton University*

OREGON

The "Oregon comeback" gained momentum during 1988. Employment reached record highs, and the growth rate of 4.1%, compared with 3.3% for 1987, was expected to continue. Unemployment stood at 5.6% for the third quarter.

Agriculture. Generally, agriculture benefited from the drought suffered in other sections of the nation. Grass-seed prices rose—for some varieties as much as 100%—and yields were high. Hay from Oregon was shipped by train, truck, and air to the South and the Midwest.

Field burning was once again an issue of public debate, as an auto accident near Albany, involving seven deaths and the destruction and burning of more than 25 cars, was blamed on smoke from burning grass-seed stubble. A moratorium was clamped on field burning for several weeks, but farmers argued that grass-seed fields must be sterilized by fire in order to prevent soil-borne diseases and insect pests.

Migrant Labor. An estimated 10,000 migrant workers were trapped in Oregon in 1988. The backlog in the paperwork required by the 1986 U.S. immigration law kept many in Oregon well past their ordinary departure date. Others lacked the funds to return home. Uncertainty over the provisions of the new law had kept many away from Oregon in 1987. The resulting labor shortage caused some farmers to deemphasize labor-intensive crops. News of 1987's shortage and a better understanding of the new law combined to attract a surplus of migrants, some, weeks before field work began. Their meager resources thus were exhausted early in the season, and a large number was destitute at season's end. While the Legislative Emergency Board granted $500,000 for the relief of migrants' needs, county requests for state funds were more than twice that amount. Local churches, clubs, and individuals conducted massive relief efforts.

Education. Forty-eight school districts fell into the "safety-net" classification. These were districts whose operating levies failed and as a result were held to 1987's budget. The federal government requires school districts to provide special services for migrant children aged 5–17. These services often cost up to $6,000 per child, yet the government provides only $500 per child. In 1988, 15,000 migrant children attended Oregon schools, and in 1989 the financial problem for districts was expected to become more critical when the law mandates services for children aged 3–21.

Elections. All congressional incumbents were returned to office. Rep. Denny Smith, Republican from the 5th District, defeated Mike Kopetski by only 665 votes. Massachusetts Gov. Michael Dukakis (D) won the state's seven electoral votes. Both houses of the Oregon legislature remained under Democratic control.

Initiatives that would mandate seat-belt use, outlaw public smoking, and tax beer, liquor, and tobacco for the benefit of college athletics were defeated. Winning initiatives would mandate full sentencing for repeating felons, designate a number of new scenic rivers for protection, and reverse a governor's executive order prohibiting job discrimination against homosexuals.

Budget. Gov. Neil Goldschmidt's budget proposal for the biennium 1989–90 called for a record $4.4 billion, of which 46% of the general-fund budget was allocated to education costs. The governor called for the abolition of the limits imposed upon state spending during the recession of the mid-1980s. Currently, the state spending growth cannot exceed the growth of Oregonians' average income.

L. CARL AND JOANN C. BRANDHORST
Western Oregon State University

OREGON • Information Highlights

Area: 97,073 sq mi (251 419 km²).
Population (July 1, 1987): 2,724,000.
Chief Cities (July 1, 1984 est.): Salem, the capital (1980 census), 89,233; Portland, 387,870; Eugene, 105,410.
Government (1988): *Chief Officers*—governor, Neil Goldschmidt (D); secretary of state, Barbara Roberts (D); *Legislative Assembly*—Senate, 30 members; House of Representatives, 60 members.
State Finances (fiscal year 1987): *Revenue,* $6,146,000,000; *expenditure,* $5,140,000,000.
Personal Income (1987): $38,245,000,000, per capita, $14,041.
Labor Force (June 1988): *Civilian labor force,* 1,454,400; *unemployed,* 84,600 (5.8% of total force).
Education: *Enrollment* (fall 1986)—public elementary schools, 308,527; public secondary, 140,780; colleges and universities, 144,801. *Public school expenditures* (1986–87), $1,760,000,000 ($4,236 per pupil).

OTTAWA

Ottawa, Canada's capital, enjoyed a rather quiet but prosperous year in 1988. One of the high points of the year was the opening of the new National Gallery of Canada building (*see* page 166). Constructed on a site overlooking the Ottawa River, it was designed by Moshe Safdie and cost C$162 million to build. The gallery's opening gave a boost to "Destination 88," a promotional program aimed at attracting more tourists, especially Americans, to the city. Tourism was up by 10% from 1987.

Federal Members of Parliament from the Ottawa area lobbied the government to establish the new Federal Space Agency in the capital area rather than in Montreal; a final decision was put off until after the federal election scheduled for November 21. Regional politicians found themselves embarrassed by a severe underestimate of between C$300–500 million for a new sewage treatment facility; it was feared the error might lead to a major hike in property taxes.

Educational politics figured prominently in 1988, due to a combination of three factors: the implementation of full provincial funding for Catholic schools; the impending creation of a French-language school (splitting the Catholic board on linguistic lines); and the transfer of surplus schools from the public to the Catholic board. In September wrangling between the English and French trustees on the separate boards over the transfer of schools from the public board reached such a point that court intervention was required to force open a French-language high school.

A proposal by the Ottawa city council to change the name of the regional government from Ottawa-Carleton to Metro-Ottawa met with strong opposition from the suburban municipalities, which feared being at the thin end of the wedge of one-tier government. Such fears were exacerbated further when city councillors proposed a plebiscite on the amalgamation of all area municipalities in the November local elections. Similarly the Ottawa Board of Education, encumbered with surplus schools, proposed amalgamation with the Carleton County Board; the latter refused this offer.

Ottawa city councillors managed to provoke a considerable public outcry by initially turning down the gift of a statue of Simón Bolívar from the Venezuelan government; one councillor objected that Bolívar had been a dictator. The statue subsequently was accepted.

Ottawa Mayor Jim Durrell was reelected in November for a further three-year term over token opposition. In sporting affairs, Ottawa hosted the 1988 Grey Cup. The Ottawa Rough Riders, however, did not participate; indeed they had one of their worst seasons ever. There were fears for the future of the franchise.

PETER J. KING, *Carleton University*

418

PAKISTAN

Pakistan experienced several dramatic events during 1988, culminating in general elections in November and the naming of Benazir Bhutto as Pakistan's first woman prime minister. The abrupt dismissal of the Mohammed Khan Junejo government in May, the death of President Mohammed Zia ul-Haq and others in an air disaster in August, floods, explosions, ethnic violence, and the signing of the Geneva accords on Afghanistan all served to make 1988 one of the most eventful years in Pakistan's four decades of independence.

Politics. A variety of growing political differences between President Zia and Prime Minister Junejo led to Junejo's dismissal on May 29. Zia also dissolved the national and provincial assemblies and announced that elections would be held later in the year. On June 15 he decreed that Islamic law *(Sharia)* would be the supreme law of the land. And in July, Zia set November 16 as the date for the national elections.

On August 17, a C-130 military transport plane exploded shortly after takeoff from Bahawalpur airport in central Pakistan. Killed were Zia, U.S. Ambassador Arnold Raphel, the chief U.S. military attaché to Pakistan, and several senior Pakistani military officers. Subsequent investigations indicated sabotage, but it remained unclear who was to blame.

Pakistan's response to this crisis was remarkably smooth and effective. In accordance with constitutional provisions, Senate chairman Ghulam Ishaq Khan became acting president. Gen. Mirza Aslam Beg became Army chief and pointedly urged the military to support the constitutional order.

President Zia had announced that the November elections would be held on a nonpartisan basis, but Pakistan People's Party (PPP) leader Benazir Bhutto—the daughter of the late Prime Minister Zulfikar Ali Bhutto, whom Zia replaced in a 1977 coup—filed a court petition challenging the ruling. Ultimately, the court and the new president agreed to hold party-based elections.

Given their first opportunity to contest elections since 1977, the parties engaged in considerable pre-poll maneuvering. The Pakistan Muslim League, which earlier had split into two factions, reunited during the campaign and became the cornerstone of the nine-party Islamic Democratic Alliance, or Islami Jamhoori Ittehad (IJI). Meanwhile, Bhutto's PPP withdrew from the Movement for the Restoration of Democracy (MRD), the coalition which had been the main opposition to Zia, and campaigned on its own. Benazir, whose marriage in 1987 appeared not to have hurt her electoral appeal, gave birth to a son in September, then resumed campaigning in October.

Although there were scattered charges of rigging, the National Assembly elections on

November 16 and the provincial polls three days later were regarded generally as fair and well-run. In the balloting for the 237 National Assembly seats, the PPP emerged with a plurality of 93 seats, the IJI was second with 55. The third largest group was the Mohajir Quami Movement (MQM), a relatively new force representing the Urdu-speaking immigrant community in Sind Province. Ultimately, the PPP and the MQM forged a coalition, which provided Bhutto the necessary majority to become prime minister. She took office on December 2.

The provincial results were mixed. The IJI won a plurality in Punjab, permitting Nawaz Sharif to form a coalition government and return as chief minister. Syed Qaim Ali Shah (PPP) became chief minister in Sind, Aftab Ahmad Khan Sherpao (PPP) in Northwest Frontier Province, and Zafarullah Khan Jamali (IJI) in Baluchistan. On December 12, Ishaq was elected to a full term as the nation's president by an electoral college consisting of the National Assembly, the Senate, and the provincial assemblies.

Violence plagued the nation throughout the year. On April 10 a munitions dump at a military camp exploded, killing 103, injuring more than 1,200, and raining projectiles on the nearby cities of Islamabad and Rawalpindi. On August 5 the prominent Shiite Muslim scholar Allama Arif Hussaini was assassinated. Ethnic conflict in Sind Province, particularly between Sindhis and Muhajirs, included a mass killing in Hyderabad City on September 30.

Economy. Pakistan's economy continued to grow, though more slowly than in the previous year. The gross domestic product (GDP) grew by 5.8% in 1987–88, only marginally below the plan target of 6.2% and the average growth over the past decade of approximately 6.0%. Agriculture grew 4.5% and manufacturing 7.6%. Exports and imports also continued to grow, although the latter increase was in part the result of higher oil prices. Inflation rose to between 6% and 7%.

AP/Wide World

Armed policemen stand guard as Pakistanis go to the polls in National Assembly elections on November 16. It was the nation's first open balloting since 1977.

Among the economic problems identified in the annual economic survey, released in June, were a growing budget deficit, a continuing high rate of population growth (3.1%), and an anticipated decline in remittances from Pakistani workers abroad. The Bhutto government also faced a growing debt burden.

Foreign Affairs. Pakistan, Afghanistan, the Soviet Union, and the United States signed agreements in Geneva on April 14 which made possible the beginning of a phased Soviet troop withdrawal from Afghanistan. The removal of 115,000 Soviet troops began on May 15 and was to be completed by Feb. 15, 1989.

Relations with India appeared to improve near the end of the year with the prospect of a democratic government in Islamabad. However, Pakistan decried India's acquisition of three Soviet nuclear submarines as a "fatal blow to denuclearization" of the subcontinent. Each country continued to raise alarms concerning the other's nuclear intentions as well as to blame each other for internal disruptions. With the hope of starting a new relationship, India's Rajiv Gandhi made a three-day visit to Islamabad—the first by an Indian prime minister in 28 years—late in December. Three agreements were signed, including one that bars attack on each other's nuclear plants.

Pakistan's relations with the United States remained strong, as a new, six-year, $4.02 billion security assistance pact took effect.

WILLIAM L. RICHTER
Kansas State University

PAKISTAN • Information Highlights

Official Name: Islamic Republic of Pakistan.
Location: South Asia.
Area: 310,402 sq mi (803 940 km²).
Population (mid-1988 est.): 107,500,000.
Chief Cities (1981 census): Islamabad, the capital, 204,364; Karachi, 5,180,562.
Government: *Head of state,* Ghulam Ishaq Khan, president (elected Dec. 12, 1988). *Head of government,* Benazir Bhutto, prime minister (took office Dec. 2, 1988). *Legislature*—Parliament: Senate and National Assembly.
Monetary Unit: Rupee (18.5 rupees equal U.S.$1, Dec. 28, 1988).
Gross National Product (1987 fiscal year est. U.S.$): $33,000,000,000.
Economic Index (1987): *Consumer Prices* (1980 = 100), all items, 159.5; food, 160.5.
Foreign Trade (1987 U.S.$): *Imports,* $5,825,000,000; *exports,* $4,090,000,000.

PARAGUAY

National elections were held on Feb. 14, 1988, and the incumbent president, Gen. Alfredo Stroessner, 75, of the Colorado Party, won an eighth term, with 88.6% of the popular vote.

Politics and Government. Prior to the balloting in the national elections, President Stroessner, a dictator who had been in office since 1954, outlawed six opposition parties, broke up political rallies, and jailed opponents. Of the two dissident parties offering token opposition, the Radical Liberty Party (PRLA) candidate won 7% of the popular vote and the Liberal Party candidate garnered only 3%. As the party finishing in first place, the Colorados automatically won two-thirds of the 108 seats in congress (36 senators and 72 deputies). The remaining places were distributed proportionally among the two losing parties. On April 1, Stroessner addressed an inaugural session of the legislative body and declared that his government would not permit outside interference in Paraguay's internal matters. Stroessner praised the nation's armed forces.

Filling the void left by an ineffective opposition was an increasingly activist Catholic Church. It attacked corruption in high places and pointed out the adverse effects of poverty. Priests condemned barriers to participation in the political process, and a lack of civil and human rights. The Stroessner government retaliated by persecuting Catholics, and on July 25, expelled a Spanish-born Jesuit priest for teaching liberation theology at the Catholic University in Asunción. After protesting students and faculty closed down the school for a day, 45,000 churchgoers marched silently through the capital's streets and gathered at the cathedral for an outdoor Mass on August 7.

Human Rights. Former Captain Napoleón Ortigoza Gomez, Paraguay's most famous political prisoner, was allowed to leave for exile in Spain on July 26, after 25 years in prison. A two-month postprison confinement had begun after his release on Dec. 17, 1987, and he was held by the authorities at a location 140 mi (225 km) outside the capital. Ortigoza then took refuge at the Colombian embassy with assistance from Hermes Rafael Saguier, an activist in the PRLA. Ortigoza had been found guilty by a military court of taking part in a coup attempt against the Stroessner regime and of participating in the murder of a cadet in 1962. A civil court previously had found Ortigoza innocent of the charges.

Economy. The gross domestic product (GDP) was expected to grow by 6%, thanks to higher yields of agricultural export crops. Soybean exports were up by more than 12% and accounted for nearly 58% of export earnings. Cotton sales abroad improved by 6.7%. The sugar harvest was up by 50%, covering domestic demand for the first time. For 1988, budget expenditures were increased by more than 36%, to 251 billion guaraníes ($285 million, at the free market exchange rate). A deficit was projected, in spite of a recommendation by the IMF to scale back public expenditures and reform taxes. The foreign debt exceeded $2 billion. In July, the guaraní was devalued by 25%, to 400 guaraníes to the dollar.

Foreign Relations. Pope John Paul II paid his first visit to Paraguay, May 16–18. In spite of official efforts to prevent his doing so, the pope went to the poorer sections of the country and met with civic leaders, as well as opposition forces in the capital. Following the pope's departure, General Stroessner traveled to New York and addressed a disarmament conference at the United Nations on June 6. The head of state returned to Asunción to prepare for a state visit to Taiwan, which he had to cancel because of a brief hospitalization in September.

LARRY L. PIPPIN
University of the Pacific

PARAGUAY • Information Highlights

Official Name: Republic of Paraguay.
Location: Central South America.
Area: 157,046 sq mi (406 750 km²).
Population (mid-1988 est.): 4,400,000.
Chief City (1982 census): Asunción, the capital, 455,517.
Government: *Head of state and government,* Gen. Alfredo Stroessner, president (took office 1954). *Legislature*—Congress: Senate and Chamber of Deputies.
Monetary Unit: Guaraní (400 guaraníes equal U.S.$1, July 1988).
Gross Domestic Product (1986 U.S.$): $3,800,-000,000.
Foreign Trade (1986 U.S.$): *Imports,* $509,000,000; *exports,* $275,000,000.

PENNSYLVANIA

During 1988, Pennsylvania was an essential state in Democratic candidate Michael Dukakis' strategy to win the presidency. In the spring he easily had won the Democratic primary, and with the enthusiastic support of popular Democratic Gov. Robert P. Casey, Dukakis counted on carrying the state in November. In the closest presidential race in Pennsylvania since 1944, however, Republican candidate George Bush won 51% of the vote. The key to Bush's narrow victory was a low turnout among black voters in Philadelphia (in response to an apparent snub by Dukakis of black Congressman William H. Gray 3d at an October breakfast as well as resentment over Dukakis' perceived ambivalence toward Jesse Jackson) and an enormous turnout in the Republican counties of central Pennsylvania. The high turnout in the heartland of the state was generated partially by attacks on Dukakis by the National Rifle Association.

In races for Congress, every incumbent up for reelection ran and won, including Republican Sen. H. John Heinz III.

Among contenders for state offices, the one major incumbent who lost was Auditor General Don Bailey, whom Republican Barbara Hafer defeated with 51% of the vote. Bailey failed to recover from allegations that he had not eliminated corruption from the office he took over from convicted former Auditor General Al Benedict. Hafer also accused Bailey of forcing his employees to contribute to his campaign. The contest for attorney general was negative from both sides. Republican Ernest D. Preate, Jr., accused Democrat Edward M. Mezvinsky of once having worked with a convicted marijuana dealer; Mezvinsky attacked Preate for, among other things, accepting campaign contributions from organized crime figures. Preate won a close race. In the third statewide race, the Democratic candidate for treasurer, Catherine Baker Knoll, became the second woman to win statewide office in 1988. In a state with no females holding statewide executive elected offices and whose legislature ranks 49th in its percentage of women, the Baker and Hafer victories were unexpected.

The percentage of women in the state legislature changed little after the election, as the composition of the legislature changed little. Only three Pennsylvania House incumbents and no state senators lost their bids for reelection. Three of the first-time winners of legislative races were women who replaced their husbands, who had died in office. Despite Governor Casey's efforts to help his party capture the Senate, the Republicans maintained a 27 to 23 advantage. In the House, the Democrats picked up one seat and had a 104 to 99 edge.

Legislation. The sharply divided legislature enacted major legislation that tightened procedures to track hazardous wastes and to begin to clean up toxic-waste dumps not covered

AP/Wide World
Pollution-control workers suction diesel fuel from the Monongahela River in downtown Pittsburgh, following the collapse of a nearby storage tank early in the year.

under the federal Superfund program. The state also progressed toward establishing a site for a repository for its low-level radioactive waste.

Economy. The economic news was mixed in Pennsylvania. For the first time since 1986, the state's unemployment percentage (5.5% in late fall) was higher than the national average. This figure, however, was lower than the 5.8% of late fall 1987. By year's end the index of leading indicators suggested a slowing of economic growth. To spur continued growth, the governors of Pennsylvania and New Jersey reached agreement on a program, including an international trade center and a ship-train-truck center, intended to revitalize Delaware River ports. Western Pennsylvania, in contrast to the prosperous Southeast, continued to suffer from problems in the steel industry and stagnation in factory jobs.

Other. The Peach Bottom nuclear plant, ordered closed in 1987 by the Nuclear Regulatory Commission because control room operators were sleeping on the job, remained closed for all of 1988. The cleanup of the damaged reactor at Three Mile Island continued.

Pittsburgh-area residents faced some adversity during the year. In early January their water supply was threatened by one of the worst inland oil spills in history, when a storage tank collapsed, pouring oil into the Monongahela River. Later, residents were saddened by the deaths of their popular Mayor Richard S. Caliguiri and the legendary founder of the Pittsburgh Steelers football team, Arthur J. Rooney, Sr.

ROBERT E. O'CONNOR
The Pennsylvania State University

PENNSYLVANIA • Information Highlights

Area: 45,308 sq mi (117 348 km²).
Population (July 1, 1987): 11,936,000.
Chief Cities (July 1, 1986 est.): Harrisburg, the capital (1980 census), 53,264; Philadelphia, 1,642,900; Pittsburgh, 387,490; Erie, 115,270; Allentown, 104,360.
Government (1988): *Chief Officers*—governor, Robert Casey (D); lt. gov., Mark Singel (D). *Legislature* —Senate, 50 members; House of Representatives, 203 members.
State Finances (fiscal year 1987): *Revenue,* $23,803,-000,000; *expenditure,* $20,571,000,000.
Personal Income (1987): $181,565,000,000; per capita, $15,212.
Labor Force (June 1988): *Civilian labor force,* 5,786,100; *unemployed;* 325,300 (5.6% of total force).
Education: *Enrollment* (fall 1986)—public elementary schools, 1,064,561; public secondary, 609,-600; colleges and universities, 545,924. *Public school expenditures* (1986–87), $7,299,000,000 ($4,752 per pupil).

PERU

Peru's worst economic crisis of the century imperiled the government of President Alan García Pérez and the nation's fragile eight-year-old democracy.

Economy and Government. With surges of 114% in September and 40.6% in October, the nation's accumulated inflation for the first ten months of 1988 reached 932.5%. As a result of the inflation along with strikes in the mining industry during the summer and fall and a scarcity of foreign exchange to buy imports essential to manufacturing, the economy was not expected to grow more than 2% for the year; some economists even predicted a 1% decline. The currency was deteriorating rapidly (the inti was valued officially at 33 to the U.S. dollar for imports but reached 207 on the black market in August); the nation's hard currency reserves were exhausted; the government could not pay its bills; and unemployment was rising.

The deteriorating economy forced President García to reshuffle his cabinet in early September. Responding to street demonstrations and public criticisms from within the cabinet itself, President García replaced Minister of Economy and Finance Cesar Robles Freyre with Abel Salinas Izaguirre, a powerful and respected figure in García's American Popular Revolutionary Alliance (APRA) party.

On September 6, just days after the cabinet shuffle, the government decided on an economic "shock" to reduce the fiscal deficit. The removal of government subsidies pushed food prices up an average of 160%, gasoline prices were increased 400%, the minimum wage was hiked 150%, and the currency was devalued by about 100%. In addition, the private sector was given ten days in which to adjust its prices, after which there would be a 120-day wage and price freeze. Anticipating high inflation for several months, many businesses raised their prices drastically, putting many products beyond the reach of consumers and throwing the economy into a sudden recession. Protesters took to the streets, and the government canceled the price freeze on all but 39 basic commodities. With the economic crisis continuing, Salinas resigned as finance minister on November 27, days after announcing a new austerity plan. He was succeeded by Carlos Rivas Davila.

In late September, Gen. Vucetich Zeballos, the chairman of the Armed Forces Joint Command, reiterated the military's support for popular sovereignty, the democratic system, and law and order. But on October 8, with President García under increasing attack for the economic situation, Gen. Victor Raúl Silva Tuesta began mobilizing senior Army officers in the north to put down what he believed was an imminent coup. When no coup materialized, General Silva—one of García's closest allies in the military—was replaced for questioning the loyalty of the army high command.

On December 20 APRA elected former Prime Minister Luís Alva Castro, a rival of García, as the party's secretary-general. It was expected that Castro would use his new post to force García to form a new cabinet.

Guerrillas and Terrorism. Exploiting the nation's economic troubles, the Sendero Luminoso ("Shining Path"), the eight-year-old Maoist guerrilla movement, emerged as a growing urban political force and joined in the January 1988 national strike and other labor activities. Although police had some success during the year in arresting high-ranking leaders of Sendero Luminoso, terrorist bombings, kidnappings, and killings of government and APRA officials continued.

On July 30 police arrested one Palestinian and two Arab members of the Abu Nidal terrorist organization based in Libya. Documents suggested that they were planning attacks on U.S., Israeli, and PLO offices in Lima. The three were deported the following week.

Foreign Affairs. In late October, President García joined other Latin American leaders of the so-called Group of Eight for meetings in Punta del Este, Uruguay, to discuss a common policy for debtor nations against industrial creditor nations of the so-called Paris Club, and to work out regional debt problems.

Earlier in the year, in August, a diplomatic delegation headed by Vice-President Luís Alberto Sánchez refused to attend the inauguration in Quito of Ecuador's new President Rodrigo Borja because he would not drop a reference in his speech calling for a revision of the Peru-Ecuador border. Peru's foreign ministry, however, dismissed the possibility of a formal diplomatic rupture.

An estimated 1.5 million people attended an outdoor Mass in a Lima park celebrated by Pope John Paul II on May 15. It was the pontiff's second visit to Peru; the first was in February 1985.

NEALE J. PEARSON, *Texas Tech University*

PERU • Information Highlights

Official Name: Republic of Peru.
Location: West coast of South America.
Area: 496,224 sq mi (1 285 220 km²).
Population (mid-1988 est.): 21,300,000.
Chief Cities (mid-1985 est.): Lima, the capital, 5,008,400; Arequipa, 531,829; Callao, 515,200.
Government: *Head of state,* Alan García Pérez, president (took office July 28, 1985). *Head of government,* Armando Villanueva del Campo, prime minister (took office May 1988). *Legislature*—Congress: Senate and Chamber of Deputies.
Monetary Unit: inti (33.0 intis equal U.S.$1, official rate, November 1988).
Gross National Product (1986 U.S.$): $19,800,000,000.
Economic Index (Lima, 1987): *Consumer Prices* (1980 = 100), all items, 11,150.4; food, 9,496.3.
Foreign Trade (1987 U.S.$): *Imports,* $3,297,000,000; *exports,* $2,577,000,000.

Philippine President Corazon Aquino is received with full military honors on arriving in Beijing in April. Major trade agreements were reached during her three-day China visit.

AP/Wide World

PHILIPPINES

Nearing the midpoint of her six-year term of office, President Corazon Aquino in 1988 experienced a brief respite from previous threats to her administration. Exiled former President Ferdinand Marcos was not allowed to return, there were no military coups, and large-scale Communist and Muslim uprisings never materialized. Although the armed resistance continued, a relatively calm year was highlighted by major land-reform legislation, modest economic growth, and political realignment.

Respite. In early May, citing "considerations of national welfare," President Aquino refused to allow President Marcos to return from exile in Hawaii to attend the funeral of his mother, Josefa Edralin Marcos. The former Philippine leader suffered another setback on October 21 when he, his wife Imelda, and eight others were indicted by a U.S. federal grand jury in New York City on six counts of fraud and racketeering. According to the indictment, they were accused of diverting $103 million from the Philippine treasury and defrauding U.S. lenders of more than $165 million.

Another enemy of the Aquino government, Col. Gregorio Honasan, the former chief security officer who had led a coup attempt in August 1987 and had been captured in December 1987, escaped with 14 guards from a navy prison ship in Manila Bay on April 2. But Honasan found too little support from the divided RAM (Reform the Armed Forces Movement) to do more than try to regroup the right-wing insurgency.

The leftist New People's Army (NPA), meanwhile, which had boasted that 1988 would be the year of major urban assaults, had its timetable drastically altered when two dozen Communist Party leaders, including Secretary-General Rafael Baylosis, were captured during raids in Manila and Cebu. José María Sison,

the party chairman released in 1986 in President Aquino's first blanket amnesty, promised more automatic weapons from funds he had been raising in Europe. Sison had his passport revoked and took refuge in countries, such as the Netherlands, that have no extradition treaty with the Philippines. Nevertheless, the revolutionary movement was beginning to separate radicals committed to random violence from moderates willing to consider cease-fires or even elective positions within the system. At the same time, the National Secretariat for Social Action, an organization of Catholic bishops, restructured itself in order to control Communist-inclined priests. Feuds also divided the Moro National Liberation Front (MNLF) from the Moro Islamic Liberation Front (MILF), neither of which found international support from the Organization of Islamic Conference after an appeal from President Aquino.

Land Reform. The months of relative calm provided the government with an opportunity to decide whether, and how much, to alter sociopolitical institutions to conform with the critical needs of the under- and middle-class. On June 10, President Aquino signed into law the Comprehensive Agrarian Reform Program (CARP), providing for the redistribution of large tracts of government-owned and private farmlands over a ten-year period. Under the measure, a total of 6.9 million acres (2.8 million ha) would be parceled out to nearly three million peasants. The first four years (1988–92) would cover unused government land and private holdings larger than 125 acres (50 ha). The next three years (1992–95) would cover private holdings ranging from 60 to 125 acres (24-50 ha). And the final three-year phase (1995–98) would involve smaller private holdings. At the end of the ten years, each landowner would be limited to a maximum of 12.5 acres (5 ha), with an additional 7.5 acres (3 ha) for each heir over age 15 who works the land. A ten-year grace

period was extended to certain private commercial and agricultural lands, such as those engaged in raising livestock, poultry, swine, fish, prawns, fruit, cut flowers, cacao, coffee, and rubber. These holdings could avoid redistribution by profit-sharing, with tenants as shareholders. The total cost of CARP over the ten years was estimated at $7 billion, but no specific funding was included in the bill.

The measure was criticized by reform advocates for what they regarded as concessions to wealthy landlords. The Philippine Peasant Movement (MMP) protested such compromises, and the Congress for a People's Agrarian Reform, with support from the Catholic Church, urged a plebiscite on the matter.

Economy and Foreign Aid. The nation's overall economic difficulties were underscored by the fact that nearly 48% of the budget and one fourth of foreign-exchange earnings went toward payments on the national debt—which exceeded $28 billion. Some help was forthcoming, however, as part of an expected multinational "mini-Marshall Plan" worth $10 billion. Substantial economic aid was pledged by both Spain ($102 million) and Saudi Arabia ($100 million), and loans were forthcoming from Italy and Switzerland after a June visit by President Aquino. Japan and 12 other nations agreed to restructure $1 billion in loan payments. Upon her return from a three-day visit to China in April, Aquino announced trade agreements worth $800 million and $3 million in rice from the People's Republic. Meanwhile, the Asset Privatization Fund planned to sell $500 million worth of government assets, including sugar facilities, mining and cement companies, and real-estate holdings in Tokyo; money from the sales would be committed to CARP.

The United States, although one of the originators of the "mini-Marshall Plan," decided to concentrate first on resolving the status of its Subic Bay Naval Station and Clark Air Base. Philippine Foreign Minister Raul Manglapus had argued for an increase in lease payments because these facilities were larger and more important than those in Greece, Turkey, or Portugal, yet were compensated for less generously. After six months of difficult negotiations, Manglapus and U.S. Secretary of State Shultz signed an interim agreement on October 17 in Washington. Under the accord, U.S. military and economic assistance was increased from $180 million annually to $481 million annually in fiscal 1990 and 1991. The United States also pledged $500 million in export credits and investment guarantees. The 41-year-old treaty between the countries would have to be renegotiated in 1991. The interim pact gave the Philippines authority to ban nuclear or chemical weapons on its territory, though it did not interfere with the U.S. policy of neither admitting nor denying the presence of nuclear weapons on its ships and planes. Philippine critics of the accord claimed that this policy was contrary to the antinuclear proliferation section of the 1987 Constitution. They also criticized Manglapus for failing to win his original demand of $1.2 billion in annual compensation.

Until the disaster of Typhoon Ruby in late October—which destroyed $45 million in crops and caused $10 million in damage to roads and bridges—1988 had been a year of sustained economic growth. Early in September, the International Monetary Fund declared the financial crisis over and offered $2 billion in extended credit. Unemployment dropped 2%, the number of strikes was down 62%; and the percentage of the population below the poverty line dropped from 70% to 55%. In agriculture, the value of copra increased fourfold. In industry, low labor costs have made the Philippines competitive with the other Pacific nations.

Investments by foreign companies also were on the rise. A Hong Kong company was

In the Philippines in late October, Typhoon Ruby took several hundred lives, destroyed $45 million in crops, and caused $10 million in damage. Many residents of the Manila suburb of Pasig, right, were forced to leave their homes and seek shelter elsewhere on higher ground.

planning two huge power plants in Manila worth $700 million. India's Birla group was investing $55 million in a rayon fiber plant. A surge in foreign and local investments beyond the $1 billion mark provided a 47% increase in capital over 1987.

In July a flood-control project was inaugurated in metropolitan Manila to divert 70% of annual overflow into the Marikina River. Three days later, in her State of the Nation address, President Aquino promised a 50% increase in the 1989 budget for rural infrastructures. The northern provinces already had been awarded $149 million for such projects as the Philippine-Japan Friendship Highway, connecting Cagayan and Ilocos Norte with the Sual seaport serving Pangasinan and La Union.

Politics. While foreign debt and land reform were sources of concern on the economic and social fronts, the unpredictable evolution of the nation's political parties also rang a note of caution. In the nation's first free local elections in 17 years, voters went to the polls on Jan. 18, 1988, to elect provincial, city, and town officials in 62 of the nation's 73 provinces; pro-Aquino candidates won two thirds of the positions. In the 11 other provinces, however, the balloting was postponed until February 8 because of violence. More than 100 people, including 39 candidates, had been killed since the start of the campaign in December 1987. Much of the violence was associated with the demise of political dynasties, deemed illegal under the Constitution; among those were the Laurels in Batangas, Ablans in Ilocos Norte, Nepomucenos and Lazatins in Pampanga, Sumulongs in Rizal, and Lopezes in Iloilo. Efforts to reestablish local fiefdoms and rearrange national loyalties prior to the 1992 presidential election exacerbated social unrest.

On June 12, the Lakas ng Bansa (People Power) and PDP-LABAN, both progovernment parties, merged to form the Lakas ng Demokratikong Pilipino Party (LDP). Speaker of the House Ramón Mitra, the head of the LDP,

began to relieve nonparty members of committee power. In a countermove, Senators Jovito Salonga and Aquilino Pimentel, along with Foreign Minister Manglapus, announced plans to create a coalition made up of the Liberal Party, a faction of PDP-LABAN, and the National Union of Christian Democrats; thus was born the Partido ng Bayan (People's Party) on September 4. Meanwhile, Vice-President Salvador Laurel, frustrated with President Aquino's refusal to resign and sensing defections within his UNIDO party, joined with Juan Ponce Enrile, the ousted secretary of defense, to form the opposition Union for National Action (UNA) in late August.

One of the consequences of all this political maneuvering was to neglect the escalating problem of corruption in government. The Office of the Ombudsman, created under the Constitution, reported to President Aquino that ten cabinet members and 30 other government officials had committed graft. And Solicitor General Francisco Chavez even leveled accusations of corruption against Ramón Diaz, the chairman of the Présidential Commission on Good Government (PCGG); Diaz resigned even though the PCGG itself is legally immune. In August, Aquino formed the Presidential Committee on Public Ethics and Accountability.

Despite losses in its leadership, the NPA sought to exploit the growing dissatisfaction with land reform and political greed. The movement gained momentum from the murder of human-rights activists across the country and especially, on June 24, the assassination of Alfonso Surigao, the regional chairman of Amnesty International in Cebu City. President Aquino had agreed to dissolve the Civilian Home Defense Force, a paramilitary national police notorious for crimes against the people, but, at the insistence of the military, created the analogous Citizens Armed Forces Geographic Units (CAFG), nominally supervised by the army's provincial commanders. Gen. Fidel Ramos, who on Jan. 21, 1988, replaced Lt. Gen. Rafael Ileto as defense minister, urged combining the Philippine Constabulary with the Integrated Police Force, as well as doubling the size of the army in order to end the 20-year-long Communist insurgency. But given the politicization of the military under and since Ferdinand Marcos, and in light of Ramos' own presidential ambitions, there was fear that the concentration of so much power in the secretary's hands might lead once more to state-supported "low-intensity" terrorism.

Cardinal Jaime Sin, speaking on June 26, warned that the February Revolution of 1986 still could be lost, urged moral rather than specific sociopolitical reforms, and called for a "New Nationalism"—one which would place "Nation first, before one's self."

LEONARD CASPER, *Boston College*
GRETCHEN CASPER, *Texas A&M University*

PHILIPPINES • Information Highlights

Official Name: Republic of the Philippines.
Location: Southeast Asia.
Area: 115,830 sq mi (300 000 km²).
Population: (mid-1988 est.): 63,200,000.
Chief Cities (1984 est.): Manila, the capital, 1,728,441; Quezon City, 1,326,035; Davao, 552,155; Caloocan, 524,624.
Government: *Head of state and government,* Corazon C. Aquino, president (took office Feb. 25, 1986). *Legislature* (unicameral)—National Assembly.
Monetary Unit: Peso (20.70 pesos equal U.S. $1, Nov. 21, 1988).
Gross National Product (1986 U.S.$): $33,100,-000,000.
Economic Index (1987): *Consumer Prices* (1980 = 100), all items, 265.5; food, 258.1.
Foreign Trade (1987 U.S.$): *Imports,* $6,811,-000,000; *exports,* $5,565,000,000.

1903–1912   1941–1943

1957–1965

1963–1966

"The Snapshot at 100: A Celebration of the First Century of the Kodak Camera" was held in Rochester, NY. The show included an 1890 photo of company founder George Eastman. Kodak models, clockwise: the No. 3A Folding Pocket, No. 3A Series III, Brownie Starflash, and Instamatic 100.

PHOTOGRAPHY

In 1988, on the eve of the 150th anniversary of photography, a plethora of auto-everything 35mm cameras was introduced that clearly indicated auto-focus (AF) is here to stay. A marketing battle was fueled in which manufacturers created cameras to appeal to specific levels of ability. The hope was that consumers would make the leap into single-lens reflex (SLR) photography and gain the creative freedom provided by interchangeable lenses. In the process, "bridge" and "new concept" cameras became part of the medium's technology and terminology.

Disposable cameras had their own mini war; Kodak's Disc camera was discontinued; video hardware proliferated; important exhibitions were held at major art institutions; a photographic auction pulled the largest-ever single draw; and Kodak introduced an astoundingly fast black-and-white film. All this occurred in the year that saw Kodak celebrate its 100th birthday.

Hardware and Software. The top SLR manufacturers made major product introductions. Minolta, which launched auto-focus photography in 1985, brought out its second-generation Maxxum, the 7000i ("i" for intelligent). It brilliantly solves many of the inherent weaknesses of SLR auto-focus and auto-exposure while providing incredible conveniences, such as the ability to add custom features. You even can program some yourself by inserting accessory electronic expansion cards into the camera body. Nikon brought out its first AF camera for professionals, the do-everything F4, as well as the fastest AF model, the N8008, with the highest shutter speed available—1/8000. Ricoh's XR-M, a full-feature multimode 35mm camera, may be the last great *non*-AF, and Yashica's Samurai indicated the resurgence of interest in half-frame cameras.

Because auto-focus and auto-exposure now allow one not to be intimidated by SLRs, a new category was born—the "bridge" camera. It combines simple, automated point-and-shoot operation with an interchangeable-lens SLR. An example is Minolta's 3000i; with this model, the user can stay with the fast 50mm or 35–80mm zoom lens designed for the camera or "bridge" into the entire line of available lenses, flash units, and accessories that a major manufacturer offers. Canon brought out two bridge AF SLRs, the EOS 750 and 850, which offer an auto built-in pop-up, pop-down flash.

Another new and exciting category is the "new concept" camera, such as Chinon's Genesis and Olympus' Infinity SuperZoom 300. These ergonomically designed cameras look like cameras for the 21st century. They have simple built-in zooms and are completely automatic.

On the optical front, at the annual Photo Marketing Association trade show, a rash of new lenses, mostly zooms, for AF SLRs was introduced. The barrage was concentrated among independent lens makers. Many electronic flashes intended for use with AF SLRs were shown in record numbers. And Durst introduced two new modular systems for the darkroom.

In the 35mm disposable film-with-camera category—in which the entire camera unit goes to the lab for processing and then is discarded

"THE SNAPSHOT AT 100"

Photos © George Eastman House

—Kodak brought out a 35mm Fling ($8.35 with f/11 lens and 1/110-second shutter). Fuji countered with a Quick Snap with a disposable flash.

The growing popularity of cheaper, easier-to-use 35mm cameras with far superior picture quality helped influence the decision to stop production of Kodak's Disc. Introduced in 1982, this mighty midget has an important place in the history of camera-film technology. It featured a wallet-thin body and 15 fingernail-size (8 x 10mm) color negatives in a flat disk—as opposed to a traditional film roll or cartridge—of Kodacolor film. The lucrative film, however, will continue to be produced.

Another Kodak classic, the Instamatic camera and accompanying Kodapak film cartridge, celebrated its 25th anniversary. In instant-print photography, Polaroid brought out a new 600-series-film instant-picture camera called the Impulse. And in the busy world of video, Canon's photoelectronic still camera, the RC760, produced the best commercially available still-video images, while Chinon's camcorder wonder with digital special effects was the EZ Movie Digital.

In software, Kodak introduced its super-secret, superspeed black-and-white film with an astounding ISO of 3200. The T-Max P3200 emulsion can be pushed to ratings as high as 25,000. Available in 36-exposure cartridges at a cost of $5.45 each, it takes advantage of technology Kodak has been developing since the early 1980s to control the shape and size of silver halide crystals.

In color films, improvements occurred in Ektachrome and Fujichrome slide films for both the amateur and professional markets, and in Kodachrome 200 for amateurs. These improvements result in better color contrast and rendition, higher saturation, and cleaner whites. Kodak's print film, the VR-G, was renamed Kodacolor Gold, and Polaroid announced its own brand of conventional color film—an acknowledgment of the declining popularity of the instant photography market. By so doing, it will be competing with Kodak and Fuji in the $7 billion world market now dominated by Kodak.

Exhibitions and Publications. The Museum of Modern Art (MoMA) in New York City sponsored a major 200-print retrospective on the work of Garry Winogrand (1930–1984), perhaps the most influential photographer of his generation, as well as a book called *Winogrand: Figments from the Real World*. Also in New York, a full-scale centennial survey of advertising photography opened at the International Center of Photography with a show, and a book called *The Art of Persuasion*. And in Washington, DC, at the Corcoran Gallery of Art, "Odyssey: The Art of Photography at National Geographic" showed how journalism sometimes jumps into the realm of art.

Photojournalism was alive and well and very visible, especially in its long tradition of operating as an instrument of social change. *Homeless in America: A Photographic Project* was a stunning example of this attempt to raise

Ergonomic, auto-everything "new concept" cameras introduced in 1988 included the Olympus Infinity SuperZoom 300, top, and Chinon Genesis. Both have built-in zooms.

Courtesy of Olympus (top) and Chinon (bottom)

A survey of advertising photography, "The Art of Persuasion," at the International Center for Photography included "Boy in Kitchen" (1939) for the Milk Marketing Board.

public awareness of the fast-increasing homeless population via a traveling show, book, and 12-minute video, plus TV and magazine coverage. And at Photokina, the international show in Cologne, West Germany, a show opened called "Eyes of Time: Photojournalism in America." The most comprehensive history assembled in years, it will tour for two years through the United States and Europe.

Photo collecting is also in fine shape, as evidenced by the spring sale at Sotheby in New York that netted $1,236,000—a worldwide record for one photo sale.

BARBARA L. LOBRON
Writer, Editor, Photographer

PHYSICS

Superconductivity, supernova neutrinos, and free-electron lasers were at the forefront of physics research during 1988.

High-Temperature Superconductors. In 1911 the Dutch physicist Heike Kamerlingh Onnes observed that when mercury was cooled below a temperature of 4 K, its electrical resistance completely disappeared—an effect called superconductivity. If an electrical current is set flowing in a superconducting ring, years later the current still will be flowing. The technological benefits of transporting electricity without loss are potentially enormous. Possible applications range from the exotic to the practical.

For example, large-scale application of magnetic levitation (super-conductors repel magnetic fields) would permit trains to travel at high speeds without friction between wheels and tracks. The combination of superconductors with current semiconductor technology (silicon and gallium arsenide) might create new opportunities in microelectronics.

Until recently, applications of superconductivity have been limited because the effect was observed only at extremely low temperatures. In the decades since Kamerlingh Onnes' discovery, low-temperature physicists have tried to raise the temperature at which a material becomes superconducting—the critical temperature, or T_c. The so-called "holy grail" of low-temperature physics was 77 K, the boiling point of liquid nitrogen. If the large and complicated devices that keep liquid helium cold could be replaced by the smaller and simpler cooling systems used for liquid nitrogen, then the expense and complexity of producing superconductivity would be reduced greatly.

A major breakthrough came in 1986, when Karl Alexander Müller and Johannes Georg Bednorz at IBM's research labs in Zürich, Switzerland, found that a ceramic compound of lanthanum, barium, and copper oxide superconducts at temperatures above the previous record of 23 K (achieved in 1973). Their results were confirmed rapidly, and researchers worldwide began using related ceramic compounds to produce superconductivity at higher and higher temperatures. In early 1987, a team of scientists led by Paul C.W. Chu of the University of Houston replaced the lanthanum with yttrium (another rare-earth metal) and achieved superconductivity above 90 K. Later that year, Müller and Bednorz were awarded the 1987 Nobel Prize in Physics.

Subsequent months saw much activity in superconductivity research, but claims of higher T_c values were unsubstantiated. It was of great interest, therefore, when in 1988 two new classes of superconductors were discovered. One class involves thallium, and another involves bismuth. The mere fact that new classes of superconducting compounds were being discovered led to optimism that progress still lay ahead, but the specific results also were very exciting. One thallium compound was confirmed to be superconducting at a record 125 K, and another was measured to carry a high current before losing its superconductivity. The latter feature is important because T_c is not the only vital parameter of a superconductor. Large electrical currents are required in many applications, and superconducting materials change to normal when currents above some critical value are passed through them. Early results on the metallic oxides had indicated that their critical currents were very small, hindering large-scale applicability. The thallium compound thereby repre-

sented a key breakthrough. The bismuth superconductors are also very encouraging because these are the first high-T_c materials which do not employ rare-earth metals.

In addition to their interest in raising T_c and increasing current-carrying capacity, scientists are paying greater attention to fabrication properties. With an ever-increasing collection of compounds to choose from, they stand a greater chance of finding materials with more advantageous properties. For example, some of the thallium superconductors are unoriented polycrystalline films, which would be quite suitable for microelectronic applications.

Superconducting Super Collider. The proposed U.S. Superconducting Super Collider (SSC), which would be the biggest and most expensive particle accelerator—or atom smasher—ever built, continued to arouse much interest and controversy in 1988. The huge machine, with its more than 50-mile (80-km) tunnel, would have countercirculating proton beams of 20 TeV each (1 TeV = 10^{12} eV) and would cost $4.4 billion or more. In September 1987, the U.S. Department of Energy (DOE) determined that 36 sites from 25 states met the qualifying criteria. The National Academy of Sciences and the National Academy of Engineering appointed a committee to evaluate the proposed sites. The committee selected eight candidates, of which one withdrew; that left Arizona, Colorado, Illinois, Michigan, North Carolina, Tennessee, and Texas. On November 10, Secretary of Energy John Herrington announced that the Texas site—located some 25 mi (40 km) south of Dallas—had been chosen.

In the meantime, the U.S. Congress allocated $100 million to continue research and development on the SSC. However, many congressional committees agonized over the project, expressing skepticism that sufficient money would be available and concern over the negative impact on other physics research. Such concerns mirrored those in the physics community and among scientists in general. The debate between champions and critics of the project is over priorities: "big" or "little" science, national leadership or international cooperation. All seem to agree that the physics would be interesting, that the Standard Model of particle physics is incomplete, and that the SSC might provide some key answers.

Supernova Neutrinos. Observation of the supernova 1987A was a major event for both elementary particle physicists and astrophysicists. Located in the nearby Large Magellanic Cloud, SN 1987A was visible to the naked eye and had been seen as an ordinary star. The unique contribution of scientific SN 1987A observations was the detection of neutrinos emitted as the star underwent gravitational collapse of its stellar core and was reborn as a neutron star. In one second, the supernova emitted more energy—most of it carried away by neutrinos—than our sun will emit in its 10-billion-year lifetime. Neutrino events were observed by neutrino detectors in both Japan and Ohio. From the spread in time among the events in the Japanese detector, the mass of the electron antineutrino was determined to be less than 20 eV. The question of whether the neutrino has a mass is crucial, since even a small mass could be sufficient for neutrinos to dominate the mass of the universe and thus determine whether the universe is closed or will continue expanding forever.

There are three known types, or "flavors," of neutrinos—electron, muon, and tau—each named after the charged particle associated with its formation or absorption. Whether or not there are more flavors is a fundamental question. The SN 1987A data imply that there can be at most only a few more flavors, since many more types of neutrinos would reduce the expected flux below the observed value.

Free-Electron Lasers. Interest in free-electron lasers has increased rapidly in recent years. As opposed to ordinary lasers, in which the emitted light appears only at frequencies specific to the atoms or molecules, free-electron lasers use electrons that are not bound into atoms or molecules and the frequency of emitted light is tunable. These devices are also capable of extremely high power.

The principle of free-electron lasers is simple. A high-energy electron beam is passed through an alternating magnetic field (called "wiggler" magnets) and, as a result of undergoing these oscillations, the electrons emit radiation at the frequency of oscillation. In the laboratory, the electrons are moving at almost the speed of light, and the resulting radiation is focused sharply in the direction the electron beam is moving. If a laser beam is sent down the electron beam, then at certain matching wavelengths the electrons radiate in phase with the laser beam. Thus, the strength of the laser beam can be modified.

Free-electron lasers offer many advantages over ordinary lasers. Tunability is one crucial advantage—in laser surgery, for example, because the absorption of light by body tissue varies by many orders of magnitude as the wavelength changes. Another crucial advantage is the capability of reaching much higher power. To a large extent, laser power is limited by the ability to dispose of the waste heat in the lasing medium. With an electron beam as the medium, waste heat is transferred at nearly the speed of light, allowing the laser to operate at very high power. The disadvantages of free-electron lasers include their high cost and difficulty of operation. Research and development now under way should improve their reliability for applications in medicine, defense, and materials science.

GARY MITCHELL
North Carolina State University

POLAND

Grave economic hardships, massive labor unrest, renewed government repression, and abortive efforts at reconciliation between the Communist regime and its opposition, led by the Solidarity movement, marked the year 1988 in Poland.

Economic Crisis. At the end of January, government decrees brought up the prices of some commodities and services by as much as 200%. Consumers faced shortages of most goods, as hoarding became a widespread response to anticipated price increases. Stores were limited in sales of butter, sugar, flour, and other staples. Food prices rose by an average of 40%, gasoline prices by about 60%, and housing costs by nearly 50%. The price of coal was slated to rise 200% by April 1. Discontent began to be felt throughout the country. The government justified the price increases as necessary to reduce wasteful subsidies and bring supply and demand into a more realistic balance. The illegal Solidarity trade union and other opposition elements viewed the increases as likely to depress drastically the living standards of workers.

A series of major strike actions began in April in transportation, steel, machinery, mining, and other sectors of the economy. In Bydgoszcz, 2,800 bus drivers won a 60% raise after a 100-hour strike paralyzed the city in late April. At the Lenin steel plant in Nowa Huta, some 12,000 workers went on strike. They demanded a 50% wage increase, recognition of Solidarity, and the release of all arrested union activists. Similar demands echoed throughout Poland.

Strike Crises. The peak of labor unrest coincided with the May Day (May 1) holiday, designated by Solidarity as a national "day of protest." Government sources admitted that as many as 12,000 people took part in antiregime demonstrations. The opposition put the figure at about 30,000. Solidarity founder Lech Walesa, the 1983 Nobel Peace Prize winner, led a strike by the shipyard workers in Gdansk, demanding wage increases, reinstatement of workers fired during the martial-law period of 1981–83, the release of political prisoners, and recognition of Solidarity.

With a $39 billion external debt, the Polish economy and especially its export industries were impaired by the labor unrest. The April strikes finally were halted by mid-May, but within three months the strike wave resumed.

The strikes of April and May were largely economic in nature. The August wave of strikes was more clearly political in character, with the recognition of Solidarity as its main objective. The government responded with the most stringent countermeasures since the imposition of martial law in 1981. Gen. Czeslaw Kiszczak, the minister of interior, announced special measures to deal with the strikes, including curfews "in areas where it may be necessary;" reinforcement of police controls in factories; and an "acceleration" of court procedures apparently intended to make it easier to detain people in custody.

In a televised speech on August 22, Kiszczak acknowledged that the port of Szczecin was closed effectively to shipping because of strikes; that 20 major enterprises, including 11 coal mines, were closed down by strikers; and that some 75,000 miners could not work because of the actions of about 6,000 strikers.

Negotiations. In the midst of the crisis, the Polish United Workers' (Communist) Party (PZPR) conducted a meeting of its Central Committee on August 27. The meeting produced a good deal of open criticism of government ineptness. It also produced the first public and official initiative in several years toward negotiating with the opposition. Kiszczak declared himself ready to talk with representatives of "various social and employee groups" and to do so without "any preconditions." As late as August 20, however, the government had rejected publicly the demand for "reactivating Solidarity."

In a tacit bargain of ending the strikes in exchange for a dialogue with the government, Lech Walesa agreed to hold talks with regime representatives on the subect of reforms and Solidarity's status. This occurred on August 31 at a meeting with General Kiszczak among others and was the first official contact between Walesa and the regime since 1982.

A six-hour meeting between Walesa and Kiszczak on September 16 resulted in an apparent agreement to hold more meetings beginning in mid-October "on the future of Poland" and presumably also on the future of Solidarity. The meeting produced some sense of hope and the possibility of future government concessions, but what appeared as the beginning of a hopeful "process" soon came to a

---

POLAND · Information Highlights

Official Name: Polish People's Republic.
Location: Eastern Europe.
Area: 120,726 sq mi (312 680 km²).
Population (mid-1988 est.): 38,000,000.
Chief Cities (Dec. 31, 1986): Warsaw, the capital, 1,664,700; Lodz, 847,400; Krakow, 744,000.
Government: *Head of state,* Gen. Wojciech Jaruzelski, chairman of the Council of National Defense and chairman of the Council of State (took office Nov. 6, 1985) and first secretary of the Polish United Workers' Party (took office Oct. 1981). *Head of government,* Zbigniew Messner, chairman of the Council of Ministers (took office Nov. 6, 1985). *Legislature* (unicameral)—Sejm.
Monetary Unit: Zloty (240 zlotys equal U.S.$1, 1987).
Gross National Product (1986 U.S.$): $259,800,000,000.
Economic Indexes (1987): *Consumer Prices* (1980 = 100), all items, 586.0; food, 687.0. *Industrial Production* (May 1988, 1980 = 100), 118.
Foreign Trade (1987 U.S.$): *Imports,* $10,379,000,000; *exports,* $11,713,000,000.

Protesting commodity price increases and demanding recognition for the Solidarity trade union, Polish workers staged strikes throughout the spring and summer. In August the Baltic port of Szczecin, right, was effectively closed to shipping because of a major strike.

AP/Wide World

grinding halt. The regime refused to negotiate further on the recognition of Solidarity. On the other hand, in early December the regime appeared to reverse its old policies by allowing Walesa to travel to France at the invitation of President François Mitterrand. In Paris, Walesa met with Andrei Sakharov and attended the 40th anniversary celebrations of the Universal Declaration on Human Rights.

In late October the government announced that the Lenin shipyard in Gdansk—birthplace of Solidarity in 1980 and Lech Walesa's workplace as well as political base—would be closed by December 1 for "economic reasons." Allegedly, it was no longer profitable.

In a surprising concession to "openness," Polish television carried a debate on November 30 between Walesa and Alfred Miodowicz, the head of the official trade union organization (OPZZ). Walesa demanded the recognition of Solidarity; Miodowicz opposed it.

Church-State Relations. The Roman Catholic Church continued to support the cause of reform in Poland. In early May church mediators proved a significant resource in negotiating strike settlements at a number of plants. Among the more prominent mediators were Andrzej Stelmachowski, chairman of Warsaw's Catholic Intellectuals' Club, lawyer Jan Olszewski, and journalist Halina Bortnowska. Following the local elections of June 19, the Roman Catholic bishops, meeting in Bialystok, issued a statement calling on Poland's Communist leaders to provide "far-sighted and courageous" reforms, both political and economic. The bishops blamed the recent wave of strikes on lack of freedom, "an insufficiency of participation that is particularly felt among the young generation of workers and students." In late August, Pope John Paul II, in a Mass celebrated in Rome, pointedly declared that no party or group can be sovereign within a state unless it bases such sovereignty on the consent of society itself.

In late October, when talks between Solidarity and the government stalled, Cardinal Josef Glemp met with party leader Gen. Wojciech Jaruzelski, apparently intending to induce concessions by the government.

Local Elections. Municipal and local elections were held on Sunday June 19 throughout Poland with multiple candidacies presented to the voters for the 109,000 seats in town, city, county, district, and provincial councils. Although 250,000 candidates competed for the available seats, all had been selected under Communist (PZPR) party control.

Solidarity called for a national boycott of the elections and several protest rallies were held in some of Poland's larger cities on June 19. The elections produced the lowest voter turnout in the history of Communist Poland. The regime had claimed that participation of half of the 26 million eligible voters would be "satisfactory" and indicated that only slightly more than 56% actually had voted.

Government Changes. The most important change in the government took place when Prime Minister Zbigniew Messner, publicly blamed for economic mismanagement, resigned on September 19. He was replaced by Mieczyslaw Rakowski, a 61-year-old Politburo member, deputy speaker of the Sejm (parliament), and a former deputy prime minister. In mid-December eight new members were appointed to the Politburo and six veterans were removed. This action increased the balance of power of the more liberal forces in the party's leadership. Stanislaw Ciosek, who had been conducting talks with Walesa, was made a party secretary as well as a Politburo member.

Environment. An Academy of Sciences report issued in late November described Poland as a country devastated by environmental pollution, with about one third of its population living in severely affected habitats.

Foreign Affairs. In mid-July, Poland hosted a meeting of the political-consultative council

431

of the Warsaw Pact, which turned into an East-bloc summit. Among the leaders attending were Mikhail Gorbachev of the Soviet Union, Nicolae Ceauşescu of Romania, Miloš Jakeš of Czechoslovakia, Bulgaria's Todor Zhivkov, Hungary's Károly Grósz, and East Germany's Erich Honecker. Poland joined with other pact members in advancing proposals for mutual North Atlantic Treaty Organization (NATO)-Warsaw Pact arms and troop reductions. The summit coincided with a special six-day visit to Poland by Soviet leader Gorbachev, who urged his hosts to advance their own version of his policies of *glasnost* (openness) and *perestroika* (restructuring). Hopes and rumors concerning Soviet willingness to withdraw parts of the two Soviet divisions stationed in Poland proved unfounded. (*See* special report, EUROPE—The Eastern Bloc, page 227.)

In early November, Margaret Thatcher, the British prime minister, visited Poland and gave strong symbolic and diplomatic support to Lech Walesa and the Solidarity movement. Thatcher told the Polish party and government leaders that any substantial further British economic and financial aid to Poland depended on the Polish regime's willingness to move in the direction of freedom and democracy and, implicitly, the recognition of Solidarity.

U.S. Deputy Secretary of State John C. Whitehead visited Poland twice during the year, discussing the problems and prospects of further normalization of relations following the removal of U.S. trade sanctions in 1987. Polish sources indicated some impatience with U.S. insistence on more political and economic reforms by the Jaruzelski regime.

At the end of September, Foreign Minister Tadeusz Olechowski and Israel's foreign minister, Shimon Perez, agreed to the exchange of independent diplomatic missions between Poland and Israel.

In December, Deputy Premier Ireneusz Sekula announced that Poland would be unable to pay all of the interest due on its debts to Western banks in 1989.

ALEXANDER J. GROTH
University of California, Davis

POLAR RESEARCH

Antarctic. Ozone layers above much of Antarctica fell to 50% below normal in October 1987, and as low as 95% below normal in some areas. During the 1987 austral spring, the ozone "hole" appeared in September but lasted longer than ever before—until December 1987. Although ozone holes are caused primarily by chlorine chemistry, their extent and duration are controlled by weather systems. Each austral winter, a vortex of strong stratospheric winds separates Antarctica from the warmer, ozone-rich air of more northern latitudes. Upper

atmosphere temperatures drop below −80°C, water vapor condenses, and polar stratospheric clouds (made of ice crystals) form. The chemical reactions that release the chlorine from long-lived, man-made chlorofluorocarbons occur on the ice-crystal surfaces. Other compounds that normally combine with chlorine and stop ozone destruction "freeze out" and fall to lower altitudes. In the spring when the sun rises, the atmosphere warms, and the depletion cycle ends as ozone-rich air gradually circulates.

Observations in spring 1988 supported this theory. Ozone levels in October were only 10% to 15% below normal. This corresponded with a 26-month tropical-wind cycle that pushes the polar vortex north, where stratospheric temperatures are higher. Because fewer polar stratospheric clouds form in the warmer atmosphere, the ozone-destruction cycle is slowed.

Near the Antarctic Peninsula, marine biologists studied the effects of decreased ozone on the marine ecosystem. As the ozone layer thins, more harmful ultraviolet radiation reaches the earth. In temperate and tropic regions, a mere 1% increase in exposure to ultraviolet radiation damages marine organisms, but the effects in Antarctica are unknown.

In January 1988 scientists launched an 11.6-million-cubic-foot (325 000-m^3) helium balloon to study Supernova 1987A. The largest high-altitude balloon ever launched in Antarctica, it carried a gamma-ray detector to an altitude of 15,000 ft (4 600 m).

In June 1988, 33 nations signed a convention to regulate mineral exploration and development in Antarctica.

Arctic. Although Arctic weather systems are similar to those in the Antarctic, Arctic temperatures remain higher, and more ozone-rich air from lower latitudes invades the stratosphere. Despite these differences, scientists believe that smaller ozone holes may form above the Arctic. Based on measurements made over the last decade, scientists have concluded that Arctic ozone levels also have dropped.

Data collected in early 1988 on ozone levels in Greenland suggested chemical reactions similar to those in Antarctica.

In October 1988 three California gray whales were trapped in unusually heavy sea ice near Point Barrow, Alaska. Despite the efforts of scientists, local residents, and government and oil-industry officials, one whale was lost. The two others were freed when a Soviet ice-breaker opened a channel in the sea ice.

During their spring summit, U.S. President Ronald Reagan and Soviet leader Mikhail Gorbachev affirmed their support for cooperative research in the Arctic. In January 1988 the United States and Canada signed an agreement on U.S. ship traffic in Arctic waters.

WINIFRED REUNING
National Science Foundation

PORTUGAL

Portugal enjoyed relative political and economic stability in 1988, although major challenges still lay ahead. A particular cause of apprehension was the approach of European Community (EC) consolidation in 1992 and the need to make Portugal more competitive with other member nations.

A major fire on August 25 destroyed Lisbon's historic Chiado district.

Politics and Government. After 15 post-revolutionary governments, Portugal appeared to have found an effective and perhaps long-lived government under the well-matched "cohabitation" of Social Democratic Prime Minister Aníbal Cavaco Silva and Socialist President Mário Soares. In July 1987, Cavaco Silva—considered an efficient technocrat—became the first prime minister since 1974 to win an absolute legislative majority, which he viewed as a mandate for his policy of opening up the economy via structural reforms. Soares is a veteran politician who has championed political and economic changes at home, while advancing Portugal's interests in foreign affairs.

Not all of Cavaco Silva's reforms have proven popular, however. Monthly opinion polls in the weekly newspaper *O Expresso* showed increasing public dissatisfaction, as his approval rating dropped from 69% in November 1987 to 43% in April 1988. The decline reflected public aversion to Cavaco Silva's rigid, no-compromise position on redrafting the constitution to allow full privatization and to remove protection for "conquests of the revolution."

Economy. The nation's economy showed new signs of flourishing in 1988, even though the stock market still was recovering from the October 1987 crash. Portugal's gross domestic product (GDP) has grown rapidly in recent years, benefiting from a tough austerity program in 1983–85, a cheap U.S. dollar, low oil prices, and EC assistance. Real domestic demand grew by about 8% in 1986 and nearly 10% in 1987, while the government anticipated a 3.75% increase in GDP for 1988. Unemployment measured 6.6% in March 1988, and the inflation rate reached 9% in July, well above the government's goal of 6%. Nevertheless, Portugal still was making up for decades of low investment in capital and human resources, a long reliance on its colonies for cheap raw materials and the purchase of its manufactured goods, and dislocations resulting from the 1974 revolution.

In March 1988 the National Assembly approved bills allowing for partial privatization and permitting the complete sale of government-owned newspapers. Pursuant to one of Cavaco Silva's strongest campaign promises, the measures were intended to facilitate payment on the public debt while improving management of many firms. On July 7 the government identified the first two state companies to be sold to the private sector. The government offered to sell 49% of Unicer, the state-owned brewery, and Banco Totta e Acores, one of nine nationalized banks, to the public. Majority shares were to be offered after an expected constitutional revision in 1989, provided that the government is able to preserve its two thirds legislative majority. The revision would allow majority stakes of state-owned companies to be privatized.

In October 1988, a year after the stock market crash, the ripple effect still had not subsided. The average daily turnover on the Lisbon exchange declined from $17 million in 1987 to only $3 million in 1988. The market was thought to be depressed because local investors had not yet regained confidence and were buying treasury bills for short-term liquidity. In addition, Portugal lacked the institutional investors—both domestic and foreign—needed to boost turnover prices. Foreign investors, while slowly moving back into the market, felt hindered by a shortage of information about companies and opportunities on the exchange.

Direct foreign investment, however, was rising dramatically. The estimated total of $460.4 million in 1987 represented a 152% increase from the previous year.

Foreign Affairs. In February, Prime Minister Cavaco Silva met in Washington with U.S. President Ronald Reagan for formal discussions on the level of U.S. compensation for the use of the military base in the Portuguese-owned Azores. Central to the talks were cuts in U.S. aid to Portugal—from $207.9 million in 1987 to $117 million in 1988. Though dissatisfied with the level of security assistance, Cavaco Silva stressed that Portugal had no intention of terminating or reducing U.S. rights to facilities in the Azores.

GEORGE W. GRAYSON
College of William and Mary

PORTUGAL • Information Highlights

Official Name: Portuguese Republic.
Location: Southwestern Europe.
Area: 35,552 sq mi (92 080 km²).
Population (mid-1988 est.): 10,300,000.
Chief Cities (1981 census): Lisbon, the capital, 807,937; Oporto, 327,368; Amadora, 95,518.
Government: *Head of state,* Alberto Mário Soares, president (took office March 1986). *Head of government,* Aníbal Cavaco Silva, prime minister (took office November 1985). *Legislature* (unicameral)—Assembly of the Republic.
Monetary Unit: Escudo (146.0 escudos equal U.S.$1, Nov. 3, 1988).
Gross National Product (1987 U.S.$): $35,000,-000,000.
Economic Indexes (1987): *Consumer Prices* (1980 = 100), all items, 347.1; food, 340.1. *Industrial Production* (1980 = 100), (Feb. 1988), 139.
Foreign Trade (1987 U.S.$): *Imports,* $13,441,-000,000; *exports,* $9,167,000,000.

POSTAL SERVICE

After signing favorable three-year union contracts in late 1987, the United States Postal Service (USPS) seemed close to realizing the financial and operational goals of the Postal Reorganization Act of 1970. Productivity was high, mail volume was booming, and the agency had had surpluses five of the last eight years. That changed, however, in December 1987 when Congress passed a budget reconciliation bill pruning expenses in order to lessen the federal deficit. Though no longer dependent on appropriations from the federal treasury, the service was ordered to reduce its expenditures $1.2 billion through fiscal years (FY) 1988 and 1989, ending Sept. 30, 1989. In addition, the legislation put a cap of $625 million in FY 1988 and $1.9 billion in FY 1989 on postal capital expenditures and blocked the $11.7 billion facilities and equipment modernization plans adopted by the USPS Board of Governors in October 1986.

Then on Jan. 5, 1988, Postmaster General (PMG) Preston R. Tisch announced his resignation, effective in the spring, to return to the family business. The system needed a new leader, he said, who could make a three-to-five-year commitment to the job, something he could not offer. In fact, a successor was named sooner than expected. On February 2, the Board of Governors announced the selection of Anthony M. Frank, head of the First Nationwide Financial Corporation, to succeed Tisch on March 1. The fifth PMG since 1985, Frank said that he proposed to remain PMG for three years or longer.

Meanwhile, realizing that the USPS might be forced to retrench despite a rapidly increasing volume of mail which reached nearly 160 billion pieces during FY 1988, the postal management had begun to target budget areas to cut. Hardest hit was the construction of new facilities and the purchase of mail-processing equipment. These were reduced by 74% for FY 1988. There was a freeze in the filling of most administrative positions as well as many part-time jobs. Window service was cut an average of half a day a week, a reduction restored in September. There were fewer mail pickups from boxes, and use of less expensive truck transport in place of movement by train or air. As expected there was some decrease in service effectiveness.

The main assistance forthcoming was in the form of postal-rate increases, requested by the USPS earlier in FY 1987. On March 3, 1988, most of these were approved by the Postal Rate Commission, to take effect on April 3. The cost of a first-class stamp rose from 22 to 25 cents, but the proportionate rise was greatest for the so-called "junk" advertising mail. There were a few reductions in favor of types of bulk mail. Taking inflation into account, U.S. first-class rates remained about where they were in 1970. They are the lowest in the world. However, rising labor and other costs, the escalation of health-care expenses, and the need to shift millions into the central federal pension system covering postal employees reduced an expected surplus to a deficit of more than $500 million.

There was still the need to modernize facilities, which averaged more than 30 years old, and to bring on-line automated equipment to handle the continually expanding volume of mail. In October 1988, PMG Frank announced a new $12.9 billion capital spending plan aimed less at facilities and more at new equipment to improve productivity. The USPS also mounted a campaign to persuade Congress to take the postal service off the formal federal budget in order not to subject it to the types of budget cuts undergone in 1988. Although such a measure was approved overwhelmingly in the House and by most of the Senate, the proposal died without action. Meanwhile, a March report by a special President's Commission on Privatization strongly recommended an end to the postal monopoly and a gradual opening up of the postal system to more competition.

Canada. After a year of much labor strife, the Canada Post Corporation entered a period of relative calm and effective development in 1988, although there was a 20-day strike beginning in August involving technicians, their supervisors, and more than 4,000 administrative and clerical staffers. First-class postal rates rose to 37 cents (Canadian) on Jan. 1, 1988, and would rise another cent on Jan. 1, 1989. But the reduction of the postal deficit to $30 million in FY 1988, ended March 31, was most impressive.

PAUL P. VAN RIPER, *Texas A&M University*

PRINCE EDWARD ISLAND

Voters in Prince Edward Island (P.E.I.) endorsed the idea of a fixed link to mainland Canada, but by less than a decisive margin. A new contract assured the island of "secure" electricity. And the legislature ratified the Meech Lake Accord.

Link to the Mainland. In a nonbinding plebiscite on Jan. 18, 1988, islanders voted in favor of the construction of a tunnel or a bridge to New Brunswick. But the margin in favor—59.9% to 40.1%—was not as overwhelming as proponents had hoped. Premier Joe Ghiz reacted by calling for a full-scale environmental study by the federal government. Environment Minister Thomas McMillan, P.E.I.'s representative in the federal cabinet, asserted that the delay caused by such a study would end the project.

The controversy flared again on September 30 when Ottawa narrowed the list of contend-

The ferry to Prince Edward Island carried a record number of visitors in 1988. Residents voted for a bridge or tunnel to the mainland, but opponents feared that the increase in tourism could disrupt the island's peaceful environment.

©Clark/Canapress Photo

ers for the crossing contract—which could be worth close to C$1 billion—to three. Five proposals were excluded from further consideration, including one from the only company that was proposing a tunnel instead of a bridge.

Fearing that a bridge might disrupt fishing spawning grounds, the province's politically powerful fishing industry demanded a new plebiscite. Premier Ghiz said that he shared the fishermen's concerns.

Meanwhile proponents of the link claimed that it would provide hundreds of new jobs and lower transportation costs. They also said that the link offered the prospect of increased tourism. But some islanders do not see this potential increase as a benefit, pointing to the more than 700,000 tourists in 1987 (up from 650,000 in 1986) and a likely 30% increase in 1988. Concern centered around the possibility that a permanent link might flood P.E.I. with tourists and transform the peaceful island's environment.

Secure Power. A perennial concern of P.E.I., secure power, was alleviated in August, when the province entered into a $150 million, six-year electricity contract with New Brunswick and Quebec. The agreement will supply 60–80% of P.E.I.'s power needs and stabilize prices. It also allows the island to lease up to $25 million of electrical capacity.

The Legislature. On May 13, Prince Edward Island became the fourth province to ratify the Meech Lake Accord, which would bring Quebec into the Canadian Constitution. The legislature's endorsement was unanimous, except for one dissenting vote cast by Liberal backbencher Nancy Guptill.

Other measures adopted at the 12-week spring session included pay-equity legislation for provincial civil servants, and an increase in the minimum wage. The 1988–89 budget imposed or increased taxes on clothing, shoes, and cigarettes.

Forest Funding. A C$24 million federal-provincial agreement signed in Charlottetown on June 23 secured funding for P.E.I.'s forestry development for an additional five years. The federal government would put up $14.2 million and the provincial government $9.9 million. About 450 jobs were expected to be created.

Fires in Charlottetown. The year 1987 and the first six months of 1988 saw 46 building fires in the capital city of Charlottetown. Most of them were caused by arsonists.

JOHN BEST, *Canada World News*

PRINCE EDWARD ISLAND
• **Information Highlights**

Area: 2,185 sq. mi (5 660 km²).
Population (June 1988): 128,500.
Chief Cities (1986 census): Charlottetown, the capital, 15,776; Summerside, 8,020.
Government (1988): *Chief Officers*—lt. gov., Lloyd G. MacPhail; premier, Joe Ghiz (Liberal). *Legislature*—Legislative Assembly, 32 members.
Provincial Finances (1988–89 fiscal year budget): *Revenues,* $577,600,000; *expenditures,* $583,500,000.
Personal Income (average weekly earnings, June 1988): $376.08.
Labor Force (August 1988, seasonally adjusted): *Employed* workers, 15 years of age and over, 55,000; *Unemployed,* 12%.
Education (1988–89): *Enrollment*—elementary and secondary schools, 24,740 pupils; postsecondary—universities, 2,300; community colleges, 1,100.
(All monetary figures are in Canadian dollars.)

PRISONS

The expansion of the U.S. prison system continued apace in 1988, with inmate populations reaching new highs across the land. Expenditures for the construction of new facilities and the personnel to staff them also continued to spiral upward, but the gradual introduction of national sentencing guidelines left little expectation that the decade-long period of rapid prison growth and overcrowding could be slowed over the next several years.

Population. In September the U.S. Department of Justice announced that the total federal and state prison population had reached another record high—604,824. This represented an increase of 4% for the first six months of the year, continuing an upward trend that had begun in the 1970s. Despite annual construction outlays in excess of billions of dollars over several years, severe overcrowding remained the norm throughout the country.

All segments of the population for which records are kept—based on gender, age, and race—showed significant increases in the rates of imprisonment. Although minority groups accounted for almost a majority of those incarcerated, some shifts in the makeup of the prison population could be noted. In recent years, the steepest percentage increase has occurred in the female population; officials attributed this rise to a sharp increase in drug convictions among women. The number of Vietnam veterans serving prison time also appeared to be growing. Although national figures are not kept, one study noted that of the 5,500 inmates in Michigan's Jackson State Prison, 1,200 (more than 20%) had served in Vietnam. Judicial and political responses to a perceived public demand for stiffer penalties across the board also have resulted in an increase in the imprisonment of white-collar criminals.

Conditions and Facilities. Published reports of the apparently more benign conditions enjoyed by wealthier inmates drew criticism during the year. Arbitrageur Ivan Boesky, sentenced in 1987 to three years in prison for trading on insider stock information, began serving his time in Lompoc, a federal prison in California that includes tennis courts. In Vermont, in response to prison overcrowding, a house-arrest program was introduced in which some inmates sentenced for nonviolent crimes could serve their time in secure housing paid for by the prisoner. When press reports revealed that John Zaccaro, Jr., the 24-year-old son of former Democratic vice-presidential candidate Geraldine Ferraro, had served parts of his four-month sentence on drug charges in a $1,500 per month luxury apartment with maid service and cable television, public outcry prompted a review of the state policy.

In an effort to control escalating labor costs associated with 24-hour-a-day staffing, some prisons began experimenting with electronic surveillance. The aim of such innovations, as stated by one official, was to allow the management of a "cheaper, better, more humane institution that does not have all the bars, yet is secure." Underground electronic cables around the perimeter of the prison detect any movement, sound alarms, and pinpoint the source of disturbance, enabling mobile patrol units to respond. In February, Justice Department officials introduced a program for monitoring a small number of parolees through electronic devices strapped to their ankles. Officers at a central location then can determine if the parolees are at home when they are supposed to be.

Sentencing Guidelines. U.S. criminal justice officials long have noted the wide differences in the length of sentences handed down for similar crimes committed in different areas of the country. Over the past decade, there has been growing demand for federal guidelines to assist judges in sentencing. In response, Congress in 1984 created a special commission to propose guidelines on uniform sentencing. The guidelines, which were submitted in April 1987 and went into effect in November 1987, increase the length of many sentences, especially for drug-related crimes, and sharply curtail the use of parole. However, the constitutionality of the new rules was challenged repeatedly—in many cases successfully—in federal court, and in June the U.S. Supreme Court agreed to review guidelines. According to many in the corrections community, the effects on the prison system and the costs of the reform, which would be borne largely by the individual states, could be catastrophic. Taking into account the new sentencing practices, projections to the year 2000 suggest a threefold increase in the number of people imprisoned.

Capital Punishment. The number of U.S. inmates awaiting execution, growing at an annual rate of 10%, exceeded 2,000 in 1988. In March, Willie Darden, who had spent 14 years on Florida's death row and lived through six stays of execution, was electrocuted. Darden had been a symbol for death-penalty opponents, who said his conviction was tainted racially. As of late 1988, a total of 37 states allowed executions, and 12 states actually were carrying them out.

Uprisings. Inmates at a medium-security state prison at Stringtown, OK, seized eight hostages in a mid-May uprising that included setting fire to a dormitory and $1.5 million in other damage. The inmates surrendered three days later. At the Coxsackie Correctional Facility in New York, 32 inmates seized five guards on August 1 and held them hostage for 15 hours.

See also CRIME.

DONALD GOODMAN
John Jay College of Criminal Justice

PRIZES AND AWARDS

NOBEL PRIZES[1]

Chemistry: Johann Deisenhofer, Howard Hughes Medical Institute (TX); Robert Huber, Max Planck Institute for Biochemistry, Martinsried, West Germany; Hartmut Michel, Max Planck Institute for Biophysics, Frankfurt/Main, West Germany; for research revealing the three-dimensional structure of closely linked proteins that are essential to photosynthesis.

Economics: Maurice Allais, École Nationale Supérieure des Mines de Paris, for "development of theories explaining market behavior and the efficient use of resources."

Literature: Naguib Mahfouz, Egyptian novelist, playwright, and screenwriter, for creating "an Arabian narrative art that applies to all mankind." (*See* page 332.)

Peace Prize: the United Nations Peacekeeping Forces, which "have, by their presence [in troubled regions], made a decisive contribution toward the initiation of actual peace negotiations."

Physics: Leon M. Lederman, Fermi National Accelerator Laboratory (IL); Melvin Schwartz, Digital Pathways Inc. (CA); Jack Steinberger, European Center for Nuclear Research, Geneva, Switzerland; for a landmark experiment which led to a theory that is a cornerstone of modern physics.

Physiology or Medicine: Sir James Black, Rayne Institute of the University of London; Gertrude B. Elion and George H. Hitchings, Burroughs-Wellcome Company (NC); for discoveries of "important principles for drug treatment . . . based on the understanding of basic biochemical and physiological processes."

[1] About $390,000 in each category.

ART

American Academy and Institute of Arts and Letters Awards
Academy-Institute Awards ($5,000 ea.): art—Christopher Brown, James DeMartino, Susan Hauptman, Albert York, Daisy Youngblood; music—Fred Lerdahl, Hale Smith, Chinary Ung, Maurice Wright
Award of Merit for Painting: Frank Lobdell
Nathan and Lillian Berliawsky Award ($5,000): The Gregg Smith Singers
Walter Hinrichson Award: Martin Boykan
Charles Ives Fellowship ($10,000): Gerald H. Plain
Charles Ives Scholarship ($5,000 ea.): Richard Argosh, Timothy Geller, Mark Kilstofte, Behzad Ranjbaran, Douglas A. Scott, David J. Vayo
Goddard Lieberson Fellowships ($10,000 ea.): David Koblitz, Anthony Korf
Richard and Hinda Rosenthal Foundation Award ($5,000): Susan Lichtman
Capezio Dance Award ($5,000): Charles (Honi) Coles
John F. Kennedy Center Honors for career achievement in the performing arts: Alvin Ailey, George Burns, Myrna Loy, Alexander Schneider, Roger L. Stevens
Edward MacDowell Medal: William Styron
National Academy of Recording Arts and Sciences
Grammy Awards for excellence in phonograph records
Album of the year: *The Joshua Tree,* U2
Classical Album: *Horowitz in Moscow,* Vladimir Horowitz, Thomas Frost (producer)
Country music song: *Forever and Ever, Amen,* Paul Overstreet and Don Schlitz (songwriters)
Jazz vocal performance: (female) *Diana Schuur and the Count Basie Orchestra,* Diane Schurr; (male) *What Is This Thing Called Love,* Bobby McFerrin
New artist: Jody Watley
Record of the year: *Graceland* (Paul Simon, artist and producer)
Song of the year: *Somewhere Out There,* James Horner, Barry Mann, Cynthia Weil (songwriters)
National Endowment for the Arts Jazz Masters
Fellowships ($20,000 ea.): Art Blakey, Lionel Hampton, Billy Taylor
National Medal of Arts: Brooke Astor, Saul Bellow, Sydney J. Freedberg, Francis Goelet, Helen Hayes, Gordon Parks, I. M. Pei, Jerome Robbins, Rudolf Serkin, Roger L. Stevens, Obert C. Tanner, Virgil Thomson
Pritzker Architecture Prize ($100,000 shared): Gordon Bunshaft and Oscar Niemeyer

Pulitzer Prize for Music: William Bolcom, *12 New Etudes for Piano*
Samuel H. Scripps/American Dance Festival Award ($25,000): Eric Hawkins

JOURNALISM

Maria Moors Cabot Prizes ($1,000 ea.): Nicholas Clark Asheshov, editor of *Lima Times,* Peru; Robert Civita, creator and publisher, *Veja,* São Paulo, Brazil; Stephen Kinzer, foreign correspondent, *The New York Times;* Hermenegildo Sabat, staff cartoonist, *Clarin,* Buenos Aires, Argentina
National Magazine Awards
Design: *Life*
Essays and criticism: *Harper's*
Feature writing: *The Atlantic*
Fiction: *The Atlantic*
General excellence: *Parents, Fortune, Hippocrates, The Sciences*
Personal service: *Money*
Photography: *Rolling Stone*
Public-interest: *The Atlantic*
Reporting (joint): *The Washingtonian, Baltimore*
Single-topic issue: *Life*
Special-interest: *Traveler* (Condé Nast)
Overseas Press Club Awards
Joseph Albright, Marcia Kuhstel, and Rick McKay, Cox Newspapers, "Stolen Childhood"
Raymond Bonner, Times Books, "Waltzing with a Dictator: The Marcoses and the Making of American Policy"
James Allen Flanery, *Omaha World-Herald,* "World Agriculture: Growing Pains"
Business Week, "Japan: Remaking a Nation"
Herbert Block, *The Washington Post,* for cartoons
Time magazine, "Gorbachev's Revolution"
David Zucchino, *Philadelphia Inquirer,* "Smothering the Flames of Black Revolution"
Brian Ellis and Walter Cronkite, CBS News, "CBS Reports: Children of Apartheid"
"NBC Nightly News" with Tom Brokaw, for Brian Ross' international drug investigations
CBS News, "Newsmark: Patrolling the Gulf"
CBS Radio, for its Persian Gulf coverage
Gary Porter, photographer, *The Milwaukee Journal,* "Empty Cradles: The Global Tragedy of Child Mortality"
Sebastiao Salgado, photographer, *The New York Times Magazine,* "An Epic Struggle for Gold"
Janet Knott, photographer, *The Boston Globe,* "Democracy: What Price?"
The Wall Street Journal, "Islam on the Move"
Margaret Ellen Hale, Gannett News Service, "AIDS: A Killer Stalks the Globe"
George Polk Memorial Awards
Career award: Murray Kempton, *Newsday*
Financial reporting: James B. Stewart and Daniel Hertzberg, *The Wall Street Journal*
Foreign reporting: Nora Boustany, *The Washington Post*
International television reporting: Gordon Manning, "Changing China" and "A Conversation with Mikhail Gorbachev," NBC
Local reporting: Ron Ridenhour, *CityBusiness,* New Orleans
Local-television reporting: Margie Nichols, "A Premium Price" and "Little Assurance," WSMV-TV (Nashville)
Magazine reporting: Roger Rosenblatt, "Enter This House and Let the Ice Melt," *Time*
Metropolitan reporting: *The Charlotte Observer* (NC)
National reporting: Mike Masterson, Chuck Cook, and Mark N. Trahant, "Fraud in Indian Country," *The Arizona Republic*
Network television reporting: CNN, "for its resourceful, uninterrupted reporting and analysis of national and international news"
Political reporting: The Washington (DC) bureau of Knight-Ridder
Radio reporting: Larry Bensky, Pacifica Radio, coverage of Iran-contra hearings
Science reporting: *Science News*
Sports reporting: Chris Mortensen, "Ignoring the Rules," *The Atlanta Journal & Constitution*
Pulitzer Prizes
Commentary: Dave Barry, *The Miami Herald*
Criticism: Tom Shales, *The Washington Post*

Editorial cartooning: Doug Marlette, *The Atlanta Journal & Constitution* and *The Charlotte Observer*
Editorial writing: Jane E. Healy, *The Orlando Sentinel* (FL)
Explanatory journalism: Daniel Hertzberg and James B. Stewart, *The Wall Street Journal*
Feature photography: Michel duCille, *The Miami Herald*
Feature writing: Jacqui Banaszynski, *The St. Paul Pioneer Press Dispatch*
General-news reporting: *The Alabama Journal*
International reporting: Thomas L. Friedman, *The New York Times*
Investigative reporting: Dean Baquet, William C. Gaines, and Ann Marie Lipinski, *The Chicago Tribune*
National reporting: Tim Weiner, *The Philadelphia Inquirer*
Public service: *The Charlotte Observer*
Specialized reporting: Walt Bogdanich, *The Wall Street Journal*
Spot news photography: Scott Shaw, *The Odessa American* (TX)

Photos AP/Wide World

Oscar winner:
Michael Douglas

Grammy winner:
Whitney Houston

LITERATURE

American Academy and Institute of Arts and Letters Awards
Academy-Institute Awards ($5,000 ea.): William Barrett, David Bottoms, Rosellen Brown, David Cope, John Clellon Holmes (posthumous), John McCormick, James Seay, William Weaver, Norman Williams
The American Academy in Rome Fellowship in Literature: Edward Hirsch
Witter Bynner Prize for Poetry ($1,500): Andrew Hudgins
Sue Kaufman Prize for First Fiction ($2,500): Kaye Gibbons
Richard and Hinda Rosenthal Foundation Award ($5,000): Thomas McMahon
Jean Stein Award ($5,000): Andre Dubus
Harold D. Vursell Memorial Award ($5,000): Jonathan Maslow
Morton Dauwen Zabel Award ($2,500): Clement Greenberg
Bancroft Prizes ($4,000 ea.): Peter R. Kolchin, *Unfree Labor: American Slavery and Russian Serfdom;* Michael S. Sherry, *The Rise of American Air Power: The Creation of Armageddon*
Canada's Governor-General Literary Awards ($5,000 ea.):
English-language awards
Drama—John Krizanc, *Prague*
Fiction—M. T. Kelly, *A Dream Like Mine*
Nonfiction—Michael Ignatieff, *The Russian Album*
Poetry—Gwendolyn MacEwen, *Afterworlds*
French-language awards
Drama—Jeanne-Mance Delisle, *Un Oiseau Vivant*
Fiction—Gilles Archambault, *L'Obsédante Obèse et Autres Agressions*
Nonfiction—Jean Larose, *La Petite Noirceur*
Poetry—Fernand Ouellette, *Les Heures*
Ruth Lilly Poetry Prize ($25,000): Anthony Hecht
National Book Awards ($10,000 ea.):
Fiction: Peter Dexter, *Paris Trout*
Nonfiction: Neil Sheehan, *A Bright Shining Lie: John Paul Vann and America in Vietnam*
National Book Critics Circle Awards
Biography/autobiography: Donald R. Howard, *Chaucer: His Life, His Work, His World*
Criticism: Edwin Denby, *Dance Writings*
Fiction: Philip Roth, *The Counterlife*
Nonfiction: Richard Rhodes, *The Making of the Atomic Bomb*
Poetry: C. K. Williams, *Flesh and Blood*
Neustadt International Prize for Literature ($25,000): Raja Rao (India)
PEN/Faulkner Award ($5,000): T. Coraghessan Boyle, *World's End*
Mystery Writers of America/Edgar Allan Poe Awards
Novel: Aaron Elkins, *Old Bones*
Critical/biographical work: Leroy Lad Panek, *Introduction to the Detective Story*
Award for lifetime achievement: Phyllis A. Whitney
Pulitzer Prizes
Biography: David Herbert Donald, *Look Homeward: A Life of Thomas Wolfe*
Fiction: Toni Morrison, *Beloved*
General nonfiction: Richard Rhodes, *The Making of the Atomic Bomb*

History: Robert V. Bruce, *The Launching of American Science 1846–1876*
Poetry: William Meredith, *Partial Accounts: New and Selected Poems*
Rea Award for the Short Story ($25,000): Donald Barthelme

MOTION PICTURES

Academy of Motion Picture Arts and Sciences ("Oscar") Awards
Actor—leading: Michael Douglas, *Wall Street*
Actor—supporting: Sean Connery, *The Untouchables*
Actress—leading: Cher, *Moonstruck*
Actress—supporting: Olympia Dukakis, *Moonstruck*
Cinematography: Vittorio Storaro, *The Last Emperor*
Costume design: James Acheson, *The Last Emperor*
Director: Bernardo Bertolucci, *The Last Emperor*
Film: *The Last Emperor*
Foreign-language film: *Babette's Feast* (Denmark)
Music—original score: Ryuichi Sakamoto, David Byrne, and Cong Su, *The Last Emperor*
Music—song: Franke Previte, John DeNicola, and Donald Markowitz (music), Franke Previte (lyrics): *(I've Had) The Time of My Life* (from *Dirty Dancing*)
Screenplay—original: John Patrick Shanley, *Moonstruck*
Screenplay—adaptation: Mark Peploe and Bernardo Bertolucci, *The Last Emperor*
Irving G. Thalberg Memorial Award: Billy Wilder
American Film Institute's Life Achievement Award: Jack Lemmon
Cannes Film Festival Awards
Golden Palm Award (best film): Bille August, *Pelle Erobreren* (Pelle the Conqueror) (Denmark)
Special Jury Prize: Chris Menges, *A World Apart* (England)
Best actor: Forest Whitaker, *Bird*
Best actress (shared): Barbara Hershey, Jodhi May, Linda Mvusi
Best director: Fernando Solanas, *Le Sud* (The South) (Argentina)

PUBLIC SERVICE

Charles A. Dana Foundation Awards for pioneering achievements in health and higher education ($50,000): Norman T. Adler; Lester Breslow; Alfred Sommer; Rev. Theodore M. Hesburgh; Mathilde Krim
General Foods World Food Prize ($200,000): Robert Flint Chandler, Jr., International Rice Research Institute
Grawemeyer Award in International Relations ($150,000 shared): Richard E. Neustadt, John F. Kennedy School of Government; Ernest R. May, Harvard University
American Institute for Public Service Jefferson Awards
National Awards ($5,000 ea.): C. Everett Koop, Marlee Matlin, Fr. Bruce Ritter, James W. Rouse
Templeton Prize for Progress in Religion ($370,000): Dr. Inamullah Khan, secretary-general of the World Muslim Congress of Karachi, Pakistan
Harry S. Truman Good Neighbor Foundation Award: Howard H. Baker, Jr.

U.S. Presidential Medal of Freedom (awarded by President Ronald Reagan on Oct. 17, 1988): Pearl Bailey, Malcolm Baldrige (posthumously), Irving Brown, Warren E. Burger, Milton Friedman, Jean Faircloth MacArthur, J. Willard Marriott, Sr. (posthumously), David Packard

SCIENCE

Bristol-Myers Award for distinguished achievement in cancer research ($50,000): George W. Santos, Johns Hopkins University

General Motors Cancer Research Foundation Awards ($130,000 ea.): Sam Shapiro, Johns Hopkins University and Philip Strax, University of Miami School of Medicine (shared): Alfred G. Knudson, Institute for Cancer Research, Philadelphia; Yasutomi Nishizuka, Kobe University School of Medicine, Japan

Louisa Gross Horwitz Prize for research in biology or biochemistry ($22,000 shared): Thomas R. Cech, University of Colorado; Phillip A. Sharp, Massachusetts Institute of Technology

Albert Lasker Medical Research Awards
Basic medical research award ($15,000): Vincent P. Dole, Rockefeller University, New York
Clinical medical research award ($15,000 shared): Thomas R. Cech, University of Colorado; Phillip A. Sharp, Massachusetts Institute of Technology

National Medal of Science (presented by President Ronald Reagan on July 15, 1988): William O. Baker, Konrad E. Bloch, D. Allan Bromley, Michael S. Brown, Paul Chu, Stanley N. Cohen, Elias J. Corey, Daniel C. Drucker, Milton Friedman, Joseph L. Goldstein, Ralph E. Gomory, Willis M. Hawkins, Maurice R. Hilleman, George W. Housner, Eric R. Kandel, Joseph B. Keller, Walter Kohn, Norman F. Ramsey, Jack Steinberger, Rosalyn S. Yalow

National Medal of Technology (presented by President Ronald Reagan on July 15, 1988): John L. Atwood, Arnold O. Beckman, Paul M. Cook, Raymond Damadian, Richard H. Dennard, Harold E. Edgerton, Clarence L. Johnson, Edwin H. Land, Paul C. Lauterbur, David Packard

TELEVISION AND RADIO

Academy of Television Arts and Sciences ("Emmy") Awards
Actor—comedy series: Michael J. Fox, *Family Ties* (NBC)
Actor—drama series: Richard Kiley, *A Year in the Life* (NBC)
Actor—miniseries or a special: Jason Robards, *Inherit the Wind* (NBC)
Actress—comedy series: Beatrice Arthur, *The Golden Girls* (NBC)
Actress—drama series: Tyne Daly, *Cagney and Lacey* (CBS)
Actress—miniseries or a special: Jessica Tandy, "Foxfire," *Hallmark Hall of Fame* (CBS)
Animated program: *A Claymation Christmas Celebration* (CBS)
Cinematography—miniseries or a special: Woody Omens, *I Saw What You Did* (CBS)
Comedy series: *The Wonder Years* (ABC)
Directing—comedy series: Gregory Hoblit, pilot episode, *Hooperman* (ABC)
Directing—drama series: Mark Tinker, "Weigh In, Way Out," *St. Elsewhere* (NBC)
Directing—miniseries or a special: Lamont Johnson, *Gore Vidal's Lincoln* (NBC)
Directing—variety or music program: Patricia Birch and Humphrey Burton, "Celebrating Gershwin," *Great Performances* (PBS)
Drama series: *thirtysomething* (ABC)
Drama/comedy special: *Inherit the Wind* (NBC)
Miniseries: *The Murder of Mary Phagan* (NBC)
Supporting actor—comedy series: John Larroquette, *Night Court* (NBC)
Supporting actor—drama series: Larry Drake, *L.A. Law* (NBC)
Supporting actor—miniseries or a special: John Shea, *Baby M* (ABC)
Supporting actress—comedy series: Estelle Getty, *The Golden Girls* (NBC)
Supporting actress—drama series: Patricia Wettig, *thirtysomething* (ABC)

Supporting actress—miniseries or a special: Jane Seymour, *Onassis: The Richest Man in the World* (ABC)
Variety, music, or comedy program: *Irving Berlin's 100th Birthday Celebration* (CBS)

Humanitas Prizes
Long-form category ($25,000): Dennis Nemec, *God Bless the Child* (ABC)
One-hour category ($15,000): Paul Haggis and Marshall Herskovitz, episode of *thirtysomething* (ABC)
One-half-hour category ($10,000): Hugh Wilson, episode of *Frank's Place* (CBS)
Children's animation category ($10,000): Mary Jo Ludin and Lane Raichert, episode of *The Flintstone Kids* (ABC)
Children's live-action category ($10,000): Joanne Lee, *The Kid Who Wouldn't Quit: The Brad Silverman Story* (ABC)
News or documentary category (nonmonetary): Marshall Frady and Helen Whitney, ABC News Closeup about the homeless mentally ill

George Foster Peabody Awards
Radio: ABC News, *Earnest Will: Americans in the Gulf;* WSM Radio, Nashville, *Of Violence and Victims;* KPAL Radio, North Little Rock, AK, full-time children's format; Mutual Broadcasting System, Arlington, VA, *Charities That Give and Take;* National Public Radio, *Weekend Edition* presentation of *Ryan Martin*
Television: NBC Entertainment, *Star Trek: The Next Generation,* "The Big Goodbye"; WCPO-TV, Cincinnati, *Drake Hospital Investigation;* KNBC-TV, Los Angeles, *Some Place Like Home;* PBS, *MacNeil/Lehrer Newshour,* "Japan Series"; WRC-TV, Washington, *Deadly Mistakes;* WCVB-TV, Boston, *Inside Bridgewater;* Cable News Network, live coverage of breaking news; CBS-TV and *Hallmark Hall of Fame,* "Foxfire" and "Pack of Lies"; NBC-TV, *LBJ: The Early Years* (Louis Rudolph Films, Brice Productions, Fries Entertainment); PBS, KQED, San Francisco, *Corridos! Tales of Passion and Revolution;* Home Box Office, *Mandela* (Titus Productions, Polymuse, Inc.); NBC and 20th Century-Fox Television, *L.A. Law;* PBS, WNET, New York, *Nature: A Season in the Sun;* CKVU-TV, Vancouver, British Columbia, *AIDS and You;* WXXI-TV, Rochester, *Safe Haven;* PBS, *Eyes on the Prize: America's Civil Rights Years* (Blackside, Inc., Boston); PBS, WGBH, Boston, and KCET, Los Angeles, *Nova: Spy Machines;* Home Box Office, *America Undercover: Drunk and Deadly* (Niemack Productions, Inc.); The Center for New America Media, Inc., New York, *American Tongues;* PBS, *One Village in China: Small Happiness: Women of a Chinese Village* (Long Bow Group, Inc., New York); PBS, WNET, New York, *Shoah;* WSMV-TV, Nashville, *4 the Family*

THEATER

Susan Smith Blackburn Prize ($5,000): Caryl Churchill, *Serious Money;* runner-up ($1,000): Elizabeth Diggs, *St. Florence*

New York Drama Critics Circle Awards
Best new play ($1,000): *Joe Turner's Come and Gone,* by August Wilson
Best foreign play: *The Road to Mecca,* by Athol Fugard
Best musical: *Into the Woods,* by Stephen Sondheim and James Lapine

Antoinette Perry ("Tony") Awards
Actor—play: Ron Silver, *Speed-the-Plow*
Actor—musical: Michael Crawford, *The Phantom of the Opera*
Actress—play: Joan Allen, *Burn This*
Actress—musical: Joanna Gleason, *Into the Woods*
Choreography: Michael Smuin, *Anything Goes*
Director—play: John Dexter, *M. Butterfly*
Director—musical: Harold Prince, *The Phantom of the Opera*
Featured actor—play: B. D. Wong, *M. Butterfly*
Featured actor—musical: Bill McCutcheon, *Anything Goes*
Featured actress—play: L. Scott Caldwell, *Joe Turner's Come and Gone*
Featured actress—musical: Judy Kaye, *The Phantom of the Opera*
Musical: *The Phantom of the Opera*
Musical—book: James Lapine, *Into the Woods*
Musical—score: Stephen Sondheim, *Into the Woods*
Play: *M. Butterfly* by David Henry Hwang
Reproduction of a play or musical: *Anything Goes*
Pulitzer Prize for Drama: Alfred Uhry, *Driving Miss Daisy*

PUBLISHING

Riding a surge of growth in the final two quarters of 1987, the U.S. publishing industries swept into 1988 with high hopes. That optimism seemed justified as revenues rose for all segments throughout the first three quarters of the year and were projected to continue to rise into 1990. The year was not without its worries, however, as steep increases in postal rates and soaring paper prices created concern across the industries. The "internationalization" of publishing continued with widespread foreign purchases of U.S. publishing companies and with two of the most expensive buyouts in publishing history by foreign-owned multinationals. Publishers invested more in technological development, as well. Desktop publishing spread, and publishers flocked to the largest trade shows ever for publishing technologies. The improved financial condition of the industries was an opportunity to attack some problems of growing urgency. At the top of publishers' lists were illiteracy and copyright. Legal issues surfaced again, too.

Books. The U.S. book publishing industry was brimming with good financial news in 1988. In the first half of the year, sales rose 9.2% to $4.923 billion, and consumer spending on books rose 9.2%. The number of books sold rose 6% to 958 million. The Book Industry Study Group predicted that growth in annual book sale revenues for 1986–90 would be 9.9%, while some investment bankers were projecting 9.4% growth in domestic sales through 1992. First-quarter sales for 1988 increased 8.5%, although publishers reported soaring return rates for paperback books. Book exports rose almost 25% in early 1988, while imports rose only 10%.

A $10 million contract between Simon and Schuster and a single author—Mary Higgins Clark—for four novels and a short-story collection underscored the increased willingness of publishers to pay large sums for promising projects. At least three other projects in 1988 involved multimillion-dollar sums for authors. Houghton Mifflin apparently broke another record when it paid $801,000 to two authors for a telling of *Swan Lake*—the largest sum ever paid for a children's book. The deal highlighted the strength of children's books in 1988. Some 56 new lines of children's books reportedly were started by major publishers.

U.S. publishing companies continued to be snapped up by overseas giants. Hachette S.A., France's largest publisher, bought Grolier (the U.S. encyclopedia publisher) for $450 million in the spring and then acquired the Spanish encyclopedia publisher Salvat. British publishing magnate Robert Maxwell spent $500 million on U.S. acquisitions in the 12 months up to March 1988. Then in the summer he spent $150 million more to buy SRA from IBM and jumped into a bidding war with the investment company of Kohlberg Kravis Roberts for control of Macmillan Publishing. In early November, Macmillan ended its months-long battle to remain independent and accepted Maxwell's offer of $90.25 per share, or $2.62 billion. In February, the British conglomerate Pearson acquired Addison-Wesley for $283 million, making Pearson one of the five largest English-language book publishers. All in all, as of late 1988, foreign owners controlled about 15% of U.S. book publishing sales volume. Some 55% of the companies that had changed hands in the previous four years went to foreign buyers.

But U.S. buyers have been active, too. Simon and Schuster topped a four-year, $1.2 billion acquisitions spree by becoming the first book publishing company in history to exceed $1 billion in annual revenues; the company reported $1.2 billion for 1987. Other companies active in acquisitions included Times-Mirror, McGraw-Hill, and Random House.

New technology continued to be an important issue, as book publishers began reassessing electronic-publishing systems. Some that had made major commitments to such systems backed off a bit, while other plunged ahead as more flexible systems became available.

The industry also was preoccupied with piracy and copyright. The U.S. Congress finally approved legislation allowing the United States to join the Berne Convention, an international copyright agreement expected to strengthen publishers' ability to deal with overseas piracy—especially in Asia. Resistance had stemmed from worries over "moral rights" granted to authors; some publishers feared that they might lead to restrictions on editing and legal difficulties over ownership. Meanwhile, U.S. Register of Copyrights Ralph Oman told publishers to expect 10–15 years of "crisis in copyright." Publishers formed the Association of Copyright Enforcement to pursue corporate copyright violations.

And publishers fretted over two bills introduced in Congress designed to implement the recommendations of the Attorney General's (Edwin Meese's) Commission on Pornography. Publishers said the bills defined obscenity and coercion so broadly that they would have to cease publishing a wide range of books, including some medical texts.

Magazines. While many U.S. magazine publishers opened 1988 worried about persistent problems in the industry—such as flat newsstand sales and a declining share of media advertising dollars—the picture brightened steadily as the year progressed. Revenues in the first half of 1988 for 156 consumer magazines were up 9.4%, while advertising pages were up 4.4%. (Revenue growth in 1987—5.5% —had been the highest in three years.) By year's end, however, advertising pages were expected to grow only 1%, as against 6.4%

growth in print media revenues and a 9.7% increase in overall media spending. Publishers expected a 5%–6% rise in ad rates, and stable or rising circulation figures. Some 20% planned increases in subscription rates, and 75% planned more auxiliary products.

Paper costs and postal rates were the biggest immediate problems in 1988. Paper mills opened the year with the third price hike in six months on Nos. 4 and 5 coated groundwood. In July prices rose another 6%–7% on lightweight coated groundwood. And more price hikes were expected late in the year. Meanwhile, fourth class postal rates rose 18%, third class rates jumped 25%, and international rates shot up 39.5%. Magazine publishers looked into pool mailing and private delivery service as alternatives. At summer's end, publishers announced advertising rate hikes of 8%–10% for 1989, reflecting higher postal rates and paper costs, they said.

Merger fever and international buyouts of magazine companies continued. The deal that sent shock waves through the entire industry was the $3 billion purchase of Triangle Publications (*TV Guide, Seventeen,* and the *Daily Racing Form*) by Rupert Murdoch in August. It was the highest price ever paid for a publishing company, and the purchase made News America Inc. the second-largest U.S. media company behind Time Inc.

The Triangle purchase overshadowed other major buys during the year. Some were by foreign concerns, such as Hachette's acquisition of Diamandis Communications for $712 million. Others were purely domestic transactions, such as the late 1987 sale of Harcourt Brace Jovanovich Publications to one of its executives for $334 million.

Several U.S. magazine publishers joined the fight against illiteracy in 1988. It was estimated that about 25 million Americans are functionally illiterate and that 60 million read at below a ninth-grade level. The number is said to be growing, and publishers worried that it would cut into magazine readership.

Both the magazine and newspaper industries breathed a sigh of relief when the U.S. Supreme Court unanimously struck down a lower court decision awarding $200,000 to the Rev. Jerry Falwell from *Hustler* magazine publisher Larry Flint for "emotional distress" caused by a cartoon. The court ruled that even outrageous "opinion" about public figures cannot be subject to libel action.

Canada in 1988 banned all cigarette advertising, and similar action was proposed in the United States. Publishers said that such a ban would hit magazines hard. The largest advertiser in U.S. magazines in 1987 was Philip Morris; the fourth largest was RJR Nabisco.

The development of regional advertising networks was one of the year's notable trends in the industry. Two networks of regional

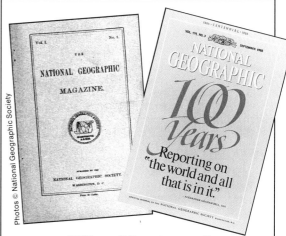

Photos © National Geographic Society

The National Geographic at 100

The National Geographic, the yellow-bordered, glossy-paged magazine published by the National Geographic Society, marked its centennial in 1988 by presenting special issues and articles. During its 100 years, the popular magazine has taken generations of armchair adventurers to the remote corners of the world and helped shape America's view of alien cultures. Today, it is distributed in 167 countries and is one of the most widely read magazines in the world.

On Jan. 13, 1888, at the Cosmos Club in Washington, DC, the 33 charter members of the National Geographic Society—scientists, educators, bankers, and lawyers—held their first meeting and declared as their mission the "increase and diffusion of geographic knowledge." The members soon agreed that the best way of accomplishing their goal was to introduce a journal, and the first issue of *The National Geographic* appeared in October 1888. In the years following, the magazine became the first to include photographs—pictures of Tibet (1905)—and the first American publication to set up its own color photo lab (1920). It also has become renowned for the quality and accuracy of its maps.

In addition to its famous magazine, the society publishes a monthly for children, *National Geographic World;* two quarterlies, *National Geographic Traveler* and *National Geographic Research;* and a variety of books for adults and children. Since its early days the society, which by 1988 was the largest membership institution in the world, with some 10.5 million members, has ventured into new realms. Its output of television programming reached 100 hours in 1988; it is developing a series of educational videodisks; and it even has produced a board game, Global Pursuit—all for the purpose of "increasing and diffusing geographic knowledge."

women's magazines were formed in 1988, one of them offering 2.2 million subscribers in ten markets.

Despite some uncertainty about the future, the number of U.S. magazine start-ups was at a record level. About 450 new consumer titles were introduced in 1987; only about 20% were expected to survive four years. The total number of business and consumer magazines was estimated to have increased 8.5% from 1982 to 1987, reaching 11,593.

Newspapers. The year proved to be financially solid for U.S. newspapers. After two years of slow growth, revenues rose 8.6% in 1987, and the U.S. Commerce Department predicted that 1988 would see gains of 9.9%. Total spending for newspaper advertising was up 8% in 1987 and was expected to rise another 5% in 1988. The Newspaper Advertising Bureau was even more optimistic, projecting an 8% jump in 1988 advertising revenues. At midyear, investment firms were projecting total expenditures for newspapers to grow 10% annually through 1992.

The most vexing problem for newspaper publishers was the decade-long decline in the percentage of the U.S. population subscribing to newspapers. Circulation was expected to rise only 1% in 1988. Studies offered publishers some hope, however, concluding that the slide in penetration may have slowed or even stopped. Other studies indicated that, since 1983, 69% of U.S. and Canadian newspapers have changed their content and 82% have changed their graphics to attract new readers.

The average price of a U.S. newspaper rose 4.1% in 1987, with almost half of all papers costing 35 cents or more in 1988. In January the 20 largest U.S. dailies upped their advertising rates by 8%.

The soaring price of paper, driven by what was expected to be a temporary shortage of newsprint, became a major concern for newspaper publishers. The price of newsprint rose from $535 per ton in 1985 to $680 per ton before year-end 1988. Newsprint accounts for 23%–25% of the cost of the average newspaper. While publishers also were concerned about U.S. postal rates, the new rate structure adopted in March was close to recommendations made by newspaper groups. Direct mail operations were particularly hard hit, which was expected to help newspapers in the long run.

International investment in the U.S. newspaper industry continued, although it was not so frantic as in other publishing segments. Early in the year, Thompson Newspapers bought nine dailies and ten non-dailies, bringing its holdings to 11 dailies with a total circulation of 1.2 million. In late 1987 and early 1988, International Thompson Organization and Hollinger Inc., owned by Canadian Conrad Black, acquired 21 dailies; Hollinger thus owned 45 dailies and 59 nondailies. The U.S.

Commerce Department predicted that foreign companies would make significant investments in U.S. newspapers over the next several years. Meanwhile, they also continued to invest in newspaper support industries. Some 14% of the firms participating in the newspaper industry's major equipment trade show were from outside the United States and Canada.

Newspaper groups (companies that own at least two papers) continued to expand their holdings. Groups owned 82% of U.S. dailies in 1988, accounting for 74% of circulation. Throughout the year, controversy swirled around a proposed joint-operating agreement between two of the ten largest U.S. newspapers, owned by the two largest newspaper groups. The *Detroit Free Press* and *Detroit News* applied for the agreement, which would permit the two publications to share expenses and equipment without antitrust prosecution by the Justice Department. Such agreements are permitted under the Newspaper Preservation Act, though some questioned whether the law was intended to protect such large corporations. The Justice Department approved the deal late in the year, although a court suit held up implementation.

Major newspaper transactions in 1988 included the February sale of the *New York Post* by Rupert Murdoch to real-estate developer Peter Kalikow for $37.6 million (after federal legislation ordered Murdoch to divest either the *Post* or a broadcast station he owned in the same market); and the sale of the *Dallas Times Herald* by William Dean Singleton's Media-News Holdings Inc. to John Buzzetta for a reported $143 million.

U.S. newspapers continued to invest heavily in new equipment and technologies. One study showed that 490 daily newspapers planned $1.6 billion in capital outlays in 1988. The use of facsimile machines increased, a satellite distribution network for newspaper advertising was expanded, and most newspapers employed "systems editors" to handle the complex electronic technologies used in the industry. *The New York Times* announced that it would spend $22 million on a network of 1,400 personal computers. *The Toronto Star* and *The Chicago Tribune* also purchased PC networks. The Knight-Ridder Company bought Dialog Information Services Inc. for $353 million, making it a major player in the computer data base industry and reestablishing its role in electronic information technologies.

Dozens of newspapers joined the battle against illiteracy. The American Newspaper Publishers Association (ANPA) joined with the International Reading Association in September to commemorate National Literacy Day, and ANPA launched a "Press to Read" campaign to combat adult illiteracy.

CHARLES C. SELF
The University of Alabama

Comic Books Are Older

On a summer night in 1933, teenage science-fiction fan Jerry Siegel was lying in bed, trying to come up with a new idea for a newspaper comic strip. Deciding to give the Hercules legend a science-fiction twist, he wrote a script about Superman, sole survivor of the planet Krypton; classmate Joe Shuster drew the illustrations. During the next five years, the adventure was rejected by every newspaper syndicate. Finally, in 1938, Superman found a home in the fledgling medium of comic books, in the first issue of *Action Comics*. The magazine was a hit, and Superman went on to star in other comics, on radio, in the movies, on television, and, ironically, in a newspaper strip. He also spawned the creation of Batman, Wonder Woman, Captain America, and other superheroes.

Superman turned 50 in 1988, and, to mark the event, there were a prime-time TV special, an exhibition of Superman memorabilia at the Smithsonian Institution, and even a cover story in *Time* magazine. Most dramatically, however, the publishers at DC Comics revamped their flagship character to bring him into the 1980s. Superman's powers were toned down considerably to make him more human, and Clark Kent was changed from a self-effacing wallflower into a yuppie workaholic. Even the supporting characters got a face-lift.

Today's Product. The changes in Superman are emblematic of an overall shift toward more realistic themes and characters in comic books. Even the name "comic book" now is frowned upon by writers and artists. No longer limited to the traditional 32-page, pulp-paper, staple-bound format, the most ambitious comics are large paperbacks. These are printed on high-quality paper and referred to as "graphic novels," a term intended to convey their legitimacy as an art form. And while garish colors and often simplistic dialogue still make it difficult for the medium to achieve the respectability of literature or motion pictures, it has a more adult orientation than ever before.

In *The Dark Knight Returns,* a 188-page graphic novel, Batman confronts middle age and the ethics of vigilantism. In *Maus,* cats and mice are used as a metaphor to recount the horrors of Nazi Germany. And in regular monthly magazines, Iron Man has had a debilitating bout with alcohol and Supergirl has died in the line of duty. Anthropomorphic animals are no longer as benign as Mickey Mouse and Bugs Bunny, but are the hip, savage Teenage Mutant Ninja Turtles. Even those perennial teenagers, Archie and his friends, have had to learn about AIDS.

Causes of the Change. Two factors have been responsible for the comic books' success in finding a more adult audience. The people who are creating comic books today grew up in the 1960s, when Marvel Comics writer-editor Stan Lee introduced the first elements of realism into the medium. The cocreator of such characters as Spider-Man and the Hulk, Lee gave his characters acne and costumes that tore during battles. Today's writers and artists have expanded the trend he began. In 1986, Marvel went so far as to introduce the New Universe, a line of comics in which the heroes have relatively modest powers and the fantasy element is kept to a minimum.

At the same time, publishers no longer have to rely solely on newsstands to sell comic books. Two thirds of comic books today are sold in the 3,000 specialty stores throughout the country that sell only comic books. The customers are buffs, and publishers feel free to experiment, knowing that fans will pay up to $2.50 for a high-quality comic book, or $12.95 or more for a graphic novel. A few fanatics also are willing to pay $28,000 for a mint-condition copy of the first issue of *Action Comics*—a magazine which originally sold for a dime.

JEFF ROVIN

PUERTO RICO

Nearly 2 million Puerto Ricans voted on Nov. 8, 1988, representing more than 80% of the island's registered voters. Gov. Rafael Hernández Colón of the Popular Democratic Party (PDP) was reelected to a second term. In the capital of San Juan, Popular Democratic Party candidate Héctor Luís Acevedo was elected mayor, the first time in 20 years his party had won in the city. Acevedo was declared the winner after a vote recount. He won by a mere 30 votes. José Granados Navedo of the pro-statehood New Progressive Party challenged the recount process in court.

The 1988 elections established some surprises and new voting trends. For the first time in Puerto Rico's electoral history, an independent candidate was selected. Santos ''El Negro'' Ortiz, mayor of the fishing and resort town of Cabo Rojo, was reelected as an independent. Earlier he had lost his renomination bid in the PDP primary. Other big election winners were Sen. Victoria ''Melo'' Muñoz of the PDP and Rep. David Noriega of the Puerto Rican Independence Party. In winning reelection to the legislature, both candidates appealed to a growing mass of voters crossing party lines and became known as mavericks.

The U.S. Democratic and Republican parties adopted platform planks on Puerto Rico's status. The Democratic Party called for empowering Puerto Rico with more political and economic autonomy. The GOP urged the support of statehood if the majority of Puerto Rican voters chose that path in a status referendum.

Economy. The Puerto Rican economy improved with a healthy 5% growth rate in 1988. Economists attributed the upswing to a weaker U.S. dollar, an improved U.S. economy, and the recovery of the construction and tourism industries. A pleasant side effect was a drop in unemployment to 14.6% by the end of the year.

Crime. The 1986 Dupont Plaza Hotel fire continued to make headlines in 1988, as charges were filed in February against three new suspects—all members of the Teamsters Union. Three other union members had been convicted of murder and arson in the fire that killed 97 persons.

Ronald Calder, a former air-traffic controller, returned to Puerto Rico from his native Iowa in January to stand trial for the murder of a local woman who was run over fatally by a car in 1981. Two Iowa governors had refused to extradite Calder, but the U.S. Supreme Court, at Puerto Rico's petition, finally overturned a 100-year-old ruling that forbade federal courts from forcing governors to extradite fugitives. Calder's charges were reduced from first-degree murder to manslaughter, and he was set free on probation.

Filiberto Ojeda Ríos, a suspected leader of an underground pro-independence group known as ''Los Macheteros,'' was brought to Puerto Rico to face charges in the shooting of an FBI agent in 1985. He was also a defendant in the $7 million Wells Fargo robbery that occurred in Hartford, CT, in 1983. Ojeda's return, shortly after being released from a U.S. prison after serving 32 months without bail, triggered some reaction from pro-independence supporters. Ojeda's bail terms were revoked, and he was sent to a federal prison in New York to await trial on the second charge.

DEBORAH RAMIREZ, *"The San Juan Star"*

QUEBEC

Quebec's political arena in 1988 was dominated by Parti Quebeçois' move to put aside its cloak of irresolution and become once again a straight-out separatist party. Quebec gave the green light for another massive hydro project although environmentalists were opposed to it.

Parti Quebeçois for Separation. Jacques Parizeau put the Parti Quebeçois (PQ) back on a clear, unambiguous Quebec-sovereignty course March 19 when he officially took over the party leadership. In a speech to about 700 party faithful in Montreal, he called on the PQ to return to its roots, saying it ''must clearly show itself to be an independence party.'' Parizeau had quit the PQ in 1985 after it began wavering on the sovereignty issue and returned to politics only after the resignation of party leader Pierre Marc Johnson in 1987. Parizeau was unopposed in his bid for the position.

The PQ lost two more seats in the National Assembly in by-elections June 20. The losses —in Roberval and Anjou—increased to 30 the number of consecutive provincial by-elections the PQ had lost since 1976.

Language Rights. On December 15 the Canadian Supreme Court struck down a provision in a Quebec law banning the posting of signs in any language but French. As French-speaking Quebecers expressed anger over the ruling, Prime Minister Mulroney appealed for ''calm reason'' on the issue of language rights.

Hydroelectric Project. Premier Robert Bourassa on March 8 announced a go-ahead for Phase 2 of the James Bay hydroelectric project —a C$7.5 billion (U.S.$6 billion), 2,500-megawatt addition to the province's power capacity. The decision to launch Phase 2 was triggered

---

PUERTO RICO • Information Highlights

Area: 3,515 sq mi (9 104 km²).
Population (mid-1988 est.): 3,400,000.
Chief Cities (1980 census): San Juan, the capital, 434,849; Bayamon, 196,206; Ponce, 189,046.
Government (1988): *Chief Officer*—governor, Rafael Hernández Colón (Popular Democratic Party). *Legislature*—Senate, 27 members; House of Representatives, 51 members.

Jacques Parizeau (center), a former provincial finance minister, was inaugurated as leader of the Parti Quebeçois on March 19. A hard-line separatist, Parizeau called for the party to adopt its traditional Quebec-sovereignty line.

Canapress Photo

by a series of agreements reached in 1987 to sell $40 billion worth of electricity to the New England states and New York in the next two decades. Although the project will create 40,000 jobs over seven years, environmentalists sought to block it because the project will destroy caribou ranges and hunting grounds of Indian and Eskimo populations. The protest had little effect.

Quebec clearly won its 12-year battle with Newfoundland over Newfoundland's demand for a greater share of the benefits from the giant Churchill Falls hydro project in Labrador. In a unanimous judgment, the Supreme Court of Canada upheld a 65-year contract signed by the two provinces in 1969. The contract allows Quebec to purchase power at rock-bottom prices—set before the mid-1970s energy crunch—and then resell it to the United States at ten times or more the price Quebec pays.

Pollution Scare. On September 10 about 3,300 residents of St. Basile-Le Grand and two neighboring communities just east of Montreal returned to their homes—two and one half weeks after a fire and explosion in a chemical warehouse forced their evacuation. The warehouse contained thousands of gallons of PCBs —polychlorinated biphenyls—a highly toxic chemical compound. It was feared that fallout from a moving cloud of smoke generated by the August 23 blaze might have contaminated the area. An international team of experts verified that there was no danger to humans, but crops in the area had to be destroyed.

Baby Bonuses. Alarmed by the province's rapidly declining birth rate, the Quebec government on May 12 inaugurated a system of cash bonuses to encourage larger families. In his budget presentation Finance Minister Gerard Lévesque announced that the province would pay $500 each for the first two children in a family, starting May 1, 1989. For each subsequent child, the payment would be $3,000, payable in eight quarterly installments.

Member of Parliament Exonerated. Conservative MP André Bissonnette, a former federal cabinet minister, was acquitted February 23 at St-Jean on four charges involving fraud, breach of trust, and conspiracy. The charges stemmed from a land deal in St-Jean in 1986. Bissonnette's political associate Normand Ouellette was involved in a series of transactions over a 100-acre (40-ha) plot of land that more than tripled in value—from $800,000 to $2.98 million —in just 11 days. Oerlikon Aerospace Inc. of Switzerland bought the land, and a few months later the company won a $600 million federal contract for a low-level air-defense system.

Ouellette, using money from a blind trust he managed for Bissonnette, previously had purchased an option on the land and made a $920,000 profit from the subsequent sale to the Swiss firm. Both men were charged with using "privileged information" to turn a profit, but Bissonnette claimed to have had no knowledge of Ouellette's investments or profits. Although Bissonnette was acquitted, Ouellette was fined $100,000 and was ordered to pay back to the Swiss firm the profit he had made on the deal. Bissonnette had been damaged politically, however; he was not nominated as a Tory candidate from St-Jean in the 1988 elections.

JOHN BEST, *"Canada World News"*

QUEBEC · Information Highlights

Area: 594,857 sq mi (1 540 680 km²).
Population (1986 census): 6,540,276.
Chief Cities (1986 census): Quebec, the capital, 164,580; Montreal, 1,015,420; Laval, 284,164.
Government (1988): *Chief Officers*—lt. gov., Gilles Lamontagne; premier, Robert Bourassa (Liberal). *Legislature*—National Assembly, 122 members.
Provincial Finances (1988–89 fiscal year budget): *Revenues,* $29,300,000,000; *expenditures,* $30,900,000,000.
Personal Income (average weekly earnings, Aug. 1988): $452.64.
Labor Force (October 1988, seasonally adjusted): *Employed* workers, 15 years of age and over, 3,078,000; *Unemployed,* 9.9%.
Education (1988–89): *Enrollment*—elementary and secondary schools, 1,134,400 pupils; postsecondary—universities, 118,400; community colleges, 159,200.
(All monetary figures are in Canadian dollars.)

RECORDINGS

The U.S. recording industry in 1988 enjoyed boom times while adjusting to the flux caused by changes in player hardware. The biggest industry story of the year was the $2 billion sale of CBS Records to Sony.

Digital Audio Tape. The sale of CBS' hugely profitable record division to Japan's leading manufacturer of home entertainment products continued a trend: the increasing expansion of hardware manufacturers into the software business. In addition, the move seemed to push the U.S. record industry one step closer to embracing the domestic sale of digital audio tape (DAT) recorders. Nevertheless, the industry continued to contend that the machine's high-tech ability to produce copies that sound as good as compact discs (CDs) will encourage the theft of copyrighted material. Foes of DAT lost a major battle when the U.S. Bureau of Standards concluded that a plan to equip the machines with spoiler chips designed to prevent the duplication of CDs would unduly impede sound reproduction.

Amid the furor, DAT machines quietly entered the U.S. market during 1988, with prices ranging from $1,500 to $2,000. Similarly, prerecorded digital audio tapes—priced in the $20 range—began to reach record stores. (Domestic production of DAT tapes mirrored the early days of CD, with independent operators handling production in lieu of the major labels.) Because of the high prices, the new technology had a negligible impact on the consumer market. As with previous consumer electronics rollouts, DATs would begin to have a major impact when prices drop.

Compact Discs. None of the market developments with regard to DAT impeded the spectacular growth of the compact disc, a trend that pushed the yearly gross income of the U.S. recording industry over the $5.5 billion mark in 1987. With the LP's (long-playing record album's) share of the market continuing to drop, CDs and cassettes accounted for two thirds of the industry's unit shipments and 80% of its dollar value. From 1986 to 1987, the dollar volume of production and shipments for all formats rose 20%, from $4.65 billion to $5.57 billion. CD consumption was up 93%, from 53 million units to more than 102 million units ($1.6 billion). Helping this growth was a gradual drop in CD prices, with many labels establishing three-tiered pricing: separate price scales for superstar releases, other new recordings, and budget-line releases from the company's catalogue. Sales of prerecorded cassettes were up 19%, to 410 million units ($2.9 billion).

American consumers have shown little resistance to the changeover from turntables to compact disc players: 4 million CD units were expected to be sold in 1988, up from 3.3 million in 1987. As of mid-1988, it was estimated that

8% of all U.S. households owned a CD player. The acceptance of CD might mitigate against demand for DAT, especially since a number of electronics firms are working on recordable CD machines that would serve the same function as a tape machine. The portability of tape machines, however, as well as their use in automobiles, gives DAT a significant advantage.

Other Formats. The introduction of other digital formats has been slower. PolyGram began to market CDV (CD Video) discs which, when played on a laser disc player designed to deliver both audio and visual signals, put pictures to music. Consumer acceptance, however, thus far has been slow. Some record labels also have begun to market 3-inch (7.6-cm) CDs, which can accommodate up to 20 minutes of music and are regarded generally as the compact disc's answer to the 45 rpm single.

Consolidation. CBS Records was not the only recording company sold in 1988. Motown Records, long the dominant black-held company in the industry, was sold to a consortium that included MCA Records, which had been distributing Motown's product in recent years. Similar consolidation took place at the retail end of the business, with chains like Musicland and Trans World Music continuing to buy smaller chains and open new outlets.

The trend toward retail consolidation does not spell the end of mom-and-pop record stores, but it does suggest that they will have to specialize. The way CD sales have been going, that specialization might well be in the vinyl LP market.

JOHN MILWARD
Free-lance Writer and Critic

REFUGEES AND IMMIGRATION

By May 1988, some 1.7 million illegal U.S. immigrants had applied for one-time amnesty under the 1986 Immigration Reform and Control Act by proving that they had resided in the United States since Jan. 1, 1982. In addition, more than 400,000 immigrants applied for amnesty under a separate program for seasonal agricultural workers. At the same time, the U.S. Immigration and Naturalization Service (INS) reported a significant decline in the number of illegal aliens apprehended at the border with Mexico. There also was evidence that employer sanctions had an impact on discouraging employers from hiring undocumented workers.

Critics of the legalization program contended, however, that it fell far short of its stated goal of bringing all eligible aliens out of their underground existence. Appeals to extend the program by six months to one year in order to give people more time to compile documentation, to save money for the application fees, and to educate people about the program were

defeated in Congress. The INS did, however, take action to deal with the stringent residence requirements which threatened to divide families of applicants who arrived at different times. It proposed to set aside 200,000 visas for illegal immigrants who did not quality for the amnesty but whose relatives did. The INS also introduced plans for the second phase of the legalization program, in which persons already granted temporary residency status could apply for permanent residency after satisfying an English proficiency and civics requirement.

Legislation was introduced in Congress in 1988 that would revamp the immigration preference system. While maintaining modified provisions for immigrants with family connections in the United States, the bill would expand the opportunities for prospective immigrants with education and skills deemed to be in short supply. The bill also would expand legal immigration to the United States by 100,000, to a new ceiling of 590,000 annually.

U.S. Refugee and Asylum Policy. Among the many illegal immigrants who decided to stay in the United States despite the loss of employment prospects are hundreds of undocumented Central Americans who arrived after Jan. 1, 1982. Many of them face worsening poverty and malnutrition. Legislation that temporarily would halt their deportation and grant them permission to work passed the House but was not acted upon by the Senate during 1988.

The 1980 Refugee Act mandates equal treatment for all refugees, based on humanitarian concern and regardless of ideology or national origin. As in previous years, however, foreign policy and ideological factors in 1988 continued to influence the adjudication of asylum claims by Central Americans. During the first nine months of 1988, 78% of Nicaraguans were granted asylum, only 2% of Salvadorans and less than 1% of Guatemalans were approved. Hundreds of Salvadorans and Guatemalans were returned home every month. In addition, the U.S. Coast Guard continued to interdict boatloads of Haitians at sea. Between 1981 when the interdiction program was instituted and 1988, more than 15,000 Haitians have been returned home forcefully, and only two Haitians have been admitted to the United States to pursue asylum claims. Large numbers of asylum seekers have been detained in isolated INS detention centers, local jails, and private-contract facilities across the country. The conditions in these centers have deteriorated. Many are overcrowded, unsafe, and provide insufficient medical care and recreational opportunities. Thousands of children were among those being held during 1988, and there were disquieting reports about their treatment. Hundreds of churches and other organizations within the Sanctuary Movement continued to provide legal, material, and moral support to Central Americans and risked criminal convictions for transporting and harboring illegal aliens. During the year, the Justice Department reviewed individually the cases of the more than 3,800 Cubans detained in prisons in Louisiana and Atlanta, GA, and denied parole to nearly one third of them.

The U.S. admissions quota for refugees worldwide in 1988 was 68,500, but that total was increased by 15,000 during the year to allow for the entry of more Soviet Armenians, Soviet Jews, and Eastern Europeans allowed to leave their home countries because of freer emigration policies. A number of developments in Southeast Asia and the Caribbean also put pressure on the United States to grant more resettlement places for refugees. The Amerasian Homecoming Act, which took effect March 21, 1988, provided for the admission of 30,000 Amerasians during the next two years. Vietnam and Laos also agreed to allow the U.S. resettlement of former political prisoners and reeducation camp detainees. In addition, a November 1987 agreement between Washington and Havana provided for the admission into the United States of 20,000 Cuban immigrants annually, 3,500 political prisoners, and some 3,000 immediate relatives of U.S. citizens. U.S. contributions to international refugeee organizations decreased significantly during the year, although in absolute terms the United States remained the largest contributor.

International Refugee Protection. Political developments regarding Afghanistan, Namibia, Cambodia, and Central America raised hopes for eventually resolving the plight of nearly half the world's current refugee population. In other respects, however, 1988 was a dismal time for the protection of refugees. Thailand forcibly turned back to sea Vietnamese boat people. Horrific accounts of pirate attacks, murders, and rapings of refugees multiplied. With rising numbers of boat people claiming asylum, Hong Kong began to treat all new arrivals as illegal immigrants subject to deportation to Vietnam. Malaysia announced that in 1989 it would close its refugee camp and accept fewer refugees. Continued violence in Sri Lanka made the return of Tamil refugees extremely difficult. Masses of Iraqi Kurds fled chemical and poison gas attacks and sought refuge in nearby Turkey and Iran. Atrocities against civilians in Mozambique at the hands of South Africa-backed Renamo forces continued to produce huge numbers of refugees. The renewal of ethnic violence in Burundi drove thousands of people into Rwanda. In the Sudan, continuing civil conflict, famine, and massive flooding put millions of people at risk. Finally, in Europe and North America, there were dramatic increases in the deportation of persons back to situations in which their security and even their lives had been threatened.

GIL LOESCHER, *University of Notre Dame*

RELIGION

Overview

A new motion picture touched off a major religious controversy in 1988. *The Last Temptation of Christ*, based on a novel of the same name by the late Nikos Kazantzakis, was denounced by conservative Christians who objected to its portrayal of Jesus making love to Mary Magdalene, being unsure of his mission, and trusting Judas. Some of the protest had a touch of anti-Semitism, as demonstrations were targeted at Jewish executives of Universal Studios and its parent company, MCA, even though the film's director (Martin Scorsese) is a Catholic and its screenwriter (Paul Schrader) a Protestant.

Interfaith relations also were strained by Pope John Paul II's June visit to the site of a World War II concentration camp in Mauthausen, Austria, during which he mentioned three Catholic victims of the Nazis but made no reference to Jewish victims. And the presentation of the Templeton Prize for Progress in Religion was postponed from its scheduled May date until September 28 because of criticisms made against the winner. Jewish leaders charged that the 1988 honoree, Inamullah Khan, secretary-general of the World Muslim Congress, had taken consistently anti-Jewish positions.

Church and State. In a major church-state ruling, the U.S. Supreme Court in June upheld a federal law that gives tax dollars to churches that counsel teenagers against pregnancy and abortion. In its 5–4 decision, the high court said the law was constitutional as long as no federal funds are used to advance a religious message. In April, the Supreme Court approved U.S. Forest Service plans to build a road near ground in California that is sacred to three Native American tribes. In that 5–3 ruling, the court said that "government simply could not operate if it were required to satisfy every citizen's religious needs and desires."

Two significant efforts to reach agreement on church-state matters occurred during 1988. Fourteen organizations of educators and clergy joined together in issuing a booklet to inform parents and teachers about constitutionally accepted ways to teach "about" religion in public schools. And some 75 leaders of government, business, religion, education, and philanthropy signed the Williamsburg Charter, a document reaffirming and expanding on the religious liberty provisions of the First Amendment.

The official celebration of the millennium of Christianity in the Soviet Union drew participants from around the world and demonstrated the far-reaching nature of General Secretary Mikhail Gorbachev's *glasnost* (openness) policy. (*See* special report, page 544.) In South Africa, churches continued to defy the law in protesting the government's apartheid policies.

The headquarters of the South African Council of Churches, a key group in the protests, were damaged by an explosion in August.

Intra-Religious Disputes. In the first major schism in the Roman Catholic Church in more than a century, dissident French Archbishop Marcel Lefebvre was excommunicated in June for defying a papal admonition against consecrating four bishops for his traditionalist movement in Econe, Switzerland. However, the Vatican did accept several dozen Lefebvre-ordained priests back into the fold without requiring them to renounce the archbishop's ultra-conservative positions.

Moves to reach compromises on such issues as ordination of homosexuals, abortion, and women bishops occupied Protestant bodies during 1988. Most notably, the Lambeth Conference of Anglican bishops endorsed the right of each of the 28 national Anglican bodies to decide whether to consecrate women bishops. In September the Rev. Barbara C. Harris, a black priest from Philadelphia, was elected suffragan bishop of Massachusetts, thereby becoming the first woman bishop in the Anglican Communion.

American Jews engaged in vociferous public debate over Israeli policy on the West Bank in putting down the continuing Palestinian uprising. The Conservative branch of Judaism adopted a written set of principles for the first time in its 143-year history and rejected a move to accept women cantors even though it has women in the rabbinate.

Barbara C. Harris, 58, was elected by the Episcopal Diocese of Massachusetts in September as the first woman suffragan (assistant) bishop in the Anglican Communion.

AP/Wide World

AP/Wide World

On April 8, six weeks after confessing to an unspecified "sin" and hours after being defrocked, the Rev. Jimmy Swaggart resigned from the Assemblies of God.

TV Evangelism. The fallout from the televangelism scandals that rocked the world of religion in 1987 continued in 1988. Jimmy Swaggart, who had been a vociferous critic of Jim Bakker during the PTL (Praise the Lord) affair a year earlier, was himself ousted from the clergy ranks of the Assemblies of God. In February, the Baton Rouge (LA)-based preacher confessed to an unspecified sin after he reportedly paid a prostitute to perform lewd acts while he watched. After a month-long jurisdictional dispute between national and Louisiana district leaders of the Assemblies over how severely Swaggart should be disciplined, he announced his resignation from the denomination in April, just hours after the word came that he was being defrocked. Swaggart later announced that God told him to return to the pulpit, and he conducted an evangelistic crusade in Indianapolis in July.

In a surprise appearance at a charismatic gathering in Charlotte, NC, during August, Jim Bakker publicly confessed that he had "sinned against the body of Christ." He also announced a bid of $172 million to buy back PTL but failed to meet a court deadline for raising the funds. In mid-December a federal bankruptcy judge ordered the assets of PTL sold to a Canadian real-estate developer for $65 million. Earlier in the month Bakker and three former associates had been indicted. Bakker was charged with defrauding contributors and diverting ministry funds for personal use.

The Rev. Jerry Falwell, who temporarily had headed PTL after Bakker's downfall, created a new television network as a profit-making venture. The company, known as FamilyNetwork Broadcasting, Inc., was headed by Falwell's associate Jerry Nims.

DARRELL J. TURNER, *Religious New Service*

Far Eastern

During an anti-Chinese riot in Lhasa, Tibet, in March 1988, at least 18 Buddhist monks were killed when they jumped or were thrown from the Jokhang Temple, Tibet's most sacred Buddhist shrine. Yuluo Dawaciren, a top Tibetan monk, was arrested on charges of instigating an anti-Chinese demonstration in Tibet in October 1987. The Dalai Lama, the Tibetan spiritual leader still living in exile in northern India, expressed regret at the violence while refusing an offer from China to return to Tibet if he would abandon his campaign for independence. The Dalai Lama advocated a "middle way" between Chinese rule and a war for independence, but he declared that "ultimately, the Chinese have to realize that Tibet is a separate country." In an interview for *Life* magazine, he said that it was not important if he returned to Tibet. "I am only concerned with the future of the Tibetan people," he said. "As a Buddhist monk, I can manage anywhere, very easily, very happily."

The largest Buddhist temple in the Western Hemisphere was dedicated in Hacienda Heights, CA, in July by the Venerable Master Hsing Yun, head of the Taiwan-based Fo Kuang Shen sect of Mahayana Buddhism. Set amid the palm trees and oil derricks of southern California, the 14-acre (5.7-ha) complex cost $15 million and includes a museum, a library, private apartments, and a temple with nearly 11,000 statues of Buddha. Fo Kuang Shen was established in 1967 by Hsing Yun, one of numerous religious leaders who fled to Taiwan when the Communist Revolution swept mainland China and gained control in 1949.

Catharine Burroughs, a Brooklyn-born mother of three, was enthroned as a reincarnate lama in September at a ceremony at the Buddhist World Prayer Center in Poolesville, MD, thus becoming the first Western woman to receive the designation. Tenzin Tethong, a special U.S. representative of the Dalai Lama, said he knew of only three or four reincarnate lamas—known as tulkus—in the Western Hemisphere. He said that it was unprecedented for a woman to be so designated.

A traditional Hindu celebration marking the death of a family member, known as the Gaj Yatra—or procession of the cows—was held in Katmandu, Nepal, after more than 700 people died in an August 21 earthquake. According to legend, the celebration originated about three centuries ago when the son of King Jaya Sthiti Malla died in a smallpox epidemic. When the king failed to console his grief-stricken wife, he asked his subjects to parade through the streets praying for the souls of the dead and then perform stunts outside the palace. In the 1988 celebration, boys in ornate cow costumes led a parade of thousands through the streets.

DARRELL J. TURNER

Islam

The interwoven nature of religion and politics in Islam manifested itself clearly in 1988. Some Muslim countries took steps to bring their governments more into line with Islamic law. In several other countries, Muslims used their religious identification to instill cohesiveness and bolster demands for equitable treatment, occasionally igniting civil disorders in the process. The government of Saudi Arabia, responsible for coordinating and overseeing the annual pilgrimage *(hajj)* to Mecca, Islam's holiest site, moved to prevent a recurrence of the politically inspired unrest that erupted in 1987.

In June the parliament of Bangladesh, 87% of whose 110 million citizens are Muslims, declared Islam to be the state religion. Although the government assured religious minorities that they could practice their faiths in "peace and harmony," thousands of non-Muslims demonstrated in protest against the new law. Elsewhere on the Indian subcontinent, Pakistan's President Mohammed Zia ul-Haq (who was killed in a midair plane explosion August 17) proclaimed the *shariah,* or Islamic law, to be the supreme law of the land. President Zia initiated this action in June, shortly after dismissing the cabinet and suspending the National Assembly on the grounds that neither had moved swiftly enough to institute Islamic policies.

Muslims in various regions of the Soviet Union also were involved in political controversies during 1988. In February and March, the Muslim population of Nagorno-Karabakh, an autonomous region surrounded by the predominantly Muslim Azerbaijan Soviet Socialist Republic, attempted to thwart efforts by the Armenian Christian majority to join the region with neighboring Armenia. The resulting civil disorder threatened to undermine reform programs advocated by the central government, leading Moscow to forceful intervention. (*See* special report, page 543.) In Central Asia, where many of the Soviet Union's 45 million Muslims (16% of the total population) reside, Muslim Tatars staged protests in the Uzbekistan capital of Tashkent during February. They did not, however, achieve their objective, which was to persuade the central government to allow them to return to their homelands in Crimea, from which they had been expelled during World War II.

At the annual meeting of the Islamic Conference Organization, held in Amman, Jordan, during March, representatives of the world's Muslim countries endorsed a proposal by Saudi Arabia to decrease by two thirds (from 150,000 to 50,000) the number of Iranian Muslims permitted to make the pilgrimage in 1988. Iran vehemently denounced the move, which was intended to minimize the likelihood of political demonstrations during the *hajj*. The following month, Iran and Saudi Arabia severed diplomatic relations, but the pilgrimage, which took place in late July, was free of any serious political incidents.

Although the Palestinian uprising against Israeli occupation of the West Bank and the Gaza Strip was primarily a political act, strong Islamic currents ran through the resistance. The entry, in January, of Israeli troops onto the grounds of the Mosque of Umar in Jerusalem, one of the most sacred shrines in the Islamic world, where they clashed with and arrested Palestinian demonstrators, embittered the Islamic world. Many of the uprising's local leaders, especially in the Gaza Strip, were affiliated with the Muslim Brotherhood or other Islamic organizations, some of which the Israeli authorities earlier had encouraged in the hope that the social aims of such groups would distract the populace from political issues. During the uprising, however, Muslim leaders placed the struggle against Israel in a religious as well as a political context.

In March, the Templeton Prize for Progress in Religion was awarded to Inamullah Khan, the 73-year-old secretary-general of the World Muslim Congress. Khan, of Burmese origin, has lived and worked in Pakistan since its creation following the partition of India. The award cited Khan's work in espousing Islamic unity and helping bring together world religious leaders. The Anti-Defamation League of the B'nai B'rith and the American Jewish Congress both criticized the decision, maintaining that Khan had taken anti-Semitic stands regarding Israel. Khan insisted that his objections to the state of Israel focused on political Zionism and not on the Jewish faith, but pressure from the two organizations postponed the awarding of the prize money until September 28.

KENNETH J. PERKINS
University of South Carolina

Judaism

The major issues facing world Jewry in 1988 were Israel's handling of Palestinian violence in Judea, Samaria, and the Gaza Strip—one consequence of which was an unexpected surge by the religious right in November Israeli elections (*see* ISRAEL and special report, pages 293–296), as well as a worldwide increase in anti-Semitism and Soviet ambivalence toward Jews. The year also was marked by events recalling the Holocaust; a statement of principles by the Conservative movement; and new attention to the issue of intermarriage.

World Issues. About 1,000 acts of anti-Jewish vandalism were reported in the United States in 1987—a 12% increase over the previous year—with the upsurge continuing in 1988; up to 1,250 such incidents were expected by year's end. Sixty U.S. congressmen ap-

In February, Britain's Chief Rabbi Immanuel Jakobovits (center) became the nation's first rabbi to be ennobled and take a seat in the House of Lords. He is flanked by Lord Young (left) of the governing Conservative Party and Lord Mischon (right) of the opposition Labour Party.

pealed to the Justice Department to take action against the "harassments, threats, and assaults against Jews and Jewish property." Perhaps the most serious incident of 1988 was the burning of five Torah scrolls at a synagogue in Brooklyn, NY, in September.

In Japan, a recent spate of anti-Semitic books caused concern in the Jewish community. The third overtly anti-Semitic novel by a popular Japanese author became an instant best-seller after its release in May. In Italy, the Jewish community was alarmed by an upsurge of anti-Semitic violence. Chief Rabbi Elio Toaff of Rome called it the worst wave of anti-Semitism there since the Fascist persecutions of a half-century earlier. Pope John Paul II caused deep resentment among world Jewish leaders by meeting with Austria's President Kurt Waldheim, an accused Nazi war criminal, and for failing to mention Jewish victims at the Nazi concentration camp in Mauthausen, Austria, the site of which he visited in June.

Early in the year, several longtime Soviet-Jewish "refuseniks"—Iosif Begun, Aleksandr Lerner, and Aleksandr Ioffe—left the USSR for Israel. And in a move to enhance Jewish worship, Soviet authorities granted exit visas to two Jews to train as a rabbi and a cantor at New York's Yeshiva University. Meanwhile, however, the regime continued to disseminate anti-Semitic literature, including the infamous *Protocols of the Elders of Zion.*

Britain's Chief Rabbi Immanuel Jakobovits —who, as the new Baron of Regent's Park, became the first rabbi to sit in the House of Lords —welcomed a resolution on interfaith relations at the Lambeth Conference of Anglican Bishops in August. The resolution included recognition of the centrality of Israel in contemporary Jewish life; rejection of all forms of anti-Semitism; and an acknowledgment that Christian teachings had helped engender traditional anti-Semitism, "culminating in the Holocaust."

Holocaust Remembrances. In an October ceremony, U.S. President Ronald Reagan un-

veiled the cornerstone of a new museum in Washington, DC, that will be dedicated to studying and remembering the Holocaust. Other events recalling that event occurred throughout the world. In April, the Jerusalem trial of John Demjanjuk—known as "Ivan the Terrible" and accused of operating Nazi gas chambers in which nearly one million Jews died during World War II—ended with a guilty verdict and death sentence. The same month, the Yad Vashem Award was presented in Amsterdam to 40 Dutch families who saved Jewish lives during the Nazi occupation. Also in April, Poland commemorated the 45th anniversary of the Warsaw Ghetto uprising. Participating in the commemoration were Polish government officials, Jewish representatives from a number of countries, and a high-level Israeli delegation. And on November 9, special ceremonies marking the 50th anniversary of Kristallnacht ("Crystal Night")—the first major, orchestrated assault on Jews and Jewish property in Nazi Germany—were held throughout Europe, the United States, and other countries.

Religious Issues. For the first time in its 143-year history, the Conservative Jewish movement in May 1988 released a formal statement of principles. The 53-page document was the result of three years of work by a committee of 35 rabbis, scholars, and laymen. The statement included a rejection of religious fundamentalism (in any faith) and called for a moderate course that preserves tradition "without resigning from the 20th century."

The perennial issue of intermarriage gained new poignancy in the United States with the presidential nomination of Gov. Michael Dukakis (D-MA), a Greek Orthodox whose wife, Kitty, is Jewish. While the prospect of a Jewish First Lady stirred pride among some Jews, others viewed it with dismay. With intermarriage by U.S. Jews estimated at 30%, many fear it as the main factor of erosion in the Jewish community.

LIVIA E. BITTON-JACKSON
Herbert H. Lehman College, CUNY

Orthodox Eastern

The Orthodox Church in the USSR celebrated its 1,000th anniversary in 1988. For the
first time in Soviet history, church services
were televised. Several church properties, including monastic centers, were returned to
church control, and all known religious prisoners, with the exception of Deacon Vladimir
Rusak, were released. During the All-Russian
Church Council held at the Danilov Monastery
in Moscow in July, various ecclesiastical regulations were revised, giving more authority to
the local clergy, and nine persons were canonized. (*See also* special report, page 544.)

The Ecumenical Patriarch of Constantinople, Dimitrios I, visited Finland, Czechoslovakia, and Poland in 1988. He refused, however, to preside over the millennial celebration
of the Russian Church because of disputes with
the Moscow patriarchate over the position of
the Church of Georgia in Orthodoxy's ecclesiastical order and the manner in which several
self-governing Orthodox churches, including
the Orthodox Church in America, would participate in the celebrations. The Moscow patriarchate granted the Orthodox Church in
America autocephalous status in 1970 and this
continues to be questioned by churches under
Constantinople's influence. Patriarch Ignatius
IV of Antioch presided at the ceremonies.

The Orthodox Church in Romania was the
target of increased antireligious activities by
the government. Church leaders, however,
continued to praise the regime publicly. The
Orthodox Church in Czechoslovakia canonized
Bishop Gorazd, who was killed by the Nazis in
1942, and Silvan, who was a monk at the Russian monastery of St. Panteleimon on Mount
Athos, was canonized by the ecumenical patriarch. The worldwide veneration of Silvan, who
died in 1938, reveals a spiritual unity among
Orthodox Christians whose churches so often
find themselves in conflict.

North America. Eastern Orthodox Christians in the United States were divided in their
response to the presidential nomination of
Massachusetts Gov. Michael Dukakis, a
Greek-American and member of the Greek Orthodox Church. Archbishop Iakovos of the
Greek Orthodox Church, which honored Dukakis at its Clergy-Laity Congress in Boston in
July, insisted the governor belonged within the
church's fold. Other churchmen criticized him
for marrying outside the church, for not being
a more active church member, and for his pro-
choice position on abortion.

The Antiochian Orthodox Archdiocese,
headed by Metropolitan Philip Saliba, continued to integrate the former Evangelical Orthodox Church into its membership. St. Vladimir's
Seminary in Crestwood, NY, celebrated its
50th anniversary.

THOMAS HOPKO, *St. Vladimir's Seminary*

Protestantism

Moves to reach compromises over such divisive issues as the ordination of homosexuals,
abortion, and women bishops occupied several
Protestant denominations in 1988.

A potential split within the worldwide Anglican Communion was averted during the 1988
Lambeth Conference, held in Canterbury, England, July 16–August 7. A measure was
adopted supporting the right of each of the 28
national Anglican bodies to decide for itself
whether to consecrate women bishops. The
resolution, which passed by a margin of 423–
28, encouraged respect between provinces that
differ on the issue and courtesy between bishops with differing opinions.

A similar compromise was reached earlier
at the triennial General Convention of the U.S.
Episcopal Church, which narrowly approved a
measure to allow parishes that reject women
bishops to call in male "episcopal visitors" to
perform sacramental functions. In September
the Rev. Barbara C. Harris, a black priest from
Philadelphia, was elected suffragan (assistant)
bishop of the Diocese of Massachusetts, becoming the first woman Anglican bishop.

Homosexuality and Ordination. The quadrennial General Conference of the United
Methodist Church voted overwhelmingly to retain language condemning homosexual practice
and barring the ordination of practicing homosexuals. On another controversial matter, the
Methodist conference adopted a new hymnal
that eliminates much of the male imagery contained in the previous volume. In perhaps the
most far-reaching action taken at the gathering,
delegates approved a new theological statement that pleased both liberals and conservatives by distinguishing doctrinal pluralism from
theological pluralism.

Ordination of homosexuals was discussed
at synodical assemblies of the new Evangelical
Lutheran Church in America, which came into
existence in 1988 through the merger of three
denominations. Three ministerial candidates at
Pacific Lutheran Theological Seminary announced that they were gay, and their ordina-
tions were postponed based on a determination
by the church's Council of Bishops that ministerial candidates must "refrain from homosexual practices."

The Orthodox Presbyterian Church left the
Reformed Ecumenical Synod to protest that
body's refusal to expel the Reformed Churches
in the Netherlands for issuing a report in 1979
that said homosexuals in faithful, loving relationships should be allowed to hold church office.

In contrast to other denominations, the
General Council of the United Church of Canada accepted practicing homosexuals as candidates for the ordained ministry, although
delegates disagreed on whether this repre-

The Most Rev. Robert Runcie (left), the archbishop of Canterbury, and Bishop Desmond Tutu, the archbishop of Cape Town, South Africa, hold an informal discussion during the 1988 Lambeth Conference. Some 500 Anglican bishops attended the decennial meeting in Canterbury, England, in the summer.

© Bob May Photographer

sented a change in policy. The church's Judicial Committee agreed to rule on the matter, which would require a vote by the 98 regional presbyteries if it were found to constitute a change in church membership provisions.

A resolution condemning homosexuality as "a chosen lifestyle" that is "a perversion of divine standards" was adopted at the annual meeting of the Southern Baptist Convention. But it did not generate as much controversy as another resolution that stressed the "role, responsibility, and authority of the pastor" and warned that the Protestant doctrine of the priesthood of the believer "can be used to justify the undermining of pastoral authority."

Abortion. Fundamentalists captured the presidency of the Southern Baptist Convention for the tenth consecutive year with the election of the Rev. Jerry Vines of Jacksonville, FL. Fundamentalist control of Southern Baptist agencies led to the resignation of the Rev. Larry Baker—whose position in favor of abortion had been criticized by conservatives—as head of the denomination's Christian Life Commission. He was succeeded by the Rev. Richard Land, an administrator at Criswell College in Dallas who strongly opposes abortion but favors capital punishment.

The American Baptist Churches replaced a 1981 statement on abortion that stressed respect for "the integrity of each person's conscience" with a new one that stresses the need to avoid abortion whenever possible. Similarly, the Episcopal Church and the United Methodist Church passed resolutions opposing abortion for the purposes of birth control or gender selection. The Presbyterian Church (U.S.A.) approved a task force to restudy its pro-choice stand on abortion, which pleased conservatives who had been trying to reopen the subject for discussion since 1983. Following an emotional

debate, the United Church of Canada voted to retain a 1980 statement calling for decriminalization of abortion, saying it should be widely available as an option.

Organizations. Two top officials of the National Council of Churches (NCC) resigned after criticizing the leadership style of the agency's general secretary, the Rev. Arie Brouwer. After J. Richard Butler resigned as head of Church World Service, the council's relief arm, and the Rev. William L. Wipfler resigned as head of the council's Human Rights Office, NCC executives worked to formulate a plan to bring Church World Service fully into the council's structure and establish clearer guidelines for staff working relationships.

The Christian Conference of Asia decided to relocate to four sites—Japan, Thailand, Hong Kong, and the Philippines—after being expelled from Singapore in late 1987 on charges of meddling in national politics. The Johannesburg headquarters of the South African Council of Churches was damaged by a bomb explosion.

DARRELL J. TURNER

Roman Catholicism

The year 1988 marked the first schism in the Roman Catholic Church in 118 years when suspended French Archbishop Marcel Lefebvre ordained four bishops on June 30 in direct defiance of Vatican orders. The Vatican threatened and then promptly excommunicated Lefebvre and the bishops, citing Canon Law which says "a bishop who consecrates someone a bishop and the person who receives such a consecration from a bishop without a pontifical mandate incur an automatic excommunication."

Although attempts at reconciling Lefebvre and his Priestly Society of St. Pius X with Sec-

Defying the Vatican, suspended French Archbishop Marcel Lefebvre ordained four bishops in Switzerland, June 30, causing a schism in the Catholic Church. On June 29, he had ordained 16 of his followers as priests, above.

ond Vatican Council teachings had seemed hopeful in May, Archbishop Lefebvre announced plans for the ordination June 15. Lefebvre and his "traditionalist" followers believe current Roman Catholic leadership is schismatic and that no pope since Pius XII, who died in 1958, has followed authentic church teachings on religious liberty, ecumenism, and use of the vernacular language at Mass. Lefebvre was suspended from his priestly ministry by Pope Paul VI in 1976 after ordaining priests against Vatican wishes.

Devotion to Mary. For most of 1988, Roman Catholics celebrated the remaining months of a Marian Year. Pope John Paul II had called for a period of special devotion to the Virgin Mary —beginning with the feast of Pentecost (June 7) in 1987 and ending with the feast of the Assumption (August 15) in 1988. Dioceses around the world designated special pilgrimage sites and held special Marian events.

Since 1981 in Medjugorje, Yugoslavia, six young visionaries have claimed to have had almost daily discussions with Mary. Although the Vatican has not recognized the authenticity of those "apparitions," Marian scholars continued to say that they are not essentials of the faith, but at most small signs meant to awaken faith. Nevertheless the number of tours to the village escalated in 1988.

The Role of Women. In 1988 both Pope John Paul II and the U.S. bishops issued statements on women and their role in the church. Neither called for women priests. The first draft of the U.S. pastoral letter, released April 11, called

for dramatic changes in the church's treatment of women to remedy what they called "the sin of sexism." Among its recommendations were: allowing female altar servers, considering ordaining women deacons, and opening all ministries and leadership positions that do not require ordination to women. The drafting committee, headed by Bishop Joseph Imesch of Joliet, IL, asked bishops to conduct local consultations on the 164-page document to aid the writing of a second draft for final consideration in November 1989.

On September 30, the pope released an apostolic letter reaffirming his stance on a male-only priesthood. The pope warned of a "masculinization" of women in an effort to achieve equality. He promised a pastoral document on the implications of the role of women in the church.

AIDS. In early January several U.S. bishops were arguing among themselves over a statement on the pastoral implications of the AIDS pandemic. Released in December 1987, the statement, "The Many Faces of AIDS: A Gospel Response," was written and approved by 50 bishops on the administrative committee of the National Conference of Catholic Bishops. Though few bishops disagreed with most of the statement, several vocal bishops and conservative Catholic groups criticized the writing for what seemed to be its tolerance of information about prophylactic devices.

Cardinal John O'Connor of New York, not a member of the administrative board, was one of the statement's strongest critics. At the bishops' summer meeting in Collegeville, MN, Cardinal Joseph Bernardin of Chicago spoke in support of the document but, acknowledging the controversy, backed the writing of a new, updated AIDS statement.

Other Developments. In May, Pope John Paul named 25 new members, including two Americans—James Aloysius Hickey of Washington and Edmund Casimir Szoka of Detroit —to the College of Cardinals. Earlier the pontiff had issued an encyclical on socio-economic development, "On Social Concerns."

In pastoral changes in the United States, Anthony J. Bevilacqua succeeded Cardinal John Krol as archbishop of Philadelphia; Donald W. Wuerl replaced Archbishop Bevilacqua as head of the diocese of Pittsburgh; and in Atlanta, Eugene Antonio Marino was installed as the nation's first black Roman Catholic archbishop.

On October 13 the church announced that three independent radiocarbon tests had disproved the authenticity of the Shroud of Turin, long revered as Jesus' burial cloth. According to the tests, commissioned by the Vatican, the shroud's material dates from the Middle Ages. However, there still was no explanation of how the image on the cloth was formed.

KEITH D. PICHER, *"The Chicago Catholic"*

Hypermarkets, combined supermarkets and discount stores that sell everything from fruits to videocassettes, have begun springing up across the United States. A typical hypermarket has some 220,000 sq ft (20 440 m²) in floor space.

RETAILING

A record merger, the $6.6 billion (C$8.2 billion) takeover of Federated Department Stores by the Campeau Corporation of Canada, hit American retailing with drastic effect in 1988. It changed the configuration of competition and market share, turned loose about 8,500 employees, and created important shifts in suppliers. (*See also* BIOGRAPHY—Campeau, Robert.)

It also generated several aftershocks. Campeau sold several of its most important divisions—Brooks Brothers to Marks & Spencer, the British retailer; Bullock's and I. Magnin in California to R. H. Macy & Company as the inducement to withdraw from the Federated bidding contest; and the Foley's chain in Texas and the Filene's fashion chain in Boston to May Department Stores Company. All these moves were aimed at producing about $2.8 billion to help Campeau pay for its big merger.

But retailers also battened down to face another windstorm, a sales slump even worse than the erratic 1987 trend. The big loser was women's apparel, the main profit generator and a spur to storewide business. The effects of the slump were mixed profits, considerable price slashing, and a drag on "comp" store sales. "Comp" stores are those at least a year old whose sales are considered widely the real barometer of consumer buying. Short skirts, first offered to a lackadaisical shopper in 1987, were blamed for the lag in women's apparel sales, but critics also cited a lack of fashion excitement. And early fall sales failed to show the anticipated pickup.

Many retail executives lost their jobs, both at the senior and middle levels. Estimates stated that some 4,500 were displaced by mergers, divestitures, and poor business. At least another 4,000 became redundant in the junior specialist, clerical, and technician ranks.

Few retailers had an outstanding year due to what was perceived as a squeeze on consumer disposable income. But hope for improvement continued.

"Beginning in spring 1987, U.S. consumers began to reduce their expenditures," observed Stacy Ruchlamer, an analyst at Shearson Lehman Hutton, New York. "We believe that the consumer is reliquifying, as indicated by current employment and personal income statistics, and perhaps retail sales will rebound. However, when the consumer does start to spend again, we do not expect the magnitude of strength of the 1983 through early 1987 period, but a more modest growth environment."

Discount stores were especially hard hit. Zayre Corporation, a dramatic success under Maurice Segall, an economist turned merchant, suffered earnings erosion and had to retrench, change divisional management, and sell stores. The latter measures included selling its discount-store division to its nearest competitor, Ames Department Stores Inc. Gold Circle stores, put on the block by Campeau in the Federated takeover, was sold for the relatively low sum of $325 million. And many Bradlees' discount stores were sold by Stop & Shop Companies.

While faltering under the slack trend in apparel, specialty store concepts continued to excite retailers. Sears, after buying several specialized chains, launched its own McKids children's wear and toy chain, using McDonald's fast-food logo and characters. Barneys New York, the country's largest single menswear store, planned to build a national chain. And in the first major retail acquisition by a Japanese firm, Jusco Limited bought Talbots, the women's apparel chain in New England.

And there was a stiffening race for size among the mass-volume chains, with K Mart creeping up on Sears' $27 billion sales and Wal-Mart Stores stealing up on K Mart's $24 billion.

In the food field, A & P continued its dramatic turnaround with consistent profits and new stores. American Stores Company, owner of the Alpha-Beta supermarkets, made a $2.5 billion offer for Lucky Stores, Inc., but ran into some legal hurdles.

ISADORE BARMASH
"The New York Times"

RHODE ISLAND

The year 1988 was one of political drama in the state, played against a backdrop of continuing economic prosperity.

Economy. The jobless rate continued to drop as the economy boomed, falling from 3.5% in January to 3% in October, well below the national average. Indeed the state was suffering an acute shortage of labor. Electric Boat, for example, the giant submarine manufacturer, had difficulty meeting its 1988 target of 500 new hirings for its Quonset plant; nevertheless, the company announced plans to hire another 500 employees by the end of 1989.

Real-estate values, especially for residential properties, continued to climb, although by the autumn observers noted some cooling. The number of sales was off only slightly, but prices were rising less steeply and offerings sold more slowly. There were signs that the condominium market was becoming glutted, but the affordability of housing for the less affluent was a growing social and political issue.

Legislature. The year in the General Assembly began with the election of Joseph De-Angelis as House speaker, replacing Matthew J. Smith, who retired to become court administrator. The 1988 session saw agreement with Republican Gov. Edward D. DiPrete on a $1.4 billion budget, including a 12% increase in spending. Legislation was enacted to increase the percentage of local educational funding from the state and on such issues as AIDS testing, campaign financing, a new job-training program, the war on drugs, housing for the homeless and those hurt by rising rents and real-estate prices, and the environment.

Politics and Elections. The hottest races in the September 14 primaries were for the Democratic nominations for general treasurer and U.S. congressman from the 1st District. Anthony J. Solomon, who held the office of general treasurer before his unsuccessful run for governor in 1984, won the party nod for that post. And in the congressional primary, 14-term incumbent Fernand St. Germain edged out Scott Wolf despite allegations that he had improperly benefited from his position as chairman of the House Banking Committee.

The local race that gained the most national coverage was for a Providence seat in the state House of Representatives. The attention focused on 21-year-old Patrick Kennedy, a son of Sen. Edward M. Kennedy (D-MA). He won.

The main focuses of attention on Election Day, however, were the races for U.S. senator, 1st District congressman, and governor. In the Senate contest, Republican incumbent John H. Chafee defeated Lt. Gov. Richard A. Licht, 54%-46%, to win a third term. In the congressional race, St. Germain, still dogged by ethical issues, lost his seat—which had been continuously Democratic for more than half a century

© Jack Spratt/NYT Pictures

Patrick Kennedy, 21-year-old philosophy student at Providence College and son of Sen. Edward Kennedy, won a seat in Rhode Island's House of Representatives.

—to political novice Ronald K. Matchley, 56%-44%. Thus, beginning in January 1989, Sen. Claiborne Pell would be the only Democrat representing a state which for decades had sent only Democrats to Washington. Rhode Island was, however, one of the ten states that supported Michael Dukakis for president.

In the gubernatorial race, Governor DiPrete enjoyed an 80% popularity rating as he began his campaign against Bruce Sundlun, whom he had defeated by a two-to-one margin in 1986. A succession of news stories during the final

weeks of the campaign, however, linked Di-Prete to an ethically questionable land deal and alleged special favors for friends and family members. He barely won.

On November 21 the Senate Democratic caucus chose David R. Carlin, Jr., of Newport as majority leader. He succeeded John C. Revens, Jr., who had not sought reelection.

ELMER E. CORNWELL, JR., *Brown University*

ROMANIA

Despite continuing critical shortages of food and energy and sporadic violent public protests, the autocratic rule of Romanian Communist leader Nicolae Ceauşescu did not seem endangered in 1988. He continued to take a hard line toward his domestic and foreign challengers.

Domestic Affairs. In 1988, Romanians suffered from the lowest standard of living and the greatest repression of human rights of any nation in Europe. A special conference of the Romanian Communist Party in December 1987 admitted some serious economic shortcomings. It promised a basic increase in pay of 10% for all workers and greater supplies of meat in 1988, but also declared that Soviet-style *perestroika* (restructuring) was not necessary and recommended the "improved application of present mechanisms" instead.

In February 1988 the state's economic plan for 1987 was declared fulfilled, with national income up 4.8%, industrial production up 5.6%, agricultural production up 3%, and foreign trade up 4.8%. The 1988 plan adopted by the Grand National Assembly predicted increases in national income of 9–10%, in industrial production of 11–12%, in agricultural production of 6–6.5%, and in foreign trade of 8–9%. Romania was proclaimed to be on its way to "the radiant summits of Communism."

The austerity program mounted by the regime to speed the repayment of Romania's

large foreign debt severely depressed living conditions and provoked open opposition in various parts of the country. In November 1987 thousands of automobile workers rioted in Braşov, shouting "Down with Ceauşescu!" and ransacking and burning party buildings. Tanks and additional police had to be called in. Rumors spread of uprisings in other cities, even Bucharest.

In January 1988, in connection with the celebration of Ceauşescu's 70th birthday, and possibly in reaction to statements by the U.S. State Department and Amnesty International accusing Romania of "a persistent pattern of human-rights abuse," the government granted amnesty to those convicted of certain specified crimes and reduced the prison terms of others.

Foreign Affairs. Romania's poor record on human rights and its alleged mistreatment of its ethnic minorities, including Jews, Hungarians, and Germans, complicated its relations with a number of other countries. In 1988 relations with Hungary worsened markedly over Romania's discrimination against some 2 million ethnic Hungarians, living mostly in Transylvania. Romania banned all Hungarian-language newspapers and periodicals, drastically reduced the number of Hungarian radio and TV broadcasts, seized food parcels sent by Hungarians to their relatives in Romania, and announced its intention of destroying some 8,000 Romanian villages, including many occupied by ethnic Hungarians. In response to mass demonstrations in Budapest and vigorous official protests from Hungary, Romania closed the Hungarian consulate in Cluj-Napoca in June 1988. In August the new general secretary of the Hungarian Socialist Workers' Party and prime minister of Hungary, Károly Grosz, met with Ceauşescu in Arad, Romania, but gained no concessions for the ethnic Hungarian minority from him.

In December 1987, West German Foreign Minister Hans-Dietrich Genscher tried unsuccessfully to convince Ceauşescu to permit the unrestricted emigration of ethnic Germans in Romania and to accept Western help to alleviate Romania's food and fuel shortages. In February 1988 the U.S. government made renewal of Romania's most-favored-nation trade status contingent on major improvement in its human-rights and emigration policies. Stung, Romania reacted sharply, announcing that it would not seek a renewal. In a more positive vein, Romania sent Foreign Minister Ion Totu to a meeting of representatives of the six Balkan states held in Belgrade, Yugoslavia, in February 1988 for the purpose of developing closer economic integration and promoting a regional ban on all nuclear and chemical weapons.

See also special report on page 227.

JOSEPH FREDERICK ZACEK
State University of New York at Albany

ROMANIA • Information Highlights

Official Name: Socialist Republic of Romania.
Location: Southeastern Europe.
Area: 91,699 sq mi (237 500 km²).
Population (mid-1988 est.): 23,000,000.
Chief Cities (July 1, 1986 est.): Bucharest, the capital, 1,989,823; Braşov, 351,493; Constanta, 327,676.
Government: *Head of state,* Nicolae Ceauşescu, president (took office 1967) and secretary-general of the Communist Party (1965). *Head of government,* Constantin Dăscălescu, prime minister (took office May 1982). *Legislature* (unicameral) —Grand National Assembly.
Monetary Unit: Leu (13.960 lei equal U.S.$1, March 1988).
Gross National Product (1986 U.S.$): $138,000,-000,000.
Foreign Trade (1986 U.S.$): *Imports,* $10,590,-000,000; *exports,* $12,543,000,000.

SASKATCHEWAN

A devastating drought, a controversial language bill, privatization policy, mineral resource development, and a quiet political scene highlighted the year in Saskatchewan.

Agriculture. The heat wave and drought that hit the U.S. Midwest and South also swept Saskatchewan in 1988, devastating its farm economy. According to most assessments, one quarter of Saskatchewan's C$4 billion annual farm economy was wiped out, with 10 million metric tons of crops killed and businesses in many rural communities facing ruin. The Progressive Conservative (PC) government of Premier Grant Devine persuaded the federal government to cover some $550 million in losses from the Western Grain Stabilization Fund, with another $390 million coming from crop insurance programs. Ironically, the decline in production caused by the drought was expected to cause farm prices to rise, something both the federal and provincial governments had been trying to accomplish for years.

Politics and Budget. With no provincial election expected until 1990, the political scene was relatively quiet. While Devine remained safely at the helm of the governing PCs, New Democratic Party (NDP) leader Roy Romanow managed to increase his party's representation in the Assembly by one seat (in a by-election). Representation then stood at 37 seats for the PCs, 26 for the NDP, and one vacancy.

Finance Minister Gary Lane's annual budget included an $80 million tax increase—spread among individuals and businesses alike—bringing the total to $3.9 billion. He predicted a deficit of $328 million for 1988–89, bringing the accumulated deficit to $3.6 billion.

Language. In April, Premier Devine's government introduced legislation to repeal a century-old statute giving French and English equal status in the province's courts and legislature. Given the vast majority of English-speaking residents and the hard economic times, Devine contended, the province could not afford to translate all of its laws into French. The federal Supreme Court ruled that the bill discriminated against Saskatchewan's 25,000 francophone residents. Ottawa finally agreed to provide $55 million to increase French-language services.

Privatization. The government continued its policy of selling publicly owned corporations and agencies to the private sector. Its biggest move in this area was to create a new, $1.6 billion corporation, CAMECO—the Canadian Mining and Energy Company—in a merger of the provincially owned Saskatchewan Mining and Development Corporation and federally owned Eldorado Nuclear Ltd. CAMECO became the largest uranium mining company in the Western world. Other operations already fully or partly privatized included the provin-

---

cial oil, gas, mineral, and power corporations, mills and mines, and a broad range of services.

Resources. The $623 million uranium and $700+ million potash industries successfully fought action in the United States that would have banned provincial exports to their biggest market. The 1987 free-trade agreement would safeguard Canadian uranium exports south of the border, while the potash industry signed a five-year agreement promising not to undercut U.S. prices. The oil industry began to recover slightly from drastic declines in world prices. New investment in the industry was expected to total $350 million in 1988, and the small but growing natural-gas industry continued to expand at a substantial rate, helped by deregulation of prices and legislation allowing producers to sell directly to consumers.

PAUL JACKSON
"Star Phoenix," Saskatoon

SAUDI ARABIA

Saudi Arabia in 1988 was relieved by the cease-fire between Iraq and Iran, but suffered a decline in the value of its oil exports.

Foreign Affairs. Although Saudi Arabia had supported Iraq both financially and diplomatically during the latter's eight-year war with Iran, the Saudis never stopped pushing for peace between the two countries. At a December 1987 meeting in Riyadh, the Gulf Cooperation Council urged the UN Security Council to impose sanctions against Iran for its refusal to accept a cease-fire. Saudi Arabia's King Fahd accused Iran of seeking to impose its power over the entire region. On April 26, 1988, Saudi Arabia broke diplomatic relations with Iran, citing the 1987 riot in the Saudi holy city of Mecca, the subsequent attack on the Saudi embassy in Tehran, and continuing Iranian attacks on oil tankers in the Persian Gulf. On April 28, King Fahd warned of reprisals—by ballistic

missile—for Iranian-sponsored bombings of Saudi property overseas or inside the country.

The Saudi government on July 29 publicly urged Iraq to compromise on a proposed UN cease-fire, which was agreed to in August.

While war tensions to their east were decreasing, the Saudis became increasingly concerned with the Arab-Israeli dispute to their north. The Palestinian uprising in the Israeli-occupied West Bank and Gaza encouraged the Saudis to play a more active role in peace efforts. Saudi Foreign Minister Prince Saud encouraged Soviet participation in an international peace conference during his visit to Moscow in January 1988—his first trip there since 1982. Saudi economic assistance was vital to the principal Arab countries and groups involved with Israel. The Palestine Liberation Organization (PLO), Jordan, Egypt, and Syria received hundreds of millions of dollars in aid from the Saudis.

Oil and Finance. While petrochemical industries became quite profitable in 1988, Saudi wealth came mostly from crude oil. Production averaged about 4 million barrels per day in 1987 and 4.2 million from January through July 1988. Oil prices and production were supposed to be set within a framework established by the Organization of the Petroleum Exporting Countries (OPEC). Saudi Oil Minister Hisham Nazer pointed out, however, that many countries had pumped more oil than their OPEC quotas permitted and had given special rebates, causing world oil prices to fall. Nazer agreed with Iran and other OPEC price "hawks" that coordination of production and pricing with non-OPEC oil-producing countries was essential, but Saudi Arabia in May 1988 opposed a suggested 5% production cut as too small to have any substantial effect. Instead, King Fahd said that full compliance with existing agreements would lead to an increase in prices. On June 14, at the end of a four-day OPEC meeting in Vienna, Nazer helped bring about a six-month extension of the existing production and pricing system, while emphasizing that Saudi Arabia would not reduce its own production so as to cut the OPEC oil surplus.

Since overproduction by other countries continued, Saudi Arabia increased its own pumping in August to about 4.9 million barrels per day, thereby hoping to maintain its share of the world market. As prices fell to $13 per barrel and then even to $10, Saudi Arabia in October increased production to 5.7 million barrels, while Nazer assured OPEC that Saudi Arabia would return to its quota as soon as the other members did.

To increase income, Saudi Arabia in 1988 reorganized its own petroleum operations and acquired an interest in a major U.S. oil company. The cost of gasoline within Saudi Arabia was doubled in November 1987, the administration of Saudi refineries was revamped, and the government-owned Aramco Services Company in June 1988 signed a letter of intent for the purchase of an interest in Texaco. The Saudis obtained a 50% share in Texaco's distribution and marketing system in 23 U.S. states. In return, the Saudis paid Texaco some $1.2 billion and guaranteed to sell up to 600,000 barrels per day of oil through their joint distribution system.

Economy and Government. Economic austerity was reflected in the new Saudi budget, announced by King Fahd on Dec. 30, 1987. Total spending in 1988 was to be $37.7 billion, down about 17% from 1987's authorized amount. For the first time since the great oil boom of the early 1970s, Saudi Arabia had to borrow money internally by selling bonds worth about $8 billion. New taxes were imposed on foreign-owned corporations, duties on some imports were raised from 7% to 12%, and government reserves held abroad were to be drawn upon to meet the projected deficit.

Governmental affairs remained steady during 1988, and there were few changes in top personnel, but the threat from Iran prompted increased internal security. Iran, however, boycotted the annual pilgrimage to Mecca. In September the death penalty for terrorism and sabotage was established.

Military. Saudi Arabia in 1988 turned away from its longtime reliance on weapons purchases from the United States because of repeated restrictions by the U.S. Congress. A new example of such limitations took place in October 1987, when the Senate voted to bar the sale of 1,600 Maverick missiles to the Saudis.

Desiring greater freedom in its military policies, Saudi Arabia turned to China and Great Britain for armaments. As early as 1985, Saudi Arabia had begun negotiations with China for the purchase of CSS-2 intermediate-range surface-to-surface missiles; secret installation of the missiles began south of Riyadh in 1987. The missiles, which had a range of about 1,600 mi (2 600 km) were discovered by the United States in January 1988. Israel was alarmed and in March hinted at possible strikes even though Saudi Arabia had pledged to use them only for

---

SAUDI ARABIA • Information Highlights

Official Name: Kingdom of Saudi Arabia.
Location: Arabian peninsula in southwest Asia.
Area: 829,996 sq mi (2 149 690 km²).
Population (mid-1988 est.): 14,200,000.
Capital (1981 est.): Riyadh, 1,000,000.
Government: *Head of state and government,* Fahd bin 'Abd al-'Aziz Al Sa'ud, king and prime minister (acceded June 1982).
Monetary Unit: Riyal (3.7505 riyals equal U.S.$1, Nov. 1, 1988).
Gross Domestic Product (1987 U.S.$): $85,000,-000,000.
Economic Index (March 1988): *Consumer Prices* (1980 = 100), all items, 95.2; food, 98.9.
Foreign Trade (1986 U.S.$): *Imports,* $19,113,-000,000; *exports,* $20,085,000,000.

defense. While the United States supported the Saudis in this dispute—and agreed in April to sell them $825 million worth of arms—the kingdom was negotiating with Great Britain for a much larger and more important commitment. A memo of understanding signed on July 3, 1988, outlined a ten-year agreement for the Saudi purchase of fighter planes, ships, weapons, and construction of air bases valued initially at $12 billion and perhaps ultimately worth up to $30 billion. It was the largest overall Middle East arms sale to date.

WILLIAM OCHSENWALD
Virginia Polytechnic Institute

SINGAPORE

Prime Minister Lee Kuan Yew's Political Action Party (PAP) won a sweeping victory in parliamentary elections September 3. Strong economic growth continued through the year.

Economy. The country continued to rebound from its 1985–86 recession. Figures released in February showed that gross domestic product (GDP) had increased 8.8% in 1987. While the government initially expected growth to slow in 1988, forecasts were revised upward after the growth rate hit 10.8% in the first quarter. Manufacturing output was up 20% in that quarter, and 20,000 new jobs were created, putting further pressure on an already tight labor pool.

A U.S. decision to withdraw its generalized system of preferences, which had allowed duty-free entry of Singaporean exports, sparked a large-scale demonstration by the National Trades Union Council in February. The United States receives annually about 30% of Singapore's exports, and the decision to withdraw the preferences (starting in 1989) reflected a view that Singapore was graduating from the ranks of developing countries. While the government sanctioned the protest, unusual for Singapore, it took no official retaliation.

Politics. In the September 3 elections, called 15 months ahead of schedule, the PAP won all

---

SINGAPORE • Information Highlights

Official Name: Republic of Singapore.
Location: Southeast Asia.
Area: 224 sq mi (580 km²).
Population (mid-1988 est.): 2,600,000.
Capital: Singapore City.
Government: *Head of state,* Wee Kim Wee, president (took office September 1985). *Head of government,* Lee Kuan Yew, prime minister (took office 1959). *Legislature* (unicameral)—Parliament.
Monetary Unit: Singapore dollar (1.997 S. dollars equal U.S. $1, Nov. 1, 1988).
Gross Domestic Product (1986 U.S.$): $18,600,-000,000.
Economic Index (1987): *Consumer Prices* (1980 = 100), all items, 116.3; food, 113.9.
Foreign Trade (1987 U.S.$): *Imports,* $32,559,-000,000; *exports,* $28,686,000,000.

---

but one of the 81 seats in parliament. After seeing a 12% drop in its share of the popular vote in the last elections, in 1984, the PAP lost just 1% in 1988, and the results were seen widely as a mandate for the government.

The victorious PAP candidates were mostly members of the party's "second generation," younger politicians who had been groomed to take over the government. Lee, who turned 65 soon after the vote and has led Singapore since 1959, was the lone member of the "old guard" to stand for reelection; and there was speculation that he, too, soon would step aside. First Deputy Prime Minister Goh Chok Tong, 46, was the immediate heir apparent, but it was thought likely that Prime Minister Lee's son, Trade and Industry Minister Lee Hsien Loong, 36, eventually would take over.

Under new rules, racially balanced teams rather than single candidates stood for election in 13 districts. The plan sparked controversy when it was adopted earlier in the year: The PAP said that it would ensure balanced representation of minorities, while opposition groups argued that it would decrease their chances because it was difficult for them to field full slates of candidates. The opposition was split into seven parties, and lack of unity was considered one reason for its weak showing in the vote. Still, some races were close. Among opposition candidates who lost narrowly was Francis T. Seow, the country's former solicitor general, who had been arrested and detained for 72 days earlier in the year.

Seow's detention had been part of a government action against what were termed threats to political security from Marxist and foreign groups. In 1987, 22 people had been arrested and charged with taking part in a Marxist plot. Most were released, but in April 1988 some charged that they had been coerced into giving false confessions. The government promised a full inquiry but dropped the plan after eight members of the group, who were arrested the day after making the charge, recanted the statement. Also arrested were Seow and another lawyer who represented the group. They were charged with conducting an "organized campaign" to discredit the government.

Foreign Affairs. Singapore's concern over outside influence in its political affairs was evident in its relations with other countries, particularly the United States. A senior U.S. diplomat was expelled May 7 on the charge that he had cultivated the opposition, specifically urging Seow to run for office and financing his efforts. The United States responded by expelling a Singapore diplomat. Tensions eased later in the year, after Singapore said that it had found no evidence of U.S. financial support and would withdraw all charges if the United States could show that it had not otherwise encouraged the opposition.

ELAINE PASCOE, *Free-lance Writer*

On October 13, President Reagan signed into law the Family Support Act, the first major revision of the U.S. welfare system. Among those on hand for the signing were the legislation's chief architect, Sen. Daniel Patrick Moynihan (D-NY), left, and Chairman of the House Ways and Means Committee Dan Rostenkowski (D-IL), right.

© Jose R. Lopez/NYT Pictures

SOCIAL WELFARE

Although the general economic prosperity of the United States continued in 1988, the quality of life for significant numbers of Americans seemed to be unaffected by the good times. A series of reports and studies by government and private groups provided evidence that tens of millions of people were living in poverty. In addition, there were strong indications that while rich Americans may or may not have gotten richer, significant numbers of poor Americans were, indeed, getting poorer.

The situation was particularly acute among inner-city blacks and rural poor of all races. Poverty among blacks in the nation's big cities was "one of the most important social issues of the remainder of the 20th century," said William Julius Williams, professor of sociology at the University of Chicago and the author of the influential 1987 book *The Truly Disadvantaged*.

As for the rural situation, the Population Reference Bureau, a private demographic group, reported that one fourth of all children outside U.S. metropolitan areas lived in poverty. Among the problems of the rural poor were high infant mortality, malnutrition, and alcoholism rates. The problems of the rural poor were compounded by the fact that many lived in isolated areas where there were few doctors and social-welfare services.

The Extent of Poverty. On the national level, the annual Census Bureau report on family income found that in 1987 some 32.5 million Americans—about 13.5% of the population— lived below the poverty line (defined as a total cash income of $11,611 for a family of four).

The national poverty rate dropped by one tenth of one percent from 1986, while the rate among blacks rose 2% to 33.1% and the rate among Hispanics climbed nearly 1% to 28.1%.

Some observers believed that the Census Bureau figures exaggerated the extent of poverty because they counted only cash income and ignored nonliquid benefits such as food stamps, housing assistance, and health care provided for under Medicaid. Including those benefits, the Census Bureau said, the poverty rate for 1987 fell in the range of 8.5%–12% of the population, depending on how the value of the benefits was calculated.

Others contended that the figures correctly mirrored the poverty situation—which they said was growing worse. "The data show that the recovery is increasingly leaving the poor behind," said Robert Greenstein, director of the nonprofit Center on Budget and Policy Priorities. "While unemployment rates returned to the levels of 1978, poverty levels are far higher than the 11.4% figure for that year, and eight million more Americans are poor. . . . The gap between rich and poor families is now at its widest level in 40 years."

Greenstein's group released a study in October that reported that black median family income in 1987 was $18,098—slightly lower than in 1978. Greenstein and others believed that the poverty problems were exacerbated by large reductions in federal spending on programs that benefit low-income persons. According to one report, federal spending on programs such as child-welfare services, energy assistance, emergency food and shelter, operating subsidies for public housing, and ·housing assistance for the elderly and handi-

capped dropped from nearly $63 billion in 1981 to some $38 billion in 1987.

A report issued by the National Urban League in May, "Black Americans and Public Policy," seconded the claim that the Reagan administration had deepened the problems of the nation's poor by sharply limiting social-welfare programs. The administration, said John Jacob, the league's president, had conducted "a disastrous eight-year experiment with government withdrawal from solutions to the problems of black people, poor people, and the cities. That experiment failed. It helped deepen the problems, not solve them."

Administration officials, on the other hand, denied that cuts in social-welfare spending were responsible for more problems among the poor. "People often equate commitment and caring with dropping planeloads of money on people," said Deputy Undersecretary of Education for Planning, Budget, and Evaluation Bruce Carnes. He denied that the administration was not committed to helping the disadvantaged. One of the government's main themes, he said, was that "the nurturing and protection of our children are the paramount duties we have as Americans."

Overhaul of the Federal Welfare System. The administration and Congress took a big step toward changing the federal and state roles in administering welfare programs in 1988. That step was the passage, after two years of debate, of a new national welfare law which *Congressional Quarterly* called "the most significant overhaul of the welfare system in half a century." The Family Support Act, which Congress passed and the president signed into law in October, was designed primarily to encourage the 3.8 million welfare parents—90% of whom were unmarried mothers—to get off the government dole and into the workforce.

The legislation has three main features. First, it requires the states to set up education, training, and other work programs aimed at helping welfare recipients find full-time jobs. Second, it guarantees a range of services—including child care and transportation support—to welfare mothers to encourage them to participate in these new training programs. Third, it establishes a series of measures to tighten child-support enforcement to try to keep families from going on welfare in the first place.

The new law was a compromise measure that ultimately received support from most liberals and conservatives on Capitol Hill and within the Reagan administration. One component of the law popular among conservatives was the requirement that one parent in two-parent welfare families participate at least two days (16 hours) per week in some form of public-service work—not just job training. Liberals, on the other hand, won provisions that require states to offer welfare benefits to two-parent families, that grant $1 billion per year

for state education and training programs, and that provide an extra year of child-care and Medicaid assistance for welfare recipients after they find full-time jobs and are no longer eligible for welfare.

Continuing Problems With the Homeless. Another group of Americans mired in poverty —the homeless—was in the news again in 1988. As in the past, there was disagreement over the extent of the homeless problem. Advocates for the homeless contended that the problem was widespread and growing worse. Those working with the homeless, such as Mitch Snyder of the Community for Creative Nonviolence in Washington, DC, estimated that 2–3 million Americans were living in the streets of the nation's cities, towns, and suburban areas. Others, including officials of the Reagan administration, said there were far fewer and that most of them were mentally ill. Secretary of Housing and Urban Development Samuel R. Pierce, for example, said that, based on a 1984 survey, he believed that there were 500,000 to 600,000 homeless Americans in 1988. Vice-President George Bush, in a Republican presidential debate, said mental illness was "the principal cause" of homelessness. The problem also was caused, he added, by poor education and "lack of shelter."

It was virtually impossible to determine exactly how many persons were without homes. But the extent of the problem could be measured by examining the situation in large cities, which had the most visible homeless populations. In Los Angeles, for example, there were an estimated 30,000 to 50,000 homeless. In Washington, DC, a group called So Others Might Eat reported serving about 1,000 homeless persons every day throughout the year. In Philadelphia, city officials estimated that there were some 15,000 homeless persons, including about 1,000 families.

The idea that mentally ill persons made up a large part of the homeless population was challenged by, among others, Robert M. Hayes, counsel to the National Coalition for the Homeless. Hayes said that, at most, 15% of the homeless were mentally unstable. As for the social makeup of the homeless population, Hayes' organization noted in a February report: "The old stereotype of the single white male alcoholic, the so-called skid row derelict, no longer applies. Increasingly, the ranks of the homeless poor are composed of families, children, ethnic and racial minorities, the elderly, and the disabled. The fastest-growing segment of the homeless population consists of families with children." A report issued in September by a National Academy of Sciences panel estimated that at least 100,000 children were among the homeless on any given night in 1988.

State, local, and private groups across the country were active during 1988 in providing a variety of services for the homeless, including

AP/Wide World

At a shelter for the homeless in Philadelphia, questionnaires are filled out in an effort to determine the number of homeless and their needs. Estimates of the U.S. homeless population in 1988 varied widely—from 500,000 to 3 million or more.

programs aimed specifically at homeless families. As for the federal government, Congress in October passed the Stewart B. McKinney Homeless Assistance Act, a two-year, $1.3 billion measure that reauthorized almost 20 programs that provided shelter, food, health care, counseling, and job training to homeless Americans. The law was named to honor the late Rep. McKinney (R-CT), a prime sponsor of the original homeless aid legislation in 1987.

Hunger and Malnutrition. Hunger and malnutrition, especially among children, also were issues during 1988. As in the case of the homeless, there was disagreement over the extent of the hunger problem. Some groups, such as the Physicians' Task Force on Hunger in America, believed that hunger was an extremely serious problem. The task force estimated that there were 20 million hungry Americans and classified the situation as a "modern-day epidemic." Rep. Leon E. Panetta (D-CA) added that the nation faced a "hunger emergency," and in March introduced a bill that would expand a range of federal nutrition programs.

Others, including such Reagan administration officials as Secretary of Agriculture Richard E. Lyng and Assistant Secretary of Agriculture for Food and Consumer Services John W. Bode, testified before Congress that there was no epidemic of hunger in America. Lyng and Bode contended that the nation had an abundance of surplus food, and that the food always was available for those who needed it. The administration said that the current level of federal spending on food stamps, about $12 billion annually, was adequate.

In August, Congress passed a version of the bill introduced by Representative Panetta. The legislation, among other things, provided slight increases in food-stamp benefits, expanded several child-nutrition programs, and required the Department of Agriculture to buy (1) significant quantities of high-protein foods for distribution through the Temporary Emergency Food Program (which would have expired in 1988), and (2) about $112 million worth of commodities over three years for distribution to emergency feeding centers.

Meanwhile, private soup kitchens and food pantries throughout the country reported helping record numbers of individuals. The Chicago-based Second Harvest National Food Bank Network, for example, distributed more than 400 million lbs (180 million kg) of donated food to some 200 food banks around the country. In New York City—where the number of soup kitchens and food pantries rose from 30 in 1981 to more than 500 in 1988—charitable groups provided more than one million emergency meals per month in 1988.

The International Situation. As dire as the social conditions were for many Americans in 1988, the situation in the United States paled in comparison with that in other parts of the world. Although several years of good crops eased the threat of famine, starvation and severe malnutrition were in evidence in parts of several African countries. The situation appeared most critical in the Sudan, where officials estimated that at least 10,000 persons died of starvation due to the effects of a growing civil war and famine in the southern part of the nation. In addition, countless men, women, and children—particularly in the big cities and rural areas of Central and South America and Asia—were leading lives of abject poverty.

Severe droughts in the United States, Canada, and China during 1988 threatened worldwide food shortages and even famine, according to a report released in October by the private nonprofit group Worldwatch Institute. Adding to the problem, the report said, were the potential for more droughts caused by the warming of the world's climate; the loss of fertile soil to erosion; the lowering of water tables due to overpumping of irrigation water; the slowdown in the development of higher-yielding varieties of major grain crops; and the exploding growth of the world's population.

MARC LEEPSON, *Free-lance Writer*

Gray Power

Of the many changes in the face of the United States during the 20th century, few have been more striking than the aging of its people. The median age of Americans keeps creeping up. At the turn of the century it was just under 23 years. In 1980 it was 30. In 1988 it was estimated at over 32 years and still rising. Not only has the birth rate been cut in half since 1900, but life expectancy is at a record high. A male infant born in 1900 could expect to live an average of 46 years, a female 48 years. By 1987 life expectancy at birth for males had increased to 71, for females to 78.

More than 30 million persons 65 years old and over now reside in the United States, a number larger than the population of all ages in 141 other countries. These Americans constitute more than 12% of the total resident population, a proportion three times higher than in 1900. Moreover, the elderly themselves are living longer. Life expectancy for someone at 65 has risen to 16.7 years on the average. Some 12 million Americans are 75 years old and over —a 60% increase since 1970 alone. Because so many people now live into their eighties, more and more elderly have surviving children who themselves are elderly.

The aging trend will continue. "We are entering the age of age," says Cynthia Taeuber, chief of the age and sex statistics branch of the U.S. Census Bureau. By the year 2020, according to bureau projections, the number of elderly likely will top 51 million, or about 17% of the population. That's roughly the same ratio currently prevailing in Florida, the state with the highest proportion of senior citizens, and Sweden, the country with the highest proportion.

Myths Debunked. Old age, long burdened with a bad name, is gaining a better reputation now that it has become the present or future lot of most Americans. To be old, it turns out, is not so bad after all. It usually confers a privileged status that is relatively new in human history: retirement, or freedom from the compulsion to work for pay. A century ago the great majority of Americans worked long hours, either on a job or at home, until they died. Two thirds of all men 65 and over held jobs in 1900; as late as 1948 nearly half of all elderly men were in the labor force. Today five out of six men 65 and over have retired from the job market, generally because they can afford to do so, thanks to Social Security, private and public pensions, and assets accumulated in a lifetime of work.

Although the average income of older people drops considerably after retirement, it is significantly better than that of retirees 30 years ago—more than twice as much in constant dollars, according to census data.

The physical health of today's elderly also exceeds that of their forebears. Alan Pifer and Lydia Bronte write in their book *Our Aging Society: Promise and Paradox:* "Most men and women over 65 today are vigorous, healthy, mentally alert, and still young in outlook." Only about one person in nine aged 65–74 reports chronic health problems that prevent performance of his or her usual activities.

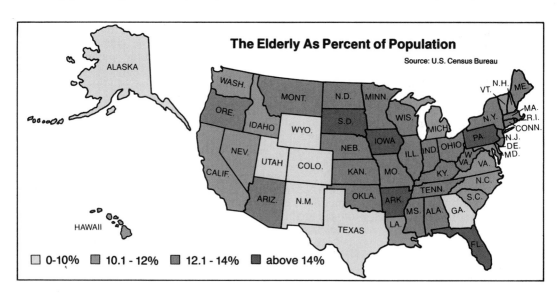

The Elderly As Percent of Population

Source: U.S. Census Bureau

ALASKA
HAWAII

0-10%   10.1 - 12%   12.1 - 14%   above 14%

So, contrary to a widespread impression, most older people generally are not poor or seriously ill. But some are; like the rest of the population, the elderly do not constitute a heterogeneous group. Lumping them together hides some key differences—and problems:

• Although three fourths of U.S. elderly are not disabled, and although most of those disabled are cared for by their families and friends, an estimated 2.3 million lived in a nursing home for at least part of 1988. Federal programs paid only about half of the $38 billion cost of nursing home care in 1986. *Consumer Reports* comments: "Most people aren't poor when they enter a nursing home but they become poor soon after."

• Although only about 12% of the elderly had incomes below the poverty level in the mid-1980s (versus 25% in 1969), the poverty rates varied widely within that group: from 7% for men aged 65–74 living in families to 73% for black women 85 and over living alone.

• Among the elderly, women outnumber men by a 3:2 ratio (5:2 among those 85 and over). Consequently, says the Census Bureau's Taeuber, the health, social, and economic problems of the elderly are problems plaguing mostly women. Their incomes are substantially lower, and they are much more likely than men to be living alone.

Voices with Clout. Confounding another stereotype, most elderly persons are not lonely, according to their testimony to researchers. Certainly as a group they are not forgotten. Both the U.S. House and Senate have special committees on aging that focus solely on their needs. An extensive network of private organizations has grown up to speak for them and to defend their interests, particularly with Congress and the numerous federal agencies having some responsibility for them.

The largest of these private groups is the American Association for Retired Persons (AARP), with an eight-story headquarters on Washington, DC's K Street, the power alley of political lobbies. AARP has 28 million members on its rolls and signs up new ones at a rate of 8,000 per day. That makes it, after the Catholic Church, the largest membership organization in the United States. Unlike the Catholic Church, AARP has its members on a centralized mailing list and runs nationwide media campaigns to get out its message. Its influence is pervasive on Capitol Hill, where it has 18 registered lobbyists, and also reaches many state capitals through volunteer lobbyists.

In the 1984 presidential election, persons 55 and older accounted for 33% of all voters; in the 1986 congressional elections they accounted for 38%. Those kinds of figures give

© Kenneth Jarecke/Contact from Woodfin Camp & Assoc.

With 28 million members, the American Association for Retired Persons (AARP) is the most powerful lobby for the U.S. elderly. In 1988 it mounted a major get-out-the-vote drive.

politicians a powerful incentive to listen to organizations like AARP, especially in election years. Though nonpartisan, AARP became involved in the 1988 presidential campaign as never before, both in the primaries and in the general election. It dedicated $8 million to a get-out-the-vote effort, including special workshops, mass mailings, magazine and television ads, and a voter's guide on elderly issues—all designed to get politicians to commit themselves on such matters as maintaining the cost-of-living index for Social Security. And indeed the candidates told AARP what it wanted to hear. Any candidate who would tamper with Social Security, said Republican Jack Kemp, is a "candidate for a frontal lobotomy."

The biggest recent legislative victory for the elderly was the establishment of nationwide "catastrophic" health insurance in 1988. Medicare, the health-insurance program for the elderly, underwent its first significant expansion by the addition of unlimited hospital care, instead of the previous 60-day limit, as well as other benefits. Mindful of the budget deficit, Congress made the measure largely self-financing. Almost all its cost will be met by persons covered under the plan through an increase in the Medicare premiums deducted from their monthly Social Security checks. Omitted from the new law was any provision of long-term care outside of hospitals, such as in nursing homes or in a patient's own home. That "challenge for the future," as the Senate Special Committee on Aging called it, remains high on the agenda of AARP and its allies.

The Gray Panthers, an 80,000-member organization with 100 local chapters throughout the United States, fights age discrimination and pressures the government on social issues ranging from health insurance to the cost of housing.

© Diana Walker/Gamma-Liaison

Who Gets and Who Pays? The heart of the challenge is budgetary, and it applies not just to possible future benefits but to present ones as well. The share of the U.S. federal budget devoted to programs for the elderly nearly has doubled since 1960, according to the Office of Management and Budget. In fiscal 1987, the estimated federal outlay for Social Security and Medicare ($280 billion) was nearly as much as that for defense ($282 billion). In each case, the outlay came to more than 27% of the federal budget, and the figures did not even include the cost of benefits for veterans and for retired civil-service employees aged 65 and over.

Because federal activities for the elderly are carried out by many government agencies, and often through different programs within those agencies, it is difficult to get a bottom line figure on costs. But the House Ways and Means Committee reported that of all the 1985 nondefense, noninterest outlays, 46% went to the elderly. Whatever the amount, it has grown large enough to become a focal point of controversy.

As is the custom in Washington, a special organization has been formed to address this issue—the Americans for Generational Equity, with James R. Jones, former House Budget Committee chairman and now a Washington lawyer, as president. "The older population," says Jones, "is going to have to reduce its rate of growth in the share of resources."

Underscoring concerns about the fate of children in a rapidly aging society, U.S. Sen. Daniel Patrick Moynihan (D-NY) points out that the United States may be the "first society in history in which a person is more likely to be poor if young rather than old." In 1987 one in five U.S. children under 18 was poor, compared with one out of eight of the elderly.

According to some experts, "intergenerational warfare" may break out as a result of the increasing burden of mandatory Social Security contributions from younger workers, many with the responsibilities of rearing children. In 1988 the Social Security tax rose from 14.3% to 15.02% on wages and salaries, up to a limit of $45,000; half is paid by the employer, half by the employee. In July 1988, when the average weekly earnings of a production worker were $324.68, his or her tax deductions included $23.21 for Social Security. That money—adding up to an annual tax of $1,207—did not go into an account for the individual who paid it but into a fund for disbursements to persons who already are retired or who soon will be.

Daniel Callahan, director of the Hastings Center, a private group in New York specializing in medical ethics, has added his voice to critics of current priorities. In his new book *Setting Limits,* he argues that the rapidly rising expenditures on health care for the elderly should be held in check. "High-technology medicine is one important place to begin," he writes. "Most of the technological advances of recent decades have come to benefit the old comparatively more than the young . . . and the older segment of the old more than any other. . . ."

U.S. Rep. Leon E. Panetta (D-CA) thinks that "there's a point at which the senior citizens themselves will say, 'Wait a minute—we can no longer afford to do this.'" Ironically, this shift might occur as a by-product of the new catastrophic insurance coverage. Its self-financing features will create tax bites as large as $848 a year starting on Jan. 1, 1989, to be deducted from the Social Security checks of the elderly it covers. And the new tax on the elderly will go up every year, at least until 1993.

ROBERT A. SENSER

SOUTH AFRICA

Over the course of 1988 the South African government was able to maintain an uneasy semblance of stability by continuing the existing state of emergency for another year, by banning or curtailing a number of black political and labor organizations, and by stifling press freedoms. Despite its stringent controls, there were national strikes, boycotts, protests by church leaders, and acts of sabotage and bombings organized by the banned and exiled African National Congress (ANC).

Government Controls and Repression. On February 24 the South African government widened its already extensive controls over black opposition groups with new regulations which severely curtailed all but administrative activities of 17 leading antiapartheid organizations, including the Congress of South African Trade Unions (COSATU) and the United Democratic Front (UDF). On March 13, despite a warning from Minister of Law and Order Adriann Vlok, church leaders organized protest services throughout South Africa. Five meetings had been planned by a newly formed committee for the Defense of Democracy, but the organization was banned by the minister only ten days after it had come into being. Archbishop Desmond M. Tutu and other church leaders called an alternative protest service at St. George's Cathedral in Cape Town.

Early in June more than 1 million black workers went on a three-day strike organized by COSATU in protest against the February crackdown on antiapartheid groups and in opposition to a labor bill that would outlaw sympathy strikes and worker boycotts. The success of the strike was a clear indication that the government was unable to prevent extra-parliamentary black opposition. Earlier in the year, on March 21, more than 1 million black workers had joined a nationwide strike to mark the 28th anniversary of the 1960 Sharpeville Massacre.

On June 9 the South African government renewed the two-year nationwide state of emergency for an additional twelve months. The first nationwide state of emergency was declared on June 12, 1986, after more than two years of unrest in South Africa.

In March the government banned the newspaper *New Nation* for three months, alleging that it was "promoting revolution" and "engendering animosity toward the security forces." This important Roman Catholic paper, with a circulation of approximately 60,000, was the first newspaper to be banned under the media restrictions added to the August 1987 renewal of the state of emergency. The newspaper's editor, Zwelakhe Sisulu, already was under detention at the time of the banning. In June the South African government announced details of a further tightening of

controls on the press. The direct impact of these measures would have been to stifle the alternative press in South Africa and all but silence free-lance or part-time journalists. Through these measures the government hoped to limit reporting on human-rights abuses. However, as a result of international criticism as well as pressure from South African newspapers, the government backed down saying that these regulations would be suspended "pending further investigation." However, early in November Minister of Home Affairs J. Christoffel Botha barred publication of the liberal *Weekly Mail* for four weeks under the censorship provision of the prevailing state of emergency.

Appeals by the "Sharpeville Six." On March 18 five African men and one African woman, known as the "Sharpeville Six," were scheduled to be hanged after they had been convicted of the 1985 murder of Jacob Khuzway Dlamini, a black township counsellor in Sharpeville. This was a controversial case because there was no evidence to link the accused directly with the death. The charge brought by the state was that they shared "the common purpose" of the 100 people who stoned the counsellor to death. On the day of execution the Supreme Court in Pretoria granted a stay of execution in the case because new evidence suggested that one of the state's witnesses might have committed perjury. However, on June 13, three months after the Sharpeville Six had been granted this reprieve, they were denied a retrial. In late November, President P. W. Botha commuted the death sentences of the six. Instead they still would serve jail sentences of from 18 to 25 years.

Political Detainees. In September, 22 black trade union leaders and antiapartheid organizers were detained and five others were restricted. At the same time there were raids on offices of trade unions and antiapartheid

---

SOUTH AFRICA • Information highlights

Official Name: Republic of South Africa.
Location: Southern tip of Africa.
Area: 471,444 sq mi (1 221 040 km²).
Population (mid-1988 est.): 35,100,000.
Chief Cities (1985 census, city proper): Pretoria, the administrative capital, 443,059; Cape Town, the legislative capital, 776,617; Durban, 634,301; Johannesburg, 632,369.
Government: *Head of state and government,* Pieter Willem Botha, state president (took office Sept. 1984). *Legislature*—Parliament (tricameral): House of Assembly, House of Representatives (Coloured), and House of Delegates (Indians).
Monetary Unit: Rand (2.4040 rands equal U.S. $1, Nov. 21, 1988).
Gross Domestic Product (1987 U.S.$): $60,000,-000,000.
Economic Index (1987): *Consumer Prices* (1980 = 100), all items, 265.1; food, 278.5.
Foreign Trade (1986 U.S.$): *Imports,* $11,980,-000,000; *exports,* excluding exports of gold, $10,860,000,000.

© Juhan Kuus/Sipa Press

South Africa's President P. W. Botha (right) and F. W. de Klerk, Transvaal National Party leader, attend a party conference in Pretoria in November. The ruling National Party suffered electoral setbacks during 1988.

groups. On September 13, Murphy Morobe and Mohammed Valli Moosa of the UDF, and Vusumuzi Phillip Kahnyile of the National Education Crisis Committee entered the U.S. Consulate in Johannesburg asking for political asylum after escaping from detention. They subsequently were joined by Clifford Ngcobo of the Soweto Civic Association who, like the other three detainees, had escaped from a nearby hospital. In October, as a result of international pressure, the South African government gave assurances that it would not arrest the former detainees when they left the U.S. Consulate.

Bombings and Sabotage. Two people were killed and 29 others were injured early in July when a car bomb exploded as 10,000 spectators were leaving the Ellis Park Sports Stadium near Johannesburg after a rugby match. On July 30 a bomb exploded in a fast-food restaurant at a shopping center in Benoni, near Johannesburg. One person was killed and at least 57 were injured. At the end of August, 23 people were injured in a bombing that destroyed Khotso House, which was the headquarters of the South African Council of Churches and a number of other antiapartheid organizations. In November the headquarters of the National Union of South African Students (NUSAS) at the University of the Witwatersrand was bombed, presumably by white extremists. During 1988, about 100 bombings took place in South Africa, many of them in Johannesburg or in adjacent towns. Except for the bombing of Khotso House and the NUSAS headquarters, most of the attacks were said to have been organized by the African National Congress.

National Council. In April, President P. W. Botha announced new constitutional plans which he stated would enable black South Africans to participate more directly in political affairs. He proposed to establish regional

authorities for blacks living outside of the Homelands and a national council to which representatives from the regional authorities would be sent. The leader of the Conservative Party, Dr. Andries Treurnicht, was highly critical of these new proposals because he feared the inclusion of blacks in the central government. Colin Eglin, at the time leader of the Progressive Federal Party, said that these proposals were inadequate because they avoided the central issue of the participation of blacks in Parliament. In June the South African government introduced the Promotion of Constitutional Development Bill to a joint session of all three South African houses, to formally institute Botha's constitutional reforms.

Inkatha-ANC Rivalries. As a result of violence between members of Chief Mangosuthu Gatsha Buthelezi's *Inkatha* movement and supporters of the United Democratic Front, 26 people died in Pietermaritzburg, Natal, early in 1988. Conflicts and tensions continued throughout the year between these two black groups which were attempting to impose their political hegemony over townships in the region.

Electorate Moves to the Right. The ruling National Party (NP) lost two important Transvaal parliamentary seats, Schweizer-Renecke and Standerton, to the right-wing Conservative Party in a March 2 by-election. President Botha dismissed the defeats and emphasized that the National Party had won 133 seats in the 178-seat all-white Parliament in the May 1987 general election.

In a third by-election, held on March 29, for the Randfontein Constituency in the Transvaal, the Conservative Party won by yet another substantial majority. Corne Mulder, son of former cabinet minister Connie Mulder, won the Randfontein seat held by his late father.

October Local Elections. Segregated municipal elections were held in October for white, black, colored, and Asian city or town councils. White councils were the most heavily contested while many black seats were either uncontested or had no candidates. Black church leaders had called for a boycott of the election by blacks. Most blacks did boycott the election; only 14% of eligible black voters turned out.

The ruling National Party once again faced strong competition from the Conservative Party, and lost heavily to the right in rural areas and in industrial parts of the country. In three of the four provinces, however, it managed to maintain control but this was not the case in the heavily populated Transvaal province. After the election conservatives controlled 60 of the 95 municipal councils in the Transvaal, but they were not able to take over the key cities of Pretoria and Johannesburg.

Group Areas Act Amendment. In July, in an apparent effort to counteract right-wing criticism, the South African government proposed

legislation that would enforce more strictly residential segregation. While the proposed new legislation would recognize some existing multiracial neighborhoods, or "gray areas," at the same time it proposed to amend the Group Areas Act to include provisions for the mandatory eviction of blacks who moved into housing in areas reserved for whites. Under existing law the state is obliged to provide alternative housing before it can evict violators. In the proposed amendment, there would be fines of more than $4,000 and penalties, including five years of imprisonment, for those found guilty of illegally occupying or owning a property designated for a different racial group. The Group Areas Amendment Bill was opposed by all major parties in the three-chamber Parliament except the right-wing Conservative Party.

Economic Conditions. Finance Minister Barend Du Plessis introduced a fiscal year 1988–89 budget to the South African Parliament on March 15, 1988. It advanced major cutbacks in all areas except defense, which received a 22% increase. Black education, which had received substantial increases in the past, received only a 10% increase. Du Plessis maintained that because of the effects of sanctions, economic growth had been held back and unemployment —particularly among blacks—had increased. Figures issued by the U.S. Department of Commerce indicated that exports from South Africa to the United States dropped by more than 40% over the first nine months of 1987. For much of 1988 the price of gold was down from its peak of $500 an ounce in late 1987.

Sanctions. In June and July, U.S. Democratic Party leaders advocated new measures which would intensify sanctions against South

Winnie Mandela's main concern was her husband, Nelson, the leader of the African National Congress. The government said that he would not go back to jail after hospital treatment but to "comfortable" accommodations.

Africa beyond the limited sanctions implemented in 1986. At that time, a coalition of Democrats and Republicans came together to override a veto by President Reagan. The new provisions included a trade embargo and an almost total ban on U.S. investment in South Africa. U.S. corporations doing business in South Africa or individuals with investments there would have a year to sell their holdings. All imports from South Africa, apart from strategic minerals and imports from businesses totally owned by blacks, would be banned as would nearly all U.S. exports to South Africa. However, these sanctions had not been acted upon by the end of the congressional session.

Nelson Mandela's 70th Birthday. Nelson Mandela, the imprisoned leader of the ANC, celebrated his 70th birthday in Pollsmoor Prison near Cape Town. The authorities had announced that he could receive a six-hour visit from his wife Winnie Mandela, his daughter Zinzi, and nine other family members. But prior to the visit Winnie Mandela, speaking on behalf of her husband, canceled the meeting. She maintained that her husband did not want any special favors from the government.

In August, Mandela was removed from Pollsmoor Prison, first to Tygerberg Hospital near Cape Town and then to a private clinic, for treatment of tuberculosis. After more than 25 years of imprisonment, Mandela remains the central symbol of black liberation in South Africa.

U.S.-Sponsored Peace Negotiations. After three months of U.S.-mediated talks, South Africa, Cuba, and Angola agreed to a cease-fire in the Angolan civil war, and South Africa began withdrawing its troops there. After further intensive negotiations, two final accords were signed on December 22. In one, South Africa agreed to surrender control of Namibia, and the timetable for Namibian independence under UN Security Council Resolution 435 was set to begin on April 1, 1989. South Africa would remove its troops from Namibia by July 1; UN-sponsored elections for a constituent assembly would be held on November 1; and independence would be achieved upon approval of a constitution by that assembly. The other accord specified a timetable for the removal of Cuban troops from Angola. (*See* ANGOLA.)

Crackdown on Antidraft Group. In 1988 resistance increased among young white English-speaking South African men against the national draft. In 1987, 23 draftees had announced that they would not serve, and one of them was sentenced to 21 months in prison. In July 1988, David Bruce argued before the courts that he would not serve in the military because it supported the racist system, but he was sentenced to six years of imprisonment. Two weeks later, 142 university students and graduates announced that they would refuse to serve.

PATRICK O'MEARA, *Indiana University*

SOUTH CAROLINA

Elections, new legislation, education issues, and a healthy economy held center stage in South Carolina during 1988.

Elections and Government. The Rev. Jesse Jackson, a native of South Carolina, sought the Democratic Party's nomination for president of the United States. He easily won the state's Democratic primary on March 12 but lost the nomination to Massachusetts Gov. Michael Dukakis. In the GOP primary one week earlier, Vice-President George Bush outpolled Sen. Bob Dole and the Rev. Pat Robertson. On Election Day, Bush won the state's eight electoral votes with 62% of the popular vote.

All incumbents—four Democrats and two Republicans—were reelected to the U.S. House of Representatives. Among them was Rep. Floyd D. Spence (R), who won a tenth term despite a double lung transplant in May and a strong Democratic challenge. Republicans gained two seats in the heavily Democratic state legislature. Voters approved constitutional amendments allowing the General Assembly to establish a state grand jury, providing for the selection of jurors from driver's license lists, and permitting the enactment of job qualifications for sheriffs.

Ethical questions brought before the legislature's judicial screening committee caused a leading candidate to withdraw from a Supreme Court race and an existing judge to give up his bid for reelection. The legislature elected state Rep. Jean H. Toal as the first woman justice of the Supreme Court.

During the year, the General Assembly enacted laws controlling the eroding coastline; permitting the confiscation of cars of multiple drunk-driving offenders; setting penalties for knowingly exposing another person to the AIDS virus; increasing the state retiree benefits, as well as those of most local government re-

tirees, by 14%; granting a 4% pay raise for state employees; adding $20 million to the medicaid program; and partly rebating the 1987 capital gains tax.

Education. The General Assembly fully honored allocation formulas for funding of public schools and approved sex-education curriculums. Overall, scores on standardized student tests improved. All schools met state standards; none were put on the special intervention list. Dropout rates declined for the eighth year in a row. Teacher salaries met Southeastern averages. In higher education, the state funding formula was raised from 87% to 93%, and separate boards were appointed for three colleges.

Economy. Unemployment was only 4.7%, with more than half of all new jobs created in rural areas. Industrial expansion was expected to outpace the $2.3 billion of 1987. Under laws permitting some existing industries to pay a "fee rate" lower than regular property taxes, several companies announced massive expan-

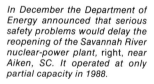

In December the Department of Energy announced that serious safety problems would delay the reopening of the Savannah River nuclear-power plant, right, near Aiken, SC. It operated at only partial capacity in 1988.

sions. Foreign investments increased significantly.

Beginning in 1989, Westinghouse will take over from DuPont as operator of the Savannah River nuclear-power plant. The last of the three reactors at the plant was shut down in August. They had been operating at partial capacity.

Reversing a longtime trend, the number of farms in the state increased. Dry weather in the spring cut corn and cotton yields but contributed to record production of small grains. Tobacco and soybean remained the chief crops.

Other. In mid-December a federal bankruptcy judge ordered the assets of the PTL ministry in South Carolina sold to a Canadian for $65 million (*see* page 449). The State Museum opened in Columbia. And bond issues were approved for an aquarium in Charleston and a performing arts center in Greenville.

ROBERT H. STOUDEMIRE
University of South Carolina

SOUTH DAKOTA

Democrats made gains at the polls, drought brought economic loss and extensive fires, and preparations for the state centennial began.

Elections. South Dakota ranked among the leading states in voter interest, with 61.5% of those eligible going to the polls. Although Vice-President Bush won the state's three electoral votes with a 53% majority, there was a general shift in preference toward Democratic candidates. The state's only U.S. congressman, Democrat Tim Johnson, won reelection with 72% of the vote. The Republican majority in the state legislature was reduced by six seats, including those of majority leader Homer Harding and the influential Sen. Peg Lamont.

Voters also cast ballots on eight referendums. They rejected limits on real-estate taxes for the second time, mandatory surface restoration by open pit mining operations, and a 4% tax on gold production by the Homestake Min-

ing Company. They approved measures to permit further telephone deregulation, to ban corporate hog farming, to allow gambling in the town of Deadwood to finance historical preservation, to divide the Board of Correction and Charities into two agencies, and to allow initiatives to go before voters without legislative approval.

Legislation. The state's appropriations (budget) act called for $1.043 billion in expenditures, of which 42.3% would derive from federal funding, 32.9% from state revenues, and the balance from private and other sources. The Department of Social Services received 21.2%, the Regents of Higher Education 18.4%, the Department of Education and Cultural Affairs (public schools, museums, historical sites, etc.) 14.6%, and the Board of Correction and Charities 5.3%. The act included an average salary increase of 3% for state employees.

The legislature increased financial support for an extended medicaid program; established closer supervision of nursing homes; legalized a three-level pricing system for telephone companies to encourage competition; allowed out-of-state holding companies to take control of banks; created a special board to mediate crises among debt-ridden farmers; increased the minimum wage for persons over 18 to $3.35; and raised the tax on motor fuels.

Economy. Service industries, government employment, and tourism-related business maintained stability in an economy shaken by rural setbacks. Farmers reported irregular crop yields, ranging from total loss to 50 bushels of soybean per acre (20 bu per ha), and nearly twice that amount for corn. Overall, South Dakotans had a better year than did neighboring states because of higher rainfall, lower unemployment, and federal farm subsidies.

Drought and Fire. In some areas parched by drought, however, fires did extensive damage. On the Rosebud Reservation, lightning started a blaze that destroyed 18,000 acres (7 300 ha) of grassland and timber. U.S. forestry officials reported twice as many fires in the Black Hills area as they had seen in any recent year; through September, 219 were caused by lightning and 39 were set by people. Nevertheless, the total area burned on public and private land in the Black Hills was only 1,800 acres (730 ha), of which more than 1,000 (400 ha) came under the management of the National Park Service.

Centennial. Nov. 2, 1988, marked the beginning of centennial observances by four states—South Dakota, North Dakota, Montana, and Washington—that entered the union through an enabling process initiated on Nov. 2, 1888. A special heritage center was opened near the capital in Pierre, and preparations for other events and facilities were under way.

HERBERT T. HOOVER
University of South Dakota

SOUTH DAKOTA • Information Highlights

Area: 77,116 sq mi (199 730 km²).

Population (July 1, 1987): 709,000.

Chief Cities (1980 census): Pierre, the capital, 11,973; Sioux Falls, 81,343; Rapid City, 46,492.

Government (1988): *Chief Officers*—governor, George S. Mickelson (R); lt. gov., Walter D. Miller (R). *Legislature*—Senate, 35 members; House of Representatives, 70 members.

State Finances (fiscal year 1987): *Revenue,* $1,241,000,000; *expenditure,* $1,281,000,000.

Personal Income (1987): $8,900,000,000; per capita, $12,550.

Labor Force (June 1988): *Civilian labor force,* 379,200; *unemployed,* 13,300 (3.5% of total force).

Education: *Enrollment* (fall 1986)—public elementary schools, 89,373; public secondary, 36,085; colleges and universities, 30,935. *Public school expenditures* (1986–87), $378,000,000 ($3,190 per pupil).

SPACE EXPLORATION

Nineteen eighty-eight, the 30th anniversary of the National Aeronautics and Space Administration (NASA), marked the return to flight of the U.S. manned Space Transportation System with missions STS-26 and STS-27, flown respectively by the shuttles *Discovery* and *Atlantis.* The year also saw a new man-in-space endurance record, with cosmonauts aboard the Soviet space station Mir living in orbit for a full year. The Soviets also carried out the initial, unmanned flight of their own space shuttle, *Buran,* and launched two spacecraft containing innovative technical and scientific instrumentation to explore Phobos, one of the two tiny moons of Mars. Sixteen years after launch and five years after leaving the solar system, the U.S. satellite Pioneer 10 continued to yield high-quality astrophysical data from a distance of more than 4 billion mi (6.4 billion km). And Israel launched its first satellite in September.

Following discussions at the U.S.-Soviet spring summit, a bilateral agreement was formulated which included a call for increased cooperation in space. Subsequent meetings in Moscow and Washington yielded substantive understandings regarding the exchange of personnel and data, the preparation of a joint publication on Venus, and a joint search for landing sites on Mars. A similar agreement was reached in November between France and the Soviet Union, with joint efforts planned in planetary exploration and studies of the Earth's environment from space.

Manned Flights. Thirty-two months after the explosion of *Challenger* and the loss of its seven crew members, the U.S. space program was recharged with the highly successful, 64-orbit flight of the shuttle *Discovery,* September 29 to October 3 (*see* pages 88–89). Flown by

Mission Commander Frederick H. Hauck and copilot Richard O. Covey, with mission specialists David C. Hilmers, John M. Lounge, and George (Pinky) Nelson, the extensively modified shuttle successfully deployed a second Tracking and Data Relay Satellite (TDRS-C), which was inserted into geosynchronous orbit by the shuttle's Inertial Upper Stage (IUS) booster. After deploying TDRS, the crew conducted science experiments and took numerous photographs of Earth for scientific and environmental study.

The second post-*Challenger* U.S. shuttle mission, STS-27 from December 2 to 6, was flown by Commander Robert (Hoot) Gibson, Pilot Guy S. Gardner, and mission specialists Richard (Mike) Mullane, Jerry L. Ross, and William M. Shepherd on the orbiter *Atlantis.* This military mission carried a classified payload reported to include a low-altitude, radar reconnaissance satellite code-named Lacrosse.

The Soviet Union broke its own record for man-hours in space on December 21, when cosmonauts Vladimir Titov and Musa Manarov, aboard the space station Mir (Peace), completed 365 days in orbit. At midyear the Soviets already had tripled their lead over the United States in total number of hours logged in space, nearly 130,000.

On June 7 the Soviet cosmonauts Viktor Savinykh and Anatoly Solovyov, and a Bulgarian, Alexander Alexandrov, were launched aboard a Soyuz TM-5 capsule bound for Mir, where they conducted a variety of scientific research projects; they returned to Earth 11 days later. On August 29, cosmonauts Vladimir Lyakhov and Valery Polyakov of the Soviet Union and Abdul Ahad Mohmand of Afghanistan were launched to Mir aboard a Soyuz TM-5 spacecraft. Polyakov remained on Mir, and the others began their return flight on Septem-

After eight days in space, cosmonauts Vladimir Lyakhov of the USSR (right) and Abdul Ahad Mohmand of Afghanistan (left) were stuck in Earth orbit for 25 hours with a dwindling supply of air. They finally managed a successful landing on September 7. Col. Lyakhov admitted error.

ber 6. After a tense, 25-hour crisis in which they were stuck in orbit with a dwindling air supply, the cosmonauts managed to land the craft safely on September 7. On November 26 a three-member crew including Frenchman Jean-Loup Chrétien was launched to Mir in a Soyuz TM-3 capsule. Chrétien returned to Earth on December 21 with the holders of the new endurance record, Titov and Manarov.

Soviet Space Shuttle. The United States was joined in shuttle deployment late in the year by the Soviet Union. On November 15 the USSR successfully initiated a new direction in its space program with the near-perfect launch and return—both at the Baikonur Cosmodrome in Central Asia—of the unmanned shuttle *Buran* (Snowstorm). The craft, very similar to the U.S. shuttle in outward appearance and many technical details, completed two orbits and was aloft for 3 hours and 25 minutes. The launch was only the second by the heavy-lift booster Energia, indicating a very high degree of confidence in what *Aviation Week* called "the most expensive and complex space mission attempted by the USSR since the launch of Sputnik." The two-stage Energia rocket is capable of launching and returning payloads significantly larger than those carried by U.S. shuttles and will be used to deliver up to ten cosmonauts into orbit, or to lift 220,000-lb (100 000-kg) civilian and military spacecraft to the space station. Eventually it will allow the space station to be used as a staging point for long-term flights to Mars, the moon, or both.

The payload size of *Buran* is about the same as that of the U.S. orbiters, but the crew cabin is significantly larger. The launch weight of *Buran* is somewhat lighter than that of the U.S. orbiters, mainly because it does not carry heavy main engines. Soviet authorities said that *Buran* will carry cosmonauts on its second or third flight in 1989, but will be launched only two to four times per year. As many as five orbiters were being built in 1988. Late in the year, the Soviets were planning test flights of a new, heavy-lift vehicle that can carry an orbiter and/or an Energia launcher-component.

Space Station. The USSR continued to use and improve its space station Mir, launched in 1986 and expanded in 1987 with the docking of the Kvant astrophysics module. Major upgrades to the station will be provided by large building-block modules, one of which underwent ground tests in 1988 and was planned for launch in 1989. The module will contain the USSR's first manned maneuvering unit (MMU), which reportedly resembles the MMUs used with the U.S. shuttle fleet. The initial module and its MMU will be utilized as a service habitat and will be nearly double the size of Mir.

The manned Soyuz and the unmanned Progress vehicles, the main transport spacecraft for Mir, also have been upgraded and improved.

For Soyuz, the major changes enhance cosmonaut comfort and visibility. For Progress, modifications allow equipment, data, and samples from the space station to be recovered intact at Earth's surface.

The proposed U.S./international space station Freedom received congressional authorization for significant but only partial funding—$900 million, with a hold on $515 million of it until May 15, 1989. Pending approval by the George Bush administration, construction of Freedom would be the next major manned-spacecraft undertaking by NASA. The project will include an international research facility and a base for the service and repair of orbiting satellites.

Space Science. Eleven science experiments were carried on board STS-26, including a protein-crystal growth experiment for medical research. The crew, which carried out the experiments in the orbiter mid-deck, also took numerous photographs of Earth for later study. Among their targets were the Erta Ale volcano in Ethiopia; the Hurricane Gilbert-damaged eastern coast of Mexico; flood-ravaged Khartoum in the Sudan; and the drought-plagued Senegal River region of Africa. Astronaut Nelson further noted ". . . indescribable views [at night] coming over South America, where we have seen huge fires in the forest."

With the success of STS-26 and STS-27, an impressive array of major scientific missions awaited shuttle launch in 1989. Among them were the deployment of the planetary probe Magellan to make a detailed radar-mapping of Venus; deployment of the Galileo probe to study Jupiter's atmosphere, with a secondary-descent vehicle that will penetrate into Jupiter's clouds; and the deployment in low Earth orbit of the Hubble Space Telescope.

The USSR conducted several scientific experiments aboard Mir during the year. The physically and mentally degraded conditions of cosmonauts Yuri Romanenko and Alexander Alexandrov following their late 1987 return to Earth after a record 326 days in orbit (for Romanenko) raised serious questions about living in space for extended periods of time. Additional information on this critical question was provided by cosmonauts Titov and Manarov after their year in orbit.

The potentially exceptional scientific benefits from the mid-July Soviet launches of two ambitious, unmanned spacecraft—Phobos-1 and Phobos-2—to explore one or both of the two tiny moons of Mars, Phobos and Deimos (as well as Mars itself, the sun, and the interplanetary environment), were diminished somewhat in September by the loss of contact with Phobos-1, owing to an unfortunate human command error. Although the Phobos-1 mission was declared lost, Phobos-2 carries sophisticated instruments, data from which will be evaluated by scientists from the Soviet

Union, United States, and 11 participating European nations. Orbital experiments include chemical and physical analysis of the material at Phobos' surface. The spacecraft also is equipped with a lander, which will make *in situ* physical and chemical measurements of the soil or rock. Phobos-2 was expected to encounter the Martian moon early in 1989, but in December the Soviets reported that it, too, was having operational difficulties.

During the year, both the Soviet Union and United States advanced long-range plans for the establishment of manned or man-tended bases on the moon, Mars, or both. The two countries continued with ambitious plans for the intensive space-based study of Earth.

Applications Satellites. The March 17 launch of an Indian weather satellite, IRS-1A, on a Vostok rocket marked the first commercial launch provided by the Soviet Union. Later that month, the San Marco D/L international atmospheric research satellite was launched on a U.S. LTV Scout. In April the third Proton launch of the year carried Cosmos 1940, an atmospheric/oceanographic research satellite, into orbit for the USSR. The Soviets launched three Cosmos Earth-resource satellites during 1988 and, after its fifth Proton launch later in the year, successfully deployed Cosmos 1946, 1947, and 1948. That completed its Glonass system, a global satellite navigation network that has been offered for international civilian use with the U.S. Navstar system.

NOAA-11, an atmosphere/environment monitoring satellite of the TIROS group, was launched by a U.S. Atlas rocket from Vandenburg Air Force Base (CA) on September 24. The TIROS satellites are used extensively for global weather forecasting; NOAA-11 also carries special equipment for measuring changes in the protective ozone layer over the Earth's surface. Also in September, a Long March 4 rocket carried China's 23rd satellite, Feng Yan 1, a weather satellite, into orbit. This was the first launch from China's third launch site.

Communications Satellites. A year that marked the 25th anniversary of the launch of the first working satellite to achieve geosynchronous orbit also witnessed the first commercial rocket launch from a U.S. government facility, when E'Prime lifted off on November 15 from Titusville, FL. The March 21 launch of the GTE Spacenet 3R satellite on an Ariane 3 rocket marked the first launch of a U.S. domestic communications satellite in two years. Pan Am's PAS 1 telecommunications platform was one of three satellites deployed from the first Ariane 4 launch on June 15. The Ariane 3 launch on September 8 was the first specifically for a U.S. customer. On September 29 astronauts aboard *Discovery* deployed the TDRS-C satellite, replacing one lost in the *Challenger* explosion (TDRS-B). With another TDRS deployment by the shuttle planned for early 1989,

the Tracking and Data Relay Satellite System will be complete, providing a global communication system (voice, television, and digital and analog signals) for the shuttle and for other low-Earth-orbiting facilities such as the Hubble Space Telescope. The first commercial flight of Ariane 4, the largest rocket ever made in Europe, carried a communications satellite and a television satellite into orbit in December.

Both France and the Soviet Union launched domestic television broadcast satellites. The Soviets launched a second Ekran satellite on the fourth Proton mission of the year, and the French deployed TDF-1 on the seventh of eight Ariane launches in 1988. With eight operational launch vehicles at their disposal, the Soviets continued the increase in launch rates observed during 1987. From early September to the end of October the Soviet Union launched 14 new spacecraft, of which ten were military satellites. During the same period, two U.S. satellites were deployed, one by *Discovery* and one by the ESA on an Ariane 3 launch vehicle, and Japan launched a communications satellite while continuing development of its H-2 launcher program.

E. Julius Dasch, *NASA Headquarters*
Pat Jones, *National Space Society*

SPAIN

In 1988, Spain's attention was focused on events to take place in 1992, when the Iberian nation will become a full member of the European Community (EC). As Spain seeks to create an integrated free market, the nation is reaching out in other ways. In 1992, Barcelona will hold the Summer Olympic Games and Seville will hold a World Exhibition.

Politics and Government. On July 8, Prime Minister Felipe González reshuffled his cabinet —firing four ministers and naming six new ones (including two women)—at a time when the Socialist administration's popularity rating had fallen to its lowest point since 1982, when it came into power. Many of the government's troubles sprang from such intractable problems as crime, unemployment, and labor unrest.

In March foreign consuls told Spanish officials that they were concerned about the security for the upcoming Olympic Games and World Exhibition. In response, the interior ministry maintained that the high crime rate had peaked. From July 1987–88 there was a decrease of 3.64% in street assaults, and a decrease of 12.35% in major crimes—such as murders, rapes, and burglaries. Relations improved with the terrorist Basque Homeland and Liberty (ETA) separatist group early in 1988, when the government announced that it would open peace talks after a four-week truce.

Civil strife erupted on May 16 when state schoolteachers—who had been striking inter-

SPAIN · Information Highlights

Official Name: Spanish State.
Location: Iberian Peninsula in southwestern Europe.
Area: 194,884 sq mi (504 750 km²).
Population (mid-1988 est.): 39,000,000.
Chief Cities (1986 est.): Madrid, the capital, 3,217,461; Barcelona, 1,756,905; Valencia, 763,-949.
Government: *Head of state,* Juan Carlos I, king (took office Nov. 1975). *Head of government,* Felipe González Márquez, prime minister (took office Dec. 1982). *Legislature*—Cortés Generales: Senate and Congress of Deputies.
Monetary Unit: Peseta (114.95 pesetas equal U.S.$1, Nov. 14,1988).
Gross National Product (1987 est. U.S.$): $282,200,-000,000.
Economic Indexes (1987): *Consumer Prices* (1980 = 100), all items, 203.8; food, 207.1. *Industrial Production* (1980 = 100), 112.
Foreign Trade (1987 U.S.$): *Imports,* $49,004,-000,000; *exports,* $34,114,000,000.

mittently for two months—voted to reject Minister of Education José María Maravall's offer of a 5% pay increase, only one third of what they had demanded. The work stoppage continued for another month, and resulted in students being given general pass certificates instead of exams.

Economy. Prime Minister González agreed to resume talks, which were suspended in 1987, with the Socialist General Union of Workers (UGT) to discuss job creation, unemployment compensation, and investment. UGT leader Nicholas Redondo insisted that pay raises were just as important as creating jobs, while González placed a higher priority on fighting unemployment. July's cabinet reorganization suggested a policy shift as two former UGT officials were given portfolios, but Economics Minister Carlos Solchaga said that González's agenda remained in place.

On December 14, more than 7 million workers out of Spain's total work force of 10 million held a one-day strike—the nation's largest since 1934—to express their dissatisfaction with the government's economic policies.

Although Spain's economy grew more quickly (5.2%) than that of any other EC member in 1987, Spain had an unemployment rate of 19.8%, the highest in Western Europe, in August 1988. The labor ministry attributed the high rate to a growing number of women entering the work force. Meanwhile labor costs were among the lowest of the industrialized nations, averaging $6.47/hour in August. Inflation was only 1.2% for the first five months of 1988—indicating that the government could be within reach of its goal of 3.9% for the year. The gross domestic product grew an estimated 4.5% to $285 billion in 1987, as the trade deficit climbed to $11.4 billion from $7.8 billion.

A merger between the Banco de Bilbao and the Banco de Vizcaya—the third- and sixth-largest banks—created the nation's largest bank, the Banco Bilbao Vizcaya. González be-

lieves the consolidation will strengthen and prepare Spain for the challenges of 1992 when all restrictions will be removed on intra-EC capital movements. This tumbling of barriers will allow citizens of member countries to open accounts—as well as for banks to lend money—throughout the community. Currently, foreign banks could have only a limited number of branches.

Economics Minister Solchaga introduced a reform bill intended to modernize the bourses to prevent Spain's stock markets from being overwhelmed by foreigners in 1992. Brokers now would be excluded from the National Stock Exchange Commission. They also would lose their monopoly of bond and share transactions, and their cartel of fixed commissions. Foreign competition promises to be challenging: From 1989 on, any EC company would be allowed to buy up to 30% of a stock market firm; in 1991, up to 50%; and in 1992, non-EC companies as well will be able to buy into Spanish firms.

Foreign Affairs. In January, to precede part of a treaty to be signed in May, the United States and Spain formally announced that the United States would honor Spain's request to withdraw, within three years, the 72 F-16 fighter bombers based at the Torrejón Air Force base near Madrid. Spain insisted on this provision to fulfill the 1986 campaign referendum to reduce U.S. presence in Spain, which González promised in exchange for his country's pledge to remain a member of NATO. Madrid also refuses to place its armed forces under NATO command. Spain, though, has offered to play an active role elsewhere in the alliance. For instance, Spain has volunteered to take responsibility for the waters between the Balearic Islands in the western Mediterranean, and the Canaries in the Atlantic; moreover, Spain will allow supplies and reinforcements to pass through its territory in order to reach the front.

Foreign aid to Spain underwent a drastic change. While the United States gave Spain $108 million in fiscal 1988, the Reagan administration submitted to Congress a foreign-aid program for fiscal 1989 that cut it off entirely.

In February, Madrid decided to end its financial support of Equatorial Guinea, Spain's only former colony in Africa. While still sending humanitarian aid, Spain made arrangements for an otherwise complete break by relinquishing its 50% share in the national bank and paying $12 million in compensation.

The year 1992 also will mark the 500th anniversary of Christopher Columbus' journey to the New World. Preparations for the commemorations have emphasized Spain's cultural and historical heritage with Latin America—a unity of *Hispanidad* (Spanishness).

GEORGE W. GRAYSON
College of William and Mary

SPORTS

© Bill Eppridge/"Sports Illustrated"

In the legally disputed 1988 America's Cup, the U.S. catamaran "Stars & Stripes" (right) sped past "New Zealand."

Overview

Streaks. A player gets "hot," a team goes "on a roll." Records are broken, championships are won. So prevalent is the phenomenon in the world of sports that a Stanford University psychologist in 1988 published a report on the subject. The apparent conclusion of the study was that streaks are a myth. "Very often," said the psychologist, "the search for explanation in human affairs is a rejection of randomness." Whatever the scholarly credentials of this researcher, sports fans in 1988 could see that hot streaks are no myth. Whatever the explanation, several memorable developments in the 1988 sports year involved teams and players who were "in a groove," "peaking at the right time," and having success that went beyond the laws of randomness.

For the city of Los Angeles, having two championship teams was a case of sheer good fortune. The Lakers did not need to play "over their heads" to win their second straight National Basketball Association (NBA) title; they were the most talented team in the league and needed only to play to their potential. The Dodgers, however, were a classic case of a team "possessed." Despite injuries, they ousted the favored New York Mets in the National League play-offs, then defeated the favored Oakland A's in the World Series. The star down the stretch was ace right-hander Orel

Hershiser, who had one of the greatest hot streaks in major-league history. In his last six starts of the regular season, he had five shutouts (plus a scoreless ten-inning nondecision) and broke Don Drysdale's "unbreakable" record of 58 consecutive scoreless innings; Hershiser ended the season with 59. He added three more victories, two of them shutouts, in postseason play. Finally, in another stroke of luck for the City of Angels, hockey superstar Wayne Gretzky—whose entire career has been a hot streak—was traded from the Edmonton Oilers to the Los Angeles Kings.

On the pro golf tour, one veteran noticed that Scotsman Sandy Lyle was on a hot streak and predicted that he would win the Masters. With a perfect shot for a birdie on the last hole, Lyle earned the green jacket and made a forecasting wizard out of his fellow competitor. In college basketball, the University of Kansas Jayhawks barely made the NCAA tournament after losing 11 games during the regular season, then got hot and rolled—inevitably it seemed —to the championship.

But if 1988 was a year of streaks and peaks, for some it was a year of slumps. Baseball's Baltimore Orioles began the season with a record 21 straight losses. And Columbia University lost its 44th straight football game—an NCAA record—before winning one (against Princeton) in October. Perhaps the laws of randomness finally did catch up.

Auto Racing

The McLaren-Honda team of France's Alain Prost and Brazil's Ayrton Senna dominated the Formula One circuit in 1988, winning 15 of 16 races and finishing 1-2 in ten of them. Senna won the world championship with eight victories, a record on the world circuit. He started from the pole position 13 times.

Rick Mears of Bakersfield, CA, became only the eighth driver to win at least three Indianapolis 500s, accomplishing the feat on May 29 at age 36. In only his tenth race at the Indy Speedway, he took the checkered flag with an average speed of 144.809 mph (231.694 km/h). Mears' victory was the seventh overall, and fourth in the last five years, for cars owned by Roger Penske.

Danny Sullivan of Louisville, KY, drove another Penske car to the CART-PPG Indy Car championship, ending Bobby Rahal's two year reign. Sullivan posted four victories and started nine of 15 races from the pole.

Bill Elliott of Dawsonville, GA, won his first Winston Cup stock-car championship, ending a two-year streak by Dale Earnhardt. Elliott and Rusty Wallace each won six races, but Elliott edged out Wallace in points, 4,488 to 4,464. Stock-car racing's most prestigious event, the Daytona 500, saw 50-year-old Bobby Allison win for the third time in his career, beating his 26-year-old son, Davey, to the finish line by two car lengths. The elder Allison was injured critically in a race on June 19 at Long Pond, PA, when his car blew a tire and was struck broadside by another racer. He missed the remainder of the season while recuperating.

STAN SUTTON, *"Louisville Courier-Journal"*

AUTO RACING
Major Race Winners, 1988

Indianapolis 500: Rick Mears
Marlboro 500: Danny Sullivan
Quaker State 500: Bobby Rahal
Daytona 500: Bobby Allison

1988 Champions

World Championship: Ayrton Senna (Brazil)
CART: Danny Sullivan
NASCAR: Bill Elliott

Grand Prix for Formula One Cars, 1988

Brazilian: Alain Prost (France)
San Marino: Senna
Monaco: Prost
Mexico City: Prost
Canadian: Senna
Detroit: Senna
French: Prost
British: Senna
West German: Senna
Hungarian: Senna
Belgian: Senna
Italian: Gerhard Berger, Austria
Portuguese: Prost
Spanish: Prost
Japanese: Senna
Australian: Prost

Baseball

The success of the Los Angeles Dodgers during the 1988 major league baseball season was a classic example of an underdog repeatedly overcoming long odds to achieve its ultimate goal. Regrouped through clever trades and free-agent additions after successive 73-89 seasons—but ignoring key injuries—the Dodgers captured the National League (NL) Western Division crown, then upset heavily favored opponents in the League Championship and World Series.

Play-Offs and World Series. For the fourth consecutive year, the regular season produced new champions in all four divisions. With their pitching staff and overall team defense bolstered by off-season deals, Los Angeles finished with a 94-67 record, good for a seven-game margin over the Cincinnati Reds in the NL West. Dodger pitchers led the league with 32 complete games, 24 shutouts, and 49 saves. The club's 2.96 earned run average (ERA) was second only to the New York Mets' 2.91 among all major league teams.

With a 100-60 regular-season record, the Mets won the NL East title by 15 games over the second-place Pittsburgh Pirates. The Mets took first place on May 3 and stayed on top for the rest of the season.

Like the Mets, the Oakland Athletics relied on home run power and solid front-line pitching to coast to a division title, in the American League (AL) West. Oakland had an early 14-game winning streak, a 50-31 road record, 64 saves (a major league record), and 104 victories —marks no other team could match in 1988.

Only in the AL East was the title chase hotly contested. The Boston Red Sox finally won, finishing one game ahead of the Detroit Tigers. The Bosox were nine games behind at the All-Star break but won the division on the strength of a .283 team batting average and 813 runs scored (both tops in the major leagues), plus an airtight defense and a vastly improved bullpen. A 24-game home winning streak—an American League record—also helped. Boston's turnaround began on July 14, when Joe Morgan replaced John McNamara as manager. The team immediately began a 12-game winning streak.

By October, however, Boston was not winning much. Their slide continued in the American League Championship Series (ALCS), as the Athletics swept the best-of-seven match— 2-1, 4-3, 10-6, and 4-1. Slugging Oakland right-fielder Jose Canseco delivered three play-off homers and relief pitcher Dennis Eckersley, who was named most valuable player (MVP) of the series, had saves in all four games.

Though the Mets (10-1 against the Dodgers during the regular season) were favored heavily to win the NLCS, they did not bank on the tenacity of ace Los Angeles starter Orel Her-

Oakland slugger Jose Canseco won American League MVP honors. His 42 home runs and 124 RBIs were tops in the majors.

shiser. The Dodger right-hander made four appearances, including a 6-0 shutout in the finale, to win play-off MVP honors. Hershiser had a win, a save, and a 1.09 ERA in the NLCS.

The teams split the first two games, both played in Los Angeles: The Mets, with three runs in the ninth, won the opener, 3-2, but the Dodgers took a 6-3 decision the following day. New York won the third game, 8-4, by scoring five runs in the eighth inning after the ejection and two-game suspension of Dodger reliever Jay Howell, who was found to have pine tar in his glove.

With Howell unavailable in Game 4, Hershiser—who had worked seven innings the previous day—came on to retire slugger Kevin McReynolds with the bases loaded and two out in the 12th inning. A Kirk Gibson homer in the top of the inning had given Los Angeles its 5-4 margin of victory. Gibson homered again in Game 5, giving the Dodgers a 7-4 win, but the Mets knotted the series by taking a 5-1 decision in Game 6. That set the stage for Hershiser's seventh-game shutout.

The 30-year-old Dodger ace continued his heroics in the World Series. After Gibson's two-out, two-run, pinch-homer off Eckersley had given the Dodgers a dramatic 5-4 win in the opener, Hershiser hurled a three-hit, 6-0 shutout in Game 2. He also got three hits himself: two doubles and a single.

In Game 3, a ninth-inning homer by Oakland's Mark McGwire off Howell gave the Athletics a 2-1 win, but rookie Tim Belcher combined with Howell to take a 4-3 decision in Game 4. Hershiser's four-hitter gave the Dodgers a 5-2 win in the decisive fifth game, and the pitcher was named World Series MVP.

Oakland had been favored heavily but was unable to muster any muscle against Dodger pitching, compiling an anemic composite average of .177. The Dodgers were able to win without the services of Gibson, whose injured hamstring had restricted him to that one productive pinch-hitting appearance. Three other key performers, outfielder Mike Marshall, catcher Mike Scioscia, and starting pitcher John Tudor, also were idled by injuries incurred during the World Series.

Regular Season. A preseason adjustment that raised the level of the strike zone several inches may have been responsible for the sharp drop in offensive production from 1987 levels. Several insiders also claimed that the lively ball of 1987 had been "dejuiced." The composite batting average in the National League dropped from .261 to .248, and in the American League from .265 to .259. The total number of home runs in the two leagues fell off 29%, from a record 4,458 in 1987 to 3,180 in 1988.

Another example of the decline in batting, especially in the National League, was the near disappearance of the .300 hitter. Only five NL players reached that plateau, and Tony Gwynn of the San Diego Padres managed to win his third batting title with a .313 average—the lowest ever for an NL batting king. Darryl Strawberry of the Mets led the NL in home runs with 39 and was second in runs batted in (RBIs) with 101; San Francisco's Will Clark had 109. But the league's MVP award went to Kirk Gibson, who inspired the Dodgers all season long and hit .290 with 25 home runs and 76 RBIs. Vince Coleman led the NL in stolen bases with 81.

In the American League, where the batting drought was not so severe, Boston's Wade Boggs hit .366 to win his fourth straight batting title and fifth in six seasons. He also led both leagues with a .476 on-base percentage, 128 runs scored, and 45 doubles. Boggs became the

first player this century to collect at least 200 hits for six consecutive seasons. The league's MVP award went to Oakland's Canseco, who led the majors with 42 homers, 124 RBIs, and a .569 slugging percentage. He also became the first player ever to hit at least 40 home runs and steal at least 40 bases in the same season. Mike Greenwell of the Red Sox produced 23 game-winning hits, an AL record, while Minnesota's Kirby Puckett led the majors with 234 hits and batted .356, the best by an American League right-handed hitter since Joe DiMaggio's .357 in 1941. Rickey Henderson of the New York Yankees stole 93 bases to win his seventh stolen base crown.

Such feats paled, however, in comparison with the year's pitching performances. Cincinnati southpaw Tom Browning hurled a perfect game against Los Angeles on September 16, eight days before Montreal's Pascual Perez posted a 1-0 no-hit victory over Philadelphia in a game shortened to five innings by rain. Major league pitchers tossed a total of 20 one-hitters during the year. The number of shutouts skyrocketed from 212 in 1987 to 292 in 1988. And overall ERAs were way down in both leagues.

For consistent exellence, no one could match the Dodgers' Orel Hershiser. His 23 vic-

Dodger ace Orel Hershiser went 23-8 and pitched a record 59 consecutive scoreless innings to win NL Cy Young honors. He also was MVP of the play-offs and World Series.

tories tied Cincinnati's Danny Jackson for NL leadership, and he ended the season by pitching a record 59 consecutive scoreless innings. That performance, which can be extended in 1989, erased Don Drysdale's 1968 mark of 58⅔ innings (later officially set at 58). Hershiser won the NL Cy Young Memorial Award for pitching excellence, while Minnesota southpaw

BASEBALL

Professional—Major Leagues
Final Standings, 1988

AMERICAN LEAGUE

Eastern Division	W	L	Pct.	Western Division	W	L	Pct.
Boston	89	73	.549	Oakland	104	58	.642
Detroit	88	74	.543	Minnesota	91	71	.562
Milwaukee	87	75	.537	Kansas City	84	77	.522
Toronto	87	75	.537	California	75	87	.463
New York	85	76	.528	Chicago	71	90	.441
Cleveland	78	84	.481	Texas	70	91	.435
Baltimore	54	107	.335	Seattle	68	93	.422

NATIONAL LEAGUE

Eastern Division	W	L	Pct.	Western Division	W	L	Pct.
New York	100	60	.625	Los Angeles	94	67	.584
Pittsburgh	85	75	.531	Cincinnati	87	74	.540
Montreal	81	81	.500	San Diego	83	78	.516
Chicago	77	85	.475	San Francisco	83	79	.512
St. Louis	76	86	.469	Houston	82	80	.506
Philadelphia	65	96	.404	Atlanta	54	106	.338

Play-offs—American League: Oakland defeated Boston, 4 games to 0; National League: Los Angeles defeated New York, 4 games to 3.

World Series—Los Angeles defeated Oakland, 4 games to 1. First Game (Dodger Stadium, Los Angeles, Oct. 15, attendance 55,983): Los Angeles 5, Oakland 4; Second Game (Dodger Stadium, Oct. 16, attendance 56,051): Los Angeles 6, Oakland 0; Third Game (Oakland Coliseum, Oakland, Oct. 18, attendance 49,316): Oakland 2, Los Angeles 1; Fourth Game (Oakland Coliseum, Oct. 19, attendance 49,317): Los Angeles 4, Oakland 3; Fifth Game (Oakland Coliseum, Oct. 20, attendance 49,317): Los Angeles 5, Oakland 2.

All-Star Game (Riverfront Stadium, Cincinnati, July 12, attendance 55,837): American League 2, National League 1.

Most Valuable Players—American League: Jose Canseco, Oakland; National League: Kirk Gibson, Los Angeles.

Cy Young Memorial Awards (outstanding pitchers)—American League: Frank Viola, Minnesota; National League: Orel Hershiser, Los Angeles.

Managers of the Year—American League: Tony LaRussa, Oakland; National League: Tommy Lasorda, Los Angeles.

Rookies of the Year—American League: Walt Weiss, Oakland; National League: Chris Sabo, Cincinnati.

Leading Hitters—(Percentage) American League: Wade Boggs, Boston, .366; National League: Tony Gwynn, San Diego, .313. (Runs Batted In) American League: Jose Canseco, Oakland, 124; National League: Will Clark, San Francisco, 109. (Home Runs) American League: Canseco, 42; National League: Darryl Strawberry, New York, 39. (Hits) American League: Kirby Puckett, Minnesota, 234; National League: Andres Galarraga, Montreal, 184. (Runs) American League: Boggs, 128; National League: Brett Butler, San Francisco, 109.

Leading Pitchers—(Earned Run Average) American League: Allan Anderson, Minnesota, 2.45; National League: Joe Magrane, St. Louis, 2.18. (Victories) American League: Frank Viola, Minnesota, 24; National League: tie, Orel Hershiser, Los Angeles, and Danny Jackson, Cincinnati, 23. (Strikeouts) American League: Roger Clemens, Boston, 291; National League: Nolan Ryan, Houston, 228. (Shutouts) American League: Clemens, 8; National League: Hershiser, 8. (Saves) American League: Dennis Eckersley, Oakland, 45; National League: John Franco, Cincinnati, 39.

Professional—Minor Leagues, Class AAA
American Association: Indianapolis
International League: Rochester
Pacific Coast League: Las Vegas

Amateur
NCAA: Stanford
Little League World Series: Tai Chung, Taiwan

Frank Viola received the AL citation. Viola, whose 24 wins led both leagues, outdistanced Oakland reliever Dennis Eckersley, who saved 45 games (one short of Dave Righetti's record). Other 20-game winners of 1988 included Dave Stewart of Oakland, Mark Gubicza of Kansas City, and David Cone of the New York Mets.

Boston's Roger Clemens failed in his bid for an unprecedented third straight Cy Young Award, but he did throw eight shutouts, tying Hershiser for the big-league lead, and strike out 291 hitters, tops in the game. Nolan Ryan of the Houston Astros won his ninth strikeout title by leading the NL with 228 whiffs at age 41 and increased his career record to 4,775. The ERA leaders were Joe Magrane of the St. Louis Cardinals (2.18) and Allan Anderson of the Minnesota Twins (2.45). Cincinnati southpaw John Franco led the NL with 39 saves.

The game's pitchers feasted on two last-place clubs, the Baltimore Orioles and Atlanta Braves, both of whom opened the season with record losing streaks and went on to lose more than 100 times. Baltimore lost its first 21 games, a major-league mark, while Atlanta lost its first ten, a modern NL record.

Though strong pitching posed yearlong problems for hitters, pitchers had difficulties of their own. Strict enforcement of the balk rule —requiring a pitcher to come to a discernible stop before releasing the ball while working from the stretch position—caused such controversy that umpires were ordered at midseason to be more lenient. By year's end, AL pitchers had yielded 558 balks and NL pitchers 366—up from 1987 totals of 137 and 219, respectively.

Superb relief by five AL pitchers enabled the Americans to take a 2-1 decision in the July 12 All-Star Game at Cincinnati's Riverfront Stadium. Oakland's Terry Steinbach, who knocked in both AL runs with a homer and sacrifice fly, was named All-Star MVP.

Other Highlights. Retired slugger Willie Stargell of the Pittsburgh Pirates was inducted into the Baseball Hall of Fame on July 31.

The Cubs hosted the Phillies in an August 8 night game, the first at Chicago's Wrigley Field, which had been without lights since its opening in 1914. The game was rained out in the fourth inning, however, and the first official night contest at Wrigley was held the next night against the Mets. (*See also* CHICAGO.)

On September 8, team owners elected NL President A. Bartlett Giamatti to succeed Peter V. Ueberroth as commissioner of baseball, effective April 1. Giamatti had enforced his reputation as a disciplinarian with a 30-day suspension of Cincinnati manager Pete Rose for shoving umpire Dave Pallone on April 30. One of the new commissioner's first tasks would be the preservation of peace between players and owners, whose Basic Agreement expires after the 1989 campaign.

DAN SCHLOSSBERG, *Baseball Writer*

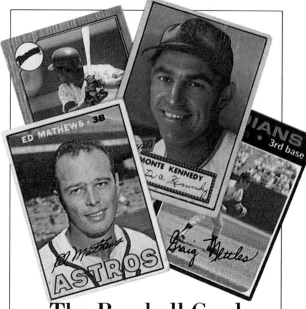

The Baseball Card Boom

Baseball cards are as American as apple pie and the national pastime, and they've been around almost as long as the game itself. Kids buy new cards for pennies, while collectors may pay hundreds or even thousands of dollars for older ones. According to one estimate, the sale of new baseball cards reached $750 million in 1987, more than double the amount spent on tickets for major-league games. Meantime, the trade in old and rare cards also has reached several hundred million dollars annually, making baseball cards a $1 billion-a-year industry.

Initially distributed in cigarette packages, the first baseball trading cards were issued during the 1880s. Today, as any 10-year-old collector could tell you, they come in packs of 15-17, with a piece of pink bubble gum, stickers, puzzles, or other items. The four major producers—Topps, Donruss, Fleer, and Sportflics—have been meeting the rise in demand by doubling their output almost every year. With the introduction of a fifth line, called Score, in 1988, total annual production was expected to reach 5 billion cards.

For collectors and investors, old and rare baseball cards have emerged as a highly lucrative market—especially since the 1987 stock market crash. Following that crash, analysts say that many investors turned to collectibles, including baseball cards, rather than stocks. During the first four months of 1988 alone, prices of such cards leaped more than 40%.

The most valuable card on the market today is the rare 1909 Honus Wagner, listed at $36,000. Among post-World War II issues, the major interest of most collectors, the prime quest is the 1952 Topps Mickey Mantle, valued at nearly $6,000. Generally, rookie cards, or first cards, of superstars are much in demand.

Basketball

The Los Angeles Lakers made basketball history in 1988 by becoming the first team in 19 years to repeat as champions of the National Basketball Association (NBA). The Lakers won the title by overcoming a difficult challenge from the Detroit Pistons in the final round of the play-offs, winning four games to three. It was the Lakers' fifth title during the 1980s and their third in four seasons.

The unsung Kansas Jayhawks overcame a season-long series of problems to register a stunning upset in the championship game of the National Collegiate Athletic Association (NCAA) men's tournament. In the title game, the Jayhawks defeated the Oklahoma Sooners, 83-79. The Connecticut Huskies won the National Invitation Tournament (NIT), and Louisiana Tech captured the women's NCAA title.

The Professional Season

The Lakers and Boston Celtics, the dominant teams in the NBA during the 1980s, once again compiled the best regular-season records in the league. Los Angeles posted the top mark, 62-20, setting an NBA record by winning at least 60 games for the fourth straight season. Boston finished with a record of 57-25. Both teams won their division championships, with the Celtics finishing 19 games ahead of the Washington Bullets and New York Knicks in the Atlantic, and the Lakers ending nine games ahead of the fast-closing Portland Trail Blazers in the Pacific.

Detroit and the Atlanta Hawks had a close race in the Central Division, but the Pistons pulled away in the final days to win the team's first title of any kind since the franchise moved from Ft. Wayne, IN, 31 years before. The Denver Nuggets were one of the league's surprise teams. Despite the lack of a dominant center, the Nuggets won the Midwest Divison, fighting off strong challenges from the favored Dallas Mavericks and improved Utah Jazz. One of the most disappointing teams was the Houston Rockets, which traded 7'4" (2.24-m) star forward-center Ralph Sampson to the Golden State Warriors during the season and finished fourth in the Midwest Division.

The most exciting—and best—player in the league was Chicago Bulls star Michael Jordan. The NBA's leading gate attraction, Jordan won his second straight scoring title, averaging 35.0 points per game to 30.7 for Atlanta Hawks forward Dominique Wilkins. Jordan was selected as the league's most valuable player (MVP) as well as its top defensive player, the first time anyone has won both honors in the same year. Just as important, Jordan was responsible in large part for the improvement in the Bulls, who added some young players and finished with a 50-32 record.

Jordan was named to the NBA all-star team, as were Earvin "Magic" Johnson of Los Angeles, Larry Bird of Boston, Akeem Olajuwon of Houston, and Charles Barkley of Philadelphia. Some new faces made the second team, including guards John Stockton of Utah and Clyde Drexler of Portland, plus New York center Patrick Ewing. Michael Cage of the lowly Los Angeles Clippers won the rebounding title, barely nosing out Charles Oakley of

PROFESSIONAL BASKETBALL

National Basketball Association
(Final Standings, 1987–88)

Eastern Conference

Atlantic Division	W	L	Pct.
*Boston	57	25	.695
*Washington	38	44	.463
*New York	38	44	.463
Philadelphia	36	46	.439
New Jersey	19	63	.232
Central Division			
*Detroit	54	28	.659
*Chicago	50	32	.610
*Atlanta	50	32	.610
*Milwaukee	42	40	.512
*Cleveland	42	40	.512
Indiana	38	44	.463

Western Conference

Midwest Division	W	L	Pct.
*Denver	54	28	.659
*Dallas	53	29	.646
*Utah	47	35	.573
*Houston	46	36	.561
*San Antonio	31	51	.378
Sacramento	24	58	.293
Pacific Division			
*L.A. Lakers	62	20	.756
*Portland	53	29	.646
*Seattle	44	38	.537
Phoenix	28	54	.341
Golden State	20	62	.244
L.A. Clippers	17	65	.207

*Made play-offs

Play-Offs
Eastern Conference

First Round	Atlanta	3 games	Milwaukee	2
	Boston	3 games	New York	1
	Chicago	3 games	Cleveland	2
	Detroit	3 games	Washington	2
Second Round	Boston	4 games	Atlanta	3
	Detroit	4 games	Chicago	1
Finals	Detroit	4 games	Boston	2

Western Conference

First Round	Dallas	3 games	Houston	1
	Denver	3 games	Seattle	2
	L.A. Lakers	3 games	San Antonio	0
	Utah	3 games	Portland	1
Second Round	Dallas	4 games	Danver	2
	L.A. Lakers	4 games	Utah	3
Finals	L.A. Lakers	4 games	Dallas	3
Championship	L.A. Lakers	4 games	Detroit	3
All-Star Game	East 139, West 133			

Individual Honors

Most Valuable Player: Michael Jordan, Chicago
Most Valuable Player (play-offs): James Worthy, L.A. Lakers
Most Valuable Player (all-star game): Michael Jordan
Rookie of the Year: Mark Jackson, New York
Coach of the Year: Doug Moe, Denver
Leading Scorer: Michael Jordan, Chicago, 35.0 points per game
Leader in Assists: John Stockton, Utah, 13.8 per game
Leading Rebounder: Michael Cage, Los Angeles Clippers, 13.03 per game
Leader in Field Goal Percentage: Kevin McHale, Boston, .604

The Los Angeles Lakers won their second straight NBA crown, defeating the Detroit Pistons in a rugged, seven-game championship series. Laker forward James Worthy (42) had 36 points and 16 rebounds in Game 7 and was named MVP of the play-offs.

Focus on Sports

Chicago, 13.03 to 13.00 per game. Stockton took the assist title (13.8 per game), handing out a league record 1,128. Boston guard Danny Ainge set a record by making 148 three-point goals. His teammate, Kevin McHale, was the top shooter, 60.4%.

The NBA once again set a new attendance record, with 12.65 million fans passing through the turnstiles. The 23 teams averaged 13,419 fans per game, and Detroit became the first franchise in league history to exceed one million (1,066,505) in home attendance for one season. The league and players' association agreed to a new collective bargaining agreement, avoiding a strike. And the NBA continued plans to expand in 1988-89 by adding teams in Miami and Charlotte, NC.

Play-Offs. Los Angeles, which already had won four titles during the 1980s, and Boston, which had won three, once again were favored to meet in the championship round of the play-offs. Both survived early scares. The Lakers needed seven games to eliminate Utah in the Western Conference semifinals, while Boston also needed seven games to beat Atlanta in the Eastern Conference semifinals. In the conference finals, the Lakers overcame a strong challenge from Dallas, finally winning Game 7, 117-102, as Magic Johnson had 24 points and 11 assists. But the Celtics were not so fortunate. In the Eastern Conference finals, Detroit used superior depth and defense to score a major upset. The Pistons grabbed an early advantage by winning in the Boston Garden for the first time in 21 games. Detroit wrapped up the series by taking Game 6, 95-90, in their home arena, the Silverdome.

That set up a championship-series pairing of the Lakers and Pistons. Detroit was playing for its first NBA title, while the Lakers were trying to become the first team in 19 years to win back-to-back league crowns. Detroit immediately took away the Lakers' home-court advantage by winning Game 1 in Los Angeles, 105-93, behind an impressive defense and 34 points from forward Adrian Dantley. The Lakers came back to win Game 2, 108-96, pulling away in the final minutes behind the playmaking of Magic Johnson.

The series then moved to Detroit, where the Lakers regained the home-court advantage with a 99-86 triumph in the Silverdome. Magic Johnson, who grew up near Detroit, celebrated his homecoming with 18 points and 14 assists, while forward James Worthy had 24 points and 9 rebounds. Detroit evened the series with a 111-86 victory in Game 4, the most physical so far. The Pistons got 27 points from Dantley and 12 assists from guard Isiah Thomas, who was playing with a bad back. In Game 5, a crowd of 41,732 poured into the Silverdome, setting an NBA play-off record. The Pistons rewarded

their fans with a 104-94 triumph, embarrassing the Lakers with a superior bench and another big game from Dantley, who had 25 points.

With Detroit leading the series three games to two, the teams returned to Los Angeles for the final two contests. The Pistons, with Thomas scoring a final-round-record 25 points in the third quarter, were leading Game 6 until the final seconds, when 41-year-old Laker center Kareem Abdul-Jabbar made two foul shots to secure a 103-102 win for Los Angeles. Thomas finished the game with 43 points despite a badly sprained ankle, while Worthy had 28 points and 9 rebounds for the Lakers. That set up Game 7, which the Lakers won by holding off late-charging Detroit, 108-105. Worthy played a sensational game, finishing with 36 points and 16 rebounds, and was named playoff MVP. Thomas tried to play on his bad ankle and limped badly throughout the game. Besides repeating as champions, the Lakers became the first NBA team to win three seven-game playoff series in the same year.

The College Season

The 1987-88 regular season in college basketball was dominated by four powerful teams: Temple, Arizona, Oklahoma, and Purdue. Temple's program, which had been rebuilt by coach John Chaney, had grown so powerful that the Owls were ranked Number 1 for much of the final part of the season, finishing with a record of 29-1. But Arizona (31-2), which had been rated Number 1 earlier in the campaign, was considered just as good, while Purdue (27-3) and Oklahoma (30-3)) also were viable contenders for the national title by the time the NCAA tournament began in March.

Indeed there was so much parity among college teams that any of more than a dozen other schools seemed good enough to win the championship. Among these were Pittsburgh (23-6), North Carolina State (24-7), Duke (24-6), Syracuse (25-8), Michigan (24-7), North Carolina (24-6), Kentucky (25-5), Illinois (22-9), Kansas State (22-8), Indiana (19-9), Nevada-Las Vegas (27-5), Loyola, California (27-3), and Brigham Young (25-5). Before the start of the season, Kansas also was rated high, mainly because of the presence of forward Danny Manning, a favorite to win player-of-the-year honors. But the Jayhawks suffered a series of injuries and academic ineligibilities and quickly fell from the national rankings. They finished the regular season with a record of 21-11 and were one of the last teams selected to play in the NCAA tournament, yet they went on to win the national championship with a stunning upset of Oklahoma. The strongest conferences were the Big Eight, Big Ten, and, to a lesser degree, the Atlantic Coast. The Big East, which had been dominant in years past, was not as strong this season.

Among individual players, Manning, who almost had passed up his senior season to join the NBA, and guard Hersey Hawkins of Bradley, the nation's leading scorer, split the major player-of-the-year awards. Hawkins was a standout in the regular season, averaging 36.3 points per game, while Manning was the dominant player in the postseason tournament. Other quality players included Arizona forward Sean Elliott, DePaul guard Rod Strickland, Duke forward Danny Ferry, Kansas State forward Mitch Richmond, Michigan guard Gary Grant, Oklahoma forward Stacey King and center Harvey Grant, North Carolina forward J.R. Reed, La Salle forward Lionel Simmons, Temple guard Mark Macon and forward Tim

Kansas forward Danny Manning had a dream season, leading his team to the NCAA title with 31 points in the final against Oklahoma and earning Player of the Year honors.

Focus on Sports

Perry, Pittsburgh center Charles Smith, Kentucky guard Rex Chapman, and Notre Dame guard David Rivers.

Tournaments. Temple, the nation's Number 1 team entering the NCAA tournament, was seeded first in the East region, while the other top-seeded squads were Purdue (Midwest), Arizona (West), and Oklahoma (Southeast). Neither Temple nor Purdue advanced to the Final Four. The Owls were upset by Duke in the East final, 63-53, and Purdue fell to Kansas State in the third round, 73-70. Arizona and Oklahoma, however, did make it all the way through the regionals. Arizona easily beat North Carolina in the West final, 70-52, while Oklahoma defeated underdog Villanova in the Southeast final, 78-59. During the early stages of the tournament, upsets were recorded by Vanderbilt (over Utah State and Pittsburgh), Murray State (over North Carolina State), and Villanova (over Illinois and Kentucky).

This was the 50th anniversary of the Final Four, held in Kansas City. In the opening game of the semifinals, heavily favored Duke, the champions of the Atlantic Coast Conference, played Kansas. Manning had an impressive game, scoring 25 points, and was supported by forward Milt Newton, who had 20. The Jayhawks' defense held the Blue Demons to just 34% shooting and won, 66-59. In the other Final Four semifinal game, considered by many the unofficial national title matchup, Oklahoma's fast break proved too strong for Arizona. The Sooners got 21 points each from Grant and King, forced Arizona to commit 15 turnovers, and registered an 86-78 victory.

That set up an all Big Eight final between Oklahoma, which won both the regular-season and tournament titles in the conference, and Kansas, considered to be the fourth-best team in the Big Eight. Oklahoma already had beaten Kansas twice during the regular season and was favored to win the title game with its high-powered, nonstop offense. The Sooners were the highest-scoring team—averaging 104 points per game—ever to reach the NCAA finals.

But Kansas in general and Manning in particular played a superb game, refusing to be intimidated by their opponents' superior talent. Surprisingly, the Jayhawks decided to run with the Sooners and were able to neutralize their quickness. Manning was dominant, scoring 31 points—including four key free throws in the final 14 seconds—and pulling in 18 rebounds; he also had five steals and two blocked shots. The 6'11" (2.1-m) senior forward was named the tournament's MVP. Just as impressive was the Kansas defense, marvelously coached by Larry Brown. Oklahoma made just 43% of its shots and rarely was able to run its fast break in the second half. Kansas handled the ball so well that the Sooners' full-court press proved ineffective. Kansas finally won, 83-79, despite 22 points from Oklahoma's Dave Sieger—who

COLLEGE BASKETBALL

Conference Champions*

Association of Mid-Continent: Southwest Missouri State
Atlantic Coast: Duke
Atlantic-10: Temple
Big East: Syracuse
Big Eight: Oklahoma
Big Sky: Boise State
Big Ten: Purdue
Colonial Athletic: Richmond
East Coast: Lehigh
ECAC Metro: Fairleigh Dickinson
ECAC North Atlantic: Boston University
Ivy League: Cornell
Metro Athletic: Louisville
Metro Atlantic Athletic: LaSalle
Mid-American: Eastern Michigan
Mid-Eastern Athletic: North Carolina A&T
Midwestern Collegiate: Xavier
Missouri Valley: Bradley
Ohio Valley: Murray State
Pacific Coast Athletic: Utah State
Pacific-10: Arizona
Southeastern: Kentucky
Southern: Tennessee-Chattanooga
Southland: North Texas State
Southwest: SMU
Southwestern Athletic: Southern U.
Sun Belt: North Carolina, Charlotte
Trans America Athletic: Texas-San Antonio
West Coast Athletic: Loyola, California
Western Athletic: Wyoming
  * Based on postseason conference
    tournaments, where applicable

Tournaments

NCAA: Kansas
NIT: Connecticut
NCAA Div. II: Lowell
NCAA Div. III: Ohio Wesleyan
NAIA: Grand Canyon
NCAA (women's): Louisiana Tech

set a title-game record with seven three-point goals—and 17 from Stacey King.

In the finals of the NIT in New York City's Madison Square Garden, the Connecticut Huskies, who finished last in the Big East, defeated Ohio State, 72-67. Phil Gamble, who was named the tournament's MVP, scored 25 points, with teammate Tate George contributing 14 points and 10 assists.

In the women's NCAA tournament, Louisiana Tech defeated Auburn, 56-54, to win its second national title. The Lady Techsters won the first women's NCAA championship in 1982 and were runners-up in 1983 and 1987. In the 1988 title contest, held in Tacoma, WA, Tech trailed by as many as 14 points in the second half before rallying for the victory. Erica Westbrooks was the outstanding player, scoring 25 points, getting 7 rebounds, and giving out 6 assists. Guard Teresa Weatherspoon contributed 8 assists and played a key role in the Lady Techsters' comeback. Leon Barmore became the first male coach ever to win a national collegiate women's title. Louisiana Tech had reached the finals with a 68-59 victory over Tennessee, avenging its final-round loss to Tennessee in 1987. Auburn advanced to the championship contest by defeating Long Beach State, 68-55.

PAUL ATTNER
National Correspondent
"The Sporting News"

Boxing

The year's big attractions in boxing involved two of the sports most popular figures, Mike Tyson and Sugar Ray Leonard.

Tyson, the 21-year-old undisputed heavyweight champion, took center stage both in and out of the ring. On June 27 in Atlantic City, NJ, he faced former champion Michael Spinks in a title bout whose media ballyhoo, television revenue, and purses were unrivaled in the history of the sport. The 31-year-old Spinks entered the ring with a perfect 31-0 career record, but Tyson launched a furious opening barrage that knocked out Spinks in just 91 seconds, making it the fourth-shortest heavyweight title bout on record. Tyson, who ran his career record to 35-0, with 31 knockouts, earned $22 million for his efforts. Spinks ended his career with a $13.5 million payday. Including all the ancillary revenue, the bout grossed more than $60 million.

The Spinks fight was Tyson's third title defense of the year. In January at Atlantic City, he stopped 38-year-old former champion Larry Holmes with three knockdowns in the fourth round. Then in March he gave Japanese fans a view of his prowess with a second-round knockout of Tony Tubbs in Tokyo.

After the Spinks fight, virtually all of Tyson's personal and business affairs were magnified by unrelenting media coverage. Much of it centered on the actress Robin Givens, whom Tyson had married in February. Eight months later, after much public name-calling and accusations back and forth, they sued each other for divorce. Givens also sued him for libel, and the champ had more legal troubles involving his promoter and his manager. In August he injured his right hand in an early morning street brawl with a fighter he already had beaten in the ring. On and on it went, making Tyson one of the most publicized champions in history.

Leonard, who had returned to the ring after a three-year absence in April 1987 to take the World Boxing Council (WBC) middleweight title from Marvelous Marvin Hagler and then retired for the fourth time, returned to the ring on Nov. 7, 1988, at Las Vegas, NV. His opponent was Canada's Donny Lalonde, with two titles on the line—the WBC's light heavyweight crown and its newly created super middleweight crown. Leonard won both championships with a ninth-round knockout, but it was not easy. In the fourth round, Leonard was knocked to the canvas for only the second time in his career and had to call on all his experience to get out of trouble. The victory made him the first fighter to win titles in five weight classes. Previously he had held the welterweight, junior middleweight, and middleweight titles. (Leonard relinquished his two new crowns shortly after the bout.)

The middleweight division was very active in 1988. Iran Barkley of New York scored an upset third-round knockout against Thomas Hearns to take the WBC title in June, and challenger Michael Nunn stopped Frank Tate in the ninth round to take the International Boxing Federation (IBF) title in July. Meanwhile, WBA champion Sumbu Kalambay of Zaire and Italy made three successful defenses during the year, unanimous decisions over Mike McCallum in March and Robbie Sims in June, and a knockout of Doug DeWitt in November.

In the welterweight division, Lloyd Honeyghan of Britain regained the WBC crown he lost to Mexico's Jorge Vaca in 1987 when he stopped Vaca in the third round of their March title bout. Honeyghan retained the crown against Yung Kil Chung of South Korea in July, when the challenger received a low blow in the fifth round and could not continue.

In the lightweight division, Julio Cesar Chavez of Mexico unified the WBC and World Boxing Association (WBA) titles by gaining a unanimous decision over WBC champion José Luís Ramirez at Las Vegas in October. The bout was stopped in the 11th round after Ramirez suffered a head butt and could not continue. Chavez, who was ahead on all the judges' scorecards, was declared the winner. Greg Haugen regained the IBF crown from the popular Vinnie Pazienza in February.

GEORGE DEGREGORIO
"The New York Times"

World Boxing Champions*

Heavyweight: World Boxing Council (WBC)—Mike Tyson, United States, 1986; World Boxing Association (WBA)—Tyson, 1987; International Boxing Federation (IBF)—Tyson, 1987.

Cruiserweight: WBC—vacant; WBA—vacant; IBF—vacant.

Light Heavyweight: WBC—vacant; WBA—Virgil Hill, United States, 1987; IBF—Charles Williams, United States, 1987.

Super Middleweight: WBC—vacant; WBA—Fulgencio Obelmejias, Venezuela, 1988; IBF—Graciano Rocchigiani, West Germany, 1988.

Middleweight: WBC—Iran Barkley, United States, 1988; WBA—Sumbu Kalambay, Zaire and Italy, 1987; IBF—Michael Nunn, United States, 1988.

Junior Middleweight (Super Welterweight): WBC—Donald Curry, United States, 1988; WBA—Julian Jackson, Virgin Islands, 1987; IBF—Robert Hines, United States, 1988.

Welterweight: WBC—Lloyd Honeyghan, Britain, 1988; WBA—vacant; IBF—Simon Brown, Jamaica, 1988.

Junior Welterweight (Super Lightweight): WBC—Roger Mayweather, United States, 1987; WBA—Juan Martin Coggi, Argentina, 1987; IBF—Meldrick Taylor, United States, 1988.

Lightweight: WBC—Julio Cesar Chávez, Mexico, 1988; WBA—Chávez, 1987; IBF—Greg Haugen, United States, 1988.

Junior Lightweight (Super Featherweight): WBC—Azumah Nelson, Ghana, 1988; WBA—Brian Mitchell, South Africa, 1986; IBF—Tony Lopez, United States, 1988.

Featherweight: WBC—Jeff Fenech, Australia, 1988; WBA—Antonio Esparragoza, Venezuela, 1987; IBF—Jorge Paez, Mexico, 1988.

Junior Featherweight (Super Bantamweight): WBC—Daniel Zaragoza, Mexico, 1988; WBA—Juan José Estrada, Mexico, 1988; IBF—José Sanabria, United States, 1988.

Bantamweight: WBC—Raul Perez, Mexico, 1988; WBA—Sung Kil Moon, South Korea, 1988; IBF—Orlando Canizales, United States, 1988.

Junior Bantamweight (Super Flyweight): WBC—Gilberto Roman, Mexico, 1988; WBA—Kaosai Galaxy, Thailand, 1984; IBF—Ellyas Pical, Colombia, 1985.

Flyweight: WBC—Kim Yong Gang, South Korea, 1988; WBA—Fidel Bassa, Colombia, 1988; IBF—Duke McKenzie, Britain, 1988.

Junior Flyweight: WBC—Jerman Torres, Mexico, 1988; WBA—Yoo Myong-Woo, South Korea, 1985; IBF—Tacy Macalos, South Korea, 1988.

Strawweight: WBC—Hiroki Ioka, Japan, 1987; WBA—Leo Gamez, Venezuela, 1988; IBF—Samuth Sithnarelpol, Thailand, 1988.

*As of Dec 31, 1988; date indicates year title was won.

Football

For the National Football League (NFL), the 1988–89 season was one of parity, change, and unpredictability. For the first time ever, neither team from the previous year's Super Bowl was able to make the play-offs, as the Washington Redskins and Denver Broncos both fell to mediocrity (finishing 7-9 and 8-8, respectively, in the regular season). The Cincinnati Bengals (12-4), Buffalo Bills (12-4), Chicago Bears (12-4), and Minnesota Vikings (11-5) each seemed dominant at various times during the season, but no one emerged clearly as "the team to beat."

Super Bowl XXIII, played at Miami's new Joe Robbie Stadium on Jan. 22, 1989, wound up as a rematch of the 1982 contest, with the Bengals of the American Football Conference (AFC) seeking revenge against the San Francisco 49ers (10-6) of the National Football Conference (NFC). In an unusually exciting Super Bowl game, the favored 49ers defeated the Bengals, 20–16, for their third title in the 1980s. The winning touchdown came on a 10-yard pass from Joe Montana to John Taylor with 34 seconds remaining. San Francisco wide receiver Jerry Rice, who had 11 receptions for a Super Bowl record of 215 yards, was voted the game's most valuable player.

In college competition, the Fighting Irish of Notre Dame, behind coach Lou Holtz, completed an undefeated (12-0) season and laid claim to the school's 14th national championship with a 34-21 victory over West Virginia (11-1) in the Fiesta Bowl. Oklahoma State's junior tailback Barry Sanders, who set National Collegiate Athletic Association (NCAA) single-season records with 2,628 rushing yards and 39 touchdowns, won the Heisman Trophy as the year's top college player.

The Canadian Football League (CFL) continued to suffer financial difficulties, as several of the league's eight teams reportedly lost money in 1988. The 76th Grey Cup game—for the CFL championship—saw the Winnipeg Blue Bombers upset the British Columbia Lions, 22-21, on a fourth-quarter field goal by Trevor Kennerd, his fourth of the game. The Bombers, who had finished second in the Eastern Division with a 9-9 regular-season record, beat the Toronto Argonauts in the Eastern play-off finals and the Hamilton Tiger-Cats in the Grey Cup semifinals.

The six-team Arena Football League completed its second season of indoor, summertime competition, with the Detroit Drive defeating the Chicago Bruisers, 24-13, in the title game.

National Football League

Not in eight years had any team managed to repeat as Super Bowl champion, and it soon became clear that the skein would run to nine, as Redskins quarterback Doug Williams—the

Final college rankings came down to Bowl Day, but the key game was played on October 15 in South Bend. Notre Dame beat Miami, 31–30, en route to a 12–0 season and a national championship; Miami (11–1) wound up Number 2.

© Jonathan Daniel/Allsport USA

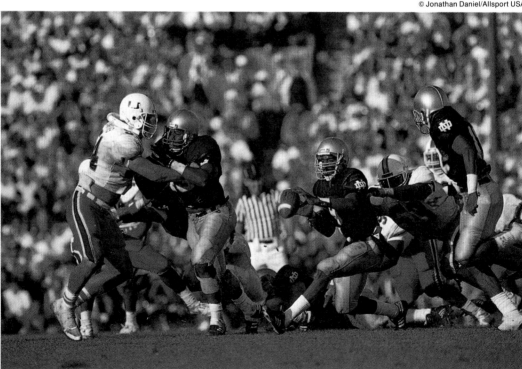

hero of Super Bowl XXII—was sidelined by injury and his team struggled. In Denver, both the explosive offense and hard-nosed defense that had carried the Broncos to the AFC title in 1986–87 and 1987–88 collapsed, and the team failed to qualify for postseason play. Perhaps most surprising and most indicative of change in 1988–89 was the lack of success by three of the game's most respected coaches: Tom Landry of the Dallas Cowboys (3-13), Chuck Noll of the Pittsburgh Steelers (5-11), and Don Shula of the Miami Dolphins (6-10).

The play-off qualifiers in both conferences included several up-and-coming teams with little postseason experience, as well as some perennial powers. In a regular season that saw countless injuries to quarterbacks, the teams that did the best generally were the ones whose first-string signal callers missed the fewest games. In the AFC, the most notable upstarts were the Bills, whose QB Jim Kelly guided them to the Eastern Division crown and their first play-off appearance since 1981 (first at home since the 1960s); and the Bengals, whose QB Boomer Esiason was the NFL's player of the year, sparked the league's highest-scoring offense (448 points), and led his team's rise from last place to first in the Central Division. The remaining AFC play-off berths went to the Western Division champion Seattle Seahawks (9-7) and the wild-card Cleveland Browns (10-6) and Houston Oilers (10-6).

In the NFC, the long-dormant Philadelphia Eagles (10-6) rose to the top of the Eastern Division behind the run-and-gun quarterbacking of Randall Cunningham. The 49ers used their own double-barreled offense—the aerial strikes of Joe Montana to Jerry Rice and the ground attack of Roger Craig—to take the Western Division crown. The Bears were the exception to the quarterback rule, as coach Mike Ditka (who suffered a mild heart attack at midseason) shuffled field generals but won his fifth straight Central Division title with the NFL's stingiest defense (215 points allowed); the Chicago wall was anchored by linebacker Mike Singletary, the league's defensive player of the year. The Vikings, who finished second to the Bears in the division race, and the Los Angeles Rams (10-6), runners-up to the 49ers in the West, qualified for the NFC play-offs as wild-card entries.

In the first weekend of postseason play, between the wild-card teams in each conference, Houston advanced in the AFC by edging out the Browns in Cleveland, 24-23, while the NFC's Vikings moved on by battering the Rams, 28-17.

An unpredictable season finally produced some predictable results in the second round of the play-offs, as all four favorites won on their home fields. Buffalo used a balanced offense and a strong defense to beat Houston, 17-10. Cincinnati stung Seattle, 21-13, with rookie running back Ickey Woods gaining 126 yards. San Francisco pounded Minnesota, 34-9, as Rice caught three touchdown passes and Craig ran for two more. And Chicago pummeled Philadelphia, 20-12, at fog-bound Soldier Field.

The AFC title game thus pitted the league's "new guard," while the NFC final matched two "establishment" teams. Neither contest was very close. Cincinnati, which held the home-field advantage throughout the AFC play-offs, turned in its best defensive performance of the year, holding Buffalo to only 181 total yards. The Bills, meanwhile, boasting the conference's top defense during the regular season, could not contain the Bengals' running game. Woods again was dominant, chalking up 102 yards and two touchdowns (the latter capped by his patented "Ickey Shuffle" celebration dance). Cincinnati advanced to the Super Bowl with a 21-10 victory. The success was especially sweet for Bengal coach Sam Wyche, who had been close to getting fired after a 4-11 record the previous year.

The NFC final was even more of a blow-out. Frigid conditions at Chicago's Soldier Field may have boded ill for the visiting 49ers, but they never seemed to notice. Despite a wind-chill factor of −26°F (−32°C), the San Francisco offense was firing on all cylinders. Montana threw for 288 yards and three touchdowns, two of them to Rice (62 yards and 27 yards). The 49er defense also left the Bears shivering, allowing but a single field goal. San Francisco advanced to the warmer climes of Miami with an impressive 28-3 win. Perhaps nothing but the final score pleased coach Bill Walsh more than his team's impeccable play: The 49ers became the first team since the Pittsburgh Steelers in the 1975 Super Bowl to go an entire play-off game without a penalty.

Outstanding individual performers during the regular season included Eric Dickerson of the Indianapolis Colts, who won his third NFL rushing title with 1,659 yards; Dallas' Herschel Walker was second with 1,514, followed by Craig of San Francisco with 1,502. The Rams' Greg Bell led the NFL with 18 touchdowns.

Cincinnati's Esiason was the league's top-rated passer, with Seattle's Dave Krieg second. (Seven out of the ten top-rated passers guided their teams to the play-offs.) Dan Marino of the Miami Dolphins led the NFL in passing yardage with 4,434, and Jim Everett of the Rams tossed a league-high 31 touchdown passes. Among receivers, Al Toon of the New York Jets caught the most passes (93), Henry Ellard of the Rams tallied the most yards (1,414), and Eddie Brown of the Bengals averaged the most yards per reception (24.0).

Buffalo kicker Scott Norwood was the NFL's leading scorer with 129 points; Detroit Lion kicker Eddie Murray was successful on 20 of 21 field-goal attempts, tying Mark Moseley's 1982 record for best percentage (.952) in a

PROFESSIONAL FOOTBALL

National Football League

Final Standings

NATIONAL CONFERENCE

Eastern Division

	W	L	T	Pct.	For	Against
Philadelphia	10	6	0	.625	379	319
N.Y. Giants	10	6	0	.625	359	304
Washington	7	9	0	.438	345	387
Phoenix	7	9	0	.438	344	398
Dallas	3	13	0	.188	265	381

Central Division

Chicago	12	4	0	.750	312	215
Minnesota	11	5	0	.688	406	233
Tampa Bay	5	11	0	.313	261	350
Detroit	4	12	0	.250	220	313
Green Bay	4	12	0	.250	240	315

Western Division

San Francisco	10	6	0	.625	369	294
L.A. Rams	10	6	0	.625	407	293
New Orleans	10	6	0	.625	312	283
Atlanta	5	11	0	.313	244	315

PLAY-OFFS

Minnesota 28, Los Angeles 17
Chicago 20, Philadelphia 12
San Francisco 34, Minnesota 9
San Francisco 28, Chicago 3

AMERICAN CONFERENCE

Eastern Division

	W	L	T	Pct.	For	Against
Buffalo	12	4	0	.750	329	237
Indianapolis	9	7	0	.563	354	315
New England	9	7	0	.563	250	284
N.Y. Jets	8	7	1	.531	372	354
Miami	6	10	0	.375	319	380

Central Division

Cincinnati	12	4	0	.750	448	329
Cleveland	10	6	0	.625	304	288
Houston	10	6	0	.625	424	365
Pittsburgh	5	11	0	.313	336	421

Western Division

Seattle	9	7	0	.563	339	329
Denver	8	8	0	.500	327	352
L.A. Raiders	7	9	0	.438	325	369
San Diego	6	10	0	.375	231	332
Kansas City	4	11	1	.281	254	320

PLAY-OFFS

Houston 24, Cleveland 23
Buffalo 17, Houston 10
Cincinnati 21, Seattle 13
Cincinnati 21, Buffalo 10

SUPER BOWL XXIII: San Francisco 20, Cincinnati 16

---

single season. The Los Angeles Raiders' Tim Brown, the 1987 Heisman Trophy winner, led the league in kick returns and set a rookie record for all-purpose yards; Philadelphia tight end Keith Jackson was another first-year standout.

Off the field, the league continued its aggressive campaign against drugs, suspending some two dozen players. Further underscoring the drug problem, however, Atlanta Falcons defensive back David Croudip died of an overdose.

One team got a new home in 1988—the Cardinals moved from St. Louis to Phoenix—and two teams got new owners—Victor Kiam in New England and Ken Behring in Seattle.

Pittsburgh Steeler owner Art Rooney, Sr., one of the founding fathers of the NFL, died in August at age 87.

On July 30 four stars of an earlier generation were inducted into the Pro Football Hall of Fame at Canton, OH: wide receiver Fred Biletnikoff of the Oakland (now Los Angeles) Raiders; linebacker Jack Ham of the Steelers; defensive tackle Alan Page of the Vikings and Bears; and tight end Mike Ditka of the Bears (whom he now coaches), Eagles, and Cowboys.

The College Season

Irish eyes were smiling on Jan. 2, 1989, as undefeated and number 1-ranked Notre Dame added another chapter to its storied gridiron history with a 34-21 thrashing of Number 3-ranked West Virginia in the Fiesta Bowl at Tempe, AZ. The victory gave Notre Dame its first national championship since 1977 and its first undefeated season since 1973. With a team made up largely of underclassmen, third-year coach Lou Holtz achieved his goal one year ahead of schedule and immediately was elevated by Irish faithful to the ranks of such Notre Dame coaching legends as Knute Rockne, Frank Leahy, Ara Parseghian, and Dan Devine.

West Virginia entered the Fiesta Bowl with its own record unblemished and seeking its first national championship. But Notre Dame was overpowering from the start. The Mountaineers' offensive line, considered one of the best in the country, was unable to protect the team's most dangerous weapon, the versatile quarterback Major Harris. The West Virginia junior signal-caller suffered a bruised shoulder early in the game, and the Mountaineers did not get a single first down until well into the second quarter. The Irish, meanwhile, moved the ball impressively. Quarterback Tony Rice threw for a career-high 213 yards, passed for two touchdowns, and ran for a third. West Virginia fell to Number 5 in the final Associated Press (AP) poll.

The other key game on Bowl Day pitted second-ranked Miami against Big Eight-champion Nebraska. Miami entered the game with a 10-1 record, their only loss coming at the hands of Notre Dame, 31-30, on October 15 in South Bend. The Hurricanes hoped that an Irish loss in the Fiesta Bowl and their own impressive victory in the Orange might persuade the pollsters to make them Number 1. Notre Dame did not follow the script, beating West Virginia in the afternoon, but Miami played its part to a tee. The Hurricanes put on a dazzling performance, overwhelming the Cornhuskers, 23-3. Steve Walsh, the latest in a line of great Miami quarterbacks (after the likes of Jim Kelly, Bernie Kosar, and Vinny Testaverde), threw two touchdown passes to the speedy Leonard Con-

COLLEGE FOOTBALL

Conference Champions	Atlantic Coast—Clemson
	Big Eight—Nebraska
	Big Ten—Michigan
	Big West—Fresno State
	Ivy League—(tie) Cornell and Pennsylvania
	Mid-American—Western Michigan
	Pacific Ten—Southern California
	Southeastern—(tie) Auburn, Louisiana State
	Southwest—Arkansas
	Western Athletic—Wyoming
NCAA Champions	Division I-AA—Furman
	Division II—North Dakota State
	Division III—Ithaca
NAIA Champions	Division I—Carson-Newman
	Division II—Westminster
Individual Honors	Heisman Trophy—Barry Sanders, Oklahoma State
	Lombardi Award—Tracy Rocker, Austin
	Outland Trophy—Rocker

Major Bowl Games

All-American Bowl (Birmingham, AL, Dec. 29)—Florida 14, Illinois 10
Aloha Bowl (Honolulu, HI, Dec. 25)—Washington State 24, Houston 22
California Bowl (Fresno, CA, Dec. 10)—Fresno State 35, Western Michigan 30
Cotton Bowl (Dallas, Jan. 2)—UCLA 17, Arkansas 3
Fiesta Bowl (Tempe, AZ, Jan. 2)—Notre Dame 34, West Virginia 21
Florida Citrus Bowl (Orlando, FL, Jan. 2)—Clemson 13, Oklahoma 6
Freedom Bowl (Anaheim, CA, Dec. 29)—Brigham Young 20, Colorado 17
Gator Bowl (Jacksonville, FL, Jan. 1)—Georgia 34, Michigan State 27
Hall of Fame Bowl (Tampa, FL, Jan. 2)—Syracuse 23, Louisiana State 10
Holiday Bowl (Tempe, AZ, Dec. 30)—Oklahoma State 62, Wyoming 14
Independence Bowl (Shreveport, LA, Dec. 23)—Southern Mississippi 38, Texas-El Paso 18
Liberty Bowl (Memphis, TN, Dec. 28)—Indiana 34, South Carolina 10
Orange Bowl (Miami, Jan. 2)—Miami 23, Nebraska 3
Peach Bowl (Atlanta, Dec. 31)—North Carolina State 28, Iowa 23
Rose Bowl (Pasadena, CA, Jan. 2)—Michigan 22, USC 14
Sugar Bowl (New Orleans, Jan. 2)—Florida State 13, Auburn 7
Sun Bowl (El Paso, TX, Dec. 24)—Alabama 29, Army 28

ley, and the defense used superior speed and strength in checking the Nebraska running game. Miami finished its season with an 11-1 record and a Number-2 national ranking; Nebraska, at 11-2, was ranked 10th.

The Florida State Seminoles, ending an 11-1 season with their 11th victory in a row, nailed down the Number-3 final ranking by defeating Auburn, 13-7, in the Sugar Bowl. Seminole running back Sammie Smith rushed for 115 yards. Auburn finished 10-2, ranked 8th in the nation.

In the 75th Rose Bowl, the Big Ten-champion Michigan Wolverines upset the Pac Ten-champion USC Trojans with a 22-14 come-from-behind win. Wolverine running back Leroy Hoard, a sophomore, scampered for 142 yards and two touchdowns. The victory gave Michigan a 9-2-1 season record and a Number-4 national ranking. USC ended up 10-2 (its other loss also coming at the hands of Notre Dame, 27-10, in the last game of the regular season) and a Number-7 final ranking.

Oklahoma State's Barry Sanders was a runaway winner in the Heisman Trophy balloting, becoming only the eighth junior ever to win college football's most coveted award. The Cowboy tailback set a total of 12 major NCAA records in 1988. In addition to the rushing and touchdown marks, he set new single-season

standards in all-purpose yards (rushing, receiving, punt returns, and kickoff returns) with 3,250 and in average all-purpose yards per game with 295.5. The latter figure broke one of college football's oldest records (246.3), set by current U.S. Supreme Court Justice Byron (Whizzer) White for Colorado in 1937.

USC quarterback Rodney Peete finished a distant second in the Heisman voting, followed by UCLA quarterback Troy Aikman. Aikman, generally regarded as the top senior passer in the college game, was expected to be the first pick in the NFL draft. The Dallas Cowboys held rights to the first selection (by virtue of the worst record in the league), and their fans got a first-hand look at their future star on Bowl Day. Aikman directed UCLA to a 17-3 triumph over Arkansas in Dallas' Cotton Bowl; it was the seventh straight bowl victory for the Bruins, setting an NCAA record.

Miami and West Virginia quarterbacks Walsh and Harris were fourth and fifth, respectively, in the Heisman balloting, followed by Michigan State offensive tackle Tony Mandarich. Among linemen, however, Auburn defensive tackle Tracy Rocker won both major awards for the year—the Outland Trophy (top interior lineman) and the Lombardi Award (top lineman or linebacker). Alabama's Derrick Thomas was awarded the Butkus Award as the nation's top linebacker; Nebraska's Broderick Thomas was the runner-up.

Notre Dame's Holtz won the Bear Bryant Award as college coach of the year. Two of the game's best-known head coaches and athletic directors resigned at season's end. Georgia's Vince Dooley stepped down voluntarily after 25 years of heading up the Bulldogs' program. Texas A & M's Jackie Sherrill, who had come under fire for alleged violations of NCAA rules, was forced to step down after seven years at the Aggie helm.

In NCAA Division I-AA competition, Furman held on for a 17-12 victory over Georgia Southern to claim the national championship. Towson State running back David Meggett won the Walter Payton Award as the year's outstanding Division I-AA player.

North Dakota State won its fourth Division II championship in six years with a 35-21 win over Portland (OR) State. Texas A & I running back Johnny Bailey won his second consecutive Harlon Hill Trophy as the top Division II performer.

Ithaca (NY) College defeated Central College (Pella, IA), 39-24, for the Division III crown.

In NAIA competition, Carson-Newman (Jefferson City, TN) romped over Adams State (Alamosa, CO), 56-21, for the Divison I championship, and Westminster College (New Wilmington, PA) beat Wisconsin-LaCross, 21-14, for the Division II title.

JEFFREY H. HACKER

© David Cannon/Allsport

Spain's Severiano Ballesteros won his third British Open, above, and six other international tournaments during 1988.

Golf

There were 11 first-time winners on the U.S. Professional Golfers' Association (PGA) Tour in 1988, leading cynics to decry the parity in the sport and traditionalists to go searching for a new hero.

They may have found one in Curtis Strange. A 34-year-old veteran of 12 years on the tour, Strange became the first player in history to win $1 million (officially $1,147,644) in one year. That also was enough to give him his third money title in four years. Strange won four tournaments, including a play-off victory against Britain's Nick Faldo in the U.S. Open for his first major championship. His overall performance earned him player of the year honors from the PGA and Golf Writers Association.

Other top men's players were Severiano Ballesteros of Spain, who won the British Open, one event on the U.S. Tour, and five tournaments in other countries and was named world player of the year by *Golf Digest* magazine; and Britain's Sandy Lyle, who won the Masters and two other tour events. The other major event, the PGA Championship, was won

PGA Tournament Winners

MONY Tournament of Champions: Steve Pate (202)
Bob Hope Chrysler Classic: Jay Haas (338)
Phoenix Open: Sandy Lyle (269)
AT&T Pebble Beach National Pro-Am: Steve Jones (280)
Hawaiian Open: Lanny Wadkins (271)
Shearson Lehman Hutton Andy Williams Open: Steve Pate (269)
Los Angeles Open Presented by Nissan: Chip Beck (267)
Doral Ryder Open: Ben Crenshaw (274)
Honda Classic: Joey Sindelar (276)
Hertz Bay Hill Classic: Paul Azinger (271)
The Players Championship: Mark McCumber (273)
K-Mart Greater Greensboro Open: Sandy Lyle (271)
Masters: Sandy Lyle (281)
MCI Heritage Classic: Greg Norman (271)
USF&G Classic: Chip Beck (262)
Independent Insurance Agent Open: Curtis Stange (270)
Panasonic Las Vegas Invitational: Gary Koch (274)
GTE Byron Nelson Golf Classic: Bruce Lietzke (271)
Colonial National Invitation: Lanny Wadkins (270)
Memorial Tournament: Curtis Strange (274)
Kemper Open: Morris Hatalsky (274)
Manufacturers Hanover Westchester Classic: Seve Ballesteros (276)
U.S. Open: Curtis Strange (278)
Georgia-Pacific Atlanta Classic: Larry Nelson (268)
Beatrice Western Open: Jim Benepe (278)
Anheuser-Busch Golf Classic: Tom Sieckmann (270)
Hardee's Golf Classic: Blaine McCallister (261)
Canon Sammy Davis, Jr. Greater Hartford Open: Mark Brooks (269)
Buick Open: Scott Verplank (268)
Federal Express St. Jude Classic: Jodie Mudd (273)
PGA Championship: Jeff Sluman (272)
The International: Joey Sindelar (17 final-round points)
NEC World Series of Golf: Mike Reid (275)
Provident Classic: Phil Blackmar (264)
Canadian Open: Ken Green (275)
Greater Milwaukee Open: Ken Green (268)
Bank of Boston Classic: Mark Calcavecchia (274)
B.C. Open: Bill Glasson (268)
Southern Open: David Frost (280)
Gatlin Brothers Southwest Classic: Tom Purtzer (269)
Texas Open Presented by Nabisco: Corey Pavin (259)
Pensacola Open: Andrew Magee (271)
Walt Disney World/Oldsmobile Golf Classic: Bob Lohr (263)
Northern Telecom Tucson Open: David Frost (266)
Nabisco Championships of Golf: Curtis Strange (279)

LPGA Tournament Winners

Mazda Classic: Nancy Lopez (283)
Sarasota Classic: Patty Sheehan (282)
Orient Leasing Hawaiian Ladies Open: Ayako Okamoto (213)
Women's Kemper Open: Betsy King (280)
Circle K'LPGA Tucson Open: Laura Davies (278)
Standard Register Turquoise Classic: Ok-Hee Ku (281)
Nabisco Dinah Shore: Amy Alcott (274)
San Diego Inamori Golf Classic: Ayako Okamoto (272)
Al Star/Centinela Hospital Classic: Nancy Lopez (210)
USX Golf Classic: Rosie Jones (275)
Sara Lee Classic: Patti Rizzo (207)
Crestar Classic: Juli Inkster (209)
Chrysler/Plymouth Classic: Nancy Lopez (204)
Mazda LPGA Championship: Sherri Turner (281)
LPGA Corning Classic: Sherri Turner (273)
Jamie Farr Toledo Classic: Laura Davies (277)
Rochester International: Mei-Chi Cheng (287)
Lady Keystone Open: Shirley Furlong (205)
McDonald's Championship: Kathy Postlewait (276)
du Maurier Classic: Sally Little (279)
Mayflower Classic: Terry-Joe Myers (276)
Boston Five Classic: Colleen Walker (274)
U.S. Women's Open: Liselotte Neumann (277)
Greater Washington Open: Ayako Okamoto (206)
Planters Pat Bradley International: Martha Nause (14 points)
Atlantic City LPGA Classic: Juli Inkster (206)
Nestle World Championship: Rosie Jones (279)
Rail Charity Classic: Betsy King (207)
Cellular One-Ping Golf Championship: Betsy King (213)
Safeco Classic: Juli Inkster (278)
Santa Barbara Open: Rosie Jones (212)
Konica San Jose Classic: Kathy Guadagnino (207)
Nichirei Ladies Cup U.S.–Japan Team Championship: Beth Daniel (139)
  (U.S. team 17 points, Japan 11 points)
Mazda Japan Classic: Patty Sheehan (206)

Other Tournament Winners

British Open: Seve Ballesteros (273)
World Match Play: Sandy Lyle
U.S. Senior Open: Gary Player (288)
General Foods PGA Seniors Championship: Gary Player (284)
Mazda Senior Tournament Players Championship: Billy Casper (278)
U.S. Men's Amateur: Eric Meeks
U.S. Women's Amateur: Pearl Sinn
U.S. Men's Public Links: Ralph Howe
U.S. Women's Public Links: Pearl Sinn
U.S. Mid-Amateur: David Eger
U.S. Women's Mid-Amateur: Martha Lang
U.S. Senior Men's Amateur: Clarence Moore
U.S. Senior Women's Amateur: Lois Hodge
NCAA Men: Individual—E. J. Pfister; Team—UCLA
NCAA Women: Individual—Melissa McNamara; Team—Tulsa

by Jeff Sluman, one of the first-time victors. Chip Beck, who had not won in nine years on the tour, won twice in 1988 and finished second on the money list with $916,818. Beck also won the Vardon Trophy with a 69.46 scoring average and was named *Golf Digest*'s most improved professional. Jim Benepe, who won the Western Open as a nonmember of the tour, was named the magazine's rookie of the year.

On the Senior PGA Tour, Gary Player won the U.S. Senior Open, the Senior PGA Championship, and three other tournaments. But Bob Charles, the New Zealand lefty, also won five times and was the leading money winner with a record $533,929. Charles also won the Byron Nelson Trophy for low scoring average with a mark of 70.05.

On the Ladies Professional Golf Association (LPGA) Tour, Hall of Famer Nancy Lopez won three tournaments and was named Rolex player of the year. Money honors went to Sherri Turner, who won the Mazda LPGA Championship and one other tournament, and pocketed a total of $350,851. Sweden's Liselotte Neumann won the U.S. Women's Open and was named rookie of the year by both the LPGA and *Golf Digest*. In the other major championships, Amy Alcott won the Nabisco Dinah Shore, and Sally Little won the du Maurier Classic. Colleen Walker won the Vare Trophy for low average at 71.26 because leader Ayako Okamoto at 70.94 did not play enough rounds to qualify.

LARRY DENNIS, *Free-lance Golf Writer*

Horse Racing

Alysheba, which as a three-year-old won the 1987 Kentucky Derby and Preakness, won a record $3,808,600 in 1988 and ran his career earnings to $6,679,242, surpassing John Henry's record. Trained by Jack Van Berg, the four-year-old son of Alydar highlighted his year by winning the $3 million Breeders' Cup Classic at Churchill Downs. (He had lost the year before by a nose to Ferdinand, the 1987 Horse of the Year.) Alysheba in 1988 also won the Charles H. Strub Stakes, Santa Anita Handicap, Philip H. Islin Handicap, Woodward Handicap, and Meadowlands Cup. In beating Forty Niner by a neck in the Woodward, Alysheba set a Belmont Park record of 1:59 2/5 seconds for 1¼ miles.

Nearly as spectacular in 1988 was Personal Ensign, which ended a perfect 13-race career by winning the Breeders' Cup Distaff by a nose over Winning Colors, the Kentucky Derby champion trained by D. Wayne Lukas. A four-year-old filly, Personal Ensign became the first American horse in 80 years to retire undefeated.

Winning Colors' victory in the Kentucky Derby spoiled Risen Star's chances for the Triple Crown. A son of Secretariat, Risen Star was retired because of a chronic injury after winning the Preakness and Belmont Stakes—as well as the $1 million bonus for the best record in the three Triple Crown races.

Other outstanding three-year-olds were Forty Niner, Seeking the Gold, and Private Terms. Among three-year-old fillies, Winning Colors was rivaled by Goodbye Halo, Gulch had an outstanding sprint season.

Hall of Fame Jockey Laffit Pincay, Jr., suffered a punctured lung and fractured ribs when thrown from a mount on August 1 at Del Mar, CA. He returned to riding in September.

Harness Racing. Herve Filion set a single-season record for victories by a driver on November 30, when he surpassed the one-year-old mark of 770 set by Michele LaChance.

Matt's Scooter posted a record time for a harness horse when he paced one mile in 1:48 2/5 at Lexington, KY, breaking Niatross' eight-year-old standard. Matt's Scooter also won the Meadowlands Pace. Armbro Goal captured the Hambletonian, the top event for trotters. BJ Scoot won the Little Brown Jug, pacing's showcase event.

STAN SUTTON
"Louisville Courier-Journal"

HORSE RACING

Major North American Thoroughbred Racers

Beldame Stakes: Personal Ensign, $332,400 (money distributed)
Belmont Stakes: Risen Star, $506,200
Breeders' Cup Classic: Alysheba, $3 million
Breeders' Cup Distaff: Personal Ensign, $1 million
Breeders' Cup Juvenile: Is It True, $1 million
Breeders' Cup Juvenile Fillies: Open Mind, $1 million
Breeders' Cup Mile: Miesque, $1 million
Breeders' Cup Sprint: Gulch, $1 million
Breeders' Cup Turf: Great Communicator, $2 million
Budweiser-Arlington Million: Mill Native, $1 milion
Budweiser International: Sunshine Forever, $750,000
Florida Derby: Brian's Time, $500,000
Haskell Invitational Handicap: Forty Niner, $500,000
Hollywood Invitational: Political Ambition, $300,000
Iselin Handicap: Alysheba, $500,000
Jockey Club Gold Cup: Waquoit, $1,063,000
Kentucky Derby: Winning Colors, $786,200
Man o' War Stakes: Sunshine Forever, $596,000
Meadowlands Cup: Alysheba, $600,000
Metropolitan Handicap: Gulch, $586,000
Mother Goose: Goodbye Halo, $237,200
Preakness Stakes: Risen Star, $536,200
Santa Anita Derby: Winning Colors, $500,000
Santa Anita Handicap: Alysheba, $1 million
Strub Stakes: Alysheba, $500,000
Surburban Handicap: Personal Flag, $380,100
Super Derby: Seeking the Gold, $1 million
Travers Stakes: Forty Niner, $1,088,050
Turf Classic: Sunshine Forever, $600,000
Wood Memorial: Private Terms, $500,000
Whitney Handicap: Personal Ensign, $270,500
Woodward Stakes: Alysheba, $831,000

Major North American Harness Races

Cane Pace: Runnymede Lobell, $583,790
Hambletonian: Armbro Goal, $1,156,800
Hambletonian Oaks: Nan's Catch, $395,300
Kentucky Futurity: Huggie Hanover, $153,818
Kentucky Pacing Derby: Totally Ruthless, $386,410
Little Brown Jug: BJ Scoot, $486,043
Meadowlands Pace: Matt's Scooter, $1,030,000
Merrie Annabelle: Peace Corps, $474,500
Peter Haughton Memorial: Keyser Lobell, $682,250
Sweetheart Pace: Concertina, $863,250
Woodrow Wilson Pace: Kassa Branca, $1,041,000

Ice Hockey

Having joined the National Hockey League (NHL) only nine years earlier, the Edmonton Oilers in 1987–88 won their fourth Stanley Cup championship. By way of comparison, both the New York Rangers and Chicago Black Hawks have won only three league titles in 62 years. With center Wayne Gretzky again leading the charge, the Oilers steamrolled the Boston Bruins in four straight games in the play-off finals to grab their fourth crown in five seasons.

Regular Season The Oilers were dethroned as the team with the best regular-season record by the Calgary Flames, who compiled 105 points en route to the Smythe Division title. The Montreal Canadiens, who topped the Adams Division, totaled 103 points, followed by the Oilers with 99 and the Boston Bruins with 94. The Detroit Red Wings (93) and New York Islanders (88) won the Norris and Patrick division races, respectively.

Gretzky's streak of seven consecutive scoring titles ended in 1987–88, as Pittsburgh center Mario Lemieux beat him by 19 points, 168-149. (Gretzky missed 16 games with injuries.) Chicago's Denis Savard was third in the scoring race with 131 points, followed by Winnipeg's Dale Hawerchuk at 121. A dozen players tallied 100 or more points, up by five from the year before.

Lemieux became only the fourth player to score 70 goals or more in one season, netting 70 in 77 games. Six other players had 50 or more goals: Craig Simpson (56) of Pittsburgh and Edmonton; Jimmy Carson (55) and Luc Robitaille (53) of Los Angeles; Joe Nieuwendyk (51) and Hakan Loob (50) of Calgary; and Steve Yzerman (50) of Detroit.

Gretzky's eight-year reign as the NHL's most valuable player (MVP) also came to an end, as Lemieux was awarded the Hart Trophy. Gretzky finished third in the voting, with Oiler goalie Grant Fuhr coming in second. Gretzky did surpass Gordie Howe to become the NHL's all-time assist leader, finishing the season with 1,086.

Play-offs. Off-the-ice incidents spiced the Stanley Cup tournament. There were two electrical blackouts—in Montreal during the first game of the Adams Division final, and in Boston during the fourth game of the Cup final. The game in Montreal continued with emergency power, but the contest in Boston was cancelled and replayed in its entirety in Edmonton; it was the first time in Stanley Cup history that a game had to be canceled. As if the blackouts were not enough, the fourth game of the Wales Conference final between New Jersey and Boston was marred by a walkout of the officiating staff. In another Stanley Cup first, a crew of amateur officials was called in to work the game.

On the ice, the Oilers got past the Winnipeg Jets, four games to one, in first-round play, and

AP/Wide World

Edmonton's Glenn Anderson celebrates an early goal in Game 4 of the Stanley Cup finals at Boston Garden. But the game had to be canceled because of a blackout, and the Oilers won the title with a 6-3 victory on home ice.

then swept the favored Flames in four straight —a series dubbed the "Battle of Alberta"—to win the Smythe Division title. Detroit cruised to the title in the Norris Division, beating the Toronto Maple Leafs in six games and the St. Louis Blues in five. In the Adams Division, the Bruins outlasted the Buffalo Sabres, four games to two, and then stunned the 1986 Cup-champion Canadiens in five games to win the division; it was the first time in 40 years that the Bruins had beaten Montreal in a play-off series. In the Patrick Division, the New Jersey Devils fashioned their own version of the Cinderella story. Having made the play-offs on the last night of the regular season, they ousted the New York Islanders in six games and the Washington Capitals in seven games.

In the Wales Conference finals, the Devils got superb goaltending from rookie Sean Burke but fell to Boston in seven games. The Bruins got equally strong play from goalie Reggie Lemelin, reaching the Cup finals for the first time since 1978. The black mark in the Devils-Bruins series was the wildcat strike by ice officials. The referee and two linesmen refused to work Game 4 because New Jersey coach Jim Schoenfeld had obtained a court injunction to stay a one-game suspension. The penalty had been levied by the NHL for verbally abusing the referee after Game 3. The Campbell Conference finals lacked such drama—both off the ice and on it—as Edmonton breezed past Detroit in five games.

The championship series also lacked some of the excitement of earlier rounds, as the Oilers were simply overpowering. In Game 1, Edmonton's Keith Acton tipped Steven Smith's shot past former Oiler goalie Andy Moog in the

third period to gain a 2-1 victory. In Game 2, Gretzky scored a breakaway goal on Lemelin with less than ten minutes to play, and Jari Kurri nailed down a 4-2 win with an empty-net goal in the final seconds.

In Game 3, Gretzky's linemate Esa Tikkanen scored three times and "The Great One" had four assists, as the Oilers erased a Boston Garden jinx—they had won there only twice in nine seasons—with a 6-3 victory. Game 4, also in Boston, was halted with 3:23 left to play in the second period—and the score tied 3-3—when the lights went out. The power was restored 30 minutes later, but there was no guarantee that the system would not quit again, so the game was scrapped (to be replayed in Boston if the series were to go to seven games).

The blackout became little more than the answer to a trivia question, however, as the Oilers whipped the Bruins, 6-3, in Edmonton. Tikkanen tallied two more goals, and Gretzky had three points—tying the NHL record of 13 in a final series. The Oiler center had a total of 43 points in postseason play and won his second Conn Smythe Trophy as play-off MVP.

Then during the summer, in a move that stunned Edmonton fans, Gretzky—who had set 43 NHL scoring records in his ten years as an Oiler—was traded to the L.A. Kings.

JIM MATHESON, *"Edmonton Journal"*

ICE HOCKEY

National Hockey League
(Final Standings, 1987–88)

Wales Conference

Patrick Division	W	L	T	Pts.	Goals For	Against
*N.Y. Islanders	39	31	10	88	308	267
*Washington	38	33	9	85	281	249
*Philadelphia	38	33	9	85	292	293
*New Jersey	38	36	6	82	293	296
N.Y. Rangers	36	34	10	82	300	285
Pittsburgh	36	35	9	81	319	316

Adams Division	W	L	T	Pts.	For	Against
*Montreal	45	22	13	103	298	238
*Boston	44	30	6	94	300	251
*Buffalo	37	32	11	85	285	305
*Hartford	35	38	7	77	249	267
Quebec	32	43	5	69	271	306

Campbell Conference

Norris Division	W	L	T	Pts.	For	Against
*Detroit	41	28	11	93	322	269
*St. Louis	34	38	8	76	278	294
*Chicago	30	41	9	69	284	328
*Toronto	21	49	10	52	273	345
Minnesota	19	48	13	51	242	349

Smythe Division	W	L	T	Pts.	For	Against
*Calgary	48	23	9	105	397	305
*Edmonton	44	25	11	99	363	288
*Winnipeg	33	36	11	77	292	310
*Los Angeles	30	42	8	68	318	359
Vancouver	25	46	9	59	272	320

*In play-offs

Stanley Cup Play-Offs
Wales Conference

First Round	Boston	4 games	Buffalo	2
	Montreal	4 games	Hartford	2
	New Jersey	4 games	N.Y. Islanders	2
	Washington	4 games	Philadelphia	3
Semifinals	Boston	4 games	Montreal	1
	New Jersey	4 games	Washington	3
Finals	Boston	4 games	New Jersey	3

Campbell Conference

First Round	Calgary	4 games	Los Angeles	1
	Detroit	4 games	Toronto	2
	Edmonton	4 games	Winnipeg	1
	St. Louis	4 games	Chicago	1
Semifinals	Detroit	4 games	St. Louis	1
	Edmonton	4 games	Calgary	0
Finals	Edmonton	4 games	Detroit	1

Championship

Edmonton	4 games	Boston	0

Individual Honors

Hart Trophy (most valuable player): Mario Lemieux, Pittsburgh
Ross Trophy (leading scorer): Mario Lemieux
Vezina Trophy (top goaltender): Grant Fuhr, Edmonton
Norris Trophy (best defenseman): Ray Bourque, Boston
Selke Award (best defense forward): Guy Carbonneau, Montreal
Calder Trophy (rookie of the year): Joe Nieuwendyk, Calgary
Lady Byng Trophy (sportsmanship): Mats Naslund, Montreal
Conn Smythe Trophy (most valuable in play-offs): Wayne Gretzky, Edmonton
Adam Trophy (coach of the year): Jacques Demers, Detroit
King Clancy Trophy (humanitarian service): Larry McDonald, Calgary

NCAA: Lake Superior State

Ice Skating

Brian Boitano of the United States and Katarina Witt (see BIOGRAPHY) of East Germany were the toasts of the figure-skating world in 1988.

Boitano, who won his fourth consecutive U.S. championship in Denver in January and thus qualified for the Olympics, regained the world title he had lost to Brian Orser of Canada in 1987. Orser, who finished second to Boitano in the Olympics, also finished second to him in the world event at Budapest in March.

Witt's performance in the world championships was flawless but conservative and left some room for Debi Thomas of the United States, her biggest rival, possibly to overtake her in the freestyle program. But Thomas, who had faltered and finished third in the Olympics, failed once again and wound up third behind Elizabeth Manley, a 22-year-old Canadian. The 21-year-old Thomas had taken the U.S. title for the second time in three years.

The pairs and dance world titles went to Soviet teams. Elena Valova and Oleg Vasiliev took their third pairs crown, and Natalya Bestemianova and Andrei Bukin were the dance champions for a fourth time.

In the U.S. championships, Jill Watson and Peter Oppegard captured the pairs crown, and Suzanne Semanick and Scott Gregory triumphed in the dance.

At Davos, Switzerland, in June, the International Skating Union voted to eliminate compulsory figures from the men's and women's singles competition starting in July 1990.

The world speed-skating overall champions were Eric Flaim of the United States and Karin Kania of East Germany.

See also SPORTS—*Winter Olympics.*

GEORGE DE GREGORIO

Scandal marred the Seoul Summer Games. Canada's Ben Johnson (left, arm raised) *won the 100-m dash, but tests later showed he had taken steroids. He was stripped of the gold medal, which was awarded to America's Carl Lewis* (far right).

The Olympic Games

Bigger and more costly than ever, the quadrennial renewal of the Olympic Games was held during 1988. The Winter Games were staged during February in Calgary, Canada, amid a refreshing Wild West atmosphere. The Summer Games were held during September-October in Seoul, South Korea, just 90 minutes from the demilitarized zone that separates the hostile countries of North and South Korea.

Both the Summer and Winter Games set records in terms of numbers of athletes and countries participating. These events have become massive undertakings, requiring enormous expenditures of money and manpower. At the same time, the "amateur" aspect of the Olympics itself is disappearing. More and more professionals are being allowed to participate, and in the future it is expected that virtually every Olympic sport will be open to all comers, amateur or professional.

The Summer Games were notable for being the first since 1972 not boycotted by a large block of nations. Beginning in 1976, when many African nations refused to attend the Games in Montreal, boycotts have marred the Olympic movement and hindered the quality of competition. The United States refused to attend the 1980 Games in Moscow, and the Soviet Union led a boycott of the 1984 Games in Los Angeles. But only five nations—most notably Cuba—followed North Korea's lead in 1988 by staying away from the Seoul Games. Otherwise, all the world's sports powers competed. The same was hoped for the 1992 Winter Games in Albertville, France; the 1994 Winter Games in Lillehammer, Norway (a break in the four-year cycle to make the Winter Games fall midway between Summer Games); and the 1992 Summer Games in Barcelona, Spain.

Competitors at both 1988 Games produced some remarkable achievements. Unfortunately, the Summer Games were rocked by the first major drug scandal in Olympic history. Canadian sprinter Ben Johnson, who set a world record while winning the 100-m dash, failed his postrace drug test, which revealed he had taken an anabolic steroid, a banned substance for Olympic competitors. Johnson lost his gold medal and his world record, and was banned from international track competition for two years. His misfortune cast a pall over the remainder of the Summer Games, even though the action by the International Olympic Committee (IOC) was hailed as a major step in cleaning up drug use among athletes.

The XXIV Summer Games

The athletic facilities—considered some of the best in the world—and municipal development projects for the Seoul Games cost some $3.1 billion in public and private funds. The South Korean government estimated, however, that the Games would generate $300 million in profit. A record 160 nations, including 9,700 athletes, and some 10,000 journalists went to Seoul, and an estimated 4 billion television viewers watched the Games worldwide.

The Soviet Union reasserted its claim as the world's leading athletic power by winning 132 total medals, including 55 gold. East Germany was second, with 102 total medals, including 37 gold; and the United States was third with 94 medals, including 36 gold. Swimmer Kristin Otto of East Germany became the queen of the Games with an impressive six gold medals, two more than any woman in one Olympics.

Track and Field. The rise and fall of Ben Johnson dominated the track and field competition, overshadowing fine efforts from Florence Griffith Joyner, Jackie Joyner-Kersee, a group of Kenyan middle-distance runners (Paul Ereng, 800 m; Peter Rono, 1,500 m; John Ngugi, 5,000 m; and Julius Kariuki, 3,000-m steeplechase), and decathlon winner Christian Schenk of East Germany.

The drama prior to the 100-m race had made it the premier event of the Olympics. This would be the ultimate showdown between Johnson, the world record holder, and Carl Lewis of the United States, who had dominated the event for years. But Johnson won this race easily, beating Lewis by five meters in a world-record time of 9.79 seconds. Three days later, the IOC announced the results of Johnson's failed drug test, and Lewis, who had won four golds at the 1984 Games, was

The star of women's track and field was Florence Griffith Joyner of the United States, who won gold medals in the 100-m dash (below), 200-m dash, and 4 x 100-m relay.

Reuters/Bettmann Newsphotos

awarded first place. He also captured the long jump in Seoul. But his quest for another four golds in these Games was thwarted when Joe DeLoach beat him by a half-stride in the 200 m. Lewis also was scheduled to run a leg on the U.S. 4 x 100-m relay team, but that quartet was disqualified in a preliminary heat for an illegal baton exchange.

As good as Lewis was, the outstanding track athlete at the Games was the glamorous Griffith Joyner. She won the women's 100 m in Olympic record time, captured the 200 m in world-record time, and picked up a third gold by running a leg on the winning U.S. 4 x 100-m relay team. She attempted to win a fourth in the 4 x 400-m relay, but the U.S. team finished second as the Soviet Union won in world-record time. Joyner-Kersee, who is Griffith Joyner's sister-in-law, broke her own world record in winning the heptathlon, and also triumphed in the long jump, setting an Olympic record.

One of the most impressive winners was tiny Rosa Mota of Portugal, who ran away with the women's marathon. In perhaps the biggest upset of the Games, American Edwin Moses failed to repeat as 400-m high hurdles champion, finishing third. Italy's Gelindo Bordin won the men's marathon on the last day of the Games. Another upset was registered by U.S. high jumper Louise Ritter, who beat the world-record holder and heavy favorite, Stefka Kostadinova of Bulgaria. Another favorite, pole vaulter Sergei Bubka of the USSR, did win, although he failed to break a world record as he had hoped.

Swimming and Diving. The United States had dominated the 1984 swimming events, but the powerful East Germans, who missed those Games, emerged as the best in the world with their showing in Seoul. Of the 31 gold medals awarded in swimming, the East Germans won 11 and the United States eight.

On the women's side, the standout performers were East Germany's Kristin Otto, a tall and extremely strong sprinter, and America's Janet Evans, a tiny and unimposing distance swimmer. Otto won both freestyle sprint events (the 50 m and 100 m), then took the 100-m backstroke and 100-m butterfly, and swam legs on the winning 4 x 100-m freestyle and 4 x 100-m medley relay teams. The diminutive Evans decisively outswam her much larger competitors to win the 400-m and 800-m freestyle events and the 400-m individual medley.

On the men's side, Matt Biondi of the United States went into the Games trying to win seven gold medals, equaling the Olympic record of Mark Spitz. Biondi won the 50-m and 100-m freestyle sprints and was on three victorious U.S. relay teams. He also had a silver in the 100-m butterfly and a bronze in the 200-m freestyle. In the 100-m butterfly, he was nosed out by Anthony Nesty of Suriname, who won that country's first-ever Olympic medal.

America's Matt Biondi, above, was the top male swimmer. His five gold, one silver, and one bronze medals were the most since Mark Spitz won seven golds in 1972.

The powerful East German swim team was led by Kristin Otto, who won six gold medals—the most ever by a woman athlete in a single Olympic Games.

In diving, America's Greg Louganis (*see* BIOGRAPHY), who won two gold medals in 1984, came back to repeat in both the springboard and platform events. But he had to struggle in each. In the springboard competition, he hit his head on the board during a preliminary dive but rallied to dominate the finals. In the platform event, he trailed 14-year-old Xiong Ni of China entering the final dive but was nearly perfect on his last attempt and pulled out the gold.

Gymnastics. One of the great controversies of the Games took place in gymnastics. The U.S. women's team was penalized a half-point when alternate Rhonda Faehn stayed on the podium during a teammate's routine instead of retreating to the floor after removing a piece of equipment. U.S. officials protested, but their appeal was denied. The U.S. women wound up losing a bronze medal to the East Germans by 0.3 points. The judge who called for the penalty was from East Germany.

In a very close contest, the Russian women wound up winning the team gold medal over the Romanians. Elena Shoushounova of the Soviet Union won the all-around by earning a perfect score of 10 on her last event, the vault, to move ahead of Daniela Silivas of Romania. But Silivas came back in the individual events, winning the balance beam, floor exercises, and uneven bars, and finishing third in the vault.

The Russian men were especially impressive, dominating all but two of their events and taking all three places in the all-around. The best of the Soviets was young Vladimir Artemov, who took the all-around title and gold medals in the horizontal bars and parallel bars; he also had a silver in floor exercise. Teammate Dmitri Bilozerchev, a former world champion, had been favored to win the all-around but finished third. He did share two gold medals in individual events.

Boxing. Once again, boxing proved one of the more controversial of Olympic sports. The worst incident came in the early days of the tournament, when bantamweight Byun Jung Il of South Korea lost on a judges' decision to Alexander Hristov of Bulgaria. His trainers and other South Korean officials, angered at the announcement, jumped into the ring and attacked referee Keith Walker of New Zealand. After Walker finally was rescued by security men, Byun sat for 45 minutes in the ring, protesting the decision.

The U.S. boxing team took advantage of the absence of the Cubans and won three gold medals: Kennedy McKinney (bantamweight), Andrew Maynard (light heavyweight), and Ray Mercer (heavyweight). South Korea had two first places.

Basketball. The Soviet Union recorded one of the big upsets of the Seoul Games by beating the United States in a men's basketball semifinal contest, 82-76. It was the first Olympic meeting between the two countries since the Soviets' controversial victory in the 1972 gold-medal matchup. The U.S. team had been favored heavily to win the gold in 1988, but the Russians played a wonderful game, never both-

ered by the Americans' pressing defense. The Soviets went on to beat Yugoslavia in the gold-medal game, with the Americans beating Australia for the bronze.

In the women's bracket, the U.S. team finished undefeated, running past Yugoslavia in the final. In the semifinals, the U.S. women had beaten the Soviet women.

Other Sports. Weight lifter Naim Suleymanoglu of Turkey, considered pound-for-pound the strongest man in the world, set six world records in winning the 132-lb (60-kg) class. Known as "Pocket Hercules," he competed for Bulgaria in 1984 as Naim Suleimanov but later defected to Turkey. Bulgaria won four weight lifting medals before withdrawing from the Games when two of the winners tested positive for drugs. The Soviets took six golds in weight lifting, four in Greco-Roman wrestling, and four in freestyle wrestling.

The Soviet Union and East Germany dominated both canoeing and kayaking and cycling, and West Germany won four of the six equestrian gold medals. Japan did poorly in judo, usually one of its strong events, capturing just one gold—one less than South Korea. East Germany picked up eight first places in rowing.

Tennis, an official Olympic sport for the first time since 1924, brought a number of top professionals to the Games. West Germany's Steffi Graf, who already had won the Grand Slam in women's tennis, added the women's singles gold medal, beating Gabriela Sabatini of Argentina in the final. Miloslav Mecir of Czechoslovakia won the men's title, beating Tim Mayotte of the United States. In some of the best team competition, the Soviets outlasted Brazil in the gold-medal soccer game. In volleyball, the United States, the top-rated squad in the world, repeated their 1984 first-place effort by beating the Soviet Union in the gold-medal match. And in water polo, Yugoslavia beat the United States in overtime in a rematch of the 1984 gold-medal game.

In a notable individual effort, Christa Rothenburger of East Germany, the gold medalist in the women's 1,000-m speed-skating event at Calgary, became the first person to win medals in both the Summer and Winter Games in the same year, when she won the silver medal in women's sprint cycling.

Overall. Despite dire predictions, the South Koreans put on an impressive Olympics free of any outside interference. These were the first Olympics since 1964 not marred by either a major boycott or such outside disturbances as civilian riots. The growing drug scandal in amateur sports did envelop the Games in its web. Ten athletes were disqualified for failing their drug tests, and the IOC pledged to crack down. By the closing ceremonies, however, IOC President Juan Antonio Samaranch was moved to declare: "These were the best and most universal Games in history."

© Dan Helms/Duomo

U.S. diver Greg Louganis, above, won the springboard event despite hitting his head on the board in the preliminaries and took the platform event with a near-perfect final dive. Soviet gymnast Elena Shoushounova, below, scored a perfect 10 on her last event to win the women's all-around title.

© P. Perrin/Sygma

The U.S. women's basketball team repeated as gold medalists by defeating Yugoslavia, 77–70, in the tournament finals.

XXIV SUMMER OLYMPICS—Gold Medalists

Archery
Men's Individual: Jay Barrs, United States
Men's Team: South Korea
Women's Individual: Kim Soo Nyung, South Korea
Women's Team: South Korea

Basketball
Men: Soviet Union
Women: United States

Boxing
Light Flyweight: Ivailo Hristov, Bulgaria
Flyweight: Kim Kwang Sun, South Korea
Bantamweight: Kennedy McKinney, United States
Featherweight: Giovanni Parisi, Italy
Lightweight: Andreas Zuelow, East Germany
Light Welterweight: Viatcheslav Janovski, Soviet Union
Welterweight: Robert Wangila, Kenya
Light Middleweight: Park Si Hun, South Korea
Middleweight: Henry Maske, East Germany
Light Heavyweight: Andrew Maynard, United States
Heavyweight: Ray Mercer, United States
Super Heavyweight: Lennox Lewis, Canada

Canoeing
Men's 500-m Kayak Singles: Zsolt Gyulay, Hungary
Men's 1,000-m Kayak Singles: Greg Barton, United States
Men's 500-m Kayak Pairs: New Zealand
Men's 1,000-m Kayak Pairs: United States
Men's 1,000-m Kayak Fours: Hungary
Men's 500-m Canadian Singles: Olaf Heukrodt, East Germany
Men's 1,000-m Canadian Singles: Ivan Klementiev, Soviet Union
Men's 500-m Canadian Pairs: Soviet Union
Men's 1,000-m Canadian Pairs: Soviet Union
Women's 500-m Kayak Singles: Vania Guecheva, Bulgaria
Women's 500-m Kayak Pairs: East Germany
Women's 500-m Kayak Fours: East Germany

Cycling
Men's 1,000-m Time Trial: Alexander Kiritchenko, Soviet Union
Men's 100-km Team Time Trial: East Germany
Men's Individual Sprint: Lutz Hesslich, East Germany
Men's 4,000-m Individual Pursuit: Gintaoutas Umaras, Soviet Union
Men's 4,000-m Team Pursuit: Soviet Union
Men's Individual Road Race: Olaf Ludwig, East Germany
Men's Individual Points Race: Dan Frost, Denmark
Women's Individual Road Race: Monique Knol, Netherlands
Women's Individual Sprint: Erika Saloumiae, Soviet Union

Equestrian
Individual 3-Day Event: Mark Todd, New Zealand
Team 3-Day Event: West Germany
Individual Dressage: Nicole Uphoff, West Germany
Team Dressage: West Germany
Individual Jumping: Pierre Durand, France
Team Jumping: West Germany

Fencing
Men's Individual Foil: Stefano Cerioni, Italy
Men's Team Foil: Soviet Union
Men's Individual Épée: Arnd Schmitt, West Germany
Men's Team Épée: France
Men's Individual Sabre: Jean-François Lamour, France
Men's Team Sabre: Hungary
Women's Individual Foil: Anja Fichtel, West Germany
Women's Team Foil: West Germany

Field Hockey
Men: Great Britain
Women: Australia

Gymnastics
Men's All-Around: Vladimir Artemov, Soviet Union
Men's Floor Exercises: Sergei Kharikov, Soviet Union
Men's Horizontal Bar: V. Artemov and Valery Lyukin, Soviet Union (tie)

Men's Vault: Lou Yun, China
Men's Parallel Bars: V. Artemov
Men's Rings: Dmitri Bilozerchev, Soviet Union; Holger Behrendt, East Germany (tie)
Men's Pommel Horse: D. Bilozerchev; Lyubomir Gueraskov, Bulgaria; Zsolt Borkai, Hungary (tie)
Men's Team: Soviet Union
Women's All Around: Elena Shoushounova, Soviet Union
Women's Balance Beam: Daniela Silivas, Romania
Women's Floor Exercises: D. Silivas
Women's Vault: Svetlana Boguinskaya, Soviet Union
Women's Uneven Parallel Bars: D. Silivas
Women's Team: Soviet Union
Women's Rhythmic Gymnastics: Marina Lobatch, Soviet Union

Handball
Men: Soviet Union
Women: South Korea

Judo
Extra Lightweight: Kim Jae Yup, South Korea
Half Lightweight: Lee Kyung Keun, South Korea
Lightweight: Marc Alexandre, France
Half Middleweight: Waldemar Legien, Poland
Middleweight: Peter Seisenbacher, Austria
Half Heavyweight: Aurelio Miguel, Brazil
Heavyweight: Hitoshi Saito, Japan

Modern Pentathlon
Individual: Janos Martinek, Hungary
Team: Hungary

Rowing
Men's Single Sculls: Tomas Lange, East Germany
Men's Double Sculls: Netherlands
Men's Quadruple Sculls: Italy
Men's Pairs With Coxswain: Italy
Men's Pairs Without Coxswain: Great Britain
Men's Fours With Coxswain: East Germany
Men's Fours Without Coxswain: East Germany
Men's Eights: West Germany
Women's Single Sculls: Jutta Behrendt, East Germany
Women's Double Sculls: East Germany
Women's Quadruple Sculls: East Germany
Women's Pairs Without Coxswain: Romania
Women's Fours With Coxswain: East Germany
Women's Eights: East Germany

Shooting
Men's Rapid-Fire Pistol: Afanasi Kouzmine, Soviet Union
Men's Free Pistol: Sorin Babii, Romania
Men's Running Game Target: Tor Heiestad, Norway
Men's Small Bore Rifle, English: Miroslav Varga, Czechoslovakia
Men's Small Bore Rifle, 3 Positions: Malcolm Cooper, Great Britain
Men's Air Rifle: Goran Maksimovic, Yugoslavia
Men's Air Pistol: Taniou Kiriakov, Bulgaria
Women's Air Rifle: Irina Chilova, Soviet Union
Women's Air Pistol: Jasna Sekaric, Yugoslavia
Women's Small Bore Rifle, 3 Positions: Silvia Sperber, West Germany
Women's Sport Pistol: Nino Saloukvadze, Soviet Union
Mixed Trapshooting: Dmitri Monakov, Soviet Union
Mixed Skeetshooting: Axel Wegner, East Germany

Soccer
Soviet Union

Swimming and Diving
Men's 100-m Backstroke: Daichi Suzuki, Japan
Men's 200-m Backstroke: Igor Polyansky, Soviet Union
Men's 100-m Breaststroke: Adrian Moorhouse, Great Britain
Men's 200-m Breaststroke: Jozsef Szabo, Hungary
Men's 100-m Butterfly: Anthony Nesty, Suriname
Men's 200-m Butterfly: Michael Gross, West Germany

Men's 50-m Freestyle: Matt Biondi, United States
Men's 100-m Freestyle: M. Biondi
Men's 200-m Freestyle: Duncan Armstrong, Australia
Men's 400-m Freestyle: Uwe Dassler, East Germany
Men's 1,500-m Freestyle: Vladimir Salnikov, Soviet Union
Men's 400-m Freestyle Relay: United States
Men's 800-m Freestyle Relay: United States
Men's 200-m Individual Medley: Tamas Darnyi, Hungary
Men's 400-m Individual Medley: T. Darnyi
Men's 400-m Medley Relay: United States
Men's Springboard Diving: Greg Louganis, United States
Men's Platform Diving: G. Louganis
Women's 100-m Backstroke: Kristin Otto, East Germany
Women's 200-m Backstroke: Krisztina Egerszegi, Hungary
Women's 100-m Breaststroke: Tania Dangalakova, Bulgaria
Women's 200-m Breaststroke: Silke Hörner, East Germany
Women's 100-m Butterfly: K. Otto
Women's 200-m Butterfly: Kathleen Nord, East Germany
Women's 50-m Freestyle: K. Otto
Women's 100-m Freestyle: K. Otto
Women's 200-m Freestyle: Heike Friedrich, East Germany
Women's 400-m Freestyle: Janet Evans, United States
Women's 800-m Freestyle: J. Evans
Women's 400-m Freestyle Relay: East Germany
Women's 200-m Individual Medley: Daniela Hunger, East Germany
Women's 400-m Individual Medley: J. Evans
Women's 400-m Medley Relay: East Germany
Women's Springboard Diving: Gao Min, China
Women's Platform Diving: Xu Yanmei, China

Synchronized Swimming
Solo: Carolyn Waldo, Canada
Duet: Canada

Table Tennis
Men's Doubles: Chen Longcan and Wei Qingguang, China
Men's Singles: Yoo Nam Kyu, South Korea
Women's Doubles: Hyun Jung Hwa and Yang Young Ja, South Korea
Women's Singles: Chen Jing, China

Tennis
Men's Doubles: Ken Flach and Robert Seguso, United States
Men's Singles: Miloslav Mecir, Czechoslovakia
Women's Doubles: Pam Shriver and Zina Garrison, United States
Women's Singles: Steffi Graf, West Germany

Track and Field
Men's 100-m: Carl Lewis, United States
Men's 200-m: Joe DeLoach, United States
Men's 400-m: Steve Lewis, United States
Men's 800-m: Paul Ereng, Kenya
Men's 1,500-m: Peter Rono, Kenya
Men's 5,000-m: John Ngugi, Kenya
Men's 10,000-m: Brahim Boutaib, Morocco
Men's Marathon: Gelindo Bordin, Italy
Men's 110-m Hurdles: Roger Kingdom, United States
Men's 400-m Hurdles: Andre Phillips, United States
Men's 3,000-m Steeplechase: Julius Kariuki, Kenya
Men's 400-m Relay: Soviet Union
Men's 1,600-m Relay: United States
Men's 20-km Walk: Jozef Pribilinec, Czechoslovakia
Men's 50-km Walk: Vyachselav Ivanenko, Soviet Union
Men's Decathlon: Christian Schenk, East Germany
Men's High Jump: Guennadi Avdeenko, Soviet Union
Men's Long Jump: C. Lewis
Men's Triple Jump: Hristo Markov, Bulgaria
Men's Discus: Jurgen Schult, East Germany
Men's Shot Put: Ulf Timmermann, East Germany
Men's Hammer Throw: Sergei Litvinov, Soviet Union
Men's Javelin: Tapio Korjus, Finland
Men's Pole Vault: Sergei Bubka, Soviet Union
Women's 100-m: Florence Griffith Joyner, United States
Women's 200-m: F. Griffith Joyner
Women's 400-m: Olga Bryzgina, Soviet Union
Women's 800-m: Sigrun Wodars, East Germany
Women's 1,500-m: Paula Ivan, Romania
Women's 3,000-m: Tatiana Samolenko, Soviet Union
Women's 10,000-m: Olga Bondarenko, Soviet Union
Women's Marathon: Rosa Mota, Portugal
Women's 100-m Hurdles: Jordanka Donkova, Bulgaria
Women's 400-m Hurdles: Debra Flintoff-King, Australia
Women's 400-m Relay: United States
Women's 1,600-m Relay: Soviet Union
Women's Heptathlon: Jackie Joyner-Kersee, United States
Women's High Jump: Louise Ritter, United States
Women's Long Jump: J. Joyner-Kersee
Women's Discus: Martina Hellmann, East Germany
Women's Shot Put: Natalya Lisovskaya, Soviet Union
Women's Javelin: Petra Felke, East Germany

Volleyball
Men: United States
Women: Soviet Union

Water Polo
Yugoslavia

Weight Lifting
Flyweight: Sevdalin Marinov, Bulgaria
Bantamweight: Oxen Mirzoian, Soviet Union

Featherweight: Naim Suleymanoglu, Turkey
Lightweight: Joachim Kunz, East Germany
Middleweight: Borislav Guidikov, Bulgaria
Light Heavyweight: Israil Arsamakov, Soviet Union
Middle Heavyweight: Anatoli Khrapatyi, Soviet Union
Heavyweight: Pavel Kouznetsov, Soviet Union
Second Heavyweight: Yuri Zakharevitch, Soviet Union
Super Heavyweight: Alexander Kourlovitch, Soviet Union

Wrestling, Freestyle
Paperweight: Takashi Kobayashi, Japan
Flyweight: Mitsuru Sato, Japan
Bantamweight: Sergei Beloglazov, Soviet Union
Featherweight: John Smith, United States
Lightweight: Arsen Fadzaev, Soviet Union
Welterweight: Ken Monday, United States
Middleweight: Han Myang Woo, South Korea
Light Heavyweight: Makharbek Khadartsev, Soviet Union
Heavyweight: Vasile Puscasu, Romania
Super Heavyweight: David Gobedjichvili, Soviet Union

Wrestling, Greco-Roman
Paperweight: Vincenzo Maenza, Italy
Flyweight: Jon Ronningen, Norway
Bantamweight: Andras Sike, Hungary
Featherweight: Kamandar Madjidov, Soviet Union
Lightweight: Levon Djoulfalakian, Soviet Union
Welterweight: Kim Young Nam, South Korea
Middleweight: Mikhail Mamiachvili, Soviet Union
Light Heavyweight: Atanas Komchev, Bulgaria
Heavyweight: Andrzej Wronski, Poland
Super Heavyweight: Alexander Kareline, Soviet Union

Yachting
Board Sailing: Bruce Kendall, New Zealand
Soling: East Germany
Flying Dutchman: Denmark
Star Class: Great Britain
Finn Class: José Luis Doreste, Spain
Tornado Class: France
Men's 470 Class: France
Women's 470 Class: United States

Final Medal Standings

Country	Gold	Silver	Bronze
Soviet Union	55	31	46
East Germany	37	35	30
United States	36	31	27
South Korea	12	10	11
West Germany	11	14	15
Hungary	11	6	6
Bulgaria	10	12	13
Romania	7	11	6
France	6	4	6
Italy	6	4	4
China	5	11	12
Great Britain	5	10	9
Kenya	5	2	2
Japan	4	3	7
Australia	3	6	5
Yugoslavia	3	4	5
Czechoslovakia	3	3	2
New Zealand	3	2	8
Canada	3	2	5
Poland	2	5	9
Norway	2	3	0
Netherlands	2	2	5
Denmark	2	1	1
Brazil	1	2	3
Finland	1	1	2
Spain	1	1	2
Turkey	1	1	0
Morocco	1	0	2
Austria	1	0	0
Portugal	1	0	0
Suriname	1	0	0
Sweden	0	4	7
Switzerland	0	2	2
Jamaica	0	2	0
Argentina	0	1	1
Chile	0	1	0
Costa Rica	0	1	0
Indonesia	0	1	0
Iran	0	1	0
Netherlands Antilles	0	1	0
Peru	0	1	0
Senegal	0	1	0
Virgin Islands	0	1	0
Belgium	0	0	2
Mexico	0	0	2
Colombia	0	0	1
Djibouti	0	0	1
Greece	0	0	1
Mongolia	0	0	1
Pakistan	0	0	1
Philippines	0	0	1
Thailand	0	0	1

The XV Winter Games

Juan Antonio Samaranch, president of the International Olympic Committee, called the XV Winter Games held Feb. 13–28, 1988, in Calgary, Alta., Canada, "the best ever." They also were the longest Winter Games in history, covering 16 days, and included 1,793 athletes from 57 countries, both records for the games. The competition itself was dominated by the Soviet Union, which won 11 gold medals and 29 total medals, and by East Germany, which won nine golds and 25 total medals. The United States picked up six overall.

Alpine Skiing. Alberto Tomba, a flamboyant 21-year-old from Italy, dominated the men's Alpine skiing by winning gold medals in the slalom and giant slalom. Tomba, a handsome, seemingly fearless man, also became one of the games' glittering stars because of his flashy manner. His successes stole the spotlight from Pirmin Zurbriggen of Switzerland, the world's best skier. Zurbriggen, who was favored to win five gold medals, finished with one gold (downhill) and one bronze (giant slalom). Franck Piccard of France took the super giant slalom, while another unheralded athlete, Hubert Strolz of Austria, won the men's combined (downhill and slalom) and finished second in the men's giant slalom. The best finisher among U.S. men's skiers was Tiger Shaw, who placed 12th in the giant slalom.

Another Swiss skier, Vreni Schneider, was the queen of the women's events. She won gold in the giant slalom and slalom, outracing two of her more famous teammates, Michela Figini and Maria Walliser. Karen Percy of Canada captured her country's first medal by ending up third in the women's downhill and becoming an instant national hero. She also was third in the super giant slalom. Edith Thys finished ninth in the super giant slalom for the best showing among U.S. women skiers.

Figure Skating. Katarina Witt (*see* BIOGRAPHY) of East Germany defended her Olympic title by winning the women's singles in figure skating. The beautiful Witt, who dominated media coverage during the games, outdueled former world champion Debi Thomas of the United States, who stumbled repeatedly during her final-night free-skating routine and wound up third behind Elizabeth Manley of Canada. Both Witt, who wants to be an actress, and Thomas skated their freestyle program to music from the opera *Carmen,* so their competition was called "The Dueling Carmens."

In another very close competition, Brian Boitano of the United States performed superbly during his free-skating program to barely edge Brian Orser of Canada for the gold medal in the men's singles. Boitano was the only American man to win a gold medal in the Olympics. Third place went to Viktor Petrenko of the Soviet Union. Not to be outdone by the women, the men's singles was billed as the "Battle of the Brians."

The most thrilling skating of the games was done by Yekaterina Gordeyeva and Sergei Grinkov of the Soviet Union. They took the gold in the pairs skating with a nearly flawless

Alberto Tomba, the high-living, 21-year-old son of a wealthy businessman from Bologna, Italy, dominated the men's Alpine skiing at the XV Winter Games in Calgary, Alta., capturing gold medals in the giant slalom and the slalom.
© 1988 Chris Speedie

© David Madison/Duomo

© Steven E. Sutton/Duomo

Women's figure skating offered drama and keen competition. East Germany's Katarina Witt (c, photo left), Canada's Elizabeth Manley (l), and Debi Thomas of the United States finished as the gold, silver, and bronze medalists, respectively. Brian Boitano, photo right, a 24-year-old Californian, outpointed Canada's Brian Orser for the men's gold.

XV WINTER GAMES—Gold Medalists

Alpine Skiing
Men's Combined: Hubert Strolz, Austria
Men's Downhill: Pirmin Zurbriggen, Switzerland
Men's Giant Slalom: Alberto Tomba, Italy
Men's Slalom: Alberto Tomba
Men's Super Giant Slalom: Franck Piccard, France
Women's Combined: Anita Wachter, Austria
Women's Downhill: Marina Kiehl, West Germany
Women's Giant Slalom: Vreni Schneider, Switzerland
Women's Slalom: Vreni Schneider
Women's Super Giant Slalom: Sigrid Wolf, Austria

Biathlon
10-kilometer Individual: Frank-Peter Roetsch, East Germany
20-kilometer Individual: Frank-Peter Roetsch
Relay: USSR

Bobsled
2-Man: USSR
4-Man: Switzerland

Figure Skating
Pairs: Yekaterina Gordeyeva and Sergei Grinkov, USSR
Men's Singles: Brian Boitano, United States
Women's Singles: Katarina Witt, East Germany
Dance: Natalya Bestemianova and Andrei Bukin, USSR

Ice Hockey: USSR

Luge
Men's Singles: Jens Mueller, East Germany
Men's Doubles: Joerg Hoffmann and Jochen Pietzsch, East Germany
Women's Singles: Steffi Walter, East Germany

Nordic Skiing
Men's 15-kilometer: Mikhail Deviatiarov, USSR
Men's 30-kilometer: Aleksei Prokourorov, USSR
Men's 50-kilometer: Gunde Svan, Sweden
Men's 40-kilometer Relay: Sweden
Men's 70-meter Ski Jump: Matti Nykaenen, Finland
Men's 90-meter Ski Jump: Matti Nykaenen
Men's 90-meter Team Ski Jump: Finland

Men's Individual Combined: Hippolyt Kempf, Switzerland
Men's Team Combined: West Germany
Women's 5-kilometer: Marjo Matikainen, Finland
Women's 10-kilometer: Vida Ventsene, USSR
Women's 20-kilometer: Tamara Tikhonova, USSR
Women's 20-kilometer Relay: USSR

Speed Skating
Men's 500 meters: Jens-Uwe Mey, East Germany
Men's 1,000 meters: Nikolai Gouliaev, USSR
Men's 1,500 meters: Andre Hoffmann, East Germany
Men's 5,000 meters: Tomas Gustafson, Sweden
Men's 10,000 meters: Tomas Gustafson
Women's 500 meters: Bonnie Blair, United States
Women's 1,000 meters: Christa Rothenburger, East Germany
Women's 1,500 meters: Yvonne van Gennip, The Netherlands
Women's 3,000 meters: Yvonne van Gennip
Women's 5,000 meters: Yvonne van Gennip

Medal Standings

	Gold	Silver	Bronze
USSR	11	9	9
East Germany	9	10	6
Switzerland	5	5	5
Finland	4	1	2
Sweden	4	0	2
Austria	3	5	2
The Netherlands	3	2	2
West Germany	2	4	2
United States	2	1	3
Italy	2	1	2
France	1	0	1
Norway	0	3	2
Canada	0	2	3
Yugoslavia	0	2	1
Czechoslovakia	0	1	2
Japan	0	0	1
Liechtenstein	0	0	1

© Steven E. Sutton/Duomo

Other highlights: U.S. speed skater Bonnie Blair, above, set a record in the women's 500 meters; Finnish ski jumper Matti Nykaenen went home with three gold medals.

© Dan Helms/Duomo

performance. Despite some stumbles in their free-skating program, Jill Watson and Peter Oppegard of the United States finished third behind the USSR's Elena Valova and Oleg Vasiliev.

The gold medal in ice dancing was won by another Soviet pair, Natalya Bestemianova and Andrei Bukin. But the most controversial pair was Isabelle and Paul Duchesnay, a brother-sister duo representing France who dared to skate to inventive music with unorthodox moves. But the judges placed them eighth in the competition.

Speed Skating. Yvonne van Gennip of The Netherlands, who once thought she never could beat the elite skaters from East Germany, won three gold medals (1,500, 3,000, and 5,000 meters) despite having foot surgery in December 1987. It was the finest Dutch Olympic effort since speed skater Ard Schenk won three gold medals in 1972. American Bonnie Blair took the women's 500 meters in world record time to become one of two American gold-medal winners. She cried on the victory stand after receiving her award. She later finished third in the 1,000 meters.

The hearts of many of the Olympic fans and spectators went out to the U.S. speed skater Dan Jansen. A favorite before the games began, he not only fell in the 500-meter and the 1,000-meter races but also lost his sister to leukemia during the competition.

Hockey and Other Events. The Soviet Union, the world's longtime dominant hockey power, easily captured the gold medal, ending rumors that it was a team on the decline. In an upset, Finland finished second; Sweden, a favorite to win the gold, was third.

Matti Nykaenen, the quiet star from Finland, solidified his position as the greatest ski jumper in history by winning both the 70- and 90-meter jumps and helping his country to win the 90-meter team competition. Of eight possible gold medals in cross-country skiing, the Soviet Union won five. East Germany captured gold in all three luge events.

Overall. Despite the lack of success by the American athletes, television ratings were impressive. But ABC television, which paid $309 million for the rights to telecast the games, still lost millions. Even though the weather presented problems—too much wind and too warm—the games ended on schedule. There were no major security incidents.

Some of the headliners at the Winter Games were the least successful athletes. Michael (Eddie) Edwards, a British ski jumper nicknamed "The Eagle," finished last in the 70-meter and 90-meter jumps. The Jamaican bobsled team had to hold fund-raisers in Calgary to pay for its expenses. Prince Albert of Monaco competed in the two-man bobsled.

PAUL ATTNER
"The Sporting News"

Skiing

Swiss skiers won the overall World Cup skiing titles in 1988 with top laurels going to Pirmin Zurbriggen and Michela Figini, but a garrulous, popular Italian, Alberto Tomba, almost prevented Zurbriggen from taking his second straight and third overall crown.

Zurbriggen, who also won the overall crown in 1984 and 1987, beat out Tomba, 310 points to 281, when the 21-year-old Tomba fell in his last two races and could not overtake the Swiss. The 25-year-old Zurbriggen, the Olympic downhill champion, had a banner season as he also won the World Cup downhill for the second year in a row and the super giant slalom title. Zurbriggen became the first skier to win consecutive World Cup downhill titles since Peter Mueller of Switzerland did it in 1980–81.

For all his bombast, Tomba, who won two Olympic gold medals, backed it up by winning nine World Cup events, including six slaloms and three giant slaloms, capturing titles in each of those disciplines. En route to his triumph, he won four straight races. Tomba, from Bologna, did not lack for braggadocio. After winning a race he told reporters at the finish line, "I feel a little bit lonely out in front all the time. Maybe the other guys should start training a little more to try and catch up." He did not, however, compete in the downhill.

Figini, who hails from the Italian region of Switzerland, clinched the overall title late in March at Saalbach, Austria, when the last race of the season, a downhill, was canceled because of warm weather. She regained the overall crown she first won in 1985 and also took the downhill and super giant slalom. She outscored another Swiss, Brigitte Oertli, 244 to 226 for the overall title. Anita Wachter of Austria was third (211). The giant slalom title among the women went to Mateja Svet of Yugoslavia, and the slalom was won by Roswitha Steiner of Austria.

Switzerland also was first in the Nations Cup standing, edging Austria 2,199 to 2,195, with the United States in ninth place with 191 points. The World Cup competition ran from November to March with events held in Europe, Canada, and the United States.

In the United States Alpine championships, Jeff Olson and Pam Fletcher were the downhill winners. Felix McGrath, who turned in the best showing by an American in the World Cup competition by finishing second and third in the men's slalom races, won the U.S. men's slalom crown; Tamara McKinney was the women's slalom winner. Tiger Shaw took the giant slalom and the combined titles. Monique Pelletier was first among the women in the giant slalom and combined; and Fletcher and Mike Brown captured the super giant slaloms.

See also SPORTS—*Winter Olympics.*

GEORGE DE GREGORIO

Soccer

In an action-packed year for international soccer, attention focused on the Olympic tournament (*see* page 494), the biennial European Championship, and club tournament play—as well as the continuing problem of fan violence. An upbeat year for American soccer was highlighted by the selection of the United States as host of the 1994 World Cup tournament.

World. The eight-team European Nations Cup tournament culminated in a final-match showdown between the Netherlands and the Soviet Union in Munich, West Germany. With goals by strikers Ruud Gullit and Marco Van Basten, the Flying Orange Dutchmen, as the team was dubbed, won their first major international soccer title, 2-0. For the flamboyant, dreadlocked Gullit, it was a banner year, as he also led his Milan team to the Italian league title and was named European player of the year.

Earlier rounds of the tournament—held in Stuttgart, Düsseldorf, Frankfurt, and Munich —were marred by bloody street brawls between English and West German fans. A total of some 1,000 rioters from both countries were arrested in less than one week. The unrest began to subside when the English team was eliminated from the tournament on June 18 and most of its fans returned home.

United States. On July 4 the International Federation of Football Associations (FIFA) accepted the U.S. bid to host the 15th World Cup tournament in 1994. As the host, the United States automatically qualifies for the month-long, 52-match tournament, to be played at 12 stadiums across the country. The United States has never hosted the event and never reached the final round. Its selection therefore was seen as a major boost for American soccer.

Another sign of the sport's U.S. revival was the debut of the new outdoor American Soccer League (ASL) in spring 1988. The ASL's ten teams, located in Eastern seaboard cities from Boston to Miami, played a 20-game schedule from April to August. The Washington Diplomats defeated the Fort Lauderdale Strikers, 3-2, to win the league's first championship.

Meanwhile, the Major Indoor Soccer League (MISL) celebrated its tenth anniversary, albeit with a sense of uncertainty. The very existence of the league was threatened when four of its 11 franchises—St. Louis, Minnesota, Tacoma, and Chicago—folded after the 1987–88 season. In July, team owners voted to play the 1988–89 season, with the remaining clubs to play a 48-game schedule.

On the field, the San Diego Sockers won their fourth MISL title in six years, defeating the Cleveland Force, four games to none, in the championship series.

In the NCAA Division 1 tournament, Indiana University defeated Howard University, 1-0, in the title match.

Swimming

The Americans Matt Biondi and Janet Evans were standout swimmers during the 1988 season, leading to their stellar performances at the Seoul Summer Olympics (*see* page 494).

At the U.S. Olympic Trials in Austin, TX, in August, Biondi and Evans both set records in their specialties. Biondi, from Moraga, CA, lowered his two-year-old world standard of 48.74 seconds in the 100-m freestyle with a clocking of 48.42—a record that held up through the Olympics. It was the third time that Biondi lowered the mark in that event. Biondi qualified for seven events in Seoul, though not all of them with first-place finishes at the Trials. In the 50-m freestyle, he was beaten by Tom Jager, who had bettered his own world record in that event with a 22.23-second clocking at the national indoor championships in Orlando, FL, during March. Then at the Olympics, Biondi claimed the record with a time of 22.14.

The 16-year-old Evans, from Placentia, CA, set a new American record (4:38.58) in the 400-m individual medley at Austin and qualified for two other Olympic events. At the national indoors in March, she shattered the world record in the 800-m freestyle by 2.41 seconds with a time of 8:17.12, and smashed her own world mark in the 1,500-m freestyle by 8.63 seconds with a clocking of 15:52.10. And Evans set her third world record of the year in Seoul with a time of 4:03.85 in the 400-m freestyle.

The men's 400-m freestyle world mark fell to Poland's Artur Wojdat, who swam 3:47.38 at the U.S. national indoors. Wojdat became the first Polish swimmer to break a world record, but his mark was bettered by East Germany's Uwe Dassler in Seoul—3:46.95.

The 100-m backstroke record fell six times during the year. Igor Polyansky of the Soviet Union turned in a 55.17 on March 15, a 55.16 the next day, and a 55.00 in July. David Berkoff, a Harvard senior from Huntington Valley, PA, swam 54.95 and 54.91 in the Olympic Trials and 54.51 in a preliminary heat at Seoul. His technique of swimming most of the first lap under water caused a sensation.

Five other men's world records fell in Seoul, three by U.S. relay teams (3:16.53 in the 400-m freestyle; 7:12.51 in the 800-m freestyle; and 3:36.93 in the 400-m medley) and two by Hungary's Tamas Darnyi in individual medleys (2:00.17 in the 200 meters and 4:14.75 in the 400 meters).

China's Yang Wenyi set a world record in the women's 50-m freestyle (24.98) in April. Canada's Allison Higson set a new standard in the 200-m breaststroke (2:27.27) in May, but East Germany's Silke Hoerner regained the record (2:26.71) at the Olympics.

George De Gregorio

Tennis

West Germany's Steffi Graf and Sweden's Mats Wilander and Stefan Edberg painted the 1988 tennis year, brightly and indelibly, in their national colors. Among them they won all four major championships for men and women, with the 19-year-old Graf sailing to the first Grand Slam in 18 years and adding an Olympic gold medal (*see* page 494).

Graf launched her successful quest for the sixth Slam in the game's history (the last being by Margaret Smith Court in 1970) by winning her first Australian Open title at the newly opened Flinders Park complex in Melbourne, beating American Chris Evert in the final, 6-1, 7-6. Swift, powerful, and nerveless, the West German repeated as French Open champion with a merciless 32-minute pounding, 6-0, 6-0, of Soviet 17-year-old Natalya Zvereva in the final. Graf, who had taken the Number 1 ranking from Martina Navratilova in 1987, wrenched away her most important crown, Wimbledon, in July 1988. Her 5-7, 6-2, 6-1 victory in the final prevented Navratilova from winning a record ninth Wimbledon singles

TENNIS

Davis Cup: West Germany
Federation Cup: Czechoslovakia
Wightman Cup: United States

Major Tournaments

Australian Open—men's singles: Mats Wilander (Sweden); men's doubles: Jim Pugh and Rick Leach; women's singles: Steffi Graf (West Germany); women's doubles: Martina Navratilova and Pam Shriver; mixed doubles: Jim Pugh and Jana Novotna (Czechoslovakia).
World Championship Tennis—Boris Becker (West Germany).
Italian Open—men's singles: Ivan Lendl (Czechoslovakia); men's doubles: Jorge Lozano (Mexico) and Todd Witsken; women's singles: Gabriela Sabatini (Argentina); women's doubles: Jana Novotna (Czechoslovakia) and Catherine Suire (France).
French Open—men's singles: Mats Wilander (Sweden); men's doubles: Emilio Sanchez (Spain) and Andres Gomez (Ecuador); women's singles: Steffi Graf (West Germany); women's doubles: Martina Navratilova and Pam Shriver; mixed doubles: Jorge Lozano (Mexico) and Lori McNeil.
U.S. Clay Courts—Andre Agassi.
Wimbledon—men's singles: Stefan Edberg (Sweden); men's doubles: Ken Flach and Robert Seguso; women's singles: Steffi Graf (West Germany); women's doubles: Steffi Graf and Gabriela Sabatini (Argentina); mixed doubles: Sherwood Stewart and Zina Garrison.
Player's International—singles: Ivan Lendl (Czechoslovakia); doubles: Ken Flach and Robert Seguso.
Player's Challenge—singles: Gabriela Sabatini (Argentina); doubles: Martina Navratilova and Helena Sukova (Czechoslovakia).
U.S. Open—men's singles: Mats Wilander (Sweden); men's doubles: Sergio Casal (Spain) and Emilio Sanchez (Spain); women's singles: Steffi Graf (West Germany); women's doubles: Gigi Fernandez and Robin White; mixed doubles: Jana Novotna (Czechoslovakia) and Jim Pugh; senior men's singles: Tom Gullikson; senior men's doubles: Marty Riessen and Sherwood Stewart; senior women's doubles: Wendy Turnbull (Australia) and Sharon Walsh Pete; boys' singles: Nicholas Pereira (Venezuela); boys' doubles: Jonathan Stark and John Yancey; girls' singles: Carrie Cunningham; girls' doubles: Meredith McGrath and Kimberly Po.
Virginia Slims Championships—singles: Gabriela Sabatini (Argentina); doubles: Martina Navratilova and Pam Shriver.
Nabisco Grand Prix Masters—singles: Boris Becker (West Germany); doubles: Jim Pugh and Rick Leach.
NCAA (Division I)—men's singles: Robby Weiss, Pepperdine; men's team: Stanford; women's singles: Shaun Stafford, Florida; women's team: Stanford.

N.B. All players are from the United States unless otherwise noted.

crown—and positioned the young German for the Grand Slam sweep. She completed her quest at the U.S. Open—on the 50th anniversary of Don Budge's original Slam—by wearing out her 18-year-old Argentine nemesis, Gabriela Sabatini, in the final, 6-3, 3-6, 6-1.

Graf's was a broader Slam than those of her predecessors (Budge, Maureen Connolly in 1953, Rod Laver in 1962 and 1969, and Court) since it was done on three surfaces: hard courts in Melbourne and New York, as well as traditional Wimbledon grass and Paris clay. Previously, the U.S. and Australian Opens had been contested on grass.

During the course of the year, Graf lost only three matches and a total of 11 sets, compiling a 73-3 match record. Two of her losses came at the hands of Sabatini. The third came in the semifinals of the Virginia Slims Championship at New York's Madison Square Garden in November, against Pam Shriver. Her 3-6, 6-7 defeat ended a 46-match winning streak. Sabatini beat Shriver in the final, 7-5, 6-2, 6-2.

In men's play, Wilander dismayed home crowds by beating local heroes for the Australian and French Open titles. His victim in Melbourne was Patrick Cash, whom he defeated 6-3, 6-7, 3-6, 6-1, 8-6 in the best of the year's major finals. In the Paris finals he beat Henri Leconte, 7-5, 6-2, 6-1; another Swede, J.B. Svensson, stopped Ivan Lendl's bid for a third successive French title in the quarterfinals, opening the way for Leconte. But for his quarterfinal defeat at Wimbledon by Czechoslovakia's Miloslav Mecir (who later won the Olympic gold medal in singles), the 24-year-old Wilander might have won a Grand Slam of his own. The hot hand at Wimbledon belonged to

The popular Andre Agassi of Las Vegas, NV, won six tournaments and rose to the Number 1 ranking among U.S. men. At age 18 he became the youngest ever to hold that position.

Photos AP/Wide World

Still only 19, West Germany's Steffi Graf completed her quest for a Grand Slam by winning the U.S. Open. She capped her dream year with an Olympic gold medal.

yet another Swede, however, the 22-year-old Edberg who rallied to beat Mecir from two sets down in the semifinals and thwarted the bid by West Germany's Boris Becker for a third title, 4-6, 7-6, 6-4, 6-2, in the final. Wilander returned to top form at the U.S. Open, where he not only deposed three-time defending champion Lendl in the final, 6-4, 4-6, 6-3, 5-7, 6-4, but also ended Lendl's three-year reign as the world's Number 1 men's player.

Like Graf, Wilander fell in an early round of his last tournament appearance of the year, the Nabisco Masters at New York's Madison Square Garden. Edberg, who defeated him 6-2, 6-2, lost to Lendl in the semifinals, who in turn succumbed to Becker in a grueling final, 7-5, 6-7, 6-3, 2-6, 6-7.

Although Navratilova won no major singles tournaments, she and Shriver combined for the Australian and French doubles titles. Evert won four tournaments, extending her all-time career record to 157; Navratilova stayed right behind by winning nine, for a total of 138.

Still vigorous at age 36, Jimmy Connors ended a four-year tournament-winning drought at Washington, DC, and Toulouse, France, advancing his men's career record to 107; Lendl's three tournament wins put him in second place with 73. But Connors was replaced as Number 1 in the U.S. rankings by Andre Agassi (winner of six 1988 tournaments), who at 18 became the youngest ever to hold that position.

BUD COLLINS, *"The Boston Globe"*

Track and Field

Florence Griffith Joyner and Jackie Joyner-Kersee, who excelled at the 1988 Summer Olympics, also were the most sensational female track and field performers during the year's regular season. Among the men, a 20-year-old world record fell by the wayside when Butch Reynolds of the United States cracked the 400-meter barrier in Zurich, Switzerland. Reynolds lowered the standard set by American Lee Evans in the 1968 Olympics by 57 hundredths of a second to 43.29.

Griffith Joyner, who is married to and coached by Al Joyner, the brother of Joyner-Kersee, excited the track and field world with a record-shattering 100-meter dash in Indianapolis on July 16 when she was timed in 10.49 and knocked 27 hundredths of a second off the 1984 mark set by Evelyn Ashford. Joyner-Kersee, regarded as the best all-around athlete in the sport, continued to dominate the heptathlon, an event in which she has held the world record since July 1986. Joyner-Kersee scored 7,215 points in Indianapolis on July 15–16 to better her 7,161 posted in August 1986. In the Olympics she lifted her score to 7,291.

Bulgarian hurdler Yordanka Donkova regained the 100-meter hurdles world record she had lost to her countrywoman, Ginka Zagorcheva, in 1987. Donkova posted a 12.21 in August to erase Zagorcheva's 12.25.

Soviet pole vaulter Sergei Bubka, who has raised the world record annually since he took it over in Rome in 1984, twice improved his marks in 1988. In June in Bratislava, Czechoslovakia, he vaulted 19′10¼″ (6.052 m) and in Nice, France, in July, the 24-year-old star registered 19′10½″ (6.058 m). Ulf Timmermann of East Germany took the world shot-put record from Alessandro Andrei of Italy with a put of 75′8″ (23.06 m). He later raised the mark 5 more inches (12.7 cm).

Galina Chrstyakova of the Soviet Union broke the long jump record of 24′5½″ (7.45 m) in June with a jump of 24′8¼″ (7.52 m). An East German, Gabriele Reinsch, broke the four-year-old discus throw record of 244′7″ (74.55 m) by Zdenka Silhava of Czechoslovakia with a throw of 252′ (76.80 m). Her countrywoman Petra Felke surpassed her javelin mark by 3′7″ (1.09 m) with a throw of 262′5″ (80.00 m).

The men's high-jump record of 7′11¼″ (2.42 m), shared by Patrik Sjöberg of Sweden and Carlo Thränhardt of West Germany, was broken by Cuba's Javier Sotomayor (7′11½″ or 2.426 m).

The 92d Boston Marathon was won by Ibrahim Hussein, a Kenyan native, and Portugal's Rosa Mota. In the New York City Marathon, Grete Waitz of Norway won the women's title for a record ninth time, and Steve Jones of Wales finished first among the men.

GEORGE DE GREGORIO

Yachting

After an unorthodox challenge broke with tradition and brought court action, the American yacht *Stars & Stripes*, a multihull catamaran skippered by Dennis Conner, turned back the challenge of a monohull, representing New Zealand, in two one-sided races off San Diego in September. The victories enabled the Americans and the San Diego Yacht Club to retain the America's Cup.

The competition took place after Michael Fay, an investment banker and chairman of the syndicate that backed New Zealand, won a suit in New York Supreme Court that ordered Conner to defend the cup three years sooner than he had intended. Conner had lost to Australia in 1983, relinquishing the cup from American hands for the first time in the history of the competition that began in 1851. But he regained the trophy in 1987 and reestablished himself as yacht racing's Number 1 tactician.

In his court challenge, Fay contended that the Deed of Gift, the document written in 1887 that governs the competition, prescribed that competing boats must be similar and that the Americans, by using a catamaran, had an unfair advantage over his monohull yacht. The Americans contended that under the current interpretation of the rules the use of any type yacht was permitted. After several hearings, the court ordered that the races take place, and in July, Justice Carmen Beauchamp Ciparick announced that she would postpone any decision on the legal ramifications of the size and type of yachts until after the races.

The races themselves turned out to be the most one-sided ever held in the competition. In the second race, Conner's 60-foot (18-m) multihull catamaran easily defeated the 132-foot (40-m) monohull *New Zealand* by 21 minutes 10 seconds over a 39-mile (63-km) course, making a sweep of the series. *Stars & Stripes* had romped to victory in the first race by 18 minutes 15 seconds.

The outcome seemed to quiet the New Zealand camp, but there was still room for a possible reversal because Justice Ciparick was expected to make a decision on whether the San Diego Yacht Club had a legal right to defend the cup in a multihull yacht. But that, too, might become academic. Hoping to avert future conflicts, a committee of cup trustees reached an agreement in September on procedures for the 28th America's Cup. The accord is intended to ensure that in future cup competition the defender and the challenger race in similar boats and that the next series be held no sooner than two years after the resolution of the court action regarding the 1988 cup.

In other 1988 yachting competition, Gary Jobson, skipper of the American entry, took the Liberty Cup with a 10-1 record.

GEORGE DE GREGORIO

SPORTS SUMMARIES[1]

ARCHERY—U.S. Target Champions: men: Jay Barrs, Tempe, AZ; women: Debra Ochs, Howell, MI.

BADMINTON—U.S. Champions: men: singles: Chris Jogis, Redondo Beach, CA; doubles: Jogis and Benny Lee, Tempe, AZ; women: singles: Joy Kitzmiller, Manhattan Beach, CA; doubles: Linda Safarik-Tong, Richmond, CA; and Linda French, San Diego; mixed doubles: Jogis and French.

BIATHLON—U.S. Champions: men: 10 km: John Ingdal, Minneapolis; 20 km: Raymond Donmrovski, Seattle; women: 5 km: Mary Ostergren, Minneapolis, 10 km: Peggy Hunter, Stowe, VT.

BILLIARDS—World Champions: men's pocket: Mike Sigel, Towson, MD; three-cushion: Torbjorn Blomdahl, Sweden; men's nine-ball classic: Earl Strickland, Richmond, KY; women's nine-ball classic: Jean Balukas, Brooklyn, NY; snooker: Steve Davis, Great Britain.

BOBSLEDDING—U.S. Champions: two-man: Brent Rushlaw, Saranac Lake, NY, and Hal Hoye, Malone, NY; four-man: Rushlaw; Hoye; Mike Wasko, Sayreville, NJ; and Bill White, Nashua, NH.

BOWLING—Professional Bowlers Association: U.S. Open: Pete Weber, St. Louis; Tournament of Champions: Mark Williams, Beaumont, TX; National Championship: Brian Voss, Seattle. **American Bowling Congress:** regular division: singles: Steve Hutkowski, Hershey, PA; doubles: Mark Lewis and Mark Jensen, Wichita, KS; all-events: Rick Steelsmith, Wichita; master's division: Del Ballard, Dallas; team: Minnesota Loons B, St. Paul, MN. **Women's International Bowling Congress:** open division: singles: Michelle Meyer-Welty, Vacaville, CA; doubles: Dee Alvarez, Tampa, FL, and Pat Costello, Merritt Island, FL; all-events: Lisa Wagner, Palmetto, FL; team: Cooks County, Chicago.

CANOEING—U.S. Champions (flatwater): men's kayak: 500 m: Mark Zollitsch, Westlake, CA; 1,000 m: Mark Hamilton, Louisville, KY; women's kayak: 500 m: Alexandra Bernhardt, Belle Harbor, NY; men's canoe: 500 m: Greg Steward, Williamsburg, OH; 1,000 m: Sandor Nyerges, Falls Church, VA.

CRICKET—World Cup: Australia.

CROSS-COUNTRY—World Champions: men: John Ngugi, Kenya; women: Ingrid Kristiansen, Norway. **U.S. Athletics Congress Champions:** men: Pat Porter, Alamosa, CO; women: Lynn Jennings, Newmarket, NH. **NCAA:** men: Robert Kennedy, Indiana; team: Wisconsin; women: Michelle Dekkers, Indiana; team: Kentucky.

CURLING—World Champions: men: Eigel Ramsfjell, Norway; women: Andrea Schopp, West Germany. **U.S. Champions:** men: Doug Jones, Seattle; women: Nancy Langley, Seattle.

CYCLING—Tour de France: men: Pedro Delgado, Spain; women: Jeannie Longo, France. **U.S. Amateur Champions:** men: road: Randy Whicker, Boulder, CO; sprint: Ken Carpenter, La Mesa, CA; pursuit: David Brinton, N. Hollywood, CA; women: road: Inga Benedict, Reno, NV; sprint: Connie Paraskevin-Young, Indianapolis.

DOG SHOWS—Westminster: best-in-show: Ch. Great Elms Prince Charming, Pomeranian owned by Skip Piazza and Olga Baker.

FENCING—U.S. Champions: men: foil: Michael Marx, Portland, OR; épée: Jon Normile, Berea, OH; saber: Peter Westbrook, New York City; women: foil: Sharon Monplaisir, New York City; épée: Xandy Brown Robinson, Redondo Beach, CA. **U.S. Collegiate:** men: foil: Mark Kent, Columbia; épée: Normile, Columbia; saber: Robert Cottingham, Jr., Columbia; team: Columbia; women: individual: Molly Sullivan, Notre Dame; team: Wayne State.

FIELD HOCKEY—NCAA: Old Dominion.

GYMNASTICS—U.S. Champions: men's all-around: Charles Lakes, Northfield, IL; women's all-around: Phoebe Mills, Chatsworth, CA. **NCAA:** men: all-around: Miguel Rubio, Houston; team: Nebraska; women: all-around: Kelly Garrison-Steves, Oklahoma; team: Alabama.

HANDBALL—U.S. Handball Association Champions: four-wall: men: Naty Alvarado, Hesperia, CA; collegiate team: Memphis State; three-wall: men: John Kendler, Concord, CA; women: Rosemary Bellini, New York City; one-wall: Joe Durso, Brooklyn, NY.

HORSE SHOWS—World Cup: Ian Millar, Perth, Ont., Canada, riding Big Ben. **U.S. Equestrian Team:** dressage: Robert Dover, Pittstown, NJ, riding Federleicht; three-day event: Bruce Davidson, Unionville, PA, riding Dr. Peaches (spring) and Molly Bliss, Rehoboth, MA, riding Hey Charlie (fall); show jumping: Chris Kappler, St. Charles, IL, riding Concorde, and Bernie Traurig, San Francisco, CA, riding May Be Forever (west).

LACROSSE—NCAA: men: Division I: Syracuse; Division II: Hobart; women: Division I: Temple; Division III: Trenton State.

LUGE—World Cup Champions: men: Marcus Prock, Austria; doubles: Yevgeny Belousov and Aleksandr Belyakov, USSR; women: Yulia Antipova, USSR. **U.S. Champions:** men: Frank Masley, Newark, DE; doubles: Joe Barile, Lake Placid, NY, and Steve Maher, Glencoe, IL; women: Bonny Warner, Mount Baldy, CA.

MODERN PENTATHLON—World Champions: Ferenc Katon, Hungary; women: Dorota Idzi, Poland. **U.S. Champions:** men: Bob Nieman, San Antonio, TX; women: Kim Arata, Tallahassee, FL.

PADDLEBALL—U.S. Champions (four-wall): men: open: Andrew Kasalo, Kalamazoo, MI; doubles: Kasalo and Andrew Mitchell, Kalamazoo, MI; women: open: Carla Teare, Flint, MI; doubles: Teare and Anna Sue Thomas, Pontiac, MI.

PADDLE TENNIS—U.S. National Open Champions: men: singles: Scott Freedman, Santa Monica, CA; doubles: Sol Hauptman, Culver City, CA, and Rick Beckendorf, Brentwood, CA; women: singles: Denise Yogi, San Gabriel, CA; doubles: Kathy Paben, Pacific Palisades, CA, and Morgan Bowman, Rancho Palos Verdes, CA.

POLO—World Cup: White Birch Farm, Greenwich, CT. **International Open:** White Birch Farm. **National U.S. Open:** Les Diables Bleus, West Palm Beach, FL.

RACQUETBALL—U.S. Champions: men: singles: Andy Roberts, Memphis, TN; doubles: Bill Sell, Huntington Beach, CA, and Brian Hawkes, Santa Ana, CA; women: singles: Toni Bevlock, Phoenix; doubles: Bevlock and Maria Bailey, Norfolk, VA. **U.S. Pro Champions:** men: Ruben Gonzalez; women: Lynn Adams, San Diego. **U.S. Collegiate Champions:** men: Mike Bronfeld, Sacramento State; women: Robin Levine, Sacramento State.

ROWING—U.S. Champions: men: elite singles: Paul Fuchs, Greenwich, CT; open singles: David Richard, Detroit; elite eight: Selection Camp A; open eight: Camp A; women: elite singles: Lauri Miller, Portland, OR; open singles: Liesel Hud, Philadelphia; elite eight: Boston R.C./Pioneer R. A.; open eight: Boston R.C. **U.S. Collegiate Champions:** men's eight: Harvard; women's eight: Washington.

SOFTBALL—U.S. Champions: men: major fast pitch: Trans-Aire, Elkhart, IN; class-A fast pitch: Stewart-Taylor, Duluth, MN; major slow pitch: Bell Corporation, Tampa, FL; class-A slow pitch: Smith Transport, Roaring Springs, PA; super division slow pitch: Starpath, Monticello, KY; modified fast pitch: Sullivan Roofing, Athens, PA; women: major fast pitch: Hi-Ho Brakettes, Stratford, CT; class-A fast pitch: San Diego Astros; major slow pitch: Anoka (MN) Spooks; class-A slow pitch: Bally, Orlando, FL.

SPEED SKATING—U.S. Champions: men: outdoor: Pat Wentland, Boston; indoor: Brian Arsenau, Chicago; women: outdoor: Elise Brinich, Lisle, IL; indoor: Wendy Goelz, Buffalo, NY.

SURFING—World Champions: men: Fabio Gouveia, Brazil; women: Pauline Menczer, Australia.

TABLE TENNIS—World Champions: men: Jiang Jialing, China; women: He Zhili, China.

TRIATHLON—Ironman Champions: men: Scott Molina, Boulder, CO; women: Paula Newby-Fraser, Encinitas, CA.

VOLLEYBALL—U.S. Champions: men's open: Molten, Torrance, CA; women's open: Chrysler Californians, Hayward, CA. **NCAA:** men: USC; women: Texas.

WATER POLO—World Champions: United States. **NCAA:** California, Berkeley.

WATER SKIING—Master's Tournament: men: overall: Sammy Duvall; women: overall: Deena Mapple.

WRESTLING (Freestyle)—U.S. Champions: 48 kg: Tim Vanni, Tempe, AZ; 52 kg: Joe Gonzalez, Tempe, AZ; 57 kg: Kevin Darkus, Cyclone Wrestling Club; 62 kg: Nate Carr, Morgantown, WV; 74 kg: Kenny Monday, Stillwater, OK; 82 kg: David Schultz, Madison, WI; 90 kg: Melvin Douglas, Minneapolis; 100 kg: Bill Scherr, Bloomington, IN; 130 kg: Bruce Baumgartner, Cambridge Springs, PA. **NCAA:** 118 lbs: Jack Cuvo, East Stroudsburg; 126 lbs: Jim Martin, Penn State; 134 lbs: John Smith, Oklahoma State; 142 lbs: Pat Santoro, Pittsburgh; 150 lbs: Scott Turner, North Carolina State; 158 lbs: Bob Koll, North Carolina; 167 lbs: Mike Van Arsdale, Iowa State; 177 lbs: Royce Alger, Iowa, 190 lbs: Mark Coleman, Ohio State; heavyweight: Carlton Haselrig, Pittsburgh-Johnstown; team: Arizona State.

[1]Sports for which articles do not appear in pages 476–506.

SRI LANKA

Amid continuing ethnic violence, the government of Sri Lanka, headed by President Junius Jayewardene, with the assistance of some 50,000 Indian troops, sought to end four years of chaos in the Northern and Eastern Provinces. Jayewardene did not run for a new term in December presidential balloting, but his proposed successor, Prime Minister Ranasinghe Premadasa of the ruling United National Party (UNP), was elected narrowly.

Politics and Unrest. The UNP held a decisive majority in the unicameral Parliament, but the party was under constant criticism for its failure to hold general elections since 1977, its alleged subservience to India, and the nation's deteriorating economic situation. Opposition parties grew in strength but had little electoral success. The UNP won majorities in all seven of the provincial elections held in April and June. These elections were boycotted by the Sri Lanka Freedom Party (SLFP), the leading opposition party; by the Patriotic People's Front, the political arm of the extremist Sinhalese People's Liberation Front (JVP); and by several smaller parties. A coalition of opposition parties that did participate, called the United Socialist Alliance (USA), won about three fourths as many seats as the UNP. In parliamentary by-elections in mid-July, the UNP retained three seats with greatly reduced majorities and lost a fourth.

Ronnie de Mal, who as finance minister for ten years had been an architect of Sri Lanka's econonic reconstruction and development program, resigned on Jan. 18, 1988.

In the troubled Tamil-majority areas of the north, Indian peacekeeping forces (IPKF) bore the brunt of efforts to implement the July 1987 Indo-Sri Lanka accord, a task made especially difficult by the armed resistance of the leading Tamil extremist organization, the Liberation Tigers of Tamil Eelam (LTTE). But the violence was widespread, mainly due to the ex-

tremist tactics of the JVP. Killings were frequent in and around Colombo; on September 12, Cabinet Minister Lionel Jayatilleke was assassinated in a nearby town. The situation in the south was so tense that the government stationed 10,000 soldiers and police there.

In spite of the continuing violence, the UNP government proceeded with plans to merge the Northern and Eastern Provinces and hold elections for a regional council, both provided for in the Indo-Sri Lanka accord. The main opponents of this election, the LTTE (which demanded more far-reaching concessions to the Tamils) and the JVP (which demanded fewer), resorted to violence and intimidation to prevent the balloting; the LTTE threatened to assassinate any Tamils who participated. Tamil groups that did decide to take part formed the Tamil Eelam Revolutionary Front, which won all 36 seats (uncontested) in the Northern Province, as well as 17 of 35 seats in the Eastern Province, in the November 19 balloting. All but one of the remaining 18 seats were won by the Muslim Congress.

The long-awaited presidential election finally was held on December 19. President Jayewardene, meanwhile, on his 82nd birthday, September 16, had announced that he would not run for reelection. The UNP accepted his choice, Prime Minister Premadasa, as its candidate; former Prime Minister Sirimavo Bandaranaike of the SLFP was Premadasa's main opponent. When the votes were counted, Premadasa was credited with a 50.4% margin, just enough to win.

General elections for Parliament, the first since 1977, were promised for February 1989.

Economy. Because of the violent and uncertain internal situation, Sri Lanka's economy continued to deteriorate in 1988. Almost all phases were affected adversely, including foodgrain production, industrial development, foreign investment, balance of trade, and tourism. Substantial foreign aid was made available to the government, including a $343 million loan by the International Monetary Fund in March. In August, Prime Minister Premadasa announced a crash program to create new jobs.

Relations with India. Opinion in Sri Lanka regarding the 1987 accord with India was divided sharply. The government defended it as a basis for ending the conflict in the north and east, while extremist Tamil and Sinhalese groups denounced it as a threat to Sri Lanka's independence. The presence of Indian peacekeeping troops exacerbated anti-Indian sentiment, which grew as the number of IPKF troops and the number of Tamil casualties mounted. The IPKF was unable to achieve its mission of forcing Tamil extremists to accept the accord and lay down their arms. In June the Indian government began a phased withdrawal.

NORMAN D. PALMER
University of Pennsylvania

SRI LANKA • Information Highlights

Official Name: Democratic Socialist Republic of Sri Lanka.
Location: South Asia.
Area: 25,332 sq mi (65 610 km²).
Population (mid-1988 est.): 16,600,000.
Chief Cities (mid-1986 est.): Colombo, the capital, 683,000; Dehiwala-Mount Lavinia, 191,000; Jaffna, 143,000; Moratuwa, 138,000.
Government: *Head of state,* R. Premadasa, president (took office Jan. 1989). *Legislature* (unicameral) —Parliament.
Monetary Unit: Rupee (32.070 rupees equal U.S.$1, July 1988).
Gross Domestic Product (1986 U.S.$): $6,300,000,000.
Economic Index (Colombo, 1987): *Consumer Prices* (1980 = 100), all items, 205.2; food, 205.2.
Foreign Trade (1987 U.S.$): *Imports,* $2,029,000,000; *exports,* $1,302,000,000.

STAMPS AND STAMP COLLECTING

The U.S. Postal Service (USPS) issued two different "Love" stamps in 1988—a 25¢ one featuring a pink rose, and a 45¢ adhesive depicting an arrangement of red and yellow roses. A "Love" folder containing blocks of both stamps also was released. The birds and the bees made their way into the stamp schedule, too. One stamp featured the saw whet owl and the rose-breasted grosbeak, while another showed a pheasant. The famed American eagle appeared on an $8.75 Express Mail stamp, and the honeybee also was honored on a stamp.

Since 1988 was an Olympic year, the United States issued two separate items hailing participation in the Winter and Summer Games. In

Siamese Cat, Exotic Shorthair Cat   Abyssinian Cat, Himalayan Cat

Maine Coon Cat, Burmese Cat   American Shorthair Cat, Persian Cat

Photos U.S.
Postal Service

continuation of the celebration of the 200th anniversary of the U.S. Constitution, there were commemoratives for several states. There also were more "flag" stamps in 1988—"Flag With Clouds" and "Flag Over Yosemite."

Another postal rate increase went into effect in March—from 22¢ for the minimum first class to 25¢. This necessitated a special "E" (Earth) stamp to be used for postage while new stamps with the added values were printed.

An historic first in the chronicles of the USPS—a three-nation stamp issuance—was hailed in worldwide philatelic circles. Finland, Sweden, and the United States issued stamps honoring the 350th anniversary of the settlement of New Sweden on the North American continent by Swedish and Finnish immigrants. All the stamps, with one basic design, were international airmails. Another combination arrangement in tribute to the founding of Australia resulted in similar stamps being issued by the United States and Australia.

A commemorative stamp booklet issued in 1988 contained five stamps depicting "Classic Cars" of the 20th century. The designs illustrated the 1928 Locomobile, 1929 Pierce-Arrow, 1931 Cord, 1932 Packard, and 1935 Duesenberg.

A block of four ornate and colorful stamps, part of the Folk Art Series, commemorated and pictured hand-carved carousels. Another block of four featured domestic cats; two cats appeared on each stamp. A quartet of Antarctic explorers were hailed on an additional block of four stamps. The heroes who first explored the ice-capped continent of Antarctica were Nathaniel B. Palmer, Charles Wilkes, Richard E. Byrd, and Lincoln Ellsworth.

A colorful, picturesque view of the famed Hearst Castle in San Simeon, CA, is seen on a postal card in the Historic Preservation Series. The sailing ship *Yorkshire,* heralded as the fastest packet ship that ever sailed, appears on an international postal card.

SYD KRONISH, *The Associated Press*

Selected U.S. Commemorative Stamps, 1988

Subject	Denomination	Date	Subject	Denomination	Date	Subject	Denomination	Date
			Pheasant	25¢	April 29	Tugboat	15¢	July 12
			Blair House (card)	15¢	May 4	Northwest Territory (card)	15¢	July 15
Georgia Statehood	22¢	Jan. 6	Samuel P. Langley Airmail	45¢	May 14	New York Statehood	25¢	July 26
Connecticut Statehood	22¢	Jan. 9	DC3 (air card)	36¢	May 14	Love	45¢	Aug. 8
Winter Olympics	22¢	Jan. 10	Flag Over Yosemite	25¢	May 20	Summer Olympics	25¢	Aug. 19
Australian Joint Issue	22¢	Jan. 26	South Carolina Statehood	25¢	May 23	Classic Cars (booklet)	25¢	Aug. 25
James W. Johnson	22¢	Feb. 2	Owl and Grosbeak	25¢	May 28	Caretta Wagon	7.6¢	Aug. 30
Cats (four)	22¢	Feb. 5	Buffalo Bill (card)	15¢	June 6	Honeybee	25¢	Sept. 2
Massachusetts Statehood	22¢	Feb. 6	Francis Ouimet	25¢	June 13	Antarctic Explorers (four)	25¢	Sept. 14
Maryland Statehood	22¢	Feb. 15	Dr. Harvey Cushing	45¢	June 17	Hearst Castle (card)	15¢	Sept. 20
Conestoga Wagon (coil)	3¢	Feb. 29	New Hampshire Statehood	25¢	June 21	Carousels (four)	25¢	Oct. 1
Knute Rockne	22¢	March 9	Igor Sikorsky (air card)	36¢	June 23	Express Mail	$8.75	Oct. 4
"E" Stamp (booklet)	25¢	March 22	Virginia Statehood	25¢	June 25	Christmas (contemporary)	25¢	Oct. 20
Stars (envelope)	25¢	March 22	Yorkshire (card)	28¢	June 29	Christmas (traditional)	25¢	Oct. 20
America the Beautiful (card)	15¢	March 28	Iowa Territory (card)	15¢	July 2	Chester Carlson	21¢	Oct. 21
New Sweden Joint Issue	44¢	March 29	Love	25¢	July 4	Mary Cassat	23¢	Nov. 4
Penalty Mail	25¢	April 11	Flag With Clouds	25¢	July 5	Gen. "Hap" Arnold Airmail	65¢	Nov. 5

In February 1988, David Ruder, chairman of the Securities and Exchange Commission, released the commission's report on the October 1987 stock-market crash. Agreeing with the findings of the presidential panel headed by Nicholas Brady, the SEC report concluded that basic negative changes in investor psychology plus computerized trading in stocks and stock-index futures contributed to the 1987 decline.

AP/Wide World

STOCKS AND BONDS

For the U.S. stock market and the investment community at large, 1988 was a year of retrenchment and recuperation from the crash that rocked the financial world the previous fall. The picture was not uniformly bleak. In fact, the Dow Jones industrial average, the best-known measure of stock-price trends, posted its seventh gain in eight years, finishing at 2,168.57, up 229.74 points, or 11.85%, from the end of 1987.

Furthermore, investment bankers and professional traders known as arbitragers were able to reap handsome earnings from a cornucopia of mergers and buyouts, including the unprecedented buyout for nearly $25 billion of RJR Nabisco in a bidding war won by the firm of Kohlberg Kravis Roberts.

But hardly anyone on Wall Street was ready to proclaim that the great bull market of 1982–87 had been revived. Trading volume in all the major markets contracted significantly from the record levels reached in 1987. At the New York Stock Exchange, the number of shares traded dropped to 40.85 billion from 47.80 billion the year before. Brokerage firms whose fortunes depend heavily on commission business found their profits slim or nonexistent. Employment in the securities industry, which had doubled from the late 1970s to the market peak in 1987, shrank by an estimated 15,000 jobs. At year's end, there was widespread talk of more layoffs in early 1989 if market conditions did not improve.

The mutual fund industry suffered as well. In the first ten months of 1988, according to the Investment Company Institute, sales of long-term funds investing in stocks, bonds, and other income-producing securities came to about $78 billion, less than half the $172 billion total reported for the comparable period in 1987. Fund sponsors did not suffer nearly as much as they had in past downturns, partly because of the continued popularity of short-term money market funds, which reached a new high in the fall of 1988. Still, few traces remained of the explosive growth the funds experienced earlier in the decade.

In the stock market, the year began with a scary aftershock from the crash on Black Monday, Oct. 19, 1987. In the late afternoon of Friday, January 8, a selling wave hit the market that left the Dow Jones industrials with a 140.58-point loss for the day. The gains that had built up in a promising rally over the year's first four sessions were wiped out, and fresh protests were raised that professionals engaged in computer-driven program trading involving stocks and futures contracts on stock indexes were threatening to wreck the market.

By early February, the New York Stock Exchange (NYSE) adopted a system known as the "collar," which effectively barred brokerage firms from using the exchange's central electronic trading apparatus for the form of program trading known as index arbitrage whenever the Dow rose or fell more than 50 points. As it turned out, the collar was an interim measure to be superseded later in the year by a proposed network of "circuit breakers" that would trigger automatic halts in stock trading for specified periods of time in wild markets.

The Brady Commission. Circuit breakers were one of several reform measures proposed in a study of the markets by a presidential commission headed by Nicholas F. Brady, an investment banker and former New Jersey senator who later in the year was appointed secretary of the treasury. But several of the Brady commission's other recommendations had yet to be acted upon as 1988 drew to a close.

The panel's main conclusion was that modern trading systems and technology had turned

the stock markets in New York and the futures markets for stock index contracts, mainly in Chicago, into "one market." As such, the commission said, it should have measures to establish some consistent relationship between the minimum margin requirements, or down payments, required to trade in the various marketplaces. In addition, the panel recommended that a single "super-regulator," possibly the Federal Reserve Board, be given power to coordinate the actions of the various organizations charged with supervising the stock and financial futures markets.

It proved difficult, however, to find a way to reconcile the margin requirements for stock trading, which were set at 50%, and those for futures trading, which were much smaller. Higher futures margins might make trading in those markets unappealing, and thus sharply restrict or even eliminate the use of index futures as a money management tool. Nobody proposed lower stock margins as a way to try to increase stability in the New York markets.

The Federal Reserve. The Federal Reserve (Fed) made clear its reluctance to assume the mantle of authority over stock trading, and no other likely candidate for the role of super-regulator could be readily found. The Fed, which oversees the nation's banking system and the progress of the economy as a whole, meanwhile had other matters on its mind. To almost everyone's surprise, the pace of business activity was not faltering in the aftermath of the crash, but instead was showing brisk growth. This came as a great relief to policymakers, business planners, workers, and consumers who had braced for a recession or something worse. But the Fed, for its part, saw strong growth as a mixed blessing.

The positives could not be ignored. The unemployment rate fell to a 14-year low. Corporate earnings flourished as industrial America, helped by a lower dollar in foreign exchange, regained some of its lost clout in the world marketplace. Improved exports helped to shrink the nation's gaping trade deficit, which had been one of the main worries cited as a cause of the 1987 crash.

With the economy beginning to show signs of straining the capacity of both its production facilities and its labor force, the Fed also saw a potential negative—the prospect of a revival of that old nemesis, inflation. The Fed began a series of steps to restrain the growth of credit, highlighted by an August 9 increase in its discount rate—the charge it imposes on loans to private financial institutions—from 6% to 6.5%. Other interest rates were on the rise as well. The prime lending rate set by banks, which began the year at 8.75%, reached 10.5% by late fall.

The Rally. By the time Wall Street reached the first anniversary of Black Monday, stocks rallied to new highs since the crash. On October 21, the Dow Jones industrial average hit a 1988 closing high of 2,183.50, more than 400 points above its low a year earlier.

The rally soon bogged down, however, in part because of the stiff competition stocks faced from interest-bearing investments. Long-term government bonds, a far less risky alternative to stocks, offered yields that fluctuated around 9%. And thanks to the tightening by the Fed, yields on short-term Treasury bills climbed to and past 8%.

As the year neared its end, the yield curve —a graphic representation of the relative levels of short- and long-term interest rates—was virtually flat. This made money-market securities especially alluring, and also prompted new worries about the economic outlook in 1989. "Inverted" yield curves, in which short-term rates exceeded long rates, are seen by many financial analysts as symptomatic of dislocations in the economy. They were linked to, or at least coincided with, recessions and stock bear markets that occurred during 1969–70, 1973–74, and 1981–82.

Leveraged Buyouts. Meanwhile, an entirely different force was depressing prices and rais-

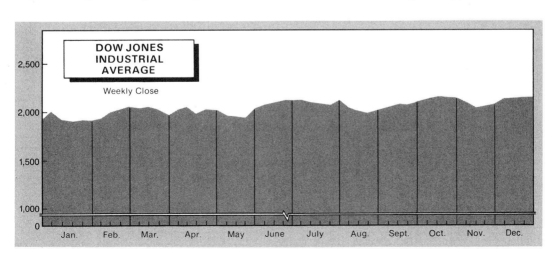

ing interest rates on corporate bonds. As the popularity of leveraged buyouts financed with high-yield, or "junk" bond debt increased, holders of existing investment-grade corporate bonds realized that they were subject to what Wall Street dubbed "event risk." In theory, almost any company, no matter how high its credit rating, could become the target of a buyout that would wind up loading the enterprise down with enormous amounts of new debt. As the battle for RJR Nabisco raged, the prices of its bonds fell sharply, and the whole corporate debt market underwent a painful reappraisal.

In response, some issuers of new corporate bonds developed features that would insulate buyers from this risk—for example, a proviso in the bond contract giving investors the right to sell the bonds back to the issuer at face value in the event of a buyout. But at year's end it still appeared that conservative investors were viewing almost all corporate bonds with a new wariness.

Controversy over leveraged buyouts extended far beyond the corporate bond market. The larger issue focused on the massive substitution of debt for equity, or stock ownership, in the financial base of corporate United States. Advocates of junk bonds long had argued that these securities promoted economic growth by giving vibrant but still-young companies access to credit they could not obtain elsewhere. Many junk-bond investors, for their part, were happy with the extra yield they received. Even with the occasional, inevitable default by one or two junk-bond issuers, studies showed, the overall return available in the junk-bond market was better than what an investor could earn from Treasury securities or top-quality bonds from the private sector.

But skeptics wondered if junk bonds, in their present vast numbers, could weather a severe economic downturn. If they could not pass that test, they might ultimately cause a slump to become much more severe than it might have been otherwise. As a new Congress convened in January 1989, it seemed very likely it would consider the question of whether junk-bond buyouts should be restricted in some way.

Savings and Loans. Along with potential problems from leveraged buyouts, some financial analysts looking to 1989 warned of the crisis posed by failures at large numbers of savings and loan institutions covered by federal deposit insurance. Estimates of the eventual cost to the country increased from $20 billion to $40 billion, and some observers said it might eventually reach $100 billion or more. (*See also* BANKING AND FINANCE.)

Response to Bush. Most Wall Streeters, with their traditional Republican views, applauded Vice-President George Bush's victory in the campaign to succeed President Reagan. Yet the Dow Jones industrial average fell nearly 79 points in the week during which Bush was elected. The trouble, analysts said, was not some sudden disillusionment with the voters' choice. Rather, they concluded, it was concern over what any administration could do to deal successfully with the budget problem. Any of the readily apparent remedies, whether tax increases or cuts in government spending, would stand to act as depressants on business activity.

International investors seemed especially concerned by these questions. After rallying a bit earlier in the year, the dollar came under renewed pressure in foreign exchange markets. Worldwide investors also had other reasons to be dissatisfied with the performance of the U.S. stock market in 1988. For the year through early December, U.S. stocks showed a gain of only 11.9%—half the 20.8% rise posted by a world index incorporating markets in nine countries.

World Markets. American stocks managed to outstrip markets in Canada, which was up 2.4%; Britain, which was up 4.5%, and Australia, which was up 10.6%. But they failed to keep pace with France, up 44.8%; Japan, up 35.9%; West Germany, up 29.4%, Hong Kong, up 23%, and Switzerland, up 19.8%.

The Japanese market, indeed, was the financial marvel of the world in 1988. When the crash hit in 1987, it suffered along with all the other industrialized countries' financial centers. It did not stay down for long, though. Within four months after Black Monday, it was back making new highs. In December, it reached a new milestone when the Nikkei index, Tokyo's counterpart to the Dow in New York, hit 30,000 for the first time.

Many American observers have long viewed Japan's bull market with a mixture of envy and skepticism. Japanese stocks persistently have traded at price-to-earnings ratios that would be considered absurdly high in the U.S. market. Many analysts argue that the numbers still represent a speculative "bubble" that must sooner or later burst. To other observers, Japanese stock prices in 1988 spoke for themselves as emblems of that nation's prodigious economic achievements.

Insider Trading. A two-year investigation into insider trading culminated with a $650 million penalty leveled against the investment banking house of Drexel Burnham Lambert Inc. Drexel admitted guilt in six felony counts of securities fraud. It was the single largest penalty ever exacted for securities fraud in the United States. (The second largest—$100 million—was levied against Ivan Boesky in 1986; Boesky was a client of Drexel.) Civil cases against Drexel were still pending at the close of 1988.

See also BUSINESS AND CORPORATE AFFAIRS.

CHET CURRIER, *The Associated Press*

SUDAN

Increased fighting in the Sudanese civil war threatened nearly 2 million people with starvation. Incessant drought followed by seasonal floods and the inundation of Khartoum, locust swarms, several coup attempts, labor strikes, and student demonstrations combined to make 1988 a dismal year for Sudan.

Civil War. By autumn 1988, hundreds of people were dying of hunger every day in areas of the southern Sudan where guerrilla war and drought had uprooted more than 1 million civilians. The war between the largely Arab and Muslim north and the African and predominantly Christian and Animist south heated up in 1988, with the south dominating during the latter part of the year.

During clandestine peace negotiations in London in December 1987, rebel leader John Garang announced three preconditions for peace: cancellation of the state of emergency, the abrogation of foreign military agreements, and the eradication of the 1983 September "Islamic" laws. The London meeting was unsuccessful and the civil war became as violent and deadly as ever.

In rebel-held territory, official government policy was not to allow food to be delivered to the starving millions. International outrage and U.S. pressure resulted in a United States-directed airlift to the famine-afflicted southern region in early October 1988. Still millions continued to suffer.

In mid-November a member of the Democratic Unionist Party and Garang signed a cease-fire agreement. The postponement of Islamic law was reported to be part of the agreement. However, Prime Minister Sadiq al-Mahdi had avoided the peace talks, and two of the three coalition parties—his own Umma Party and the Islamic National Front—opposed it. Parliament rejected the peace plan in December, and Garang vowed to continue fighting.

Economy. The civil war was costing Sudan's collapsing economy about $1 million per day. Sudan's foreign debt had reached $12 billion by February 1988. A government layoff of 1,500 airline workers led to a widespread 24-hour general strike Nov. 17, 1987. On Nov. 25, 1987, Sudan requested its foreign creditors to facilitate loan repayments or write them off altogether. Only Sweden responded by writing off $20 million of Sudan's debts in March 1988. Sudan has failed to meet debt repayment deadlines in full since the early 1980s.

Domestic Issues. Student strikes and demonstrations broke out throughout the country at the end of 1987. The strikes were mounted in protest against price increases, food shortages, an unpopular debt restructuring agreement with the International Monetary Fund (IMF), and laws regulating student behavior.

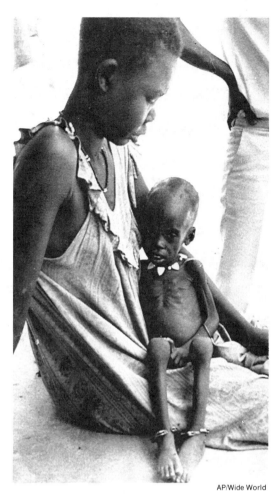

AP/Wide World

Nearly 2 million Sudanese, including the mother and two-year-old child, above, *members of the Dinka tribe, were threatened with starvation caused by the nation's civil war.*

In December 1988, after the government announced price increases on a variety of consumer goods, protest strikes and demonstrations spread throughout Khartoum. The unrest continued even after the price hikes were rescinded, and on December 29 police opened fire on demonstrators, killing one.

Several coup attempts were reported early in the year. On Jan. 18, 1988, the *Voice of Lebanon* reported an alleged unsuccessful coup attempt against the government of Prime Minister Sadiq al-Mahdi. On January 25 the government extended the six-month-old state of emergency for six more months.

Foreign Affairs. Sudanese-Ethiopian relations remained hostile as each side accused the other of supporting dissident forces residing in and operating out of their respective territories. On Dec. 17, 1987, Ethiopian soldiers, fighting alongside Sudanese rebels, were captured around Shali. On Oct. 8, 1988, Ethiopian air raids on Sudanese territory caused the government to cease spraying locust swarms plaguing the eastern Sudan.

SUDAN • Information Highlights

Official Name: Republic of the Sudan.
Location: Northeast Africa.
Area: 967,494 sq mi (2 505 810 km²).
Population (mid-1988 est.): 24,000,000.
Chief Cities (1983 census): Khartoum, the capital, 476,218; Omdurman, 526,287; Khartoum North, 341,146.
Government: *Head of state,* Ahmad al-Mirghani, chairman, State Council (took over May 6, 1986). *Head of government,* Sadiq Siddiq al-Mahdi, prime minister (took over May 6, 1986). *Legislature* (unicameral)—National People's Assembly.
Monetary Unit: Pound (4.5 pounds equal U.S.$1, July 1988).
Foreign Trade (1986 U.S.$): *Imports,* $961,000,000; exports, $333,000,000.

Relations with Libya improved. On March 17, 1988, Libyan leader Muammar el-Qaddafi announced that he would permit Sudanese nationals to enter his country without passports or other official documents.

The United States remained the Sudan's largest aid donor. On Oct. 12, 1988, the Sudan agreed to a $100 million U.S. food airlift to the starving millions in the south, doubling the aid that the Sudan annually receives from the United States.

See also AFRICA.

JOHN P. ENTELIS and ŌMER K. ALPTEKIN
Fordham University

SWEDEN

In elections for a new Parliament held on Sept. 18, 1988, the Social Democratic Party saw its representation reduced from 159 to 156 seats. However, it was able to retain a slim majority in the 349-seat legislature with the support of the Communists' 21 seats. The nonsocialist parties—Moderates (also called Conservatives), Liberals, and the Center Party—held on to 152 seats, a loss of 19 seats in all. The Greens Party, the first new party to enter the Riksdag in 70 years, garnered a respectable total of 20 seats. There was no indication of how the Greens would fit into the traditional left-right scheme in Swedish politics.

Prime Minister Ingvar Carlsson, in a speech at the opening of the 1988–89 session of Parliament on October 4, emphasized that the economy, full employment, and welfare would serve as bases for future development. New efforts would be required in the country's energy and environmental policies as well as in the fields of taxation and social and cultural life. Sweden also would intensify its cooperation with the European Community to the extent compatible with its policy of neutrality.

A number of cabinet changes were announced following the election. Thage G. Peterson was elected new speaker of parliament to succeed Ingemund Bengtsson, who retired after holding the post since 1979.

The Palme Case. The still unsolved murder of Prime Minister Olof Palme in February 1986 had repercussions in 1988. During the summer a Parliamentary Standing Committee on the Constitution conducted public hearings on the efforts of a Swedish businessman, Ebbe Carlsson, to conduct a private investigation of Palme's death. The committee criticized his action, saying it contravened Swedish legal principles. Among those involved were Sweden's chief of police, Nils Erik Åhmansson, and Anna-Greta Leijon, the minister of justice; both resigned. In December, Carl Gustav Christer Pettersson, a suspect in the Palme case, was arrested. By year's end, he was still in custody, but no charges had been filed.

Antarctic Research. The largest Swedish research expedition ever mounted to Antarctica and the South Pole left Stockholm in December 1988. The 50-member expedition was to conduct research in the fields of glaciology, geology, oceanography, and marine biology. An already existing Swedish research station in Antarctica, located 310 mi (500 km) inland in Queen Maud Land, was to be joined by a new and larger research station to be constructed 75 mi (120 km) inland, where new habitation systems for frigid climates would be tested.

On September 21 at a meeting in Paris, Sweden and Spain became members of the 22-nation group which, according to the Antarctic Treaty, supervises all Antarctic activities.

Foreign Affairs. On January 13 Prime Minister Carlsson and Nikolai Ryzhkov, chairman of the Soviet Union's council of ministers, signed an agreement settling a 19-year-old dispute regarding the two countries' joint boundary in the Baltic Sea. The dispute concerned a 8,400-sq mi (22 000-km²) economic zone east of the island of Gotland. Sweden claimed that the boundary ought to be drawn halfway between Gotland and the coastline of the Soviet Baltic Republics, while the USSR had held out for a center line between the two mainlands, with

SWEDEN • Information Highlights

Official Name: Kingdom of Sweden.
Location: Northern Europe.
Area: 173,730 sq mi (449 960 km²).
Population (mid-1988 est.): 8,400,000.
Chief Cities (Dec. 31, 1987 est.): Stockholm, the capital, 666,810; Göteborg, 431,521; Malmö, 230,838; Uppsala, 159,962.
Government: *Head of state,* Carl XVI Gustaf, king (acceded Sept. 1973). *Head of government,* Ingvar Carlsson, prime minister (elected March 12, 1986). *Legislature* (unicameral)—Riksdag.
Monetary Unit: Krona (6.187 kronor equal U.S.$1, Nov. 1, 1988).
Gross Domestic Product (1986 U.S.$): $105,500,-000,000.
Economic Indexes (1987): *Consumer Prices* (1980 = 100), all items, 167.0; food, 191.1. *Industrial Production* (1980 = 100), (1986) 110.
Foreign Trade (1987 U.S.$): *Imports,* $40,649,-000,000; *exports,* $44,447,000,000.

the exception of the territorial waters around Gotland. It was agreed that 75% of the disputed area be allotted to Sweden and the rest to the Soviet Union. Also, for 20 years Soviet fishermen will be entitled to make catches of up to 18,000 tons annually in the Swedish zone, while Swedes may catch up to 6,000 tons each year in the Soviet zone. The quotas will be reviewed and renegotiated after 20 years.

During 1988 the Swedish and U.S. peoples celebrated the 350th anniversary of the founding of the New Sweden colony. Located in what are now parts of the U.S. states of Delaware and Pennsylvania, the colony was established by the Swedish government and flourished from 1638 to 1655, when it was taken over by the Dutch. The U.S. festivities were attended by King Carl XVI Gustaf and Queen Silvia of Sweden and called attention to the contributions Swedes have made to U.S. life.

The king and queen also made a state visit to New Zealand February 13–16 at the invitation of Governor-General Paul Reeves. It was the first such visit by a Swedish head of state to that nation and served to cement the very friendly relations between the two countries.

ERIK J. FRIIS
"The Scandinavian-American Bulletin"

SWITZERLAND

Escalating concern over Switzerland's future relations with the European Community and an incipient political scandal involving the only woman member of the Federal Council were major issues in Switzerland during 1988.

Relations with the European Community. In 1992 the European Community (EC) is scheduled to remove all remaining internal trade barriers and end individual national trade agreements negotiated by its member states. Switzerland, as a member of the European Free Trade Association, currently enjoys considerable trade benefits with the EC without having to provide reciprocal privileges. In addition, it has negotiated some 130 special trade agreements with EC nations.

All this seems likely to end in 1992, and Swiss business and banking interests have reacted with alarm. Joining the EC is not seen as a viable alternative, given Swiss traditions of neutrality and independent decision-making. Swiss firms and banks therefore moved in 1988 to ensure a major investment of capital inside the EC. Perhaps the most publicized action was the hostile takeover of the British firm Rowntree in June by Nestle; this followed Nestle's acquisition of the Italian food conglomerate Buitoni in March. Other Swiss industries representing chemicals, engineering, food, transportation, banking, and insurance made concerted attempts to improve their position inside the EC.

SWITZERLAND • Information Highlights

Official Name: Swiss Confederation.
Location: Central Europe.
Area: 15,942 sq mi (41 290 km²).
Population (mid-1988 est.): 6,600,000.
Chief Cities (Jan. 1, 1987 est.): Bern, the capital, 137,134; Zurich, 349,549; Basel, 173,160.
Government: *Head of state,* Pierre Aubert, president (took office Jan. 1987). *Legislature*—Council of States and National Council.
Monetary Unit: Franc (1.4995 francs equal U.S.$1, Nov. 1, 1988).
Gross National Product (1986 U.S.$): $126,200,-000,000.
Economic Indexes (1987): *Consumer Prices* (1980 = 100), all items, 126.0; food, 132.0. *Industrial Production* (1980 = 100), (1986) 108.
Foreign Trade (1987 U.S.$): *Imports,* $50,609,-000,000; *exports,* $45,487,000,000.

Other Economic Concerns. A report released April 19 indicated that Switzerland continued to have the highest labor costs of any major industrialized nation, with an average wage rate of $19.83 per hour. In conjunction with other European states, Switzerland raised interest rates in August in an effort to stem the decline in the value of European currencies against a strengthening U.S. dollar.

Of historical import was the decision by the Soviet Union to enter the European bond market for the first time since the 1917 Bolshevik Revolution. To gain permission for Swiss banks to handle the sale of $78 million in Eurobonds, the Soviet government had to agree to pay off debts owed to Switzerland by the prerevolutionary czarist government—obligations which the Bolshevik regime had renounced in 1917.

Swiss banks again found themselves involved in the continuing U.S. Iran-contra arms scandal. On March 16 a U.S. grand jury indicted Lt. Col. Oliver North and three others on several charges, including "wire fraud," involving the electronic transfer of monies in and out of Swiss bank accounts. This allegedly was done in order to hide the diversion to Nicaraguan contras of profits from Iranian arms sales.

Political Controversies. Justice Minister Elizabeth Kopp found her political career jeopardized as a result of her husband's financial and business affairs. Until his resignation on October 27, her husband was associated with a Lebanese-controlled firm that was under investigation for money laundering. On December 12, Mrs. Kopp announced that she would give up her post, effective in February 1989. Five days earlier parliament had elected her vice-president, and under the nation's rotating system she would have become president in 1990.

Olympic Success. All Swiss rejoiced in the success of their athletes at the Winter Olympics. *See* SPORTS—*The XV Winter Games,* page 500.

PAUL C. HELMREICH
Wheaton College, MA

SYRIA

Despite obvious and perhaps growing problems both domestic and external, the Baath Party regime of President Hafiz al-Assad still was firmly in power in Syria during 1988.

Domestic Affairs. Assad has a seemingly slender power base, in that he and nearly all the leading figures of his government are members of the small Alawi Muslim sect, who number no more than one tenth of the population of Syria and are regarded by the predominantly Sunni Muslims in Syria as a near-heretical sect. But even if the government lacks legitimacy in the eyes of many Syrians, it is a strong regime. About two thirds of the country's budget is spent on the army and security services.

In 1988 the economy certainly was limping badly. A cabinet reshuffle at the beginning of the year perhaps signaled a search for solutions. There were sporadic shortages of many basic commodities. State-owned industry functioned at about 50% of capacity, and there was hardly any new private investment. The International Monetary Fund (IMF) has pointed out that subsidies to keep down prices of essential goods have crippled the economy, yet these may be politically untouchable. Syria has defaulted on interest payments on loans from several East-bloc countries. On the other hand, rains were good in 1988 and therefore the harvests were better. Another point on the credit side was the growing production of oil. U.S. oil companies were allowed to recommence work in Syria in 1987, and British oil concerns have operated without interruption. Some new discoveries have given Syria an exportable surplus of oil. The government also claims a small overall balance-of-payments surplus.

Foreign Relations. Some part of Assad's success in maintaining his power must be attributed to his role as champion of the Arab cause in general. He has figured as probably the most implacable enemy of Israel.

In 1988, Syria's ambition of virtually controlling Lebanon—of turning it into a kind of Syrian viceroyalty, which had seemed possible two or three years earlier—receded from Syria's grasp. The politics of Lebanon became progressively more frustrating and uncontrollable by Syria or, indeed, anyone, as Lebanese unity eroded. Syria had some 30,000 troops in Lebanon, but could not secure the post of president for either its first or second choices in the fall of 1988; Syria's actions here were generally thought to show serious errors of judgment. In a strange twist in the second half of the year, the hard-line Christian (Maronite) forces in East Beirut were being aided by Iraq, Israel, and the Palestine Liberation Organization (PLO) forces loyal to Yasir Arafat (who was detested by Assad), thus frustrating the hopes of Syria and the United States for a unified and functioning Lebanon.

One of the more curious developments of 1988 was the emergence of an informal, but close and cordial, working relationship between the United States and Syria, symbolized by a number of visits to Damascus by Secretary of State George Shultz and Assistant Secretary Richard Murphy. This change was facilitated by Syria's "good grades" on terrorism—no terrorist actions for two years past having been laid at Syria's door—and by Assad's generally more moderate policies. There was a general resumption of normal relations with Syria by Western countries. Also, Syrian relations with its moderate neighbor Jordan were excellent.

When Khalil Wazir, Arafat's second-in-command, was slain in Tunis on April 16, supposedly by Israeli forces, he was buried in Damascus. Arafat, not present at the funeral, visited Damascus on April 25 and met his enemy Assad for the first time since 1983. No formal statement was issued afterward.

Syria was the sole important supporter of Iran throughout the Iran-Iraq war, and Syria and Iraq, the two neighboring Baath Party regimes, were in any event bitter enemies before the war. Therefore, it was assumed widely in the aftermath of the August cease-fire that Syria stood exposed to some kind of retaliatory action by a well-armed Iraq that just had fought Iran to a standstill. Apart, however, from Iraq's proxy actions in Lebanon, nothing of the kind happened within the year.

In July it was reported that China had concluded a deal to sell new M-9 short-range missiles to Syria over the next 18 months. Israel regarded this as ominous. It also was reported, in August, that the Soviet Union was expanding its naval base at Tartus, on the Syrian coast. The new construction would enable the Soviet Mediterranean fleet to be maintained without frequent returns to the Black Sea.

See also MIDDLE EAST.

ARTHUR CAMPBELL TURNER
University of California, Riverside

TAIWAN

For Taiwan, 1988 was a year of change unprecedented in scope during the 40 years since the Kuomintang (KMT), or Nationalist Party, established itself there in the wake of its civil war with the Chinese Communists.

Politics and Government. The year began with the death of President Chiang Ching-kuo on January 13. Chiang had served in that office for ten years, having succeeded his father, Chiang Kai-shek. Though much more accessible a politician than his father, the younger Chiang was a part of the same conservative and staunchly anti-Communist political constituency that his father was. Although the substantial democratization of the political system that took place during 1988 came in the months that followed his death, it was he who initiated the process in the last months of his life.

Among Chiang Ching-kuo's last liberalizing acts was to engineer the election of Lee Teng-hui as his vice-president. Born on Taiwan, Lee represents the 85% of the population who, unlike Chiang and his fellow "mainlanders," did not arrive on the island with the KMT forces in 1949. Although most observers predicted that Lee would succeed Chiang as president, they thought his tenure would be short and that he would be unable to secure a position in the KMT commensurate with his position as head of state. Lee proved them wrong. Not only did he take over the presidency on January 13, but within two weeks he had consolidated his position in the party sufficiently to be named acting chairman by its Central Standing Committee. He did so, apparently, against the opposition of Premier Yü Kuo-hua, who had the support of Chiang Ching-kuo's once highly powerful stepmother, Madame Chiang Kai-shek. Lee's appointment was confirmed by the full Party Congress in July.

This 13th session of the Congress itself was emblematic of the opening up of the political process as a whole. For the first time the party's Central Committee was elected, rather than appointed, and nominations were ac-

© Alvin Chung/Sygma

Lee Teng-hui, 64, became the first native of Taiwan to be sworn in as the nation's president. He took office immediately upon the death of Chiang Ching-kuo on Jan. 13, 1988.

cepted from delegates to the Congress as well as from the retiring Central Committee. In the contest that ensued, a number of establishment nominees, including Premier Yü himself, received fewer votes than did nonestablishment nominees. Though the premier retained his position on the Central Committee and in the newly appointed Cabinet, it was assumed widely that his position had been weakened seriously.

The position of Taiwanese members of the party leadership was enhanced significantly by the Congress. Taiwanese made up 40% of the Central Committee, a majority of the Standing Central Committee, and 50% of the new Cabinet. The average age of members of these bodies dropped from 70 to 60.

Relations with the Mainland. While the new president had to move with caution, lest he undermine his efforts at nurturing a new, independent political base, he made it clear that he intended to proceed along the path of reform opened by his predecessor. At his instigation, the Congress adopted a new set of guidelines for relations with the mainland. Although authorization to visit the mainland was not extended to persons without relatives there, the existing authorization remained in place, and more than 100,000 Taiwanese citizens took advantage of it during the year.

Trade and investment with the mainland were authorized by the Congress, with the

---

TAIWAN • Information Highlights

Official Name: Taiwan.
Location: Island off the southeastern coast of mainland China.
Area: 13,892 sq mi (35 980 km²).
Population (mid-1988 est.): 19,800,000.
Chief Cities (Dec. 31, 1986): Taipei, the capital, 2,575,180; Kaohsiung, 1,320,552; Taichung, 695,562; Tainan, 646,298.
Government: *Head of state,* Lee Teng-hui, president (installed Jan. 1988). *Head of government* Yü Kuo-hua, president, executive yuan (premier) (took office, June 1984). *Legislature* (unicameral) —Legislative Yuan.
Monetary Unit: New Taiwan dollar (28.10 NT dollars equal U.S.$1, Dec. 1, 1988).
Gross National Product (1986 est. U.S.$): $72,600,-000,000.

proviso that they be carried on through third parties, most of them located in Hong Kong. Official indirect trade was projected at $2.5 billion for the year. A number of wholly owned and joint ventures in the mainland's Fujian and Guangdong provinces were set up by Taiwan investors interested in availing themselves of low labor, plant, and raw material costs there.

Paradoxically, it was individuals to the political right of President Lee who attempted to go much further in dealing with the Chinese Communists. At the July Congress, conservative "mainlanders" proposed making a $10 billion grant-in-aid to the Beijing government in exchange for its pledge to abandon Communism and to renounce the use of force in its attempt to reunify with Taiwan. The proposal met with little support. Three months later another conservative "mainlander," Hu Chiu-yuan, 78, was expelled from the party for having engaged in unauthorized negotiations on the subject of reunification with political authorities in Beijing.

The political opposition, gathered but not unified under the banner of the Democratic Progressive Party (DPP), took advantage of the new political climate to organize an unprecedented number of political demonstrations during the year—more than 1,000 by one count. While still polling more than 20% support in public opinion surveys, DPP members were divided deeply on a range of issues, most importantly the question of what an "independent Taiwan" might mean. Some argued that it should mean a loose confederation with the mainland that preserves Taiwanese control over domestic politics and the economy. Others favored a wholly independent state under Taiwanese administration. And a third group held that Taiwan's future should be determined by a plebiscite of its citizens. According to the official line of the KMT, advocating independence is tantamount to sedition.

Economy. The Taiwan economy continued to grow in 1988, albeit somewhat more slowly than in 1987. Projections for the rate of growth stood at 7.2%, down from 11% the previous year. Taiwan continued to enjoy a trade surplus with the United States and most of its other trading partners. Total foreign reserves topped $75 billion, second only to those of Japan.

JOHN BRYAN STARR, *Yale-China Association*

TANZANIA

Tanzania built on 1987's impressive economic performance and became one of the few countries in Africa whose economic growth (3.9%) was more rapid than the growth in its population (3.5%). President Ali Hassan Mwinyi's economic challenges were compounded, though, as regional tensions between his native

---

TANZANIA · Information Highlights

Official Name: United Republic of Tanzania.
Location: East coast of Africa.
Area: 364,900 sq mi (945 090 km²).
Population (mid-1988 est.): 24,300,000.
Chief City (1985 est.): Dar es Salaam, the capital, 1,096,000.
Government: *Head of state,* Ali Hassan Mwinyi, president (took office Nov. 1985). *Head of government,* Joseph S. Warioba, prime minister (took office Nov. 1985). *Legislature* (unicameral)—National Assembly, 233 members.
Monetary Unit: Tanzanian shilling (97.283 shillings equal U.S.$1, Aug. 1988).
Gross Domestic Product (fiscal year 1987 U.S.$): $4,900,000,000.
Foreign Trade (1986 U.S.$): *Imports,* $780,000,000; *exports,* $346,000,000.

Zanzibar and the mainland reached new heights.

Economy. In July, 24 international donors met in Paris to recommit themselves to Tanzania's economic-recovery program sponsored by the International Monetary Fund (IMF). The "Paris Club" pledged $800 million, up from 1987's $740 million, of which only 66% had been distributed. Nearly 45% of the new aid will cover an expansion in imports. In line with the IMF, Tanzania continued to liberalize its economy and raise agricultural producer prices. For its part, the IMF agreed to finance long-term development projects in certain social sectors.

Tanzania's transport network also received significant international assistance. The aging Tazara Railroad linking Tanzania with Zambia secured $145 million of a projected $250 million ten-year rehabilitation project, with the United States alone contributing $45 million. The Tanzam highway, parallel to the railroad, also was being resurfaced, and an Italian-financed $27 million bitumen asphalt plant was being built.

In February, Malawi and Tanzania signed a trade agreement which focused on the $100 million rehabilitation of the "Northern Corridor" trade routes between the two countries. Rehabilitation of the port of Dar es Salaam also is a major priority. Due to regional unrest, Tanzania now handles 25% of all southern Africa's external trade, 80% of Zambia's imports, and 45% of its exports.

Tension with Zanzibar. On January 26 the popular though independent Zanzibari Chief Minister, Seif Shariff Hamad, was fired by his president, Idris Abdul Wakil. He was replaced by Omar Ali Juma. Following a demonstration by more than 10,000 Hamad supporters, during which government forces opened fire and killed two persons, Hamad and seven colleagues were expelled from the ruling Chama Cha Mapinduzi Party. While Zanzibari membership in the party has dropped by some 80%, Wakil is thought to have operated with the blessings of party chief Julius Nyerere.

WILLIAM CYRUS REED, *Wabash College*

TAXATION

The mounting U.S. budget deficit increased pressure to raise taxes, but the campaign promise of Republican presidential candidate George Bush not to do so was a key factor in his election victory. Major tax-reform legislation was introduced or enacted in a number of countries, including Japan, West Germany, Canada, and Great Britain.

United States

Federal. The U.S. federal government collected $909.0 billion in revenues—including $401.2 billion in individual income taxes (up 2.2%) and $94.2 billion in corporate income taxes (up 12.2%)—during fiscal year (FY) 1988, ending September 30. Despite a 6.4% increase over 1987 collections, the government was left with a budget deficit of $155.1 billion, which exceeded the 1987 figure by $5.4 billion. With the budget deficit representing more than 3.3% of the gross national product (GNP), pressure to raise taxes continued to mount.

Several factors, however, mitigated against raising taxes or taking other major action to offset the budget deficit. First, since 1988 was an election year, legislation to raise taxes was politically untimely. The budget "summit" between the Reagan administration and Congress, called in the wake of the stock market crash of Oct. 19, 1987, worked out a two-year deficit reduction plan that conveniently postponed tax manipulation during an election year. The summit deliberations ultimately led to the Revenue Act of 1987, which called for $8 billion and $14 billion in new tax revenues for FY 1988 and FY 1989, respectively.

Secondly, the public still was absorbing the impact of the Tax Reform Act of 1986, which radically changed the tax code for individuals and corporations. Since many of the provisions of the 1986 Act are staggered over five years, its full effects will not be realized until 1990 or later. Another major tax act in 1988 would not have been able to gain enough political momentum, particularly if it involved increasing the income-tax rates established by the 1986 act.

The third and perhaps most important reason why there was no major deficit-reduction legislation in 1988 was the appointment of the National Economic Commission (NEC) late in 1987 to address the deficit problem. The 14-member bipartisan panel, comprised of business, labor, and congressional leaders appointed by the president and Congress, was not scheduled to report its preliminary recommendations until March 1989. Many analysts did not expect major action to reduce the deficit until well after the NEC releases its final recommendations. Also, any prospects for a tax increase may be jeopardized by President-elect Bush's pledge not to raise taxes and his campaign declaration that he would not support any tax-increase proposals by the commission.

The most important piece of tax legislation passed during the year was the Technical and Miscellaneous Revenue Act of 1988 (TAMRA), signed by President Reagan on November 10. TAMRA ended a two-year-long battle to correct substantial drafting errors in the 1986 legislation which bestowed unexpected benefits upon some taxpayers while imposing unintended liabilities on others. TAMRA also extended certain tax preferences that were due to expire and created several modest tax breaks for certain groups. The act also established the first "Taxpayer's Bill of Rights" for dealing with the Internal Revenue Service (IRS).

The extension, modification, and creation of tax breaks were expected to yield a revenue loss of $4.1 billion, to be offset by $4.1 billion in revenue increases over three years. Among those who benefit from the legislation are farmers, writers and artists, banks, and workers who receive education assistance from their employers. Key provisions include: extension of the states' authority to issue qualified tax-exempt mortgage bonds; extension of the 20% tax credit allowed for research expenditures incurred in carrying on trade or business; extension of the tax exclusion for employer-provided educational assistance for 1988; extension of business energy tax credits; extension of the targeted jobs tax credit; modification of mutual-fund shareholder expenses to exempt them from taxation; modification to expand the low-income rental housing tax credit; modification allowing farmers to take deductions for farm animals they breed before the animal is born; and modification allowing writers and artists to deduct expenses on works before they sell them.

Almost one third of TAMRA's $4.1 billion revenue increase will come from defense contractors, from whom $1.3 billion will be extracted over three years. The revenue will be generated by a provision that restricts a tax-deferral accounting technique known as the "completed contract" method. Other major revenue-enhancing provisions accelerate payments of corporate estimated taxes; curb limited-premium life-insurance policies; and restrict loss transfers by Alaskan native corporations.

Another important provision included in TAMRA was the removal of limits on the amount of long-term bonds that the U.S. Treasury can issue. This provision was sought by the Reagan administration to help finance the national debt, which reached more than $2.6 trillion by the end of FY 1988.

The Taxpayer's Bill of Rights allows a taxpayer to be represented before the IRS by a certified public accountant (CPA), attorney, or other authorized professional; requires the IRS to establish formal guidelines for what consti-

tutes a reasonable time and place for a taxpayer interview; prohibits the IRS from evaluating the performance of employees involved in collection on the basis of quotas or goals based on amounts assessed or collected; gives taxpayers a 30-day grace period before the IRS can seize a bank account or property; gives the IRS authority to allow installment tax payments if the agreement would facilitate collection; and extends the jurisdiction of the tax court.

On October 13, President Reagan also signed into law the Family Support Act of 1988. While the main purpose of the legislation was to reform the federal welfare system, it also will have a major tax impact on many taxpayers because a portion of the legislation's $3.3 billion cost will come from changes in the tax code. The largest share of funding will come from extending for five years an expiring IRS program under which debt owed to the government is deducted from income-tax returns.

With the signing of the Omnibus Trade Bill on August 23, the Crude Oil Windfall Profit Tax of 1980 was repealed. Manufacturers and consumers alike were expected to benefit, since the windfall profit tax was viewed as a disincentive to exploration and production of domestic crude and as posing burdensome record-keeping expenses on producers.

Another major piece of legislation enacted in 1988 was the Medicare Catastrophic Coverage Act of 1988, signed into law on July 1. The benefits contained in the legislation, estimated to cost about $31 billion between 1988 and 1993, will be paid for primarily by the people who are expected to be the beneficiaries. Payment is made in the form of (1) increased income taxation of Medicare-eligible individuals (called the "supplemental" premium), and (2) increased part-B monthly premium rates (called the "flat" premium). Many tax analysts consider the new supplemental premium a marginally disguised progressive tax increase, since it will boost the amount the nation's higher-income senior citizens owe the IRS by 15% (as much as $1,600 per couple) in 1989 and 28% (up to $2,100) in 1993; poor seniors will pay as little as $96 a year per couple. All in all, the Catastrophic Coverage Act will require senior citizens to pay an additional $19 billion over the next five years.

State and Local. U.S. state and local governments collected $421.8 billion in taxes during the 12 months ending March 1988, an increase of 8%, or $31.2 billion, over the same period one year earlier. State tax collections totaled $259.7 billion, up 8.3%, and local government taxes amounted to $162.1 billion, a 7.5% rise. Thirty-four states witnessed tax increases, largely on motor fuel, tobacco, alcoholic beverages, and general sales. The fiscal condition of many states improved in 1988, primarily because of a stronger-than-expected national economy and various tax increases enacted in 1987. However, a few large states experienced severe revenue shortfalls and deficits.

Supreme Court. During its 1987–88 term, the U.S. Supreme Court decided ten tax cases. Seven of them involved federal taxes, and in all but one the court sided with the federal government. In the most important case, *South Carolina v. Baker,* the justices ruled that Congress is free to tax all interest on state and local government bonds. And in another case with potentially wide-ranging consequences, *D.H. Holmes Co. v. Louisiana Secretary of Revenue and Taxation,* the court ruled unanimously that the application of Louisiana's use-tax to merchandise catalogues ordered from out-of-state and shipped to prospective customers within the state does not violate the Commerce Clause of the U.S. Constitution.

International

Japan. Japan's ruling Liberal Democratic Party introduced a major tax-reform measure that was passed by the lower house of the Diet (parliament) in November and by the upper house in December. The package slashes income-tax and excise-tax rates, but introduces a controversial 3% national sales tax. Other major changes include a new capital-gains tax, corporate tax-rate reductions to 37.5% (from 42%) by 1990, and a reduction in the number of income-tax brackets from 12 to five. The new tax rates range from 10% to 50%, compared with the previous range of 10.5% to 60%.

West Germany. The Tax Reform Act of 1990 in the Federal Republic of Germany, approved July 8, 1988, reduces income-tax rates for both corporations and individuals. The highest individual rate was reduced from 56% to 53%, with corporate rates cut from 56% to 50%. The reform focuses largely on personal taxes and aims to spur savings and investment by cutting U.S.$10.67 billion from the national tax bill.

Canada. The Canadian Tax Reform of 1988, which became law on September 13, reduces the number of personal income tax brackets from ten to three—17% on the first C$27,500 of taxable income, 26% on the next C$27,500, and 29% on all taxable income above C$55,000— and converts most personal exemptions to tax credits. The law also lowers the general corporate-tax rate from 36% to 28% and reduces the rate for manufacturing companies from 30% to 23% by 1991.

Great Britain. A major tax overhaul introduced on March 15, Britain's annual Budget Day, went into effect in June. The simplification plan reduces the number of rates from six to two. The basic rate was reduced from 27% to 25%. The upper rate, for people who make more than U.S.$35,700, was set at 40%; under the old system, the top rate of 60% applied to people who earned more than U.S.$72,600.

PAUL G. MERSKI, *Tax Foundation*

Jane Seymour and Sir John Gielgud were two of the stars in ABC's epic television adaptation of novelist Herman Wouk's "War and Remembrance." The 32-hour, $110 million miniseries was the sequel to "The Winds of War," broadcast in 1983.

TELEVISION AND RADIO

In what *The New York Times* called an "up-heaval . . . just below the surface" of the U.S. television landscape, ratings statistics showed that while the total audience for all forms of television programming grew in 1988, the Big Three networks' share of it shrank again by another point, to 43%. The other sectors of TV —independent stations, superstations, and cable programmers—increased their share. Blamed in part for the networks' woes was what *Variety* called "one of the most severe droughts of advertising revenue in recent history." The 22-week strike by the Writers Guild of America also was responsible for the poor network ratings of the 1987–88 season, in which the National Broadcasting Company (NBC) continued its domination of recent seasons, followed by the American Broadcasting Companies (ABC), and the Columbia Broadcasting System (CBS) in only its second-ever last-place finish. The strike fragmented the start-up of the 1988–89 season schedules and pushed them into the late fall.

Time magazine also chimed in with a forecast of television changes, proclaiming that "the networks face the most troubled fall of their history" and supporting it with a report that cable reached 53% of American homes, four times as many as in 1978. *Time* dubbed Herman Wouk's *War and Remembrance*—at 32 hours and $110 million the longest and costliest TV production ever—"the event that TV historians may one day call the Last Gasp of the Miniseries." Although praised for its moments of fearlessness—naked corpses shown

tumbling into a mass grave, for example—the World War II epic faced low ratings and financial losses for ABC at its December midpoint.

Critics sensed a sea change of viewing patterns and tastes, also reflected in abysmal ratings for coverage of the presidential conventions. *Variety* observed in the midsummer convention season: "Video stores around the country reported a surge in rentals as obviously bored viewers voted for theatrical movies over political theater." Even proven stars could not assure success on the changing TV landscape: Dick Van Dyke and Mary Tyler Moore, one of the most beloved TV couples of the 1960s, bombed in their separate fall vehicles for CBS.

Network Programming. The success of ABC's *Thirtysomething,* the winner of the 1988 Emmy Award for best dramatic series, opened the floodgates for 1988–89 programming aimed at so-called baby boomers. CBS' *Almost Grown* traced three decades in the life of a New Jersey couple, beginning with high-school dating in the 1960s with that era's ever-popular Motown soundtrack. ABC's *The Wonder Years* looked at the charged and pivotal year of 1968 through the eyes of a 12-year-old boy. The personal dilemmas of young professional women were explored in CBS' *Murphy Brown,* starring Candice Bergen as a television reporter; and in NBC's *Baby Boom,* Kate Jackson extended Diane Keaton's film role of a single, working mother. *Tattinger's,* set in a posh New York restaurant, attempted to capitalize on the "yuppie" cuisine craze, combining the *L.A. Law* style of ensemble drama with the glitz of such nighttime soap operas as *Knots Landing.* The ABC comedy *Roseanne* swam against the

Stand-up comedienne Roseanne Barr (second from left) brought her brand of humor to the arena of the television sitcom in ABC's new series "Roseanne." The popular show also starred John Goodman (right) as Roseanne's good-natured husband.

baby boomer current with its unstylishly over-weight working-class couple, and got off to a fast ratings start in 1988–89.

With more programs stretching the tradi-tional sitcom format to encompass both com-edy and drama, the hybrid word "dramady" became an established term of TV industry slang. Such topics as AIDS, drugs, and sexual problems frequently were addressed.

Dropped by ABC after 30 years, *American Bandstand* was picked up immediately by NBC, with ageless Dick Clark expected to con-tinue as host. Another veteran star, Peter Graves, returned in a new edition of the CBS 1960s classic, *Mission: Impossible. Later,* an irreverent talk format with Bob Costas, sought to extend NBC's talk dominance (*Tonight* with Johnny Carson, *Late Night* with David Letter-man) even further into the late night-early morning time slot.

Wrapping up a distinguished six-year run, the NBC hospital drama *St. Elsewhere* con-cluded with a controversial episode—termed by one critic "a wacko . . . wonderful Easter egg hunt for in-jokes"—that poignantly framed the entire series as though it had been the fan-tasy of an autistic child. Fantasy sequences, in fact, were seen as a widespread TV innovation, playing important roles in such series as *Moon-lighting* and *Thirtysomething.* CBS' *Beauty and the Beast,* to one analyst, also satisfied a national yearning for fantasy and pristine, old-fashioned romance. But explicit material—

sometimes praised as candid, more often con-demned as exploitative—was more prevalent, as announced in the *USA Today* newspaper under the headline, "Network Censors Are Re-laxing Their Grips." Competition from racier cable services was cited as one reason, and *De-signing Women* was mentioned as a frequent subject among the shrinking staff of CBS cen-sors.

A classic stage drama, rare for commercial TV adaptation—NBC's *Inherit the Wind—* won Emmys for best drama special and best actor in a special (Jason Robards).

Fox Broadcasting, after a season-and-a-half still the butt of jokes on late-night talk shows for its middlebrow programming, finished 1988 with $90 million in losses but surprised many industry executives by climbing into double-digit ratings. Praising the intelligent police drama *21 Jump Street* and such bright come-dies as *The Tracey Ullman Show* and *It's Garry Shandling's Show, Time* magazine dubbed Fox "the little network that might."

Cable, Syndicated, and Public TV. The Public Broadcasting Service (PBS), rich in acclaim but always financially poor, encountered yet another stumbling block in the form of Sen. Daniel Inouye (D-HI), chairman of the Senate Subcommittee on Communications. Because Inouye believed, in the words of *Variety,* that "PBS can't be trusted" with government funds, he inserted language in the network's 1991–93 funding bill which, if approved, would

TELEVISION | 1988
Some Sample Programs

The Attic: The Hiding of Anne Frank—TV-movie adaptation of Miep Gies' book about how she helped hide the Frank family from the Nazis. With Mary Steenbergen, Paul Scofield. CBS, April 17.

Baby M—A two-part TV movie based on Mary Beth Whitehead's fight to retain custody of the child she had agreed to bear by artificial insemination for pay. With JoBeth Williams. ABC, May 22.

The Black Tower—A six-part *Mystery* dramatization of P. D. James' novel about a nursing home plagued by a series of murders. With Roy Marsden. PBS, April 30.

The Bourne Identity—A two-part TV-movie adaptation of Robert Ludlum's spy thriller about an amnesiac who searches for his identity and his role in a mysterious conspiracy. With Richard Chamberlain, Jaclyn Smith. ABC, May 8.

Cause Célèbre—A two-part *Mystery* adaptation of Terence Rattigan's play based on a 1930s case of a woman who, with her teenaged lover, murdered her husband. With Helen Mirren, David Morrissey. PBS, Oct. 15.

David—TV movie dramatizing the story of six-year-old David Rothenberg, whose seemingly devoted father set him on fire. With Bernadette Peters, John Glover, Matthew Lawrence. ABC, Oct. 25.

David Copperfield—A five-part *Masterpiece Theatre* adaptation of Charles Dickens' novel. With David Dexter, Colin Hurley, Simon Callow. PBS, March 27.

Destined to Live—Documentary about women who have recovered emotionally and physically from breast cancer. Host: Jill Eikenberry. NBC, Oct. 12.

Drugs: A Plague Upon the Land—*ABC News Special* focusing on the heavy cost of drug use to society and individuals. Host: Peter Jennings. ABC, April 10.

Favorite Son—A three-part political thriller made for TV revolving around the rise to fame of a freshman senator after he was wounded during the assassination of a Nicaraguan contra leader. With Harry Hamlin, Linda Kozlowski, Robert Loggia. NBC, Oct. 30.

Four Days in November—*CBS Reports* look at how the network covered the 1963 assassination of President John F. Kennedy. CBS, Nov. 17.

God Bless the Child—TV movie about a homeless mother who finds it increasingly difficult to support her child or break out of the cycle of poverty. With Mare Winningham. ABC, March 21.

Inherit the Wind—TV-movie version of the Broadway play about the controversy over the teaching of evolution in public schools in the 1920s. With Kirk Douglas, Jason Robards. NBC, March 20.

Irving Berlin: 100th Birthday Celebration—Carnegie Hall gala featuring Frank Sinatra, Ray Charles, Rosemary Clooney, and others performing the songs of Irving Berlin, who was born May 11, 1888. CBS, May 27.

Jack the Ripper—A two-part TV movie retelling the story and claiming to solve the mystery of the Victorian murderer's identity. With Michael Caine, Armand Assante, Ray McAnally. CBS, Oct. 21.

Joseph Campbell and the Power of Myth—A series of six discussions between journalist Bill Moyers and mythologist Joseph Campbell on the continuing need of human beings for myths in order to feel "the rapture of being alive." PBS, May 23.

Kristallnacht: The Journey from 1938 to 1988—Documentary compiled from 1930s films and modern interviews about the night of Nov. 9–10, 1938, when Nazis murdered hundreds of German Jews and destroyed their homes, businesses, and synagogues. PBS, Nov. 9

Laura Lansing Slept Here—TV movie about a famous novelist who, to prove she has not lost touch with ordinary people, moves in with a suburban family. With Katharine Hepburn. NBC, March 7.

Liberace—TV-movie biography of the flamboyant pianist, "authorized" by his estate. With Andrew Robinson, Rue McClanahan. ABC, Oct. 2.

Maybe Baby—TV movie about the doubts and joys of a couple who have waited until middle age to have a baby. With Dabney Coleman, Jane Curtin. NBC, Dec. 5.

The Mind—A nine-part probe of "what the brain does"; topics include mental disorders and the workings of the mind in daily life. PBS, Oct. 12.

The Murder of Mary Phagan—A two-part TV movie based on the 1913 Georgia case of Leo Frank, a Jew accused of murdering a young factory worker. With Jack Lemmon, Peter Gallagher, Richard Jordan. NBC, Jan. 24.

My Father, My Son—TV movie based on Elmo Zumwalt III's relationship with his father, whose authorization as naval chief of staff of the use of Agent Orange in Vietnam probably caused his son's cancer. With Keith Carradine, Karl Malden. CBS, May 22.

Nixon in China—*Great Performances* telecast of the Houston Grand Opera's production of an opera by John Adams about President Nixon's historic 1972 visit to mainland China. PBS, April 15.

An Ocean Apart—A seven-part documentary series about 20th-century Anglo-American relations. PBS, May 16.

Perfect People—TV-movie comedy about a middle-aged couple who go to extremes of diet, exercise, and cosmetic surgery to recapture their youth. With Perry King, Lauren Hutton. ABC, Feb. 29.

A Perfect Spy—A seven-part *Masterpiece Theatre* adaptation of John le Carré's autobiographical spy novel focusing on an agent's relationship with his con-man father. With Peter Egan, Ray McAnally. PBS, Oct. 16.

Promised a Miracle—TV movie based on fact about a couple who withhold insulin shots from their diabetic son because they believe God will cure him. With Rosanna Arquette, Judge Reinhold. CBS, May 19.

Race for the Superconductor—*Nova* documentary examining the quest to perfect a chemical compound to conduct electricity with no resistance. PBS, March 29.

Racism 101—*Frontline* documentary on racism on college campuses. PBS, May 10.

A Report on Foster Care—*ABC News Closeup* about case overload and other problems in foster-care programs in the United States. Reported by Rebecca Chase. ABC, Aug. 30.

Rivera in America—*American Masters* portrait of the controversial Mexican artist Diego Rivera, focusing on his visit to the United States in 1930–31. PBS, Aug. 29.

Roots: The Gift—Special, set in Christmas 1775 and featuring characters from the 1977 miniseries, about the Underground Railroad. With Louis Gossett, Jr., LeVar Burton, Avery Brooks. ABC, Dec. 11.

Side by Side—TV-movie comedy about three elderly friends who go into business together manufacturing clothing for other senior citizens. With Milton Berle, Sid Caesar, Danny Thomas. CBS, March 6.

Stones for Ibarra—*Hallmark Hall of Fame* dramatization of Harriet Doerr's novel about an American couple who move to Mexico to reopen his father's copper mine. With Keith Carradine, Glenn Close. CBS, Jan. 29.

Stressed to Kill—*NBC News Special* about the causes, manifestations, and treatment of stress in daily life. Host: Connie Chung. NBC, April 25.

Struggles for Poland—A nine-part history of 20th-century Poland. Narrated by Roger Mudd. PBS, July 12.

The Tenth Man—*Hallmark Hall of Fame* production of a Graham Greene novel about a wealthy Frenchman's unusual deal to escape a Nazi firing squad. With Anthony Hopkins, Derek Jacobi. CBS, Dec. 4.

This Honorable Court—A two-part documentary on the U.S. Supreme Court. PBS, May 2.

Toscanini: The Maestro—*Great Performances* profile of the legendary conductor. Host: James Levine. PBS, Jan. 8.

The Trial of Bernhard Goetz—Two-part *American Playhouse* dramatization of the trial of New York City's "subway vigilante," with dialogue taken from the trial transcripts. With Peter Crombie. PBS, May 11.

Voices and Visions—A 13-part series on American poets and their careers. PBS, Jan. 28.

The Wall Within—*CBS Reports* episode on post-traumatic stress disorder (PTSD), suffered by many Vietnam veterans. With Dan Rather. CBS, June 2.

War and Remembrance—Adaptation of Herman Wouk's novel in seven episodes and 18 hours, looking at World War II through the eyes of one American family. With Robert Mitchum, Polly Bergen, Jane Seymour, Victoria Tennant, John Gielgud, Hart Bochner. ABC, Nov. 13.

A Week in Israel—A week of *Nightline* broadcasts from Israel, including a "town meeting" between Israeli and Palestinian representatives. Host: Ted Koppel. ABC, April 25.

Who Lives, Who Dies—Critical analysis of the increasing costs of health care in the United States. Narrated by James Earl Jones. PBS, Jan. 5.

Talk Shows

UPI/Bettmann   AP/Wide World   UPI/Bettmann   UPI/Bettmann

MORTON DOWNEY   **OPRAH WINFREY**   **GERALDO RIVERA**   **SALLY JESSY RAPHAEL**   **PHIL DONAHUE**

As the popularity of television talk shows reached an all-time high in 1988, their intelligence and integrity reached—in the minds of some observers—all-time lows.

At the center of controversy was Morton Downey, Jr. Described as "The Pit Bull of Talk-Show Hosts" by *Time* Magazine, a "yahoo messiah" by *Rolling Stone,* and "rude and overbearing" by his own proud admission, Downey came snarling and swaggering onto the U.S. scene with a right-wing agenda and a gift for inflaming the passions of his audience.

Seen as a throwback to Joe Pyne and other confrontational broadcast commentators of the 1960s, the 55-year-old Downey began 1988 as an obscure journeyman with a checkered broadcast career of racial and ethnic slurs. But *The Morton Downey Jr. Show*—symbolized by a caricature of Downey's toothy, wide-open mouth—was so popular during its first few months on the New York/New Jersey superstation, WWOR-TV, that it went into national syndication on Memorial Day. It was offered to stations for an unusual no-obligation test period of 15 weeks because of, in the words of one newspaper, "the show's inherent violence."

And sometimes the violence went beyond "inherent." While yelling and verbal abuse—spurred on by a heavily male, blue-collar studio audience—were routine on the show, Downey physically ejected a journalist and two horror-movie producers from the set and was arraigned for allegedly slapping a gay activist after a taping. A critic for the *New York Daily News* called him "a disgrace to television," but Downey, the son of a famous Irish tenor, exhibited an uncanny appeal to conservatives of all ages. "They like me because I give them rock 'n' roll without the music," he said.

If Downey was an embarrassment to many in the television industry, it was three daytime talk-show rivals—Sally Jessy Raphael, Geraldo Rivera, and Oprah Winfrey—who had the reddest faces of 1988. After they had hosted two persons claiming to be patients from various forms of sex therapy, the "patients" revealed that they were Chicago actors who had staged a hoax to reveal that purportedly serious talk shows are "mere entertainment." The unmasked hoaxers, Wes Bailey and Tani Freiwald, returned to Ms. Raphael's show to be told by the livid host, "You have made me and, much more important, the audience, a laughingstock." Ms. Winfrey threatened legal action.

Regarding the new daytime talk landscape, Don Merrill of *TV Guide* opined: "The frequent emphasis on salacious subjects doesn't speak well for what it takes to attract an audience these days. . . ."

In late-night programming, Johnny Carson calmly continued his preeminence on NBC's *The Tonight Show,* despite the strike by the Writers' Guild of America (*see* TELEVISION AND RADIO) and a continuing onslaught of competition. In the midst of the strike, Carson made headlines with a decision to write his own comedy material. Some observers were surprised to hear a more middlebrow, nightclub-style humor than Carson's writing staff is known for. His latest competition came from hosts with opposite styles: the high-strung Downey, whose show a number of stations carried in the late-night slot; and the vanilla-smooth Pat Sajak of *Wheel of Fortune* fame, who was tapped by CBS for a projected talk show to debut in 1989 and overlap with both the Carson and David Letterman time slots.

DAN HULBERT

rechannel money to the individual PBS stations. Inouye and his allies called for an extensive review of the network, claiming that it was in danger of becoming redundant with such cable services as The Discovery Channel, Bravo, and the Arts & Entertainment Network —which were starting to outbid PBS for cultural and educational programming.

Explosive results were expected in some quarters from Turner Network Television (TNT), a new cable network specializing in classic films. Part of the Atlanta-based Turner Broadcasting System that also includes Cable News Network, TNT was at the center of a controversy over the colorization of old black-and-white films, with TNT president Ted Turner as the most colorful proponent. A TNT remake of *A Man for All Seasons,* starring Charlton Heston and Vanessa Redgrave, was cited as the kind of prestigious, high-gloss programming in which cable now could compete with the three major commercial television networks.

In a front-page article, *The New York Times* reported that, sparked by its 1984 deregulation, the price of cable-TV service increased much faster—by 13.6%—than the overall rates of inflation for the year ended in October.

The Chicago Tribune reported that, further eroded by widespread disillusion in the wake of the scandals surrounding the Rev. Jimmy Swaggart and the Rev. Jim and Tammy Bakker, the viewership for syndicated big-time evangelical programs continued to decline. A. C. Nielsen ratings showed that from 1986 to 1988, Swaggart and the Bakkers lost 51% of their audience, the Rev. Oral Roberts 39%, and the Rev. Jerry Falwell 38%.

TV News and Sports. The smoldering public resentment against what one critic termed "the imperial news organizations" and their perceived liberal bias was detonated on Jan. 25, 1988, when Vice-President George Bush became openly combative under aggressive questioning by *CBS Evening News* anchor Dan Rather. Bush, trying to shed his "wimp" image as presidential candidate, some observers believed, deflected questions about his role in the Iran-contra scandal by invoking a notorious 1987 gaffe in which Rather stormed out of a live broadcast because of an internal CBS dispute. The vice-president received the largest share of viewer support for standing up to an "ambush interview."

A brawl in the literal sense—resulting in host Geraldo Rivera's nose being broken by a thrown chair—erupted in front of the cameras of *Geraldo* between right-wing "skinheads" and black activists led by Roy Innis. The shocking melée was cited by critics as the most blatant example of "trash journalism": inflammatory talk shows and sensationalism thinly disguised as documentary. (*See* special report, page 524).

World Monitor, a new 30-minute newscast prepared under the auspices of *The Christian Science Monitor* and shown on cable TV's Discovery Channel, generally was praised as a vanishing species of responsible broadcast journalism. On the other hand, *USA Today: The Television Show,* an attempt to apply the lighter, speedier approach of that newspaper to a syndicated TV newsmagazine, premiered to bruising criticism and what one industry executive called "catastrophic ratings."

NBC's surprise choice of Michael G. Gartner, an Iowa newspaper veteran with no TV experience, to replace Larry Grossman as the head of its news division, was seen as a sign of the new, belt-tightening times. *Variety* commented that Gartner's "skills of managing slow-growth enterprises—the kind which have faced newspapers for years but only recently have afflicted TV news organizations" impressed NBC owner General Electric Company, which decreed that the news division must pay its own way instead of absorbing its customary loss.

NBC's coverage of the 1988 Summer Olympics in Seoul, South Korea, was a critical success but a surprising ratings disappointment, yielding only a marginal profit. Still, the network agreed to pay $401 million for broadcast rights to the 1992 Summer Olympics in Barcelona, Spain—25% more than the network shelled out for the 1988 Games.

Radio. AM radio, which commanded three fourths of all radio listeners in 1972, saw its audience share drop to one fourth by 1988. In an effort to regain listeners, AM stations were exploring more and more specialized formats. WFAN in New York offered 24-hour sports; K-PAL in Little Rock, AR, broadcast only children's programming; WWNN, or "Winner's Radio" in Pompano Beach, FL, was devoted entirely to self-help and motivational programming; and by year's end, four stations were playing nothing but the 642-song library of Elvis Presley. The all-sports WFAN replaced WNBC-AM at 660 on the New York dial after the latter—NBC's flagship station for 62 years—went off the air October 7.

In what some industry observers saw as a wave of the future, International Cablecasting Technologies of Chicago announced a mid-1989 launch date for ten cable radio channels capable of carrying the full compact-disc sound quality that is partially lost in conventional radio broadcasts. The system also includes a pay-per-listen option for live concerts.

The 50th anniversary of the fabled *War of the Worlds* radio drama by Orson Welles and the Mercury Theatre on the Air brought many commemorative rebroadcasts. An all-star radio remake with Jason Robards also went out over the airwaves on the October 30 anniversary.

DAN HULBERT
"The Atlanta Journal and Constitution"

TENNESSEE

Sen. Albert Gore, Jr., Tennessee's candidate for the Democratic presidential nomination, did well in several of the March 1988 "Super Tuesday" primaries, but subsequently lost out to Massachusetts Gov. Michael Dukakis. Tennessee voters backed the Republican Bush-Quayle ticket in the November elections, while generally favoring Democrats in other contests. Economically, the year showed a mixed picture: Agriculture and tourism suffered because of drought, but unemployment was low and economic growth was strong.

Elections. Tennesseans for the eighth time in the last ten presidential elections voted for a Republican candidate for president, as Vice-President Bush polled a majority in all of the congressional districts. In other political races, Democrat Jim Sasser was elected to a third term as U.S. senator over negligible opposition. In the 2nd District, John J. Duncan, Jr., who had won a special election earlier in the year to succeed his late father in the U.S. House, captured a full term in November. Other incumbent congressmen, except for Ed Jones of the 8th District, were reelected. Jones chose not to run and was replaced by State Representative John Tanner, a Union City Democrat. As usual, a Democratic majority was returned to the state House of Representatives and Senate.

Economy. The hottest and driest summer in more than three decades cut crop production and otherwise caused problems throughout the state. Corn was hardest hit, with production in some areas being reduced to 15% of normal.

Tourism, Tennessee's second largest industry, wilted under the summer heat and failed to meet expectations. Nevertheless, more Tennesseans were finding jobs than ever before, and at midyear the state's unemployment rate had declined to 5.3%—the lowest monthly rate since October 1979. Services and manufacture of durable goods accounted for nearly 750,000 jobs. Urban areas had the lowest unemployment: Nashville and Davidson County were at 3.8%; but rural Johnson in east Tennessee was at 25%.

Despite the low unemployment rate, bankruptcy judges complained in late summer of the state's "astonishing, ever-growing" number of bankruptcies. Included among those filing was the financially plagued Nashville Symphony Association, which ceased operation early in the year but made serious efforts at revival on a reduced-size basis at the year's end.

Tennessee climbed to tenth place among the 50 states in economic growth, according to research published in *Inc*, a nationally circulated magazine. A state's position on the list reflects the relative success of its economy over a four-year period in job generation, new business creation, and young company growth. Japa-

nese companies continued to find Tennessee appealing; more than 60—one tenth of the national total—have established plants there.

While public school enrollment in grades one through 12 remained steady, college and university matriculations increased sharply—despite a 6% decline at the University of Tennessee at Knoxville.

The Japanese population has become so large in Tennessee that Meiji Gakiun University of Tokyo purchased a defunct military college campus at Sweetwater, 40 mi (64 km) south of Knoxville, and was developing a branch there for children of Japanese families. The program of study planned will ensure that the children receive an education accredited by the Japanese system.

ROBERT E. CORLEW
Middle Tennessee State University

TERRORISM

Terrorism continued to plague many nations in 1988. Although the United States was spared throughout much of the year, many Americans were aboard a Pan American flight that crashed over Lockerbie, Scotland, in December. Some 270 lives were lost in the tragedy, which experts said was caused by a bomb. By year's end no one had been charged in the case.

Nevertheless, the year began with yet another American being taken hostage in Lebanon. In February, Lt. Col. William Higgins, the chief of staff of the United Nations Truce Supervision Organization, was kidnapped in southern Lebanon by Iranian-backed Shiite extremists. A number of hostages were freed during the year, including Mithileshwar Singh, an Indian citizen with permanent-resident status in the United States, but the fate of several others remained in doubt as 1988 ended.

The 31 remaining hostages aboard a Kuwaiti airliner were released by hijackers on April 20, after a 15-day ordeal that took the plane to Iran, Cyprus, and finally Algeria.

Pro-Iranian terrorists also were responsible for the longest and most publicized hijacking of 1988. A Kuwaiti airliner en route from Bangkok, Thailand, to Kuwait with 112 people aboard was hijacked on April 5. After forcing the plane to land in Iran—where heavier arms reportedly were provided—the hijackers diverted the Boeing 747 to Lebanon. But control tower officials in Beirut refused to give landing clearance, and the plane continued on to Cyprus—where the hijackers killed two Kuwaiti passengers. The 15-day ordeal finally ended in Algeria, where the hijackers released the 31 remaining hostages and were allowed safe passage out of the country. Kuwait had refused the hijackers' demand that it release 17 Shiite terrorists being held for the 1983 bombings of the U.S. and French embassies.

In December, four gunmen in the southern Soviet Union seized a bus full of schoolchildren, whom they exchanged for a plane and money. With the hijackers and a crew of eight on board, the plane was flown to Israel, where the gunmen surrendered. Israel agreed to a Soviet request for their return.

The major terrorist incident at sea during 1988 occurred in Greece, where Arab gunmen opened fire indiscriminately and threw grenades aboard a Greek ferry loaded with nearly 500 tourists; 11 people were killed and 98 wounded. In a related incident, a car loaded with explosives blew up at the port where the ship was to have anchored, killing the occupants of the car. A group calling itself the Organization of the Martyrs of the Popular Revolution in Palestine claimed responsibility for the massacre on the ship and the explosion of the car. Greece also was the site of the June 28 car-bombing assassination of the U.S. military attaché in Athens, Capt. William Nordeen, by members of the November 17 Revolutionary Organization.

Drug-related terrorism continued to grow in Latin America, where two sticks of dynamite exploded along a road on which U.S. Secretary of State George Shultz was traveling in Bolivia on August 8. Four vehicles in the motorcade were damaged, but there were no injuries. Shultz had gone to Bolivia to deliver a speech condemning international drug trafficking. Earlier in the year, Colombia's Attorney General Carlos Hoyos Jimenez was kidnapped and murdered by drug traffickers who had declared war on government officials trying to extradite them to the United States.

One unresolved incident of 1988 was the midair explosion of a plane carrying Pakistan's President Mohammad Zia ul-Haq on August 17. Also killed were U.S. Ambassador Arnold L. Raphel, the chief U.S. military attaché to Pakistan, five Pakistani generals, and 22 other persons. U.S. investigators concluded that the crash probably was caused by a malfunction in the aircraft and not by a bomb or missile. However, Pakistani investigators ruled out mechanical failure and cited sabotage or some other criminal act as the cause of the crash.

Among the terrorist groups most active during the year were Sikh extremists in the Punjab in India, where massacres and assassinations became a regular occurrence. In May, Sikh separatists once again seized the Golden Temple at Amritsar, where hundreds of people were killed in a 1984 confrontation with Indian troops. This time the troops did not enter the temple, and most of the militants eventually surrendered. Nevertheless, sporadic gunfire killed 26 people.

The Irish Republican Army (IRA) also was active in 1988, extending its attacks beyond Northern Ireland. The IRA struck targets in England, Belgium, and the Netherlands. In March, three IRA members were killed by British commandos in Gibraltar, touching off a cycle of violence that included shootings during funeral processions.

JEFFREY D. SIMON, *The RAND Corporation*

TEXAS

Presidential politics, a crisis in the state's banking industry, the awarding of a major scientific research project, and the 25th anniversary of the assassination of President John F. Kennedy in Dallas focused national attention on Texas during 1988.

Politics. The 1988 U.S. presidential election held special interest for Texans. The Republican candidate, Vice-President George Bush, claimed Texas as his native state and ultimately delivered his victory speech in Houston. The importance of the state's 29 electoral votes to the Democratic Party was evidenced by Gov. Michael Dukakis' selection of Sen. Lloyd Bentsen as his vice-presidential running mate. Although the Republican tide proved too strong for the Democratic ticket—with Bush-Quayle winning 56%-44%—the popular Bentsen easily won his fourth term in the U.S. Senate, defeating Rep. Beau Boulter, 60%-40%. James Baker, a former Houston lawyer and Reagan cabinet official, acted as Bush's campaign manager and was appointed secretary of state in the new administration.

Despite the solid GOP victory in the presidential race, the Democrats gained two more seats in the state's U.S. congressional delegation—increasing its majority to 19-8—and retained control of both houses of the state legislature.

Economy. The Texas economy remained stagnant during 1988. World oil prices continued to slide, and the uncertain political situation in the Middle East only compounded the problem. Real-estate values continued to decline, though not as steeply as in prior years. These two factors contributed to the greatest banking collapse in state history. Well over 100 commercial banks and savings and loan associations (S&Ls) failed, including some of the largest in Houston and Dallas. Federal rescue efforts and merger arrangements eased the crisis somewhat, but the potential for further dislocation remained. (*See also* BANKING AND FINANCE.) Finally, although there was some improvement during the year, unemployment continued to run at a rate slightly above the national average.

Judicial Issues. The Texas State Supreme Court came under widespread criticism. Many legal scholars disagreed with its refusal in November 1987 to hear Texaco's request to throw out Pennzoil's $10.3 billion judgment against it —a judgment that led to Texaco's bankruptcy. The court's image was tarnished further when it was revealed that the principal attorney for Pennzoil had made substantial campaign contributions to some of the justices. Shortly thereafter Chief Justice John Hill resigned, stating that the judiciary should be appointed rather than elected. Six spots on the Supreme Court were contested in the November election —the most ever on the ballot at one time—and business interests spent $1 million to help elect a conservative majority. Republican Tom Phillips was elected chief justice; the six seats were divided equally among Democrats and Republicans.

Taxation. Texas remained one of the few states in the nation without a state income tax. Although the legislature was not scheduled to convene until January 1989, committees were hard at work considering new sources of revenue. A proposal for a state income tax already encountered strong opposition from Gov. William Clements and Speaker of the House Gibb Lewis on the grounds that it would discourage new business ventures from locating in Texas. Opposition to the proposed income tax led advocates of a state lottery to surface again, even though such a plan was defeated in the legislature. Backers pointed to the enormous profits generated by lotteries in such states as Florida and California, and the allocation of any lottery profits to education made the proposal attractive to many Texans.

Education. SAT scores for college admission improved somewhat in Texas in 1988, but educators hoped for a greater rate of advancement. Adequate funding for education is a major obstacle. Only three states have a lower resident college tuition rate than Texas, but attempts to raise tuition have met with opposition from students and parents.

Super Collider. On November 10, U.S. Secretary of Energy John Herrington and Governor Clements announced that Texas had been chosen as the site of the proposed $4.4 billion U.S. Superconducting Super Collider. The particle accelerator—or atom smasher—would be the largest and most costly scientific instrument in the world. To be located near Waxahachie in Ellis County, it is expected to create some 8,000 area jobs. (*See also* PHYSICS.)

STANLEY E. SIEGEL, *University of Houston*

TEXAS • Information Highlights

Area: 266,807 sq mi (691 030 km²).

Population (July 1, 1987): 16,789,000.

Chief Cities (July 1, 1986 est.): Austin, the capital, 466,550; Houston, 1,728,910; Dallas, 1,003,520; San Antonio, 914,350; El Paso, 491,800; Fort Worth, 429,550; Corpus Christi, 263,900.

Government (1988): *Chief Officers*—governor, William Clements (R); lt. gov., William P. Hobby (D). *Legislature*—Senate, 31 members; House of Representatives, 150 members.

State Finances (fiscal year 1987): *Revenue,* $24,038,000,000; *expenditure,* $21,717,000,000.

Personal Income (1987): $232,783,000,000; per capita, $13,866.

Labor Force (June 1988): *Civilian labor force,* 8,596,700; *unemployed,* 685,800 (8.0% of total force).

Education: *Enrollment* (fall 1986)—public elementary schools, 2,317,454; public secondary, 892,061; colleges and universities, 776,019. *Public school expenditures* (1986–87), $10,672,000,000 ($3,584 per pupil).

THAILAND

After nearly eight-and-a-half years in office, Prime Minister Prem Tinsulanonda in July 1988 declined a new term and was replaced by Acting Deputy Premier Chatichai Choonhavan. The new government would seek to extend Thailand's economic boom and announced that it would try to improve relations with Vietnam when the latter carries out its promise to withdraw its forces from Cambodia.

Politics. Facing the threat of a no-confidence vote, Prime Minister Prem in late April dissolved parliament and his cabinet, and called for elections on July 24. Chatichai's Thai Nation Party, which won the most seats (87) in the 357-member parliament, formed a majority coalition with four other parties. The coalition offered Prem another term, but the 67-year-old former general unexpectedly declined, citing "personal reasons."

The coalition turned to Chatichai, a 66-year-old former general and diplomat (who presided over the reestablishment of relations with China in 1975) and close political supporter of Prem. Unlike Prem, Chatichai won a seat in parliament and thus became Thailand's first elected prime minister in 12 years.

As usual, the election campaign centered on personalities and economic issues. Prem had decided to dissolve parliament and call an election after one of his opponents threatened to discuss his personal life in public. The fact that Prem was not an elected member of parliament became a key issue in the brief campaign, which was marked by strikes, student demonstrations, and a petition to King Bhumibol Adulyadej by 99 leading professionals. The petitioners claimed that Prem was not behaving in a properly neutral manner as caretaker head of government during the campaign. The choice of an elected member of parliament to succeed Prem was hailed by many Thai intellectuals as a step forward for democracy.

Rumors of a military coup were fostered during the election campaign by Thai Army commander Gen. Chaovalit Yongchaiyut, who called for *patiwat*, or peaceful revolution. Some saw this as Chaovalit and several other senior or retired generals positioning themselves openly as possible future prime ministers. After the election, Chatichai quickly moved to consolidate the support of the military by giving Chaovalit and other service chiefs a free hand in promotions. Chatichai's cabinet also granted amnesty to those who had taken part in an abortive 1985 coup.

Nevertheless, the new government faced its first challenge just two months after taking office. The attack came from the opposition coalition in parliament rather than from the military. The opposition tried to drive a wedge between the two main parties in the government coalition—the Thai National and Social Action parties—by accusing a Social Action minister of impropriety. Chatichai came to his minister's defense and the attack failed, but one of Chatichai's enemies accused him of planning to sell Senate seats to wealthy businessmen.

Economy. The economic boom allowed the government to enhance its popularity by granting pay increases to the nation's 1.5 million civil servants, policemen, and soldiers. In an effort to gain the support of labor, Chatichai said he planned to raise the minimum wage and support a badly needed social security pension law. Clearly, however, there would be limits on what his government could spend without overheating the economy and creating serious inflation.

Meanwhile, public-sector workers in railroads and public utilities continued to clamor for a greater share of the country's prosperity. Concern by these workers over government plans to transfer some public enterprises to the private sector—and abolish many unnecessary jobs—led to railroad and other strikes just before the election.

Foreign Relations. Foreign Minister Siddhi Savetsila remained in office under the new government, but it remained to be seen how well he and Prime Minister Chatichai could work together. Siddhi was one of the main architects of the policy of opposing Vietnamese control over Cambodia by backing the Cambodian resistance. When the new prime minister announced his goal of turning Indochina "from a battleground into a trading market," Siddhi replied that he had no problem with this goal—but only after Vietnam withdraws its troops from Cambodia.

Earlier in the year, in mid-February, Thailand and Laos agreed to a truce in a three-month-old border conflict over a small, sparsely populated area claimed by both countries.

PETER A. POOLE
Author, "The Vietnamese in Thailand"

┌───┐
THAILAND · Information Highlights

Official Name: Kingdom of Thailand (conventional); Prathet Thai (Thai).
Location: Southeast Asia.
Area: 198,456 sq mi (514 000 km²).
Population (mid-1988 est.): 54,700,000.
Chief City (Dec. 31, 1986 est.): Bangkok, the capital, 5,468,915.
Government: *Head of state*, Bhumibol Adulyadej, king (acceded June 1946). *Head of government*, Chatichai Choonhavan, prime minister (took office July 1988).
Monetary Unit: Baht (25.47 baht equal U.S.$1, July 1988).
Gross National Product (1986 U.S.$): $41,800,-000,000.
Economic Index (Bangkok, 1987): *Consumer Prices* (1980 = 100), all items, 134.0; food, 119.1.
Foreign Trade (1987 U.S.$): *Imports*, $12,849,-000,000; *exports*, $11,546,000,000.
└───┘

Andrew Lloyd Webber's musical "The Phantom of the Opera" began its New York run in early 1988. The London-born smash hit starred Michael Crawford in the title role.

THEATER

There was a recovery—albeit a phantom one, perhaps—in the Broadway season of 1987–88. With the huge success of *The Phantom of the Opera* and a few other smash musicals masking the general sluggishness of the scene, particularly with regard to plays, Broadway recorded its second straight season of attendance increase in the midst of decades-long declines. The League of American Theatres and Producers reported that attendance rose 16% to 8.1 million, or 76% of capacity, over 1986–87. Swiftly climbing ticket prices (a $50 weekend "top" for certain musicals) helped explain the all-time ticket sales record of $253 million. In a season (June 1, 1987 to June 1, 1988) of just 32 new productions—12 musicals, 8 new plays, 7 revivals, and 5 special attractions—it was surprising to see two important, beautifully crafted plays make their premieres on Broadway without any development in the nonprofit theater and then beat the overwhelming odds for box-office success. They were David Mamet's *Speed-the-Plow* and David Henry Hwang's *M. Butterfly*. *Plow* continued Mamet's journey into the predatory world of American business (*American Buffalo, Glengarry Glen Ross*), lacerating the ethics of two crass Hollywood producers (played by Joe Mantegna and Ron Silver) with bitter hilarity. Ticket sales began to wane late in the year, however, after the departure of Madonna from her controversial Broadway-debut role as an enigmatic secretary, and it closed December 31. *M. Butterfly* won the 1988 Tony Award for best play. Staged with tingling suspense by John Dexter (*Equus*), it was a dark fable about East and West as partners in a ritualized charade of imperialistic and sexual manipulation, based on the true story of a French diplomat (played by John Lithgow) who discovers that the Chinese opera singer he has been having an affair with for 20 years is actually a male spy. B. D. Wong's stunning dual-gender role won the Tony for best supporting actor.

Glenda Jackson salvaged a sharp, interesting reading of Lady Macbeth, opposite an oddly subdued Christopher Plummer, in a disappointing production of Shakespeare's ever-beleaguered "Scottish play." Blythe Danner, likewise, took the best of the mixed notices for her Blanche Dubois in Tennessee Williams' *A Streetcar Named Desire* at the resident company, Circle in the Square.

Among the season's noble failures were Lee Blessing's *A Walk in the Woods*, starring Sam Waterston and Robert Prosky as American and Soviet arms negotiators trying to humanize superpower politics; *Joe Turner's Come and Gone*, a suspense drama of uprooted former slaves in August Wilson's continuing play-cycle on black history; and Hugh Whitemore's London import, *Breaking the Code*, a vehicle for the dazzling performance of Derek Jacobi as the English mathematician who broke the Nazi war code but was persecuted for his homosexuality.

Capturing the trendy tastes of the time with its opulent Maria Bjournson designs and lavishly romantic pop score, *The Phantom of the Opera* came from London amid great hype and fanfare and instantly became New York's least available ticket. Critics were grudgingly receptive of the overrated show, which did contain a dazzling comeback staging by Hal Prince (*Evita*) and a brilliant, universally acclaimed performance by Michael Crawford in the title role. Crawford's award for best actor in a musical was one of the show's seven Tonys.

Phantom may have represented the last salvo, at least temporarily, in the so-called British Invasion of blockbuster musicals (the continuing hits *Cats, Me and My Girl, Les Misérables,* and *Starlight Express*), as the two following salvos turned out to be big, costly duds. They were *Carrie*, the Royal Shakespeare Company's high-tech treatment of the Stephen King horror novel, and *Chess*, a love triangle story set across a superpower chess championship. *Phantom*, joining *Cats* and *Starlight*,

gave composer Andrew Lloyd Webber (*see* BI-OGRAPHY) an unprecedented three hits running simultaneously in London and New York.

The American-made musical hits of 1987–88 were *Into the Woods*, with composer-lyricist Stephen Sondheim and author-director James Lapine of *Sunday in the Park* teaming again for a witty, adult sequel to popular fairy tales; and a sleek revival of Cole Porter's 1934 tunefest *Anything Goes*, starring Patti LuPone. *Sarafina!*, by rock songwriter Hugh Masekela, was exhilaratingly performed by black teenagers in the roles of South African students who boycott their Soweto schools. In the category of noble failure was writer-director Lee Breuer's *The Gospel at Colonus*, which framed Greek mythology in a black church service but had lost its edge after successful nonprofit engagements across the country.

In the slow-starting 1988–89 season, the only big-scale musical to arrive before Jan. 1, 1989, was *Legs Diamond*, the Broadway debut of Australian composer-star Peter Allen as a song-and-dance gangster of the 1930s. Although kept afloat by a big advance sale, the show bombed with critics when it opened late in December.

Straight plays, ironically, got off to a somewhat more promising 1988–89 start. In *Spoils of War*, Michael Weller captured the emotional currents of the 1950s—much as he had captured the 1960s in *Moonchildren* and the 1970s in *Loose Ends*. A classically constructed American family drama centering on a boy's heartbreaking attempt to reconcile his estranged parents, *Spoils* provided Kate Nelligan with the big, magnetic role she long had deserved and raised Weller to the front rank of American dramatists. Previewing in December was *Eastern Standard*, the breakthrough play for Richard Greenberg, which managed to synthesize observations about AIDS, the homeless, and yuppies in a witty and sharply contemporary comedy-drama. The entertaining hit production transferred intact from off-Broadway's Manhattan Theatre Club.

But the highly anticipated *Rumors*, Neil Simon's first new play since his career-topping trilogy of 1983–87, was considered a disappointing lowbrow farce in many quarters.

Among national touring companies, a big surprise was Robert Goulet in *South Pacific*, which kept adding cities to its itinerary by popular demand. Satellite companies of *Les Misérables* settled in for long runs in Philadelphia and Los Angeles.

Off-Broadway. In 1987–88, their third full season as artistic director and executive producer, Gregory Mosher and Bernard Gersten decisively banished the 20-year jinx of Lincoln Center, winning high critical marks and filling houses with solid, popular fare. In the fall of 1988, the Lincoln Center hits *Sarafina!* and Mosher's wire-taut staging of *Speed-the-Plow*

continued their runs in Broadway houses, while on Lincoln Center's New House stage a limited run of *Waiting for Godot*—directed by Mike Nichols and starring comedians Steve Martin and Robin Williams—was a sellout before the mixed notices ever appeared. Since *Anything Goes* kept sailing on Lincoln Center's Beaumont stage, Broadway's Lyceum Theatre was leased as a satellite house. The first offering there, Mosher's spare and haunting staging of *Our Town*, seemed to define the Americana character of his company. While Mosher was careful not to claim Lincoln Center as a "national theater," he was on his way to realizing that long-cherished, long-frustrated dream.

At New York's other leading nonprofit institution, the New York Shakespeare Festival (NYSF), producer Joseph Papp was realizing his own dream—the first full year of the Shakespeare Marathon, a projected six-year cycle of all the Bard's works. Audiences were delighted by a fanciful, South American-flavored *Midsummer Night's Dream*, with F. Murray Abraham as an ebullient Bottom in NYSF's Public Theatre; and Kevin Kline and Blythe Danner were perfectly matched for the romantic parries of *Much Ado About Nothing* in Central Park. The series' most original and daring entry, at the Public, was a spare, spiky, explosive staging of *Coriolanus* by the fast-rising British actor-director-playwright Steven Berkoff. It featured the long-awaited Shakespearean coup of Christopher Walken in the title role.

The first New York International Festival of the Arts included dozens of early-summer performances all over Manhattan by world-renowned companies. Highlights included Sean O'Casey's *Juno and the Paycock* by the Gate Theatre of Dublin; and a twin bill of Eugene O'Neill classics in repertory—*Ah, Wilderness!* and *Long Day's Journey Into Night*—which reunited America's two leading O'Neill interpreters, Colleen Dewhurst and Jason Robards.

Some of the important but unfortunately short-lived productions of the 1987–88 season were *The Road to Mecca*, another moving drama from the great South African playwright Athol Fugard, featuring Amy Irving; and Tom Griffin's moving study of retarded adults, *The Boys Next Door*, with Josh Mostel leading a superb ensemble. Carry-over hits from the previous off-Broadway season, well-crafted as well as popular, included Barbara Lebow's *A Shayna Maidel*, Terrence McNally's *Frankie and Johnny in the Clair de Lune*, and Alfred Uhry's 1988 Pulitzer Prize-winner, *Driving Miss Daisy*.

New off-Broadway entries were thin in the early part of the 1988–89 season. But two leading resident companies introduced interesting plays: Circle Repertory Company presented Craig Lucas' revised version of his dark com-

edy, *Reckless;* and Playwrights Horizons premiered Wendy Wasserstein's *The Heidi Chronicles,* tracing three decades in the lives of contemporary young women.

Forbidden Broadway, Gerard Alessandrini's wickedly witty, long-running spoof of the New York theater scene, reopened in a new, updated edition—more wildly popular than ever—at the off-off Broadway cabaret, Theatre East.

Resident Theaters. There was a movement among theater artists to drop the outmoded term "regional theater" ("It sounds tributary to New York," said Robert Brustein, artistic director of American Repertory Theatre in Cambridge, MA) and instead refer to those institutions consistently as resident, nonprofit theaters. In 1987–88, for the third straight theatrical season, League of Resident Theaters (LORT) contracts logged more workweeks for Actors Equity members than did contracts for Broadway and commercial tours, indicating that the preponderance of professional work was outside New York and that the LORT houses, indeed, had outgrown their old tributary role.

But many of the same factors afflicting Broadway—rising production costs and competition from VCRs and other entertainment media—challenged the financial and artistic health of the resident nonprofit system. Theatre Communications Group (TCG), the system's information clearinghouse, reported that in 1987, for 188 theaters surveyed, total attendance reached a five-year high of 14.6 million; but in a core sample group of 48 leading theaters, 22 gained in attendance over 1986 while 26 lost ground. Eighty-five of the 188 theaters

---

BROADWAY OPENINGS | 1988

MUSICALS

Ain't Misbehavin' (revival), music by Fats Waller; lyrics by Andy Razaf and others; directed by Richard Maltby, Jr.; with Nell Carter, Armelia McQueen, Ken Page, Andre De Shields, Charlaine Woodard; Aug. 15–.

Carrie, music by Michael Gore; lyrics by Dean Pitchford; book by Lawrence D. Cohen, based on a novel by Stephen King; directed by Terry Hands; with Betty Buckley, Linzi Hateley, Gene Anthony Ray; May 12–15.

Chess, music by Benny Andersson and Bjorn Ulvaeus; lyrics by Tim Rice; book by Richard Nelson and Tim Rice; directed by Trevor Nunn; with Judy Kuhn, David Carroll, Philip Casnoff; April 28–June 25.

The Gospel at Colonus, music by Bob Telson; book and lyrics by Lee Breuer; from a play by Sophocles; directed by Lee Breuer; with Isabell Monk, Morgan Freeman; March 24–May 15.

Legs Diamond, music and lyrics by Peter Allen; book by Harvey Fierstein and Charles Suppon; directed by Robert Allan Ackerman; with Peter Allen, Julie Wilson, Joe Silver, Randall Edwards; Dec. 26–.

Mail, music by Michael Rupert; book and lyrics by Jerry Colker; directed by Andrew Cadiff; with Michael Rupert, Mara Getz; April 14–May 15.

The Phantom of the Opera, music by Andrew Lloyd Webber; lyrics by Charles Hart, additional lyrics by Richard Stilgoe; book by Richard Stilgoe and Andrew Lloyd Webber from a novel by Gaston Leroux; directed by Harold Prince; with Michael Crawford, Sarah Brightman; Jan. 26–.

Romance/Romance, music by Keith Herrmann; book, lyrics, and direction by Barry Harman; with Scott Bakula, Alison Fraser; May 1–.

Sarafina!, music by Mbongeni Ngema and Hugh Masekela; lyrics and book by Mbongeni Ngema; directed by Mbongeni Ngema; With children from South African townships; Jan. 28–.

PLAYS

Ah, Wilderness!, by Eugene O'Neill; directed by Arvin Brown; with Colleen Dewhurst, Jason Robards, Elizabeth Wilson, George Hearn; June 23–July 23.

Checkmates, by Ron Milner; directed by Woodie King, Jr.; with Denzel Washington, Paul Winfield, Ruby Dee, Marsha Jackson. Aug. 4–Jan. 1, 1989.

The Devil's Disciple, by George Bernard Shaw; directed by Stephen Porter; with Philip Bosco, Victor Garber, Roxanne Hart, Rosemary Murphy, Remak Ramsay; Nov. 13–.

Joe Turner's Come and Gone, by August Wilson; directed by Lloyd Richards; with Ed Hall, Delroy Lindo, Mel Winkler, L. Scott Caldwell; March 27–June 27.

Juno and the Paycock, by Sean O'Casey; directed by Joe Dowling; with John Kavanagh, Donal McCann; June 21–July 2.

Long Day's Journey into Night, by Eugene O'Neill; directed by José Quintero; with Colleen Dewhurst, Jason Robards, Jamey Sheridan; June 14–July 23.

Macbeth, by William Shakespeare; directed by Kenneth Frankel; with Christopher Plummer, Glenda Jackson; April 21–July 3.

M. Butterfly, by David Henry Hwang; directed by John Dexter; with John Lithgow, B. D. Wong, Lori Tan Chinn, George N. Martin, Rose Gregorio; March 20–.

The Night of the Iguana, by Tennessee Williams; directed by Theodore Mann; with Jane Alexander, Nicholas Surovy, Pamela Payton-Wright, Maria Tucci; June 26–Sept. 4.

Our Town, by Thornton Wilder; directed by Gregory Mosher; with Spalding Gray, Penelope Ann Miller, Eric Stoltz; Dec. 4–.

Paul Robeson, by Philip Hayes Dean; directed by Harold Scott; with Avery Brooks; Sept. 28–Oct. 9.

Rumors, by Neil Simon; directed by Gene Saks; with Christine Baranski, Ron Leibman, Andre Gregory, Mark Nelson, Jessica Walter; Nov. 17–.

Serious Money, by Caryl Churchill; directed by Max Stafford-Clark; with Kate Nelligan, Allan Corduner; Feb. 9–20.

Speed-the-Plow, by David Mamet; directed by Gregory Mosher; with Joe Mantegna, Ron Silver, Madonna. May 3–Dec. 31.

Spoils of War, by Michael Weller; directed by Austin Pendleton; with Kate Nelligan, Jeffrey De Munn, Christopher Collet; Nov. 10–Dec. 10.

A Streetcar Named Desire, by Tennessee Williams; directed by Nikos Psacharopoulos; with Blythe Danner, Aidan Quinn, Frances McDormand, Frank Converse; March 10–May 22.

A Walk in the Woods, by Lee Blessing; directed by Des McAnuff; with Sam Waterston, Robert Prosky; Feb. 28–June 26.

OTHER ENTERTAINMENT

Canciones de mi Padre; revue of mariachi songs and dances; with Linda Ronstadt; July 12–30.

Jackie Mason's "The World According to Me!" (revival); a comedy revue; with Jackie Mason; May 2–Dec. 31.

Michael Feinstein in Concert; with Michael Feinstein. April 19–June 12 and Oct. 5–Nov. 6.

Oba Oba—"The Brazilian Experience"; dance revue; March 29–May 15.

Stand-Up Comedy: A Twentieth Century Art, one-man show; with Robert Klein; July 4.

John Lithgow (right) and B. D. Wong won acclaim for their roles in "M. Butterfly," a fact-based Broadway drama about the strange 20-year love affair between a French diplomat and a Chinese male spy who poses as a female Beijing Opera diva.

ended 1987 in the red, but that number continued its five-year pattern of improvement. TCG president Peter Zeisler decried an "artistic deficit," a general trend toward safer, budget-balancing fare.

Steppenwolf Theatre Company, a pacesetter of the exciting Chicago theater scene, mounted a big, nationally acclaimed adaptation of John Steinbeck's *The Grapes of Wrath*. Two other theaters drew good national notices, too, for sharply contemporary Shakespearean stagings: the Old Globe Theatre in San Diego for its John Hirsch mounting of *Coriolanus*, and the Hartford Stage Company for *A Midsummer Night's Dream* under artistic director Mark Lamos.

American Theatre magazine noted a wave of "Marx Mania": The Arena Stage in Washington mounted a smash revival of the Marx Brothers' 1920s Broadway vehicle *The Cocoanuts;* and the Huntington Theatre of Boston and the Alliance Theatre Company of Atlanta coproduced, in the two cities, a delightful revival of *Animal Crackers*.

The first National Black Arts Festival, the only national-scale arts festival entirely administered by blacks, was held in Atlanta, GA, July 30–August 7. Among the prestigious world premieres at the biennial, $1.5 million fest was

the Negro Ensemble Company's *Sally*. The drama about the emancipation of Southern slaves was by Charles Fuller, the Pulitzer Prize-winning author of *A Soldier's Play*.

New artistic director Josephine Abady began the revitalization of the long-invisible Cleveland Play House with such high-profile productions as *Born Yesterday*, with Ed Asner and Madeline Kahn, and *On the Waterfront*, adapted from a classic screenplay by Budd Schulberg.

The first Fund for American Plays, cosponsored by American Express and the John F. Kennedy Center for the Performing Arts, distributed $336,000 to eight theaters for the debut of selected plays; one of the surprise recipients was the feisty Hip Pocket Theatre of Fort Worth, TX, for the American premiere of *Widows*, by Chilean political dissident Ariel Dorfman.

South Coast Repertory of Costa Mesa, CA, known for its development of such new playwrights as Craig Lucas *(Three Postcards)*, was awarded the 1988 Special Tony Award for resident-theater achievement by the American Theater Critics Association. (*See also* PRIZES AND AWARDS.)

DAN HULBERT
"The Atlanta Journal and Constitution"

TRANSPORTATION

Congestion, safety, financing, and corporate restructuring drew major attention in the transportation industry in 1988. U.S. government policies for control of the business practices of transportation companies (often called economic regulation) were also subjects of debate and attempted change during the year.

Congestion and Safety Issues. Road and air transport experienced severe congestion in numerous countries. U.S. motor vehicle traffic approached two trillion mi (3.24 trillion km) per year, up more than 27% from 1977. Yet, total U.S. capacity (or mileage) increased less than 1% in the same period. Traffic volumes also continued to rise without significant increases in road capacity in Western Europe, Japan, and other nations.

A series of operational errors by air traffic controllers in the face of dense traffic caused the Federal Aviation Agency (FAA) to reduce landings at Chicago's O'Hare International Airport from 96 to 80 per hour. Capacity problems also plagued other major U.S. airports. In Boston, a proposal to reduce peak period demand by restricting private (general aviation) air traffic in preference to scheduled commercial flights drew strong protests from various interest groups. Lack of a unified European air traffic control system, coupled with strong traffic growth, caused unprecedented numbers of delayed and cancelled flights and air-terminal crowding in Britain, West Germany, France, and other countries during the summer vacation travel season.

In April, the crew of an Aloha Airlines early model Boeing 737 landed it following in-flight separation of a portion of the plane's upper fuselage and the death of a flight attendant. The event focused increased attention on the structural conditions of aging commercial jet aircraft by the FAA, airlines, and aircraft manufacturers.

On November 14, U.S. Secretary of Transportation James Burnley issued rules requiring five different phases of drug testing—pre-employment, periodic, random, reasonable cause, and post-accident—for operating and maintenance personnel in air, rail, water, interstate truck and bus, urban transit, and pipelines engaged in natural gas and hazardous liquids movement.

Concern over drug use also contributed to enactment of the Rail Safety Improvement Act (RSIA) of 1988 on June 22. It required the Federal Railroad Administration (FRA) to implement within 18 months a program for federal licensing of locomotive engineers. The act also strengthened the FRA's power to enforce previously enacted federal railroad safety laws.

Railroads. Preliminary 1988 data for freight traffic on U.S. railroads showed increases over 1987 of about 4.5% in the total number of cars loaded and approximately 6.5% in revenue freight ton-miles. Intermodal traffic—freight in truck trailers and containers carried on railway flatcars—rose about 8% from 1987 levels. In response to continuing strong competition from trucking, French and West German rail carriers announced plans for improving service quality by various means, including increases in freight train speeds to between 70 and 100 mph (113 and 161 km/hr).

Rail passengers carried by Amtrak between Oct. 1, 1987, and Sept. 30, 1988, increased 5.16% over the previous 12-month period. This growth helped raise Amtrak's revenues to 69% of its operating costs, thus requiring lower government subsidy. However, the growth also pressed Amtrak's equipment fleet so severely that the company turned away business in some markets. As a partial solution, Amtrak ordered 100 new passenger cars and eight used

During the morning rush hour on December 12, a crowded commuter train in south London slammed into the back of another one stopped on the track. A third train then ploughed into the wreckage. Thirty-three people were killed, 113 injured. The accident was blamed on a "technical fault" in signals on the line, which were being replaced in a modernization program.

locomotives. Amtrak also began testing new trains that would travel the New York-Boston routes at much higher speeds.

Several European countries continued to make heavy investments in rail track and equipment designed for fast, frequent operation. French National Railways (SNCF) moved ahead with planning and construction of addition TGV (very high-speed train) lines designed for a speed range of 150-210 mph (240-340 km/hr). The German Federal Railway (DB) opened part of its new high-speed (150 mph or 240 km/hr) Hannover-Wurzburg line, with full opening scheduled for 1991. Construction also progressed on a second new DB high-speed line between Mannheim and Stuttgart, targeted for completion in the same year. In addition, planning was undertaken to raise maximum passenger train speed on various existing mainlines to 120 mph (190 km/hr). The national rail carriers of Spain and Italy also pursued plans to increase passenger service speeds.

A major change in corporate structure within the U.S. rail-freight industry occurred on August 9, when the Interstate Commerce Commission (ICC) approved purchase of the 12,798-mi (20 596-km) Southern Pacific Transportation Company by the 2,248-mi (3 618-km) Denver & Rio Grande Western Railroad. The newly merged carrier, which took the name Southern Pacific, became the fifth-largest U.S. rail carrier in terms of route-miles. Earlier, on May 18, the ICC approved the merger of the 3,150-mi (5 069-km) Katy Railroad into the 20,924-mi (33 674-km) Union Pacific. The merger, completed on August 12, created the nation's largest railroad as measured by route mileage.

From the early 1980s through 1987, a boom developed in the sale of light density line segments by large railroads to short-line and regional railway firms. The boom was halted in 1988 by court decisions stemming from railway unions' dissatisfaction with labor protection and representation terms applicable to such sales. However, a few transactions occurred despite this opposition. The largest took place on July 19, when CSX Transportation sold 340 mi (547 km) of line to the newly formed Buffalo & Pitttsburgh Railroad for $30 million.

Another regional rail carrier, the Chicago, Missouri & Western (CM&W), filed for bankruptcy on April 1. The carrier had begun operation on April 28, 1987, when it purchased 631 mi (1 015 km) of line between Joliet, IL, St. Louis, and Kansas City from the Illinois Central Gulf Railroad. CM&W's revenues were insufficient to pay interest on money borrowed to finance its line purchase. The company continued to provide service under the direction of a court-appointed trustee. On June 20 another railway, the 1,200-mi (1 931-km) Delaware & Hudson, which operates in parts of the Northeast, filed for bankruptcy.

In September the U.S. Senate Committee on Commerce, Science and Transportation stalled legislation intended to restore greater government regulation over the pricing of rail-freight service. The legislation had been sought by various freight shippers who expressed dissatisfaction with rail carriers' rate-making practices following partial deregulation of the industry by the Staggers Rail Act of 1980.

Major changes in the economic regulation of all modes of transport took effect in Canada on January 1. In general, the changes were intended to increase competitiveness between carriers, which presumably would result in lower freight rates and passenger fares and improved service.

Trucking. The intensely competitive rate-cutting that reduced earnings of U.S. LTL motor carriers (trucking firms that generally move shipments smaller in lot size than a full truckload) moderated somewhat. However, some truckers continued to experience heavy operating deficits. One of them, American Carriers, Inc., filed for bankruptcy in August and ceased all LTL freight operations. It had been among the 15 largest U.S. trucking firms in terms of gross revenues.

On October 28, Roadway Services, Inc., the nation's second-largest trucking firm, completed the purchase of Viking Freight, Inc., a West Coast regional LTL carrier. Also in October, five TL motor carriers (carriers that generally move full truckload lot-sized shipments) were sold to a new company named Landstar System, Inc., thus forming one of the largest TL carriers in the nation (with approximately $580 million in annual gross revenue).

To reduce traffic congestion and pollution, the city of Los Angeles proposed that truck deliveries be limited by requiring truck operators to buy a special permit for deliveries made during rush hours. Also, a delivery tax would be imposed on businesses not open for nonrush hour deliveries.

On July 15 the U.S. Department of Transportation (DOT) issued a final rule establishing standards for the testing and licensing of interstate and intrastate truck and bus drivers. The DOT also began a two-year fleet test program to evaluate antilock braking systems for heavy trucks. Legislaton was passed requiring the DOT to study the effects of existing hours-of-service limits for commercial drivers, and to begin formulating rules for use of onboard computers for the recording of drivers' time in service.

On June 7 the Interstate Commerce Commission (ICC) approved a request by Greyhound Lines, Inc., for permanent authority to acquire and operate scheduled intercity bus routes and certain related assets from Trailways, Inc. Greyhound had been operating the Trailways routes under temporary ICC authority since July 1987.

British experts concluded that the crash of a Pan Am 747 jet over Lockerbie, Scotland, on December 21 was caused by a powerful plastic explosive device. All 259 people on board, and 11 others on the ground, were killed. In the aftermath, the U.S. government announced strict new security measures for flights of U.S. airlines from 103 airports in Europe and the Middle East.

AP/Wide World

Shipping. Water carriers on the Mississippi and Ohio rivers suffered severe economic losses when summer drought conditions forced reductions in the size of barge tows and load limits of individual barges. Operations improved during the fall as dredging and new rainfall increased the depth of navigation channels.

Decline in value of the U.S. dollar and revival of the steel industry helped to produce an 800% increase in export steel shipments on the Great Lakes/St. Lawrence Seaway System. Growth in movements of raw materials for steelmaking resulted in the operation of more dry bulk-carrying vessels on the Great Lakes than in any year since 1984.

The declining U.S. dollar also affected ocean freight traffic patterns. Imported goods carried on containerships between the Far East and the United States declined to the point where capacity on eastbound ships exceeded cargo by more than 10%. Westbound trans-Pacific traffic increased, as U.S. exports to Asia grew. On the North Atlantic, eastbound traffic increased relative to westbound traffic, as exports to Europe increased.

Airlines. Air passenger traffic growth and the aging of existing fleets caused a surge in orders for new aircraft. The combined order backlog of the world's three largest aircraft builders—Boeing, McDonnell-Douglas, and Airbus Industries—rose above 2,000 airplanes, an all-time high.

Unlike most air carriers, Eastern Airlines suffered traffic losses and acted to reduce or eliminate service at 14 cities and to lay off about 10% of its work force. On October 12, Eastern agreed to sell its profitable shuttle operations in the Washington-New York-Boston corridor to a newly created carrier, Trump Airlines.

European air carriers sought corporate combinations and efficiencies that would enable them to meet conditions expected to result from full integration of the European Community in 1992. Scandinavian Air System agreed to purchase a 10% interest in Texas Air Corporation to gain access to U.S. passenger markets.

Congressional Action. Legislation appropriating $3.15 billion for federal funding of U.S. urban transit was enacted on September 30. The appropriation, which covers federal fiscal year 1989, was 1.9% below that of fiscal year 1977 and $1.6 billion more than the Reagan administration requested.

Transit industry representatives indicated in congressional testimony that it might not be possible to meet the 1991 emissions standards set by the Environmental Protection Agency for diesel bus engines.

Congress earmarked $54 million to assist with construction of a new 18-mi (29-km) St. Louis area light rail transit line. Engineering and design contracts for a 27.5-mi (44-km) light rail transit line serving the Baltimore area were approved on May 18.

JOHN C. SPYCHALSKI
Pennsylvania State University

TRAVEL

The decline of the U.S. dollar attracted foreign visitors to the United States in record numbers in 1988, but it did not keep Americans at home. The growth of outbound travel slowed but did not stop, as U.S. travelers found ways to get the most out of their travel dollars overseas. Many Americans, it seemed, no longer considered travel a nonessential expense—and the pool of potential globe-trotters was growing as the baby boom generation moved into the prime age group for international travel.

For overseas visitors to the United States, the dollar exchange rate proved as irresistible as the reverse situation had been for Americans a few years prior. Europeans crossed the Atlantic in record numbers, and in the opposite direction the rapidly expanding Japanese market made seats on transpacific flights hard to come by. Tourism, in fact, became one of the few areas in which the United States could point to a trade surplus with Japan and West Germany.

U.S. Domestic Travel. In their own country, Americans in 1988 logged some 1.25 billion "person trips"—trips of more than 100 miles (160 km) from home—according to the U.S. Travel Data Center. That represented an increase of 5% over 1987.

The trend of the past several years toward shorter vacations, but more of them, continued; while the number of vacation trips jumped by 9% during the first seven months of the year, actual vacation nights fell by 2.3%. Americans had not abandoned the traditional two-week vacation, but obviously many of them were taking shorter trips—either instead of or in addition to longer vacations. Weekend vacations, in fact, grew at a rate of about 11% and were especially popular with younger travelers; 55% of all "person trips" by those in the 18-to-34 age bracket took place over a weekend or extended weekend, compared with 42% for those 35 and over.

Amtrak had its busiest summer ever and recorded increases of 8% in the number of train passengers, 12% in revenue, and 15% in passenger miles for its fiscal year ended in September 1988. Demand exceeded supply on the rail system, and even in the off-season it took a lead time of four to six weeks to ensure first-class space on Amtrak trains. Space was sold out months ahead for summer travel.

For the first time in six years, vehicular travel grew at a faster rate than air travel within the United States. Statistics for the first half of the year showed a 5.2% increase in passenger miles by vehicle, while passenger miles on domestic air routes dropped .6%.

An influx of foreign visitors from overseas, Canada, and Mexico—a total of 33.5 million, 13% over 1987, boosted domestic tourism. Of that total, some 12.6 million visitors were from overseas, 20% more than in 1987. Some 5.85 million Europeans (up 25%) visited the United States in 1988 to take advantage of dollar exchange rates in their favor. Another strong source of overseas visitors was Asia and the Middle East, with 3.8 million arrivals, for a 20% increase over 1987. The rate of increase from Japan alone was expected to be more than 25% when final statistics were tabulated.

Canada remained the number one source of visitors, accounting for 13.5 million—up 8%. Mexico sent some 7.5 million visitors to the United States in 1988, an unexpectedly strong 12% increase over the previous year.

Americans Going Abroad. While overseas travel by Americans slowed to single-digit rather than double-digit growth percentages, some 14.2 million still traveled overseas—4% more than in 1987. For some 6.25 million of them, Europe remained the destination of choice, according to European Travel Commission estimates—up 5% from the previous year.

To offset the decreased spending power of their dollars, Americans seemed to be budgeting more carefully, going down a rank in amenities at their destination, using public transportation more, and buying prepaid travel packages in greater numbers than usual. European promotional efforts in the United States emphasized ways to stretch the dollar, and France in particular seemed to benefit from an advertising campaign highlighting travel packages and air fares.

The Pacific-Asia region was expected to show a growth rate of 5% to 6% for travel from North America when the year's final statistics were compiled. Travel from the United States to Japan declined as a result of the strong yen, and vacation travel to the region as a whole was affected by the weakened dollar. Still, business ties to the Pacific continued to grow, offsetting the crimp in leisure travel.

Travel to Mexico slowed somewhat but still showed a 5% increase, with 13.7 million Americans going there. And some 13.4 million Americans visited Canada, up 1% from 1987.

Trends. Change was in the air, quite literally, in 1988. Smoking was banned on all U.S. commercial flights of two hours or less under a law that went into effect in April. Northwest Airlines extended the ban to all its North American flights. And more and more hotels were setting aside no-smoking rooms.

Technological innovations in some locales were a preview of things to come. Video kiosks installed in such places as city shopping malls made it possible to book travel packages on the spot. And in some cases, prospective travelers who had personal computers with modems could obtain travel information from a travel agent's computer and make bookings from their own homes—at any hour of the day.

See also feature article, page 73.

PHYLLIS ELVING, *Free-lance Writer*

TUNISIA

After removing President for life Habib Bourguiba from office in a constitutional coup on Nov. 7, 1987, President Zine El Abidine Ben Ali began consolidating his power while actively pursuing the democratization of state and society. In foreign affairs, the new president strongly has advocated greater regional cooperation, and has reestablished close ties with Libya, from which Tunisia was estranged under Bourguiba; he also has ʼsought to strengthen links to the Communist and Afro-Asian countries while maintaining good relations with the West.

Domestic Affairs. In July the National Assembly approved new constitutional rules that abolished the life presidency, limiting the president to two consecutive five-year terms; the rule that made the prime minister the president's automatic successor also was scrapped.

In the areas of human rights and civil liberties broad changes were introduced to protect individual freedoms. More than a dozen political parties were allowed to apply for legal certification. The press was allowed greater leeway, and freedom of opinion was guaranteed constitutionally so long as Tunisia's basic Islamic, Arabic, and national character were not attacked or compromised.

The government proposed a National Pact with five priorities: cultural and national identity (and the role of Islam); sovereignty and political independence; society and citizen rights; economic development with social justice; and joint Arab action in foreign relations.

Also in July, Ben Ali announced a sweeping cabinet reshuffle in which he dismissed most of the old Bourguiba appointees. The new ministers were largely younger technocrats and the reshuffle strengthened the government team and consolidated support for the president. The prime minister continued to be Ben Ali's trusted ally, Hedi Baccouche.

On economic matters, Tunisia has moved away from strict state control, but according to current thinking, the state still has a role where the private sector cannot carry out the job, where social factors come into account, or where the national interest requires government to control a particular activity. In 1988 a combination of poor weather and locust plagues limited farm production, and industrial investment slipped somewhat. Tourism provided the only bright spot with a spectacular increase in foreign tourists as compared with 1987.

In early October the World Bank approved a $150 million loan for two years to support the country's liberalization program. World Bank officials expressed satisfaction with Tunisia's efforts to reduce the trade deficit by encouraging private-sector exports. In the next stage of this liberalization the government would priva-

tize some 100 state-run enterprises and take gradual steps toward making the dinar a convertible currency.

Foreign Affairs. President Ben Ali has been particularly active in promoting regional cooperation with his Maghrebi (North African) neighbors. With the opening of the Tunisian-Libyan border, thousands of Libyans poured into Tunisia to purchase the many consumer items so desperately lacking at home. On August 6, Ben Ali made an official visit to Libya. One important result was the resolution of the vexing dispute over oil rights in the critical Gulf of Gabes. Both countries agreed to set up a joint company to exploit the region's offshore reserves. For its part Libya allowed some 30,000 Tunisian workers back into the country, about the same number as were expelled in 1985 when diplomatic relations were severed. Meanwhile, regular contacts and trade continued to reinforce Tunisia's relations with Algeria and Morocco.

In September, Ben Ali made his first visit to France as Tunisian president. His three-day stay reinforced previous ties and resulted in numerous economic, social, and cultural agreements. Although he cancelled a scheduled trip to Washington, U.S.-Tunisian relations continue to be close.

JOHN P. ENTELIS, *Fordham University*

TURKEY

Inflation and high-level contacts with Greece captured public attention in Turkey in 1988.

Internal Developments. The most important domestic issue continued to be the economy. Prime Minister Turgut Ozal's second government was installed at the beginning of the year, but despite the absolute majority of his Motherland Party in the Assembly, he was unable to enact policies to stem inflation. Near year's end inflation was estimated to be running at an annual rate of 78%. In response, in September,

Turkish voters decisively rejected (65% to 35%) a government-backed constitutional referendum on advancing the date of local elections that was regarded widely as a vote of confidence (or no-confidence) in the government.

Ozal nonetheless reaffirmed his determination to pursue a policy of rapid growth and increased exports. He did have some success, including an overall growth rate of nearly 7.5%; significant increases in exports, especially to Middle East and Third World countries; and advances in expansion of energy facilities, communications to remote areas, and urban infrastructure. The government also continued to press its bid for eventual admission to the European Community, and several European missions visited Turkey to make assessments and recommendations.

The Kurdish insurgency also continued to take up much of the government's attention. In eastern Turkey fighting continued between Kurdish separatists and government forces. One of the worst incidents took place in May, when guerrillas killed 25 civilians in two villages. There was thus some surprise when in September, Turkey offered temporary asylum to an estimated 70,000 Iraqi Kurdish refugees who crossed the border in flight from the Iraqi army, which had been freed from other duties by the cease-fire in its war with Iran. The Turkish government said that this was done as a humanitarian gesture, and it won favorable comment from many countries. In regard to the Iraq-Iran War, Turkey steadfastly maintained neutrality, and after the cease-fire joined other nations in contributing to the United Nations observer force.

In June, Prime Minister Ozal survived an assassination attempt by an escaped murderer who was rumored to have been a member of the defunct neo-fascist National Order Party before 1980.

In July a second bridge was opened spanning the Bosporus between Europe and Asia.

© Argyropoulos/Sipa

Turkey's Prime Minister Turgut Ozal (right) and his Greek counterpart, Andreas Papandreou (left), met in Athens in June. Their talks were held in a "constructive spirit."

It was built by a consortium of Japanese, Italian, and Turkish firms at an estimated cost of $550 million.

In an important gesture to world public opinion, in January, Turkey signed the European Convention for the Prevention of Torture and Inhuman or Degrading Treatment or Punishment.

Foreign Affairs. Both President Kenan Evren and Prime Minister Ozal again visited several foreign countries, and travel by other senior government officials and members of the Turkish parliament continued to be very frequent. Evren's visit to the United States in late June was the first official U.S.-Turkish contact at that level in 21 years. The visit had been planned for 1987 but had been postponed because of differences on several issues, including U.S. trade policy. Relations improved, however, and among other things a "side letter" to the Defense and Economic Cooperation Agreement was ratified to expand U.S.-Turkish military cooperation. Turkey continued to be the third-highest recipient of U.S. military aid. In July, President Evren visited Britain, returning a visit by Prime Minister Margaret Thatcher in April. He also traveled to West Germany, Algeria, and Kuwait.

Ozal's travels took him to Egypt, Iraq, Iran, Libya, the United States, Italy, and in July to Saudi Arabia, where he also made the pilgrimage to Mecca.

TURKEY • Information Highlights

Official Name: Republic of Turkey.
Location: Southeastern Europe and southwestern Asia.
Area: 301,382 sq mi (780 580 km²).
Population (mid-1988 est.): 52,900,000.
Chief Cities (1985 census): Ankara, the capital, 2,235,035; Istanbul, 5,475,982; Izmir, 1,489,772.
Government: *Head of state,* Gen. Kenan Evren, president (took office Nov. 10, 1982). *Head of government,* Turgut Özal, prime minister (took office Dec. 13, 1983). *Legislature*—Grand National Assembly.
Monetary Unit: Lira (1,676 liras equal U.S. $1, Nov. 2, 1988).
Gross National Product (1986 U.S.$): $58,100,-000,000.
Economic Index (1987): *Consumer Prices* (1982 = 100), all items, 528.3; food, 507.8.
Foreign Trade (1987 U.S.$): *Imports,* $14,161,-000,000; *exports,* $10,140,000,000.

Heads of government paying official visits to Turkey in 1988 included Egyptian President Hosni Mubarak, Indian Prime Minister Rajiv Gandhi, and Yugoslav Prime Minister Branko Mikulíc.

A historic development was contact with Greece. Ozal and Greek Prime Minister Andreas Papandreou met in Davos, Switzerland, in January in efforts to ease long-standing hostility. They agreed to establish better channels of communication, including meetings at the prime-ministerial level at least once a year. Meetings of Greek-Turkish friendship and political committees took place, and Ozal visited Greece in June—the first Turkish prime minister to visit Greece in 36 years. But both sides warned against excessive optimism, and indeed little of substance was agreed upon.

UN efforts to settle the Greek-Turkish dispute over Cyprus again were fruitless. There was also no settlement of Turkey's dispute with Bulgaria over the treatment of ethnic Turks there, although relations between the two states improved in other areas.

WALTER F. WEIKER, *Rutgers University*

UGANDA

During his second year in office, Yoweri Museveni continued to pursue a dual strategy of bringing antigovernment rebel leaders into the government's National Resistance Army and basing Uganda's economic reconstruction on agricultural exports. These tasks were made all the more difficult since the areas of heaviest fighting also contain some of Uganda's most fertile land.

The Economy. The government's most pressing challenges of 1988 were to resettle those areas where fighting had stopped and to convince farmers to grow coffee, tea, and other crops for export, rather than food crops for sale in the urban areas. To this end, the government increased producer prices for major export crops between 25% and 90% in January and by nearly 150% in June. These massive increases were offset quickly by inflation, officially reported at 120% but thought to be twice that figure, and by another massive currency devaluation. Following a 72% devaluation in 1987, the Uganda shilling was devalued again from 60 Uganda shillings to 150 Uganda shillings per one U.S. dollar. The devaluation was not expected to affect the unofficial exchange rate of 600 Uganda shillings to U.S.$1.

During 1988, famine relief in the northeast, refugee resettlement, and the staging of an international trade summit conference in the capital city of Kampala were cited as reasons for massive reductions in social spending. The 1988–89 budget was announced in July. While public spending was to double, it would fail to keep up with inflation. Museveni remained committed to the recovery plan put forth by the International Monetary Fund (IMF) in May 1987. In spite of dramatic increases in taxes and in the price of basic items, including sugar, petroleum, and kerosene, the deficit was expected to approach 30% of total spending.

Internal Affairs. In the north, the United People's Democratic Army (UDPA) signed a treaty with the National Resistance Army of the Uganda government. As part of the treaty, the NRA promised constitutional changes ushering in elections for local and district councils, which will elect representatives to the National Resistance Council. The treaty also divided the exiled UDPA leaders who oppose the treaty from the domestic rank and file who negotiated it. Attempts to unite rebels in the east were thwarted.

In February, Museveni reshuffled his cabinet for the first time since attaining office in 1986. His most important move was to create three deputies to his ailing but popular prime minister, Samson Kisekka. The former minister of state in the prime minister's office, Eriya Kategaya, was appointed first deputy, while the second and third posts went to former Interior Minister Paul Ssemogerere and former Information Minister Abubakar Mayanja. Kategaya, a Westerner like Museveni, is very close to the president; Ssemogerere is the leader of the Democratic Party, which represents the Buganda and other important southern groups.

External Relations. Relations with Kenya remained tense since the exchange of gunfire on their border in December 1987. Goods vital to Uganda's survival were allowed into Uganda from Kenya, however.

Uganda continued to receive the enthusiastic support of the Western financial community, especially the IMF. Many non-Western nations, including Algeria, North Korea, Libya, Cuba, Bulgaria, and Egypt provided Uganda goods on a barter basis. Between 1986 and 1988, Uganda signed more than 20 barter agreements totaling more than $450 million. Due to inadequate production, Uganda found meeting such commitments difficult.

WILLIAM CYRUS REED, *Wabash College*

UGANDA • Information Highlights

Official Name: Republic of Uganda.
Location: Interior of East Africa.
Area: 91,135 sq mi (236 040 km²).
Population: (mid-1988 est.): 16,400,000.
Chief Cities (1980 census): Kampala, the capital, 458,423; Jinja, 45,060.
Government: *Head of state,* Yoweri Museveni, president (Jan. 29, 1986). *Head of government,* Samson Kisekka, prime minister (Jan. 30, 1986). *Legislature* (unicameral)—National Assembly.
Monetary Unit: Uganda shilling (150 shillings equal U.S. $1, July 1988).
Foreign Trade (1986 est. U.S.$): *Imports,* $309,500,000; *exports,* $394,900,000.

USSR

The year 1988 was the most turbulent to date of General Secretary Mikhail Gorbachev's four years in power. It represented a turning point in his program of *perestroika,* or restructuring of the Soviet system, as well as a time of internal crises and tragedy. By the end of 1987, Gorbachev's reforms had passed through several phases. By 1988 he had begun to heed advice that the pace of change was too slow, that reform would fail unless it went deeper and faster. Evidence was abundant of the vast bureaucracy quietly trying to contain and domesticate *perestroika,* and Gorbachev responded by radicalizing the reform process.

Simultaneously, the period was fraught with mounting open challenges to Gorbachev and his reforms from both the right and left. The conservative opposition came into the open with a pointed attack on many of his policies in the central press. The major "liberal" challenge arose from the smaller union republics to the south and north, where impassioned ethnic groups advanced their own agendas for social change, outstripping Moscow's intentions and testing Gorbachev's patience and tolerance.

The year was not, however, without its successes. For the time being at least, Gorbachev managed to curb his conservative critics within the leadership and forge ahead by gathering more power into his own hands. He also continued to build on his image as a statesman.

By year's end, however, even the most tumultuous and unprecedented political events of the preceding months were eclipsed by nature's fury, as an enormous earthquake visited great tragedy on the southern republic of Armenia.

Domestic Affairs

Throughout 1988—in meetings of the party's Central Committee, at the 19th Communist Party Conference in June, and in talks with foreign leaders—General Secretary Gorbachev continued campaigning for *perestroika.* Given the extensive internal television coverage of these occasions, it became apparent that Gorbachev was using his domestic and foreign conferees as the medium through which to promote the virtues of his reforms to the broad Soviet public. The basic message remained the same: *glasnost,* or openness, is intended as a catalyst to "democratization," and the two together, along with "new thinking" in foreign policy, would help lever the behemoth bureaucracy toward economic reform.

Economic "Perestroika." Although great progress had been made in *glasnost,* democratization, and foreign policy, the *raison d'être* of *perestroika*—the economy—remained stalled. In an unprecedented announcement in late Oc-

AP/Wide World

While in New York in December, Soviet General Secretary Gorbachev (right) met for some 2½ hours with President Reagan and President-elect Bush on Governors Island.

tober, Finance Minister Boris I. Gostev acknowledged that the Soviet Union had been running large budget deficits for years and that the deficit for 1988 was projected at 36.3 billion rubles (about $58 billion). Gostev said that the deficit was not alarming by Western standards but that it did reflect the nation's economic difficulties and could contribute to inflation—another newly acknowledged problem. Grain production was an estimated 205 million metric tons, according to the U.S. Department of Agriculture, down some 3.0% from 1987—contributing to already chronic shortages of food. All in all, the situation with regard to consumer goods and services was, if anything, a little worse in 1988 than in previous years.

The lack of economic progress and the obstruction of reform was blamed, in large measure, on the huge, hydra-headed state and party bureaucracy. With a self-sustaining interest in

AP/Wide World

The Nuroyans of Leninakan, Armenia, were one of the thousands of families devastated by an enormous December earthquake. The tragedy took a minimum of 25,000 lives.

resisting change and continuing business as usual, the Soviet bureaucracy had the power to make departmental regulations interpreting (and often distorting) national legislation, and the authority to issue "state orders" (production contracts) that override the new rights of individual production enterprises (under reform legislation that went into effect on Jan. 1, 1988).

Gorbachev's response was to radicalize economic and ancillary reforms. While the 1987 law on individual enterprise and cooperative businesses was working, the several hundred thousand people engaged in these new ventures (such as beauty shops, restaurants, and private taxis) fell well short of initial expectations. The party had the same experience with the opportunities for private initiative offered in the agricultural sector. Few peasants were availing themselves of the right to subcontract land from collective farms and take up family farming. Understandably, part of the problem was a population long averse to risk-

taking, but local bureaucratic red tape also was "braking" the entrepreneurial process. Gorbachev reacted by pushing through a much broader business law with a far less confiscatory "corporate" tax structure and by offering the hesitant peasantry the prospect of leaseholds for up to 50 years. These initiatives, it was hoped, would prime the food and services sectors.

Although the 1987 "Law on the State Enterprise" had shifted 60% of Soviet industry to a self-financing basis, blockage quickly became apparent. Much of the responsibility lay with the deferral of price reform until the 1990s. The continued imposition of centrally-set prices hemmed in enterprise directors, making it difficult for them to exercise more meaningful autonomy. Added to the structural difficulties was the bureaucratic factor. Feedback from managers in the field indicated that economic bureaucrats and central planners were resisting implementation of the enterprise law in various ways.

The Gorbachev regime proposed a variety of measures for dealing with the stalled industrial reform. Reflecting his great belief in the efficiency of legal action, Gorbachev promised yet more laws, including ones to circumscribe departmental rule-making and restrict the power of central planners. For instance, to encourage the faster infusion of foreign capital and technology as a way of leapfrogging the bureaucracy, Prime Minister Nikolai Ryzhkov proposed radically revising the new joint-venture law to give foreign firms majority control and ease the task of repatriating profits. Western European firms and governments responded during the year with a number of deals and credits, but U.S. firms continued to proceed cautiously and slowly. On the need to decontrol prices, however, the Soviet leadership showed little inclination to step up its timetable. If anything, the experience during 1988 of other socialist countries where partial decontrol of prices yielded inflation and unrest may have caused some apprehension.

Political Changes. By far, Gorbachev's most dramatic response to his flagging economic reforms and to conservative opposition within the regime was to extend radical *perestroika* into the political process so as to gain more power.

In the previous three years, Gorbachev had made no secret of the fact that *perestroika* faced internal opposition in the party as well as the state bureaucracy. It was the familiar post-Stalin struggle between reformers and conservatives, and in 1988 those who resisted change pushed the issue to the breaking point.

In March, just as Gorbachev was leaving for a visit to Yugoslavia, the conservatives launched a major public attack on his policies, thinly disguised as the position of an ordinary citizen. Yegor Ligachev, then second-in-com-

Members of the Politburo vote on October 1 to remove Andrei Gromyko (center, front row), who served as foreign minister (1957–85), as president. Under a new executive-legislative system, General Secretary Gorbachev became head of state.

mand to Gorbachev as well as the leader of the conservative faction, arranged for the March 12 publication in *Sovetskaya Rossiya* of a highly critical open letter. It was a blunt attack on *glasnost,* democratization, and the denigration of Stalin and the Soviet past. The widely reprinted letter was applauded in dozens of party organizations as a welcome change of course. On April 5, *Pravda* published a sharp rebuttal reaffirming General Secretary Gorbachev's reformist program.

At the June party conference, called by Gorbachev to accelerate the tempo of change, he sprung on the 5,000 delegates—and the entire nation—the idea of a strong political executive to head the state and a substantially renovated working legislature. Predictably, despite the opposition of conservatives, Gorbachev's initiative was endorsed by the party. Relevant amendments to the constitution of 1977 were proposed in October, and, in spite of unexpectedly vigorous opposition in several republics and pointed criticism by others—such as the noted dissident and 1975 Nobel Peace Prize winner Andrei Sakharov—the amendments were approved in late November.

The new executive-legislative setup comprises a strong, single-seat chief executive and a two-tiered legislature. Elections for the 2,250 seats in the new Congress of Soviets were scheduled for early 1989, after which the Congress would elect a smaller, working legislative body, the Supreme Soviet, and the chairperson of its standing Presidium. Proportional representation rules, however, would ensure Com-

munist Party control over both the Congress and Supreme Soviet.

Despite the party's endorsement of Gorbachev's sweeping political reform at the June conference, infighting at the highest level continued until late September—when Gorbachev again took the initiative. Under the pretext of restructuring the party, he radically reorganized the Secretariat and displaced the principal conservatives on the Politburo. Ligachev was shunted to the agricultural portfolio, Viktor Chebrikov lost his KGB chairmanship, and President Andrei Gromyko was retired. Proreform figures were promoted.

The departure of Gromyko opened the way for Gorbachev to become head of state under the new executive-legislative system. Because the Communist Party will retain ultimate control over both legislative bodies, Gorbachev's assumption of executive authority frees him of the party Politburo's collegial rule and supplements his position as party general secretary with a virtual "imperial presidency." Paradoxically, then, Gorbachev had engineered a recentralization of power to effect a decentralization of the Soviet system. Sakharov's criticism therefore expressed what many proponents of change were thinking—that Gorbachev's strategy was "a campaign to achieve democratic change through nondemocratic means."

Social Reforms. During 1988 further progress was made in extending *glasnost* and expanding democratization. The Soviet press and public continued to enlarge upon their already

The Millennium of the Russian Orthodox Church

One thousand years ago, on a broad river bank at the edge of European civilization, Prince Vladimir of Kiev played out a drama that marked the introduction of Christianity in what is now the Soviet Union. Under the prince's order, a pagan people overturned their wooden idols and floated them down the River Dnieper before crowding into the water for a mass baptism.

In 1988, reflecting the new openness *(glasnost)* of the atheistic Soviet state, General Secretary Mikhail Gorbachev recognized the millennium of that event by meeting with leaders of the Russian Orthodox Church and allowing live television and radio broadcasts of the religious observances. The millennium was celebrated in Moscow by a series of liturgies, conferences, and other special events during the week of June 5–12. The celebration moved to Kiev the following week, where Russian Orthodox leaders were joined in the observances by Christian delegations from all over the world.

Although the life of the Russian Orthodox Church is relatively short—half the total span of Christianity and centuries less than that of Christianity almost everywhere else in Europe—the faith of its adherents long has remained fervent. Behind the trappings of the ''state religion,'' and despite decades of repression, some 50–90 million Soviet citizens today practice the Russian Orthodox faith.

Christianity in what is now the USSR has survived through centuries of nationalistic and political conflict. In the 10th century there was no ''Russia,'' only the city-state of ''Kievan Rus,'' the power of which would be shattered 300 years later by the invasion of the Asiatic Golden Horde. The center of the civilization moved north to Muscovy, later to be called ''Russia,'' and then west, to what became Belorussia. Kiev itself gradually expanded, eventually becoming the Ukraine, the focus of a fierce nationalism. After the Communist Revolution, the Kremlin came to have an intense fear of Ukrainian nationalism. Stalin, playing cunningly on Russian nationalism, engaged the Orthodox Church to absorb the Ukrainian Orthodox Church and later the Eastern-Rite Catholic Church. Both are still illegal today, though the latter has up to four million clandestine members. In 1988, Ukrainian Catholics could play no role in the millennium celebrations, and the focus of the observances in Moscow rather than Kiev was a clear assertion of Russian nationalist supremacy.

AP/Wide World

A June 12 procession at the newly renovated Danilov Monastery, Moscow's oldest, culminated a week of celebrations marking the millennium of the Russian Orthodox faith.

The Russian Church always has had a special veneration for the suffering and humiliated Christ and it helped prepare the church for the extermination suggested by Lenin and all but carried out by Stalin in the 1930s. Following a revival during World War II, the church underwent further persecution during the Khrushchev and Brezhnev regimes. Although Gorbachev has undergone no Constantinian conversion, his recognition of the millennium gave Soviet Christians reason to rejoice. Basic repressive measures remained in force—such as the outlawing of the Ukrainian Church and the 70-year-old laws barring the Russian Church from educating, printing literature, contesting the closure of churches, and securing its own administration against state infiltration and control. Nevertheless, Soviet believers could await new laws with some optimism, because, whatever insecurities the future may hold, the emergence of the Russian Church in June 1988 was perhaps no less dramatic than Prince Vladimir's baptismal drama of 988.

MICHAEL BOURDEAUX

extensive *de facto* rights of speech and assembly while awaiting promised legislative confirmation.

Journalistic *glasnost,* which had startled the Soviet public with a litany of previously concealed social problems, in 1988 revealed the existence of male as well as female prostitution and the nation's first case of an AIDS-related death. Cultural *glasnost* broke new ground by publishing works by George Orwell and the Stalinist prison camp stories of Varlam Shalamov. In the spirit of economic *glasnost,* inflation and the budget deficit were acknowledged for the first time. A public criticism of his institution by Chairman of the Soviet Supreme Court V.I. Terebilov greatly expanded the revelations of legal *glasnost.* Criticism of Stalin and posthumous rehabilitation of his victims accelerated under historical *glasnost;* the full rehabilitation of Nikolai Bukharin, the most prominent Old Bolshevik to have been purged, was the high-water mark of this process. Within the purview of military *glasnost,* the mishaps as well as the successes of the Soviet space program continued to receive exposure. Finally, further advances were recorded in political *glasnost,* as even the KGB engaged in public self-criticism. In sharp contrast to the paucity of public information on the Chernobyl nuclear accident in 1986, *glasnost* produced unprecedented coverage of the Armenian earthquake in December 1988.

But the advance of *glasnost* was not without differentiation, unevenness, and outright lapses. Journalistic, cultural, and economic openness progressed rapidly, while *glasnost* on matters of history, the military, and high party politics remained relatively tentative. Notable lapses in the spirit of openness concerned Gorbachev's election as head of state and the passage of controversial constitutional amendments enhancing his power. Indeed, 1988 witnessed the first visible limits imposed "from above" on *glasnost.* In a speech in January, Gorbachev set the tone: "We are for *glasnost* without reservations, without limitations, but for *glasnost* in the interests of socialism." Throughout the year Gorbachev, fellow Politburo member Alexander Yakovlev, and the new ideological secretary, Vadim Medvedev, criticized the press periodically for exceeding the bounds of permissible *glasnost,* leaving no doubt as to who was determining the "interests of socialism."

The process of democratization also made gains and met limits in 1988. The gains were of two kinds—planned and spontaneous. In the first category were the new electoral law, promised new legislation on religion, and, to a lesser extent, human-rights policy.

Changes brought about by the new election law included multiple candidacy for elective office, mandatory secret balloting, and limited terms of office. In the area of religion, Gorbachev used the occasion of the millennium of the Christianization of the Ukraine and Russia (*see* special report, page 544) to promise new, more enlightened legislation on state-church relations. Progress in the area of human rights generally was mixed. The apparent freeze on political arrests and trials in the Moscow and Leningrad regions continued to hold, but in provincial areas out of sight of the Western press, repression continued. A commission recodifying Soviet criminal law was still at work as the year drew to a close, and a spirited internal discussion on the rephrasing of two articles long used to repress dissidents appeared to be under way.

The spontaneous aspect of democratization was seen in the continuing formation of independent groups throughout the Soviet Union which advocate and lobby on a variety of causes from environmental issues to ethnic concerns. In the first half of the year, more than 250 unauthorized demonstrations by these groups were recorded, including large ethnic turnouts in nine of the 15 union republics. The regime's response was twofold: Legislation regulating demonstrations and providing stiff penalties for noncompliance was passed, and a special corps of riot police was created within the Ministry of Internal Affairs. Although a law on informal groups still was pending, Gorbachev and the Moscow leadership indicated the boundaries of official tolerance: no opposition parties, no changes of internal borders, and no advocacy of racial or ethnic hatred.

Ethnic Unrest. The statement that Moscow would not tolerate racial or ethnic hatred came in the context of interethnic violence, as well as a growing challenge to the Soviet system, in the southern republic of Armenia (*see* special report, page 546).

But Armenia was not the only region in which demands for greater autonomy by ethnic groups reached crisis proportions during 1988. Uprisings also were mounted in the Baltic re-

---

USSR • Information Highlights

Official Name: Union of Soviet Socialist Republics.
Location: Eastern Europe and northern Asia.
Area: 8,649,498 sq mi (22 402 200 km²).
Population (mid-1988 est.): 286,000,000.
Chief Cities (Jan. 1, 1986 est.): Moscow, the capital, 8,703,000; Leningrad, 4,901,000; Kiev, 2,495,000.
Government: *Head of government,* Nikolai I. Ryzhkov, chairman of the USSR Council of Ministers (took office Sept. 1985). General secretary of the Communist Party, Mikhail S. Gorbachev (elected March 11, 1985). *Legislature*—Supreme Soviet: Soviet of the Union Soviet of Nationalities.
Monetary Unit: Ruble (0.621 ruble equals U.S.$1, August 1988—noncommercial rate).
Gross National Product (1986 U.S.$): $2,356,-700,000,000.
Economic Indexes (1986): *Consumer Prices* (1980 = 100), all items, 106.5; food 114.2. *Industrial Production* (1980 = 100), 126.
Foreign Trade (1987 U.S.$): *Imports,* $96,061,-000,000; *exports,* $107,874,000,000.

Armenia and the Armenians

© Manouk/Sipa Press

In the Armenian capital of Yerevan, the president of the Supreme Soviet Committee, Hrant Voskanian, answers questions at a September rally. The cause of Armenian nationalism was frustrated repeatedly during the course of the year.

Armenia is one of the 15 union republics of the Soviet Union. It is located in the southern part of the country, in the Transcaucasian region along with Azerbaijan and Georgia. The population of Armenia is about 3.3 million and relatively homogeneous. Although the USSR is officially an atheist state, the Armenians historically are Orthodox Christians. The Armenian nation today has a profound sense of ethnic consciousness, reinforced by strong bonds of national cohesion.

The year 1988 began with a resurgence of Armenian nationalism and ended with an epic tragedy. The focus of the ethnic resurgence was a small, predominantly Armenian enclave called Nagorno-Karabakh, located just inside Azerbaijan. In 1923, in response to Turkish diplomatic pressure on behalf of their Islamic brothers, the Azeris, the young Soviet state had transferred jurisdiction of the enclave from Armenia back to Azerbaijan.

Beginning in 1986, in the context of Mikhail Gorbachev's program of *glasnost* (openness) and democratization, Armenian ethnic activists began lobbying Moscow for annexation of the Karabakh. By February 1988 the issue had caught the imagination of the broad Armenian public. Pro-annexation rallies in the Armenian capital of Yerevan exceeded 500,000 people.

In Azerbaijan, authorities defended the status quo. Moscow tried to resolve the issue politically, promising greater economic and

cultural freedom for the Armenian majority in Karabakh but refusing border changes. This merely intensified Armenian demands and Azeri resistance. The first major violence broke out on February 28 in the Azerbaijani city of Sumgait, where mobs of Azeris attacked resident Armenians; 32 people were killed. Moscow deployed troops in the region.

During the spring and summer, the Armenians took their case to Moscow through constitutional channels but were rebuffed. A sense of betrayal by Gorbachev incensed the Armenians, and the conflict escalated. Communal violence during the fall caused more than 150,000 people to flee their homes—Azeris from Armenia, Armenians from Azerbaijan. By now large numbers of Soviet troops were deployed, and many cities were under martial law. But as the bitterness deepened on both sides, the death toll continued to mount.

Then came calamity. On December 7, Armenia was struck by the worst earthquake in the Caucasus in 1,000 years, leveling three dozen communities and killing more than 25,000 people. But not even a tragedy of this magnitude abated the tension. When riot troops were pulled out of Azerbaijan to help in the rescue effort, Azeris attacked homes in Armenian neighborhoods. Conversely, even as Gorbachev toured the devastated areas, Armenians lobbied him on the Karabakh issue.

ROBERT SHARLET

gion in the north. During the spring, Moscow permitted formation of a "People's Front" political organization, outside of party control, in the republic of Estonia. The front quickly attracted tens of thousands of Estonians seeking an opportunity to pursue their long-suppressed ethnic agenda. Similar organizations were established in nearby Latvia and Lithuania. During the summer, all three fronts began to generate a series of demands concerning historical rectification and greater cultural autonomy. By early fall, the fronts had gained thousands of members. The Estonians were the boldest, calling for their own currency, diplomatic missions abroad, and the right to control immigration into their territory. Moscow conceded many of the cultural demands and offered more economic autonomy, but it dismissed the more radical proposals.

It was in this context that the party leadership issued its draft constitutional amendments on the new executive-legislative system, and the conflict with Estonia quickly flared. Fearing the loss of its newly gained autonomy under *perestroika,* the People's Front vigorously opposed the proposed constitutional changes. Failing in their efforts, the Estonian Supreme Soviet amended the republic's own constitution in open defiance of Moscow's authority, asserting the right to refuse to implement Soviet legislation unless it was deemed to be in the republic's interest. Not surprisingly, Gorbachev marshaled federal constitutional authority to overrule the Estonian action. Then in December, the Estonians announced their rejection of Moscow's ruling on their "declaration of sovereignty," raising the tension even higher.

Facing one crisis after another, Gorbachev grew increasingly concerned over the uncompromising tenor of ethnic challenges to Moscow and began to castigate them as willful efforts to sabotage *perestroika.* His statements to that effect, however, did little more than alienate and antagonize the ethnic legions, further fanning the flames of unrest.

Foreign Affairs

In a roller-coaster year on the domestic front, Gorbachev's only consistent area of success was foreign policy. Although he began to resemble a beleaguered politician at home, his stock as a statesman achieved ever higher levels in 1988. Gorbachev chalked up a string of major and minor diplomatic successes, some of which played well as media events at home and distracted a population increasingly frustrated over *perestroika's* failure to deliver the economic goods.

The main triumphs were two summits—one major and one "mini"—with the United States, the latter crowned by Gorbachev's remarkable speech to the UN General Assembly on December 7. Although the two summits— the first in Moscow from May 29 to June 1, the second in New York from December 6 to 8— produced no significant new agreements, they did underscore the continuity of the improving U.S.-Soviet relationship and further institutionalized the process of annual summits to maintain the dialogue on disarmament, human rights, and regional conflicts. The less consequential New York minisummit was of course important to Gorbachev for the opportunity to make his first official contact with U.S. President-elect George Bush. The visit was most notable, however, for Gorbachev's major address to the UN, in which he impressively presented a radically restructured Soviet foreign policy. With this speech, the more parochial "socialist internationalism" became a thing of the past, at least rhetorically, as Gorbachev abandoned the Marxist-Leninist class approach to international relations and embraced universal internationalism. Most newsworthy were his renunciation, at least theoretically, of the use of force in foreign policy and his unilateral decision to cut Soviet conventional arms in Europe and Asia. The first was foreshadowed by the Soviet decision to withdraw its troops from Afghanistan, a process that began on May 15, and represented a further retreat from the "Brezhnev Doctrine" used to justify military intervention in Eastern Europe. The arms announcement was of particular interest to China, Hungary, Czechoslovakia, East Germany, and the NATO states, and it clearly gave the USSR a propaganda advantage during the transition from the Reagan to the Bush presidencies. The UN speech also included a major debt-relief proposal aimed primarily at the Third World.

Other provisional successes of 1988 included China's long-sought agreement to hold a summit with the USSR in 1989, and some further progress in Moscow's campaign to secure the West's agreement on a mandated international human-rights conference in Moscow during 1991. These high-profile foreign-policy achievements, however, ultimately must be judged on how they contribute to solving the real problems of domestic *perestroika* in the USSR. Gorbachev's reform program got mixed reactions among its Eastern European allies, testing the unity of the Communist bloc (*see* special report, page 227).

As the year drew to a close, the Soviet Union suffered a calamitous natural disaster, the devastating earthquake in Armenia. Cutting short his New York visit, Gorbachev returned home to assume leadership of the Soviet and international relief effort. In the spirit of his new commitment to global interdependence, this was the first time since World War II that the USSR accepted international humanitarian assistance.

ROBERT SHARLET, *Union College*

Norway's Ambassador to the United Nations Tom Eric Vraalsen (right) congratulates Secretary General Javier Pérez de Cuéllar following the announcement that the UN peacekeeping forces had been awarded the 1988 Nobel Peace Prize.

UNITED NATIONS

Thanks largely to a new level of cooperation between the superpowers, the United Nations in 1988 achieved several major successes in resolving regional conflicts. In his annual report to the General Assembly in September, Secretary General Javier Pérez de Cuéllar declared that the organization's successes offered to "millions around the world a gratifying demonstration of [the UN's] potential."

In the Afghanistan conflict, UN mediators helped broker an agreement, signed on April 14, for a Soviet troop withdrawal scheduled to be completed by Feb. 15, 1989.

A UN cease-fire between Iran and Iraq took effect on August 20, exactly 13 months after the Security Council ordered the two countries to end their war that began in 1980. On August 25 they began negotiations under the auspices of Pérez de Cuéllar for a permanent peace settlement. The Security Council dispatched a team of 350 observers, known as the UN Iran-Iraq Military Observer Group (UNIIMOG) to monitor compliance with the cease-fire and to supervise the eventual withdrawal of all forces to internationally recognized boundaries.

Morocco and Polisario Front rebels on August 30 agreed to a UN plan to end their 13-year-old war over Western Sahara. On October 19, Pérez de Cuéllar appointed a special representative to make arrangements for monitoring a cease-fire and supervising a referendum in Western Sahara in 1989.

After months of negotiation, South Africa, Angola, and Cuba signed two U.S.-brokered agreements on December 22 which provide for the independence of Namibia and the withdrawal of Cuba's 50,000 troops from Angola. The accords, if implemented, mean that the UN Security Council's ten-year-old plan for Namibian freedom would take effect in 1989. As a first step, the Council voted on December 20 to send a 70-member UN observer force to Angola to oversee the Cuban withdrawal.

And in both Cambodia and Cyprus, the peace process edged forward. Vietnam, under pressure from the UN General Assembly and from its Soviet allies, announced in May that it would withdraw 50,000 of its 120,000 occupation troops from Cambodia by the end of 1988. That was expected to pave the way for a UN peace plan involving a UN force to oversee a cease-fire, free elections, and guarantees that the former Pol Pot leadership would be barred permanently from power. In Cyprus, Pérez de Cuéllar persuaded leaders of the Greek and Turkish communities to resume direct negotiations and to try to reach an overall settlement by June 1, 1989.

By September, as a result of these developments, an air of euphoria enveloped the UN. A major tribute to the organization came on September 29, when the Nobel Peace Prize was awarded to the UN peacekeeping forces, the 10,000 blue-helmeted soldiers from nations around the world who monitor regional trouble spots. "They represent the manifest will of the community of nations to achieve peace through negotiations," the Nobel Committee said, "and the forces have by their presence made a decisive contribution toward the initiation of actual peace negotiations."

Ironically, the UN's achievements helped precipitate a new financial crisis for the organization. Pérez de Cuéllar estimated that if all

the regional conflicts are resolved, the cost of UN peacekeeping operations could rise from $235 million in 1987 to between $1.5 billion and $2 billion, or twice the UN's regular budget.

At the end of the year another crisis loomed. In violation of its host-country agreement to admit all UN invitees, the United States refused to grant a visa to Palestine Liberation Organization (PLO) leader Yasir Arafat, despite the fact that he was invited to address the General Assembly. In an unprecedented rebuke to the United States, the outraged Assembly moved to Geneva for three days in December. The Reagan administration's subsequent decision to open talks with the PLO helped placate angry UN members, but Third World delegates warned that unless Washington observes its treaty with the UN, the organization will conduct more and more of its business in Geneva.

General Assembly. The 42nd General Assembly, which had begun in 1987, reconvened three times in 1988 to protest a U.S. effort to close down the PLO observer mission to the UN. That issue was resolved on June 29, when a U.S. federal judge ordered the Justice Department to uphold the headquarters treaty with the UN and allow the PLO mission to function freely.

For the third time in a decade, the Assembly held a special session on disarmament. The 159 member states labored from May 31 to June 26 to reach a consensus on a document that would set out their aims and priorities. In the end, however, they proved unable to agree on a final declaration, failing to bridge North-South and East-West disagreements over such issues as the relationship between disarmament and development, the UN's role, the relative importance of conventional versus nuclear arms cuts, and prevention of an arms race in outer space.

The 43rd regular session of the General Assembly opened on September 20 and elected Dante Caputo, Argentina's foreign minister, as its president. Among the world leaders who addressed the session was Soviet General Secretary Mikhail Gorbachev, the first Soviet head of state to address the Assembly since Nikita Khrushchev's famous shoe-banging speech in 1960. In his December 7 address, Gorbachev announced that the USSR would unilaterally reduce its military forces by 500,000 troops and 10,000 tanks and would work with the new U.S. administration for further arms cuts in 1989. He called for "deideologizing" international relations, pledged to broaden Soviet civil rights, and reiterated his desire to strengthen the UN and enhance its role.

In another historic address, Arafat, appearing before the Assembly when it convened in Geneva on December 13, declared that the PLO would seek a "comprehensive settlement" with Israel on the basis of Security Council resolutions 242 and 338. He urged the UN to convene an international conference on Palestine and to put the Israeli-occupied territories temporarily under the supervision of a UN force. Following his speech, the Assembly adopted a resolution calling for an international conference, Israel's withdrawal from the occupied territories (including Jerusalem), and UN supervision of those territories. The vote demonstrated the isolation of the United States and Israel on this issue, as 138 members supported the resolution, Canada and Costa Rica abstained on it, and the United States and Israel opposed it.

Most of the Assembly's resolutions in 1988 were similar to those of previous years. More than 60 dealt with disarmament and security, including the perennial calls for complete disarmament; bans on all nuclear, chemical, and biological weapons; reductions in military budgets; and the establishment of nuclear-free zones.

Sixteen resolutions on South Africa included a call for a special General Assembly session on apartheid in 1989. The Assembly also reiterated its call on the Security Council to impose mandatory sanctions against South Africa and singled out the United States and Great Britain as opponents of sanctions. A resolution favoring "support for armed struggle" on behalf of Namibian independence was criticized by Western nations for its failure to take into account the successful South African-Angolan-Cuban negotiations for Namibian independence. In a notable departure from the past, the Assembly's annual resolution on Afghanistan was adopted by consensus; reflecting the progress that was achieved during the year, it called for "faithful implementation of the Geneva accords."

Also for the first time, the Assembly invited the leaders of North and South Korea—neither of them full members of the UN—to address the body; South Korea's President Roh Tae Woo spoke on October 18; a lower-level North Korea official spoke the next day. And for the first time since 1946, it approved a budget by consensus. The new spending program, which covers 1990 and 1991, incorporates many of the administrative and budgetary reforms demanded by the United States and other industrialized countries. Estimated at $1.76 billion, the two-year budget is slightly smaller than the revised budget for 1988 and 1989.

Finally, the Assembly elected five nonpermanent members of the 15-nation Security Council: Colombia, Ethiopia, Canada, Malaysia, and Finland. In all the Assembly adopted 324 resolutions, 187 of them by consensus. The delegates recessed on December 22, deferring consideration of half a dozen items until 1989.

Security Council. Two issues dominated the Security Council's year: the Persian Gulf War and the Palestinian uprising. In the former, the

five permanent Council members followed up the July 1987 passage of Resolution 598 (demanding that Iran and Iraq lay down their arms) with an ongoing joint effort to end the war.

Iraq had accepted Resolution 598, but Iran stalled and the USSR and China resisted a U.S. effort to punish the Iranians by imposing military sanctions. During the summer of 1988, Iran's military losses forced the Tehran regime to agree to a truce, but at that stage the Iraqis raised obstacles. Finally in August, intense diplomatic pressure and fear of sanctions brought both sides to the peace table. During the rest of the year, the Security Council guided Pérez de Cuéllar's efforts to persuade Iran and Iraq to reach a permanent settlement.

Early in 1988, shortly after the Palestinian uprising began, Pérez de Cuéllar proposed that the Big Five extend their joint diplomacy to the Arab-Israeli conflict. At that time, however, the United States still refused to deal with the PLO and a joint approach was not possible.

Israel's harsh response to the uprising angered Security Council members, and on January 5 the body unanimously called on the Jerusalem government to refrain from deporting Palestinian civilians, citing the Geneva Convention. The affirmative U.S. vote represented the first time since 1981 that Washington had supported a resolution criticizing Israel. On January 14 the United States abstained on a similar resolution, and when the Council again tried to censure Israel—five more times from January to December—the U.S. delegation vetoed each resolution. On April 25 it abstained on a resolution tacitly blaming Israel for the assassination of the PLO's chief of military operations, Abu Jihad.

In other votes, the Security Council twice condemned the use of chemical weapons in the Iran-Iraq war; expressed "deep distress" over the July 3 downing of an Iran Air passenger plane by a U.S. warship in the Persian Gulf; condemned South African attacks on Botswana; called on South Africa to commute the death sentences of the "Sharpeville Six"; and extended the mandates of the UN peacekeeping forces in Lebanon, the Golan Heights, and Cyprus.

Secretariat. In his seventh year as secretary-general, Javier Pérez de Cuéllar established himself as one of the UN's most successful chiefs. In addition to his efforts in mediating conflicts, he set in motion a major restructuring of UN management and finances. With a series of reforms in his pocket, he went to Washington on July 15 and appealed to the White House to pay some of the United States' back dues. Washington agreed to repay $144 million, enabling the UN to avert the immediate fiscal crisis, but by year's end the United States was still in arrears by close to $402 million.

The Secretariat's financial experts predicted a major crunch in 1989, when the UN would need to finance a large peacekeeping force for Namibia's transition to independence. In anticipation of that, Pérez de Cuéllar asked the General Assembly to consider "both new methods of raising money, such as voluntary contributions or interest-free loans, and also such fundamental measures as changes in the scale of assessments."

During the course of the year, 168 UN staff members were arrested, detained, or abducted in 16 countries or territories. Pérez de Cuéllar told the General Assembly that the situation was "totally unacceptable" and that member governments must be responsible for the safety of the UN staff. He also issued a number of urgent appeals for the release of Lt. Col. William Higgins, an American serving as chief of the UN observer group in Lebanon who was kidnapped there on February 17.

Agencies. Among the UN specialized agencies concerned with health matters—the World Health Organization (WHO), the UN Children's Fund (UNICEF), the UN Development Program (UNDP), and the UN Population Fund—the year's dominant concern was AIDS (Acquired Immune Deficiency Syndrome). WHO coordinated the UN's prevention and control activities through its Special Program on AIDS (SPA), which provided assistance to more than 100 countries in developing national programs for blood screening and improved diagnostic and treatment facilities. WHO, UNDP, the Red Cross, and the Red Crescent also began an effort to help poor countries develop safe blood supplies.

The UN Fund for Drug Abuse Control and UNDP joined forces to develop programs to reduce poppy and coca cultivation in poor agricultural countries through crop substitution programs.

The UN Environment Program (UNEP), together with the World Meteorological Organization and the International Council for Scientific Unions, began an assessment of the causes and potential effects of world climatic change. Their objective was to coordinate governmental policies "to prevent, limit, delay, or adapt to this change."

The UN Conference on Trade and Development (UNCTAD) in September called for a "once-and-for-all" effort to ease the debt burden of developing countries. The International Monetary Fund and the World Bank welcomed a proposal by the Group of Seven industrial nations to reduce interest on loans to the poorest countries and partially forgive their debts. UNICEF's year-end report on the state of the world's children said that after 40 years of progress, 500,000 children died in 1988 because of cuts in services for the poor by debt-ridden governments in developing countries.

JANE ROSEN, *"Manchester Guardian"*

ORGANIZATION OF THE UNITED NATIONS

THE SECRETARIAT

Secretary-General: Javier Pérez de Cuéllar (until Dec. 31, 1991)

THE GENERAL ASSEMBLY (1988)

President: Dante M. Caputo, Argentina
The 159 member nations were as follows:

Afghanistan	Cape Verde	German Demo-	Laos	Papua New	Suriname
Albania	Central African	cratic Republic	Lebanon	Guinea	Swaziland
Algeria	Republic	Germany, Federal	Lesotho	Paraguay	Sweden
Angola	Chad	Republic of	Liberia	Peru	Syria
Antigua and	Chile	Ghana	Libya	Philippines	Tanzania
Barbuda	China, People's	Greece	Luxembourg	Poland	Thailand
Argentina	Republic of	Grenada	Madagascar	Portugal	Togo
Australia	Colombia	Guatemala	Malawi	Qatar	Trinidad and Tobago
Austria	Comoros	Guinea	Malaysia	Romania	Tunisia
Bahamas	Congo	Guinea-Bissau	Maldives	Rwanda	Turkey
Bahrain	Costa Rica	Guyana	Mali	Saint Christopher	Uganda
Bangladesh	Cuba	Haiti	Malta	and Nevis	Ukrainian SSR
Barbados	Cyprus	Honduras	Mauritania	Saint Lucia	USSR
Belgium	Czechoslovakia	Hungary	Mauritius	Saint Vincent and	United Arab Emirates
Belize	Denmark	Iceland	Mexico	The Grenadines	United Kingdom
Belorussian SSR	Djibouti	India	Mongolia	São Tomé and	United States
Benin	Dominica	Indonesia	Morocco	Principe	Uruguay
Bhutan	Dominican	Iran	Mozambique	Saudi Arabia	Vanuatu
Bolivia	Republic	Iraq	Nepal	Senegal	Venezuela
Botswana	Ecuador	Ireland	Netherlands	Seychelles	Vietnam
Brazil	Egypt	Israel	New Zealand	Sierra Leone	Western Samoa
Brunei Darussalam	El Salvador	Italy	Nicaragua	Singapore	Yemen
Bulgaria	Equatorial Guinea	Ivory Coast	Niger	Solomon Islands	Yemen, Democratic
Burkina Faso	Ethiopia	Jamaica	Nigeria	Somalia	Yugoslavia
Burma	Fiji	Japan	Norway	South Africa	Zaire
Burundi	Finland	Jordan	Oman	Spain	Zambia
Cambodia	France	Kenya	Pakistan	Sri Lanka	Zimbabwe
Cameroon	Gabon	Kuwait	Panama	Sudan	
Canada	Gambia				

COMMITTEES

General. Composed of 29 members as follows: The General Assembly president; the 21 General Assembly vice-presidents (heads of delegations or their deputies of Bahrain, China, Cyprus, Denmark, Ecuador, El Salvador, France, Guinea-Bissau, Ivory Coast, Libya, Malta, Nepal, São Tomé and Principe, Swaziland, Thailand, USSR, United Kingdom of Great Britain and Northern Ireland, United Republic of Tanzania, United States, Vanuatu, Yugoslavia); and the chairmen of the main committees at right, which are composed of all 159 member countries.

THE SECURITY COUNCIL

Membership ends on December 31 of the year noted; asterisks indicate permanent membership.

Algeria (1989)	Finland (1990)	USSR*
Brazil (1989)	France*	United Kingdom*
Canada (1990)	Malaysia (1990)	United States*
China*	Nepal (1989)	Yugoslavia
Colombia (1990)	Senegal (1989)	(1989)
Ethiopia (1990)		

THE ECONOMIC AND SOCIAL COUNCIL

President: Andrés Aguilar (Venezuela)
Membership ends on December 31 of the year noted.

Bahamas (1991)	Iran (1989)	Saudi Arabia (1990)
Belize (1989)	Iraq (1991)	Somalia (1989)
Bolivia (1989)	Ireland (1990)	Sri Lanka (1989)
Brazil (1991)	Italy (1991)	Sudan (1989)
Bulgaria (1989)	Japan (1990)	Thailand (1991)
Cameroon (1991)	Jordan (1991)	Trinidad and Tobago
Canada (1989)	Kenya (1991)	(1990)
China (1989)	Lesotho (1990)	Tunisia (1991)
Colombia (1990)	Liberia (1990)	Ukrainian Soviet
Cuba (1989)	Libyan Arab	Socialist Republic
Czechoslovakia	Jamahiriya (1990)	(1991)
(1991)	Netherlands (1991)	USSR (1989)
Denmark (1989)	New Zealand (1991)	United Kingdom
France (1990)	Nicaragua (1991)	(1989)
Germany, Federal	Niger (1991)	United States (1991)
Republic of (1990)	Norway (1989)	Uruguay (1989)
Ghana (1990)	Oman (1989)	Venezuela (1990)
Greece (1990)	Poland (1989)	Yugoslavia (1990)
Guinea (1990)	Portugal (1990)	Zaire (1989)
India (1990)	Rwanda (1989)	Zambia (1991)
Indonesia (1991)		

First (Political and Security): Douglas Roche (Canada)
Special Political: Eugeniusz Noworyta (Poland)
Second (Economic and Financial): Hugo Navajas Mogro (Bolivia)
Third (Social, Humanitarian and Cultural): Mohammad A. Abulhasan (Kuwait)
Fourth (Decolonization): Jonathan C. Peters (Saint Vincent and the Grenadines)
Fifth (Administrative and Budgetary): Michael George Okeyo (Kenya)
Sixth (Legal): Achol Deng (Sudan)

THE TRUSTEESHIP COUNCIL

President: Jean-Michel Gaussot (France)

China[2] France[2] USSR[2] United Kingdom[2] United States[1]

[1] Administers Trust Territory. [2] Permanent member of Security Council not administering Trust Territory.

THE INTERNATIONAL COURT OF JUSTICE

Membership ends on February 5 of the year noted.

President: José María Ruda (Argentina, 1991)
Vice-President: Kéba Mbaye (Senegal, 1991)

Roberto Ago (Italy, 1997)	Kéba Mbaye (Senegal, 1991)
Mohammed Bedjaoui (Algeria, 1997)	Ni Zhengyu (China, 1994)
Taslim O. Elias (Nigeria, 1994)	Shigeru Oda (Japan, 1994)
Jens Evensen (Norway, 1994)	Stephen Schwebel (United States, 1997)
Gilbert Guillaume (France, 1991)	Mohamed Shahabuddeen (Guyana, 1997)
Robert Y. Jennings (United Kingdom, 1991)	Nikolai Konstantinovich Tarassov (USSR, 1997)
Manfred Lachs (Poland, 1994)	one vacancy

INTERGOVERNMENTAL AGENCIES

Food and Agricultural Organization (FAO); General Agreement on Tariffs and Trade (GATT); International Atomic Energy Agency (IAEA); International Bank for Reconstruction and Development (World Bank); International Civil Aviation Organization (ICAO); International Fund for Agricultural Development (IFAD); International Labor Organization (ILO); International Maritime Organization (IMO); International Monetary Fund (IMF); International Telecommunication Union (ITU); United Nations Educational, Scientific and Cultural Organization (UNESCO); United Nations Industrial Development Organization (UNIDO); Universal Postal Union (UPU); World Health Organization (WHO); World Intellectual Property Organization (WIPO); World Meteorological Organization (WMO).

UNITED STATES

There were no official government ceremonies, no presidential speech, no congressional proclamation. Yet in the U.S. capital and in cities across the country, Americans did not need such reminders to pay public and private tribute to the memory of the late President John F. Kennedy on Nov. 22, 1988, the 25th anniversary of his assassination. A nation that cannot forget John F. Kennedy's youthful vitality and stirring rhetoric paused on this occasion to ponder the meaning of his presidency for the present and the future.

Critics claimed that he had raised expectations that neither he nor any other president could fulfill and thus blamed him for contributing to the current sense of national frustration with problems at home and abroad. But others contended that a closer study of the young president's deeds and words would reveal a realistic insight into the limits of American destiny which would serve the country's current leadership well. "If America was self-deluded in the Kennedy years, it was not Kennedy's fault," wrote *Washington Post* columnist Philip Geyelin. ". . . Kennedy had come painfully to realize by November 1963 . . . we have only lately come to realize—that our reach has exceeded our grasp."

Domestic Affairs

The Reagan Administration. Certainly in 1988, with American power and influence in the world no longer as dominant as in the past, and with the economy's yield no longer seemingly boundless, there was plenty of evidence to support that sobering judgment. To be sure President Ronald Reagan characteristically sought to put the best face on the nation's problems. "If anyone expects just a proud recitation of the accomplishments of my administration, I say let's leave that to history," Reagan told a joint session of Congress in his seventh State of the Union Address on Jan. 25, 1988. "We're not finished yet. So my message to you tonight is put on your work shoes, we're still on the job."

The president pointed with pride to his administration's accomplishments. "Our record is not just the longest peacetime expansion in history but an economic and social revolution of hope, based on work, incentives, growth, and opportunity." And he looked ahead with confidence. "We Americans like the future, and like making the most of it. Let's do that now." And he went on to list a now familiar agenda for cuts in government spending and restraints in government power. "It's time for Washington to show a little humility," he declared.

But the president was now a lame duck, with the political campaign to choose his successor already under way. His prestige, while relatively high compared to his predecessors in the closing scenes of their presidencies, had been diminished somewhat by the taint of the Iran-contra scandal and by the shadow of the huge budget deficit. And Democrats were quick to make clear that if anyone in Washington should be more humble, it was the president himself.

"The dark side of the Reagan years has only begun to loom," warned Democratic Senate leader Robert Byrd of West Virginia, delivering the opposition party's rebuttal to the president's address. "Instead of a balanced budget, he has presided over a doubling of the national debt in seven years. Our record budget and trade deficits . . . have now forced the government to default on its most fundamental promises, like education and health."

And even though Reagan rejected such grim assessments, his own budget proposal submitted to the Congress February 18 reflected the strictures under which the government was forced to operate. Reagan's $1.09 trillion 1989 budget included retrenchment measures designed to conform to the deficit-reduction agreement reached with Congress following the October 1987 stock market crash, which had underlined the urgency of the nation's fiscal difficulties. Consequently, the president acknowledged that the budget "does not fully reflect my priorities." For example, his $299.5 billion proposal for defense spending amounted to the smallest boost in Pentagon outlays since he entered the White House. Other deficit-trimming proposals, which the president was less reluctant to make, included an 11% cut in outlays for the Environmental Protection Agency and a number of plans for converting government programs to private operation.

But despite these economy moves, the president's projected deficit of $129.5 billion was about $50 billion too low, according to the Congressional Budget Office, which relied on different economic assumptions. And even by the president's reckoning, just more than $150 billion of 1989 outlays, or nearly 15% of the total, would go to pay interest on the national debt, which would reach $2.15 trillion in 1989.

Four months later, on June 6, the Senate completed action on the congressional version of the 1989 budget. The nonbinding $1.1 billion spending resolution called for no new taxes and postponed any other stringent deficit cutting measures until the election year had passed. The congressional plan projected a deficit of $135.3 billion which also was criticized as being overly optimistic. As it turned out, at year-end the deficit was estimated at more than $150 billion.

The deficit aside, the administration had to cope with a broad range of other problems dur-

As president and vice-president for eight years, Ronald Reagan and George Bush (left) lunched together regularly. During his own successful campaign for the White House, the vice-president emphasized his "loyalty" to President Reagan.

ing 1988. One that attracted considerable public attention was a self-inflicted embarrassment. This was the disclosure by former White House chief of staff Donald Regan that astrology had played a significant role in the timing of White House events, because of Nancy Reagan's reliance on astrological advice. That revelation, contained in Regan's book *For the Record: From Wall Street to Washington,* was part of a broad picture the author painted of a presidency dominated by Mrs. Reagan, who had helped to force him from his job as chief of staff in February 1987. He charged that the first lady seemed to believe that the office that had been bestowed upon her husband by the people somehow fell into the category of worldly goods covered by the marriage vows. The White House denied that any policy decision had been influenced by astrology, which assumes that human affairs are influenced by the alignment of the stars and planets. But it did not refute Regan's contention that astrology had been a factor in scheduling the president, apparently because of Mrs. Reagan's anxiety about her husband's safety following the assassination attempt against him in March 1981.

A more substantive concern for the administration was the Pentagon procurement scandal that broke in June, with raids by the Federal Bureau of Investigation and the National Identification Service on offices of some of the nation's largest defense contractors and on homes of former key defense officials. Targets included McDonnell Douglas Corp., Northrop Corp., Teledyne Inc., Pratt & Whitney Aircraft Co., and Unisys Corp. A two-year investigation, which included wiretaps, pointed to a massive conspiracy in which defense contractors bribed Defense Department officials to get profitable military contracts. U.S. Attorney Henry E. Hudson of Alexandria, VA, director of the probe, told Congress that "tens of billions of dollars" could be involved.

Democrats blamed the scandal on the administration's massive defense buildup and Republican Sen. Charles Grassley of Iowa charged that the Justice and Defense Departments had ignored evidence of massive fraud. But Attorney General Edwin Meese claimed credit for unearthing the wrongdoing. The investigation led by Hudson continued through the year with further disclosures and some indictments expected in 1989. Meanwhile transition advisers to President-elect George Bush emphasized that reform of the Pentagon procurement system was a high priority for the incoming administration in order to restore public confidence.

The president had to deal with charges of misconduct that struck closer to home, as a result of a continuing probe into the affairs of Edwin Meese, his attorney general and longtime friend. Reagan himself continued to express confidence in Meese. But on March 29 two of Meese's top subordinates at Justice, Deputy Attorney General Arnold I. Burns and Assistant Attorney General William F. Weld, resigned, after reportedly telling White House Chief of Staff Howard Baker that they believed the investigations of Meese were damaging public confidence.

On April 1, James C. McKay, the special prosecutor heading the investigation, announced that so far the probe into Meese's connections with a $1 billion Iraqi pipeline project

and his investment in telephone company stock had not provided the basis for a criminal indictment. McKay previously had made a similar statement about his probe into Meese's ties to Wedtech Corp., a controversial defense contractor. Nevertheless criticism of Meese continued, not just from Democrats but also from Republicans who regarded him as a political liability in an election year. On July 5, Meese abruptly announced that he was resigning, claiming that he had been "completely vindicated" because McKay had filed a report on the 14-month investigation without recommending criminal charges. On July 12, President Reagan announced the nomination of Richard Thornburgh, former Republican governor of Pennsylvania and former federal prosecutor, to replace Meese. He was confirmed easily by the Senate.

Meanwhile, the legal fallout from the Iran-contra scandal confronted the administration with new dilemmas. On March 16 a federal grand jury in Washington filed conspiracy and other charges in the case against former National Security Council staff member Oliver North, former National Security Adviser Rear Adm. John M. Poindexter, retired Air Force Maj. Gen. Richard V. Secord, and Albert Hakim, an Iranian-American businessman. A week earlier another former Reagan administration official, Robert McFarlane, had pleaded guilty to federal misdemeanor charges.

North was scheduled to stand trial first early in 1989. Meanwhile President Reagan faced strong pressure from conservatives, including some members of Congress, to issue a pretrial pardon for the much decorated Marine combat veteran, whom many Americans regarded as a hero because of his role in the scandal. But on December 1 the president announced that he would not pardon North or the other Iran-contra defendants because this "would leave them under the shadow of guilt for the rest of their lives." But on another and more complex issue the president said that "duty requires him" to suppress certain classified documents which might be needed for North's trial to go forward. North and his lawyers contended that without such materials he cannot get a fair trial. But Reagan contended that the information he decided to withhold would threaten national-security interests if it were released.

In addition, the administration was faced with a devastating drought that afflicted half of the nation's farm counties, according to the Department of Agriculture. Farm experts called it the driest spring since the dust bowl of the 1930s. The drought, which gripped the Midwest and the South, sent commodity prices soaring and grain stocks plunging and slowed the farm belt's recovery from a ten-year depression. In August, Congress passed a sweeping relief measure, estimated to cost nearly $4 billion, which provided aid to stricken growers and livestock owners.

Congress. In its second session the 100th Congress confronted no overriding national crisis and passed no single law of historic implication. Yet in the judgment of longtime observers on Capitol Hill the lawmakers turned in a remarkable performance in terms of overall productivity, managing to make significant contributions across the board of public policy. Much of the credit for these accomplishments probably was owed to the Democrats, who had established a broad legislative agenda after their party gained control of the Senate in the

The new B-2 Stealth bomber, said to be virtually invisible to radar and considered a milestone in military technology, was unveiled in Palmdale, CA, in late November. Each such bomber has an estimated price tag of at least $500 million.

A large sign at the Veterans Administration Building in Washington marks the creation of the 14th cabinet-level post, the Department of Veterans Affairs.

© Terry Ashe/"Time" Magazine

1986 elections. But President Reagan played a role, too, notably by making possible what many thought was the Congress' most portentous achievement, Senate ratification of the treaty with the Soviets banning intermediate range missiles.

Here are the areas of notable achievements:

• National Security. By a 93-5 vote on May 27, the Senate ratified the Intermediate Nuclear Forces Treaty (INF), the first major arms control pact it had approved in 16 years. The pact bans ground-launch missiles with ranges of 300 to 3,400 mi (500 to 5 000 km). (See ARMS CONTROL.) Congress also enacted provisions that had the effect of barring Strategic Defense Initiative (SDI) tests in outer space and of preventing further weapons buildups over the limits set in the never ratified SALT II Treaty.

• Social Services. The enactment of catastrophic health care insurance expanded Medicare to protect 33 million elderly and disabled beneficiaries against staggering medical bills due to serious injury or illness. The legislation also ultimately will cover up to 80% of the cost of prescription drugs after deductibles are reached. The costs will be borne by beneficiaries, through higher premiums or a surtax on those with incomes high enough to pay income taxes. Just as significant, Congress passed the first major revision of welfare laws in half a century, requiring states to set up work and training programs for welfare recipients and establishing the first federal work requirement for some welfare recipients. An omnibus drug bill created a cabinet-level drug czar, authorized more spending for drug treatment and rehabilitation, and permitted the death penalty for major drug traffickers.

• Civil Rights. Congress gave the Department of Housing and Urban Development broad new authority to crack down on discrimination in the sale and rental of housing, the first antibias law in the housing field passed in 20 years. Along with strengthening safeguards against racial discrimination, the new law also bans housing bias against the handicapped and families with young children. On the education front, Congress overturned the controversial Supreme Court Grove City decision, that held antidiscrimination prohibitions covered only the specific programs at an educational institution that received federal aid. The new law makes clear that discrimination is prohibited in the entire institution.

• Trade. The omnibus trade bill, passed after three years of hot debate, gives the president added power to retaliate against unfair trade practices and provides relief to U.S. industries hurt by imports if they make themselves more competitive. Congress also enacted statutes clearing the way for implementation of a trade agreement between the United States and its largest trading partner, Canada.

The Congress also established a cabinet department of veterans affairs and passed new tax legislation. For all its many accomplishments Congress put off some major problems for the 101st Congress. These included the liquidity crisis of the savings and loan industry, the soaring costs of entitlement programs, the inequities of campaign-financing regulations, and the need for long-term commitments to cleaning up the environment.

In still other areas the will of the Congress was frustrated by the president. Reagan pocket vetoed legislation that would have limited advertising during children's television shows on grounds that this violated constitutional guarantees of free expression. He also pocket vetoed legislation tightening restrictions on lobbying by former government officials and

UNITED STATES · Information Highlights

Official Name: United States of America.
Location: Central North America.
Area: 3,618,770 sq mi (9 372 614 km²).
Population (Jan. 1, 1988 est.): 244,427,098.
Chief Cities (July 1, 1986 est.): Washington, DC, the capital, 626,000; New York, 7,262,700; Los Angeles, 3,259,300; Chicago, 3,009,530; Houston, 1,728,910; Philadelphia, 1,642,900; Detroit, 1,086,220.
Government: *Head of state and government,* Ronald Reagan, president (took office for second term, Jan. 20, 1985). *Legislature*—Congress: Senate and House of Representatives.
Monetary Unit: Dollar.
Gross National Product (third quarter 1988, current dollars): $4,909,200,000,000.
Merchandise Trade (1987): *Imports,* $406,200,000,000; *exports,* $254,100,000,000.

imposing them on members of Congress, contending that such restrictions would make it more difficult to recruit well-qualified persons into federal service.

Several members of the House had to face accusations of personal misconduct of varying degrees of severity. The most prominent target of such charges was House Speaker James Wright of Texas who came under investigation by the House Ethics Committee. One question the panel was looking into had to do with the unusually high royalties Wright received from a published collection of his reflections, many copies of which were bought by his political supporters, in what critics charged was a violation of campaign-finance rules. Other areas of inquiry in the probe which began in June and would continue into 1989 concerned Wright's intervention with federal bank regulators on behalf of bankers in his state, his use of a Fort Worth condominium, and his oil-well holdings.

In August, Rep. Mario Biaggi of New York resigned from the House after being convicted of taking a bribe from the defense contractor Wedtech Corp. The House Ethics Committee found Democratic Rep. Charles Rose of North Carolina guilty of borrowing campaign funds for his personal use, but recommended no punishment because he had returned the funds. Congressmen under scrutiny in ethical cases who went down to defeat in November included Georgia Republican Pat Swindall, who was indicted on charges that he lied to a grand jury about his knowledge of a money laundering scheme; Rhode Island Democrat Fernand St. Germain, chairman of the House Banking Committee, who had been the subject of a long investigation regarding his role with lobbyists from the savings and loans industry; and Florida Democrat Bill Chappell, Jr., who was under investigation for his role with defense contractors. Rep. Harold Ford (D-TN), who was under indictment for fraud and conspiracy, won reelection. On November 21, New York Rep. Robert Garcia (D) was indicted in the continuing Wedtech investigation.

With the record of the 100th Congress now part of history, the 101st Congress began preparing for its role by picking its leaders. Senate Democrats selected Maine Sen. George J. Mitchell, a former federal judge with a reputation as a liberal, as their new leader replacing West Virginia's Robert Byrd. The West Virginia senator was giving up the post, which he had held since 1977, to become chairman of the Senate Appropriations Committee. Sen. Alan Cranston (CA) won an unprecedented seventh term as Democrat whip.

On the Republican side the three Senate leaders were reelected—Robert Dole of Kansas as minority leader, Alan Simpson of Wyoming as assistant leader, and William Armstrong of Colorado as chairman of the Republican Policy Committee.

The House Democrats returned their top leaders by acclamation—Speaker Jim Wright, Majority Leader Thomas Foley (WA), and Majority Whip Tony Coelho (CA). William H. Gray III of Pennsylvania was selected as the new chairman of the House Democratic caucus. On the GOP side of the House, Robert H. Michel (IL) was returned as minority leader; Dick Cheney (WY) was chosen to succeed Senator-elect Trent Lott (MS) as minority whip; and Jerry Lewis (CA) was picked as conference chairman.

The Transition. Vice-President George Bush's election to the presidency on November 8 (*see* feature article, page 24) meant that the president and the president-elect were of the same political party for the first time since 1928 when Republican Herbert Hoover was chosen to succeed Republican Calvin Coolidge. Since the burdens and powers of the presidency have increased enormously in the past 60 years, the Reagan-Bush transition presented a unique situation so far as the modern presidency was concerned. On the one hand the situation created the potential threat to President-elect Bush of being overshadowed by the incumbent chief executive, since tact demanded that he be cautious about appearing to challenge Reagan's authority. On the other hand Bush was presented with a friendly environment in which to test his presidential wings. Bush took full advantage of the latter circumstance to offset any problems that the former might have caused him.

President Reagan helped smooth the way for his successor, repaying Bush for the loyalty he had shown as vice-president. Two days after the election, Reagan asked his cabinet to resign to give Bush the flexibility to decide which of them he wished to retain. From then on Bush moved swiftly to select his top advisers, thus commanding attention for his government-in-waiting. (*See also* UNITED STATES—*The Bush Cabinet,* page 561.)

ROBERT SHOGAN
Washington Bureau, "Los Angeles Times"

The Reagan Legacy

Pete Souza/The White House

Ronald Reagan's first political hero was Franklin Delano Roosevelt, the modern U.S. president with whom all successors have been compared. It seemed appropriate, then, that as Reagan prepared to leave office, many scholars contended that his presidency had had more impact on the nation than any since that of his onetime liberal idol.

Like Roosevelt, Reagan took the helm of a deeply troubled nation, raised its spirits, and improved its material well-being. Like his Democratic predecessor, Republican Reagan made the United States a stronger presence on the international stage. And also like Roosevelt, Reagan relied heavily on two natural gifts—an appealing temperament and a talent for communicating.

For all the similarities, it would be unfair to measure Reagan's achievements against those of FDR. For one thing, Reagan had to contend with the structure of institutions and beliefs about government which Roosevelt had forged in more than three terms in the White House, a structure which many believed Reagan actually helped consolidate simply because he felt obliged to. "Reagan proved once and for all that it is impossible to dismantle the domestic public sector," said University of Texas political scientist Walter Dean Burnham. "He may have rolled back the Great Society, but he has preserved the New Deal." Thus, such New Deal

inventions as Social Security and unemployment insurance remained inviolate during Reagan's two terms.

The 40th president also had to contend with obstacles to leadership which had developed since Roosevelt's tenure. At home, political parties were weaker and society in general more fragmented. Abroad, the United States, which had been a rising power in Roosevelt's day, now was fighting against decline. For these reasons, any assessment of Reagan's performance turns out to be a balance sheet on which triumphs are offset by disappointments.

Some historians believe that Reagan will be remembered and respected mainly for his intangible accomplishments. Taking power from a president who declared the republic to be in a state of malaise, Reagan with his buoyant optimism and firm convictions made Americans feel better about themselves and their country. Yet because of some problems he helped create, such as the budget and trade deficits, and others that he did not solve, such as the soaring costs of health care and higher education, the president also left his countrymen with a sense of uneasiness about the future. For the first time in the modern era, Americans no longer could feel assured that life would be better for their children than it had been for them.

Yet another intangible success—and one that even his opponents conceded—was that Reagan's early accomplishments as chief executive increased public regard for the office he held. "Whatever the wisdom of his policy, Ronald Reagan has restored the presidency as a vigorous, purposeful instrument of national leadership," declared liberal Democratic Sen. Edward M. Kennedy (MA) a few months after the 1984 election. Two years later, however, the Iran-contra scandal cast a cloud over Reagan's reputation. Though he left office with his personal popularity still high, his uncertain handling of that fiasco revived questions about whether any president could lead the nation effectively.

Just as the verdict on Reagan's symbolic accomplishments is mixed, so are the judgments of his performance in the major areas of public affairs.

The Economy. The biggest grievances against Reagan's immediate predecessor in 1980 were high inflation and high interest rates. The new president slashed the inflation rate to one third of what it had been when he took office, which helped bring interest rates well below the high double-digit levels of the Carter era. Unemployment dropped to a 14-year low. Personal income climbed, and more than 15 million new jobs were created. In one of his first major legislative victories, President Reagan effected deep across-the-board cuts in tax rates. And in his second term, he helped push through massive tax reform, closing loopholes and eliminating inequities which had caused citizen resentment for decades. He left his successor the longest sustained economic expansion since the 1960s.

But the Reagan tax cuts led to a federal budget deficit in the range of $150 billion. This helped drive the total national debt to more than $2 trillion, with interest payments of about $150 billion annually. "I happen to think we have a time bomb, a Frankenstein monster," said former President Gerald R. Ford of the budget deficit. The tide of red ink swamped all proposals for dealing with such everyday citizen concerns as health care, child care, and education. Moreover, many economists felt that the huge budget deficit had helped produce the staggering trade deficit, which soared to a record $170 billion in 1987. The trade imbalance transformed the United States into a debtor nation, making it harder for Americans to maintain control of their own economy. "We are today more vulnerable economically than at any time in recent history," Brookings Institution fellow Thomas Mann told a conference on the Reagan legacy at the University of California, Davis, in June.

International Affairs. Some scholars believe that foreign affairs gave the president his greatest triumphs and the clearest vindication for his beliefs. Reagan took office convinced that getting tough with the Soviet Union was the only way to reach agreement with the world's other superpower. He launched a massive military buildup and labeled Moscow the center of an "evil empire." But in his second term, the president reached a historic agreement with the Soviets on eliminating intermediate-range nuclear missiles and won major concessions in the field of human rights. "Reagan challenged the Soviet Union and established new terms of cooperation," said Condoleezza Rice, a Stanford University specialist in Soviet affairs, at the Davis conference. "In doing so, he has broadened the bipartisan consensus for arms control."

On the debit side, the president's decision to deploy U.S. Marines in Lebanon on a hazily conceived "peacekeeping" mission led to the deaths of 240 of them in a 1983 terrorist bombing. Then there was the ill-conceived effort to improve relations with so-called "moderates" in Iran by selling them arms in return for the release of hostages; profits from the arms sales were diverted secretly to "contra" guerrillas fighting the leftist regime in Nicaragua.

By sending troops to Grenada in 1983 to stifle a potential threat from a left-wing regime, Reagan demonstrated that in the post-Vietnam era the United States still was willing to use force to protect its interests. But his major effort to combat the threat of Communism in the Western Hemisphere—aiding the contras—produced division at home and at best inconclusive results in Central America.

Politics. When the Democrats convened in Atlanta in July 1988 to nominate Gov. Michael Dukakis for president, they heaped scorn and abuse on the Republican standard-bearer, George Bush. But they had few harsh words for the incumbent Republican president, Ronald Reagan. Indeed, in accepting his party's nomination, Dukakis had some praise for the chief executive. "President Reagan has set the stage for deep cuts in nuclear arms," said Dukakis, "and I salute him for that."

The gentlemanly treatment of Reagan was a reflection of the extent to which he had come to dominate national politics during his eight years in the Oval Office. Not only did Reagan win two landslide election victories, but he seemed to exercise a veto power over the national agenda. For all the promise of change they offered at the convention, the Democrats generally avoided saying what Reagan had done that they would undo. The tax cut, for example, the cornerstone of Reaganomics and

once a favorite target for Democratic denunciations, barely was mentioned at the convention or during the campaign. Even Dukakis promised that he would raise taxes only as "a last resort."

But President Reagan had only limited success in extending his personal esteem and support to his party and to his successor. The Democrats controlled the House of Representatives all through his presidency and in 1986 took back the Senate, which Reagan had helped the Republicans carry in 1980. Though his presidential legatee, George Bush, won an impressive victory in his own right against Dukakis, the GOP lost ground in Congress and Bush himself was unable to maintain Reagan's level of support among young voters, the middle class, and independents.

But the most serious criticism of Reagan's presidency and political priorities was that, while he reduced the government's ability to raise money, he failed to use his personal prestige and political influence to curb the public's

appetite for government spending and services. President Reagan himself called the deficits "one of my greatest disappointments." But he blamed them on what he called an "iron triangle" of Congressmen, lobbyists, and the press. Special-interest groups, Reagan said, pressure lawmakers with campaign contributions into funding various programs, while the press fails to report the administration's opposition. As a result, the chief executive went on, the "constitutional balance" had been tilted.

Critics, however, held Reagan at least partly accountable for the government's being in arrears. "The president has permitted his relentless optimism to blind him to a unique opportunity," wrote John Palmer, editor of the Urban Institute's *Perspectives on the Reagan Years*. "The American people apparently found Reagan's personality so appealing they would have swallowed some unpleasant truths from him."

ROBERT SHOGAN

The Economy

It was the year when the worst did not happen—when the stock market did not crash again, when the federal budget deficit did not grow substantially larger, or the trade deficit worsen. Inflation did not burn up the economy, nor did recession put it on ice. And yet, fears of such reversals were pervasive throughout 1988, affecting the behavior of Americans at all levels of the economic scale. The attitude of the Federal Reserve was typical, with chairman Alan Greenspan indicating strongly that if the Fed erred, it desired to do so on the side of restraint.

The Trends. While apprehension was a constant factor in decisions, economic activity was strong, and even robust. More than 4 million jobs were created, housing construction retained its strength, more than 10 million domestic and foreign cars were sold once again, corporate profits and personal income rose, and so did stocks.

While it remained a serious problem, the unruly deficit showed some improvement, falling to just more than $10 billion in October, thanks to a sharp decline in imports. While exports also fell, Commerce Secretary William Verity observed that nearly one half of U.S. economic growth in the first ten months of 1988 came from a 28% surge in exports and only an 8% rise in imports. While the federal budget deficit remained high at $153 billion for fiscal 1988 and presented a formidable challenge if it is to be reduced to zero in 1993, as prescribed by law, it was $70 billion lower than the high of

$220 billion in fiscal 1986. The direction, at least, was right.

In spite of such trends, the economic mood of America was one of great unease. The announcement of good news was discounted as quickly as business and academic economists could contact the media. Fears were most pronounced about inflation and recession. Repeatedly throughout the year warnings were issued that falling unemployment and more intense usage of factory capacity would produce upward pressure on wages and prices.

While the inflation-recession scenario never unfolded, it never ceased to be present. It was an eccentricity, a peculiarity of 1988, perhaps based in the fear that expansions just did not last much longer than the six years that this one would achieve by November. When November retail sales rose an unexpectedly strong 1.1%, for example, it was viewed widely as evidence of overheating. But rather typically, less attention was given to a simultaneous report showing producer prices in the same month rose only 0.3% for the third month in a row.

By the numbers, the consumer price index rose just more than 4% for the year, while the gross national product (GNP) price deflator, a broader measure, finished the year about 3.5% higher in real terms. While these levels could not be ignored—4% inflation for five years cuts buying power by one quarter—there was little evidence of the runaway inflation that had plagued the 1970s.

Monitoring the situation, the Federal Reserve allowed interest rates to rise throughout the year. The prime commercial lending rate

rose steadily from a first-quarter average of 8.6% to 10.5% in December. Fixed-rate home mortgages, which began the year at about 10%, were closer to 10.5%, and in many instances well above that, as the year closed.

Disposable personal income, adjusted for inflation, rose about 3.5%, and total personal income topped $4 trillion for the first time. Business income was unusually strong: After-tax profits soared more than 10.5% to about $158 billion; and dividends, rising about 9%, topped $100 billion.

The stock market reflected the business condition more realistically than in the pre-crash days of 1987. As always, the Dow Jones industrial average had its ups and downs, but it averted the convulsions that marred 1987 and that many financial people feared were in store for 1988. On the first trading day of the year, the Dow closed at 2015.25 points, and it closed the year at 2,168.57. (*See* STOCKS AND BONDS).

Manufacturing companies were particularly strong, continuing their comeback from years of competitive decline. While the falling U.S. dollar aided many manufacturing companies by reducing their export prices, there was more to it than that. Some companies had spent years paring their costs through the elimination of nonproductive jobs, the closing of inefficient plants, and the employment of labor-saving equipment and techniques. After two decades of decline, U.S. manufactured goods again were competing in the world marketplace.

Foreign Buying. Whatever reluctance they still might have had about American goods, foreigners continued to be eager purchasers of U.S. assets. Japanese and British individuals and companies were especially active. Their interest and abundant funds pushed up prices not just of corporations and corporate stocks and bonds, but of real estate and art. The intense foreign interest was viewed, as had become the habit, with mixed feelings and viewpoints. Some saw it as additional evidence of an American decline; others considered it an indication of America's attractiveness. In the first in-stance, the U.S. trade deficit was seen as leav-ing so many dollars abroad that the country could, in effect, suffer an economic and finan-cial invasion. At the extreme, editorial writers screamed that foreigners would own every-thing. What if these foreigners suddenly sold off their U.S. assets? Why, it was said, Ameri-can markets would collapse. But many others, including Milton Freidman, the conservative economist, saw it differently. To them, foreign investment was evidence that smart people viewed the United States as a good investment. To them, it was a sign of faith in the American economy.

Takeovers. There was also unusual interest in American assets from a source closer to home. Wealthy corporations became the ob-jects of well-financed raiders who felt they could improve shareholder values or, if not, sell off individual pieces for a high price. Some of the takeover attempts, financed largely by so-called junk bonds, involved corporate offi-cers who sought companies for themselves by bidding for the shares of existing shareholders.

The New Year hardly had begun when an unaccepted $4 billion takeover bid for Sterling Drug opened the floodgates of a record year of mergers, takeovers, acquisitions, and lever-aged buyouts. In the first nine months, such transactions amounted to $198 billion, or 35% ahead of the 1986 record pace. The ultimate deal involved the firm of Kohlberg, Kravis Roberts & Co. buying RJR Nabisco for about $25 billion. It was the largest corporate pur-chase in American history.

The level of such activity and the enormous consequences to employees, communities, bondholders, shareholders, and the entire economy generated intense interest in Con-gress, and seemed likely to lead to legislation in 1989. (*See also* BUSINESS AND CORPORATE AFFAIRS.)

A Look Ahead. As 1988 ended, it appeared that taxpayers might have to contribute heavily to paying off the multibillion dollar obligations of failed savings and loan associations. The shaky condition of many banks also was on the agenda, as well as the problem of how to deal with Third World debt. Solutions could not be put off indefinitely on any of these issues with-out risking even more delicate, intricate, and perplexing difficulties. (*See also* BANKING AND FINANCE.)

President-elect George Bush knew this. Clearly, he was inheriting an economy with many strengths, some of them bound to pay off during his administration. Just as clearly, there were weaknesses—the deficits, for example—and issues, such as the stability of the dollar. In typical 1988 style, he was being warned about the negatives. Apprehension, it seemed, was destined to continue for at least another year.

JOHN CUNNIFF, *The Associated Press*

The U.S. Economy—Some Key Indicators

Consumer Price Index (November 1988, 1982–84 = 100): 120.3

Corporate After-Tax Profits (third quarter 1988): $169,100,000,000.

Gross National Product (third quarter 1988, 1982 dollars): $4,009,400,000,000; (current dollars): $4,909,200,000,000.

Industrial Production (October 1988, 1977 = 100): 139.2; percent change from October 1987: 5.1%.

Personal Income (October 1988, seasonally adjusted at annual rate): $4,185,000,000,000.

Prime Rate (November 1988): 10–10.5%.

Retail Sales (November 1988): $138,100,000,000.

Unemployment Rate (1988): 5.4%.

Weekly Earnings, Average (private nonagricultural industries, October 1988): $328.51; percent change from October 1987): 4.1%.

THE BUSH ADMINISTRATION

As president-elect, George Bush began to assemble his administration. His appointments included John Sununu as White House chief of staff, Richard G. Darman as director of the Office of Management and Budget, and Brent Scowcroft as national security adviser. His cabinet nominees, profiled here, included three from the Reagan cabinet. All others faced confirmation by the Senate.

Department of Defense: John Tower was named amid controversy over his personal life and his ties, as a consultant, to the defense industry. The 63-year-old Houston native spent 24 years in the U.S. Senate (1961–85), chairing the Armed Services Committee for the last four. In 1986 he was named by President Reagan to head a three-member panel to study the National Security Council's role in the Iran-contra affair. He has a bachelor's degree from Southwestern University and a master's from Southern Methodist University.

Department of Health and Human Services: The appointment of Dr. Louis W. Sullivan, 55, pleased those who wanted a black in the cabinet but angered the pro-life lobby, who are opposed to his tacit approval of abortion. Born in Atlanta, Sullivan received his medical degree from Boston University (1958), where he later was co-director of hematology. A former professor and dean at Morehouse School of Medicine, he became its president in 1985. His research specialty is blood disorders related to vitamin deficiencies.

Department of Justice: Richard L. (Dick) Thornburgh, who was sworn in as the nation's 76th attorney general on Aug. 12, 1988, was asked to remain in the post. After taking degrees at Yale and Pitt, Thornburgh practiced law in his native Pittsburgh (1959–69). He was U.S. attorney for western Pennsylvania (1969–75) and head of the Justice Department's criminal division (1975–77). The 56-year-old former governor of Pennsylvania (1979–87) served briefly as director of the Institute of Politics at Harvard's Kennedy School of Government.

Department of Transportation: Samuel K. Skinner had been chairman of the nation's second-largest mass transportation system, the Regional Transportation Authority of Northeastern Illinois, since 1984. The 50-year-old Chicago native attended the University of Illinois and has a law degree from De Paul. He served as an assistant U.S. attorney (1968–75) and U.S. attorney (1975–77) before going into private practice. Skinner, a licensed pilot, was Illinois cochairman of the Bush presidential campaigns of 1980 and 1988.

Department of Agriculture: Clayton Yeutter, 58, served as President Reagan's special trade representative beginning in 1985. Prior to that he was president of the Chicago Mercantile Exchange for seven years, deputy special trade representative in the Ford administration, and assistant secretary of agriculture in the Nixon administration. Yeutter, who raises cattle and corn on the family farm in his native Nebraska, holds a law degree and a doctorate in agricultural economics from the University of Nebraska. He was in the Air Force (1952–57).

Department of Education: Lauro F. Cavazos, the first Hispanic to serve in the U.S. cabinet, remains in the post to which President Reagan appointed him in August 1988. Cavazos, 61, grew up on a Texas ranch and served with the Army during World War II. He earned bachelor's and master's degrees from Texas Tech and a doctorate in physiology from Iowa State. Cavazos has taught at the Medical College of Virginia and at Tufts University, where he also was dean, and was president of Texas Tech (1980–88).

Department of Housing and Urban Development: Jack F. Kemp completed nine terms as a member of the U.S. House from Buffalo, NY, in January 1989. As a House member, he had a conservative voting record and was a key advocate of supply-side economics. He opposed Bush for the 1988 GOP presidential nomination. Born in Los Angeles on July 13, 1935, Kemp was graduated from Occidental College in 1957 and played professional football (1957–70). He cofounded the American Football League Players Association in 1965.

Department of Labor: A Salisbury, NC, native, Elizabeth H. Dole holds a bachelor's degree from Duke and master's and law degrees from Harvard. The 52-year-old former Democrat was a deputy director of the White House Office of Consumer Affairs (1971–73), a member of the Federal Trade Commission (1973–79), President Reagan's assistant for public liaison (1981–83), and secretary of transportation (1983–87). Her husband, Senate Minority Leader Robert Dole, had opposed the president-elect for the Republican nomination.

Department of the Treasury: Nicholas F. Brady was renamed to the position which he had assumed on Sept. 16, 1988. Born in New York City on April 11, 1930, he received degrees from Yale and Harvard. He joined the investment firm of Dillon, Reed & Co. in 1954, becoming chairman and chief executive officer in 1982. A director of various corporations, Brady served as U.S. senator from New Jersey, filling the unexpired term of Harrison Williams in 1982. He was chairman of the presidential task force that examined the 1987 stock-market crash.

Department of Commerce: Robert A. Mosbacher, a longtime friend of George Bush, has spent his career as an independent oil and gas producer in Texas. Born in White Plains, NY, on March 11, 1927, he was graduated from Washington and Lee University in Lexington, VA. He was chief fundraiser for Bush's 1980 and 1988 presidential campaigns, as well as for Gerald Ford's 1976 campaign. An international yachting champion, Mosbacher has served on the advisory boards of various educational and cultural organizations.

Department of Energy: Retired Navy Adm. James D. Watkins, 61, has had extensive training in nuclear technology and engineering. He is a former nuclear-submarine commander and was a member of Adm. Hyman Rickover's program to design, build, and operate nuclear-powered ships. He served as commander-in-chief of the Pacific Fleet (1981–82), chief of naval operations (1982–86), and head of President Reagan's Commission on AIDS (1987–88). He has degrees from the U.S. Naval Academy (1949) and Naval Postgraduate School (1958).

Department of Interior: Manuel Lujan, Jr., was born on May 12, 1928, in San Ildefonso, NM. A graduate of the College of Santa Fe, he worked as a broker in his family insurance business. The first and only Hispanic Republican to serve in the U.S. House of Representatives (1969–89), he was the ranking Republican on the House Interior and Insular Affairs Committee (1981–85) and on the Science, Space, and Technology Committee (1985–89). Lujan had wanted to be interior secretary during the Reagan administration.

Department of State: James A. Baker III, 58, served as White House chief of staff during President Reagan's first term and treasury secretary during his second term. He resigned the latter post in August 1988 to become campaign manager for Bush, a longtime associate. He also had managed the presidential campaigns of Reagan in 1980 and Gerald Ford in 1976, as well as Bush's unsuccessful Senate bid in 1970. Born to a wealthy Houston family, he earned degrees from Princeton University and the University of Texas law school.

Department of Veterans Affairs: Edward J. Derwinski would face the challenge of turning the Veterans Administration into an "efficient but streamlined new bureaucracy" when the agency becomes the 14th cabinet department on March 15, 1989. After service in the U.S. Army (1945–46), he was graduated from Loyola University in 1951. Derwinski was a member of the Illinois General Assembly (1957–58) and the U.S. House (1959–83). Since 1983 he had served in the State Department. He is a member of various veterans organizations.

The fourth summit meeting between U.S. President Reagan and Soviet leader Mikhail Gorbachev, May 29–June 2 in Moscow, included the exchange of formal documents of ratification of the INF treaty. It was Reagan's first visit to the USSR.

Foreign Affairs

The final year of a U.S. presidential administration often is marked by efforts to resolve outstanding foreign-policy problems and to shape the agenda for the next administration. The Reagan administration, which had begun in 1981 with strongly ideological rhetoric about the Soviet Union as the source of "evil" in world politics, ended its final full year in office in 1988 with agreements and a highly pragmatic approach in dealing with Moscow. Progress on arms control was achieved, and several Third World military conflicts which had festered since the end of the Carter administration finally moved toward resolution, at least in part because of U.S.-Soviet consultation. Yet a series of important international problems, particularly in the economic area, persisted. The fate of the "Reagan Doctrine," dedicated to undermining Soviet-sponsored states in the Third World, remained in doubt, and the administration suffered an embarrassing setback in a failed attempt to oust Panamanian strongman Manuel Noriega, a former U.S. client.

Foreign-policy initiatives were spurred in part by changes within the administration during its final year. The president's disengaged management style, a certain disdain for legal restrictions on executive action, and contradictions between stated antiterrorist policies and actual bargaining for hostages had been exposed embarrassingly by the Iran-contra affair in 1986–87. This led to replacements in the National Security Council staff and a determination to salvage the administration's reputation. In addition, the departure of Secretary of Defense Caspar Weinberger in November 1987 and of other White House "hard-liners," together with the emergence of Soviet General Secretary Mikhail Gorbachev, opened the way for more fruitful dialogue between the superpowers.

Soviet Relations and Arms Control. Major progress on arms control and Third World conflicts was achieved at two Reagan-Gorbachev summit conferences, in Washington in December 1987 and in Moscow in May-June 1988. Soviet concessions on the destruction of an entire class of intermediate- and short-range nuclear missiles in Europe, and the limitation of those based in Asia, led to the completion of the Intermediate Nuclear Forces (INF) Treaty, including provisions for on-site inspection. The Soviets in turn gained the elimination of U.S. missiles in Europe capable of reaching the USSR. However, certain battlefield-range nuclear forces, as well as the considerable British and French arsenals, remained outside the agreement.

While the United States and USSR in 1988 also discussed a chemical-weapons accord and agreed in principle on a 50% reduction in long-range strategic nuclear weapons, details of where the cuts would be made and of reliable verification remained for further negotiation. Nuclear-arms control in Europe also alerted both sides to the importance of agreement on the size of conventional force deployments; some progress was made on the definition of forces on both sides, but actual limits were far from resolved.

The U.S. interest in these agreements centered on NATO's "dual track" strategy, in which a European nuclear buildup was begun in the 1980s in hopes of convincing the Soviets to dismantle their own weapons. In essence this was achieved, although with considerable controversy among the allies about the wisdom of continued reliance on nuclear versus conventional deterrence. Strategic weapons limitations also would make the task of defending against nuclear attack at least theoretically easier if the U.S. Strategic Defense Initiative (SDI) is continued in the next administration. Moscow in 1988 continued to press strongly

against deployment of SDI and the erosion of the existing Anti-Ballistic Missile (ABM) Treaty. The Soviets saw arms control as a way of saving defense costs, diminishing the threat of a first strike against Soviet nuclear forces, and building East-West trust for more comprehensive agreements.

President Reagan and President-elect Bush met briefly with Gorbachev during the general secretary's December visit to New York.

Regional Conflicts. Among the major conflicts on which progress was made in 1988, the most prominent was the Iran-Iraq war. Although a cease-fire was reached in August, progress on an overall Iran-Iraq peace agreement remained very slow. The American naval presence in the Persian Gulf, first escorting U.S.-flagged Kuwaiti oil tankers and extending similar protection to vessels of other nations, had both positive and negative effects. The political mission of the U.S. fleet remained ill-defined, but evidently the fleet's presence did convince Iran of the dangers of U.S. military support for Iraq, and at least somewhat reassured Arab Gulf states of the reliability of U.S. commitments. Tragically, however, it also resulted in the downing of an Iranian civilian airliner in July with the loss of 290 lives. The White House apologized for the error and offered compensation to the aggrieved families. Controversy in Washington over the sale of sophisticated arms to Kuwait and Saudi Arabia also diluted the positive effects of the U.S. Gulf commitment, and led the Saudis to conclude one of the largest arms purchases in recent history with Great Britain. A U.S.-Kuwaiti arms agreement followed shortly thereafter.

Despite considerable effort by U.S. Secretary of State George Shultz, little progress was made on the other major Middle Eastern conflict, involving the Israelis, Palestinians, and other Arab states. As Israel struggled to suppress a prolonged Palestinian uprising in the occupied territories, Washington applied mild pressure on the Israelis to negotiate with influential moderate Palestinians. In August, Jordan's King Hussein cut ties and surrendered claims on the West Bank, further complicating President Reagan's long-standing hope of involving him in peace negotiations with Israel. In November the Palestine Liberation Organization (PLO) declared an independent state in the occupied territories and implicitly recognized the existence of Israel. Washington at first reacted coolly but in mid-December agreed to hold talks with the PLO.

The United States and Soviet Union, along with Pakistan and Afghanistan, basically came to terms on a Soviet withdrawal from Afghanistan. A phased withdrawal over a period of 18 months was begun in May. No actual settlement of the Afghan civil war was achieved, however, and disagreements persisted over continued superpower aid to the warring parties. U.S. policy in the area was complicated in August, when Pakistan's President Zia ul-Haq was killed, along with the U.S. ambassador and other officials, in a midair explosion possibly caused by sabotage.

Throughout most of the Reagan years, Undersecretary of State Chester Crocker toiled to produce an agreement between South Africa and its "frontline" black African neighbors. In mid-1988, these efforts, in conjunction with U.S.-mediated talks involving Cuba, South Africa, and Angola, bore some fruit on the issues of Namibia (currently Southwest Africa, under South African administration) and Angola. The framework of an agreement emerged in which South Africa, hard pressed by Cuban forces, withdrew its troops from Angola. Under the accord, this would open the way for Namibian independence, although there was no clear specification of the type of government to be permitted. Such independence would depend on the withdrawal of Cuban troops from Angola. Late in the year negotiators for the three nations reached agreement on a timetable for the Cuban pullout—to take place over 27 months —and independence for Namibia. UNITA guerrillas in Angola were not part of the agreement and vowed to continue fighting.

In a year of proposed troop withdrawals, Vietnam formally announced in May that it would begin a phased pullout from Cambodia, where the United States and China had been supporting a coalition of guerrilla fighters. As in the Persian Gulf, Angola, and Afghanistan, the United Nations attempted to provide its good offices for mediating the settlement, but the prospect of a coalition government for Cambodia remained a problem, and U.S.-Vietnamese relations remained bitter.

The United States also confronted instability in South Korea, as youthful protesters, critical of U.S. involvement, called for quick reunification with the North. With Seoul playing host to the Olympic Games, talks between North and South were renewed, though without much prospect for an early settlement.

In contrast to hopes for negotiated settlements in other regions, prospects in Central America, especially in Nicaragua and El Salvador, dimmed as 1988 progressed. Unlike many Democrats, the Reagan administration lacked enthusiasm for the Oscar Arias peace plan of 1987, in which the Costa Rican president outlined terms for Central Americans to settle their own differences. In fact, the U.S. administration imposed harsh trade and loan terms on Costa Rica and continued to press Congress for contra aid to oppose the Nicaraguan government. The approach of U.S. elections, however, effectively postponed the fight for contra aid until the next administration. Prospects for the U.S.-backed El Salvador government also worsened with the serious illness of President José Napoleón Duarte and

with guerrilla attacks in various parts of the country.

Trade Issues, World Debt, Foreign Aid. President Reagan was involved in another major summit meeting in mid-1988, among the seven major industrial democracies. The 14th annual summit, held in June in Toronto, produced few substantive agreements on issues such as the U.S. budget deficit, trade imbalances, international debt relief, agricultural subsidies, and South African apartheid. U.S. and Western European leaders pressed Japan to limit export subsidies and increase imports, while Australians made similar requests of the United States and Europeans. President Reagan proposed to phase out all farm subsidies by the year 2000, while the Europeans favored less specific targets. Japan was under pressure as well to contribute more foreign aid to the Third World, and to shoulder more responsibility for the defense of strategic points in Asia and the Middle East. While Congress was passing assertive trade legislation, the administration was able to conclude agreements with Japan on cooperation in science and technology and on increased Japanese imports of beef and citrus fruits.

The summit leaders did hammer out some common principles for dealing with the debt problems of the most impoverished Third World countries. A variety of options for debt relief could be exercised, including extending repayment periods (favored by the United States) or debt forgiveness. Poorer states obtaining debt relief would have to accept the market-driven economic policies favored by the major industrial powers, thus limiting their ability to plan their own economies. The debt

The leaders of the seven major industrial democracies met in Toronto, June 19–21, for their 14th annual economic summit. The meetings produced few substantive agreements.

AP/Wide World

of larger Third World states, such as Brazil and Mexico, was not covered under the agreement and constituted a continued threat to world financial markets and political stability. In October, Washington announced a major loan program for Mexico.

U.S. foreign aid, both military and economic, totaled $14.4 billion in 1988, a decline from prior years and below the levels recommended by world organizations. Moreover, most of the aid was concentrated in a few states thought to be strategically important (e.g. Israel, Egypt, and Pakistan). The United States also remained in arrears in its UN assessments. Because of doubts about the effectiveness of U.S. foreign assistance in raising living standards abroad, a bipartisan congressional coalition cosponsored the Global Poverty Reduction Act, which would instruct the president to "develop a plan to ensure that United States development assistance contributes measurably to eradicating the worst aspects of absolute poverty by the year 2000." The bill still was pending when Congress adjourned and would be a focus of debate in 1989.

Late in the year, the administration also concluded negotiations with the Philippines on aid levels and the future of U.S. military bases there. The agreement extended U.S. military presence until a basic renegotiation of the agreements in 1991. Terms of U.S. financial compensation, however, did not fully satisfy critics of the Philippine government.

Prospects. The Bush administration would inherit the task of adjusting to a new U.S. role in international politics and economics. While still the world's largest single economy and one of the two predominant military powers, the United States has seen a decline in its control of international affairs, and Washington appears to have recognized the need for multilateral approaches to ending world conflicts.

The highly competitive technologies of Japan and Europe will provide a continuing challenge. At the same time, Americans are concerned by growing foreign investment in U.S. enterprises, brought on by attractive interest rates and the financial strains of federal budget deficits. The administration will be tested in its ability to generate the investment funds needed for technological research, development, and production while finding a way to keep its own budget in order.

Meanwhile, Western Europe and Japan will be exploring their own alternate defense and technological strategies, adjusting to uncertainties about the depth of U.S. military commitments, to a more outward-reaching Soviet regime, and to the costs of maintaining defense industries. U.S. policy will be tested in responding constructively to these trends and alliance pressures.

FREDERIC S. PEARSON
University of Missouri, St. Louis

URUGUAY

The 1989 presidential contest started early —actually before the end of 1987.

Politics and Government. Since it was impossible for incumbent President Julio María Sanguinetti of the official, centrist Colorado Party to run for reelection, names of other Colorado political figures began to surface early. One aspirant was Jorge Pacheco Areco, who had served as president from 1967 to 1971. Vice-President Enrique Tarigo was another likely candidate. As for the opposition National Party (Blanco), the first candidates to appear were Alberto Zumarán and Luís Alberto Lacalle. A third political force, the leftist Broad Front (FA), was unable to name a candidate because of uncertainty over who its integral parties would be. The newly organized National Liberation Movement (MLN) of former Tupamara guerrillas wanted to join the FA, and its socialist and Communist members welcomed them. However, incorporation of the MLN would force the Christian Democrats to abandon the Front. MLN leader Raúl Sendic indicated that his party would not put up any candidates in 1989 contests.

A key political issue concerned a petition signed by thousands of Uruguayan citizens requesting a referendum to overturn a year-old amnesty law for military officers accused of human-rights violations during the country's 1973–85 dictatorship. Whether the referendum would take place, and its outcome, were still conjecture in late 1988.

Economy. Economic measures implemented in the latter part of 1987 and continued in 1988 stagnated economic activity and left half of the public disapproving of President Sanguinetti's performance. According to a poll published in September, only 20% of the residents of Montevideo approved of the regime. Some 59% of those polled found the economy to be in worse shape than a year earlier. In the latter part of 1987 the government had taken unpopular steps to cool down an overheated economy, including credit restrictions, higher interest rates, currency devaluations, curbs on public expenditure, and wage hikes below the increased cost of living. Economic and finance ministers were called to parliament in August and September 1988 to defend their policies. Both ministers survived censure motions.

On Sept. 12, 1988, Sanguinetti, speaking in Tacuarembo department, pointed to signs of recovery—including higher exports, salary increases, and reduced unemployment. A favorable trade balance of $100 million was projected. Salary adjustments on June 1 were limited to 90% of the inflation rate, which was 21% for the first five months of the year. More than 10% of the work force was idle.

A rescheduling of $1.8 billion of a total foreign indebtedness of $5.4 billion was finalized

AP/Wide World

Uruguay's President Julio María Sanguinetti (left) welcomed Brazil's José Sarney (right) and other Latin American leaders for an October meeting of the Group of Eight.

in March 1988. Debt swaps of $60 million involving two hotels, a textile mill, a citrus-juice plant, two forest projects, and a pharmaceutical project were approved. Uruguay was to finance the transaction through the sale of treasury bonds for 80% of the project cost. Loans of $66.5 million were obtained in May from the Inter-American Development Bank, to be used for agriculture.

Foreign Relations. Reflecting an expanded role for Uruguay in international affairs, the first state visit by a Uruguayan head of state to the Soviet Union was made from March 21–23. During his sojourn in Moscow, President Sanguinetti met with both Soviet leader Mikhail Gorbachev and Supreme Soviet President Andrei Gromyko. Topics considered in bilateral conversations were the crisis in Central Amer-

---

URUGUAY • Information Highlights

Official Name: Oriental Republic of Uruguay.
Location: Southeastern coast of South America.
Area: 68,039 sq mi (176 220 km²).
Population (mid-1988 est.): 3,000,000.
Capital (1985 census): Montevideo, 1,246,500.
Government: *Head of state,* Julio María Sanguinetti, president (took office March 2, 1985). *Legislature* —National Congress: Senate and House of Deputies.
Monetary Unit: Peso (416.00 pesos equal U.S.$1, Nov. 11, 1988).
Gross Domestic Product (1987 est. U.S.$): $6,900,-000,000.
Foreign Trade (1987 U.S.$): *Imports,* $1,130,000,-000; *exports,* $1,189,000,000.

ica and increased commercial, economic, and cultural ties between the two countries. Bilateral trade, which amounted to only $40 million in 1987, was to be increased to $200 million by 1990. While in Europe, Sanguinetti criticized growing trade protectionism, and pleaded with the European Community to modify its program of farm subsidies.

Before accepting the presidency of the Inter-American Development Bank in March, Foreign Minister Enrique Iglesias oversaw the establishment of relations with the People's Republic of China (PRC) and the severing of diplomatic ties with Taiwan. A five-year trade agreement was reached under which the PRC would raise its purchases of Uruguayan goods from $80 million to $150 million. Sanguinetti was scheduled to visit Beijing and possibly Shanghai for ten days during November.

Luís Barrios Tassano, former ambassador to Argentina, became foreign minister on March 9.

LARRY L. PIPPIN
University of the Pacific

UTAH

Elections, tax initiative referenda, and a criminal case concerned Utahns in 1988.

Elections. In federal races, Utah voters remained solidly Republican with one exception. The Bush-Quayle team won 66% of the vote, about 9% below the 1984 percentage of the Reagan-Bush ticket. Sen. Orrin Hatch (R) was reelected with 67% of the vote; Rep. James Hansen (R) was reelected in the 1st District with 60% of the vote; and Rep. Howard Nielson (R) was reelected in the 3rd District with 67% of the vote. The exception was Rep. Wayne Owens (D) who won reelection in the 2nd District with 57% of the vote.

At the state level, the three-way gubernatorial contest overshadowed all other races. The incumbent governor, Norman Bangerter, was challenged by Democrat Ted Wilson, former mayor of Salt Lake City, and Independent Merrill Cook, a local businessman. Wilson was favored heavily, according to public opinion polls, by leads of 30–35% a year before the election. During the year, Cook embraced the popular tax-revolt cause and provided a serious challenge to the other candidates. Governor Bangerter waged a strong personal campaign and narrowly won reelection with 40% of the vote (a 12,000-vote victory margin among 645,000 voters) over Ted Wilson. Cook was rewarded with nearly 21% of the votes.

Democrats won only one state office when Democrat Paul Van Dam, a former Salt Lake County attorney, defeated incumbent Republican David L. Wilkinson for attorney general. There was virtually no change in the Republican-dominated state legislature. There was a

---

UTAH • Information Highlights

Area 84,899 sq mi (219 889 km²).
Population (July 1, 1987): 1,680,000.
Chief Cities (1980 census): Salt Lake City, the capital (July 1, 1986 est.), 158,440; Provo, 74,108; Ogden, 64,407.
Government (1988): *Chief Officers—*governor, Norman H. Bangerter (R); lt. gov., W. Val Oveson (R). *Legislature—*Senate, 29 members; House of Representatives, 75 members.
State Finances (fiscal year 1987): *Revenue,* $3,400,000,000; *expenditure,* $3,262,000,000.
Personal Income (1987): $19,095,000,000; per capita, $11,366.
Labor Force (June 1988): *Civilian labor force,* 750,800; *unemployed,* 35,600 (4.7% of total force).
Education: *Enrollment* (fall 1986)—public elementary schools, 308,389; public secondary, 107,605; colleges and universities, 106,213. *Public school expenditures* (1986–87), $961,000,000 ($2,455 per pupil).

---

net Democratic gain of one seat in the House and the loss of one seat in the Senate, leaving Republican majorities of 47-28 in the House and 22-7 in the Senate.

Tax Initiatives. Utah voters were asked to vote on three tax-limitation proposals. Initiative A: The "People's Spending and Limitation Amendment" would have limited residential property taxes to ¾ of 1% of fair-market value and 1% of other property; Initiative B: The "People's Tax Reduction Act" would have repealed the tax increases (income, gas, sales, cigarettes) passed in 1987; and Initiative C: The "Family Choice in Education Act" would have given tuition tax credit for enrollment in private and home schools. Proponents argued that savings realized by passage of the initiatives could be absorbed by state and local government agencies and education. Opponents argued that the anticipated loss of revenue ($330 million) would result in curtailment of vital services and would have disastrous effects on education. All three initiatives were defeated.

Crime. The John Singer family of Summit County again was involved in a confrontation with police. John Singer was slain on Jan. 18, 1979, in a standoff with police seeking to arrest him for contempt of court. In mid-January 1988, Singer's widow, Vickie, his son-in-law, Addam Swapp, and 12 other persons were surrounded by 150 law-enforcement officers after the bombing of a Mormon church. The 13-day siege ended with the killing of police officer Freddie Floyd House in a gun battle. Addam, his brother Jonathan, and Vickie's son, John Timothy Singer, were indicted and found guilty in federal court of attempted murder of federal officers, the bombing, and resisting arrest. Vickie also was convicted of resisting arrest. The three men also were charged with second-degree murder in the killing of House. In Utah state court in December, Addam and John were convicted of manslaughter and Jonathan of negligent homicide.

LORENZO K. KIMBALL, *University of Utah*

VENEZUELA

Former President Carlos Andres Pérez won reelection to the presidency December 4 after being out of power ten years. But Pérez faced a new challenge—an economic crisis involving a deteriorating balance of trade and a decline in the value of the bolívar.

Pérez Defeats 22 Rivals. Pérez, the 66-year-old candidate of the left-of-center Democratic Action Party (AD), won almost 55% of the votes of the 7.8 million citizens who went to the polls—an 85% turnout. His nearest rival, Eduardo Fernández of the Social Christian Party (COPEI) took about 40% and the remaining vote was split among 21 other candidates. AD won 22 seats in the 49-member Senate and took 97 of the 201 seats in the Chamber of Deputies. COPEI took 23 Senate seats.

Pérez, who nationalized foreign oil holdings in his 1974–79 presidency, is the first president in three decades of democratic elections to win a second five-year term. Presidents are barred from immediate reelection. During the campaign, Pérez said he planned to seek "decent repayment terms" on the nation's $33 billion foreign debt. He also pledged to address poverty, establish day-care centers, and fund low-cost housing.

On election night, Pérez extolled the orderly voting of his own nation and criticized the rebellion of a group of Argentine troops as "a new uprising by groups that have not calmed down and have not learned that the time has passed for dictatorship in Latin America."

Outgoing President Jaime Lusinchi, also of the AD, was embarrassed by two events during the year. He obtained the resignation of José Manzo González March 28 amidst reports Manzo had organized a secret police unit to infiltrate narcotic rings; the unit then sold captured drugs and weapons and pocketed the profits. Lusinchi's divorce from his wife of 39 years also damaged his image.

The government had to cope with protests in four cities over the October 29 Army patrol shooting of 14 Venezuelan and Colombian "fishermen" on the Colombian border. Three students died in the protests and more than 50 students and police were injured. The riots were caused, in part, by a belief that the military was covering up discrepancies about the incident. Lusinchi and Gen. Humberto Camejo Arias claimed that ten of the "fishermen" carried Colombian and Venezuelan citizenship papers, that seven had police records as members of two Colombian guerrilla groups, and that seven were involved in an October 21 kidnapping attempt on a retired Army colonel.

To stem future cross-border incidents, Venezuelan and Colombian officials signed agreements in June and August to exchange information to prevent kidnappings and the smuggling of arms and drugs across the frontier.

Economic Problems. International monetary reserves declined from $9.4 billion in December 1987 to $8.2 billion in July 1988. Oil-export revenues declined from $9.1 billion in 1987 to an estimated $7.1 billion for 1988. Debt-service payments amounted to $5 billion in 1988. In response to the economic conditions Lusinchi called a September 19 meeting with AD candidate Pérez, the cabinet, and other officials to establish guidelines for Venezuela's foreign-debt restructuring. The government owed $25.7 billion and the private sector owed $6 billion. At year's end Lusinchi suspended payments on part of the nation's foreign debt.

Lusinchi resisted several other economic-policy changes in late 1988 in order to ensure AD's electoral chances. But the government announced in late October that the exporters of nontraditional goods would receive bolívares at the Central Bank at the free-market rate rather than a 14.5-bolívares-to-the-dollar rate in effect since December 1986. (The free-market rate had crept up from around 30 in January to 37.5 at the time of the announcement.)

Imports were expected to reach $9 billion in 1988, up from $8.8 billion in 1987 and $7.9 billion in 1986. On the other hand, oil revenues—90% of Venezuela's export earnings—were down. Average oil production was 1.6 million barrels per day (bpd) during the first six months of 1988 compared with 2.6 million bpd in 1987. Venezuela exported an average of 1 million bpd of crude oil and 561,000 bpd of other oil products the first half of 1988—slightly above its quota under Organization of the Petroleum Exporting Countries (OPEC) agreements. The average price from January to June was $13.83 per barrel compared with $17.57 in 1987.

Foreign Policy Matters. Several Panamanian and Haitian politicians found refuge in Venezuela during the year. After the ouster of Haitian President Leslie Manigat June 9, Lusinchi withdrew Venezuelan military units engaged in several housing and public-works projects.

NEALE J. PEARSON, *Texas Tech University*

VENEZUELA • Information Highlights

Official Name: Republic of Venezuela.
Location: Northern coast of South America.
Area: 352,143 sq mi (912 050 km²).
Population (mid-1988 est.): 18,800,000.
Chief Cities (1987 est., incl. suburbs): Caracas, the capital, 3,247,698; Maracaibo, 1,295,421; Valencia, 1,134,623.
Government: *Head of state and government,* Jaime Lusinchi, president (took office Feb. 2, 1984). *Legislature*—National Congress: Senate and Chamber of Deputies.
Monetary Unit: Bolívar (37.10 bolívares equal U.S.$1, Dec. 22, 1988).
Gross Domestic Product (1986 U.S.$): $53,900,-000,000.
Economic Index (Nov. 1987): *Consumer Prices* (1984 = 100), all items, 177.9; food, 243.7.
Foreign Trade (1987 U.S.$): *Imports,* $7,951,000,000; *exports,* $8,402,000,000.

VERMONT

By a narrow popular margin, 51%-49%, Vermont gave its three electoral votes to Vice-President George Bush in the November 1988 election. The election results reflected the state's 30-year tradition of ticket splitting. Democratic Gov. Madeleine Kunin and Lt. Gov. Howard Dean won reelection handily, while Republican Rep. James Jeffords trounced Democrat William Gray (69% to 31%) for a U.S. Senate seat. For Vermont's lone House seat, former Republican Lt. Gov. Peter Smith prevailed (42%) over Burlington's Socialist Mayor Bernard Sanders (39%) and Democratic State House leader Paul Poirier (19%). Democrats retained their lead in the State Senate, while losing their House majority.

Legislation and the Economy. For the second consecutive year, Vermont recorded a $60 million surplus, which inspired the 1988 legislature to vote the largest spending increase in state history. Major beneficiaries were state aid to education, human services, sewage-treatment improvements, and farm assistance. (Vermont is the only state to have voted a dairy subsidy on top of federal-price supports.)

The most important work of the legislative session was a growth-control law, enacted with Governor Kunin's strong backing after statewide hearings by the Commission on Vermont's Future, to supplement Vermont's renowned Act 250 with stronger state and regional planning of land use and development. A new Human Rights Commission also was created with greater powers than any previous comparable state agency.

By the fall of 1988 the official unemployment rate had dropped to 1.7%, believed to be the lowest rate for any state since 1976.

Court Cases and Protests. Judgments of judicial improprieties from previous years were newsworthy as a former assistant judge was convicted of perjury and sentenced to 45 days. Also, the state Judicial Conduct Board requested the Vermont Supreme Court to discipline a retired Supreme Court justice for five instances of misconduct.

The former school superintendent of Bennington, Vermont's largest school union, was found guilty of embezzlement in the state's largest-ever instance of public corruption. By late 1988, four persons had been convicted of wrongdoing, 17 faced civil charges, and others had lost their teaching licenses in the case.

John Zaccaro, Jr., son of former vice-presidential candidate Geraldine Ferraro, figured in a public protest over a prison-release program through which Zaccaro, performing public service while renting a $1,500-a-month apartment, served a drug-trafficking sentence. The protest persuaded Governor Kunin to bar drug-law offenders from the program.

Both the University of Vermont and Goddard College experienced student protests. University of Vermont students blockaded administrative offices to demand greater efforts to recruit minority students and faculty. Later in the year, Goddard College students closed the college for two days by barricading themselves in administration offices to issue demands ranging from changes in college-administrative procedures to ending homelessness.

Abenaki-Indian efforts to gain tribal recognition were highlighted when the police chief of the town of Swanton briefly impounded Abenaki Chief Homer St. Francis' car for bearing Abenaki rather than Vermont license plates. The Abenaki tribal court subsequently fined the police chief $500 for illegally seizing the car and harassing St. Francis.

ROBERT V. DANIELS AND SAMUEL B. HAND
University of Vermont

VERMONT · Information Highlights

Area: 9,614 sq mi (24 900 km²).
Population (July 1, 1987): 548,000.
Chief Cities (1980 census): Montpelier, the capital, 8,241; Burlington, 37,712; Rutland, 18,436.
Government (1988): *Chief Officers*—governor, Madeleine M. Kunin (D); lt. gov., Howard Dean (D). *General Assembly*—Senate, 30 members; House of Representatives, 150 members.
State Finances (fiscal year 1987): *Revenue,* $1,294,000,000; *expenditure,* $1,153,000,000.
Personal Income (1987): $7,840,000,000; per capita, $14,302.
Labor Force (June 1988): *Civilian labor force,* 299,800; *unemployed,* 7,600 (2.5% of total force).
Education: *Enrollment* (fall 1986)—public elementary schools, 63,392; public secondary, 28,720; colleges and universities, 32,460. *Public school expenditures* (1986–87), $370,000,000 ($4,459 per pupil).

VETERANS

The 27.4 million veterans of the United States had reason to celebrate in 1988: A new Cabinet-level department of Veterans Affairs was established; an antiquated law preventing veterans from hiring lawyers and challenging the government in court was overturned; and major new health-care and job-training proposals became realities.

Cabinet Department. Veterans' organizations had pushed for a Cabinet-level department for decades. They argued that including one of the largest federal bureaucracies in the president's Cabinet was important to the nation as a whole. Proponents pointed out that the Veterans Administration (VA)—the independent agency that has overseen veterans' affairs since 1930—is involved in a range of activities that touch American society. And with an annual budget of nearly $30 billion and more than 240,000 employees, the VA is surpassed in size only by the Defense Department and U.S. Postal Service.

Furthermore, at a time of budget deficits, when federal agencies are competing ferociously for funds, many veterans' advocates said that the VA ought to be allowed a seat at the Cabinet table so that it could fight for its share of the money. Opponents argued that veterans already have plenty of friends in Congress looking out for their interests. In November 1987, President Reagan unexpectedly endorsed the idea. The weight of the endorsement, along with Congress' desire to appease a large veteran constituency during an election year, translated into success for the initiative. The new department would come into existence on March 15, 1989. President-elect George Bush would name its first secretary.

Other Legislation. In July the Senate passed judicial-review legislation for the fifth time in the past ten years. The previous four times, the legislation had died in the House Veterans' Affairs Committee. But in 1988, after pressure to move a bill was applied by high-ranking liberals in the House of Representatives, a compromise judicial-review measure passed in October. The law created a new federal court to handle veterans' appeals. It also killed a Civil War-era statute that effectively precluded veterans from hiring lawyers by capping their fees at $10. Prior to passage, the VA was the final arbiter of all disputes.

In April, Congress passed a measure establishing new health-care programs, including an outpatient entitlement, a mobile clinic pilot program, compensation for travel to and from VA medical facilities, and incentives for retention of nurses. Also enacted in 1988 was a job-training measure aimed primarily at veterans who served in the Korean and Vietnam wars and are chronically unemployed.

RICHARD COWAN, *"Congressional Quarterly"*

VIETNAM

During 1988, the death of Vietnam's premier and the election of his successor were the main political events. Most leaders of the party and government were committed to the policy of economic reform—allowing more market forces to operate and trying to attract Western capital. But they could not agree on the pace of reform, and Vietnam's economy remained weak.

Politics. Premier Pham Hung died in March and was replaced temporarily by Vo Van Kiet, a former mayor of Ho Chi Minh City, who shared the reformist views of Communist Party Chairman Nguyen Van Linh. Although the party congress in 1986 endorsed a program of liberalizing the tightly controlled economy, Linh and Kiet often met resistance from party bureaucrats and military leaders who believed that national security (and their own vested interests) dictated a much slower pace of reform.

VIETNAM • Information Highlights

Official Name: Socialist Republic of Vietnam.
Location: Southeast Asia.
Area: 127,243 sq mi (329 560 km²).
Population (mid-1988 est.): 65,200,000.
Chief Cities (1985 est.): Hanoi, the capital, 2,000,000; Ho Chi Minh City (1986 est.), 4,000,000.
Government: Communist Party secretary, Nguyen Van Linh.
Monetary Unit: Dong (18.000 dongs equal U.S.$1, July 1988).
Gross National Product (1986 U.S.$): $12,400,-000,000.

Vo Van Kiet had the misfortune of becoming acting premier just in time to be blamed for two major disasters—a serious famine in the north and runaway inflation. The Communist Party chose a conservative party functionary, Du Muoi, to be premier. But the national assembly members from Ho Chi Minh City insisted on nominating Vo Van Kiet to run against Muoi. So Vietnam had its first contested election for the position of head of the national government.

Muoi's election was assured when party chairman Linh threw his support to him. Linh may have supported Muoi in order to ensure that the conservative faction in the party helped implement the reform program.

Economics. For most Vietnamese, runaway inflation produced great hardship. Government officials, whose fixed salaries were equal to only a few dollars a month, were forced to moonlight at one or even two extra jobs to support their families. Only a small number of businessmen took advantage of the government's policy of allowing certain forms of private enterprise. Finally, despite efforts to attract Western investors, only a few minor joint ventures were begun.

Foreign Relations. The announcement that Vietnam would withdraw almost half its troops from Cambodia during 1988 and the rest during 1989 was aimed clearly at ending the economic boycott that the Western countries imposed when Vietnam invaded Cambodia in 1978. Vietnam had sought openly to end its diplomatic and economic isolation from much of the Western world. In November 1988, in a rapprochement effort with the United States, Vietnam returned 23 sets of remains thought to be those of U.S. soldiers who had lost their lives in the Vietnam War. The remains of 38 other Americans were returned in December.

The Soviet Union, which was Vietnam's main source of aid, undoubtedly influenced Vietnam's decision to leave Cambodia and improve its ties with the West. The Soviets could not afford to keep the Vietnamese economy afloat, and they were seeking to improve relations with China and the Southeast Asian nations which support a neutral Cambodia.

PETER A. POOLE
Author, "Eight Presidents and Indochina"

VIRGINIA

Virginians in 1988 approved a gambling initiative for the second year in a row, elected the state's most prominent politician to the U.S. Senate, and pioneered a breakthrough technique for convicting serious criminals.

Elections. More than 2 million Virginians went to polls in November and collectively split their tickets right down the middle. They voted solidly for the Republican presidential candidate and the Democratic Senate nominee, and elected five Republicans and five Democrats to the U.S. House of Representatives.

In a referendum question on whether the state should allow pari-mutuel gambling at horse-racing tracks, the western half of the state voted "no" and the eastern half voted "yes." The eastern half contains the state's most populous cities and counties, so pari-mutuel wagering was approved with 56% of the vote. The horse-racing vote came in the first year of the Virginia lottery.

Former Gov. Charles S. Robb, son-in-law of the late President Lyndon Johnson, took 71% of the vote in his Senate race against Republican Maurice A. Dawkins, the state's first black Senate candidate in modern history.

All ten incumbents were returned to the House of Representatives. Among them were Democrat Lewis F. Payne, Jr., of the 5th District. Payne had won a special election earlier in the year to fill the seat of Dan Daniel, who had died in January during his tenth term.

Criminal Court. Timothy Wilson Spencer was the first serial killer in the United States, and the first criminal defendant in Virginia, to be convicted through the use of DNA testing, or "genetic fingerprinting."

Spencer, who is from Arlington but was known as Richmond's "Southside Strangler," was sentenced to death twice—once in a Richmond trial and once in Arlington—for slaying two women in separate incidents. He also was charged in two other capital murder cases in the Richmond area. All of the victims were raped and strangled to death during a period in which Spencer was living in a prison halfway house in Richmond. Genetic fingerprinting matched the DNA found in semen at the murder scenes with DNA found in Spencer's blood.

The Legislature. The State General Assembly passed legislation that would make it legal for motorists to drive 65 mi/hr (105 km/hr) on 800 mi (1 287 km) of rural interstates, require truckers to cover their dangerous loads, and ensure that children will receive sex education in specially designed school classes. The so-called "family life" curriculum for public schools, which would include a sex-education program for each grade, was passed only after opponents won a mandate that parent input be allowed in each school system's program.

VIRGINIA • Information Highlights

Area: 40,767 sq mi (105 586 km²).
Population (July 1, 1987): 5,904,000.
Chief Cities (July 1, 1986 est.): Richmond, the capital, 217,700; Virginia Beach, 333,400; Norfolk, 274,800; Newport News, 161,700; Chesapeake, 134,400.
Government (1988): *Chief Officers—*governor, Gerald L. Baliles (D); lt. gov., L. Douglas Wilder (D). *General Assembly—*Senate, 40 members; House of Delegates, 100 members.
State Finances (fiscal year 1987): *Revenue,* $11,174,000,000; *expenditure,* $9,693,000,000.
Personal Income (1987): $97,515,000,000; per capita, $16,517.
Labor Force (June 1988): *Civilian labor force,* 3,170,400; *unemployed,* 120,600 (3.8% of total force).
Education: *Enrollment* (fall 1986)—public elementary schools, 673,237; public secondary, 301,898; colleges and universities, 308,318. *Public school expenditures* (1986–87), $3,466,000,000 ($3,809 per pupil).

The Assembly rubber-stamped Gov. Gerald L. Baliles' $22.5 billion budget recommendations. These included massive infusions of education aid to localities, extra funds for mental health, a housing loan fund, child-care money, and funds to continue the Chesapeake Bay cleanup.

Battlefield. President Ronald Reagan ended an eight-month battle between preservationists from across the country and Virginia developers by signing a bill allowing the federal government to seize a 542-acre (219-ha) tract of land and add it to the Manassas National Battlefield Park. The developers had wanted to build a mall on land on which two major Civil War battles had been fought. (*See* page 87.)

ED NEWLAND
"Richmond Times-Dispatch"

WASHINGTON

In 1988, Washington began a yearlong celebration of its 100th birthday, with commemorative events to continue through Nov. 11, 1989 —a century after President Benjamin Harrison signed Washington's admission into the Union.

Elections. Washington was one of the ten states that backed Democrat Michael Dukakis in November 1988. Republican Slade Gorton recaptured a seat in the U.S. Senate, narrowly defeating Democratic Congressman Mike Lowry. Gorton won the seat vacated by Republican Sen. Dan Evans, a former three-term Washington governor who left the senate after one term. Gorton had been defeated for reelection in 1986 by Democrat Brock Adams. Gov. Booth Gardner, a Democrat, won reelection to a second term, defeating Bob Williams, a Republican state representative.

State voters approved a strict new law requiring industry to pay more for cleanup of toxic wastes and turned down a more flexible

alternative, supported by the legislature, which would have allowed greater use of public funds in toxic-waste cleanups. A state law banning "exit polls" of voters at polling places by the media was declared unconstitutional by a federal appeals court prior to the election.

Economy. The Boeing Company marked a record sales year both in the number and value of commercial airplanes sold. The state's top cash crops and their estimated 1987 values were milk ($475 million), cattle and calves ($325 million), apples ($312 million), wheat ($308 million), and potatoes ($244 million).

Environment. The federal Energy Department decided not to reopen its 25-year-old, plutonium-producing N Reactor at the Hanford Nuclear Reservation in eastern Washington. Closure of the problem-plagued reactor was expected to mean the loss of 2,500 jobs. The Centers for Disease Control began a study of possibly radiation-related health problems in surrounding communities.

Crime. Stella Nickell of Auburn became the country's first person brought to trial under a new federal charge of causing a death through product tampering. In May a federal-court jury found her guilty of killing her husband and another woman by putting cyanide in capsules of a commercial pain reliever. She was sentenced to 90 years in prison.

An increase in drug-related crime in Seattle and Tacoma, blamed on an influx of gang members from Los Angeles, prompted the creation of a federal-local task force to stem the spread of street gangs.

Downtown Seattle. The $186 million Washington State Convention and Trade Center opened in June over Interstate 5 in downtown Seattle. Completion of the 55-story Washington Mutual Tower in Seattle highlighted a year which saw 1 million sq ft (92 900 m²) of office space added to the downtown area, with another 1.8 million sq ft (167 220 m²) scheduled to be ready in 1989.

WASHINGTON • Information Highlights

Area: 68,139 sq mi (176 479 km²).
Population (July 1, 1987): 4,538,000.
Chief Cities (July 1, 1986 est.): Olympia, the capital (1980 census), 27,447; Seattle, 486,200; Spokane, 172,890; Tacoma, 158,950.
Government (1988): *Chief Officers*—governor, Booth Gardner (D); lt. gov., John A. Cherberg (D). *Legislature*—Senate, 49 members; House of Representatives, 98 members.
State Finances (fiscal year 1987): *Revenue,* $11,575,000,000; *expenditure,* $9,982,000,000.
Personal Income (1987): $70,795,000,000; per capita, $15,599.
Labor Force (June 1988): *Civilian labor force,* 2,363,900; *unemployed,* 144,200 (6.1% of total force).
Education: *Enrollment* (fall 1986)—public elementary schools, 521,333; public secondary, 240,095; colleges and universities, 242,450. *Public school expenditures* (1986–87), $2,699,000,000 ($3,808 per pupil).

After 30 years of planning, debate, and legal struggles, the $250 million Westlake Center opened. The center, intended to revitalize Seattle's retail core, combines a 21-story office tower, one-acre park, and 95 retail shops.

In early September the downtown area was subjected to a three-day power outage caused by a cable fire, closing businesses and leaving residents without air conditioning in the midst of a record heat wave.

JACK BROOM, *"The Seattle Times"*

WASHINGTON, DC

In the November 1988 general election, the Democratic Party won handily in the District of Columbia, led by Democratic presidential candidate Michael S. Dukakis, who won the District's three electoral votes, receiving 83% of the votes cast. Walter E. Fauntroy (D) won reelection to a tenth term as the District's nonvoting delegate to the U.S. House of Representatives, receiving nearly three fourths of the votes cast; and incumbent Democrat John Ray won a third four-year term as at-large City Council member. The races for four ward seats also were won easily by the Democratic incumbents John A. Wilson, Charlene Drew Jarvis, H. R. Crawford, and Wilhelmina J. Rolark.

Independent William P. Lightfoot, Jr., a lawyer, won his first elected office as a citywide member of the City Council. On the nonpartisan 11-member school board, Karen Shook, a Parent Teacher Association president, narrowly ousted an incumbent to win a citywide seat. Incumbent David H. Eaton, a prominent city minister, won reelection to an at-large position, and newcomer Erika Landberg won a ward-based seat on the board.

Legislation. Congressional intervention in local legislation was evident in 1988. Congress voted to cut off all federal funds and prohibit the city from spending local tax-generated monies for abortions, except in cases where the mother's life was endangered. The Congress also directed the council to repeal the 1986 law that prohibited insurance companies from denying coverage to persons who tested positive for the AIDS virus. In addition, Congress directed the council to adopt legislation permitting nonresidents to work for the city.

The council replaced the strict residency requirement with one giving preference in hiring to city residents. Congress ordered the council to exempt religious educational institutions from the District's Human Rights Act that barred discrimination against homosexuals. The council filed suit, and a U.S. District Court judge ruled that the Congress had acted unconstitutionally.

The council voted to increase the annual salaries of its members to $69,500, and to maintain the $85,000 salary of the mayor.

© Carol M. Highsmith

The $181 million restoration of the 1907 beaux arts Union Station was completed in the fall. The building will serve as Washington's largest shopping area, with many stores, restaurants, and movie theaters, as well as a rail terminal.

Other News. James A. Hickey, the Washington Roman Catholic diocese archbishop, was named a cardinal in May.

Late in the year Washington Mayor Marion S. Barry, Jr., came under federal investigation for possible drug use, obstruction of justice, and involvement in municipal corruption. The mayor denied committing any crimes.

MORRIS J. LEVITT, *Howard University*

WEST VIRGINIA

West Virginia's citizens suffered through another year of economic misery and frustration in 1988 and vented some of their anger on election day by turning out veteran Republican Gov. Arch A. Moore, Jr., who was seeking an unprecedented fourth term. They replaced him with political newcomer Gaston Caperton, a Charleston insurance executive.

Election Results. Caperton and U.S. Sen. Robert C. Byrd led a Democratic sweep that saw the party capture all four U.S. House of Representatives seats, majorities in the state legislature, and most statewide elective offices. Five of the state's six electoral votes went to Democratic presidential candidate Michael Dukakis. One vote was cast for his running mate, Lloyd Bentsen, as a protest against the Electoral College system.

Cleve Benedict of Lewisburg, the last Republican to serve in Congress from the state (1981–83), won the secretary of agriculture post. But Glen Gainer, Jr., a leading critic of Moore's fiscal policies, was reelected as auditor, while Secretary of State Ken Hechler, Attorney General Charlie Brown, and Treasurer A. James Manchin all were unopposed.

Byrd, who never has lost an election since his entry into politics in 1946, won his sixth term in the Senate. Representatives Alan Mol-

lohan, Nick Joe Rahall, and Bob Wise, Jr., all won reelection by decisive margins, while Harley O. Staggers, Jr., was unopposed. Margaret Workman became West Virginia's first woman on the Supreme Court, and Thomas Miller was reelected to the other vacancy.

Budget and Tax Fights. The legislature adopted a "budget that pleased no one," but failed to find solutions to the state's recurrent problems of an inadequate tax base, chronic unemployment of near 9%, and a growing list of unpaid bills. Perhaps the most unpopular piece of legislation passed during 1988 was a "temporary" 1% increase in the sales tax.

Political foes waged a running battle over tax-revenue estimates and projections. Payments to county-school boards were sometimes dangerously late. The Public Employees Insurance Fund was running up to eight months behind on reimbursement to hospitals and physicians (the state's Medicare shares were so far behind that several small hospitals were considering closing). Some income-tax refunds were not received until autumn.

WEST VIRGINIA • Information Highlights

Area: 24,232 sq mi (62 760 km²).
Population (July 1, 1987): 1,897,000.
Chief Cities (1980 census): Charleston, the capital, 63,968; Huntington, 63,684; Wheeling, 43,070.
Government (1988): *Chief Officers*—governor, Arch A. Moore, Jr. (R); secy. of state, Ken Hechler (D). *Legislature*—Senate, 34 members; House of Delegates, 100 members.
State Finances (fiscal year 1987): *Revenue,* $3,965,000,000; *expenditure,* $3,884,000,000.
Personal Income (1987): $20,907,000,000; per capita, $11,020.
Labor Force (June 1988): *Civilian labor force,* 736,000; *unemployed,* 65,000 (8.8% of total force).
Education: *Enrollment* (fall 1986)—public elementary schools, 243,538; public secondary, 108,299; colleges and universities, 76,781. *Public school expenditures* (1986–87), $971,000,000 ($2,959 per pupil).

The New Legislature. The 1989 legislature promised to be especially challenging as a result of various financial emergencies left over from 1988. It also would be a legislature with more than the usual share of new faces; at least eight newcomers were elected to the 17 vacant Senate seats; and at least 38 new (out of 100) members will be seated in the House of Delegates, because incumbents retired or ran for other offices. Democrats had controlled the Senate 27-7 and the House 79-21 before the election.

The Radiotelescope Disaster. The U.S. National Radio Astronomy Observatory Telescope, located in Green Bank, WV, collapsed Nov. 15, 1988. The cause of the disaster was unknown. Built in 1962 for $850,000, the 300-ft (91-m) wide-dish antenna was instrumental in the discovery of the first pulsars. Scientists estimated that the loss would set back U.S. astronomy for several years because of its role as a "screening" device that surveyed large areas of the sky.

DONOVAN H. BOND
West Virginia University

WISCONSIN

In significant events in Wisconsin in 1988, the state elected a new U.S. senator, the city of Milwaukee chose a new mayor, and its citizens got a lottery.

Elections. When William Proxmire, U.S. senator for 31 years, announced that he would not seek another term, there was an immediate scramble among office-seekers. Proxmire, a Democrat, had prided himself on winning office without spending much money: In his 1982 reelection campaign he spent $145.10. That was not the case for his would-be successors, and the race became the costliest in state history. Making his first bid for public office, Herbert Kohl, 53-year-old multimillionare owner of the Milwaukee Bucks basketball team, set the pace. Kohl declined special-interest funds, instead spending some $6 million, largely for TV advertising. Kohl defeated such well-known figures as Anthony Earl, a former governor, and Ed Garvey, a candidate in 1986, in the Democratic primary, then went on to defeat Susan Engeleiter, GOP minority leader in the state Senate, in the general election.

Massachusetts Gov. Michael Dukakis carried the state by a 52%-48% margin over Vice-President George Bush. All incumbent U.S. representatives (5D-4R) were reelected, and the legislature remained basically the same, with a 56-43 Democratic margin in the Assembly and a 20-13 Democratic edge in the Senate.

In a notable election in Milwaukee, John Norquist, a Democratic state senator, became mayor, succeeding Henry Maier, who had held the office for 28 years. In his first major accom-

---

WISCONSIN • Information Highlights

Area: 56,153 sq mi (145 436 km²).
Population (July 1, 1987): 4,807,000.
Chief Cities (July 1, 1986 est.): Madison, the capital, 175,850; Milwaukee, 605,090; Green Bay (1980 census), 87,899.
Government (1988): *Chief Officers*—governor, Tommy G. Thompson (R); lt. gov., Scott McCallum (R). *Legislature*—Senate, 33 members; Assembly, 99 members.
State Finances (fiscal year 1987): *Revenue,* $12,167,000,000; *expenditure,* $9,427,000,000.
Personal Income (1987): $70,862,000,000; per capita, $14,742.
Labor Force (June 1988): *Civilian labor force,* 2,581,800; *unemployed,* 103,300 (4.0% of total force).
Education: *Enrollment* (fall 1986)—public elementary schools, 509,584; public secondary, 258,235; colleges and universities, 283,653. *Public school expenditures* (1986–87), $3,194,000,000 ($4,701 per pupil).

plishment, Norquist got the Common Council to agree to a city budget that cut taxes and reduced spending.

Legislative Action. Property-tax relief was the goal of two legislative sessions in the spring, but it was not achieved due to considerable wrangling between the Democratic-controlled legislature and Gov. Tommy G. Thompson, a Republican. The governor vetoed the bills passed by the legislature, and the bills sponsored by Republicans were not passed. The legislature approved two resolutions to amend the constitution to provide property-tax relief, but the measures would have to be passed during another legislative session.

Elsewhere on the agenda, lawmakers passed a measure to allow pari-mutuel betting on horse and dog racing, and the tracks were expected to be operational in the fall of 1989. The legislature also approved a bill to ban hardcore, violent pornography. Although opposed by business interests, a bill was approved to require businesses with 50 or more employees to grant workers up to six weeks of unpaid leave for the birth or adoption of a child, and two weeks to care for a sick family member.

State Lottery. After many years of debate, and with the state constitution changed by voters in a referendum, a state lottery went into effect on September 14. The lottery garnered $50 million in the first six weeks, and provided $17.5 million for property-tax relief. Under the law, half of the lottery's gross revenues must be paid back in prizes.

Economy. Growth continued with manufacturing employment expected to increase by 22,200 to 553,000 in 1988. This increase of 4.2% followed a 2.3% gain in 1987. Personal-income growth was expected to post a gain of 6%, an addition of $4.26 billion over 1987. The drought had severe ramifications on the farm economy, however, and conservative estimates indicated that farm income would be off by nearly 25%.

PAUL SALSINI, *"The Milwaukee Journal"*

Benazir Bhutto became the first woman leader of a Muslim country after her Pakistan People's Party won that nation's November 16 parliamentary elections. The 35-year-old prime minister, who gave birth to a child in September, is the daughter of late Prime Minister Zulfikar Ali Bhutto.

WOMEN

A U.S. Supreme Court ruling that opened the doors of all-male clubs to women was among several advances in equal rights in 1988. But in politics and other areas, women saw little change.

Politics. In contrast to 1984, when Geraldine Ferraro ran on the Democratic ticket as the first female U.S. vice-presidential candidate, women were not highly visible in the 1988 presidential race. Rep. Patricia Schroeder (D-CO) briefly entered the field of Democratic hopefuls but withdrew before the race picked up steam. Women, however, did play important roles as campaign managers and aides. Prominent in this group was Susan Estrich, a Harvard law professor who was campaign manager for Democratic candidate Michael Dukakis. A "gender gap" was evident in the presidential vote, with 50% of women and 57% of men choosing the victorious Republican ticket.

Two women, both Republicans, were defeated in bids for U.S. Senate seats: Susan Engeleiter in Wisconsin, and Maria M. Hustace in Hawaii. Hawaii also featured a congressional race between two women; incumbent Patricia Saiki (R) defeated Democrat Mary Bitterman. Among other incumbent representatives who retained their seats were Schroeder, Barbara Vucanovich (R-NV), and Liz Patterson (D-SC). In New York, Democratic challenger Nita Lowey defeated incumbent Joseph DioGuardi in one of the year's most expensive House races. Gov. Madeleine M. Kunin (D) of Vermont won a third term handily, while Democratic challenger Betty Cooper Hearnes failed to unseat Gov. John Ashcroft of Missouri.

For the most part, women's issues were not in the forefront of the 1988 campaign. One major exception was abortion, on which the parties split. The Republican platform included a right-to-life plank, while the Democratic stand was pro-choice. In referendums, voters in Michigan, Colorado, and Arkansas approved measures banning state funding for abortions.

Employment. U.S. Census Bureau figures showed the gap between male and female earnings closing. Women's average annual earnings rose from 59% of men's in 1979 to 64% in 1986. Analysts said that the numbers represented losses by men as well as gains by women. And with the government projecting that job growth in the 1990s would come mainly in low-paying and female-dominated clerical and service work, women's salaries were not expected to continue growing at the same pace.

Equal Rights. On June 20 the U.S. Supreme Court unanimously upheld a New York City law banning sex discrimination in many private clubs. The prestigious Century Association and three other all-male groups had challenged the law, which was aimed at clubs where members meet to "network" and do business. Entry in such clubs, the court found, amounts to a commercial opportunity and thus falls under anti-discrimination laws. But the court indicated that clubs not used for business or professional purposes might be exempted.

One group that hoped for such an exemption was the Young Women's Christian Association (YWCA), which voted on June 27 to continue to bar men from membership. The YWCA, long a champion of women's rights, faced several charges of discrimination against men. The latest involved a dispute with its Tacoma, WA, branch, which had hired a man as executive director.

In other rights issues, the U.S. Equal Opportunity Commission ruled that employers could not fire or refuse to hire women on the ground that exposure to chemicals or radiation on the job might someday cause reproductive damage. And the National Organization for Women (NOW) renewed its calls for an equal rights amendment to the U.S. Constitution. Bills on day care and parental leave, also supported by NOW and other women's groups, died in the Senate at the end of the 1988 session.

ELAINE PASCOE, *Free-Lance Writer*

WYOMING

With a population of less than half a million, Wyoming ranks as the smallest of the 50 U.S. states. Since 1980 it has experienced an out-migration of nearly 10% of its population, reflecting the sluggish condition of its mineral and energy industry. Agriculture and tourism, two other important sectors of the economy, were affected adversely in 1988 by drought conditions in northern parts of the state and by forest fires which burned through Yellowstone Park and adjoining national forests. Unprecedented in their extent and duration, the fires finally were brought under control in late October.

Legislation. The state legislature met in its 20-day budget session in February, confronting a revenue shortfall of about $100 million in funding for general operations, education, and local government. Lawmakers attacked the problem with fund transfers and a drawdown of reserves, finally approving an overall biennial appropriation (including state and federal funds) of $1.43 billion—about 3% less than Gov. Mike Sullivan (D) had requested.

Two legislative questions dominated the session. One was the legal drinking age. Among the 50 states, only Wyoming had not yet raised the age from 18 to 21. Continued failure to meet this federal mandate would cost the state an estimated $8 million in federal highway funds, but the threat to local autonomy sparked heated debate. The lure of federal dollars finally prevailed, and the drinking age was raised to 21. The other major issue facing the legislature was a 1987 ruling by the Wyoming Supreme Court that the state's multilevel property-tax system was unconstitutional. In a bipartisan action, lawmakers in 1988 passed a law to meet the court's deadline and then contrived a device by which the essentials of the existing system could be retained. The law established a flat-rate system in which all types of property would be taxed equally. The legislators then passed a constitutional amendment (approved

in the November elections) which, in effect, negated the flat-tax law and established a three-tiered system of property rates. In another action, touted as a boon to the state's mineral reserves, the legislature approved a low-interest loan of $250 million for construction of a natural-gas pipeline to California.

Politics. With about twice as many registered Republicans as Democrats, Wyoming voted overwhelmingly, 61% to 39%, for Vice-President George Bush over Gov. Michael Dukakis in the November presidential election. The U.S. senate race pitted two-term incumbent Malcolm Wallop (R) against challenger John Vinich (D) in a campaign that dominated the state media. Vinich, a state legislator for 14 years, had scored a mild upset in the primary by defeating State School Superintendent Lynn Simons and University of Wyoming law professor Peter Maxfield. In the general election, Vinich focused on local issues (jobs and economic development) and his record in the state legislature. Wallop stressed his service in the Senate and his conservative philosophy. The strong early favorite, Wallop finally won by less than one percentage point. For Wyoming's only seat in the U.S. House, incumbent Dick Cheney (R) won 68% of the vote and a sixth term in office, defeating Wheatland attorney and businessman Bryan Sharratt (D). The GOP retained control of the state legislature, 41 to 23, although the Democrats did gain three seats. The Senate remained unchanged at 19 Republicans and 11 Democrats.

H. R. DIETERICH, *University of Wyoming*

YUGOSLAVIA

In 1988, mass discontent with economic conditions and unrestrained ethnic hostilities threatened Yugoslavia with total collapse. The country had not faced such turmoil since World War II.

Domestic Affairs. More than 1 million people were unemployed, about 14% of the total population. The annual rate of inflation passed 200%, and the standard of living was 20% below the 1987 level. Labor productivity and exports sagged, and the country faced an accumulated foreign debt of about $21 billion. Workers vented their anger in widespread strikes and violent demonstrations. The government reported that there had been 1,570 strikes in 1987, involving about 350,000 people. In 1988, workers actually stormed the building of the Federal Assembly (parliament) in Belgrade.

In January 1988 the Assembly approved an optimistic economic development plan for the country that envisioned an annual increase in social product of 2%, in employment of 1%, in labor productivity of 1%, in industrial production of more than 2%, in agricultural produc-

---

WYOMING • Information Highlights

Area: 97,809 sq mi (253 326 km²).
Population (July 1, 1987): 490,000.
Chief Cities (1980 census): Cheyenne, the capital, 47,283; Casper, 51,016; Laramie, 24,410.
Government (1988): *Chief Officers*—governor, Mike Sullivan (D); secretary of state, Kathy Karpan (D). *Legislature*—Senate, 30 members; House of Representatives, 64 members.
State Finances (fiscal year 1987): *Revenue,* $1,802,000,000; *expenditure,* $1,630,000,000.
Personal Income (1987): $6,231,000,000; per capita, $12,709.
Labor Force (June 1988): *Civilian labor force,* 239,400; *unemployed,* 11,500 (4.8% of total force).
Education: *Enrollment* (fall 1986)—public elementary schools, 72,239; public secondary, 28,716; colleges and universities, 24,357. *Public school expenditures* (1986–87), $598,000,000 ($6,229 per pupil).

Ethnic tensions reached a high pitch in Yugoslavia's Kosovo autonomous province. The Belgrade government also faced widespread strikes and demonstrations over the perilous state of the nation's economy.

AP/Wide World

tion of 4%, in exports of 4.9%, and in imports of 7.6%. But in March, the government of Prime Minister Branko Mikulić barely survived a vote of no confidence brought over its economic policies by the Slovenian and Croatian representatives in the Assembly. In May the government's appeal to the International Monetary Fund (IMF) and other creditors for a rescheduling of its foreign-debt payments and a grant of additional monetary credits was successful. In return, it had to agree to a new austerity program, lifting basic price controls, freezing wages, and devaluing the dinar by 24%. But late in the year, Parliament refused to pass a law needed to ensure continued IMF support, and on December 30—for the first time since the Communist Party took over after World War II—the government resigned.

Ethnic tensions reached their highest level since 1981, primarily over the alleged mistreatment of the Serbian and Montenegrin ethnic minorities in the Kosovo autonomous province by the ethnic Albanian majority. They provoked a wave of nationalism among Yugoslavia's Serbs, numbering nearly one third of the population and led by a rising strongman, Slobodan Milosević, chief of the Serbian League of Communists. This set off nationalist reactions among Slovenes, Croats, and the Muslims of Bosnia-Herzegovina.

YUGOSLAVIA • Information Highlights

Official Name: Socialist Federal Republic of Yugoslavia.
Location: Southeastern Europe.
Area: 98,764 sq mi (255 800 km²).
Population (mid-1988 est.): 23,600,000.
Chief Cities (1981 census): Belgrade, the capital, 1,470,073; Osijek, 867,646; Zagreb, 768,700.
Government: *Head of state,* collective state presidency, Lazar Mojsov, president (took office May 1987). *Legislature*—Federal Assembly: Federal Chamber and Chamber of Republics and Provinces.
Monetary Unit: Dinar (4,095.57 dinars equal U.S.$1, Nov. 28, 1988).
Gross National Product (1986 U.S.$): $145,000,-000,000.
Economic Indexes (May 1987): *Consumer Prices* (1980 = 100), all items, 2,382.9; food, 2,454.8. *Industrial Production* (1980 = 100), 117.
Foreign Trade (1987 U.S.$): *Imports,* $12,626,-000,000; *exports,* $11,474,000,000.

From July on, hundreds of thousands of Serbs and Montenegrins took to the streets all over Yugoslavia in antigovernment and antiparty demonstrations. In October, they caused the resignation of the head of government and the entire party politburo in the autonomous province of Vojvodina and almost toppled government and party leaders in the Montenegrin republic. The federal authorities responded by sending special police units into Kosovo and arresting and trying growing numbers of ethnic Albanians for crimes of "nationalism and separatism." Many sought asylum abroad. The Communist parties of Kosovo and the republic of Macedonia ,were purged, and a number of Serbian officials were dismissed for failing to deal with the ethnic problem effectively. Some Croats and Slovenes also were arrested for disseminating antigovernmental propaganda. There were rumors of a planned military coup in Slovenia and a revival of the Fascist Ustasha movement in Croatia.

The Federal Assembly approved draft constitutional changes that would increase federal authority over the republican and provincial governments. Milosević introduced a proposal for a constitutional revision that would abolish the autonomy of Kosovo and Vojvodina and integrate them completely into the Serbian republic. An emergency session of the Central Committee of the League of Communists of Yugoslavia held in October adopted no new initiatives and proposed no new solutions; it merely voiced its approval of introducing a greater measure of free-market economics and loosening one-party control, and promised broad economic and political changes.

Foreign Affairs. In February, Belgrade hosted a conference of the foreign ministers of the six Balkan states to discuss economic integration and the establishment of a nuclear-weapon-free zone in the region. In March, Soviet leader Mikhail Gorbachev visited Yugoslavia. He officially accepted Soviet blame for the split with Yugoslavia's venerated leader, Tito, in 1948, and pledged no interference in Yugoslavia's internal affairs.

JOSEPH FREDERICK ZACEK
State University of New York at Albany

YUKON

Yukon's economy continued to grow in 1988, following a 1987 upsurge in which all sectors expanded. Forecasts for the year indicated a rate of growth much higher than the Canadian average, but below that of 1987.

Mining. Yukon's top industry produced C$440 million in minerals during 1987, a 250% increase over 1986. Gold continued to be favored by the mining industry as production increased by C$39 million to almost C$100 million. Silver more than doubled to C$40 million, while lead values increased more than fourfold to C$106 million. Zinc production increased from C$62 million in 1986 to C$197 million in 1987.

Indian Land Claims. After more than 15 years of negotiations, a "framework agreement" was initialed in July between the federal and territorial governments and the Council for Yukon Indians, representing the territory's 12 Indian bands. It is to be used as a basis for a comprehensive final agreement expected by about 1990. According to the settlement under negotiation, the Indians would receive 16,000 sq mi (41 500 km²) of land and more than C$230 million over 18 years.

Government. An early 1989 territorial election was expected to be called as the ruling socialist New Democratic party (NDP) approached its fourth year in power. Standings in the 16-seat Yukon legislature as 1988 ended included nine New Democrats, six Progressive Conservatives, and one Liberal.

Northern Accord. In the summer, the federal and territorial governments signed an Agreement in Principle on a Northern Accord that identifies the principles under which oil and gas resource management and revenues are negotiable. It provides for the phased transfer to the territorial government of legislative responsibility for managing and regulating onshore oil and gas resources, a share of those revenues, and a commitment to future sharing, as well as regulation and management of offshore northern oil and gas resources in the Beaufort Sea.

DON SAWATSKY, *Whitehorse*

ZAIRE

Zaire's economy continued in a precarious state despite reforms forced on President Mobutu Sese Seko by the International Monetary Fund in 1985. Although corruption at the highest levels was lessened and much unnecessary government spending curtailed, there was still a significant difference between income and expenditure in this potentially richest state in sub-Saharan Africa.

Domestic Affairs. Inflation increased more than 100% during 1987 and the price of consumer goods, already high, rose 35% between January and May 1988. The official rate of exchange for Zaire's currency fell continuously. During the fiscal year it had depreciated 90% relative to the U.S. dollar and 220% compared to the Belgian franc.

Mining and agriculture improved in 1988. Small-scale gold and diamond mining was worth $154.9 million for the first seven months of the year, an increase of 13% over the previous year. The sale of diamonds in August was double that of August 1987.

In the political sphere, Mobutu and his MPR party continued unchallenged in control of the state. All other parties were ineffectual and were forced to operate outside Zaire. There was a women's demonstration in Kinshasa in April 1988 but it was primarily symbolic. Mobutu continually reorganized his cabinet to deny potential rivals a power base.

Foreign Policy. President Mobutu continued his eclectic policy of dealing with states hostile to one another while attempting to act as a mediator between them. He continued to support friendly nations such as Morocco. Zaire trained commandos for Chad. Mobutu defused his most serious problem with Angola, which had charged Zaire with supporting UNITA rebels by providing bases in Zaire for the rebels and allowing the United States to fly supplies to them. Zaire signed an agreement with Angola in June 1988 to strengthen security along the 2,100-mi (3 380 km) common border. Problems with Zambia were minimized in June by the creation of a joint commission for the exchange of prisoners.

HARRY A. GAILEY, *San Jose State University*

YUKON • Information Highlights

Area: 186,660 sq mi (483 450 km²).
Population (Sept. 1988): 25,400.
Chief cities (1986 census): Whitehorse, the capital, 15,199.
Government (1988): *Chief Officers*—commissioner, J. Kenneth McKinnon; government leader, Tony Penikett (New Democratic Party). *Legislature*— 16-member Legislative Assembly.
Public Finance (1988–89 fiscal year budget est.): *Revenues,* $307,047,000; *expenditures,* $302,-280,000.
Personal Income (average weekly earnings, June 1988): $532.89.
Education (1988–89) *Enrollment*—elementary and secondary schools, 5,000 pupils.
(All dollar amounts expressed in Canadian currency)

ZAIRE • Information Highlights

Official Name: Republic of Zaire.
Location: Central equatorial Africa.
Area: 905, 564 sq mi (2 345 410 km²).
Population (mid-1988 est.): 33,300,000.
Chief City (1987 est.): Kinshasa, the capital, 2,500,000.
Government: *Head of state,* Mobutu Sese Seko, president (took office 1965). *Legislature* (unicameral)—National Legislative Council.
Monetary Unit: Zaire (200.5 zaires equal U.S.$1, July 1988).
Foreign Trade (1986 U.S.$): *Imports,* $884,000,000; *exports,* $1,092,000,000.

ZIMBABWE

In 1988, significant political realignments took place in Zimbabwe. A new government was announced on January 2 following the merger of President Robert Mugabe's ruling Zimbabwe African National Union (ZANU) and Joshua Nkomo's Zimbabwe African People's Union (ZAPU) at the end of 1987. Joshua Nkomo (who formerly was opposed to Mugabe's rule) was appointed vice-president and second secretary of the newly minted Zimbabwe African National Unity Party. Former Deputy Prime Minister Simon Muzenda was named as the other vice-president and second secretary. Bernard Chidzero was chosen as finance minister and Maurice Nyazumbo was chosen as minister in charge of political affairs.

On April 2, ZAPU held a special congress in order to ratify the agreement. At this meeting, more than 5,000 delegates voted unanimously to confirm the unity agreement. The ZAPU meeting was followed by a special congress of ZANU on April 9. It was anticipated that a unity congress of the combined two parties would be set up in the future to open the way for a one-party state. Because of the unity agreement, Mugabe controlled 99 of the 100 seats in the Zimbabwe parliament. Prior to the agreement, ZAPU had controlled 15% of the seats. As a result of the unity between the two parties, there was a significant decline in violence in the southern province of Matabeleland. For more than five years dissident followers of ZAPU had been involved in acts of sabotage and in killings because of the decline in the party's political prominence.

Early in the year, on January 21, Zimbabwe's new united parliament, nonetheless, had renewed the controversial state of emergency which gives extensive powers to the government, including the right to detain people indefinitely without trial.

Espionage. In January, five white Zimbabweans were arrested on charges of sabotage. The accused were charged with numerous acts of sabotage, which included blowing up an army munitions dump in 1981, destroying Zimbabwean aircraft at the Thornhill Air Base in 1982, bombing offices and a residence of the (South) African National Congress in 1986, and several other incidents. Under Zimbabwean law, all of the accused face the death penalty for such offenses. At the beginning of July an effort to rescue the five by South African commandoes was foiled when it was discovered that Zimbabwe security forces knew about the plan.

In another case the Zimbabwe government withdrew charges of espionage against six whites who were accused of spying for South Africa. The six had been detained in September of 1987 when one of the accused, Ivor Harding, was caught driving into Zimbabwe from South Africa with sophisticated surveillance equipment. Charges were dropped August 1 because there was insufficient evidence to convict the six. However, they remained under detention under Zimbabwe's emergency powers act. Ivor Harding had been chief secretary of the government's Post and Telecommunications Corporation, while two others had worked as engineers for the corporation.

Return of Zimbabwean Boy to Africa. Early in January the U.S. State Department asked the U.S. Supreme Court to remove an order blocking the return to Zimbabwe of a nine-year-old boy who allegedly had been beaten by his father, Floyd Karamba, a Zimbabwean diplomat to the UN in New York. In December 1987, Terrence Karamba had become the center of an intense diplomatic incident when New York child welfare officials took him into custody, charging that he was an abused child. His father had been ordered to leave the United States because of acts of child abuse. In requesting that the Supreme Court lift the stay on the return of Terrence Karamba to Zimbabwe, the State Department emphasized that delays "would pose a serious threat to the international relations of the United States." It also emphasized that the Department of Social Welfare in Zimbabwe would assign a special caseworker who would be responsible for the young Karamba. Later in the month Terrence Karamba was permitted to leave the United States and return to Zimbabwe.

Papal Visit to Zimbabwe. Zimbabwe was the first stop on Pope John Paul II's September 1988 visit to southern Africa. While in Harare, the capital city, he mentioned that Zimbabwe could become a model for all of Africa. In particular, he said that President Mugabe was unlike other Third World leaders because he had brought about ideological change without large-scale appropriations of private property. The pope also emphasized President Mugabe's policy of national reconciliation following the liberation war and praised the considerable freedom of worship allowed in Zimbabwe.

PATRICK O'MEARA, *Indiana University*

ZIMBABWE • Information Highlights

Official Name: Republic of Zimbabwe.
Location: Southern Africa.
Area: 150,803 sq mi (390 580 km²).
Population (mid-1988 est.): 9,700,000.
Chief Cities (1983 est.): Harare (formerly Salisbury), the capital, 681,000; Bulawayo, 429,000; Chitungwiza, 202,000.
Government: *Head of state and government,* Robert Mugabe, executive president (sworn in Dec. 31, 1987). *Legislature*—Parliament: Senate and House of Assembly.
Monetary Unit: Zimbabwe dollar (1.847 Z dollars equal U.S.$1, July 1988).
Economic Indexes (Nov. 1987): *Consumer Prices* (1980 = 100), all items, 262.0; food, 279.8. *Industrial Production* (1980 = 100), 116.
Foreign Trade (1986 U.S.$): *Imports,* $985,000,000; *exports,* $1,019,000,000.

ZOOS AND ZOOLOGY

Completely redesigned and rebuilt zoos opened in the hearts of two of the United States' metropolitan areas in 1988. On June 12, the New Indianapolis (IN) Zoo, constructed on 64 acres (25.9 ha) on the west bank of the White River in downtown Indianapolis, made its debut. The $64 million park displays more than 2,000 animals representing wildlife from four major regions of Earth—the waters, the plains, the temperate forests, and the deserts. The Waters Complex features the world's largest fully enclosed Whale and Dolphin Pavilion. The 74,000-sq-ft (6 880-m²) structure houses false killer and beluga whales and bottle-nosed dolphins. Also in the aquatic region are California sea lions, walruses, polar bears, puffins, and penguins; a coral reef complete with myriad colorful creatures; and an Amazon River exhibit inhabited by caimans, anacondas, and armored catfish. The Plains are roamed by giraffes, lions, baboons, elephants, zebras, and elands from Africa, as well as red kangaroos, wallabies, and emus from Australia. Siberian tigers, lesser pandas, Japanese macaques, bald eagles, and Kodiak bears inhabit the 1.5-acre (.61-ha) Temperate Forest. And the huge, acrylic-domed Desert Conservatory features giant palms and cactus, small free-ranging reptiles, and free-flying birds.

At 5.5 acres (2.23 ha), New York City's Central Park Zoo is the United States' smallest zoo. It is also the country's oldest and one of its most heavily visited. Established in 1864 by donations from well-meaning citizens and government officials, the collection was housed in 1934 in a quadrangle of brick buildings with a sea lion pool as its centerpiece. Today, nearly 125 years after the zoo's modest beginnings, most of the old outdated barred cages have been demolished and replaced. The new Central Park Zoo, now operated by the New York Zoological Society, opened on August 8. A series of naturalistic habitats display more than 450 animals of 100 species from three of the world's major climatic zones—the tropics, the temperate regions, and the polar reaches. In the Temperate Territory, the Sea Lion Pool—still the zoo's centerpiece—has been redesigned and enlarged. Now visitors can watch these playful pinnipeds swim and frolic from above and below the water. Japanese snow monkeys, lesser pandas, muntjacs (tiny deer), and river otters also live in this region. Upon entering the Tropic Zone, visitors are immersed in a dense, moist jungle of towering trees, trailing vines, colorful birds, and leaping colobus monkeys. In the Polar Circle, the Edge of the Icepack building houses chinstrap and gentoo penguins as well as tufted puffins, and outdoors are polar bears; all of these cold-adapted animals can be seen from above and below water, too.

Elsewhere, new exhibits enhanced a number of U.S. zoos. San Diego (CA) Zoo's Tiger River, which opened in the spring, focuses on tropical rain forests. It features tigers, of

The $64 million New Indianapolis Zoo, covering 64 acres (26 ha) in the city's downtown area, displays more than 2,000 animals in four general sections: the Waters Complex, below; Plains; Temperate Forest; and domed Desert Complex.

After a major face-lifting, New York City's 125-year-old Central Park Zoo—the nation's oldest—was reopened on August 8. Barred cages were replaced by naturalistic habitats representing the world's major climatic zones: tropics, temperate regions, and polar reaches.

© Melanie Stetson Freeman/"The Christian Science Monitor"

course, as well as Malayan tapirs, fishing cats, Chinese water dragons, and pythons. Also present are brilliantly colored birds such as azure-winged magpies, red-wattled lapwings, white-breasted kingfishers, and milky storks. Tiger River is part of a large reorganization project to transform the San Diego Zoo's exhibits into ten bioclimatic areas—that will take more than 15 years to complete.

Already well-known for its black-and-white killer whales and gray dolphins, Marine World Africa USA, in Vallejo, CA, added vibrant color with its spring opening of Butterfly World. Orange-and-black African monarchs, yellow western tiger swallowtails, and green malachites are among 600 butterflies flying free in a 6,000-sq-ft (558-m²) greenhouse complete with a waterfall and tropical plants and flowers. The greenhouse also features pools inhabited by carp, alligators, and snapping turtles, and a covey of button quail stalking insects.

At Zoo Atlanta (GA), Willie B., a male gorilla, had lived by himself for 27 years in a glass, concrete, and tile cage. But in June, Willie B. got a new home and some companions. The gorilla habitat now encompasses 1.5 acres (.61 ha) of rolling forested hills and hidden moats, and zoogoers are the ones confined—to enclosed walkways and platforms from which they can watch Willie B. and the other gorillas "knuckle walk," groom one another, and rest on shady knolls.

Wildlife Conservation Programs. In an effort to help save the last 3,500 black rhinos left on Earth, Wildlife Conservation International, a division of the New York Zoological Society, established the Rhino Rescue Fund. In 1970, there were an estimated 65,000 black rhinos in Africa, but hunters in search of valuable rhino horns have decimated the species. Monies collected by the fund are being used to set up new sanctuaries for black rhinos in Tanzania and Kenya; to expose the smuggling network

that ships rhino horn to Asia (where it is ground up and used in medicines); and to relocate threatened rhino populations in West Africa to refuges.

On April 29 the world's first captive-bred California condor hatched at the San Diego Wild Animal Park. Named Molloko, an Indian word for condor, the chick brings to 28 the number of California condors in existence—all of them in captivity. Efforts to save the species rest with captive-breeding programs at the Wildlife Park and at the Los Angeles Zoo. The last known wild California condor was brought into captivity in April 1987.

In a cooperative project between zoos in Indonesia and the United States, 20 pairs of Bali mynas—striking white starlings with black tail and wing tips—have been sent from ten U.S. zoos to Indonesia for a captive-breeding and release program. Offspring from these birds will be released into Barat Bali National Park on the species' native island of Bali. Only about 70 of the birds now remain in the wild. It is hoped this project will ensure the species' survival.

The Sumatran rhino hangs onto existence by a thread. Only about 800 of these prehistoric-looking creatures remain in the wild; about 700 of them are in Sumatra, where many of the animals are too isolated by habitat destruction to breed. In order to help the Indonesian government save the species on Sumatra, the Bronx, Cincinnati, Los Angeles, Miami, and San Diego zoos have formed the Sumatran Rhino Trust. The trust has mounted a capture expedition on Sumatra and has trapped three wild rhinos—all females—that will become part of a captive-breeding project. The trust hopes to acquire enough Sumatran rhinos to set up two breeding pairs in Indonesia and five pairs in North America.

DEBORAH A. BEHLER
Associate Editor, "Animal Kingdom"

Statistical and Tabular Data

NATIONS OF THE WORLD

A Profile and Synopsis of Major 1988 Developments

Nation, Region	Population in millions	Capital	Area Sq mi (km²)	Head of State/Government
Antigua and Barbuda, Caribbean	0.1	St. John's	170 (440)	Sir Wilfred E. Jacobs, governor-general Vere C. Bird, prime minister

Antigua and Barbuda joined other Caribbean island countries in expressing concern over drug trafficking in the region and appealing to the United Nations for adoption of a new international convention on drugs. Gross Domestic Product (GDP) (1985): $173 million. Foreign Trade (1986): Imports, $181 million; exports, $25 million.

Bahamas, Caribbean	0.2	Nassau	5,382 (13 940)	Sir Henry Taylor, governor-general Lynden O. Pindling, prime minister

Prime Minister Lynden O. Pindling was the subject of a U.S. grand jury investigation prompted by allegations that he had been involved in drug trafficking. Pindling dismissed the inquiry as baseless. GDP (1986): $2.1 billion. Foreign Trade (1986): Imports, $3.29 billion; exports, $2.7 billion.

Bahrain, W. Asia	0.5	Manama	239 (620)	Isa bin Sulman Al Khalifa, emir Khalifa bin Salman Al Khalifa, prime minister

Bahrain announced in January that it had uncovered a terrorist plot to blow up the country's oil facilities. Three men, an Iranian teacher and two Bahraini engineers, were arrested. Because of its strategic location, the country was granted an exception to a U.S. ban on sales of Stinger missiles in the Persian Gulf region. GDP (1987 est.): $3.77 billion. Foreign Trade (1987): Imports, $2.42 billion; exports, $2.05 billion.

Barbados, Caribbean	0.3	Bridgetown	166 (430)	Sir Hugh Springer, governor-general Erskine Sandiford, prime minister

At a January meeting of the Caribbean Community and Common Market in Bridgetown, Barbados joined other Caribbean nations in criticizing the Haitian government for thwarting democratic elections late in 1987. The CARICOM members declined, however, to impose sanctions against Haiti, which is not a member of the group. GDP (1986): $1.23 billion. Foreign Trade (1987): Imports, $515 million; exports, $156 million.

Benin, W. Africa	4.5	Porto Novo	43,483 (112 620)	Mathieu Kérékou, president

The United States accused Benin of allowing Libyan terrorists to use its territory as a base for their activities. The U.S. protests followed the February 20 arrest of Libyan agents who had flown from Benin to Senegal carrying explosives. In May, President Kérékou was reported to have contracted to accept French nuclear waste, which was to be buried near the village of a leading opposition figure. The contract was canceled when publicity raised a furor. Gross National Product (GNP) (1986 est.): $1.4 billion. Foreign Trade (1986): Imports, $329 million; exports, $131 million.

Bhutan, S. Asia	1.5	Thimphu	18,147 (47 000)	Jigme Singe Wangchuck, king

In November, Bhutanese celebrated the official wedding of King Jigme Singe Wangchuck and his four wives, who in fact had been married privately for the preceding nine years. At the same ceremony, eight-year-old Prince Jigme Gesar Namgyal Wangchuck officially was named crown prince. The purchase of the country's first passenger jet in November was expected to improve tourism and communication with the outside world. GDP (fiscal year 1986): $300 million. Foreign Trade (fiscal year 1985): Imports, $69.4 million; exports, $15.1 million.

Botswana, S. Africa	1.3	Gaborone	231,803 (600 370)	Quett Masire, president

In a raid on a suburb of Gaborone March 28, South African troops killed four persons it said were terrorists belonging to the African National Congress. Botswana protested the attack. In June, two South African soldiers were captured in a second, unsuccessful raid. President Masire received minor injuries when an engine on his plane exploded during a flight to Luanda, Angola, in August. The plane made an emergency landing in central Angola. In September, Pope John Paul II visited Gaborone. Foreign Trade (1985): Imports, $535 million; exports, $653 million.

Brunei, S.E. Asia	0.3	Bandar Seri Begawan	2,228 (5 770)	Sir Muda Hassanal Bolkiah, sultan and prime minister

Two leaders of a small political party, which had been formed at the government's instigation, were arrested in March after they criticized the government and called for parliamentary democracy. The party was dissolved. Ten days of celebrations marked the Sultan's 42nd birthday on July 15. GDP (1986): $2.94 billion. Foreign Trade (1985): Imports, $615 million; exports, $2.97 billion.

Burkina Faso, W. Africa	8.5	Ouagadougou	105,869 (274 200)	Blaise Compaoré, president

A major contribution to the economy came from the more than 1 million Burkina Faso citizens who continued to work abroad in Ghana and Ivory Coast in 1988. Burkina Faso worked with the World Bank in an effort to iron out financial difficulties, including the cost of operating its main rail link to the African coast. As a result of a dispute with Ivory Coast, the country was forced early in 1988 to assume full control of its leg of the railway, which had been operated jointly by the two countries. GDP (1985): $1.2 billion. Foreign Trade (1986): Imports, $405 million; exports, $83 million.

Burundi, E. Africa	5.2	Bujumbura	10,745 (27 830)	Pierre Buyoya, president

In August an outbreak of violence between the Tutsi, who control the government, and the Hutu, who form the majority of Burundi's citizens, left 5,000 people dead. Most of the violence was concentrated in the northern hill country. Reports indicated that the Hutu may have begun the killing after hearing rumors that the largely Tutsi army intended to conduct a pogrom against them; there were also reports, denied by the government, that army troops sent to restore order killed hundreds of Hutu in reprisals. More than 35,000 Hutu were said to have fled to neighboring Rwanda. GDP (1986 est): $1.33 billion. Foreign Trade (1987): Imports, $212 million; exports, $86 million.

Cameroon, Cen. Africa	10.5	Yaoundé	183,568 (475 440)	Paul Biya, president

President Biya, running unopposed, was reelected on April 29. Voter turnout was lower and there were more blank ballots cast than in the previous election, in 1984. Biya announced several new economic programs after the election. Sixty students were killed in December when a stampede occurred in a school building, triggered by rumors the building was about to collapse. GDP (fiscal year 1987 est.): $12.6 billion. Foreign Trade (1987): Imports, $1.75 billion; exports, $829 million.

Nation, Region	Population in millions	Capital	Area Sq mi (km²)	Head of State/Government
Cape Verde, W. Africa	0.3	Praia	1,556 (4 030)	Aristides Pereira, president Pedro Pires, prime minister

Along with many other countries of North and West Africa, Cape Verde was threatened by the worst infestation of locusts to appear in the region in 30 years. Foreign Trade (1985): Imports, $59.1 million; exports, $3 million.

Central African Republic, Cen. Africa	2.8	Bangui	240,533 (622 980)	André-Dieudonne Kolingba, president of the Military Committee for National Recovery

The death sentence of former self-proclaimed emperor Jean-Bedel Bokassa, who was convicted of murder and theft in 1987, was commuted in February to life imprisonment in solitary confinement. In August, President Kolingba ordered an investigation into charges that government officials had agreed to permit the dumping of European industrial and pharmaceutical wastes in Central African Republic in exchange for a $500,000 fee. GDP (1984): $764 million. Foreign Trade (1986): Imports, $252 million; exports, $131 million.

Comoros, E. Africa	0.4	Moroni	838 (2 170)	Ahmed Abdallah Abderemane, president

Comoros was among several small African nations that were reported to have established trade and other links with South Africa, where the white government was seeking ways to evade the effects of any sanctions that larger nations might impose against it. The country established formal diplomatic relations with the Seychelles in June. GNP (1986 est.): $163 million. Foreign Trade (1986): Imports, $42 million; exports, $22.8 million.

Congo, Cen. Africa	2.2	Brazzaville	132,046 (342 000)	Denis Sassou-Nguesso, president Ange Edouard Poungui, prime minister

A furor broke out over a plan to allow European toxic wastes to be stored in the scenic Diosso Gorge, near the port of Pointe Noire. In July, Congo canceled contract negotiations in the matter and dismissed two government ministers who were responsible for the plan. Security forces put down a rebellion and killed its leader, Pierre Anga, on July 4. Anga had been close to former President Joachim Yhomby-Opango, who remained under house arrest. GDP (1984): $1.8 billion. Foreign Trade (1985): Imports, $751 million; exports, $1.08 billion.

Djibouti, E. Africa	0.3	Djibouti	8,494 (22 000)	Hassan Gouled Aptidon, president Barkat Gourad Hamadou, premier

GDP (1986): $333 million. Foreign Trade (1986): Imports, $197 million; exports, $96 million.

Dominica, Caribbean	0.1	Roseau	290 (750)	Clarence A. Seignoret, president Mary Eugenia Charles, prime minister

In March, the House of Assembly ratified a tax information exchange agreement with the United States, giving the United States easier access to Dominica's records. The Dominica Labor Party had opposed the agreement. GDP (1986 est.): $91 million. Foreign Trade (1985): Imports, $57 million; exports, $28.4 million.

Dominican Republic, Caribbean	6.9	Santo Domingo	18,815 (48 730)	Joaquin Balaguer, president

Sharp increases in the cost of living touched off strikes and demonstrations in February. Labor groups described as inadequate the government's decision to raise the minimum wage 33%. In other news, Defense Secretary Maj. Gen. Antonio Imbert Barera was dismissed June 17 following rumors that the armed forces intended to stage a coup. Elias Wessin y Wessin, a retired general, was named in his stead. In August the government closed 36 private financial companies that were threatened with failure and took over administration of their assets. GDP (1986 est.): $5.6 billion. Foreign Trade (1987): Imports, $1.51 billion; exports, $718 million.

Equatorial Guinea, Cen. Africa	0.3	Malabo	10,830 (28 050)	Teodoro Obiang Nguema Mbasogo, president Cristino Seriche Bioko, premier

In an effort to lessen involvement with its former colony, Spain arranged in February to withdraw from Equatorial Guinea's national bank. GNP (1986): $75 million. Foreign Trade (1982): Imports, $41.5 million; exports, $16.9 million.

Fiji, Oceania	0.7	Suva	7,054 (18 270)	Sir Penaia Ganilau, president Sir Kamisese Mara, prime minister

With civilian rule nominally restored after his 1987 coup, Col. Sitiveni Rabuka continued to hold considerable power as military commander and home affairs minister. France restored aid to Fiji, and the country moved toward establishing better relations with Britain, Australia, and other countries. Australia's discovery of an illegal shipment of arms bound for Fiji led the Fijian government to arrest 22 people, mostly of Indian descent, and to impose emergency restrictions that were lifted in November. GDP (1986): $1.18 billion. Foreign Trade (1987): Imports, $379 million; exports, $307 million.

Gabon, Cen. Africa	1.3	Libreville	103,348 (267 670)	El Hadj Omar Bongo, president Léon Mébiame, premier

In June, some 3,500 people from neighboring countries were arrested as illegal immigrants. GNP (1986): $3.3 billion. Foreign Trade (1985): Imports, $976 million; exports, $1.97 billion.

Gambia, W. Africa	0.8	Banjul	4,363 (11 300)	Sir Dawda Kairaba Jawara, president

A coup plot was discovered in late January, and 20 people were arrested. In June, three were convicted of plotting against the government, and officials alleged that Libya had been involved. Gambia also adopted heavy penalties for people convicted of illegally importing toxic wastes. GDP (1985): $125 million. Foreign Trade (1986): Imports, $100 million; exports, $35 million.

Ghana, W. Africa	14.4	Accra	92,100 (238 540)	Jerry Rawlings, chairman of the Provisional National Defense Council

In an effort to block the illegal entry of toxic wastes, Ghana formed a task force of chemical experts to assist customs officials. The nation launched a major project to improve its cocoa production, Ghana's major source of foreign-exchange earnings. In June three men were convicted of a plot to overthrow the government. GNP (1986 est.): $5.7 billion. Foreign Trade (1986): Imports, $783 million; exports, $862 million.

Grenada, Caribbean	0.1	St. George's	131 (340)	Sir Paul Scoon, governor-general Herbert A. Blaize, prime minister

Grenada faced political and economic difficulties, with the ruling coalition headed by Herbert Blaize increasingly torn by dissension and with tourism and exports of nutmeg falling below expectations. Appeals dragged on in the case of 17 leftists convicted of killing former Prime Minister Maurice Bishop. Elections were expected early in 1989. GDP (1986): $129 million. Foreign Trade (1986): Imports, $83 million; exports, $28 million.

Nation, Region	Population in millions	Capital	Area Sq mi (km²)	Head of State/Government
Guinea, W. Africa	6.9	Conakry	94,927 (245 860)	Lansana Conté, president

The country adopted strict penalties for people convicted of illegally importing toxic wastes. President Conté reshuffled his cabinet in February. Nine state secretariats were abolished and seven new or reconstituted ministries were created. GNP (1986): $1.7 billion. Foreign Trade (1986 est.): Imports, $511 million; exports, $538 million.

Guinea-Bissau, W. Africa	0.9	Bissau	13,946 (36 120)	João Bernardo Vieira, president

A plan to import European toxic wastes was canceled after international aid workers leaked copies of the contract and the public reacted strongly against the proposal. GDP (1984): $190 million.

Guyana, N.E. South America	0.8	Georgetown	83,000 (214 970)	Desmond Hoyte, president Hamilton Green, prime minister

GDP (1986): $519 million. Foreign Trade (1985): Imports, $255 million; exports, $207 million.

Ivory Coast, W. Africa	11.2	Yamoussoukro	124,502 (322 460)	Félix Houphouët-Boigny, president

Ivory Coast, the world's leading cocoa producer, attempted to bolster falling cocoa prices by announcing that it would not sell its 1988 crop for less than $2 a kilogram, about 50 cents higher than the prevalent market price. As a result, cocoa sales were late and low, and the country missed payments on its foreign debt. South African President P. W. Botha visited Ivory Coast in October. Ivory Coast adopted strict laws governing the disposal of toxic wastes. GDP (1987): $10.4 billion. Foreign Trade (1986): Imports, $2.05 billion; exports, $3.33 billion.

Jamaica, Caribbean	2.5	Kingston	4,243 (10 990)	Florizel Glasspole, governor-general Edward Seaga, prime minister

(See page 169.) GDP (1986): $2.4 billion. Foreign Trade (1987): Imports, $1.21 billion; exports, $657 million.

Kiribati, Oceania	0.06	Tarawa	277 (717)	Ieremia Tabai, president

GDP (1985): $20 million. Foreign Trade: Imports (1986), $11.7 million; exports, $1.4 million.

Lesotho, S. Africa	1.6	Maseru	11,718 (30 350)	Moshoeshoe II, king Justin Lekhanya, chairman, council of ministers

The visit of Pope John Paul II to Maseru on Sept. 14 prompted a terrorist incident in which a group of antigovernment rebels hijacked a bus and held 69 Roman Catholic pilgrims aboard hostage, demanding to see the pope and King Moshoeshoe II. A South African antiterrorist squad stormed the bus; three of the terrorists and one hostage were killed and 11 other hostages were wounded in the fight. GDP (1985): $247 million. Foreign Trade (1986): Imports, $343 million; exports, $325 million, including remittances from Lesotho workers in South Africa.

Liberia, W. Africa	2.5	Monrovia	43,000 (111 370)	Samuel K. Doe, president

Two U.S. businessmen were arrested in July and accused of plotting with J. Nicholas Podier, a former Liberian official, to overthrow President Doe. Podier reportedly was shot; the Americans were charged with treason in September, although they were not Liberian citizens. In another case, ten people, including former presidential candidate Gabriel Kpollah, were convicted in October of plotting to overthrow the government. Four others also charged in the alleged plot remained at large. GDP (1986): $711 million. Foreign Trade (1986): Imports, $259 million; exports, $408 million.

Liechtenstein, Cen. Europe	0.03	Vaduz	62 (160)	Franz Josef II, prince Hans Brunhart, prime minister

On July 26, Liechtenstein marked the 50th year of Prince Franz Josef's rule.

Luxembourg, W. Europe	0.4	Luxembourg	998 (2 586)	Jean, grand duke Jacques Santer, prime minister

GNP (1986): $4.6 billion. (Luxembourg's foreign trade is recorded with Belgium's.)

Madagascar, E. Africa	10.9	Antananarivo	226,656 (587 040)	Didier Ratsiraka, head of government Victor Ramahatra, premier

An epidemic of malaria in the rural highlands killed some 100,000 people and prompted aid from various countries. The disease added to Madagascar's economic problems, which included widespread deforestation. Former Minister of Public Works Victor Ramahatra was appointed premier after Desire Rakotoarijaona retired in February, citing poor health. The change was thought to be an attempt to ease domestic discontent. Some 245 members of an underground kung fu organization were tried on internal security charges; on March 5, 18 were sentenced to prison, ten were given suspended sentences, and the rest were acquitted. The group had been broken up and its leader killed in 1985. GDP (1986): $2.7 billion. Foreign Trade (1986): Imports, $353 million; exports, $304 million.

Malawi, E. Africa	7.7	Lilongwe	45,745 (118 480)	Hastings Kamuzu Banda, president

Social services in Malawi were stressed by the presence of more than 600,000 refugees from civil war in neighboring Mozambique. The country also faced a drought and an infestation of mealybugs, which damaged cassava crops. GDP (1986): $1.23 billion. Foreign Trade (1987): Imports, $296 million; exports, $276 million.

Maldives, S. Asia	0.2	Male	116 (300)	Maumoon Abdul Gayoom, president

A November 3 coup attempt staged by Tamil mercenaries and rebels was put down with the help of Indian troops. About 30 people were killed in the fighting, and 70 mercenaries were captured. President Gayoom was reelected for a third term on September 26, having run unopposed. The country prospered from tourism but faced a shortage of fresh water and danger from ocean flooding. Foreign Trade (1986): Imports, $52 million; exports, $22.5 million.

Mali, W. Africa	8.7	Bamako	478,764 (1 240 000)	Moussa Traoré, president

Agriculture and forest preservation programs were threatened by a severe outbreak of locusts. President Traoré was named chairman of the Organization of African Unity (OAU) on May 24 and made a state visit to the United States in October. GDP (1985): $1.1 billion. Foreign Trade (1987): Imports, $476 million; exports, $260 million.

Malta, S. Europe	0.4	Valletta	124 (320)	Paul Xuereb, president Eddie Fenech Adami, prime minister

GDP (1986): $1.5 billion. Foreign Trade (1987): Imports, $1.14 billion; exports, $603 million.

Mauritania, W. Africa	2.1	Nouakchott	397,954 (1 030 700)	Maaouiya Ould Sid Ahmed Taya, president and prime minister

Multicandidate elections for local councils were held for the first time since independence. Mauritania was threatened by the worst infestation of locusts in 30 years. Foreign Trade (1987): Imports, $382 million; exports, $428 million.

Nation, Region	Population in millions	Capital	Area Sq mi (km²)	Head of State/Government
Mauritius, E. Africa	1.1	Port Louis	718 (1 860)	Sir Veerasamy Ringadoo, governor-general Anerood Jugnauth, prime minister

Led by clothing manufacturing, the country's diversified economy continued to grow, and Mauritius relaxed exchange controls and made plans to open a stock market in an effort to attract more capital. Economic links to South Africa brought sharp criticism from other African nations, prompting the Mauritian representative to walk out of an OAU meeting in May. GDP (fiscal year 1987): $1.5 billion. Foreign Trade (1986): Imports, $675 million; exports, $675 million.

Monaco, S. Europe	0.03	Monaco-Ville	0.7 (1.9)	Rainier III, prince M. Jean Ausseil, minister of state

In elections on January 24, all 18 seats in the National Council went to the National and Democratic Union.

Mongolia, E. Asia	2.0	Ulan Bator	604,247 (1 565 000)	Jambyn Batmonh, chairman of the Presidium Dumaagiyn Sodnom, chairman, Council of Ministers

Nauru, Oceania	0.008	Nauru	8 (20)	Hammer DeRoburt, president

GNP (1985): $160 million. Foreign Trade (1984): Imports, $73 million; exports, $93 million.

Nepal, S. Asia	18.3	Katmandu	54,363 (140 800)	Birendra Bir Bikram, king Marich Man Singh Shrestha, prime minister

On August 20, a severe earthquake in the eastern part of the country killed more than 700 people and destroyed almost 18,000 buildings. Earlier in the year, on March 13, more than 90 people were killed in a stampede at a soccer game in Katmandu. GDP (fiscal 1987): $2.4 billion. Foreign Trade (fiscal year 1987): Imports, $365 million; exports, $130 million.

Niger, W. Africa	7.2	Niamey	489,189 (1 267 000)	Ali Saibou, president Mamane Oumarou, prime minister

In an extensive reshuffling of the cabinet in mid-July, Prime Minister Hamid Algabid was replaced by Mamane Oumarou. Niger received offers to store European chemical wastes. The country also shared a regional threat from locusts. GDP (1985 est.): $1.2 billion. Foreign Trade (1985): Imports, $309.4 million; exports, $250.6 million.

Oman, W. Asia	1.4	Muscat	82,031 (212 460)	Qaboos bin Said, sultan and prime minister

GDP (1986 est.): $7.5 billion. Foreign Trade (1986): Imports, $2.6 billion; exports, $2.8 billion.

Papua New Guinea, Oceania	3.7	Port Moresby	178,259 (461 690)	Sir Kingsford Dibela, governor-general Rabbie Namaliu, prime minister

Prime Minister Paias Wingti's government fell in July on a vote of no confidence in parliament, and Rabbie Namaliu formed a new coalition government, becoming the country's fourth prime minister since independence in 1975. He promised constitutional reforms that would make such changes less frequent. After Indonesian troops were reported to have crossed into Papua New Guinea from Irian Jaya in pursuit of rebels of the Free Papua Movement, Foreign Minister Michael Somare went to Jakarta in November for talks on the border situation. GDP (1985): $2.4 billion. Foreign Trade (1986): Imports, $931 million; exports, $1.05 billion.

Qatar, W. Asia	0.4	Doha	4,247 (11 000)	Khalifa bin Hamad Al Thani, emir and prime minister

Seeking to match the military buildup of its neighbor Bahrain, Qatar reportedly made a secret purchase of 13 U.S.-made Stinger missiles from Iran. GDP (1987): $5.4 billion. Foreign Trade (1987): Imports, $890 million; exports, $1.9 billion.

Rwanda, E. Africa	7.1	Kigali	10,170 (26 340)	Juvénal Habyarimana, president

More than 35,000 Hutu refugees were reported to have fled to Rwanda to escape intertribal violence in neighboring Burundi. GDP (1985 est.): $1.84 billion. Foreign Trade (1987): Imports, $353 million; exports, $113 million.

Saint Christopher and Nevis, Caribbean	0.04	Basseterre	139 (360)	C. A. Arrindell, governor-general Kennedy A. Simmonds, prime minister

GDP (1986 est.): $70 million. Foreign Trade (1986): Imports, $63.4 million; exports, $33.5 million.

Saint Lucia, Caribbean	0.1	Castries	239 (620)	Sir Vincent Floissac, governor-general John Compton, prime minister

Tourism and banana exports helped St. Lucia achieve an economic performance that was above average among the Caribbean island states. GDP (1986): $158 million. Foreign Trade (1986): Imports, $141 million; exports, $24.3 million.

Saint Vincent and the Grenadines, Caribbean	0.1	Kingstown	131 (340)	Henry Williams, acting governor-general James F. Mitchell, prime minister

GDP (1986 est.): $95 million. Foreign Trade (1986): Imports, $87 million; exports, $68 million.

San Marino, S. Europe	0.023	San Marino	23 (60)	Co-regents appointed semi-annually

São Tomé and Principe, W. Africa	0.1	São Tomé	371 (960)	Manuel Pinto da Costa, president Celestino Rocha da Costa, prime minister

A new government was formed January 29, with Celestino Rocha da Costa taking the post of prime minister. About 40 rebels invaded São Tomé by canoe March 8 but failed in their attempt to overthrow the government. The country continued to move away from its previous socialist stance, forming ties with Western countries and increasing private control of agriculture. GDP (1986 est.): $37.7 million. Foreign Trade (1986 est.): Imports, $2.6 million; exports, $9.8 million.

Senegal, W. Africa	7.0	Dakar	75,749 (196 190)	Abdou Diouf, president

President Diouf was reelected February 28 in an election that also saw one fifth of the seats in parliament going to various opposition groups. Street riots broke out when charges of fraud circulated after the vote, and 13 people, including opposition leader Abdoulaye Wade, were arrested in connection with the violence. The government continued a program of economic austerity and reform. Ties with Libya, broken in 1980, were restored in November.

Nation, Region	Population in millions	Capital	Area Sq mi (km²)	Head of State/Government
Seychelles, E. Africa	0.1	Victoria	176 (455)	France Albert René, president

Seychelles established formal diplomatic relations with Mauritius and Comoros in late June. The move was intended to cement good relations and improve cooperation between the countries.

Sierra Leone, W. Africa	4.0	Freetown	27,699 (71 740)	Joseph Momoh, president

GDP (fiscal year 1987): $965 million. Foreign Trade (1987): Imports, $137 million; exports, $132 million.

Solomon Islands, Oceania	0.3	Honiara	10,985 (28 450)	Sir Baddeley Devesi, governor-general Ezekiel Alebua, prime minister

GDP (1986): $115 million. Foreign Trade (1986): Imports, $59 million; exports, $65 million.

Somalia, E. Africa	8.0	Mogadishu	246,200 (637 660)	Mohamed Siad Barre, president

In April, Ethiopia and Somalia agreed to settle their border dispute and end support for rebels in both countries. However, as Somali rebels who had been based in Ethiopia returned home, widespread fighting broke out in the northern regions during the summer. More than 300,000 Somalis fled to Ethiopia to escape the violence.

Suriname, S. America	0.4	Paramaribo	63,039 (163 270)	Ramsewak Shankar, president Henck Arron, vice-president and prime minister

On January 12, the National Assembly elected Ramsewak Shankar as president and former premier Henck Aaron as vice-president. However, Lt. Col. Desire Bouterse, who had overthrown the government in 1980 and since then headed a military government, was expected to retain much power. With the return to civilian rule, the country sought improved relations with the Netherlands and the United States. GDP (1986): $904 million.

Swaziland, S. Africa	0.7	Mbabane	6,703 (17 360)	Mswati III, king

Pope John Paul II visited Swaziland in September on a tour of southern African nations. GDP (1986 est.): $478 million.

Togo, W. Africa	3.3	Lomé	21,927 (56 790)	Gnassingbé Eyadéma, president

Tonga, Oceania	0.1	Nuku'alofa	270 (700)	Taufa'ahau Tupou IV, king Prince Fatafehi Tu'ipelehake, premier

GDP (1985): $100 million. Foreign Trade (1986): Imports, $40 million; exports, $6 million.

Trinidad and Tobago, Caribbean	1.3	Port-of-Spain	1,981 (5 130)	Noor Hassanali, president Arthur Robinson, prime minister

Declines in oil output and prices prompted the government to adopt an austerity budget and pledge to cut its work force by 15%. Prime Minister Robinson survived a no-confidence vote in parliament on May 2. GDP (1986): $5 billion. Foreign Trade (1987): Imports, $1.22 billion; exports, $1.46 billion.

Tuvalu, Oceania	0.008	Funafuti	10 (26)	Sir Tupua Leupena, governor-general Tomasi Puapua, prime minister

Tuvalu's public transportation system, consisting of a single aged ship which linked the eight islands, was expected to improve with the arrival of a new ship, purchased by Britain.

United Arab Emirates, W. Asia	1.5	Abu Dhabi	32,278 (83 600)	Zayid bin Sultan Al Nuhayyan, president Rashid bin Sa'id Al Maktum, prime minister

An offshore oil facility owned by the United Arab Emirates was raided by Iranian gunboats in April, as part of the wider conflict in the Persian Gulf. GNP (1987 est.): $22 billion.

Vatican City, S. Europe	0.001	Vatican City	0.17 (0.438)	John Paul II, pope

In October, the Vatican announced that it had posted a record deficit of $63.8 million in 1987.

Vanuatu, Oceania	0.2	Port-Vila	5,699 (14 760)	George Ati Sokomanu, president Walter Lini, prime minister

Prime Minister Lini expelled the opposition from parliament in July. Five opposition leaders, including Barak Sope, Lini's chief rival, were dismissed on July 25 on charges that they had incited antigovernment riots in May; the riots had begun as a protest over land policy. The remaining 18 opposition members were dismissed three days later for failing to appear in the legislature. The country's supreme court upheld the legality of the action. Lini, meanwhile, was said to be recovering from a stroke. A government power struggle broke out in December but Lini said he would not yield power. GDP (1986): $84 million. Foreign Trade (1987): Imports, $70 million; exports, $18 million.

Western Samoa, Oceania	0.2	Apia	1,104 (2 860)	Malietoa Tanumafili II, head of state Tofilau Eti, prime minister

General elections February 26 resulted in a close vote, with Prime Minister Vaai Kolone the apparent victor. However, while a recount was in progress, Kolone's coalition chose Tofilau Eti as leader in his place. Eti formed a new government in April. GDP (1986 est.): $102 million. Foreign Trade (1986): Imports, $43 million; exports, $10.5 million.

Yemen, North, S. Asia	6.7	San'a	75,290 (195 000)	Ali Abdallah Salih, president Abdel Aziz Abd al-Ghani, prime minister

North Yemen joined the ranks of oil-producing countries with exports that reached 175,000 barrels a day in mid-1988. On July 5, the country held its first elections for a new 159-seat legislative council (31 members were appointed by the president). The council elected President Salih to his third five-year term on July 17. GDP (1986): $3.2 billion. Foreign Trade (1986): Imports, $1.12 billion; exports, $8 million.

Yemen, South, S. Asia	2.4	Aden	128,560 (332 970)	Haydar Abu Bakr al-Attas, president

South Yemen was one of six nations listed by the U.S. State Department as supporting international terrorism. Relations with North Yemen remained strained. Foreign Trade (1986): Imports, $483 million; exports, $29 million.

Zambia, E. Africa	7.5	Lusaka	290,583 (752 610)	Kenneth David Kaunda, president K. Musokotwane, prime minister

President Kaunda was reelected on October 26, having run unopposed as the candidate of the country's only political party. Nine persons were detained for alleged subversive activities in the weeks before the election. GDP (1986 est.): $2.1 billion. Foreign Trade (1986): Imports, $581 million; exports, $461 million.

WORLD MINERAL AND METAL PRODUCTION

ALUMINUM, primary smelter (thousand metric tons)

	1986	1987
United States	3,037	3,343
USSR[e]	2,300	2,400
Canada	1,364	1,540
Australia	882	1,024
Brazil	758	844
West Germany	765	738
Norway	712	725
China[e]	510	540
Venezuela	423	440
Spain	350	341
France	322	323
United Kingdom	276	297
Netherlands	266	269
India	257	253
Other countries[a]	3,218	3,130
Total	15,440	16,207

ANTIMONY, mine[b] (metric tons)

	1986	1987
China[e]	18,000	20,000
Bolivia	10,243	10,635
USSR	9,500	9,600
South Africa	6,816	6,299
Canada	3,805	3,575
Mexico	3,337	2,839
Turkey	1,978	1,451
Guatemala	1,898	1,405
Thailand	1,019	1,300
Australia	1,131	1,228
Czechoslovakia[e]	1,000	1,000
Other countries[a]	3,831	3,865
Total	62,558	63,197

ASBESTOS[c] (thousand metric tons)

	1986	1987
USSR[e]	2,400	2,400
Canada	662	660[e]
Brazil	204	210[e]
Zimbabwe	164	164[e]
China[e]	150	150
South Africa	139	135
Italy	115	120
Other countries[a]	216	215
Total	4,050	4,054

BARITE[c] (thousand metric tons)

	1986	1987
China[e]	1,000	1,000
USSR[e]	540	540
United States	269	406
Mexico	321	404
India	344	270
Turkey[e]	175	175
Brazil[e]	150	150
Ireland	128	150
Other countries[a]	1,798	1,567
Total	4,725	4,662

BAUXITE[d] (thousand metric tons)

	1986	1987
Australia	32,384	34,206
Guinea	12,130	13,400[e]
Jamaica	6,944	7,775
Brazil	6,544	7,250[e]
USSR[e]	6,185	6,188
Yugoslavia	3,459	3,394
Hungary	3,022	3,101
Guyana	2,600	2,785
China[e]	2,650	2,750
India	2,322	2,685
Suriname	3,847	2,581
Greece	2,230	2,472
Sierra Leone	1,242	1,390
France	1,379	1,271
Other countries[a]	2,875	3,236
Total	89,813	94,484

CEMENT[c] (thousand metric tons)

	1986	1987
China	161,560	179,868
USSR	135,119	137,400
United States	72,499	72,122
Japan	71,246	71,604
India	36,400	36,980
Italy	35,340	35,748
South Korea	23,403	25,662
Brazil	25,297	25,470
West Germany	26,580	25,248
France	21,588	23,560
Spain	22,008	23,016
Mexico	19,751	21,996
Turkey	20,004	21,980
Other countries[a]	324,981	336,734
Total	995,776	1,037,388

CHROMITE[c] (thousand metric tons)

	1986	1987
South Africa	3,907	3,789
USSR[e]	3,150	3,150
Albania	850	830
Finland	678	710[e]
Turkey	543	600[e]
Zimbabwe	533	540[e]
India	616	520
Brazil[e]	200	225
Philippines	183	173
Other countries[a]	521	545
Total	11,181	11,082

COAL, anthracite and bituminous[c] (million metric tons)

	1986	1987
China	870	920
United States	739	760
USSR	588	595
Poland	192	193
India	171	186
Australia	170	176
South Africa	175	175
United Kingdom	112	107
West Germany	87	82
Canada	58	60
North Korea	48	55
Other countries[a]	182	187
Total	3,392	3,496

COAL, lignite[c][f] (million metric tons)

	1986	1987
East Germany	311	309
USSR	163	165
West Germany	114	109
Czechoslovakia	101	101
Poland	67	73
United States	67	70
Yugoslavia	68	60
Australia	38	38
Other countries[a]	233	234
Total	1,162	1,159

COPPER, mine[b] (thousand metric tons)

	1986	1987
Chile	1,399	1,418
United States	1,147	1,256
Canada	699	767
USSR[e]	620	630
Zambia	513	527
Zaire	503	500
Poland	434	437
Peru	397	392
China[e]	220	260
Mexico	182	247
Australia	248	238
Papua New Guinea	178	218
Philippines	223	215
South Africa	203	194
Other countries[a]	1,104	1,072
Total	8,070	8,371

COPPER, refined, primary and secondary (thousand metric tons)

	1986	1987
United States	1,480	1,561
USSR[e]	975	987
Japan	943	980
Chile	942	945
Zambia	487	509
Canada	493	491
Belgium	413	407
West Germany	422	400
China[e]	350	400
Poland	388	390
Peru	225	218
Zaire	218	210
Australia	184	208
South Africa	159	155
Spain	158	151
Other countries[a]	1,609	1,634
Total	9,446	9,646

DIAMOND, natural (thousand carats)

	1986	1987
Australia	29,211	30,333
Zaire	23,304	23,350
Botswana	13,110	13,207
USSR[e]	10,800	12,000
South Africa	10,228	9,053
Namibia	1,010	1,020
China[e]	1,000	1,000
Brazil	625	645
Other countries[a]	2,468	2,421
Total	91,756	93,029

FLUORSPAR[g] (thousand metric tons)

	1986	1987
Mexico	767	824
Mongolia[e]	790	800
China[e]	650	650
USSR[e]	560	560
South Africa	334	317
Spain	282	255
France	198	200[e]
Italy	145	147[e]
Other countries[a]	1,022	1,009
Total	4,748	4,762

GAS, natural[h] (billion cubic feet)

	1986	1987
USSR	24,200	25,700
United States	16,791	17,155
Canada	2,696	2,803
Netherlands	2,808	2,587
United Kingdom	1,474	1,470[e]
Algeria	1,320	1,320[e]
Mexico	1,175	1,194
Indonesia	1,113	1,188
Romania[e]	1,120	1,120
Other countries[a]	11,313	11,800
Total	64,010	66,337

GOLD, mine[b] (thousand troy ounces)

	1986	1987
South Africa	20,514	19,228
USSR[e]	8,850	8,850
United States	3,739	4,966
Canada	3,365	3,788
Australia	2,414	3,472
Brazil[e]	2,300	2,300
China	2,100	2,300
Philippines	1,296	1,071
Colombia	1,286	851
Other countries[a]	5,756	5,655
Total	51,620	52,481

GYPSUM[c] (thousand metric tons)

	1986	1987
United States	13,973	14,163
Canada	8,803	8,811
Iran[e]	8,400	8,400
China[e]	6,500	7,200
Japan	6,355	6,500
Spain[e]	5,500	5,500
USSR[e]	5,000	5,000
France	4,384	4,508
United Kingdom[e]	3,200	3,200
Thailand	1,666	3,030
Mexico	2,625	2,457
West Germany	1,896	1,900[e]
India	1,549	1,861
Australia	1,569	1,600
Other countries[a]	15,078	15,315
Total	86,498	89,445

IRON ORE[c] (thousand metric tons)

	1986	1987
USSR	249,959	251,000
Brazil	132,288	131,600
Australia	94,135	100,368
China[e]	90,000	100,000
India	47,800	52,000
United States	39,486	47,568
Canada	36,167	37,550
South Africa	24,483	21,998
Sweden	20,489	19,627
Venezuela	19,125	17,780
Liberia	15,295	13,742
France	12,436	10,911
Other countries[a]	86,729	79,322
Total	868,392	883,466

IRON, steel ingots (thousand metric tons)

	1986	1987
USSR	160,550	162,000
Japan	98,275	98,513
United States	74,032	80,261
China	51,960	56,000
West Germany	37,134	36,248
Italy	22,872	22,900[e]
Brazil	21,234	22,231
France	17,844	17,726
United Kingdom	14,811	17,425
Poland	17,144	17,148
South Korea	14,554	16,782
Czechoslovakia	15,108	15,420
Canada	14,076	14,832
Romania[e]	14,000	14,000
India	11,427	12,105
Spain	11,976	11,760
Belgium	9,744	9,600[e]
South Africa	9,144	8,700[e]
East Germany	7,967	8,244
Mexico	7,170	7,510
Other countries[a]	79,828	79,999
Total	710,850	729,404

LEAD, mine[b] (thousand metric tons)

	1986	1987
Australia	448	476
USSR[e]	440	440
Canada	349	413
United States	353	319
China	227	252
Mexico	207	200[e]
Peru	194	192
North Korea[e]	110	110
Yugoslavia	117	98
Other countries[a]	931	942
Total	3,376	3,442

LEAD, refined, primary and secondary[i] (thousand metric tons)

	1986	1987
United States	995	1,084
USSR[e]	770	780
West Germany	367	343
Japan	361	338
United Kingdom	328	338
China[e]	240	240
Canada	258	226
Australia	171	217
France	230	213
Yugoslavia	155	142
Other countries[a]	1,708	1,709
Total	5,583	5,630

MAGNESIUM, primary (thousand metric tons)

	1986	1987
United States	126	124
USSR[e]	89	90
Norway	57	50[e]
France[e]	14	14
Italy	12	11
Japan	8	8
Canada	7	7
China	7	7
Other countries[a]	9	11
Total	329	322

MANGANESE ORES[c] (thousand metric tons)

	1986	1987
USSR	9,300	9,300
South Africa	3,719	2,892
Brazil[e]	2,600	2,400
Gabon	2,510	2,400[e]
Australia	1,649	1,853
China[e]	1,600	1,600
India	1,213	1,303
Other countries[a]	1,099	975
Total	23,690	22,723

MERCURY (76-pound flasks)

	1986	1987
USSR[e]	66,000	67,000
Spain	42,653	43,000[e]
Algeria	22,000	22,000
China[e]	20,000	20,000
Mexico	10,008	10,000[e]
Other countries[a]	18,602	16,800
Total	179,263	178,800

MOLYBDENUM, mine[b] (metric tons)

	1986	1987
United States	42,627	34,073
Chile	16,581	16,700[e]
Canada	11,251	11,580
USSR[e]	11,400	11,500
Mexico	3,350	3,630
Peru	3,484	3,500[e]
Other countries[a]	3,607	3,615
Total	92,300	84,598

NATURAL GAS LIQUIDS (million barrels)

	1986	1987
United States	566	578[e]
USSR	180	190
Saudi Arabia	150	150[e]
Mexico	129	132[e]
Algeria[e]	122	125
Canada	120	117
Other countries[a]	378	385
Total	1,645	1,677

NICKEL, mine[b] (thousand metric tons)

	1986	1987
Canada	164	188
USSR[e]	185	185
Australia	77	74
New Caledonia	62	62
Indonesia	53	58[e]
Cuba[e]	33	34
South Africa[e]	32	34
China	25	25
Other countries[a]	127	127
Total	758	787

NITROGEN, content of ammonia (thousand metric tons)

	1986	1987
USSR[e]	19,600	20,000
China[e]	15,500	14,500
United States	10,432	12,051
India	5,410	5,300[e]
Canada	3,540	2,742
Netherlands	2,153	2,828
Romania[e]	2,900	2,800
Indonesia	2,299	2,364
France	2,022	2,029
West Germany	1,570	1,931
Other countries[a]	24,722	26,459
Total	90,148	93,004

PETROLEUM, crude (million barrels)

	1986	1987
USSR	4,520	4,590
United States	3,168	3,047
Saudi Arabia	1,841	1,544
China	954	978
Mexico	886	946
United Kingdom	884	861
Iran	686	849
Iraq	617	785
Venezuela	654	650[e]
Canada	537	547
United Arab Emirates	500	547

PETROLEUM, crude (cont'd)

	1986	1987
Indonesia	507	509
Kuwait	519	497
Nigeria	534	455
Libya	389	368
Other countries[a]	3,239	3,234
Total	20,435	20,407

PHOSPHATE ROCK[c] (thousand metric tons)

	1986	1987
United States	38,710	40,954
USSR[e]	33,900	34,100
Morocco	21,178	20,955
China[e]	6,700	9,000
Jordan	6,249	6,801
Tunisia	5,951	6,390
Brazil	4,509	4,777
Israel	3,673	3,798
Togo	2,314	2,644
South Africa	2,920	2,623
Other countries[a]	12,636	13,106
Total	138,740	145,148

POTASH, K$_2$O equivalent basis (thousand metric tons)

	1986	1987
USSR	10,200	10,400
Canada	6,752	7,465
East Germany	3,485	3,500[e]
West Germany	2,161	2,140
France	1,617	1,650
Israel	1,255	1,300
United States	1,202	1,202
Other countries[a]	2,086	2,155
Total	28,758	29,812

SALT[c] (thousand metric tons)

	1986	1987
United States	33,296	33,142
China	17,299	18,000[e]
USSR[e]	16,100	16,100
West Germany	13,102	13,200[e]
India	10,118	11,002[e]
Canada	10,332	9,990
France	7,084	7,161
United Kingdom[e]	7,000	7,000
Australia[e]	6,200	6,200
Poland	5,421	6,168
Mexico	5,927	6,000[e]
Romania	5,355	5,400
Netherlands	3,763	3,979
Italy	4,033	3,880
Other countries[a]	31,550	35,401
Total	176,580	182,623

SILVER, mine[b] (thousand troy ounces)

	1986	1987
Mexico[e]	75,200	75,000
Peru	61,916	66,000[e]
USSR[e]	48,200	48,200
Canada	34,979	40,180
United States	34,524	39,790
Australia	32,882	32,762
Poland	26,653	26,500[e]
Chile	16,078	15,800[e]
Japan	11,294	9,040
Sweden	7,555	6,912
South Africa	7,145	6,691
Spain	5,697	5,709
Other countries[a]	52,361	54,419
Total	414,484	427,003

SULFUR, all forms[j] (thousand metric tons)

	1986	1987
United States	11,087	10,538
USSR[e]	9,275	9,550
Canada	6,543	6,668
Poland	5,120	5,220[e]
China[e]	3,100	3,100
Mexico	2,220	2,399
Japan	2,371	2,221
West Germany	1,573	1,625
Saudi Arabia[e]	1,300	1,400
France	1,306	1,252
Spain	1,310	1,120
Other countries[a]	8,869	9,128
Total	54,074	54,221

TIN, mine[b] (thousand metric tons)

	1986	1987
Malaysia	29,135	30,388
Brazil	25,200	28,900
Indonesia	24,049	27,000
USSR[e]	23,500	24,000
Thailand	17,066	15,006
China[e]	15,000	15,000

TIN, mine (cont'd)

	1986	1987
Australia	8,470	9,000[e]
Bolivia	10,479	7,000[e]
Other countries[a]	26,478	23,419
Total	179,377	179,713

TITANIUM MINERALS[k] (thousand metric tons)

ILMENITE

	1986	1987
Australia	1,252	1,392
Norway	804	852
Malaysia	415	500[e]
USSR	450	455
China[e]	145	145
India[e]	140	140
Other countries[a]	189	207
Total	3,395	3,691

RUTILE

	1986	1987
Australia	216	257
Sierra Leone	97	113
South Africa	55	55
Other countries[a]	24	25
Total	392	450

TITANIFEROUS SLAG

	1986	1987
South Africa	435	1,085
Canada[e]	850	900
Total	1,285	1,985

TUNGSTEN, mine[b] (metric tons)

	1986	1987
China[e]	15,000	18,000
USSR[e]	9,200	9,200
South Korea	2,455	2,500[e]
Portugal	1,637	1,500
Mongolia[e]	1,500	1,500
Austria	1,387	1,250[e]
Australia	1,600	1,150
North Korea	1,000	1,000
Brazil	875	672
Thailand	475	660
Peru	593	600[e]
Bolivia	1,095	500
Other countries[a]	5,839	1,700
Total	42,656	40,232

URANIUM OXIDE (U$_3$O$_8$)[l] (metric tons)

	1986	1987
Canada	13,789	14,696
United States	6,123	5,900
South Africa	5,443	4,717
Australia	4,900	4,445
Namibia	3,900	3,810
France	3,828	3,800
Niger	3,629	3,447
Other countries[a]	1,819	1,805
Total	43,431	42,620

ZINC, mine[b] (thousand metric tons)

	1986	1987
Canada	1,291	1,500
USSR[e]	810	810
Australia	662	733
Peru	598	592
China[e]	396	425
Mexico	271	304
Spain	223	235[e]
United States	216	233
North Korea	180	225
Sweden	214	200[e]
Poland	190	190
Ireland	182	177
Other countries[a]	1,596	1,520
Total	6,829	7,144

ZINC, smelter, primary and secondary (thousand metric tons)

	1986	1987
USSR[e]	1,005	1,015
Japan	708	665
Canada	571	611
West Germany	371	378
China	336	375
United States	316	343
Australia	310	314
Belgium	285	285
France	288	266
Italy	229	256
Spain	202	213
Netherlands	196	207
Mexico	174	180[e]
Poland	179	177
Other countries[a]	1,591	1,745
Total	6,761	7,030

---

[a] Estimated in part. [b] Content of concentrates. [c] Gross weight. [d] Includes calculated bauxite equivalent of estimated output of aluminum ores other than bauxite (nepheline concentrate and alunite ore). [e] Estimate. [f] Includes coal classified in some countries as brown coal. [g] Gross weight of marketable product. [h] Marketed production (includes gas sold or used by producers; excludes gas reinjected to reservoirs for pressure maintenance and that flared or vented to the atmosphere which is not used as fuel or industrial raw material, and which thus has no economic value). [i] Excludes bullion produced for refining elsewhere. [j] Includes (1) Frasch process sulfur, (2) elemental sulfur mined by conventional means, (3) by-product recovered elemental sulfur, and (4) elemental sulfur equivalent obtained from pyrite and other materials. [k] Excludes output in the United States, which cannot be disclosed because it is company proprietary information. [l] Excludes output (if any) by Albania, Bulgaria, China, Czechoslovakia, East Germany, Hungary, North Korea, Mongolia, Poland, Romania, and Vietnam.

Compiled by Charles L. Kimbell primarily from data collected by the U.S. Department of Mines, but with some modifications from other sources.

UNITED STATES: 101st CONGRESS
First Session

SENATE MEMBERSHIP

(As of January 1989: 55 Democrats, 45 Republicans). Letters after senators' names refer to party affiliation—D for Democrat, R for Republican. Single asterisk (*) denotes term expiring in January 1991; double asterisk (**), term expiring in January 1993; triple asterisk (***), term expiring in January 1995. [1] Appointed to fill vacancy.

Alabama
* H. Heflin, D
** R. C. Shelby, D

Alaska
* T. Stevens, R
** F. H. Murkowski, R

Arizona
*** D. DeConcini, D
** J. McCain III, R

Arkansas
** D. Bumpers, D
* D. H. Pryor, D

California
** A. Cranston, D
*** P. Wilson, R

Colorado
* W. L. Armstrong, R
** T. E. Wirth, D

Connecticut
** C. J. Dodd, D
*** J. I. Lieberman, D

Delaware
*** W. V. Roth, Jr., R
* J. R. Biden, Jr., D

Florida
** B. Graham, D
*** C. Mack, R

Georgia
* S. Nunn, D
** W. Fowler, Jr., D

Hawaii
** D. K. Inouye, D
*** S. M. Matsunaga, D

Idaho
* J. A. McClure, R
** S. Symms, R

Illinois
** A. J. Dixon, D
* P. Simon, D

Indiana
*** R. G. Lugar, R
** D. Coats, R [1]

Iowa
** C. E. Grassley, R
* T. R. Harkin, D

Kansas
** R. J. Dole, R
* N. L. Kassebaum, R

Kentucky
** W. H. Ford, D
* M. McConnell, R

Louisiana
* J. B. Johnston, D
** J. B. Breaux, D

Maine
* W. Cohen, R
*** G. J. Mitchell, D

Maryland
*** P. S. Sarbanes, D
** B. A. Mikulski, D

Massachusetts
*** E. M. Kennedy, D
* J. F. Kerry, D

Michigan
*** D. W. Riegle, Jr., D
* C. Levin, D

Minnesota
*** D. F. Durenberger, R
* R. Boschwitz, R

Mississippi
* T. Cochran, R
*** T. Lott, R

Missouri
*** J. C. Danforth, R
** C. S. Bond, R

Montana
* M. Baucus, D
*** C. Burns, R

Nebraska
* J. J. Exon, Jr., D
*** R. Kerrey, D

Nevada
** H. Reid, D
*** R. H. Bryan, D

New Hampshire
* G. J. Humphrey, R
** W. B. Rudman, R

New Jersey
* B. Bradley, D
*** F. R. Lautenberg, D

New Mexico
* P. V. Domenici, R
*** J. Bingaman, D

New York
*** D. P. Moynihan, D
** A. D'Amato, R

North Carolina
* J. Helms, R
** T. Sanford, D

North Dakota
*** Q. N. Burdick, D
** K. Conrad, D

Ohio
** J. H. Glenn, Jr., D
*** H. M. Metzenbaum, D

Oklahoma
* D. L. Boren, D
** D. L. Nickles, R

Oregon
* M. O. Hatfield, R
** B. Packwood, R

Pennsylvania
*** J. Heinz, R
** A. Specter, R

Rhode Island
* C. Pell, D
*** J. H. Chafee, R

South Carolina
* S. Thurmond, R
** E. F. Hollings, D

South Dakota
* L. Pressler, R
** T. A. Daschle, D

Tennessee
*** J. R. Sasser, D
* A. Gore, Jr., D

Texas
*** L. Bentsen, D
* W. P. Gramm, R

Utah
** E. J. Garn, R
*** O. G. Hatch, R

Vermont
** P. J. Leahy, D
*** J. M. Jeffords, R

Virginia
* J. W. Warner, R
*** C. S. Robb, D

Washington
** B. Adams, D
*** S. Gorton, R

West Virginia
*** R. C. Byrd, D
* J. D. Rockefeller IV, D

Wisconsin
** R. W. Kasten, Jr., R
*** H. Kohl, D

Wyoming
*** M. Wallop, R
* A. K. Simpson, R

HOUSE MEMBERSHIP

(As of January 1989, 259 Democrats, 174 Republicans, 2 vacancies). "At-L." in place of congressional district number means "representative at large." * Indicates elected Nov. 8, 1988; all others were reelected in 1988.

Alabama
1. H. L. Callahan, R
2. W. L. Dickinson, R
3. vacant
4. T. Bevill, D
5. R. G. Flippo, D
6. B. Erdreich, D
7. C. Harris, Jr., D

Alaska
At-L. D. Young, R

Arizona
1. J. J. Rhodes, III, R
2. M. K. Udall, D
3. B. Stump, R
4. J. L. Kyl, R
5. J. Kolbe, R

Arkansas
1. W. V. Alexander, Jr., D
2. T. F. Robinson, D
3. J. P. Hammerschmidt, R
4. B. F. Anthony, Jr., D

California
1. D. H. Bosco, D
2. W. W. Herger, R
3. R. T. Matsui, D
4. V. Fazio, D
5. N. Pelosi, D
6. B. Boxer, D
7. G. Miller, D
8. R. V. Dellums, D
9. F. H. Stark, Jr., D
10. D. Edwards, D
11. T. P. Lantos, D
12. *T. J. Campbell, R

13. N. Y. Mineta, D
14. N. D. Shumway, R
15. T. Coelho, D
16. L. E. Panetta, D
17. C. J. Pashayan, Jr., R
18. R. H. Lehman, D
19. R. J. Lagomarsino, R
20. W. M. Thomas, R
21. E. W. Gallegly, R
22. C. J. Moorhead, R
23. A. C. Beilenson, D
24. H. A. Waxman, D
25. E. R. Roybal, D
26. H. L. Berman, D
27. M. Levine, D
28. J. C. Dixon, D
29. A. F. Hawkins, D
30. M. G. Martinez, Jr., D
31. M. W. Dymally, D
32. G. M. Anderson, D
33. D. Dreier, R
34. E. E. Torres, D
35. J. Lewis, R
36. G. E. Brown, Jr., D
37. A. A. McCandless, R
38. R. K. Dornan, R
39. W. E. Dannemeyer, R
40. *C. Cox, R
41. W. D. Lowery, R
42. *D. Rohrabacher, R
43. R. Packard, R
44. J. Bates, D
45. D. L. Hunter, R

Colorado
1. P. Schroeder, D
2. D. Skaggs, D

3. B. N. Campbell, D
4. H. Brown, R
5. J. M. Hefley, R
6. D. Schaefer, R

Connecticut
1. B. B. Kennelly, D
2. S. Gejdenson, D
3. B. A. Morrison, D
4. C. Shays, R
5. J. G. Rowland, R
6. N. L. Johnson, R

Delaware
At-L. T. R. Carper, D

Florida
1. E. Hutto, D
2. B. Grant, D
3. C. E. Bennett, D
4. *C. T. James, R
5. B. McCollum, Jr., R
6. *C. B. Stearns, R
7. S. M. Gibbons, D
8. C. W. Young, R
9. M. Bilirakis, R
10. A. Ireland, R
11. B. Nelson, D
12. T. Lewis, R
13. *P. J. Goss, R
14. *H. A. Johnston II, D
15. E. C. Shaw, Jr., R
16. L. J. Smith, D
17. W. Lehman, D
18. C. D. Pepper, D
19. D. B. Fascell, D

Georgia
1. R. L. Thomas, D
2. C. F. Hatcher, D
3. R. B. Ray, D
4. *B. Jones, D
5. J. R. Lewis, D
6. N. Gingrich, R
7. G. Darden, D
8. R. Rowland, D
9. E. L. Jenkins, D
10. D. Barnard, Jr., D

Hawaii
1. P. F. Saiki, R
2. D. K. Akaka, D

Idaho
1. L. Craig, R
2. R. H. Stallings, D

Illinois
1. C. A. Hayes, D
2. G. Savage, D
3. M. Russo, D
4. *G. Sangmeister, D
5. W. O. Lipinski, D
6. H. J. Hyde, R
7. C. Collins, D
8. D. Rostenkowski, D
9. S. R. Yates, D
10. J. E. Porter, R
11. F. Annunzio, D
12. P. M. Crane, R
13. H. W. Fawell, R
14. J. D. Hastert, R
15. E. R. Madigan, R
16. L. M. Martin, R
17. L. Evans, D

18. R. H. Michel, R
19. T. L. Bruce, D
20. R. Durbin, D
21. *J. Costello, D
22. *G. Poshard, D

Indiana
1. P. J. Visclosky, D
2. P. R. Sharp, D
3. J. P. Hiler, R
4. vacant
5. J. P. Jontz, D
6. D. L. Burton, R
7. J. T. Myers, R
8. F. McCloskey, D
9. L. H. Hamilton, D
10. A. Jacobs, Jr., D

Iowa
1. J. Leach, R
2. T. T. Tauke, R
3. D. R. Nagle, D
4. N. Smith, D
5. J. R. Lightfoot, R
6. F. L. Grandy, R

Kansas
1. C. P. Roberts, R
2. J. C. Slattery, D
3. J. Meyers, R
4. D. Glickman, D
5. B. Whittaker, R

Kentucky
1. C. Hubbard, Jr., D
2. W. H. Natcher, D
3. R. L. Mazzoli, D
4. J. Bunning, R
5. H. D. Rogers, R
6. L. J. Hopkins, R
7. C. C. Perkins, D

Louisiana
1. R. L. Livingston, Jr., R
2. C. C. Boggs, D
3. W. J. Tauzin, D
4. *J. McCrery, R
5. T. J. Huckaby, D
6. R. H. Baker, R
7. J. A. Hayes, D
8. C. C. Holloway, R

Maine
1. J. E. Brennan, D
2. O. J. Snowe, R

Maryland
1. R. P. Dyson, D
2. H. D. Bentley, R
3. B. L. Cardin, D
4. C. T. McMillen, D
5. S. H. Hoyer, D
6. B. B. Byron, D
7. K. Mfume, D
8. C. A. Morella, R

Massachusetts
1. S. O. Conte, R
2. *R. E. Neal, D
3. J. D. Early, D
4. B. Frank, D
5. C. G. Atkins, D
6. N. Mavroules, D
7. E. J. Markey, D
8. J. P. Kennedy II, D
9. J. J. Moakley, D
10. G. E. Studds, D
11. B. J. Donnelly, D

Michigan
1. J. Conyers, Jr., D
2. C. D. Pursell, R
3. H. E. Wolpe, D
4. F. S. Upton, R
5. P. B. Henry, R
6. B. Carr, D
7. D. E. Kildee, D
8. B. Traxler, D
9. G. Vander Jagt, R
10. B. Schuette, R
11. R. W. Davis, R
12. D. E. Bonior, D
13. G. W. Crockett, Jr., D
14. D. M. Hertel, D
15. W. D. Ford, D
16. J. D. Dingell, D
17. S. M. Levin, D
18. W. S. Broomfield, R

Minnesota
1. T. J. Penny, D
2. V. Weber, R
3. B. Frenzel, R

4. B. F. Vento, D
5. M. O. Sabo, D
6. G. Sikorski, D
7. A. Stangeland, R
8. J. L. Oberstar, D

Mississippi
1. J. L. Whitten, D
2. M. Espy, D
3. G. V. Montgomery, D
4. *M. Parker, D
5. *L. Smith, R

Missouri
1. W. L. Clay, D
2. J. W. Buechner, R
3. R. A. Gephardt, D
4. I. Skelton, D
5. A. D. Wheat, D
6. E. T. Coleman, R
7. *M. Hancock, R
8. W. Emerson, R
9. H. L. Volkmer, D

Montana
1. P. Williams, D
2. R. C. Marlenee, R

Nebraska
1. D. Bereuter, R
2. *P. Hoagland, D
3. V. Smith, R

Nevada
1. J. H. Bilbray, D
2. B. F. Vucanovich, R

New Hampshire
1. R. C. Smith, R
2. *C. J. Douglas III, R

New Jersey
1. J. J. Florio, D
2. W. J. Hughes, D
3. *F. Pallone, Jr., D
4. C. H. Smith, R
5. M. S. Roukema, R
6. B. J. Dwyer, D
7. M. J. Rinaldo, R
8. R. A. Roe, D
9. R. G. Torricelli, D
10. *D. Payne, D
11. D. A. Gallo, R
12. J. Courter, R
13. H. J. Saxton, R
14. F. J. Guarini, D

New Mexico
1. *S. H. Schiff, R
2. J. R. Skeen, R
3. W. B. Richardson, D

New York
1. G. J. Hochbrueckner, D
2. T. J. Downey, D
3. R. J. Mrazek, D
4. N. F. Lent, R
5. R. J. McGrath, R
6. F. H. Flake, D
7. G. L. Ackerman, D
8. J. H. Scheuer, D
9. T. J. Manton, D
10. C. E. Schumer, D
11. E. Towns, D
12. M. R. Owens, D
13. S. J. Solarz, D
14. G. V. Molinari, R
15. B. Green, R
16. C. B. Rangel, D
17. T. Weiss, D
18. R. Garcia, D
19. *E. L. Engel, D
20. *N. Lowey, D
21. H. Fish, Jr., R
22. B. A. Gilman, R
23. *M. R. McNulty, D
24. G. B. Solomon, R
25. S. L. Boehlert, R
26. D. Martin, R
27. *J. T. Walsh, R
28. M. F. McHugh, D
29. F. Horton, R
30. L. M. Slaughter, D
31. *L. W. Paxon, R
32. J. J. LaFalce, D
33. H. J. Nowak, D
34. A. Houghton, R

North Carolina
1. W. B. Jones, D
2. T. Valentine, D

3. H. M. Lancaster, D
4. D. E. Price, D
5. S. L. Neal, D
6. H. Coble, R
7. C. Rose, D
8. W. G. Hefner, D
9. J. A. McMillan, R
10. C. Ballenger, R
11. J. McC. Clarke, D

North Dakota
At-L. B. L. Dorgan, D

Ohio
1. T. A. Luken, D
2. W. D. Gradison, Jr., R
3. T. P. Hall, D
4. M. G. Oxley, R
5. *P. E. Gillmor, R
6. B. McEwen, R
7. M. DeWine, R
8. D. E. Lukens, R
9. M. C. Kaptur, D
10. C. E. Miller, R
11. D. E. Eckart, D
12. J. R. Kasich, R
13. D. J. Pease, D
14. T. C. Sawyer, D
15. C. P. Wylie, R
16. R. Regula, R
17. J. A. Traficant, Jr., D
18. D. Applegate, D
19. E. F. Feighan, D
20. M. R. Oakar, D
21. L. Stokes, D

Oklahoma
1. J. M. Inhofe, R
2. M. Synar, D
3. W. W. Watkins, D
4. D. McCurdy, D
5. M. Edwards, R
6. G. English, D

Oregon
1. L. AuCoin, D
2. R. F. Smith, R
3. R. Wyden, D
4. P. A. DeFazio, D
5. D. Smith, R

Pennsylvania
1. T. M. Foglietta, D
2. W. H. Gray, III, D
3. R. A. Borski, Jr., D
4. J. P. Kolter, D
5. R. T. Schulze, R
6. G. Yatron, D
7. W. C. Weldon, R
8. P. H. Kostmayer, D
9. B. Shuster, R
10. J. M. McDade, R
11. P. E. Kanjorski, D
12. J. P. Murtha, D
13. L. Coughlin, R
14. W. Coyne, D
15. D. L. Ritter, R
16. R. S. Walker, R
17. G. W. Gekas, R
18. D. Walgren, D
19. W. F. Goodling, R
20. J. M. Gaydos, D
21. T. J. Ridge, R
22. A. J. Murphy, D
23. W. E. Clinger, Jr., R

Rhode Island
1. *R. K. Machtley, R
2. C. Schneider, R

South Carolina
1. A. Ravenel, Jr., R
2. F. D. Spence, R
3. B. C. Derrick, Jr., D
4. E. J. Patterson, D
5. J. M. Spratt, Jr., D
6. R. M. Tallon, Jr., D

South Dakota
At-L. T. Johnson, D

Tennessee
1. J. H. Quillen, R
2. J. J. Duncan, R
3. M. Lloyd, D
4. J. Cooper, D
5. B. Clement, D
6. B. J. Gordon, D
7. D. K. Sundquist, R
8. *J. S. Tanner, D
9. H. E. Ford, D

Texas
1. J. Chapman, D
2. C. Wilson, D
3. S. Bartlett, R
4. R. M. Hall, R
5. J. W. Bryant, D
6. J. L. Barton, R
7. B. Archer, R
8. J. M. Fields, R
9. J. Brooks, D
10. J. J. Pickle, D
11. J. M. Leath, D
12. J. C. Wright, Jr., D
13. *B. Sarpalius, D
14. *G. Laughlin, D
15. E. de la Garza, D
16. R. D. Coleman, D
17. C. W. Stenholm, D
18. M. Leland, D
19. L. E. Combest, R
20. H. B. Gonzalez, D
21. L. S. Smith, R
22. T. D. DeLay, R
23. A. G. Bustamante, D
24. M. Frost, D
25. M. A. Andrews, D
26. R. K. Armey, R
27. S. P. Ortiz, D

Utah
1. J. V. Hansen, R
2. D. W. Owens, D
3. H. C. Nielson, R

Vermont
At-L. *P. P. Smith, R

Virginia
1. H. H. Bateman, R
2. O. B. Pickett, D
3. T. J. Bliley, Jr., R
4. N. Sisisky, D
5. *L. F. Payne, Jr., D
6. J. R. Olin, D
7. D. F. Slaughter, Jr., R
8. S. Parris, R
9. F. C. Boucher, D
10. F. R. Wolf, R

Washington
1. J. R. Miller, R
2. A. Swift, D
3. *J. Unsoeld, D
4. S. W. Morrison, R
5. T. S. Foley, D
6. N. D. Dicks, D
7. *J. McDermott, D
8. R. Chandler, R

West Virginia
1. A. B. Mollohan, D
2. H. O. Staggers, Jr., D
3. R. E. Wise, Jr., D
4. N. J. Rahall, II, D

Wisconsin
1. L. Aspin, D
2. R. W. Kastenmeier, D
3. S. C. Gunderson, R
4. G. D. Kleczka, D
5. J. Moody, D
6. T. E. Petri, R
7. D. R. Obey, D
8. T. Roth, R
9. F. J. Sensenbrenner, Jr., R

Wyoming
At-L. D. Cheney, R

AMERICAN SAMOA
Delegate, E. F. H. Faleomavega, D

DISTRICT OF COLUMBIA
Delegate, W. E. Fauntroy, D

GUAM
Delegate, Ben Blaz, R

PUERTO RICO
Resident Commissioner
J. B. Fuster, D

VIRGIN ISLANDS
Delegate, Ron de Lugo, D

589

UNITED STATES: Major Legislation Enacted During the Second Session of the 100th Congress

SUBJECT	PURPOSE
Memorial to Blacks	Allows a memorial to blacks who fought against the British in the Revolutionary War to be built in Washington's main tourist district. Signed March 25. Public Law 100-265.
Korean War Memorial	Approves the location of the Korean War Memorial. Signed March 28. Public Law 100-267.
Discrimination	Overturns 1984 Supreme Court decision regarding Grove City College (see page 225). Presidential veto was overridden on March 22. Public Law 100-259.
Contra Aid	Provides $47.9 million for aid to the Nicaraguan contras, Nicaraguan children injured by the war, and support for the Central American peace process. Signed April 1. Public Law 100-276.
INF Treaty	Ratifies the U.S.-USSR treaty on intermediate-range nuclear-force (INF) missiles, which was signed by President Reagan and Soviet General Secretary Mikhail Gorbachev on Dec. 8, 1987. Ratified June 1.
Maritime Museum	Establishes the National Maritime Museum in San Francisco, CA. Signed June 27. Public Law 100-348.
Catastrophic Health Insurance	Expands Medicare to provide coverage of unlimited hospital stays and to impose a cap on out-of-pocket medical costs of covered services, including outpatient prescription drugs, in a given year. Signed July 1. Public Law 100-360.
Welfare	Reauthorizes for two years authority for the states to use federal Work Incentive Program funds for demonstration programs operated through state welfare program departments. Signed July 11. Public Law 100-364.
Plant Closings	Requires employers of more than 100 workers to give notice of 60 days of a plant closing or a layoff lasting more than six months. Enacted without President Reagan's signature on August 4. Public Law 100-379.
Japanese Americans	Authorizes $1.25 billion in reparations and a formal apology from the U.S. government to Japanese Americans interned during World War II. Signed August 10. Public Law 100-383.
Drought Relief	Provides financial assistance to farmers and ranchers whose livelihoods have been affected by 1988's drought conditions. Signed August 11. Public Law 100-387.
Omnibus Trade	Extends presidential authority to negotiate trade agreements abroad; requires the president to retaliate against certain unfair trade practices; expands benefits to farms and workers harmed by imports and other dislocations; streamlines controls on export of high technology to East-bloc nations; encourages export promotion and training programs. Signed August 23. Public Law 100-418.
Forest Fires	Assists fire fighters dealing with fires raging in the West; permits the United States to enter into an agreement with Canada, whereby the United States would reimburse Canada for fire-fighting equipment and services. Signed September 9. Public Law 100-428.
Housing	Strengthens enforcement of law banning housing discrimination; establishes a procedure by which the government may impose fines on those who discriminate in the sale or rental of housing. Extends protection to the handicapped and those with children. Signed September 13. Public Law 100-430.
Defense	Appropriates $282.4 billion for defense for fiscal 1989; authorizes $27.14 million in new humanitarian aid for the Nicaraguan contras. Signed October 1. Public Law 100-463.
Endangered Species	Revises and reauthorizes the 1973 Endangered Species Act for five years. Signed October 7. Public Law 100-478.
Welfare Reform	Establishes a new welfare program (see page 462). Signed October 13. Public Law 100-485.
Military Bases	Establishes a mechanism for closing out-of-date or underutilized military bases. Signed October 24. Public Law 100-526.
Veterans	Establishes the U.S. Department of Veterans Affairs as a cabinet post. Signed October 25. Public Law 100-527.
Medical Wastes	Requires the Environmental Protection Agency to develop a system for tracking medical wastes. Signed November 1. Public Law 100-582.
Government Ethics	Provides for the reauthorization of appropriations for the Office of Government Ethics. Signed November 3. Public Law 100-598.
Genocide Convention	Enables the United States to ratify the Genocide Convention; amends the U.S. criminal code to make genocide a federal offense. Signed November 4. Public Law 100-606.
Gambling	Allows certain privately run, nonprofit gambling enterprises, e.g., church-sponsored bingo games, to advertise on radio and television and through the mail. Signed November 7. Public Law 100-625.
Homeless	Renews homeless-assistance legislation enacted in 1987; authorizes $1.3 billion for the homeless for two years. Signed November 5. Public Law 100-628.
Taxation	(See page 519.) Signed November 10. Public Law 100-647.
Ocean Dumping	Curbs ocean pollution by ending all dumping of sewage sludge after 1991. Signed November 18. Public Law 100-688.
Drug War	(See page 43.) Signed November 18. Public Law 100-690.
Insider Trading	Raises the federal penalties for insider trading. Signed November 19. Public Law 100-704.

Contributors

ADRIAN, CHARLES R., Professor of Political Science, University of California at Riverside; Author, *A History of City Government: The Emergence of the Metropolis 1920–1945;* Coauthor, *A History of American City Government: The Formation of Traditions, 1775–1870, Governing Urban America:* CALIFORNIA; LOS ANGELES

ALPTEKIN, OMER, Fordham University: SUDAN

ALTER, STEWART, Editor, *Adweek:* ADVERTISING

AMBRE, AGO, Economist, Office of Economic Affairs, U.S. Department of Commerce: INDUSTRIAL PRODUCTION

ARNOLD, ANTHONY, Visiting Scholar, Hoover Institution, Stanford, CA; Author, *Afghanistan: The Soviet Invasion in Perspective, Afghanistan's Two-Party Communism: Parrham and Khalq:* AFGHANISTAN

ATTNER, PAUL, National Correspondent, *The Sporting News:* SPORTS—*Basketball, The Olympic Games*

BARMASH, ISADORE, Business-Financial Writer, *The New York Times;* Author, *Always Live Better Than Your Clients, More Than They Bargained For, The Chief Executives:* RETAILING

BATRA, PREM P., Professor of Biochemistry, Wright State University: BIOCHEMISTRY

BECK, KAY, School of Urban Life, Georgia State University: GEORGIA

BEHLER, DEBORAH A., Associate Editor, *Animal Kingdom* magazine: ZOOS AND ZOOLOGY

BEST, JOHN, Chief, *Canada World News:* NEW BRUNSWICK; PRINCE EDWARD ISLAND; QUEBEC

BITTON-JACKSON, LIVIA, Professor of Judaic and Hebraic Studies, Herbert H. Lehman College of the City University of New York; Author, *Elli: Coming of Age in the Holocaust, Madonna or Courtesan: The Jewish Woman in Christian Literature:* RELIGION—*Judaism*

BOND, DONOVAN H., Professor Emeritus of Journalism, West Virginia University: WEST VIRGINIA

BOULAY, HARVEY, Systems Manager, Rogerson House; Author, *The Twilight Cities:* MASSACHUSETTS

BOURDEAUX, REV. MICHAEL A., General Director, Keston College; Coauthor, *Ten Growing Soviet Churches;* Recipient, Templeton Prize for Progress in Religion (1984): USSR—*The Millennium of the Russian Orthodox Church*

BOWER, BRUCE, Behavioral Sciences Editor, *Science News:* ANTHROPOLOGY; ARCHAEOLOGY

BRAMMER, DANA B., Director, Public Policy Center, University of Mississippi: MISSISSIPPI

BRANDHORST, L. CARL, and JoANN C., Department of Geography, Western Oregon State College: OREGON

BROOM, JACK, Reporter, *The Seattle Times:* WASHINGTON

BURANELLI, VINCENT, Free-lance Writer and Editor; Author, *Edison, The Trial of Peter Zenger, Louis XIV;* Coauthor, *Spy/Counterspy: An Encyclopedia of Espionage:* ESPIONAGE

BURKS, ARDATH W., Professor Emeritus Asian Studies, Rutgers University; Author, *Japan: A Postindustrial Power:* JAPAN

BUSH, GRAHAM W. A., Associate Professor of Political Studies, University of Auckland; Author, *Local Government & Politics in New Zealand;* Editor, *New Zealand—A Nation Divided?:* NEW ZEALAND

BUTTRY, STEPHEN, National/Mid-America Editor, *The Kansas City Times:* MISSOURI

CASPER, GRETCHEN, Department of Political Science, Texas A&M: PHILIPPINES

CASPER, LEONARD, Professor of English, Boston College; Past Recipient of Fulbright grants to lecture in the Philippines: PHILIPPINES

CASTAGNO, ANTHONY J., Energy Consultant; Manager, Nuclear Information, Northeast Utilities: ENERGY

CHALMERS, JOHN W., Historical Society of Alberta; Editor, *Alberta Diamond Jubilee* Anthology: ALBERTA

CHRISTENSEN, WILLIAM E., Professor of History, Midland Lutheran College; Author, *In Such Harmony: A History of the Federated Church of Columbus, Nebraska:* NEBRASKA

CLARKE, JAMES W., Professor of Political Science, University of Arizona; Author, *American Assassins: The Darker Side of Politics:* ARIZONA

COLE, JOHN N., Founder, *Maine Times;* Author, *In Maine, Striper, Salmon, House Building:* MAINE

COLLIER, VIRGINIA P., Professor, Department of Curriculum and Instruction, George Mason University; Coauthor, *Bilingual and ESL Classrooms: Teaching in Multicultural Contexts:* EDUCATION—*Bilingualism*

COLLINS, BUD, Sports Columnist, *The Boston Globe:* SPORTS—*Tennis*

COLTON, KENT W., Executive Vice-President and Chief Executive Officer, National Association of Home Builders, Washington, DC: HOUSING

CONRADT, DAVID P., Professor of Political Science, University of Florida; Author, *The German Polity, Comparative Politics, Modern European Politics:* GERMANY

COOPER, MARY H., Staff Writer, *Editorial Research Reports:* INSURANCE, LIABILITY

CORLEW, ROBERT E., Dean, School of Liberal Arts, Middle Tennessee State University: TENNESSEE

CORNWELL, ELMER E., JR., Professor of Political Science, Brown University: RHODE ISLAND

COSSER, ANNE, Free-lance Journalist: ICELAND

COWAN, RICHARD, *Congressional Quarterly:* VETERANS

CUNNIFF, JOHN, Business News Analyst, The Associated Press; Author, *How to Stretch Your Dollar:* UNITED STATES— *The Economy*

CUNNINGHAM, PEGGY, *The Evening Sun,* Baltimore, MD: MARYLAND

CURRIER, CHET, Financial Writer, The Associated Press; Author, *The Investor's Encyclopedia, The 15-Minute Investor;* Coauthor, *No-Cost/Low-Cost Investing:* STOCKS AND BONDS

CURTIS, L. PERRY, JR., Professor of History, Brown University: IRELAND

DANIELS, ROBERT V., Professor of History, University of Vermont; former Vermont state senator; Author, *Russia: The Roots of Confrontation:* VERMONT

DARBY, JOSEPH W., III, Reporter, *The Times-Picayune,* New Orleans: LOUISIANA

DASCH, E. JULIUS, National Aeronautics and Space Administration; Author of more than 100 papers and abstracts in geology and geochemistry: SPACE EXPLORATION

De GREGORIO, GEORGE, Sports Department, *The New York Times;* Author, *Joe DiMaggio, An Informal Biography:* SPORTS—*Boxing, Ice Skating, Skiing, Swimming, Track and Field, Yachting*

DELZELL, CHARLES F., Professor of History, Vanderbilt University; Author, *Italy in the Twentieth Century, Mediterranean Fascism, Mussolini's Enemies:* BIOGRAPHY—*Ciriaco de Mita;* ITALY

DENNIS, LARRY, Golf Writer, Creative Communications: SPORTS—*Golf*

DIETERICH, H. R., Professor of History, University of Wyoming: WYOMING

DUFF, ERNEST A., Professor of Politics, Randolph-Macon Woman's College; Author, *Agrarian Reform in Colombia, Violence and Repression in Latin America, Leader and Party in Latin America:* COLOMBIA

DUIKER, WILLIAM J., Professor, Department of History, The Pennsylvania State University; Author, *The Communist Road to Power in Vietnam, Vietnam Since the Fall of Saigon, China and Vietnam: The Roots of Conflict:* ASIA

DYMALLY, MERVYN M., Member, United States Congress; Author, *The Black Politician: His Struggle for Power;* Coauthor, *Fidel Castro: Nothing Can Stop the Course of History:* BLACK AMERICANS: AN UPDATE

EADINGTON, WILLIAM R., Professor of Economics, University of Nevada, Reno; Author, *Gambling Research, The Gambling Studies, The Gambling Papers:* GAMBLING

ELKINS, ANN M., Fashion Director, *Good Housekeeping Magazine:* FASHION

ELVING, PHYLLIS, Free-lance Travel Writer: SMOOTH SAILING FOR THE CRUISE INDUSTRY; TRAVEL

ENSTAD, ROBERT H., Writer, *Chicago Tribune:* CHICAGO; ILLINOIS

ENTELIS, JOHN P., Professor, Department of Political Science, Fordham University: MOROCCO; SUDAN; TUNISIA

EWEGEN, ROBERT D., Editorial Writer, *The Denver Post:* COLORADO

FAGEN, MORTON D., AT&T Bell Laboratories (retired); Editor, *A History of Engineering and Science in the Bell System,* Vol. I, *The Early Years, 1875–1925,* and Vol. II, *National Service in War and Peace, 1925–1975:* COMMUNICATION TECHNOLOGY

FISHER, JIM, Editorial Writer, *Lewiston Morning Tribune:* IDAHO

FRANCIS, DAVID R., Economic Columnist, *The Christian Science Monitor:* INTERNATIONAL TRADE AND FINANCE

FRIIS, ERIK J., Editor and Publisher, *The Scandinavian-American Bulletin:* DENMARK; FINLAND; SWEDEN

GAILEY, HARRY A., Professor of History, San Jose University: CHAD; MOZAMBIQUE; NIGERIA; ZAIRE

GANS, CURTIS B., Director, The Committee for the Study of the American Electorate: U.S. ELECTIONS: *Voter Turnout*

GEIS, GILBERT, Professor, Program in Social Ecology, University of California, Irvine; Author, *On White Collar Crime:* CRIME

GIBSON, ROBERT C., Regional Editor, *The Billings Gazette:* MONTANA

GOODMAN, DONALD, Associate Professor of Sociology, John Jay College of Criminal Justice, City University of New York: PRISONS

GORDON, MAYNARD M., Editor, *Motor News Analysis;* Author, *The Iacocca Management Technique:* AUTOMOBILES

GRAYSON, GEORGE W., John Marshall Professor of Government and Citizenship, College of William and Mary; Author, *The Politics of Mexican Oil, The United States and Mexico: Patterns of Influence, Oil and Mexican Foreign Policy:* BRAZIL; PORTUGAL; SPAIN

GREEN, MAUREEN, Free-lance Writer, London: LITERATURE— *English*

GREENE, ELAINE, Free-lance Design Reporter; Contributing Editor/Design, *House Beautiful:* INTERIOR DESIGN

GROTH, ALEXANDER J., Professor of Political Science, University of California, Davis; Author, *People's Poland;* Coauthor, *Contemporary Politics: Europe, Comparative Resource Allocation, Public Policy Across Nations:* POLAND

HACKER, JEFFREY H., Free-lance Writer and Editor; Author, *Government Subsidy to Industry, Franklin D. Roosevelt, Carl Sandburg, The New China:* BIOGRAPHY—*Michael Eisner, Katarina Witt;* SPORTS—*Overview, Football*

HADWIGER, DON F., Professor of Political Science, Iowa State University; Coauthor, *World Food Policies: Toward Agricultural Interdependence:* AGRICULTURE; FOOD

HALLER, TIMOTHY G., Professor, Department of Political Science, University of Nevada, Reno: NEVADA

HAND, SAMUEL B., Professor of History, University of Vermont: VERMONT

HANDELMAN, GLADYS, Free-lance Writer and Editor: ART— *Today's Antique Market;* BIOGRAPHY—*Robert Campeau, Christian Lacroix;* GREAT BRITAIN—*The Arts;* HOUSING—*The Remodeling Trend*

HART, MARION H., Free-lance Writer: ENGINEERING, CIVIL

HARVEY, ROSS M., Assistant Deputy Minister, Department of Culture and Communications, Government of the Northwest Territories: NORTHWEST TERRITORIES

HELMREICH, ERNST C., Professor Emeritus of History, Bowdoin College; Author, *The German Churches under Hitler: Background, Struggle, and Epilogue:* AUSTRIA

HELMREICH, JONATHAN E., Professor of History, Allegheny College; Author, *Belgium and Europe: A Study in Small Power Diplomacy, Gathering Rare Ores: The Diplomacy of Uranium Acquisition, 1943–54:* BELGIUM

HELMREICH, PAUL C., Professor of History, Wheaton College; Author, *Wheaton College: The Seminary Years, 1834–1912; From Paris to Sèvres: The Partition of the Ottoman Empire at the Peace Conference of 1919–1920:* SWITZERLAND

HINTON, HAROLD C., Professor of Political Science and International Affairs, The George Washington University; Author, *Korea under New Leadership: The Fifth Republic, Communist China in World Politics, The China Sea: The American Stake in Its Future:* KOREA

HOLLOWAY, HARRY, Professor of Political Science, University of Oklahoma; Coauthor, *Public Opinion: Coalitions, Elites, and Masses, Party and Factional Division in Texas:* OKLAHOMA

HOOVER, HERBERT T., Professor of History, University of South Dakota; Author, *The Yankton Sioux, To Be an Indian, The Chitimacha People, The Sioux, The Practice of Oral History:* SOUTH DAKOTA

HOPKO, THE REV. THOMAS, Assistant Professor, St. Vladimir's Orthodox Theological Seminary: RELIGION—*Orthodox Eastern*

HOYT, CHARLES K., Senior Editor, *Architectural Record;* Author, *More Places for People, Building for Commerce and Industry:* ARCHITECTURE; BIOGRAPHY—*Moshe Safdie*

HUFFMAN, GEORGE J., Assistant Professor, Department of Meteorology, University of Maryland: METEOROLOGY

HULBERT, DAN, *Atlanta Journal & Constitution:* TELEVISION AND RADIO; TELEVISION AND RADIO: *Talk Shows;* THEATER

HUTH, JOHN F., JR., Reporter (retired), *The Plain Dealer,* Cleveland: OHIO

JACKSON, PAUL CONRAD, Journalist, *Saskatoon Star-Phoenix:* SASKATCHEWAN

JEWELL, MALCOLM E., Professor of Political Science, University of Kentucky; Coauthor, *American State Political Parties and Elections, Kentucky Politics:* KENTUCKY

JONES, H. G., Curator, North Carolina Collection, University of North Carolina at Chapel Hill; Author, *North Carolina Illustrated, 1524–1984:* NORTH CAROLINA

JONES, PAT, National Space Society, Washington, DC: SPACE EXPLORATION

JUDD, DENNIS R., Professor of Political Science and Interim Director, Center for Metropolitan Studies, University of Mis-

souri at St. Louis; Author, *The Politics of American Cities: Private Power and Public Policy:* CITIES AND URBAN AFFAIRS

JUDD, LEWIS L., Director, National Institute of Mental Health: MEDICINE AND HEALTH—*Mental Health*

KARNES, THOMAS L., Professor of History Emeritus, Arizona State University; Author, *Latin American Policy of the United States, Failure of Union: Central America 1824–1960:* BIOGRAPHY—*Manuel Antonio Noriega;* CENTRAL AMERICA; CENTRAL AMERICA—*Focus on Panama*

KIMBALL, LORENZO K., Professor Emeritus, Department of Political Science, University of Utah: UTAH

KIMBELL, CHARLES L., Senior Foreign Mineral Specialist, U.S. Bureau of Mines: STATISTICAL AND TABULAR DATA—*Mineral and Metal Production*

KING, PETER J., Professor of History, Carleton University, Ottawa; Author, *Utilitarian Jurisprudence in America:* ONTARIO; OTTAWA

KINNEAR, MICHAEL, Professor of History, University of Manitoba; Author, *The Fall of Lloyd George, The British Voter:* MANITOBA

KISSELGOFF, ANNA, Chief Dance Critic, *The New York Times:* DANCE

KOZINN, ALLAN, Free-lance Music Writer; Contributor, *The New York Times, Opus, Keynote:* MUSIC—*Classical*

KRAUSE, AXEL, Corporate Editor, *International Herald Tribune,* Paris: BIOGRAPHY—*Michel Rocard;* FRANCE

KRONISH, SYD, Stamp Editor, The Associated Press: STAMPS AND STAMP COLLECTING

LAI, DAVID CHUENYAN, Associate Professor of Geography, University of Victoria, British Columbia: HONG KONG

LANCASTER, CAROL, Director, African Studies Program, Georgetown University; Coeditor, *African Debt and Financing:* AFRICA

LAWRENCE, ROBERT M., Professor of Political Science, Colorado State University; Author, *Strategic Defense Initiative: Bibliography and Research Guide:* ARMS CONTROL; MILITARY AFFAIRS

LEE, STEWART M., Chairman, Department of Economics and Business Administration, Geneva College; Coauthor, *Personal Finance for Consumers:* BUSINESS AND CORPORATE AFFAIRS; CONSUMER AFFAIRS

LEEPSON, MARC, Free-lance Writer: WAR ON DRUGS; MEDICINE AND HEALTH—*Problems of Alcohol;* SOCIAL WELFARE

LEVINE, LOUIS, Professor, Department of Biology, City College of New York; Author, *Biology of the Gene, Biology for a Modern Society:* BIOTECHNOLOGY; GENETICS; MICROBIOLOGY

LEVITT, MORRIS J., Professor, Department of Political Science, Howard University; Coauthor, *Of, By, and For the People: State and Local Government and Politics:* WASHINGTON, DC

LEWIS, JEROME R., Director for Public Administration, College of Urban Affairs and Public Policy, University of Delaware: DELAWARE

LOBRON, BARBARA L., Writer, Editor, Photographer: PHOTOGRAPHY

LOESCHER, GIL, Associate Professor of International Relations, University of Notre Dame; Author, *Calculated Kindness: Refugees and America's Half-Open Door, Refugees and International Relations, The Moral Nation: Humanitarianism and U.S. Foreign Policy:* REFUGEES AND IMMIGRATION

LUBENOW, GERALD C., London Bureau Chief, *Newsweek:* GREAT BRITAIN

LYNCH, MARY JO, Director, Office for Research, American Library Association: LIBRARIES

MABRY, DONALD J., Professor of History, Mississippi State University; Author, *Mexico's Acción Nacional, The Mexican University and the State;* Coauthor, *Neighbors—Mexico and the United States:* BIOGRAPHY—*Carlos Salinas de Gotari;* MEXICO

MARCOPOULOS, GEORGE J., Associate Professor and Deputy Chair, Department of History, Tufts University: CYPRUS; GREECE

MATHESON, JIM, Sportswriter, *Edmonton Journal:* SPORTS—*Ice Hockey*

MATTHEWS, WILLIAM H., III, Professor of Geology, Lamar University; Author, *Fossils: An Introduction to Prehistoric Life, Exploring the World of Fossils:* GEOLOGY; GEOLOGY—*Dinosaurs: A New Look at Some Old Bones*

McCORQUODALE, SUSAN, Professor of Political Science, Memorial University of Newfoundland: NEWFOUNDLAND

McFADDEN, ROBERT D., Reporter, *The New York Times;* Coauthor, *No Hiding Place;* Recipient, New York Press Club's Byline Award: NEW YORK CITY

McGILL, DAVID A., Professor of Marine Science, U.S. Coast Guard Academy: OCEANOGRAPHY

McMAHON, JAMES J., Formerly, SUNY Buffalo/ITM, Malaysia; Lockheed Fellowship—Stanford University, Institute of Management of Science Conference Project Evaluation, "A Cost Benefit Analysis of a Tourism Project in Puerto Rico": MALAYSIA

MELIKOV, GREG, State News Desk, *The Miami Herald:* FLORIDA

MERSKI, PAUL G., Director of Special Studies, Tax Foundation Inc.; Author, *Facts and Figures on Government Finance, 1988–89:* TAXATION

MICHAELIS, PATRICIA A., Curator of Manuscripts, Kansas State Historical Society: KANSAS

MICHIE, ARUNA NAYYAR, Associate Professor of Political Science, Kansas State University: BANGLADESH

MILWARD, JOHN, Free-lance Writer and Critic: IRVING BERLIN AT 100: STEALING AN EXTRA BOW; MUSIC—*Popular;* RECORDINGS

MITCHELL, GARY, Professor of Physics, North Carolina State University: PHYSICS

MORTIMER, ROBERT A., Professor, Department of Political Science, Haverford College; Author, *The Third World Coalition in International Politics:* ALGERIA

MORTON, DESMOND, Professor of History and Principal, Erindale College, University of Toronto; Author, *A Short History of Canada, Bloody Victory: Canadians and the D-Day Campaign, Working People: An Illustrated History of the Canadian Labour Movement, A Military History of Canada, Winning the Second Battle: Canadian Veterans and the Return to Civilian Life, 1915–1930:* CANADA

MURPHY, ROBERT F., Reporter, *The Hartford Courant:* CONNECTICUT

NAFTALIN, ARTHUR, Professor Emeritus of Public Affairs, University of Minnesota: MINNESOTA

NASH, NATHANIEL C., Reporter, Washington Bureau, *The New York Times:* BANKING AND FINANCE

NEUMANN, JIM, *The Forum,* Fargo, ND: NORTH DAKOTA

NEWLAND, ED, Assistant State Editor, *Richmond Times-Dispatch:* VIRGINIA

NORBOM, ELLEN, Free-lance Writer: NORWAY

OCHSENWALD, WILLIAM, Professor of History, Virginia Polytechnic Institute; Author, *The Hijaz Railroad, Religion, Society, and the State in Arabia:* SAUDI ARABIA

O'CONNOR, ROBERT E., Associate Professor of Political Science, The Pennsylvania State University; Author, *Politics and Structure: Essentials of American National Government:* PENNSYLVANIA

OLSEN, MICHAEL L., Professor, New Mexico Highlands University: NEW MEXICO

O'MEARA, PATRICK, Director, African Studies Program, Indiana University; Coeditor, *Africa, International Politics in Southern Africa, Southern Africa, The Continuing Crisis:* ANGOLA; SOUTH AFRICA; ZIMBABWE

PALMER, NORMAN D., Professor Emeritus of Political Science and South Asian Studies, University of Pennsylvania; Author, *Westward Watch: The United States and the Changing Western Pacific, The United States and India: The Dimensions of Influence, Elections and Political Development: The South Asian Experience:* INDIA; SRI LANKA

PARKER, FRANKLIN, Distinguished Visiting Professor, Center for Excellence in Education, Northern Arizona State University; Coauthor, *Education in the People's Republic of China, Past and Present: An Annotated Bibliography, U.S. Higher Education: A Guide to Information Sources:* EDUCATION

PASCOE, ELAINE, Free-lance Writer and Editor; Author, *Racial Prejudice:* BIOGRAPHY—*Raisa Gorbachev, Jesse Jackson;* ETHNIC GROUPS; FAMILY; INDONESIA; SINGAPORE; WOMEN

PEARSON, FREDERIC S., Professor of Political Science and Fellow, Center for International Studies, University of Missouri-St. Louis; Recipient, Ford Foundation Research Award, in Great Britain; Author, *International Relations: The Global Condition in the Late Twentieth Century; The Weak State in International Crisis:* UNITED STATES—*Foreign Affairs*

PEARSON, NEALE J., Professor of Political Science, Texas Tech University: CHILE; PERU; VENEZUELA

PERETZ, DON, Professor of Political Science, State University of New York at Binghamton; Author, *The West Bank—History, Politics, Society & Economy, Government and Politics of Israel, The Middle East Today:* EGYPT; ISRAEL; ISRAEL—*The Palestinian Issue*

PERKINS, KENNETH J., Assistant Professor of History, University of South Carolina: LIBYA; RELIGION—*Islam*

PICHER, KEITH D., *The Chicago Catholic:* RELIGION—*Roman Catholicism*

PIPPIN, LARRY L., Professor of Political Science, University of the Pacific; Author, *The Remón Era:* ARGENTINA; PARAGUAY; URUGUAY

PLATT, HERMAN K., Professor of History, Saint Peter's College: NEW JERSEY

POOLE, PETER A., Author, *The Vietnamese in Thailand, Eight Presidents and Indochina:* CAMBODIA; LAOS; THAILAND; VIETNAM

RALOFF, JANET, Policy/Technology Writer, *Science News:* ENVIRONMENT

RAMIREZ, DEBORAH, Reporter, *San Juan Star:* PUERTO RICO

REBACK, MARILYN A., Associate Editor, *The Numismatist:* COINS AND COIN COLLECTING

REED, WM. CYRUS, Professor, Department of Political Science, Wabash College: KENYA; TANZANIA; UGANDA

REUNING, WINIFRED, Writer, Polar Program, National Science Foundation: POLAR RESEARCH

RICHTER, LINDA K., Associate Professor, Department of Political Science, Kansas State University; Author, *Land Reform and Tourism Development: Policy-Making in the Philippines, The Politics of Tourism in Asia:* BURMA

RICHTER, WILLIAM L., Professor and Head, Department of Political Science, Kansas State University: PAKISTAN

RIGGAN, WILLIAM, Associate Editor, *World Literature Today,* University of Oklahoma; Author, *Picaros, Madmen, Naïfs, and Clowns, Comparative Literature and Literary Theory:* LITERATURE—*World*

ROBINSON, LEIF J., Editor, *Sky & Telescope:* ASTRONOMY

ROSEN, JANE K., Contributor, *Manchester Guardian:* LAW—*International;* UNITED NATIONS

ROSS, RUSSELL M., Professor of Political Science, University of Iowa; Author, *State and Local Government and Administration, Iowa Government and Administration:* IOWA

ROVIN, JEFF, Free-lance Writer; Author, *A Pictorial History of Science Fiction Films, The Fabulous Fantasy Films, The Films of Charlton Heston, From Jules Verne to Star Trek:* BIOGRAPHY—*Cher, Linda Ronstadt, Andrew Lloyd Webber;* PUBLISHING—*Comic Books Are Older*

ROWEN, HERBERT H., Professor Emeritus, Rutgers University, New Brunswick; Author, *The Princes of Orange: The Stadholders in the Dutch Republic:* NETHERLANDS

RUBIN, JIM, Supreme Court Correspondent, The Associated Press: BIOGRAPHY—*Anthony M. Kennedy;* LAW

RUFF, NORMAN J., Assistant Professor, Department of Political Science, University of Victoria, B.C.; Coauthor, *The Reins of Power: Governing British Columbia:* BRITISH COLUMBIA

SALSINI, PAUL, Staff Development Director, *The Milwaukee Journal:* WISCONSIN

SAVAGE, DAVID, Free-lance Writer: CANADA—*The Arts;* LITERATURE—*Canadian*

SAWATSKY, DON, Free-lance Writer/Broadcaster; Author, *Ghost Town Trails of the Yukon:* YUKON

SCHAEFER, MARILYN L., Professor, New York City Technical College: ART

SCHLOSSBERG, DAN, Baseball Writer; Author, *The Baseball IQ Book, The Baseball Catalog:* BIOGRAPHY—*Dave Winfield;* SPORTS—*Baseball*

SCHROEDER, RICHARD, Former Washington Bureau Chief, *Visión;* Syndicated Writer, various U.S. newspapers: BOLIVIA; CARIBBEAN; CARIBBEAN—*Jamaica;* ECUADOR; HAITI; LATIN AMERICA

SCHWAB, PETER, Professor of Political Science, State University of New York at Purchase; Author, *Ethiopia: Politics, Economics, and Society:* ETHIOPIA

SEIDERS, DAVID F., Chief Economist and Senior Staff Vice President, National Association of Home Builders, Washington, DC: HOUSING

SELF, CHARLES C., School of Communication, University of Alabama: PUBLISHING

SENSER, ROBERT A., Free-lance Labor Writer, Washington, DC: LABOR; LABOR—*Benefits in Flux;* SOCIAL WELFARE—*Gray Power*

SETH, R. P., Professor of Economics, Mount Saint Vincent University, Halifax: CANADA—*The Economy;* NOVA SCOTIA

SEYBOLD, PAUL G., Professor, Department of Chemistry, Wright State University: CHEMISTRY

SHARLET, ROBERT, Professor of Political Science, Union College; Coeditor, *P. I. Stuchka: Selected Writings on Soviet Law and Marxism, The Soviet Union Since Stalin, Pashukanis: Selected Writings on Marxism and Law:* USSR; USSR—*Armenia and the Armenians*

SHEPRO, CARL E., Professor, University of Alaska: ALASKA

SHOGAN, ROBERT, National Political Correspondent, Washington Bureau, *Los Angeles Times;* Author, *A Question of Judgment, Promises to Keep:* THE U.S. ELECTIONS; BIOGRAPHY—*Lloyd Bentsen, George Bush, Michael Dukakis, J. Danforth Quayle;* UNITED STATES—*Domestic Affairs, The Reagan Legacy*

SIEGEL, STANLEY E., Professor of History, University of Houston; Author, *A Political History of the Texas Republic, 1836–1845, Houston: Portrait of the Supercity on Buffalo Bayou:* TEXAS

SIMON, JEFFREY D., The Rand Corporation, Santa Monica, CA: TERRORISM

SMITH, REX, Albany Bureau Chief, *Newsday:* NEW YORK

SNIDER, LEWIS W., Associate Professor of International Relations and Government, Claremont Graduate School; Author, *The Emergence of Lebanon: Reality or Illusion?;* Coauthor, *Middle East Foreign Policy:* LEBANON

SNODSMITH, RALPH L., Garden Editor, "Good Morning America"; Host, "Garden Hotline"; Author, *Ralph Snodsmith's Tips from the Garden Hotline, Garden Calendar and Record Keeper 1985–1988:* GARDENING AND HORTICULTURE

SPYCHALSKI, JOHN C., Chairman and Professor of Business Logistics, College of Business Administration, The Pennsylvania State University; Editor, *Transportation Journal:* TRANSPORTATION

STARR, JOHN BRYAN, Executive Director, Yale-China Association; Author, *Continuing the Revolution: The Political Thought of Mao;* Editor, *The Future of U.S.-China Relations:* CHINA; TAIWAN

STERN, JEROME H., Associate Professor of English, Florida State University; Editor, *Studies in Popular Culture:* BIOGRAPHY—*Toni Morrison;* LITERATURE—*American*

STEWART, WILLIAM H., Associate Professor of Political Science, The University of Alabama; Author, *Concepts of Federalism, Alabama Government and Politics:* ALABAMA

STOUDEMIRE, ROBERT H., Distinguished Professor Emeritus, University of South Carolina: SOUTH CAROLINA

SUTTON, STAN, Sportswriter, *The Courier-Journal,* Louisville, KY: SPORTS—*Auto Racing, Horse Racing*

SYLVESTER, LORNA LUTES, Associate Editor, *Indiana Magazine of History,* Indiana University: INDIANA

TABORSKY, EDWARD, Professor of Government, University of Texas at Austin; Author, *Communism in Czechoslovakia, 1948–1960, Communist Penetration of the Third World:* CZECHOSLOVAKIA

TAYLOR, WILLIAM L., Professor of History, Plymouth State College: NEW HAMPSHIRE

TESAR, JENNY, Science and Medicine Writer; Author, *Parents as Teachers:* HEADACHES: THE NUMBER ONE PAIN PROBLEM; COMPUTERS; COMPUTERS—*Computer Viruses;* MEDICINE AND HEALTH; MEDICINE AND HEALTH—*Aspirin, The Nursing Shortage*

THEISEN, CHARLES W., Assistant News Editor, *The Detroit News:* MICHIGAN

TRIEGEL, LINDA, Free-lance Writer and Editor: OBITUARIES—*Louis L'Amour;* TELEVISION AND RADIO—*Some Sample Programs;* THEATER—*Broadway Openings 1988*

TURNER, ARTHUR CAMPBELL, Professor of Political Science, University of California, Riverside; Coauthor, *Ideology and Power in the Middle East:* IRAN; IRAQ; IRAN AND IRAQ—*The Gulf War;* JORDAN; KUWAIT; MIDDLE EAST; SYRIA

TURNER, CHARLES H., Free-lance Writer: HAWAII

TURNER, DARRELL J., Associate Editor, Religious News Service: RELIGION—*Overview, Far Eastern, Protestantism*

VAN RIPER, PAUL P., Professor Emeritus and Head, Department of Political Science, Texas A&M University: POSTAL SERVICE

VOLSKY, GEORGE, Center for Advanced International Studies, University of Miami: CUBA

WEIKER, WALTER F., Professor of Political Science, Rutgers University: TURKEY

WILLIAMS, C. FRED, Associate Vice Chancellor for Educational Programs, University of Arkansas at Little Rock; Author, *Arkansas: An Illustrated History of the Land of Opportunity, Arkansas: A Documentary History:* ARKANSAS

WILLIS, F. ROY, Professor of History, University of California, Davis; Author, *France, Germany and the New Europe, 1945–1968, Italy Chooses Europe, The French Paradox:* EUROPE

WILMS, DENISE MURCKO, Assistant Editor, *Booklist Magazine,* American Library Association: LITERATURE—*Children's*

WOLF, WILLIAM, New York University; Author, *The Marx Brothers, The Landmark Films, The Cinema and Our Century:* MOTION PICTURES

YOUNGER, R. M., Journalist and Author; Author, *Australia and the Australians, Australia! Australia! A Bicentennial Record:* AUSTRALIA AT 200: A LAND WORTH LIVING IN; AUSTRALIA—*Historical Chronology;* AUSTRALIA

ZACEK, JOSEPH FREDERICK, Professor of History, State University of New York, Albany; Author, *Palacky: The Historian as Scholar and Nationalist:* ALBANIA; BULGARIA; EUROPE—*The Eastern Bloc;* HUNGARY; ROMANIA; YUGOSLAVIA

Index

Main article headings appear in this index as bold-faced capitals; subjects within articles appear as lower-case entries. Both the general references and the subentries should be consulted for maximum usefulness of this index. Illustrations are indexed herein. Cross references are to the entries in this index.